THE AFRICAN DIASPORA EXPERIENCE

EXPERIENCE

—FOURTH EDITION—

Edited by

Glenn O. Phillips

Tapestry Press, Ltd.
Littleton, Massachusetts 01460

Acknowledgments:

Pp. 3–10: "The Dynamics of the Global African Diaspora," by Joseph E. Harris. The Walter Prescott Webb Memorial Lectures Committee, The University of Texas at Arlington. All rights reserved.

Pp. 11–14: "Defining and Studying the Modern African Diaspora" by Colin Palmer. From *Perspectives, American Historical Association Newsletter*, 6, vol. 36, (September 1998). Reprinted by permission.

Pp. 15–26 : "Shifting Paradigms in the Study of the African Diaspora and of Atlantic History and Culture" by Kristin Mann from *Slavery and Abolition: A Journal of Slave and Post Slave Studies*, Vol. 22, No. 1 (April 2001), pp. 3–21. All rights reserved.

Pp. 27–33: "The Hamitic Hypothesis: Its Origin and Functions in Time Perspective" by Edith R. Sanders from *The Journal of African History*, Vol. 10, No. 4 (1969), pp. 9–17. All rights reserved.

Pp. 39–49: "The Emergence of Mankind in Africa," by David W. Phillipson. From *African Archaeology*, by David W. Phillipson, © 1993. Reprinted by permission of Cambridge University Press via the Copyright Clearance Center.

Pp. 50–62: "Origin of the Ancient Egyptians," by Cheikh Anta Diop. From *Egypt Revisited* by Ivan Van Sertuisa. © 1989 by Cheikh Anta Diop. Reprinted by permission of Transaction Publishers.

Pp. 63–68: "African Civilizations" by G. O. Ogunremi from *Fundamentals of General Studies*, Chapter 19, Lagos State University (Lagos, Nigeria: L.S.U. Press), pp. 253–262. All rights reserved.

Pp. 69–73: "A Survey of Early African History" by Hakeem Tijani from *Fundamentals of General Studies*, Chapter 20, Lagos State University (Lagos, Nigeria: L.S.U. Press), pp. 263–269. All rights reserved.

Pp. 74–79: "The Land, Early Nubian Cultures and Egypt," by John H. Taylor. From *Egypt and Nubia* by John H. Taylor. Reprinted by permission of British Museum Publications.

Pp. 80–88: "The Great Empires of Medieval Sudan" by Robert W. July. Reprinted by permission of Waveland Press, Inc. from *A History of the African People*, Fifth Edition by Robert W. July. Long Grove, IL: Waveland Press, Inc., 1998. All rights reserved.

Pp. 93–106: "Toward an Understanding of the Ancient View of Blacks," by Frank M. Snowden, Jr. Reprinted by permission of the publisher from *Before Color Prejudice: The Ancient View of Blacks* by Frank M. Snowden, Jr., pp. 61–108, Cambridge, Mass.: Harvard University Press, Copyright © 1983 by the President and Fellows of Harvard College.

Pp. 107–122: "European Dimensions of the African Diaspora" by Allison Blakely, from *Africa in World History: Old, New, and Now* edited by Leonard Plotnicov and Michael W. Coy, Jr. *Ethnology Monographs*, No. 16 (1995). Reprinted by permission of Ethnology.

Pp. 123–134: From *The Revolt of African Slaves in Iraq in the 3rd/9th Century* by Alexander Popovic. Markus Wiener Publishers, Princeton, NJ. Copyright © 2000. All rights reserved.

Pp. 135–149: "Black Slaves in the Mediterranean World: Introduction to a Neglected Aspect of the Black Diaspora," from John O. Hunwick, *Slavery and Abolition*, 5, 1978, Pp. 10–30. Reprinted by permission of Frank Cass Publishers.

Pp. 150–159: "African Presence in Iran: Identity and Its Reconstruction in the 19th and 20th Centuries" by Behraz A. Mirzai from *Traites et Esclavages: Vieux Problems, Neau Velles*, ed. O. Petre-Grenovilleau (Paris: Societe Francaise d'Outre-Mer, 2002), pp. 231–246. All rights reserved.

Pp. 165–176: "The 19th Century Islamic Slave Trade from East Africa: Alternate Census," by Ralph A. Austen in *The Economics of the India Ocean Slave Trade in the Nineteenth Century* by William Gervase Clarence-Smith. Reprinted by permission of Frank Cass Publishers.

Pp. 177–190: "The Ethiopian Diaspora to India: The Role of Habshis and Sidis from Medieval Times to the End of the Eighteenth Century" by Richard Pankhurst from *The African Diaspora in the Indian Ocean*, ed. Shihan de Silva, Jayasuriya, Richard Pankhurst (Trenton, NJ: Africa World Press, 2003), pp. 189–212. All rights reserved.

Pp. 191–201: "The African Presence in Portuguese India" by Ann M. Pescatello from *Journal of Asian History*, XI (1977). Reprinted by permission of the Journal of Asian History.

Pp. 202–217: "Anti-Black Racism in Post-Mao China" by Barry Sautman from *The China Quarterly*, No. 138 (June 1994), pp. 413–437. All rights reserved.

Pp. 221–225: "The Origin of Negro Slavery," by Eric E. Williams. From *Capitalism and Slavery* by Eric Williams. Copyright © 1944, by the University of North Carolina Press, renewed 1972 by Eric Williams. New introduction by Colin A. Palmer © 1994 by the University of North Carolina Press. Used by permission of the publisher. www.uncpress.unc.edu

Pp. 226–231: "The Life of Olaudah Equiano, or Gustavus Vassa the African," by Olaudah Equiano. From *The Interesting Narrative of the Life of Olaudah Equiano or Gustavas Vassa, The African*, Longman, 1793. All rights reserved.

Pp. 232–238: "Measuring the Immeasurable: The Atlantic Slave Trade," by David P. Henige. From the *Journal of African History*, 1986. Reprinted by permission of Cambridge University Press via the Copyright Clearance Center.

Pp. 239–251: "Enslaved Africans and Their Expectations of Slave Life in the Americas: Toward a Reconsideration of Models of 'Creolosation'" by Paul E. Lovejoy and David Trotman. From *Questioning Creole: Creolization Discourses in Caribbean Culture*, edited by Verene A. Shepard and Glen L. Richards, Ian Randle Publishers, Ltd. Copyright © 2002. Reprinted by permission of the publisher.

Pp. 255–261: From *Narrative of the Life of Frederick Douglass, an American Slave* by Frederick Douglass. All rights reserved.

Contents

clearer picture of the ongoing dialogue and debates among scholars about the African Diaspora experience.

I wish to also thank my ever faithful supporters of all my projects, including my wife Ingrid, daughter Mariette, brother Dion and his son, Ernest Phillips, for all the encouragement they gave me as I pondered this fourth attempt and prepared this edition for publication.

Glenn O. Phillips
September 2007

Preface to Fourth Edition

This fourth edition is designed to accomplish two goals. First, it seeks to present many of the essential writings and seminal essays that will capture the fundamental concepts that are involved in clearly understanding the interdisciplinary nature of the study of the African Diaspora experience. Second, this volume acknowledges the limitations of the earlier editions that included a high percentage of ground-breaking essays, and includes a number of more recent essays that extend the dialogue and create further debate based on these pioneering views about the African Diaspora experience.

Consequently, this edition will break new ground and introduce to its readers many of the new paradigms that authors from a wide variety of fields have introduced in the last ten years. On the other hand, all the materials included are intended to serve as the background from which students interested in the study of the African Diaspora experience from a historical perspective will clearly understand the wide range and impact of the movements of generations of persons of African descent globally over a period of roughly six thousand years.

Nevertheless, this edition has not radically restructured the main sections formed in the third edition. Some of the sections have been rearranged. A number of essays in the earlier editions have been replaced, shortened, or relocated. It is hoped that the changes, additions, and improvements in this edition will assist both the beginning students and general readers to more adequately grasp the essentials of African Diaspora history and the various approaches scholars used to discuss this fascinating subject.

The major challenge in producing this fourth edition was deciding on the number of new essays to include and still maintain a balanced collection of authoritative essays in a wide variety of academic fields. I believe that this collection of essays will still meet the needs of college students who are studying this subject for the first time. At the same time it acknowledges that there are many excellent essays that could not be included because of space constraints. It is hoped that the essays included would so stimulate readers about this subject that they will be encouraged to seek other works that satisfy their evolving interest in the African Diaspora experience.

Each of these editions owes its existence to many of the same educators and collaborators, but like the earlier editions, there are a few new faces and voices who in some way provided very valuable insights, suggestions, materials, or in other ways contributed to this work. Not in all cases could we include all the materials suggested by many interested participants in the process of evaluating the last edition.

We acknowledge the ongoing support of Dr. Burney J. Hollis, Dean of the College of Liberal Arts, Dr. Annette Palmer, Chairperson of the Department of History and Geography, and Dr. Raymond Winbush, Director of the Institute for Urban Research at Morgan State University, without whose support this fourth edition would not be possible.

We are also grateful to all the members of the Morgan State University's Department of History African Diaspora teaching committee who made many valuable suggestions, and these include Drs. Arthur Burt, Jeremiah Dibua, Debra Newman Ham, Perry Kyles, Hakeem Tijani, and Aubrey Thompson as well as lecturers Homer Fleetwood, Derick Hendricks, and Gloria Marrow.

The ongoing support and understanding of Michael Miskin, President of Tapestry Press in the publication of this fourth edition was critical for its completion. Equally helpful are those who helped locate sources or typed some section or parts of the manuscript, and these include my daughter, Mariette Phillips, Patricia Thomas of the Institute for Urban Research, and Joyce Nibbs of the Department of History. My graduate assistants, Amber Simon and Marcus Allen, helped obtain hard copies of new essays along with Maggie Wanza, Associate Director of the Soper Library at Morgan State University, Donald Matthews, coordinator of Soper's interlibrary loan system, Ava Colbert of the Circulation Desk, Edith Murungi and Elizabeth Grossmont of the Davis Room Collection at the Soper Library at Morgan State University.

We wish to also thank Sara Hofeldt, editor-in-chief, who again superbly managed the entire production process and Elizabeth Pulcini, manuscript editor, for her excellent editing work.

We trust that this fourth attempt to highlight the important themes, issues, and complexities involved in the study of the African Diaspora will continue to give readers and students a

Introduction to the African Diaspora Experience

Glenn O. Phillips

Over the last decade an increasing number of scholars and writers from numerous fields have turned their attention to examining various aspects of the interdisciplinary field of African Diaspora studies. This wider acceptance of African Diaspora themes by scholars in the more established fields, organizations, and institutions of higher learning has given a certain legitimacy to the field. From its infancy in the 1980s, the study of the African Diaspora has now emerged as a distinct field of academic pursuit encamping the fields of African studies, African American studies, Caribbean studies, World History, World migrations, interdisciplinary studies and other related themes. An increasing number of colleges and universities are now offering courses that focus on the study of the African Diaspora. At the same time, the expanding discussion and debate regarding what constitutes the essentials of African Diaspora thought and interpretation have undergone a second round of both interdisciplinary and methodological analysis. The result is that many new paradigms essentially have emerged from the Post Modern and the Deconstruction methods of analysis used by recent scholars. Consequently both the impressive volume and the easy accessibility of numerous works on a multitude of African Diaspora themes make the selection process for determining what to include in an African Diaspora experience primer more challenging than in previous years.

Presently, numerous publishing houses and presses have introduced readers to a wider range of closely related themes in journals, monographs as well as in their multivolume encyclopedic publications that converge on the new interpretations of the African Diaspora. They have also republished older works that have been out of print for decades. The increasing availability of a growing number of online sources makes it much easier to obtain the latest information on current studies related to most African Diaspora focused subjects. Nevertheless, students need to be reminded that there are materials available on the Internet system, that are provocative, persuasive, insightful, and authoritative, yet they contain mostly inaccurate, unreliable, and undocumented information that cannot withstand careful academic evaluation.

It is, therefore, the main goals of this edition to include in each section a combination of essays from across the disciplines that reflect a balanced portrayal of the various historical components of the African Diaspora experience. This volume adequately covers the essential issues around the basic themes that impacted Africa, Africans, and persons of African descent from earliest times to the present. Like earlier editions, this volume includes some of the seminal essays that are still insightful, provocative, and generate considerable debate among more recent scholars. Also included are new essays that articulate new and critical insights and unfolding dimensions of the African Diaspora experience. Most sections have been redesigned to call attention to many new inquiries about that theme yet not neglecting to make readers become fully aware of the fundamental issues involved in understanding the total African Diaspora experience.

There are a number of current insights and perspectives about the study of the African Diaspora that this edition will address that were ignored in the previous editions. Among these are articles that focus on the latest trends that have emerged in the new waves of migration of persons of African descent to leading countries in Europe and Asia. Another new feature will be to examine the ethnic identity of women of color and the ongoing impact of African religions in shaping the early and recent African Diaspora experience.

Within the eleven major sections of this edition, students will encounter narratives that incorporate exciting new approaches to many of the legitimate questions about the most critical components that comprise and played a major role in the formation and flourishing of African communities. Some essays will examine the identities of persons of African descent within and outside the African continent, while analyzing their encounters with various groups around the world.

A.   What is the African Diaspora?

The African Diaspora experience traces the many centuries of migration by the peoples of African descent from their motherland to all parts of the world.[1] While the diaspora concept was probably first recorded by the writer of Deuteronomy in the Bible's Septuagint translation (c. 280 B.C.) to describe the forced migration of Jews from their homeland into Babylonian captivity by Nebuchadnezzar II in 597 B.C., the term is currently used to denote and characterize the various experiences of exile groups throughout history. Many of the earliest writings about diaspora dealt primarily with the Jewish experience. Nevertheless, there were many nineteenth-century authors who wrote about the manifestations of the African Diaspora. These include William F. Mavor in his *History of the Dispersion of Jews . . . and of African Nations* (1802), Robert B. Lewis's *Light and Truth, Collected From Ancient and Modern History* (1844), Alexander Crumwell's *The Future of Africa* (1862), James Horton's *West African Countries and Its peoples* (1868), and Edward Wilmot Blyden's *Christianity, Islam and the Negro Race* (1887). Some early twentieth-century scholars who also captured the concept in their writings included W. E. B. DuBois in *The Negro* (1915), and *Black Folk Then and Now: An Essay in the History and Sociology of the Negro Race* (1939), and Carter G. Woodson in *African Myths* (1928) and *The African Background Outlined* (1935). However, the term "African Diaspora" was first used by more recent scholars in the mid-1960s, at the peak of the Black consciousness movement that grew out of the Civil Rights movement in the United States, to characterize the collective African experience both inside and outside of Africa.

There were at least four leading influences that contributed to this new interest in the study of the African Diaspora experience. Clearly the rhetoric of the most vocal proponents of Black nationalism and Pan-Africanism revolved around many of the issues and the themes they advocated. The growing numbers of newly politically independent African countries beginning with Ghana in 1957, sparked a rebirth of worldwide interest in the continent and the future of its peoples. There was a far larger community of Black academics (as compared to earlier times) who felt compelled to study and write about various aspects of the African Diaspora experience. Finally, the expanding and more meaningful collaboration of Black intellectuals from around the world sharing ideas and calling for a reexamination of their peoples' past also contributed to the increased interest. Some of these mid-twentieth century exchanges transpired at the first and second Congress of Black World Writers and Artists in London during 1956 and in Rome in 1959. UNESCO's decision in 1964 to support the research and publication of a general history of Africa also kept alive interest on the continent and its peoples. Finally, the 1978 Conference on the Slave Trade and Its Impact contributed further discussion and debate, promoting new intellectual exchanges regarding the relationship between Africa and those who left the motherland over the centuries. Over the last ten years, numerous conferences have been held in the Caribbean, Latin America, Europe, and around the U.S. on the theme, most recently commemorating the bicentenary of the ending of the trans-Atlantic Slave Trade.

Over the last eight years, the recently established Association for the Study of the World-wide Diaspora has held biennial conferences that have attracted a wide range of scholars. The Association's 2005 conference was held in Brazil, and their fourth was convened in Barbados, October 9–12, 2007 on the theme "Memories, Meanings and Migrations."

The main objective in studying the African Diaspora experience include the critical examination of a wide range of ideas and issues that focus on both the voluntary and involuntary movements of Africans across the African continent and beyond, into the Mediterranean, the Middle East, Europe, Asia, the Pacific, and the Americas. Among the issues involved in studying the major implications of these movements are the viewing of Africa as the "ancestral motherland"; the validity of using an Afrocentric approach to evaluate circumstances, examining the ramifications of both the pull and push factors for African migration; and the changing ideas of Africa in the minds and lives of the exiled Africans. Other themes include the debate regarding the extent of preservation, survival, and assimilation of African folkways and the factors related to linkages and communication among Africans within the African Diaspora as well as the challenges. Finally, the impact and contributions of the

---

[1]The word "diaspora" can be traced from the Greek language into the Old German and is the root of many English verbs including "spread," "sprawl," and "sprout" and nouns like "sperm" and "seed," suggesting the creation of a distinctly new life and experience.

A.   What is the African Diaspora?

The African Diaspora experience traces the many centuries of migration by the peoples of African descent from their motherland to all parts of the world.[1] While the diaspora concept was probably first recorded by the writer of Deuteronomy in the Bible's Septuagint translation (c. 280 B.C.) to describe the forced migration of Jews from their homeland into Babylonian captivity by Nebuchadnezzar II in 597 B.C., the term is currently used to denote and characterize the various experiences of exile groups throughout history. Many of the earliest writings about diaspora dealt primarily with the Jewish experience. Nevertheless, there were many nineteenth-century authors who wrote about the manifestations of the African Diaspora. These include William F. Mavor in his *History of the Dispersion of Jews . . . and of African Nations* (1802), Robert B. Lewis's *Light and Truth, Collected From Ancient and Modern History* (1844), Alexander Crumwell's *The Future of Africa* (1862), James Horton's *West African Countries and Its peoples* (1868), and Edward Wilmot Blyden's *Christianity, Islam and the Negro Race* (1887). Some early twentieth-century scholars who also captured the concept in their writings included W. E. B. DuBois in *The Negro* (1915), and *Black Folk Then and Now: An Essay in the History and Sociology of the Negro Race* (1939), and Carter G. Woodson in *African Myths* (1928) and *The African Background Outlined* (1935). However, the term "African Diaspora" was first used by more recent scholars in the mid-1960s, at the peak of the Black consciousness movement that grew out of the Civil Rights movement in the United States, to characterize the collective African experience both inside and outside of Africa.

There were at least four leading influences that contributed to this new interest in the study of the African Diaspora experience. Clearly the rhetoric of the most vocal proponents of Black nationalism and Pan-Africanism revolved around many of the issues and the themes they advocated. The growing numbers of newly politically independent African countries beginning with Ghana in 1957, sparked a rebirth of worldwide interest in the continent and the future of its peoples. There was a far larger community of Black academics (as compared to earlier times) who felt compelled to study and write about various aspects of the African Diaspora experience. Finally, the expanding and more meaningful collaboration of Black intellectuals from around the world sharing ideas and calling for a reexamination of their peoples' past also contributed to the increased interest. Some of these mid-twentieth century exchanges transpired at the first and second Congress of Black World Writers and Artists in London during 1956 and in Rome in 1959. UNESCO's decision in 1964 to support the research and publication of a general history of Africa also kept alive interest on the continent and its peoples. Finally, the 1978 Conference on the Slave Trade and Its Impact contributed further discussion and debate, promoting new intellectual exchanges regarding the relationship between Africa and those who left the motherland over the centuries. Over the last ten years, numerous conferences have been held in the Caribbean, Latin America, Europe, and around the U.S. on the theme, most recently commemorating the bicentenary of the ending of the trans-Atlantic Slave Trade.

Over the last eight years, the recently established Association for the Study of the World-wide Diaspora has held biennial conferences that have attracted a wide range of scholars. The Association's 2005 conference was held in Brazil, and their fourth was convened in Barbados, October 9–12, 2007 on the theme "Memories, Meanings and Migrations."

The main objective in studying the African Diaspora experience include the critical examination of a wide range of ideas and issues that focus on both the voluntary and involuntary movements of Africans across the African continent and beyond, into the Mediterranean, the Middle East, Europe, Asia, the Pacific, and the Americas. Among the issues involved in studying the major implications of these movements are the viewing of Africa as the "ancestral motherland"; the validity of using an Afrocentric approach to evaluate circumstances, examining the ramifications of both the pull and push factors for African migration; and the changing ideas of Africa in the minds and lives of the exiled Africans. Other themes include the debate regarding the extent of preservation, survival, and assimilation of African folkways and the factors related to linkages and communication among Africans within the African Diaspora as well as the challenges. Finally, the impact and contributions of the

---

[1]The word "diaspora" can be traced from the Greek language into the Old German and is the root of many English verbs including "spread," "sprawl," and "sprout" and nouns like "sperm" and "seed," suggesting the creation of a distinctly new life and experience.

Introduction to the African Diaspora Experience

Glenn O. Phillips

Over the last decade an increasing number of scholars and writers from numerous fields have turned their attention to examining various aspects of the interdisciplinary field of African Diaspora studies. This wider acceptance of African Diaspora themes by scholars in the more established fields, organizations, and institutions of higher learning has given a certain legitimacy to the field. From its infancy in the 1980s, the study of the African Diaspora has now emerged as a distinct field of academic pursuit encamping the fields of African studies, African American studies, Caribbean studies, World History, World migrations, interdisciplinary studies and other related themes. An increasing number of colleges and universities are now offering courses that focus on the study of the African Diaspora. At the same time, the expanding discussion and debate regarding what constitutes the essentials of African Diaspora thought and interpretation have undergone a second round of both interdisciplinary and methodological analysis. The result is that many new paradigms essentially have emerged from the Post Modern and the Deconstruction methods of analysis used by recent scholars. Consequently both the impressive volume and the easy accessibility of numerous works on a multitude of African Diaspora themes make the selection process for determining what to include in an African Diaspora experience primer more challenging than in previous years.

Presently, numerous publishing houses and presses have introduced readers to a wider range of closely related themes in journals, monographs as well as in their multivolume encyclopedic publications that converge on the new interpretations of the African Diaspora. They have also republished older works that have been out of print for decades. The increasing availability of a growing number of online sources makes it much easier to obtain the latest information on current studies related to most African Diaspora focused subjects. Nevertheless, students need to be reminded that there are materials available on the Internet system, that are provocative, persuasive, insightful, and authoritative, yet they contain mostly inaccurate, unreliable, and undocumented information that cannot withstand careful academic evaluation.

It is, therefore, the main goals of this edition to include in each section a combination of essays from across the disciplines that reflect a balanced portrayal of the various historical components of the African Diaspora experience. This volume adequately covers the essential issues around the basic themes that impacted Africa, Africans, and persons of African descent from earliest times to the present. Like earlier editions, this volume includes some of the seminal essays that are still insightful, provocative, and generate considerable debate among more recent scholars. Also included are new essays that articulate new and critical insights and unfolding dimensions of the African Diaspora experience. Most sections have been redesigned to call attention to many new inquiries about that theme yet not neglecting to make readers become fully aware of the fundamental issues involved in understanding the total African Diaspora experience.

There are a number of current insights and perspectives about the study of the African Diaspora that this edition will address that were ignored in the previous editions. Among these are articles that focus on the latest trends that have emerged in the new waves of migration of persons of African descent to leading countries in Europe and Asia. Another new feature will be to examine the ethnic identity of women of color and the ongoing impact of African religions in shaping the early and recent African Diaspora experience.

Within the eleven major sections of this edition, students will encounter narratives that incorporate exciting new approaches to many of the legitimate questions about the most critical components that comprise and played a major role in the formation and flourishing of African communities. Some essays will examine the identities of persons of African descent within and outside the African continent, while analyzing their encounters with various groups around the world.

African Diaspora peoples in the host countries, as well as the motherland, from ancient times to the present, is a fundamental theme.

This volume is designed primarily to meet the needs of students taking the introductory undergraduate survey course in the study of the African Diaspora history at Morgan State University. This accumulation of essays is the consequence of teaching this course for many years and, in the process, discovering authoritative essays on critical themes that are written in a manner to stimulate meaningful classroom discussion. Over these years, it has been difficult to find one text that covers this wide historical sweep and maintains interdisciplinary yet primarily historically oriented materials. This collection of essays seeks to meet this need while at the same time it must be acknowledged that there are many excellent essays on related themes that could not be included because of space constraints.

The study of the African Diaspora experience is a broad and demanding subject. It covers centuries of history and is global in scope. The aim of this volume is to bring together a collection of the most practical, balanced, concise essays that portray many of the important issues that scholars and writers from different fields and perspectives have prepared in the most readable manner. The essays are not all written by historians and include narratives authored by anthropologists, curators, linguists, demographers, journalists, and activists. These interpretive articles begin with an examination of the methodology used in the study of the subject, deal with African preliterate societies, and include a few primary sources and eyewitness accounts, while striving to focus on many of the relevant issues of the African Diaspora discussion as we enter the twenty-first century.

Within the body of readings exists a careful mix of topics, themes, and issues, in chronological order, that should supplement and enrich the lectures and discussions presented in the classroom. The selections expose students to a wide range of historical writings and methodologies. Students are encouraged to view these essays with an eye to better understanding the many tools that historians and other scholars use in presenting their views on the African Diaspora experience.

B. Highlight of Chapters

This collection of essays is divided into eleven sections. This fourth edition includes an additional section on "African Religions in the Diaspora." Many teachers have requested that we include essays on this very important theme that is clearly an integral part of the African Diaspora experience over the centuries. Within the other sections, we have deleted a number of essays and replaced them with more up-to-date or insightful materials with the object of making this edition even more relevant to the expanding need for students to obtain the sources for their study of this subject. We have therefore introduced twenty new essays that reflect the ongoing dialogue among scholars across the discipline.

Our first section, "An Examination of African Diasporan Themes" seeks to present to our readers some of the methodological issues that students of this subject need to know. The first essay is by Joseph E. Harris entitled "The Dynamics of the Global African Diaspora" and remains a standard overview essay that highlights many of the important issues involved in the study of the African Diaspora experience. It is followed by three other essays that argue and investigate some of the more recent views by scholars about what is really involved in a careful examination of various aspects that constitute African Diaspora studies across the disciplines. Colin A. Palmer's "Defining and Studying the Modern African Diaspora" will assist in giving a clear focus to the various thematic streams within the widening field. Kristin Mann's "Shifting Paradigms in the Study of the African Diaspora and of Atlantic History and Culture" warns against scholars having a "too narrow" view of what the African Diaspora is about, and she suggests that more creative approaches to studying this Diaspora will enable scholars to recognize the many "regional and temporal variations in its development" beginning in Africa. She suggests that "There is no single slave-trade, rather there were a number of more specific slave trades." In the final essay of this section, Edith R. Sanders' "The Hamitic Hypothesis, Its Origins in Time" has been requested by many instructors who teach this course. This essay carefully traces how ancient writers and scholars, especially in the Western World, have attempted to perpetuate in their writings baseless negative stereotyping of persons of African descent.

Section two, entitled "The Formation of Early African Societies" contains a number of new essays yet retains two very important ones. This section includes essays that deal with early African history and the extremely lively debate about the Origins of earliest Mankind, the Africannest of Ancient Egypt, and the extent of the sophistication of the Ancient Sudanic Empires of West Africa. The first essay is the archaeological study of David W. Phillipson entitled "The Emergence of Mankind in Africa." It gives valuable background on the archaeological evidence unearthed regarding the earliest human findings across East Africa in Tanzania, Kenya, and Ethiopia. The second essay focuses on the crowning work of Cheikah Anta Diop as he gives a clear series of arguments challenging the limited, negative view of Africa and Africans regarding their presence in Ancient Egyptian history. The emergence of early African societies in helping to shape the Ancient World is outlined by G. O. Ogunremi. It describes in short, masterful paragraphs Africa's role in creating its own ancient civilization. It is followed by Hakeem Tijani, "Survey of Early African History" that is most suitable for students who have not studied this subject before. Also included is John H. Taylor's "Land, Early Nubian Cultures and Egypt" that continues to demonstrate to readers the integral relationship that existed over Sub-Sahara Africa and Ancient Egypt. Robert July's "The Great Empires of Medieval Sudan" remains an important essay that gives important insights into the ascendancy of West African societies centuries before the Atlantic Slave trade began to dominate this region.

Section three, "The Early Interactions of Africa with Other Societies: From Antiquity to the Middle East" covers over a millennium of history and relationships between Africans and their neighbors to the North and East of the African Continent. Four of the five essays were retained from the third edition. These are Frank M. Snowden's "Towards An Understanding of the Ancient View of Blacks," which is still considered by classical scholars a "balanced pioneering work" on the interaction of the ancients of Greece and Rome with the contemporary Africans who lived in the Mediterranean world. Allison Blakely's "The European Dimension of the African Diaspora" investigates the wide variety of evidence that clearly indicates the persistent African presence in Europe from the early eighth century C.E. and the existence of folklore and religious thought about Africa in northern Europe from the early Middle Ages. Alexandre Popovic's "The Revolt of African Slaves in Iraq in the 3rd /9th Century" was finally translated into English from French and gives a clear insight into one of the most significant African slave revolts that transpired outside of Africa prior to those that occurred in the Americas between the sixteenth and nineteenth centuries. John O. Hunwick's "Black Slaves in the Mediterranean World" leads readers to a precise understanding of the magnitude and significance of the sub-Sahara slave trade that blossomed and existed for numerous centuries whereby African slaves became an integral part of the social, economic, political, and religious life in Middle Eastern and Islamic lands around the Mediterranean Basin.

The last essay in this section is new and the work of a young scholar, Beharaz A. Mirzai, who has studied the African presence in the Iranian empire for many years. It is entitled "The African Presence in Iran: Identity and Its Reconstruction in the 19th and 20th Centuries" indicating that Africans were held in slavery in this most easterly of Middle East countries.

Section four, "Africans in Northern and Eastern Societies: From India to Recent China" is comprised of four essays. Three of these essays are appearing for the first time. The first essay has been retained because of its importance in allowing students to obtain a careful study of the African slave trade during one of its most critical periods.

The Asian continent is the home of two of the world's largest civilizations that today account for population centers with more than a billion inhabitants each, China (1.321) and India (1.136) as of mid-2007. For at least ten centuries from the coast of East Africa, African, Arab and Swahili traders transported African slaves into the Persian Gulf and beyond, on to the Asian continent and into the islands of Southeast Asia. Some estimates suggest that between 7 to 10 million Africans arrived in lands across the Indian and Pacific Oceans over the centuries. African slaves were taken to China from at least the sixth century C.E., during the Tang Dynasty (618–907 A.D.). Scholars have conducted far too few studies on this region of the African Diaspora experience. While there is little trace of Africans in mainland China today, small communities of African Asians live in the present-day countries of Bangladesh, Bhutan, India, Nepal, Pakistan, and Sri Lanka. Other African Asians can also be traced in many countries of Southeast Asia from Indonesia to the Philippines, Papua New Guinea and Fiji, to

Australia and Hawaii. We have selected a wide cross-section of essays covering this vast region of the world and centuries of history.

Our first essay is Ralph A. Austen's important work "The 19th Century Islamic Slave Trade from East Africa (Swahili and Red Sea Coast): A Tentative Census." Austen carefully reviews all the available evidence regarding the volume of Africans leaving the East African coast during the pivotal nineteenth century for areas of the Middle East and some Asian countries.

Richard Parkhurst's "The Ethiopian Diaspora to India: The Role of Habshis and Sidis from Medieval Times to the Edge of the Eighteenth Century" covers the essentials of Africans migrating to various parts of the Indian Subcontinent. Ann Pescatello's "The African Presence in Portuguese India" shows how Africans followed the Portugese to India and how they lived as part of Portugal's control of coastal regions of India, while contributing to the economy of this region.

Barry Sautman's "Anti-Black Racism in Post Mao China" examines the reactions of large numbers of Chinese to the more recent African presence in the seaports and around universities and communities where Africans lived at the end of China's cultural revolution. China had, during the Cold War, engaged a growing number of African students to study at their universities, but in more recent conservative times, Africans living in these areas found the Chinese not as welcoming as they had appeared in earlier times.

Section five, "The Impact of the Atlantic Slave Trade: The Middle Passage" is comprised of four very different essays covering a wide spectrum of issues and regions, and is not limited to the Atlantic slave trade. The first essay is Eric Williams's "Origin of Negro Slavery," taken from his monumental work *Capitalism and Slavery* (1944, 1990), which argues for the significant role of economics in the establishment and profitability of the Atlantic slave trade over three centuries. The second essay is probably the most vivid account on record of an African, Olaudah Equiano, who experienced the infamous Middle Passage. It is considered the classic autobiography of one African who experienced the voyage across the Atlantic and lived to explain to the world what it was like. It was written to counter the impression given at the time by many Europeans that the African slave trade was a justifiable act of compassion. The third essay in this section, David P. Henige's "Measuring the Immeasurable: The Atlantic Slave Trade," captures the sentiment and discussion of numerous scholars who have been debating the issues of determining the actual volume of the Atlantic slave trade over the many centuries of this clandestine and illegal practice. The discussion about the actual size of the population taken from Africa to the Americas is still evoking extensive debate among scholars. Our fourth essay in this section is written by Paul E. Lovejoy and David V. Trotman entitled "Enslaved Africans and Their Expectations of Slave Life in the Americas: Towards a Reconsideration of the Models of 'Creolization'," includes a review of creolization literature on slaves. This essay deals with the changing expectations of slaves after the Middle Passage experience and their adoption and adjustment to slave environments.

The sixth section, "Comparative Slavery in the Americas" contains six articles that deal with a wide variety of issues involving the comparative history approach to slavery in the Caribbean and the Americas. The articles deal with the vital systems that held Africans in slavery from the seventeenth to the nineteenth centuries. They examine slavery that was operated by English, Portuguese, and Spanish slaveholders. They consider the many faces of the institution of manumission in Brazil, where the largest numbers of Africans existed in the Americas and where African slavery existed for the longest period, ending in 1888. They examine the unique pressure placed on slave families in the United States. This section includes essays that describe the heart and fabric of African slavery across the Caribbean region and in two South American countries, Peru and Argentina.

This section begins with selected passages from the compelling autobiography of Frederick Douglass, the most well-known American slave, whose personal experiences opened the eyes of the rest of the world to the great injustices of African slavery in the Americas, particularly in the United States. This section continues with the vivid perspective of Franklin W. Knight in his assessment of Caribbean slave society. He provides a balanced picture of the overriding elements of the slave community in the Caribbean. Knight's narrative is taken from *The Caribbean, The Genesis of a Fragmented Nationalism* (1990), which examines and highlights much of the most recent research on Caribbean slave life as well as the problems of nation-building in more contemporary times. Katia M. de Queiros Mattoso's "The Charter of Freedom in Brazil"

xvi Introduction to the African Diaspora Experience

seeks to give the reader a vivid picture of the nature and experience of African slaves in Brazil, where the institution of slavery held more Africans and for a longer time (1440–1880) than any other country in the Americas. This essay is at the heart of de Queiros Mattoso's *To Be a Slave in Brazil 1550–1880* (1986) and explains the illusive nature of freedom for Brazil's slaves over the centuries. The third essay in this section is from Andrew Billingsley's early study *Black Families in White America,* first published in 1968. Billingsley is a sociologist by training, but he reviews the history of the African American family during slavery in his second chapter entitled "Historical Backgrounds of the Negro Family." He suggests that the African American slave family experienced a very different treatment from other slave families in the Caribbean and Latin America. Peter Blanchard gives us a clear picture of another kind of slave life in the newly independent Andean Republic of Peru, the native home of the ancient Incas. Although African slaves formed a small percentage of the republic's population, African slavery ended decades after this Spanish colony received its political independence. This essay is from Blanchard's longer work *Slavery and Abolition in Early Republic Peru* (1992). George Reid Andrews's "Black Legions of Buenos Aires," taken from his book *The Afro-Argentines of Buenos Aires 1800–1900* (1980), carefully describes the critical role that the descendants of Argentine's slaves played in defending the new republic and destroys the long-held myth that most persons of African descent had disappeared after Argentina achieved its independence.

At the foundation of section seven, is one essay entitled "The Role of Women in the African Diaspora" that is a holdover from the first edition. That essay is Rosalyn Terborg-Penn's prudent analysis of the scholarship that has taken place in Women's Studies and that is now at the heart of many outstanding works regarding the reevaluation of women's role in world history. The other accompanying essays were selected to give the reader a wide perspective of the important and vital role women played during slavery in the Caribbean, Latin America, and the United States. Barbara A. Bush's "The Economic Role of Slave Women" is one of the significant pioneering essays on the many strengths that slave women contributed to the institution of slavery, with a focus on the former British West Indies between 1660 and 1838. Robert Olwell's "Slave Women in the Eighteenth-Century Charleston Marketplace" gives an interesting perspective to the dominant role of female slave marketers in a southern American city who tried "to escape the limitation of their condition in such a public way." The essay by Robert W. Slenes, "Perceptions of Slave Women in Nineteenth-Century Brazil," is a most insightful reexamination of writings about slave society in Brazil that had previously suggested that sexual promiscuity was an overwhelming feature of Brazilian slave women and affected their family unit. The final essay by Cheryl Johnson-Odin is entitled "Actions Louder Then Words: The Historical Task of Defining Feminist Consciousness in Colonial West Africa." Johnson-Odim is an authority on African feminism and argues for using a non-Western interpretation to better understand the struggles of women in West Africa.

The new addition in this section is Ula Y. Taylor's "Negro Women are Great Thinkers As Well As Doers: Amy Jacques-Garvey and Community Feminism in the United States 1924–1927." This essay illustrates the presence of numerous essays and books published in the last ten years that shed new light and multiple insights on the very important role women of African descent played in the shaping of the African Diaspora experience.

Section eight highlights the impact that "Slave Resistance and Abolition" played in the slave colonies of the Americas. These articles cover a wide variety of issues and experiences that confronted slaves in the Caribbean and the Americas. This edition includes Robert N. Anderson's "The Quilombos of Palmares, A New Overview of a Maroon State in 17th century Brazil." This essay calls attention to one of the largest Maroon societies during the century of African enslavement in the Americas. Patrick Carroll's "Mandinga: The Evolution of a Mexican Runaway Slave Community 1735–1827" sheds light on the early and large African slave population in Mexico and their attempts at resistance for decades. David P. Geggus articulates a most insightful and compact description of "The Haitian Revolution." In spite of the treatment of this subject by many scholars, Geggus's essay presents one of the best, relatively brief, but wide-ranging discussions on this slave revolt that led to the first politically independent country of former slaves in the Western hemisphere. Michael L. Conniff and Thomas J. Davis's "The Abolition of the Atlantic Slave Trade" details the great struggle by Europeans and Africans, but especially by the British from 1807, to bring an end to one of the most lucrative, clandestine, and illegal business enterprises undertaken by the European nations and their Arab and African collaborators. The essay also points out some of the reasons why this very profitable and deadly trade ended. Rebecca J. Scott in "Gradual Abolition and the Dynamics of Slave Emancipation in Cuba 1868–1886" focuses on the incremental processes undertaken to bring an end to the institution of slavery in areas of the largest slave population in the Americas. Scott examines the particular circumstances that led to the granting of freedom to some Cuban slaves during the Ten Years War and the subsequent emancipation of all Cuban slaves in 1886. She expands on her position in her work *Slave Emancipation in Cuba: The Transition to Free Labour 1860–1899* (1985). The final essay in this section, Kim D. Butler's "Abolition and the Politics of Identity in the Afro-Atlantic Diaspora: Toward a Comparative Approach," calls for a broadening of scholars' views on how to evaluate the changing identity of the newly freed Africans in the Americas and gives special attention to Afro-Brazilians.

Section nine, "The Role of Religions in the African Diaspora" is a new theme included in this fourth edition. A growing number of scholars have been calling our attention to the ongoing significance and impact of African religions on the slave society and have demonstrated its ongoing importance generations after African slavery in the Americas was abolished. A wide range of scholars from various fields from Anthropology to Religious Studies and Sociology have continued to examine the major African Religions in the Americas from Vodouns in Haiti to Santeria in Cuba, Candomble in Brazil, Garifunia in Belize and Honduras, Shango in Trinidad, and Rastafari in Jamaica, and in their diasporas to North Atlantic metropolitan areas.

We have included five essays about the emergence and ongoing influence of five of these religions. Most of these essays are highly descriptive in nature and are prepared by leading authorities based on their early studies of these religions. Among the goals in creating this group of essays on this theme is to show the adaptation and ongoing effectiveness of all these and other African religions in the past and present societies where persons of Africa have lived fulfilling lives with their families for centuries.

This group of essays begins with Sidney Mintz and Michel-Rolph Trouillot's "The Social History of Haitian Vodou." These leading scholars of the Caribbean wrote this essay for general audiences. William Basom clearly outlines the essentials of Cuba's major African religion in "The Focus of Cuban Santeria." Abril Trigo's "Candomble and the Reterritorialization of Cultures" shows the major readjustments made within Brazilian society that indicate the expanding role of this, the most widely observed of African religions in the Americas. Anthropologist Frances Henry presents a clear description of Trinidad's Shango religion in "The Orisha Religion in Trinidad Today." Michael Barnett's "Rastafarianism as An African Diaspora Phenomenon" describes the historical roots of this religion that emerged in Jamaica during the early 1930s. Another anthropologist, Martin Holbraad, examines the recent outstanding appeal of Ifa Cults in socialist Cuba to a new kind of worship in his "Religious Speculation: The Rise of Ifa Cults and Consumption in Post Soviet Havana" indicating the excitement that Ifa cultists created in present-day Cuba.

The tenth section, "The Challenges of Freedom and Liberty" examines three of the major themes that captured the imagination of the newly emancipated populations of African descent through the latter half of the nineteenth century and the first half of the twentieth. The emerging leaders within the African Diaspora from Brazil to Canada recognized that although slavery was over, their people were not truly free. Consequently, the ideas of Black Nationalism, the Back to Africa movement and Pan-Africanism were extremely attractive and appealing to many activists and became part of an important dialogue that forced segments of the various scattered populations within the African Diaspora to listen and respond, based on their particular experience within their host country. While the purveyors of these ideas did not often have broad-based support and wide appeal within communities, their messages and actions were taken seriously by authorities and policy-makers, and in many ways moved the reluctant leaders of the wider community to make significant concessions that greatly benefited the entire African Diaspora community.

There are seven essays in this section. The first essay portrays the view and work of Hilary Teage, who was the editor of the *Liberia Herald* from 1834 to 1850. The author, Carl Patrick Burrowes, describes the issues that Teage promoted to move the West African colony of former African American slaves toward its gaining of political independence in 1847. The second essay is taken from the autobiography of Booker T. Washington, *Up from Slavery* and his famous 1895

Atlanta speech, and gives insight into the views of one of the most influential African Americans at the turn of the twentieth century. Next, Jeremiah Dibua and Colin Legum examine the circumstances around the creation and flowering of the Pan-African movement during the early twentieth century. Colin Legum's "Back to Africa, 1958–1962" concentrates on the later developments and activities that had always characterized the Pan-African Congresses but that focused on improving socioeconomic and political conditions in Africa. The next pair of essays deals with the views and activities of the two most prominent and effective Black Nationalist leaders of the twentieth century, Marcus Mosiah Garvey and Malcolm X. Tony Martin, one of the leading authorities on the life of Garvey and Garveyism, makes many compelling points in "Marcus Garvey, the Caribbean and the Struggle for Black Jamaican Nationhood." He describes the enormous impact of Garvey's ideas and work during his lifetime even after the actual decline of his organization, the Universal Negro Improvement Association. Martin suggests that Garvey's views eventually led to many meaningful social, economic, and political changes. The second narrative on Black Nationalism comprises selected excerpts from the autobiography of Malcolm X. These passages capture the times, moods, and wide range of experiences that engulfed the life of one of the most charismatic Black Nationalists of the 1960s. These paragraphs are among the most revealing and insightful passages in his autobiography, and highlight some of the extremely critical views that he espoused.

Our final entry is a brief but insightful essay by W. Arthur Lewis, entitled "Colonial Relations." This article is clearly written and describes how European powers used the colonial system to their advantage in areas where there were large populations of persons of African descent.

The eleventh and final section, "Africans in the Global Community: Reaching Back," comprises six provocative essays prepared by scholars from various disciplines. This subject considers some of the most significant issues with which African Diaspora populations have had to wrestle for most of their existence. Edwin Dorn and Walter Carrington's "Three Centuries Removed: Black Americans and Their African Connections" points to attempts made over this period by Africans in the Diaspora to contribute and help shape the destiny of the African motherland. The second essay is by A. Mazrui. His short discourse "Islam and the Black Diaspora: The Impact of Islam migration" examines the growing trend for significant numbers of Africans in the Diaspora to become followers of Islam and examines its implications for the future. Ethan Miachaeli's "Another Exodus: The Hebrew Israelites from Chicago to Dimona," written by a reporter for the *Chicago Defender*, traces the experiences of an African American group who emigrated from the United States in the late 1960s to Liberia, and later, to the state of Israel, where the mostly African American immigrants settled in a land that they consider to be located in northeast Africa. Keith Richburg's "American in Africa: A Black Journalist's Story" returns the focus to examining Africa. The essay, published before his longer autobiography, raises a number of issues that are important for students of the African Diaspora in their attempts to better understand contemporary Africa. Richburg, a leading African American journalist for the *Washington Post*, witnessed and made critical observations regarding a number of human tragedies that are often not dealt with so forthrightly in the public arena by authors of African descent. The next essay, authored by Molefi Kete Asante, deals with one of the most hotly debated subjects related to the African Diaspora experience in recent years. Asante's "The African American Warrant for Reparations: The Crime of European Enslavement of Africans and Its Consequences" outlines the major arguments that are under discussion in these debates. He also seeks to justify the necessity for all segments of the American public to get involved in the discussion and resolve this matter that has been around for more than a century and a half.

The final entry in this fourth edition is a strident letter written to the editor of the *Washington Post* in August 2007 regarding the growing number of Western activists who are involved in numerous African causes including the struggles to end the genocide in the Darfur region of the Republic of Sudan. The young American novelist of Nigerian parents, Uzo Dinma Iweala's, "Stop Trying to 'Save' Africa" illustrates that the younger generation, born in the African Diaspora, continue to view Africa as the homeland and are deeply concerned about the repercussions of Western involvement there. These essays represent serious attempts by persons and groups of the African Diaspora community to return to the motherland and become part of the dialogue about the African Diaspora experience.

There are seven maps on the first pages of this book that highlight the close relationship between the geography and history of Africa and those of the Diaspora from ancient to contemporary times. The maps show Africa during pre-colonial times and during the European occupation of Africa prior to World War I. The third map identifies the trans-Sahara African trade routes as well as those taken by Africans who migrated to the Mediterranean basin, Europe, the Middle East and parts of the Far East. One of the most revealing maps highlights the major areas along the African coast from where Africans were taken and the Middle Passage route, as well as where the largest percentages arrived and settled in the Caribbean and across the Americas. The fifth map identifies the many nations in the Caribbean and Latin America where a significant percentage of the peoples of African descent presently live. The sixth map shows the wide distribution of the African American population across the United States, and the final map gives the borders and dates of the present-day independent African States.

MAPS OF AFRICAN DIASPORA

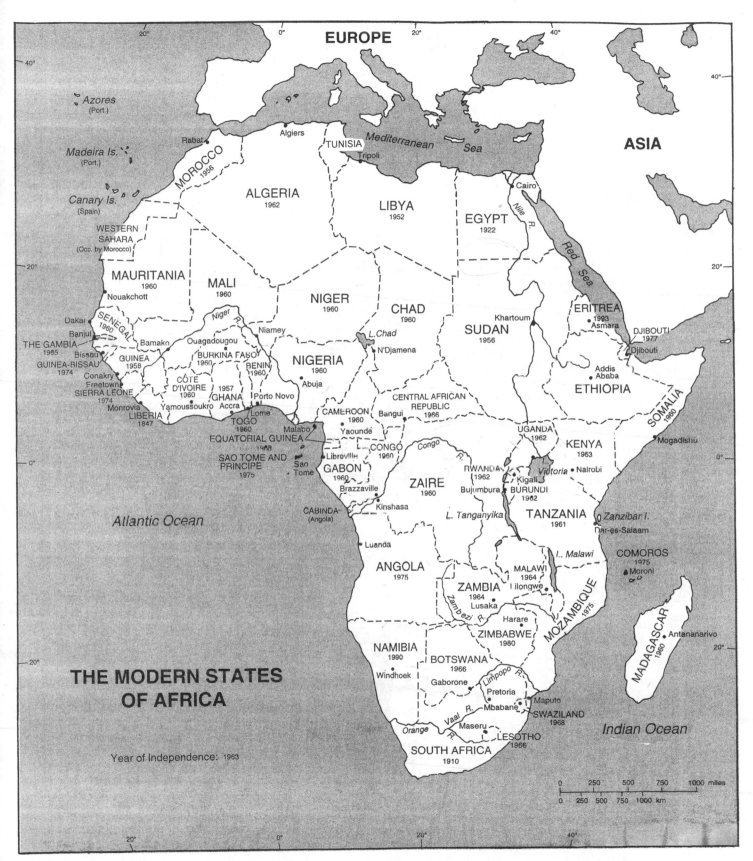

THE MODERN STATES
OF AFRICA

Year of Independence: 1963

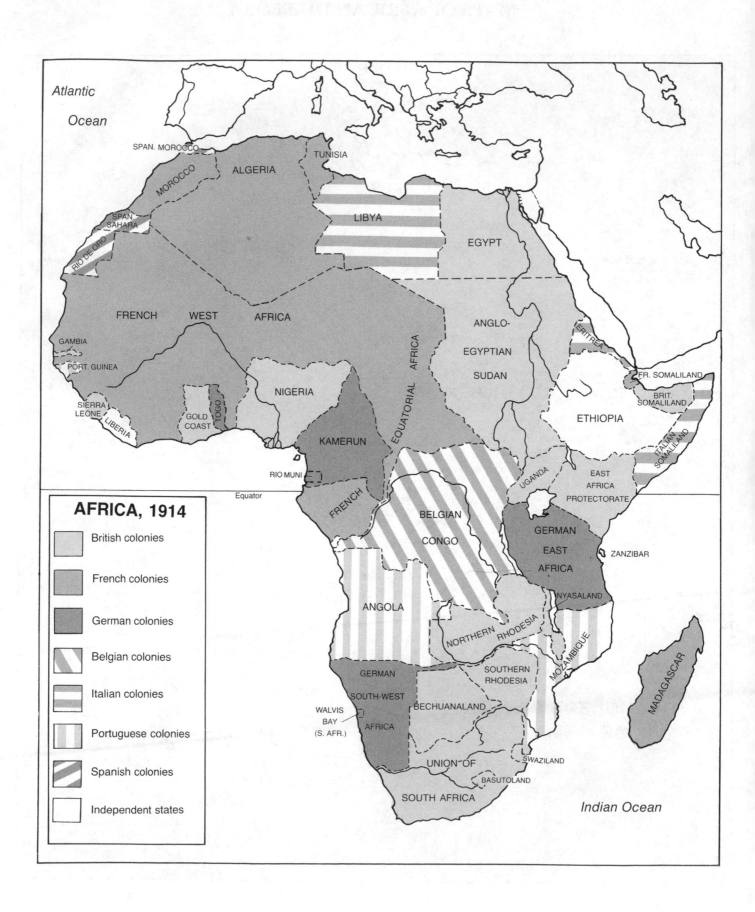

Atlantic

Ocean

SPAN. MOROCCO

MOROCCO

TUNISIA

ALGERIA

LIBYA

EGYPT

SPAN
SAHARA

RIO DE ORO

FRENCH   WEST   AFRICA

ANGLO-
EGYPTIAN
SUDAN

ERITREA

GAMBIA

PORT. GUINEA

NIGERIA

EQUATORIAL AFRICA

FR. SOMALILAND

BRIT.
SOMALILAND

SIERRA
LEONE

LIBERIA

GOLD
COAST

TOGO

KAMERUN

ETHIOPIA

ITALIAN
SOMALILAND

RIO MUNI

FRENCH

Equator

BELGIAN

CONGO

UGANDA

EAST
AFRICA
PROTECTORATE

GERMAN
EAST
AFRICA

ZANZIBAR

AFRICA, 1914

British colonies

French colonies

German colonies

Belgian colonies

Italian colonies

Portuguese colonies

Spanish colonies

Independent states

ANGOLA

NORTHERN   RHODESIA

SOUTHERN
RHODESIA

NYASALAND

MOZAMBIQUE

MADAGASCAR

GERMAN
SOUTH-WEST
AFRICA

WALVIS
BAY
(S. AFR.)

BECHUANALAND

UNION OF

SWAZILAND

BASUTOLAND

SOUTH AFRICA

Indian Ocean

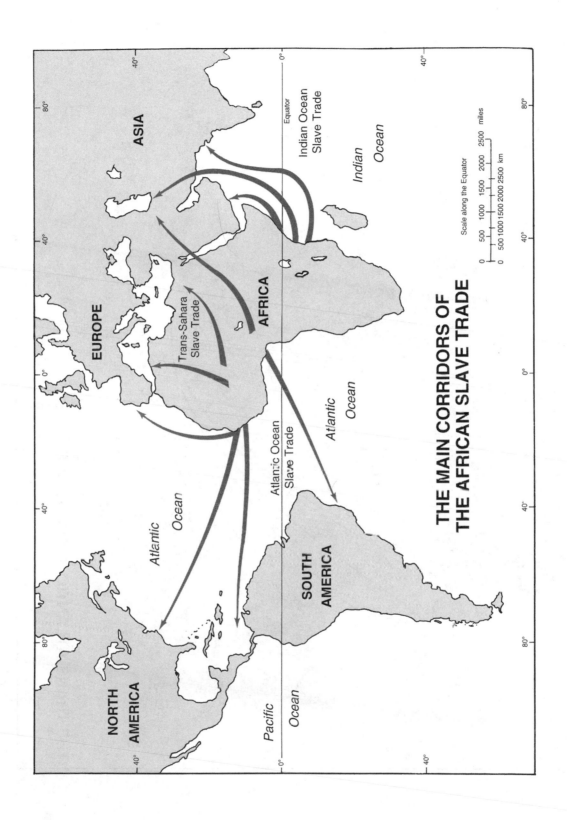

THE MAIN CORRIDORS OF
THE AFRICAN SLAVE TRADE

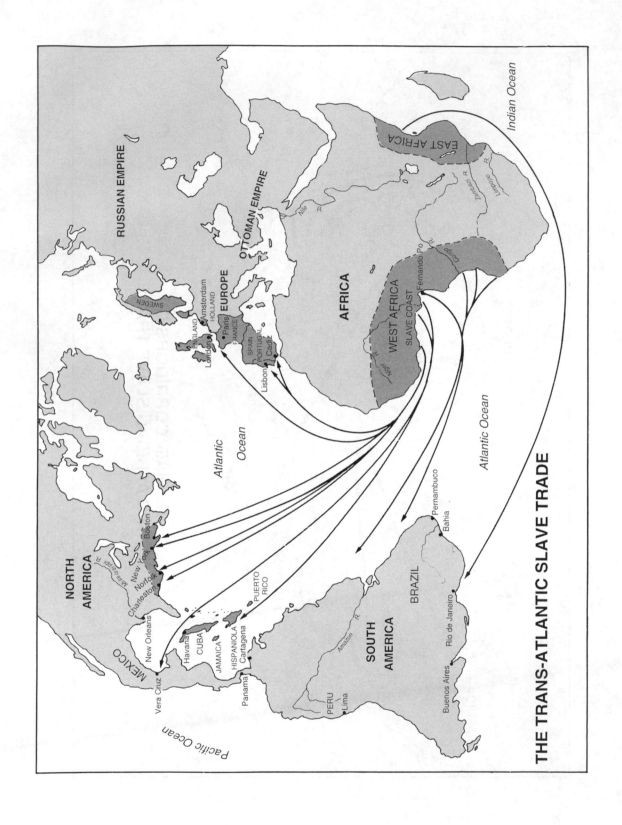

THE TRANS-ATLANTIC SLAVE TRADE

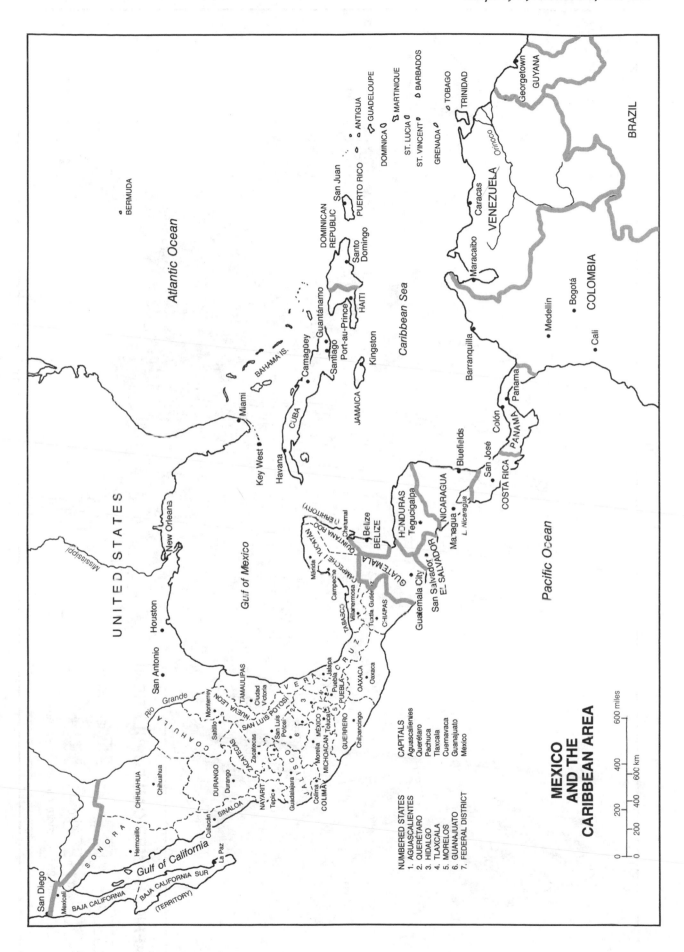

MEXICO
AND THE
CARIBBEAN AREA

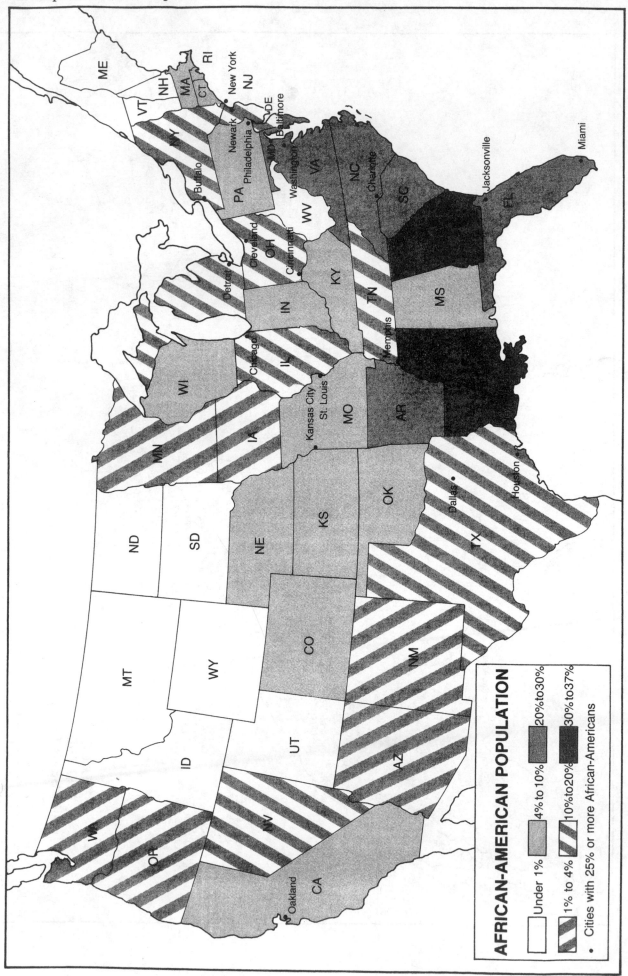

AFRICAN-AMERICAN POPULATION

Under 1%

4% to 10%

1% to 4%

10%to20%

20%to30%

30%to37%

• Cities with 25% or more African-Americans

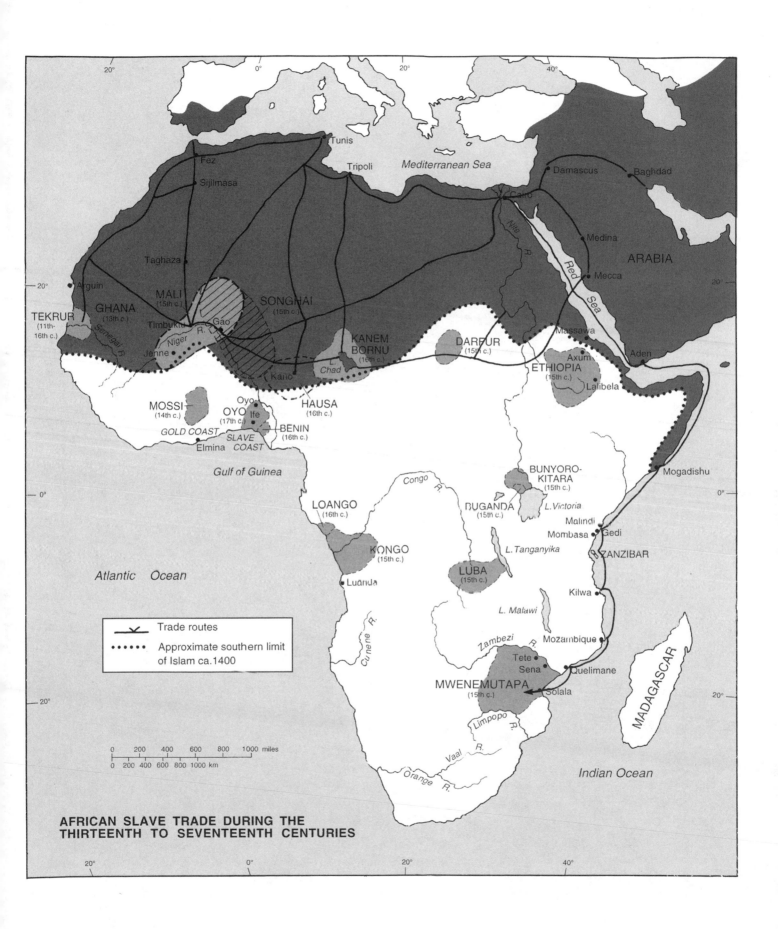

**AFRICAN SLAVE TRADE DURING THE
THIRTEENTH TO SEVENTEENTH CENTURIES**

SECTION ONE:
AN EXAMINATION OF
AFRICAN DIASPORA THEMES

Introduction

Since the recent proliferation of articles, monographs, and conferences on various aspects and issues related to the study of the African Diaspora experience, a wide range of scholars have expressed their views and given new insights into what they consider appropriate perspectives and methodologies for the widening field of African Diaspora Studies. The main objective of this first section is to include published and clearly written critical essays that raise new questions, and suggest new directions for the methodological approaches that scholars should use in researching and writing about this theme.

The first essay in this section is probably among one of the earliest articles to clearly outline the fundamental parameters for studying and researching African Diaspora themes. The author is Joseph E. Harris of Howard University who is widely acknowledged as one of the leading pioneers of the Modern African Diaspora Studies movement. In this essay, Harris emphasizes the historical magnitude, the geographic scope as well as a heritage worth preserving under the topic "The Dynamics of the Global African Diaspora." Although this essay was first delivered over two decades as a lecture and later appeared in Harris's 1982 edited work *Global Dimensions of the African Diaspora*, its treatment of the theme for general readers has not been surpassed. Furthermore, Harris's views at the time reflect the early focus of the early African Diaspora at Howard University in the summer of 1979, where scholars from Africa, Europe, Latin America, the Caribbean, and the United States participated. He retired as Distinguished Professor of African History at Howard after teaching history at Northwestern University and was a visiting professor of History at the University of Nairobi in Kenya. His many publications include *The African Presence in Asia: Consequences of the Early African Slave Trade* (1971); *Africa and Africans* (1981); *Africans and Their History* (1987); *African Americans' Reactions to the War in Ethiopia 1936–1941* (1994); *and Global Dimensions of the African Diaspora* (1982, 1993).

The second essay is written by Colin A. Palmer who reexamines more closely the various approaches to the study of the African Diaspora. He argues that in order to adequately study any aspect of the African Diaspora, one should begin with and relate it to the history of Africa. He further declares any study related to the African Diaspora experience should "be subjected to the same methodological rigor as any other area of knowledge, free from romantic condescension, essentialism, and distracting fads."

Palmer is Dodge Professor of History at Princeton University and has authored a wide range of works on various aspects of the African Diaspora experience. He was also distinguished Professor of History at the Graduate School and University Center of the City University of New York as well as Chairperson of the Department of History at the University of North Carolina, Chapel Hill. His publications include *Passageways: An Interpretative History of Black America* (1998*); Africa's Children: The Black Experience in the Americas; Human Cargoes: The British Slave Trade to Spanish America, 1700–1739* (1981); and *Slaves of the White God: Blacks in Mexico, 1570–1650* (1976). He is the recent author of *Eric Williams and the Making of the Modern Caribbean* (2006).

The third essay is Kristin Mann's "Shifting Paradigms in the Study of the African Diaspora and of Atlantic History and Culture" that was published in 2001 in the journal, *Slavery and Abolition*. It is one of many similar essays that encourages scholars to expand their view of what should be considered as appropriate areas of inquiry with the discipline. Mann is professor of History at Emory University and has interest in social and economic African history as it relates to gender, marriage, and the family. She is the author of many works on West Africa, especially Nigerian Colonial history on the following topics: *Marrying Well: Marriage, Status and Social Change Among the Educated Elite in Colonial Lagos*, co-editor of *Law in Colonial Africa and Rethinking the African Diaspora: The Making of a Black Atlantic World in the Bight of Benin and Brazil*.

The final essay in this section seeks to outline to students of the African Diaspora the age-old debate regarding the long held views about the inferiority of persons of African descent. The author, Edith R. Sanders, in "The Hamitic Hypothesis: Its Origin in Time," traces the negative views that both ancient and modern Western writers used to portray Africans as naturally inferior to other world groups. This essay appeared in *The Journal of African History* and has been repeatedly requested by a number of our classroom instructors who felt that students needed to read about the long and varied history of the "Hamitic Hypothesis." Sanders was an anthropologist who received her Ph.D. from Columbia University and taught at Fairleigh Dickinson University in New Jersey and Fordham University in New York City.

The Dynamics of the Global African Diaspora

Joseph E. Harris

The African diaspora is a triadic relationship linking a dispersed group of people to the homeland, Africa, and to their host or adopted countries. Diasporas develop and reinforce images and ideas about themselves and their original homelands, as well as affect the economies, politics, and social dynamics of both the homeland and the host country or area. Diasporas are therefore significant factors in national and international relations.

In recent years the term *diaspora* has become increasingly common in studies of African, Chinese, Indian, and other communities outside their original homelands. These communities reside in and have loyalty to their adopted country but also identify with and maintain connections to their country of origin. This relationship helps explain the depth of complexity in the dynamics between the people in these communities, their homelands, and their host countries. Thus, it is important that we understand the historical development and impact of the linkages between Africa and its diaspora communities. Historically, the Jews and Irish have received considerable attention as diaspora communities with influence abroad. However, the study of diasporas is especially timely today because of the current fragmentation and displacement of people throughout the world: in Eastern Europe, for example, the former Yugoslavia and the Soviet Union; South and Southeast Asia, especially India, Vietnam, and Cambodia; and Africa, notably Ethiopia, Somalia, and Rwanda. More recent and urgent for Americans is the mass immigration of Haitians, Cubans, Mexicans, Vietnamese, and Chinese into the United States. These diaspora groups share characteristics of ethnic identity, marginality, and homeland linkage, and one cannot understand them without an examination of their original homelands and the root causes and specific contexts within which they were dispersed.

The case of Africans and their descendants abroad is especially complex, with a long history of international dispersion, stereotypes, and myths that continue to obstruct policies and practices to guarantee freedom and justice. The facts in this instance are fairly well-known and are rooted in centuries of Africans being characterized as inferior, destined to be slaves, incapable of developing complex societies, lacking a meaningful cultural history, and uncivilized and thus having made no contribution to world civilization; this list could be expanded. These myths and variations of them persist in spite of evidence to the contrary. Yet recent research amply demonstrates the dynamic and rich heritage of Africa and its diaspora: abundant evidence of African achievements in continuing archaeological discoveries, the reconstruction of ancient and complex societies in Africa and their impact on other parts of the world; the commercial relations of Africans, Arabs, and Asians in the Indian Ocean since ancient times; the creative art of Benin, Dogon, and other African societies; the literary accomplishments of Africans in pre- and early Islamic Arabia; the roles Africans played in the rise and expansion of Islam and Christianity; the early relations between Mali, Kongo, and other African states with Portugal prior to the slave trade; and the many accomplishments of Africans and their descendants in Europe and the Americas.

This essay, then, will examine the global dispersion of African peoples since ancient times, making a distinction between the historical and modern diasporas, will provide evidence of the continuity of their consciousness of and identity with Africa, and will assess the gradual transformation from African to African American and the implications of that development. Although primary focus on the African diaspora has been placed on the slave trade, one should remember that Africans traveled voluntarily throughout much of the world long before the slave trade existed. In ancient times they traveled as merchants and sailors, many of whom settled in Europe, the Middle East, and Asia. Some came as soldiers and remained permanently. There are many examples of Africans engaged in sports and the arts in the Middle East and Europe, and some of these people became residents. Others served as missionaries for Islam and Christianity and settled in the Middle East, Asia, and Europe. Several Ethiopian monks accompanied European Crusaders to Rome, in the Middle Ages. Free Africans also participated in the exploration and development of the Americas: Canada, the Caribbean and Central America, and North and South America. Long before the Age of European Exploration, Africans, like other people, traveled abroad as free persons and often settled in their host countries.

It was, however, the slave trade that made the African presence essentially global. For at least fifteen hundred years prior to the European-conducted trade in African slaves, Arabs conducted a slave trade across the Sahara Desert, the Mediterranean Sea, the Red Sea, and the Indian Ocean, and they took Africans to Arabia, India, and the Far East. Enslaved Africans worked in the Persian Gulf in salt mines, coconut groves, and date plantations; in Arabia and India as domestics and field hands; and throughout much of the Muslim world as concubines and eunuchs.

Today discrete communities of African descent can be found in Iran (Bander Abbas, Jiruft, Shiraz, and Tehran), in Iraq (Baghdad and Basra), in Pakistan (Karachi, Lahore, and Baluchistan), and in India (Hyderabad, Ahmadabad, Surat, Cutch, and Gujarat). Many people of African origin reside in communities of mixed descent throughout Asia. Little evidence has appeared to identify contemporary African descendants in China and Japan dating from this period, although the historical record shows that Africans were taken to Macao, Hwangchou, and Nagasaki in the sixteenth century.

The largest number of enslaved Africans were settled in India. Known as Siddis and Habshis, Africans served as administrators, guards, sailors, and farm hands. Large numbers of enslaved and free Africans served in Muslim armies in Gujarat in the thirteenth century, and in India today there remains the Habshi Kot, an Ethiopian fort with tombs of African soldiers and nobles. During the Medieval period Europeans and Arabs captured and sold Africans in the Mediterranean area. Africans were shipped from Tunis and Cyrenaica to Barcelona, Genoa, Naples, Turkey, and the Middle East. Indeed, Africans were settled along wide stretches of the northern Mediterranean coast.

It was the European Age of Exploration in the fifteenth century, however, that led to the greatest dispersion of Africans in history. Although occurring in a shorter time-frame than that of the Arabs, the European-conducted slave trade enveloped the continent. In 1444 a company was established in Lagos, Portugal, to engage in the slave trade. That year some 240 bonded Africans were appropriated by Prince Henry, the church of Lagos, the Franciscans of Saint Cape Vincent, and some merchants. By 1448 a regular trade in goods and Africans had been established between Arguim and Portugal. Africans worked in the mines, at construction, on farms, and as guards, soldiers, domestics, couriers, stevedores, concubines, and factory workers. Slave communities were established in Lisbon, Barcelona, Cadiz, Seville, and Valencia. Africans were also taken to the Spanish possession of The Netherlands.

In spite of the fact that Queen Elizabeth I in 1556 observed that there were too many "blackamoores" in England and that they should be returned to Africa, their numbers continued to grow, so that by the nineteenth century there were some fifteen thousand in England. Slavery also emerged in France, despite a royal proclamation prohibiting it. Both enslaved and free Africans lived in the cities of Anjou, Lyon, Orleans, Nantes, Marseilles, Toulon, and Paris, where they worked as servants, menial laborers, pages, and entertainers.

Other parts of Europe also became home for Africans, both enslaved and free. Some joined the small communities of Ethiopian monks in Venice, Rome, and neighboring cities along the northern Mediterranean rim; others settled along the southern Adriatic coast of what today is Yugoslavia. The city of Ulcinj in particular had a number of Africans who in the sixteenth and seventeenth centuries worked as seamen in the straits of Otranto. Of eastern Europe we know very little, except for the great-grandfather of Aleksander Pushkin, who was reexported from Turkey to Russia.

When the Europeans defeated the Arabs and took control of the Indian ocean trade routes, they developed their own slave trade from Zanzibar and other regions of Africa's eastern coast to Asia. Europeans also took Africans from what today are Kenya, Tanzania, Mozambique, and Madagascar along the southern route, around the Cape of Good Hope to Buenos Aires in Argentina, Montevideo in Uruguay, and Rio de Janeiro in Brazil. Africans were marched overland from Buenos Aires and Montevideo through the passes of the Andean Mountains to enslavement in Santiago and Valparaiso in Chile; from Rio de Janeiro through Paraguay and Bolivia to Lima and Callao in Peru.

The northern route from East Africa extended around the cape to northern Brazil and into the Caribbean, where some Africans were sold and others were transported to North American cities such as Mobile, Charleston, and Richmond. Cartegena in Colombia became a major port from which enslaved Africans were taken overland to the Pacific coast of Choco. Others were transported to and across Panama to the Pacific coasts of Ecuador, Peru, and Chile.

The well-known Guinea coast of West Africa was the area from which European slave dealers took most of the Africans enslaved in Europe and the Americas. As early as the 1440s Africans were taken from Arguim to Portugal and sold. Enslaved Africans became more common in Spain, France, and England during the sixteenth century. Gradually the Portuguese developed tropical plantations on the offshore African islands of Cape Verde, Sao Tome, and Principe, thereby establishing a relationship between the plantation economy and enslaved African labor, both of which they transferred to the Americas.

The other major area of intensive slave trading was around the mouth of the Congo River in Zaire and upper Angola, which supplied large numbers of captive Africans to Brazil and the Caribbean Islands, as well as North America. Again, most of the Africans who reached North America were transported via the Caribbean, where they were first "seasoned."

Although not part of the slave trade, the convict labor system used by the British to populate a number of their colonial possessions constituted another means of African dispersion abroad. Convict labor drew from the prison population, which included debtors, thieves, and other criminals. The Africans in this group were usually vagrants who could not find employment in a racially biased society. At least several hundred of the original Australian settlers were Africans.

There is no way to know the exact number of Africans who were transported and enslaved abroad, but the best estimates are those for the Americas: a total of between 12 and 25 million Africans reached the American hemisphere; many others perished during the trans-Atlantic voyage. Of the arrivals, most went to Brazil, followed by the British Caribbean, the French Caribbean, Spanish American areas, and North America.

Despite the inhumane nature of the capture and enslavement of Africans, cultural continuities persisted for years in multiple ways throughout the diaspora. Africans who arrived abroad continued to speak and practice their native languages and traditions, especially during the early years and in the privacy of their quarters, homes, and social groups: they sang and danced as their cultures had taught them, referred to themselves as Africans and Ethiopians, and gave their children African names. Neither the Middle Passage nor the slave system broke their awareness of their history. This is revealed in their religious practices (Candomble and Santeria especially), songs, and oral traditions. Their culture and aspirations for freedom were expressed in different forms (songs, poetry, religion) and were sometimes employed to solidify mass followings in resistance movements, such as the ninth-century revolt in Iraq, in which Rihan Ibn Salib established an autonomous community that replicated African traditions; the sixteenth-century revolt in Mexico, in which Yanga sought to replicate Guinea; the seventeenth-century revolt led by Zumbi in Brazil, in which Palmares adopted

African traditions and remained autonomous for most of that century; the eighteenth-century revolt in Haiti initiated by the African-born Boukman and the Christian, diaspora-born Toussaint L'Ouverture, and which resulted in independence; and the abortive nineteenth-century revolt in Virginia, led by the African Gullah Jack and diaspora-born Nat Turner. All of these freedom movements incorporated traditional symbols and ceremonies around which Africans rallied.

As important as was the struggle for freedom, it must be emphasized that Africans did much more than think about their enslavement. They were primarily occupied with daily life, which necessitated creativity and a degree of accommodation to local conditions. These Africans were concerned about family and community life, with such social organizations as churches, lodges, and mutual aid and burial groups. They learned European languages and culture; in time some converted to Christianity. In Asia they learned Arabic, Farsi, Gujarati, Urdu, and other languages, and some of them converted to Islam. Throughout Europe and Asia they distinguished themselves as artists, writers, poets, teachers, and inventors. This gradual transformation from African to African American or African European, for example, helps to explain the complexity and dialectical contradictions in the relations between the African diaspora and the homeland, the phenomenon behind W. E. B. Du Bois's concept of "double consciousness."

This necessarily brief discussion of the historical diaspora confirms a global dispersion and settlement of Africans, who settled abroad voluntarily and involuntarily and maintained a consciousness of their homeland and their identity while adapting to new societies. This phase of the diaspora was largely a heritage of the slave trade and enslavement, but it was also a period of abolitionism and the establishment of colonial rule in Africa itself during the nineteenth century. The convergence of these two phenomena resulted in the globalization of black economic and political dependence on Europeans with the consequent global entrenchment of the age-old negative images, myths, and stereotypes about Africans and their descendants.

The abolition of the slave trade reinforced African hopes to return to their homeland and increased efforts by Europeans and Americans to return them to Africa. Efforts by the former were poorly financed, encountered many obstacles, and in fact only drew from the small free community; efforts by the latter were more successful and encouraged a number of slave owners to free Africans with the stipulation that they return to Africa. Slave ships were intercepted and captive

Africans were freed and initially settled at selected points outside of Africa: Florida, briefly, for the Atlantic trade, and India, Aden, and the Seychelles for the Indian Ocean trade.

These temporary stations were replaced by permanent resettlement efforts as missionary and business groups in England and the United States realized that diaspora Africans could serve as a means to rid Europe and America of unwanted blacks and at the same time establish communities that could both expand the Christian faith and commerce and also be regarded as humanitarian. Thus it was that Sierra Leone in 1787 and Liberia in 1821 became permanent resettlement communities in West Africa for ex-slaves from the Atlantic Ocean countries, and Freretown in Kenya became the resettlement point in 1873 for ex-slaves from the Indian Ocean areas. While some African descendants abroad opposed "return to Africa" movements, others saw these projects as a means to achieve freedom, launch the redemption of the African continent, and establish themselves as viable members of the world community.

When Sierra Leone and Kenya became British colonies, the diaspora sentiment was muted, although not destroyed; Liberia, however, declared its independence in 1847 and became the second independent African country, after Ethiopia, until well into the twentieth century. By 1867 some twenty thousand African Americans had settled in Liberia and many of them had been free in the United States and returned voluntarily with material resources. Liberia thus became a symbol of hope for the regeneration of Africans on the continent and in the diaspora. Its Declaration of Independence took note of the plight of African peoples abroad and committed the country to "provide a home for the dispersed children of Africa." Although these returnees carried with them ideas of superiority taught in the United States, they did identify with Africa, which they hoped to redeem and lead into the modern world.

This return movement from the United States coincided with a growing consciousness of and identification with Africa by African Americans. A number of their church and social groups had already adopted "African" as a label and engaged in activities in the Caribbean and Africa. Indeed, although they were influenced by white denominations, black churches provided the principal opportunities for the development of sustained and meaningful links with Africa and the diaspora and the outside world.

Thus a common social condition and origin, stemming largely from the centuries-old slave trade and slavery, became more deeply embedded in the black consciousness of the diaspora. Europeans and Americans regarded enslaved Africans as chattel and free blacks as inferior beings. One of the best illustrations of this situation occurs in the American Declaration of Independence and the Constitution, in which both the concepts of freedom and inhumanity are embedded. The former portrays European settlers as victims who escaped political and economic inhumanity in Europe and who established a refuge for liberty in the American colonies, while the Constitution defines Africans as three-fifths of a white person. Other provisions of that document allowed "fugitive" (African) slaves to be tracked down like animals and treated as property. Subsequently, in 1858 the Supreme Court declared that blacks had no rights that whites had to respect.

While amendments to the Constitution have declared citizenship rights for former slaves, there never has been a constitutional recognition of the horrendous European and Euro-American inhumanity to Africans in Africa and their descendants abroad, nor has there been a strong, sustained effort by the government or the people as a whole to establish and protect African American humanity since liberation—abolition and civil rights movements notwithstanding. Stereotypes and myths about black physical and mental incapacity persist and continue to obstruct equity and justice for African Americans as a group.

A determining factor in the relations between Africans in Africa and their descendants abroad stemmed from decisions made by Europeans at the Berlin Conference of 1884–85, which essentially established the boundaries of the African states. This partition of Africa divided peoples and cultures into different countries, making them "citizens" by fiat. It initiated a new phase of population displacement and division, created an internal diaspora, and led to irredentist movements that plague the continent today.

The colonial-era partition and dispersion of Africans was marked by an accelerated gravitation of Africans to and settlement in major cities of the colonial powers: France for the Senegalese, Malians, Ivoriens, Haitians, Martinicans, Guadeloupeans, and others from French-speaking areas; England for the Ghanaians, Nigerians, Kenyans, South Africans, Jamaicans, Trinidadians, Barbadians, and others in English speaking areas; Portugal for the Angolans, Mozambicans, Cape Verdans, and Brazilians; the Netherlands for the Surinamese; Belgium for the Zairians; and the United States during the late colonial period and especially after World War II. The major cities of the Western powers thus became loci for the gathering of diverse ethnic and political groups of African origin, facilitating the development of an international network linking Africa to its diaspora; this network may be called a mobilized diaspora.

The critical factor about the earlier, primarily involuntary diaspora is that it occurred prior to the partition of Africa and therefore had no consciousness of the boundaries established during the era of colonial rule. Although the dispersion during the colonial era did begin to internalize a consciousness of the colonial territory, most Africans did not directly or fully confront the colonial presence. When the colonial era ended, after less than a century in most cases, the colonial identity had not fully matured. Consequently, until the 1960s most Africans in Africa retained a primary ethnic allegiance, while their descendants abroad constituted a "stateless" diaspora without a common county of origin, language, religion, or culture. The strength of the connection between Africans and the African diaspora remained essentially their common origin in Africa as a whole and a common social condition (social, economic, and political marginalization) throughout the world.

It was this combination that paved the way for the development of an effective international network by the mobilized African diaspora, namely, descendant Africans with a consciousness of the identity of their roots, occupational and communication skills, social and economic status, and access to decision-making bodies in their host country. For blacks this meant the mobilization of their communities around race or ethnicity for the exertion of political pressure on elected officials. In time they elected members of their own group to offices at virtually all levels of local, state, and national government.

From the early years of the twentieth century, African American migration from southern states resulted in the gradual emergence of large segregated communities in such northern American cities as Washington, Philadelphia, New York, Detroit, and Chicago. This pattern of migrations increased significantly after World War I. In these cities African Americans found better educational and employment opportunities, which also attracted black immigrants from Caribbean countries, notably Jamaica, Barbados, Trinidad, and Panama. New York City was the principal recipient of this emerging international community of blacks.

A somewhat similar development was expanding with immigrants primarily from Jamaica, Barbados, and Trinidad. London had long been a place where blacks from the West Indies, the United States, and Africa were familiar as abolitionists, businessmen, journalists, scholars, and travelers. As early as 1900 Henry Sylvester Williams of Trinidad and W. E. B. Du Bois of the United States had convened the first Pan-African Congress to mobilize African people in a coordinated international effort against racism in the African colonies and communities of blacks in the diaspora.

Although the Congress demonstrated that Africans and their descendants abroad shared common interests and were prepared to seek a common means to satisfy their concerns, it was not until after World War I that the Pan-African movement would have a sustained impact. Du Bois revived the movement and convened four congresses (in 1919, 1921, 1923, and 1927) with similar objectives of human rights for African peoples.

Marcus Garvey, a Jamaican, arrived in the United States in 1916 after having traveled widely in the Caribbean and South America, where he protested against white exploitation of blacks. In the United States he organized the Universal Negro Improvement Association (UNIA), with branches throughout much of the African world. His newspaper, *The Negro World*, appeared in English, French, and Spanish and made a strong appeal for black unity, pride, and organization. His Black Star Line was organized not only to transport blacks who wanted to go to Africa but also to initiate commercial relations between Africa and its diaspora. Although his projects failed and he was deported from the United States, Garvey contributed immeasurably to the development of a consciousness of Africa in the diaspora and to racial pride and organization. Garveyites continued his tradition by maintaining branches of UNIA and participating in numerous organizations dedicated to black progress.

Du Bois and Garvey were giants of their time, but there were many others who contributed significantly to the cause of Africa and its diaspora between the two World Wars: Casely Hayford and Kwame Nkrumah of Ghana, Ladipo Solanke and Nnamdi Azikiwe of Nigeria, Duse Mohammed of Sudan, Jomo Kenyatta of Kenya, Candace Gratien of Guadeloupe, Leopold Sedar Senghor of Senegal, Leon Damas of Guyana, Aimee Cesaire of Martinique, Jean Price-Mars and Dantes Bellegarde of Haiti, Ras Makonnen of Guyana, and George Padmore and C. L. R. James of Trinidad.

A number of less well-known but important leaders and organizations either joined the better-known groups or organized their own to mobilize African peoples worldwide: William Leo Hansberry and William R. Steen organized the Ethiopian Research Council in the United States; Malaku Bayen, an Ethiopian, organized the Ethiopian World Federation in the United States; Max Yergen, W. E. B. Du Bois, and Paul Robeson organized the International Committee on Africa, which became the Council for African Affairs; C. L. R. James organized the International Friends of

Ethiopia in London, with branches in the United States and the Caribbean; George Padmore, a Jamaican, and Ras Makonnen, a Guyanan, organized the International African Service Bureau in London; and Alioune Diop, a Senegalese, organized the Society for African Culture in France, while John A. Davis and others organized an affiliate in the United States, the American Society for African Culture. In short, members of the mobilized diaspora pioneered the establishment of international organizations promoting African consciousness and solidarity in what essentially became a foreign relations movement. Prevented from being actors in state foreign affairs, these leaders established their own nonstate mechanisms for the conduct of foreign affairs in the interests of Africans and their descendants abroad.

The Congressional Black Caucus in 1960 represented a major step toward the official participation of blacks in the foreign affairs of its country. Mobilized black voters elected three congressmen who became the founding members of the Caucus. The membership increased to forty in 1992 and gave the organization significant political influence. Caucus leaders soon realized that their impact on foreign policy centered on African world issues, and, without conceding their right to input on foreign affairs generally, they embraced Africa and the Caribbean as their special domain. Members of their staffs followed by forming the African Forum on Foreign Affairs, which soon evolved into TransAfrica, the established lobby for African and Caribbean issues in the United States. Its influence on U.S. policy regarding South Africa and Haiti in particular has legitimized it as a force in world politics for Africa and its diaspora.

The dynamics of black nationalism in the African world during the last generation has transformed the meaning of identity in Africa and the diaspora. Whereas the diaspora of the slave trade era was essentially "stateless," relying primarily on an Africa remembered, the post-independence diaspora promotes a consciousness of new nations, sometimes with new names and ideologies that challenge the older diaspora to make choices between conflicting interests not only within the diaspora community, but also between it and particular African countries. The existence of over fifty African countries with varying social and political conditions and different international interests further complicates the relationship between Africa and its diaspora. Moreover, the legacy of colonial internal division and dispersion of ethnic groups form a kind of diaspora that African states must confront also.

In the United States, diverse interests and ideologies are evident, and they are complicated by the continuous influx of continental Africans and Americans of African descent from the Caribbean and increasingly from South American countries. Consequently, the geographical area of focus for African Americans has been expanded to include French-, Spanish-, and Portuguese-speaking areas of the Americas.

Noteworthy in this modern phase of the diaspora is that whereas prior to independence continental Africans and African Americans used nongovernmental networks (churches, social groups, schools, etcetera) as the principal conduit for the promotion of their ideas and policies, independent African leaders must negotiate their interests through governments and their representatives, thereby excluding effective nongovernmental agencies of the diaspora. While this approach maximizes economic dimensions for African states, it minimizes the cultural and social dimensions that continue to sustain the mutual identity between them and their diaspora, a significant political force in time of need.

If direct and effective relations are to be cultivated, Africa and its diaspora must devise other structures to achieve their goals. This could take the form of a non-political organization or foundation that reaches across national boundaries and that represents African governments and private organizations and diaspora groups for broad consultative purposes and humanitarian assistance. The African world would benefit greatly from having this kind of international structure with the financial capability to initiate and fund programs without reliance on outside financial or political support. Such autonomy would enable Africans and their descendants abroad to sustain their political presence and work with greater confidence in alliance with other groups interested in their social, political, and economic well-being.

Such a form of Pan-Africanism is better described as Trans-Africanism, best demonstrated in the 1930s when Ethiopia resisted Italian aggression. Organized groups of Americans of African descent in the United States mobilized efforts and contributed money, supplies, and advisers to assist the Ethiopians during and after the war. These groups also ventured into private diplomacy: developing a code, communicating directly through their network with Haile Selassie, and persuading him to appoint a representative to the United States. These efforts demonstrated the strength the diaspora could display when compelled to action by African issues. In addition, the reciprocal involvement of Ethiopians with these groups heightened the political consciousness of African Americans and contributed to their greater participation in the democratic process of their country.

A particular problem that has prevented the fuller development of this trend has been the diversity of the groups involved and the scope of issues African Americans have attempted to address internally while pursuing issues under the rubric of Pan-Africanism or Trans-Africanism. The independence of over fifty African countries and a dozen in the Caribbean continue to divert attention and limited material resources.

The last decade of the twentieth century is marked by countries and cultures being pulled closer together by technology, world health issues, and international trade. Moreover, the United States has emerged as the lone superpower and is thus obliged to respond to issues of world significance. As the preeminent country of mobilized diasporas, the United States can enhance its role by enlisting its diasporas as bridges to troubled lands—as teachers, scientists, technicians, and emissaries for peace and development.

Over the centuries African Americans, by their sustained struggle for justice, have contributed significantly to the positive international image of this country's potential for real democracy. They have remained in the vanguard of struggles of human rights for minorities, women, and other under-represented groups. From the abolitionist travels and egalitarian appeals of Frederick Douglass and others in the nineteenth century to Martin Luther King and Malcolm X in the twentieth and to the adoption by Africans, Asians, and Europeans in freedom struggles of the anthem "We Shall Overcome," African Americans have aligned the United States with struggles against racism and colonialism. It is no accident that two of the five black Nobel Peace Laureates—Ralph Bunche and Martin Luther King—are African Americans; the other three—Albert Luthuli, Bishop Tutu and Nelson Mandela—are South Africans, whose heritage in many ways parallels that of African Americans.

Blacks in the United States are conscious of their relationship to the global African presence; they have a long and steadfast tradition of association not only with African people, but also with other minorities, with the poor and disadvantaged, and with women. African Americans have remained in the vanguard of the struggle for human rights and since the 1930s have increasingly asserted themselves in international affairs. The twenty-first century may well witness the convergence of this heritage and the skills of the diaspora with the political and economic development of Africa and thus the full participation of the African world in international affairs.

---

[1]St. Clair Drake, *Black Folk Here and There*, 2 volumes (Los Angeles: Center for Afro American Studies, 1986, 1990) is a major source for a study of the global presence of African peoples; Joseph E. Harris, ed., *Global Dimensions of the African Diaspora* (Washington, D.C.: Howard University Press, 1993) includes essays on various regions, concepts, and themes relevant to the African diaspora.

[2]Bernard Lewis, *Race and Slavery in the Middle East* (New York: Oxford University Press, 1990); Joseph E. Harris, *The African Presence in Asia: Consequences of the East African Slave Trade* (Evanston, Ill.: Northwestern University Press, 1971); Harris, "Scope of the African Diaspora" (Silver Spring, Md.: African Diaspora Maps, 1990).

[3]See *The African Slave Trade from the Fifteenth to the Nineteenth Century* (Paris: UNESCO, 1979); Ibrahim B. Kake, *Les Nôtres do la Diaspora* (Libreville, Gabon, 1978); Leslie Rout, *The African Experience in Spanish America* (Cambridge: Cambridge University Press, 1976); Folarin Shyllon, *Black People in Britain* (London: Oxford University Press, 1977).

[4]Philip D. Curtin, *The Atlantic Slave Trade: A Census* (Madison: University of Wisconsin Press, 1969), although dated, remains a valuable source; Joseph Inikori, *Forced Migration* (New York: Africana 1982) is an excellent study that revises much of Curtin's work.

[5]For cultural manifestations in the Americas, see Robert Farris Thompson, *Flash of the Spirit* (New York: Vintage, 1984). For revolts, see Alexandre Popovic, *La Révolte des Esclaves en Iraq au III"/IX' Siècle* (Paris: P. Geuthner, 1976); Colin Palmer, *Slaves of the White God: Blacks in Mexico, 1570–1650* (Cambridge: Cambridge University Press, 1976); Manuel Carneiro da Cunha, *Negros, Estrangeiros* (São Paulo, Brazil: Brasiliense, 1985); C. L. James, *Black Jacobins* (New York: Vintage, 1963); Frederico Brito Figueroa, *Venezuela Colonial: Las Rebelliones De Esclavos Y La Revolucion Francesa* (Caracas, Venezuela: CUHALC, 1989); and Harris, *Global Dimensions of the African Diaspora*.

[6]W. E. B. DuBois, *Souls of Black Folk* (New York: Fawcett, 1961).

[7]Arthur T. Porter, *Creoledom: A Study of the Development of the Freetown Society* (London: Oxford University Press, 1963); Akintole Wyse, *The Krio of Sierra Leone: An Interpretive History* (Washington, D.C.: Howard University Press, 1991); Tom Shick, *Behold the Promised Land: A History of Afro-American Settler in Nineteenth Century Liberia* (Baltimore: Johns Hopkins University Press, 1980); Harris, *Repatriates and Refugees in a Colonial Society: The Case of Kenya* (Washington, D.C.: Howard University Press, 1987).

[8]A. I. Asiwaju, *Partitioned Africans: Ethnic Relations Across Africa's International Boundaries, 1884–1994* (Lagos: Lagos University Presse, 1985).

non political organizations and foundations to reach across national boundaries and that represent African govts for conservative purposes and humanitarian assistance,

[9]See Vincent Thompson, *Africa and Unity* (New York: Humanities Press, 1969); W. E. B. DuBois, *The World and Africa* (New York: 1947); J. Ayodele Langley; *Pan-Africanism and Nationalism in West Africa, 1900–1945* (Oxford: Clarendon Press, 1973); Ras Makonnen, *Pan-Africanism From Within* (New York: Oxford University Press, 1973); and Drake, "Diaspora Studies and Pan-Africanism," in Harris, ed., *Global Dimensions of the African Diaspora*, pp. 451–514.

Defining and Studying the Modern African Diaspora

Colin Palmer

As a field of study, the African diaspora has gathered momentum in recent times. This is reflected in the proliferating conferences, courses, PhD programs, faculty positions, book prizes, and the number of scholars who define themselves as specialists. But, as far as I know, no one has really attempted a systematic and comprehen-sive definition of the term "African diaspora," although the concept has been around since the 19th century and the term has been used since the 1960s, if not earlier. Does it refer simply to Africans abroad, that is to say the peoples of African descent who live outside their ancestral continent? Is Africa a part of the diaspora? Is the term synonymous with what is now being called the Black Atlantic?

The concept of a diaspora is not confined to the peoples of African descent. For example, historians are familiar with the migration of Asians that resulted in the peopling of the Americas. Sometime between 10 and 20 thousand years ago, these Asian peoples crossed the Bering Strait and settled in North and South America and the Caribbean islands. The Jewish diaspora, perhaps the most widely studied, also has very ancient roots, beginning about two thousand years ago. Starting in the eighth century, Muslim peoples brought their religion and culture to various parts of Asia, Europe, and Africa, creating communities in the process. European peoples began their penetration of the African continent in the 15th century, a process that in time resulted in their dispersal in many other parts of the world, including the Americas. Obviously, these diasporic streams, or move-ments of specific peoples, were not the same in their timing, impetus, direction, or nature.

The study of the African diaspora, as mentioned at the outset, represents a growth industry today. But, there is no single diasporic movement or monolithic diasporic community to be studied. For the limited purposes of this discussion, I identify five major African diasporic streams that occurred at different times and for different reasons. The first African diaspora was a consequence of the great movement within and outside of Africa that began about 100,000 years ago. This early movement, the contours of which are still quite controversial, constitutes a neces-sary starting point for any study of the dispersal and settlement of African peoples. To study early humankind is, in effect, to study this diaspora. Some scholars may argue, with considerable merit, that this early African exodus is so different in character from later movements and settlements that it should not be seen as constituting a phase of the diasporic process. This issue ought to be a subject for a healthy and vigorous debate among our colleagues and students.

The second major diasporic stream began about 3000 B.C.E. with the movement of the Bantu-speaking peoples from the region that is now the contemporary nations of Nigeria and Cameroon to other parts of the African continent and to the Indian Ocean. The third major stream, which I characterize loosely as a trading diaspora, involved the movement of traders, merchants, slaves, soldiers, and others to parts of Europe, the Middle East, and Asia beginning around the fifth century B.C.E. Its pace was markedly uneven, and its texture and energy varied. Thus the brisk slave trade conducted by the Muslims to the Mediterranean and Middle Eastern countries starting after the seventh century was not a new development but its scope and intensity were certainly unprecedented. This prolonged third diasporic stream resulted in the creation of communities of various sizes composed of peoples of African descent in India, Portugal, Spain, the Italian city-states, and elsewhere in Europe, the Middle East, and Asia long before Christopher Columbus undertook his voyages across the Atlantic. In his important study of blacks in classical antiquity, for example, Frank Snowden notes that while the "exact number of Ethiopians who entered the Greco-Roman world as a result of military, diplomatic, and commercial activity is difficult to determine ... all the evidence suggests a sizable Ethiopian element, especially in the population of the Roman world." In the parlance of the time, the term "Ethiopian" was a synonym for black Africans. The aforementioned three diasporic streams form what I shall call the premodern African diaspora.

The fourth major African diasporic stream, and the one that is most widely studied today, is associated with the Atlantic trade in African slaves. This trade, which began in earnest in the 15th century, may have delivered as many as 200,000 Africans to various European societies and 11 to 12 million to the Americas over time. The fifth major stream began during the 19th century particularly after slavery's demise in the Americas and continues to our own times. It is characterized by the movement of Africans and peoples of African descent among, and their resettlement in, various societies. These latter two diasporic streams, along with several substreams and the communities that emerged, constitute the modern African diaspora. Unlike the premodern diaspora, "racial" oppression and resistance to it are two of its most salient features.

The five major diasporic streams (or four if the first is excluded) that I have identified do not constitute the only significant movements of peoples of African descent within or outside of the African continent. Scholars, depending on their perspectives, should identify other major streams or substreams, such as that resulting from the desiccation of the Sahara between 2500 B.C.E. and 2300 B.C.E., or the movement of peoples from East Africa to the Middle East and Asia during the era of the Atlantic slave trade and after. They should make sure, however, that these streams are not conflated in terms of their timing, scope, and nature. It should be stressed that it is these diasporic streams—or movements of specific peoples to several societies—together with the communities that they constructed, that form a diaspora. The construction of a diaspora, then, is an organic process involving movement from an ancestral land, settlement in new lands, and sometimes renewed movement and resettlement elsewhere. The various stages of this process are interrelated, yet discrete.

Although diasporas involve the movement of a particular people to several places at once or over time, a migration is usually of a more limited scope and duration, and essentially is the movement of individuals from one point to another within a polity or outside of it. The boundaries between the two processes are, to be sure, very elastic because diasporas are the products of several migratory streams. Thus, the contemporary movement of Jamaicans to England is a migration, but it also constitutes a part of the fifth diasporic stream identified in this essay.

Diasporic communities, generally speaking, possess a number of characteristics. Regardless of their location, members of a diaspora share in emotional attachment to their ancestral land, are cognizant of their dispersal and, if conditions warrant, of their oppression and alienation in the countries in which they reside. Members of diasporic communities also tend to possess a sense of "racial," ethnic, or religious identity that transcends geographic boundaries, to share broad cultural similarities, and sometimes to articulate a desire to return to their original homeland. No diasporic community manifests all of these characteristics or shares with the same intensity all identity with its scattered ancestral kin. In many respects, diasporas are not actual but imaginary and symbolic communities and political constructs; it is we who often call them into being.

It is also useful in this context to remind ourselves that the appellation "African" was a misnomer until very recent times. Because, generally speaking, the peoples of Africa traditionally embraced an ethnic identification in contradistinction to a trans-ethnic, regional, or continentally based one, it is more historically accurate to speak of Yoruba, Akan, or Malinke diasporas for much of the period up to the late 19th century or even later. The issue becomes even more complicated when one recognizes that individuals also moved from one society in Africa to another for a variety of reasons including being captured in war. Because an African or trans-ethnic consciousness did not exist, the people who left their ethnic homeland were, strictly speaking, residing "abroad." Should such internal movements of specific peoples in Africa be considered parts of a diasporic stream? Can we speak of all African diaspora before the late 19th or 20th century since the subjects of our study did not define themselves as African but as Yoruba, Wolof, Igbo, or other? Equally impor-tant, what demographic, temporal, or other boundaries should be imposed on the concept?

Clearly, a major problem that scholars of the modern African diaspora confront is how to make a case for the contours and nature of their subject. This may not be very easy, as the preceding observations suggest. The difficulty notwithstanding, I hope to initiate a scholarly debate by attempting a definition of the modern African diaspora because it is the one that is currently receiving the most attention. This diaspora possesses some of the characteristics that I mentioned, but as the following tentative definition implies, it has its unique features.

The modern African diaspora, at its core, consists of the millions of peoples of African descent living in various societies who are united by a past based significantly but not exclusively upon "racial" oppression and the struggles against it; and who, despite the cultural variations and political and other divisions among them, share an emotional bond with one another and with their ancestral continent; and who also, regardless of their location, face broadly similar problems in constructing and realizing themselves.

This definition rejects any notion of a sustained desire to emigrate to Africa by those of its peoples who currently live outside of that continent's boundaries, although groups such as the

Rastafarians sometimes articulate such a desire. The desire to return to Africa, to be sure, was articulated by many of the enslaved who were removed from that continent, and thousands of free African Americans left for Liberia during the 19th century. Men such as Henry Highland Garnet, Henry McNeal Turner, Marcus Garvey, and others actively embraced emigration to Africa at various times but the appeal of the continent as a place to reestablish roots seems to have waned over time.

Methodologically speaking, the study of the modern African diaspora should, in my opinion, begin with the study of Africa. The African continent—the ancestral homeland—must be central to any informed analysis and understanding of the dispersal of its peoples. Not only must the programs that are designed promote an understanding of the history and nature of the variegated African cultures, but it must be recognized that the peoples who left Africa and their ethnic group, coerced or otherwise, brought their cultures, ideas, and worldview with them as well. Africa, in all of its cultural richness and diversity, remained very much alive in the receiving societies as the various ethnic groups created new cultures and recreated their old ways as circumstances allowed. Consequently, the study of the modern African diaspora, par-ticularly the aspect of it that is associated with the Atlantic slave trade, cannot be justifiably separated from the study of the home continent.

Scholars must be careful not to homogenize the experiences of the diverse peoples of the modern diaspora. There are obviously certain commonalities, but there are fundamental differences born of the societal context, the times, the political, economic, and "racial" circum-stances, and so on. North American scholars in particular must avoid the temptation to impose paradigms that reflect their own experiences upon other areas of the diaspora. I am, in effect, suggesting that we ask different kinds of questions that will more accurately inform our understanding of the peoples of a diaspora who are simultaneously similar but yet different. Scholars of the modern diaspora must also make a methodological distinction between studying the trajectory of a people and the trajectory of the nation-state in which they reside. In many cases, including the United States, England, and Canada, the history of marginalized blacks who occupy a minority status is not coterminous with the history of the nation-state. The history of black America is certainly not a carbon copy of that of the larger polity. In the case of those societies in which peoples of African descent constitute the majority or exercise political and other forms of power, the issues are more complex. The scholar not only has to examine how a people realized

themselves over time in specific contexts but how they began the task of constructing nation states as well. Obviously, the histories and experiences of peoples of African descent in such societies as Jamaica, Haiti, and Barbados, where they comprise the overwhelming majority, cannot be conflated with those of their counterparts in England, Germany, Canada, or Mexico, where they form a distinct minority. The differences are too vast. In societies such as Brazil and Cuba where the peoples of African descent may be in the majority but do not exercise political power commensurate with their number, the questions that are asked must be appropriate to their circumstances. Finally, we must be careful not to paint a static and ahistorical picture of what was and is a very dynamic set of processes at work everywhere.

Historians and other scholars should also adopt with the utmost caution the term "Black Atlantic" (recently popularized by Paul Gilroy) as a synonym for the modern African diaspora. Not only does this appellation exclude such societies as those in the Indian Ocean that are not a part of the Atlantic basin, but there are fundamental differences in the historical experiences of the peoples of the North Atlantic and the South Atlantic and within those zones as well. If the appellation Black Atlantic is to be adopted, scholars must resist any tendency to homogenize and conflate the histories of these variegated peoples whose memories are still haunted by the ocean that is so associated with the travail of their ancestors. Not too long ago, some scholars used the term "Plantation America" to characterize the peoples of African descent in the Americas, in contrast to those who were called Euro-Americans and Indo-Americans. Unlike the Caucasians and the Indians, blacks as people were rendered invisible by this terminology and defined according to a particular economic arrangement. Although the adjective "Black" suggests that people are included in the "Black Atlantic" construct, I am still concerned that the term lends itself to some of the same kinds of criticisms that were leveled at the use of "Plantation America." In addition, if a general nomenclature is needed for the peoples of African descent living in the Atlantic basin, it should emerge from their complex and unique internal experiences, their sinews and deep structures. Seen in this light, the Atlantic Ocean is of questionable value as the signifier of a people's trajectory and the core of their history. Similarly, if a "Black Atlantic" exists, is there an oppositional "White Atlantic," and if so, what are its animating features? The term "Africology" that is now being embraced by some to mean the study of the peoples (of African descent also suggests a kind of "racial" or ethnic essentialism that should be questioned. Obviously, the temptation to reify "race" or ethnicity as the impetus for a people's motions in a diaspora as opposed to deeper and more universal structural forces should be avoided.

The point that I should like to emphasize is that new fields require new methodologies, and it is unacceptable for scholars to see the modern African diaspora as a replica of other diasporas or is black American, black British, or Caribbean history writ large. The field must embrace disciplinary and interdisciplinary orientations and must, perforce, be comparative in its methodological dimensions. Scholars, arguably, cannot and should not define themselves as diaspora specialists if their area of expertise is confined to one society, or worse, to one small corner of that society. More than anything else, we need at this stage new and provocative questions that seek to illuminate the processes at work among the peoples of African descent who are still continuing to construct themselves and command their destinies. African diaspora studies, as we shape this developing field, must be subjected to the same kind of methodological rigor as any other area of knowledge, free from romantic condescension, essentialism, and distracting fads. For a start, let us see if we can arrive at a broad agreement on the meaning of the modern African diaspora, and then we can embrace and promote our diverse interpretive stances.

[1] For a discussion of the African origins issue, see Christopher Stringer and Robin McKie, *African Exodus: The Origins of Modern Humanity* (New York: Henry Holt and Company, 1996).

[2] Frank M. Snowden Jr., *Blacks in Antiquity: Ethiopians in the Greco-Roman World* (Cambridge: Harvard University Press, 1970), 184. See also St. Clair Drake, *Black Folk Here and There*, 2 vols. (Los Angeles: Center for Afro-American Studies, 1990).

[3] This definition owes a great deal to the efforts of my students at the Graduate School of the City University of New York, who enrolled in my spring 1997 course, "Social Movements in the African Diaspora during the Twentieth Century."

[4] This question was originally raised by Samuel K. Roberts Jr., a graduate student at Princeton.

Shifting Paradigms in the Study of the African Diaspora and of Atlantic History and Culture

Kristin Mann

Historians of Africa and the Americas have recently discovered one another and begun to glimpse the benefits of closer cooperation in their efforts to document and interpret the development of the African diaspora. Yet differences of opinion on how to conceive of the diaspora can quickly dominate their conversations with one another, inhibiting meaningful exchange. This essay begins by introducing two dominant paradigms on which the discourse has drawn, and then argues that the opposition that has been posited between them is neither necessary nor any longer intellectually fruitful. The work seeks to demonstrate that a way around the conceptual impasse lies in recovering the longer, richer and more complex history of the diaspora. From this history, even as briefly and incompletely surveyed here, a new and more heuristically powerful paradigm begins to emerge.[1] The article concludes by introducing ideas from the rapidly developing field of Atlantic history and culture and examining their usefulness for the study of the African diaspora. It shows, at the same time, how research on the diaspora also demands that we recast dominant ideas about the Atlantic world.

It should be stressed at the outset that the idea of the African diaspora developed first among Africans and their descendants, a point not sufficiently recognized in most academic discussions of the subject. Traditions of thought on both sides of the Atlantic about the connections between Africa and the Americas date to the era of the slave-trade. Joseph Miller recounts the belief of West Central Africans in Mwene Puto, the Lord of the Dead living in the west, whose people "took their nourishment from the flesh of the blacks they so avidly sought" and burned the bones of slaves to produce the gunpowder needed to procure fresh captives.[2] Edna Bay argues, [in this volume] that the ruling elite in the Fon kingdom of Dahomey used the slave-trade to exile political and military rivals and were themselves occasionally exiled through it. There is ample evidence that during the middle passage and in the Americas African-born slaves believed death would free them to return home and that some committed suicide to hasten the transition.[3] During the slave insurrection in Bahia in 1807,

participants are said to have intended to capture ships in the harbour to sail back to Africa.[4]

Given the importance of ancestors in the religions of many of the cultures from which slaves came, it would be interesting to know more about how first-generation slaves imagined their relationship to their deceased forebears following export from Africa. Sterling Stuckey and Margaret Creel have both argued that shared belief in the religious importance of ancestors helped promote unity among slaves in the United States and contributed to the development of nationalist sentiment among them.[5] By the time of abolition in West Africa, if not before, descendants of liberated slaves there were conscious of themselves as belonging to a black world that spanned the Atlantic, and they strove to establish and maintain ties with their brethren in the Americas. Robert A. Hill has argued that indigenous West African myths of exile and diaspora stemming from the slave-trade provided the assimilating nexus of Garveyism and its reception in Africa.[6] Far too little is known about these early African-American popular ideas of the diaspora and about their legacy. Much work remains to be done on these subjects.

But beyond popular or folk ideas, academic discourse on the diaspora developed first in North America among persons of African descent. In his short history *The Negro*, published in 1915, W. E. B. Du Bois conceived his subject in global terms, preceding two chapters on Latin America, the West Indies, and the United States by eight on Africa.[7] That same year Carter G. Woodson founded the Association of Negro Life and History, whose serial *The Journal of Negro History* defined "Negro" in global terms, and in its first 30 years took a diasporic perspective. Du Bois sought, through his work with the Pan-Africanist movement, to draw together "Negroes in all parts of Africa and other parts of the world." Consistent with this orientation, in 1945 he applied his conviction that "the problem of the twentieth century is the problem of the color-line" to an analysis of the African situation, asking "what in truth is going to be the future of black folk" there.[8] In the United States, however, the ideas of these and other early African-American intellectuals had little impact on the production of knowledge by members of the white academic establishment until the 1970s, and even since then relatively few scholars, black or white, have adopted their diasporic perspective, as Earl Lewis has recently shown.[9]

In Anglo-America, academic discourse on the origins of African-American culture, and by extension on the diaspora, has long been dominated by anthropologists. In the 1920s, Melville Herskovits began to study vestiges of African cultures that had survived in the Americas, and over the course of a long career he passionately promoted the view that African "traditions, attitudes, and institutionalized forms of behavior" had been retained in the New World in both secular and religious life.[10] In the 1970s, Richard and Sally Price, with their mentor and often co-author Sidney Mintz, developed a model of the diaspora that emphasized innovation and adaptation within black cultures of the New World and argued for the development of hybrid creole culture.[11] While they acknowledged that blacks sometimes drew on African influences, they understood these not primarily as retentions of specific traditions—slaves derived from too many different places for that—but as deep-level cultural principles shared by all Africans despite their disparate origins.[12] As Karen Olwig has observed, the emphasis in Mintz and Price's approach was on "cultural mixture and blend, rather than particular, retained African cultural traits and traditions."[13] Other perspectives have developed, but since the 1970s the creolist interpretation has predominated among those subscribing to the idea that African slaves had a meaningful impact on the cultures of the Americas.

A creative new way of conceiving the relationship between Africa and the Americas has more recently inspired the Diaspora from the Nigerian Hinterland Project, a major international collaborative research effort. Its organizers have called for a shifting of the point of origin, in the study of the diaspora, from the Americas to Africa, in an effort to transcend what they perceive as the common disjunction between the study of the history of Africa and of the African diaspora. Law, Lovejoy, and Soumonni have developed a conception of the diaspora that follows slave routes—beginning with the enslavement of specific cohorts of peoples in Africa and tracing their movement not only to the coast and west across the Atlantic, but also north across the Sahara to destinations in the Arab world. They urge us to look at the ways in which these slaves helped shape the societies and cultures that they entered throughout the diaspora.

The Project assumes that persons born in Africa carried with them into slavery not only their culture but also their history, and that if we understand the experiences of slaves and the histories of the societies from which they came, then we will be able to trace these influences into the diaspora. The organizers of the Diaspora from the Nigerian Hinterland Project have sought to implement this idea by linking the study of two regions from which slaves were exported—the Bights of Benin and Biafra and their hinterlands—and the places in the Americas, North Africa, and the Middle East to which they were displaced. The focus in this research moves beyond Herskovits's earlier quest for African "survivals," disconnected from time, by situating African influences in specific historical contexts and viewing them as part of "continuous historical experience."[14] At their boldest, Law and Lovejoy have argued for extending "the boundaries of 'African history' to include the history of Africans in the diaspora."

This call for the extension of African history into the diaspora has met with mixed response among Americanists. Many students of slave culture in Latin America, the Caribbean, and the United States have in fact anticipated it and have for some time been seeking to better understand the impact of African history and culture on the world the slaves made. For Brazil one need note only Mary Karasch's innovative study of slave culture in Rio de Janeiro, João Reis's pioneering work on the 1835 Muslim uprising in Bahia, and Stuart Schwartz's essay on the role of West Central African institutions in the creation of Palmares.[15] For the Caribbean, Monica Schuler's perceptive studies of myalism and Akan rebellion in Jamaica, Roderick McDonald's study of slave material culture on the same island, and George Brandon's research on Cuban Santeria adopt a similar perspective.[16] In the United States, John Blassingame's *The Slave Community*, Eugene Genovese's *Roll, Jordan, Roll*, Peter Wood's *Black Majority*, Lawrence Levine's *Black Culture and Black Consciousness*, and Albert Raboteau's *Slave Religion* led the way in the 1970s, while since then Margaret Creel's *"A Peculiar People"* and Gwendolyn Hall's *Africans in Colonial Louisiana* have lifted the project to new heights.[17] Most recently, Michael Gomez has carried the initiative to its logical conclusion by turning his training as an Africanist to the study of communities of African descent in the southern United States.[18] For Africanist historians wanting to extend the purview of their discipline across the Atlantic, it is indeed fortuitous that so many Americanists want to talk to us at precisely the moment when we want to talk to them.

Yet the reception by Americanists has not been universally enthusiastic. Philip D. Morgan, for example, has expressed frank skepticism about the kinds of close linkages between Africa and the Americas that the Diaspora from the Nigerian Hinterland Project posits. He thinks that creolization theory, with its emphasis on heterogeneity, fluidity, and hybridity, comes closer to capturing the experiences of persons of African descent in the New World.[19] Even among Americanists concerned with African influences, the cultural background of slaves is usually understood in very general terms and, for most, acculturation remains the dominant paradigm.[20]

In my view, the opposition that has emerged between proponents of the Africanist and creolist models has reached the limits of its usefulness. Surely, the goal is not to prove that Old or New World influences were more important in shaping the experiences of slaves, but rather to understand the relationship between them in specific historical contexts. What slaves brought with them from Africa and what they encountered in the Americas were both relevant. What we need to understand is how, when, and why slaves were able to draw on material, social, ideological, and other resources from one or other traditions, or from both, to fashion communities for themselves and cope with the demands of bondage. In the remainder of this essay, I will argue that one way around the Africanist-creolist impasse lies in developing a fuller and richer understanding of the history of the diaspora.

Regardless of the history of ideas about it, the diaspora itself began in Africa. It started with the movement of slaves north across the Sahara, west across the Atlantic, and in different directions across Africa itself. Robert A. Hill has argued that diasporas in fact existed on the continent prior to the growth of the European slave-trade, and that the Atlantic crossing should be seen as simply another extension of the moving African frontier. The fact that in modern times persons of African descent throughout the Atlantic world have sought, for their own purposes, to reconstitute Africa should not, in Hill's view, be allowed to subvert this basic historical reality.[21]

Granting its African origins, we need a conception of the diaspora that recognizes regional and temporal variations in its development. Thinking now about the Atlantic world only, it is clear that shifts in systems of slave-supply and demand had a major impact on the direction and timing of the movement of African peoples and cultures into the diaspora. Work on the slave-trade during the past three decades has shown that well-established commercial networks operating in particular regions of the African interior delivered slaves to specific places on the coast.[22] There these African commercial networks intersected specialized European ones that over time developed "market power" at particular places on the African coast and delivered slaves from those places to different markets in the Americas.[23] The regional distribution of both sources of slave-supply and locations of slave-demand shifted over time, moreover, with the exception that West Central Africa and Brazil always dominated. In short, there was no single slave-trade; rather there were a number of more specific slave-trades.

Thanks to this new research, we now know much more than we did before about where slaves came from, where they went, and how that changed historically. This work, when coupled with new knowledge about the African past produced during the last 30 years, enables us to say more than we once could about the history and culture that slaves took with them to particular regions of the Americas. Whereas it was once believed that slaves came to the Americas in heterogeneous and amorphous "crowds" rather than in more specific groups,[24] the reverse now appears to have been true. As Paul Lovejoy has observed, we are beginning to be able to dissect the diaspora into a number of "different population dispersals and regroupings."[25] Differences in the numbers, identities, and age and gender ratios of slaves entering specific regions of the Americas at particular moments in time all need to be taken into account when thinking about the historical development of the diaspora. Conditions that slaves encountered in the Americas also varied regionally and temporally and shaped the development of the diaspora. Of these, the labour demands of specific systems of commodity production were perhaps the most important. Stuart Schwartz has observed, "the nature of labour demands varied considerably in different slave regimes according to the kind of economic activity and the level of technology available. The variety of work requirements was a primary element that determined the nature of slave life."[26] Philip D. Morgan has stated succinctly: "Work was the most important determinant of a slave society."[27] Michael Mullin has shown the impact that the requirements of sugar production in Barbados and Jamaica, wheat and tobacco production in the Chesapeake Bay region, and rice and indigo production on the Carolina low-country had on the assertion and recognition of ethnicity among slaves.[28] Within Brazil, Katia Mattoso, Stuart Schwartz, and others have explored the impact on slave culture of the requirements of sugar production in the northeast, mining in Minas Gerais, and coffee and cotton production in both the south and north.[29] In British mainland North America, Ira Berlin delineated three different slave systems during the seventeenth and eighteenth centuries—one in the non-plantation north and the other two in the distinctive plantation regions around the Chesapeake Bay and in the Carolina and Georgia low-country. More recently, Gwendolyn Hall identified a fourth system in the frontier region of French colonial Louisiana.[30] Both Berlin and Morgan have explored with depth and imagination the differences that work, ecology, and related ways of life made in the world of slaves.[31] On the comparatively small island of Saint Domingue, over a period of only about 30 years between 1763 and the slave revolt of 1792, David Geggus has found that differences in patterns of work, age of settlements, and dictates of geography "made for significant differences in the composition of the slave labor force" and helped shape the different social worlds of the coastal plains and mountain forests. The African presence, he concludes, was "much stronger in the highlands than in the plain and also more homogeneous."[32]

Demographic regimes, cultural and moral constraints imposed by law and religion, and characteristics of the population beyond the plantation also affected the experiences of slaves, in addition to the demands of labour. If we are to understand fully the historical development of the diaspora, we must take into account not only who the slaves were and what they brought with them to the Americas, but also what they found there and how those things helped or hindered them in drawing on their African cultural resources to construct new worlds for themselves.

If differences existed across regions of the Americas, conditions within particular regions also changed, and this too shaped the development of the diaspora. The different timing of the growth of plantation economies across the British Caribbean affected their character and hence the experience of their African slaves.[33] Plantation regimes in British colonial North America were in important respects different than they would become in the antebellum United States, with important implications for African-American life.[34]

Events in Bahia in the late eighteenth and early nineteenth centuries aptly illustrate the need to bring time into an analysis of the formation of the diaspora. The expansion of the Bahian economy between the 1780s and 1820s, coupled with a demographic regime which dictated that the slave population needed to be continually replenished with new imports, led to the introduction of large numbers of African-born. slaves from the Bight of Benin during those years. This influx occurred at a time when increased numbers of Hausa and Nagô (Yoruba) slaves,

many of them Muslim, were being exported from the region. Jodo Reis has shown that the introduction of these African-born slaves into Bahia led to the spread of new religious beliefs and practices, both Muslim and non-Muslim, that combined with local conditions to produce a tradition of slave rebellion culminating in the Muslim uprising of 1835.[35] Paul Lovejoy has argued that the experience of the Hausa and Nagô slaves with religiously inspired revolt and holy war in Africa prior to export contributed to the rise of a slave community in Bahia that was capable of sustaining a tradition of resistance.[36] A depression in Bahia in the 1820s and 1830s led to the sale of slaves from there to Rio de Janeiro and other parts of Brazil and contributed to the spread of Candomblé and Islam to other parts of the country.[37] Susan Socolow's research on patterns of slave migration from Rio to Montevideo suggests the possibility of the further extension of the diaspora from the Bight of Benin into the interior of South America.[38] The proportion and identity of African-born slaves in any population was a highly significant variable that changed with time.

The work of Reis and other Brazilianists on slave religion perfectly illustrates the point that knowledge only of what slaves brought from Africa will not suffice to explain the formation of their communities in the Americas. João Reis has documented, in research on a Jeje religious centre in Bahia, both continuity in Fon and Yoruba religious beliefs in the involvement of spirits in the world of the living, and transformation in the ritual practices of African priests.[39] In his study of slave culture in Rio, Robert Slenes has shown that West Central Africans drew on religious and linguistic commonalities from the Old World to construct a cosmology unknown and unknowable to their masters. But in the process, they changed the meaning of West Central African religious practices.[40] The importance of both specific, retained African beliefs and practices and fusion with New World (and explicitly Christian) faith also emerges from Schuler's work on myalism and Creel's on Gullah religion.[41] All of this work clearly demonstrates that focusing on neither New World adaptations nor specific, retained African traditions alone will suffice in the study of slave cultures. Both are necessary. What we need to understand is the relationship between the two in specific regional and historical contexts.

Beyond beginning in Africa and tracing the introduction and transformation of culturally and historically specific African influences in the Americas, the study of the diaspora needs also to incorporate an appreciation of the reciprocal effects of the Americas on Africa. People, goods, beliefs and practices flowed not only east to west, but also in the reverse direction in the era of the slave-trade and after abolition. Nowhere have these reciprocal connections been stronger than between the Bight of Benin and Bahia. Robin Law and I have argued that during the period of the slave-trade Brazilians of different origins, from white and mulatto slave-traders to freed slaves and indeed slaves themselves, lived on West Africa's Slave Coast—settling there of their own initiative or brought by their owners. These persons established and maintained economic, social, and cultural ties that spanned the Atlantic in sufficient numbers and with such density that by the end of the eighteenth century they formed part of an "Atlantic community."[42] From the 1830s, of course, sizeable numbers of freed slaves from Brazil and smaller numbers from Cuba, the West Indies, and the United States returned to the Slave Coast and its interior, heightening and diversifying New World influences. Immigrants from the Americas brought with them not only a transatlantic economic orientation but also new ideas about ethnicity that had been forged abroad and new religious institutions and practices, both Catholic and Muslim, as Olabiyi Yai and Robin Law show in their contributions to this volume. They also introduced new material culture and aesthetic values.[43]

The reciprocal influences of the Americas on Africa during the era of slavery are well known, if not yet fully understood. Less commonly appreciated is the fact that the diaspora was not bilateral but multilateral. As a consequence, we need a model of it that is not two-dimensional but three-dimensional. Influences moved not only back and forth between specific regions of Africa and the Americas but also between different parts of Africa and of the Americas. Indeed, they circulated in flows of differing reach and proportion all around the Atlantic basin. In Africa, itself, the arrival of Europeans on the west coast in the fifteenth and sixteenth centuries spawned ocean-borne trade in cloth, slaves and other commodities among different peoples.[44] Throughout this period, the Gold Coast imported many more slaves than it exported.[45] The diaspora that slaves liberated at Sierra Leone created, when they returned to their homelands or moved elsewhere to trade or work, has been widely studied.[46] Less familiar is the diaspora connecting Hausa and Nupe slaves or their descendants on the coast with their communities of origin or with Hausa ex-slaves who returned to West Africa from Brazil following the Malé uprising of 1835.

In the Americas, Ira Berlin has argued, "charter generations" of "Atlantic creoles" whose origins lay along the littoral of Africa, Europe, and the Americas and who were cosmopolitan in the fullest sense, knowing the commerce, languages, and cultures of the Atlantic, flourished prior to the triumph of plantation production.[47] But nothing illustrates the movement of Africans and their descendants around the Atlantic world better than the experiences of black sailors. Equiano gained a transatlantic perspective and acquired valuable maritime skills while the slave of a British naval captain. Later he engaged in trade and accumulated capital to free himself while a slave on a ship sailing among the islands of the Caribbean.[48] In his book *Black Jacks*, Jeffrey Bolster has shown the importance of black sailors in the development of networks of communication and consciousness of shared identity among eighteenth and nineteenth century African-Americans.[49] Denmark Vesey may have developed a "Pan-African" outlook that inspired him to want to overthrow slavery while working as a cabin-boy on a ship sailing between Charleston, South Carolina, and the West Indies.[50] Nor were black sailors confined to the English-speaking Americas. In 1775, half of all the sailors so important to transportation and communication in the sugar-producing Recôncavo region of Bahia were slaves, and many of them would have been African-born.[51]

Black soldiers were not as mobile as black sailors, but they too moved around the Atlantic world carrying information, fostering exchanges, and promoting the development of new identities. Michael Mullin has noted that when revolution swept through France and the islands of the Caribbean around the turn of the nineteenth century, black soldiers began to be recruited into West Indian regiments.[52] Troops from the British force created in this way were stationed in Lagos, on the West African coast, during the colonial conquest, where Hausa ex-slaves who had run away from their local owners were also recruited.[53] The fate of these recruits is not known, but presumably some of them left with their regiment when it was transferred elsewhere. By the second half of the nineteenth century, the British West Indian Regiment then consisted of Caribbean-born former slaves or their descendants and newly-freed slaves from West Africa, who were deployed as needed throughout Britain's Atlantic empire. The existence and movement of this force suggest fascinating possibilities for the circulation of peoples, cultures, and ideas throughout black populations in the English-speaking Atlantic world. As documented by all of these data on the circulation of peoples of African descent around the Atlantic world, historically the diaspora consisted not of discrete sets of bilateral networks that connected particular regions of Africa with others in the Americas, but rather of a complex web of multilateral and intersecting networks that linked different parts of the black Atlantic world.

To this point, my analysis has focused primarily on the era of slavery. Yet, formative though studies of slavery and the slave trade have been, we must not allow them to "enslave" research on the development of the diaspora, as Earl Lewis has argued they did for many years the history of African-Americans.[54] The diaspora linking Africa and the Americas has not been static: it was not constituted in the era of slavery and then passed on unchanged to subsequent generations. Rather it has been forged and reforged until the present as successive generations of Africans and persons of African descent all around the Atlantic basin have reconstituted their sense of themselves and their relationship with one another.[55] A number of the papers presented at the conference "Rethinking the African Diaspora: The Making of a Black Atlantic World in the Bight of Benin and Brazil," some of them published here, demonstrated fruitful new lines of inquiry into the ongoing transformation of the relationship between two pivotal regions in the history of the diaspora. Ubiratan Castro de Araujo's perceptive analysis of the last slave cargo from Lagos to Salvador served as a reminder that the commerce in labour between the Bight of Benin and Bahia ended in the middle of the nineteenth century and, by extension, that we need to know more about the impact of abolition and the rise of the new palm-produce trade with Europe on the commercial and familial networks that had been so central to the formation and maintenance of the Brazilian diaspora. Trade between the Bight of Benin and Brazil in such goods as palm oil, cotton cloth, kola nuts, black soap, ritual objects, tobacco, aguardente, food, cigars, and other items survived following abolition, and continued to foster communication and exchange across the Atlantic, as João Reis, Kim Butler and J. Lorand Matory have shown.[56] But it was nowhere near as economically important to the interior of the Bight of Benin as the new commerce with Europe, and apparently it declined absolutely over the second half of the nineteenth century.[57] While some of the old Brazilian slave-traders or their families on the coast made the transition to the palm-produce trade, and in the process shifted their cultural as well as economic orientation at least in part away from Brazil and to Europe, others experienced decline.[58]

Religious beliefs, associations, and practices—African, Muslim, and Christian—bridged the Atlantic, linking the Bight of Benin and Brazil after, as well as before, the end of slavery. When the economic ties between the two parts of the world weakened, the religious connections remained strong. Matory has demonstrated that, in Candomblé, influences flowed in both directions, and he and Butler have argued that the dominance and prestige of the Nagô (Yoruba) houses in late nineteenth and early twentieth century Bahia owed much to the movement across the Atlantic of travellers, priests and priestesses, who helped promote not only a belief that certain religious practices were African and pure but also a sense of transatlantic national identity.[59] Muslims returning to the coast from Brazil following the Malé rebellion of 1835 founded a predominantly Hausa quarter and built the first mosque in Ouidah under the patronage of the famous Brazilian slave-trader F. F. da Souza. In Lagos and Porto Novo, they established new mosques, which in the latter town precipitated a split along ethnic lines within the local Muslim community—"Brazilian" versus indigenous Yoruba.[60] Olabiyi Yai's essay in this volume looks at the role of "Aguda," as the freed slaves returned from Brazil were called on the Slave Coast, in the establishment of a variety of local, non-missionary Catholicism. In contemporary times, certainly, religious specialists and ritual authorities have been in the forefront of movement around the Atlantic world, helping to connect communities and construct identities in Africa, Brazil, Cuba, and the United States.

A number of scholars have begun to study the construction and transformation of transatlantic nations or identities since abolition, and they have looked as well at their importance in political mobilization in Brazil and West Africa. Robin Law, J. Lorand Matory and Maria Inês Côrtes de Oliveira have examined the emergence of new ethnic identities—defined in Matory's view as "nations"—in Brazil during the era of slavery and their movement back to Africa with returned former slaves in the second half of the nineteenth century, where they acquired local as well as transatlantic significance.[61] Kim Butler has demonstrated that following emancipation Afro-Bahians used representations of Africa as symbols and signifiers in their struggle to transform their identities and negotiate greater access to political power in Brazil.[62] In this volume, Yai links the Aguda's ancestral tradition of resistance to slavery in Brazil with successful resistance to French colonialism in Dahomey in the 1930s. J. M. Turner, Bellarmin Codo and Elisée Soumonni have shown the relationship between shifting constructions of Brazilian identity in the southern Republic of Benin and struggles for control of the state before and after independence.[63]

In the discipline of history, it has been fashionable for some time to consider the Atlantic basin as a single integrated unit of analysis, and I want to conclude by suggesting that this idea has great relevance to the study of the African diaspora. A recent discussion by Bernard Bailyn of the emergence of the idea of Atlantic history since World War II is replete with references to the fruitfulness of thinking about the construction of Atlantic civilization as a joint enterprise of the New World and the Old; of conceiving the Atlantic ocean as a basin around which a new Atlantic civilization formed; and of understanding the unitary character of the entire Atlantic world.[64] There has long been, and still is in some quarters, however, an extraordinary myopia about how the Atlantic basin is formed. Bailyn mentions Africa only twice in his essay, once in a brief discussion of the role of the slave-trade in transoceanic labour flows and the second time in a quotation linking white South Africa with western Europe and the two Americas in the creation of an "Atlantic civilization."[65] For the most part, his essay reads as if the Atlantic Ocean washed the shores of only three continents—Europe, North America, and South America. It might be argued, in Bailyn's defence, that his article deals not with the making of Atlantic history but with the history of ideas about it. In response, I would return to a point with which I began this article. Embedded in the writings of early African-American intellectuals about the African diaspora is the notion that it is an Atlantic phenomenon. There is a history of ideas about Atlantic history and culture that brings Africa and peoples of African descent to the centre of the story, but to find it one must examine the work of black, not white, intellectuals.

Views of the Atlantic world outside African and African American history are changing, to be sure, but slowly. Within the mainstream of the discipline many, perhaps most, historians are still unable to conceive the history of the Atlantic basin in ways that adequately recognize African contributions to it. Two facts illustrate this point. The first is well known by now, if insufficiently appreciated, and the second is startlingly new. David Brion Davis and Philip D. Curtin made us aware some time ago that, as Davis put it: "If one takes the New World as a whole, one finds that the importation of African slaves far surpassed the flow of European immigrants during the first three and one-third centuries of settlement."[66] More recently, David Eltis has shown, using the Du Bois Consolidated Slave Trade Database, that before 1800 "it is likely that at least 80 per cent of the females, and well over 90 per cent of the children sailing to the Americas were not European."[67] The majority of these were Africans. Yet most historians are far from able to conceptualize the early history of the Americas in ways that recognize the experiences and contributions of all these African men, women and children. The history of the Americas is certainly not normally taught in ways that do justice to the truth of their peopling.

There has been for a number of years an influential counter-hegemonic approach to the study of Atlantic history and culture, best exemplified by the now defunct Program in Atlantic History, Culture and Society at Johns Hopkins University. This approach integrates Africa and Africans, along with indigenous peoples of the Americas, into the study of "the linked pasts and common experiences of societies bordering the Atlantic."[68] Focusing as it did on the development of the Atlantic system from the sixteenth through the eighteenth century, the Hopkins programme brought slavery and the slave-trade to the centre of its concerns. Although it was the product of a partnership between history and anthropology, the programme was heavily influenced by the tradition of anthropological study of African Americans descending from Herskovits and then led by Mintz, one of the founders of the Hopkins programme, that I discussed earlier. The Hopkins programme was absorbed in 1993 into a reconstituted and broader Institute for Global Studies in Culture, Power and History. This was done, in part, to free the project of studying the linked pasts and common experiences of the world's societies and cultures in ways that grant agency to "people without history" from the temporal constraints imposed by focusing on a particular historical epoch. The new programme sought thereby to encourage an examination of the continuing rearrangement of the relationship between the local and the global. But the reorganization also reflected the growing dominance of the globalization paradigm within the academy.[69]

While there is a clear need to unshackle temporally the study of connections among cultures and of peoples previously left out of historical narratives, as I have already argued, much remains to be gained by retaining a geographic focus on the Atlantic world. For if not isolated from broader global influences in the modern or, for that matter, early modern era, the societies and polities of the Atlantic stood in closer relationship to one another—demographically, economically, intellectually, institutionally, religiously, and culturally—than they did to other parts of the world. They formed part, as Bailyn has argued, of an integrated whole.

A third tradition of scholarship on Atlantic history and culture began to emerge in the 1990s from the field of cultural studies. It is perhaps best exemplified by Paul Gilroy's book *The Black Atlantic*, which views the Atlantic as "one single, complex unit of analysis," and one in which blacks are "perceived as agents" equally with whites. Gilroy conceives the Atlantic as "continually crisscrossed by the movements of black people—

not only as commodities but engaged in various struggles toward emancipation, autonomy, and citizenship."[70] Yet his starting point is not Africa, but the North Atlantic, and more specifically modern Anglo-America. He is concerned with the rise there of a "transnational and intercultural perspective" and its relationship to rhetorics of race, culture, nationality, and ethnicity. Africa itself figures in Gilroy's work as an object of retrospective rediscovery, rather than as an active agent. Moreover, Gilroy ignores both the rich and dense world of the predominantly Lusophonic and Spanish South Atlantic and the roots of the transnational, intercultural black perspective in the pre-modern era.

Despite their limitations, if one culls the best from each of these traditions of scholarship on the Atlantic world and combines them with what is beginning to be known about the history of the African diaspora, then a new paradigm for understanding both begins to emerge. The idea of the Atlantic world as a single integrated unit of analysis that peoples from four continents have had agency in shaping demands that we bring Africa and Africans to the centre of the story as equal players. Moreover, it frees those of us in North America from our, too common, narrow preoccupation with the Anglo-American tradition. So far as the African diaspora itself is concerned, what we know about the past now requires a model that begins in Africa, traces the movement of specific cohorts of peoples into the Americas and examines how, in regionally and temporally specific contexts, they drew on what they brought with them as well as borrowed from what they found in the Americas to forge new worlds for themselves. In the process, persons of African descent contributed to the making of broader regional and eventually national histories and cultures, forging the wider Atlantic civilization. New awareness of the Atlantic as a single, complex and integrated unit of analysis helps us recognize that influences not only have flowed reciprocally forwards and backwards from Africa to the Americas but also have circulated around the Atlantic world. This knowledge, too, needs to feed back into and enrich our conceptualization of the history and culture of the Atlantic basin. Finally, the scholarship on Atlantic history and culture reminds us of the need to remember the *longue durée* and look not only at the eras of slavery and abolition, but also at the ongoing reconstitution of the diaspora. The contributions of Africa and persons of African descent to the wider Atlantic story lie in this more modern period as much as in the earlier one. If we bear these principles in mind, they will help us in our quest to represent the African diaspora beyond simple oppositions, unitary models and static constructions to more varied, complex and fluid accounts that come closer to capturing the unfolding experiences of Africans and their descendants throughout the Atlantic world. At the same time, they will challenge us to rewrite Atlantic history and rethink Atlantic culture.

Notes

Two fruitful collaborations undertaken simultaneously with different colleagues at Emory University contributed greatly to the writing of this essay. They were an undergraduate colloquium on "The African Background to Atlantic Culture" team-taught with Leslie Harris, an American historian, and the conference organized with Edna G. Bay for which this essay was first written. I am deeply indebted to Leslie and Eddy, as well as to the students in the colloquium, for the development of this essay. James L. Roark and Bruce Fort provided helpful advice about the literature on slavery in the United States.

1. The Diaspora from the Nigerian Hinterland Project, based at York University in Toronto, led by Paul E. Lovejoy, David Trotman, Robin Law, and Elisée Soumonni, and funded largely by the Social Science and Humanities Research Council of Canada, has played a leading role in fostering closer cooperation among Africanists and Americanists interested in the African diaspora. I am grateful for past support from this project, as well as ongoing participation in it. The ideas expressed in this essay are my own, however, and the project bears no responsibility for any shortcomings in them.
    Other recent initiatives, too numerous to mention here, also reflect the new interest of Americanists and Africanists in each other's work. A few further examples include the ongoing "Black Atlantic/African Diaspora Seminars" at Rutgers University, the "Transatlantic Slaving and the African Diaspora" conference convened at the Omohundro Institute of Early American History and Culture at William and Mary College in September 1998, and the recent Call for Papers on "Africans and the Roots of Early American Culture" by the *Radical History Review*.

2. J. Miller, *Way of Death: Merchant Capitalism and the Angolan Slave Trade, 1730–1830* (Madison: University of Wisconsin Press, 1988), pp. 4–5.

3. T. Phillips, "A Journal of a Voyage Made in the Hannibal," in A. Churchill and J. Churchill, *A Collection of Voyages and Travels*, 3rd ed. (London: H. Linot and J. Osborn, 1746), p. 219; excerpts from Sloane, Leslie, and Lewis in R. D. Abrahams and J. F. Szwed, *After Africa: Extracts from British Travel Accounts and Journals of the Seventeenth, Eighteenth, and Nineteenth Centuries Concerning the Slaves, their Masters, and Customs in the British West Indies* (New Haven: Yale University Press, 1983); A. J. Raboteau, *Slave Religion: The "Invisible Institution" in the Antebellum South* (New York: Oxford

University Press, 1978), p. 32; M. Mullin, *Africa in America: Slave Acculturation and Resistance in the American South and the British Caribbean, 1736–1831* (Urbana: University of Illinois Press, 1994), pp. 35, 69.

4. J. J. Reis, *Slave Rebellion in Brazil: The Muslim Uprising of 1835 in Bahia* (Baltimore: Johns Hopkins University Press, 1993), p. 42. P. D. Morgan, *Slave Counterpoint: Black Culture in the Eighteenth-Century Chesapeake and Lowcountry* (Chapel Hill: University of North Carolina Press, 1998), p. 446, also refers to slaves speaking of returning home and acting on their words.

5. S. Stuckey, *Slave Culture: Nationalist Theory and the Foundations of Black America* (New York: Oxford University Press, 1987), pp. 3–97; M. W. Creel, *"A Peculiar People": Slave Religion and Community-Culture Among the Gullahs* (New York: New York University Press, 1988), pp. 308–22.

6. R. A. Hill, "Race and Transitional Phenomena" (paper presented to the Graduate Institute of the Liberal Arts, Emory University, 1998); personal communication, 1998.

7. W. E. B. Du Bois, *The Negro* (1915; reprint, with an introduction by G. Shepperson, New York: Oxford University Press, 1970).

8. W. E. B. Du Bois, *The World and Africa* (New York: Viking Press, 1947), pp. 227, 236.

9. E. Lewis, "To Turn as on a Pivot: Writing African Americans into a History of Overlapping Diasporas," *American Historical Review*, 100 (1995), pp. 765–87.

10. M. J. Herskovits, *The Myth of the Negro Past* (Boston: Beacon Press, 1958), p. 143.

11. S. Hawkins and P. Morgan, "Patterns of Cultural Transmission: Diffusion, Destruction, and Development in the African Diaspora" (paper presented at the conference "The African Diaspora and the Nigerian Hinterland: Towards a Research Agenda," York University, Toronto, 2–3 Feb. 1996), p. 5.

12. S. W. Mintz and R. Price, *The Birth of African-American Culture: An Anthropological Perspective* (Boston: Beacon Press, 1992).

13. K. F. Olwig, "African Cultural Principles in Caribbean Slave Society: A View from the Danish West Indies," in S. Palmier (ed.), *Slave Cultures and the Cultures of Slavery* (Knoxville: University of Tennessee Press, 1995), p. 26.

14. R. Law, P. E. Lovejoy and E. Soumonni, "The Development of an African Diaspora: The Slave Trade of the 'Nigerian' Hinterland, 1650–1900" (paper presented at the UNESCO "Slave Route Project" conference, Cabinda, Angola, 4–6 April 1996), pp. 2–3. J. Thornton, *Africa and Africans in the Making of the Atlantic World, 1400–1680* (Cambridge: Cambridge University Press, 1992), in certain ways anticipated this approach.

15. M. C. Karasch, *Slave Life in Rio de Janeiro, 1808–1850* (Princeton: Princeton University Press, 1987); Reis, *Slave Rebellion*; S. B. Schwartz, *Slaves, Peasants, and Rebels: Reconstructing Brazilian Slavery* (Urbana: University of Illinois Press, 1992), pp. 103–36.

16. M. Schuler, "Akan Slave Rebellions in the British Caribbean," *Savacou*, 1 (1970), pp. 373–86, and "Myalism and the African Religious Tradition in Jamaica," in H. Beckles and V. Shepherd (eds.), *Caribbean Slave Society and Economy* (New York: The New Press, 1976), pp. 295–303; R. A. McDonald, *The Economy and Material Culture of Slaves: Goods and Chattels on the Sugar Plantations of Jamaica and Louisiana* (Baton Rouge: Louisiana State University Press, 1993); G. Brandon, *Santeria from Africa to the New World: The Dead Sell Memories* (Bloomington: Indiana University Press, 1993).

17. J. W. Blassingame, *The Slave Community: Plantation Life in the Antebellum South* (New York: Oxford University Press, 1972); E. D. Genovese, *Roll, Jordan, Roll: The World the Slaves Made* (New York: Vintage Books, 1972); P. H. Wood, *Black Majority: Negroes in Colonial South Carolina from 1670 through the Stono Rebellion* (New York: Alfred A. Knopf, 1974); L. W. Levine, *Black Culture and Black Consciousness: Afro-American Folk Thought from Slavery to Freedom* (New York: Oxford University Press, 1977); Raboteau, *Slave Religion*; Creel, *"A Peculiar People"*; G. M. Hall, *Africans in Colonial Louisiana: The Development of Afro-Creole Culture in the Eighteenth Century* (Baton Rouge: Louisiana State University Press, 1992).

18. M. A. Gomez, *Exchanging Our Country Marks: The Transformation of African Identities in the Colonial and Antebellum South* (Chapel Hill: University of North Carolina Press, 1998).

19. P. D. Morgan, "The Cultural Implications of the Atlantic Slave Trade: African Regional Origins, American Destinations and New World Developments," *Slavery and Abolition*, 18 (1997), pp. 122–45; also Hawkins and Morgan, "Patterns of Cultural Transmission," p. 14. This perspective underpins *Slave Counterpoint*, as, for example, in ch. 10.

20. Stuckey, *Slave Culture*; Mullin, *Africa in America*; Olwig, "African Cultural Principles."

21. Hill, "Race and Transitional Phenomena" (personal communication, 1998).

22. A. J. H. Latham, *Old Calabar, 1600–1891: The Impact of the International Economy upon a Traditional Society* (Oxford: Clarendon Press, 1973), pp. 25–30; P. D. Curtin, *Economic Change in Precolonial Africa: Senegambia in the Era of the Slave Trade* (Madison: University of Wisconsin Press, 1975), pp. 153–96; D. Northrup, *Trade without Rulers: Precolonial Economic Development in South-eastern Nigeria* (Oxford: Clarendon Press, 1978), pp. 50–176; P. Manning, *Slavery, Colonialism and Economic Growth in Dahomey, 1640–1960* (Cambridge: Cambridge University Press, 1982), pp. 10–11, 31–50; P. E. Lovejoy, *Transformations in Slavery: A History of Slavery in Africa* (Cambridge: Cambridge University Press, 1983); Miller, *Way of Death*, pp. 3–244 passim; K. O. Dike and F. Ekejiubua, *The Aro of South-eastern Nigeria, 1650–1980: A Study of*

Socio-economic Formation and Transformation in Nigeria (Ibadan: Ibadan University Press, 1990); R. Law, *The Slave Coast of West Africa, 1550–1750: The Impact of the Atlantic Slave Trade on an African Society* (Oxford: Clarendon Press, 1991), pp. 182–91.

23. S. D. Behrendt and D. Eltis, "Competition, Market Power, and the Impact of Abolition on the Transatlantic Slave Trade: Connections between Africa and the Americas" (paper presented at the annual meeting of the American Historical Association, New York, Jan. 1997); S. D. Behrendt, D. Eltis, and D. Richardson, "The Bights in Comparative Perspective: The Economics of Long-term Trends in Population Displacement from West and West-central Africa to the Americas before 1850," in P. E. Lovejoy (ed.), *Identifying Enslaved Africans: The "Nigeria" Hinterland and the African Diaspora* (Proceedings of the UNESCO/SSHRCC Summer Institute, York University, Toronto, 1977), pp. 47–63.

24. Mintz and Price, *The Birth*, pp. 14–18.

25. P. E. Lovejoy, "The African Diaspora from the Nigerian Hinterland: Patterns for the Research Agenda" (paper presented at a conference on "The African Diaspora and the Nigerian Hinterland Towards a Research Agenda," York University, Toronto, 2–3 Feb. 1996), p. 6.

26. Schwartz, *Slaves, Peasants*, p. 39. See also I. Berlin and P. D. Morgan, "Introduction," in I. Berlin and P. D. Morgan (eds.), *Cultivation and Culture: Labor and the Shaping of Slave Life in the Americas* (Charlottesville: The University of Virginia Press, 1993), pp. 1–45.

27. Morgan, *Slave Counterpoint*, p. xxi.

28. Mullin, *Africa in America*, pp. 13–33.

29. K. M. Mattoso, *To Be a Slave in Brazil, 1550–1888* (New Brunswick, New Jersey: Rutgers University Press, 1986), pp. 40–54, 93–6; S. B. Schwartz, *Sugar Plantations in the Formation of Brazilian Society: Bahia, 1550–1835* (Cambridge: Cambridge University Press, 1985), pp. 98–159; Schwartz, *Slaves, Peasants*, pp. 39–63.

30. I. Berlin, "Time, Space, and the Evolution of Afro-American Society in British Mainland North America," *American Historical Review*, 85 (1980), pp. 44–78; Hall, *Africans*, especially chs. 1, 5, 7 and 8.

31. I. Berlin, *Many Thousands Gone: The First Two Centuries of Slavery in North America* (Cambridge: Harvard University Press, 1998), extends the analysis in his earlier essay and also discusses the Lower Mississippi Valley; Morgan, *Slave Counterpoint*.

32. D. P. Geggus, "Sugar and Coffee Cultivation in Saint Domingue and the Shaping of the Slave Labor Force," in Berlin and Morgan (eds.), *Cultivation and Culture*, p. 94.

33. Mullin, *Africa in America*; H. S. Klein, *African Slavery in Latin American and the Caribbean* (New York: Oxford University Press, 1988), pp. 50–6, 92; J. R. Ward, *British West Indian Slavery, 1750–1834: The Process of Amelioration* (Oxford: Clarendon Press, 1988), pp. 8–37, 119–232; F. W. Knight (ed.), *The Slave Societies of the Caribbean* (London: UNESCO, 1997), pp. 6–7, and chs. 3, 4, 6; and essays in V. A. Shepherd and H. M. Beckles (eds.), *Caribbean Slavery in the Atlantic World: A Student Reader* (Kingston, Jamaica: Ian Randle, 2000).

34. P. Klochin, *American Slavery, 1619–1877* (New York: Hill and Wang, 1993). I am aware of no broad synthesis that analyses regional variations in slave societies within the nineteenth-century United States in the depth that Berlin, *Many Thousands Gone*, does for the earlier period. However, Berlin himself probed some of the differences between colonial and antebellum slavery in "The Plantation Revolution and the Historicization of Slavery in the United States" (paper presented at the annual meeting of the Southern Historical Association, Atlanta, Nov. 1997). Among the many fine local studies that illuminate antebellum slavery are B. J. Fields, *Slavery and Freedom on the Middle Ground: Maryland during the Nineteenth Century* (New Haven: Yale University Press, 1985); J. C. Inscoe, *Mountain Masters, Slavery, and the Sectional Crisis in Western North Carolina* (Knoxville: University of Tennessee Press, 1989); P. A. Coclanis, *The Shadow of a Dream: Economic Life and Death in the South Carolina Low Country, 1670–1920* (New York: Oxford University Press, 1989); M. A. McLaurin, *Celia, a Slave* (Athens: University of Georgia Press, 1991); J. P. Reidy, *From Slavery to Agrarian Capitalism in the Cotton Plantation South: Central Georgia, 1800–1880* (Chapel Hill: University of North Carolina Press, 1992); and C. B. Dew, *Bond of Iron: Master and Slave at Buffalo Forge* (New York: W. W. Norton, 1994). Morgan, *Slave Counterpoint* and Berlin, *Many Thousands Gone*, as well as many other studies of slavery in the colonial and revolutionary periods, also emphasize the importance of changes wrought by time.

35. Reis, *Slave Rebellion*.

36. P. E. Lovejoy, "Background to Rebellion: The Origins of Muslim Slaves in Bahia," *Slavery and Abolition*, 15 (1994), pp. 151–80.

37. Mattoso, *To Be a Slave*, pp. 44–6; Karasch, *Slave Life*, pp. 284–7; and Alberto da Costa e Silva's contribution to this collection.

38. S. M. Socolow, "From Brazil to the Rio de la Plata: Patterns of Slave Migration in South America" (paper presented at the conference "Rethinking the African Diaspora: The Making of a Black Atlantic World in the Bight of Benin and Brazil," Emory University, Atlanta, 17–18 April 1998).

39. J. J. Reis, "Magia Jeje na Bahia: A Invasao do Calundu do Pasto de Cachoeira, 1785," *Revista Brasileira de Historia*, 8 (1988), pp. 57–81. Reis also emphasized the need to understand both Old and New world influences on slaves in "Slave Resistance in Brazil" (paper presented to the Department of History, Emory University, 16 April 1998).

40. R. W. Slenes, "'Malungu, ngoma vem!': África coberta e descoberta do Brasil," *Revista USP*, 12 (1991–92), pp. 48–67. I am grateful to Frank T. Proctor, a graduate student in Emory University's Department of History, for providing me with English summaries of this article and the one cited in the previous note.

41. Schuler, "Myalism"; Creel, *"A Peculiar People."*

42. R. Law and K. Mann, "West Africa in the Atlantic Community: The Case of the Slave Coast," *William and Mary Quarterly*, 54 (1999), pp. 308–34.

43. On the return of freed Brazilian slaves to West Africa and their impact on its culture see P. Verger, *Trade Relations between the Bight of Benin and Bahia from the 17th to 19th Century* (Ibadan: Ibadan University Press, 1976); J. M. Turner, "Les Bresiliens—The Impact of Former Brazilian Slaves upon Dahomey" (PhD diss., Boston University, 1975); M. C. da Cunha, *Negros, estrangeiros: Os Escravos Libertos e sua Volta à Africa* (Sao Paulo: Editora Brasiliense, 1985); M. and M. C. da Cunha, *From Slave Quarters to Town Houses: Brazilian Architecture in Nigeria and the People's Republic of Benin* (Sao Paulo: Nobel, 1985); and M. Guran, *Agudás: Os "Brasileiros" do Benim* (Rio de Janeiro: Editora Nova Fronteira, 1999).

44. A. F. C. Ryder, *Benin and the Europeans, 1485–1897* (Harlow: Longmans, 1969), pp. 24–75; Law, *The Slave Coast*, pp. 56–8, 116–18, 148–50, 192–8, 219–24.

45. R. A. Key, *Settlements, Trade, and Polities in the Seventeenth-Century Gold Coast* (Baltimore: Johns Hopkins University Press, 1982), pp. 20, 110, 197–200; T. C. McCaskie, *State and Society in Pre-colonial Asante* (Cambridge: Cambridge University Press, 1995), pp. 25–6.

46. J. H. Kopytoff, *A Preface to Modern Nigeria: The "Sierra Leonians" in Yoruba, 1830–1890* (Madison: University of Wisconsin Press, 1965); K. Mann, *Marrying Well: Marriage, Status and Social Change among the Educated Elite in Colonial Lagos* (Cambridge: Cambridge University Press, 1985), pp. 25–34; M. Lynn, "Technology, Trade, and 'a Race of Native Capitalists': The Krio Diaspora of West Africa and the Steamship, 1852–1895," *Journal of African History*, 33 (1992), pp. 421–40; and M. Dixon-Fyle, *A Saro Community in the Niger Delta, 1912–1984: The Potts-Johnsons of Port Harcourt and their Heirs* (Rochester: University of Rochester Press, 1999).

47. I. Berlin, "From Creole to African: Atlantic Creoles and the Origins of African-American Society in Mainland North America," *William and Mary Quarterly*, 53 (1996), p. 254; see also Berlin, *Many Thousands Gone*, pp. 29–63.

48. O. Equiano, *The Life of Olaudah Equiano, or Gustavus Vassa the African* (Harlow: Longmans, 1989), pp. 29–105; J. Walvin, *An African's Life: The Life and Times of Olaudah Equiano* (London: Cassell, 1998), pp. 31–41, 63–77.

49. W. J. Bolster, *Black Jacks: African American Seamen in the Age of Sail* (Cambridge: Cambridge University Press, 1997); see also P. Linebaugh and M. Rediker, "The Many-Headed Hydra: Sailors, Slaves, and the Atlantic Working Class in the Eighteenth Century," *Journal of Historical Sociology*, 3 (1990), pp. 225–52.

50. Stuckey, *Slave Culture*, p. 44.

51. Schwartz, *Sugar Plantations*, p. 76.

52. Mullin, *Africa in America*, p. 223.

53. Public Record Office, Colonial Office Original Correspondence, Lagos Colony, CO 147/6, Freeman to Newcastle, 6 May 1864. On the origins of the West Indian Regiments see R. N. Buckley, *Slaves in Red Coats: The British West Indian Regiments, 1795–1815* (New Haven: Yale University Press, 1979). S. C. Ukpabi, "West Indian Troops and the Defence of British West Africa in the Nineteenth Century," *African Studies Review*, 17 (1974), pp. 133–50, discusses their wider involvement in West Africa.

54. Lewis, "To Turn as on a Pivot," p. 766.

55. J. E. Harris (ed.), *Global Dimensions of the African Diaspora*, 2nd ed. (Washington: Howard University Press, 1993), has led the way in emphasizing the reciprocal and dynamic character of the African diaspora.

56. See the essays by Reis and Butler in this volume; also J. L. Matory, "The Trans-Atlantic Nation: Reconsidering Nations and Transnationalism" (paper presented at the conference "Rethinking the African Diaspora: The Making of a Black Atlantic World in the Bight of Benin and Brazil," Emory University, Atlanta, 17–18 April 1998).

57. Da Cunha, *Negros, Estrangeiros*, pp. 108–20.

58. D. A. Ross, "The Career of Domingo Martinez in the Bight of Benin, 1833–64," *Journal of African History*, 6 (1965), pp. 88–9; Law and Mann, "West Africa in the Atlantic Community," p. 333.

59. J. L. Matory, "Return, Race, and Religion in a Transatlantic Yoruba Nation" (paper presented at the annual meeting of the African Studies Association, San Francisco, Nov. 1996); also Butler's essay in this volume.

60. R. Law, "Islam in Dahomey: A Case Study of the Introduction and Influence of Islam in a Peripheral Area of West Africa," *Scottish Journal of Religious Studies*, 7 (1986), pp. 95–122; S. Y. Boadi-Siaw, "Brazilian Returnees of West Africa," in Harris (ed.), *Global Dimensions of the African Diaspora*, pp. 421–39; Guran, *Agudás*, pp. 96–104.

61. R. Law, "Ethnicity and the Slave Trade: 'Lucumi' and 'Nagô' as Ethnonyms in West Africa," *History in Africa*, 24 (1997), pp. 205–19; Matory, "The Trans-Atlantic Nation" and M. I. Côrtes de Oliveira, "Minas et Jejes de Bahia: Qui étaient-ils en Afrique" (papers presented at the conference "Rethinking the African Diaspora: The Making of a Black Atlantic World in the Bight of Benin and Brazil," Emory University, Atlanta, 17–18 April 1998). See also M. I. Côrtes de Oliveira, "La grande tente Nagô: rapprochements ethniques chez les

africains de Bahia au XIXe siécle," in Lovejoy (ed.), *Identifying Enslaved Africans*, pp. 286–301.

62. K. D. Butler, *Freedoms Given, Freedoms Won: Afro-Brazilians in Post-Abolition São Paulo and Salvador* (New Brunswick: Rutgers University Press, 1998), chs. 2 and 6.

63. J. M. Turner, "Democratic Instincts in Dahomey (Benin Republic), 1920–1930 and 1989–1996: Afro-Brazilian Political Behavior on the Benin Gulf" (paper presented at the annual meeting of the African Studies Association, San Francisco, Nov. 1996); B. C. Code, "Les 'Brésiliens' en Afrique de l'ouest: Hier et Aujourd'hui," in Lovejoy (ed.), *Identifying Enslaved Africans,* pp. 428–37; and E. Soumonni's essay in this volume.

64. B. Bailyn, "The Idea of Atlantic History," *Itinerario,* 20 (1996), pp. 19–41.

65. Ibid, pp. 26, 33.

66. D. B. Davis, *Slavery and Human Progress* (New York: Oxford University Press, 1986), p. 51. Perhaps no historian has done more than P. D. Curtin to promote the study of the forced migration of Africans to the Americas. His relevant publications are too numerous to cite, but two of the most influential have been *The Atlantic Slave Trade: A Census* (Madison: University of Wisconsin Press, 1969); and *The Rise and Fall of the Plantation Complex: Essays in Atlantic History* (Cambridge: Cambridge University Press, 1990).

67. D. Eltis, "Gender and the Slave Trade in the Early Modern Atlantic World" (paper presented at the conference "Transatlantic Slaving and the African Diaspora," Omohundro Institute, Williamsburg, 11–13 Sept. 1998), p. 13.

68. "'The Legacy of the Atlantic Program,' a Conversation with Sidney W. Mintz," *Crosscurrents,* 1 (1993).

69. See the programme description on its webpage, which begins with a quote from E. R. Wolf, author of *Europe and the People without History* (Berkeley: University of California Press, 1983).

70. P. Gilroy, *The Black Atlantic: Modernity and Double Consciousness* (Cambridge: Harvard University Press, 1993), pp. 6, 15–16.

The Hamitic Hypothesis: Its Origin and Functions in Time Perspective[1]

Edith R. Sanders

The Hamitic hypothesis is well-known to students of Africa. It states that everything of value ever found in Africa was brought there by the Hamites, allegedly a branch of the Caucasian race. Seligman formulates it as follows:

> Apart from relatively late Semitic influence...the civilizations of Africa are the civilizations of the Hamites, its history the record of these peoples and of their interaction with the two other African stocks, the Negro and the Bushman, whether this influence was exerted by highly civilized Egyptians or by such wider pastoralists as are represented at the present day by the Beja and Somali....The incoming Hamites were pastoral "Europeans"—arriving wave after wave—better armed as well as quicker witted than the dark agricultural Negroes.[2]

On closer examination of the history of the idea, there emerges a previous elaborate Hamitic theory, in which the Hamites are believed to be Negroes. It becomes clear then that the hypothesis is symptomatic of the nature of race relations, that it has changed its content if not its nomenclature through time, and that it has become a problem of epistemology.

In the beginning there was the Bible. The word "Ham" appears there for the first time in Genesis, chapter five. Noah cursed Ham, his youngest son, and said:

> Cursed be Canaan;
> A servant of servants shall he be unto his brethren.
> And he said,
> Blessed be Jehovah, the God of Shem; And let Canaan be his servant.
> God enlarge Japhet,
> And let him dwell in the tent of Shem; And let Canaan be his servant.

Then follows an enumeration of the sons of Noah: Shem, Ham, Japhet, and their sons who were born to them after the flood. The Bible makes no mention of racial differences among the ancestors of mankind. It is much later that an idea of race appears with reference to the sons of Noah; it concerns the descendants of Ham. The Babylonian Talmud, a collection of oral traditions of the Jews, appeared in the sixth century A.D.; it states that the descendants of Ham are cursed by being black, and depicts Ham as a sinful man and his progeny as degenerates.[3] Thus, early tradition identified the Hamites with Negroes and endowed them with both certain physiognomical attributes and an undesirable character. This notion persisted in the Middle Ages, when fanciful rabbinical expansions of the Genesis stories were still being made. Ham, some of them said, was supposed to have emasculated Noah, who cursed him thus:

> "Now I cannot beget the fourth son whose children I would have ordered to serve you and your brothers! Therefore it must be Canaan, your firstborn, whom they enslave. And since you have disabled me...doing ugly things in blackness of night, Canaan's children shall be borne ugly and black! Moreover, because you twisted your head around to see my nakedness, your grandchildren's hair shall be twisted into kinks, and their eyes red; again because your lips jested at my misfortune, theirs shall swell; and because you neglected my nakedness, they shall go naked, and their male members shall be shamefully elongated! Men of this race are called Negroes; their forefather Canaan commanded them to love theft and fornication, to be banded together in hatred of their masters and never to tell the truth."[4]

Scholars who study the Hebrew myths of the Genesis claim that these oral traditions grew out of a need of the Israelites to rationalize their subjugation of Canaan, a historical fact validated by the myth of Noah's curse. Talmudic or Midrashic explanations of the myth of Ham were well known to Jewish writers in the Middle Ages, as seen in this description by Benjamin of Tudela, a twelfth-century merchant and traveller south of Aswan:

> There is a people...who, like animals, eat of the herbs that grow on the banks of the Nile and in their fields. They go about naked and have not the intelligence of ordinary men. They cohabit with their sisters and anyone they can find...they are taken as slaves and sold in Egypt and neighbouring countries. These sons of Ham are black slaves.[5]

Ideas have a way of being accepted when they become useful as a rationalization of an economic fact of life. As Graves and Patai put it: "That Negroes are doomed to serve men of lighter color was a view gratefully borrowed by Christians in the Middle Ages; a severe shortage of cheap manual labor caused by the plague made the reinstitution of slavery attractive."

The notion of the Negro-Hamite was generally accepted by the year 1600. In one of the earliest post-medieval references found, Leo Africanus, the great Arab traveller and one-time protégé of Pope Leo X, wrote about Negro Africans as being descended from Ham. His translator, the Englishman John Pory, followed the text with his own commentary in which he stressed the *punishment* suffered by Ham's descendants, thus reinforcing the myth in modern times.[6]

Some seventeenth-century writers[7] acquaint us with notions current in their time by citing European authors, known or unknown today, who wrote, directly or indirectly, about the low position of Negro-Hamites in the world. This was further strengthened by European travellers who went to Africa for reasons of trade[8] or curiosity.[9] Concurrently, there existed another point of view, in which the term "Hamite" denoted a sinner of some sort, not necessarily a Negro, although the characteristics of the Hamite were the same negative ones variously attributed to the Negro.[10]

The idea of a Negro-Hamite was not universally accepted. Some individuals[11] believed that the blackness of the Negro was caused by the soil on which he lived together with the extreme heat of the sun. Others doubted that either the climate theory or the efficacy of Noah's curse were responsible for the Negro's physiognomy, but reasoned that "their colour and wool are innate or seminal, from their first beginning. . . ."[12]

By and large, however, the Negro was seen as a descendant of Ham, bearing the stigma of Noah's curse. This view was compatible with the various interests extant at that time. On the one hand, it allowed exploitation of the Negro for economic gain to remain undisturbed by any Christian doubts as to the moral issues involved. "A servant of servants shall he be" clearly meant that the Negro was preordained for slavery. Neither individual nor collective guilt was to be borne for a state of the world created by the Almighty. On the other hand, Christian cosmology could remain at peace, because identifying the Negro as a Hamite—thus as a brother—kept him in the family of man in accordance with the biblical story of the creation of mankind.

The eighteenth century saw an efflorescence of scientific inquiry, which directed its efforts to the understanding of man's place in the world. Modern science had developed a century earlier and had attempted to establish order in the universe; the nature of man, however, was not part of scientific investigation, but remained in the province of theology. This state of affairs became unsatisfactory to the later scholars, namely the *philosophes* of the Enlightenment, who tried to apply scientific methods to the study of man and whose theories as to the origin of the race often came into direct conflict with the Scriptures.

The Negro's place in nature was the subject of great debate at that time. One of the crucial issues of this debate was the question of unity in mankind, or monogenism, as opposed to the separate creation of races or polygenism.[13] The concept of the Negro-Hamite was steadily losing ground because theological interpretation of the peopling of the world did not satisfy the men of the Enlightenment. The myth was now kept alive mainly by the clergy, who tried to keep their hold on the laity by discrediting the savants as infidels.[14]

The polygenist theories led to a widespread belief that the Negro was subhuman and at the same time de-emphasized his relationship to the accursed Ham. The monogenist theories attempted to explain Negro physical characteristics by natural rather than mythical causes. The conservative theologians still clung to the now classic exegesis of the Old Testament and discouraged any attempt at a different interpretation.[15] At the end of the eighteenth century, many famous men espoused and popularized one of two views regarding the Negro. One was that he was the result of "degeneration" due to various environmental conditions.[16] The other and more frequent view was that he was a separate creation, subhuman in character.[17]

The Western world, which was growing increasingly rich on the institution of slavery, grew increasingly reluctant to look at the Negro slave and see him as a brother under the skin. Some writers[18] feel that the image of the Negro deteriorated in direct proportion to his value as a commodity, and the proudly rational and scientific white man was impatient to find some definitive proof for the exclusion of the Negro from the family of man and for ultimate denial of common ancestry.

The catalyst which made this possible was an historical event, namely Napoleon's invasion of Egypt in 1798. Because Napoleon shared the passion for science and antiquities that was the hallmark of the Enlightenment, he invited archaeologists and other scientists to join him. The experts who had accompanied him discovered treasures that led them to found the new science of Egyptology and an institute on Egyptian soil. These discoveries were to revolutionize history's view of the Egyptian and lay the basis for a new Hamitic myth.

Napoleon's scientists made the revolutionary discovery that the beginnings of Western civilization were earlier than the civilizations of the Romans and the Greeks. Mysterious monuments, evidences of the beginnings of science, art, and well-preserved mummies were uncovered. Attention was drawn to the population that lived among these ancient splendours and was presumably descended from the people who had created them. It was a well-mixed population, such as it is at the present time, with physical types running from light to black and with many physiognomical variations. The French scholars came to the conclusion that the Egyptians were Negroids. Denon, one of Napoleon's original expedition, describes them as such: "... a broad and flat nose, very short, a large flattened mouth ... thick lips, etc."[19]

The view that the Egyptians were "Negroid" and highly civilized apparently existed before the French expedition to Egypt. Count Volney, a French traveller to the Middle East, spent four years in Egypt and Syria and wrote in a well-known book:

> How are we astonished ... when we reflect that to the race of negroes, at present our slaves, and the objects of our contempt, we owe our arts, sciences, and ... when we recollect that, in the midst of these nations, who call themselves the friends of liberty and humanity, the most barbarous of slaveries is justified; and that it is even a problem whether the understandings of negroes be of the same species with that of white men![20]

In spite of the deserved respect which Volney enjoyed, his opinions on this subject were not accepted.

Nevertheless, the Egyptian expedition made it impossible to hide that seeming paradox of a population of Negroids who were, once upon a time, originators of the oldest civilization of the West. The conflicting ideologies which existed in the West made it difficult for the various proponents of these ideologies to deal with the notion as it stood. Such a notion upset the main existing tenets; it could not be internalized by those individuals on both sides of the Atlantic who were convinced of the innate inferiority of the Negro, nor by those who adhered to the biblical explanation of the origin of races. To the latter such an idea was blasphemous, as Noah's curse condemned the Hamites to misery and precluded high original achievement.

Egypt became the focus of great interest among the scientists as well as among the lay public. The fruits of this interest were not long in coming. A few short years after the Egyptian expedition, there appeared a large number of publications dealing with Egypt and Egyptians. Many of these works seemed to have had as their main purpose an attempt to prove in some way that the Egyptians were not Negroes. The arguments which follow brought forth the questions of language, migration, ancient writers, and the existence of mummies.[21] The polygenist theories of race postulated that as each race was created separately, so it was endowed with its own language. Because the Coptic language was clearly related to Arabic, it was convenient to draw the conclusion that the nations who spoke related languages must have proceeded from one parental stock. Since the Ethiopians, Nubians and other allied peoples were declared not to be Negro by European travellers, the Egyptians could not be said to be of African (Negro) race, as all of these peoples were colonists from Syria or Arabia Felix. Since ancient writers were silent on the subject of the Negroid physiognomy of the Egyptian, it was understood that in effect Egyptians were not Negroid, as such a fact would have startled the ancients into a detailed description. Herodotus himself ran the argument, and described them in comparative not absolute terms. Thus "black and woolly haired" meant black as compared to the Greeks and woolly haired as compared to the Greeks. Some said that the existence of the mummies itself constituted sufficient proof that these people were non-Negro; to W. G. Browne the "... prescience of that people concerning errors into which posterity might fall, exhibits irrefragable proof of their features and of the colour of their skin...."[22] clearly implying, therefore, that the ancient Egyptians knew they could be mistaken for Negroes, and so left their bodies in evidence to refute such an allegation.

Browne insisted that the Egyptians were white. Although he himself did not call them "Hamites," he paved the way for his successors who were to identify the Egyptians as such.

Modern times showed their influence on theological writings as well. The new Hamitic concept made its appearance quite early in the nineteenth century, spearheaded by the clergy. If the Negro was a descendant of Ham, and Ham was cursed, how could he be the creator of a great civilization? It follows logically that the theologians had to take another look, both at the Bible and at its explanation of the origin of the races of man. The veracity of the Scriptures obviously could not be denied. New interpretations of the meaning of Scriptures were offered. Egyptians, it was now remembered, were descendants of Mizraim, a son of Ham. Noah had only cursed Canaan-son-of-Ham, so that it was Canaan and his progeny alone who suffered the malediction. Hain, his other sons, and their children were not included in the curse.

For example, the Reverend M. Russell took up the issue of the Hamites and the Egyptians:

> In the sacred writings of the Hebrews it [Egypt] is called Mizraim . . . the name which is applied to Egypt by the Arabs of the present day. The Copts retain the native word "Chemia" which perhaps has some relation to Cham, the son of Noah; or as Plutarch insinuates, may only denote that darkness of colour which appears in a rich soil or in the human eye.[23]

He admits that there is a peculiarity of feature common to all the Copts, but asserts that neither in countenance nor personal form is there any resemblance to the Negro.

He and other scholars re-read the Book of Genesis focusing on the genealogy of the three ancestors of mankind, and especially Ham. The histories of the sons of Ham were discussed, particularly those of Cush and Mizraim. The question was raised then whether it was Hain who had been cursed after all, or was it only Canaan?[24] It was indeed Canaan who was cursed, but the rest of the progeny of Ham went on to prosper.

So it came to pass that the Egyptians emerged as Hamites, Caucasoid, uncursed and capable of high civilization. This view became widely accepted and it is reflected in the theological literature of that era. A survey of Biblical dictionaries of the period is quite revealing as to the wide acceptance of the new Hamites. *Cyclopedia of Biblical Literature,* published in 1846 by John Kitto, D.D., F.S.A., has a long article under the name *Ham.* It is stressed that the curse of Noah is directed only against Canaan. The general opinion is stated that all southern nations derive from Ham. However, the article admits difficulties in tracing the history of the most important Hamitic nations—the Cushites, the Phoenicians and the Egyptians—due to their great intermixture with foreign peoples. Thus, the early decades of the nineteenth century greeted a new Hamitic myth, this time with a Caucasoid protagonist. At the same time the scientific bases of the new Hamitic myth were being devised and, allegedly, substantiated.

Perhaps because slavery was both still legal and profitable in the United States, and because it was deemed necessary and right to protect it, there arose an American school of anthropology which attempted to prove scientifically that the Egyptian was a Caucasian, far removed from the inferior Negro. As Mannheim said, each intellectual stand is functionally dependent on the "differentiated social group reality standing behind it."[25] Such workers as Dr Morton,[26] assisted in various ways by Josiah Nott[27] and George Gliddon,[28] collected, measured, interpreted and described the human crania. The comparative studies made of these crania led Morton to believe that the Egyptian osteological formation was Caucasian, and that it was a race indigenous to the Nile Valley. He also postulated fixity of species, considering it a primordial organic form, permanent through time. Nott and Gliddon, who acted as Morton's apostles, also bolstered his interpretation by explaining the Negroid admixture of the Egyptians as being a population which descended from numerous Negro slaves kept by Egyptians in ancient days. These theories attempted to include the Egyptians in the branch of the Caucasoid race, to explain their accomplishments on the basis of innate racial superiority, and to exclude the Negro from any possibility of achievement by restating his alleged inferiority and his position of "natural slave." The conclusions of American scholars found a receptive audience in Europe, where craniology was considered to yield positive and meaningful data, a point of view expressed by two scientists of world renown, the Drs. Retzius of Sweden and Broca of France. The intellectual vogue of the day was the stress on "facts," not abstract theories, in all disciplines. Craniology provided a seemingly concrete "fact," thus fitting in neatly with the prevailing academic attitudes. Again, there was no complete consensus among anthropologists. The most prominent opponent of the American school of anthropology was James Prichard of England,[29] who was not convinced that the Egyptians belonged to the Caucasian race.

The science of philology added weight to the new Hamitic theory. This young science was developing at a time when language and race were considered to be inextricably bound together, an approach which lent itself to polygenist theories. Bunsen,[30] a philologist and an Egyptologist, reported two branches of cognate languages, the Semitic and what he called the Iranian. Khamitic or Egyptian he postulated to be anterior to Semitic and antedeluvian. Here was irrefutable proof, it seemed, that the Hamitic language belonged to the Caucasoid peoples, and it was eagerly adopted by scholars and theologians. The new Hamitic myth was gaining momentum.

The late nineteenth century provided two new ideologies which utilized and expanded the concept of the Caucasoid Hamite: colonialism and modem racism. Both shaped the European attitude to Africa and Africans. The travellers found a variety of physical types in Africa, and their ethnocentrism made them value those who looked more like themselves. These were declared to be Hamitic, or of Hamitic descent, and endowed with the myth of superior achievements and considerable beneficial influence on their Negro brothers. John Hanning Speke[31] was seminal to the Hamitic hypothesis which we know today. Upon discovery of the kingdom of Buganda with its complex political organization, he attributed its "barbaric civilization" to a nomadic pastoralist race related to the Hamitic Galla, thus setting the tone for the interpreters to come. The Hamites were designated as early culture-bearers in Africa owing to the natural superiority of intellect and character of all Caucasoids. Such a viewpoint had dual merit for European purposes: it maintained the image of the Negro as an inferior being, and it pointed to the alleged fact that development could come to him only by mediation of the white race.[32] It also implied a self-appointed duty of the "higher" races to civilize the "lower" ones, a notion which was eventually formulated as "the white man's burden." At this point in time the Hamite found himself in an ambiguous position. On the one hand he was considered to be Caucasoid, that is superior. On the other hand he was a native, part of the "burden," a man to benefit from European civilization. Here the Teutonic theory of race showed its adaptability. Having devised a hierarchy within the Caucasian race, the builders of the theory placed the Teutonic Anglo-Saxon on top of the ladder with the Slavs on the lowest rung. But an even lower position could always be added, and the Hamites filled the space admirably. "Politics and race theories seemed natural allies",[33] they provided a seemingly cogent ideological framework for colonial expansion and exploitation.

The beginning of the twentieth century saw the Caucasoid-Hamite solidly established. Science supplanted theology as the alpha and omega of truth. Racial "scientific" classifications, which had to face the physical diversity of the various "Hamites," established a separate Hamitic *branch* of the Caucasian race, closely following the creation of a linguistic entity called a family of Hamitic languages. Linguistic typologies were based on racial types and racial classifications on linguistic definitions. The confusion surrounding the "Hamite" was steadily compounded as the terms of reference became increasingly overlapping and vague. The racial classification of "Hamites" encompassed a great variety of types from fairskinned, blonde, blue-eyed (Berbers) to black (Ethiopians). Two early racial typologies were devised by Sergi[34] and Brinton.[35] Sergi called certain populations Hamitic chiefly on the basis of their linguistic characteristics. Among these were the inhabitants of the Sahara, the Berbers, and even such people "who have wholly, or partially, lost

their language," like the Egyptians, Watusi and Masai. They were divided into the Eastern branch, and the Northern branch. The Eastern branch included the ancient and modern Egyptians (excluding the Arabs), Nubians, Bejas, Abyssinians, Gallas, Danakil, Somali, Masai and Watusi (or Wahuma). The Northern branch included the Berbers, Tebus, Fulbes (Fulani) and the Gaunches of the Canaries.[36] Brinton denoted Lybians, Egyptians and the East African groups as Hamitic, and remarked that each of these groups is distinguished by physical and linguistic differences.[37] He went on to state that "the physical appearance of the Libyan peoples distinctly marks them as members of the white race, often of uncommonly pure blood. As the race elsewhere, they present the blonde and brunette type, the latter predominant, but the former extremely well marked." Because Brinton also considered the Iberians to be Hamites, and not Basques, his description of the Libyans seems to imply that the Libyans are a sort of half-way house of the "Hamitic" race, because they combine elements of the blonde Hamites (of Europe) and the brunette Hamites (of East Africa). This reasoning appears to be no more logical than that of Sergi, who first bases a racial group on its linguistic characteristics and then includes in it people who have "wholly or partially" lost the language!

Linguistic classifications were based on geography, racial characteristics and occupation, rather than on rigorous methodology pertaining solely to language. Grammatical gender became the main diagnostic of the so-called Hamitic languages. Although grammatical gender exists in many unrelated languages of the world, it was not found in the languages of the "true" Negro (racial category again). Thus linguistic typologies had racial bases just as racial typologies were based on linguistics.[38]

Because the Hamites discovered in Africa south of the Sahara were described as pastoralists and the traditional occupation of the Negro was supposedly agriculture, pastoralism and all its attributes became endowed with an aura of superiority of culture, giving the Hamite a third dimension: cultural identity.

The historians who began to compile histories of Africa wrote with an often unconscious racial bias, and accepted the dicta of the discoverers of that continent as indisputable proven facts and presented them as historical explanations of the African past.[39]

Much of anthropology gave its support to the Hamitic myth. Seligman found a cultural substratum of supposedly great influence in Africa.[40] In 1930 he published his famous *Races of Africa*, which went through several editions and which was reprinted in 1966 still basically unchanged. He refined the Sergi-devised classifications of Hamitic peoples, adding the category of Nilotes or "half-Hamites." Every trace and/or sign of what is usually termed "civilized' in Africa was attributed to alien, mainly Hamitic, origin. In such a way, iron-working was supposed to have been introduced to the Negroes by pastoral Hamites, along with complex political institutions, irrigation and age-grade systems.[41] Archaeological findings of any magnitude were also ascribed to outside influences, and kept the Negro African out of his own culture history.[42] In the eyes of the world the Negro stood stripped of any intellectual or artistic genius and of any ability at all which would allow him, now, in the past, or in the future, to be the master of his life and country.

The confluence of modern nationalism and the ensuing modern racism evolved from earlier nineteenth-century national romanticism and developed through theories of de Gobineau and adaptations of the Darwinian revolution. It was echoed in all Western nations, culminating finally in the ideology of Nazi Germany. Because that leading exponent of racism became the enemy of most of Europe and of the United States during World War II, German-championed ideology seemed to have lost some of its popularity. The Hamitic myth ceased to be useful with African nations which have been gaining their independence one by one, and the growing African nationalism drew scholarly attention to Africa's past. Many of the scholars were unencumbered by colonial ties; some of them were themselves African. They began to discover that Africa was not a *tabula rasa*, but that it had a past, a history which could be reconstructed; that it was a continent that knew empire builders at a time when large areas of Europe stagnated in the Dark Ages; that it knew art and commerce.

Some writers started to throw doubts on the Hamitic hypothesis by discovering indigenous Negro achievement of the past,[43] while others attempted to explode it.[44] Still the myth endures, is occasionally subverted by new terminology (such as "Southern Cushites")[45] and stubbornly refuses to give way and allow an unbiased look at what can be validly ascertained from African culture history. It would be well-nigh impossible to point to an individual and recognize in him a Hamite according to racial, linguistic, and cultural characteristics to fit the image that has been presented to us for so long. Such an individual does not exist. The word still exists, endowed with a mythical meaning; it endures through time and history, and, like a chameleon, changes its colour to reflect the changing light. As the word became flesh, it engendered many problems of scholarship.

Summary

The anthropological and historical literature dealing with Africa abounds with references to a people called the "Hamites." "Hamite," as used in these writings, designates an African population supposedly distinguished by its race—Caucasian—and its language family, from the Negro inhabitants of the rest of Africa below the Sahara.

There exists a widely held belief in the Western world that everything of value ever found in Africa was brought there by these Hamites, a people inherently superior to the native populations. This belief, often referred to as the Hamitic hypothesis, is a convenient explanation for all the signs of civilization found in Black Africa. It was these Caucasoids, we read, who taught the Negro how to manufacture iron and who were so politically sophisticated that they organized the conquered territories into highly complex states with themselves as the ruling elites. This hypothesis was preceded by another elaborate Hamitic theory. The earlier theory, which gained currency in the sixteenth century, was that the Hamites were black savages, "natural slaves"—and Negroes. This identification of the Hamite with the Negro, a view which persisted throughout the eighteenth century, served as a rationale for slavery, using Biblical interpretations in support of its tenets. The image of the Negro deteriorated in direct proportion to the growth of the importance of slavery, and it became imperative for the white man to exclude the Negro from the brotherhood of races. Napoleon!s expedition to Egypt in 1798 became the historical catalyst that provided the Western World with the impetus to turn the Hamite into a Caucasian.

The Hamitic concept had as its function the portrayal of the Negro as an inherently inferior being and to rationalize his exploitation. In the final analysis it was possible because its changing aspects were supported by the prevailing intellectual viewpoints of the times.

Notes

[1]This topic has been explored in detail in E. R. Sanders "Hamites in Anthropology and History: A Preliminary Study," unpublished manuscript, Columbia University, 1965.

[2]C. G. Seligman, *Races of Africa* (1930), 96. All subsequent editions make the same statement (1957, 1966).

[3]T. F. Gossett, *Race—the History of an Idea in America* (1963), 5.

[4]R. Graves and R. Patai, *Hebrew Myths* (1964), 121.

[5]R. Hess. "Travels of Benjamin of Tudela," *J. Afr. Hist.* vi, I (1965), 17.

[6]J. Pory, *Translation of Leo Africanus, Hakluyt Society,* xcii–xciv (London, 1896).

[7]For instance, the Italian philosopher Campanella and a Mr. Mede who was cited by seventeenth-century authors (see below) but whose own writings I was unable to find.

[8]Richard Jobson, *The Golden Trade* (1623).

[9]Sir Thomas Herbert, *Some Years of Travels into Divers Parts of Africa* (1677).

[10]E. Pagitt, *Heresiography or a Description of the Hereticks,* printed by W. W. for W. Lee (London, 1646).

[11]Herbert, op. cit. 27.

[12]Cited by T. Bendyshe, The History of Anthropology: Memoir read before the *Anthropological Society of London* I (1863–4), 371.

[13]Some of the outstanding monogenists were Linnaeus, Buffon and Blumenbach. Some outstanding polygenists were Voltaire, Lord Karnes and Charles White (an English physician and author of *An Account of the Regular Gradations in Man and in Different Animals* (London, 1799)).

[14]Lord Bolingbroke, an English friend of Voltaire, attempted a different interpretation of Genesis which was answered by a book by Robert Clayton, Bishop of Clough, entitled *A Vindication of the Histories of Old and New Testament,* in 1753.

[15]For instance, the Rev. Samuel Stanhope Smith, a professor at Princeton, then called College of New Jersey, an institution founded in 1746 to train Presbyterian ministers. He wrote *An Essay on the Causes of the Variety of Complexion* (Philadelphia, 1787).

[16]Buffon, cited by L. Eiseley, *Darwin's Century* (1961), 35–46; and Dr Benjamin Rush (American physician and son-in-law of Benjamin Franklin), cited by J. Greene, "The American debate on the Negro's place in nature, 1780–1815," *Journal of History of Ideas,* xv (1954), are examples of this school of thought.

[17]Voltaire, *The Works of Voltaire: A Contemporary Version* modernized by W. J. Fleming (New York, 1901); and Lord Kames, *Sketches of the History of Man* (Edinburgh, 1780), are examples of this group.

[18]E. Williams, *Capitalism and Slavery* (University of Carolina Press, 1944); P. D. Curtin *Image of Africa* (New York, 1964).

[19]V. Denon. *Travels in Upper and Lower Egypt* (London, 1803).

[20]Volney, *Travels through Syria and Egypt 1783 1784–1785* (1787), 83.

[21]The arguments presented here are those of W. G. Browne, a British traveller to Egypt, who was representative of this type of thinking; he was one of the first to have his ideas published. These ideas contained the seeds of the new Hamitic myth that was to emerge in the very near future. W. G. Browne, *Travels in Africa, Egypt and Syria* (London, 1806).

[22]W. G. Browne, op. cit. 170–5.

[23]M. Russell, *View of Ancient and Modern Egypt* (New York, 1831), 27.

[24]It was the same doubt which had been formulated by Lord Bolingbroke 100 years before. But now the doubt was general, and the answer much different from that given by Bishop Clayton.

[25]K. Mannheim, *Essays in Sociology of Knowledge* (1952), 190,

[26]Samuel George Morton, American physician and professor of anatomy, author of several books on the human crania, such as *Crania Americana* and *Crania Egyptica* (1844).

[27]Josiah Clark Nott, an American scientist and collaborator with Gliddon on *Types of Mankind* (1854).

[28]George R. Gliddon, an American vice-consul in Cairo and an admirer of Dr. Morton, whom he supplied with Egyptian skulls.

[29]J. Prichard, *The Natural History of Man* (London, 1855).

[30]C. K. J. Bunsen, *Egypt's Place in Universal History* (London, 1848–67).

[31]J. H. Speke, *Journal of the Discovery of the Source of the Nile* (New York, 1964).

[32]With respect to the role played by such theories in English colonial expansion see E. Sanderson, *Africa in the Nineteenth Century* (London, 1898); F. D. Lugard, *The Rise of Our East African Empire* (Edinburgh, 1898); J. Scott Keltie, *Partition of Africa* (London, 1895); W. L. Langer, *The Diplomacy of Imperialism, 1890–1902* (New York, 1935).

[33]J. Barzun, *Race: A Modern Superstition* (New York, 1965), 33.

[34]G. Sergi, *The Mediterranean Race* (New York, 1901).

[35]D. G. Brinton, *Races and Peoples* (New York, 1890).

[36]Sergi, op. cit. 40–41.

[37]V. Brinton, op. cit. 115.

[38]Early work on the Hamitic language family was done by R. N. Cust, *A Sketch of African Languages* (London, 1883); also Lepsius and Meinhof.

[39]See A. R. Atterbury, *Islam in Africa* (New York, 1899); J. W. Gregory, *The Foundation of British East Africa* (London, 1901); K. Johnston, *Africa* (London, 1884); J. Scott Keltie op. cit.; E. Sanderson, op. cit.; Capt. C. H. Stigand, *The Land of Zinj* (London, 1913); and A. S. White, *The Development of Africa* (London, 1890).

[40]"Some Aspects of the Hamitic Problem in the Anglo-Egyptian Sudan," *Journal of Royal Anthropological Institute,* LIII, 1913.

[41]S. Cole, *The Prehistory of East Africa* (Hammondsworth, 1954); K. Oberg in *African Political Systems,* M. Fortes and E. Evans-Pritchard (eds.); D. Westermann, *The African Today and Tomorrow* (Oxford, 1949), are only a few of a long list of examples.

[42]See early writings on Great Zimbabwe: D. B. MacIver, *Mediaeval Rhodesia* (New York, 1906); W. C. Willoughby, *Race Problem in New Africa* (Oxford, 1923); E. Naville, "The Land of Punt and the Hamites," *Journal of Transactions of the Victoria Institute,* LVII (1925).

[43]G. Caton-Thompson, *The Zimbabwe Culture: Ruins and Reactions* (Oxford, 1931); J. P. Crazzolara, *The Lwoo, Missioni Africane* (Italy, 1950); two instances of such discoveries.

[44]See, for example, D. Apter, *Political Kingdom in Uganda* (Princeton, 1961), 63; L. Fallers, *Bantu Bureaucracy,* East African Institute of Social Research (1956), 27–9; J. H. Greenberg, *Studies in African Linguistic Classifications* (New Haven, 1955); I. Wallerstein, *Africa, the Politics of Independence* (New York, 1961), 12–13; D. McCall, *Africa in Time Perspective* (Boston, 1964), 136–138.

[45]E.g., G. P. Murdock, *Africa, Its Peoples and Their Culture History* (New York, 1959).

SECTION TWO:
THE FORMATION OF
EARLY AFRICAN SOCIETIES

Introduction

African Diaspora Studies by its very nature traverses a broad range of fields and disciplines. The second section seeks to further introduce students to the wide range of disciplines related to understanding early African history and, in the process, uses research from the fields of anthropology, archaeology and paleontology. The recent debate on early African history requires this kind of interdisciplinary focus. Nevertheless, these writers present the main arguments in their essays in a very accessible manner for the nonspecialist reader.

Many scholars place the African continent and its peoples at the center of their quest to understand what happened to persons of African descent over millennia. Consequently, they recognize the continents of Africa as the "motherland" for these peoples. Furthermore, they argue that Africa is the home of earliest man and the place where all civilization began. This second section continues to deal with these ongoing debates regarding the origins of humans in Africa, the earliest developments of civilization in the region of the Nile Valley (particularly the area of Nubia), and the "Nile Valley Scholars" discussions regarding the Africanness of Ancient Egypt as well as the state of West Africa prior to the Atlantic Slave Trade.

The six readings in this section examine these important issues related to the understanding of the early African experience. The essays lay the groundwork for the view that the African continent is the motherland for all peoples of African descent.

The first essay is David W. Phillipson's insightful explanation of the existence of earliest man in Africa. This essay establishes many of the arguments that support the "Out of Africa" theory, which suggests that man first lived in Africa before migrating to other parts of the globe. Phillipson presents an authoritative survey on African archaeology that suggests that the origin of humans is in Africa. There is an ongoing debate on the origins of humans among humanist scholars. Beginning with Charles Darwin's *The Origin of the Species* (1859), his later *The Descent of Man* (1871), and the subsequent search by humanists, there has been a long list of discoveries supporting evidence for the earliest Homo sapiens emerging from Africa. Raymond Dart's 1940's work in South Africa; Louis and Mary Leakey's 1950's work at Olduvai Gorge in Tanzania; Donald Johanson, Timothy Gray, Berhane Asfaw, and Timothy White's 1980's work at Hadar, Ethiopia; and others in the early 1990s all support the "Out of

Africa" theory. On the other hand, the proponents of "The Multiregional Continuity Hypothesis," with the striking 1989 discoveries in Hubei Province, China; the 1991 Republic of Georgia (in the former Soviet Republic) fossil find; and others in a wide distribution of regions across the world are supported by an equally impressive group of scholars. Some of the leading scholars in this group include Carl O. Swisher and Carness H. Curtis of UCLA's Institute of Human Origins. These and others, like Milford Wolpoff and Rachel Caspari, have suggested that man evolved in other parts of the world at the same time that the process took place in Africa. Phillipson's essay "The Emergence of Mankind in Africa" is taken from his work African Archaeology, in which he clearly outlines the evidence in support of the "Eve," or "Out-of-Africa" hypothesis.

Phillipson is Curator of the Museum of Archaeology and Anthropology, and Reader in African Prehistory at the University of Cambridge, England. His African Archaeology (1993), first published in 1985, but updated in 1993 with the latest findings at the time of publication, makes a very strong case for the "Eve," or "Out-of-Africa," hypothesis. Since the publication of Phillipson's outstanding work in 1993, there has been a growing number of paleontological discoveries in East Africa that continue to validate the "Eve," or "Out-of-Africa," hypothesis. These discoveries include the Australopithecus afarensis in Afar, Ethiopia in 1994, who scholars believe lived about 3.9 million years ago. Maeve Leakey of the National Museums of Kenya identified the Australopilthecus anamensis in Kenya, which is believed to have existed about 4.1 million years ago. The most recent unearthed remains from the Northeast region of Africa was obtained in July 2000. Paleontologists made the discovery in Galilo in Ethiopia's northeastern Afar region and believe the remains to be about 3.4 million years old. On the other hand, the proponents of the opposing view, called the "Regional Continuity Hypothesis," still argue that Homo erectus developed in various regions of the world from China to Europe to southeast Asia, and not only in Africa. The debate regarding exactly where on earth modern humans first evolved will continue in the years to come among humanists, evolutionists, and other scholars. However, more experts are now having greater confidence in supporting the "Eve," or "Out-of-Africa," hypothesis because of the overwhelming evidence that has come to light in the last decade.

The second essay in this section is taken from Cheikh Anta Diop's controversial "Origin of the Egyptians" treatise, which is an excellent summation of his arguments on the long-standing argument regarding the Africanness of Ancient Egypt. Diop was one of the leading scholars who had been seriously engaged in this discussion for many years. Other supporters of this argument include W. E. B. DuBois, Carter G. Woodson, Joel A. Rogers, Chancellor Williams, George James, Louis B. Leakey, Basil Davidson, Martin Bernal, Ivan Van Sertima, Asa G. Hilliard, and many others. Diop was a leading Senegalese scholar who was educated at the Sorbonne in the mid-1950's. He returned to West Africa to become director of the Radio Carbon Dating Center at the University of Dakar, now called the Cheikh Anta Diop University. For decades, he researched and wrote on African themes, constantly arguing that Africa was the cradle of all civilizations. His four major works that shed light on his views about Ancient African and Ancient Egypt are Nations négres et culture: de l'antiquité Nége Egyptienne aux problemes *cultureis de l'Afrique noire d'aujourd'hui* (1954), *The African Origin of Civilization* (1974), *Precolonial Black Africa* (1967), and *Civilization or Barbarism* (1988).

The third essay in this section was written by a leading Nigerian scholar, G. O. Ogunremi, Professor of African History at Lagos State University, where he taught and conducted extensive studies on early African history, and gives us a clear sweep of Africa's early documented history.

The fourth essay entitled "A Survey of Early African History" was prepared by Hakeem Ibikunie Tijani, Associate Professor of History at Morgan State University since the fall of 2006. Tijani received his education in Africa and Europe in African History. He graduated from Lagos State University with BA (Hons), MA from University of Lagos, Ph.D., University of London, and Ph.D. in African History from the University of South Africa. His publications include two recent books, *Britain, Leftist Nationals and the Transfer of Power in Nigeria 1945–1965* (2006) and *Nigeria's Urban History: Past and Present* (2006).

The fifth essay is by the English author John H. Taylor, who focuses on the ancient land of Nubia in northeast Africa, which for centuries was the earliest and main commercial link between sub-Saharan Africa, Egypt, and the Mediterranean. Taylor concentrates on three important archaeological expeditions and their findings about the earliest Nubians. He discusses with great clarity their contacts and relationships with Ancient Egyptian society. This essay suggests that there was more direct Nubian influence between these regions than previously considered by earlier Egyptologists. John H. Taylor is Curator in the Department of Egyptian Antiquities of the British Museum in London, England. His earlier insightful work, *Egyptian Coffins* (1989) dealt with the rulers of Ancient Egypt.

The sixth and final essay in this second section was prepared by Robert W. July, an Africanist who spent decades studying African history. July's narrative comes from his widely acclaimed publication entitled *A History of the African People* (1970, 1998) for which he received the 1970 Anisfield-Wolf Award in Race Relations. July describes in a vivid and detailed manner the vast empires that occupied the regions of West Africa from which a significant percentage of the Africans who were transported to the Americas to become slaves originated. He highlights the socioeconomic and political activities that made the empires of Ancient Ghana, Mali, and Songhay successful. July taught history at Columbia University; City University of New York; Hunter College; University of Ibadan, Nigeria; and University of Nairobi, Kenya. He was also the author of numerous essays on African history, literature, and thought. His other works on African history include *The Origins of Modern African Thought* (1967), and *Precolonial Africa: An Economic and Social History* (1975).

The Emergence of Mankind in Africa

David W. Phillipson

Precursors of the Hominids

The story of the emergence of mankind extends far back into geological time (fig. 2.1). The modern species of Old World and New World monkeys, apes and humans are all classed as members of the Anthropoidea sub-order of the order Primates (fig. 2.2). Other members of this order, with which we are not here concerned, include such animals as tarsiers and tree-shrews. Fossil remains of early primates have been recovered at many sites in the Americas, Europe and Asia as well as in Africa, extending back in time as far as the end of the Cretaceous period about 70 million years ago.

The modern Old World Anthropoidea are believed to be descended from small but ape-like primates, notably that named *Aegyptopithecus*, whose remains are best known from deposits in the Fayum Depression of Egypt, dating from the Oligocene period of between 36 and 23 million years ago (Simons, 1985; Szalay and Delson, 1978).

By the beginning of the subsequent Miocene, it appears that primate evolution had proceeded sufficiently far to permit the differentiation of lines of descent that have led, on the one hand, to the modern monkeys, and on the other to the great apes and modern people. On the latter (hominoid) line, some of the most important fossils are those from western Kenya attributed to the genus *Dryopithecus*, which show important developments in skull, teeth and wrist. *Dryopithecus* probably lived in the forests that were widespread in East Africa in Miocene times, before the completion of the great earth movements which resulted in the formation of the Rift Valley. Fossils attributed to the same genus are also recorded from Europe and south-eastern Asia. *Dryopithecus* limb bones show that these creatures could use their fore-limbs as arms and also walk on all four limbs, while the teeth suggest that fruit may have been an important part of the diet.

In later Miocene times, between about 14 and 10 million years ago, further evolutionary development took place which eventually led to the emergence of the hominid family to which all human types, past and present, belong. With greater geographical spread, resulting in the colonization of new environments and subsequent isolation, several distinct early hominoid species now developed; of greatest relevance to the study of human origins are those attributed to the genus *Ramapithecus*. The faces of these creatures were less snout-like than those of their ancestors, the jaws were more massive and the teeth were further adapted to use as grinders. One type of ramapithecine has been found at Fort Ternan in Kenya, but most of the other significant discoveries come from south-east Europe and from southern Asia. Other fossils from the same sites indicate that these creatures favored open savanna woodland environments in contrast with the forest habitat of *Dryopithecus*. This adaptation to a less circumscribed habitat, doubtless linked (as the teeth indicate) with the adoption of a more omnivorous diet, may have been a major step in the evolutionary processes which led to the emergence of mankind (Simons, 1977). It was at one time suggested that *Ramapithecus* should be classified as the earliest known hominid, but the evidence now suggests a closer affinity with the great apes.

Between about 10 million years ago and some time between 5.0 and 4.0 million years ago there is a major gap in the available fossil evidence for human ancestry. This covers the end of the Miocene and early Pliocene periods. Fossil-bearing deposits of this time are relatively rare in Africa, for reasons that are not fully understood; and in those that have been investigated primate remains are extremely uncommon. When the fossil record resumes, in the second half of the Pliocene, it is exclusively in eastern and southern Africa that fossils of true hominids are found; and they occur with an abundance that contrasts markedly with the earlier periods. Despite the wide Old World distribution of the ramapithecines, the evidence currently available suggests that it was probably in Africa that mankind first evolved.

The Earliest Hominids

It is clear from the results of recent research that it was in the period between about 6.0 and 4.0 million years ago that the first creatures generally acknowledged as hominids developed. Virtually all the important fossils which illustrate this process have been recovered from sites in eastern and southern Africa. Before discussing these sites it is first necessary to describe the different types of hominid that have been recognized in this crucial time-span, and the theories that have been put forward concerning their inter-relationships.

Million years ago	Geological period	African hominoids
0	Pleistocene/Recent	Homo
2	Pliocene	
4		Australopithecus
6		
8		
10		Ramapithecus
12		
14	Miocene	
16		
18		Dryopithecus
20		
22		
24		
26		Oligopithecus
28	Oligocene	and
30		Aegyptopithecus

2.1 The geological periods of the last thirty million years, showing the ages of the principal hominoid types attested in the fossil record

There can now be little reasonable doubt that, by about 2.0 million years ago if not before, several distinct types of hominid were co-existing in broadly similar environments. The exact number of parallel hominid lineages and their relationship to each other are subjects of controversy. This is partly because many of the fossils are fragmentary, and also because it is not known how much variation may have existed between the sexes and individuals of a single species or genus at any one time.

The most widely accepted classification of the early hominids places them in two distinct genera (Tobias, 1978a, 1980; Bilsborough, 1986; Klein, 1989). Of these, the earliest to evolve was *Australopithecus*. The first australopithecines were of a lightly built, or gracile, type, which first appeared at least 4.5 million years ago. The earlier East African fossils of this type—before about 3.4 million years ago—are generally classed as *Australopithecus afarensis*, the later ones as *A. africanus* (Johanson and White, 1979; Day *et al.*, 1980). However, the diversity of East African hominid fossils has led some scholars to propose that certain large-jawed australopithecines of about 2.5 million years ago should be regarded as representing a distinct species, *A. aethiopicus* (Klein, 1989). The gracile australopithecines were probably extinct by about 2.0 million years ago in South Africa, perhaps surviving rather later further to the north. In both areas more heavily built, or robust, forms—*A. robustus* in South Africa and *A. boisei* in East Africa—are attested between 2.0 and 1.0 million years ago, and may be regarded as descendants of *A. aethiopicus*.

It is instructive briefly to compare an australopithecine both with a modern person and with a modern great ape, such as a gorilla (fig. 2.3). *Australopithecus africanus* is here taken as an example. The first point that one notices is the small size of the australopithecine: an adult stood less than 1.5 m high and weighed only 33 to 67 kg (McHenry, 1988). Comparison of the skulls shows that the jaws and teeth of *Australopithecus,* despite the creature's small overall size, were actually larger than those of a modern person. The brain, on the other hand, was only about one-third as large, at about 450 cubic centimeters. This is approximately the same size as the modern gorilla's brain. In the gorilla the brain is placed behind the face, and the neck-muscle attachment is at the back of the skull. In people, the brain extends over the face, with the development of a true forehead, and the muscle is attached to the base of the skull. In both respects, the australopithecine occupies a position intermediate between the gorilla and a modern person. In two important ways, *Australopithecus* was, however, clearly much closer to a person than to a gorilla: the posture was completely upright, and the canine teeth were much reduced in size. A gorilla's molar teeth serve essentially a crushing function: in people and the australopithecines they are primarily grinders.

Although these characteristics are true of all types of australopithecine, there were nevertheless significant differences between them (Tobias, 1967; Bilsborough, 1972, 1986; Klein, 1989). The front teeth (incisors and canines) of *A. africanus* were appreciably larger than those of its robust counterparts; this is in contrast to the generally more substantial build of the latter species. While *A. africanus* was essentially omnivorous, *A. robustus* may have evolved a specialized predominantly

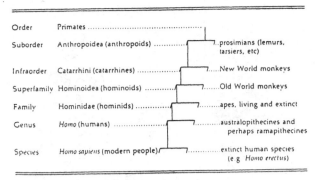

Order	Primates	
Suborder	Anthropoidea (anthropoids)	...prosimians (lemurs, tarsiers, etc)
Infraorder	Catarrhini (catarrhines)	....New World monkeys
Superfamily	Hominoidea (hominoids)	.......Old World monkeys
Family	Hominidae (hominids)	..........apes, living and extinct
Genus	*Homo* (humans)	.........australopithecines and perhaps ramapithecines
Species	*Homo sapiens* (modern people)	..............extinct human species (e g *Homo erectus*)

2.2 The classification of the hominids within the order Primates

vegetarian diet to which large grinding molar teeth were well suited (Grine, 1988). To this feature may be linked also the massive musculature, especially that of the jaw, which in turn gave rise to the large ridges of bone to which the muscles were attached. This was the sole function of the "sagittal crest" of bone running along the top of the skull from front to back, a feature which both *A. robustus* and *A. boisei* shared with the modern male gorilla. There was also significant postcranial variation, as yet imperfectly understood, between skeletons of the different australopithecine species.

The earliest representatives of the genus *Homo*, to a single species of which all types of modern humans belong, may be dated somewhat earlier than 2.0 million years ago. *Homo* probably evolved from a gracile australopithecine (Tobias, 1978a; Klein, 1989). The earliest known specimens are of the type designated *Homo habilis*; the more advanced *H. erectus* first appeared around 1.8 million years ago. One way in which the early hominid types may have been related to one another is shown in figure 2.4. It should be stressed that there is much controversy concerning the relationship between *Australopithecus africanus* and the earliest members of the genus *Homo* (J. T. Robinson, 1967; Wood, 1978; Tobias, 1978a; R. E. Leakey and Walker, 1976; Walker and Leakey, 1978; Delson, 1985; Klein, 1989). Some authorities even deny that two genera are represented, regarding *H. habilis* as a gracile australopithecine. The dispute serves to show how difficult it is to describe evolutionary processes in "Linnaean" terms, which were originally designed to classify modern genera and species (Campbell, 1978; but see Bilsborough, 1986).

Specimens attributed to *Homo habilis* differ from those accepted as australopithecine most importantly in their larger brain size—averaging about 640 cubic centimeters, which is 45 percent greater than the equivalent figure for *A. africanus* (fig. 2.5). The teeth also more closely resemble those of modern people, as do the bones of the hand. The posture of *H. habilis* seems to have been completely upright and there is no evidence for such massive muscles, with bony ridges for their attachment, as

were characteristic of the contemporary *A. boisei* and the individuals now classed as *A. aethiopicus*. As more fossils are discovered, it is becoming apparent that the *Homo* population at this time was extremely diverse (Wood, 1985). At Koobi Fora in northern Kenya there is evidence for a contemporary or variant of *H. habilis* with an even larger brain, best represented by the "1470" specimen (fig. 2.5): this creature may have been the direct ancestor of the *Homo erectus* types that are attested in East Africa from about 1.5 million years ago.

The Oldest East African Discoveries

It must be emphasized that the distribution of fossil discoveries is controlled not only by the former geographical extent of the relevant species, but also by the presence or absence of conditions suitable for their preservation, survival and eventual recovery. These conditions have occurred in both East and South Africa, but in very different situations (fig. 2.6). In East Africa the lake basins of the Rift Valley provided favored habitats for the early hominids and their associated faunas. Rapid sedimentation rates ensured their preservation and the volcanic activity of the area provided materials that can be dated, notably by potassium/argon analysis. Lastly, more recent developments have often led to the erosion of the fossil-bearing deposits, thus exposing their contents for collection or excavation and subsequent study. In South Africa, on the other hand, bones accumulated in limestone caves, in deposits that were consolidated by minerals carried down by water seepage. They have subsequently been exposed, for the most part, in the course of mining operations. Direct dating of these cave deposits has not yet proved possible, but study of the faunal remains has enabled them to be set in sequence and tentatively correlated with the dated East African succession (Howell, 1982; H. B. S. Cooke, 1984).

In both regions where remains of *Australopithecus* have been found, open savanna conditions with patches of woodland are indicated. This represents a further shift in preferred habitat

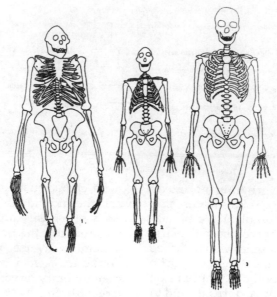

2.3 Skeletons, to the same scale, of 1 – gorilla, 2 – *Australopithecus africanus* 3 – *Homo sapiens*

away from the denser woodland frequented by the Miocene ramapithecines.

It is important to realize that in both South and East Africa, but especially in the latter region, the majority of the fossil discoveries have been made within recent years. Study of many is as yet at a preliminary stage, and there is often considerable controversy about their attribution to named species and, on occasion, their dating. Likewise, new finds are steadily being announced, and these may mean the modification or abandonment of existing theories. Any account of the current state of research must, therefore, be both tentative and provisional.

2.4 A tentative 'family tree' of African hominids during the last four million years. *Australopithecus robustus* and *A. boisei* are regarded as regional races, found in South and East Africa respectively. Likewise, *A. afarensis* appears to be the East African equivalent of the earliest South African examples of *A. africanus*

The earliest hominid fossils are very fragmentary and come from Miocene and early Pliocene sites west and south of Lake Turkana in northern Kenya. At Lothagam a jaw fragment is dated to some 5.5 million years ago, while the

Chemeron Formation near Lake Baringo has yielded a skull fragment from a somewhat more recent context. Little can confidently be said about this scanty material, but it is similar to specimens of rather late date which are attributed to the genus *Australopithecus* (Howell, 1982).

Additional, more abundant, remains attributed to *Australopithecus* of between 4.0 and 3.0 million years ago (Walter and Aronson, 1982) come from two sites in eastern Africa: Hadar in the Afar Triangle of Ethiopia 500 km north-north-east of Addis Ababa, and Laetoli (formerly known as Laetolil) on the western side of the Rift Valley in northern Tanzania. The larger collection comes from Hadar where lacustrine and river-delta deposits are separated by a series of volcanic tuffs: at one locality the remains of thirteen early hominids, including four juveniles, were found together. The most informative discovery, however, is a 40 percent complete skeleton of a female, popularly known as Lucy. Her pelvis and leg bones indicate a well developed upright posture. Her original height was probably about 1.2 m (Taieb *et al.*, 1974; Johanson *et al.*, 1978; Johanson and White, 1979; Johanson and Edey, 1981). At Laetoli, aeolian tuffs have yielded remains which consist mainly of jaws and teeth, allowing detailed comparisons to be made (M. D. Leakey *et al.*, 1976; Johanson and White, 1979; M. D. Leakey and Harris, 1987). The same deposits included layers of hardened ash-covered mud in which were preserved a remarkable series of footprints of hominids and other creatures. The hominid spoor provides further evidence for a fully bipedal gait (M. D. Leakey and Hay, 1979; White, 1980).

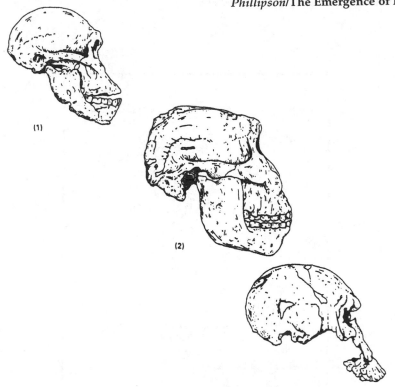

2.5 Skulls of 1 – *Australopithecus africanus* from Sterkfontein, 2 – *A. boisei* from Olduvai, 3 – large-brained *Homo*, cf. *H. habilis* (1470), from Koobi Fora

Because of their physical similarity and near contemporaneity, it seems likely that the Laetoli and Hadar hominid fossils should be regarded as representatives of the same species. Conflicting attributions have been proposed, but most researchers now agree that these finds belong to *Australopithecus afarensis*, a relatively lightly built or gracile species showing several features, principally in the teeth and face, which serve to distinguish it from the later australopithecines (Johanson and White, 1979; Day *et al.*, 1980). The Hadar discoveries are additionally important as providing the best sample of postcranial remains belonging to any australopithecine population.

No artifacts have been recovered from the Laetoli deposits, but at Hadar small numbers of apparently artificially flaked cobbles (fig. 2.7) are reported in contexts provisionally dated to some 2.6 million years ago (H. Roche and Tiercelin, 1980; J. W. K. Harris, 1983). These specimens and their associations await full investigation; should preliminary accounts be confirmed, these occurrences are by a substantial margin the earliest known incidence of hominid-made artifacts, although it should be emphasized that they are not associated with, and are considerably more recent than, the Hadar hominid fossils. (See also Kalb *et al.*, 1982; J. D. Clark *et al.*, 1984.)

To this same general period belongs the beginning of the long sequence of fossil-bearing deposits in the Omo Valley of southern Ethiopia (Howell, 1976; Howell and Coppens, 1976; Howell *et*

al., 1987). The Omo River, flowing into the northern end of Lake Turkana, has exposed a complex series of deposits that were laid down at intervals during the last 4.0 million years in a variety of lakeside and riverine environments (Brown *et al.*, 1985a). These deposits have yielded abundant fossil material, mostly very fragmentary. The hominid remains consist for the most part of isolated teeth. The oldest of these specimens are probably almost as ancient as those from Laetoli, but they are of relatively little value in illustrating the evolution of the various hominid species.

In the Omo Valley, artificially chipped stone tools occur in deposits which may be dated to just before 2.0 million years ago. These specimens, the earliest artifacts known from the Lake Turkana basin, are simple flakes struck from small nodules of quartz, which was the only suitable material available in the area (fig. 2.7). The characteristics and significance of these artifacts are discussed below.

Olduvai and Koobi Fora

Discoveries of great richness and importance come from the parts of the Lake Turkana basin which lie within the modern Kenya. Those from the Koobi Fora area on the north-east shore of the lake are best known (M. G. and R. E. Leakey, 1978; Coppens *et al.*, 1976; Wood, 1991). The focus of research has recently shifted to the western shore (J. M. Harris *et al.*, 1988), where highly significant sites have been located, so far known only from

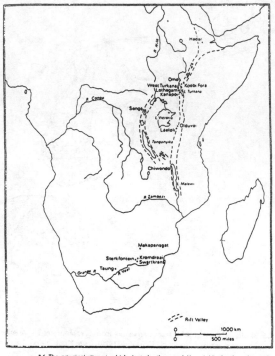

2.6 The principal sites at which *Australopithecus* and *Homo habilis* fossils and/or well-dated Oldowan artefacts have been discovered

preliminary publications. Lake Turkana lies in a closed basin and has no outlet except an overflow channel to the Nile, which functions only when its waters reach a very high level (Butzer, 1980; Harvey and Grove, 1982). The height and size of the lake have thus fluctuated considerably; it and its feeder rivers have laid down a deep and complex series of sediments in which hominid and other fossils are exceptionally well preserved. The sediments with which we are concerned form part of the Koobi Fora Formation, and they are separated into various members by horizons of consolidated volcanic debris known as tuffs, the most important being that known as the KBS Tuff. Although formerly the subject of much controversy, the age of the KBS Tuff is now well established at about 1.8 million years, and the fossil-bearing deposits at Koobi Fora appear to span the period from rather more than 2.0 million until about 1.2 million years ago. Detailed studies of the deposits have succeeded in demonstrating the local circumstances in which they were laid down, and thus the immediate environments where the various species represented in the fossil assemblages lived and died. Concentrations of artifacts are also preserved at Koobi Fora, but unfortunately they are rarely in direct association with the hominid fossils (fig. 2.8). Artifacts have also been recovered at sites of this period on the west

side of Lake Turkana, but details have not yet been published (Klein, 1989).

At least two, and almost certainly three, hominid lines are represented at Koobi Fora (Walker and Leakey, 1978; M. G. and R. E. Leakey, 1978; Wood, 1985; Walker *et al.*, 1986). There is a robust form of *Australopithecus*, (*A. aethiopicus or A. boisei*), and possibly the gracile species *A. africanus*. The genus *Homo* also occurs throughout the sequence. The early form, which some would attribute to a large-brained form of *H. habilis,* is best represented by the fossil skull generally known by its registration number, 1470. Virtually complete, the skull comes from a context below the KBS Tuff which is securely dated to about 2.0 million years ago. The rounded skull-vault with a well-developed forehead housed a brain which, at about 800 cubic centimeters, was some 70 percent larger than those of the contemporary robust australopithecines. The skull crest and massive muscle attachments of the latter species were likewise not present in 1470. Robust australopithecines were present as long ago as 2.5 million years at West Turkana (Walker *et al.*, 1986). Subsequently they became significantly more common, representing about half of the total hominid sample. By about 1.5 million years ago, an even more advanced hominid is attested in the fossil record by a partial skeleton from West

Turkana and by skulls from Koobi Fora which may confidently be attributed to *Homo erectus*. These creatures had even larger cranial capacities than their predecessors, and thus presented a striking contrast with the robust australopithecines, their only hominid contemporaries, the gracile form having by this time become extinct. There may be a tendency at Koobi Fora for remains of *Homo* to occur predominantly in old lakeside environments, and those of *Australopithecus boisei* in riverine situations (Behrensmeyer, 1976).

Further confirmation for the existence, side by side, of early *Homo* and a robust australopithecine comes from the famous site of Olduvai Gorge in northern Tanzania. Here, natural erosion has exposed a deep series of superimposed beds which contain abundant artifact and fossil assemblages covering the greater part of the last 1.8 million years (L. S. B. Leakey, 1965; M. D. Leakey, 1971; Hay, 1976; Johanson *et al.*, 1987). In the lowest horizon, Bed I, laid down in lakeside conditions around 1.75 million years ago, are found the remains both of the gracile but large-brained *Homo habilis*, and of the robust *Australopithecus boisei*. Both have been found in association with concentrations of stone tools. Both hominids are unlikely at the same time to have been engaged in the manufacture of identical tools; and we assume that the artifacts were the work of *H. habilis*, who was physically, and presumably also intellectually, the more advanced of the two species.

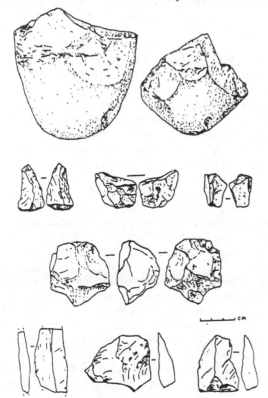

2.7 Stone artefacts: top row from Hadar (after Roche and Tiercelin, 1980); remainder from the Omo Valley (after H. V. and J. P. S. Merrick, 1967)

Only at Olduvai and Koobi Fora have concentrations of the earliest stone artifacts been investigated *in situ*. Although artifacts have occasionally been found in earlier contexts, the most informative occurrence is the "KBS site" at Koobi Fora, dated to about 1.8 million years ago (Isaac *et al.*, 1976; Isaac and Harris, 1978). The KBS site appears to have been originally located in the sandy bed of a seasonal stream and its area was perhaps restricted by the availability of shade. Shortly after the site's apparently brief occupation, volcanic activity covered the area with a thick deposit of fine ash, thus ensuring its preservation in a virtually unmodified state. The traces of hominid activity cover an area 12 to 15 m across. It may be calculated that between 400 and 500 stone artifacts were originally abandoned on the site. The assemblage contains a few core-tools—choppers, discoid cores and a scraper—but most of the artifacts are flakes, up to 6 or 7 cm long, very few of which showed any signs of intentional trimming. The presence of very tiny chips and splinters shows that the tools were made on the spot, not brought to the site from elsewhere, although the lava from which they were made must have been carried from about 5 km away. Broken animal bones were also discovered on the site, including those of porcupine, pig, waterbuck, gazelle, hippopotamus and crocodile. An interesting feature of this list is that it includes animals obtained as prey or carrion from several different environments: hippopotamus from the lake, and gazelle from the drier inland plains, for example. The significance of these observations has been the subject of much controversy. Some prehistorians consider that the bone accumulations at such sites owe little to hominid agency, and that their association with stone tools merely indicates that several species, including hominids, frequented the same place for some purpose such as getting water (Binford, 1981; Potts, 1986). However, the different source-areas of the species represented in the KBS bone accumulation strongly suggest that the early hominids used the site as a homebase and brought back to it carcasses or joints of meat that they obtained elsewhere, from more than one source. This observation is of great importance, for it suggests that one of the most basic features of human behavior, the transport of food in order to share it, had probably already been developed (Isaac, 1976, 1978; but see also Potts, 1984).

If the KBS site was a home-base, this was not the only type of site that has been left behind by the earliest tool-making hominids of the Koobi Fora area. Only 1 km to the south, in a similar ash-filled stream channel, were found many bones representing the remains of a single hippopotamus. These were mixed with over a hundred stone

Million years ago	Stratigraphy	Principal discoveries
1 4		
	Chari Tuff .	
		Karari industry 3733 *Homo erectus*
1.9		
	KBS Tuff	
		KBS site and stone industry 1470 *Homo habilis*
3.2		
	Toroto Tuff	

2.8 Simplified stratigraphy of the Koobi Fora Formation and principal archaeological discoveries at Koobi Fora

artifacts, mostly flakes, essentially similar to, but less varied than, those from the KBS site. Whether or not the hippopotamus was killed by hominids, there can be little doubt that it was butchered, and that stone tools were manufactured on the site for this purpose. Here, then, was a second type of site, showing that the early hominids on occasion made use of temporary butchery sites for the dismemberment or consumption of carcasses too large to be transported entire to their homebase. Similar butchery sites, but incorporating elephant skeletons, have been investigated in Bed I at Olduvai.

Several sites at Olduvai in Bed I and the lower part of Bed II provide possible evidence for the former existence of some simple type of shelter. This evidence takes two forms, the more obvious being a setting of stones which may have served as the foundation of some kind of windbreak and which enclosed the densest part of the artifact scatter on one particular site (fig. 2.9). A similarly confined scatter is suggestive of such structures also on other sites, where no other traces have survived.

The artifacts from the lower part of the Olduvai sequence clearly bear a close technological resemblance to those from the KBS and contemporary sites at Koobi Fora. There are, however, some significant differences. Whereas unretouched flakes predominate at Koobi Fora, at Olduvai there is a higher proportion of cores or core-tools, including cobbles from which a few flakes have been removed as if to produce a cutting or chopping edge. Flake tools, some of remarkably small size, are also a feature of assemblages from Olduvai (fig. 2.10). The very simple stone-working represented at Olduvai Bed I and other sites described in this chapter have been designated "mode 1" in J. G. D. Clark's (1969) comparative study of stone-tool technology.

The artifact occurrences of this period are generally attributed to the "Oldowan industry," defined with reference to material from Bed I at Olduvai Gorge. Occurrences from Hadar, Omo and Koobi Fora are sufficiently similar to justify their inclusion. The variations in artifact size and morphology may largely be explained by reference to the different raw materials from which

the artifacts were made. The most important characteristic of the Oldowan, in contrast with all later stone industries, is the absence of standardization (Isaac, 1984, 1986; Toth, 1985a). It appears that the basic technique employed was the striking of sharp flakes from which could be selected artifacts suited for a particular need: on occasion the flake might receive simple retouch, or the core itself might be employed. Since there was no reservation of particular types for special purposes, it is only through study of traces of wear on the flakes that we can discover the uses to which they were put. Such studies on Oldowan stone flakes from Koobi Fora (Keeley and Toth, 1981) have yielded evidence for the cutting of wood, meat and bone. The last of these uses is also demonstrated by cut marks on bones recovered at several sites (Bunn and Kroll, 1986).

Faunal material from the Olduvai sites includes a high proportion of remains of small creatures and fish, the collecting of which may have been a major subsistence activity. However, the previously held belief that such small creatures were more abundantly represented in the oldest sites at Olduvai, being then gradually supplanted by larger species, is not supported by recent investigations.

There has been until recently a tendency for prehistorians to assume that the bones recovered on Oldowan (or later) sites are necessarily those of animals that were hunted for food. It must be stressed that this is an unjustified assumption. Several studies of the mechanics of bone accumulation have shown that hominid activities need not always have been responsible. Furthermore, animal food was not necessarily obtained by hunting. There is an increasing body of evidence that the early hominids generally obtained their meat by scavenging (Shipman and Rose, 1983; Bunn, 1986; Blumenschine, 1986; O'Connell *et al.*, 1988). Animals killed by other carnivores seem to have been obtained by the early hominids and either butchered on the spot or removed for consumption elsewhere. The range of species eaten is thus more indicative of wild carnivores' predation abilities than of hominid hunting skills. It is important also not to underestimate the significance of vegetable foods in early hominid diets; unfortunately traces of such foods are hardly ever preserved in the archaeological record.

Central and South-Central Africa

Although early hominid fossils have only been recovered from sites in East and (as will be shown below) South Africa, artifacts of Plio/Pleistocene age have been discovered at two places in the intervening regions. These are at Senga on the Semliki River of easternmost Zaire (J. W. K. Harris *et al.*, 1987) and in the Chiwondo Beds south of Karonga on the north-western shore of Lake Malawi (Kaufulu and Stern, 1987). Although the Plio/Pleistocene Chiwondo Beds have yielded abundant faunal material, hominid remains have not yet been recovered there. These recent discoveries in Zaire and Malawi serve to emphasize the large part played by chance in securing the preservation of the earliest archaeological remains, and also the extent to which future research may radically alter our present knowledge.

South Africa

Remains of *Australopithecus* have been found at five sites in South Africa. The sites are all limestone caves where fossil bones have become incorporated in earthy deposits which have since hardened to produce the hard rock-like material known as breccia. The first discovery was made during quarrying operations at Taung, near the Harts River north of Kimberley, in 1924. It consisted of a magnificently preserved complete skull of a juvenile hominid who had perhaps been about six years old at death. Publication of the find (Dart, 1925) stressed the view that the specimen belonged to a previously unknown creature intermediate between apes and modern humans. It was on the basis of this single, immature specimen that *Australopithecus africanus* was named. Its discovery made surprisingly little impact upon archaeological thinking at that time, because southeast Asia and Europe were believed to have been the main areas where the early stages of human evolution had taken place. A further problem was that, at Taung, there were no associated finds other than animal bones and, given the state of knowledge at that time, there was no way in which the absolute age of the site could be estimated (cf. Peabody, 1954; Butzer, 1974b).

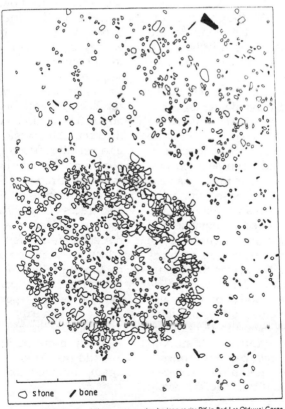

○ stone / bone

2.9 Plan of a stone circle on an occupation horizon at site DK in Bed I at Olduvai Gorge (after M. D. Leakey, 1971). This may represent the base of a shelter constructed of branches

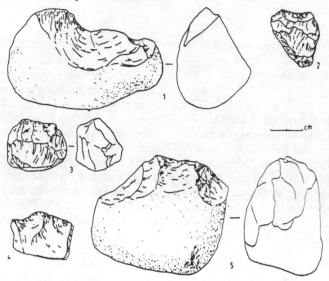

2.10   Oldowan artefacts from site DK in Bed I at Olduvai Gorge (after M. D. Leakey, 1971):
        1 – unifacial chopper/core, 2 – flake scraper, 3 – light-duty chopper, 4 – utilised flake,
        5 – bifacial chopper/core

From 1936 onwards, however, further discoveries began to be made in South Africa, first at the sites of Sterkfontein, Swartkrans and Kromdraai in the Blaawbank Valley near Krugersdorp, and then at Makapansgat in the northern Transvaal (Brain, 1958, 1976; J. T. Robinson and Mason, 1962; Inskeep, 1978 and references; Klein, 1989 and references). Between them these sites have yielded the remains of well over one hundred australopithecines. Although over the years a bewildering variety of species and genera has been proposed, it is now generally believed that they all belong to the two species *A. africanus* and *A. robustus* (Tobias, 1978b).

There has been considerable controversy over the precise nature of these Transvaal sites and how the bone concentrations, amongst which the australopithecine remains occurred, came to be accumulated there. It was at one time believed that many of the animal bones had been selected and taken to the sites by *Australopithecus* for use as tools (Dart, 1957). This argument was based upon the seemingly standardized fractures on many of the bones. This view, which involved acceptance of a tool-making status for *Australopithecus*, is not generally held today; for the breakage patterns may be paralleled at other sites where there is no possibility of hominid agency (Brain, 1967). The differential representation of body parts is also equivalent to that which occurs at leopard lairs, where carcasses are often deposited in trees, out of reach of scavengers, for consumption at leisure. In the same way, over prolonged periods, bones—including those of the australopithecines—probably accumulated gradually in the Transvaal caves (Brain, 1969a, 1978, 1981).

Despite several attempts and experiments, no satisfactory method has yet been devised for directly dating the South African australopithecine sites. There are no volcanic deposits such as have yielded potassium/argon dates for the early hominid sites in East Africa. On the basis of comparisons of the faunal assemblages as a whole with those of the relatively well dated East African sequence, it has however proved possible to show that the South African sites fall within the period between 3.0 and 1.4 million years ago (fig. 2.11). The earliest occurrences are those at Makapansgat and in the earlier part of the Sterkfontein (Type Site) sequence. Significantly, in both these deposits *Australopithecus africanus* is the only hominid represented, and there are no stone tools. An age of about 3.0 million years seems probable for this material. After what may have been a substantial gap in the South African sequence come the occurrences at Sterkfontein Extension Site and in the Older Breccia at Swartkrans. Here, *A. robustus* is the only australopithecine species present; there are also traces of a creature who has been attributed to the genus *Homo*, possibly *H. habilis*. Both these sites have yielded a few stone artifacts (Clarke, 1988) which are accepted by most archaeologists as akin to those of Bed II at Olduvai. The finds from Kromdraai also probably belong to this same general period—perhaps about 2.0 million years ago or shortly thereafter. By this time *Australopithecus africanus* was almost certainly no longer present in South Africa (Tobias, 1976). The Swartkrans Younger Breccia is much younger again, and need not be discussed here.

Million years ago	Makapansgat	Sterkfontein	Swartkrans	Kromdraai	Taung
0.5					
1.0					
1.5		⋮			
2.0		⋮	⋮	⋮	
2.5		⋮			⋮
3.0	⋮	⋮			

2.11 Chronological chart showing the probable ages of the South African australopithecine sites

Conclusions: The Earliest Tool-Makers

As has been shown, incontrovertible archaeological evidence for the earliest recognizable stages of human culture comes almost exclusively from eastern Africa, and dates to between 3.0 and 2.0 million years ago. Broadly contemporary sites in South Africa have yielded hominid fossils but no conclusive evidence for tool-making. The picture is made more complex by the presence in both regions at this time of different hominids which most authorities believe to represent more than one genus. It is clearly important to determine whether *Australopithecus* or *Homo* (or both) was the maker of the earliest artifacts.

Olduvai is the only site where hominid fossils and very early stone tools have been found in direct association with each other (M. D. Leakey, 1978), but it should be noted that from about 1.8 million years ago onwards such tools only occur on sites where the presence of early *Homo* is also indicated. In fact, the sole plausible candidates for pre-Homo artifacts are at the earliest occurrences at Hadar and in the Omo Valley. It may thus be argued that neither the gracile nor the robust variety of *Australopithecus* was a regular maker of stone tools. Such a hypothesis would explain the absence of such tools on the earliest South African hominid sites, for there only *Australopithecus* has been found.

It must be stressed, however, that the recognizably artificial Oldowan tools probably represent a late stage of a prolonged process of development. We have noted the absence of standardized tool-types and suggested that sharp flakes were selected for particular purposes. Such selection may previously have been applied to stones which had not been artificially fractured and which it would be virtually impossible for the archaeologist to recognize. Other tools, long-since perished, may have been made of wood, for it is significant that some Oldowan stone flakes were evidently used for working that material. The development from tool-use to tool-making may have been long and hesitant. We know that tool-use today is not a prerogative of the hominids, so this development may be one which stretched far back into Pliocene or even earlier times where no archaeological record has yet been recovered. The earliest tools will only be properly understood when we know the uses to which they were put, and research to this end is only just beginning.

Our knowledge of the early hominids is, and will presumably always remain, very incomplete. We can learn something of these creatures' appearance and physical abilities from their fossil remains. We can learn about the places they frequented and the food that they ate. Their tools, when made of imperishable materials, can tell us something about their technology. Taken together, these factors allow us to reconstruct a very limited view of their life. The list of what we do not know is far longer. What was the social basis for the groups of hominids that left remains such as those at the KBS site? Was there any socio-political unit larger than such a group? Were such associations permanent? How did they exploit the seasonally shifting and changing resources of their African homeland? All these questions, like the all-important ones of intellect and communication, are ones that research is only now beginning to address.

Origin of the Ancient Egyptians

Cheikh Anta Diop

The general acceptance, as a sequel to the work of Professor Leakey, of the hypothesis of mankind's monogenetic and African origin, makes it possible to pose the question of the peopling of Egypt and even of the world in completely new terms. More than 150,000 years ago, beings morphologically identical with the man of today were living in the region of the great lakes at the sources of the Nile and nowhere else. This notion, and others which it would take too long to recapitulate here, form the substance of the last report presented by the late Dr. Leakey at the Seventh Pan-African Congress of Pre-History in Addis Ababa in 1971.[1] It means that the whole human race had its origin, just as the ancients had guessed, at the foot of the Mountains of the Moon. Against all expectations and in defiance of recent hypotheses it was from *this place* that men moved out to people the rest of the world. From this two facts of capital importance result:

(a) of necessity the earliest men were ethnically homogeneous and negroid, Gloger's law, which would also appear to be applicable to human beings, lays it down that warm-blooded animals evolving in a warm humid climate will secrete a black pigment (eumelanin).[2] Hence if mankind originated in the tropics around the latitude of the great lakes, he was bound to have brown pigmentation from the start and it was by differentiation in other climates that the original stock later split into different races;

(b) there were only two routes available by which these early men could move out to people the other continents, namely, the Sahara and the Nile valley. It is the latter region which will be discussed here.

From the Upper Paleolithic to the dynastic epoch, the whole of the river's basin was taken over progressively by these negroid peoples.

Evidence of Physical Anthropology on the Race of the Ancient Egyptians

It might have been thought that, working on physiological evidence, the findings of the anthropologists would dissipate all doubts by providing reliable and definitive truths. This is by no means so: the arbitrary nature of the criteria used, to go no farther, as well as abolishing any notion of a conclusion acceptable without qualification, introduces so much scientific hair-splitting that there are times when one wonders whether the solution of the problem would not have been nearer if we had not had the ill luck to approach it from this angle.

Nevertheless, although the conclusions of these anthropological studies stop short of the full truth, they still speak unanimously of the existence of a negro race from the most distant ages of prehistory down to the dynastic period. It is not possible in this paper to cite all these conclusions: they will be found summarized in Chapter X of Dr. Emile Massoulard's *Histoire et protohistoire d'Egypte* (Institut d'Ethnologie, Paris, 1949). We shall quote selected items only.

> Miss Fawcett considers that the Negadah skulls form a sufficiently homogeneous collection to warrant the assumption of a Negadah race. In the total height of the skull, the auricular height, the length and breadth of the face, nasal length, cephalic index and facial index this race would seem to approximate to the negro; in nasal breadth, height of orbit, length of palate and nasal index it would seem closer to the Germanic peoples; accordingly the Pre-Dynastic Negadians are likely to have resembled the negroes in certain of their characteristics and the white races in others. (pp. 402–3)

It is worth noting that the nasal indices of Ethiopians and Dravidians would seem to approximate them to the Germanic peoples, though both are black races.

These measurements, which would leave an open choice between the two extremes represented by the negro and the Germanic races, give an idea of the elasticity of the criteria employed. A sample follows:

> An attempt was made by Thomson and Randall MacIver to determine more precisely the importance of the negroid element in the series of skulls from El'Amrah, Abydos and Hou. They divided them into three groups: (1) negroid skulls (those with a facial index below 54 and a nasal index above 50, i.e. short broad face and broad nose); (2) non-negroid skulls

50

(facial index above 54 and nasal index below 50, long narrow face and narrow nose); (3) intermediate skulls (assignable to one of the two previous groups on the basis of either the facial index or on the evidence of the nasal index, plus individuals marginal to either group). The proportion of negroids would seem to have been 24% of men and 19% of women in the early Pre-Dynastic and 25% and 28% respectively in the late Pre-Dynastic.

Kieth has disputed the value of the criterion selected by Thomson and Randall MacIver to distinguish the negroid from the non-negroid skulls. His opinion is that if the same criteria were applied to the study of any series of contemporary English skulls, the sample would be found to contain approximately 30% of negroid types. (pp. 420–1)

The converse of Kieth's proposition could also be asserted, namely, that if the criterion were applied to the 140 million negroes now alive in black Africa a minimum of 100 million negroes would emerge whitewashed.

It may also be remarked that the distinction between negroid, non-negroid and intermediary is unclear: the fact is that "non-negroid" does not mean of white race and "intermediary" still less so.

"Falkenburger reopened the anthropological study of the Egyptian population in a recent work in which he discusses 1,787 male skulls varying in date from the old Pre-Dynastic to our own day. He distinguishes four main groups" (p. 421). The sorting of predynastic skulls into these four groups gives the following results for the whole predynastic period: "36% negroid, 33% Mediterranean, 11% Cro-Magnoid and 20% of individuals not falling into any of these groups but approximating either to the Cro-Magnoid or to the negroid." The proportion of negroids is definitely higher than that suggested by Thomson and Randall MacIver, though Kieth considers the latter too high.

"Do Falkenburger's figures reflect the reality? It is not our task to decide this. If they are accurate, the Pre-Dynastic population far from representing a pure bred race, as Elliot-Smith has said, comprised at least three distinct racial elements—over a third of negroids, a third of Mediterraneans, a tenth of Cro-Magnoids and a fifth of individuals crossbred—to varying degrees" (p. 422).

The point about all these conclusions is that despite their discrepancies the degree to which they converge proves that the basis of the Egyptian population was negro in the Pre-Dynastic epoch. Thus they are all incompatible with the theories that the negro element only infiltrated into Egypt at

a late stage. Far otherwise, the facts prove that it was preponderant from the beginning to the end of Egyptian history, particularly when we note once more that "Mediterranean" is not a synonym for "white," Elliot-Smith's "brown or Mediterranean race being nearer the mark." "Elliot-Smith classes these Proto-Egyptians as a branch of what he calls the brown race, which is the same as Sergi's 'Mediterranean or Eurafrican race.'" The term "brown" in this context refers to skin color and is simply a euphemism for negro.[3] It is thus clear that it was the whole of the Egyptian population which was negro, barring an infiltration of white nomads in the proto-dynastic epoch.

In Petrie's study of the Egyptian race we are introduced to a possible classification element in great abundance which cannot fail to surprise the reader.

Petrie . . . published a study of the races of Egypt in the Pre-Dynastic and Proto-Dynastic periods working only on portrayals of them. Apart from the steatopygian race, he distinguishes six separate types: an aquiline type representative of a white-skinned Libyan race; a "plaited-beard" type belonging to an invading race coming perhaps from the shores of the Red Sea; a "sharp-nosed" type almost certainly from the Arabian Desert; a "tilted nose" type from Middle Egypt; a "jutting beard" type from Lower Egypt; and a "narrow-nosed" type from Upper Egypt. Going on the images, there would thus have been seven different racial types in Egypt during the epochs we are considering. In the pages which follow we shall see that study of the skeletons seems to provide little authority for these conclusions. (p. 391)

The above mode of classification gives an idea of the arbitrary nature of the criteria used to define the Egyptian races. Be that as it may, it is clear that anthropology is far from having established the existence of a white Egyptian race and would indeed tend rather to suggest the opposite.

Nevertheless, in current textbooks the question is suppressed; in most cases it is simply and flatly asserted that the Egyptians were white and the honest layman is left with the impression that any such assertion must necessarily have a prior basis of solid research. But there is no such basis, as this chapter has shown. And so generation after generation has been misled. Many authorities skate around the difficulty today by speaking of red-skinned and black-skinned whites without their sense of common logic being in the least upset. "The Greeks call Africa 'Libya,' a misnomer *ab initio* since Africa contains many other peoples besides the so-called Libyans, who belong among the whites of the northern or Mediterranean periphery and hence are many steps removed from the brown (or red) skinned whites (Egyptians)."[4]

In a textbook intended for the middle secondary school we find the following sentence: "A Black is distinguished less by the colour of his skin (for there are black-skinned 'whites') than by his features: thick lips, flattened nose . . ."[5] It is only through these twistings of the basic definitions that it has been possible to bleach the Egyptian race.

It is worthwhile calling to mind the exaggerations of the theorists of anthropo-sociology in the last century and the beginnings of the present one whose minute physiognomical analyses discovered racial stratifications even in Europe, and particularly in France, when in fact there was really a single and by now practically homogeneous people.[6] Today Occidentals who value their national cohesion are careful to avoid examining their own societies on so divisive a hypothesis, but continue unthinkingly to apply the old methods to the non-European societies.

Human Images of the Protohistoric Period: Their Anthropological Value

The study of human images made by Flinders Petrie on another plane shows that the ethnic type was black: according to Petrie these people were the Anu whose name, known to us since the protohistoric epoch, is always "written" with three pillars on the few inscriptions extant from the end of the fourth millennium before our era. The natives of the country are always represented with unmistakable chiefly emblems for which one looks in vain among the infrequent portrayals of other races, who are all shown as servile foreign elements having reached the valley by infiltration (cf. Tera Neter[7] and the Scorpion king whom Petrie groups together: "The Scorpion King . . . belonged to the preceding race of Anu, moreover he worshipped Min and Set.").[8]

As we shall see later Min, like the chief gods of Egypt, was called by the tradition of Egypt itself "the great negro."

After a glance at the various foreign types of humanity who disputed the valley with the indigenous blacks, Petrie describes the latter, the Anu, in the following terms:

> Besides these types, belonging to the North and East, there is the aboriginal race of the Anu, or Annu, people (written with three pillars) who became a part of the historic inhabitants. The subject ramifies too doubtfully if we include all single pillar names, but looking for the Annu written, with the three pillars, we find that they occupied southern Egypt and Nubia, and the

name is also applied in Sinai and Libya. As to the southern Egyptians, we have the most essential document, one portrait of a chief, Tera Neter, roughly modeled in relief in green glazed faïence, found in the early temple at Abydos. Preceding his name, his address is given on this earliest of visiting cards, "Palace of the Anu in Hemen city, Tera Neter." Hemen was the name of the god of Tuphium. Erment, opposite to it, was the palace of Annu of the south, Annu Menti. The next place in the south is Aunti (Gefeleyn), and beyond that Aunyt-Seni (Esneh).[9]

Amélineau lists in geographical order the fortified towns built along the length of the Nile valley by the Annu blacks.

The common ancestor of the Annu settled along the Nile was Ani or An, a name determined by the word ‒ (khet) and which, dating from the earliest versions of the "Book of the Dead" onwards, is given to the god Osiris.

The wife of the god Ani is the goddess Anet who is also his sister, just as Isis is the sister of Osiris.

The identity of the god An with Osiris has been demonstrated by Pleyte;[10] we should, indeed, recall that Osiris is also surnamed by (?) the Anou: "Osiris Ani." The god Anu is represented alternatively by the symbol ۱ and the symbol ۱ . Are the Aunak tribes now inhabiting the upper Nile related to the ancient Annu? Future research will provide the answer to this question.

Petrie thinks it possible to make a distinction between the predynastic people represented by Tera Neter and the Scorpion King (who is himself a Pharaoh even at that date as his head-dress shows) and a dynastic people worshipping the falcon and probably represented by the Pharaohs Narmer,[11] Khasekhem, Sanekhei and Zoser.[12] By reference to the faces reproduced in the figure it is easily perceived that there is no ethnic difference between the two lots, and both belong to the black race.

The mural in tomb SD 63 (Sequence Date 63) of Hierakonpolis shows the native-born blacks subjugating the foreign intruders into the valley if we accept Petrie's interpretation: "Below is the black ship at Hierakonpolis belonging to the black men who are shown as conquering the red men."[13]

The Gebel-el-Arak knife haft shows similar battle scenes: "There are also combats of black men overcoming red men." However, the archaeological value of this object, which was not found *in situ* but in the possession of a merchant, is less than that of the preceding items.

What the above shows is that the images of men of the protohistoric and even of the dynastic period in no way square with the idea of the Egyptian race popular with Western anthropologists. Wherever the autochthonous racial type is represented with any degree of clearness, it is evidently negroid. Nowhere are the Indo-European and Semitic elements shown even as ordinary freemen serving a local chief, but invariably as conquered foreigners. The rare portrayals found are always shown with the distinctive marks of captivity, hands tied behind the back or strained over the shoulders.[14] A protodynastic figurine represents an Indo-European prisoner with a long plait on his knees, with his hands bound tight to his body. The characteristics of the object itself show that it was intended as the foot of a piece of furniture and represented a conquered race.[15] Often the portrayal is deliberately grotesque as with other proto-dynastic figures showing individuals with their hair plaited in what Petrie calls pigtails.[16]

In the tomb of king Ka (first dynasty) at Abydos, Petrie found a plaque showing an Indo-European captive in chains with his hands behind his back.[17] Elliot-Smith considers that the individual represented is a Semite. The dynastic epoch has also yielded the documents illustrated in Pls 1.9 and 1.14 showing Indo-European and Semitic prisoners. In contrast, the typically negroid features of the Pharaohs (Narmer, first dynasty, the actual founder of the Pharaohic line; Zoser, third dynasty, by whose time all the technological elements of the Egyptian civilization were already in evidence; Cheops, the builder of the Great Pyramid, a Cameroon type;[18] Menthuhotep, founder of the eleventh dynasty, very black;[19] Sesostris I; Queen Ahmosis Nefertari; and Amenhophis I) show that all classes of Egyptian society belong to the same black race.

Pls 1.15 and 1.16, showing the Indo-European and Semitic types, have been included deliberately to contrast them with the quite dissimilar physiognomies of the black Pharaohs and to demonstrate clearly that there is no trace of either of the first two types in the whole line of Pharaohs if we exclude the foreign Libyan and Ptolemaic dynasties.

It is usual to contrast the negresses on the tomb of Horemheb with the Egyptian type also shown. This contrast is surely a false one: it is social and not ethnic and there is as much difference between an aristocratic Senegalese lady from Dakar and those antique African peasant women with their horny hands and splay feet as between the latter and an Egyptian lady of the cities of antiquity.

There are two variants of the black race: (a) straight-haired, represented in Asia by the Dravidians and in Africa by the Nubians and the Tubbou or Tedda, all three with jet-black skins; (b) the kinky-haired blacks of the Equatorial regions. Both types entered into the composition of the Egyptian population.

Melanin Dosage Test

In practice it is possible to determine directly the skin color and hence the ethnic affiliations of the ancient Egyptians by microscopic analysis in the laboratory; I doubt if the sagacity of the researchers who have studied the question has overlooked the possibility.

Melanin (eumelanin), the chemical body responsible for skin pigmentation, is, broadly speaking, insoluble and is preserved for millions of years in the skins of fossil animals.[20] There is thus all the more reason for it to be readily recoverable in the skins of Egyptian mummies, despite a tenacious legend that the skin of mummies, tainted by the embalming material, is no longer susceptible of any analysis.[21] Although the epidermis is the main site of the melanin, the melanocytes penetrating the derm at the boundary between it and the epidermus, even where the latter has mostly been destroyed by the embalming materials, show a melanin level which is non-existent in the white-skinned races. The samples I myself analyzed were taken in the physical anthropology laboratory of the Musée de l'Homme in Paris off the mummies from the Marietta excavations in Egypt.[22] The same method is perfectly suitable for use on the royal mummies of Thutmoses III, Seti I and Ramses II in the Cairo Museum, which are in an excellent state of preservation. For two years past I have been vainly begging the curator of the Cairo Museum for similar samples to analyze. No more than a few square millimeters of skin would be required to mount a specimen, the preparations being a few um in thickness and lightened with ethyl benzoate. They can be studied by natural light or with ultra-violet lighting which renders the melanin grains fluorescent.

Either way let us simply say that the evaluation of melanin level by microscopic examination is a laboratory method which enables us to classify the ancient Egyptians unquestionably among the black races.

Osteological Measurements

Among the criteria accepted in physical anthropology for classifying races, the osteological measurements are perhaps the least misleading (in contrast to craniometry) for distinguishing a black man from a white man. By this criterion, also, the Egyptians belong among the black races. This study was made by the distinguished German savant Lepsius at the end of the nineteenth century and his conclusions remain valid: subsequent methodological progress in the domain of physical anthropology in no way undermines what is called the "Lepsius canon" which, in round figures, gives the bodily proportions of the ideal Egyptian, short-armed and of negroid or negrito physical type.[23]

Blood-Groups

It is a notable fact that even today Egyptians, particularly in Upper Egypt, belong to the same Group B as the populations of western Africa on the Atlantic seaboard and not the A2 Group characteristics of the white race prior to any crossbreeding.[24] It would be interesting to study the extent of Group A2 distribution in Egyptian mummies, which present-day techniques make possible.

The Egyptian Race According to the Classical Authors of Antiquity

To the Greek and Latin writers contemporary with the ancient Egyptians the latter's physical classification posed no problems: the Egyptians were negroes, thick-lipped, kinky-haired and thin-legged; the unanimity of the authors' evidence on a physical fact as salient as a people's race will be difficult to minimize or pass over. Some of the following evidence drives home the point.

(a) Herodotus, "the father of history,"-480 (?) to -425. With regard to the origins of the Colchians[25] he writes:

It is in fact manifest that the Colchidians are Egyptian by race . . . several Egyptians told me that in their opinion the Colchidians were descended from soldiers of Sesostris. I had conjectured as much myself from two pointers, firstly because they have black skins and kinky hair (to tell the truth this proves nothing for other peoples have them too) and secondly and more reliably for the reason that alone among mankind the Egyptians and the Ethiopians have practiced circumcision since time immemorial. The Phoenicians and Syrians of Palestine themselves admit that they learnt the practice from the Egyptians while the Syrians in the river Thermodon and Pathenios region and their neighbors the Macrons say they learnt it recently from the Colchidians. These are the only races which practice circumcision and it is observable that they do it in the same way as the Egyptians. As between the Egyptians themselves and the Ethiopians I could not say which taught the other the practice for among them it is quite clearly a custom of great antiquity. As to the custom having been learnt through their Egyptian connections, a further strong proof to my mind is that all those Phoenicians trading to Greece cease to treat the pudenda after the Egyptian manner and do not subject their offspring to circumcision.[26]

Herodotus reverts several times to the negroid character of the Egyptians and each time uses it as a fact of observation to argue more or less complex theses. Thus to prove that the Greek oracle at Dodona in Epirus was of Egyptian origin, one of his arguments is the following: " . . . and when they add that the dove was black they give us to understand that the woman was Egyptian."[27] The doves in question—actually there were two according to the text—symbolize two Egyptian women who are said to have been carried off from the Egyptian Thebes to found the oracles in Greece at Dodona and in Libya (Oasis of Jupiter Amon) respectively. Herodotus did not share the opinion of Anaxagoras that the melting of the snows on the mountains of Ethiopia was the source of the Nile floods.[28] He relied on the fact that it neither rains nor snows in Ethiopia "and the heat there turns men black."[29]

(b) Aristotle, -389 to -332, scientist, philosopher and tutor of Alexander the Great.

In one of his minor works, Aristotle attempts, with unexpected naïveté, to establish a correlation between the physical and moral natures of living beings and leaves us evidence on the Egyptian-Ethiopian race which confirms what Herodotus says. According to him, "Those who are too black are cowards, like for instance, the Egyptians and Ethiopians. But those who are excessively white are also cowards as we can see from the example of women, the complexion of courage is between the two."[30]

(c) Lucian, Greek writer, +125 (?) to +190.

The evidence of Lucian is as explicit as that of the two previous writers. He introduces two Greeks, Lycinus and Timolaus, who start a conversation.

Lycinus (describing a young Egyptian): "This boy is not merely black; he has thick lips and his legs are too thin . . . his hair worn in a plait behind shows that he is not a freeman."

Timolaus: "But that is a sign of really distinguished birth in Egypt, Lycinus. All freeborn children plait their hair until they reach manhood. It is the exact opposite of the custom of our ancestors who thought it seemly for old men to secure their hair with a gold brooch to keep it in place."[31]

(*d*) Apollodorus, first century before our era, Greek philosopher.

"Aegyptos conquered the country of the black-footed ones and called it Egypt after himself."[32]

(*e*) Aeschylus, -525 (?) to -456, tragic poet and creator of Greek tragedy.

In *The Suppliants*, Danaos, fleeing with his daughters, the Danaïds, and pursued by his brother Aegyptos with his sons, the Aegyptiads, who seek to wed their cousins by force, climbs a hillock, looks out to sea and describes the Aegyptiads at the oars afar off in these terms: "I can see the crew with their black limbs and white tunics."[33]

A similar description of the Egyptian type of man recurs a few lines later in verse 745.

(*f*) Achilles Tatius of Alexandria.

He compares the herdsmen of the Delta to the Ethiopians and explains that they are blackish, like half-castes.

(*g*) Strabo, -58 to about +25.

Strabo visited Egypt and almost all the countries of the Roman empire. He concurs in the theory that the Egyptians and the Colchoi are of the same race but holds that the migrations to Ethiopia and Colchoi had been from Egypt only.

"Egyptians settled in Ethiopia and in Colchoi."[34] There is no doubt whatever as to Strabo's notion of the Egyptians' race for he seeks elsewhere to explain why the Egyptians are darker than the Hindus, a circumstance which would permit the refutation, if needed, of any attempt at confusing "the Hindu and Egyptian races."

(*h*) Diodorus of Sicily, about -63 to +14, Greek historian and contemporary of Caesar Augustus.

According to Diodorus it was probably Ethiopia which colonized Egypt (in the Athenian sense of the term, signifying that, with overpopulation, a proportion of the people emigrate to new territory).

The Ethiopians say that the Egyptians are one of their colonies,[35] which was led into Egypt by Osiris. They claim that at the beginning of the world Egypt was simply a sea but that the Nile, carrying down vast quantities of loam from Ethiopia in its flood waters, finally filled it in and made it part of the continent . . . They add that the Egyptians have received from them, as

from authors and their ancestors, the greater part of their laws.[36]

(*i*) Diogenes Laertius.

He wrote the following about Zeno, founder of the Stoic School (-333 to -261): "Zeno son of Mnaseas or Demeas was a native of Citium in Cyprus, a Greek city which has taken in some Phoenician colonists." In his *Lives*, Timotheus of Athens describes Zeno as having a twisted neck. Apollonius of Tyre says of him that he was gaunt, very tall and black, hence the fact that, according to Chrysippus in the First Book of his Proverbs, certain people called him an Egyptian vine-shoot.[37]

(*j*) Ammianus Marcellinus, about +33 to +100, Latin historian and friend of the Emperor Julian.

With him we reach the sunset of the Roman empire and the end of classical antiquity. There are about nine centuries between the birth of Aeschylus and Herodotus and the death of Ammianus Marcellinus, nine centuries during which the Egyptians, amid a sea of white races, steadily crossbred. It can be said without exaggeration that in Egypt one household in ten included a white Asiatic or Indo-European slave.[38]

It is remarkable that, despite its intensity, all this crossbreeding should not have succeeded in upsetting the racial constants. Indeed Ammianus Marcellinus writes: " . . . the men of Egypt are mostly brown or black with a skinny and desiccated look."[39] He also confirms the evidence already cited about the Colchoi: "Beyond these lands are the heartlands of the Camaritae[40] and the Phasis with its swifter stream borders the country of the Colchoi, an ancient race of Egyptian origin."[41]

This cursory review of the evidence of the ancient Graeco-Latin writers on the Egyptians' race shows that the extent of agreement between them is impressive and is an objective fact difficult to minimize or conceal, the two alternatives between which present-day Egyptology constantly oscillates.

An exception is the evidence of an honest savant, Volney, who traveled in Egypt between +1783 and +1785, i.e. at the peak period of negro slavery, and made the following observations on the true Egyptian race, the same which produced the Pharaohs, namely, the Copts:

All of them are puffy-faced, heavy-eyed and thick-lipped, in a word, real mulatto faces. I was tempted to attribute this to the climate until, on visiting the Sphinx, the look of it gave me the clue to the enigma. Beholding that head characteristically Negro in all its features, I recalled the well-known passage of Herodotus which reads: "For my part I consider the Colchoi are a colony of the Egyptians because, like them, they are black-skinned and kinky-haired." In other words the ancient Egyptians were true negroes of the same stock as all the autochthonous peoples of Africa and from that datum one sees how their race, after some centuries of mixing with the blood of Romans and Greeks, must have lost the full blackness of its original colour but retained the impress of its original mould. It is even possible to apply this observation very widely and posit in principle that physiognomy is a kind of record usable in many cases for disputing or elucidating the evidence of history on the origins of the peoples...

After illustrating this proposition citing the case of the Normans, who 900 years after the conquest of Normandy still look like Danes, Volney adds:

> but reverting to Egypt, its contributions to history afford many subjects for philosophic reflection. What a subject for mediation is the present-day barbarity and ignorance of the Copts who were considered, born of the alliance of the deep genius of the Egyptians and the brilliance of the Greeks, that this race of blacks who nowadays are slaves and the objects of our scorn is the very one to which we owe our arts, our sciences and even the use of spoken word; and finally recollect that it is in the midst of the peoples claiming to be the greatest friends of liberty and humanity that the most barbarous of enslavements has been sanctioned and the question raised whether black men have brains of the same quality as those of white men![42]

To this testimony of Volney, Champollion-Figeac, brother of Champollion the Younger, was to reply in the following terms: "The two physical traits of black skin and kinky hair are not enough to stamp a race as negro and Volney's conclusion as to the negro origin of the ancient population of Egypt is glaringly forced and inadmissible."[43]

Being black from head to foot and having kinky hair is not enough to make a man a negro! This shows us the kind of specious argumentation to which Egyptology has had to resort since its birth as a science. Some scholars maintain that Volney was seeking to shift the discussion to a philosophic plane. But we have only to re-read Volney: he is simply drawing the inferences from crude material facts forcing themselves on his eyes and his conscience as proofs.

The Egyptians as They Saw Themselves

It is no waste of time to get the views of those principally concerned. How did the ancient Egyptians see themselves? Into which ethnic category did they put themselves? What did they call themselves? The language and literature left to us by the Egyptians of the Pharaonic epoch supply explicit answers to these questions which the scholars cannot refrain from minimizing, twisting or "interpreting."

The Egyptians had only one term to designate themselves: $\mathit{n\check{c}}$ =kmt=the negroes (literally).[44] This is the strongest term existing in the Pharaonic tongue to indicate blackness; it is accordingly written with a hieroglyph representing a length of wood charred at the end and not crocodile scales.[45] This word is the etymological origin of the well-known root kamit which has proliferated in modern anthropological literature. The biblical root kam is probably derived from it and it has therefore been necessary to distort the facts to enable this root today to mean "white" in Egyptological terms whereas, in the Pharaonic mother tongue which gave it birth, it meant "coal black."

In the Egyptian language, a word of assembly is formed from an adjective or a noun by putting it in the feminine singular. "Kmt" from the adjective =km=black; it therefore means strictly negroes or at the very least black men. The term is a collective noun which thus described the whole people of Pharaohic Egypt as a black people.

In other words, on the purely grammatical plane, if one wishes to indicate negroes in the Pharaonic tongue, one cannot use any other word than the very one which the Egyptians used of themselves. Furthermore, the language offers us another term, kmtjw=the negroes, the black men (literally)=the Egyptians, as opposed to "foreigners" which comes from the same root km and which the Egyptians also used to describe themselves as *a people as distinguished from all foreign peoples*.[46] These are the only adjectives of nationality used by the Egyptians to designate themselves and both mean "negro" or "black" in the Pharaonic language. Scholars hardly ever mention them or when they do it is to translate them by euphemisms such as the "Egyptians" while remaining completely silent about their etymological sense.[47] They prefer the expression $\mathit{Rmt\ kmt}$=the men of the country of the black men or the men of the black country.

In Egyptian, words are normally followed by a determinative which indicates their exact sense, and for this particular expression Egyptologists suggest that km=black and that the color qualifies the determinative which follows it and which signifies "country." Accordingly, they claim, the translation should be "the black earth" from the color of the loam, or the "black country," and not "the country of the black men" as we should be inclined to render it today with black Africa and white Africa in mind. Perhaps so, but if we apply this rule rigorously to ⸗kmit, we are forced to "concede that here the adjective 'black' qualifies the determinative which signifies the whole people of Egypt shown by the two symbols for "man" and "woman" and the three strokes below them which indicate the plural." Thus, if it is possible to voice a doubt as regards the expression

⸗kme, it is not possible to do so in the case of the two adjectives of nationality kmt and kmtjw unless one is picking one's arguments completely at random.

It is a remarkable circumstance that the ancient Egyptians should never have had the idea of applying these qualifications to the Nubians and other populations of Africa to distinguish them from themselves; any more than a Roman at the apogee of the empire could use a "color" adjective to distinguish himself from the Germani on the other bank of the Danube, of the same stock but still in the prehistoric age of development.

In either case both sides were of the same world in terms of physical anthropology, and accordingly the distinguishing terms used related to level of civilization or moral sense. For the civilized Romans, the Germans, of the same stock, were barbarians. The Egyptians used the expression =nahas to designate the Nubians; and nahas[48] is the name of a people, with no color connotation in Egyptian. It is a deliberate mistranslation to render it as negro as is done in almost all present-day publications.

The Divine Epithets

Finally, black or negro is the divine epithet invariably used for the chief beneficent gods of Egypt, whereas all the malevolent spirits are qualified as de-srêt=red; we also know that to Africans this form applies to the white nations; it is practically certain that this held good for Egypt too but I want in this chapter to keep to the least debatable facts.

The surnames of the gods are these:

⸗Kmwr=the "Great Negro" for Osiris[49]

⸗km=the black=the name of the god[50]

⸗kmt=the black + the name of the goddess[51]

The km (black) qualificative is applied to Hathor, Apis, Min, Thoth, etc.[52]

set kmt=the black woman=Isis.[53] On the other hand "seth," the sterile desert, is qualified by the term desrêt=red.[54] The wild animals which Horus fought to create civilization are qualified as desrêt=red, especially the hippopotamus.[55]

Similarly the maleficent beings wiped out by Thoth are Des= =dèsrtjw=the red ones' this term is the grammatically converse of Kmtjw and its construction follows the same rule for the formation of "nisbés."

Witness of the Bible

The Bible tells us: ". . . the sons of Ham [were] Cush, and Mizraim [i.e. Egypt], and Phut, and Canaan. And the sons of Cush; Seba, and Havilah, and Sabtah, and Raamah, and Sabtechah."[56]

Generally speaking all Semitic tradition (Jewish and Arab) classes ancient Egypt with the countries of the blacks.

The importance of these depositions cannot be ignored, for these are peoples (the Jews) which lived side by side with the ancient Egyptians and sometimes in symbiosis with them and have nothing to gain by presenting a false ethnic picture of them. Nor is the notion of an erroneous interpretation of the facts any more tenable.[57]

Cultural Data

Among the innumerable identical cultural traits recorded in Egypt and in present-day black Africa, it is proposed to refer only to circumcision and totemism.

According to the extract from Herodotus quoted earlier, circumcision is of African origin. Archaeology has confirmed the judgment of the Father of History for Elliot-Smith was able to determine from the examination of well-preserved mummies that circumcision was the rule among the Egyptians as long ago as the protohistoric era,[58] i.e. earlier than -4000.

Egyptian totemism retained its vitality down to the Roman period[59] and Plutarch also mentions it. The researches of Amélineau,[60] Loret, Moret and Adolphe Reinach have clearly demonstrated the existence of an Egyptian totemic system, in refutation of the champions of the zoolatric thesis.

If we reduce the notion of the totem to that of a fetish, usually representing an animal of a species with which the tribe believes it has special ties formally renewed at fixed intervals, and which is carried into battle like a standard; if we accept this minimal but adequate definition of a totem, it can be said that there was no country where totemism had a more brilliant reign than in Egypt and certainly nowhere where it could better be studied.[61]

Linguistic Affinity

Walaf,[62] a Senegalese language spoken in the extreme west of Africa on the Atlantic Ocean, is perhaps as close to ancient Egyptian as Coptic. An exhaustive study of this question has recently been carried out.[63] In this chapter enough is presented to show that the kinship between ancient Egyptian and the languages of Africa is not hypothetical but a demonstrable fact which it is impossible for modern scholarship to thrust aside.

As we shall see, the kinship is genealogical in nature.

We have the following correspondence between the verb forms, with identity or similarity of meaning: all the Egyptian verb forms, except for two, are also recorded in Walaf.

EGYPTIAN	COPTIC	WALAF
𓊘 =keſ=to grasp, to take a strip (of something)[64]	(Saïdique dialect) keh=to tame[65]	keſ=seize a prey

PRESENT	PRESENT	PRESENT
keſ i	keh	keſ na
keſ ek	keh ek	keſ nga
keſ et	keh ere	keſ na
keſ ef	keſ ef	
keſ es	keh es	keſ ef na
		keſ es
keſ n	keh en	keſ nanu
keſ ton	keh eterû	keſ ngen
keſ sen[66]	keh ey	keſ naĥu

PAST	PAST	PAST
keſ ni	keh nei	keſ (on) na
keſ (o) nek	keh nek	keſ (on) nga
keſ (o) net	keh nere	keſ (on) na
keſ (o) nef	keh nef	keſ (on) ef na
keſ (o) nes	keh nes	keſ (on) es
keſ (o) nen	keh nen	keſ (on) nanu
keſ (o) n ten	keh netsten	keſ (on) ngen
keſ (o) n sen[67]	keh ney[68]	keſ (on) naĥu

EGYPTIAN	WALAF
𓂋𓏏 =ſeh=go away	ſeh=rush off

EGYPTIAN	WALAF
ſeh-ef	ſeh-ef
ſeh-es	ſeh-es
ſeh-n-ef	ſeh-ôn-ef
ſeh-n-es	ſeh-ônes
ſeh-w	ſeh-w
ſeh-weſ	ſeh-w-ef
ſeh-w-es	ſeh-w-es
ſeh-w-n-ef	ſeh-w-ôn-ef
ſeh-w-n-es	ſeh-w-ôn-es
ſeh-in-ef	ſeh-il-ef
ſeh-in-es	ſeh-il-es
ſeh-t-ef	ſeh-t-ef
ſeh-t-es	ſeh-t-es
ſeh-tyſy	ſeh-ati-fy
ſeh-tysy	ſeh-at-ef
ſeh-tw-ef	mar-tw-ef
ſeh-tw-es	mar-tw-es
ſeh-kw(i)	ſahi-kw
ſeh-n-tw-ef	ſeh-an-tw-ef
ſeh-n-tw-es	ſeh-an-tw-es
ſeh-y-ef	ſeh-y-ef
ſeh-y-es	ſey-y-es

EGYPTIAN	WALAF
𓌻𓏤 =mer=love	mar=lick[69]
mer-ef	mar-ef
mer-es	mar-es
mer-n-ef	mar-ôn-ef
mer-n-es	mar-ôn-es
mer-w	mar-w
mer-w-ef	mar-w-ef
mer-w-n-ſ	mar-w-ôn-ef
mer-w-n-es	mar-w-ôn-es
mer-in-ef	mar-il-ef
mer-in-es	mar-il-es
mer-t-ef	mar-t-ef
mer-t-es	mar-t-es
mer-tw-ef	mar-tw-ef
mer-tw-es	mar-tw-es
mer-tyſy	mar-at-ef
mer-r-tysy	mar-at-es
	mar-aty-sy
	mar-aty-sy
mer-kwi	mari-kw
mer-y-ef	mar-y-ef
mer-y-es	mar-y-es
mer-n-tw-ef	mar-an-tw-ef
mer-n-tw-es	mar-antw-es
	mar-tw-ôn-ef
	mar-tw-ôn-es

Egyptian and Walaf Demonstratives

There are the following phonetic correspondences between Egyptian and Walaf demonstratives.

EGYPTIAN	WALAF
	cp→w
◦◗ = pw	p→b
(ipw)→bw	w→w
◦◗" = pwy	p→b́
(ipw)→bwy	w→2
	y→y
◦̲ = pn bané	p→b́
(ipn)→	n→n
balé	p→b́
	n→l [70]
◦̲ = pſ bafe	p→b
(ipſ)→	f→f
◦̲◣ = pſ3→baſa	p→b́
	f→f
	3→a
◦̲" = pſy	p→b́
(ipſy)→baſy	f→f
	y→y
ⅩⅩ◣ = p3→bá	p→b
	3→á
◖◗ = iptw→baɾw	p→b
	ɩ→ɩ
	w→w
◖◦̲ = iptn→batné	p→b
	ɩ→ɩ
Batalé	n→n
	n→l·
◖◦̲ = iptſ	
= iptſ→bataſé	p→b́
	ɩ→ɩ
	f→f

These phonetic correspondences are not ascribable either to elementary affinity or to the general laws of the human mind for they are regular correspondences on outstanding points extending through an entire system, that of the demonstratives in the two languages and that of the verbal languages. It is through the application of such laws that it was possible to demonstrate the existence of the Indo-European linguistic family.

The comparison could be carried to show that the majority of the phonemes remain unchanged between the two languages. The few changes which are of great interest are the following.

(a) The correspondence n (E)→ l (W)

EGYPTIAN	WALAF
n	l
◥ ɪ◦◖ = nad = ask	laɗ = ask
◌̄◡ = nah = protect	lah = protect
◢–◗◖ = ben ben = wellup	belbel = well up
◌◖◖ = teni = grow old	talé = important
◡◯◖ = teſnwt = the goddess born of Ra's spittle	teſnit = 'spit out' a human being. teſlit = spittle teſli = spitter
◗◖◣ = nebt = plait	let = plait náb = to plait hair temporarily

(b) The correspondence h (E)→g (W)

EGYPTIAN	WALAF
h	g
◖◿–= hen = phallus	gen = phallus
◖±◗ = hwn = adolescent	gwné } = adolescent goné }
◖◦◣ = hor = Horus	gor = vir (? male ?)
◣◖±◗ = hor gwn = the youth Horus	gor gwne = young man (m.à.m)

It is still early to talk with precision of the vocalic accompaniment of the Egyptian phonemes. But the way is open for the rediscovery of the vocalics of ancient Egyptian from comparative studies with the languages of Africa.

Conclusion

The structure of African royalty, with the king put to death, either really or symbolically, after a reign which varied in length but was in the region of eight years, recalls the ceremony of the Pharaoh's regeneration through the Sed feast. Also reminiscent of Egypt are the circumcision rites mentioned earlier and the totemism, cosmogonies, architecture, musical instruments, etc., of Africa.[71] Egyptian antiquity is to African culture what Graeco-Roman antiquity is to Western culture. The building up of a corpus of African humanities should be based on this fact.

It will be understood how difficult it is to write such a chapter in a work of this kind, where euphemism and compromise are the rule. In an attempt to avoid sacrificing scientific truth, therefore, we made a point of suggesting three preliminaries to the preparation of this volume, all of which were agreed to at the plenary session held in 1971.[72] The first two led to the holding of the Cairo Symposium from 28 January to 3 February 1974.[73] In this connection I should like to refer to certain passages in the report of that symposium. Professor Vercoutter, who had been commissioned by Unesco to write the introductory report, acknowledged after a thorough discussion that the conventional idea that the Egyptian population was equally divided between blacks, whites and half-castes could not be upheld. "Professor Vercoutter agreed that no attempt should be made to estimate percentages, which meant nothing, as it was impossible to establish them without reliable statistical data." On the subject of Egyptian culture: "Professor Vercoutter remarked that, in his view, Egypt was African in its way of writing, in its culture and in its way of thinking."

Professor Leclant, for his part, "recognized the same African character in the Egyptian temperament and way of thinking."

In regard to linguistics, it is stated in the report that "this item, in contrast to those previously discussed, revealed a large measure of agreement among the participants. The outline report by Professor Diop and the report by Professor Obenga were regarded as being very constructive."

Similarly, the symposium rejected the idea that Pharaonic Egyptian was a Semitic language. "Turning to wider issues, Professor Sauneron drew attention to the interest of the method suggested by Professor Obenga following Professor Diop. Egyptian remained a stable language for a period of at least 4500 years. Egypt was situated at the point of convergence of outside influences and it was to be expected that borrowing had been made from foreign languages, but the Semitic roots numbered only a few hundred as compared with a total of several thousand words. The Egyptian language could not be isolated from its African context and its origin could not be fully explained in terms of Semitic, it was thus quite normal to expect to find related languages in Africa."

The genetic, that is, non-accidental relationship between Egyptian and the African languages was recognized: "Professor Sauneron noted that the method which had been used was of considerable interest, since it could not be purely fortuitous that there was a similarity between the third person singular suffixed pronouns in Ancient Egyptian and in Wolof, he hoped that an attempt would be made to reconstitute a palaeo-African language, using present-day languages as a starting point."

In the general conclusion to the report it was stated that: "Although the preparatory working paper sent out by Unesco gave particulars of what was desired, not all participants had prepared communications comparable with the painstakingly researched contributions of Professors Cheikh Anta Diop and Obenga. There was consequently a real lack of balance in the discussions."

A new page of African historiography was accordingly written in Cairo. The symposium recommended that further studies be made on the concept of race. Such studies have since been carried out, but they have not contributed anything new to the historical discussion. They tell us that molecular biology and genetics recognize the existence of populations alone, the concept of race

being no longer meaningful. Yet whenever there is any question of the transmission of a hereditary taint, the concept of race in the most classic sense of the term comes into its own again, for genetics tells us that "sickle-cell anemia occurs only in negroes." The truth is that all these "anthropologists" have already in their own minds drawn the conclusions deriving from the triumph of the monogenetic theory of mankind without venturing to put them into explicit terms, for if mankind originated in Africa, it was necessarily negroid before becoming white through mutation and adaptation at the end of the last glaciation in Europe in the Upper Paleolithic; and it is now more understandable why the Grimaldian negroids first occupied Europe for 10000 years before Cro-Magnon Man—the prototype of the white race—appeared (around -2000).

The ideological standpoint is also evident in apparently objective studies. In history and in social relations, it is the phenotype, that is, the individual or the people as that individual or people is perceived, which is the dominant factor, as opposed to the genotype. For present-day genetics, a Zulu with the "same" genotype as Vorster is not impossible. Does this mean that the history we are witnessing will put the two phenotypes, that is, the two individuals, on the same footing in all their national and social activities? Certainly not—the opposition will remain not social but ethnic.

This study makes it necessary to rewrite world history from a more scientific standpoint, taking into account the Negro-African component which was for a long time preponderant. It means that it is now possible to build up a corpus of Negro-African humanities resting on a sound historical basis instead of being suspended in mid-air. Finally, if it is true that only truth is revolutionary, it may be added that only *rapprochement* brought about on a basis of truth can endure. The cause of human progress is not well served by casting a veil over the fact.

The rediscovery of the true past of the African peoples should not be a divisive factor but should contribute to uniting them, each and all, binding them together from the north to the south of the continent so as to enable them to carry out together a new historical mission for the greater good of mankind; and that is in keeping with the ideal of Unesco.

Note by the Editor of *General History of Africa* (Unesco, 1981): The opinions expressed by Professor Cheikh Anta Diop in this chapter are those which he presented and developed at the Unesco symposium of "The peopling of ancient Egypt" which was held in Cairo in 1974. The arguments put forward in this chapter have not been accepted by all the experts interested in the problem.—Gamal Mokhtar.

[1] *Proceedings of the Seventh Pan-African Congress of Pre-History and Quaternary Studies,* December 1971.

[2] M. F. A. Montagu, 1960, p. 390.

[3] The study of this race's pigmentations can be carried farther by the method described; actually Elliot-Smith often found patches of skin on the bodies and the mummification methods which cause skin deterioration were not yet in use.

[4] D. P. de Pedrals, p. 6.

[5] *Géographie,* classe de 5°, 1950.

[6] In his "Lutte des races" (1883) L. Gumplovicz asserts that the diverse classes making up a people always represent different races, of which one has established its domination over the others by conquest. G. de Lapounge in an article published in 1897 postulated no less than a dozen "fundamental laws of anthropo-sociology" of which the following are typical: his "law of distribution of wealth" posits that, in countries of mixed European-Alpine populations, wealth is greater in inverse proportions to the cephalic index; the "law of urban indices" given prominence by Ammon in connection with his research on Badener conscripts asserted that town dwellers exhibit greater dolichocephaly than the people in the adjacent countryside; the "law of stratification" was formulated in the following terms: "the cephalic index decreases and the proportion of dolichocephalics rises the higher the social class, in each locality." In his "Sélections sociales" the same writer has no hesitation in asserting that "the dominant class in the feudal epoch belongs almost exclusively to the variety "Homo Europaeus" so that it is not pure chance which has kept the poor at the foot of the social ladder but their congenital inferiority."

We thus see that German racism was inventing nothing new, when Alfred Rosenberg asserted that the French Revolution must be deemed a revolt of the brachycephalics of the Alpine stock against the dolichocephalics of the Nordic race." (A. Cuvillier, p. 155).

[7] W. M. F. Petrie, 1939, Fig. 1.

[8] ibid., p. 69.

[9] ibid., p. 68.

[10] E. Amélineau, 1908, p. 174.

[11] Pl. 1.2.

[12] Pl. 1.3.

[13] W. M. F. Petrie, 1939, p. 67.

[14] Pl. 1.11.

[15] Pl. 1.5.

[16] Pl. 1.8.

[17] Pl. 1.7. I know that "Indo-European" is usually said to be a language, not a race, but I prefer this term to "Aryan" wherever its use causes no confusion.

[18] Pl. 1.12.

[19] Pl. 1.13.

[20] R. A. Nicolaus, p. 11.

[21] T. J. Pettigrew, 1834, pp. 70–71.

[22] C. A. Diop, 1977.

[23] M. E. Fontane, pp. 44–5 (see reproduction: T).

[24] M. F. A. Montagu, p. 337.

[25] In the fifth century before our era, at the time when Herodotus visited Egypt, a black-skinned people, the Colchians, were still living in Colchis on the Armenian shore of the Black Sea, east of the ancient port of Trebizond, surrounded by white-skinned nations.

The scholars of antiquity wondered about this people's origins and Herodotus in "Euterpe," the second book of his history on Egypt, tries to prove that the Colchians were Egyptians, whence the arguments we quote. Herodotus, on the strength of commemorative stelae, erected by Sesostris in conquered countries, asserts that this monarch had got as far as Thrace and Scythia, where stelae would seem to have been still standing in his day (Book II, 103).

[26] Herodotus, Book II, 104. As with many peoples in black Africa, Egyptian women underwent excision of the clitoris: cf. Strabo, *Geography,* Book XVII, Ch. I.

[27] Herodotus, Book II, 57.

[28] Seneca, *Questions of Nature,* Book IV, 17.

[29] Herodotus, Book II, 22.

[30] Aristotle, *Physiognomy,* 6.

[31] Lucian, *Navigations,* paras 2–3.

[32] Apollodorus, Book II, "The family of Inachus," paras 3 and 4.

[33] Aeschylus, *The Suppliants,* vv. 719–20. See also v. 745.

[34] Strabo, *Geography,* Book I, ch. 3, para. 10.

[35] My italics.

[36] Diodorus, *Universal History,* Book III. The antiquity of the Ethiopian civilization is attested by the most ancient and most venerable Greek writer, Homer, in both the *Illiad* and the *Odyssey:* "Jupiter followed today by all the gods receives the sacrifices of the Ethiopians" (*Illiad,* I, 422). "Yesterday to visit holy Ethiopia Jupiter betook himself to the ocean shore" (*Illiad,* I, 423).

[37] Diogenes Laertius, Book VII, i.

[38] The Egyptian notables liked to have a Syrian or Cretan female slave in their harems.

[39] Ammianus Marcellinus, Book XXII, para. 16 (23).

[40] Pirate gangs who worked from small ships called *Camare.*

[41] Ammianus Marcellinus, Book XXII, para. 8 (24).

[42] M. C. F. Volney, *Voyages en Syrie et en Egypte,* Paris, 1787, Vol. I, pp. 74–7.

[43] J. J. Champollion-Figeac, 1839, pp. 26–7.

[44] This important discovery was made, on the African side, by Sossou Nsougan, who was to compile this part of the present chapter. For the sense of the word see *Wörterbuch der Aegyptischen Sprache,* Vol. 5, 1971, pp. 122 and 127.

[45] ibid., p. 122.

[46] ibid., p. 128.

[47] R. O. Faulkner, 1962, p. 286.

[48] Wörter buch der ägyptischen Sprache, p. 492.

[49] ibid., p. 124.

[50] ibid., p. 125.

[51] ibid., p. 123.

[52] It should be noted that set=kem=black wife in Walaf.

[53] Wörter buch der ägyptischen Sprache, p. 492.

[54] ibid., p. 493.

[55] Desrêt=blood in Egyptian; deret=blood in Walaf: ibid., p. 494.

[56] Genesis, 10: 6–7.

[57] C. A. Diop, 1955, pp. 33ff.

[58] E. Massoulard, 1949, p. 386.

[59] Juvénal, *Satire* XV, vv. 1–14.

[60] E. Amélineau, *op. cit.*

[61] A. Recnach, 1913, p. 17.

[62] Often spelled Wolof.

[63] C. A. Diop, 1955, pp. 33ff.

[64] R. Lambert, 1925, p. 129.

[65] A. Mallon, pp. 207–34.

[66] A. de Buck, 1952.

[67] ibid.

[68] A. Mallon, pp. 207–34.

[69] By extension=love intensely (hence the verb marmaral) after the fashion of a female animal licking the cub which she has just borne. This sense does not conflict with the other notion which the determinative may convey of a man raising hand to mouth.

[70] See below for the explanation of this important law.

[71] See C. A. Diop, 1967.

[72] See *Final Report of the First Plenary Session of the International Scientific Committee for the Drafting of a general History of Africa*, UNESCO, 30 March-8 April 1974.

[73] Symposium of "The peopling of ancient Egypt and the deciphering of the Meriotic script." Cf. Studies and Documents No. I, UNESCO, 1978.

African Civilizations

G. O. Ogunremi

Introduction

It is apt to quote right from the start of this section a veteran scholar, an Africanist, L. S. B. Leakey, who says:

> These critics of Africa forget that men of science today are with few exceptions, satisfied that Africa was the birthplace of man himself, and that for many hundreds of centuries thereafter Africa was in the forefront of all world progress (Leakey, 1969).

Leakey's remark is certainly not an exaggeration, otherwise by now it would have been so reduced to nothing that it would not be more than a mere platitude. Rather, more researchers have ascertained the legitimacy of the scholar's assertion. Perhaps no work gives this testimony more than the UNESCO's *General History of Africa* series, especially Volumes I to V, i.e., from pre-history to about the eighteenth century. Volume I, "Methodology and African Pre-history" and Volume II, "Ancient Civilization of Africa," in particular, give a distinctive feature of African civilizations from the earliest times.

Therefore, anyone who said that Africa had no history said so purely out of ignorance of available evidence on the ancient history of Africa. Even now, archaeological evidence on which the early history is based is not uniformly spread throughout the length and breath of Africa. In many cases the evidence is slender and fragmentary, leading to suppositions and over-concentration on the area around the Nile valley from Bahrel Chazal in the south to the Mediterratican in the north, which is unique for Africa's well-dated original sources, which enable us to follow its history from the end of the Neolithic period—around 3000 (B.C.)—to the seventh century of our era (A.D.) (Mokhtar, 1981). This means that the early history of the area south of the Sahara is limited in scope.

Our emphasis in this section, therefore, will be on the civilizations in Egypt, Nubia, Kush, Aksum, and to some extent on west Africa. Rather than concentrating heavily on each of the areas mentioned above, it will be pertinent to emphasize the spread of civilization from one area to another. Indeed, treating this topic in a small chapter here is like touching, not even scratching, a tip of an iceberg. Each of the items is a big chapter in *General History of Africa* Vol. II (1981). Readers who are interested in knowing the details of the history of these ancient kingdoms and regions must consult this monumental work.

The Importance of Nile

We can hardly talk of the ancient civilization of Africa without attributing it to the existence and importance of the River Nile. The Nile with its source from Lake Victoria in East Africa runs northwards and enters the Mediterranean Sea. This makes it unique, being one of the longest rivers in the world and certainly the longest in Africa. More importantly, it gives Eygpt its unique position as an ancient centre of civilization. But for the Nile, Egypt would be like the other North African countries, a desert country. Hence the old saying, "no Nile No Egypt" is as true today as many centuries ago.

If we go deeper into the very ancient history of Egypt we know that it did not, in the early times, depend on the Nile for its subsistence. This was so as at the end of the Neolithic age around 3300 to 2400 B.C. Then the whole northwestern area enjoyed a relatively wet climate. Egypt and the neighbouring kingdoms had a virile agriculture and supported a considerable cattle raising. Indeed, tax payment to the central autority was based more on cattle than on farm products.

However, with the desiccation of the Sahara and the whole of northwestern Africa, Egypt found itself in a dry land. This is where the role of Nile became pertinent. Although it had always been in existence, the Nile did not play such an important role until after the desiccation. The essential and fundamental achievement of the ancient civilization of Egypt and the entire Nile Valley depended on the River Nile. The seasonal flood of the Nile must be controlled in order to avert disaster that the flood could cause. For example, if uncontrolled, the flood of the Nile would destroy villages, cattle and farmland. It was therefore necessary to build dikes and dams. This control eventually led to irrigation which was of paramount importance to agriculture.

The survival of all the peoples in the Nile Valley depended and still depends on cattle rearing and farming which in turn depended on the water and alluvia provided by the Nile which flooded the valley every year. However, making use of the flood for irrigation was not an easy job. It tasked the ingenuity of the people and led to a considerable amount of work on their part. After each flood the embarkments of the Nile must be repaired, the cross-dams strengthened and the canals cleared. This was done by the communities, perhaps at the village level, and supervised by the central government. All this must be done in good time before the arrival of another flood and alluvia. This natural order to a large extent, dictated the political order which must also be stable. Political instability might cause delay in preparation for agriculture leading to wastage of the flood which might also destroy existing structures and finally lead to catastrophic famine, hunger and death.

Apart from making the best use of the Nile, efforts were also made to prepare for lean years. The Nile flood was never regular in volume. In some years there could be over-flooding while as little as half of the expected flood might occur in some years. Therefore, efforts had to be made to stockpile in the year or years of plenty and also consume less grains in order to save for time of inadequate or excessive flood. Thus, the central government, by effective planning took over from the natural order. This explains the statement that "Egypt is not only a gift of the Nile; it is, above all, a creation of man."

Egypt's Relations with the Rest of Africa

Scholars in archaeology and pre-history as well as in anthropology have done a considerable study of the Egyptian civilization. One important factor that the studies have revealed is the spread of its civilization to the other parts of Africa. However, while the studies have concentrated on and have been quite definitive in the area of the Nile Valley, they have not been so certain in the areas south of Meroe. This may be due to the problem of relevant data with which to construct the history.

We have some rather fragmentary and inconclusive evidence that a few Egyptian objects were discovered in its southern parts. For instance, a statue of Osiris dating from the seventh century B.C. was found in Zaire, on the banks of River Lualaba. Also, a statue of Thutmose III (1440–1468 B.C.) was found south of the Zambezi. It was also discovered that certain cultures which occurred in modern Ghana especially among the Akans were thought to be influenced by the Egyptian cultures. For example, the vulture as a symbol of self-creation and also the serpent cult which were found in Ghana were probably traceable to Egypt.

It is, however, certain that Egypt had attracted its neighbours because of its needs for agricultural labourers and military men. Egypt also looked towards its neighbours for resources which it could obtain from them. Lower Nubia, for example, interested the Egyptians on account of the gold it produced and to the southern Nilotic regions because of the routes leading to the interior of Africa through the white Nile or the Saharan routes or Darfur. Egypt cherished these southern routes and did everything to preserve them.

One reason for the Egyptian interest in the southern routes was to obtain human resource from Sudan. It also looked up to the Sudanese livestock and minerals. Also, the Nubians were needed in Egypt because of their fame for archery and so were required in the Egyptian army. Besides, the Nubians were also brought into Egypt as agricultural labourers. The Egyptian interaction with the south including the Sudan was so close that Egypt appointed a governor, known as the Governor of the South to guard the southern gate of Egypt, organise commercial exchanges and facilitate the circulation of trading expeditions.

Nubian Civilizaion

Africa's ancient civilisation is by no means limited to Egypt. It even transcended the Nilotic region to Western Sudan and also to eastern, central and southern Africa. However, since history is based on facts we can for now only properly account for regions that have been excavated or where documentary or artistic evidence abounds. Nubia is one of such lucky areas. It was strategically positioned between Central Africa and the Mediterranean. This position enabled Nubia to serve as a link between the ancient civilizations of Egypt and the Mediterranean on the one hand and the black Africa on the other. This makes Nubia one of the regions of Africa where contacts were easy, not just between the north and the south but also between east and west. In the southern part the Ethiopian highlands, the Red Seas and the Indian Ocean could easily be reached through the Blue Nile, the Atbara and their tributaries. Westwards, the chad depression and the valley of the Niger and West Africa could also be linked through the Nile between the Third and Fourth Cataracts and with the Kordafan and Darfur Plains.

We can therefore see Nubia as an African crossroad, and a meeting-place for civilizations from the east and west and also from the north and south of Africa. ... An important significance of this is that Nubia was able to acquire some peoples' cultures and transfer them to others. Such interactions could he through trade or warfare. They could also be through reciprocal visits by the Nubians and their neighbours.

It is known, for example, that the Egyptians carried their culture to Nubia through their troops. The Egyptians tried to bring the Nubians under their control for at least two reasons. First, they wanted to control Nubia so as to have easy access to the Nubian wood and other raw materials which Egypt needed but did not possess. Second, Egypt invaded Nubia so as to be able to keep open the passage leading southwards from where incense, gum, ivory, ebony, and ponthers were obtained. To this end, the Egyptian soldiers carried not only their war weapons to Nubia but also their culture. One such acquisition was the smelting techniques which the Egyptians (not necessarily soldiers) introduced in the upper Nile Valley. The Nubians gained this metallurgy technique, and by 2000 B.C. were able to make copper objects as well as to handle gold.

Through the "Nubian Corridor," the Egyptians were also able to reach Africa south of the Sahara. Apart from the references made to Zaire and modern Ghana, a dwarf was also found in Egypt. This dwarf had been associated with the pygmy in the tropical forest. It can therefore be assumed that there had been contacts between Egypt and Central Africa as early as the sixth dynasty (c. 2750–2200 B.C.). It must be noted that apart from all the civilizations that passed through Nubia to the other parts of Africa, Nubia also had its civilizations which it channelled to the rest of Africa.

The Civilization of Napata and Meroe in Kush Kingdom

In the political organisation of Napata and Meroe the king was the head and the system monarchical. One important feature of the political system was the choice of a new leader by election and as ordered in the end by the oracle. The priests first selected whoever they regarded the best candidates from the royal lineage; and the people, going through the god chose the king who was immediately honoured as if he were a god since the kingdom was entrusted to him by the will of the divinity. This method of selecting a new king was peculiar to Napata and Meroe in contrast to the situation in Egypt or the oriental political system, where succession normally followed the father-son hereditary pattern. The choice of a king was far from being arbitrary. The initiative in choosing a new king came from the military leaders, high officials, clan chiefs and the queen-mother.

In many cases, successors were brethren of the deceased king but there were a few usurpers who later on managed to legitimize their positions. Once accepted the king was absolutely powerful, at least in theory. In real practice his power was limited by the customary law and taboos. Indeed, as it happened much later in the history of the Oyo empire in modern Nigeria, the priests could order an unpopular king to commit suicide. This went on in Kush kingdom till about 250 B.C. when a king who had a Greek education not only stopped the practice but also killed some high chiefs.

The king occupied an essential position in the administrative system. Generally, he was an absolute, autocratic ruler whose word was law and who neither delegated his power nor shared it with anyone. To help in the administration were officers such as the chief of the treasury, seal bearers, heads of archives, chiefs of granaries, and scribes. There were also military leaders. It was likely that most of the officers were the king's brothers from the royal lineage. With the king they lived in the capital, Napata.

There were also provincial officers who administered areas further away from the seat of the king. When the Meroitic kingdom was at its height, it was so vast and the means of communication became so poor that provincial governors also had to decentralize authority for the administration to function.

The kingdom of Kush depended on a wide variety of economic activites. However, animal husbandry and agriculture predominated. The people kept long- and short-horned cattle as well as sheep, goats, and to some extent horses, and also donkeys which were used as beasts of burden. At the end of the first century B.C., camels were introduced. Cattle breeding was very important and it often led to movement from areas where grazing was difficult to where it was easy. For example, this was the main reason why the capital of Kush kingdom moved from Napata to Meroe, a better grazing area, being in the south where rainfall was better. When this transfer took place in the fourth century B.C., cattle breeding was given a new impulse.

In both Napata and Meroe areas, agriculture was also important. However, irrigation was not practised as in Egypt owing to the scarcity of fertile land in the narrow valley of the Nile. This is not to say that they did not have the knowledge of an irrigation system. When the capital moved to Meroe, agriculture improved and at the peak of the Meroitic kingdom the Island was highly cultivated. The network of canals and irrigation basins attest to this.

Among the crops cultivated were barley, wheat and especially sorghum and lentils. Cotton was another major crop cultivated. Its cultivation most likely began in the empire of Kush because it was unknown in ancient Egypt. In the fourth century B.C., cultivation of cotton and the knowledge of its spinning and even weaving in Meroe reached a very high level. Indeed, the export of textiles was one of the sources of wealth of Meroe.

The empire of Kush and especially the area of Meroe has been described as one of the richest areas in the world. Kush was one of the gold-producing centres in the ancient world. It was exported to near and far distances, and it greatly influenced foreign relations with Rome and Egypt in particular. It has been calculated that during the ancient times Kush produced about 1,600,000 kilogrammes of pure gold. There were other minerals such as carbuncle, hycinth, beryl, and amethyst. However, it is important to note that since Meroe was a crossroad and a hub some articles of trade which were not produced there passed through the Meroitic trade channels and so increased the fame of Meroe as one of the richest countries in the ancient world.

Another important mineral that is worth mentioning is iron. Because of the abundance of iron slags found around Meroe, the place was declared the "Birmingham of an ancient Africa" in 1911 by a scholar, A. H. Sayce. This declaration has now been challenged by scholars who recently did more work on iron metallurgy in Meroe. It is now argued that the slag heaps of Meroe were remains of industries rather than iron, and that if the dumps were the slags of iron, the areas around Meroe should be littered with iron-smelting furnaces. But no traces of such have been found. It has, however, been argued also that there is no conclusive evidence to show that the knowledge of iron smelting was unknown in Meroe or in some other parts of Africa.

Meroitic towns were also important centres of crafts and trade. Although the Egyptian influences were notable, there was no doubt that the people freed themselves of foreign influences in their artistic work. They created a highly original and independent artistic tradition. Of all the works of craft, pottery was the most famous product of the Meroitic civilization. The pottery was famous in particular for both its texture and decoration. There were two types: one was the handmade pottery made by women, and they were remarkable for their style which reflected a deep-rooted African tradition. The other was the wheel-turned wares made by men. These varied and were responsive to changes.

Other works of art included jewellery in forms of necklaces, bracelets, earrings, and finger-rings. Also, ivory carving was done on a large scale. But unlike the jewelery which had some Egyptian influence, ivory carving was purely Meroitic.

The empire of Kush was an ideal entrepôt for trade because of its location between the Red Sea, the Upper Nile and the Nile-Chad savannah. This is why foreign trade played such an important role in the Meroitic economy and politics. Caravan routes to Egypt, for example, indicated the magnitude and antiquity of the trade. Since ancient times the major exports from Nubia generally were gold, incense, ivory, ebony, oils, ostrich feathers, and leopard skins. Some of these traded goods originated in Meroitic territory while the origins of the others were certainly from countries to the south.

Apart from trading with Egypt, the Mediterranean world was another major area of foreign trade. The main trade route was the Nile, but there was also a land route which crossed the savannah, especially between Meroe and Napata, and between Napata and Lower Nubia. The Island of Meroe was criss-crossed by many caravan routes, and it was also the starting-point for caravans to the Red Sea region, Northern Ethiopia, Kordofan and Darfur. Because of the nomads who often raided the routes, fortresses were erected at strategic points for protecting the caravans; and wells were dug for them too at strategic centres.

This trade declined from the beginning of the first century B.C. One reason for this was that the main route was transferred from the Nile axis to the Red Sea. This reduced the volume of trade directly exported from Meroe because many traded goods could be obtained from Northern Ethiopia where Aksum had just started to rise. Also, the last centuries of the Meroitic kingdom coincided with the crisis of the Roman empire which led to a sharp decline and interruption of trade relations between Meroe and Egypt. Indeed, many towns which were dependent on the trade were ruined. In addition, neither Rome nor Meroe was capble of defending the trade routes against some nomads who persistently raided the caravans.

The Aksumite Civilization

In the fifth century B.C. some form of civilization of the Arabian influence was established on the northern Ethiopian plateau. It was largely an agrarian culture which prospered during the fifth and fourth centuries B.C. Although the civilization declined, some of its characteristics were preserved in the Aksumite civilization.

However, unlike the empire of Kush whose history is deeply rooted in antiquity, that of Aksum belongs mainly to our era (i.e., A.D.). It is only in the second and third centuries A.D. that historical sources record the rapid rise of Aksum as a new African power. It was Claudius Ptolemy, writing around the middle of the second century A.D. who first mentioned the Aksumites as one of the peoples of Ethiopia. By the beginning ot the third century A.D., it had certainly become a powerful kingdom. It waged war in Yemen and occupied some of its territories. At the end of the third and in the early years of the fourth centuries, Azhah, an Aksumite king, also waged wars in Southern Arabia. By about 270 A.D. the fame of Aksum had reachcd Persia; and it was regarded as one of the four greatest empires of the world.

The political structure of Aksum was partly based on its military efforts. Right from its beginning, it had to establish its power over the segmentary states of Northern Ethiopia and to encompass them into one kingdom. Success depended largely on the Aksumite king's strength and the degree to which it exceeded that of other princes in ancient Ethiopia. Sometimes, a new ruler had to inaugurate his reign by having a countrywide campaign to enforce a formal submission on the provinces. For example, at the outset of his reign, King Ezana, a very popular ruler, asserted his authority by doing so. From the end of the second century up to the beginning of the fourth, Aksum was involved in the diplomatic struggles among the states of Southern Arabia. Also, the Aksumites subjugated the regions between the Tigre Plateau and the Valley of the Nile. In the fourth century they, in fact, conquered the Meroe Kingdom which by that time had declined.

The kingdom was divided into Aksum proper, and its provincial kingdom had rulers that were subject to the Aksum almighty king to whom tributes were paid. The king appointed his relations to assume the direction of affairs of the state. For example, military expeditions were led by the king or his brother or other kinsmen. Around this king of kings were court officials who also constituted an armed retinue in wartime. These court officials carried out in peacetime such functions as serving as envoys and guards. Probably due to the military government, the administration of Aksum was highly centrally organized around the king of kings.

Economically, the Aksumites were engaged in agriculture and stock-breeding. The mountain slopes were terraced and irrigated by the water of mountain streams channelled into the fields. The Aksumites kept large herds of cattle, sheep, and goats while elephants were captured and domesticated.

Crafts and trades were also well developed. There were highly skilled blacksmiths, metal-workers, potters, builders, stone-masons and carvers. An important technical innovation was the use of iron-tools which became widespread in the first millennium B.C. This innovation influenced the development of agriculture, trade, and military science.

Aksum was remarkable for being a first-rate trading power as evidenced by the minting of its own gold, silver, and copper coinage. It is regarded as the first state in tropical Africa to introduce coins. The minting of coins, especially gold, was not just an economic advancement; it was also a political measure. It proclaimed to the whole world the independence and prosperity of the Aksum state. However, it was the king more than anyone else who enjoyed the commercial ventures of the kingdom. Also, the nobility and the entire privileged social group of Aksumites benefited from the profits of trade.

The kingdom of Aksum has been linked with the Jewish faith before Christianity reached there. One Frumentius was closely linked with the introduction of Christianity and he later became the first bishop of Aksum in 315 A.D. But the kings found it difficult to divorce themselves from their traditional gods and saw themselves as the almighty. Among the first rulers to accept Christianity was King Ezana who was baptized between 350 and 360 A.D.

Conclusion

This chapter delved into the remote past of African history. We have seen that in Africa the earliest civilization recorded is in the lower and upper Valley of the Nile, with Egypt predominating in the Lower valley and the Kush empire in the Upper part. We have seen the importance of the Nile in the history of Africa. One of the longest rivers in the world, the Nile, originates and ends in Africa. The waters and alluvia it carries on its journey have been a great blessing to all the settlements it passes through from generation to generation.

As a result of paintings, engravings and writings that have been done in the Nile valley, and as a result of the climate that was conducive to preservation of materials, much history of the area has been written. However, the role of archaeology cannot be over-stressed. Quite a lot of archaeological evidence has been used to construct the history of the area. This is why much is known of the Meroitic civilization.

It has been discovered that by the time of the decline of Meroe, the kingdom of Aksum had developed properly. What is important to note, however, is that by the fourth century A.D. when it declined, a reasonable part of the culture of Meroe which either originated there or was transferred there had also been passed to its south and west.

One of such was iron-smelting technology. Most likely, the best known of the iron age societies in West Africa is that of Nok. It is certain that the Nok people were located in the south-west of the Jos Plateau in modern Nigeria. It has been discovered that these men of the Nok culture were smelting iron and making terra-cotta scruptures of high quality as early as the fifth century B.C. or even earlier. It is possible that the culture reached the southern parts of modern Nigeria, especially Ife and Benin, and some other ancient Yoruba towns. This possibility is based on the similarities between the Nok and Ife art works.

Also the Igbo Ukwu excavations clearly show that iron-working in Southeastern Nigeria is at least as early as the ninth century A.D. It has been found that particular, exclusive lineages were involved in iron smithing. The most famous of the

Igbo smiths are those from Awka, east of Onitsha. They worked the iron ore obtained from the Igbo smelters of Udi, and it was only much later that they received supplies of European iron. And, of course, there were other iron-working areas among the Igbo.

The most important significance of iron smelting in all parts of Africa was the development of agriculture. The smelted iron was forged by the blacksmiths into agricultural implements such as hoes, cutlasses and knives. That encouraged a more elaborate production of food which in turn led to greater population which became urbanized with time. Besides, iron was also forged into war weapons. This might be destructive because it often encouraged internecine warfare purely for expansion of empires. For example, we know that the possession of iron-pointed spears enabled the ancient empire of Ghana to fight expansionist wars and enlarge the empire by controlling weaker neighbouring settlements which had no iron to fight with. It can therefore be said that iron was an empire destroyer and empire builder.

Finally, it must be noted that the question of diffusionist theory is a nagging one which has always engaged the attention of scholars. It cannot be precisely said where a particular culture had originated. Neither can it be said that one culture is older than another until after a thorough archaeological investigation has been carried out. We strongly believe, however, that every society possessed one type of civilization, culture, and technology or the other. We also believe that the civilization was dynamic—changing according to the growth and needs of the society.

A Survey of Early African History

Hakeem Tijani

Introduction

The work of the historian is not only to record, but to analyse and evaluate available facts. He is not expected to be partial in his write-up, nor is he expected to blow his facts beyond proportion; hence, the history we read may turn out not to be factual, but "series of accepted judgements."[1]

E. H. Carr was more succinct when he wrote that "the function of the historian is not to love the past nor to emancipate himself from the past, but to master and understand it as the key to the understanding of the present."[2] Suffice it to say that early African history, and indeed the history of any group, could broaden the student's imaginative capability and also bestow on him an analytical and objective orientation, as well as, critical reasoning as a result of his daily use of evidence that must be critically tested. The study of history will therefore afford us the opportunity to understand the present realities better by our ability to cast a glance back into the past for an illumination on the problems of today. And that is why history has been defined as the distilled experience and wisdom of the past. This chapter is thus divided into three parts; Sources of Early African History; Western View of Early Africa History; and Man in Africa.

Sources of Early African History

The historian by training derives his material from a great many sources. Evidence for the past comes from sources both written and unwritten. The unwritten sources are derived from the work of scholars in a variety of disciplines, including archeaology anthropology linguistics, art history, botany, zoology, ethrography, and of course, oral accounts. Written source, however, could be divided into two groups, library material (books and printed reports), and archival material (manuscripts). The library material includes historical reconstructions contained in the books and articles of scholars; early works of history and geography; travellers' accounts, autobiographies, and other literary works and reports usually of an official nature. For the professional historian archival materials often provide much more importance than any other source partly due to its reliability and safety.

In most African states, for instance, the archives established by the colonialists, have proved a great repository for any historian interested in African past. The Public Record Office in the United Kingdom, Late Patrice Lumumba Centre in the Soviet Union National Archives and Record Administration, as well as the Washington Research Centre in the United States of America, are examples. The regional offices of the National Archives at Ibadan, Enugu, and Kaduna in Nigeria have been of significance to professional and nonprofessional historians.

Oral traditions[3] remain one of the vital sources of early African history. These are accounts given by eye witnesses, usually a chain of transmissions. Oral traditions may be divided into three different categories, i.e., myths, legends, folktales and popular history. Recent works, both African and European, have revealed the wealth of oral tradition in certain localities and demonstrated convincingly the degree of detail that can be achieved in the reconstuction of the more recent past.

Archeaology is another important source of historical information, particularly in Africa. It could be defined as that science that probes the human past by studying fossil remains. According to Professor Thurstan Shaw, "archeaology is a science which is able to discover large parts of the story of man's un-written past by studying the material objects he had left behind."[4] Therefore, Robin Hallet is right when he said "for the remote past archeaology is naturally of paramount importance."[5] Through the carbon 14 dating, and the principle of stratigraphy (or relative dating), the archeaologist could detemine the dates for a particular fossil of man. That is, the use of radio carbon, the proportion of radio active isotope of C14 to ordinary C12 with charcoal could give a rough date of a sample being analysed. It is, however, important to state that carbon dates are not exact dates, but are often expressed as statistical probabilies.

Anthropology and sociology on the other hand have been primarily concerned with the variations of physical types, gathering information on the range of a people's material culture, some aspects of which may be of special concern to art historians, and investigating thought processes, religious and philosophical ideas, tracing the complex structure of a society and describing its form of law and government. They usually ask questions about the past, despite the fact that their major concern is the contemporary. This is because they are conscious of the historian's dictum of the present being part of the past which cannot be delineated from one another.

Linguistics[6] is an extremely arduous discipline, many branches of which the historian may find himself ill-equipped to understand. But, he cannot ignore the fact that every language represents an important historical document and that certain aspects of its study, notably the nature of its relationship with other languages and the derivations of its loanwords, may provide the historian with the material from which to construct valuable hypotheses about the past. Taken by itself, the evidence from linguistics can never appear completely convincing, but it can prove an invaluable auxillary in the reconstruction of the broad lines of development in distant periods of the past. Professor Greenberg's analysis of Africa south of the Sahara is quite relevant here. Through his analysis, it is now known that Africans have intelligible phonetics. Perhaps of more importance is the linguistic discovery of Bantu dispersion from present day Eastern Nigeria.

Zoology has also proved to be an important source of early Africa history. Although, the study of the plants and animals are primarily the concern of the botanist and zoologist, such aspects of their research are of great interest to the historian as well. To know the exact area of the original domestications of a plant or animal, to be able to trace the routes by which it came to be more widely diffused, to possess some account of the fauna and flora of a particular region at a particular period in the past, represents an extremely valuable contribution to the stock of historical knowledge.

The Arabs, as well as the Europeans, have also contributed in the reconstruction of the African past. A number of scholars writing in Arabic devoted themselves to the history of Egypt, Andulasia, Maghreb, Western and Central Sudan. Noteworthly are Al Bakri, Ibn Bathuta, at-Farsari, al-Yarqubu, al-Maghrisi, al-Maghili, Ibn Fartua and so on. For the reconstruction of the history of the people north of the Sahara, for instance, Arabic sources have proved to be very useful. In fact, it was on such that European travellers depended during their travels in Africa. Importantly, in the course of their journeys they came up with their own accounts of the geography, peopling, and socio-political situation within Africa.

Periplus of the Eritrean Sea and Strabo's account are invaluable in the reconstruction of East and Southern Africa. It is interesting to note that the late fifteenth century saw the opening of a new age of European interest in Africa. Many of the European authors, particularly in West Africa, were traders, missionaries, and few adventurers. The writings of travelers such as the Scotman, James Bruce in Ethiopia, the Englishman, Richard Burton in Somalia and East/West Africa, the German, Heinrich Barth in the Western and Central Sudan,

the Frenchman Emile Granduier in Madagascar, may well be regarded as foundations of modern African studies.[7]

In recent time, the use of interdisciplinary approach has also become an important source of writing the African past. The most germane description of this source could be deduced from the work of Robin Hallet, who once wrote:

> ...one cannot make a hard and fast distinction between different disciplines and especially between anthropologists, geographers, and historians, for their studies are complementary. Ideally, the anthropologist needs to acquire the time perspective of the historians, the historian to develop that awareness of the complexity of society possessed by the anthropologist, while both ought to possess that sense of the importance of the physical environment that comes naturally to the geographers....[8]

Western View of Early African History: Stereotypes, Racism and Hamitic Hypothesis

The history of Africa is relevant to the history of black people throughout the world. This is partly because persons of African ancestry are dispersed throughout the world, and partly because of the general derogatory image Africans and black people everywhere have inherited from Western history. Hence, historians of Africa are faced with the multitude of stereotypes and myths fashioned by Europeans of yesteryears. The denigration of Africans can be traced back to antiquity (before Christ) and in later times, anyone who wished to employ degrading stereotypes about black people could easily establish a reference point in classical times, when scholars and writers such as Herodotus described Africans as strange and primitive creatures.

Herodotus, in attempting to explain African culture which was different from his, sowed seeds of racial prejudice that shaped black-white images over the centuries. He frequently referred to Africans as "barbarians" and "savages." In fact, Pliny the elder also said that, "by report," Africans, "had no heads but mouth and eyes both in their chest," and others "who crawled instead of walking."

The most decisive derogatory racial tradition stems from the biblical interpretation of Noah's course of Ham, where descendants of Ham were referred to as blacks. The image of Africans as inferior was reinforced by arguments of several Christian missionaries, ministers, etc., who explained that an African was better off a slave in a Christian society than free in "African savagery." This, perhaps, was used to justify European slave trade, and subsequently the partitioning and colonialism of Africa.

Hegel, in his *Philosophy of History* also made the same unabashed remark about Africa. As he noted:

> ...it is manifest that want of self-control distinguishes the character of the Negroes. This condition is capable of no development or culture.... At this point, we leave Africa, not to mention it again. For it is no historical part of the World.[9]

A great landmark in this historical drama occurred during the nineteenth century when modern nationalism in Europe and imperialism abroad contributed to the development of ideologies that sanctioned the idea that whites are natural donors, and blacks recipients. That is, the wrong idea that Africa has no civilisation, whatever landmark in the continent was due to external forces. In fact, Egypt with its civilisation was excluded from Africa and merged with the Middle East. Thus, the emergence of Social Darwinism which synthesized the old ideas and provided new zeal for old and erroneous beliefs. We can briefly summarise the Western stereotype here by highlighting the views of its modern exponents, i.e., Karl Popper and C. G. Seligman, and Cheikh Anta Diop's remarkable response to them and their cronies.

C. G. Seligman applied the Concept of Social Darwinism to African ethnography which amounted to the attribution of absolute values to white and black physical types, with the latter occupying the lower rung of advancement. According to him, "the Hamites—who are Europeans, belong to the same great branch of mankind as the whites who civilized Africa, the civilisations of the Hamites, its history, etc., is the record of these people and their interaction with the two other African stocks, the Negro and the Bushman." The stamp of racism thus made its indelible imprint not only on the history of Africa, Africans, and all black people, it also prejudiced scholarly studies of black people for many centuries. To a great extent, the institution of colonialism and apartheid system could be dated to this era.

Two other stereotypes, i.e., tribe and native, need be considered here. The term "tribe" denotes a person of a lower order, while "native" denotes subordinate units. The "tribe" was regarded as a more primitive unit which in time evolved into a civilized one. In brief, the terms are general derogatory labels for Africans that prejudged their historical experience. They have, however, been discredited by Africanists in view of their long historical association with the concept of black inferiority.

However, through rigorous historical scholarship and the use of multidisciplinary approach, attempts were made, and are still being undertaken to reconstruct the erroneous views. What is important here, therefore, is that scholars like Cheikh Anta Diop have criticized this position. Drawing evidence from eye-witness accounts of Herodotus and others, he concluded that Egyptians were black, and their contributions to the World are black peoples' contribution. As he maintained:

> It remains...true that Egyptian experiment was essentially Negro, and that all Africans can draw the same moral advantage from it that Westerners draw from Gracci-Latin Civilisation.[10]

Evolution of Man

One of the controversial issues in historical and evolutionary sciences is that of the origin of man as we know him today. Some Europeans based on their bias towards the historical significance of Africa maintain that the origin and evolution of man should be sought in the Far East or Asia. Not until Leakey's discovery at Olduvai Gorge in Tangayika did many scholars begin to think positively about the African origin of man. Although Charles Darwin in his *Descent of Man,* 1871, had projected that man must have originated in Africa, subsequent European scholars did not subscribe to this.

Apart from the controversy regarding the origin of man, there is also the debate of his evolution. Religious and secular theorists are divided on this issue. While the former believe in the biblical injunction of the creation of heaven, earth and man by the omnipresent (God) in seven days, the latter, led by Charles Darwin opine that man evolved through evolutionary means—that is, from animal to a primate with high intellectual capability. Hence, the history of man involves changing his environs to suit his needs. Man belongs to the primates and his family is the *hominidae,* but a definition of when a hominid became man has caused some difficulty. It has been earlier defined as a period when man began to make tools in regularly set patterns. However, recent research showed that chimpanzees meet that requirement. Consequently, a more recent definition is that man emerged at that stage of evolution when his carriage or posture became erect (*Homo Erectus*) as he walked on two legs, and he possessed the ability to make cutting tools for future use (*Homosapien*).

The Olduvian culture discovered by Leakey and his assistants suggest the origin of man to be in

Africa. A skull which was located at the Gorge when finally pieced together, was a *hominid* type, subsequently named *Zinjathropus* or Man of Zinj, the latter being the term for the East Africa coast in early history. Zinjathropus, also called *Nutcracker Man* because of its large molars, was found in proximity to primitive store tools which, under the earlier definition, suggested that this was man. In 1960, a second discovery named *Homohabilis*, was made. Both were seen as contemporaries. However, Homohabilis is said to have possessed a great brain capacity. In addition, while Zinjathropus had teeth adapted for a coarse vegetable diet, Homohabilis had teeth more adapted to meet a dut which would have required greater reliance on the making and use of tools. The latter also had hands with opposable thumb and forefinger (an adaptation which facilitated tool-making), a much more necessary technique for the survival of Homohabilis as a meat eater than for Zinjathropus, although the nature of the latter's hand is not known. Hence, Homohabilis is associated with the Olduvian culture, the fully established stone age culture.

Homohabilis seems to be the direct ancestor of man, dating back to about two million years. Homoerectus, the main human type, emerged about three-fourths of a million years ago, when the man had migrated to Asia, Europe, and possibly elsewhere. Early man evolved a nomadic life. Although he hunted for game, he remained a scavenger and gatherer of wild fruits and vegetables. It has been posited that between 50,000 and 100,000 years ago, man in Africa became a regular user of fire. The benefit of this was increased potential for collecting, producing and cooking food. The use of fire therefore contributed greatly to better nourishment, comfort, and security of man.

The movement from a gathering and hunting culture, to cultivating and harvesting of crops for consumption is referred to as the *Neolithic Revolution*. By this period man had evolved a sedentary life, based on a food-producing community. The Nile, Delta, Fayum, Taruga and Yobe are examples of places in Africa where man excelled. The Nachikufu revealed tools associated with vegetable foods, and are dated from about 4300–250 B.C. The Nok culture is dated between 2000–1000 B.C. while the Fayum economy is dated from about 6000 B.C. In fact, the anthropologist George Mardeck (*Africa: Its Culture and Peoples*) has credited Africa with a much larger number of indigenous beans, cotton and yams. A species of rice, *orza glaberimma*, was said to have been cultivated by the people of Nok.[12]

The discovery of iron-ore and the knowledge of iron metallurgy enhanced greatly the development of the agricultural sector of the economy. Iron-ore are smelted into various forms which are used in catching game, as farm implements, etc. As Joseph Harris puts it, "the appearance of iron-ore culture that greatly accelerated developments in farming and led to decisive changes in the lives of Africans." The acquisition and knowledge of iron-smelting techniques spread throughout Africa at different times. In Egypt it has been dated from 2000 B.C. It was probably developed about 500 B.C. at Meroe. Between 300–200 B.C. iron-making appeared along the plateau area of the Niger-Benue rivers in central Nigeria. While the knowledge of iron smelting appeared in the area of the Zambezi by the first century A.D., the various excavations at these sites have debuked the diffusionist theory, which denies Africans (blacks in particular) any ingenuity. The question of who disseminated the knowledge of iron-making/smelting is no more being asked, but rather how effective was its discovery in revolutionalizing the life of Africans. This is where state formation in Africa takes it root.

As hunting groups became larger, weapons more deadly and with longer firing range, competition for game more intense, specialization more advanced and longer conditions for settlement more necessary, the pressures increased for the organisation of food production and distribution, the regulation of relationships of individuals in the group and protection of life and property brought about state formation and evolution of a well organised social organisation in Africa.

Apart from the development of iron knowledge, there was also that of artistic ingenuity. In North Africa, chipped figures of animals have survived on rock walls in the Atlas Mountains and in Nigeria, rock paintings are found in the Sahara regions of Tasili, Ahaggar and Tibestic. Other rock paintings appear in Rhodesia, Zambia, and South Africa. All these paintings and engravings not only attest to the prehistoric Africa's artistic knowledge and style as well as his developments with durable paints, but in addition, valuable data are thus provided about Africans and their environment during and after the Neolithic age.

We should consider the desertification of the Sahara at this juncture. This is in view of its importance in African pre-history. Between 200–50 B.C., the Sahara which used to be a green and fertile land, began to dry up. Its green leaves and alluvian soil turned sandy and became a desert. The consequence was migration of people towards the sub-saharan area. The desertifications of the Sahara and its migrational consequence is often used by the diffusionists to justify their belief that the idea of iron-making and cultivation of crops, as well as state formation, came from the North, where the hamites (white skins) had interacted with the black Africans.

In conclusion, it is not tenable that Africans have no history. We now know that the sense of history, and the use of history are parts of the whole process of African development.

References

1. See, Walsh W. H. *Introduction to the Philosophy of History*.
2. See, Carr, E. H. *What Is History*, London, 1963.
3. See, Vansina, J. *Oral Tradition: A Study in Historical Methodology*, Chicago, 1965. Henige D. P. *The Chronology of Oral Tradition: The Quest for Chimera*, Oxford, 1974.
4. See Thurstan Shaw (ed.) *Nigerian Pre-history and Archaelogy*, Ibadan, 1969.
5. Robin Hallet, *Africa to 1875*, London, 1966.
6. Anstrong, R. G. "The Use of Linguistic and Ethnographic Data on the Study of Idoma and Yoruba History," in Vansina et al. (eds.), *The Historian in Tropical Africa*, Oxford, 1964.
7. A critique of their historiography can be found in Toyin Falola, "The Sources of Nigerian History," in Falola T. and Adediran A., *A New History of Nigeria for Colleges*, Book One, John West Publications, 1986.
8. Robin Hallet, op. cit.
9. Hegel, *Philosophy of History*.
10. See, Childe Golden, *What Happened in History*, London, 1965.
11. For a detailed study, see *UNESCO Volume 1*.
12. See, George Murdock, *Africa: Its Peoples and Culture*, 1960.

The Land, Early Nubian Cultures and Egypt

John H. Taylor

1

The Land of Nubia and Its Inhabitants

The ancient land of Nubia, which is today divided between Egypt and the Republic of the Sudan, consisted in essence of the stretch of the Nile valley immediately south of Egypt. This was the only continuously occupied tract of land linking sub-Saharan Africa with the Mediterranean world, a position which was a crucial factor in shaping the course of Nubia's history.

In earlier times many different states and kingdoms flourished there and the region has been known by several names. Ironically, the name given to it by the earlier indigenous inhabitants is unknown. The Egyptians at different times called it *Ta-sety* ("Land of the Bow," a reference to the weapon most closely associated with the Nubians), "the Southern Lands," or "Kush." To the Greeks and Romans, it was part of Ethiopia ("Land of Burnt Faces"), a vaguely defined region stretching from India to West Africa. The name "Nubia," which first occurs in the Roman period, poses problems of interpretation, for while it is tempting to see it as a derivative of *nbw*, the Ancient Egyptian word for gold, its etymology has not been established conclusively. Although no political entity exists under this name today, the term "Nubia" is still used to define the region between Aswan and Debba in which the Nubian languages are spoken. In ancient times, the peoples who spoke these languages and who were ethnically and culturally related, inhabited the entire area from Aswan to Khartoum and beyond. It is in this wider sense that the term "Nubia" is used in this book.

The Nile is the single most important feature of the Nubian landscape and, as in Egypt, its life-giving water was vital to the development of human settlement. On its northward journey from Khartoum the river passes through a constantly changing environment. For most of its course it flows over a soft sandstone bed which is periodically interrupted by rocky barriers of granite, forming the cataracts, where the channel is broken into dangerous and unnavigable rapids. Between the six main cataracts which lie between Khartoum and Aswan are contrasting landscapes. Areas with relatively rich alluvial deposits, such as the Dongola Reach and Lower Nubia, and the

grasslands of the Shendi Reach, favored human settlement and, predictably, it was here that the greatest cultural advances took place. The cataracts and the barren rocky stretches of the Batn el-Hagar ("Belly of Rocks") and the Abu Hamed Reach were only sporadically inhabited. As barriers to navigation they tended to become frontier zones, and important land routes developed to avoid them. The Batn el-Hagar marks the principal division into Upper and Lower Nubia, the southern and northern regions of the land respectively.

Today Nubia has one of the world's most extreme environments. Daytime temperatures can reach 52°C, rainfall is almost unknown north of Dongola, and harsh erosive winds blow all year round from the Sahara Desert. In antiquity it was not quite so forbidding; the climate was moister and in Upper Nubia savannah-like vegetation—which has now retreated further south due to increasing desiccation—flourished as long ago as the fifth millennium BC. Against this backdrop emerged some of the earliest urbanized and culturally advanced societies in northeast Africa.

The historical importance of Nubia was primarily economic and stemmed, on the one hand, from the rich natural resources—chiefly gold, copper and stone but also semi-precious stones such as cornelian, jasper and amethyst—which were obtainable within easy reach of the Nile and more significantly, from the strategic location of the land itself as virtually the only reliable link between the lands of tropical Africa and the Mediterranean. It was along this "corridor" that the wealth of Africa passed in trade: ivory, ebony, incense, exotic animals, slaves, and a host of other luxuries.

Because of these factors the Nubians were in close contact with their neighbors for long periods of their history, often profiting from their position as commercial middlemen, at other times being subjected to the domination of stronger powers. This was the pattern of their relationship with the Egyptians who, through their efforts to exploit and dominate the southern land, left a lasting impression on Nubian cultural development. In the long term, the relationship was reciprocal. Nubian culture influenced that of Egypt at several important periods and culminated in the domination of the northern kingdom by Nubian rulers at the end of the eighth century BC.

Egypt was not the only influence, however. Nubia's position made it a meeting-place of different cultures, and her own cultural makeup reflects a constantly changing mixture of indigenous and outside elements—on the one hand are the southern traditions which reflect the Nubians' links with the people of central Africa, and on the other the influence of the Mediterranean cultures with which they came into contact from time to time.

The modern Nubians are probably the direct descendants of the ancient inhabitants, since the physical characteristics of the people appear to have changed little over the millennia. The varying environmental conditions along the enormously long inhabited strip of the Nile valley are accurately reflected in the gradual if superficial change in the physical characteristics of the population from north to south, skin becoming darker in color, facial features flatter, hair more tightly curled and skeletons increasingly slender. The ancient Egyptians observed these differences and faithfully reproduced them in painting and sculpture, distinguishing the "brown"-skinned inhabitants of Lower Nubia from the black people living further to the south. The ancient Egyptians and the Nubians were closely linked in ethnic background, but the languages they spoke were unrelated. Whereas Ancient Egyptian was an Afro-Asiatic language (a family found in North and East Africa and in Western Asia), the Nubian tongues belonged to the Nilo-Saharan group, found only in the central part of the continent.

Archaeological excavation has made the largest contribution to our understanding of the history of Nubia. Three major archaeological surveys and many independent campaigns have been conducted, mainly in Lower Nubia, since the beginning of this century. The most ambitious enterprise, however, was the Unesco rescue campaign of 1960–80, organized in response to the construction of the Aswan High Dam, which resulted in the permanent flooding of Lower Nubia. Involving the systematic excavation of scores of archaeological sites and the physical removal and re-erection of the temples destined to be submerged beneath the waters of Lake Nasser, it emphasized the necessity of salvaging cultural heritage, and has made the archaeology of Lower Nubia probably the best documented of any comparable area in the world.

Written evidence is rare. No Nubian language was written down until the second century BC, when the Meroitic script was devised (see below). Since even this remains largely untranslatable, the ancient Nubians cannot speak for themselves, and the scholar is forced to view them through the writings of the various foreigners with whom they came into contact. The majority of the textual sources, therefore, incorporate a degree of bias and, even when not actually hostile to the Nubians, are often confused or exaggerated.

The first synthesis of Nubian cultural development was devised in the early years of this century by the American archaeologist George Andrew Reisner, of the Harvard University-Museum of Fine Arts, Boston Expedition, who distinguished the different phases by names such as "A-Group," "B-Group" and "C-Group." The basis of this division was the changes observable in material culture, but Reisner's use of the term "group" reflected an erroneous belief that the alterations in customs and types of artifact were accompanied by physical changes in the population. The emergence of each new phase was seen as the result of an incursion or migration of "new" people, whose culture ousted that of their precursors. In place of Reisner's "Groups" some recent scholars prefer to substitute "phases," "sequences" or "horizons." The emphasis on cultural continuity which this approach entails undoubtedly clarifies the picture of Nubian history, but the terms "A-Group" and "C-Group" have now become so well established in the archaeological literature as a means of distinguishing assemblages of material remains that they have been retained in this book.

2
Early Nubian Cultures and the Egyptian Old Kingdom

In the late Palaeolithic period, from c. 25,000 BC, both Egypt and Nubia were inhabited by nomadic bands who lived in small temporary camps close to the Nile and depended for their survival on hunting wild animals and fishing in the abundantly stocked river. The principal material remains of these earliest inhabitants are their stone tools and numerous drawings on the rocks along the valley, showing the animals they hunted: giraffe, antelope, elephant and gazelle.

By the Mesolithic and Neolithic periods there was a trend towards the establishment of settled societies, and numerous localized cultures arose in different parts of Egypt and Nubia. A notable development which occurred at this time was the beginning of pottery production, itself an indication of an increasingly sedentary society. Knowledge of ceramics first became established in the Khartoum and Shendi regions of the Nile valley towards 6000 BC with a culture known as the Khartoum Mesolithic. The handmade ceramics of these people are unpainted globular vessels decorated with wavy line and dotted zigzag motifs, impressed into the clay with a fishbone or rocker-stamp. These techniques became more sophisticated in the succeeding Khartoum Neolithic phase, and the surface of the pottery was usually burnished.

Whereas their precursors had subsisted by hunting and fishing, the Khartoum Neolithic people were the first in this region to keep domesticated cattle and to cultivate cereal crops. These methods of subsistence were apparently introduced into the Nile valley from the eastern Sahara and were being practiced at the important site of Kadero, north of Khartoum, as early as c. 4000 BC. Although other cultures with a related ceramic tradition continued to flourish in adjacent areas like the eastern Sudan, the Khartoum Neolithic culture itself came to an end in the early third millennium BC and the central Nile valley was apparently left unoccupied for over two thousand years. It is in Lower Nubia that the next important cultural developments can be most clearly traced.

Food production and the domestication of animals may have been practiced in Lower Nubia as early as the fourth millennium BC, though the evidence is not conclusive. The early cultures there seem to have had more in common with those of Upper Egypt than with the Khartoum region, and it was perhaps from Egypt that they learned about the new subsistence methods. Some of the early Lower Nubian cultures had a definite influence on the development of important stages of early Upper Egyptian culture at this time. Comparison between the pottery of the Abkan Culture of the Second Cataract area and that of the Badarian, the dominant culture of Upper Egypt between c. 5000 and c. 4500 BC, indicates that both were closely related, an impression reinforced by the similarity of their methods of making tools and the sources they used for raw materials. Conversely the Nagada Culture of Upper Egypt was influential in northern Nubia, as seen in the presence of Nagada objects in Lower Nubian graves and similarities in pottery design.

The first widespread indigenous Nubian culture, the A-Group, developed between c. 3500 and c. 3000 BC. It extended throughout Lower Nubia from Kubanieh, north of Aswan, to the Second Cataract region and it owed a great deal both to the earlier cultures which had existed in the same area, notably the Abkan Culture, and to those of predynastic Egypt.

The A-Group Nubians, like their predecessors, lived a semi-nomadic life. Communities probably consisted of a few families dwelling in temporary camps of reed or grass huts, and moving with the seasons. It is likely that they lived close to the banks of the Nile for most of the year, moving back to the edge of the floodplain when the river overflowed its banks during the annual inundation. Rock-shelters were also used, and towards the end of the fourth millennium permanent settlements, sometimes with stone houses, were becoming increasingly common.

During the A-Group period agriculture became more widespread. Cereals and leguminous plants were grown on the floodplain and grinding stones of sandstone or quartzite were used to prepare the grain. Animal husbandry may also have been practiced, though the scarcity of firm evidence makes it hard to assess its importance. Sheep and goats and a few cattle were probably the main animals kept, but hunting, gathering and fishing were still an important means of obtaining food.

The close contacts which existed between the inhabitants of southern Egypt and northern Nubia at this period must have been based largely on trade. Before the end of the fourth millennium BC Egyptian craftsmen were already working ivory and ebony to produce figurines, amulets, ornamental containers and furniture fittings, and much of the raw materials presumably came from the south. The main Egyptian market for this trade was probably on the island of Elephantine at Aswan. The very name of the place (in Egyptian, Abu, "Elephant Town," translated into "Elephantine" by the Greeks) indicates that it was a major emporium for traffic in ivory and doubtless for other African products. The A-Group Nubians probably acted as middlemen in this trade, and the contents of their graves provide information on the kinds of goods which the Egyptians supplied in return. Egyptian beer- and wine-jars are frequently found, suggesting that these drinks—probably not made in Nubia—were much sought after. Food products, such as cheese, oil and honey, as well as linen cloth were doubtless also traded. Copper axes and adzes of Egyptian type are found in the richer graves, and smaller metal implements such as awls and needles may also have come from Egypt. Some graves are remarkable for the richness of their contents. The best-known example is the grave at Sayala in which were found two gold handled ceremonial maces, copper chisels and fine stone vessels and palettes of Egyptian type. It is conjectured that this grave may have been that of a chief who had received presents from Egyptian trading partners. While the degree of variation in A-Group graves and their contents is insufficient to suggest the existence of a truly stratified society, the Sayala burial was not the only one which contained rich goods. A cemetery of this period at Qustul, near Faras, which yielded exceptionally rich goods, may be the burial place of other chiefs who profited by trade with Egypt.

The A-Group graves were usually oval or rectangular pits with circular stone superstructures.

They are the first in Lower Nubia in which objects were buried with the dead, and in the absence of written records their contents tell us most of what is known about the beliefs and lifestyle of the people. Items of personal adornment are commonly found: necklaces, amulets and pendants were made from shell, ivory, bone, faience and stone. Bracelets and anklets were usually of bone or stone, though sometimes of ostrich-eggshell or ivory. As in Egypt, green eye-paint made from malachite was used by both sexes; many graves have yielded the rhomboidal quartzite palettes and the pebbles which were used to grind the pigment. A few graves contained simple garments such as belts and leather loincloths. Feathers were worn in the hair and sometimes leather caps are found.

The most attractive class of objects found at A-Group sites is the pottery. Ceramics were generally more highly valued by the Nubians than the Egyptians throughout the period covered by this book, a circumstance which is reflected in the technical and artistic superiority of Nubian pottery. The handmade ceramics of the A-group include pots with a polished red exterior and a shiny black interior and rim, the surfaces often decorated with a rippled finish. The finest type, however, is the "eggshell" pottery. Examples are mostly open bowls and cups, with very thin walls (3–5 mm), decorated on the outside with geometric patterns or designs derived from basketry, painted in red ochre. Vessels of this type are relatively rare and must have been highly prized.

A-Group craftsmen also produced clay figurines of humans and animals, which represent a considerable advance in artistic expression and are among the earliest examples of sculpture in the round from Nubia. The human figurines, probably intended to fulfill some magical role, are steatopygous females with attenuated limbs and very summary facial features. Linear markings on the abdominal area and on the thighs are thought to represent some form of body decoration such as tattooing.

Because of the harsh environment of Lower Nubia the population remained small and scattered; consequently development towards an urbanized and stratified society was slow. Egypt, in contrast, experienced a rapid rise to a high level of cultural development during the late fourth millennium BC. With the unification of the country under a single ruler in c. 3100 BC, Egypt emerged as a hierarchical society with a centralized government, a written language and expanding commercial interests abroad. As territorial boundaries became more firmly defined, the First Cataract came to be regarded as a political frontier between Egypt and Nubia. With growing Egyptian prosperity and cultural sophistication, demand for southern luxury goods increased and rulers turned more and more to aggression in order to obtain what had formerly been acquired through trade. Raids into Nubia took place in the First Dynasty and seem to have increased in frequency and scale during the Old Kingdom (c. 2686–2181 BC). The A-group chiefs who had profited by acting as intermediaries in the trade now found themselves bypassed as the Egyptians sought to make contact directly with the markets further south.

The A-Group culture, which had reached its peak in the Egyptian First Dynasty (c. 3100–2890 BC), came to an end in the early third millennium, and the following centuries are almost a blank in the archaeological record of northern Nubia. Thinly scattered groups of indigenous people perhaps continued to occupy the region as late as the Fourth or Fifth Dynasty but the majority of inhabitants of Lower Nubia seem to have abandoned the Nile valley and retreated to the desert edges, forced to leave their homes by a deterioration in the climate and the effects of the change in Egyptian policy from a mutually beneficial exchange system to one of exploitation.

The Egyptians' new aggressive attitude also entailed the establishment of permanent settlements to exploit Nubia's natural resources more effectively. The earliest one yet identified is a walled town situated north of the Middle Kingdom fortress of Buhen, which flourished during the Fourth and Fifth Dynasty, though perhaps founded earlier. Copper was smelted there, as the remains of furnaces, crucibles, ingot molds and quantities of slag and ore found on the site show. At the same period diorite and possibly cornelian was being extracted from quarries in the desert west of Toshka.

During the Egyptian Sixth Dynasty (c. 2345–2181 BC) Lower Nubia was resettled by a new culture, known as the C-Group (the existence of a "B-Group," once thought to be the successor to the A-Group, has now been disproved). The C-group culture remained dominant in the north until the people there were encouraged to adopt Egyptian customs in the sixteenth century BC. Though stemming from the same cultural tradition as the A-Group, the C-Group did not develop directly from the earlier phase; the precise origins of the people who reoccupied northern Nubia at this time are uncertain, but it is probable that they had moved in from the Western Desert.

The early C-Group people, while practicing agriculture and hunting, were more strongly orientated towards cattle-herding than their predecessors. Though this has to be deduced from relatively isolated circumstances—the carving of long-horned cows on "stelae" or grave markers, on pottery and on rocks, the burying of ox-skulls in cemeteries, and the use of cow-dung to temper pottery—there can be little doubt of the importance of cattle to these people. Sheep and goats were also kept.

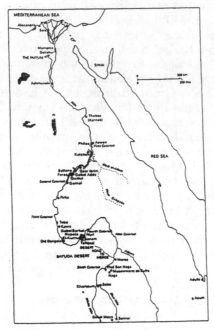

While occupying much the same area as the A-Group, they enjoyed a more settled life. Important C-Group sites like Aniba, Faras and Dakka show long-term occupation over many generations. Huts and tents, seasonally occupied, were gradually replaced by houses consisting partly of drystone walls with the upper parts of wattle and the rood supported by beams.

The burial practices of the C-Group were similar to those of the A-Group. The bodies were laid in round or oval pits in a semi-flexed position, and over these were built superstructures consisting of rings of stone filled with gravel. In some important cemeteries, such as that at Aniba, stone slabs were planted vertically in the ground to serve as stelae. The grave goods reveal both continuity and change in the customs of daily life. Clothing continued to consist chiefly of leather garments and sandals, while jewelry was confined mainly to necklaces and bangles, but the cosmetic palettes and pebbles, so characteristic of A-Group and early Egyptian graves, are absent.

The pottery of the C-Group is highly distinctive and, though handmade, shows high technical excellence. Some of it has clear affinities with Egyptian types, such as the black-topped red ware, also associated with the A-Group and the Kerma and Pan-Grave Cultures. The manufacture and decoration of other types, however, display African influence more strongly. An example is the "polished incised ware." These vessels are mainly round-bottomed bowls, probably used to hold food and drink, whose surfaces present a contrasting mosaic of smooth areas or stripes, and areas filled with hatched lines, criss-cross or herringbone patterns, the early examples probably deriving from basketwork designs. They were fired so as to leave a black or occasionally red lustrous surface, and white pigment was rubbed into the incisions to make the pattern stand out. C-Group graves also yield clay figurines of women and cattle.

About the time of the resettlement of Lower Nubia the character of Egyptian activity in the area changed. Operations at the Toshka quarries and the town at Buhen ceased in the late Fifth Dynasty (c. 2400 BC) and the settlements seem to have been abandoned. No doubt the appearance of settlers obliged the Egyptians to adopt a different approach, as they now needed the cooperation of the C-Group to obtain Lower Nubian goods and to pass through on their way to trade with regions further south. It was to the provincial governors of Aswan that responsibility for maintaining this traffic now fell. These men acted as expedition-leaders, and the accounts of their exploits, inscribed in their tombs at Qubbet el-Hawa, provide an illuminating glimpse of conditions in Lower Nubia in this period. Three distinct regions are mentioned—Wawat, Irtjet and Satju—the chiefs of which probably traded cattle with the Egyptians, who also mounted expeditions to Wawat to obtain timber for shipbuilding and recruits for the Egyptian armies. Since the inhabitants of these regions posed a potential threat to the security of expeditions, the Egyptians tried to maintain good relations with the chiefs, though conflict did occasionally take place. In the late Sixth Dynasty, Pepinakht, governor of Aswan, raided Wawat and Irtjet and brought many prisoners away.

During the Sixth Dynasty some rudimentary political development seems to have occurred in Lower Nubia. The autobiography of Harkhuf, governor of Aswan, reveals that about the time of the Egyptian king Merenre, Wawat, Irtjet and Satju all came under the rule of one man. This may even have led to the existence of a short-lived monarchy in northern Nubia; rock inscriptions of this period attest local rulers who adopted Egyptian-style royal titularies, but were certainly not Egyptian kings. It has been suggested that Lower Nubia was on the verge of becoming a state at this time, but the material culture of the C-Group does not suggest that a significant level of social stratification had yet been attained, and it is likely that political development in the region was intermittent.

Egyptian records of the Sixth Dynasty show that the main goal of expeditions at this time was a region known as the Land of Yam, which lay to the south of Wawat, Irtjet and Satju. Harkhuf made four journeys there, using donkey caravans to avoid the laborious portages which would have been necessary to get boats past the Second Cataract. The account of the products he brought back, which included ebony, incense, oil, leopard-skins, elephant-tusks and throwsticks, show that he was making contact with the African luxury trade. These goods were highly valued, but far more interesting to Harkhuf's master, King Pepy II, was a dancing dwarf which the intrepid governor had acquired on his fourth expedition. In a letter from the court, which Harkhuf proudly had inscribed on the façade of his tomb, the boy-king charged him to take every precaution to ensure that the dwarf arrived safely at Memphis, adding, "My Majesty desires to see this dwarf more than the products of Sinai or of Punt!" Punt, a land of indeterminate origin thought to be near the Red Sea coast, supplied Egypt from time to time with a wide range of exotic products.

Harkhuf's descriptions make it clear that Yam was ruled by a powerful chieftain who controlled the traffic in trade goods arriving from the south and west. The Egyptians were probably only one among many peoples who obtained permission to participate in this trade, and their donkeys doubtless brought presents for the ruler before being loaded with goods for the return trip. The power of this ruler commanded respect in Lower Nubia; the presence of a Yamite escort with Harkhuf's men on one return journey guaranteed him good treatment by the northerners.

It is generally believed, on the grounds of calculations based on the length of Harkhuf's journeys (each one took seven to eight months), and details of the goods he obtained, that Yam lay in the Dongola Reach and that its ruler resided at the site of Kerma. Excavation revealed that a very advanced indigenous culture flourished at the site as early as the twenty-fifth century BC.

The Great Empires of Medieval Sudan

Robert W. July

The great empires of the medieval Sudan have sometimes been regarded as ephemeral political entities without great intrinsic unity and lacking even frontiers to delineate the extent of their authority. In a purely temporal sense it seems unreasonable to impute weakness to states that lasted as long as Ghana's minimum four centuries, Mali's effective existence from the advent of Sundiata in 1230 A.D. until the capture of Jenne by Sunni Ali over two hundred years later, the unbroken thousand-year reign of the ruling *mais* of Kanem-Bornu, or the long-lived stability of the Mossi states. Furthermore, the test of political vitality in these African kingdoms must be in terms of Africa's own traditional social institutions which made for an administration and political structure rather different from modern concepts of national entity.

"Ghana, the golden land," remarks the Arab astronomer, al-Fazari, saying little but suggesting much in wealth, and by implication, in power. This first external notice of the state of Ghana dates from the late eighth century; what came before the rise of Ghana can be reconstructed only indirectly from archaeology, linguistic analysis, and surviving bits of tradition.

It seems reasonable to suppose that African peoples moving generally southward from the encroaching desert lived simply in small groups—herders whose social and political organization centered on family-owned cattle, farmers inhabiting village communities made up of lineage groups related by blood to a common ancestor. Supplementary ties, no doubt, emerged to neutralize lineage competition, in some cases a central structure of government culminating in a ruler and his council drawn from heads of lineages; in others, age groupings made of successive generations, or hierarchies of titles, that cut clearly across lineage loyalties. On occasion quasi-religious secret societies imposed a further check on the governance of a ruler who in any case probably based his own authority on a supernatural sanction as magician and priest.

Government was simple among these modest populations of farmers and pastoralists, for they were content to invent devices sufficient to their needs and no more. What characterized them all, however, was their firm basis, not so much in law as in a web of personal relationships like the feudal societies that emerged in Europe over much the same period of time. Land occupation and utilization was the ultimate objective of political organization among people whose survival depended upon control of a territory and its products. Nonetheless there were no such things as national boundaries; even the kingdom had no name, and visitors from the Arab and European worlds typically misused the name and title of the ruler to identify his domain.

The large kingdoms of the savanna seem to have developed naturally from these smaller, simpler states, in effect a petty kingdom writ large. In time some communities grew complex, developing clans that divided along social or economic lines. A vigorous head of a warrior or royal clan, or perhaps the leader of an age set might have succeeded in imposing his fiat on a growing number of neighboring villages, partly relying on interconnecting loyalties but also utilizing military force. Such authority varied inversely with distance, but communication was relatively easy across the open savanna, and after the introduction of North African horses, an energetic conqueror like the Songhai ruler Sunni Ali could and did maintain his hegemony, though it necessitated an almost ceaseless regimen of military conquest. Such activity eventually posed problems of administration and of succession. Remote districts, difficult to control, were often left in the hands of tribute-paying local chieftains. Alternatively, rulers assigned members of the royal clan to positions as regional viceroys, a dangerous device that invited revolt and led to the alternative institution of non-royal provincial governors, especially chosen because they had no legitimate claim to princely succession.

After the rise of Islam, the arrival of Arab and Berber merchants from North Africa introduced a new element that greatly strengthened the large savanna states. Along with their commerce the northern traders brought their religion and their literacy, both of which helped consolidate imperial administration. Muslim scribes and advisors were widely employed while the religion of the Prophet, slowly adopted by the savanna nobility, introduced administrative standards for such activities of scale as the policing of markets or the levying and collecting of taxes.

It was, however, the trans-Saharan trade and the wasteland it traversed that were the main engines responsible for the emergence of the great states that bordered the desert. The peoples of the Sahel and savanna, both north and south, had long been in contact with the desert dwellers, sometimes peacefully, sometimes in contention. Possessing the camel, the nomads of the desert were not always content to confine their raids to one another's herds or to prey only upon passing trans-Saharan caravans. Tuareg and Teda, for example, recruited their domestic slaves through regular forays upon savanna farming villages; more generally, the desert people maintained a symbiosis with the more settled areas, varying from peaceful seasonal migration to large-scale warfare and conquest. During cycles when the rains were normal and water holes remained productive, the pastoralists abandoned the desert only for the dry months, the Bedouins moving into the Atlas highlands to graze their flocks on the mountain pasture, the southern nomads conducting a similar infiltration of the Niger River valley. In difficult times, however, when the rains failed and the wells ran dry, these pacific movements converted to armed invasion, sometimes in the form of hit-and-run raids and sometimes as more permanent conquest and occupation.

Indeed, the desert nomads were bound up in a vast rhythm of history with the peoples who lived to the north and to the south of them. At moments of stress when conditions became severe and the savanna or Mediterranean regions were weakened, the desert encroached on the settled areas and the desert people predominated. Conversely, when the savanna organized and unified itself under a strong central regime, the settled area extended farther into the desert, and it was the nomadic peoples who were forced back and obliged to pay allegiance to the more powerful authority.

More important still was the impact of the trans-Saharan trade. The great value of the West African gold mines was easily recognized; more generally, it was apparent that those who controlled the trade to the north commanded great wealth, but control implied political organization to insure the peaceful passage of caravans and the orderly conduct of business in the marketplace. While the sovereigns of the savanna states failed in their attempts to seize the mines of Wangara, they did succeed in taxing the trade both through the appropriation of all gold nuggets and with tariffs levied on caravans arriving at the major savanna entrepôts. In return they provided their celebrated "pax savanna" which, at its best, insured honest dealings in the markets and enabled strangers and local people alike to travel throughout the realm without fear of molestation. When the savanna states could no longer provide protection, the trade moved elsewhere as their strength atrophied; thus it was with the eventual demise of Ghana or the desert

march of the Moroccans that later settled the fate of Songhai.

The Kingdom of Ghana

The earliest known kingdom of the Sudan was Ghana, and its history well exemplified the ancient conflict between the Sahara and the savanna, involving both the religious asceticism of the desert and the desire for gold that has infected all peoples. Its origins have been lost, but by the time it had come to the notice of Arab commentators in the eighth century, Ghana was already a thriving state headed by black African Soninke kings and renowned for its wealth in gold. Traditions speak of various founding dynasties, including nonblack northerners, doubtless a reflection both of Ghana's close contact with neighboring Berbers and of later attempts by West African Muslims to associate Sudanic states with Islamic and Arabic antecedents. By the ninth century Ghana was approaching the fullest extent of its power and influence with territory extending to the south as far as the upper reaches of the Niger and Senegal, to the north into the desert and eastward to the Niger bend.

Control over the gold commerce assured the prosperity of Ghana's kings, but Ghana suffered from the competition of Awdaghost lying to the west, which was held by Sanhaja Berbers and which was pressing its own claim to become the major terminus for the commerce across the western Sahara. The vexation of the Awdaghost competition was temporarily laid to rest in 990 A.D., however, when the Soninke of Ghana captured the rival city during a period of internal dissension among the Sanhaja. This was the peak moment of glory. The market city of Kumbi Saleh became the chief mercantile and intellectual center in the Sudan and its king was renowned for his wealth and the splendor of his court. When he held audience, he appeared resplendent in garments of fine cloth and ornaments of gold, while his retainers and even the royal animals were similarly bedecked. His tariffs filled the royal treasury, his armies kept the peace across his vast domain, and his fame spread far to the north where people spoke of "the king of Ghana ... the richest monarch in the world."

Such prosperity was difficult to maintain. During the eleventh century, the Sanhaja experienced a profound religious revival led by a particularly puritanical Muslim sect, the Almoravids, and the white heat of religious fervor was soon converted into a jihad with repercussions as far as Morocco and the states of Andalusia. In the Sahel, this holy war took the shape of a campaign against Ghana. Authorities differ over the consequences. Some say Kumbi fell to the Almoravid jihad as Ghana was forcibly converted to Islam. Others contend that the conversion was voluntary. In either case the Almoravids extended their control of the desert trade at Ghana's expense, and the Soninke kingdom, though subsequently cooperating with the Almoravids, gradually declined in power and wealth. The ensuing power vacuum was soon occupied by the Soso chieftaincy of Kaniaga, a former vassal state which had already revolted successfully, and now moved to capture Ghana under the leadership of Sumaguru Kante. In 1203 Kumbi was sacked and the independent kingdom of Ghana ceased to exist. The merchants of Kumbi, no longer able to pursue their affairs at the old site, moved north toward the desert to the rising commercial center of Walata.

The Rise and Fall of Mali

The exploits of Sumaguru seemed to be the beginning of a new power centering on the Soso, but in fact the heir to Ghana's authority lay in another quarter. South of Kaniaga along the upper reaches of the Niger, were Mandinka blacks occupying fertile farm land near the source of West Africa's gold supply, and these people were subdued by Sumaguru after his victory over Ghana. According to one tradition, Sumaguru put all the sons of the Mandinka ruler to death save one who was spared as an inconsequential cripple. This sole survivor, Sundiata, overcame his weakness, rallied local support, and fashioning a guerrilla army, eventually defeated and killed Sumaguru in 1235. The Soso were quickly absorbed, whereupon Sundiata advanced northward, sacked and annexed the remnants of Ghana in 1240, at the same time taking control of the gold trade routes and the port cities of the Saharan commerce. This was the genesis of the empire of Mali which, in a few short years, had established itself, extending its hegemony to include all of the former sphere of influence of Ghana.

Although the early Mandinka princes were said to be Muslims, it seems likely that Sundiata was a pagan, and it was on the traditional relationships within clans and lineage groups that he built his administration. Securing these relationships by force and persuasion before confronting the Soso, Sundiata established his capital, possibly at his ancestral village of Niani, from where he and his successors ruled their extensive empire. Mali was an agricultural community but this by no means meant a neglect of the commercial possibilities of the trans-desert traffic. In addition to the gold supplies in the south, Mali reached out to control the salt trade of Taghaza as well as Saharan copper, and it was during the period of Mali's growth during the thirteenth century that Timbuktu began its development within the new kingdom as an entrepôt for desert caravans.

The precise extent of the empire under Sundiata is not known, but after his death in 1255 additional conquests were made by Mansa Uli and by Sakura, a freed slave of the royal household who seized power during a period of weakness within the ruling dynasty. Either Sundiata or Uli first brought Songhai under Mali suzerainty and Sakura was apparently responsible for campaigns against Tekrur in the west as well as for the capture of Gao in the east. Nevertheless, until recently many of these conquests had been attributed to Mansa Musa (1312–1337), partly because Musa's devotion to Islam attracted the praise of Muslim historians and partly because of the fame of his glittering pilgrimage to Mecca.

The progress of Musa's caravan has been recorded and savored by historians—the five hundred slaves bearing golden staffs, the hundred camels each loaded with three hundred pounds of gold, the spending spree in the bazaars of Cairo, and the scattering of bounty with such a lavish hand as to force a serious depreciation of gold on the Cairo exchange. So too has his sponsorship of as-Sahili, a poet and architect from Andalusia, who returned from Mecca with Musa's entourage to introduce an Arabian style to the religious and secular architecture of the Sudan. These events, along with the number of Muslim scholars he brought back from the Middle East, emphasized Musa's Islamic persuasion and doubtless pleased Muslim historians who thereby may have tended to underestimate the accomplishments of Musa's royal predecessors. Moreover, they may have overlooked the degree to which the king, for all his devotion to Islamic religion and civilization, continued to rely upon traditional institutions for the administration of his realm. For example, when the propagation of the true faith threatened gold production in pagan Wangara, proselytizing was quickly abandoned. Moreover, despite the might and glory of Mali's great rulers, the integrity of local chieftaincies was scrupulously observed, and no attempt was made to eliminate traditional ritual at the royal court. Describing the audiences of the mansa a few years after Musa's death, Ibn Battuta approvingly commented on evidence of Islamic practice, but he was also obliged to observe the importance of customary usage—the mansa seated amid the many traditional articles symbolic of royal authority, the elaborate ceremony with its liberal reliance on ritual magic, the rigid demands on time-honored protocol tendering homage to the ruler through prostration and dusting, and the royal Mandinka decorations for distinguished service which took the form of trousers of exceptional width.

The splendor of Mali reached during the reign of Musa continued for several decades, but by the late years of the fourteenth century the problem of dynastic succession had intruded a fatal weakness into the government. Palace quarrels encouraged outside attack. As the fifteenth century opened, the Mossi were raiding the middle Niger having earlier sacked Timbuktu. This luckless entrepôt was occupied by Tuareg in 1433–1434, and in 1468 Sunni Ali of the growing power of Songhai captured the city with great loss of life, five years later reducing the supposedly impregnable town of Jenne. The rise of Songhai put an effective end to Mali's hegemony in the eastern Niger region, but its power lingered on fitfully in the west. Gradually deteriorating, however, it was finally snuffed out in the middle of the seventeenth century with the appearance of the Bambara states of Kaarta and Segu. Thus, after four hundred years, the great Mali empire had finally returned to the original status of a small chieftaincy on the upper Niger.

The Empire of Songhai

By the time of Mali's final demise, Songhai, its imperial successor in the Sudan, had experienced its own brief moment of ascendancy—a century and a half that saw a rapid expansion across the western savanna, a short period of stability, and then an equally rapid decline into extinction. All this came as a climax to a long era of much more modest development.

The point of origin for the Songhai people seems to have been those reaches of the Niger River downstream from the great bend, centering on the town of Kukiya. Here the Za dynasty presided over an agricultural community, giving way to the Sunni line at a time when Mali was still ascendant throughout the Niger country. North of Kukiya lay Gao, a market town on the Sahel edge, like Timbuktu under Malian control, and attracting traders from south and west as well as from North African points. Toward the end of the fourteenth century, as Mali began to suffer internal decay, the Sunnis of Kukiya sensed their opportunity to share in the lucrative trade of the Gao area, probably occupying the river port about the time Timbuktu fell to the Tuareg.

It was a step that initiated the trans-formation from insignificant principality to major Sudanic empire. First, Songhai began to enjoy the riches of its improved trading position, an expanding wealth that meant growing influence and widening authority. Next, control of Gao placed Songhai astride the east-west route of the Niger bend, a strategic position that offered the possibility of a thrust westward toward Timbuktu and beyond. It was Gao, moreover, that moved the Songhai into close contact with Islamic civilization, bringing at least a measure of conversion to the royal house if not to the general population.

In the days of Mansa Musa, Songhai had been subject to Mali; now during the fifteenth century an independent Songhai began to acquire territory at the expense of its former master, at first pushing westward into Mema and adjacent Sahelian provinces beyond the Niger bend. The main imperial expansion came, however, with the long reign of Sunni Ali which began in 1464. With furious energy he overran the whole Niger country, capturing Jenne after his occupation of Timbuktu, pushing back the Tuareg to the north and punishing the Mossi states on his south after they had sacked Timbuktu and besieged Walata. During twenty-eight years of almost incessant campaigning, Ali created, then protected, an empire along the Niger that dominated the trade routes and the great grain-producing region of the Niger's inland delta.

Under Ali, the administration of the Songhai state seems to have been delegated largely to military commanders backed by Ali's own mobility and martial energy. He maintained a fleet on the river, controlled the overland route through the Hombori Mountains south of the Niger bend, established several "capitals" the better to control his domains, and placed distant provinces in the hands of local rulers responsible to him for maintaining order and collecting taxes. His armies apparently consisted of a core unit of troops under his personal command along with special levees raised for particular campaigns.

Much of the information concerning Sunni Ali and his activities comes from Muslim accounts which have pictured him as a ruthless, bloodthirsty conqueror, as well as an unbeliever, a reaction to his savage persecution of Timbuktu Muslims, particularly those associated with the Sankore mosque. Ali argued that his persecution of the Sankore adherents was purely political, occasioned by their support for his Tuareg foes. After his occupation of Timbuktu, Ali did not molest other Muslims in the town and in general maintained good relations with the Islamic community throughout his lands. It is true that Ali bore his Islamic faith lightly, and local tradition emphasizes his position as a great magician who followed many indigenous practices, for example, worshipping idols and consulting diviners and sorcerers. It would seem that Sunni Ali's actions were indeed largely political and economic. The Songhai state was created through conquest and sustained primarily through force, but there was necessarily an element of persuasion. At least nominally Muslim, Ali could command the loyalty of most true believers, while concurrently he remained an African priest-king sensitive to the spiritual interest of his pagan people.

Sunni Ali died in a drowning accident in 1492, and the following year the throne was usurped by Muhammad Toure, governor of the Hombori region and founder of the succeeding Askia dynasty. Sunni Ali had established the basis for the Songhai empire. Under Askia Muhammad it was greatly expanded and institutionalized.

As with Sunni Ali, Askia Muhammad's objectives were strategic and economic, although his tactics were far different, at once more comprehensive and more subtle. Concerned that Ali's war making had disrupted the Saharan gold trade, Muhammad moved to stabilize the western empire, campaigning against the Mossi in 1498–1499, and soon thereafter probing westward to Diara in ancient Ghana. His conquest of Air in 1501–1502 secured the trade routes to Tripoli and Egypt while his absorption of the Taghaza mines brought control of the salt and gold trade of the western Sudan.

Military action, however, was balanced with diplomacy. Only three years after taking power, Muhammad undertook a pilgrimage to Mecca, the purpose certainly involving religious piety, but it was also a move to cement relations with important Muslim commercial circles in both North and South Africa. Again, Askia Muhammad placated the Muslims of Timbuktu and cultivated the celebrated North African cleric, al-Maghili, achieving the double objective of gaining Muslim support, at the same time obtaining al-Maghili's verdict that Sunni Ali had been a pagan and therefore an appropriate objective for legitimate military takeover.

Muhammad also effected basic admini-strative reforms. He created a professional army of slave soldiers, ruling over his domains, partly through tribute-paying local chieftains, partly through hereditary royal title holders, and partly with the help of Muslim advisers and officials, relying often on Islamic sanctions regarding such matters as taxation and trade. Nonetheless these changes were less than fundamental. Askia Muhammad conducted no jihads against infidel neighbors, retained numerous traditional customs at court, and acknowledged indigenous authorities at the village level. Staunch Muslim though he was, he realized like Sunni Ali that much of his authority stemmed from Songhai tradition from which he could stray too far only at his peril.

One element of effective administration that eluded Askia Muhammad was the matter of orderly succession. After a long reign the Askia had declined in health and energy when in 1528 he was deposed in a rebellion engineered by his sons. This was the first of a series of coups that ensued over a sixty-year period, undermining the state, almost invariably bringing disunity and weakness, and leading to its final disintegration which came abruptly at the end of the sixteenth century. Over this period no less than eight askias reigned in Songhai. One of these, Daud (1549–1582), was an able and successful ruler, but his success only underscored the shortcomings of the others.

During the second half of the sixteenth century, Songhai came under increasing pressure from the Sadian kingdom of Morocco, intent upon gaining access to the rich trans-Saharan traffic, particularly through control over the salt mines of Taghaza. The move may have been occasioned by the new sea routes around Africa that diverted European commerce away from the Mediterranean; in any event Morocco saw opportunity to the south. Taghaza and other desert oases were periodically attacked and plans were made for an advance on Songhai in the hopes of gaining control of its gold supply.

Although these Moroccan threats were well known in Songhai, its rulers felt secure in the protection of the desert; indeed, for all its belligerency, Morocco had not been able to hold Taghaza, let alone march on the Niger. Nevertheless, in 1591 a column of four thousand soldiers led by an Andalusian, Judar Pasha, succeeded in crossing the desert and appeared at Tondibi on the Niger above Gao. It was a much smaller force than the Songhai army but it contained a large proportion of European Muslim converts equipped with muskets, which, in addition to superior discipline, were decisive against the bows and spears of the ill-organized enemy. Songhai, already weakened by civil war, was easily defeated, its army put into full retreat, and the Niger country rendered defenseless against the invaders.

Military defeat was quickly followed by political collapse. Morocco gained small recompense from its adventure, for it found little of the wealth it sought and was unable to occupy and exploit Songhai. Nevertheless the invasion spelled the end of the Songhai empire. Gao and Timbuktu were occupied, the latter permanently, for the Moroccan soldiers eventually settled along the Niger bend ruling the region first as a protectorate, and then as they gradually became absorbed into the local population, establishing an independent, albeit politically feeble, state. Elsewhere Songhai split into its components. The Songhai themselves retreated down river to the Dendi home whence they had originally come and where they succeeded in eluding the Moroccans. In Masina and Dirma, the Fulani raided the local farming people, the Jenne region was attacked by the Bambara, while Tuareg visited their usual devastation all along the Niger bend.

Political disintegration was followed by famine, and famine by plague. When some semblance of stability finally returned, political cohesion had been reduced to a much more modest scale than that which had characterized the apogee of the great Sudanic kingdoms. Raiding by nomadic and warrior groups combined with internecine struggles to keep states small, weakened, and defensive; hence, larger units did not reappear until the emergence in the eighteenth century of the Bambara kingdoms of Segu and Kaarta. Trade, too, suffered from the political fragmentation, although in general merchants managed to keep the trans-Saharan traffic moving at its former levels despite the vigorous interference of desert raiders. As for the civilization that Islam had introduced by way of the northern trade routes, these were not years of growth, and the indifference that the true faith encountered both at court and in the countryside was to build frustrations leading to the religious upheavals that engulfed the western and central Sudan during the early nineteenth century.

Kanem-Bornu and the Hausa States

The pattern of population movements, economic growth, and political centralization that had characterized the western Sudan was repeated with variations in Kanem-Bornu and Hausaland. Here, too, the drying out of the Sahara forced ancient negroid hunting and fishing societies south into the more congenial latitudes of the savanna, where they turned gradually to a sedentary farming life, leaving the increasingly arid desert to nomadic herders. In its time, the trans-Saharan commerce arose to bind the central Sudan to the markets of North Africa, and to stimulate the appearance of Sudanic states concerned in part to protect that commerce. Finally, Islamic theology and culture spread its influence in the central Sudan, as it had in the west, coming across the desert to gain the allegiance of royalty, but failing by and large to extend its sway beyond the limited populations of the market cities.

Judging from the present-day linguistic configuration, those migrants who descended into the regions directly west of Lake Chad spoke languages comprising the Chadic subdivision of the Afro-Asiatic linguistic classification, those to the east belonged to the quite different Saharan branch of the Nilo-Saharan grouping, while south of the lake were Benue-Congo speakers of the Niger-Congo family. These migrations very likely involved a variety of folk filtering into an indigenous population, a process that gave rise during the first millennium after Christ to a heterogeneous mixture of herders, farmers, and fisherfolk. Traders visiting the region introduced their own names and these eventually became permanent—Zagawa to identify the people and

Kanem for the loose collection of local states bordering the lake.

Kanuri tradition credits an Arab leader, Saif ibn Dhi Yazan, with unifying these diverse peoples and establishing the ruling Saifawa dynasty of the Kanuri mais or kings, a probable myth designed to gain legitimacy for the Kanem rulers by linking them with the name of a great Arab hero. In any event, the Saifawa dynasty, probably founded in the ninth century, was to survive for a thousand years, an unusual longevity during which the state of Kanem emerged and endured, developing other qualities that added an idiomatic flavor to its basic vitality. To begin with, the mai was regarded as divine, and as a god remained aloof from the profane gaze of his people, speaking from behind a screen and always taking his meals in solitude. The institution of a divine, ritually secluded monarch, widely practiced among traditional African societies, was joined by characteristics more typically Kanuric—an elaborate, highly centralized palace hierarchy, royal descent in the male line combined with important and powerful positions for the queen mother or *Magira* and other female members of the mai's household, and a minutely regulated provincial administration and military organization based upon feudal rights and obligations.

There is repeated evidence of the continuing influence on state affairs by the women of the royal household, an influence apparently originating in pre-Islamic times—that is, before royal conversion in the eleventh century—but nevertheless continuing in spite of Islamic injunctions concerning the position of women. One chronicle reports a Magira as actual ruler; another testifies to the imprisonment of a ruling mai by his mother because of an alleged mismanagement of royal justice. Still another eulogizes a queen mother as the holder of extensive fiefs as well as "owner of a thousand thrones and five hundred gunmen."

It was trade that stimulated the centralizing efforts of the Saifawas, responding to the growing number of merchants from North Africa who sought to organize and control the Saharan commerce after the rise of Islam in the seventh and eighth centuries. The northerners were primarily interested in slaves for soldiering and domestic service in the Middle East and these they purchased with fabrics and metals, chiefly copper and bronze. Though merchants, they were also active proselytizers for Islam, and toward the end of the eleventh century the Saifawa royal house was converted in the person of Mai Hume. Succeeding mais built upon this beginning by establishing closer relations with Muslim states to the north and east and encouraging the *hajj*, or pilgrimage, to

Mecca, a policy that presumably had commercial as well as religious objectives.

These political and institutional developments were accompanied by the gradual expansion of Kanem beyond its homeland just east of Lake Chad to form an empire that spread as far west as Kano, its eastern territories taking in the region of Wadai but not reaching as far as Darfur. By the middle of the thirteenth century, under Mai Dunama Dibalami, Kanem had also extended its control northward into the Fezzan, thereby securing its position as a major African state dominating the central Sudanic regions. Even at this moment of maximum strength, however, Kanem began to feel the effect of disruptive forces which eventually brought about the disintegration of this first Kanuri empire.

Partly, the trouble was internal, involving wasting dynastic struggles within the expanding Saifawa family. Beyond this, throughout the fourteenth century, there were difficult wars, first with the So people located south of Lake Chad, and then during the second half of the century with the Bulala, these formidable antagonists attacking the Kanuri so successfully that they finally precipitated the evacuation of Kanem.

There was probably another, largely economic, reason. As Kanem expanded, reaching out for a growing share of the Saharan trade, its pastoralism and oasis farming could not sustain the military cost of defending its desert commerce. The long distance trade began to bypass Kanem, moving directly from Bornu to the Sahara, a potential disaster for the state which could only be averted by moving the court to occupy its Bornu province on the western side of Lake Chad. Late in the fourteenth century, under the leadership of Mai Umar ibn Idris, the ruling house abandoned its old territory and reestablished itself in Bornu, parts of which had previously fallen under Kanuri control. For about a hundred years the state remained weak, its armies faring poorly, its mais following one another in quick succession, victims both of assassination and of enforced exile. Toward the end of the fifteenth century, a measure of stability at last returned, and with this renaissance came the beginning of the second Kanuri empire.

The individual responsible for the upturn in Kanuri fortunes was Ali Ghaji who, as mai during the last quarter of the century, put an end to the power struggles within the palace, checked the aggressions of the Bulala, and founded a new capital in Bornu, the walled city of Gazargamu, which became the first fixed seat of government since the remove from Kanem a century earlier. Ali's son and successor, Idris Katakarmabi, temporarily liberated Kanem through two successful campaigns against the Bulala, and later

mais extended Bornu domination to the Saharan region of Air, possibly in connection with diplomatic and commercial relations that were concurrently established with the Ottoman rulers of Tripoli.

Such successes, however, were but a prelude to the reign of Mai Idris Aloma (1571–1603) under whom Kanem-Bornu reached the height of its power. During much of his long tenure Idris was preoccupied with military campaigns through which he both consolidated the triumphs of his predecessors and added fresh conquests of his own. Thus, he subdued dissidents in Bornu and secured a long-lived peace with the Bulala who remained a quasi-autonomous people in Kanem. His campaigns as far as Kano assured his suzerainty in Hausaland, while with the aid of camel-mounted cavalry he routed the Tuareg and Teda on his northern frontiers, thus protecting his commercial ties with North Africa. Indeed, much of Idris Aloma's military success was due to his introduction of new weapons and tactics—greater mobility through improved transport, an effectively drilled standing army to supplement the traditional feudal levies, flexibility of battle plans altered to suit the idiosyncrasies of terrain and foe, and, perhaps most of all, the introduction of firearms against adversaries limited to their traditional bowmen and lancers.

Idris was by no means exclusively preoccupied with conquest, however. A devout Muslim, he made his pilgrimage to Mecca and established hostels in that holy city for the shelter of Bornu pilgrims, built brick mosques in the capital city of Gazargamu in lieu of the older reed structures, and began to replace customary law and traditional tribunals with courts under Muslim magistrates following the dictates of Quranic law. His reforms extended to moral as well as juridical questions for he took a strong stand against adultery and obscenity. "So he wiped away the disgrace," observed a contemporary, "and the face of the age was blank with astonishment."

Military conquest and the encouragement of Muslim law seem to have been accompanied by no great change in the traditional political administration of the empire. The same complex hierarchy of officials aided the mai in governing; if anything, the system was more rigid than ever, based upon a pattern of fiefs granted to nobility and royal servants in return for both their loyalty and material assistance to the crown. The economy, moreover, had changed little from earlier days. The basic productivity of the land was agricultural, and the basic labor force was the peasantry supplemented by substantial numbers of slaves. Slaves were also an important commodity in the lively trans-Saharan trade, the Kanuri continuing their time-honored custom of raiding to the south for slaves to be shipped to North Africa—eunuchs and young girls were a specialty—in return for the horses of Barbary.

By the end of the eighteenth century, the Kanem-Bornu empire had declined from the greatness of the Aloma era. Succeeding mais became less aggressive, preoccupying themselves with Muslim piety as subject neighbors gathered strength and slipped away one by one. When a new crisis arose early in the nineteenth century, the Saifawa were no longer equal to the need for vigorous leadership. The Fulani armies that had already overrun Hausaland attacked Bornu and compelled the ancient kingdom to embark on a new period of reform and reconstruction in order to forestall disintegration and annexation by the new power that threatened it. As for the Hausa, the Fulani occupation brought revolutionary changes to a way of life that in many ways had been typical of the civilization of the savanna.

For long centuries the Hausa had occupied the area between Songhai and Kanem-Bornu. Their tradition postulated the familiar theme of a ruler who came from the north—in this case, Bayajidda, son of the king of Baghdad, who slew the serpent harassing the people and married the local queen, and whose grandsons became the kings of the major Hausa states of Gobir and Daura, Katsina and Zazzau (Zaria), Kano and Rano, and finally Biram. Such a tradition seems to suggest southward migrations of Saharan hunters and fisherfolk who filtered into the savanna with the onset of desiccation. Indeed, although Hausaland undoubtedly absorbed such migrations, the Bayajidda legend appears to have been a later development, antedated by early population movements and the emergence of the Hausa city-states.

Like their neighbors, the Hausa were agriculturalists. The broad, flat plains of their countryside were well suited for the cultivation of corn, barley, rice, and cotton, while livestock fatted on the rich grass and citrus fruit grew wild in the low, wooded hills. Most of the people lived in small farming villages but in time walled towns like Kano and Katsina had established themselves as centers of trade and of religious and secular thought. Like Kanem-Bornu, the Hausa states engaged in a brisk exchange with North Africa across the Sahara, the chief southern products being slaves and kola nuts, the latter always in great demand as one of the few stimulants permitted Muslims. Katsina and Kano rose to be the major Hausa entrepôts, but the other states also contributed to the trade in a well-conceived division of labor—Zaria to the south served as the slave raider, Rano was a center for industry, and

Gobir on the edge of the desert protected Hausaland against the raids of the desert nomads.

Islamic culture and religion entered Hausaland gradually via the urban centers, probably having been first introduced through contacts with Bornu. Kano and Katsina were under Islamic influence by the late fourteenth century, but the degree of commitment was modest both among the general population and within the ruling class. Other states were even more lightly touched. Gobir was still pagan in the sixteenth century and Zaria was not converted until the nineteenth century jihad of Usuman dan Fodio. Indeed, dan Fodio's religious war was precipitated by his perception of a general laxness in Islamic practice, both at court and on the countryside. Theology aside, the impact of Islamic civilization was considerable, especially in the cities. When Timbuktu was enjoying a peak in the fifteenth and sixteenth centuries, a number of its scholars visited Hausaland, living and working in Kano and Katsina—for example, al-Hajj Ahmad, who taught theology in Kano; Muhammad ibn Ahmad, a Sankore scholar who became a magistrate in Katsina; and al-Maghili, who wrote an essay on the art of governing, advising Muhammad Rimfa (1463–1499), the king of Kano, that, "the eagle can only win his realm by firm resolve.... Kingdoms are held by the sword, not by delays."

Until the Fulani achieved unity in Hausaland, good advice and firm resolve had never been sufficient to bring together the Hausa states under a single ruler. This is surprising because the Hausa during much of their history were under pressure from powerful states—Mali and Songhai in the west and Kanem-Bornu to the east—and from time to time put forward resourceful local rulers like Sarkin Kanajeji who reportedly introduced iron helmets and chain mail to the armies of Kano.

Another such ruler was Queen Amina of Zaria, whose many exploits have become the stuff of legend as well as history. In either event, as with Kanem-Bornu, her activities point out the importance of women in savanna state governments. She is credited with widespread conquests in Hausaland and the encouragement of walled defenses in her domains and beyond. Other notable royal women were the mothers of Kano kings, their names and occasionally their activities cited in the chronicles—in one instance as a co-ruler, in others as important players in palace politics.

Despite these shows of strength, outside pressure usually meant periodic Hausa vassalage, now to Songhai at the time of Askia Muhammad, now to Kebbi during its sixteenth century ascendancy under the *kanta* or king, Kotal, or from time to time to Kanem-Bornu, whereas regional leaders were generally unable to achieve more than the strengthening of their own state in relation to the others in the Hausa complex. Intramural rivalry dominated Hausa affairs over the years. Kano and Katsina were chronically at war with each other over which would dominate the southern end of the Sahara trade, and during the eighteenth century Gobir enjoyed a period of strength which it put to use largely in attacking its fellow Hausa states. It was in Gobir, on whose kings Islam had made little impression, that Usuman dan Fodio served as tutor to the royal princes, and eventually set in motion the forces of the Fulani jihad that was to bring ultimate political unity to Hausaland at the beginning of the nineteenth century.

SECTION THREE:
THE EARLY INTERACTIONS OF AFRICANS WITH OTHER SOCIETIES: FROM ANTIQUITY TO THE MIDDLE EAST

Introduction

For millennia, Africans have been migrating and settling in the adjunct and neighboring lands and in societies both north and east of their homeland, that is, in Europe and the Middle East. While they have remained for much of this time a minority population, they often made a significant impact on these societies and helped shape the inhabitants' views about African and Africans. In recent years, there are an increased number of works that help us to better understand the interaction between the African and the populations in their host countries. Two of the pioneering seminal works that deal with the African presence during the period of Classical Antiquity when Greece and Rome ruled the world, roughly during the 9th century B.C. to the 5th century A.D. were prepared by Frank M. Snowden, Jr. His two major publications of the theme were the result of fifty years of careful study and research, and published by Harvard University Press. These works are *Blacks in Antiquity: Ethiopians in the Greco-Roman Experience* (1970) and *Before Color Prejudice: The Ancient Views of Blacks* (1983). The first essay "Toward An Understanding of the Ancient View of Blacks" is from his first work, *Before Color Prejudice* and captures some of his significant insights into the relationships that existed between Africans and the citizens of Greece and Rome. Later scholars have objected to some of Snowden's observations and others have approached the relationship between these peoples with different perspectives. Among the most controversial works, Martin Bernal's multivolume *Black Athena: The Fabrication of Ancient Greece 1785–1985* (1987) that won the 1987 Socialist Review Book Award and the second volume *Black Athens: The Afro-Asiatic Roots of Classical Civilization* (1991) the1990 American Book Award.

Snowden, who died in February 2007, was Professor Emeritus of Classics at Howard University for decades and won the American Philological Association's Goodwin Award for his pioneering scholarly work on the African presence during the period. Classical scholars continue to credit his pioneering work in this field. Snowden based his views on the available literary, epigraphical, papyrological, numismatic and archaeological evidence during the time of his research. He focused on the historical and social perceptions that these Ancients had of Africans. He stated that the Greeks and the Romans referred to the Africans they encountered as Ethiopians and regarded them without "the color prejudice" that emerged regarding Africans after the Atlantic Slave trade.

The second essay in this section confronts the presence of Africans in Europe up to the early 1990s. Until relatively recent, there were very few works that dealt with Africans living and settling on the continent of Europe, especially in Northwestern Europe north of the Iberian peninsular. While there are numerous works that shed light on the African presence in Europe during and after the eighth century Moslem invasion, there have been few works that call attention to the consistent presence of Africans in Europe. One of the earliest recent works is A. C. Saunders' *A Social History of Black Slaves and Freedmen in Portugal 1441–1555* (1982). Another very useful work is the recent publication edited by Kate Lowe and T. F. Earle entitled *Black Africans in Renaissance Europe* (2006). We have retained Allison Blakely's "European Dimensions of the African Diaspora" in this edition because of the broad scope and approach it uses to capture the changing view of Africans across Europe over decades. Blakely examines the commercial, cultural, and political relationships that existed over centuries between Africa, Africans, and Europeans. He deals with the existence and endurance of African imagery in Europe and shows how and when attitudes changed towards the African. Blakely is one of the pioneering and prolific African American writers on this subject having written dozens of articles over the last thirty years. These include his *Russia and the Negro: Blacks in Russian History and Thought* (1986) and almost a decade later *Blacks in the Dutch World: The Evolution of Racial Imagining in a Modern Society* (1994). Since 2001 Blakely is the George and Joyce Wein Professor of African American Studies and European and Comparative History at Boston University. A growing number of scholars have been documenting the African presence in Europe that for decades remained a largely ignored theme in modern historiography

Some of the relatively recent works on this theme include Edward Scobie's *Black Britannia: A History of Blacks in Britain* (1972), James Walvin's *Black and White: The Negro and English Society 1555–1945* (1973), Peter Mark's *Africans in European Eyes* (1974), Folarin Shelton's *Black People in Britain 1555–1833* (1977), Hans W. Debrunner *Presence and Prestige Africans in Europe: A History of Africans in Europe Before 1918* (1979), Nigel Fibe and Chris Power's *Black Settlers–Britain 1555–1958* (1981), Reinhold Grimur and Jost Hermand (eds.) *Blacks and German Culture* (1986), and Peter Fryer's *Black People in the British Empire* (1988).

The three remaining essays in this sector focus on the African presence in the western section of Asia, referred to as the Middle East. The first is Alexandre Popovic's "The Revolt of African Slaves in Iraq in the 3rd / 9th century." Today's students find this essay very revealing for few were aware that Africans had migrated to the country that has been in the American and world news since U.S. troops invaded the land in the early years of the twenty-first century.

This fourth essay is truly a pioneering work about the Black experience and as slaves in the Islamic world from the seventh century to mid-nineteenth century. Although more recent works have been published on this subject, this essay gives a clear overview of this aspect of the African Diaspora.

John Hunwick is professor of African History at Northwestern University. He is author of *Sharia in Songhay, Timbukutu and the Songhay Empire* and more recently *West Africa, Islam and the Arab World* (2006).

The fifth essay in this section deals with Africans living during the nineteenth and twentieth centuries within Iran, formerly known as Persia. Miezai narrates the establishment of Afro-Iranian communities as a result of a vibrant slave trade conducted by Arabs, Persians, and Indians around the Persian Gulf She shows how these Africans to some extent retained their African culture but also developed a new identity.

Behnaz Mirzai Asl received her early education in Iran. Her first degree is in Iranian and Islamic History from the Sharaid Beheshi University in Tehran, Iran, graduating in 1990. She earned two Masters degrees, the first in 1994 from Azad University in Tehran, Iran and the second from York University in 1999. She received the Ph.D. in history from York University in Canada and her dissertation was "The Abolition of the Slave Trade and Slavery in Iran 1848–1928." Her research shows that Persian slavery existed before the sixth century BC and included Turkish slaves as well as in later centuries, African and Indian slaves. However, by the early nineteenth century after the ban of Turkish slaves to Persia, East Africans became the main source of slaves entering Iran to be part of the mostly domestic slave system in the Persian state. She has been co-editor of *Islam, Slavery and Diaspora* with Paul Lovejoy and Ismael Musah, author of "The Slave Trade and the African Diaspora in Iran" in Abduf Sheriff (ed.) *Monsoon and Migration: Unleashing Dhow Synegies* (2005), "The 1848 Abolitionist Farman: A Step Towards Ending the Slave Trade in Iran," in *Abolition and Its Aftermath in Indian Ocean, Africa and Asia* (2005). She is presently Assistant Professor of History at Brock University in St. Catharines, Ontario, Canada.

Toward an Understanding of the Ancient View of Blacks

Frank M. Snowden, Jr.

Color prejudice has been a major issue in the modern world. W. E. B. DuBois called it the "problem of the twentieth century,"[1] and D. B. Saddington, among others, notes that racial difficulties are at their worst when associated with differences in skin color.[2] Notable, therefore, is the fact that the ancient world did not make color the focus of irrational sentiments or the basis for uncritical evaluation. The ancients did accept the institution of slavery as a fact of life; they made ethnocentric judgments of other societies; they had narcissistic canons of physical beauty; the Egyptians distinguished between themselves, "the people," and outsiders; and the Greeks called foreign cultures barbarian. Yet nothing comparable to the virulent color prejudice of modern times existed in the ancient world.[3] This is the view of most scholars who have examined the evidence and who have come to conclusions such as these: the ancients did not fall into the error of biological racism;[4] black skin color was not a sign of inferiority;[5] Greeks and Romans did not establish color as an obstacle to integration in society;[6] and ancient society was one that "for all its faults and failures never made color the basis for judging a man."[7]

To some commentators, however, a few ancient texts suggest color prejudice, or at least the germ of anti-black bias. Some, for example, regard as pejorative statements in classical authors that point to a preference for northern or "white" rather than for southern or "dark" beauties. Such interpretations, however, do not mention that the ancients themselves recognized that the criteria for beauty varied from nation to nation, and that those in the predominantly white societies of Greece and Rome having preference for "black" beauty did not hesitate to say so. Parenthetically, it is questionable whether individuals should be called "racist" because they accept aesthetic canons prevailing in their country.

There has also been at times a tendency to read modern racial concepts into ancient documents and to see color prejudice where none existed. Scholars have made these observations: the ugliness of the Negro seems to have appealed alike to sculptor, engraver, and painter;[8] "plastic" vases are always best when the subject, like the Negro's head, is itself grotesque;[9] or Negroes in classical art are often near caricatures or outright examples of the comic.[10] But those scholars who have allowed ancient art to speak for itself argue that the so-called ugliness or comic exists primarily in the minds of the modern beholders, not in the eyes of the ancient artists, and that Negro subjects are among some of the finest and most sympathetically executed pieces to have come from the workshops of ancient artists.[11] The view of blacks as the equivalent of slaves or savages has sometimes given rise to an unwillingness to accept the implication of the ancient evidence. In spite of the widespread repute of blacks as mercenaries in antiquity, for example, Xerxes' black contingent in the Persian Wars has been described as a "humble and almost grotesque auxiliary."[12] A remarkable incredulity appears in the following observation on the rule of the Twenty-fifth Ethiopian Dynasty in Egypt: "In the place of a native Egyptian pharaoh or of the usurping Libyans the throne of Egypt was occupied by a Negro king from Ethiopia! But his dominion was not for long."[13]

In general, the pattern of black-white relations in the ancient world differed markedly from that of later societies which have attached great importance to skin color. The probable reasons for the attitudes toward blacks in antiquity have never been adequately explored. Such an inquiry is in itself worth undertaking, but an examination of the ancient black-white racial pattern in the light of modern research on the origin and nature of prejudice is also instructive. Though social, economic, and demographic factors have obviously differed in many respects, some comparisons of racial attitudes in the ancient and modern world are not without value. The perception of blacks, for example, in modern northwest Africa (the Maghreb), a region where blacks and whites have encountered each other for centuries, has been similar in some respects to that of the ancient world, while the view of blacks in countries that have lacked the experience of Mediterranean societies has often been negative. Thus a consideration of the experience of blacks in dissimilar milieus may provide a key to understanding attitudes toward color in antiquity and may throw some light on why color, in itself neutral and meaningless, has come to assume such great importance in the self-image of many peoples.

The Size of the Black Population

The proportion of blacks in predominantly white societies is often included among factors that have contributed to the development of color prejudice. An appropriate starting point for this analysis, therefore, is a consideration of the size of the black element in the population of ancient Mediterranean societies.

The exact ratio of blacks to whites in various parts of the ancient world is not known and, because of the lack of overall statistics, cannot be precisely determined. We would be better informed as to the number of blacks and their descendants if the ancients had considered color of sufficient significance to mention it more frequently in referring to blacks and their families. In general, ethnic tags were applied in antiquity to persons of pronounced Negroid characteristics much less often than in many postclassical societies, and only occasionally to mulattoes and others of mixed black-white extraction. In spite of the shortcomings of the evidence, a number of factors suggest that blacks were much more numerous than has been recognized. Frequent notices in ancient documents attest that for centuries blacks were well-known types in Mediterranean regions. The few instances that provide figures in the hundreds or thousands are valuable for general estimates of blacks in similar cases in which numbers are not given.[14] It would be hazardous to generalize on the basis of such small samples, but in view of the scope of the military operations in which blacks participated—the centuries-old employment of mercenaries in Egyptian armies, the encounters of Meroïtes with the Ptolemies and Romans, the presence of Ethiopians in the Persian and Cathaginian forces and in other military conflicts in northeast and northwest Africa—the few available figures take on greater significance.

Iconographical evidence has not been given enough weight in the assessment of the black population. The tendency has been to give attention only to the so-called pure Negro and to ignore almost entirely blacks of less pronounced Negroid characteristics, with the result that the picture of blacks in antiquity has been as unrealistic and distorted as a study of the black population in the United States or Brazil would be if restricted to a consideration of "pure" Negroes. The works of artists that have come down to us are only a small fraction of what must have existed: all the more significant, then, are the large number and wide variety of Negroid types that have survived from every major period of ancient art. If it is also kept in mind how often it is possible to relate the blacks of ancient artists to specific facts or historical events, it is apparent that the value of iconography has been greatly underestimated. Though obviously much larger in Egypt than elsewhere, the black population in other Mediterranean areas, especially in northwest Africa and Italy, was probably also greater than traditional estimates.

Several scholars have maintained that the small size of the black population in the ancient world was a factor in minimizing racial hostility. Illustrative of these views are the following: blacks were few in number except in Egypt and, hence, there was no political or economic competition between whites and blacks; hostility would have arisen if there had been more blacks, even though free; the population of blacks in Rome did not correspond to the threshold of intolerance that some modern sociologists attempt to define.[15] These opinions are in themselves debatable; and more so if my interpretation of the evidence as to size of the black population is correct. Further, with respect to the question of numbers, the importance of Egypt is often overlooked: people from three continents often formed their views of blacks on the basis of what they saw and heard in Egypt, where for centuries the black element in the population was obviously sizable. Observations of Greeks and Romans who resided in or visited Egypt show no indication of hostility toward blacks: in fact, writers like Diodorus, the historian of the second half of the first century B.C., and Origen, the Christian author of the third century A.D.,[16] did much to further a highly favorable image of blacks.

In antiquity the black population was at least large enough to satisfy what P. L. van den Berghe considers the most important necessary condition for the development of racism: "the presence in sufficient numbers of two or more groups that look different enough so that at least some of their members can be easily classifiable."[17] Still, intense color prejudice did not arise. The evidence from the ancient world seems to confirm the views of scholars who hold that the "numbers theory" of the origin of color prejudice must be used with care.[18] Philip Mason cautions against "attempting to fix any exact proportion at which certain results will follow." The state of Bahia, though located in a section of northeastern Brazil where Negroes have been most numerous, is the region in which prejudice against colored peoples has been, in the opinion of many Brazilian specialists, the slightest, while in regions of São Paulo, where Negroes are proportionately fewer, color prejudice has been more pronounced.[19] The ancient pattern as a whole would seem to have resembled that of modern northwest Africa, where, in spite of a sizable black element in the population, color has not played as significant a role in the white man's vision of blacks as in some other areas of the modern world.[20] The argument that color prejudice is an inevitable consequence of numbers finds little support in the experience of the ancient world.

First Impression of Blacks

An inclination to discriminate on the basis of readily observable physical differences, it has been suggested, is lessened in white societies that have always had blacks in their midst.[21] The hypothesis that a feeling of common humanity is generated by white-black familiarity over the years merits consideration because in the ancient world, as in later northwest Africa, several predominantly white peoples had prolonged contacts with blacks.

We have seen that populations of dark pigmentations were nothing novel to ancient Mediterranean peoples. Negroes were present in Egypt as early as the middle of the third millennium B.C.; black mercenaries lived in upper Egypt not far from Thebes (Luxor) at the beginning of the second millennium B.C. and, farther north, shortly thereafter. And outside Africa the Negroid type was known in Crete early in the second millennium B.C. In the ninth century B.C., Zerah and his Kushites and later Taharqa led black troops into Asia. Blacks were among the first foreign peoples whom many Greek colonists and mercenaries encountered in the sixth century B.C.; and they were known to the Romans as early as the Carthaginian Wars. The inhabitants of Egypt during the Pharaonic, Ptolemaic, and Roman periods not only developed an acquaintance with blacks in Egypt itself but also, through regular contacts of various sorts with the south, acquired a knowledge of Nubia and its populations. White-black contacts, however, were not limited to northeast Africa. The ancients, and especially the Romans, were also well acquainted with dark-skinned peoples living in northwest Africa.

In short, in the Mediterranean world the black man was seldom a strange, unknown being. In this respect the ancient situation differed strikingly, for example, from that in countries such as England, where the powerful impact the Africans' color made upon sixteenth-century Englishmen resulted from the abrupt nature of their contacts with blacks: one of the fairest nations on earth was suddenly brought face to face with one of the blackest of mankind.[22] In England color became the basis for discrimination. In the Maghreb, on the other hand, with its long history of black-white contacts, bitter hostility toward blacks did not arise. The pattern of the ancient white-black encounters, therefore, may have been a factor in the formation of attitudes toward blacks in antiquity.

First impressions often have a significant role in the formation of images, sometimes an effect of considerable duration. Among the earliest blacks depicted by artists of the Old Kingdom were prisoners of war, some of the first in a long line of black warriors to resist Egyptian aggression in Kush or to serve in pharaonic armies at various periods from 2000 B.C. on. The experience of Egyptians with black soldiers was not unique. Warriors were among the first blacks encountered not only by Egyptians but also by Asiatics and Europeans. A majority of the first blacks whom many whites came to know both inside and outside Africa were not "savages" or slaves but, like the whites themselves, soldiers protecting their own territory against foreign invasion or pursuing their national or personal interests in other lands. Nothing in these initial contacts points to a pejorative view of blacks. On the contrary, black soldiers commanded the respect of peoples beyond Nubia at various times from the second millennium B.C. until the early Roman Empire. Among many Mediterraneans the first and continuing image of blacks was that of a respected ally or an enemy, often a formidable foe.

Another first impression of tremendous importance in its impact on attitudes toward blacks in the Greek and Roman world was the Homeric image of Ethiopians. The influence of Homer's blameless Ethiopians, the most distant of men, favorites of the gods, is the subject of B. M. Warmington's penetrating observation on the first Ethiopians in European literature: "It cannot be said what dim memory of the Bronze Age lies behind Homer's few but much discussed lines about the 'blameless Ethiopians' ... Their real importance, given the place of the Homeric epics in the Greek consciousness, lies in the fact that they were there at all; it was inevitable that in later Greek times, geographers and philosophers would discover what would explain and amplify the Homeric references, and in particular the religious practices which would account for the favor of the gods. The fact that these as recorded are in no way remarkable, and that some Ethiopians lived in a state of savagery, made no difference to the generally favorable judgment."[23] Whatever the origin and full significance of Homer's blameless Ethiopians, and whatever their precise physical characteristics, Ethiopian-Olympian consortia and pious, just Ethiopians were not forgotten, with vestiges of these Ethiopians appearing in late classical and early Christian authors as well. The initially favorable view of Ethiopians was reinforced long after African Negroes had become an everyday reality, in environmental explanations of racial differences, in ideas of the unity of mankind, and in the exegeses of Christian writers. And there was nothing in the daily experiences of blacks as slaves, freedmen, or freemen that did not confirm formal and informal expressions of these views.

In striking contrast was the attitude toward blacks and their color in some later societies where first impressions derived from different circumstances. An account of the first English voyages to Africa in the mid-sixteenth century, for example, described Negroes as a people of "beastly living, without a God, laws, religion, or common wealth; and so scorched and vexed with the heate of the sunne that in many places they curse it when it riseth"[24]—obviously vastly different from the descriptions of Ethiopians in Homer, Herodotus, or Agatharchides. The Negro's color became in the English mind, W. D. Jordan has observed, the identification of a native of a distant continent of African peoples radically defective in religion, libidinous, bestial, a source of slaves.[25] An early, partly fictional and partly factual response to Africa characterized much of the Englishman's understanding of Africa for two hundred and fifty years. In England the myths of Africa, James Walvin emphasizes, were "to prove more resilient and influential than its truths."[26]

In antiquity slavery was independent of race or class, and by far the vast majority of the thousands of slaves was white, not black. The identification of blackness with slavery did not develop. No single ethnic group was associated with slave status or with the descendants of slaves. The Negro as slave or freedman was in a no more disadvantageous position than anyone else unfortunate enough to be captured as a prisoner of war or to be enslaved for some other reason. It has often been noted that anti-black racism developed or increased in intensity after black and slave had become synonymous. In the New World, after the emergence of the doctrine that "a slave cannot be a white man" and of color as the token of slave status,[27] "the most powerful and persistent claims were put forward," as M. I. Finley has pointed out, "for the 'naturalness' of slavery, with ample quotation from the Bible, and moral arguments for the *abolition* of slavery were fully mustered for the first time."[28]

In fact, it no doubt was an important stage in the beginning of the end of slavery when slavery became identified with the Negro only. "When the definition of slavery was symbolized by the Negro," W. L. Westermann remarks, "it spelled the death knell of slavery itself within the European cultural area."[29] A new issue arose: Why the Negro only? Answers to this question gave rise to all kinds of theories as to the innate inferiority of Negroes and to racial stereotypes nonexistent in ancient society. In attempts to justify slavery, later Christians maintained, Roger Bastide notes, that God punished Negroes with a black skin and, against a background of black-white symbolism, "invented causes for the malady, intended to justify in their own eyes a process of production based upon the exploitation of Negro labor."[30] Such a use of black-white symbolism was completely alien, as we shall see, to the spirit of the formidable exegesis in which early Christians made the Ethiopians representative of the totality of Gentiles.

To summarize this point, the ancient world never developed a concept of the equivalence of slave and black; nor did it create theories to prove that blacks were more suited than others to slavery. The importance of this difference was underscored early in the century by the Earl of Cromer, who raised the question of whether "a differentiation between the habits of thought of moderns and ancients may, in some degree, be established on the ground that the former have only enslaved the colored races, whereas the latter doomed all conquered people indiscriminately to slavery." The close identification of slavery with difference of color encouraged the idea of white supremacy and fostered racial antipathy.[31]

Images of Nubia in Contemporary Societies

In the modern world the image of Africans in the minds of whites has often been considered a major factor in the development of color prejudice. Edward Shils, for example, has observed that one of the simplest and most obvious reasons for the great importance color has assumed in the self-imagery of many peoples is that it is an easy means of distinguishing "between those from the periphery and those from the center of particular societies and of the world society." "Differences of pigmentation," Shils continued, "symbolize or indicate contemporaneous differences between present wealth and power and present poverty and weakness, between present fame and present obscurity, between present eminence in intellectual creativity and present intellectual unproductiveness."[32] This observation on color as the focus of complex sentiments provides another useful basis for looking at the images of blacks in antiquity. What was the image of Nubia in contemporary Mediterranean societies? What were common opinions of Nubia's material resources, military and political position, its cultural and intellectual attainments?

Nubia's natural resources were items in great demand among the inhabitants of the Nile Valley, who sought access to products within Nubia itself or available to Nubia indirectly through the control of traffic in goods from east or central Africa. Wishing to profit as middlemen in the flow of trade, Nubians responded to the commercial or imperial ambitions of their northern neighbors by a variety of countermeasures. During periods of Egypt's internal military or political difficulties, Nubia often took advantage of Egyptian disunity to promote its own commercial and military interests, meeting with substantial success as early as the Second Intermediate Period. About the age of the composition of the Homeric poems and the time of the traditional founding of Rome, the Napatans were already emerging as a successful and triumphant people: in Robin Hallett's words, "for the first and indeed the only time in history, a state based on the interior of Africa played an active part in the politics of the Mediterranean."[33] Thus it is not surprising that Isaiah describes the Kushites as a great and formidable nation, or that historians like Herodotus and Diodorus looked back to Sabacos as a model king, or that in retrospect Taharqa appeared to Megasthenes and Strabo as a great conqueror.[34] The Ethiopian military presence continued to be felt in the Ptolemaic world. At various times during the occupation of Egypt until late in the sixth century A.D., the Romans found southern opposition a threat to their boundaries, as the Egyptians and Ptolemies had earlier.

In short, the Napatan-Meroïtic Kingdom of Kush, though experiencing foreign occupation from time to time in its thousand-year history, was able to maintain its territorial integrity with remarkable success against powerful nations. The contemporaries of Nubia, far from regarding that country as materially poor or politically and militarily weak, were clearly aware of its resources and its role in the politics of the day. In addition, some Greek and Roman authors wrote sympathetically of Ethiopia's freedom-loving independence and hatred of foreign aggression.[35]

Another factor responsible for the importance of color in the self-imagery of peoples has been the view of blacks as culturally backward. It is instructive, therefore, to refer briefly to cultural highlights of the Napatan and Meroïtic Kingdoms of Kush. The rulers of the Twenty-fifth Dynasty regarded themselves as perpetuators of the pharaonic traditions. They patronized Egyptian gods and shrines, renovated existing temples, built new structures, and restored ancient texts. To many Egyptians, Napatans appeared "Egyptian," not foreign. The later Meroïtes, though heavily indebted to the Egyptians throughout their history in language, religion, and art, gradually developed their own distinctive writing, worshipped their own gods, and created their own style in architecture, sculpture, and pottery.[36] As early as the fifth century B.C. Herodotus described Meroë as a great city, the capital of the other Ethiopians.[37] Meroë at the time of the ruler Ergamenes in the third century B.C. was a Nubian Alexandria, which saw a renaissance of temple building paralleling the outburst of construction in Ptolemaic and Roman Egypt.[38] As late as the first century B.C. Ethiopians were presented to the Greco-Roman world by Diodorus as among civilization's "pioneers," and by writers of the early Roman Empire as renowned for their wisdom and for their fame in astrology.[39]

It is clear that Nubia, though located on the geographic periphery of the ancient world, was neither considered culturally backward nor sufficiently different from central Mediterranean societies to warrant the extreme contrasts between blacks and whites that Shils links to the development of color prejudice in the modern world. In the eighteenth and nineteenth centuries, as a result of the cultural differences perceived by whites of European stock between themselves and black colonials whom they ruled, many whites associated poverty, inefficiency, and backwardness with non-whites and attached strong emotions to physical differences.[40] Among the ancients, similar associations of color with material poverty, military weakness, political insignificance, and cultural unproductivity did not exist.

Awareness of Color

No single ancient document treats in detail the attitudes of whites toward the color of the black man's skin. Greek and Roman sources, however, are instructive on this subject, particularly when they are examined in the light of modern research on color awareness, standards of beauty, and color symbolism.

The Egyptians, whose contacts with Nubia dated back to the Old Kingdom, did not usually designate Kushites by color terms. Though the monarchs of the Twenty-fifth Dynasty had their skin painted dark-brown in reliefs and their Nubian features clearly delineated by the sculptors,[41] they mentioned neither their own color nor that of the lighter-skinned Egyptians. Piye, for example, in his triumphal stele made no reference to color: he apparently did not regard himself as a champion of black peoples who had overturned their former white masters. Egyptians and Nubians had for centuries been accustomed to the gradations in skin color among the inhabitants of the Nile Valley and hence saw nothing unusual in the differences.

The first to call special attention to the Nubian's blackness were peoples living outside Africa: the color of the Kushites gave rise to a proverb in the Old Testament, and the Greeks invented a color term to describe the Nubians. Though obviously aware of the Nubians' color, however, neither the writers of the Old Testament nor classical authors attached any basic significance to it. Ethiopians do not astonish Greeks because of their blackness and their different physical appearance: such a fear, Agatharchides wrote, ceases at childhood.[42] This statement was not only an accurate assessment of

Greek reaction to the Ethiopians' color, but also a sound observation on as aspect of child behavior that has been studied by modern psychologists. "Four-year-olds," according to Gordon Allport, "are normally interested, curious, and appreciative of differences in racial groups."[43] Alan Marsh, in a study on the awareness of racial differences in British and West African children living in Britain, found that the critical age of racial curiosity seems to be around three to three and half years for the children he studied.[44] In other words, it is perfectly normal for a white child living in a predominantly white society to notice the color of blacks. The reaction of an African child, upon first contacts with whites, is similar and equally innocent. Reporting on his experience in African villages previously unvisited by Europeans, the explorer David Livingstone wrote that the moment a child met them he would "take to his heels in agony of terror" and that the mother, alarmed by the child's wild outcries, would rush out of the hut and dart back again "at the first glimpse of the same fearful apparition."[45]

An initial reaction, even of fear, is normally short-lived in children, according to social psychologists, and may not necessarily have a bearing upon the patterns of later attitudes. There is a strong indication, Marsh concludes, that "whilst the development of 'race values' in children is logically contingent upon knowledge of racial differences, the obverse is not necessarily true. That is to say, children can *know* all about racial differences but do not *necessarily* attach value judgments to them, especially those leading to the formation of racial stereotypes, *unless* they are exposed to socializing forces characterized by overt racial consciousness and/or hostility."[46] In the setting of his study, Marsh noted that "such socializing forces were absent . . . overt race values, beyond those affective bonds formed in personal relationships, were also absent in children."[47] Likewise, Greek and Roman children lived in an atmosphere in which the Negroid type was well known but in which marked hostility to blacks was not a characteristic of the society; there was no reason for a child or even a parent to attach special significance to differences in color or to think that blacks were *fundamentally* different.

In Marsh's investigation a British foster parent of an African child, when his own child remarked for the first time that his African foster brother was still dirty after a bath, explained that his visitor had come from a hot country where the strong sunshine made everyone black.[48] It is possible that a Greek or Roman parent, in response to a child's curiosity about an Ethiopian's color, gave either a mythological or a "scientific" explanation, perhaps both: the story of Phaethon who lost control of his father's chariot and, by coming close to earth, blackened the skin and curled the hair of the Ethiopians; or some version of the environment theory setting forth the effects of climate on northern and southern peoples.[49] Such explanations would have satisfied the curiosity of a Greek or Roman child as effectively as the British answer in Marsh's study: no serious value judgment would have been attached to the Ethiopian's blackness.

In summary, by his observation that fear of Ethiopians ceased at childhood, Agatharchides was merely recording an aspect of child behavior noted by many psychologists since his time—the normal reaction of young children to differences in skin color. He was not setting forth, as Albrecht Dihle has suggested, a theory of aversion to the black man's color rooted in childhood.[50]

The Somatic Norm Image

The Greeks and Romans, like other peoples before and after them, had narcissistic canons of physical beauty. In referring to ethnocentric standards for judging beauty, H. Hoetink uses the term "somatic norm image," which he defines as "the complex of physical (somatic) characteristics which are accepted by a group as its norm and ideal," pointing out that each group considers itself aesthetically superior to others.[51] As an illustration of the somatic norm image, Hoetink mentions a central African creation myth in which the Negro regards himself as perfectly cooked but the white man as underdone because of a defect in the Creator's oven where people were fashioned from clay.[52] Similarly, the Greeks and Romans noted that criteria of beauty varied from people to people. Philostratus remarked that Indians esteemed white less than black because, he implied, black was the color of Indians.[53] Dio Chrysostom's discourse on beauty raised the question as to whether there was not a foreign type of beauty just as there was a Hellenic type.[54] Sextus Empiricus noted that men differed in definitions of beauty—Ethiopians preferring the blackest and most flat-nosed; Persians, the whitest and the most hooked-nose; and others considering those intermediate in color and features as the most beautiful.[55]

What were the Greek and Roman "canons" and their significance for attitudes toward the Ethiopians? The combined Platonic, Lucretian, and Ovidian statements of the classical norm image indicate, in general, a preference for a middle point between the extremes.[56] Lovers in classical poetry seem to prefer their own complexion to that of the extremely fair Germans and of dark-hued Africans; their darker hair and eyes to the blond hair and blue eyes of Germans; their noses to those of the hooked-nosed Persians or flat-nosed Africans. In view of the Greco-Roman aesthetic criteria, there was nothing unusual about the inclusion of color in judgments of beauty.[57] In short, like other people white and black, in their expressions of aesthetic preference the Greeks and Romans used their own physical traits as a yardstick. It is often overlooked, however, that there were whites as well as blacks who did not measure up to the Greco-Roman norm image. This omission in some modern interpretations results in an emphasis on blackness that distorts the classical view of the Ethiopians' color.

Particularly important in an assessment of the Greco-Roman reaction to the color black is the fact that in predominantly white societies there were those who emphasized the subjectivity of their criteria, others who extolled the beauty of blackness, and still others with preferences for blacks who had no hesitancy in saying so. Herodotus, the first European to express an opinion about the physical appearance of Ethiopians, described them as the most handsome of all men.[58] A poem of Philodemus to a certain Philaenion, short, black, with hair more curled than parsley and skin more tender than down, concludes: "May I love such a Philaenion, golden Cypris, until I find another more perfect."[59] Asclepiades praises the beauty of one Didyme: "Gazing at her beauty I melt like wax before the fire. And if she is black, what difference to me? So are coals, but when we light them, they shine like rose-buds."[60] Theocritus reminds those who call his Bombyca sunburned that to him she is honey-brown and charming and adds that violets and hyacinths are dark but are the first flowers chosen for nosegays.[61] Terence, perhaps of Negroid extraction, was freed by his master, according to Suetonius, because of his talent and his good looks: he was *fuscus* (dark).[62] Vergil explained his preference for a dark Amyntas (*fuscus*) by saying that violets and hyacinths are dark (*nigra*) and warned the fair Alexis (*candidus*) not to have too much faith in his color for white privets fall but dark (*nigra*) hyacinths are picked.[63] Ovid's Sappho tells Phaon that she is not fair but reminds him that Andromeda, dark (*fusca*) with the hue of her native Ethiopia, captivated Perseus by her beauty.[64] Martial writes that, though he was sought by a girl whiter than a washed swan, than silver, snow, lily, or privet, he pursued a girl blacker than an ant, pitch, jawdaw, or cicada.[65]

One poem in praise of blackness, because it brings together several relevant themes, merits detailed analysis. The sixth-century poet Luxorius paid a tribute to Olympius, a famous black animal fighter, a Hercules in strength and a favorite of the people, which reads in part:

O wonderful, O bold, O swift, O spirited O always ready! Not at all does your swarthy body harm you because of its blackness. So did nature create black precious ebony. So does the purple deeply placed in the tiny murex gleam, so do violets of deepest shade bloom in the soft grass, so does a certain grace set off gems of somber hue, so does the huge elephant please because of its dusky limbs, so do black Indian incense and pepper give pleasure. Finally, you are as beautiful in the great love the people bear you as another man, handsome without strength, is ugly.[66]

Vergil's rejection of the prevailing aesthetic standard had included only violets and hyacinths as examples of dark beauty. The later poet retained Vergil's dark violets but, in order to emphasize the natural beauty of Ethiopian blackness, added more—precious luxury goods highly prized in antiquity. Luxorious, however, was not only writing of black physical beauty but was expressing another important idea: excellence is found among all men, whatever their race. Menander had said that natural bent, not race, determines nobility;[67] Agatharchides, that success in battle depends not upon color but upon courage and military science.[68] Similarly, for Luxorius, it was Olympius' strength and skill in the ampitheater that mattered. There is nothing in this tribute to justify a view that the references to color in the poem are pejorative. At the end of the classical period Luxorius, in an extravagant but still serious fashion, was using an ancient symbolism—black in a society with a somatic norm image of white—to emphasize the inconsequent of color in evaluating men.

What the majority of the people of Carthage thought about Olympius' intrinsic worth is suggested by Luxorius' epitaph to him:

Animal fighter who brought us great joy and often delighted us with your skill against the wild beasts—quick, pleasant, most brave, daring—who, as a boy that had not yet reached the age of young men, used to perform all feats with mature effort, who gave to others the privilege of winning with you, although you could give great pleasure to the spectators and win acclaim by yourself—so great were the rewards of your remarkable physique that after your death your companions are still awed by you and praise you.

Alas, now this tomb contains you carried off so unexpectedly by envious death, you whom the walls and towers of Carthage could not bear when you triumphed in the arena. But you lose nothing among the shades because of this bitter death. The fame of your glory will live everlastingly after you, and Carthage will always say your name![69]

A tribute by Luxorius to another invincible black athlete also refers indirectly to the champion's color, but only to praise him in glowing terms. Associating a famed black charioteer with mythological greats, Luxorius writes that he has the swiftness of Aeolus and Zephyrus; the color of Night, his mother, and of Memnon, but that unlike the great ally of the Trojans he will not meet death at the hands of Achilles.[70]

Thus "white" was for many in the ancient world a basic element in the somatic norm image, as it has usually been in predominantly white societies. The number of implied or expressed preferences in classical literature for white beauty exceeds slightly those for black or dark beauty. About this there is nothing strange. But what is unusual was the number of those in the Greco-Roman world who rejected the norm of whiteness and openly stated their rejection. As far as the Greeks and Romans were concerned, it seems the matter was basically one of individual preference. As Propertius observed, a tender beauty, white or dark, attracts,[71] and, as we have seen, the dark were inclusive—from *fuscae* to *nigerrimae*.

Art and the Somatic Norm Image

A valuable source of information on attitudes toward the physical appearance of blacks is the copious evidence of art. Works of artists from Egyptian to Roman times confirm in a most striking manner written evidence of interracial mixture[72] and provide convincing testimony that the white somatic norm image was not always observed. These artists demonstrate clearly that some scholars have read nonexistent anti-black sentiment into Greco-Roman preferences which in fact merely reflected the prevailing norms, and were no more "racist" than the preferences of blacks for their ideals of beauty. Ancient artists have not left a record of their own feelings about the Negroes who served as their models. Suggestions as to their views, however, have not been lacking. Modern opinions have often been based on an examination of small samples because only recently has an extensive gallery of Negroes in art of the ancient world become available for study. We need a fresh look at modern interpretations of the ancient evidence.

Some scholars have seen an aesthetic antipathy to the Negro among ancient artists; C. T. Seltman stresses the appeal of the ugliness of Negroes;[73] W. N. Bates concludes that on Greek vases as a rule the Negro is most absurdly drawn;[74] Martin Robertson observes that Memnon was represented as white because of a Greek aversion to Negroid features;[75]

and others have seen primarily caricature or the comic in ancient portrayals of blacks.[76] Some Negroes, but far from the majority, appear in scenes that may rightly be classified as comic or caricatural—a fourth-century B.C. Negroid Nike and Heracles from Cyrenaica, for example, or blacks in Kabeirion episodes such as a Negroid Circe and Odysseus on a skyphos in the British Museum. In some cases, a belief in the supposed apotropaic charm of Negroes may have also been a factor, but some critics have seen apotropaic, grotesque, and comic where none existed. Still there is no reason to conclude that classical artists who depicted blacks in comic or satirical scenes were motivated by color prejudice. Whites of many races—even gods and heroes—appeared in comic or satirical scenes. Why should blacks have been excluded? If Negroes had been depicted only as comic or grotesque, or if satirical scenes had been the rule and not the exception, there might be some justification for a pejorative interpretation of the Negro in classical art. In the absence of ancient evidence to support such views, however, these suggestions must be regarded as the opinions of modern critics, not of the artists themselves.

Classical artists, according to other interpretations, worked from Negro models for no such motives as those cited above, but for many of the same reasons as they selected whites, and often with remarkable success. The Negroid Spinario (Boy Pulling Out a Thorn) from Priene, which some have regarded as comic,[77] R. A. Higgins has described as a "creation of unusual charm" and "transformed by the coroplast into a human document, a sympathetic study of a racial type."[78] The vitality of the tiny Hellenistic bronze head of a Negro in Florence was one of the qualities that Herbert Read had in mind when he referred to the piece as "a great work of art, even the greatest work of art in the world."[79] The terracotta of the sleeping emaciated boy in the Ashmolean,[80] according to A. J. Evans, "for life-like realism and true pathos is probably without a rival amongst Greek terra-cottas."[81] D. G. Mitten ranks the Hellenistic bust of a Negro in Providence with that of "the Pergamene Gauls as one of the most penetrating depictions of hostile or captive ethnic types achieved by Hellenistic artists."[82] Deschamps finds in the blacks of classical art an astonishing diversity and vividness, and a grace that bespeaks an absence of prejudice.[83] A common view is that the treatment of blacks was in general sympathetic and that their continued popularity among the Greeks and Romans was motivated by the artistic challenge of the physical types, an impulse to realism, and pure aesthetic delight.[84]

Of the various foreign populations in the classical world, the Negro attracted artists over a longer period of time than any other alien type—long after the initial excitement and curiosity about a novel element in the population had abated. One of the reasons was aesthetic. In his rejection of conventional explanations of blacks in Greek art, J. D. Beazley emphasizes the aesthetic attractiveness of the Negro: "The black man gets in not because he has strong prophylactic properties, nor because he is more addicted to wine, or perfume, than the white man, nor because there were both perfumes and black men in Egypt, but because it seemed a crime not to make negroes when you had that magnificent black glaze."[85] Aesthetic quality seems also to be the basis of Henri Metzger's observation that the black man had an uncontestable attraction for Greek artists.[86] The features of the Negro presented a challenge to the skill of the artist to represent, by texture and paint, the black man and especially his hair. Jenifer Neils has pointed out that the painters of the "Negro alabastra" were particularly successful in delineating the Negro's features by using black outline drawing on a white ground, effectively representing the woolly hair by black dots, reminiscent of the plastic points of head-vases, and contrasting the black skin with the white ground.[87] The problem of painting blacks on a black background was effectively met by the Niobid Painter's depiction of Cepheus' Ethiopian attendants, with their mass of woolly hair strikingly rendered in white.[88]

In addition, the presence of different Negroid and mixed types in their midst presented opportunities for a diversity in physical types, black-white contrasts, and artistic experimentation. Egyptian artists were the first to make effective contrasts of blacks and whites—a motif frequently employed in portraying pharaonic triumphs over Negroes and Asiatics.[89] We may note further the varied concepts of Negroid types in illustrations of the Andromeda and Busiris legends, the effective contrast of blacks and whites in the plastic head-vases, and in the Herculaneum frescoes of the Isiac worship.[90] When motifs "in white" such as the Boy Blowing a Fire, the Spinario, or Eros had run their course, resourceful artists varied traditional themes by turning for models to "pure" Negroes or mulattoes.[91]

The attitude of ancient artists toward their models is a matter that must be based on a careful examination of the ancient works themselves. Regardless of the varied interpretations of modern scholars, it is difficult to deny that the artists found in their Negro models interesting, if not in some instances aesthetically attractive, examples of non-Greek and non-Roman types. In discussing the image of the Negro in European art of a much later period, D. B. Davis has pointed out that, in spite of the esteem of poets and painters for fair complexions, Sir Thomas Browne, Sir Joshua Reynolds, and Lord Kames considered standards of beauty a matter of custom, and the "Europeans were by no means blind to the physical beauty of Negroes."[92] Davis in this observation is describing circumstances not unlike those in which the classical image of blacks developed. We do not know how many Greeks and Romans accepted the somatic norm image of whiteness, stated or implied in some authors, but in assessing the overall ancient view it is important not to overlook the rejection of such a criterion as attested by the iconographical evidence for substantial racial mixture and by the aesthetic appeal of Negroid types to classical artists.

Color Symbolism

Among the Greeks and Romans, white was generally associated with light, the day, with Olympus and victims sacrificed to the higher gods, with good character and good omens; black with night and darkness, with the Underworld, death, and chthonian deities, with bad character and ill omens.[93] In this the Greeks and Romans resembled people in general who, according to research on color symbolism, have a basic tendency to equate blackness with evil and white with goodness. Recent studies point out that there seems to be a "widespread communality in feelings about black and white," that among both Negroes and whites the color white tends to evoke a positive and black a negative reaction, and that both colors figure prominently in the areas of human experience concerned with religion and the supernatural.[94] C. N. Degler's observations on this subject underline the similarities between ancient and modern reactions to color: "It is surely more than a coincidence that in Africa and Asia as well as in Europe, black is associated with unpleasantness, disaster, or evil. Black undoubtedly evokes recollections of the night—that time when men, with their heavy dependence upon sight, are most helpless and in greatest danger. White, on the other hand, is the color of light, which emanates principally from the sun, which in turn is the source of warmth and other conditions that support life. Night is not only dark, but cold and therefore a threat to life. Is it any wonder that white is seen everywhere as the symbol of success, virtue, purity, goodness, whereas black is associated with evil, dirt, fear, disaster, and sin?"[95]

It was obviously because of a deeply rooted tradition linking blackness with death and the Underworld that some writers of the early Roman Empire put dark-skinned peoples—Ethiopian, Egyptian, Garamantian—in ill-omened contexts. An Ethiopian was reported to have met troops of Cassius and Brutus as they were proceeding to battle.[96] At the time of Caligula's death, according to

Suetonius, a nocturnal performance was in rehearsal in which scenes from the lower world were enacted by Egyptians and Ethiopians.[97] The events foreshadowing the death of Septimius and Severus included the sight of an Ethiopian soldier carrying a garland of cypress boughs.[98] A metrical inscription from Hadrumetum (Sousse in southern Tunisia) deserves to be cited in full: "The dregs of the Garamantes have come up into our region and the black slave rejoices in his pitch-black body. If the voice issuing from his lips did not make him sound human, the grim ghost would be frightening upon sight. Hadrumetum, may ill-omened Tartarus carry off your monster for itself! The abode of Dis should have him as a guardian."[99]

Although the Greek and Roman association of the color black with death and the Underworld had in origin nothing to do with skin color, the introduction of dark-skinned peoples into such contexts was a natural development. Homer's and Vergil's underworlds were dark and murky; the god of the Underworld himself was often black;[100] and the ferryman Charon, son of Erebus and Night, was gloomy, grim, and terrible in his squalor.[101] The biographer of Septimius Severus was continuing this tradition when he noted the presence of an Ethiopian in the vicinity of the emperor on the eve of his departure to the dark Underworld whose presiding deity was black. Drawing on the language of Vergil's lower region, the Hadrumetum inscription is a *jeu d'esprit* on the common theme of the blackness of death and the Underworld. The pitch-black Garamantian (*piceo . . . corpore . . . niger*) of the Hadrumetum inscription is reminiscent of Vergil's grim warden Charon (*portitor . . . horrendus*), guardian of black Tartarus (*nigra Tartara*); and the door of black Dis (*atri ianua Ditis*) in Vergil's Underworld[102] is echoed in the Hadrumetum inscription—the grim ghost (*horrida larva*) who should be the guardian of Dis. The intent is clear in both cases: mindful of widespread beliefs in the blackness of death and the nether realms, the biographer of Septimius Severus was aiming at complete coverage by including the Ethiopian in his catalogue of omens preceding the death of Septimius Severus—dreams, falling statues, black sacrificial victims; and the primary aim of the piece on the Garamantian was to echo traditional descriptions of the Underworld.

Interpretations that have seen a significant anti-black sentiment in the ancient association of Ethiopians with death and the Underworld are questionable. In the first place, the association seems to have been due primarily to the basic tendency of peoples, African Negroes included, to equate blackness and evil. Second, recent research in the social sciences has raised the question of whether individuals who react negatively to the color black also develop an antipathy toward dark-skinned people and suggests that, though such a reaction is in theory plausible, the evidence is far from conclusive.[103] It is doubtful, for example, that expressions such as blackball, blacklist, black mark, or black-hearted would in themselves have given rise to serious anti-Negro sentiments in the modern world in the absence of such phenomena as Negro slavery and colonialism.

In view of the overall attitude toward blacks in antiquity it is unlikely that the association of dark-skinned peoples with omens of evil in the early Roman Empire had an adverse impact on day-to-day reactions to blacks: the favorable image of Ethiopians had long been firmly established, and the unbiased environmental explanation of racial differences had been deeply rooted since the fifth century B.C. At the same time that the notion linking dark-skinned people and omens of disasters was being circulated, proponents of the environment theory were setting forth unprejudiced explanations of physical differences; the ancient image of just Ethiopians was being reinforced; and Christian authors were developing a rich black-white imagery emphasizing the black man's membership in the Christian brotherhood.[104]

---

[1]W. E. B. DuBois, *The Souls of Black Folk: Essays and Sketches* (New York, 1965), p. 23.

[2]D. B. Saddington, "Race Relations in the Early Roman Empire," in H. Temporini, ed., *Aufstieg und Niedergang der römischen Welt*, II. 3 (Berlin, 1975), p. 112.

[3]On the importance of distinguishing between ethnocentrism and racism, see P. L. van der Berghe, *Race and Racism: A Comparative Perspective* (New York, 1967), p. 12, and "Racism," *New Encyclopedia Britannica* (1976), XV, 360. For the absence of color prejudice in the ancient world in general, see S. Davis, *Race-Relations in Ancient Egypt: Greek, Egyptian, Hebrew, Roman* (London rpt., 1953), p. 54, and van der Berghe, "Racism," pp. 361–362; and in Egypt, J. A. Wilson, in H. and H. A. Frankfort, J. A. Wilson, T. Jacobsen, and W. A. Irwin, *The Intellectual Adventure of Ancient Man: An Essay on Speculative Thought in the Ancient Near East* (Chicago, 1946), pp. 33–34, 37.

[4]W. den Boer, review of Snowden, *Blacks in Antiquity*, in *Mnemosyne* 24 (1971), 438 [Review of *Blacks in Antiquity*, hereafter *RBA*].

[5]M. Cebeillac-Gervasoni, *RBA*, in *L'Antiquité classique* 44 (1975), 781–782.

[6]B. M. Warmington, *RBA*, in *African Historical Studies* 4 (1971), 386.

[7]W. R. Connor, *RBA*, in *Good Reading: Review of Books Recommended by the Princeton University Faculty* 21 (May, 1970), 3.

[8]C. T. Seltman, "Two Heads of Negresses," *American Journal of Archaeology* 24 (1920), 14.

[9]A. Lane, *Greek Pottery*, 3rd ed. (London, 1971), p. 55.

[10]D. von Bothmer, "A Gold Libation Bowl," *Bulletin of the Metropolitan Museum of Art* 21 (1962–63), 161, finds

the Negroes on the Panagjurishte phiale "almost caricatures." See fig. 39a-b, above.

[11] See below, "Art and the Somatic Norm Image."

[12] G. H. Beardsley, *The Negro in Greek and Roman Civilization: A Study of the Ethiopian Type* (Baltimore, 1929), p. 53.

[13] G. Steindorff and K. C. Seele, *When Egypt Ruled the East*, rev. K. C. Seele (Chicago, 1957), p. 271.

[14] Since the figures of black combatants or captives are usually derived from non-Nubian sources, the numbers must be regarded with caution. Sneferu, for example, claimed 7,000 prisoners in his Nubian campaign, *ARE* I, 66, sec. 146. Strabo in his account (17.1.54) of Petronius' Ethiopian campaign states that the Romans forced 30,000 Ethiopians to flee, and Pliny (6.35.186) writes that Meroë used to furnish 250,000 armed men.

[15] R. Mauny, *RBA*, in *Journal of African History* 12 (1971), 159; Warmington, *RBA*, p. 385; J. Desanges, "L'Antiquité gréco-romaine et l'homme noir," *Revue des études latines* 48 (1970), 94.

[16] Diodorus 3.2–7; on Ethiopians as an element in the motley population of Alexandria, see Dio Chrysostom *Orationes* 32.40; and below, notes 216–226.

[17] P. L. van den Berghe, *Race and Racism: A Comparative Perspective* (New York, 1967), p. 13.

[18] P. Mason, *Race Relations* (New York, 1970), p. 147.

[19] C. N. Degler, *Neither Black nor White: Slavery and Race Relations in Brazil and the United States* (New York, 1971), pp. 99–100; F. Fernandes, "The Weight of the Past," in J. H. Franklin, ed., *Color and Race* (Boston, 1968) [hereafter *Color and Race*] p. 282.

[20] L. C. Brown, "Color in Northern Africa," in *Color and Race*, pp. 186–194. Brown makes these points: in north Africa the black-white pattern is not comparable to that in the United States; there has never been anything approximating segregation on the basis of color; there has been no color bar; north Africa, though not color-blind, has not been color-conscious.

[21] Ibid., p. 190.

[22] W. D. Jordan, *White over Black: American Attitudes toward the Negro, 1550–1812* (Baltimore, 1969), p. 6. J. Walvin, *Black and White: The Negro and English Society, 1555–1945* (London, 1973), p. 19, states that the African's blackness and nakedness impressed Englishmen deeply and that these two characteristics placed Africans at opposite physical and social poles to Elizabethan Englishmen, with the result that blacks came to be seen as a "dramatic inversion of their most deeply cherished social and cultural values." G. K. Hunter, "Elizabethans and Foreigners," in *Shakespeare in His Own Age*, ed. A. Nicoll [hereafter *Shakespeare Survey*] (1964) XVII, 37–52.

[23] Warmington, *RBA*, p. 385.

[24] "The second voyage to Guinea . . . in the yere 1554. The Captaine whereof was M. John Lok," in Richard Hakluyt, *The Principal Navigations, Voyages, Traffiques, and Discoveries of the British Nation* (London and New York n.d. [Everyman's Library]) IV, 57.

[25] Jordan, *White over Black*, pp. 3–34.

[26] Walvin, *Black and White*, pp. 5–8, 28.

[27] O. and M. F. Handlin, "The Southern Labor System," in R. W. Winks, *Slavery: A Comparative Perspective: Readings on Slavery from Ancient Times to the Present* (New York, 1972), p. 49.

[28] M. I. Finley, "The Extent of Slavery," ibid., p. 13.

[29] W. L. Westermann cited in F. Tannenbaum, *Slave and Citizen: The Negro in the Americas* (New York, 1947), p. 110.

[30] R. Bastide, "Color, Racism, and Christianity," in *Color and Race*, p. 36.

[31] The Earl of Cromer [Evelyn Baring], *Ancient and Modern Imperialism* (London, 1910), pp. 140–142. In commenting on the beauty and vitality of blacks in Hellenistic and Roman art, D. B. Davis in his review of *The Image of the Black in Western Art*, vols. 1 and 2 (*New York Review of Books*, Nov. 5, 1981, 0. 40), writes that "such individualized and humanistic representations would have been inconceivable in later slave societies founded on the premise of racial inferiority. In late antiquity the image of the black was one expression of the infinite diversity of a common human nature."

[32] E. Shils, "Color, the Universal Intellectual Community, and the Afro-Asian Intellectual," in *Color and Race*, p. 2.

[33] R. Hallett, *Africa to 1875: A Modern History* (Ann Arbor, 1970), p. 82.

[34] Isaiah 18:2, Herodotus 2.137, 139; Diodorus 1.65; Megasthenes cited by Strabo 15.1.6.

[35] E.g. Herodotus 3.20–21 and Seneca *De ira* 3.20.2.

[36] F. and U. Hintze, *Civilizations of the Old Sudan: Kerma, Kush, Christian Nubia* (Amsterdam, 1968), p. 27; Hintze, *Africa in Antiquity*, pp. 89–98; Wenig, *Africa in Antiquity*, II, 65–99. Adams, "Ceramics," *Africa in Antiquity*, pp. 129–130.

[37] Herodotus 2:29.

[38] M. I. Rostovtzeff, *Social and Economic History of the Roman Empire*, rev. P. M. Fraser I (Oxford, 1957), pp. 302–305.

[39] Diodorus 3.2.1–3.7; Pliny *Naturalis historia* 2.80.189; Plutarch *Septem sapientium convivium* 151 b-c; Lucian *De astrologia* 3.

[40] P. Mason, "The Revolt against Western Values," *Color and Race*, pp. 50–51.

[41] Cf. Wenig, *Africa in Antiquity*, II, 18–19; cf. Leclant, *Image of the Black*, pp. 89–104.

[42] Agatharchides *De Mari Erythraeo* 16 GGM I, 118.

[43] G. W. Allport, *The Nature of Prejudice* (Boston, 1964), p. 304.

[44] A. Marsh, "Awareness of Racial Differences in West African and British Children," *Race* 11.3 (1970), 289–302.

[45] D. and C. Livingstone, *Narrative of an Expedition to the Zambesi and its Tributaries and of a Discovery of the Lakes Shirwe and Nyassa, 1858–1864* (New York, 1866), p. 199. Cf. the fifteenth-century Venetian explorer Alvise da Cadamosto, who reported that the Negroes in a Senegalese village "touched my hands and limbs and rubbed me with their spittle to discover whether my whiteness was dye or flesh. Finding that it was flesh they were astounded"—in G. R. Crone, *The Voyages of Cadamosto and Other Documents on Western Africa in the Second Half of the Fifteenth Century* (London, 1937), p. 49.

[46] Marsh, "Awareness of Racial Differences," p. 301.

[47] Ibid., pp. 301–302.

[48] Ibid., p. 297.

[49] Ovid *Metamorphoses* 2.235–236; see below, note 109.

[50] A. Dihle, "Zue hellenistischen Ethnographie," in H. Schwabl et al., Fondation Hardt, Entretiens sur l'antiquité classique, vol. 8, *Grecs et barbares: six exposés et discussions* (Vandoeuvres-Genève, 1962), pp. 214–215.

[51] H. Hoetink, *The Two Variants in Caribbean Race Relations: A Contribution to the Sociology of Segmented Societies,* trans. E. M. Hookykaas (New York, 1967), p. 120.

[52] Ibid., p. 126.

[53] Philostratus *Vita Apollonii* 2.19. If the reading, *hi pudore,* (Detlefsen suggested *Hypsodores*) in Pliny *Naturalis historia* 6.35.90 is correct, Pliny's statement that the Mesanches, an Ethiopian tribe, covered themselves with red because they were ashamed of their blackness differs from the usual Greco-Roman view of the somatic norm image (e.g. Philostratus *Vita Apollonii* 2.19 and Sextus Empiricus *Adversus mathematicos* xi.43.) J. Balsdon, *Rome and Aliens* (London, 1979), p. 219, suggests that Pliny may have been wrong as to motive but right as to the Ethiopian practice. Herodotus 7.69 provides an explanation of such a custom when he notes that Ethiopians, upon going into battle, painted their bodies half with chalk and half with vermilion.

[54] Dio Chrysostom *Orationes* 21.16–17.

[55] Sextus Empiricus *Adversus mathematicos* xi.43.

[56] Plato *Respublica* 5.474 DE; Lucretius 4.1160–1169; Ovid *Ars amatoria* 2.657–662; *Remedia amoris* 327. Cf. Martial 4.62, 7.13. For a somewhat similar "intermediate" standard of beauty in Jewish thought, see S. W. Baron, *A Social and Religious History of the Jews,* II: *Christian Era, The First Five Centuries,* 2nd ed. (New York and London, 1952), p. 238, who points out that Rabbi Ishmael was proud of the fact that Jews were "like an ebony tree," i.e., of an intermediate color, neither as fair as Germans nor as dark as Negroes. The canon of an ideal intermediate color may have influenced the Midrashic interpretation of Noah's curse on Canaan (Genesis 9.25) e.g. *Midrash Rabbah, Genesis (Noach)* xxxvi.7 [p. 293 in Midrash Rabbah I (Genesis), trans. H. Freedman (London, 1939)], which states that Ham's seed would be "ugly and dark-skinned." W. D. Jordan, *White over Black: American Attitudes toward the Negro, 1550–1812* (Baltimore, 1969), p. 18, contrasts the difference between the Christian and Talmudic-Midrashic interpretation of Noah's curse. The church fathers, Jordan points out, cited the curse in reference to slavery but not to Negroes, whereas Talmudic and Midrashic sources suggested the curse as the origin of blackness in Ham and his descendants. The criterion of an intermediate color appears also in Arabic and Muslim writers: *Jahiz* of Basra (ca. 776–869) described inhabitants of cold countries as undercooked, of hot countries as burned; ibn al-Faqih (ca. 902/3) stated that the Iraqis were intermediate in color, neither "half-baked dough" like northerners nor "burned crust" like southerners—B. Lewis, *Race and Color in Islam* (New York, 1971), pp. 33–34.

[57] J. Desanges, "L'Afrique noire et le monde méditerranéen dans l'Antiquité Éthiopiens et Gréco-romains)" *Revuew française d'histoire d'outre-mer* 62.228 (1975), sees an aesthetic prejudice (pp. 410–411) in a sixth-century poem of Luxorius, who contrasts an ugly Garamantian and a pretty Pontic girl (no. 43 in M. Rosenblum, *Luxorius: A Latin Poet among the Vandals* (New York, 1961); and sees anti-black sentiment in another poem of Luxorius in praise of a black charioteer (Rosenblum, no. 67) and in a third-century epitaph, found in Egypt (E. Bernand, *Inscriptions métriques de l'Egypte gréco-romaine: Recherches sur la poésie épigrammatique des grecs en Egypte* [Besançon and Paris, 1969] no. 26, pp. 143–147) in which a master memorializes a slave by contrasting his black color and his white soul. D. S. Wiesen, "Juvenal and the Blacks," *Classica et Mediaevalia* 31 (1970) 132–150, interprets some of the same passages cited by Desanges as well as others in Juvenal as indicative of a pejorative view of blacks. Juvenal's juxtaposition of *Aethiopem albus* (2.23), *Gaetulum Ganymedem* (5.59), and *Aethiopem Cyncnum* (8.33), for example, is evidence to Wiesen that the Negro in Juvenal is a "kind of insult to nature and nature's proper product—the white man" (p. 143) and proof that the satirist despised the physical being of Negroes and attached "a special stigma to the physical attributes of blacks and finds in them faults which are neither of their own making nor capable of being corrected" (p. 149). For a different view of Juvenal's attitude toward Negroes and other non-Romans, see W. J. Watts, "Race Prejudice in the Satires of Juvenal," *Acta Classica* 19 (1976) 83–104, who believes (p. 86) that Juvenal is more concerned with cultural than physical differences and that (p. 95) the satirist felt no hostility to any one non-Italian group, except perhaps the Egyptians. Cf. J. Ferguson, *Juvenal: The Satires* (New York, 1979), pp. 128–129 on 2.23 and p. 211 on 6.600. Juvenal, of course, must be read with caution because he lashes out at all foreigners regardless of the color of their skin.

As a corrective for some modern interpretations of Juvenal, a look at other writers of the early Roman Empire is appropriate. Seneca (*De ira* 3.26.2), for example, observes that the color of the Ethiopian among his own people is not notable and that among the Germans red hair gathered into a knot is not unbecoming a man. And, Seneca adds, apparently rejecting a common Roman view, one is to consider nothing in a man odd which is characteristic of his nation. Martial, Juvenal's contemporary, states (*Spectacula* 3.9–10) that present at the opening of the Colosseum were Sygambrians with their hair twisted in a knot and Ethiopians with their hair twisted in another way. Like this reference, Martial's other mentions of Ethiopians or dark "beauties" are similarly without judgment (e.g. 1.115). What both Desanges and Wiesen overlook in their interpretations is that the passages they cite as evidence of anti-black sentiment merely reflect a somatic norm image, something found in all societies, black included. Juvenal (13.163–173) himself recognizes such a standard when he says that women in Meroë with large breasts (bigger than their fat babies) and Germans with their blue eyes and yellow hair (greasy curls twisted into a horn) evoke no astonishment in their own countries because their physical traits are common. Similarly, the satirist adds, no one would laugh at Pygmies in their native land because the whole population is no taller than one foot. These important points are seldom mentioned in some modern interpretations of attitudes toward blacks in antiquity: (1) The frequent classical references to the extreme fairness, blue eyes, and light hair of northerners are often omitted while the Ethiopian's blackness is pointed out, an emphasis of modern and not of ancient commentators—cf. J. Balsdon, *Romans and Aliens*, p. 215, who refers to something of a Roman "colour prejudice" against palefaced men—i.e., there were whites as well as blacks who did not conform to classical canons. (2) The Greeks and Romans also designated as dark or black peoples other than Ethiopians, such as Egyptians, Indians, Moors, and Garamantes (one of the passages cited above by Wiesen refers to a Gaetulian and one by Desanges to a Garamantian). (3) There were in the ancient world those who questioned the validity of the classical somatic norm image, others who extolled the beauty of blackness (as Luxorius, no. 67 in Rosenblum), and still others who stated their preferences for black beauty.

[58]Herodotus 3.20.

[59]Philodemus in *Anthologia Palatina* 5.121 (Loeb I.184).

[60]Asclepiades, ibid. 5.210 (Loeb I.232).

[61]Theocritus 10.26–29.

[62]Suetonius *Vita Terenti* 5.

[63]Vergil *Eclogues* 10.37–39, 2.16–18.

[64]Ovid *Heroides* 15.35–38.

[65]Martial 1.115.

[66]Luxorius, *Anthologia Latina*, ed. F. "Bücheler and A. Riese, I, fasc. 1 (Leipzig, 1894), pp. 277–278, no. 353; trans. Rosenblum, p. 151.

[67]Menander, Fragment 612 in A. Koerte, 2nd ed. (Leipzig, 1959); Kock, Frg. 533.

[68]Agatharchides *De Mari Erthraeo* 16 GGM I, 118.

[69]Luxorius, *Anthologia Latina*, 278, no. 354; trans. Rosenblum, pp. 151–153.

[70]Ibid., p. 251, no. 293; trans. Rosenblum, pp. 114–115.

[71]Propertius 2.25.41–42.

[72]See *Image of the Black*, e.g., figs. 169, 176, 197, 275, 286, 334.

[73]C. T. Seltman, "Two Heads of Negresses," *American Journal of Archaeology* 24 (1920), 14.

[74]W. N. Bates, "Scenes from the Aethiopis on a Black-Figured Amphora from Orvieto," *Transactions of the Department of Archaeology*, University of Pennsylvania Free Museum of Science and Art (Philadelphia, 1904), I and II, 50.

[75]M. Robertson, *Greek Painting* (Geneva, 1959), p. 67.

[76]E. Riefstahl, "A Wounded Warrior," *Bulletin: The Brooklyn Museum* 17.4 (1956) 6, states that it is rare to find Negro types caricatured in Egyptian art of the pharaonic period, and that while Egyptian artists noted carefully the physical features of blacks, they did not regard Negroes as ludicrous or grotesque. For a view of Negroes as caricature, see R. Winkes, "Physiognomonia: Probleme der Charakterinterpretation römischer Porträts," in H. Temporini, ed., *Aufstieg und Niedergang der römischen Welt*, I.4: *Von den Anfangen Roms bis zum Ausgang der Republik* (Berlin and New York, 1973), pp. 908–913; and note 10 above. For interpretations of the Negro as comic, see next note.

[77]G. H. Beardsley, *The Negro in Greek and Roman Civilization*, pp. 37–38, 39, 47, 65, 81; C. M. Havelock, *Hellenistic Art: The Art of the Classical World from the Death of Alexander the Great to the Battle of Actium* (London, 1971), p. 136; *Image of the Black*, fig. 268 and p. 206.

[78]R. A. Higgins, *Greek Terracottas* (London, 1967), p. 120; *Image of the Black*, figs. 262–263. For a marble head of a Negroid youth of about 100 B.C. in Toronto, which perhaps belonged to a Spinario, see N. Leipen, "Grotesque Head of a Young Man," *Antike Kunst* 23 (1980), pp. 154–158, figs. 1–2, and plates 41–42.

[79]H. Read, *A Coat of Many Colours: Occasional Essays* (London, 1945), pp. 2, 5. See fig. 28 above and *Image of the Black*, fig. 242.

[80]*Image of the Black*, figs. 262–263 and p. 206.

[81]A. J. Evans, "Recent Discoveries of Tarentine Terra-Cottas," *Journal of Hellenic Studies* 7 (1886), 37–38; *The Image of the Black*, I, figs. 262–263.

[82]D. G. Mitten, *Classical Bronzes: Catalogue of the Classical Collection*, Museum of Art, Rhode Island School of Design (Providence, 1975), p. 62. See fig. 24 above and *Image of the Black*, fig. 239.

[83]H. Deschamps, *RBA*, in *Africa: Journal of the International African Institute* 41 (1971), p. 68.

[84]Cf. G. Becatti, *The Art of Ancient Greece and Rome from the Rise of Greece to the Fall of Rome* (New York, 1967), p. 274; D. M. Buitron, "Greek Encounters with Africans," *Walters Art Gallery Bulletin* 32 (Nov. 5, 1980), 1: "In general Greek representatives of Ethiopians are of high quality."

[85]J. D. Beazley, "Charinos: Attic Vases in the Form of Human Heads," *Journal of Hellenic Studies* 49 (1929), 39.

[86]H. Metzger, *RBA*, in *Revue des études anciennes* 73 (1971), 498.

[87]J. Neils, "The Group of the Negro Alabastra: A Study in Motif Transferal," *Antike Kunst* 23 (1980), 22.

[88]*Image of the Black*, figs. 174–175 and p. 155.

[89]See, for example, the footstool decorated with black and Asiatic captives from Thebes, the tomb of Tutankhamun in *Image of the Black*, fig. 37; and the Asiatic (carved in ivory) and black (in ebony) captives bound to the handles of a ceremonial walking stick, also from Tutankhamun's tomb, in E. D. Ross, ed. *The Art of Egypt through the Ages* (London, 1931), p. 43 and plate 195.

[90]For examples of "pure" Negroes in Andromeda scenes, see *Image of the Black*, figs. 174–175, and for mixed black-white types, see fig. 176; and Snowden, *Blacks in Antiquity*, fig. 26. For illustrations of several Negroid types in the Busiris legend, see *Image of the Black*, figs. 167–173. For late sixth-century kantharoi of conjoined black and white heads, see *Image of the Black*, fig. 160, and *Blacks in Antiquity*, fig. 12. For the frescoes from Herculaneum, see figs. 60–61 below and, in color, *Image of the Black*, figs. 288–289, in which black Isiac cultists are contrasted with white worshipers; the brilliance of the white tunics of the blacks emphasizes the ebony hue of their heads and shoulders.

[91]For a Negro Spinario, see above, notes 77–78. The Negro boy has been interpreted as an adaptation of the well-known *Boy Blowing a Fire*, of the Hellenistic painter Antiphilus (Pliny, *Historia naturalis* 35.40.138); see K. Herbert, *Greek and Latin Inscriptions in The Brooklyn Museum* (Brooklyn, 1972), pp. 14–16 and plate 5. For a capital (second half of the first century B.C.) in the shape of youthful Eros with broad nose, thick lips, and curly hair, found in underwater excavations near Mahdia off

the Tunisian coast, see A. Lézine, "La 'Maison des chapiteaux historiés' à Utique," *Karthago* 7 (1956), plates 6–7 and p. 20.

[92] D. B. Davis, *The Problem of Slavery in Western Culture* (Ithaca, 1966), p. 449. Davis, in his review of the first two volumes of *The Image of the Black in Western Art*, in *New York Review of Books*, considers the pictorial image of blacks from the pharaohs to Emperor Charles V most impressive because of the interest and delight in diversity, the dignity with which artists portrayed most blacks, and their enduring capacity for empathy and human expression; and he concludes that, in spite of the complexities of the black image, "the artistic heritage from Egyptian and Hellenistic times to the great portraits by Memling, Bosch, and Rembrandt presents an unanswerable challenge to the later racist societies that have relied on dehumanizing caricature as an instrument of social and economic oppression" (p. 42).

[93] See *melas* and compounds in H. G. Liddell and R. Scott, *A Greek-English Lexicon*, rev. H. S. Jones and R. McKenzie (Oxford, 1968), and *niger* and compounds in P. G. W. Glare, *Oxford Latin Dictionary* (Oxford, 1976) V, p. 1176; J. André, *Étude sur les termes de couleur dans la langue latine* (Paris, 1949), pp. 57, 362–364; A. Hermann, s.v. "Farbe" in T. Klauser, ed., *Reallexikon für Antike und Christentum*, 7 (Stuttgart, 1969), cols. 358–447; E. Irwin, *Colour Terms in Greek Poetry* (Toronton, 1974), pp. 158–193.

[94] K. J. Gergen, "The Significance of Skin Color in Human Relations," in *Color and Race*, pp. 120, 112–125; for examples of recent studies on the colors black and white and for the findings cited, see also Davis, *The Problem of Slavery*, pp. 447–452; Jordan, *White over Black*, pp. 4–20; Degler, *Neither Black nor White*, pp. 207–211; J. E. Williams and J. K. Morland, *Race, Color, and the Young Child* (Chapel Hill, 1976), pp. 33–45; D. Zahan, "White, Red and Black; Colour Symbolism in Black Africa," in A. Portmann and R. Ritsema, eds., *The Realms of Colour* (Leiden, 1974), pp. 365–396, esp. 364, 373.

[95] Degler, *Neither Black nor White*, p. 211.

[96] Appian *Bella civilia* 4.17.134; Florus 2.17.7.7–8; Plutarch *Brutus* 48.

[97] Suetonius *Caligula* 57.4

[98] SHA, *Septimius Severus* 22.4–5.

[99] *Anthologia Latina*, I, fasc. 1, no. 183, pp. 155–156.

[100] For *niger Jupiter* and *niger Dis*, see Seneca *Hercules Oetaeus* 1705; Statius *Thebais* 2.49, 4.291; Ovid *Metamorphoses* 4.438.

[101] Vergil *Aeneid* 6.298–299.

[102] *Aeneid* 6.128, 134–135, 298–299.

[103] Gergen, "The Significance of Skin Color," p. 121.

[104] For examples of the environment theory in the early empire, see Diodorus 3.34.7–8; Pliny, *Naturalis historia* 2.80.189; Vitruvius *De architectura* 6.1.3–4; Ptolemy *Tetrabiblos* 2.2.56. Illustrations of "just" Ethiopians in the early empire appear in Diodorus 3.2.2–3.3.1; Seneca *De ira* 3.20.2; Pausanias 1.33.4; Heliodorus *Aethiopica* 9.21, 26; 10.39.

European Dimensions of the African Diaspora

Allison Blakely

Dr. Blakely traces economic, cultural, and political ties linking Africa and Africans with the histories of Europe and southwestern Asia. He describes where and how the African Diaspora formed in the Eastern Hemisphere from pre-Islamic times to post Soviet conditions, and makes the important point that a racist perception of Africa and Africans was absent prior to the Crusades. The European view of Africa as the dark and mysterious continent developed subsequently.

There is a saying of uncertain origin that "Europe ends at the Pyrenees." Regardless of the accuracy of this statement in general, it has real merit for viewing the European dimensions of the African Diaspora in their proper historical perspective. Regarding Spain and Portugal during the period when they played their major role on the historical stage, it is useful to look upon the Iberian Peninsula as an extension of Africa rather than an arm of Europe. In the thirteenth and fourteenth centuries neither Muslims nor Christians recognized the Mediterranean Sea as a line defining their realms; each intended to control a world bridging the waterway history was later to leave as a virtual moat between them. Ancient trade route patterns reveal that there was much traffic between Africa and Europe, even before Greek and Roman times, and later led by the Arabs from the one side and the Italian city-states from the other. The Greek and Roman World included North Africa and the Iberian Peninsula; there were trans-Saharan branches to the commerce; and in all of this process over the centuries there was some infusion of Africans into Europe.

In the eighth century A. D., a branch of Islam conquered much of the Iberian Peninsula, bringing Black Africans among their military units, and continuing to include them in their slave trading during the centuries of occupation there. Other slaves were acquired by the Christian inhabitants of Iberia during these centuries, at first through Moslem traders in North Africa and later directly from West Africans themselves. This was possible because Iberia had the advantage of being part of the Atlantic World as well as the Mediterranean. If we use a new perspective when looking at the Atlantic as connecting Europe, Africa, the Americas, and the countless islands between, rather than as separating them, we can better understand the ease with which peoples of African descent spread to all of these regions over the centuries, especially after global explorations and European expansion generated a demand for a massive labor supply in the Americas.

It is also important to note that Blacks were not just passive pawns in these developments: they participated as rulers, merchants, seamen, soldiers, and free laborers, as well as slaves. With respect to the main thrust of this essay, focusing on Europe, it should be pointed out that the first Africans who went to the Americas with the Portuguese were from Europe, not Africa. Blacks were in Spain and Portugal in high numbers in the fifteenth and sixteenth centuries, with many assimilated into the population. Thus it was to be expected that they would be present in the Spanish and Portuguese empires in the entire Atlantic World; that is, Europe, Africa, and the Americas. During the early centuries of European expansion in the Americas the African presence would be greater in the Spanish and Portuguese possessions than in those of the other European powers; that is, the Dutch, English, French, and Scandinavian.

The African Diaspora's penetration into Eastern Europe was just another facet of the same story that encompasses southern, western, northern, and central Europe. It will be seen, for example, that although Russia was not directly involved in the African slave trade, Blacks also came into the territories that would become Russia as a result of the ancient trading routes, the extension of the Moslem world into some of those territories, and through Russia's contacts with other parts of Europe and the Americas.

The Iberian World to the Seventeenth Century Moorish Iberia

In Islamic Iberia, Moslem rule began when Tariq ibn-Ziyad and his Moorish legions crossed over from North Africa, defeated the Gothic armies, and consolidated rule in the Iberian Peninsula in the early eighth century (711 to 716). These troops included Black Africans. Most were probably mercenaries and slaves, brought across Tunisia by the ruling Omayad dynasty. The slaves in Islamic Spain, however, as compared to those in the later Atlantic slave trade, were in a limited type of bondage, often allowing for emancipation. Especially after the launching of the first Christian

Crusades at the end of the eleventh century, concerted efforts to defeat Islam in Europe as well as the Holy Land were repeatedly mounted by European religious and political leaders. By 1250 Moorish rule was terminated in the Portuguese kingdom. By that time the caliphate was in a hopeless position and only the stronghold of Granada on the southern edge of the peninsula was left. This remnant of Moorish power would be completely broken in 1492.

How did Blacks fare in Moorish Iberia? By all accounts it was a mixed experience. Al-Hakam I (796–822) appointed some Blacks to positions as palace guard, and some as *mawla*, a military-religious prayer leader. In contrast, Abd-al-Rahman III (912–961) had thousands of Berber and Black slave soldiers, but limited them to labor battalions and did not allow them promotion. Al-Hakam II (961–975) used many slave troops of all types and had a Black honor guard. Yusef ibn-Tashufln, founder of the Berber Almoravid dynasty in Iberia, made a practice of exchanging Black African boys for White Christian boys with slave traders, in an effort at demoralizing the Christian armies he faced by throwing blue-eyed troops against them. An unintentional result was a wider dispersal of Blacks in Europe.

There were also many Black women slaves, used as domestics and concubines. Some mulatto offspring received favored treatment, and attained middle class and even aristocratic status. On the whole the Blacks were not limited to servile roles; but they were also not really influential as a group. It does appear that they continued to stand out as different from the majority. Some Arab accounts tend to distinguish them as a separate part of the population, referring to them by the term slaves *(abid)* or as "Blacks from the Sudan." There is less information available on Blacks in the Christian areas of the peninsula during the Moorish period. It is clear, however, that the new Christian kingdom of Portugal emerging upon the ouster of the Moslems had a labor shortage due to the resultant flight of Moslems to Granada, their remaining stronghold. This was one reason why Black workers were welcomed in Portugal. Some Black slaves were sold by Moorish traders in Portugal as early as 1258. The Christians would eventually refer to them as Black Moors to distinguish them from the rest. But they were still too expensive to be a good labor supply in the Christian realm until the Portuguese military victories in North Africa in the early fifteenth century gave them direct links with the trans-Saharan trade. Soon afterward they gained access to direct trade with West Africa by sea.

The Christian Atlantic World

In his recently published book, *Africa and Africans in the Making of the Atlantic World, 1400–1680,* John Thornton presents a definition of the Atlantic World which brings even broader perspective on how people, commerce, and ideas moved about than the one presented here thus far. He notes how the Atlantic World was linked to river routes penetrating into the interior in both Africa and the Americas. These formed a vital linkage to the ocean for societies and states which often lay hundreds of kilometers from the coast; for example, the Senegal, Gambia, Niger, and Congo rivers. Thus Africa can be viewed as having river zones of penetration similar to the access provided by the Mediterranean and North Sea for Europe. In the Americas the Amazon and Mississippi served a comparable role.

Thornton divides the expansion into two "wings." The first was the African, seeking mainland products such as slaves, gold, and pepper; the second sought land producing wild products or suitable for agriculture. This second would lead, in stages, to the discovery of the new continents. The main initial activity in the first type of expansion consisted of limited raiding for immediate profit. The second type of expansion, that first developed its patterns in the nearby Atlantic islands, quickly came to include colonization and a demand for labor-intensive products (initially coffee and cotton) which increased the attractiveness of slave labor.

Although there is still some controversy concerning when the first links became established between West Africa and the Americas, it is certain when sustained contacts began in the modern period. Arabic accounts note early accidental visits to West Africa; but all these travelers had to return home by overland routes because they did not yet know how to go North with the prevailing currents. Only in the fifteenth century did they learn the way back by sea, and this was on circuitous routes leading through the Canaries, Madeira, and the Azores. The distinctive feature of the Iberian contribution to exploration was the role of royal patronage. In the actual exploration, the English, French, Polish, and Italians also contributed ships and were initially furnishing the capital under a charter/license provided by the Portuguese or Spanish rulers. By 1504 there were 14 ships which were officially royal ships along with others renting trading rights, except for the gold trade.

The Canary Islands, the Azores, and Madeira were the islands which first helped whet an appetite for and then helped establish capital for ventures further West and South. The Canaries, the only ones inhabited when the Europeans came, were also an early region to raid for slaves (its inhabitants were a Berber people), and later for use of African slave labor. The Catalans, Portuguese, and Castilians were the leaders in this. By 1250 Castilian Spanish colonization had expanded agriculture and sheep herding in the Canaries to produce sugar, wines, and sheep and dairy products. This brought constant European commerce closer to Africa and provided a firmer launching base for expansion there. The uninhabited Cape Verde Islands were colonized in the 1460s, and Sao Tome in 1485. On Madeira the labor for clearing the land and raising wheat was obtained from Europe and from attacks on the Canaries. The large exports of wheat, some in the form of bread, went to Europe, Morocco, the Saharan coast, and West Africa. Wine was the big profit maker. The Canarians were employed slave labor especially in the sugar industry. There was thus a dress rehearsal for the New World economy, here with only part of the labor Black.

Since the Europeans brought nothing that Africa did not already produce, the commerce was controlled mainly by the Africans, who initially viewed the European contribution as only supplemental, not vital. Early European visitors described the West African city of Benin as follows:

> [It] was a stronghold twenty-five miles in circumference, protected by a wall and natural defenses, containing an elaborate royal palace and neatly laid out houses with verandas and balustrades, and divided by broad avenues and smaller intersecting streets. The power of the oba was apparent in his wealth, his divinity, his domination over commercial transactions, and his large and lavish court. In this prosperous society, the wealthier classes dressed and lived very well. Beef, mutton, chicken, and yams were staples, while the less well-to-do made do with yams, dried fish, beans and bananas. (July 1980: 4)

Africa imported European iron, in some instances because it was more easily obtainable and cheaper than theirs, but the European iron was not always better. This was even more true of cloth. Africans exported hides, copper, gold, gum, ivory, slaves, and pepper, but at times also imported some of these. The European trade was attractive to the Africans mainly for its variety, and its prestige value. This was similar to the European import of African slaves into Europe as curiosities in regions where there were already enough servants and serfs.

By 1650 Africans were the majority of new settlers in the new Atlantic World, including the Americas. By then in Africa part of the coastal trade from Sierra Leone to Cape Mount was dominated by Mulatto settlers who had ties, often family, with local African rulers. As early as the sixteenth century Blacks had worked alongside White sailors with no difference in pay, but were restricted to lower ranks. Some vessels had Black interpreters for dealing with African princes, merchants, and other necessary contact persons. Beginning as early as 1520 the state of Benin began to restrict the slave trade, finally cutting it off by around 1550. This seemingly reflected a rising need in Africa for labor in the cloth and pepper industries. Kongo cut off its export of slaves in the early seventeenth century. Its cloth exports gave it something to satisfy the need to exchange something for what it wished from abroad. Meanwhile the Gold Coast imported slaves from its neighbors, and from the Portuguese, sometimes paying in gold.

The Africans were at times successful in repulsing the Europeans. The Portuguese found eventually that it was more profitable to maintain diplomatic relations with the various African states, and send presents to rulers. They came to learn that there was an intricate commercial economy already established which they could buy into without force. Meanwhile, African Kings, for example Afonso I of Kongo, enforced customs rules along the coast by capturing European vessels engaged in illegal trade. Thus the Africans held the key to development of the Atlantic World on both sides of the Ocean, since on the one they long dictated the terms in European commerce, and on the other they were the bulk of the labor force, and at times the main fighting force for the Europeans in their struggle with native and rival European forces there.

The Impact of the Atlantic Expansion on Iberia

A few illustrations of how the role of Africans in the early developments in the Americas directly affected the Iberian expansion will be useful for our discussion. Among the 168 Spaniards in the expedition of Francisco Pizarro which seized the Inca emperor Atahuallpa at the town of Cajamarca in the northern Peruvian highlands in 1532 were at least three Blacks. Their profiles provide graphic evidence of the extent to which Blacks played an integral role in the exploitation of the so-called New World. Two were artisans. There was a Spanish practice of having the criers (i.e., public announcers) be Blacks or mulattoes. These often also served as executioners, auctioneers, and constables. The crier of the expedition that conquered Peru was Juan Garcia Pregonero, who doubled as a piper. He was a foot soldier at the action at Cajamarca, although it should be noted that the term soldier was not used of these adventurer/conqueror/ treasure seekers in such expeditions.

The second artisan, Juan Garcia Pregonero, who had the job of weighing much of the gold and silver for the party at Cajamarca, was a dark mulatto, born in Spain. Part of the illiterate minority in the expedition, he was still apparently considered lower class upon return to Spain. Records show, however, that he was apportioned shares of gold and silver in Peru which would make him a wealthy man back in Spain, although he was not given one of the larger shares. He functioned basically as an equal to the Spaniards on the expedition. He was later one of the founders of Spanish control of Cuzco in 1534 and lived there for a few months before returning to Spain in 1536 by way of Lima and the Ithmus. It appears that one reason he left Cuzco is that he could not fit into settled society in such a high position with his color. In less formal frontier society more was possible. As society took more formal shape it took on the hierarchical characteristics of the home country.

Another member of the expedition, Miguel Ruiz, was a mulatto horseman, born in Seville to a Black or mulatto mother. He was considered to be on a higher social standing than Juan Garcia Pregonero, as horsemen were ranked in the upper third among the conquerors. Ruiz received a larger share of gold and silver, although he had to share this with a notary who actually owned the horse. Ruiz later died in battle while riding south after Cajamarca with the forces of Hernando de Soto in 1533. There was also noted a mulatto captain of artillery in Pizarro's army at the battle of Salinas in 1538; but for some reason he was hanged sometime thereafter.

The Negroes of Peru (they could not be simply called Africans, since some were born in Spain, Portugal, and the Indies) had little choice but to become rather Spanish in culture, because they were too diverse in origins to maintain any group identity and had no other natural allies in Peru. They therefore tended to more or less fit into the Spanish scheme of things. After all, a sizable minority of them was from Spain. They did maintain such cultural traits as the dances. The Negroes in Peru were often willing partners of the Spaniards, playing a crucial role, and while subordinated, were not brutalized as in the plantation economies. Furthermore, for the first half-century of the conquest, the Indians tended to view the Blacks as "Whites," and even described them as "Black Whites," just as the "blackamoors" were linked to the Moors in Iberia. Later, when more Blacks arrived as slaves, the Indians in some regions considered Blacks to be inferior to them as a result of this status.

We can now return to the question of the impact on Spain and Portugal of the Atlantic World expansion in general. As mentioned earlier, by the early fifteenth century Blacks were purchased in North Africa from Moslems by Christians and sold in Spain. However, those obtained in Cadiz, for example, were very expensive. By the sixteenth century they could also be purchased more cheaply from the Portuguese who brought them to Valencia, Barcelona, and Seville. Treaty agreements of the time allowed Spain to go only as far as the Canary Islands along the African coast. As many as 100,000 Black slaves may have been imported into Portugal and its Madeira Islands from the region of the rivers and Gulf of Guinea (the Portuguese had first raided coastal Berbers for slaves). The new slave population was around 10 per cent; they worked in agriculture and fishing. Records also show free Blacks living in Loule and Lagos in the southern edge of Portugal. They owned houses, worked as day laborers, midwives, bakers, and servants. Eventually there were slaves in Portugal owned by the king, the nobility, the Church, artisans, and working people. Most were domestic servants, laborers (including those on ships and river craft), and petty tradesmen. Free Blacks, especially women, could become innkeepers.

One possible explanation for the apparent greater acceptance of Blacks in Portugal than in other parts of Europe, which was generally short of labor in the wake of the Bubonic plague of the preceding century, is that Iberia had already experienced centuries of a Black presence, and at an exceptionally high level during the Moorish rule. In reflecting upon the significance of all of this for Europe proper, it is important to remember that during the sixteenth and seventeenth centuries the German Hapsburg family ruled Spain and its possessions as part of its Holy Roman Empire. Spain also held Portugal between 1580 and 1640. Thus, as our look at the African and American dimensions of the empire has shown, developments in the Iberian World could have very wide-ranging influence.

This could even be seen as far as Asia. But it was especially true in other parts of Europe. With respect to the Black Diaspora, an example of this connection can be seen in the southern part of the Netherlands, where Black slaves and servants were also conspicuous in Antwerp. There in 1550 a street was named "Moriaanstraat" (Moor Street). Later under the name "Kleine Moriaanstraat" (Little Moor Street), it came to feature a series of houses bearing names such as "Coninck van de Mooren" (King of the Moors), "Coninginne van de Mooren" (Queen of the Moors), "Moriaens hooft (Moor's Head), "Knit van den Moriaen" (Child of the Moors), "Slave van den Moriaen" (Slave of the Moors), and "slavinne van den Moriaen" (Woman Slave of the Moors). This can best be attributed to Antwerp's prominent role in world trade at the time. One house on "Moriaanstraat" was occupied for a time by representatives of the Hanseatic League, and some merchant families there had Moors' heads in their coats of arms.

But it was in Portugal that the Black population was most noticeable. Antwerp's Black population was the second largest in Europe after Lisbon's. In Portugal "Blacks" were defined as *preto* or *negro*. This applied to all Negroid people or people of mixed Negroid and Caucasoid descent, with a few exceptions. "Negro" was often used as an offensive term. By 1550 Blacks had replaced Moors as the main ethnic group among a slave population comprising about 10 per cent of the population of Lisbon and other towns. Between 1450 and 1505 about 140,000 slaves were imported into Europe from Africa. Of the population of approximately 100,000 of Lisbon in 1551, 10,000 were slaves; in 1573 there were around 70,000 in the kingdom as a whole which had a population of 1.2 million. Lisbon was described by a French traveler of the period as a "city of Africa."

White Christian slaves existed in Europe until the sixteenth century. There were eight categories of slaves in Spain by the end of the fifteenth century; Jewish, Moorish, one called Turkish (which was really Egyptian), Syrian, Lebanese, White Christian (Sardinians, Greeks, Russians, Spaniards), Guanche (Canary Islanders), and Sub-Saharan African. In the fifteenth century the main term for slave was *maura* (Moor); Black slaves were first called *mouros negros* (blackamoors). White Moorish slaves still came in the sixteenth and seventeenth centuries as a result of the continuous conflict in the Mediterranean between Spain and the Turks and their allies the Barbary Pirates, which produced prisoners of war. But the Blacks eventually proved to be the easiest attainable and easiest to justify. This rested first on Papal Bulls of Nicholas V (1454) and Calixtus III (1456), which in effect said enslavement of pagans in general was beneficial because they could be Christianized. Prince Henry also had expressed this. The Blacks fit better than the Moors and Moriscos (the term for supposedly Christianized Moors) who remained more suspect because of their ambivalence concerning Christianity.

A Spanish city in which the Black population was especially prominent, a counterpart of Lisbon, Portugal, was Seville. With the establishment of the slave trade to the Americas in the sixteenth century, Seville became second only to Lisbon as a conduit through Europe. By the end of the sixteenth century there were around 100,000 slaves in Spain, half of these in Andalusia (mainly Seville). Some observers then said that Seville had almost as many Negro and Moorish slaves as free citizens. Much earlier, at the end of the fourteenth century, the Church had established the Hospital of Our Lady of the Angels in the parish of San Bernardo to serve the Negro population. The custom of city officials in Seville appointing a Black as *mayoral* (steward) over the rest, with authority to defend them against their masters, before the courts, and settle disputes, was just one of the privileges aimed at allowing a degree of collective freedom. Dance and feast celebrations were also permitted. There was also one type of institution formed by Blacks, with official sanction, in Barcelona, Valencia, and Seville in the mid-fifteenth century. This was the religious brotherhoods (*cofradias*). They served social and recreational functions, and also procured burial grounds. Blacks and mulattoes were denied access to normal ones in Spain and Portugal.

As in Portugal, Blacks in Spain served as stevedores, factory workers, farm laborers, footmen, coachmen, and butlers. Male and female domestics apparently lived well compared to other lower-class people. Slaves could work in all the crafts, for example, sword making, but could not join the guilds. There were limitations on assembly by slaves and Moriscos and on the bearing of arms apart from the masters. Normally free Blacks were engaged in the same types of work as slaves. There were some prominent Blacks in Spain. Most were mulattoes. A few examples are Cristobol de Meneses, a Dominican priest; the painters Juan de Pareja and Sebastian Gomez; and Leonardo Ortiz, a lawyer.

Among the few notable dark-skinned Blacks who achieved high status was Juan Valladolid, appointed by Ferdinand and Isabella chief and judge over the Black population in the town and archdiocese of Seville. Another was Juan Latino, a slave from Africa who through his master's benevolence was able to become educated, earning degrees at the University of Granada. But he then experienced racial prejudice, as his name was placed last on the graduation list for no reason; and he had to fight racism in his academic career, never receiving an official appointment although teaching at the University. There were, however, also some other signs of respect for Blacks during these centuries. In 1306 an Ethiopian delegation came to Europe to seek an alliance with the "King of the Spains" against the Moslems. Thus it was not only the Europeans who sought a "Prester John." King Anfos IV of Aragon considered arranging a double marriage with the Negus of Ethiopia in 1428. And the Portuguese crown sent Pedro de Corvilhao to Ethiopia in 1487 on a similar mission.

In considering further the impact of expansion on Iberian society, it is also important to note the role of returnees from America. Slaves now returned with wealthier masters, who did better in Spanish society. The returnees to Portugal during the period from the sixteenth to the eighteenth centuries included free mulatto students, gentlemen, free and slave household servants, and sailors from Brazil and Africa. Those returning to Spain included successful colonists bringing back slaves and mixed race children; there were also free mulattoes who came as students, clerics, and sailors.

Images of Blacks in Europe

Images of Blacks were present in Europe long before there was a significant physical presence. Folklore and religious thought of the Middle Ages provide a fascinating array of vivid illustrations of this. They resulted not only from the fact that Europe was contiguous to North Africa and contained a strong Moorish influence, but also because of the general confrontation unfolding between Europe and the wider world. The visual arts, epics, and legends from the period provide a means of recapturing some of this imagery. By the fourteenth century European painters were frequently portraying Black Africans, based in part on the renewed contacts between the two continents and in part on popular religious and classical secular themes. There were even earlier forms of iconography based more on the imagination than on real life.

Images from the World of the Mind

Adoration of the Magi. The Adoration of the Magi was the single most popular religious theme featuring Blacks in European art; it was featured in thousands of works. As early as the late fourteenth and fifteenth centuries in Italy and Germany this iconography developed to include Asians and Blacks among the wise kings and their retinue. The Black king was usually depicted as the youngest, presumably symbolizing Africa as the continent just beginning to participate in world affairs. The Black king was also often strikingly handsome. Dutch artists executed some of the most distinctive of these. The practice also extended into Eastern Europe.

Baptism of the Ethiopian eunuch. Another biblical theme was that surrounding the baptism of the Ethiopian eunuch in a passage of the Book of Acts. This theme can best be approached by reference first to a passage in the Old Testament (Jeremiah 13: 22–25):

> Can the Nubian change his skin, or the leopard its spots?
> And you? Can you do good, you who are schooled in evil?
> Therefore I will scatter you like chaff driven by the desert wind.
> This is your lot, the portion of the rebel, measured out by me,
> says the Lord,

because you have forsaken me and trusted in false gods.

This passage, in which a Nubian's (or more popularly translated as Ethiopian's) skin color is mentioned in a discussion of sin and punishment, came down in the popular lore of Western civilization as a stigma against black skin color. It may well be, as Frank Snowden (1983: 7) surmised in his study of the ancient view of Blacks, that the reference here was simply to color as a neutral, immutable trait, and not to racial or moral qualities. He further points out that Origen, St. Augustine, and other Patristic Church Fathers articulated an interpretation of scripture using Ethiopia as a symbol of the mission to spread the faith. This culminated with Theodoret, who explained the baptism of the Ethiopian eunuch by Philip the Deacon in the Book of Acts as affirmation that it was, indeed, possible for the Ethiopian to "change his skin," at least figuratively, through Christianity.

However, in its travel through the Greek and Roman World and into early modern Europe, the inescapable negative implications of this proverb also persisted. After all, the celebrated "cleansing" also reiterates the "evil stain." It became a popular theme in Christian iconography from the third century forward and became an extremely popular one in European art, especially for the fifteenth to the seventeenth centuries (Davis 1984: 37). Many artists executed more than one version. The "Ethiopian" varied in his physical features; at times definitely Negroid, at others Cushitic or somewhat Asiatic. Like the Adoration theme, that concerning Baptism symbolized inclusion of Blacks in the civilized and Christianized world. Baptism related to the "Ethiopian," which in Early Modern Europe was used to describe Negroes in general as well as Ethiopians, actually suggested two different biblical injunctions which were in some respects contradictory. The one was the philanthropic evangelical charge, the other the Old Testament negative use of an Ethiopian's color in an analogy concerning salvation. It is difficult to say which of these meanings these paintings conveyed to the public. Another occasionally illustrated biblical event with a Black is the rescue of the prophet Jeremiah from a dungeon by the Ethiopian eunuch Ebed Melech.

The Hamitic legend. A related and even older religious theme bearing a negative connotation for Blacks was that concerning the Hamitic legend. Based on varying interpretations of a chapter of the Old Testament book of Genesis in which Noah supposedly condemned the descendants of one of his sons to perpetual servitude, this theme enjoyed intermittent popularity over the centuries in later Moslem and Christian traditions as well as the

Judaic. In European art it was conventional to depict Ham's descendants as Negroid.

Since slavery in modern European history came to mean almost exclusively enslavement of Black Africans, the Hamitic legend played an especially important role in the shaping of perceptions of Blacks. The convergence of this legend (as well as that on the Ethiopian baptism) with the historic advent of the African slave trade represents just the type of historical fusion that can help explain the depth of modern racism's roots; that is, myth seemingly confirmed by experience. This is true notwithstanding the inconsistency of the Hamitic legend. It is illogical because the relevant biblical text states that Noah placed a curse on the descendants of only one of Ham's sons, Canaan. This became distorted and confused in later lore and literature (Davis 1984: 43). Illustrations done for Bibles and paintings on this theme usually focused on Noah and his sons and therefore only hinted at a different sort of progeny for Ham by giving him curlier hair and darker complexion than his brothers.

The Queen of Sheba. A more famous story is the biblical visit of the Queen of Sheba to King Solomon. It was depicted in Europe in various art forms, including paintings, tapestry, and sculpture. In one piece attributed to the school of Hieronymus Bosch, the Queen is White, but her attending maid is Black. The *Hours of Catherine of Cleves,* a work executed in Utrecht in 1440, also shows the Queen of Sheba as White, but accompanied by a Black servant woman. In a painting by Erasmus Quellinus, *The Queen of Sheba Offering Gold and Precious Stones to King Solomon,* the Queen is Black, as also in later versions found in Dutch art. In the Christian and Islamic traditions, the Queen has usually symbolized ministry to those outside the faith. In the Judaic tradition she has also been viewed in some instances as a demonic, occult figure.

The Black saints. Black saints were proclaimed in parts of medieval Europe. The statue of St. Maurice in the chapel of St. Kilian at Magdeburg and the seventeenth-century bust and older relics of St. Gregory the Moor at the church of St. Gereon in Cologne testify to the strength of these notions. These legendary figures, both allegedly Roman martyrs to the Christian cause centuries earlier, were of ambiguous origins until the thirteenth century, but thereafter they were frequently featured as Black. The 15 October celebration called *Das Mohrenfest* is said to be based upon the commemoration of the battle to the death of Gregory and his 318 Moorish companions in the third century. In this celebration, which was depicted in later German paintings, people dress in masks or costumes meant to be suggestive of Africa.

This special recognition aimed not only to acknowledge the contribution of African martyrs to the Christian cause, but also to affirm the relevance of Christianity to all peoples and races. Hence the Holy Roman Emperors, beginning with Charles IV's ascension in 1346, adopted Blacks into the iconography of their realm, including the depiction of St. Maurice as a Black and the touting of Gregory the Moor as the major protector of the city of Cologne (Devisse and Mollat 1979: 22–58). Becoming part of the Empire after Philip the Good acquired Holland and Zeeland in 1428 Brabant and Limburg in 1429, and the bishopric of Utrecht in 1455, the Low Countries too witnessed these symbols along with popularization of depiction of one of the Magi as Black. Then Africans first appeared in Flemish and Dutch paintings in the fifteenth century.

Other biblical motifs. Illustrations for other biblical stories which did not specifically mention Blacks also included some Black figures. As has been shown earlier, they also appeared in illustrations in bibles and prayer books themselves. One theme popular throughout Europe was the scene with Bathsheba in her bath, often featuring a Black servant girl. Rubens and Cornelisz van Haarlem are among artists in the Low Countries who depicted this theme.

Josephus's *History of the Jews* featured some distinctively Black figures. The story of Moses and the Egyptians is the prime example. On this same theme, Moses's marriage to an Ethiopian woman, described in the Book of Numbers, inspired one of the most powerful paintings involving Blacks in all of European art: Jordaens's sixteenth-century *Moses en Zippora.* The crucifixion of Christ depicted by C. Engebrechtsen in the sixteenth century features a prominent Black spectator.

Secular imagery. There were also secular allegorical pieces, joining mythology and history. Examples can be seen in the work of artists such as Hendrik Goltzius in the sixteenth century and Abraham Hondius in the seventeenth, whose works featuring Black figures include themes about the cosmos. A. Quellenius's piece on the gable of the seventeenth-century Amsterdam City Hall, symbolizing the wealth of the world being brought to Holland, illustrates how the depictions of Blacks contributed to the definition of the roles of national, ethnic, and religious groups. The Europeans, riding the wave of their world conquests, were of course pre-eminent in such works.

Images from the World of Experience

The Moor in heraldry. The origin of the widespread European adoption of the Moor's head as a symbol for family and town coats of arms is highly obscure. It is not surprising to encounter it in such places as fifteenth-century arms of the islands of Sardinia and Corsica when we consider that they sit in the middle of the Mediterranean, belonging to the African and Moslem world as well as the European, and washed by centuries of foreign conquest from all directions. Much harder to explain is the apparent greater popularity of this symbol in northern Europe than in Spain or Italy. The theme of the Moor first appeared in Dutch heraldry as early as the thirteenth century. By the time heraldry reached the peak of its development in the fourteenth and fifteenth centuries, this symbol could be found in the far reaches of northern and eastern Europe as well as the Mediterranean region.

Many prominent families in Nuremberg in the late fifteenth century used the Moors' head emblem. In the sixteenth century it formed the center of the family crest of the painter Albrecht Durer. Later it could be found as far north as the small community of Marken in North Holland. The Brotherhood of the Black Heads based in Riga had the image of St. Maurice on many of its artifacts. The city's crest also included Moors' heads. Thus this emblem was spread to the most distant Baltic ports. The most frequent line of explanation views this symbol as a form of trophy, celebrating the victory of Christendom over the Moslems in various battles. However, it appears to have been more popular in Germany than in France, which played a larger role in the Crusades (Devisse and Mollat 1979: 7–58).

Epics, legends, and literature. Other imagery concerning Blacks drawn more from the historical experience than from imagination was expressed in epics, legends, and literature. In light of the early presence of imagery concerning Blacks in folklore and art, it is not surprising that similar elements also appeared in literature from its very beginnings. As in the folklore and art, it is once again through the pervasive theme of the Moor that Blacks entered the literature. The first well-known work is of course the *Song of Roland (Chanson de Roland)*. This epic tale, based on events in the eighth century, and first written down some three centuries later, perpetuated two lasting, contrasting stereotypes of the Moors, who were often thought of as Black, although only a minority of their total number were. On the one hand the tale depicted them as fierce and cruel. At the same time, when one confronted by a brave Frenchman cries, "Let's get out of here!" the poem continues:

> And at that work a hundred thousand run.
> No matter who may call, they won't come back.
> Thus the Saracens, as they are also called, are cowardly as well.

Another famous work from the period is Wolfram von Eschenbach's *Parzifal*, drawn from the legend of King Arthur and his court, which evolved for centuries in England, France, Germany, and the Netherlands. A distinctive innovation of Wolfram's adaptation of this part of the legend, which was based most directly on an unfinished novel by Chretien de Troyes, was his expansion of the Grail society to include non-Whites, by introduction of Africans as central characters and incorporation of the themes of interracial love and marriage. The images of the Blacks in the story are at times positive and at others negative, sometimes noble, at others ridiculous. Also, foreshadowing a familiar theme of the present day, the males have uncontrollable sexual appetites. In the story Parzifal accidentally meets his half-brother, Feirefiz, whose speckled-black-and-white skin color is the result of the parentage of their father Gahmuret and a Moorish princess prior to his return to Europe where he married Parzifal's mother, a Christian queen.

This infusion of the Africans into this venerable myth was surely an allusion to recent real life experiences of European knights during the Crusades. It was also probably more than coincidence that it was precisely in Wolfram's thirteenth-century Germany that the saints Gregory and Maurice were first portrayed as Black. In both instances historical developments were clearly making an impact on the choice of imagery.

Further evidence of an historical progression of what we might call Black awareness is apparent in the fourteenth century Dutch version of the Parzifal story, which came to be titled *Morien* because of its Black hero. In the Dutch version, which appears to have been based on an earlier French one different from the one Wolfram used, Feirefiz was rather than speckled. In the first encounter between the two brothers he is described as follows:

> He was black, . . . his head, his body, and his hands were all black, saving only his teeth. His shield and armour were even those of a Moor, and black as a raven. . . . Had they not heard him call upon God no man had dared face him, deeming that he was the devil or one of his fellows out of hell. . . . (Nutt 1970: 29)

Here it can be seen that the religious distinctions are very important. However, even more notable is the perception of the black skin color as sinister. It should also be noted that not only had Feirefiz become totally Black by the fourteenth century, he had also become Christian. This paralleled the growing European familiarity with actual African peoples, and the European determination to Christianize all of Europe as well as the rest of the world. Wolfram's Feirefiz also fathered the legendary Prester John through a European woman. Prester John was the mythical Christian African ruler whom the Europeans had dreamed of and sought as an ally against Islam since the time of the Crusades. Another possible explanation of why Wolfram's Feirefiz is half-White is that to the European mind noble bearing and civilized behavior were more palatable if European ancestry could be seen to account for it.

The Grail Society of the Arthurian legend, accessible only to those disposed to goodness, justice, and human understanding, was symbolic of much that has continued to characterize the ideals of Western Civilization. These ideals have likewise often stood in tension with historical reality, just as those of the Grail did with King Arthur's Camelot. The attitude toward Blacks suggested by the imagery considered here reflects a similar ambivalence between good and evil. Examples of its validity can be seen in the fact that among Satan's titles in literature and folklore were "black knight," "black man," "big Negro," "black Jehovah," and "black Ethiopian." The notion of the black knight as an irreconcilable enemy, harking back to Charlemagne's campaigns against Moors, became especially popular. The depiction of Blacks as tormentors and sexual symbols was also popular.

Yet, such figures as Ruprecht and Black Pete (*Zwarte Piet*), the sometimes benevolent bogeymen who accompany the Saint Nicholas figure in the Christmas celebrations in Germany and the Netherlands show that the ambivalence persists. *Zwarte Piet* and *Sinterklaasi* are an example of the joining of religion and folklore. They also demonstrate how this ambivalent attitude of Whites toward Blacks in Western culture has continued to be the main posture on down to the present. As with Wolfram's Black characters, racial harmony in most places and times in Western Civilization ever since have frequently involved just a marriage of convenience, often very temporary.

The Black Presence and Attitudes Toward Blacks in Europe

As indicated earlier, images of Blacks were present in Europe long before there was a significant physical presence. These were expressed in the folklore and religious thought from the early Middle Ages. Many of these same themes persisted to the present time, evolving into various forms which have been captured in the visual arts. At the same time, as we move into the seventeenth century and beyond, we find a growing physical presence as well as that in the European imagination. This resulted from the same pattern of developments discussed earlier concerning the entry of thousands of Blacks into Spain and Portugal from their maritime empire in the earlier centuries.

Those coming to Europe were servants (both slave and free), sailors, various types of laborers, mulatto students from the colonies, and other colored family members of Europeans. By the seventeenth century they also came to play similar roles, in smaller numbers, in the Netherlands, England, France, Germany, and Scandinavia. In the modern period the largest number came to England, where some estimates count as high as 30,000 by the end of the eighteenth century. There were several thousand in France by that time, a few thousand in the Netherlands, and perhaps a few hundred scattered through Germany and Scandinavia. In the twentieth century, of course, the numbers have reached the hundreds of thousands in the major countries mentioned.

Returning again to the outline of the African Diaspora, consider the proximity of Africa to Europe. Recall once more the historical background of the presence of Blacks in Europe, both in European thought and the actual physical presence; that is, the commercial and other linkages between Europe and Africa going back to ancient times. Remember that, contrary to what is generally thought, the Black presence in Europe long predated that in the Americas which has grown so much larger, and which has monopolized attention in the African Diaspora. In view of all this, why is it that the African presence in Europe is not much greater? Viewing this in historical perspective, I would submit that it is because after a certain point the European societies deliberately limited entry of Africans into Europe, although they found it expedient to employ a massive labor force of Africans in the Americas. Nevertheless, the genesis of this relatively small Black presence in Europe proper is an interesting story and one which may provide useful insight for understanding the historical evolution of racial attitudes related to color. A sampling of this story for northern, central, and eastern Europe can be gained from an outline of its developments in the Netherlands and Russia.

Blacks in the Dutch World

The Dutch entry into the African slave trade, beginning in the seventeenth century and eventually accounting for the removal of around half-a-million Africans to the Americas, made the single greatest impact on the subsequent image of Blacks in Dutch culture. The image of Blacks as a servile race eventually eclipsed all the others earlier in Dutch society. This became all the more reinforced as the practice of slavery in the Dutch colonies led to an actual presence of hundreds of Black servants and slaves in the Netherlands by the mid-eighteenth century. They served as house servants, coachmen, and in various roles as laborers. While the earlier images were based on concepts, the new derived from more direct experience. Since the focus of the present essay is Europe, attention will center here on Blacks in the European part of the Dutch World, although they were clearly more numerous in the empire abroad.

So little is known about free Blacks in the Netherlands before the twentieth century who were not servants that there is a general false impression that there were none. There was, in fact, a significant though small number present for centuries. They engaged in various occupations, but especially in those related to the maritime industry, and from the eighteenth century in the military as well. The absence of record-keeping practices in the maritime service which would offer detailed descriptions of sailors employed makes a count impossible. However, the presence of Black seamen in the service of the Dutch is recorded in works of art and in other historical materials.

A Black presence in Dutch ports such as Amsterdam and Rotterdam was also assured by visits of British, French, and American vessels with Black seamen. It is surprising that there is no record of small communities of Black cities, such as developed, for example, in some British ports. Perhaps one reason there is so little awareness of a Black population, even of descendants of servants, is that there was intermarriage with the rest of the population at times. When subsequent generations were light-complexioned they might never be referred to again as "Negro." In general the designation as "Black" was reserved for those of dark color, rather than the broader definition based on Black African ancestry.

There were a few fairly prominent Black figures in Dutch history who at least briefly caught the public eye. The earliest was the former slave Jacobus Capitein, who mastered several European languages and became a predicate after completing theological training at the University of Leiden in 1742. He became famous as the author of a treatise which defended slavery as an avenue to redemption for the Africans. This saw four printings and his portrait, usually accompanied by didactic poetry, circulated widely advertising that Blacks could be transformed by Christianity and Western Civilization. Prior to going off to what proved a disastrous mission in his homeland on the Gold Coast, he preached in Holland to audiences who flocked to see this novelty.

Another interesting figure who passed through the Netherlands in the eighteenth century was Anthony William Amo, who gained fame in Germany. Born on the Gold Coast around 1700, he also arrived in Holland as a boy. The West India Company brought him to Amsterdam when he was about ten years old and presented him to the Duke of Wolfenbuttel. He was baptized in Wolfenbuttel in 1707 and given the names Anton and Wilhelm in honor of the reigning duke and his son. A grant from the Duke allowed him to be educated to a point where he was able to enter the universities at Halle in 1727 and Wittenberg in 1730, where he became skilled in Latin, Greek, Hebrew, French, German, and Dutch and concentrated on Philosophy. In 1729 he held a public disputation on the subject *De iure Maurorum in Europa* (*Concerning the Law of the Moors in Europe*).

In 1730 he gained the degree of Master of Arts in Philosophy at Halle. In 1734 he was awarded the doctorate degree from the University of Wittenberg with a dissertation on *De humanae mentis apatheia* (*On Apathy in the Human Mind*). In his philosophical work he was a rationalist, and devoted special attention to mathematical and medical knowledge in the context of Enlightenment thought. He became a lecturer at the University of Halle and later at the University of Jena. By some accounts, the Court at Berlin awarded him the title of Counsellor of State. However, due to his declining fortunes in Europe, possibly related to loss of favor from his patron and affiliation with intellectual circles also out of favor, he returned to obscurity in the Gold Coast around the 1750s.

One more eighteenth-century Black personality who enjoyed fleeting fame among the Dutch public was Granman Quassie, who lived in Suriname most of his life, but twice visited the Netherlands. Whether born on the coast of Guinea and transported to Suriname as a child, as one version on his origins goes, or actually born in Suriname, he first gained status as an intermediary between the Dutch and the Maroons in Suriname. The Saramaka tribe called him Kwasimukamba. In 1730 Jan van Sandick, a member of the Policy Council at Paramaribo awarded him a gold breastplate with the inscription "Quassie, faithful to the Whites." Governor Mauricius bought him in 1744 and used him both as a scout and emissary to the Maroons. The governor also had him teach his own youngest son the Sranan, Carib, and Arawak languages.

In 1755 Quassie was given his freedom as a reward for his military services in particular. He also became a renowned herbalist and healer, the discoverer of a popular bitter stock which controlled fever, and which was therefore later name Quassi-bitter by Linnaeus in his honor. In Suriname some Europeans, as well as Blacks and Indians, believed that he had miraculous powers. In fact when accompanying Dutch forces into battle against the

Maroons, he would sell charms promising invincibility to the Black troops of the Free Corps and Black Rangers placed under his command for the occasion. In 1776 he was received at court in the Hague by William V. and awarded a medal for his service to the Dutch authorities in Suriname. Other gifts included a goldlaced coat and hat with white feather, a large gold medal, and a gold-headed cane and silver gilt hanger. It was in this costume that he was captured in the John Stedman portrait that served as the basis for the famous engraving of him in his eighties by William Black, later published in Stedman's (1796) book on Suriname.

By the nineteenth century Blacks from her colonies also began to appear in the Netherlands for professional training. One additional specific case from the nineteenth century is that of Aquasi Boachi, son of the Ashanti king, Kwaku Dua. He came to the Netherlands in 1837 for training as a mining engineer in Delft. Kwame Poku, a cousin, also came. The two boys were given a typical middle-class education, including courses in French, German, history, geography, science, and religion. They moved in the highest social circles, including that of the royalty. In 1850 Boachi decided not to return to Africa. Instead he gained a post as a miner in the government service in Dutch East India and spent the rest of his career there.

It is clear, then, that the Dutch public did have some, albeit rare, alternative images of Blacks in contrast to those of the traditional role of slave and servant. The role of Blacks in the Dutch military also showed further variety. Materials related to Africans recruited by the Dutch for the colonial armies provide an interesting glimpse at some of the popular reaction to these troops in Holland. In the course of the nineteenth century, beginning in the 1830s, approximately 4,000 African soldiers were taken by the Dutch from West Africa directly to service in Java and Sumatra. However, after their tours of duty were completed those who elected to return to Africa usually came through Holland, laying over briefly until they could gain passage on a boat destined for the Gold Coast. They usually stayed in Harderwijk, the main training center in Holland for European recruits for the colonial armies. A few of the African soldiers achieved distinction in their military careers. The most famous was Jan Kooi, who earned the *Militaire Willems Ordre* (the highest decoration category) for valorous action in 1878 in the Atyeh War.

After emancipation the number of Blacks in the higher circles in the colonies increased. The tremendous economic boom brought by the introduction of oil refineries in Curaçao and other islands in the 1920s made the trip to Holland more affordable for Antilleans. However, it was only after World War II that Antilleans systematically replaced Dutchmen in the highest posts, those necessitating formal advanced education. Such students were the single largest category of Blacks going to the Netherlands in the late nineteenth and early twentieth centuries from the Dutch American colonies. Others came in connection with the firms they worked for. The students often remained in the Netherlands after their studies, marrying lighter-complexioned mates and becoming doctors, lawyers, or teachers. For some their assimilation of the European culture and values was so complete that they thought of Holland as true home, a virtual promised land. However, many others going there felt like a people in diaspora, longing for their native American or Indonesian shores, not the African clime of their ancestors. The colored elite often found better treatment from Europeans in the Netherlands than at home. The character of their experience in Europe appeared to be based mainly on their economic and social status, not their race per se.

In the twentieth century the subject peoples would pass out of the control of the European powers into their own, rather than simply falling to other European domination as before. By mid-century Dutch East India would take this path; a quarter of a century later Suriname would follow; and the Netherlands Antilles, amid discussions of independence, has become more a part of the kingdom of the Netherlands. The empire is, therefore, all but over. However, it left a permanent mark on the makeup of Dutch society. In a way the popular mood might be symbolized by the world's fairs held throughout the Western world in the late nineteenth century, with Amsterdam hosting one in 1883. The representatives of the Suriname population (including eleven Blacks) transported with great effort for the fair could be placed on display in their "proper" place along with all the other exhibits celebrating the achievements of Western industry and progress. The onlooking crowds did not yet realize that these dark guests were part of Dutch society. This would not become fully manifest until most of the other vestiges of empire were gone, but representatives of its various peoples remained.

For present purposes the most important change which the ending of the Dutch empire brought was a massive shift in the distribution of the Black population, especially that from the colonies to the "mother country." The most dramatic shift, of course, was that which came after 1970, with the more than 225,000 emigrants from Suriname and the Netherlands Antilles moving to the Netherlands. The shift on a much more modest scale that had begun in the late nineteenth century had produced a population of several thousand new arrivals by the mid-twentieth century. This new level of frequent contacts in a new setting has had a profound mutual impact on perceptions and relations between Blacks and Whites in Dutch society. In the historical evolution of the perception of Blacks by Europeans this was even more important than the transition from the period when most knowledge about Blacks shaping Dutch perceptions was vicarious to when contacts first increased, mainly abroad. Now there was even greater pressure on the Dutch to think of Blacks as equals.

It is not surprising that with the heavy migration of the 1970s racial discrimination became pronounced and persistent within the Netherlands, as the declining economy, rising unemployment, and increased strain on limited space and resources fostered in the minorities a growing demand for employment, education, health, welfare, and social services, and in the majority increasing prejudice and discrimination. While the evidence belies a popular perception that the minority presence is responsible for the unemployment, housing shortage, deficiencies in education, and other problems such as rising crime rates, the belief persists that the minorities are being given preferential treatment detrimental to the rest of society. Thus for the Dutch the same process of modernization which created empire with its wealth has in its further course ended the empire and attenuated both the physical and social boundaries which had separated its component parts, leaving the Dutch to grapple with a dilemma they earlier thought existed only in other societies.

Blacks in Russia and Eastern Europe

The pattern of the Diaspora of African peoples and of ideas about them in eastern Europe and Russia resembled those in Spain, Portugal, and northern and central Europe. In Russia too there was imagery related to Africans and Africa in religious themes, folklore, art, and literature, especially the stereotypes. Much of it in fact was borrowed directly from the West. For example, the Russian painter Karl Briulov in the nineteenth century portrayed the biblical theme concerning Bathsheba at her bath while working for a while in Italy, just as many of his Spanish, German, and Dutch counterparts had earlier.

The major difference between the African Diaspora in eastern Europe and Russia and that in the West stemmed from the fact that Russia had fewer direct contacts with Black Africa. Especially significant is that She was not involved in the African slave trade and its consequent feeding of African population into those European countries which were. There was the one brief attempt at establishing a colony at Djibouti in 1889, and some attempt to unite the Russian and Ethiopian churches, both of which are Eastern Orthodox. Since there was such limited direct contact, there was far less awareness of Africa and Africans in Russia than in the West and the actual Black population numbered only in the thousands over the centuries. Nevertheless, this dimension of the African Diaspora contains fascinating episodes which may be instructive when added to the rest of the picture.

The native Negro population in tsarist Russia was comprised of scattered small settlements in the Caucasus mountains near the Black Sea. The existence of these African descendants went unnoticed even by the Russian public until the first decade of the twentieth century. During the period articles appeared in some Russian newspapers concerning a group of about 500 Negroes found living in villages in a part of Georgia called Abkhazia. Only within the past two decades have Russian scholars begun devoting further attention to the origin of these people. The current consensus is that they were mainly descendants of African slaves of Turkish or Georgian lords of the eighteenth century. However, English (1959) speculates that these Abkhazians might actually trace their roots far back to the Black Colchians described by the ancient Greek historian Herodotus as living in this region in the fifth century B.C.

There seems little doubt that African Negroes have been present in the general area since ancient times. The ancient Greeks, the Roman Empire, the Arabs, Genoese, and Turks all had colonies on the Black Sea coast where slave trading was common. It is also known that many Negroes, both slaves and freemen, came to Constantinople in the sixth and seventh centuries. Furthermore, there were Blacks in Iraq in the ninth century; a seventeenth-century Arab traveler, E. Chlebi, observed Blacks in the Crimea; and today there are still small settlements of African Negro descendants in Yugoslavia and Iran (Lopashich 1958). Future Russian Middle-Eastern anthropological and ethnographic studies should help clarify the origins of all these groups. In any case, it can be seen that Negroes have for centuries been part of the population of the area that came to be southern Russia.

Beginning at least as early as the seventeenth century, three other categories of Negroes began arriving in Russia. The first consisted of servants and slaves; the second was ships' crews; and the third was sundry visitors. The Russian nobility began to participate in the general European fashion of maintaining a few Black house servants for decoration. At first they were acquired through such ports as Constantinople and Amsterdam. Some came as slaves, some as freemen. Since chattel slavery was passing out of usage at the time, at least in the Russian parts of the empire, those brought as slaves simply became servants.

The first Negro to attain high recognition in Russia was Abram Hannibal, the African slave who became a favorite of Tsar Peter the Great and was the maternal great-grandfather of the nineteenth-century poet Alexander Pushkin, the most revered figure in all of Russian culture. Brought to Russia at the beginning of the eighteenth century in a group of young Negro prospective servants, Hannibal, under the tsar's sponsorship, went on to attain a high level of education and eventually to advance to the rank of general in the army engineers. One of his sons, Ivan, also had an illustrious military career rivaling his father's and is considered the founder of the city of Kherson on the Dnieper River. Two other sons, Peter and Osip, also had respectable careers in the military and civil service. The Hannibals married into the Russian nobility and became completely assimilated into Russian high society (Blakely 1979). Although this family's experience is exceptional and not representative of what Negroes could aspire to in Russia, the Hannibal chronicle does show a high degree of freedom of movement for Negroes within Russian society, which contrasts sharply with contemporary Negro experience in the Americas.

From the eighteenth century to the end of Imperial Russia the tsars kept a permanent staff of Black servants at court, numbering about twenty. When one left or died, another would be obtained. Some came from Africa, but others came from the Americas. The U.S. Minister to Russia in 1894, Andrew Dickson White, was surprised to discover that one of these Negroes, whom he had been told were Nubians, was from Tennessee. U.S. Customs Bureau records in the National Archives reveal that a main channel of access of Negroes into Russia was their frequent role as seamen on commercial vessels. One famous Black seaman who made the trip to Russia more than once was Matthew Henson, who later became the first known man to reach the North Pole in Robert Peary's 1909 expedition (Henson 1912). Henson sailed to Russia twice in the 1880s as a cabin boy. As Black seamen sailed to Russia from several American ports and from many foreign countries, it is clear that Negroes were not an uncommon sight in at least the major port cities.

Besides the Black natives of the Caucasus, the slaves or servants brought to Russia, and ships' crewmen, the visitors of various types, including artists, athletes, and foreign service officials, comprised another category of Negroes in Russia. Some of these visitors actually stayed for several years, some permanently. Ira Aldridge, the renowned Negro Shakespearean actor, toured Russia for about five years in the 1860s and lies buried in Poland. The great jockey Andy Thomas, who won two Kentucky Derbies, moved to Russia and established a comparable record there. When Richard Greener, a Black lawyer and politician, became the chief American consular official in Vladivostok in 1898, he was surprised to find another American Negro already working there as a handyman. At the same time, in another Siberian city, a Negro singer was the resident performer at the hotel.

One of the most interesting examples of all is the American Negro named George Thomas, who arrived in St. Petersburg in the 1890s as a valet. He eventually managed to make a small fortune by engaging in various amusement enterprises. By the First World War he owned a large amusement complex in Moscow, including at least one restaurant and hotel. He had to leave Russia when the Bolsheviks took power in 1917, however, because he was considered a capitalist enemy. Undaunted, he escaped to Istanbul, where he hosted another restaurant; then later to Paris where he opened yet another (Johnson 1969: 64–65). One other enigmatic figure at the end of tsarist Russia was Sergeant Major Marcel Pliat. This crewman on a Sikorsky bomber was of mixed African and French descent, and was serving in the Russian air force in 1916 when he won the St. George's Cross for gallantry for exploits against the Germans.

In the Soviet era Negroes from Africa and the Americas have been conspicuously present from the beginning and have had a special significance owing to the emphasis Soviet Marxist ideology placed on oppressed peoples and developing nations. Even as early as the Russian Civil War, there were some Negroes, in addition to those in Abkhaza, fighting in the Red Army. One of them, a dashing cavalry officer who died in battle, inspired a poem entitled *Moia Afrika (My Africa)* by Boris Kornilov. The 1920s saw several American Negroes and Africans among foreigners invited to attend special schools established to train Communist Party leaders for various parts of the world (Haywood 1978: 148ff).

Negroes who went to the Soviet Union for specifically ideological reasons were only a small segment. Most went simply out of curiosity or to seek a better life. The poet Claude McKay was the first prominent Negro to visit the Soviet Union on his own, without party affiliation. When he arrived in 1922 he was welcomed as a poet, not a politician. However, because the one Black American delegate to the fourth Comintern Congress, who happened to be native Dutch Guianese Otto Huiswood, turned out to have a very light complexion, the Soviet leaders wanted McKay, who was very dark, to represent the American Negro to the Russian public. He was, therefore, photographed with the leaders of the Communist International, introduced to other such luminaries as the poet V. Mayakovsky, to Leon Trotsky, and to Lenin's wife Krupskaya, who was representing her ill husband. He was also made an honorary member of the Moscow City Council, and was treated to a brief airplane ride while on an inspection of the Red Army (McKay 1937: 206).

From the late 1920s and 1930s, through the late 1940s, the Soviet government encouraged any Americans with technical skill to come to Russia. Trotsky told McKay in 1923 of a proposal he had for training a group of Negroes as Red Army officers. In 1945 the *Chicago Defender* newspaper reported that V. Kuznetsov, chairman of the Central Council of Trade Unions of the USSR, had extended an invitation to the pilots of the Negro 99th Squadron to come to the Soviet Union for postwar jobs as pilots. The Soviet government also paid special tribute to American Negroes during this period through special awards such as the selection of the novelist Arna Bontemps for the Pushkin Prize in 1926.

Especially in the late 1920s and 1930s, the Soviet Union played the role of a kind of mecca of human rights for some and an escape from the Great Depression for others. One observer writing on the subject of Negroes in Russia in 1932 estimated that several hundred had visited Russia since the Revolution. They came primarily from the United States and the West Indies. Few of these remained permanently. Those who did stay often married Russians and raised families. Of the hundreds of American Negroes who have visited Russia, only several dozen actually settled. Some left in disillusionment with Soviet life, others simply out of homesickness, or because material conditions had improved in the United States. There is no evidence of many Negroes emigrating to the Soviet Union since the Second World War.

Nonetheless, Negroes have continued to enjoy prominence there. Others besides McKay were elected to the Moscow city Council; and a mountain was named after Paul Robeson (Duberman 1988). In keeping with the commitment to aid developing nations, the Soviet Union hosted thousands of American students in Soviet higher educational institutions since the late 1950s. This has accounted for a fairly large, constant, Negro population up to the present. Some of these students are enrolled in programs requiring as long as six years to complete. A native Afro-Soviet journalist in 1992 estimated that there are hundreds of mulattoes in Moscow, and smaller numbers elsewhere who consider themselves Russian Blacks.

Attitudes Toward Blacks

Focusing now briefly on attitudes toward Blacks in the areas treated here, it can be seen that a persistent pattern has survived over the centuries. Both Christian and Islamic society showed some color prejudice. The standard Western stereotypes about Blacks also were reflected in Spain, with skin color depicted as an indelible stain in drama and literature and Blacks shown as servile by nature. The following quote from the visiting Flemish humanist Clenardus who left us his impression from first seeing the large number of slaves in Portugal in 1535, while an outsider's view, dramatizes the fact that the Black presence was striking, and troubling to some Europeans:

> Truly, when I first arrived in Evora I thought that I had come to some city of evil demons: everywhere there were so many blacks whom I so loathe that they may just be able to drive me away from here. (Saunders 1982: 1)

One of the main objectives of the present essay is to trace the source of such intense negative feeling among some Europeans, including educated intellectuals, of this era. To Clenardus's credit, it should be added that he did teach three Black slaves Latin so that they could assist him in his school at Evora. Moreover, he acknowledged their assistance by titling his Latin grammar, *Grammafica Aethiopica*.

Blacks clearly captured the imagination of the Spanish and Portuguese as well as of visitors such as Clenardus. There are Black characters throughout the literature and folklore of the fifteenth and sixteenth centuries. They could be encountered in songs about Blacks and in fairy tales where even giants were presumed to have Black servants. There were also references to Blacks in sayings and figures of speech. Some popular dances in Spain were probably first introduced by slaves from Africa. The early Portuguese and Spanish experience of the Black Diaspora is of special interest for understanding all of the European dimension because the patterns established during the first century of contact between Europe and Black Africa continued up to the nineteenth century.

With regard to the Atlantic slave trade and the relegation of Black people to servitude or positions of inferior status in countries ruled by Whites, it was in Portugal that large numbers of Blacks were first subjected to White rule and there that many features of their status common to all European societies were first defined. There also continued the debate over the justness of slavery that had begun in the ancient world. In the Islamic and Christian Iberian World, and in the Atlantic World there was endless diversity of experiences, with Blacks functioning on all levels in the social, economic, and political structures, and present in the arts as well. There seemed as much basis for the development of positive attitudes toward Blacks in Europe as for negative. The question is: why is it that strong negative attitudes have persistently dominated? The answer to this must be sought in a fuller study of the early evolution of perceptions of Blacks in Europe which has been traced here only in outline.

The dominant images of Blacks in Dutch culture by the end of the nineteenth century can be viewed in broad terms as an amalgamation of the negative associations with darkness present in many world societies; a touch of xenophobia combined with fascination; and a sense of superiority stemming from the dominance of Western Civilization in the modern world. While there were some positive concepts concerning Blacks throughout the centuries treated here, the negative ones clearly predominated as time progressed. Tracing the course of their evolution, the most positive images existed before extensive contacts between Dutchmen and Blacks, a time when one might rather suppose that only the most fantastic notions would occur. The most negative images then developed precisely during the Enlightenment and scientific age.

As a reflection of this, in the course of the nineteenth century industries throughout the Western world began to adopt trademarks featuring Blacks: for example, those for tobacco products, cleansers, coffee, liquor, rice, shoe and metal polish, and tooth paste. Those for raw materials and foods were especially prominent. This seems to reflect an association of Blacks with the primitive and often with the sensuous. This commercial use of Blacks as symbols tended to reinforce a dehumanization of Blacks in societies where the actual Black population was extremely small. These trademarks were additional embellishment of imagery already manifested in the popular culture in literature, song, and story. While a trend toward denigration of Blacks was obviously related to the contemporary African slave trade and slavery, it should be noted that the negative stereotypes reached their fullest expression after abolition in the late nineteenth century.

In comparing the experience of Blacks in Russia and eastern Europe in this regard, it is interesting to note that the broad patterns were very similar, but compressed into a narrower time frame. The case of Soviet Russia illustrates this point especially well. In this colossal experiment in social engineering which might be viewed as one logical conclusion to which the ideals of the eighteenth-century Enlightenment might be taken, and a society which worships science, there is considerable evidence that the undercurrents of racial conflict seem to have survived just as strong in spite of the fact that they are prohibited by law and official ideology. Future needed studies on this question will have to address the reasons that the ambivalence noted here in the early centuries was succeeded by an increasingly more negative picture during the past three centuries. The concept of progress so popular in Western Civilization, the Enlightenment, and the Scientific Revolution seemed to reinforce rather than dispel racial bias.

Bibliography

Blakely, A. 1979. "Gannibal, Abram Petrovich." *Modern Encyclopedia of Russian and Soviet History*, Vol. 12. Gulf Breeze FL.

———1986. *Russia and the Negro: Blacks in Russian History and Thought*. Washington, D.C.

———1993. *Blacks in the Dutch World: The Evolution of Racial Imagery in a Modern Society*. Bloomington, IN.

Davis, D. B. 1984. *Slavery and Human Progress*. New York.

Devisse, J., M. Mollat. 1979. *The Image of the Black in Western Art II: From the Early Christian Era to the "Age of Discovery,"* vol. 2, Africans in the Christian Ordinance of the World (Fourteenth to the Sixteenth Century), Cambridge.

Duberman, M. 1988. *Paul Robeson*. New York.

English, P. 1959. "Cushites, Colchians, and Khazars." *Journal of Near Eastern Studies* 18: 45–53.

Haywood, H. 1978. *Black Bolshevik*. Chicago.

Henson, M. 1912. *A Negro Explorer of the North Pole*. New York.

Johnson, J. 1969. *Jack Johnson is a Dandy*. New York.

July, R. W. 1980. *A History of the African Peoples*. New York.

Lopashich, A. 1958. *Negro Community in Yugoslavia*. Man 58: 169–73.

McKay, C. 1937. *A Long Way from Home*. New York.

Nabokov, V. 1964. *Pushkin, Eugene Onegin*, vol. 3. New York.

Nutt, D. 1970 (1901), *Arthurian Romances Unrepresented in Malory's Morte D'Arthur*, vol. 5, Morien, transl. J. L. Weston. New York.

Robinson, R. 1988. *Black on Red: My 44 Years in the Soviet Union*. Washington, D.C.

Saunders, A. C. de C. M. 1982. *A Social History of Black Slaves and Freedmen in Portugal 1441–1555*. Cambridge.

Smith, H. 1954. *Black Man in Red Russia*. Chicago.

Snowden, Jr., F. M. 1983. *Before Color Prejudice: The Ancient View of Blacks*. Cambridge.

Stedman, J. 1796. *Narrative of a FiveYears' Expedition Against the Revolted Negroes of Surinam, in Guiana, on the Wild Coast of South America*. London.

Thornton, J. 1992. *Africa and Africans in the Making of the Atlantic World, 1400–1680*. Cambridge.

---

[1]The Canaries were rediscovered by Malocello in the early fourteenth century. The Azores were reached by Diago de Silves in 1427.

[2]In his recent book, Thornton notes that the guns-for-slaves cliché is not valid since guns did not really prove decisive in most African wars because of the state of development of the weapons and the conditions of warfare. As late as in the mid-eighteenth century, the Lunda state still considered guns as cowards' weapons.

[3]Pareja was an assistant to the painter Velasquez and himself an outstanding religious painter.

[4]For fuller discussion of all these issues related to the Dutch experience see Blakely (1993).

[5]On Pushkin's relationship to his African heritage see Blakely (1986: 50–56) and Nabokov (Appendix, 1964).

[6]Vivid accounts of the experiences of these immigrants can be found in the autobiography of Langston Hughes, who went in 1932 with a party of twenty young men and women invited by the Comintern to participate in an anti-racism propaganda film project. Even fuller treatments of Negro life in the USSR appear in Smith (1954) and Robinson (1988).

The Revolt of African Slaves in Iraq in the 3rd/9th Century

Alexandre Popovic

Chapter 1
Origins of the Revolt

The Abbasid Empire was founded in 750, by Abû al-'Abbâs al-Saffâh (descendant of 'Abbâs, uncle of the Prophet Muhammad) who, with the aid of Persian troops, seized power and put an end to the Umayyad dynasty (661–750). Baghdad, founded in 762, became their residence. The caliphs, thirty-seven in number, reigned until 1258, when Hûlâgû, a grandson of Genghis Khân, brought their empire to an end. Their chief interest was in the Asian part of the empire, for, as soon as they arrived to power, first Spain had slipped from their grasp and then North Africa, where only the Ifriqiyya (Tunisia and the eastern part of Algeria) remained nominally submitted to them. In the time of Hârûn al-Rashîd, the Abbasid Empire was one of the principal centers of world civilization, and Baghdad dazzled the world with its splendor and prosperity. Nevertheless, following troubles brought on by Turkish mercenaries, the seat of the caliphate was moved, in 836, to Sâmarrâ which remained the capital until the year 892. At the beginning of the tenth century, continuing domestic troubles and growing decadence obliged the caliph to yield temporal power to a sort of "palace mayor," while the governors became practically independent of the central power . . . Temporal power then passed into the hands of the Seljuk sultans (Turks) until February 10, 1258, the day Hûlâgû's Mongols seized and devastated Baghdad, putting an end to the Abbasid dynasty, whose last caliph was strangled to death.

However, at the time of the revolt of the Zanj (869–883), the Abbasid Empire was still a great world power which reigned *de facto* or *de jure* (mostly through semi-independent governors) over vast territories from Tunisia to Central Asia and from the Caspian Sea to Yemen, but actually over hardly more than Iraq, Mesopotamia, and western Persia.

I. Geography

Two provinces of the Abbasid Empire were affected by the Zanj revolt: Iraq and Ahwâz (the Khuzistân). Hostilities, which did not extend beyond Jarjarâyâ and Râmhurmuz, raged mostly in southern Iraq and western Ahwâz. Tremendous rivers crossed the provinces, facilitating navigation and transport and, along with caravan routes, the hundreds of canals that linked up the waterways favored intense movement of people and goods. Of special interest to us are two regions that contributed greatly to the insurrection because of the nature of their soil. They are al-Batîha and Maysân, Lower Iraq's canal region.

Al-Batîha.—The "Marshes" is the name for a basin with prairies that are almost constantly filled with mud due to regular flooding, more or less. In the Middle Ages Arab authors employed the term al-Batîha and its plural al-Batâ'ih specifically to designate Lower Iraq's swamp region, located roughly between Kûfa and Wâsit in the north and Basra in the south. These swamps were the result of annual flooding and had existed from earliest antiquity because the waters of the Tigris and the Euphrates frequently overran the extremely flat terrain and often changed course. Assyrians, Greeks, Romans, Sassanids, and Arabs had built dams, dikes, and canals in the region, but "a stable hydrographic network was impossible in the extensive flatlands of southern Mesopotamia where there were no elevations to offset the malleability of alluvion-formed soil, all the more so since the system of irrigation canals was subject to economic and political fluctuations."

Enormous growths of reeds and rushes, often several meters tall, covered the vast surface across which ran a great many more or less wide but often very shallow canals. Most of the time, they could be navigated only by small, flat boats, and this made access to al-Batîha very difficult. As a result, the region was always a perfect location for brigands, rebels, or settlements who needed observation posts from which they could keep an eye on trade and other activities. But it could be a dangerous area. Ibn Battuta, the famous fourteenth-century Arab traveler, notes:

> . . . And, in a region known as Idhâr, we went along the Euphrates. It is a forest of reeds surrounded by water, and inhabited by Arabs, known for their excesses. They are bandits of the sect of 'Ali [that is to say Shiites]. They attacked a troop of *fakirs* (poor people) who had fallen behind our caravan and stripped them of their sandals and goblets. They fortify themselves in these swamps and defend

themselves against pursuers. There are many ferocious beasts in that place.

Al-Batîha's ordinary inhabitants engaged in tilling plots of land, and their chief crops were rice, barley, yellow corn, sorghum, millet, lentils, melons, watermelons, and onions. The reeds and rushes growing wild in the region were also gathered and put to many uses.

Fish of various kinds were plentiful and there were other fauna such as buffalo, sheep, and cows, without mentioning various types of waterfowl: gulls, wild duck, geese, swans, etc. Lions, leopards, jackals, wolves, lynx, and wildcats were also found. "Herds of wild boar still wallow in the swamp. The countless swarms of mosquitoes and gnats are a terrible scourge and the source of endemic diseases such as malaria, which must have been one of the principal causes of the region's decline."

Inaccessibility, a readily available food supply, and climate which Abbasid troops found difficult and unhealthy are features which made this an ideal location for the insurgents.

II. The Population (the Zutt, the Zanj)

Among the population of very diverse origins inhabiting these regions in the ninth century, two ethnic groups attract our particular attention: the Zutt and the Zanj.

The Zutt.—The Zutt lived in the swamps and engaged in violent robbery and even open revolt. They fought government troops on several occasions during the reign of al-Ma'mûn (Abbasid caliph, 813–833), disrupting communications between Baghdad and Basra. Al-Mu'tasim (Abbasid caliph, 833–842) managed to subdue them, but not without difficulty. He resettled them on the northern border of Syria, but we do not know much more about the Zutt or these events.

The Zanj.—"Jâhiz (a very important Arab prose-writer) distinguishes four categories of Zanj. Qunbula, Lanjawiyya, Naml, and Kilâb [*Bayân*, III, 36, we were not able to identify these names] were Negroes from the east coast of Africa who had been imported as slaves, at an indeterminate date."

Origins of the name "Zanj."—This name is not Arabic, even though the Arabs have treated it as a word of their language. Its composition in three letters, Z, n, j, made it easy for the Arabs to adapt. They use it as a collective word with the value of a plural, which they can also denote by the form *zonoûdj*, just as from *hind*, the singular collective denoting Hindus, they form the plural *Honoûd*.

Since the word Zanj is not of Arabic origin, there are several explanatory hypotheses for it, and opinions are very divided. L. M. Devic thinks it is a borrowed Ethiopian word: "It is obviously a foreign word. The Ethiopian lan-guage, sister of Arabic, has a verb *zanega,* mean-ing to prattle, to stammer, to barbarize with the noun *Zengua,* confused, absurd speech, and these words are probably etymologically related to the name of the Zendj people; but we can presume that the latter produced the Ethiopian verb and noun."

Others, such as G. Ferrand, A. Werner, and Philip K. Hitti believe in a Persian origin, but G. F. Hourani questions it. As for M. Dunlop, he writes: "The name itself has been explained as having come from the Persian *Zang, Zangî* (Pahlawi Zoroastrian *zangîk* "Negro"), but it is perhaps of local origin." This is close to the view held by W. Fitzgerald who, speaking of Zanzibar, writes: "The name is derived from two terms, one Persian, the other Indian, *viz. Zanzibar,* which means 'Country of the Black Man'."

Some authors, among whom are A. Müller and the same G. F. Hourani, believe that the name is related to the Greek "Zingis"; but they remain extremely guarded, as for example, C. H. Becker: "The name Zandj goes back to early antiquity; Ptolemy, the famous Greek astronomer, mathematician and geographer of the second century, knew *Zingis akra* and Kosmas Indicopleustes (merchant and traveler of the sixth century) spoke of *tò Zingion.* The name itself is unexplained."

Opinions are also divided as far as interpretation of the word is concerned. L. M. Devic hesitates between Zinj, Zanj, or Zenj, therefore between *fatha* and *kasra*. F. al-Sâmir believes that three readings are possible: Zanj, Zinj, and Zunj; therefore *fatha, kasra,* and *damma.* Ibn Manzûr (author of a famous Arab dictionary, who lived in the thirteenth and fourteenth centuries) indicates only two: Zanj and Zinj, therefore, *fatha* and *kasra.* And we find the same thing in E. W. Lane's work. On the other hand, Ibn Durayd (Arab philologist, 837–933), who lived at the time of the revolt, is of a different opinion altogether and says clearly: "The Zanj are a well-known people; as for the pronunciation Zinj, it is incorrect."

D'Herbelot was the first to point out that "Rîh" instead of "Zanj" is sometimes found in texts.

> Masoudi had undertaken research into the cause of this lightmindedness, this carelessness and extreme inclination to cheerfulness, but the only solution he found was to mention the remark by Galen and al-Kendi, according to which this character is due to a weakness of the brain from whence would come a weakness of intelligence. This explanation is worthless and proves nothing ... (*Prolegomenes,* p. 176–77).

There are a number of pages of this type in the work of Devic, that is to say, among Arab authors of the Middle Ages, and even among those who came later. They contain explanations for these characteristics, for the planets that govern the destinies of the blacks, as well as all sorts of essays and proverbs.

Here is a summary of these pages. Among other things, the Zanj are: evil, "they surpass brute animals in their unfitness and their perverse natures"; cannibals, "there are among them tribes of men with sharp teeth who eat one another"; ugly, ". . . they are so hideous and so ugly that they appear to be the most horrible thing in the world to see. The women of this island are the ugliest in the world"; idolaters, evil and cruel; they have soothsayers remark-able for their accuracy in predicting the future; most of the time they go naked; they are great fighters, "Without the deserts and the branch of the Nile that flows into the sea, which is a natural protection for the Abyssinian frontier, the Habacha, would not have been able to remain in their country because of the numerous and violent troops of these Negroes"; they go into combat mounted on oxen; they have themselves tattooed; they have their nose pierced for the very uncommon needs due to their manner of waging war among themselves; they venerate the Arabs; they eat various kinds of millet, maize, bananas, meat, honey; they adore dates, etc.

Their political organization is simple. They have a king, who is the chief of one or several tribes, and they wage war on another.

On the other hand we can find:

The Zanj are very eloquent, and have orators who address the people in their language. Often one of the country's religious men stands in the middle of a large crowd and urges them to make themselves pleasing to God and follow his commandments, pointing out to them the punishments to which their disobedience exposes them and, reminding them of the example of their ancestors and former kings. The Zanj have no religious code; their kings confine themselves to a few traditions which lay down certain obligations of the people towards their ruler, and a few rules that the prince must observe in regard to his subjects.

In studying the objects of creative activity of the language, that-is-to-say the literary monuments, al-Jâhiz remains faithful to his comparative method which he considers indispensable in other cases (*Bayân,* II, 56). He knows the literature of other peoples, not only that of the Greeks and Persians, but also that of the Hindus and the Zanj.

These passages must have referred above all to the Zanj in their country of origin because, as Devic emphasizes: "Besides the reason we have given for explaining the diversity of judgments concerning the Zanj, we must consider that some of the peoples of this name had undergone the civilizing influence of the Muslims settled on their coasts, while others continued to live in a savage state."

The Zanj in Arab Countries.—We know that blacks were much appreciated as slaves in Muslim countries. From time immemorial, they constituted a large part of the population and were to be found at every level of Islamic society. The Zanj were imported as slaves at an indeterminate date, and it is not at all easy to understand this importation phenomenon in a real-life situation without being faced with the disadvantage of the "particular case." F. al-Sâmir emphasizes that the slave trade was not of Arab origin and that it was well-known at the time of the pharaohs. He insists on having it conceded that the Arabs themselves did not capture the Zanj, but acquired them from tribal chiefs. There is no doubt that the slaves were acquired in different ways and that it is impossible to generalize as to just how they were obtained. That is why we prefer the opinion of Bernard Lewis, who flatly states, ". . . they were largely Negroes from East Africa, where they had been captured, bought or obtained from subject states as tribute."

As for just when the Zanj were introduced into Iraq, it is practically impossible to give anything close to an exact date. Devic believes that the Arabs had visited Zanguebar since the new era, and in any case, from the beginning of Islam. F. al-Sâmir suggests 720 as the date for the Muslim trading posts in East Africa, and the first century of the Hegira (622–722) for date of Arab arrival in Iraq. As we have seen, Charles Pellat more cautiously prefers "an indeterminate date." That seems to us the only plausible solution. If Arab historians report Zanj revolts in 70/689–90 and 75/694–5, which proves that the Zanj had arrived at an even earlier date, there is no doubt that the boats and caravans transporting them were still arriving in the period that interests us.

Arab Opinions of the Zanj.—In a preceding section (characteristics and way of life), we dealt with the Zanj in their land of origin. Now we turn to the opinions of medieval Arab authors on the Zanj in "Islamic country."

Before citing any author at all, we wish to direct attention to a certain number of points. First of all, we should eliminate the revolt and its consequences (all later judgments are known in advance); we must not forget that there are Zanj and Zanj, that some had been settled (and Islamized?) for a century or more, and some had just arrived; we should never lose sight of their condition of absolute physical and moral destitution; we must reflect on their transplantation from an archaic culture to civilization, and on the language barrier; finally, we must not forget that, if there are no Zanj who are not black, there are many blacks who are not Zanj.

We have already said that the Zanj were highly valued as rural labor; on the other hand, they were considered to have many flaws. According to a common proverb: "The hungry Zanj steals; the sated Zanj rapes"; the Zanj was, as we would say today, stereotyped: he is stupid; he is cheerful for no apparent reason; he is a thief; he does not speak Arabic; he has no memory; he is the cheapest slave in the market, etc. . . .

Two passages from al-Jâhiz summarize the general opinion, which emerges from the texts:

We know that the Zanj are the least intelligent of men, the least discerning, and the least concerned with the future. If their generosity came only from their lack of intellect and intelligence, and knowledge, it would be agreed that the Persians were greedier than the Byzantines . . .

. . . He was in the habit of saying, "I have never eaten dates with pleasure, except in the company of the Zanj and the people of Esfahan. The Negro does not choose, while I choose; as for the inhabitant of Esfahan, he takes a handful and finishes it before touching any other dates.

Few texts are favorable to them. Ahmad Amîn's attempt to group together complimentary descriptions of them concerns only a few actual or presumed individual Zanj. As for the famous treatise by al-Jâhiz, Charles Pellat is definite: "Al-Jâhiz mentions them often but certainly did not have them in mind when he was writing his letter on the merits of the blacks."

It must be pointed out that "racism," as the term is understood today, was never an important factor in the Muslim world of the Middle Ages. From time to time, there might be violent eruptions against unassimilable groups, such as the despised and mistreated Zutt and Zanj, but if for no reason other than the occurrence of significant intermixing among the populations, we can say that racial separation, in the strict sense, did not exist.

Some Arabs displayed loathing for the Zanj. Taous al-Yemani, who was a lieutenant of Abdallah, son of Abbâs, refused to eat the meat of any animal killed by a Zanj, in his words, a hideous slave; and the Caliph Rhadi Billah (d. 940), son of al-Moktadir, shared this aversion to such an extent that he would accept nothing from a black man's hand. Nevertheless, there were undoubtedly special reasons for these

feelings since, in general, the Arabs harbor no sentiments of repugnance for Negroes.

Be that as it may, the conditions of Zanj slaves in Iraq were wretched, and there were two uprisings before the great revolt.

The Insurrection of 70/689–90.—A first uprising occurred under the government of Halid Mus'ab b. al-Zubayr (governor of Iraq for the Umayyads). For the most part, it involved small gangs engaged in pillage and is of little impor-tance. The government's army broke them up easily, beheading the prisoners taken and hanging their corpses on the gibbet. F. al-Sâmir, in speaking of this revolt, points out that in this early period the Zanj were already living under appalling social conditions.

The Insurrection of 75/694.—The second revolt seems to have been more important and, above all, better prepared. The Zanj had a leader, the Lion of the Zanj, and the authorities were obliged to undertake two operations to crush them. This revolt was more complicated than the first, but we have very little information about it:

A few years later, in 75/694–5, thanks to a revolt led by 'Abd Allâh ibn al-Jârûd, against al-Hajjâj (celebrated Umayyad governor), a large number of Zanj chose a certain Rabâh (Riyâh?), known as Shîr Zanjî (Lion of the Zanj) to be their leader and revolted. They even defeated a troop that was sent against them, and it was not until Ibn al-Jârûd's rebellion was suppressed that al-Hajjâj succeeded in reestablishing order . . . The true nature of this movement cannot be determined from the information we have; it would seem that it did not break out spontaneously and that the Zanj had been stirred up by propaganda, but the movement was short-lived because almost two centuries passed before the Zanj were heard from again. Not without interest on this subject, [adds the author in a note] are the lines of a maulâ (client or freed slave) of the qurayshite tribe of the Banû Sâma ibn Lu'ayy, named Sulaih ibn Riyâh in which he praises the Negroes and mentions a certain number of sons of Negro women such as Ziyâd ibn 'Amr al-'Atakî and 'Abd Allâh ibn Khâzim as-Sulamî. These lines would have been composed after the first revolt . . .

Other References to the Zanj in Muslim History before the Great Revolt of 255/869.—Apart from the two early insurrections and without mentioning texts concerning true or false Zanj personalities, historical sources record only an incident in 132/749–50. Under 'Abû l-'Abbâs al-Saffâh's caliphate, a government force of four-thousand men strong was sent to put down an uprising of the inhabitants of al-Mawsil (present-day Mosul, Iraqi city in northern Mesopotamia). It distinguished itself by its fierceness and massacred, it was said, more than ten-thousand people, men, women, and children.

The Huge Spawning Grounds of the Revolt.—Our information about the sites on which the Zanj worked is very limited. Everything that has been written on the subject is based on a few bits of information found in the work of al-Tabarî (a great Arab historian, 838–923, who lived at the time of the revolt) and on a passage from *Kitâb al-'Uyûn.* (By al-Qayrawânî, Arab author of the eleventh and twelfth centuries).

According to Tabarî, our principal source, the rebels were employed as laborers *(kassâhîn)* to prepare land of Lower-Mesopotamia, removing the *sebâkh* and piling it in mounds, so that the nitrous lands of the Shatt al-'Arab could be cultivated.

. . . They were recruited from among imported Negro slaves and local peasants, and grouped in camps of 500 to 5,000 workers, packed in without family or hope, given a few handfuls of flour, semolina and dates as their only food. From contact with the Islam of their masters, these wretches learned through the phenomenon of spiritual induction that they had a right to existence and minimum justice; the influence of Muslim religious from the neighboring hermitages of 'Abbâdân (city southwest of Basra, not far from the sea) perhaps had something to do with it.

These work camps were reportedly located at Furât al-Basra and on the other side of the Dujayl. It is generally believed that they were east of Basra and part of a small section of Khûzistân. Given the number of slaves employed on them, they must have been very large, and only rich persons or wealthy merchants are thought to have owned such camps. The number of slaves they employed was certainly very large; al-Tabarî's figure of fifteen thousand has been repeated by other historians, but it is obvious that no figures can be verified. As already mentioned the labor in these camps was composed of Zanj and other blacks, of different names, from other regions, including probably a certain number of peasants. The task was to remove the crust of natron from the surface of the land, take it away on mules, and pile it in heaps "as large as mountains." It was hard work and overseers appointed from among emancipated slaves, eager to justify their promotion, made it even more grueling.

The situation is all the more striking since slavery in Islamic countries in the Middle Ages (contrary to slavery in Rome at the time of Spartacus) was essentially domestic servitude and not much employed for large rural projects. The conditions under which the Zanj slaves lived were unquestionably unusual for medieval Muslim society.

Basra's growth was a brief, intense crisis in the rise of Arabism, as studied by Ibn Khaldûn. Basra was destined to furnish the first example of the destructive social crisis of the city in Islam, when social restraints were broken, when usury, indirect taxes, government borrowing were rampant, and the opposition was exasperated by the luxury of the wealthy; slaves for luxury and luxuriousness, expensive clothes and jewelry, African ivory, pearls from the Gulf, precious wood from India made a mockery of the working proletariat's misery on the plantations (canonically, the lands of Basra were "amwât" ("dead lands"), under their original crust of unproductive natron or *sebâkh*), "revived" by the coolie labor of Zanj, kassâhîn, shûrjîyîn, who were refused their claim to freedom following their conversion. In the third century of the hegira, while in other Muslim cities, the social crisis was only among large bourgeois corporations and the small craftsmen of the guilds, between 'hostile gangs' of financiers carving up the latifundia, and serfs of the land ambitious to become landowners, in Basra it ended in a fight to the death between the privileged elite of the City that wanted everything for itself, and the starved proletariat of the plantations and sand-filled oases who pounced on the City to destroy it. Babel, which was alive as long as it was a place where the exogamous exchange of values and language was carried on, became Sodom, and burned.

Chapter 2
'Alî b. Muhammad

We know little about the life of 'Alî b. Muhammad, the man who instigated the revolt of the Zanj. Only a few phrases dealing with his birth, parents, and family have come down to us. There is even less information on the period he spent at the court of Samârrâ (city of Iraq on the left bank of the Tigris, north of Baghdad). There are a few more details, but still they are insufficient to allow us to make a definitive statement about his sojourns in Bahrayn, Basra, and Baghdad. Even for the periods covered by pages and pages devoted to his exploits in war, we have only fragmentary information or disparate details. Tabarî's nine pages and a passage in Safadî's work represent just about all we know about the person responsible for the Zanj uprising.

'Alî b. Muhammad's Birth, His Name, His Parents, His Ancestors.—The leader of the Zanj was apparently born in a village in the vicinity of al-Rayy called Warzanîn. His true name was probably 'Alî b. Muhammad b. 'Abd al- Rahîm, and he would have been of the tribe of 'Abd al-Qays. There are two different versions of his parental background, but the one that is known and that later historians have repeated is from Tabarî.

His mother's name was Qurra bint 'Alî b. Rahîb b. Muhammad b. Hakîm. She was of the Banû Asad b. Khuzayma tribe and lived in Warzanîn, where he was born and grew up. It has been recorded that, in speaking of his family, he maintained that his maternal grandfather, Muhammad b. Hakîm, lived in the town of Kûfa. With Zayd b. 'Alî b. al-Husayn, he was a member of the Kharijites against Hishâm b. 'Abd al-Malik. When Zayd died, Muhammad fled Iraq and went to al-Rayy, where he settled in Warzanîn.

Alî's paternal grandfather, 'Abd al-Rahîm, was of the 'Abd al-Qays tribe. Born in al-Tâliqân (Tâlaqân?), he settled in Iraq and bought a Sindian slave. The son she bore him named Muhammad would be our 'Alî's father.

Safadî's version is much longer and disagrees with the one above:

His mother, Qurra bint 'Abd al-Wâhid b. Muhammad al-Shâmî, recounted that her father went on the pilgrimage every year and passed through Medina where he stayed with a shaykh of Abû Talib's family who received him with honor and respect and to whom he brought gifts from Rayy every year. One year when he went on the pilgrimage carrying his gifts, the shaykh's son, Muhammad (future) father of 'Alî, was (then) ten years old, the shaykh was dead when my father arrived and only his son was left to receive my father as best he could. My father suggested that he come with him, but he refused, saying: "My father and my sister prevent me from doing so." My father continued on the pilgrimage and on his return found them dead (both of them), he (then) brought Muhammad back to the village of Warzanîn with him and suggested that he marry me. At first he refused saying: "In a dream I saw myself urinating, and my urine burned half the world"; (after the dream) my father forbade me to marry him. Never-theless, he did marry me later, and I bore him two daughters who died at an early age. My father died. Then I brought 'Alî b. Muhammad into the world. After that Muhammad ['Alî's father]

spent my fortune and squandered it and I separated from him because of a slave he had bought. Then he left me and took his son with him and for several years I had no news of them. Then my child came back and told me of his father's death. For a certain period, he stayed with me in Rayy and endlessly pursued everyone who knew the *adab* (necessary general culture) and the *riwâya* (the traditions, the "narratives"), after that he left for Khurâsân and was away two or three years. He returned, (again) stayed a little while, then left again and disappeared. (It was during this absence) that I received a letter from him from Basra, telling me what he had become and that he possessed wealth, but I did not believe (this news) because of what I knew about him, for sure.

'Alî, Master of the Zanj states: "When I was young, I was stricken by a serious illness. My father came to visit me and found my mother sitting at my bedside. She said to him, 'He is going to die.' He replied, "If he dies who will lay waste to Basra?" That remained engraved in my heart (mind) until the moment I rebelled there."

The Sojourn in Samârrâ.—After having spent his childhood in Warzanîn, 'Alî b. Muhammad went to Samârrâ where he became poet (panegyrist) at the court of Caliph al-Muntasir (861–862). There he was in contact with people attached to the Caliph's family and with, among others, Gânim al-Shatranjî, Sa'îd al-Sagîr and Yusr al-Khâdim. He earned a living in the capital from his poetry and from teaching children the art of writing, grammar, and astronomy.

The Sojourn in Bahrayn.—In 249/863–864, he left Samârrâ for Bahrayn, where he claimed to be an 'Alid with the following genealogy: 'Alî b. Muhammad b. al-Fadl b. al-Hasan b. 'Ubayd Allâh b. al-'Abbâs b. 'Alî b. Abî Tâlib.

It was at Hajar that he began his movement by asking the residents of the town to follow him. Some of the population joined him, and some would not. Relations between the two factions became acrimonious, causing many deaths in both camps. Following these events, 'Alî b. Muhammad left Hajâr for al-Ahsâ' and went first to the tribe of Banû Tamîm, then to the Banû Sa'd, of the Banû Shammâs branch, among whom, it is said, he was considered such a prophet that the population paid taxes to him.

He exercised great influence over the popu-lation and succeeded in stirring up some of the people against the Caliphate's forces. Not everyone approved of his actions, however, so he changed his location again and went into the desert with his most loyal supporters. Among those who accompanied him were a measurer of grains from al-Ahsâ', named Yahyâ b. Muhammad al-Azraq known by the nickname al-Bahrânî (who was a *mawla*, a client, an emancipated man), from the Banû Dârim; a merchant from Hajar, Yahyâ b. Abî Tha'lab; and finally a black man, a *mawla*, from the Banû Hanzala named Sulaymân b. Jâmi'. They went from one tribe to another in the desert. Alî b. Muhammad claimed to have received supernatural revelations in the form of verses of the Qur'an. He did not know how he had learned them, but they rolled off his tongue straight-away; and while he was complaining about the laxness of the desert's inhabitants, he heard a voice from heaven, in the thunder, ordering him to go to Basra.

It is said that, on arriving in the desert, he claimed to be Yahyâ b. 'Umar Abû l-Husayn. With desert-dwellers who joined him, he pushed on to al-Radm, where he was defeated and a great number of his followers were killed. At this juncture, the Bedouins with him withdrew and fled. In 254/868, he returned to Iraq and went to Basra.

We have scant information on the five years he spent in Bahrayn.

Bernard Lewis writes: "after a first attempt to win support in Bahrayn where he would have had family connections...." He also says: "after several aborted attempts at sedition in different places...." Faysal al-Sâmir's statements contribute nothing new. This is even more the case since they ignore a passage from Mas'ûdî that went completely unnoticed by Arab authors (except for A. Olabi), but which was already known to de Goeje.

As a matter of fact, speaking of the cities of al-Bahrayn, Mas'ûdî writes: "Al-Zahrân and al-Hasâ, residences of the Temimite tribe of Sa'd;—al-Juwata, placed under the command of al-'Uryân, son of al-Haytham the Rebiite. It is from him that we hear of the leader of the black slaves, 'Alî, son of Muhammad, who revolted in the province of Basra, and who, in a poem composed at the moment he took up arms in the Bahrayn at the head of Temimite, Kilâbite, Numayrite, and other tribes, before going to Basra, claimed to be a descendant of Abû Tâlib. With the tribes of 'Abd al-Qays, of 'Âmir son of Sa'sa'a, of Muhârib, son of Khasafa, son of Qays, son of Aylân and others, al-'Uryân had attacked him; after several battles, he had forced him to leave Bahrayn and the vicinity, having inflicted great losses on him. In Sammân, 'Alî b. Muhammad had noticed a little bird and had written a poem that begins as follows:

> Oh, bird of Sammân, what are you doing there all alone? Did you come to find consolation near me, or did an accident separate you from your friend?

During this piece, he says:

> May my noble horses be taken from me if I do not bring them back (to Bahrayn) mounted by armored horsemen of noble race;
> Mounted by the men of Temîm headed by the glorious, valiant men of Kulayb, son of Yarbû;
> Sa'd forming the center; Numayr and the excellent swords of Kilâb on the flanks!
> If no accident prevents me, I will surprise 'Âmir and Muhârib in the morning with a blow that will smash them.
> Does 'Uryân think that I forget my horsemen who fell on the day of the attack near the dike, when death hung from them?

In another piece, the same poet, speaking of 'Abd al-Qays's tribe, says:

> Does 'Abd al-Qays think that I have forgotten him? I will never forget him and I will not renounce my vengeance.

De Goeje speaks of this passage and draws conclusions above all about the Qarmats, which takes us away from the subject. W. Caskel summarizes the period: "During the year 249–254 (863–868), an 'Alid or a pseudo 'Alid rebelled in Bahrayn. He tried his luck first in Hadjar then with the Sa'd in al-Ahsâ'. Finally, he went to the desert and gathered an army of Tamîm and tribes recently arrived from the West. Al-'Uryân and other 'Abd al-Qays princes had difficulty driving away the rebel who, before long, would set in motion the great Zanj revolt in Basra."

The First Sojourn in Basra. —In Basra, he stayed with the Banû Dubay'a. Some of the tribe, among whom were 'Alî b. Abân al Muhallabî (who will be mentioned a great deal in the pages that follow) and his two brothers, Muhammad and Halîl, rallied to him.

At this time the city was in turmoil because of the struggle between two tribal groups: the Balâlites and the Sa'dites. In an attempt to draw one of the parties into his camp, 'Alî b. Muhammad sent four of his men—Muhammad b. Salm al-Qassâb al-Hajarî, Buraysh al-Quray'î, 'Alî al-Darrâb, and Husayn al-Saydanânî, all faithful supporters since Bahrayn—to preach in front of the 'Abbâd mosque. Their mission was unsuccessful, and the governor of the city, Muhammad b. Rajâ al-Hidârî, drove them out.

Accompanied by Muhammad b. Salm, Yahyâ b. Muhammad, Sulaymân b. Jâmi', and Buraysh al-Quray'i, 'Alî b. Muhammad left the city and fled to Baghdad. His supporters in Basra, people who had joined his ranks and certain members of his family, were thrown into prison on orders from the governor. Among his companions who were jailed were Yahyâ b. Abî Tha'lab and Muhammad b. al-Hasan al-Iyâdî. Members of his household who were imprisoned included his wife, his oldest son, his daughter, and her servant.

The Sojourn in Baghdad.—The fugitives were captured while crossing al-Batîha and taken before the governor of Wâsit, Muhammad b. Abî 'Awn. 'Alî b. Muhammad managed to extricate himself and his men from their precarious situation, and he went on to Baghdad where they remained for a year. At that time, he was claiming to be a descendant of Ahmad b. 'Isâ b. Zayd. In addition, he again invoked the supernatural: he claimed to know what every one of his men was doing and thinking and to have received a message that was written auto-matically on a wall, in handwriting that was invisible.

During his stay in Baghdad, his supporters increased in numbers. Among his new supporters were Ja'far b. Muhammad al-Sûhânî, Muhammad b. al-Qâsim, and two of Yahyâ b. 'Abd al-Rahmân b. Khaqân's *gulâm* (young servants or freed slaves) named Mushriq and Rafîq. To Mushriq, 'Alî b. Muhammad gave the name Hamza Abû Ahmad, and to Rafîq that of Ja'far Abû al-Fadl.

Return to the Basra Region.—Meanwhile, Muhammad b. Rajâ, who had been dismissed as governor of Basra, left the city. Anarchy and disturbances broke out immediately thanks to the Balâlite and Sa'dite agitators who opened the doors of the prisons and freed the inmates. As soon as he learned of this, 'Alî b. Muhammad returned to the Basra region. This was in the month *Ramadân* 255/August–September 869, and among the supporters who accompanied him were 'Alî b. Abân al-Muhallabî (who had joined the ranks during the time in Baghdad), Yahyâ b. Muhammad, Muhammad b. Salm, Sulaymân b. Jâmi', Mushriq, Rafîq, and a deserter from the army named Abû Ya'qûb who took the name Jurbân. When they arrived at Furât al-Basra, they settled at Qasr al-Qurashî, located at Bi'r Nakhl on the 'Amûd b. al-Munajjim Canal, in the saltpeter region. Now, 'Alî b. Muhammad passed himself off as a business man from a princely family and the manager of a *sabâkh* sale for one of al-Wâthiq's children. This brought him into close contact with the Zanj, and he began preparing the uprising.

The first person in the region to join him was a man named Rayhân b. Sâlih. While engaged in his usual work transporting flour from Basra for distribution to the Zanj laborers in the area, he was captured near Bi'r Nakhl and taken to 'Alî b. Muhammad who questioned him about the situation in the city. He was unable to provide the rebel leader with any information. 'Alî b.

Muhammad then asked him about the workers in the saltpeter sites; he wanted to know how they were fed. He urged Rayhân to speak to the workers on his behalf and promised him a good reward and command of any he succeeded in recruiting. After having sworn to return and not to reveal to anyone 'Alî b. Muhammad's where-abouts, Rayhân was allowed to continue on his way. When he had made his delivery, he returned to 'Alî b. Muhammad and became one of his followers.

Rafîq, whom 'Alî b. Muhammad had sent to Basra, returned accompanied by a *dibs* merchant named Shibl b. Sâlim. He also brought with him the silk that 'Alî b. Muhammad had ordered him to purchase to make a flag. It was to be inscribed in red and green letters, with an entire verse from the Qur'an, beginning with: "Allâh purchased from believers their persons and their possessions, in exchange for a gift from the Garden. They fight in the path of Allâh. . . ." 'Alî's name and that of his father were also inscribed on the flag.

Proclamation of the Revolt.—The revolt was probably declared on Wednesday, 26 *Ramadân* 255/September 7, 869. Rebels intercepted a group of fifty slaves who were on their way to work. After binding the leader hand and foot, they went on to another work site where they did the same thing. Five-hundred slaves, including a certain Abû Hudayd, are reported to have joined them, then another 150 slaves, among whom were Zurayq and Abû l-Hanjar, and yet another 80 slaves, among whom were Râshid al-Magribî (Mugrabî?) and Râshid al-Qurmatî. Such occur-rences were constantly repeated, and the ranks of the insurgents continued to grow.

In due time, 'Alî b. Muhammad called together and addressed all of the men who had joined his cause. After promising them improve-ment in their conditions with much wealth, he solemnly swore that he would never deceive them or fail to support them.

Turning towards the slaveholders, he reminded them that they deserved death for the way they had behaved towards their slaves and for doing things forbidden by God. They replied that the slaves would leave him before long and offered him money to return them. 'Alî b. Muhammad ordered the slaves to beat their masters and overseers, and when each had received 500 blows, he released them after making them take a solemn oath not to reveal to anyone his whereabouts or the number of his troops. One of the slave owners crossed the Dujayl and went to warn the overseers of the large camps where 15,000 slaves were working.

As for 'Alî b. Muhammad, he left the region after the prayer of the *'asr*. He crossed the Dujayl with his men and settled on Maymûn Canal. The mosque in the middle of the market overlooking the canal housed his headquarters.

At that time (middle of *Shawwâl* 255/September, 869), he was claiming to be 'Alî b. Muhammad b. Ahmad b. 'Alî b. Isâ b. Zayd b. 'Alî b. al-Husayn b. 'Alî b. Abî Talib.

Chapter 3
The Revolt and the Beginning of the War (Spread of the Insurrection)

There were two distinct periods in the Zanj revolt. The first (255–66/869–79) was the period of success and expansion. During this time, internal and external reasons prevented the central power from effectively suppressing the revolt. The second (266–70/879–83) was the slow agony before final defeat. In this period, the Caliphate made crushing the rebellion its chief order of business.

I. Riot Against Neighboring Villages and "the People of Basra" (255/869)

At the beginning, the insurrection appeared to be totally local. Masses of slaves had been stirred up against their masters, and their chief priorities were food and weapons. Confronting them were villagers trying to protect their property and the large landowners of Basra who were determined to use every means possible to regain repossession of their slaves. In the am-bushes and battles between slaves and freemen that ensued, the Zanj usually got the upper hand. One after the other, successive detachments sent out by "the people of Basra" were defeated and freed slaves swelled the ranks of the insurgents. The villages either surrendered or were sacked. Confused attempts were made to form coalitions against the rebels, but finally, just when a heavy offensive against them was on the verge of success, the Master of the Zanj managed to turn imminent defeat into victory. The residents of Basra were terrified by the bloody debacle, and they wrote to the Caliph to appeal for help. Meanwhile, the Zanj set up their new camp.

Tabarî gives many details of these events, and it should be possible to form a precise idea of what was a short period (about a month and a half). For reasons to be mentioned later, this is not the case.

The First Battles.—Rebel headquarters were set up on Maymûn Canal. On the Fast Breaking Day in 255/September 869, 'Alî b. Muhammad assembled his followers, whose numbers continued to grow, under the flag for prayer. In an address to them, he spoke of their miserable condition and assured them that God had chosen him to be the instrument of their deliverance. He also told them that he, 'Alî b. Muhammad, wanted to improve their lot so that one day they, too, might have beautiful homes and slaves. After the oath, and before leaving, he asked those who had understood to translate for anyone who did not speak Arabic.

Later, the rebels won their first significant victory. They defeated al-Himyarî and his men, and their ranks were swelled by three-hundred Zanj and their leader who rallied to their cause. Their numbers grew constantly. 'Alî b. Muhammad appointed officers and promised that any man they recruited would be assigned to them. Some authors claim that he did not name leaders until a little later, after the events in Bayân.

A troop of four-thousand men attacked the rebels. The Zanj "army" was poorly equipped to fend them off with only three sabers in its arsenal. One rebel was seen dashing into battle carrying only his plate as a weapon. Never-theless, the Zanj won another victory and put the enemy to flight. One member of the attacking force was killed; others died of thirst. On orders from 'Alî b. Muhammad, prisoners were be-headed. The Zanj carried away the severed heads on their own mules.

On the way back from the encounter, one of the blacks was killed by a resident of the village of al-Qâdisîya. 'Alî b. Muhammad would not give his men permission to sack the village and look for the culprit. He wanted to find out to what extent all villagers had been involved in the murder and whether or not they supported the assassin. When the rebels returned to Maymûn, they stuck the severed enemy heads on pickets and put them on display.

The next day, the Zanj headed for al-Ja'farîya, a village on al-Sîb Canal. There was no violence as they crossed the territory of al-Karkh and Jubbâ, where they found shelter. A resident of Jubbâ offered 'Alî b. Muhammad a horse. At the time, the Master of the Zanj had neither saddle nor bridle, so he improvised with a cushion of palm-tree stuffing and a cord. The Zanj entered Ja'farîya. The villagers had been warned of their imminent arrival and had already fled. The rebels took their first booty: 250 dinars, 1,000 dirhams, 3 horses, and many weapons.

The following day 'Alî b. Muhammad learned that an army under the joint command of three leaders, Rumays, al-Himyarî, and 'Aqîl was on its way to attack him. He sent 500 men, under Yahyâ b. Muhammad, against them. The Zanj won another victory, and seized weapons and a small boat. The next day 'Alî b. Muhammad signed a peace agreement with the inhabitants of al-Ja'farîya and then headed for al-Madhâr. Crossing al-Sîb, he encountered Rumays and his men in the village of al-Yahûd. In the battle that ensued, Rumays suffered a new defeat and considerable losses. The Zanj sank a small boat and beheaded its rower. They moved on to Jabal al-Shayâtîn where

Rumays offered 'Alî b. Muhammad five dinars for each slave returned and promised to let the Master of the Zanj leave the territory without any difficulty. 'Alî b. Muhammad violently rejected the offer.

lbrâhîm b. Ja'far al-Hamadânî joined the insurgents. The future general explained to 'Alî b. Muhammad why he thought that instead of going toward al-Madhâr, it would be preferable to march to the south of the Ahwâz, where the people were ready to accept him and the Balâlites were even waiting for him.

Both Rumays' proposal and lbrâhîm's words caused considerable unrest among the Zanj. Disturbances erupted and some men fled. 'Alî b. Muhammad reacted immediately. That very night he assembled his men and, through an interpreter, swore that none of them would ever be returned to their former masters. "May some of you remain with me and kill me if you feel that I am betraying you." Then he called together those who spoke Arabic and solemnly promised to lead them in battle personally and risk his life with them. He assured them that it was not for the wealth and honor of this world that he had rebelled. The Zanj were calmed down by his words.

The next day, there were new and bloody battles on al-Sîb Canal. When 'Alî b. Muhammad met with the inhabitants of al-Ja'farîya and attempted to avoid fighting by requesting safe passage from the villagers and reminding them of their peace agreement, they responded with stones and arrows. The Zanj killed several people in retaliation. The prisoners they took were reprimanded and then released. 'Alî b. Muhammad guaranteed the village that it would be protected and told his men that any pillaging would be punished. He engaged Rumays and his allies in battles, and his Zanj forces captured four small boats and their crew. From the prisoners he learned that Rumays and the others had been promised substantial rewards by the villagers and slave owners. After inquiring about two of his own men, he ordered all the prisoners, except one, decapitated, the boats put to the torch, and the flags and severed heads removed.

The Zanj were well received by the residents of the Banû 'Ijl village and again by inhabitants of al-Karkh. 'Alî b. Muhammad spent the night in conversation with a Jew who claimed to have found a passage about him in the Torah. At the time wine was not forbidden in the army.

According to one inhabitant of al-Karkh, a large enemy army was coming their way. It would bar 'Alî b. Muhammad's path across the bridge over al-Maymûn Canal and make it impossible for him to return to his camp. The hostile force consisted of Rumays, leading inhabitants of al-Maftah and neighboring villages; 'Aqîl, (accompanied by people from al-Ubulla); so-called al-Dabîlâ (a people of Dravidian origin, the original population of India), and al-Himyarî (one of the commanders of anti-Zanj forces) with people from al-Furât. 'Alî b. Muhammad checked their positions and prepared an ambush in which many of the enemy were killed. The twenty-two prisoners taken were decapitated and their heads kept, as was the custom. With the help of a man who knew the area, the Zanj crossed the river and returned to their camp, where they displayed the severed heads on pickets.

Rumays pursued the Zanj. Informed of the situation by spies, 'Alî b. Muhammad sent a thousand men against the pursuers and wrote to 'Aqîl, reminding him of the peace agreement signed with the inhabitants of al-Ubulla. He also reminded Rumays of the agreement they had entered into at al-Sîb Canal.

From their camp on Maymûn Canal, the Zanj headed in the direction of their vanguard. Along the way, 'Alî b. Muhammad gave orders to sack the villages of al-Qâdisîya and al-Shifîyâ because they had refused to hand over the man who had previously killed one of his soldiers. The villages were sacked and the inhabitants placed in captivity. The assassin was beheaded. 'Alî b. Muhammad stopped the Zanj troops when they began drinking the wine looted from al-Qâdisîya and reminded them that they still had battles to fight.

Rumays' and 'Aqîl's men established a foothold on the left bank of the Dujayl, and the Dabîlâ boats occupied the river. 'Alî b. Muhammad prepared for battle by drawing up his troops and consulting an astrolabe. When his Zanj troops attacked, they were victorious; a great number of their opponents were killed; others fled without looking back. Enemy boats blown closer to the shore by the wind were seized and their occupants massacred. A reward of one dinar and command of a one-hundred-man troop of blacks was promised to any one of 'Alî b. Muhammad's men

According to an insurgent named Rayhân, he and 'Alî b. Muhammad quarreled over a *jubba* (a man's dress) during the pillage. Zanj forces later captured al-Zaynabî's garrison, which was on the right bank of al-Qindal Canal and guarded by two-hundred men, many of whom were killed during the siege. The Zanj spent the night in the garrison.

The next day, the rebels pillaged the village of Mundhirân, where they found many Zanj. The blacks rallied to the rebel cause, and 'Alî b. Muhammad divided them among his officers. Boats headed for Dubbâ were captured next, and some claim that it was only at this point that 'Alî b.

Muhammad appointed commanders of his rebel army.

A native of Basra, a certain Muhammad b. Ja'far al-Muraydî, was found in the area and taken to 'Alî b. Muhammad, who questioned him about the Balâlites. He claimed that they were interested in knowing the conditions for joining the insurgents. 'Alî b. Muhammad gave al-Muraydî assurances of goodwill and an escort as far as al-Fayyâd. After waiting four days for the Basrian to return, he inspected the region himself and noticed a group of more than six-hundred Bedouin horsemen. Muhammad b. Salm was sent out to reconnoiter the situation. He returned with his report, and 'Alî b. Muhammad, suspecting an enemy ruse, gave orders to attack the horsemen. His suspicions were justified. The Bedouins unfurled a black flag (official flag of the Abbasids); al-Zaynabî's brother Sulaymân (soon to become commander of an anti-Zanj army of Balâlites and Sa'dites from Basra) was among them.

The Zanj finally reached Dubbâ, where they slaughtered sheep and spent the night. The next day, in the al-Amîr Canal region, they attacked troops under the command of Shihâb b. al-'Alâ' al-'Anbârî, who managed to escape with a small number of men, though most were massacred. A group of six-hundred slaves (*shûrjiyya*) encountered by the Zanj, who killed their *wakîl*, rallied to 'Alî b. Muhammad. In the Basra Canal region, the Zanj stopped in the vicinity of al-Dinârî Canal. After giving his men orders not to rush to attack the big city and to wait for a signal from him, he sent them to pillage the surrounding area.

Battles in the Vicinity of Basra.—The Zanj reached al-Riyâhî Canal. Informed of the enemy's presence, 'Alî b. Muhammad dispatched 'Alî b. Abân and a detachment of three-thousand men to engage them and promised to send reinforcements if necessary. He was told that people were approaching from the direction of al-Ja'farîya, and he sent Muhammad b. Salm along that route. A member of the expedition named Rayhân left a detailed account of how it unfolded. Fighting was fierce, but the Zanj were finally victorious, and the enemy (the *jund*, or the regular army, the Bedouins, the Balâlites, and the Sa'dites) suffered five-hundred casual-ties. Muhammad b. Salm carried the severed heads back to 'Alî b. Muhammad. A Balâlite prisoner who was brought back was able to give information about the enemy troops and name their commanders, but as far as their exact number was concerned, he could only say that it was large.

The real battle took place the next day, 12 *Dhû l-Qa'da* 255. 'Alî b. Muhammad, who had drawn up his troops after having forbidden them, once again, to attack the city, sent reinforcements. With boats carrying his supporters' wives and loaded with beasts of burden, he himself headed for the al-Kathîr Canal bridge. After a terrible battle, the Zanj were defeated and routed. Many perished in battle; others drowned in the canal. 'Alî b. Muhammad himself narrowly escaped death after trying to organize his retreat and fighting alone while separated from his men. He returned to a place called al-Mu'allâ, on the right bank of the Shaytân Canal, with the remnants of his army. Most of his men were scattered or in flight. Attempts were made to rally the five hundred or so who remained but there was no response to the usual signal. Small groups did return during the night, and Rayhân was sent on a scouting mission to the area around the Harb Canal bridge, but he found nothing. The "people of Basra" had seized and looted Zanj boats.

The next morning, 13 *Dhû l-Qa'da* 255, 'Alî b. Muhammad took a count of his men; a thousand had come back during the night. He reprimanded a certain Shibl, whose flight and return with ten deserters has been described in different versions, and questioned him about the other runaways. He sent Muhammad b. Salm to the bridge of the Kathîr Canal to speak to the "people of Basra" and explain the reasons for the revolt. Sulaymân b. Jâmi' and Yahyâ b. Muhammad accompanied the emissary as far as the river. When he was killed, they returned with the news to 'Alî b. Muhammad, who ordered them not to tell anyone. He himself told his men, after the al-'asr prayer, and promised that Muhammad b. Salm's death would be avenged the next day by the death of ten-thousand Basrians. Then he sent Zurayq to make sure that no one crossed the river.

Three boats loaded with fighters and scores of unarmed people left Basra on 14 *Dhû l-Qa'da* 255, guided by an experienced sailor. As soon as scouts reported this activity, 'Alî b. Muhammad, who was on the Shaytân Canal, prepared his defense: two ambushes, one on each bank of the river, and a third, commanded by 'Alî b. Abân, facing the enemy. Zanj women were given the task of supplying their warriors with rocks. The Basrians suffered an overwhelming defeat. Attacked from all sides, many drowned as they tried to flee, or were killed the minute they set foot on land. 'Alî b. Muhammad said that he was aided by supernatural forces that sent great white birds to capsize the enemy boats. Many prominent Basrians lost their lives in the battle. The Zanj put some of their foes' severed heads on display and loaded the rest on boats to Basra.

The day has remained known as "Yawm al-shadhâ" (from the type of boats used) and is celebrated by poets. It was the beginning of a great deal of renewed strength for 'Alî b. Muhammad and his struggle. The panic-stricken residents of

Basra wrote of their defeat to the Caliph, who responded by sending the Turk, Ju'lân, to their aid. Abû l-Ahwas al-Bâhilî was named *wâlî* of al-Ubulla, and the Turk, Jurayh, was appointed his assistant.

'Alî b. Muhammad's troops were eager to attack Basra, and he had to restrain them. "It is up to them to seek you out," he told them. He established a new camp on the *sabkha* (salt marsh) of Abû Qurrâ and in a friendly place, surrounded by date palm trees and prosperous villages, ordered his men to build huts. The Zanj dispersed throughout the region, killing and plundering everything in their path and seizing cattle.

Black Slaves in the Mediterranean World: Introduction to a Neglected Aspect of the African Diaspora

John O. Hunwick

The Trading of Slaves

During the pre-modern period in the Muslim world (for the purposes of this paper before the mid-nineteenth century), slaves of many and varied origins poured into the Mediterranean basin and the Near East. Many were purchased by sultans and princes to serve in their armies, to act as bodyguards and to staff their palaces. Among the rest of the population it was generally only the middle and upper bourgeoisie—government servants, teachers, merchants and the like—who could afford the expense of purchasing a slave. There were, of course, cheap as well as highly expensive slaves, the black male (unless an Ethiopian, a eunuch or possessing some outstanding skills) generally being among the cheapest. Thus in certain times and places when supply was abundant and prices consequently lower than normal, artisans, tradesmen and even peasants might be able to afford such a purchase. Although the majority of the population in the areas under consideration was Muslim, slave owning was not confined to them. Jews and Christians, though legally second-class citizens in the lands of Islam, were permitted to own domestic slaves, though they could not own slaves who had converted to Islam. It was also possible in Islamic law jointly to own a slave with one or more other persons. Joint ownership most frequently came about through the precise requirements of Islamic inheritance law, though there was nothing to stop two individuals sharing in the price of a slave, if neither could afford the slave by himself, and then to apportion his labor. In the case of a female slave neither owner would have rights of concubinage.

In the first century of Islam slaves were acquired by the Arabs during the period of the great Islamic conquests which expanded the borders of the Dar al-Islam, the abode of Islam, westwards to as far as the R. Douro in northern Spain, eastwards to the Indus valley and northwards to the R. Oxus. The conquered people, however, soon began to adopt Islam *en masse* and it became necessary to look farther afield for sources of slaves. The jurists, basing their views on the reality of the situation, declared that what lay beyond the Dar al-Islam was Dar al-Harb, the abode of war, which the Muslims should attempt to gain control of by agreement or by force and incorporate into the Dar al-Islam. Although the Qur'an and the Traditions of the Prophet give no support and the jurists are silent on the issue, it became commonly accepted that since the peoples of the Dar al-Harb were non-Muslims and hence liable to be attacked in a *jihad*, they were also all potential slaves. Hence, any of them the Muslims could lay hands on, whether by actual *jihad* (probably the least common method), by raiding on sea or land or by purchase, could be taken as slaves.

The Muslims of the Mediterranean basin obtained slaves from all three continents of the Old World. Firstly from Europe, notably from the populations of central and northern Europe and the west of what is now the Soviet Union. These were the so-called "Slavs" (*saqaliba*) obtained largely through the agency of Jewish and Christian merchants and purchased by the Muslims at certain northern Mediterranean seaports and through the ports of the Black Sea. This source dried up by the twelfth century as Europe began to emerge from its Dark Ages, but piratical activity by North African corsairs along the northern shores of the Mediterranean and the Atlantic coasts of Europe continued down to the end of the eighteenth century. A second important source of slaves was Central Asia, the home of diverse nomadic tribes speaking Turkic languages. These warrior slaves were in great demand from the middle of the ninth century when the caliphs of Baghdad first began recruiting forces of Turkish guards to form a buffer between themselves and their regular Arab and Persian troops. Later, the great Manduk dynasty of Egypt (1250–1517) was to derive its sultans and all its senior officers of state from, at first, Central Asian slaves (Turkic and Mongol tribes) and later from Circassian slaves from the Caucasus. Indeed, their very name—Mamluk—means "possessed" in Arabic.

The third great human reservoir, and the one which mainly concerns us in this paper, was sub-Saharan Africa, which was one of the first to be drawn upon and the last to dry up. The Nile Valley and the Red Sea provided relatively easy channels of communication between the Mediterranean region and certain areas of the continent. The conquest of Egypt soon brought the Arabs into direct contact with black Africa in the shape of the Nubian kingdoms that bordered Upper Egypt. An agreement was soon made with the Nubians that in exchange for the annual tribute of 360 slaves the Muslims would leave the Christian Nubians in peace. The name given to this agreement, the *baqt*, appears to be an arabicization of the Greek *pakton* (or Latin *pactum*); thus the Arabs would merely have become heirs to an arrangement that has been in existence for long. Up the Red Sea came slaves from Ethiopia, the Horn of Africa and the East African coast; slaves from these regions were also taken to ports of the Persian Gulf and some were re-exported from there to India. From newly established towns in North Africa Arab and Berber merchants soon discovered routes leading across the Sahara to the polities of the Sahelian belt. The primary lure there was gold from the western Sudanic regions, but from a very early period slaves also formed a significant item in the trade especially along the central Sudanic route via the Fazzan to Kanem, just to the north of Lake Chad, for this region produced no gold. The slaves were provided by local rulers, at first non-Muslims but from the eleventh century onwards increasingly Muslims, who exchanged slaves they had taken in raids and wars for a wide variety of Mediterranean goods. Barbary horses were among the more valuable commodities imported into the Sahel and these were typically bartered against slaves in the ratio of 10–15 slaves (depending on age and sex) against one horse. The trans-Saharan slave trade diminished in the nineteenth century as the North African states, one by one (beginning with the French in Algeria after 1830), abolished first the trade in and then the ownership of slaves, though slaves were still being clandestinely brought across to Benghazi via the Tibesti and Kufra as late as 1910. Among the Tuareg in the central Sahara a form of slavery existed until at least the 1950s.

When the slave-dealer (commonly known as a *jallab*, "importer" or *nakhkhas*, "goader/cattle-dealer") brought his human merchandise to a commercial center within the Dar al-Islam, he handed them over to a broker (*dallal*) who either put them up for sale in a public slave-market or, if they were more highly prized, arranged for their sale privately. The brokers were also responsible for slave resales, for during this period of captivity a slave might be sold many times over. The *muhtasib* had to keep a close eye on brokers and ensure that certain stipulations were observed. Among these were that the broker know to whom a slave was being sold and should record the slave's name and description (important in case the slave turned out to be a free man or stolen property); he also had to find out any conditions imposed at first sale and ensure that no Muslim slave was sold to a non-Muslim. A male slave might be inspected above the navel and below the knees; the purchaser of a female slave might only see her hands and her face (in point of fact African slaves were often much more scantily clad), but if women were present and he took the slave girl to his house with them he might see her entire body in their presence. A woman who had children under the age of seven could not be separated from them. The purchaser was allowed a period of three days trial with his new slave before the deal was ratified. If he found defects in a slave that were not apparent at the time of sale he could return the merchandise. Not surprisingly, brokers had a considerable stock of artifices for making their female slaves look more attractive. A twelfth-century Spanish manual for the *muhtasib* describes the cosmetic treatment given to black girls:

> They anoint their faces, their arms and legs with oil of violets and perfume to improve their appearance. They blacken their hair with oil of myrtle, oil of fresh walnut and poppy oil and wash it with a decoction of myrobalan. They make the hair curl tightly with [extract of] lotus, myrtle and azerderac. They remove body odor by making a paste of white lead and rose-water which they make into tablets and store inside a rose until it dries out.

The same author also warns against the wiles of slave brokers who take advantage of the trial period allowed by law clandestinely to hire out slave girls for prostitution.

By the time the black African slave reached the slave market in North Africa or the Middle East he or she was already a nominal Muslim. This was ensured by the slave-dealers themselves who had male slaves circumcised when necessary and both male and female slaves given Arabic names. These names were often peculiar to slaves and tended to have meanings which were redolent of happiness, good fortune and favor from God; for males Khayr Allah (goodness of God), Jar Allah ("neighbor" of God), Kafar (camphor), 'Anbar (ambergris), Murjan (gem); for females Umm al-khayr (mother of goodness), Bakhita (fortunate), Mabruka (blessed), Mahbuba (beloved), Sa'ida (happy), Za'faran (saffron) etc. Under more pious masters favorite slaves were taught to pray and read the Qur'an; on the other hand some (perhaps many) retained their original religious and cosmological beliefs and gave an Islamic veneer (sometimes very thin) to ceremonies that derived from their African past.

Most large towns in the Islamic Mediterranean world had a special hall or courtyard within their market area devoted to the sale of slaves. The Dutch scholar C. Snouck Hurgronje, who spent the year 1884–5 in Mecca, describes the slave market there:

> All kinds of African slaves were obtainable in large quantities through the brokers. The slaves of both sexes exposed in the slave market (a large hall near the mosque gate called Bab Derebeyah) are partly fresh arrivals and partly offered for sale by masters who no longer need them. On the benches near the wall sit girls and women, the adults lightly veiled; before them sit or stand on the ground male slaves of riper years; in the middle play dozens of children. Some slave-brokers converse on their living merchandise. One of the spectators is giving special attention to a small black boy. The broker charged with the sale of this boy calls him up and shows his teeth and tongue and meanwhile praises his style and skill. If the customer is a sensible man he now addresses the slave himself, for no slave deceives a person who might ever become his master about his own merits . . . The broker does not delay to show the part of the boy's body where he has small-pox marks (the surest inoculation against recurrence) . . . If the customer is still doubtful he goes to a doctor who examines slaves for money. If he is very pious he has recourse to what is called *istikhara*, that is he leaves the choice to God by performing certain religious ceremonies and then going to sleep and letting the decision depend on his dreams, or if he is superstitious, he goes to a divinely illuminated sheikh or to a sand-diviner. Before the deal is closed, the customer asks the slave: "Are you willing to serve me?" . . . [for] no one would buy a male slave against his will, and still less a female slave against her will.

Since the sale of a slave was a binding contract in law, the purchaser had to take great care that he was not duped. As the above passage points out, there were special doctors who examined slaves to spot physical defects or tell-tale signs of debilitating diseases. Some of them wrote treatises on the examination process (*al-taqlib*), while the tenth-century Christian physician of Baghdad, Ibn Butlan, in his treatise also included sections giving the current wisdom on the qualities and dispositions of slaves of various ethnic origins as well as a warning against the wiles of the brokers.

As mentioned above, the purchaser had (as with other merchandise) a period of three days in which to uncover hidden defects. In the case of a woman destined to be a concubine the law demanded that she undergo a period of waiting to determine if she were pregnant (*istibra'*). She was to be kept in the household of a trustworthy third-party until she menstruated, unless she were sold while actually menstruating, but this precaution was not uncommonly ignored.

Slave Occupations in the Islamic Mediterranean World

Al-Saqati, whose manual for the *muhtasib* has already been alluded to, summed up the principal occupations for male slaves as follows: "In regard to males, Indians and Nubians are suitable for looking after property and persons, Zanj and Armenians are good for heavy labor and service which is rewarded, while Turks and Slavs are suitable for war and acts of bravery." His categories: domestic and commercial service, unskilled labor (both agricultural and industrial) and soldiering do in fact represent the three major types of occupation to which male slaves were put in the Mediterranean world. Contrary to his ethnic type-casting, however, we find that black African slaves served in all three of his categories. Although we lack any statistical basis for such an assertion, it is probably safe to say that over the eleven or twelve centuries of the black slave experience in the Islamic Mediterranean, the largest number of such slaves were used in the domestic and commercial sphere and the least in the industrial and agricultural, while military service only absorbed large numbers in certain specific times and places.

Female slaves were uniquely reserved for domestic tasks: cooking, cleaning, washing, waiting on the ladies of the house, acting as nursemaids or wet-nurses for their children and, if they were the property of one of the males of the household, sharing the bed of their master as and when he desired. There was a generally recognized "pecking order" for female slaves and a stereotyping of their qualities and abilities. In nineteenth-century Egypt (and other times and places roughly reflect its preferences) white females were at the top of the hierarchy and often married their masters or their masters' sons. Next came the Ethiopian women *habashiyyat*—usually Oromo [Galla] who were too proud to serve white women and were usually concubines of middle-class males and did only minor household chores. At the bottom of the list were the African women other than Ethiopians who did heavier household chores and were concubines of lower middle-class males. They were reckoned to be too proud to serve Ethiopians, but were willing to serve white women.

The situation in nineteenth-century Mecca was evidently somewhat similar. According to Snouck Hurgronje, non-Ethiopian black women (presumably mainly East Africans and southern and western Sudanese) were considered the strongest of African women and were used for housework in the kitchen or the living rooms, though sometimes also as concubines. Ethiopian women, who were generally considered to have more delicate constitutions, were reserved mainly for concubinage and were highly prized by Meccan males. The same observer goes on:

> If the ordinary Mekkan followed his inclination (rather than his social obligations), he would unite himself only to Abyssinians... The aim of the Abyssinian woman is a lasting connection with a Mekkan to whom she, if her good intellectual and moral gifts have not been spoilt by her upbringing, becomes a true life companion... The well brought up Abyssinian women are excellent housekeepers, modest, unpretending women, and they put all their good qualities at the service of their lord. The high esteem in which they are held by Mekkan men is most clearly shown in the many cases in which an Abyssinian woman has borne him from five to twelve children, and the children are the best pledge of the continuance of their parents' happiness. As mother of one or more Mekkans she belongs to Mekkan society as a virtually free member, though nominally her slavery continues.

Lane paints a rather similar picture of domestic bliss involving Ethiopian women and Egyptian males in the earlier years of the nineteenth century and points out that the situation of a concubine who has borne her master children was, indeed, more secure than that of a free wife, for the latter could be divorced unilaterally whereas the slave mother could not be sold or given away and was free on her master's death. Concubinage thus provided a means of integration into society for both the woman and her children, lineage rather than skin color being the principal determinant of social status.

Concubinage and a settled domestic life were, however, not necessarily the lot of all female slaves. Those who were taken into the harems of large households, even if they were maintained in a state of physical well-being, were, with the exception of passing favorites, treated merely as objects of physical pleasure who might see their master but rarely and can have had little feeling of attachment. Those who did not produce at least one child were liable to be sold, while those whose attractions had diminished through child-bearing would find themselves no longer in their master's favor unless they had unusual intellectual or musical talents. In the big harems of the Turkish officials all concubines except the favorites of the hour were subject to the tyranny of their keepers, the black eunuchs, who compensated for their robbed masculinity by bullying and cajoling the females under their command. Nor, of course, were all female slaves taken as concubines. Some were not considered attractive enough for the role and were destined to a lifetime of household drudgery. Even this was not the worst that could happen to a female slave. Though we have no clear indication of how common it was for such women to be prostituted, the fact that writers on *hisba* warn the *muhtasib* to be on the watch for it, indicates that it cannot have been uncommon. At the hands of a slave dealer prostitution was but a passing, though inevitably degrading, experience. Among the Ibadis of Jabal Nafusa in Libya in the twelfth century, however, it seems to have been a regular practice, while in Egypt in the nineteenth century the *ghawazi*—popular singers, dancers and prostitutes—sometimes kept their own black female slaves, the profits of whose prostitution they took for themselves. Reports from the Sudan in the same century also indicate that slave prostitution was not uncommon.

As indicated above, male slaves were also used for domestic tasks and to assist their master in his commercial dealings or other means of livelihood. In a society where there was normally a rigid partitioning between those areas of the house where the females lived and worked and those which might be used only by the male members of the household and their guests, it was necessary to have males (either slaves or servants—the latter more rare) to look after the public and private rooms, to prepare the master's pipe and coffee and to attend to the needs of master and guests for refreshments. Slaves also had the task of attending to horses or donkeys and, in the richer households of nineteenth-century Egypt, to carriages. They normally accompanied their master when he rode out, clearing the way for him in the narrow, crowded streets, defending him against aggressors or thieves and taking charge of his mount at his destination. They were also sent out independently to carry messages, to make purchases in the market and to fetch goods needed for the master's business. In the households of rulers or other eminent persons (*a'yan*) there might be scores of male slaves, including a number of eunuchs, whose tasks were highly specialized and whose positions were fixed according to a strict hierarchy.

Some interesting glimpses of the condition of the black slave in medieval Egyptian society are afforded us by the scattered entries in the great biographical dictionary of the fifteenth century compiled by al-Sakhawi. The period he was writing of was, of course, one dominated by men of slave origin, though the reigning Mamluks were of white, Circassian origin. Nevertheless, it is likely that, in general, a slave origin might have been an advantage rather that a disadvantage. The main rungs of the ruling estate were filled by Circassian Mamluks as were most subordinate positions in the households of the sultan and the emirs. Some of the latter positions (as well as positions in the households of great Egyptian merchants) were filled by black slaves, mainly Ethiopians, about one third of those well-known enough to reach the pages of al-Sakhawi's work being eunuchs. Many of these rose quite rapidly to positions of responsibility within the sultan's household or in the households of related families; but often just as rapidly they were dismissed or banished on their master's whim or because he suspected them of embezzlement or other malfeasance. One such Ethiopian became customs collector for the port of Jeddah, another (a eunuch) was made governor of Aden, while a third (also a eunuch) was sent on a mission to his home country, though he was subsequently removed from office as Commander of the Sultan's Mamluks (muqaddam al-mamalik) and banished. More fortunate Ethiopians retained enough of the wealth they gained through office to retire comfortably, to pursue the Islamic sciences and to build mosque-colleges (madrusa). Those belonging to merchants were often allowed to trade and travel in their own right. One, who was freed by his master, combined commercial acumen with piety and learning and on his former master's death married his widow.

The second major use to which male black slaves were put was military service. On the one hand they were used in the militia or bodyguards of petty rulers, while on the other they often formed a distinct corps in the professional armies of North Africa and Egypt. Slave soldiers were a common phenomenon in the Islamic world, at least during the sixteenth century when the Ottomans established themselves in the Levant, Egypt and much of North Africa. In the eastern provinces of the Islamic empire these were mainly Turks recruited from the nomadic tribes of Central Asia. In Egypt, too, Turkish troops were commonly used from the late ninth century down to the mid-fourteenth century when they finally ceded to Circassians, while free "Turks" (often, in fact, Greeks, Bosnians, Albanians or other south-east European peoples) made up the military during the Ottoman period (1517–1798). Black slave troops were first introduced into Egypt during the period of the Turkish governor, Ahmad b.Tulun (868–84) and a special quarter was built for them in the barrack town established for foreign troops. In the following century, the Ikhshidids, successors to the Tulunids, also employed black troops, while under

their successors, the Fatimids (969–1171), large battalions of black troops were raised to counterbalance the powerful Berber and Turkish contingents. There were many violent clashes between these three great military divisions and on several occasions the Turks and Berbers united against the blacks. In the final and greatest clash, which took place in 1169, an estimated 50,000 black troops fought valiantly against their hostile colleagues in arms before being defeated and driven out of Cairo to seek refuge in southern Egypt. The Fatimids' successors, the Ayyubids, did not revive the tradition of using black troops and, indeed, it was not until the early nineteenth century under Muhammad Ali that they were used again.

In North Africa and Andalusia both African and European slave troops were used, the Africans being called by the generic name sudan ("blacks") and the Europeans by the generic name saqaliba ("Slavs"), use of the latter dying out by the twelfth century. Black troops were first used under the Aghlabid dynasty of Ifriqiya (roughly modern Tunisia) in the ninth century, possibly from very early on in their reign, though this has been disputed. The need here, as with Turks in Baghdad and blacks in Egypt at a similar period, was to counteract the potentially rebellious tendencies of local troops by creating a corps which had no local attachments and which was made up of men who owed their very existence to the ruler and hence whose loyalty could be counted upon. The Aghlabids' successors, the Fatimids, first slaughtered the blacks who had served the Aghlabids and then raised another corps of blacks which would have no loyalty but to them. When the Fatimids removed the seat of their dynasty to Cairo in 969, their lieutenants in Ifriqiya, the Zirids, continued to use black slave troops and, on occasion, we find these troops becoming involved in dynastic struggles. After the Hilalian migration in the mid-eleventh century black troops appear to have been little used; the Hilali Arabs quickly took over their role, hiring their services to any party that offered them the opportunity for enrichment.

In the "farther Maghrib" (al-maghribal-aqsa— roughly modern Morocco), black troops are not in evidence until the reign of the Almoravid ruler Yusuf b.Tashfin (1061–1106) who established a bodyguard of some two thousand, as well as a corps of European slave troops recruited in Spain. The Almoravids' successors, the Almohads, also made use of black troops to a limited extent. The most intensive use of black troops—indeed, the supreme example of the use of such troops in the Mediterranean world—came in the reign of the second 'Alawid sultan, Mulay Isma'il (1672–1727), himself the son of a black concubine. Early in his reign he took the decision to create an exclusively black slave army which would constitute the instrument of his very personal rule. A small black slave corps had been formed some eighty years earlier from slaves brought back from Timbuktu following the conquest of the Middle Niger by troops of the Sa'dian sultan al-Mansur in 1591. Early in his reign Mulay Isma'il ordered the seizure of all male blacks in his kingdom, whether slave or free, including "naturalized" blacks known as *haratin* who lived in regions bordering the Sahara and occupied a serf-like position *vis-à-vis* the Arab and Berber tribes. The blacks thus rounded up were subsequently augmented by expeditions into the Sahara and, no doubt, by the direct conduit of the trans-Saharan slave trade.

Isma'il also looked to the natural process of reproduction to maintain his army and to provide his household with the services it required and he set up a training and reproductive program tailored to his precise needs. In some ways this resembled the Mamluk system in Egypt in the period 1250–1517, as may be seen from this account by al-Nasiri:

> In the year 1100/1689 the sultan ordered those slaves to bring him all their sons and daughters over the age of ten. When they were brought he divided up the girls among the matrons (*'arifat*) of his household—one group per palace—to be educated and taught good manners. He divided the boys up among the builders and carpenters and other craftsmen to serve them and work with them and sent others to drive donkeys and to learn how to ride them. A year later they were transferred to driving mules which carried bricks, tiles, wood, etc., and after a further year they were transferred to the service of the central palace to make prefabricated blocks. The following year they were transferred to the first rank among the soldiery and were given uniforms and trained in the martial arts. After a further year they were given horses which they had to ride bareback and bring out to the arena to learn how to handle them. In the last year of their training, when they had mastered their mounts, they were given saddles to ride on and were taught how to charge and withdraw, how to be skillful in thrusting with lances and how to hurl javelins from on horseback. After this they were enrolled in the army of active service. Then he brought forth the girls who had come with them earlier and married one to each of them, giving each man ten *mithqal-s* [of gold] as dowry for his bride and each girl five *mithqal-s* for her trousseau. One of their older male relatives would be given charge of them

> and he would be given sufficient funds to build a house for him and huts for his companions. Then he would send them off to join the army after their names had been recorded in the army register.

Isma'il thus created a self-perpetuating black slave army which may have numbered as many as one hundred and fifty thousand men at its height. Following his death they became king-makers over the coming thirty years, enthroning and deposing during the period no less than seven of Isma'il's estimated five hundred sons. When, finally, in 1737 a stronger ruler, Mulay Muhammad III, came to the throne, he recruited an Arab army and dispersed the black regiments, some of whom were then enslaved by the Arab soldiers. A small number of those who remained in Morocco were reintegrated into the 'Alawid army at the end of the eighteenth century, while as late as the 1880s a 5,000-strong army of black slaves served the ruler of the small independent principality of Iligh in southern Morocco.

The third category of employment for black male slaves, and the one which is encountered least in the sources, is agricultural and industrial labor. It is difficult to say just how widespread the use of slave labor in these sectors of production was, since our sources, both Arab and European concern themselves chiefly with urban rather than rural conditions. One thing seems clear, however. Plantation-style slavery, such as was the norm in the New World, was not common in the Mediterranean world. When the Arabs conquered the Near East and North Africa in the seventh century they were not pushing into vast tracts of virgin land. They were taking control either of lands unsuitable for cultivation—such as deserts and mountains—or of agricultural lands of relatively limited extent which had been cultivated by indigenous populations for centuries. As nomads, the Arabs had little interest in settling on the land (and were, indeed, banned from so doing by the Caliph 'Umar) and adopted the more realistic policy of leaving the land in the hands of its owners and taxing them on its produce. Land-owning was generally on a peasant small-holding basis (even estates—*iqta'at*—were conglomerations of small-holdings rather than united agricultural terrains) and there were few areas where crops suitable to a large-scale production (for example, cotton, rice, sugar, dates) could be grown. It is, however, precisely in those areas where such non-perishable (and hence "exportable") produce could be grown that we do find evidence of plantation slavery. Sugar, for example, was being produced with the help of slave labor in the Ahwaz province of western Persia in the late ninth century. Slaves from this area joined in the great Zanj revolt when slaves of East African origin who were clearing marsh lands for cultivation in southern Iraq defied the forces of the 'Abbasid caliphate for a full fifteen years from 868 to 883. In the tenth century we also hear of large numbers of slaves being employed in the date groves of al-Ahsa' in the north-east of the Arabian peninsula near Bahrain and in Saharan oases where date growing forms an important source of revenue, slaves were commonly used, both in date production and for cultivating grain and vegetables. In nineteenth-century Egypt, when there was a high world demand for cotton and the supply of slaves from the Sudan was abundant, slave labor was used for a period to boost production. Saharan nomads, "Moors" in the west and Tuareg in the central Sahara, have traditionally made use of black slave labor for herding flocks, hewing wood, drawing water and as a general work force in their encampments. Slave labor was also used in working the salt pans of Taghaza and later Taodeni in the western Sahara (modern Mali), in the extraction and smelting of copper of Tegidda (modern Niger) and in exploitation of the gold mines of Wadi 'Allaqi in Egyptian Nubia until the mines became exhausted in the fourteenth century.

There remains one aspect of slavery in the Mediterranean Muslim world that has only so far been referred to in passing and to which, despite its distasteful nature, fuller reference must now be made: the eunuch (*tawashi*, or, euphemistically, *kaddim*—"servant," *fata*—"young man," *agha*—"chief," or *ustadh*—"teacher"). Castration of male slaves, although the maintenance of large harems by Muslim potentates undoubtedly encouraged the practice, had not been unknown in earlier cultures. It was practiced in ancient Persia and medieval China, for example. The practice seems to have been unknown, however, in ancient Arabia and does not appear in the Islamic Mediterranean until well into the second century of Islam. Early Muslims seem to have revolted against this practice and other abuses of slaves, for a saying was put into the mouth of the Prophet: "Whoever kills a slave, him will we kill. Whoever cuts off the nose of a slave, his nose will we cut off, and whoever castrates a slave, him also shall we castrate.". In fact, although Muslims were quite prepared to make use of eunuchs and to pay very high prices to obtain them, those of the Mediterranean lands at any rate were generally scrupulous about observing the prohibition on mutilation themselves. Thus European slaves destined for sale as eunuchs in the Muslim lands of the Mediterranean in the Middle Ages were operated on at Prague or Verdun; those coming from central Asia were operated upon in Kharazrn close to the Caspian Sea and those from southern Russia in Armenia. In Africa eunuchs were produced in several different locations. Ethiopia was for long a provider of eunuchs; all eunuchs mentioned by al-Sakhawi in his biographical dictionary of fifteenth century Egypt bear the *nisba* al-Habashi, though this term probably referred to a wider geographical area than present-day Ethiopia. Eunuchs were also produced, at least from the seventeenth century onwards, in Baghirmi, a nominally Muslim state to the south-east of L. Chad. From there they were sent across the Sahara to the Libyan coast or to Egypt, many crossing the Mediterranean to join service in the Ottoman sultan's harem; others were sent directly to Mecca with pilgrim caravans to serve in the mosque of the Ka'ba there or in the Prophet's mosque in Medina. Some eunuchs may also have reached the Mediterranean world from distant Nupe, since this kingdom is said to have begun sending eunuchs to Kano in the fifteenth century. Morocco, too, must have had a source of its own, since Mulay Isma'il is said to have owned upwards of two thousand, though whether their source was in West Africa or somewhere in Morocco cannot be definitely ascertained. There was also in the early nineteenth century (and no doubt before this) an operating center in Egypt itself, though it was run by Christians, not by Muslims. At the monastery of Deir al-Jandala, near Abu Tig in Upper Egypt some two to three hundred eunuchs were produced annually by monks who, despite their alleged skills, could not, apparently, prevent two out of every three operated upon from dying. As observed above, it was service in the harems of rulers and rich notables that created the demand for eunuchs. Once in such a position the eunuch could acquire considerable power, since he alone knew the intimate secrets of the household. The great harem of the Ottoman sultan in Istanbul was policed entirely by black eunuchs from the beginning of the seventeenth century. The status and power of the chief eunuch (the *Kislar Agha*) has been described by Penzer in his classic account of the harem:

> He became commander of the corps of *baltaji* or halberdiers, held the rank of Pasha with three tails, was confidential messenger between the Sultan and the Grand Vizier, was alone entitled to have both eunuchs and girls as slaves, was allotted as many as three hundred horses for his personal use, could alone approach the Sultan at all times of day and night, and was described as "the most illustrious of the officers who approach his August Person, and worthy of the confidence of monarchs and of sovereigns," was the most feared, and consequently the most bribed, official of the Ottoman Empire.

Not only did the eunuchs acquire power by virtue of the positions they were put in, but rulers often deliberately chose them for confidential positions and those involving stewardship of money or property because the eunuch had no family whose loyalty might challenge his loyalty to his master and no sons to whom he might think of bequeathing wealth or whose interests at court he might seek to promote. This did not necessarily stop eunuchs from acquiring wealth by fair means and foul, for in the absence of virility the most tangible evidence they could provide of their self-worth was the rich clothes they wore, the fine horses they rode, the elegant dwellings they lived in or the mosque-colleges they endowed..

It might be thought that their mutilated physical state (which revealed itself publicly through lack of secondary sexual characteristics and other physical peculiarities), would have made them objects of general derision. But this does not seem to have been the case. On the contrary, perhaps on account of their belonging to the most powerful households and always appearing in public richly dressed and finely mounted, they were held in awe by the common man. Perhaps, too, their rare and anomalous status enshrouded them in an air of mystery. The Swiss traveler Burckhardt, who visited Medina in 1829, described the function and status of the black eunuchs there, the leader of whom (shaykh al-haram) was a former Kislar Agha:

> The police of the mosque [of the Prophet], the office of washing the Hedjra [an inner covered court] and the whole of the building, of lighting the lamps etc., etc., is entrusted to the care of forty or fifty eunuchs, who have an establishment similar to that of the eunuchs of the Beitulla [the Ka'ba] at Mekka; but they are persons of greater consequence here; they are more richly dressed, though in the same costume; usually wear fine Cashmere shawls, and gowns of the best Indian silk stuffs, and assume airs of great importance. When they pass through the Bazar, everybody hastens to kiss their hands; and they exercise considerable influence in the internal affairs of the town. They have large stipends, which are annually sent from Constantinople by the Syrian Hadj caravan; they also share in all donations made to the mosque, and they expect presents from every rich hadjy, besides what they take as fees from visitors to the Hedjra. They live together in one of the best quarters of Medina, to the eastward of the mosque, and their houses are said to be furnished in a more costly manner than any others in the town. The adults are all married to black or Abyssinian slaves . . . The

eunuch of the mosque would be highly affronted if he were so termed by any person. Their usual title is Aga. Their chief takes the title of Highness, or Sadetkon [sa'adatkum], like a Pasha or the Sherif of Mecca..

It is a curious irony that while the female slave's best chance of a life of ease and respect was through the exploitation of her female sexuality as a concubine and ultimately as a mother, the male slave's surest road to prosperity and power lay in having his own sexuality sacrificed through a transformation whose physical and emotional pain can better be imagined than described.

Manumission and the Lot of the Freed Slave

As already observed, Islamic ethics encouraged the manumission of slaves while Islamic law provided the juristic framework within which the injunctions of the Qur'an and Hadith could find practical expression. There were several ways in which a slave might obtain his freedom. Firstly, the master might free his slave as an act of piety at any time and masters did evidently celebrate important family events, such as marriages or deaths by acts of manumission.. According to Morell, writing of Algeria in the 1850s, "scrupulous Musselmans think themselves bound to offer liberty after nine years' good service, because it is thought that after that time they have paid their value in labour.". Manumission at the expiry of a given term, or on repayment of the slave's value was also common. The slave could enter into a written contract with his master (kitaba) to buy his freedom installmentally and after this had been agreed upon he could not be disposed of. He was generally then granted the status of a ma'dhri—one "granted permission" to conduct business on his own behalf. Slaves also commonly obtained their freedom on their master's death, either by the master writing this condition into his will (as part of the one-third of his estate not subject to formal division) or in the case of a concubine who had borne him a child (the so-called umm walad), by the automatic process of enfranchisement that such a status guaranteed her on her master's death. The umm walad and the slave who had been promised freedom on his master's death (al-mudabbar) could not be disposed of thereafter since they were already conditionally free.. When a master freed a slave during his lifetime he was under an unwritten obligation to see that the freedman was able to establish himself independently. In nineteenth-century Egypt a freed slave was given a sum of money equivalent to about half of his replacement value to set himself up in a craft or trade.. A female slave would not be freed unless she could be found a marriage partner, in which case the master acted as her marriage guardian (*wali*).

Although manumission meant that the former slave henceforth enjoyed all the rights and privileges of a free-born person (as well, of course, as his liabilities and responsibilities), he nevertheless remained in thrall to his former status through the institution of clientship (*wala*).. This was a two-edged weapon. On the one hand, he enjoyed a link with the family which had roots in the society and a social position within it. Thus, however distantly, the freedman vicariously enjoyed something of the social status of his former master and might use the "family name" (*nisba*), while his descendants might adopt a fictive genealogy which integrated them into the family line. A similar process took place in the first century of Islam when non-Arabs (*mawali*) who converted to Islam had to become clients of Arab tribes and eventually made the tribal *nisbas* their own. On the other hand, this link with the former owning family had its liabilities, since under certain circumstances the former master might have the right to a share in his freedman's estate. If the freedman died without heirs the former master inherited his entire estate. If he was married but without children his wife inherited a quarter of the estate while the former master inherited the remaining three quarters. In the case of a married female slave without children, the husband and her former master inherited equal shares of her estate. If the former master was dead, the three quarters of one half of the estate in the two cases mentioned above went to the Public Treasury (*bayt al-mal*)..

This brings us to what is, perhaps, the most interesting question- or series of questions—with respect to black Africans in the Mediterranean world. What became of the millions of black Africans who were taken as slaves into the Mediterranean domains of Islam over the centuries? Is it the case that, in Bernard Lewis's words, "[T]here is nothing in the Arab, Persian and Turkish lands that resembles the great black and mulatto populations of North and South America"?. There are two answers to this. First, it is true in the sense that there do not appear to be any massive concentrations of black Africans, no ghettoes, no visible struggles for civil rights, etc. Yet, the evidence presented below and that contained in the writings of others would suggest that, at least in regard to North Africa and Arabia, the slave trade may have left behind a not inconsiderable residuum. If this is so, then it must therefore be asked whether it is the lack of contemporary visibility of such populations that makes it seem that they do not exist. A possible answer to this may be that descendants of freed slaves occupy such lowly rungs on the socio-economic ladder that they

are quite marginalized both socially and physically.. Dispersal or confinement to remoter suburbs and rural villages would likely result in lack of social coherence and, combined with a depressed social and economic status, make it the more difficult for social protest to emerge and attention to be focused.

If, on the contrary, there is no residuum, at least in certain Mediterranean lands into which black slaves were formerly imported, then this raises some very interesting questions. Lewis offers two suggestions for the absence of large black populations: first, the high proportion of eunuchs among black males; second, the high death rate and low birth rate among slaves. The first suggestion seems to me unlikely, given the very high price of eunuchs. and the restricted call for their specific services (viz. as guardians of harems in large households). The second suggestion is more plausible, if we are to judge by the data presented by Walz for nineteenth-century Egypt. If, as now seems to be the case at least for the nineteenth century, female slaves imported outnumbered males by perhaps as much as 2:1, then it is little surprise if black populations were unable to maintain themselves. A fair proportion of the females would have been integrated into households in receiving societies through concubinage and their offspring would have been biracial and succeeding generations perhaps more genetically mixed. Those women who did not become concubines but remained in service may not have been allowed to marry, or perhaps only to marry when they were manumitted at an age already past that of child-bearing. Male slaves may have had little chance to marry, or at least to marry women young enough to bear children. Additionally, as both Lewis and Walz point out, epidemic diseases often carried off a disproportionate percentage of the slave population due to their lower standard of health care compared with the free population and their genetic unpreparedness for diseases not prevalent in their lands of origin.. An alternative hypothesis would be that there are no large identifiable black populations because there has been successful social integration including intermarriage. If this is so, one would like to understand better the particular social dynamics that brought this about.

It is important to stress, however, that there is simply not enough (not *nearly* enough) data at our disposal at present to make any general statements about the existence or size of residual black communities in the Mediterranean world or the extent to which freed slaves and their descendants have been integrated into host societies or have remained separate, endogamous and unequal. It is equally important to stress that such questions must be looked at on a culture by culture, community by community, case by case, basis and no assumptions made based on single cases or single cultures, much less on the assumption that the egalitarian principles of Islam were automatically put into practice in former slave-owning societies.

To date little work has been done on such questions, but they clearly offer a very rich field for the historian and the sociologist. Without trying to offer any answers, however, it may be instructive to conclude this survey of the Mediterranean dimension of the black diaspora by looking briefly at two contrasting images of former African slaves in the Mediterranean world: first, the image that appears in the writings of nineteenth-century European travelers in the Arabian peninsula, and second, the image that emerges from the writings of French administrators and anthropologists working in the Maghrib. Both of these images result from what may be termed uncontextualized "snapshots," but they may serve to illustrate both the diversity of the black experience in the Mediterranean lands and the complexity of the issues involved.

In the Arabian peninsula there are, or there have been until very recent times, considerable numbers of blacks of slave origin who seem to have been integrated into local society with fair success. Important though patrilineal descent is in Arabia as an indicator of social status, the adoption of a lineage through clientage has always been recognized as a legitimate way for a male to belong to a descent group, while for females the "adoption" process came about more commonly through concubinage or marriage. Both Palgrave and Doughty, traveling in the deserts and oases of Arabia in the 1860s and 1880s respectively, remarked on the numerous communities of African descent, both pure and mixed, and were evidently surprised at the extent to which these ex-slaves had become "arabianized." Palgrave found that the treasurer of Faysal, the great Wahhabi ruler, was "jet-black, a negro, in fact, though not a slave, having obtained his freedom from Turkee, the father of the present king." He also found in and around Riyad, the Wahhabi capital, a considerable number of men of mixed race known as *khudayriyya*, or "little green ones" ("green" being often in Arabic a synonym of black), who were merchants, shopkeepers and government servants and he offered the following reflection on the situation of the emancipated African slave:

> The number of negro slaves in these provinces (sc. eastern and central Arabia) gives rise to a second stage of existence for the black, common in the East, though not equally compatible with his condition in the West. I mean that not of

emancipation only, but of social equality also, with those around him—not by Act of Parliament or of Congress, but by individual will and public feeling ... These new possessors of civil liberty soon marry and are given in marriage. Now, although an emancipated negro or mulatto is not at once admitted to the higher circles of aristocratic life, nor would an Arab chief of rank readily make his daughter over to a black, yet they are by no means under the ban of incapacity and exclusion which weighs upon them among races of English blood. Accordingly, negroes can without any difficulty give their sons and daughters to the middle or lower classes of Arab families, and thus arises a new generation of mixed blood here denominated "Khodeyreeyah" or "Benoo-Khodeyr," the which being interpreted means "The Greens" or "the sons of the green one" ... These "green ones" again, marry, multiply and assume various tints ... Like their progenitors they do not readily take their place among the nobles or the upper ten thousand, however, they do end by doing even this in the process of time; and I have myself while in Arabia been honoured by the intimacy of more than one handsome "Green-man," with a silver-hilted sword at his side, and a rich dress on his dusky skin, but denominated Sheykh or Emeer, and humbly sued by Arabs of the purest Ismaelitic or Kahtanic pedigree.

Doughty also claimed that the position of the freed black in Arabia was a prosperous, even a favored, one for they were "rich men's children by adoption, where the poor disinherited Arabs must hire themselves to every man's task as day labourers." Snouck Hurgronje also gave a glowing account of the situation of freed blacks in Mecca in the 1880s:

> There is hardly an office or position that is unattainable to such freedmen. They compete with the freeborn on a footing of perfect equality, and the result shows that they are not the worst equipped for the struggle as they are numerously represented among the influential burghers and the owners of houses and business establishments.

These views of outsiders undoubtedly need to be compared with the view which Arabs of Arabia themselves held about their former slaves and the view those ex-slaves had of their own social and economic status, though in the present state of our knowledge sources for such studies cannot readily be identified.

The situation of the persons of slave ancestry in Morocco and Algeria is, or at least was in the recent past, somewhat in contrast to that of the reasonably integrated situation of the black freedmen of Arabia. Here we find distinct communities of black Africans, living in towns and oases, largely endogamous and continuing to practice non-Islamic possession cults, such as the Hausa *bori* or the Songhay *holey*, or cults of purification and healing through sacrifice, such as those of the "Seven Springs" (*sab' 'uyun*) in Algiers and the lightly islamized pseudo-Sufi cults of the Diwan Sidi Bilal in various Algerian locations and the Gnawa cult of Morocco.. There are also Sufi orders of a more recognizable variety, such as the 'Isawa (Aissaoua) and the Hamadsha in Morocco which indulge in bloodletting and self-mutilation in a state of ecstatic frenzy. They are thought to owe some of their sacrificial practices to the influence of sub-Saharan African cults introduced by ex-slaves and have attracted large black memberships.. The existence of distinct and separate communities whose members continue to adhere to beliefs and rituals of their lands of origin, or who established or helped to promote essentially syncretic manifestations of the religion of former slave owners would seem to suggest that emancipation has not been accompanied by any great degree of social integration. Economically, too, blacks have tended to work in low status occupations—butchers, sweepers, unskilled laborers, jugglers, dancers, street musicians; only in exercising their talent as exorcisers of evil jinns do they find themselves looked up to by some members of the Berbero Arab communities they live among and who acknowledge their skill in this art. The close connection between the oppression of slavery, the depressed social and economic state of the freedman and the adoption of heterodox forms of religion has been summed up by Emile Dermenghem who has also provided some of the most detailed eyewitness descriptions of the ceremonies of these cults:

> The cruel situation, at least as regards its origin, of the blacks of North Africa has favoured the life of their brotherhoods and the maintenance of a Sudanic ritual adapted to Islam; and it is the liturgical activity of the brotherhoods which has favoured the maintenance of racial consciousness and mutual self-help. The religious phenomena characterized by the words *zar* and *bori* (spirit possession) and by *diwan* (assembly) are widespread in Abyssinia, North Africa, Hausaland and among the Bambara and Songhay . . . Under the symbolism of the spirits the deeper goals, beyond the social effects, are a catharsis, a

> purification of the [psychic] forces, the curing of illnesses of nervous origin and the calming of the soul through ecstasy. This is the form which can easily be taken by the mysticism of an uprooted, exiled and oppressed minority which has accommodated itself to Islam in Africa, just as it did to Christianity in America..

Although Dermenghem is one of the most recent writers to describe the black brotherhoods in North Africa, it is nevertheless over thirty years since he wrote. It would certainly be interesting to know how much of what he describes of these cults still exists and to what extent the creation of an independent and socialist-oriented Algeria has provided blacks with opportunities for upward social and economic mobility which would tend to break up the old communities..

Some Concluding Observations

There is little point, given the present state of research in this field, in trying to make any generalizations. At the moment we still lack detailed studies of the institution of slavery as a whole in the lands of Islam. and only when some steps have been taken in this direction shall we be able more clearly to discern the particular problems of the black slave and the black freedman within such societies. Nevertheless, in the nineteenth century, slavery and black slavery became synonymous—or almost so—in such areas as North Africa, Egypt and the Arabian peninsula. In these areas it should be possible to undertake fruitful research on the black diaspora, not only since "slave" meant "black," but because the records are likely to prove far more abundant for the nineteenth century than for earlier periods. For many areas there are two kinds of records for much of the century: the correspondence and reports drawn up by colonial powers or European nations crusading for abolition, and the indigenous records—official and personal correspondence and, most importantly, the judicial records which document slave sales, taxes on slaves, runaway slaves, the enslavement of "free Muslims," the emancipation of slaves and inheritance matters.. In addition there is an extensive travel literature for North Africa and Egypt, as well as for the Sahara and those areas of sub-Saharan Africa from which the slaves were exported. Finally, there remains for the sociologist and the anthropologist a considerable field of inquiry among the surviving black communities of North Africa and Turkey in particular, and perhaps also Egypt and the Arabian Peninsula, though sensitivities over the issue of slavery and skin color in such countries present the researcher with inherent difficulties..

[1] On Jewish slave-owning in medieval Egypt, see S. D. Goitein, *A Mediterranean society*, Vol. I, *Economic Foundations*, University of California Press, 1967, 130–47 *et passim*.

[2] Lewis, *Race and Slavery*, 148, gives a translation of a fifteenth-century *fatwa* from North Africa which makes slavery a punishment for "unbelief": "slavery is a humiliation and a servitude caused by previous or current unbelief and having as its purpose to discourage unbelief."

[3] On the sources of slaves and routes of the trade in medieval times, see M. Lombard, *L'Islam dans sa première grandeur*, Paris, 1971, 194–202.

[4] The Muslims also bound themselves to send the Nubians a quantity of cereals and textiles as part of the agreement, see F. Lokkegard, art. "Bakt" in *EI*, 2, i, 966.

[5] See Harris, *African Presence in Asia*, 19–23; J. Burton Page, art. "Habashi" in *EI*, 2, iii, 14–16.

[6] The pilgrimage to Mecca was also taken advantage of by West Africans for the sale of slaves. Such slaves were often sold in different locations to defray the expenses of the journey and to purchase goods to take back across the Sahara; see Taqi 'l-Din al-Maqrizi, *K. al-suluk fi ma'rifat duwal al-muluk*, tr. in J. F. P. Hopkins & N. Levtzion, *Corpus of Early Arabic Sources for West African History*, Cambridge, 1981, 356 (examples from the years 1351, 1416 and 1439). See also Fisher and Fisher, *Slavery and Muslim Society in Africa*, 121–4, 128–9.

[7] Leo Africanus, *Description de l'Afrique*, ii, 480; Duarte Pacheco Pereira, *Esmeraldo de situ Orbis*, tr. George H. T. Kimble, London, 1937, Hakluyt Soc., (2nd ser., 79), 78, 92; G. R. Crone, ed. & tr., *The Voyages of Cadamosto and other documents on Western Africa in the second half of the fifteenth century*, London, 1937, Hakluyt Society, (2nd ser., 80), 17; G. F. Lyon, *A Narrative of Travels in Northern Africa in the Years 1818, 19 and 20*, London, 1821, 154; Morell, *Algeria*, 340.

[8] Hans Vischer, *Across the Sahara from Tripoli to Bornu*, London, 1910, 148; A. A. Boahen, *Britain, the Sahara and the Western Sudan, 1788–1861*, Oxford, 1964, 158.

[9] See J. Nicolaisen, *The Ecology and Culture of the Pastoral Tuareg*, Copenhagen, 1963, 439–46; Jeremy Keenan, *The Tuareg; People of Ahaggar*, London, 1979, 95–100. For a historical summary, see Priscilla E. Staratt, "Tuareg slavery and the slave trade," *Slavery and Abolition*, 2, 1981, 83–113.

[10] Ibn al-Ukhuwwa, *Ma'alim al-qurba.*, loc. cit.; G. S. Colin & E. Lévi-Provençal, *Un Manual hispanique de hisba. Traité de Abu Abd Allah Muhammad b. Abi Muhammad as-Sakati de Malaqa*, Paris, 1931, 47.

[11] Colin & Lévi-Provençal, op. cit., 51.

[12] See below, 28–9.

[13] For a description of the slave market of Cairo, see Terence Walz, "Wakalat al-Gallaba: the market of Sudan goods in Cairo," *Annales Islamologiques*, 13, 1977, 217–45. For that of Istanbul, see Alan W. Fisher, "The sale of slaves in the Ottoman empire. Markets and state taxes on slaves: some preliminary considerations," *Bogazici Universitesi Dergisi*, Beseri Bilimler, 6, 1978, 151–6.

[14] C. Snouck Hurgronje, *Mekka in the Latter Part of the Nineteenth Century*, Leiden, 1931, 14.

[15] Ibn Butlan, *Risala fi shira al-raqiq wa-taqlib al-abid* in "Abd al-Salam Muhammad Harun, ed., *Nawadir al-makhtutat*, iv, Cairo, 1954, 333–89. In the same volume is another treatise purely on the medical examination of slaves by a seventeenth or eighteenth-century writer, Muhammad al-Ghazali, *Hidayat al-murid fi taqlib al-abid*, 391–410.

[16] *Mukhtasar*, 164–5; *Risala*, 196 and comm. of al-Nafrawi, *al-Fawakih al-dawani*, Cairo, 1374/1955, ii, 96; Brunschvig in *EI*, 2, i, 28.

[17] Colin & Lévi-Provençal, *Un Manuel hispanique de hisba*, 50.

[18] Ibid, 49–50; Ibn Butlan, op. cit., 376–84.

[19] See Samuel W. Baker, *Exploration of the Nile Tributaries of Abyssinia*, Hartford, 1868, 533–4. On the Ethiopian slave trade in the nineteenth century see Mordechai Abir, "The Ethiopian slave trade and its relation to the Islamic world" in J. R. Willis (ed.), *Slaves and Slavery in Muslim Africa*, ii, 123–36.

[20] Lane, *Modern Egyptians*, 183–4; G. Baer, "Slavery and its abolition" in his *Studies in the Social History of Modern Egypt*, Chicago, 1969, 163. An earlier version of this article was published in *Journal of African History*, 8, 1967, 417–41.

[21] Hurgronje, *Mekka in the Latter Part of the Nineteenth Century*, 109.

[22] *Modern Egyptians*, 185.

[23] G. Tournès, *Les Eunuques en Egypte*, Geneva: Imprimerie Vaney, 1869, 20–1.

[24] J. L. Burckhardt, *Arabic Proverbs*, London, 1830, 176; Lane, *Modern Egyptians*, 38.

[25] R. Hill, *On the Frontiers of Islam*, OUP, 1970, 183; J. L. Burckhardt, *Travels in Nubia*, 2nd ed., London, 1822, 301–2.

[26] Muhammad b. Abd al-Rahman al-Sakhawi, *al-Daw' al-lami li-ahl al-qarn al-tasi'*, 12 vols., Cairo, 1353–5/1934–6.

[27] Op. cit., 3: No. 877 (customs collector), 10: No. 684 (governor of Aden), 6: No. 839 (emissary to Ethiopia).

[28] Ibid, 3: No. 70.

[29] For references to the use of black troops in medieval Egypt, see S. Lane-Poole, *A History of Egypt in the Middle Ages*, London, 1901, 63, 86–9, 132–3, 141, 145, 168, 192.

[30] J. F. P. Hopkins, *Medieval Muslim Government in Barbary*, London, 1958, 72–3. Michael Brett (in *The Cambridge History of Africa*, 2, 1978, 529) argues that the terminology used in the sources does not distinguish the color of the slaves used in the Aghlabid army in the early period and that they may just as easily have been Europeans. Only towards the end of the ninth century is there mention of sudan—"blacks."

[31] Idris, *La Berbérie Orientale sous les Zirides*, 530–1.

[32] Hopkins, *Medieval Muslim Government*, 76.

[33] Idem, 78.

[34] See Magali Morsy, "Moulay Isma'il et l'armée de métier," *Revue d'histoire modern et contemporaine*, 14, 1967, 97–122; Allan Meyers, "The Abid al-Bukhari: slave soldiers and state-craft in Morocco, 1672–1790," Ph.D. diss., Cornell University, 1974.

[35] M. Delafosse, "Les débuts des troupes noires au Maroc," *Hespéris*, 3, 1923, 1–12.

[36]Some were evidently urbanized, see A. A. Batran, "The *'ulama'* of Fas, Mulay Isma'il, and the issue of the haratin of Fas" in J. R. Willis, ed., *Slaves and Slavery in Muslim Africa*, ii, 1–15.

[37]al-Nasiri, *K. al-istiqsa'*, vii, 76.

[38]Moroccan sources (al-Nasiri, *K. al-istiqsa'*, vii, 61; Abu-Qasim b. Ahmad al-Zayyani, *al-Turjuman al-mu'rib 'an duwal al-mashriq wa 'l-maghrib*, ed. O. Houdas, Paris, 1886, 16) puts the total of the *'abid al-Bukhari* at 150,000 at their height, though this figure may include a large number assigned to public works as well as military duties. Allan Meyers in his article "Class, ethnicity and slavery: origins of the Moroccan *"abid"* (*Int. J. African Hist. Stud.*, 10, 1977, 427–42) displays some uneasiness at this large figure, but seems to accept it, *faute de mieux*. Lewis, *Race and Slavery*, 69, says they were "said to number 250,000," but it is not clear where he got this figure from or how much credence he gives it. Abdullah Laroui (*The History of the Maghrib*, Princeton University Press, 1977, 273) gives a figure of only "thirty to fifty thousand" for the size of the army at its height, though he does not indicate how he arrived at this. A figure of 150,000 sounds on the face of it exaggerated, though it is said to be based on the ledgers (*kunnashat*) of the sultan's chief secretary. These ledgers—or at least some of them—are still preserved in Morocco and it is therefore possible that one day more accurate figures may become available.

[39]Oscar Lenz, *Timbouctou. Voyage au Maroc au Sahara et au Soudan*, Paris, 1886, ii, 355–6.

[40]See T. Lockhart, art. "Ahwaz" in *EI*, 2, i, 305.

[41]On the Zanj revolt, most recently, see the study of Alexandre Popovic, *La révolte des esclaves en Iraq au IIIe/IXe siècle*, Paris, 1976.

[42]See W. Madelung, art. "Karmati," in *EI*, 2, iv, 664.

[43]Baer, "Slavery and its abolition," 165–6.

[44]Ibn Battuta, *Voyages (Tuhfat al-nuzzar)*, texte arabe accompagné d'une traduction par C. Defrémery et B. Sanguinetti (new ed. with preface and notes by V. Monteil, Paris, 1969), iv, 378 (Eng. tr., Said Hamdun & Noel King, *Ibn Battuta in Black Africa*, London, 1975, 23); René Caillié, *Travels through Central Africa to Timbuctoo*, London, 1830, II, 119; Lenz, *Timbouctou*, ii, 73–4.

[45]Ibn Battuta, *Voyages*, IV, 441 (Hamdun and King, *Ibn Battuta in Black Africa*, 58).

[46]G. Wiet, art. "al-'Allaki," in *EI*, 2, i, 418; see also L. E. Kubbel and V. V. Matveev, *Arabskiye Istochniki VII-X bekob*, Moscow, 1960, 41–2 (account of al-Ya'qubi, d. 897).

[47]For a detailed study of eunuch terminology and of the Saqaliba eunuchs, see D. Ayalon, "On the eunuchs in Islam," *Jerusalem Studies in Arabic and Islam*, 1, 1979, 67–124. On the making and employment of eunuchs in sub-Saharan Africa, see Fisher and Fisher, *Slavery and Muslim Society in Africa*, 143–8. See also art. "Khasi" by Ch. Pellat in *EI*, 2, iv, 1087–92.

[48]Quoted in 'Abduh Badawi, *al-Shu'ara al-sud*, 203; see also A. J. Wensinck & J. P. Mensing, *Concordance et indices de la tradition musulmane*, Leiden, 1943, ii, 38.

[49]According to the Maliki school of law, a slave had to be freed if he or she were mutilated, see *Risala*, 229; *Mukhtasar*, IV, 60; *Qawanin*, 408. See further Muhammad b. 'Umar al-Tunsi, *Tash 'hidh al-adh'han bi-sirat bilad al-*'arab wa 'l-sudan*, ed. Khalil Mahmud 'Asakir & Mustafa Muhammad Mus'ad, Cairo, 1965, 233–4. Al-Tunisi gives the title of a treatise forbidding the employment of eunuchs at the Prophet's tomb by Jalal al-Din al-Suyuti (d. 1505)—*Hurmat khidmat al-khisyan li-darih sayyid wuld 'Adnan*, but I have been unable to locate a copy of it.

[50]Lombard, op. cit., 196–7.

[51]Ibid, map on p. 198 where a center of castration is also indicated near Cordoba, i.e. in Muslim territory. According to Ibn Hawqal. *Opus Geographicum (K. Surat al-ard)*, ed. J. H. Kramers, Leiden, 1939, 110, Jewish merchants were said to perform the operation in Andalusia in the tenth century.

[52]Ibn Fadl Allah al-'Umari (d. 1349), tr. M. Gaudefroy-Demombynes, *L'Afrique moins l'Egypte*, Paris, 1927, 16–17.

[53]Fisher & Fisher, op. cit., 145–6.

[54]See the anon. "Kano Chronicle" in H. R. Palmer, *Sudanese Memoirs*, Lagos, 1928, iii, 108–10. Kano began to appoint eunuch officials in the second half of the fifteenth century and other West African kingdoms such as Songhay, Dagomba, Bagirmi, Darfur and Borno later did so.

[55]al-Zayyani, *al-Turjuman al-mu'rib*, 15 (Arabic text). A late eighteenth century European traveler in Morocco, and sometime physician to the royal harems reported that the source of Moroccan eunuchs was the "kingdom of Bambara" (i.e. the state based on Segu, a little upstream from the inland delta of the Niger) and he estimated that in 1789 they numbered no more than one hundred in the entire 'Alawid kingdom, see W. Lemprière, *A Tour from Gibraltar to Tangier, Sallee Mogadore, Santa Cruz. Tarudant and thence over Mount Atlas to Morocco*, 3rd edn., London, 1804, 357. Lenz, op. cit., i, 395, reported that in nineteenth century Morocco some masters castrated their own slaves and used them as concubines.

[56]Louis Frank, "Mémoire sur le commerce des nègres au Kaire et sur les maladies auxquelles ils sont sujets en y arrivant," *Mémoires sur l'Egypte*, Paris, 1800–1803, iv, 132ff.; O. Meinardus, "The Upper Egyptian practice of making eunuchs in the eighteenth and nineteenth century," *Zeitschrift für Ethnologie*, 94, 1969, 47–58; Tournés, *Les eunuques en Egypte*, 9ff.

[57]N. Penzer, *The Harem*, London, 1936, 129. On these royal eunuchs, see also M. Izeddin, "Les eunuques dans le palais ottoman," *Orient*, 6 (24), 1962, 103–21; Ehud Toledano, "The imperial eunuchs of Istanbul: from Africa to the heart of Islam," *Middle East Studies*, 20, 1984, 379–90; Alev L. Croutier, *Harem: the World of the Veil*, New York, 1989, 125–42, partly based on Penzer and other published sources, but with some personal and family reminiscences. A scathing denunciation of the black eunuchs of the Ottoman sultan's harem has been published in Cenzig Orhonlu, "Dervis Abdullah'in Darussaade Agarli hakkinda bir Eseri. Risale-i Teberdariye ff ahval-i Daru's-saade" in *Ismail Hakki Uzunçarsulu Armagani'ndan ayribasim*, Ankara: Turk Tarih Jurumi Basimevi, 1975, 225–49. I am grateful to Max Kortepeter for providing me with a summary translation of the document contained in this article.

[58]On the physical appearance and character traits of eunuchs, see al-Jahiz, *K. al-Hayawan*, Cairo, 1938, i, 106ff.; Ibrahim al-Bayhaqi (fl. 920), *K. al-mahasin wa 'l-masawi*, ed. Ibrahim Muhammad Abu 'l-Fadl, Cairo,

1961, ii, 390–3; Sir Richard Burton, *Personal Narrative of a Pilgrimmage to al-Madinah and Mecca*, Memorial ed., London, 1893, i, 372; Tournès, op. cit., 16–18; Drs. Hikmet & Félix Regnault, "Les eunuques de Constantinople," *Bulletin et Mémoires de la Société d'Anthropologie de Paris*, sér. v, 2, 1901, 234–40.

[59]J. L. Burckhardt, *Travels in Arabia*, London, 1829, 142–4. On the institution under the Mamluks, see S. E. Marmon, "The Eunuchs of the Prophet: space, time and gender in an Islamic society," Ph.D. diss., Princeton University, 1990.

[60]See, for example, *Letters Written during a Ten Years' Residence at the Court of Tripoli*, 3rd edn., London, 1819, i, 100, 174, 231; Palgrave, *Personal Narrative*, 271.

[61]Morell, *Algeria*, 342; see also Walz, "Black slavery in Egypt," quoting E. F. Tugay, *Three Centuries: Family Chronicles of Turkey and Egypt*, London, 1963, to the effect that white slaves in the imperial Ottoman service were customarily freed after nine years, while black slaves were freed after seven. Shi'i jurists recommended freeing Muslim slaves after seven years, see Brunschvig in *EI*, 2, i, 31.

[62]On the various paths to manumission according to Maliki law, see *Risala*, 220–9; *Mukhtasar*, iv, 59–72; *Qawanin*, 407–16; "Code de l'esclavage chez les musulmans," 340–4.

[63]Walz, "Black slavery in Egypt," 18.

[64]Brunschvig in *EI*, 2, i, 30–1; *Risala*, 228–9; *Mukhtasar*, iv, 73–4; *Qawanin*, 410–11; Levy, *Social Structure of Islam*, 81.

[65]Walz, op. cit., 27.

[66]*Race and Slavery*, 84.

[67]Almost twenty-five years ago Leon Carl Brown remarked: "A disproportionately large number of black men are likely to be found, for example, working as unskilled laborers at a construction site or on a work-gang building a highway . . . The ill-defined and often ignored position of the black man in North Africa has been interpreted as indicating a greater social mobility and less resistance along color lines than prevail in black-white relations in most of the world. Such an interpretation may be too optimistic—a king of over-reaction to the more clear-cut segregation pattern that characterizes white-black relations in the English-speaking world." See his "Color in North Africa," *Daedalus*, 96, 1967, 480, n. 12.

[68]Up to seven times the price of an uncastrated male; see, by way of example, Magali Morsy, *North Africa 1800–1900*, London, 1884, 63, who gives figures for Tripoli in the 1820s; A. G. B. Fisher & H. J. Fisher, *Slavery and Muslim Society in Africa* (London, 1970, 164) who give figures for sales in the market of Kuka (Bornu) in the 1870s.

[69]Louis Frank, a doctor who had experience of Egypt, remarking on the visibility of black Africans in Tunis, noted that this was because there was a lesser incidence of "plague" in Tunis than in Egypt and because the people of Tunis were in the habit of freeing their slaves and the latter generally preferred to remain in Tunis rather than return home where they might again be enslaved. See his *Tunis. Description de cette Régence in L'Univers pittoresque*, Paris, 1850, 116.

[70]Not the least of these issues is the ideological framework within which the various commentators viewed the topic they were discussing. Even in the late nineteenth century there were those who were still ready to defend black slavery and claim it was a way of "civilizing the savage." See Lewis, *Race and Slavery*, 82–4.

[71]Palgrave, *Personal Narrative*, 272.

[72]Ibid, 270–1.

[73]C. Doughty, *Travels in Arabia Deserta*, London: Jonathan Cape, 1923, i, 554.

[74]Op. cit., 13.

[75]An eighteenth-century African Muslim scholar, however, found cause to complain of Meccan attitudes, and he had never been a slave. Muhammad b. Muhammad al-Kashnawi al-Fullani, writing in 1733 remarked: "In general the people of this land love no one—least of all those of our Sudanic race—unless it be for the satisfaction of some need of theirs, without any true affection or friendship." See his *al-Durr al-manzum wa-khulasat al-sirr al-maktum fi'l-sihr was 'l-talasim wa 'l-nujum*, Bombay, 1303/1885–6, 2. This book was, in fact, written at the request of a Meccan scholar.

[76]The essential reference on sub-Saharan religious influence in North Africa is Emile Dermenghem, *Le Culte des saints dans l'Islam maghrébin*, Paris, 1954, 253ff. Specifically on the bori cult in Tunis and Tripoli, see A. J. H. Tremearne, *The Ban of the Bori*, London, 1914, and the indignant polemic of Ahmad b.Abi Bakr al-Tunbuktawi, (1804), *Hatk al-sitr 'amma 'alayhi sudan Tunis min al-kufr* in Abdeljelil Temini, *Les Affinités culturelles entre la Tunisie, la Libye, le Centre de l'ouest de l'Afrique à l'époque moderne*, Tunis: Publications de la Revue d'Histoire Maghrébine, 7, 1981; on the "seven springs," see J. D. Andrews, *Les Fontaines des génies (seba aioun). Croyances soudanaises d'Alger*, Algiers, 1903; on the Gnawa, V. Pâques, *L'Arbre cosmique dans la pensée populaire et dans la vie quotidienne du nord-ouest africain*, Paris, 1964, and her "Le monde des gnâwa" in *L'Autre et l'ailleurs. Hommage à Roger Bastide*, Paris, 1976, 169–8.

[77]See René Brunel, *Essai sur la confrérie des Aissaoua au Maroc*, Paris, 1926; V. Crapanzano, *The Hamadsha: a Study in Moroccan Ethnopsychiatry*, University of California Press, 1973.

[78]Emile Dermenghem, *Le Culte des saints*, 260. A recent doctorial thesis by Gerasimos Makris (London School of Economics, University of London, 1991) on the Tumbura cult in northern Sudan suggests that former slaves used this very adaptive possession and healing cult in support of their endeavor to cross boundaries from "paganism" to Islam, from non-Arabness to Arabness and from "savagery" (as perceived by northern Sudanese Muslims) to "civilized" norms. Such cults, then, would represent less a revolt against a new culture forced upon the alienated or an attempt to hold on to a severed past, but the negotiation of an entry into a new identity.

[79]A recent article indicates there has been little change in the Saharan regions of Algeria at any rate. See L. Blin, "Les noirs dans l'Algérie contemporaine," *Politique africaine*, 30, 1988, 22–31.

[80]An exception is the recent monograph by Ehud R. Toledano, *The Ottoman Slave Trade and its Suppression* (1982), though as its title indicates its main emphasis is the trade itself and its abolition rather than the social and economic role of slaves before and after emancipation. Lewis, *Race and Slavery*, vi, comments on "the remarkable dearth of scholarly work on the subject . . . The documentation for a study on Islamic

slavery is almost endless; its exploration has barely begun."

[81]For different areas the volume and nature of local records will, of course, vary. For Egypt, Walz has observed: "The *mahkama* archive holdings show that an in-depth study of slavery in Egypt can be—and deserves to be—written"; see his "Black slavery in Egypt," 137. For an example, albeit much more microcosmic, from a Muslim society south of the Sahara, see Alan Christelow, "Slavery in Kano, 1913–14: evidence from the judicial records," *African Economic History*, 14, 1985, 57–74.

[82]Among the studies which do exist are the following: G. Zadowski, "Le rôle des nègres parmi la population tunisienne," *En Terre d'Islam*, 1942, 146–52; A. Lopashich, "A negro community in Yugoslavia," *Man*, 58 (231), 1958, 169–73; P. N. Boratav, "Les noirs dans le folklore turc et le folklore des noirs de Turquie," *J. Soc. des Africanistes*, 28, 1958, 7–23; Z. Komorowski, "Les descendants des soudanais en Algérie et leurs traditions," *Africana Bulletin* [Warsaw], 15, 1971, 43–53; A. Destro, "Habs el 'Abid: il quartiere africano di Gerusalemme," *Africa* [Rome], 39, 1974, 193–212; Blin, "Les noirs dans l'Algérie contemporaine" (see above nt. 79).

African Presence in Iran: Identity and Its Reconstruction in the 19th and 20th Centuries[*]

Behnaz A. Mirzai

Abstract: *The establishment of Afro-Iranian communities was to a great extent due to the slave trading activities of Arabs, Persians and Indians in the Persian Gulf, in the 15th century. The questions on how various socio-economic elements function within the Afro-Iranian communities and how their cultural representations perpetuate and develop among both their members and outsiders underline the significance of the study of African Diaspora in Iran which assist us to appreciate that African displacement could not totally erase their heritage, however, rather reconstruct a new identity influenced by both Africa and Iran as well.*

In his article on *Africans in Asian History*, Joseph Harris mentions that: "there are virtually no published materials available in English or French about African communities in Iran."[1] That statement signifies that important work needs to be done to fill in the gap. But research on this theme is problematic in the sense that black communities who were mostly imported through enslavement in different periods are dispersed in different parts of Iran and do not know their precise origins. To address this problem, this paper makes use of the works of authors who have been among Afro-Iranians, and familiar with their situation. Persian sources, which significantly contribute in this research, comprise of three categories including historical, musicological and travelers' accounts. For example, Kababi's works, besides illuminating the socio-economic history of Bandar 'Abbas and the Persian Gulf, give some important information on Afro-Iranians in the mid 19th and early 20th centuries. The significance of Muqaddam's account lies in his close observation of the status of Africans in Baluchistan in the 20th century. The cultural representation of Afro-Iranians, in particular, spirit possessions in the modern period were examined by Riyahi and Sa'idi. Morever, primary English sources including Sheil's contain brief but useful information about the status of Afro-Iranians in Persia. Since the history of the African Diaspora is tied to the slave trade, the study of the archival documents in Iran and England relating to slavery has been significant. On the other hand, my interviews with the local people of Bandar 'Abbas, Minab, and Qishm played a crucial role in

appreciation of the concepts of self-identification, ethnic awareness, and linguistic and cultural continuity of Afro-Iranians. It is hoped that this short survey on Afro-Iranian communities will contribute to the historiography of both Iran and the African Diaspora.

This paper examines the African presence in Iran in the 19th and 20th centuries by surveying its geographical dispersal, socio-economic status, culture and rituals. Attention is drawn to the fact that Afro-Iranians were scattered in various coastal regions of southern Iran in different periods. It is also argued that some elements associated with the African homeland were preserved by the Afro-Iranians, and such cultural heritage, which includes common rituals such as *Zar*, not only unified their communities but also led to the reconstruction of a new identity in the host land. The recognition of this identity will assist us to appreciate the continuity of African history in relation to the diaspora.

Trade and the Diaspora

Historians, archeologists and anthropologists put different interpretations on the question of the timing of the African presence in Iran. Since there has been a constant traffic between Iran and Africa, it is difficult to determine the timing of Africans' migration to Iran. Afshar states that in the ancient period black skinned people were living in Khuzistan, but after the arrival of black slaves from Muscat and Zanzibar, a new ethnic group of blacks emerged there.[2] Some researchers believe that at the time of the migration of Aryans[3] to Iran (about 3,000 B.C.), the indigenous people of the coastal areas of the Persian Gulf and Oman were black people or Habashis.[4] In this regard Sykes refers to the archeological research that:

"Dieulafoy and de Morgan, who both headed expeditions to Elam, and who studied the question most exhaustively on the spot, concur in the opinion that there was a very ancient occupation of the Susian plain by Negritos, and that, so far as is known, these were the original inhabitants. In support of this view Herodotus writes: "The Ethiopians from the direction of the sunrising (for the Ethiopians were in two bodies) had been appointed to serve with the Indians, being in no way different in appearance from the other Ethiopians, but in their language and in the nature of their hair only; or the Ethiopians from the East are straight-haired, but those of Libya have hair more thick and woolly than that of any other men. Again, there is the fact that in the most ancient bas-reliefs, figures of Negritos appear with frequency. More especially is this the case in the famous stele of Naramsin, referred to in the next chapter, where the monarch, who is of Semitic type, is portrayed as leading Negritos to victory."[5]

Field examined different ethnic groups in Iran in the context of the anthropological research. He refers to the various theories in analyzing the idea of blacks as being the natives of Persia. "Brinton considers that the alleged primitive Dravidian or Negritic Black race as depicted on the monunents at Susa are more likely to have been portraits of slaves or captives than of an old resident population."[6] Regarding the existence of an African population in Iran, Field states that: "In Iran the presence of Negroid features may be due to an ancient strain in the population or to the infiltraion due to slaves or sailors. The important fact is that evidence of Negroid blood was recorded among the modern population examined."[7] However, the timing of the blacks' settlement in Iran, and the possible link between blacks and Africans may remain controversial, and the development of commercial activities should be regarded as the major cause for Africans' migration to Iran.

The historical connection between Iran and Africa was established through trading activities. Significant consequences of such commercial and geographical linkage include cultural exchanges and population movements in both directions. Merchants established trading contacts through the sea routes from the Iranian ports in the Persian Gulf to Somalia, Kenya, and Tanganyika. Iranian merchants in the port of Gung were exporting dates and salt from Qishm Island to Kenya, and Tanganyika. In return, they sought other goods, especially mangrove, (in Persian Chandal).[8] Mangrove is native to Africa and was used together with palm branches in the making of ceilings for houses in parts of southern Iran such as Kharg and Qishm Islands and 'Abbasi and Lingah ports.[9] Trade in mangrove dates back to hundreds of years ago. Istakhri (d. 933 A.D.) refers to the usage of mangrove in the construction of houses in the city of Siraf.[10] I visited Qishm Island where the imported mangrove from Africa had been used in the construction of houses more than a hundred years

ago, but such structures still survive up to the present day. Iranian traders exported ceramics made in Firozah, a village in southern Iran, to Zanzibar.[11] Lari, a currency minted in Lar, a city in the Fars province, was extensively used for payment in commercial relations in Muscat and some African cities.[12] Slaves, ivory, teakwood, ambergris, tortoise shell, and gold, comprised the most important part of trade from East Africa to Iranian ports.[13]

The consequences of external trade for Africa include the deportation of a slave population from the continent. As in other parts of the world, such as the Americas, involuntary migration of Africans through the slave trade was the main reason for the presence of Africans and the establishment of their communities in Iran. Inevitably, trade connection also led to cultural exchange and population displacement in both Iran and Africa.

Various ethnic groups have been enslaved due to commercial, political, and military upheavals in Iran in different periods. By 634 A.D. when the Arabs invaded Persia, war captives including some of the indigenous people, formed a distinctive social group of *Bandagan* (slaves) used in mining and agricultural plantations. In the ninth century, Turkish slaves were imported from Transoxiana to serve in the military, and gradually, they played a very crucial role in the socio-political system of Iran. Besides trade in white Turkish slaves, Africans and Indians were also imported into Iran. In the period of the Great Shah 'Abbas (1588–1629), Georgian slaves, both female (kaniz) and male (ghulam), were imported and used in the *harams*, but the latter formed the permanent body of the army. Through the 1828 Treaty of Turkomanchay, a large area of northern Iran was lost to Russia, which subsequently suppressed the importation of white, Georgian slaves into Iran. As a result, in the 19th century, slaves in Iran were mostly from eastern and northeastern African countries such as Tanganyika, Kenya, Somalia, Sudan, and Ethiopia. Kababi (d. 1943), who served as a government official, indicated some instances of African slaves originally from Mozambique in Bandar 'Abbas.[14] It is worth noting to consider the enslavement of different ethnic groups within Iran, such as Kurds or Turkomans who were sold in Baluchistan, or people of Bojnurd who served as slaves in Astirabad. Meanwhile, Persians were also sold in other countries, for example Baluchi people who served as government soldiers in Oman and on the coast at places like Bagamoyo. They were the most vulnerable ethnic group who were also sent as slaves from Iran to Oman and East Africa.

According to Lovejoy, the total number of slaves exported from East Africa, in the 19th century, was about 718,000, out of which 347,000 were exported to Arabia, Persia, and India.[15] Martin and Ryan's estimates demonstrate that in the 19th century, the highest number of slaves exported from East Africa to Arabia, Persia, and India occurred during the years of 1850–1873, and at the same time, the average annual import of slaves to the former countries was about 6,500.[16] Based on Sheil's report in 1850, the number of slaves imported into the ports of Iran was around 2,000–3,000 per year.[17] Based on the above figures, we may conclude that from 1850 to 1873, from the total average annual export of East Africans to Arabia, Persia, and India, 38% of slaves embarked in the Persian Ports, and at the same period, with regard to the total number of exported slaves from East Africa to all different countries, 18% imported to Persia.

Though rather low, this number was large enough that after a considerable period of time led to the formation of identifiable African communities in several districts in southern Iran. More likely the demographic pattern of African communities can be explained based on the gender difference of imported slaves. The gender ratio of African slaves according to Issawi demonstrates the dominance of males:

> "The number of boats arriving at Kharg in August–October 1841 was put at 117, with 1,217 slaves. And an answer to a questionnaire stated that some 3,000 slaves (two-thirds male and one-third female) arrived in Busheir each year, of whom only 170 or 180 were sold in that town, the rest being sent on to Muhammarah and Basra; Bandar-Abbas took about one-quarter as many as were sold in Bushire, and a small number was also sold in Lingah and Congoon."[18]

African slaves were imported to Iran either by desert from the western frontier or by sea from the south in the Persian Gulf. People of various ethnic groups, such as Arabs, Iranians, and Indians, were involved in the slave trade in different periods. A few number of slaves were bought by Persian pilgrims at markets in Mecca, Medina, or Karbala.[19] Mary Sheil in her reports stated that the port of Bandar 'Abbas and the city of Bushihr were receiving the largest number of slaves from Africa.[20] Muqaddam quotes from the local people in Baluchistan on how Africans were imported and sold in that area.

> "Since a long time ago, black ghulams and kanizes[21] were living in Baluchistan. Arab merchants were traveling to Zanzibar and the coastal area of Africa by ship; and kidnapping

or buying them [Africans], then were selling them to the prosperous Baluchis."[22]

The point here, however, is that the presence of Africans in Iran through enslavement was mainly a result of commercial activities, and also this massive involuntary migration and displacement of Africans that occurred before the abolitionist movement in the 19th century.

Ethnicity & Geographic Boundary

Afro-Iranian communities are widely scattered from southwest Iran through the coastal areas of the Persian Gulf to the southeastern region of the country. Black communities are also settled in the provinces of Sistan va Baluchistan, Hurmuzgan, Bushihr and Khuzistan, including the Southern Islands of Qishm, Kharg, and Kish. At present, there is no indication of an African presence in northern cities such as Tehran. Although, in the 19th century, African slaves were living in cities such as Shiraz and Tehran, where they were mainly employed as domestics, such as, lala[23] or daya,[24] dowry, or concubines in the harams, of the well-to-do, it is most likely that they have been completely assimilated into the host population, and have disappeared as a distinguishable ethnic group. Southern Iran is the only part of the country in which Afro-Iranian communities are visible. Perhaps the difference in the total numbers of imported African slaves in various areas was one of the significant reasons for such complete social assimilation. Thus more slaves were retained in southern Iran, where they were involved in various economic sectors and created Afro-Iranian communities in the region.

The pattern of population settlement and social and ethnic structure among African-Iranians varies in each geographical area. As this demographic pattern suggests in some cases Africans are identifiable as a social group of slave descent; and in some cases their equal membership in the host society provided them opportunity for social assimilation. The formation of different patterns of African communities was necessitated by socio-economic considerations peculiar to each region.

Social and economic structure in some cities like Bandar 'Abbas, Qishm Island, and Minab facilitated Africans' assimilation into the host society. Kababi refers to manifestations of ethnic boundaries in religious issues when he observes that liberated African slaves performed Islamic ceremonies in places separated from other ethnic groups in Bandar 'Abbas in the early 20th century.[25] Yet despite the segregated geographical location of black communities in some districts in Bandar 'Abbas, their marriage with indigenous people gradually assisted in breaking down ethnic boundaries and led to the absorption of Africans into the host population. One of the consequences of marrige with the local people was the increase in the population of mulattos and the corresponding decline in the number of pure blacks, and perhaps the gradual loss of ethnic identity. The reason for this could be found in the geographical location of Baluchistan as against Bandar 'Abbas and others. The latter districts were located closer to India, Africa, the Arab countries and the Indian Ocean world. Because of this, they were more exposed to foreign influence making room for an alternative worldview.[26]

In Baluchistan, Afro-Iranians live together; they are described as descendants of slaves whose identity depends upon the position of their masters and the condition imposed by the local situation. In Baluchistan marriage restrictions play a crucial role in generating ethnic boundaries, thereby preventing socio-economic movement. Salzman refers to the marriage condition among Baluchis that: "There were general categories of people who were proscribed as ineligible spouses for Sarhadi baluch, Ghulamzai, the descendants of slaves, and Luri, the small groups of itinerant blacksmiths."[27] The *ghulams* can only marry the *kanizes,* and most of the *kanizes* become the wives of the *ghulams. Suryat* is when an owner has a relationship with his *kaniz;* the child born of their union is regarded as free. If a *ghulam* marries a *kaniz* belonging to another slave owner, the *ghulam* will be recognized as a new slave for the latter. In this case, there is no right for the owner to protest. But, if the marriage occurs between a *ghulam* and a *kaniz* of two different tribes, such as Zihiha and another tribe, the owner of the *kaniz* has to buy the *ghulam* from his owner.[28] *Ghulam* and *kaniz* can be inherited by the children of the owner, or can be given as dowry to their daughters. In Sirik, in southern Iran, the recognition of ethnicity created boundaries, which separated African descendants from other social groups. After the abolition of slavery, this distinct slave society was transformed from slavery to servitude. The social position of Africans was not changed; rather they became servants who depended upon their masters. The social hierarchy in Sirik was so strict that any socio-economic mobility was hard to achieve; thus Afro-Iranians remained marginalized. Their ethnic identification as outsiders became apparent in inter-marriage restrictions. So in this area, Africans defined their membership in the host society as a subordinate ethnic group.[29]

In general, in all societies, stereotypes and racial designations prevent the formation of a new identity for Africans in the host society. This state of affairs had been maintained through marriage restrictions which prevented the absorption of the black population within society especially in some parts of Iran. However, marriage could be effected between Muslims of two different schools of *Sunni* and *Shi'ite.*[30] It rarely happened between blacks and whites; white men usually could marry black women, but it could not occur the other way around.[31] Breaking ethnic boundaries is difficult, while racial difference generates barriers over time for further generations. This racial difference could prevent Afro-Iranians' children from socio-economic promotion. In the rural area of Buti, in Baluchistan it seems that Afro-Iranians were illiterate.[32] The children of *ghulams* were not educated; only in 1966, for the first time, were two or three of their children sent to school.[33] In Iran, stereotypes and racism that had rooted in a traditional view was gradually losing its significance in the late 20th century.

The significant feature of Iranian society is its composition of diffrent ethnic groups, such as Turks, Arabs, Baluchis, Kurds, and Lurs as well as Persians. In essence, Africans were dispersed into a heterogeneous society that was composed of various ethnic groups. Afshar asserts that inhabitants of Khuzistan are Arabs, Lurs, and Turks; and various mixed ethnic groups such as Farsis, Baluchis, Arabs, and blacks (Africans) live in Bandar 'Abbas and the province of Hurmuzgan.[34] Various ethnic groups such as Hindus, Asuris, Afghanis, and Africans are also settled in Mukran in Sistan va Baluchistan, Hurmuzgam and Jask.[35] Curzon refers to the port of Lingah and its mixed population of Arabs, Persians, and Africans.[36] Bampur, one of the Baluchistan's villages, had a mixed population of blacks and whites.[37] Kababi refers to two villages of Chil and Balad al-'od in the Hingam Island and that its 500 population was composed of mixed people of black and white.[38]

The emergence of different patterns of language structure was one of the significant consequences of these diverse ethnic groups. Each geographical region is recognized as having its own specific local dialect and language spoken by the majority ethnic group of that particular area. As a result of the deep historical connections between southern Iran and India, Arabia and Africa, there was a huge linguistic interaction. According to Afshar, southern Iran has deep historical connections with India, Arab countries and Africa that consequently resulted in cultural and linguistic influence.[39] The main language in the province of Hurmuzgan is Farsi (Persian) but it has been mixed with Arabic, Swahili, and very limited words in English, Polish, Portuguese, and Hindi.[40] Over time, the language structure and dialect of each area greatly influenced the Africans. Significantly, they absorbed the language of local people such as Arabic, Baluchi, Luri, Abbasi, Lari, or Mukrani while they, nevertheless, maintained and conveyed Swahili words in their daily lives. During my fieldwork, I recorded my interviews with Afro-Iranians who spoke Arabic, Persian, as well as Swahili languages. Due to the constant traffic of people from both sides of southern Iran and the eastern coasts of Africa, Swahili became a lingua franca for the western Indian Ocean, especially, the Gulf, the Oman-Bandar and the southern Iran sub-region. However, more research is required in order to have a full appreciation of this mutual linguistic impact.

Socio-economic Status

Members of the African diaspora are influenced by specific linguistic and socio-economic patterns, as well as cultural practices of the host society of each particular region that they were settled in. Those Africans who live in ports and commercial cities such as Bandar 'Abbas and Qishm Island have had more opportunities in terms of their assimilation with the host society and improvement of their socio-economic status. In fact, commercial cities facilitate cultural, technical, and ideological interaction. In all cities and remote villages there was actually no chance for socio-economic movement, since people as a whole—both indigenous and Africans—lived in poverty, so blacks remain subordinate in this atmosphere.

Based on the collected reports on the tribal condition in Iran in 1934, Field provides useful information on the status of Africans in Iran. He refers to the socio-economic structure of Baluchistrin based on feudalism and the fact that the local chiefs, called *Sardars* or *Mirs*, besides having the prime power, owned a number of slaves.[41] According to Field the population of Bint, one of the villages of the Mukran district in Baluchistan, was composed of some Baluchi and about 2000 slaves for whom date plantations were the major economic activity.[42] Muqaddam, who spent some time in Baluchistan, provides very useful information on the socio-economic status of people in different villages of this area. Based on Muqaddam's report, around 1965, the total population of Ghulam, Muhammad Bazar, a rural area in Baluchistan, was about 250, of whom 10 were *ghulams* and 12 *kanizes*, all Africans of slave descent.[43] Among the total population of 5,000 in the village of Dashtyari, some were Africans of slave descent. "Most of them [Afro-Iranian in Baluchistan] are inhabitants of Dashtyari, a few in Rasak, most of the inhabitants of Turshab are slave descendants, but none of them live in Sarbaz."[44] From the headman of Dashtyari, Muqaddam was informed that:

"some people of Dashtyari are blacks; our fathers brought them from Zanzibar, or bought them from Arab merchants in Chahbahar,

Kinarak, and Kirichi. Men are *ghulams*, and women are *kanizes*, it is an old tradition, of course, now, they are the same (as us), and there is no difference between a *ghulam* and a Baluch.[45]

The pattern of social organization in the Sarhad Baluch suggests general egalitarian only among the tribesmen, while categorized Afro-Iranians as the descendants of slaves and the lowest social class.[46] They were easily identifiable from the Blauchis through the colour of their cloths which were in muted hues of blue and dusty rose.[47]

In Dashtyari, Afro-Iranians were working on wheat plantations, and after harvesting, they could take part of the produce.[48] In his visit to the rural area of Buti, Muqaddam met an old man called Jidgaly, the owner of 5 to 6 *ghulams*. He describes the situation of the *ghulams* as follows:

"previously, their fathers were slaves; our ancestors were buying them from the captain of the Arabs' ships in Karachi. Now, they are no longer slaves, they are working for us, and live in Kapar[49] where their fathers were living."[50]

That statement reveals that in fact there was neither social nor geographic mobility for the descendants of slaves. In Buti, Afro-Iranians worked in agriculture, tilling, sowing, and threshing corn in order to get a portion of the products. They were also involved in cutting the branches of trees, weeding, and feeding cattle. *Kanizes*, or female slaves, were involved in milking, making dairy products, baking, spinning, weaving, and baby-sitting, among others.[51]

In Hichan, a village in Baluchistan, tribal hierarchy was an essential characteristic feature, so each tribe played a specific role in terms of their function in socio-economic activities. Mubarakis and Raisis tribes were the owners of land, cattle, water, and houses. The headman of Hichan village was from the Raisi tribe. The people of Durazi tribe were cultivators of palm trees and could keep a portion of the produce. They were not landowners; the property of some of them consisted of one or two goats. But Durazis were free people. Originally the people of the Dawudis tribe were Lur. Their occupation consisted of playing music such as drums, and dancing at weddings or different ceremonies. Dawudis also worked as artisans and performers. At the bottom of this hierarchical system were servants or slave descendants who constituted a deprived social group which had no property. Muqaddam quotes the headman of Hichan village: "Previously, they [the servants] were *ghulams* and *Kanizs*; our fathers were buying them. Now, that slavery is abolished, they are servants."[52] After the abolition of slavery in 1928, all *ghulams* and *kanizes* were emancipated. They chose a family name for themselves, although these names came as a reminder of slave origins, such as Shanbih Azadi (Saturday freedom), or Jumah Azadi (Friday freedom), and obtained identity cards.[53]

In the coastal areas such as Bandar 'Abbas, lack of sufficient water and fertile soil prevent the involvement of people in agriculture. On the other hand, the conditions of northern regions are much more suitable for agriculture than areas close to the coast.[54] So, fishing comprises the main economic activity of people in the coastal area of southern Iran, and the Africans were equally employed in this sector.

In my interview with one of the local people in Bandar 'Abbas, I was told that in the past, the conditions of blacks in northern Bandar 'Abbas differed from those in the southern city. For instance, in the north blacks served the headman as his agents. Among other activities, slaves were involved in announcing news and had access to people's houses. Through their acquired power derived from the headman, blacks in northern Bandar 'Abbas could improve their socio-economic status. In the south, blacks who were living in the marginal area of Bandar 'Abbas were treated as *ghulams* and *kaniz* of the lowest social group.[55] Kababi states that in 1898 the population of Africans in Bandar 'Abbas was about 300 and was comprised of slave descendants. "They were minstrels, stone breakers, woodcutters, and the area they were living in the northwest of the city was called Blacks' Quarter."[56] He states that a very limited number of Africans were also involved in rope weaving.[57] Two separate quarters still exist as the heritage of blacks' isolation in the past: "Manbar-i Siyahan"(Blacks' pulpit), and "Pusht-i Shahr" (Behind the city).

Since Bandar 'Abbas has been one of the biggest cities and a significant port for Iran, its logistical situation and maritime facilities brought it in close contact with the world through the Persian Gulf. In the 20th century, the development of maritime technology gradually changed the socio-economic status of Afro-Iranians in that area and brought people of various ethnic groups and societies together.

Perpetuation of Identity

Afro-Iranians in each province tend to perceive themselves in term of communities rooted in the local region and emphasizing discontinuities with their homeland. Khusrud states that in Kharg Island an African from Zanzibar proudly identified himself as an Iranian.[58] In my interviews with Afro-Iranians in Bandar 'Abbas and Qishm Island, they identified themselves as Iranian, and in some cases even rejected any connection with Africa. On the other hand, the majority of Persians also do not know the homeland of the blacks as Africa; rather they consider them as inhabitants of the regions and as one of the local ethnic groups in southern Iran. Besides emphasizing their nationality as being Iranian, the identification with Islam was also strong among Afro-Iranians. Islam is the religion of the majority, and most people in Baluchistan are *Sunni Hanafite*. Initially, Africans were identified as infidels, but their conversion to Islam assisted in maintaining their communities.[59] In Baluchistan, Afro-Iranians identify themselves as Baluch and speak Baluchi; they have no knowledge of their background, ancestors or historical connection to the homeland.[60] Afro-Iranians were not able to determine their origins due to the formation of new identities in the host society. They, however, unconsciously remained an agent for the continuation and survival of their cultural links to Africa. In this regard, scholars who have knowledge of African history can play a significant role in determining their cultural linkage with Africa.

Cultural expression among Afro-Iranians should be regarded as the most significant constituent of their association with Africa. Curzon states that due to the large importation of slaves from Muscat and Zanzibar, considerable African elements exist in Baluchistan.[61] Riyahi who has traveled to Baluchistan refers to the circumcision of girls among one particular ethnic group of blacks as the result of the influence of African culture. He states that these people are related to the Kikoyo[62] in Africa. "Until a few years ago, a specific group of blacks were circumcising their daughters on the rocks close to the sea in a region of Chahbahar in the southwest of the city beside the tomb of Khazar. But today they do it rarely and only in secret."[63] It is much more likely that the custom entered Afro-Iranian society from the Horn, where it a prevalent among the Somali and many Ethiopian peoples.

The development of different features of African cultures is regarded as an important component of African identity in the diaspora. Afro-Iranians' roots are easy to perceive through their skin colour and cultural elements associated with their homeland.

Kababi refers to the use of black tobacco, or *Totoon* among the people of low social groups in Bandar 'Abbas.[64] The custom of using the edible tobacco in southern Iran can also be traced to Africa, and the Swahili people who mix tobacco with saltpeter and then chew it like gum. Playing the *Gammam*, (a kind drum) that is also found among Afro-Indians in Gujarat, the sickness of the *Zar* are all elements of African influences.[65]

Cultural continuity was an essential reaction and a form of resistance to slavery in which Africans generated a defensive mechanism to protect and unify themselves in the host country. Enslaved Africans defined their membership in their own communities by developing sub-cultures in the context of the host country. One of the significant cultural traits of African heritage is the practice of spirit possessions such as *Zar* among the African diaspora in Iran. Africans provided a common cultural core such as the widespread practice of the *Zar* spirit possession cult through which they could preserve their unity. Africans in the diaspora created a sub-cultural society by performing their music, song, and ritual practices independently of the host country. Afshar states that:

"during the night, in order to diminish their grief and sorrows, blacks were gathered all together, playing and singing in the tradition of their native land. In virtue of the combination of the Africans' music with that of the indigenous, gradually, the traditional music of Hurmuzgan and the whole coastal area of the south were born."[66]

People believe in metaphysical forces throughout the southern part of Iran from Khuzistan to Baluchistan. Based on the interviews and evidences I collected from southern Iran, without doubt the *Zar* practice is very common among Afro-Iranians.[67] However, I encountered a few instances of young people, who believed that *Zar* was a mysterious and dangerous force, and were so scared of being involved in this rite. The characteristic feature of spirit possession is evident in its multiple aspects. The association of music and dance is crucial in spirit possession. Instead of belief in the efficacy of medicine, *Zar* adherents trace many ailments to malicious winds, so they perform their ceremony by singing special songs and beating the 'dohol' supported by rhythmic movements of head and body to ward off evil spirit from the body.[66] Constantinides refers to the practice of *Zar* in other countries that: "In Egypt, the Sudan, Ethiopia, the Saudi Arabian peninsula, the Persian Gulf states, Iran and Turkey, both the category of spirits and the cult of healing are called zar."[69]

The African cultural heritage was transferred into a new land and combined with Islamic elements. Darvishi states that spirits are divided into five: *Zar*, Bad (wind), Jinn, Div (daemon), and Mashayakh, and he concludes that there are 15 different kinds of *Zars*, 12 different Bads, and a few jins.[70] According to Sa'idi, there are more than 72 kinds of *Zars*.[71] He mentions that the influence of Islamic elements caused the division of winds into evil (includes different kinds of *Zars*) and good (includes different kinds of Mashayikhs).[72] There is a belief that *Zar* is the most dangerous and widespread wind brought from Africa into southern Iran.[73] Poor mulattos and blacks such as fishermen and farmers are the most vulnerable social group influenced by *Zar*, and those who were possessed by one of the winds called Ahl-la Hava (air-inhabitant). The performers of the *Zar* ritual, who are all blacks, are called *"Baba"* or *"Mama."*

In Baluchistan, *Gowat* means wind or air, and *Gowati* is the term used for a person whose body is possessed by *Gowat*. Darvishi states that all Blacks whom he encountered in Baluchistan were possessed by the evil wind at least once.[74] The Baluchi people believe that music is the only way to force the evil spirits out of the body. This music should be performed along with rhythmic movements of the body.[75] The *Gowati* songs comprise of praising Abdul Qadir the founder of the *Qadiriyya sufi* order and L'l-i Shahbaz, one of the Iranian sufi leaders.[76]

"In Baluchistan, the *Gwat-yi Mat* is the person who deals the healing. When the *Gwat-yi Mat* recognizes what kind of *Zar* has possessed the body, then he starts the process of healing. *Kanizes* and *ghulams* sit around the sick person, and begin singing, playing drums, tanborah,[77] and cane. Each *Zar* has a specific song and melody. They [Afro-Iranians] play for three days and nights, sometimes five or six nights, then they sacrifice a kid; after cooking, everybody including the sick person must eat it."[78]

The *Gwati* ritual has different performance styles and utilizes various types of Baluchi musical instruments, such as Tamborah, Sarangi, Nay (cane), Dohol (drum), Qarani or Zomir, and Bambo.[79] But in the *Zar* ceremony, the only instrument that is used is the Dohol.

Song, music and dance in the province of Hurmuzgan and southern Iran are widely influenced by Africa.[80] Hamidi suggests that the presence of dramatic, ritualistic, and mythological elements in music is evidence of an African cultural influence.[81] "The chief form of music in this area is ritualistic music, especially the 'Zar' and the 'Noban'. This ritual is a kind of a music with curing quality; it is called 'Gwati' or 'damal' in Baluchistan."[82]

Edward Alpers describes in detail the diasporic cultural transformation of Africa in different countries in the Indian Ocean, and refers to the influence of African arts in Oman as follows:

"two of these arts—at-tanburah (an-nuban) and az-zar—derive ultimately from northeast Africa, which we know was a source of slaves for Oman in the 19th century, although these performance styles may also have entered Oman from Zanzibar."[83]

In southern Iran, *Nuban* is considered a Muslim and sacred wind. Tambirah or Tambora, which is considered a holy instrument, is the only instrument to be used in the *Nuban* ritual. This is an instrument of Sudanese origin and is also being used in Ethiopia which is named *Krar*.[84] It consists of six strings attached to a big wooden bowl, which is covered by the goatskin. Tambirah is one of African musical instruments that Hamidi believes was brought to the southern part of Iran about one or two centuries ago.[85] Darvishi refers to his visit with BabaDarvish, a performer of *Zar* and *Nuban* rituals in the Qishm Island, who inherited his Tambireh from his ancestors who brought it from Hamura[86] in Africa.[87] According to Alpers, *Nuban* as a feature of African cultural influence is being practiced in Dubai, and the United Arab Emirates in the Persian Gulf.[88] Alpers quotes Racy that: "This ritual, which is connected with spirit possession and healing, is associated with an African instrument, the lyre, and it has *Nuban* roots."[89] As in other countries in the Persian Gulf, the significant point about *Nuban* ritual in Iran is its association with Tambirah.

Afshar refers to *Liwa* employing the earliest African musical instruments such as big drums (Dohol) and some sort of reedy instruments.[90] In general, *Liwa* is one of the famous rituals associated with spirit possession and amusement. According to the local people, nowadays, *Liwa* is being performed in ceremonies such as weddings.

"Many people, about 60–80, participate in the play of *Liwa*. They gather in a big square or field. Whoever is possessed by a wind or depressed participates in *Liwa*. In addition to Dohols (drums), Korna, a kind of big trumpet whose sound reaches as far as hills and villages is used. When people hear that sound, they come to participate in Liwa. The Dohol, which is being used in Liwa, is the same as Pepe."[91][92]

Alpers also refers to the prevalence of *Liwa* among the people in Sohar, Zanzibar, Dubai, and Bahrain.[93]

Al Ahmad, who observed "Shaykh Faraj," a dance specific to Afro-Iranians in Kharg, calls it similar to "*Dammam*," a dance among Afro-Iranians in Bushihr.[94]

"They were performing this dance at weddings, and parties, everybody was gathering in the house of the headman and playing different kinds of drums, one by one, they were standing up to dance. When all were standing up, they shook, and danced until they fell on the ground powerless."[95]

Khusravi who traveled to Kharg in 1962, states that Salmin, an African from Mombassa performed the *Zar* using two drums called "Shaykh Faraj."[96]

According to Afshar, *Sabalu* is a song influenced by African music in southern Iran. People who want to perform *Sabalu* gather in a place, sit in a circle, play the tamborine, and shake their shoulders from right to left.[97] *Sangali* is also another type of traditional song performed by a group of sailors and seamen while rowing or loading the goods.[98] In addition, the Swahili songs are also used in the *Zar* ritual in southern Iran.[99]

While there are many other African elements in Afro-Iranian culture, tracing each particular cultural trait is not the main aim of this paper. This essay rather serves its purpose in drawing attention to the African presence in Iran.

Conclusion

What was highlighted in this paper is that Africans in Iran had different experiences depending on different local conditions. The socio-economic, geographic, and ethnic component in each region influenced their identity in society and the way they formed different types of communities. Their ethnic characteristics have changed over generations. In some big cities they have been socially assimilated, while in some areas, their identity is a reminder of slavery, which legitimated their status as servile and marginalized people. Nevertheless, Afro-Iranians successfully transformed their cultural heritage in the new land. The significance of their cultural heritage lies in the mutual influence of Africa and the host society. Music, dance, song, spirit possession, and language were significant cultural characteristics of the African diaspora in Iran that is influenced by Islamic and cultural elements of the society on the one hand, and was transformed by indigenous practices on the other. This mutual impact facilitated the continuity of the African heritage by making it a significant part of Iranian society.

Notes
I wish to thank professors Edward A. Alpers, Houchang Chehabi, and Sydney Kanya-Forstner for their significant scholarly criticism and comments on this paper.

1. Joseph E. Harris, "Africans in Asian History" in Joseph E. Harris, ed., *Global Dimensions of the African Diaspora* (Washington, 1993), 325.
2. Iraj Afshar Sistani, *Khuzistan va Tamadun-i Dirini-yi An* (Tihran, 1373), vol. 1,474.
3. Aryan-speaking Nordic nomads from eastern Russia assimilated original inhabitants of Persia in some areas as early as 2000 B.C. (Henry Field, *Contributions to the Anthropology of Iran* [Chicago, 1968], 608.)
4. Hasan Pirniya, *Iran Bastani* (Tihran, 1362), 144.
5. Sir Percy Sykes, *A History of Persia*, (London, 1969), 51.
6. Field, *Contributions to the Anthropology*, 108.
7. Field, *Contributions to the Anthropology*, 531.
8. Husayn Nurbakhah, *Bandar Gung*, (Bandar 'Abbas, 1359), 126; Jalal Al Ahmad, *Jaziri-yi Kharg, Dorr-i Yatim-i Khalij-i Fars*, (Tihran, 1376), 87; Husayn Nurbakhah, *Jaziri-yi Qishm va Khalij-i Fars* (Tihran,1369), 475.
9. Al Ahmad *Jaziri-yi Kharg,* 79; Muhammad Ali Kababi, *Bandar 'Abbas va Khalij-i Fars* (Tihran, 1368), 119.
10. Abu Ishag-I Istakhri, *Masalik va Mamalik* (Tihran, 1368), 113.
11. Kababi, *Bandar 'Abbas*, 12.
12. Ahmad Iqtidari, "Zabanha-yi Mahalli va Fulklur-i Khalij-i Fars," *Majmua-yi Maqalat-i Khalij-i Fars* (Tihran, 1369), 139; Kababi, *Bandar 'Abbas,* 57.
13. Thomas M. Ricks, "Persian Gulf Seafaring and East Africa: Ninth–Twelfth Centuries," *African Historical Studies,* 3/1 (1970), 343.
14. Kababi, *Bandar 'Abbas,* 361.
15. Paul E. Lovejoy, *Transformations in Slavery,* (Cambridge, 1997), 150.
16. Martin B. Esmond and T. C. I. Ryan, "A Quantitative Assessment of the Arab Slave Trade of East Africa, 1770–1896," *Kenya Historical Review,* 5/1 (1977), 79.
17. Lady [Mary] Sheil, *Glimpses of Life and Manners in Persia* (New York, 1973), 245; Charles Issawi, *The Economic History of Iran, 1800–1914* (Chicago, 1971), 125.
18. Issawi, *The Economic History*, 125.
19. Sheil, *Glimpses of Life,* 245.
20. Sheil, *Glimpses of Life,* 244.
21. *Ghulam* and *Kaniz* are Persian words; *ghulam* applies to male and the latter to female African slaves.
22. Mahmmud Zand-i Muqaddam, *Hikayat-i Baluch* (Tihran, 1370), 439.
23. Male slaves employed to tutor children.
24. Female slaves employed to look after children.
25. Kababi, *Bandar 'Abbas,* 158.
26. This a based on my observations during my fieldwork and so are many of the following descriptions.
27. Philip Carl Salzman, *Black Tents of Baluchistan* (Washington and London, 2000), 241.
28. Muqaddam, *Hikayat-i Baluch,* 440.
29. My interview with Mr. Ja'fari, one of the officials of the *Sazman-i Irshad-i Islami* in Bandar 'Abbas, November 2000.
30. Khusru Khusravi, *Jaziri i-yi Kharg* (Tihran, 1342), 105.
31. In my interview with Mr. Ja'fari, he referred to his father's will suggesting that the marriage between a white girl and a black should be prohibited. November 2000.
32. Muqaddam, *Hikayat-i Baluch*, 212.
33. Muqaddam, *Hikayat-i Baluch*, 201.
34. Iraj-i Afshar, *Shinakht-i Ustan-i Hurmuzgan* (Tihran, 1378), 302.
35. Afshar, *Shinakht-i Ustan-i Hurmuzgan,* 303.
36. George N. Curzon, *Persia and the Persian Question* (London,1892), Vol. 2, 409.
37. Muqaddam, *Hikayat-i Baluch,* 24.
38. Kababi, *Bandar 'Abbas,* 131.
39. Afshar, *Shinakht-i Ustan-i Hurmuzgan,* 201.
40. Afshar, *Shinakht-i Ustan-i Hurmuzgan,* 304; Iqtidary, *Zabanha-yi Mahalli,* 143.
41. Field, *Contributions to the Anthropology,* 236.
42. Field, *Contributions to the Anthropology,* 238.
43. Muqaddam, *Hikayat-i Baluch,* 164.
44. Muqaddam, *Hikayat-i Baluch,* 311.
45. Muqaddam, *Hikayat-i Baluch,* 169.
46. Salzman, *Black Tents of Baluchistan,* 9.
47. Salzman, *Black Tents of Baluchistan,* 37.
48. Muqaddam, *Hikayat-i Baluch,* 197.
49. A house made of the palm branches and mat.
50. Muqaddam, *Hikayat-i Baluch,* 211.
51. Muqaddam, *Hikayat-i Baluch,* 212.
52. Muqaddam, *Hikayat-i Baluch,* 45.
53. Muqaddam, *Hikayat-i Baluch,* 441.
54. Ghulam Husayn Sa-idi, *Ahl-i Hava* (Tihran, 1535), 22.
55. My interview with Mr. Ja'fari, Bandar 'Abbas, November 2000.
56. Kababi, *Bandar 'Abbas,* 157.
57. Kababi, *Bandar 'Abbas,* 162
58. Khusravi, *Jaziri-yi Kharg,* 110.
59. Muqaddam, *Hikayat-i Baluch,* 212.
60. Muqaddam, *Hikayat-i Baluch,* 211–12.
61. Curzon, *Persia and the Persian Question,* 259.
62. Kikoyo refers to the Gikuyu.
63. Ali Riyahi, *Zar va Bad va Baluch* (Tihran, 1977), 3.
64. Kababi, *Bandar 'Abbas,* 163.
65. Muhammad Husyan Adammyyat, "Uza'a-i Ijtima'i-yi Khalij-i Fars," *Khalij-i Fars,* 2 (1342), 149.
66. Afshar, *Shinakht-i Ustan-i Hurmuzgan,* 327.
67. A documentary videotape about the *Zar* in Bandar 'Abbas demonstrates that it is a common practice among Afro-Iranians. My thanks to Musa Kamali for providing me a copy if it.
68. Husayn Hamidi, *Hasht Bihisht* (Tihran, 1375), 20.
69. Pamela Constantinides, "The History of Zar in the Sudan: Theories of Origin, Recorded Observation and Oral Tradition" in I. M. Lewis, Ahmad Al-Safi and Sayyid Hurreiz, eds., *Women's Medicine* (Edinburgh, 1991), 83.
70. Muhammad Riza Darvishi, *Aynah va Avaz* (Tihran, 1376), 34.
71. Sa'idi, *Ahl-i Hava,* 64.
72. Sa'idi, *Ahl-i Hava,* 40.
73. Afshar, *Shinakht-i Ustan-i Hurmuzgan,* 317.
74. Muhammad Riza Darvishi, *Musiqi va Khalsah* (Tihran, 1378), 19.

75. Hamidi, *Hasht Bihisht*, 17.
76. Darvishi, *Aynah va Avaz*, 34.
77. Tamborah or Tanborah is a kind of lute that is one-meter length, and consists of a bowl with three strings attached to it.
78. Muqaddam, *Hikayat-i Baluch*, 212.
79. Riyahi, *Zar va Bad va Baluch*, 5.
80. Riyahi, *Zar va Bad va Baluch*, 327.
81. Hamidi, *Hasht Bihisht*, 20.
82. Hamidi, *Hasht Bihisht*, 20.
83. Edward A. Alpers, "The African Diaspora in the Northwestern Indian Ocean: Reconsideration of an Old Problem, New Directions for Research," *Comparative Studies of South Asia, Africa and the Middle East*, 17/2 (1997), 69.
84. Cynthia Tse Kimberlin, "The Music of Ethiopia" in Elizabeth May, ed., *Musics of Many Cultures* (Los Angeles, 1983), 237.
85. Hamidi, *Hasht Bihisht*, 63.
86. The geographical location of Hamura is not clear.
87. Darvishi, *Aynah va Avaz*, 137.
88. Alpers, "The African Diaspora," 70.
89. Ibid.
90. Afshar, *Shinakht-i Ustan-i Hurmuzgan*, 327.
91. Pepe refers to upepo which is a Swahili word meaning wind.
92. Sa'idi, *Ahl-i Hava*, 93.
93. Alpers, "The African Diaspora," 70.
94. Al Ahmad, *Jaziri-yi Kharg*, 81.
95. Al Ahmad, *Jaziri-yi Kharg*, 82.
96. Khusru Khusravi, *Jaziri-yi Kharg* (Tihran, 1342), 109.
97. Iraj Afshar Sistani, *Maqalat-i Iranshinasi* (Tihran, 1369), 499.
98. Ahmad Iqtidari, Khalij-i Fars (Tihran, 1536), 251; my interview with Isam'il Mubarak, an Afro-Iranian in the Qishm Island, November 2000.
99. Darvishi, *Aynah va Avaz*, 175.

SECTION FOUR:
AFRICANS IN NORTHERN AND
EASTERN SOCIETIES:
FROM INDIA TO RECENT CHINA

Introduction

One of the most fascinating windows into understanding the extent of the African Diaspora experience is fathoming the global scope of the African presence centuries ago as well as in today's society. Persons of African descent continue to migrate and settle in lands distant and very different from their native land.

Numerous studies and writings over many centuries have indicated that Africans migrated and settled for generations on all the surrounding islands and continents including the Mediterranean, Europe, and Asia.

For dozens of generations, Africans lived among the people who inhabited the islands and lands adjacent to the Mediterranean Sea. Large populations of Africans lived under the governance of Greek and Roman rule. Some individuals of African descent made important contributions that recent scholars have identified.

Scholars have in more recent years argued convincingly that there were a series of migration waves out of Africa towards mainland Asia, Southeast Asia, Australia, and the Pacific islands that began at least 60,000 years ago. Among the many scholars who have promoted this view is the research team led by A. Silvanna Santachuara-Benercetli from the University of Pavia in Italy who in their 1999 study showed that based on samples taken from populations living in Africa, Asia, and the Middle East, the "Mitochondia with the DNA" evident within these populations indicate a common ancestry dozens of generations earlier.

Over the last hundred years, writers have presented a wide range of evidence that indicates that there was an African presence in many of the centers of Asia and Asian civilization. While this aspect of African migration has been the least carefully researched, understood and written about, scholars have presented enough evidence that indicates the validity of this view. In earlier editions we provided readers with essays that highlighted the presence of African slaves living in parts of China during the Tang and Ming Dynasty 618–1644 AD. In this volume, we have introduced a more contemporary view of the African presence in China.

Over the last thirty-five years the Chinese government has won acceptance at the international level after the 1971 U.N. General Assembly resolution and has, according to a 207 International Monetary Fund, placed their country at the helm of all countries including the U.S. for projected economic growth measured at 11.2% as compared to 20% for the U.S. Interestingly, the Chinese government has, since the 1960s, encouraged and fostered meaningful Sino-African relations by encouraging African students to attend their universities to receive training in many urban universities. Consequently, a small number of persons of African descent as well as others have written about their experiences in Chinese urban cities. A review of these sources indicate that there have been racial tensions and evidence of outright prejudice and discrimination towards the recent Africans who reside in China. One case that has been carefully documented was the Nanjing Anti-African Mass Protest and Demonstration that was held in late 1988 and early 1989 against some African students who attended the Hehai University. The major concerns of the demonstrators were the financial benefits that some African students were receiving while attending Chinese universities that were not granted to Chinese students. Other concerns centered on the perceived attachment of some female Chinese college students to some of the African students. Chinese government officials eventually dealt with this sensitive situation, and the intercultural relationships between Africans living in urban Chinese regions have since improved. The present Chinese government seeks to develop closer ties with African governments and therefore has a policy of allowing small numbers of persons of African descent to settle in China.

At present, there are thousands of first generation African immigrants living in a few of the Chinese vast urban centers. Some African students seem to have remained after finding employment in China. The largest percentages of these are from South Africa, Nigeria, and Ethiopia. One enclave that has attracted wide positive attention by the Chinese population has been the creation of an African football team in Beijing that has been competing in the city's football league for about ten years. The Afrika Limited Football Club has been very successful under Coach Kagsliam, originally from Tanzania and recently a documentary file was produced about the team entitled "African Boots of Beijing."

Over the last decade the Chinese government has also made significant strides in developing extensive training ties with the various African nations. In November 2006, the China government hosted fifty African heads of state and pledged to increase Chinese aid to U.S. $42 billion and to extend their foreign direct investment which, according to one source, is already estimated at U.S. $8 billion. Additionally, a growing number of Chinese professionals and workers have been migrating to work in various African countries at the invitation of these countries. These include acupuncturists, agriculturalists, nurses, businessmen, architects, construction worker and so on. A group of Chinese medical personnel have been involved in instituting preventive measures to stop the spread of diseases like AIDS and malaria. The Holley Pharmaceutical (Chongging) Co., Ltd., a leading Chinese anti-malaria drug manufacturer, has been operating with various African countries over the last ten years.

already estimated at U.S. $8 billion. Additionally, a growing number of Chinese professionals and workers have been migrating to work in various African countries at the invitation of these countries. These include acupuncturists, agriculturalists, nurses, business men, architects, construction worker and so on. A group of Chinese medical personnel have been involved in instituting preventive measures to stop the spread of diseases like AIDS and malaria. The Holley Pharmaceutical (Chongging) Co., Ltd, a leading Chinese anti-malaria drug manufacturer has been operating with various African countries over the last ten years.

There are four essays in this section dealing with the African presence in societies east of the African continent. The first essay in this section introduces us to the debate that continues to rage among scholars regarding the extent and significance of the African Slave Trade from the east coast of Africa to the regions of the Persian Gulf and beyond, including the southern Indian subcontinent and possibly regions of Southeast Asia. Ralph A. Austen's 1989 essay, "19th Century Islamic Slave Trade from East Africa (Swahili and Red Sea Coast): A Tentative Census," was part of his early ongoing examination of the volume issue. Austen reevaluates some of the earliest observations he and other scholars made in estimating the volume of the East African Slave Trade. He suggests that for that specific region and for that century the number of African slaves leaving for the East appears to be just under one million persons.

Ralph A. Austen is a Professor of African History at the University of Chicago and has written extensively on the African-Islamic Slave Trade in the Indian Ocean. He is author of many earlier essays, including "The Islamic Trade Out of Africa (Red Sea and Indian Ocean): An Effort at Quantification" (1977); "The Islamic Red Sea Trade: An Effort at Quantification;" and other related essays, including one in David Eltis and James Walvin's *The Slave Trade and Abolition Impacts on Africa, the Americas, and Europe*.

Western scholars have always found this part of the world more difficult and far more culturally and racially complex than other regions of the globe. Nevertheless, there has been an ongoing debate for decades about the African presence in this vast geographical region. Howard Barry Fell (1917–1994), zoologist, anthropologist, linguist and oceanographer, grew up in New Zealand and lived among the native Maoris. He was a graduate of Wellington and Victoria University Colleges and earned a Ph.D. at the University of Edinburgh, Scotland, in 1941. Fell undertook a careful pioneering study of "native" New Zealanders. He researched this society at Harvard University and concluded that there was a direct connection between the Maoris' alphabet in New Zealand and the language of one of the Libyan peoples, which is a western dialect of Ancient Egypt. His findings have created extensive controversy, as has the work of George F. Carter of Texas A&M University. Carter's "Egyptian Gold Seekers and Exploration of the Pacific," in which he translates Heinrich Quirling's 1952 work "Die Goldinsel Des Isador Von Sevilla, Aegypter Der 20 Dynastie Als Entdecker und Kulturbringer in Ostasien," claims that the Ancient Egyptians were familiar, from as early as the fifth dynasty, with the Red Sea and beyond, and that in later dynasties the Ancient Egyptians had traveled through the Indian Ocean and to the western fringes of the Pacific Ocean, especially some areas of the China Sea. Other equally provocative essays can be found in Ivan Van Sertima and Runoke Rashidi's edited work, *African Presence in Early Asia* (1985, 1988). The essays in this volume include Walter A. Fairservis' "The Script of the Indus Valley Civilization," John G. Jackson's "Krishna and Buddha of India: Black Gods of Asia," Gershorn Williams' "Ancient Kuskite Roots of

India: A Survey of the Works of Godfrey Higgins" and James E. Brunson's "African Presence in Early China."

Further afield and following the more conventional approach is the work of Catherine H. and Ronald M. Berndt, anthropologists at the University of Western Australia. They have interpreted the early history of Australian Aborigines in a very insightful manner. Other recent conventional studies that highlight most of early prehistoric East Asian societies are included in works like M. Graves and R. C. Green's *The Evolution and Organization of Prehistoric Society in Polynesia* (1993).

A review of these and other essays and works will indicate to the careful reader the use and misuse of historical evidence and also point out some of the many complexities one encounters in seeking to obtain a well-balanced yet multi-ethnic perspective regarding the African presence in Asia. There appears to be a wealth of information waiting to be uncovered regarding the African presence in this part of the world.

The second essay in this section is Richard Pankhurst's "The Ethiopian Diaspora to India: The Role of Habshis and Sidis from Medieval Times to the End of the Eighteenth Century." Pankhurst dedicated decades of his studies to understanding Ethiopian history and wrote extensively about this outstanding Ancient African Kingdom. His published work on Ethiopian history spans over forty years beginning in 1957 and includes over twenty monographs. Among his best known early work on Ethiopian history is his 1961 *An Introduction to the Economic History of Ethiopia from Early Times to 1800* (1961). The article included here is from his *The African Diaspora in the Indian Ocean* (2001).

The third essay is Ann M. Pescatello's "The African Presence in Portuguese India" and was a chapter in Patrick Manning's *Slave Trades, 1500–1800: Globalization of Forced Labour* (1996). Pescatello has also been researching and writing on closely related African Diaspora themes for over twenty-five years. Her first publication in this venture was the edited work, *The African in Latin America 1492–1972* (1975); another is *Old Roots in New Lands: Historical and Anthropological Perspectives, the Black Experience in the New World* (1977). Her more recent works include the edited, *Power and Pawn: The Female in Iberian Families, Societies and Cultures* (1977) and the narrative *Charles Seeger: A Life in American Music* (1992).

The final essay in this section is Barry Sautman's "Anti-Black Racism in Post-Mao China." Sautman has been studying and writing about Chinese international relations for some time. He is Associate Professor of Social Science at the Hong Kong University of Science and Technology. He earned his many degrees at a number of American universities in various fields from Political Science to Library and Information Sciences. He earned a J.D. degree in Law at the University of California, Los Angeles, and a Ph.D. in Political Science at Columbia University in 1990. He has taught at the University of Utah, California State University as well as at Northridge and The Johns Hopkins-Nanjing University Center for Chinese and American Studies in Nanjing, China. His most recent books include *Cultural Genocide and Asian State Peripheries* (2006) and the co-edited *Contemporary Tibet: Politics, Development and Society in a Disputed Region* (2007).

The 19th Century Islamic Slave Trade from East Africa (Swahili and Red Sea Coast): A Tentative Census[1]

Ralph A. Austen

Efforts to estimate the number of slaves taken by Muslims out of the various regions of East Africa began during the nineteenth century as part of an evangelical and colonialist assault upon Islam by contemporary Europeans. The endeavour has continued, in more recent and restrained scholarly writings, to produce considerable controversy.[2] Clearly no definitive census of this trade is possible, since any research must depend to a large extent upon the same suspect observations which are the subject of the initial dispute.

The present study attempts to minimize such problems by laying out its evidence in detailed tabular form (see Table I).[3] Thus the sources can be subjected to critical analysis and re-evaluation. A second set of basic tables (see Table V) present data on slave demography and deployment in the areas of Arabia, the Persian Gulf and South Asia to which East African slaves were sent. While this material is even less numerically precise than the direct slave trade documentation, it independently provides a scale of possible African presence in these receiving zones against which calculations of the trade can be checked.

None of these efforts can fully overcome the difficulties inherent in Islamic slave trade assessments. The individual observations remain questionable, not only on ideological grounds but also because even the most dispassionate ones tend to be less real statistical statements than what Philip Curtin has called "capacity estimates," i.e. figures reflecting only the levels possible under optimal trading conditions instead of the average over a normal range of time.

Some of the observations are based upon customs reports, which represent the closest evidence we have to the working records from which the best economic history statistics (including studies of the Atlantic slave trade) are derived. However, unlike the accounts of merchants themselves, customs records only reflect that portion of a trade visible to government officials and we are dealing here with regions where governments had only limited control over private-sector activities. Moreover, for the best set of customs figures in these tables, those from the Swahili Coast in the mid-nineteenth century, we only learn about that portion of the trade which was legal and this, after 1846, excluded all exports outside of East Africa i.e. the very subject of the present study. The Red Sea evidence is not as reliable, but it is also less problematic for present purposes and thus subject to less historiographic controversy.[4]

1. The Swahili Coast

The African area usually labelled "Swahili Coast" extends from Southern Tanzania to Northern Kenya, encompassing both mainland and off-shore islands. This zone, with its nineteenth-century commercial centre of Zanzibar, will be the focus of the present analysis, but the term will also be extended to northern Mozambique and Madagascar to the south, and to southeastern Somalia (the Brava Coast) to the north.

For the nineteenth century Islamic slave trade in this area the most reliable information available to us deals with the traffic from Kilwa to Zanzibar and (either directly or via Zanzibar) the Kenya-Brava coasts. These data are critical for indicating the general level of slave commerce in the region, but do not immediately reveal anything about exports to the external Islamic zones. This last trade was clearly smaller than that involved in supplying servile labour within East Africa, and was only a residual of the latter. Indeed there seems to have been no extensive movement of slaves to Arabia, the Persian Gulf and India from the points of direct access to the East African interior (Kilwa and northern Mozambique) but only a secondary (and for most of the period clandestine) shipment from Zanzibar, the Kenya-Brava coasts, and Madagascar. Nonetheless, the main coastal slave trade of the nineteenth century was quite large, so that its overflow out of the region could still have been quite significant. To estimate this external trade we must both look for direct evidence concerning it and also determine the probable residuals from the various local trades.

165

Table I. Selected Slave Trade Observations

Date	Quantity	Comments	Original Source	Reference
A. Swahili Coast				
1. 1811		Zanzibar exports 6–10,000 slaves p.a. to Muscat, India, Isle de France	Smee, British naval officer	Burton, 1872, 11, p. 493
2. 1812	2,000	calculations from Kilwa customs data; formerly exported "many thousands" now Arabs "do not take many"	Prior, British naval officer	Freeman-Grenville, 1962, pp. 210–211
3. 1817–19	25,000	Zanzibar imports; 13,000 from Kilwa; some skepticism	Albrand, French scholar, official	Nicholls, 1971, p. 213
4. 1822	8,000	Zanzibar imports; seen as decline	Moresby, British India official	Nicholls, 1971, p. 207
5. 1826		export from Zanzibar domains "very trifling"	British official report	Sheriff, 1987, p. 35
6. 1853		20 Arab ships seen at Mogadishu smuggling slaves to Arabia	Krapf, German missionary	Krapf, 1860, p. 112
7. 1861	400	350–450 slaves from Zanzibar to Red Sea	Oldfield, British naval officer	PP 1863, p. 173
8. 1861	10,000	estimate of no. of slaves shipped north (includes Kenya, Somalia)	Walker, British admiral	PP 1863, p. 172
9. 1865	6,000	Zanzibar exports 5–7,000 to Arabia, Red Sea	Ropes, U.S. consul	Bennett/Brooks, 1965, p. 54
10. 1866	6,000	40 dhows leave for Gulf, estimated to hold 150 slaves each	Pasley, British naval officer	PP 1867–68, (A) C. 4,000 no. 81
11. 1868	9,000	6,000 from Zanzibar, Pemba, 1,000 from N. coast, 2,000 stolen, all to Arabia	Churchill, British consul, Zanzibar	PP 1868–69, (B), no. 85
12. 1873–4	7,000	slaves seen Dec. 1873–March 1874 on land route from Kilwa	Elton, British vice-consul	Elton, 1879, pp. 94, 104
13. 1874	40,000	overland exports from Kilwa (high mortality, most to northern coast)	Holmwood, British vice-consul	PP 1876, LXX, p. 7
14. 1875	12,000	1,500 p. month to Kilwa; 1,000 continue north	Ward, British naval officer	PP 1877, LXVIII, pp. 31–32
15. 1876	24,000	overland exports north	Kirk, British consul	PP 1877, LXVIII, pp. 251–252
16. 1877		overland slave trade from Kilwa suppressed	Kirk, British consul	PP 1878, LXVIII, pp. 271–72
17. 1902	700	Sur ships take on slaves at Mozambique, captured by Portuguese	British official reports	Busch, 1967, p. 171
B. Persian Gulf				
1. 1830	1,550	Muscat customs records 1,400–1,700 $^3/_4$ Swahili; $^1/_4$ Ethiopian	Wilson, British Gulf official	Sheriff, 1987, pp. 38–39
2. 1841	1,337	Kharq ships recorded plus Sheriff projection	Kemball, British Gulf official	Sheriff, 1987, p. 39
3. 1841	2,887	estimate of slaves to upper Persian Gulf, based on No. 2 above	Robertson, British official, Kharq	Kelly, 1968, p. 416
4. 1847	3,488	Total upper Gulf imports seen as low	Kemball, British Gulf official	FO 84/692
5. 1852	435	landed on Trucial Coast; probably undercounted	British agent, Sharjah	Kelly, 1968, p. 610
6. 1852	1,200	imported into one region of Trucial Coast	Kemball, British Gulf agent	Kelly, 1968, p. 610
7. 1865	1,400	estimate for various small Omani ports	British agents, Muscat	PP 1867–68, LXIV, no. 124
8. 1866	900	small N. Oman ports import 700–1,100 Swahili slaves for local date cultivation	Disbrowe, British agent, Muscat	PP 1867–68, LXIV, pp. 787–88
9. 1896		100 Suri dhows fly French flag, presumedly slavers	British naval report	Beachey, 1976, p. 239
C. West Arabian Ports				
1. 1856	8,650	total W. Arabian ports; includes 2,500 Swahili	Lambert, French consul, Jiddah	Ewald, 1987, p. 11
2. 1859	5,000	1,900 p. annum via Hajj, etc. to Jiddah, 3,000+ to other Arabian ports	Rosseau, French consul, Jiddah	MAE, Turquie: Djedda, 2, p. 358
3. 1864	5,000	total for all Arabian ports based on "active research"	Pelessier, French consul, Jiddah	MAE, Turquie: Djedda, 3, pp. 118–19
4. 1869	4,250	total for all West Arabian ports	Raby, British consul, Jiddah	FO 84/1305a, fol. 271
5. 1878	2,000	minimum total of Red Sea trade to Arabia	Malcolm, British official	FO 541/22, p. 17
6. 1880	700	slaves seen at one time at Hodeidah	Burrel, British official	Ewald, 1987, p. 10
7. 1880	3,000	imports into Hejaz	Burrel	Ewald, 1987, p. 10

Europeans made many estimates of slave exports from the Swahili coast to the Persian Gulf during the nineteenth century but most of them are quite obviously out of the range of plausibility. Even the figures retained here (I/A/8–11) have to be treated as exaggerations; their value is rather to indicate that some external trade, on a yet undetermined scale, was taking place. For the middle and later part of our period, the few observations which can be taken more literally (I/A/6, 7, 17) suggest where we may look for the trade but do not provide a basis for any serious calculations.

We can attempt our own estimates of the export trade from the accounts of the Kilwa and Zanzibar slave trade for the first three decades of the nineteenth century, before clove plantations in Zanzibar and Pemba and other commercial crops on the Kenya and Brava coasts had begun to absorb very large numbers of slaves for local use.[5] Alpers and Sheriff have argued that the Asian demand for Swahili coast slaves was always low; that a rise in demand was created by French initiatives in the later eighteenth century, first at Mozambique and then Kilwa; and that with the withdrawal of the French during the Napoleonic wars the demand for slaves again declined until the growth of coastal plantations (as well as further traffic to the French Mascarenes and new Mozambique–Brazil trade) revived the system.[6] The problem with this argument lies not in its explanation of the greatly expanded general East African slave trade of the nineteenth century, but rather in its perspective on the continuity of the more modest external Islamic element within this trade. This lesser trade is described directly in a few early nineteenth-century documents but these must also be linked to the evidence for pre-nineteenth century slave exports from the region.

The reports in I/A/1–5 describe a slave trade from Kilwa and Zanzibar during the interim between French and local plantation demands. All observers but one state that the trade is small, declining, or less than reported. As indicated by the various quantitative references in Prior (I/A/2), however, the concepts of scale in these comments ("many thousands") seem to be based upon the Atlantic or earlier and later European exports from East Africa, and could minimize a quite substantial trade in Islamic terms. The figures actually given for local trade are indeed probably too high (except possibly for Prior, whose customs revenue coefficient of $8 per slave is unusually large, thus reducing what may be the actual number of individuals sold) but they suggest a very substantial export to the Persian Gulf and India of several thousand.

If we also consider the figures and descriptions of the Muslim East African slave trade during the sixteenth and seventeenth centuries (not presented here), we can assume that such a level would be normal even without the stimulus of France's eighteenth century intervention. Moreover the emphasis in these earlier data on exports from Madagascar suggests a pattern which has to be sought again in the nineteenth century, when the local Islamic slave trade to Madagascar became especially active.[7]

For the major portion of the nineteenth century, we can estimate the external Islamic slave trade only as a residual of local trades. In the case of Madagascar, this cannot presently be done with any precision, since the data presented in the other papers of this collection do not provide the necessary documentation. We may safely assume such a trade, of modest but steady proportions, from both earlier precedent, the continuing Persian Gulf connections of Arabs engaged in the Mozambique–Madagascar slave trade,[8] and one piece of substantial direct evidence for such trade at the beginning of the twentieth century (I/A/17).[9] Finally, what all the evidence about sailing routes and the use of Portuguese and French flags suggests is that illegal Arab slave traders could most easily have evaded British naval patrols by taking the route from Madagascar to the Persian Gulf.

The more precise customs data on the legal Kilwa–Zanzibar–northern coast slave trade during the nineteenth century provide a potential basis for calculating exports out of East Africa from the demography of local slave retention. In the previous work of Ryan and Martin and Sheriff, most of this effort has been concentrated on Zanzibar and Pemba, which had both the best recorded slave imports and the largest slave populations. However, once the exaggerated figures of nineteenth-century abolitionists have been discredited, this effort does not yield very specific results. The number of slaves leaving Zanzibar directly for the north was obviously not very large and thus cannot be linked closely to the quite substantial resident slave population. The figures for Zanzibar slave imports and Kilwa exports to Zanzibar are thus important only to demonstrate that a sufficiently large renewal of the resident slave population was taking place for the illegal exports recorded in such documents as I/A/10, 11 to be plausible. Dhows from the Gulf did come regularly to Zanzibar and even so sceptical an analyst as Sheriff assigns a rounded (and reduced from the British estimates) number of 1,010 per year to their slave smuggling.

We can, I think, get more mileage out of the smaller customs figures for Kilwa trade to points other than Zanzibar and Zanzibar legal exports, since these must be correlated with the absorptive capacities of the smaller urban and agricultural centres along the coast. I have made such correlations in rough form and presented their results in Table II, although they suffer particularly from lack of attention to temporal variants within the larger period under question. However, my calculations do provide a basis for determining how much of the coastal slave trade might eventually have leaked out to the external Islamic world. This trade appears to be smaller than the Kilwa non-Zanzibar exports but, nevertheless, remains significant.

Table II represents the calculations for the period during which the slave trade within the Swahili coast region was still legal. Items I/A/ 12–16 describe a final overland surge of the Kilwa export trade after Britain outlawed all maritime carriage of slaves within the region. While one cannot treat any of these figures as literally accurate, they are based upon enough direct observations to indicate at least a large continuing traffic. Some proportion of these northbound slave caravans would again enter external channels, although at a reduced rate given the more urgent needs of coastal plantations, including a sugar-plantation sector just developing around Pangani in northern Tanzania.[10]

By 1877, after Britain imposed further abolitionist measures on the Sultan of Zanzibar and interior slave traders realized that their coastal market was no longer what it had been, the flow of slaves through Kilwa seems to have ended. After that time only small and sporadic supplies of slaves are reported coming to the coastal plantations, usually from local Tanzanian and Kenyan sources.[11] Exports from this part of the coast must thus have been reduced to a trickle.[12] For the last quarter of the nineteenth century, only Madagascar and Mozambique could continue to provide any significant supply of slaves to the Persian Gulf.

2. The Persian Gulf and South Asia

The most solid evidence we have for slave exports from East Africa to the Persian Gulf and India comes not from the Swahili Coast but rather the receiving points. By far the most significant of these is the Persian Gulf where, as will be shown below, there was a major, possibly even a growing, demand for African labour in the nineteenth century.

Sheriff bases much of his argument for a very low slave trade out of East Africa on the scrutiny of two fairly precise reports of slave imports into the Persian Gulf (I/B/1, 2). As with all of Sheriff's work, the evidence presented by these documents forces us to deflate many of the larger figures given by British and other observers of Persian Gulf imports, but it does not define the full scale of slave intake into this region.

For the Lower Gulf (Oman and Trucial Oman [present day United Arab Emirates] we must double Sheriff's figure of 500 because it is based only on southern Oman (see I/B/5–8). For the Upper Gulf (the only destination of boats passing Kharq Island) Sheriff's figures are also probably too low, since not all shipping for this region could be observed from Kharq.[13] The calculations in I/B/3, 4 also have to be given consideration and even if only the lower one is accepted and treated as an upper limit capacity estimate, we still have an import level which, if adjusted for the various items in the conclusion of Table II, provides confirmation of the export figures used for the coast. There is no more quantitative evidence from the Gulf for the period after the maritime trade in East Africa became illegal (1873) but items I/A/17, B/9, even when allowances are made for British ideological distortions of the latter, provide some evidence for the continuation of such slave movements. It has further been argued that the commitment of Persian Gulf shipping to slave trading and other contraband activities was increased during this period because of the loss of "legitimate" cargo to British steam vessel competition.[14]

I have also included in Table II/F a brief analysis of Gulf shipping capacity to indicate that even at the lowest level derived from Royal Navy capture data, enough shipping would have been available to take 4,000 slaves per annum from East Africa. The bottom limits of this scale do not, in any case, describe most of the relevant shipping since larger vessels, capable of dealing with rougher open seas, also appeared better able to elude British patrols by keeping farther away from East African coastal watch points.[15] The very small Gulf boats in II/F/4 also played an important role in the slave trade, but they were so numerous that their capacity does not limit the scale of aggregate slave imports into the region.

South Asia (especially its northwest coast) played a minor although steady role in the Indian Ocean slave trade during the first five decades of the century. By the mid-1840s, however, the very British scrutiny indicated by the extensive documentation of this traffic seems to have brought the import of East Africans to a virtual end. As will be seen below, this evidence matches that for black slave demand within South Asia.

Table II. Swahili Coast Slave Trade Calculations

A. Coastal Exports		per annum
1. Kilwa Exports, non-Zanzibar, 1859–1870		4,000[1]
2. Zanzibar exports to northern coast 1861–1873		7,403
3. Northern coastal retention (1860s–70s)		
Pemba		2,180
Mrima/Pangani		500[2]
Mombasa		1,000[3]
Malindi		1,000
Lamu		2,000[4]
Benadir		2,175[5]
total		8,855

4. Exports out of Africa	per annum	total
Zanzibar/Kilwa 1800–1846 (legal)	4,000	188,000
Zanzibar, 1847–1874 (smuggling)	1,000	28,000
residual ex Kilwa, 1847–1874 (legal)		
total p.a. exports 4,000		
coastal absorption 1,500[6]		
residual export	2,500	70,000
Kilwa, Mozambique, 1847–1874 (smuggling)	500	14,000
[total exports 1847–1874	4,000]	
General smuggling, 1875–1899	500	12,500
Total for nineteenth century		313,000

B. Persian Gulf Imports (1830–1866)	
1. Oman, Lower Gulf retention	1,000
2. Muscat exports to Upper Gulf	1,500–2,000
3. Sur exports to Upper Gulf	500
subtotal	3,000–3,500
adjusted total[7]	2,700–3,100
C. Red Sea Imports	500[8]
D. South Asia Imports	500
E. Total Imports	3,700–4,100

F. Slave Shipping Capacities	vessels	average cargo	no. vessels for 4,000 slaves
1. Leaving Zanzibar 1867–70 (for N. Swahili coast)[9]	551	56	71
2. Captured 1868–70 (en route to E. Af., Arabia)[10]	109	29	138
3. Captured 1873–96 (en route to E. Af., Arabia)[11]	600	14.5	276
4. Shipping of 2 small N. Oman ports, 1866[12]	19–24	6.5–11	364–615

[1] The computed average for the figures in this column of Table II is 3,813; however the figure of 3,000 for the last three years appears stereotyped; assuming that it is indicative of a decline for the first year and a return to almost normal previous levels (average 4,300) for subsequent years, the total average would be around 4,000.

[2] J. Glassman reveals that extensive use of slave labor for commercial agriculture did not begin in this area until the mid-1870's.

[3] Mombasa and Malindi retention from Cooper, 1977, p. 88.

[4] Martin and Ryan, 1980, p. 112

[5] Ibid, p. 114.

[6] surplus of total coastal absorption over Zanzibar export.

[7] down 20% for Red Sea slaves; up 10% for mortality at sea.

[8] based on table I/A/7 (and other evidence not cited here).

[9] British report based on customs records in Sheriff, 1987, p. 241.

[10] Lloyd, 1949, p. 278.

[11] C. Glassman (see endnote 10), p. 9.

[12] Disbrow, British agent, Muscat, PP 1867–68, XIV, pp. 787–88.

Table III. Competing Swahili Coast Slave Trade Estimates

	per annum	subtotal]1	total
A. Martin and Ryan, 1977			
1800–1829	2,500	75,000	
1830–1839	3,500	35,000	
1840–1849	4,000	40,000	
1850–1873	6,500	156,000	
1874–1896	400	9,200	
			314,200
B. Sheriff, 1987			
1800–1874	3,000	225,000	
[1875–1899	400	12,500]1	
			237,500

1 Sheriff's study ends in 1873 but in order to compare his results with the others, I have extended his main period by one year and assigned him the lower of the two projections for the post-abolition period.

3. The Red Sea

The evidence on slaves leaving Africa via the Red Sea during the nineteenth century is less complicated than that for the Swahili coast. Slave cargoes at the maritime ports of the Nilotic Sudan (Suakin), Ethiopia (Massawa, Northern Danikil) or northern Somalia (the Gulf of Aden) were not bound for some other point on the continent but rather destined directly for Arabia. Some of these data come from customs records but most of them

are based upon anecdotal "literary" observations. We are thus forced to arbitrate between the probable understatement of the former figures and the tendency towards exaggeration and capacity estimates of the latter. The method for calculating the scale of this trade is thus relatively simple although incapable of producing anything like exact results. As shown in Table IV, I have broken down the trade for each port or set of ports into sub-periods where uniform conditions seemed to prevail, established plausible annual averages for these smallest units, multiplied them into subtotals for each, and added together the results. Whatever the shortcomings in these calculations (and I find it difficult to specify a margin of error), they represent the results of considerable refinements as well as augmentation[16] of observations previously used and at least on this basis are more reliable.

The Gulf of Aden was the most important source of Red Sea slaves during the course of the nineteenth century, largely because it was closest to the sources of Somali and Oromo slaves as well as to the Ethiopian Shoan state which so successfully expanded in this era. The official figures from this area indicate extremes in this trade, while the numerous capacity estimates do not place such

Table IV. Red Sea Slave Trade Estimates

	per annum	subtotal	total
A. Gulf of Aden			
1800–1884	3,000	235,000	
1885–1890	1,500	9,000	
1891–1899	500	4,500	
total			250,000
B. Massawa			
1800–1810	1,000	11,000	
1811–1875	1,500	97,500	
1876–1899	100	2,500	
total			111,000
C. Northern Danikil			
1877–1888	2,000	24,000	24,000
D. Suakin			
1800–1859	1,200	72,000	
1860–1879	1,000	20,000	
1880–1899	500	5,000	
total			107,000
Grand Total			492,000

E. Correlation with West Arabian Imports

	import Arabia	export Suakin	export Massawa	export Aden Gulf	export Danikil	export total
1856	8,659	1,500	1,500	3,000		(6,000)
1859	5,000	1,500	500	3,000		(5,000)
1864	5,000	1,000	1,200	3,000		(5,200)
1869	4,250	1,000	1,200	3,000		(5,200)
1878	2,000	1,000	100	3,000	2,000	(6,100)
1880	4,000	500	100	1,500	1,000	(3,600)

polar indications in mutually separate periods. The figure of 3,000 which I have assigned to the slave trade from this area for the period up to 1885 may be just a little too high, so I have lowered the resulting subtotal by 20,000.

The Northern coastal ports of Massawa and Suakin (particularly the latter) drew on a population which was also exploited by the flourishing Nile Valley slave trade. Janet Ewald has argued that with the decline of the trade into Egypt during the 1870s, the number of slaves entering the Red Sea via Massawa and Suakin should have increased.[17] However I am not convinced by specific evidence for the two ports during this decade that such a diversion occurred on any significant scale.

The documentation for Massawa is actually quite complex, because both official and capacity estimate reports indicate periodic fluctuations in its slave trade during the course of the nineteenth century. I have been somewhat more conservative here than with the Gulf of Aden, especially for the period after 1875, because the sudden emergence of the Northern Danikil as a major export area implies a long-term decline in Massawa's role. Finally, for Suakin, which faced very active competition from the lower Nile (both Egypt and the Northern Sudan) during the periods when it is reported as most actively exporting slaves, I have also been conservative in my calculations.

The final result of just under half a million slaves exported via the Red Sea is over 50 per cent lower than the only other estimate, that of Pankhurst. However, Pankhurst does not pretend to the kind of precision or thoroughness attempted in Martin and Ryan or Sheriff's Swahili Coast quantifications, and himself confesses that the figure he arrives at is improbably high.

It is impossible to correlate this overall result with a similar figure for the West Arabian coast, since most of the direct observations for this region deal only with fragments of total annual imports. The more general figures upon which Ewald has placed perhaps too much reliance tend to the same kind of exaggerations found in estimates of the Swahili Coast external trade. For the six years where reliable aggregate figures are available (see I/C), I have made comparisons (IV/E) with the relevant African export projections. In half of these years the figures match reasonably closely. The discrepancy for 1856 indicates a typical, if relatively moderate, exaggeration by a Jiddah consul; his figure of 2,500 for Swahili Coast imports is clearly off by at least 2,000 (cf. I/A/7). The 1869 difference goes in the other direction but not by enough for it not to be explained by, for instance, the omission of

slaves sent from the Red Sea to the Persian Gulf. In 1878 the Jiddah count really seems too low; perhaps the official prohibition of the slave trade by the Ottoman Sultan made imports into Arabia so clandestine as to escape the scrutiny of European consuls.

In any case both the 1880 estimate and the observations of Hurgronje (who entered Mecca disguised as a Muslim pilgrim)[18] suggest that the decline had not been as precipitous as perceived in the late 1870s. Ewald has also described the various ways in which the demand for slaves in and through western Arabia continued during the late 1870s and 1880s. At the same time, contrary to Ewald's implications, there was decline: the suppression of the Egyptian slave imports seems to have been paralleled, rather than compensated for, by the Red Sea trade in the last quarter of the nineteenth century.[19]

4. Deployment of East African Slaves

In the absence of really hard statistical information on slave exports from Eastern Africa, much of the argument concerning their quantity has centred around questions of deployment. Sheriff as well as Jwaideh and Cox[20] have noted the incompatibility of the absorptive capacity of the receiving Islamic areas with the huge scale sometimes projected for the Indian Ocean slave trade. Information of this kind does not provide a firm demographic base for slave trade statistics; it can, however, establish boundaries of plausibility for such a trade and may also indicate whether established niches for black slaves within external Islamic economies and societies were expanding or contracting during the nineteenth century.

The demographic observations in Table V/A contain very little in the way of real census data. I have included here references where the only occupational indication was domestic service, which Sheriff very reasonably argues created a limited demand in an area with such low urban concentrations as the Persian Gulf.[21] Entry V/A/1 does, however, remind us that a major factor in the Islamic slave trade was the constant need to replace existing black slaves of all kinds, who did not reproduce themselves either biologically or socially in the countries where they entered the general population.[22]

For Arabia, the figures here provided no precision, but the trend is strong enough to suggest that in the southern portion of the Peninsula blacks were considerably more evident than in the areas surveyed by Jwaideh and Cox. South Asia is again a minor factor, with most of the observations referring to slaves imported before the nineteenth century.[23]

The Persian Gulf offers the best demographic data for both the medieval period and the nineteenth century. While such British estimates as V/A/2, 3 are clearly exaggerations, the judgements of Landen (A/4) and especially the survey by Lorimer (A/5) must be taken seriously. The 10 per cent-plus projection for Lorimer's total Gulf population is conservative, since it falls below the percentage of black population calculated in several areas (and even these did not include slaves living in their masters' homes and listed as "uncounted"). A black population of this size would need a significant slave trade to reach and maintain it. Indeed, if we follow Sheriff's 10 per cent replacement rule, the trade would be far larger than any plausible direct evidence allows us to believe. However, much of the black population described here was free and presumably locally born, while the trade had been considerably reduced by the time the observations were made, so we cannot establish any precise ratio of population to immigration or imports.

It will also be noted when we turn to V/B that the areas of the Gulf in which blacks were most concentrated were also those with economic activities which would require African labour. Finally, the absence of reference in this or the following tables to inland Iran should be balanced against the argument of Ricks, that the Iranian plateau did receive a significant black servile population from the nineteenth century Gulf trade.[24]

At the centre of the arguments about demand for African slaves in Arabia and the Persian Gulf is the question of their role as economically productive labourers. The Muslim areas in question contained no large-scale plantation systems rivalling those of the New World or even those of Muslims and Europeans in the Western Indian Ocean where, as already shown, the most intensive regional demand for slaves existed. However, as indicated in V/B, agriculture and pearl fishing on both sides of the Arabian peninsula did employ significant bodies of African labour during the nineteenth century.

Agriculture in the receiving areas never regained the brief peak of the ninth century which is conventionally cited as the "exception that proves the rule" of non-economic Muslim slavery. However, the date plantations of the Persian Gulf are consistently reported (V/B/1, 2) as employing slave labour—although it also has to be noted that indigenous Arabs themselves did the work of maintaining irrigation systems in the less commercialized interior oasis zones. The reports by Lorimer (V/A/5) of major black populations in Hasa and Trucial Oman (United Arab Emirates) can only be explained by agriculture since these were not urbanized or pearl fishing centres. The potential high point for slave use in western Arabian agriculture would have been the era of the Yemen coffee boom in the seventeenth and early eighteenth centuries but we presently have no data on labour relations in this region. However, the late nineteenth and twentieth centuries do provide some indications (V/B/3–5) that slaves were active here as well as in other local agriculture. Given the sex ratios and price differentials of slave cargoes in all of the areas, it would be important to know whether female slaves were employed alongside, or even instead of, males in agricultural labour.

We may assume that agriculture in most regions of Arabia and Iran grew during the nineteenth century as a general response to the expansion of trade in the region and the Pax Britannica. However, there is no precise evidence at present to challenge Sheriff's belief that the departure of the Omani Sultan for Zanzibar led to economic decline in his home region.[25] For pearl fishing, on the other hand, there are definite indications of growth. The Persian Gulf fleets described in V/B/6–9, 14, 15 become increasingly larger over time, while Red Sea pearl fishing on a noticeable scale appears to be an innovation of the later nineteenth century. Pearl fishing demands might account for some of the young males found in Sheriff's evaluation of Persian Gulf slave cargoes, since this was a skilled profession to which workers needed to be trained from a young age. It is likely that black slaves were a less significant portion of pearling crews in earlier times when the labour demand was not as great. Again, we need more studies of this industry as a particularly sensitive indicator of the integration between sectors of the greater Indian Ocean economy.

Not much can be said about the few reports on slaves in nineteenth century seafaring contained in V/B. In South Asia, this was again mainly a residue of past slave trading. For the Gulf one may argue that increased demands in this occupation, which do seem to have occurred, would place a further premium on younger male slaves, who could be more easily trained than adults to the necessary skills.

As revealed by Table V/C, military and political service was one form of slave deployment which had clearly declined well before the beginning of the nineteenth century. The only place where black abid still provided Muslim elites with major public support was in Arabia. But even here, the bands of servile retainers around local chiefs did not match the Abyssinian armies of medieval Yemeni dynasties. In India, where Habshi troops, commanders and ministers had played such an important role in early Muslim regimes, the rise of the Mughal hegemony in the seventeenth century had reduced them to a very minor position which motivated no new recruitment in the 1800s. Despite the extensive importation of both Swahili and Abyssinian slaves into the Persian Gulf, military forces built around them (never very large even in their heyday) seem entirely absent. Instead, the Omani rulers brought Baluchi mercenaries from the Gulf to support their newly established position in East Africa! Despite (or perhaps because of, given its outcome) Muhammad Ali's massive recruitment of Sudanese slaves into his modernized Egyptian army, the nineteenth century Middle East no longer seems to have had a major role for the black servile soldier. Other forces of European-inspired change, particularly economic ones, stimulated increased demand for slaves; but the state, often seen as the most recalcitrant institution in the Muslim world, had shifted its base of support to its own subjects. The effect on demand for slaves from Africa was more than offset by the increasing urban wealth and rural production which did require more involuntary migration of African men, women, and children.

Table V. Selected Data on Blacks and Slaves in Receiving Areas

Date	Quantity	Comments	Original Source	Reference
A. General Population				
1. 950–1,500		African slaves common in core Islamic world but climate causes ill health	various medieval slave manuals	Mueller, 1980, passim
2. 1831		Bahrein population 50% slave or slave descent	Wilson, British Gulf official	PP 1837–38, LI, #697, p. 10
3. 1835		Oman more than 1/3 African	not given	Coupland, 1938, p. 31
4. 1870's	33,000	15–50,000 Africans in Oman	various British, French sources	Landen, 1967, p. 151
5. c. 1904		survey of Persian Gulf	Eyewitness and various reports	Lorimer, 1908, pp. 241–1,537
		Basra: blacks "fairly numerous"; total pop. = 58,000		p. 276
	11,000+	Bahrein: 6,000 slaves, 5,000 free blacks, plus others uncounted; total pop. = 100,000		p. 241
		Hasa: blacks fairly numerous; total pop. = 67,000		p. 645
	4,000	Kuwait: 4,000 blacks; total pop. = 35,000		p. 1,051
	1,500	Lingeh Town: 1,500 blacks; total pop. = 12,000		p. 1,097
		Oman: "large" black pop.; total pop. = 471,000		p. 1,391
	5,500+	Qatar: 4,000 slaves, 1,500 blacks, plus others uncounted; total pop. = 27,000		p. 1,531
		Trucial Oman: blacks "exceptionally numerous" on coast; total pop. = 72,000		p. 1,537
	90,000	Approximate total black pop. of Gulf (total pop. of areas mentioned = 868,000; black pop. = 10%+)		
B. Labor Force				
1. 1821		Muscat has many slaves, employed on coastal plantations	Fraser, British traveller	Fraser, 1825, pp. 6–18
2. 1870–1904		Slaves brought to main cultivation areas of Oman	British, French reports	Landen, 1967, pp. 151–152
3. 1876		slaves in date, coffee cultivation, Hijaz and Yemen	Wylde, British consul, Jiddah	FO 541/21, fol. 6
4. 1960's		N. Yemen and S. Saudi: large landowners employ numerous black slaves	Serjeant, British Arabist/traveller	Serjeant, 1987, p. 3
5. 1970's		Abid, dark-skinned descendents of slaves, in Yemen coffee area	Gerholm, Swedish anthropologist	Gerholm, 1977, p. 132
6. c. 1825		2,000 boats in Arabian Gulf ports plus Persians; slave crews; unhealthy	Buckingham, British traveller	Buckingham, 1830, II, pp. 299–301
7. 1830's		Total Persian Gulf pearl fleet 4,300 boats, c. 30,000 men	Wellsted, British naval officer	Wellsted, 1842, p. 182
8. 1831		Bahrein pearl fishers 1/3 slaves plus freeborn Swahilis	Wilson, British Gulf official	PP 1837–38, LI, p. 9
9. 1856		Total Persian Gulf pearl fleet 3,000 boats, c. 27,000 men	Bombay govt. report	Fryer, 1909, p. 364
10. 1863–76		"considerable numbers" of black slaves among Queseir, Jiddah, etc. crews (100's)	Klunziger, German resident, Queseir	Klunziger, 1878, pp. 311–315
11. 1878		High slave mortality in Red Sea pearl fishing	Malcolm, British AST agent, Egypt	FO 541/22, p. 48
12. 1880's		widespread use of slaves as divers (3–4 per boat) in Red Sea	Wylde, British consul, Jiddah	Wylde, 1888, pp. 247–248

Table V. Selected Data on Blacks and Slaves in Receiving Areas (continued)

Date	Quantity	Comments	Original Source	Reference
13. 1882–83		Several Sudani pearl divers among slaves seeking protection	Moncrieff, British consul, Jiddah	FO 541/25, pp. 79–85
14. 1890's		High slave mortality in Persian Gulf pearl fishing	Prideaux, British consul, Jiddah	Harris, 1971, pp. 37–38
15. 1905–07		Total Persian Gulf pearl fleet, 4,500 boats, 74,000 men ("mainly poor Arabs and free negroes or negro slaves")	observations and British reports	Lorimer, 1915, I, pp. 2,220–61
		Bahrein: 917 boats, 17,633 men		
		Kuwait: 461 boats, 9,200 men		
		Lingeh Town: 72 boats, 1,306 men		
		Qatar: 815 boats, 12,890 men		
		Trucial Oman: 1,215 boats, 22,045 men		
16. 1832		Malabar, Conora elite use Abyssinians for general service, navigation	Baber, British administrator	PP 1834, XLIV, p. 181
17. 1833		Mandavie (Kutch) fleet of 20 ships manned by Africans	Tod, British traveller	Tod, 1839, p. 450
18. 1860's		African "domestic slaves" as major element in dhow crews	British naval reports	Lloyd, 1949, p. 105
C. Military and Political Service				
1. 1806	600	1,000-man Yemeni army mainly black	Valentia, British traveler	Valentia, 1809, III, p. 328
2. 1809	1,500	"Abada" (presumedly black slaves) mobilized by Yemeni slave sultan	Salt, British traveler	Salt, 1814, p. 127
3. 1880's		Sherif of Mecca recruits soldiery from Ethiopia	Doughty, British traveller	Doughty, 1923, p. 71
4. late 1920's		Bedouin chiefs maintain black slave troops; self-reproducing	Raswan, German traveler	Raswan, 1934, pp. 145, 152
5. 1931		black slave soldiers throughout Hadramaut, Yemen; 100 in one village	Dutch, German travelers	Meulen, Wissmann, 1932, pp. 19–150, passim
6. 1756	500	Muscat black military now 500, formerly 4,000	Dutch EIC report	Floor, 1979, pp. 178–79

5. Conclusion

My progress in the study of Islamic slave trades out of Africa has been marked by two contradictory tendencies: the discovery of additional data and the awareness of greater limitations in the type of data available. For the Swahili Coast trade, the second tendency has been stronger, as it is now clear that the part of the trade which we can best estimate is that remaining within East Africa and its off-shore islands. For the Red Sea trade, the increased data come mainly from the Arabian receiving areas and are thus without precision, but nevertheless helpful in pulling together irregular, if better, observations from the export centres.

The effect of this new research on my bottom line estimates for the two trades has also varied. In the case of the Swahili Coast I am coming down somewhat closer to the figures of Sheriff, with whom I was originally in dispute. On the Red Sea exports, I remain basically with my original figures despite the arguments of Ewald and others. In any case, the work establishes the reasonableness of a certain range of estimates shared by most scholars working on this topic. What may be at least as valuable as the quantitative results of such work is the reflection it stimulates upon the role of the slave trade and slavery in the development of, and connections between, African and external Islamic societies.

Bibliography
(for references in tables only)

Abbreviations:

MAE = Ministère des Affaires Etrangères, Affaires Politiques (France), archival files

PP = Parliamentary Papers (Great Britain, House of Commons)

Bennett, Norman and George Brooks. 1965. *New England Merchants in Africa.* Boston: Boston University.

Buckingham, J.S. 1830. *Travels in Assyria, Media and Persia.* London: Colburn & Bentley.

Burton, Richard. 1872. *Zanzibar: City, Island Coast.* 2 vols. London: Tinsley.

Busch, Britin Cooper. 1967. *Britain and the Persian Gulf.* Berkeley: University of California.

Cooper, Frederick. 1977. *Plantation Slavery on the East Coast of Africa.* New Haven: Yale University Press.

Coupland, Reginald, 1938. *East Africa and Its Invaders.* Oxford: The Clarendon Press.

Doughty, Charles M. 1923. *Travels in Arabia Deserta.* London: J. Cape.

Elton, James Frederick. 1879. *Travels and Researches among the Lakes and Mountains of Eastern and Central Africa.* London: J. Murray.

Floor, Willem M. 1979. "A Description of the Persian Gulf and its Inhabitants in 1756," *Persica*, 8, pp. 163–179.

FO/84, Great Britain, Public Records Office, Foreign Office files, Slave Trade.

FO/541, Great Britain, Foreign Office, Confidential Prints.

Fraser, James. 1825. *Narrative of a Journey into Khorasan.* London: Longman et al.

Freeman-Grenville, G.S.P. 1962. *The East African Coast: Select Documents from the first to the earlier nineteenth century.* Oxford: Clarendon.

Fryer, John. I W9. *A New Account of East India and Persia.* London: Hakluyt Society.

Gerholm, T. 1977. *Market, Mosque and Mufraq: Social Inequality in a Yemeni Town.* Stockholm: U. of Stockholm.

Harris, Joseph E. 1971. *The African Presence in Asia.* Evanston: Northwestern University Press.

Kelly, John Barret. 1968. *Britain and the Persian Gulf, 1795–1880.* Oxford: Clarendon Press.

Klunzinger, Karl B. 1878. *Upper Egypt, Its People and Its Products.* Glasgow: Blackie & Sons.

Krapf, J. Lewis [Ludwig]. 1860. *Travels, Researches and Missionary Labors.* London: Trübner.

Lloyd, Christopher. 1949. *The Navy and the Slave Trade.* London: Longmans, Green.

Lorimer, J.G. 1908. *A Gazetteer of the Persian Gulf, Oman and Central Arabia. II. Geographical.* Calcutta (reprinted, Farnborough: Gregg International, 1970).

Lorimer. J.G. 1915. *Gazetteer . . . I., Historical.* Calcutta (reprinted, Farnborough: Gregg International, 1970).

MAE, Turquie: Consulats: Hodeida.

MAE, Turquie: Consulats: Djedda.

Martin, Esmond B. and T.C.I. Ryan. 1980. "The Slave Trade of the Bajun and Benadir Coasts," *Transafrican Journal of History*, 9, 112, pp. 103–32.

Meulen, D. van der and H. von Wissmann. 1932. *Hadramaut: Some of its Mysteries Unveiled.* Leyden: J. Brill.

Mueller, Hans, 1980. *Die Kunst des Sklavenhandels nach arabischen, persischen and türkischen Ratgebern vom zehnten bis zum achzehnten Jahrhundert.* Freiburg: Klaus Schwartz.

Nicholls, C.S. 1971. *The Swahili Coast, 1798–1856.* London: Allen and Unwin.

PP 1844, XLIV, Accounts and papers, no. 174, Papers relative to slavery in India.

PP 1837–38, LI, no. 697, Slave Trade (East India).

PP 1863, LXXI, no. 126, Slave Trade.

PP 1868–69, LVI, Correspondence . . . Slave Trade.

PP 1867–68, LXIV, Correspondence . . . Slave Trade.

PP 1876, LXX, c. 1588, Correspondence . . . Slave Trade.

PP 1877, LXVIII, c. 1829, Correspondence . . . Slave Trade.

PP 1878, LXVIII, c. 2319, Correspondence . . . Slave Trade.

Raswan, Carl. 1934. *Im Land der schwarzen Zelten: mein Leben unter den Bedouinen.* Berlin: Ullstein.

Salt, Henry, 1814. *A Voyage to Abyssinia.* London: Rivington.

Serjeant, Robert Bertram. 1987. "Some Observations on African Slavery in Arabia." SOAS Conference.

Tod, James. 1839. *Travels in Western India.* London: W.H. Allen.

Valentia, George Viscount, 1809. *Voyages and Travels to India, Ceylon, the Red Sea, Abyssinia, and Egypt.* 3 vols. London: W. Miller.

Wylde, Augustus, 1888. *'83 to '87 in the Sudan.* London: Remington.

---

[1]The present essay represents an advanced but not yet final stage of work initiated in several earlier papers: Ralph A. Austen, "The Islamic Slave Trade out of Africa (Red Sea and Indian Ocean): An Effort at Quantification." Conference on "Islamic Africa: Slavery and Related Institutions," Princeton University, 14 June, 1977; ibid., "The Islamic Red Sea Slave Trade: An Effort at Quantification," *Proceedings of the Fifth International Conference on Ethiopian Studies* (Chicago: U. of Illinois, 1979), pp. 443–67; and "From the Atlantic to the Indian Ocean: European Abolition, African Slave Trade and Asian Economic Structures," in David Eltis and James Walvin, *The Slave Trade and Abolition: Impacts on Africa, the Americas and Europe* (Madison: U. of Wisconsin, 1981), pp. 117–39. I hope eventually to combine these Indian Ocean studies with a refined version of earlier research on the Mediterranean Islamic slave trade out of Africa "The Transsaharan Slave Trade: A Tentative Census," in H. Gemery and J. Hogendorn, *The Uncommon Market: Essays in the Economic History of the Atlantic Slave Trade* (New York: Academic, 1979), pp. 23–76 to produce a general book on this subject.

[2]My own estimates cited above have challenged and/or been challenged by Richard Pankhurst, "The Ethiopian Slave Trade in the Nineteenth and Early Twentieth Centuries: A Statistical Inquiry," *Journal of Semitic Studies*, Vol. 9 (1964), 220–2; Esmond B. Martin and T.C.I. Ryan "A Quantitative Assessment of the Arab Slave Trade of East Africa, 1774–1896," *Kenya Historical Review*, 5.1 (1977), 71–91; and especially Abdul Sheriff, *Slaves, Spices & Ivory: Integration of an East African Commercial Empire into the World Economy* (London, 1987); for a comparison of findings, see Table III.

[3]Considerations of space do not allow complete tables to be published here; the present tables only display observations specifically referred to in the text.

[4]It is perhaps revealing that at the 1987 SOAS conference, Swahili Coast specialists continued to argue that I had overestimated the external slave trade while Red Sea experts believed that my then figures were too low.

[5]For the beginnings of the Zanzibar and Pemba plantations see Sheriff, pp. 45–54.

[6]Edward A. Alpers, *Ivory and Slaves: Changing Patterns of International Trade in East Africa to the Later Nineteenth Century* (Berkeley, 1975), pp. 151, 185–6; Sheriff, pp. 41ff.

[7]José Capela, "The 'Mujojos' Slave Trade in Moçambique," SOAS Conference, 1987; see also, José Capela and Eduardo Medeiros *O trafico de escravos de Moçambique para as ilhas do Indico, 1770–1902* (Maputo, 1987).

[8]José Capela, p. 1; see also interviews in 1876 with such slave traders by British consul James Frederick Elton, *Travels and Researches* (London, 1879), pp. 170–2.

[9]See also Portuguese naval documents on this incident cited in José Capela, p. 4 and unspecified references to a small Madagascar-Persian Gulf trade in Stephen Ellis,

"Madagascar's Place in the International Slave Trade in the Nineteenth Century," 1987 SOAS Conference, p. 13.

[10]Jonathan Glassman, "The Development of Plantation Slavery on the Northern Mrima," unpublished dissertation chapter.

[11]Carla Glassman, "The Illegal Seagoing East African Slave Trade, 1873–1900: a Strategic Approach," unpublished paper, Trinity College, Cambridge, n.d.; J. Glassman, pp. 34–5; Frederic Rodger Morton, "Fugitives and Freedom on the Kenya Coast, 1873–1903," unpublished dissertation, University of Syracuse, 1976, pp. 12–18.

[12]Slaving vessels captured by the British navy after 1873 were overwhelmingly involved in local rather than long-distance trade, C. Glassman, pp. 14–15; for examples of Omani Slave smuggling from Zanzibar under the French flag in this period, see R.W. Beachey, *The Slave Trade of Eastern Africa* (ICY., 1976), pp. 238–41.

[13]This critique of Sheriff was already made in Cooper, 1977, p. 43.

[14]Robert Geran Landen, *Oman since 1856* (Princeton, 1967), p. 150.

[15]C. Glassman, pp. 8–9.

[16]Total observations: Austen, 1977 = 55; Austen, 1979 = 71; Austen, 1988 = 102.

[17]Janet Ewald, "The Nile Valley System and the Red Sea Slave Trade, 1820–1880," 1987 SOAS Conference; in response to the critique which follows, Ewald has revised her argument as reflected in the version of her paper which appears in this volume.

[18]C. Snouck Hurgronje, *Mekka* (The Hague, 1889), 11, pp. 12–24.

[19]Ewald, pp. 16f.; cf. William Ochsenwald, "Muslim-European Conflict in the Hijaz: the Slave Trade Controversy," *Middle Eastern Studies*, 16, 1 (1980), pp. 115–26.

[20]Albertine Jwaideh and J. W. Cox, "The Black Slaves of Turkish Arabia and the North Arabian Desert during the Nineteenth Century," 1987 SOAS Conference (in this volume).

[21]Abdul Sheriff, "Localisation and Social Composition of the East African Slave Trade," 1987 SOAS Conference (in this volume).

[22]This point has been specified for the Nile Valley slave trade in Terence Walz, "Black Slavery in Egypt during the Nineteenth Century as Reflected in the Makhama Archives of Cairo," in John Ralph Willis (ed.), *Slaves and Slavery in Muslim Africa*, II, (London, Cass, 1985), pp. 137–60.

[23]However it should be noted that in the midst of the 1987 SOAS Conference, BBC reports of Benazir Bhutto's wedding celebrations in Pakistan singled out the role of local African-descended communities.

[24]Thomas M. Ricks, "Slaves and Slave Traders in the Persian Gulf, 18th and 19th Centuries: an Assessment," 1987 SOAS Conference (in this volume); this paper is largely undocumented but Ricks elaborated his arguments in oral presentation.

[25]There is reference to a decline in trade at this time, but also a good deal of conflicting evidence (unfortunately not well-documented) about expanding commercial date production from the 1840s in Calvin H. Allen Jr., "Sayyids, Shets, and Sultans: Politics and Trade in Masqat under the al-Busaidis, 1785–1914," unpublished dissertation, University of Washington, passim.

The Ethiopian Diaspora to India: The Role of Habshis and Sidis from Medieval Times to the End of the Eighteenth Century

Richard Pankhurst

Commercial contacts between Ethiopia and India, which were much facilitated over the centuries by the Trade Winds blowing between Africa and Asia, date back to early times. The scope and extent of such relations are indicated in the *Periplus of the Erythraean Sea*, a Graeco-Egyptian commercial manual written around the 1st century AD. This work shows that the Aksumite port of Adulis, on the Red Sea coast of Africa, traded extensively with various parts of Western India, which supplied Ethiopia with both textiles and spices. Aksumite exports consisted mainly of ivory and rhinoceros horn, but, the Roman writer Pliny says, also included slaves. The latter were also shipped, according to the *Periplus*, from Opone, later known as Ras Hafun, a promontory on the Indian Ocean coast of Africa, ninety miles south of Cape Guardafui.[1]

Aksumite trade with the East was an on-going affair in ancient times, as evident from an early sixth century Graeco-Egyptian text, the *Christian Topography* of Kosmas Indikopleustes. It states that the Aksumites were at that time trading with India and Taprobane, i.e. Ceylon, as well as Arrabia and Persia.[2]

The coming of Ethiopian, and other East African, slaves to India a millennium or so later is abundantly documented in Indian, and in particular Gujarat, records. These refer to such slaves mainly by three more or less alternative names: Habshis, Sidis, and Kaffirs.

The term Habshi was a corruption of Habash, the Arabic name for Abyssinia. This name is believed to have derived from Habashat, the name of a Semitic people located in northern Tegray in present-day Ethiopia, and a neighboring stretch of Eritrea. They are believed by many to have migrated in ancient times from Yaman.[3]

The word Habshi, as its derivation implies, doubtless at first applied primarily to Abyssinians (or, in modern parlance, Ethiopians), but was later used more widely for any Africans. However, most slaves taken from Africa to India would, for geographical reasons, have originated on the eastern side of the continent. For much of the time covered in this paper they would probably have included a substantial, if not a predominant, proportion of Abyssinians.

The term Sidi by contrast was a corruption of the Arabic Saiyid, or "master."[4] The word, as Edwardes notes, had "an honourable import" when first assumed, but, in common parlance, had become "rather an appellation of reproach than distinction."[5] This is confirmed by the Frenchman François Pyrard of Laval, who, reporting on a visit to the Maldives in 1607, observed that "the greatest insult that can be passed upon a man is to call him a cisdy," i.e. Sidi.[6]

The term Kaffir was derived from the Arabic Kafir, originally an Infidel, or Unbeliever in Islam. The word tended to be used in India for any non-Muslim, and was in many, though not all, cases applied to African immigrants and descendants.[7]

Ethiopian and other African slaves taken to India (or indeed Arabia, their first port of call) were for the most part converted to Islam. This change of religion sometimes occurred even on the boats transporting the captives across the sea. After conversion they almost invariably abandoned their pre-Muslim names, in favour of Islamic ones. This was unfortunate from the historical point of view, for it destroyed the possibility of identifying the slaves' places of origin from their personal or family names.

Slaves in Islamic India, on the other hand, benefited from their conversion, in that it facilitated their integration into Indian Muslim society. Unlike Negro slaves in the New World, slaves in Muslim India were largely free from racial discrimination. They differed from slaves in America and the West Indies, moreover, in that they were not subjected to plantation labour. Many slaves in India entered the personal service of rulers and other politically important personalities, in not a few instances as palace guards. This enabled them, like such functionaries in many lands, to exercise immense power, not only as king-makers, but, after successful *coups d'etat*, as kings themselves.

From the Early 13th to the Late 15th Century

The first Ethiopian slaves arriving in the Indian sub-continent may have come early in the Christian era. This would appear probable, in view of the antiquity of the Horn of Africa's slave exports, and the extensive trade between Ethiopia and India indicated in the *Periplus of the Erythraean Sea*.

Documentation on African slaves in India is, however, scarcely available for over a millennium, until the early 13th century.

The North and West: Delhi, Gujarat, the Gulf of Cambay, and Malabar

The first Habshi of whom there is a historical record was probably Jamal al-Din Yaqut, a royal courtier in the kingdom of Delhi, in the north of the sub-continent. A handsome and most likable individual, he won the favour of the then reigning sovereign Queen Radiyya (1236–1240). This incurred him much jealousy at court, on which account he was eventually murdered by his rivals.[8]

Habshis, it is evident from 14th century reports, were then also prominent in several other parts of India. The largest concentrations of slaves was apparently found in the north-west, facing Africa: in Gujarat, and, immediately to the east, around the Gulf of Cambay. Both areas had been in close commercial contact, across the Arabian and Red Seas, with Ethiopia and the Horn of Africa.

Evidence of an Ethiopian slave presence in the sub-continent is provided by the famous Moroccan traveller Ibn Battuta. Describing the situation between 1333 and 1342, he recalls that on embarking on a ship at Qandahar, or Gandhar on the west coast of India, he found on board "fifty Abyssinian men-at-arms," and adds, with admiration: "these latter are the guarantors of safety on the Indian Ocean; let there be but one of them on a ship and it will be avoided by the Indian pirates and idolaters."[9] Half a century later, in 1375–6, Gujarat was reported as paying a tribute of 400 slaves, described as "children of Hindu chiefs and Abyssinians."[10]

A sizable number of Habshis were also found much further south, at Calicut, which also faced the African continent, and traded with Ethiopia. Ibn Battuta tells of a ship owner's agent at the port, who, when going ashore, was "preceded by archers and Abyssinians with javelins, swords, drums, trumpets and bugles."[11]

Habshis were likewise in evidence further south again, at Colombo, in Ceylon, where Ibn Battuta reports that Jalasti, "the wazir and ruler of the sea," had "about five hundred Abyssinians."[12]

The North: Alapur and Jaunpur

Habshis were also reported in the interior of northern India. Ibn Battuta recalls that at Alapur, north of Delhi, the governor was "the Abyssinian Badr..., a man whose bravery passed into a proverb." He was "continually making raids on the infidels alone and single-handed, killing and taking captive, so that his fame spread far and wide and the infidels went in fear of them." Gossip had it that he had retained some non-Indian ways: according to Ibn Battuta he used to eat "a whole sheep at a meal," and, "following the custom of the Abyssinians," would, after consuming it, drink a pound and a half of ghee, or clarified butter.[13]

Later in the century a slave called Malik Sarwar, described as a Habshi, was appointed further north as governor of Jaunpur. He was succeeded by his son Mubarak Shah, who struck coins in his own name, and was succeeded in turn by his brother Ibrahim Shah. The latter reigned for almost forty years, and is remembered as a patron of literature and the arts.[14]

The North-East: Bengal

Numerous Habshis and other foreign slaves were likewise politically very prominent in 15th century Bengal, a region in north-east India which also enjoyed extensive trade with Ethiopia and other parts of Africa. The then Bengali ruler, Sultan Rukn al-Din (1450–1474), reportedly had no less than 8,000 African slaves, some of whom rose to positions of considerable importance.[15] Such slaves were particularly influential during the ensuing reign of Jalal al-Din Fath Shah (1481–1487). This caused the modern Indian historian Sir Jadu-Nath Sarkar, a stern critic of the Habshis, to remark:

"The Abyssinians...presented a serious problem...they had captured most of the high positions and now swarmed in the palace and in the city. Power made them arrogant and like the Turks in the employ of the later Abbaside Caliphs, they behaved with the citizens with increasing violence. The more defiant of them, according to Firishta, were consequently punished 'with the scourge of justice.'"[16]

The Habshis were in fact so powerful in Bengal that a group of them, including the chief eunuch, conspired to overthrow Jalal al-Din Fath. Taking advantage of the absence on campaign of the loyal Habshi commander-in-chief, Amir al-Umara Malik Andil, the Habshi commander of the palace guards, Sultan Shahzada, assassinated Jalal al-Din. "From protectors of the dynasty," one historian wrote, "the Abyssinians became masters of the kingdom."[17]

Shahzada duly assumed the throne, in 1486, and adopted the name of Barbak Shah.[18] He was, however, soon afterwards killed by the Habshi Amir al-Umara who in his turn made himself king, with the name Sayf al-Din Firuz (1487–1490). A kind man, he is said to have confounded his treasury officials by the largesse of his gifts to the poor. His reign was, however, short, for he was replaced only three years later by an infant king. Real power, however, fell into the hands of another Habshi, Habash Khan, who was later killed by yet another Habshi, Sidi Badr "the madman," who had the young king put to death. Badr then seized the throne, under the name of Shams al-Din Muzaffar Shah, and instituted a reign of terror. His cruelty, however, provoked strong opposition against him, and by extension against Habshi domination. His army, which included no less than 5,000 well-armed Habshis, was besieged for three months, at the end of which he died.[19]

The Habshis, who had thus shown themselves so formidable in the bloody struggles of the time, were then banished from Bengal. Many sought refuge further north, in Delhi and Jaunpur, after which they drifted to the Deccan and Gujarat, where many of their number had earlier lived.[20] The memory of their immense power in Bengal was nevertheless so strong that the early 16th century Portuguese traveller Tomé Pires observed, with truth, that for three-quarters of a century it had "always been Abyssinians—those who are very near the king"—who had reigned.[21]

The South: The Deccan

The Deccan, in south-western India, was another area in which the Habshis gained prominence, and, as elsewhere, became involved in many conflicts of the day. At the beginning of the 15th century the local Bahmani ruler, Sultan Firuz (1397–1422), had many Habshi slaves as his personal attendants, as well as in his bodyguard, and *harem*. He incurred the enmity, however, of his brother Ahmad, who subverted the Habshi bodyguard, by one of whom Firuz was assassinated. Ahmad, though brought to power by the Habshis, feared their growing strength, and placed his trust instead in Persians, Turks and other foreigners of the Shiah faith. The Habshis and local Deccanis, both of whom were Sunni, thus both lost favour.[22]

Ahmad, unlike the rulers of Bengal, did not, however, banish the Habshis, who therefore continued to be both prominent, and powerful. During the subsequent reign of Ala-ud-Din Ahmad (1436-1458), they stood for example on the left of the throne, though the other foreigners were assigned the more prestigious position on the right. This did not, however, prevent Habshis from continuing to play a major role in political affairs, as when Ala-ud-Din's son and successor, Humayan "the tyrant," was stabbed to death by a Habshi maid-servant, in 1461.[23]

Several other notable Habshis feature in the Deccan annals of the time. One, named Khudavand Khan, served as governor of Mahur, while another, an eunuch called Dastur Dinar, ruled Gulbarga. Habshis thus governed two out of the four Bahmani provinces. A third Habshi, Mahmud, was keeper of seals, while a fourth, Jauhur, is on record as executing one of the principal nobles, who had been accused, perhaps falsely, of disloyalty to the ruler.[24]

Ethiopian and other African slaves were at this time probably arriving in India in considerable numbers. The *Gazetteer of the Bombay Presidency,* a generally reliable compilation, states that around "the middle of the 15th century . . . the fashion arose of bringing to western India large numbers of Abyssinian and other East Africans," i.e. Habshis or Sidis. Turning to the political role of these immigrants, the *Gazetteer* concludes: "Though most Habshis came to India as slaves, their faithfulness, courage, and energy often raised them to positions of high trust in the Bahmani court."[25]

The influence of Habshis in the Deccan at this time was also emphasised by a British historian of the Mogul Empire, Robert Orme. He observes that the slaves "gained ascendance" over a king of Bijapur, and were "exalted by him to highest employments in the state . . . they gathered all of their own country they could procure either by purchase or invitation, and even the Coffrees [kafirs, or blacks] of other parts of Africa." On the skill with which the Sidis involved themselves decisively in the political life of their country of adoption, he adds: "The natural courage of these people, not unmixed with ferocity, and always foremost in battle, awed the envy of their rivals, however indignant from the pride of their ancient descent, although the Siddees had likewise taken their religion."

The first marriages, of the Habshis, Orme continues, "were with natives of India," but later ones were largely "among their own families, which preserving their nationality, in time formed a numerous community, distinct in figure, colour, and character from all the other races of Mahomedans; which nevertheless could not have subsisted, if the body of the people amongst whom they had intruded, had not been, as themselves, Mahomedans. Later, during the reigns of Nizam (1461–1463) and Mahomed III (1463–1482) the Habshis regained influence, and in the latter reign in particular they shared in the offices of state."[26]

During the subsequent reign of Mahmud Shah (1482–1518), another Habshi, Dilavar Khan, became finance minister, but was later ousted by Malik Hassan, a Muslimised Hindoo, who then made himself dictator. Dilavar Khan tried to assist Mahmud against the latter, but, failing, was obliged to flee the country. The unfortunate king later appealed for help to the Habshi Dastur Dinar to free him of the usurper, but Dastur, despite strenuous efforts, proved unable to do so.[27]

The kingdom of Deccan, torn apart by continuous strife, was by then beginning to decline. In 1490 Ahmadnagar, Bijapur and Berar declared their independence of Bihar, where a Turkish minister, Qasim Barid-ul-Mamalik, usurped power. Almost immediately afterwards the Habshi Dilavar Khan returned from exile to assist Mahmud, but was defeated and killed. Qasim Barid-ul-Mamalik then consolidated his position, and in 1495 demoted Dastur Dinar, who was then governor of western Telingana, and appointed him governor of Gulbarga. The Habshi leader resisted this demotion, but was defeated. He was, however, subsequently reinstated in Gulbarga, but as a result of further strife was later driven from the city, and eventually killed, in 1504.[28]

The conflict in Bijapur between the factions nevertheless continued. A stern decree was issued in 1510 prohibiting Deccanis, Habshis, or even their children, from holding office.[29] This law was, however, later reversed by Ibrahim Adil Shah (1534–1558), who restored the Sunnis to power, in 1537. He then divided offices of state between the Habshis and Deccanis, and thus brought an end to Shiah paramountcy.[30]

Several other Habshis were nevertheless prominent during the ensuing period of strife. They included Khudavand Khan's two sons, Shaza Khan and Ghalib Khan, and Dastur Dinar's son Jahangir Khan.[31]

The importance of the Habshis of this time is further evident from the fact that a hill outside the capital city of Bidar, where once they had their stronghold—and where many of them were buried—is to this day known as Habshi Kot.[32]

The West Coast

Habshis at this time were also prominent at several points along India's western coast. They were particularly powerful at the island fort of Janjira, and in the nearby creek of Danda-Rajpuri, where they were almost invariably referred to as Sidis.[33]

There are different accounts as to how the Sidis established themselves at Janjira. According to a history of Ahmadnagar, one of the kings of that state, Malik Ahmad (1490–1508), entrusted the island to his Abyssinian slave Yaqut, and established the Sidis as the latter's captains.

Another story holds that the Habshis made their appearance when one of their number, Perira Khan, and a group of other "Abyssinians" in the service of Malik Ahmad disguised themselves in 1489, as merchants. They obtained permission from Ram Patil, the chief of the island, to land 300 large boxes supposedly containing wine and silk. Ram Patil gave them leave, after which they regaled the garrison with wine. When the men had drunk to excess, the Habshis opened their boxes, in which armed soldiers were hidden. Taking advantage of their opponents' surprise, they then easily captured the fort.[34]

Other versions of the story suggest that the Habshis gained control of Janjira somewhat later, possibly in the early 16th century. There is, however, no denying that they remained in effective charge of the island, as we shall see, for the next two hundred years.[35]

Further north, at Daman, on the coast of Ahmadnagar facing Africa, the governor at the time of the Portuguese occupation in 1530 was a Habshi chief called Sayf al-Mulk Miftah, who had a force of 4,000 fellow Habshis.[36] To the south meanwhile, at Goa, Habshis were also prominent. In 1493, the Bahmani admiral Sidi Yaqut is said to have been sent with a fleet of 20 vessels against the Gujarat fort of Mahim near Bombay, and succeeded in capturing it.[37] Habshis were likewise to the fore at Calicut, the population of which, according to the modern Indian historian K. M. Panikkar, continued to include many people from Abyssinia.[38]

Cambay

Cambay, to the north-west of the sub-continent, at this time still also had a considerable Habshi population. Some made their way into the interior, including Mandu, whose sultan, Shah Khalji (1469–1500) reportedly had "five hundred Abyssinian slave girls dressed in male attire." Known as the Habiwash band, they were armed with swords and shields.[39] A decade or so later, the Portuguese traveller Tomé Pires recalled that the Cambay rulers had "many" warriors, among them Abyssinians, with whose assistance they were "constantly fighting with the neighbouring kingdoms."[40] The importance of such Habshis as fighters is likewise recognised by the Bombay *Gazetteer*: it claims that they were "among the most skillful and daring soldiers and sailors in Western India."[41]

The Habshis of Cambay were, however, not only soldiers, but also included many people engaged in the agate trade. One of their traditions, cited in the Bombay *Gazetteer*, holds that early in the 16th century "an Abyssinian merchant came to Gujarat, and established an agate factory at Nandod in Rajpila." The merchant reportedly died at Nandod, and was buried near the tomb of Baba or Bawa Ghor by the river Narboda.

Another tradition asserts that the shrine was actually raised in honour of the merchant. It is said that "while wandering from place to place as a religious beggar, he did business in precious stones, and, becoming skilled in agate, set up a factory at Nimodra," where he "prospered and died rich."[42] The British ethnographer R. E. Enthoven, who refers to him as "an Abyssinian saint and great merchant," states that he came to be venerated by the Sidis, "many" of whom were "imported to work in these mines."[43] According to the modern Indian scholar D. K. Bhattacharya, the supposed Abyssinian trader was the only such holy man "revered generally by all the Sidi."[44]

The 16th Century: The Rise of Imam Ahmad Ibn Ibrahim, or Grañ, and Its Aftermath

The advent of fire-arms in the Red Sea and Gulf of Aden region led, in the late 15th and early 16th centuries, to major changes in the balance of power in the Horn of Africa. One of the most important of these developments was the rise of the Muslim state of Adal, in the east of what is now Ethiopia, bordering the Gulf of Aden. This was followed, in the late 15th and early 16th century, by some twenty-four years of instability, in which Imam Mahfuz, the Muslim ruler of the Gulf of Aden port of Zaila, carried out annual slave-raiding expeditions from Adal into the Ethiopian interior. Such raiding resulted in a considerable expansion in the slave trade, and in particular to the export of numerous Ethiopian slaves to Arabia, India and elsewhere.[45]

The importance of this slave trade, the source at this time of most of India's Habshis, was noted by the Portuguese traveller Francisco Alvares, who travelled widely in Ethiopia in the early 1520s. He observes that slaves from Damot, in the south-west of the Ethiopian empire, were especially "much esteemed by the Moors," i.e. Muslims. He adds that "all the country of Arabia, Persia, India, Egypt, and Greece," was "full" of such slaves, who reportedly made "very good Moors and great warriors."[46]

Slave-raiding was subsequently intensified by Mahfuz's more famous son-in-law Imam Ahmad ibn Ibrahim, better known in Ethiopia as Imam Ahmad Grañ, or the Left-handed. A charismatic leader of Adal, and a man of no small military ability, he rose to prominence immediately after Alvares's departure. In 1527 he began a series of expeditions which took him much further into the Ethiopian interior than Mahfuz had ever gone. In the course of these military operations Ahmad captured innumerable slaves, and thereby gave an immense new fillip to the slave trade. This resulted in a vast, but incalculable, increase in the number of Ethiopian, or Habshi, slaves arriving in the Indian sub-continent, and in particular Gujarat.

The prominence acquired in India by persons of Ethiopian, or other African, origin in the aftermath of Imam Ahmad's campaigns is confirmed by foreign travellers of the time. Towards the middle of the 16th century the Portuguese mariner Joam de Castro for example declared that Ethiopian slaves, serving in India as soldiers, were "strong and valiant to such a degree that there was a proverb throughout India that good soldiers or *ascaris*, or servants, must be Abyssinian." Such men, he adds, were "so well regarded in Bengal, Cambaia, Ballagate and other places [in India] that all those who command the armies or have a rank there are taken from among this race."[47]

The Habshi presence in India was also discussed last quarter of the century by the Dutch traveller John Huyghen Van Linschoten. Referring to slaves from the country of Prester John, i.e. the Christian empire of Ethiopia, he states, in an old English translation, that there were "divers men" there who sent slaves and free-men into India who served as "Sailors in the Portugalles ships."[48] He also observes:

"There are many Arabians and Abexiins in India . . . the Abexiins some are Mahometans, some Christians after their manner, for they are of Prester John's land. . . . There are many of them in India that are slaves and captives, both men and women which are brought (thither) out of Aethiopia, and sold like other Oriental Nations . . . the Abexiins that are Christians have their faces 4 burnt markes in the manner of a Crosse, one over their nose in the middle of the forehead, betweene (both their) eyes, on each of their cheekes one, betweene their eies, and their eares, and one under their neather lip, (down) to the chin."[49]

Linschoten, who published "pictures of the Arabians and Abexijns with their wives, as they goe in India," also reports a significant foreign slave presence in Goa. Its population at this time, he states, included, "many Persians, Arabians, and Abexijns, some (of them) Christians and some (of them) Moores."[50]

Gujarat

The relationship between Imam Ahmad ibn Ibrahim's expeditions and the influx of Habshi slaves was evident to the contemporary Gujarat scholar Abdallah Muhammad ibn Omar al-Makki, al-Asafi, Ulugh Khan, generally known as Haji ad-Dabir. He mentions the impact of the fighting in Abyssinia in his Arabic *History of Gujarat*, completed around 1605. His observations are significant because he was particularly well aware of things Habshi. He was in fact successively in the service of two Gujarat Habshi noblemen: first Muhammad Yaqut Ulugh Khan, from 1559 to 1573, and later Abdul Kerim Sayfud Muhammad Fulad Khan, in 1599–1600.[51]

Haji ad-Dabir considered Imam Ahmad's fighting so central to the experience of north-west India that he included in his *History of Gujarat* long excerpts from the chronicle of the Imam's Yamani scribe Shihab ad-Din Ahmad ibn al-Qader, also known as Arab-Faqih.[52]

In his Gujarat *History* Haji ad-Dabir thus quotes from the Yamani writer's account of the Adal ruler's many victories over the Christian Ethiopians. He reports that many of the latter, taken prisoner at the battle of Dir, or Ad Dayar, and elsewhere, were sent to Amir Salman of Zabid, in the Yaman, and were handed over to him at the Yamani offshore island of Kamaran. Amir Salman, it is said, selected the most promising Abyssinians, who are referred to as Rumikhanis, and put the rest to death. Those spared were obliged to embrace Islam, but were otherwise treated kindly and, significantly, received a training in arms as well as letters.[53]

Amir Salman was murdered, in 1529, after which his slaves from Abyssinia were inherited by his nephew Mustafa ibn Bahram. The latter received orders in 1531 from his father in Constantinople to proceed at once to India to help the Gujarat sultan Bahadur (1526–1537) in his conflict with the Portuguese. Mustafa immediately set out, taking with him the newly captured slaves, by then irrevocably converted to Islam.[54]

The significance of the arrival of such large numbers of Abyssinians in Gujarat was emphasised by Haji ad-Dabir. He claims that they were as good as Arabs in everything except descent, but were often disliked by ordinary Indians, who were sometimes incited to murder them.[55] There were later, he adds, no less than 5,000 Habshis at Ahmadabad, and 1,500 in Baroda, in 1561–2. When the Mogul Emperor Akbar (1556–1605) subsequently entered Gujarat in 1572 there were likewise 700 Habshi horsemen on the scene.[56]

The importance of this influx of slaves from war-torn Ethiopia was not lost on the British historian of India, Denison Ross. Recalling the bitter fighting on the Horn of Africa, the resultant extensive capture of slaves, and their subsequent political importance on the sub-continent, he observes: "the Habshis who rose to such prominence in Gujarat in the 16th century were for the most part the prisoners or sons of the prisoners captured during the Muhammadan invasion of Ethiopia." It was "in this manner," he adds, "that these Abyssinians came to Gujarat," and "the manner in which many of them rose to prominence and independence forms one of the most interesting features of this story."[57]

Elaborating on the above theme, he declares that in the disorders in India which began with the accession of Mahmud III (1537–1554), the Abyssinian slaves, i.e. those captured in Imam Ahmad's wars, "found a scope for rising to favour and prominence," though "their rivalry with the local nobility, and with the leaders of other foreign mercenaries, brought about a state of dissension which enabled Akbar to conquer Gujarat almost without a blow."[58]

The above-mentioned wave of Habshi immigration, though crucially important was, it should be emphasised, only one phase in an on-going, and largely involuntary, movement of population from East Africa to Western India. Discussing migration to Gujarat, Ross observes that "from the end of the 13th century to the end of the 17th . . . soldiers, traders, and slaves kept flocking into Gujarat by land and sea." Immigrants, he adds, included Abyssinians and Arabs, as well as persons of many other races. Emphasising the cultural significance in particular of the Habshis, he concludes: "A close study of the history of Gujarat in the 15th and 16th century has led me to the conclusion that European historians, following in the wake of Muhammedan chroniclers, who no doubt had their prejudices, have failed to attach sufficient importance to the part played by the Habshis in the history of that country."[59]

Most of the Habshis who arrived in Gujarat in the aftermath of Imam Ahmad's expeditions in Ethiopia and the Horn of Africa lived a life of near anonymity, and scarcely feature in records of the time. A number of their leaders, however, attained prominence, and deserve mention.

Three notable Habshis were accorded the honorific title of Ulugh Khan.

The first Habshi to hold this title was Mandal Dilawar Khan, who attracted the attention of Sultan Mahmud III, and was appointed captain of the latter's bodyguard in 1553, but died in battle in the same year.

The second Habshi Ulugh Khan was Sultan Mahmud's vizier Yaqut Sibit Khan Habshi, also known as Yaqut Begi Sultani, who, on the death of Mandel Dilawar Khan, succeeded to his title and military commands. He commanded a Habshi force under Imad-ul-Mulk Arslan, and obtained the latter's rank when Imad became chief minister to Sultan Ahmad II (1554–1562). On the death of Yaqut, in 1558, he was buried at Sarkhej, beside Bilal Jhujhar, another famous Habshi of the day. The latter, like other Habshis of that name, was probably named after the Prophet's first *muezzin* Bilal, the son of an Abyssinian slave woman in Arabia. Muhammad had spoken of him with appreciation as "the first fruit of Abyssinia."[60]

The third Habshi bearing the title of Ulugh Khan was Yaqut's son Muhammad, also known as Shams ud-Dawlah Muhammad al-Habshi, who served as vizier to his father from 1543–4 to 1557–8. Also called Khayrat Khan, he also held the title of al-Majlis al-Ashraf al-Ali, and is remembered, as we have seen, as one of the patrons of the Gujarat historian Haji ad-Dabir. Muhammad Ulugh Khan appointed as his vizier yet another Habshi, Bilal Falah Khan, and, according to the Indian historian M. S. Commissariat, "secured the same devotion as his father had enjoyed from the Habshi troops in Gujarat and was thus able to take an active part in the confused politics of the time." He sided sometimes with Itimad Khan and sometimes with Imad-ul-Mulk Arslan, but after Akbar's conquest of Gujarat ended his days in captivity, and was buried at Sarkhej beside the graves of his father Yaqut and his son Ahmad.[61]

The prestigious title of Jhujhar Khan, as Commissariat notes, was likewise successively held, by "two Abyssinian commanders" of Gujarat. The first was Bilal Habshi, who was appointed in 1538–9, and was governor of Burhanpur under Mubarak Shah of Khandesh (1537–1566). He was subsequently killed in battle before the great commercial town of Surat in 1558–9, and was buried at Sarkhej. His son, Aziz Khan, and grandson, Amin Khan, both acquired some prominence in Gujarat.

The second Habshi with the title of Jhujhar Khan was Bilal Habshi's son Marjan Sultani Habshi, who held the fiefs of Bahmanul and Munda. The adopted brother of Yaqut Ulugh Khan, he died in 1573, when he was executed by being trampled on by an elephant.[62]

Other prominent Habshis of this time included Said Safar Salami, who, after Bahadur's death in 1537, became governor of Surat with the title of Khudavand Khan; Bilal Falah Khani Habshi, vizier to Muhammad Ulugh Khan, who subsequently became an independent chieftain with the title of Khayrat Khan and died in 1563–4; and Fulad Khan Sandal, who ruled the town of Jamud, until his death in 1569–70.[63]

Yet another important Habshi of Gujarat was Shaik Said al-Habshi Sultani. Originally a slave of Rumi Khan, he later entered the service of Sultan Mahmud III. On the latter's death in 1554 he joined the great Habshi captain Jhujhar Khan, and, after a long and distinguished military career, received valuable fiefdoms from the latter, who reportedly regarded him as a brother. Shaik Said managed his land efficiently, and acquired great wealth. He collected a fine library, and had over a hundred slaves, probably mainly or entirely Habshis, as well as numerous horses and camels. Until Emperor Akbar's conquest of Ahmadabad, he dined daily in the company of many nobles and divines, and maintained a public kitchen, which distributed food daily to nearly a thousand destitute persons. He died in 1576;[64] and is perhaps best remembered as the builder of a famous mosque, known by his name, in Ahmadabad.[65]

Akbar's conquest of Gujarat had major consequences for the Habshis, as well as for others, in the territory. Most of the nobles, among them two Habshis, Muhammad Ulugh Khan and Marjan Jhujhar Khan, were obliged to submit. The latter, who had uttered abusive words against Akbar, was punished, as we have seen, by being thrown under an elephant and crushed to death. His son Walil Khan was on the other hand given a command in the Akbar's Gujarat army. Another Habshi, Abdul Kerim Sayfud Muhammad Fulad Khan, the son of the afore-mentioned Fulad Khan, was the ruler of Songir under the kings of Khandesh. He subsequently transferred his allegiance to Akbar, who responded by reaffirming his possession of Songir. He later became, as we have seen, Haji ad-Dabir's second patron.[66]

Bijapur

Habshis in this period after Imam Ahmad's campaigns continued to be prominent further south of the sub-continent, in Bijapur, where their power was bitterly, and almost continuously, contested by other military factions.

Ibrahim Adil Shah's old policy of dividing power between the Habshis and Deccanis, both of them Sunnis, was reversed by his son Ali (1558–1580). He once more dismissed the Habshis and other Sunnis, in favour of the Shiates. Later, however, during the reign of Ibrahim Adil Shah II (1580–1627), a Deccani nobleman seized the dowager queen Chand Bibi, and made himself master of the realm. Three Habshi nobles, Ikhlas Khan, Hamid Khan and Dilavar Khan—the second Habshi of that name—nevertheless soon afterwards drove him from the capital. Ikhlas, who is clearly depicted in a contemporary picture as being of African descent, or at least a man of dark colour,[67] became regent for a short time. He was, however, shortly afterwards dismissed by

Chand Bibi, but later resumed his dictatorship which was, however, soon challenged by the other foreigners.

The more northerly Kingdom of Ahmadnagar, taking advantage of these serious dissensions, attacked Bijapur in 1567. The Habshis, realising that they could not defend their city alone, thereupon tended their resignation to Chand Bibi. This, in the view of the British historian Wolseley Haig, provided "the only example of self-denying patriotism to be found in this strife of factions." The Shiah foreigners then rallied to the defence of the city, and the Ahmadnagar army was forced to withdraw, whereupon the struggle at Bijapur was, however, renewed. Ikhlas Khan attacked his fellow Habshi Dilavar Khan, but was defeated by the latter, who became the supreme ruler from 1582 to 1591. In the latter year he was defeated in a battle with the Ahmadnagar army, as a result of which his power in Bijapur collapsed. He thereupon fled to Ahmadnagar where he found service with Burhan II, who had by then seized control there. The ruler of Bijapur complained at this employment of the former Habshi dictator, but Burhan replied by declaring war. He was, however, unsuccessful, and was obliged to make peace. The Deccanis then rebelled against him, and found a ready leader in Dilavar's old rival the Habshi Ikhlas Khan who failed, however, to capture Ahmadnagar.[68]

Burhan was succeeded by Ibrahim Nizam Shah (1595–1596), whose mother had been a Habshi. His chief minister, a Deccani, allowed Ikhlas Khan to return to Ahmadnagar. Ikhlas then persuaded the king, against his minister's advice, to declare war on Bijapur. Ibrahim was killed, and a further struggle for succession ensued. Ikhlas Khan proposed the accession of one prince, while two other Habshis, Ahang Khan and Habashi Khan, supported another.

The above struggles, in which the Habshis, as so often, thus played major roles, immediately preceded the conflict between Ahmadnagar and the Mogul empire which led to the latter's decisive victory in 1597.[69]

Sailors

Numerous Habshis were meanwhile employed as sailors in Indian waters. The Dutchman Linschoten recalls that besides Arabs there were also "Abexiins" serving as sailors around India, where they were replacing the Portuguese, who considered such work incompatible with their prestige. "These Abexiins and Arabians, such as are free," he declares, "doe serve in all India for Saylers and sea faring men, with such merchants as saile from Goa to China, Japan, Bengala, Mallaca, Ormus, and all the

oriental coast. . . . These Abexiins and Arabians serve for small money, and being hyred are very lowlie (and subiect), so that often times they are (beaten and) smitten, not as slaves, but like dogs, which they bear very patientlie, not (once) speaking a word."[70]

Some Habshis sailed even further east. They travelled indeed as far as Siam, where the Portuguese mariner Ferdinand Pinto told of "Turks, Abyssins and Moors" engaged in fighting in 1548.[71]

The 17th and 18th Centuries

Indian trade with the Red Sea, Gulf of Aden and Eastern coast of Africa continued to flourish in the 17th century, and was accompanied by many further shipments of slaves. The number arriving in India seems, however, to have been significantly less than at the time of Imam Ahmad, with the result that Habshis on the whole began to play a diminishing role in Indian political affairs.

Travellers to India in the 17th century, however, still report a significant Habshi presence. The Englishman Edward Terry noted for example early in the century that there were "many Abissines" in "Indostan."[72] His compatriot the historian W. H. Moreland, writing of the time of the death of Emperor Akbar in 1605, agrees that "Abyssinians were in much demand," and "sometimes" rose to "very responsible positions."[73]

The demand for Habshi slaves was likewise subsequently reported by the early 17th century British envoy Thomas Roe. He recalls that he was requested by the Mogul Emperor Jahanger (1605–1627) "to buy three Abassines (for fortie Rupias a man) whom they suppose all Christians," but he refused, declaring, "I could not buy men as slaves."[74]

Later in the 17th century another Englishman, William Crooke, stated that Habshis, or "Syddies" as he called them, were raised to some of "the Chief Employments" in the land, with the result that "Frizled Woolly-paled Blacks" rose to "great Preferments."[75]

Habshis were still in demand in the 18th century, at the close of which J. H. Grose, a British traveller, declared that the "Moors," i.e. Indian Muslims, were "fond of having Abyssinia slaves, known in Indian by the name of Habshee Coifrees," i.e. Kafirs, or Africans. Such slaves, he believed, came mainly from the Ethiopian region via the Red Sea and Arabian ports. The slaves' principal place of origin, he thought, was the southern Ethiopian province of Enarya, bordering upon what was "commonly called Negroeland, in the heart of Africa." It was from Ethiopia, he claims, that such slaves were "selected, and a great traffic made of them, all over the Mogolistan and Persia." As for the character of these slaves, he observes that they were "highly valued for their courage, fidelity, and shrewdness; in which they so far excel, as often to rise to posts of great trust and honor, and are made governors of palaces; when they take the title of Siddees," i.e. Sidis.[76]

Though there was still a considerable demand for Habshi slaves, as Grose suggests, most, by the 18th century, were probably descendants of immigrants imported into Ethiopia earlier rather than immigrants themselves.

Malik Ambar, and Other Prominent Habshis

The best known Habshi of the early 17th century was probably Malik Ambar (1549–1626), an "Abyssinian" slave purchased in Baghdad, who became chief minister in the shrunken kingdom of Ahmadnagar. He won renown in 1601 by defeating the Mogul forces in south-west Berar, and subsequently established Murtaza Nizam Shah (1603–1630) as the nominal ruler of the land. He also reorganised the tax system, and improved the training of the soldiers.[77] The Mogul court chronicler, Mutamid Khan, wrote: "This Ambar was a slave, but an able man. In warfare, in command, in sound judgment, and in administration he had no rival or equal."[78]

On the death of Malik Ambar his son, Fath Khan, submitted to the Moguls, but soon afterwards joined Murtaza Nizam Shah in attacking them. The latter, however, subsequently appointed another Habshi, Hamid Khan, to the post of minister, and fell completely under his influence and that of the latter's wife. She became the recognised means of communication between the monarch and his subjects, and on occasion even assumed control of the army. In 1626 she overcame the army of Bijapur, which, however, in the following year decisively defeated her husband.[79]

Meanwhile another Habshi, Yaqut Khudavand Khan, led a group of fellow Habshis over to the Mogul Emperor Jahanger in protest against the influence of Hamid Khan and his wife. The defectors, however, soon deserted the Emperor, whose forces then hunted them down. The Habshis fought bravely, and reportedly "gathered together like ants and locusts," but were defeated. Hamid Khan's grandsons, realising the futility of the struggle, later made their submission to Jahanger, who in return granted them fiefs in the Deccan.[80]

Hamid's defeat had fatal consequences. Malik Ambar's son Fath Khan, uncertain of his influence over Murtaza, killed him, and replaced him by the latter's son Husayn Nizam Shah III (1630–1633).

Randola Khan, a prominent Habshi general in Bijapur, then persuaded Fath Khan to join in the struggle against the Moguls, but the two Habshis were eventually defeated. Fath Khan nevertheless received honourable treatment from the victors, and was allowed to live in Lahore with an ample pension.[81]

Several other Habshis held important positions later in the century. They included Atish Habshi (d. 1651), sometime governor of Bihar and later of the Deccan;[82] Habsh Khan Sidi Miftah Habshi, who was honoured by Emperor Aurengzeb, and attracted the interest of the German scholar Hiob Ludolf, who reproduces his portrait in his *Relatio nova de Hodierno Habessinae Statu*; Habsh Khan's son Ahmad Khan;[83] Dilavar Khan (d. 1702–3), another sometime governor of the Deccan, who was in turn succeeded as its ruler by another Habshi;[84] and Malik Marjan, Ibrahim Adil's governor of Bidar.[85] Mention may also be made of an unidentified Habshi of Breampur, who, according to the Frenchman Pierre du Jarric, was "a very brave captain," and one of the principal guardians of the fortress of Asirgath.[86]

Hyderabad

There was at least one prominent Habshi in 18th century Hyderabad, in the interior of central India. He was Rahut Jung, also known as Sidi Asud Ula (died 1796), an infantry commander, described by the historian J. Clunes as "a native of Abyssinia."[87]

The Indian West Coast, and Janjira

Though the influence of the Habshis in the sub-continent was as a whole declining, they continued to hold power at the island of Janjira, on the west coast, where they were almost invariably referred to as Sidis. They were also prominent in the Nizam Shahi fleet of Ahmadnagar. In the early 17th century, during the reign of Malik Ambar for example, two Habshis, Habash Khan and Sidi Ambar, served as admirals of this fleet, while a third, Sidi Bulbul, was in command of Rairi.[88]

The Sidis played a notable role in the struggle between Emperor Aurengzeb and the Maratha leader Shivaji (1674–1680). No less than "three of the principal provinces" of Bijapur, according to Orme, were then governed by Sidis. One of them was the admiral of the Bijapur fleet, and had under his jurisdiction a "considerable" stretch of coast both north and south of Janjira.[89] Shivaji took the offensive in 1659 when he attacked Janjira, but failed to capture it. He nevertheless succeeded in seizing the nearby fort of Danda-Raipuri.

Several mutually irreconcilable accounts of this struggle are extant. One author, Muhammad Hashim Khan, claims that Fath Khan, the then ruler of Janjira, had "three Abyssinian slaves, Sidi Sambal, Sidi Yaqut, and Sidi Khariyat, each of whom had ten Abyssinian slaves, which he had trained and drilled." They were so well organised that "the management of the island and many domestic concerns" fell into their hands. Learning that Fath Khan intended to surrender the island to the Muslim leader Shivaji, they reportedly plotted together to forestall the betrayal. They succeeded in taking Fath Khan prisoner, and made Sambal ruler in his stead, after which they appealed to Aurengzeb's imperial armies for help.[90]

Conflict between Shivaji and the Habshis, according to this account, later "grew more violent." The Maratha leader collected forty or fifty warships to use against the Habshis, after which "there were frequent naval fights between the opposing forces, in which the Abyssinians were often victorious." Sidi Sambal was then given the title of commander of nine hundred, and, before his death, appointed Sidi Yaqut his successor, and "enjoined all the other Abyssinians to pay him a loyal and cheerful obedience." Yaqut, it is said, was distinguished for his "courage, benignity and dignity," and "strove more than ever to collect ships of war, to strengthen the fortress and to ward off naval attacks. Armed and ready night and day, he frequently captured ships of the enemy, and cut off the heads of many Marathas." He and Sidi Khariyat later launched a surprise attack, with scaling ladders, on Danda Rajpuri, in the course of which its powder magazine caught fire, and the Habshis made themselves masters of the area.[91]

Another, rather different, version of the story, cited by Orme, and elaborated upon in the Bombay *Gazetteer*, claims that the Sidis on the mainland, faced with Shivaji's growing strength, escaped to Janjira. Several Sidis were then "in high military command" there. One of them, Sidi Joreh, an admiral of the Bijapur fleet, was sent on an expedition against Shivaji, but, failing in his mission, was suspected of treachery and put to death. His successor, Sidi Sambal, and a group of other Sidis then opened negotiations with Emperor Aurengzeb's generals in Gujarat and the Deccan. The Sidis offered them their services, and the support of Janjira fort and the entire Bijapur fleet. They nevertheless reserved the right to rule at Janjira, and to recapture whatever former Sidi property in Bijapur they could.

Aurengzeb, according to this account, accepted the Sidi proposals, and Sambal was duly appointed a Mogul admiral. He was raised to the dignity of a commander of nine hundred, and given "a large stipend on the revenues" of the town of Surat, whence he afterwards received continuous support against Sevaji.[92]

The Sidis, we are told, were at this time rich, and reportedly gained as much from their trade as from a stipend from Aurengzeb. Their administrative organisation, which was in some ways unusual, is described by Orme, who observes:

"Reverence to the higher family, and to the Mogul's choice, had given the pre-eminence of command to Siddee Sambole; but the other captains preserved the distinct command over their own crews and dependents, and an aristocratical council determined the general welfare of this singular republic; in which the lowest orders from their skill and utility, maintained some influence, and proud of their importance, merited, by the alacrity of their service, in so much that they excelled all the navigators of India, and even rated themselves equal to Europeans; and indeed the onset of their sword was formidable in boarding, and on shore."[93]

A similar picture is drawn by the 18th century British writer R. O. Cambridge. He asserts that the Sidis beside possessing "many vessels of force," "carried on a considerable trade."[94]

Sidi Sambal's appointment as admiral resulted, according to Orme in Sidi Kassim becoming commander of Janjira, and Sidi Khariyat ruler of Danda-Rajpuri. Kassim subsequently succeeded Sambal as admiral in 1677, after which he expanded his fleet, and captured many Maratha ships, while Sidi Khariyat became governor of Janjira, and held this position until his death in 1696.[95]

Though some details of the above events are obscure, and differently reported, there can be no denying that the Sidis were in "constant war with the Marathas," between 1673 and 1707, as the Bombay *Gazetteer* states. "Sometimes laying waste large tracts of Maratha territory," they were "at other times stripped of their own lands," and only "with difficulty" held on to their island of Janjira."[96]

The Habshi admirals of the Mogul empire, it should be noted, enjoyed an influence far beyond Janjira. The Indian seas, as Cambridge noted in the mid-18th century, had long been "infested to an intolerable degree by pirates," and it was for this reason that "the Mogul appointed the Siddee, who was chief of a colony of Coffrees to be his admiral." The Mogul rulers, who were "equally moved by zeal for the Mahometan religion, and concern for the interests of commerce," were then every year sending a large vessel to the Red Sea. In return for its protection by the Sidis of Janjira, the Mogul authorities granted the latter's admiral a revenue called *tanka*, valued at three *lak*, or 300,000 rupees, annually. This sum was raised partly from the revenues of Surat, and partly on rents from adjacent lands.[97]

After advent of the British in Bombay, the Sidis of Janjira appealed to them for help against Shivaji, in 1672. The British, however, refused, and instead adopted a policy of strict neutrality. For the next seven years the Sidis nevertheless made their way to Bombay, where, with or without leave, they passed the monsoon. Their object was to use the port, as Rawlinson explained, as a base for operations along the coast against the Marathas.[98]

Half a century or so later, in 1733, the British concluded an offensive and defensive alliance with the Sidis.[99] The death of the Sidi leader Yaqut in the following year, was followed, however, by a dispute over the succession. This weakened afterwards the power of the Sidis, after which the Peshwa seized many of their forts.[100]

The power of the Sidis was by then fast declining. Their ships, as the Bombay *Gazetteer* notes, proved "no match for the Maratha fleets," and were therefore unable to protect the shipping of Surat.[101]

Sidi Massut, who had been denied some of his revenue from Surat, nevertheless sailed there with fleet in 1759, and remained there throughout the monsoon period. During this time the Sidis "not only retained the government of the castle," as Cambridge asserts, but also "greatly encroached on that of the town": they appropriated no less than one-third of its revenues.[102]

The British shortly afterwards, in 1761, gave the Sidis their support, and forced the Marathas to restore part of the Sidis' former land in Konkan. A new dispute over the Sidi succession nevertheless occurred in 1784, whereupon the Marathas attempted once again, though unsuccessfully, to capture Janjira.[103]

The Sidis thus held their own at Janjira throughout the seventeenth and eighteenth centuries. They had been engaged, as Clunes noted in 1828, "in constant wars, by sea and land," until only 15 or 20 years previously, and their principality, "though circumscribed in its limits," still maintained its independence.[104]

The Deccan

The continued prevalence of Habshis, further south, in the Deccan, was noted in the early 17th century by the British traveller William Fitch. He recalls that one of the generals of the king of the area was an "Abashad," i.e. Abyssinian, or Habshi, who had with him "some ten thousand of his owne coste (caste), all brave soldiers."[105]

Two generations later another Englishman, William Crooke, told, in racist terms, of a Portuguese at Barvi in the Deccan, who had "a bloody Leash of Coiferies," i.e. Kafirs. Crooke also refers to a certain Khawas Khan, an Itoby Caphir," i.e. Ethiopian Kafir, who had been "made a free Denizen and Naturalised." He was allegedly "so terrible" to Shivaji's followers that they declared that these Habshis, with their swords, were able to "cut down Man and Horse" alike.[106]

Elaborating on the position of Habshi slaves in the Deccan, Crooke observes that the "Coiferies," on their first arrival as slaves, became "endeared to their Master" who accorded them the "first places of Honour and Trust." His only Proviso was that they should be "faithfully obliged to their Lord," in which their newly acquired Muslim faith "rarely failed them." Self-interest moreover taught them to be "true to him that raised them," for only those who were not raised "at the Will of their Master, are tied to their Good Behaviour."[107]

Western Coastal Areas

Habshis were also to the fore in several other areas along the western coast of India.

In the Bombay area, the southern part of Kalyan province was controlled in 1648, according to James Duff, by an "Abyssinian" called Jaghi. He had the responsibility of maintaining a naval force, for the protection of trade, as well as of pilgrims travelling to Mecca. His appointment was not hereditary, but "conferred on the most deserving Abyssinian of the fleet," who was styled wazir. Many of his crews were reportedly Abyssinians, who had created "a small African colony" in the Konkan area.[108] The same was apparently true at the two fortified rocks of Henara and Canara, at the mouth of Bombay harbour. Both, Grose noted in 1722, had until recently been in Sidi hands.[109]

Goa in the 17th century, according to Crooke, likewise had a sizable population of "Cofferies," though these, according to François Pyrard of Laval, by then came largely from Mozambique, rather than from Abyssinia. This is largely confirmed by Crooke, who observes that "most" of these slaves then originated in Mozambique and Mombasa (rather than, we may comment, in Abyssinia, as formerly). The Portuguese, he adds, ran a school, where they were "taught to sound on Trumpets," and produce "Loud Musick."[110]

Further north, in Kathiawar, the port and small territory of Jafarabad were handed over to one of the Habshis, Sidi Hilol, then admiral of the Mogul fleet, in 1731. Sidi claims to the area were later confirmed by the British in 1759, after which Sidi control of the area continued for many years.[111]

Sailors and Pirates

Habshi sailors, of often uncertain origin, meanwhile, continued to be active in Indian waters. Indian boats from the islands of the East, according to the mid-17th century Dutchman Gautier Schouten, were "full of Blacks," armed with spears, swords, shields, and muskets. One such sailor, the 17th century Englishman Peter Mundy reports, was his interpreter, Antonio, a "Capher Eathiopian Abissin, or Curled head," who had defected from the Portuguese to join the Chinese.[112]

Slaves from Africa, as Mundy suggests, travelled widely. They were reported as far away as Bassein, in Burma, where the Portuguese, according to Crooke, liked to display their wealth by the number of their slaves as well as by the number of their umbrellas. Such slaves were at times apparently unruly, for Crooke claims that it was "dangerous to walk late for fear of falling into the Hands of those Pilfering Abusive Rascals."[113]

There was also at this time a sizable number of Sidi pirates operating along the Western Indian coast. They were described by Clunes as "terrible," and "more dreaded, than all others, on the pirate coast." Their presence is confirmed by the Bombay *Gazetteer,* as far as the Thane, north of Bombay is concerned.[114]

The Decline of the Slave Trade

The Ethiopian slave trade, which apparently reached its peak after the fighting and slave raiding at the time of Imam Ahmad ibn Ibrahim, in the first half of the 16th century, thereafter significantly declined.

Later evidence nevertheless suggests that slave exports from Ethiopia and the Horn of Africa in the first two-thirds of the 19th century was by no means inconsiderable. Such exports (which were destined for Arabia and other areas as well as India) were then running at close on ten thousand a year, i.e. almost a hundred thousand per decade, or nearly a million per century. The average annual break-down of slaves was as follows:[115]

From Tajura and Zayla: 6,000 slaves
From Massawa: 1,750 slaves
From Beilul: 1,500 slaves
Total: 9,250 slaves

Such figures indicate that though the number of slaves entering the Indian sub-continent probably fell substantially in the 18th century, the slave trade had by no means fully dried up. This would in turn suggest, as far as the Indian sub-continent is concerned, that there was probably still a not insignificant influx of slaves from Ethiopia and the Horn of Africa, and that they would have at least partially replenished the ranks of the long-established Habshi population.

Habshis, or their descendants, continued in fact to be reported in various parts of the sub-continent, and the comprehensive investigation of their descendants, by social scientists, and linguists, no less than by historians, should prove rewarding.

Notes

[1]R. Pankhurst, *An Introduction to the Economic History of Ethiopia* (London, 1961), pp. 16–24.
[2]J. W. McCrindle, *The Christian Topography of Cosmas Indicopleustes* (London, 1929), pp. 365–6, 368, 372.
[3]On the Habashat see C. Conti Rossini, "Sugli Habas at," *Rendiconti della Reale Accademia dei Lincei* (1906), XV, 39–50; J. S. Trimingham, *Islam in Ethiopia* (London, 1952), pp. 32–3; E. Ullendorff, *The Ethiopians. An Introduction to Country and People* (London, 1973), pp. 48–9.
[4]H. Yule and A. C. Burnell, *Hobson-Jobson* (London, 1886), p, 806; *Gazetteer of the Bombay Presidency,* XI, 433.
[5]J. C. G. Duff, *A History of the Marattas* (London, 1921), I, 111.
[6]A. Gray, *The Voyage of François Pyrard of Laval to the East Indies, the Maldives, the Moluccas and Brazil* (London, 1888), I, 173.
[7]Yule and Burnell, *Hobson-Jobson,* pp. 140–2.
[8]J. Briggs, *History of Mohomedan Power in India till the Year A.D. 1612, translated from the Original Persian of Mohomed Kasim Ferishita* (London, 1829), I, 220; E. Thomas, *Chronicles of the Parthan Kings* (London, 1871), p. 106; S. Lane-Poole, *Medieval India under Mohomedan Rule (A.D. 412–1764)* (London, 1903), pp. 75–6; *The Cambridge History of India,* edited by Sir Wolseley Haig (Cambridge, 1928), III, 60; R. C. Mujumdar, H. C. Raychaudhuri and K. Datta, *An Advanced History of India* (London, 1956), p. 286.
[9]H. A. R. Gibb, *Ibn Battuta, Travels in Africa and Asia, 1324–1354* (Cambridge, 1962), pp. 229–30.
[10]K. K. Basu, *The Tarikh-i-Mubarak Shadi* (Calcutta, 1932), p. 139: Lane-Poole, *Medieval India,* p. 147.
[11]Gibb, *Ibn Battuta,* p. 236.
[12]Gibb, *Ibn Battuta,* p. 260.
[13]Gibb, *Ibn Battuta,* p. 224.
[14]J. Burton-Page, "Habshi," *Encyclopedia of Islam,* p. 14.
[15]Majumdar and others, *Advanced History,* p. 345; *Cambridge History,* III, 268.
[16]Jadu-Nath Sarkar, *The History of Bengal, II The Muslim Period 1200–1757* (Ramma, Dacca, 1948), p. 137.
[17]Sarkar, *History of Bengal,* II, 139.
[18]Majumdar and others, *Advanced History,* pp. 345–6; J. C. Powell-Price, *A History of India* (London, 1955), p. 208.
[19]Sarkar, *History of Bengal,* II, 139; Majumdar and others, *Advanced History,* p. 346; C. Stewart, *The History of Bengal* (London, 1913), pp. 102–3, 106–7, 208; Lane-Poole, *Medieval India,* p. 154; Powell-Price, *History,* pp. 189, 202, *Cambridge History,* III, 269–70.
[20]Stewart, *History of Bengal,* p. 111; *Cambridge History,* III, 271.
[21]A. Cortesão, *The Summa Oriental of Tomé Pires* (London, 1944), p. 80.

[22]Powell-Price, *History of India*, pp. 195, 197.

[23]*Cambridge History*, III, 412.

[24]*Cambridge History*, III, 412–14, 417–20; Cortesão, *Summa Oriental*, p. 51.

[25]*Gazetteer of the Bombay Presidency*, XI , 433.

[26]R. Orme, *Historical Fragments of the Mogul Empire* (London, 1782), p. 80.

[27]*Cambridge History*, III, 422–5. See also G. Yazdani, *Bidar: its History and Monuments* (Oxford, 1947), p. 11.

[28]*Cambridge History*, III, 428–31.

[29]*Cambridge History*, III, 434.

[30]*Cambridge History*, III, 439–40.

[31]*Cambridge History*, III, 458

[32]Yazdani, *Bidar*, pp. 180–4, and plate CXIX.

[33]Duff, *History of the Marattas*, I, 111.

[34]*Gazetteer of the Bombay Presidency*, I, part II, 34, XI, 434–5; J. Clunes, *Appendix to the History of Western India* (Bombay, 1828), p. 24; Duff, *History of the Marattas*, I, 110.

[35]Burton Page, "Habshi," p. 15.

[36]Burton Page, "Habshi," p. 16.

[37]*Gazetteer of the Bombay Presidency*, XI, 434.

[38]Pannikar, *Malabar and the Portuguese*, p. 11.

[39]R. Skelton, "The Ni'mat nama: a Landmark in Malwa Painting," *Marg* (1959), XX, no. 3, p. 34.

[40]Cortesão, *Summa Oriental*, p. 34.

[41]*Gazetteer of the Bombay Presidency*, XI, 434.

[42]*Gazetteer of the Bombay Presidency*, VI, 206. See also J. Copeland, "Account of the Cornelian Mines of the Neighbourhood of Baroach," *Transactions of the Literary Society of Bombay* (1819), I, 289.

[43]R. E. Enthoven, *The Tribes and Castes of Bombay* (Bombay, 1922), III, 332. See also *Gazetteer of the Bombay Presidency*, IX, part II, p. 12; M. S. Commissariat, *A History of Gujarat* (London, 1938), I, 269–70.

[44]D. K. Blattacharya, "Indians of African Origin," *Cahiers d'Etudes Africaines* (1970), X, 580.

[45]C. F. Beckingham and G. W. B. Huntingford, *The Prester John of the Indies* (Cambridge, 1961), II, 410–15.

[46]Beckingham and Huntingford, *Prester John*, II, 445.

[47]A. Kammerer, *Le routier de Dom Joam de Castro* (Paris, 1936), p. 80.

[48]P. A. Tiele, *The Voyage of John Huyghen Van Linschoten to the Indies* (London, 1855), I, 34.

[49]Tiele, *Voyage*, I, 264–5.

[50]Tiele, *Voyage*, I, 222, 276–7.

[51]Commissariat, *History of Gujarat*, I, 471; E. Denison Ross, *An Arabic History of Gujarat* (London, 1910–28), I, vii.

[52]Denison Ross, *Arabic History*, I, 584–9, 503–8.

[53]Denison Ross, *Arabic History*, II, xxxiii.

[54]Denison Ross, *Arabic History*, II, xxxiv; Commissariat, *History of Gujarat*, I, 470.

[55]Denison Ross, *Arabic History*, II, *Arabic History*, 407; Commissariat, *A History of Gujarat*, I, 470.

[56]Denison Ross, *Arabic History*, I, 447, 455, II, xxxvii; Commissariat, *A History of Gujarat*, I, 470.

[57]Denison Ross, *Arabic History*, II, xxxiii–iv; Commissariat, *History of Gujarat*, I, 470.

[58]Denison Ross, *Arabic History*, II, xxxiii–iv; Commissariat, *History of Gujarat*, I, 470.

[59]Denison Ross, *Arabic History*, II, xxii, xxxviii.

[60]W. Muir, *The Life of Mahomet* (London, 1878), p. 64.

[61]Denison Ross, *Arabic History*, I, xiv; Commissariat, *A History of Gujarat*, I, 471, 495.

[62]Denison Ross, *Arabic History*, I, xiv–xv; Commissariat, *History of Gujarat*, I, 471, 495–6.

[63]Denison Ross, *Arabic History*, I, ii, xv.

[64]Commissariat, *History of Gujarat*, I, 502–3.

[65]Commissariat, *History of Gujarat*, I, 502–3; *Gazetteer of the Bombay Presidency*, I, part II, p. 34; *Cambridge History*, III, 616.

[66]Denison Ross, *Arabic History*, I, ii, xv; M. S. Commissariat, *History of Gujarat*, I, 495–6; H. Beveridge, *The Akhbarnama of Abul-l-Fasl* (Calcutta, 1903–10), III, 46, 76.

[67]British Library, Ad. MS. Orient 5,234, folio 34. See also Orient 22, 282, folios 16, 20.

[68]*Cambridge History*, III, 458–61.

[69]*Cambridge History*, III, 464–6.

[70]Tiele, *Voyage*, I, 265–7. See also *Gazetteer of the Bombay Presidency*, I, part II, p. 62.

[71]*The Voyage and Adventures of Ferdinand Mendez Pinto* (London, 1663), p. 179.

[72]W. Foster, *Early Travels in India 1583–1619* (London, 1921), p. 307.

[73]W. H. Moreland, *India at the Death of Akbar* (London, 1820), p. 26.

[74]W. Foster, *The Embassy of Sir Thomas Roe to the Court of the Great Mogul 1615–1619* (London, 1889). On slaves at Goa, see also Gray, *Voyage*, II, 65.

[75]W. Crooke, *A New Account of East Indies and Persia being Nine Years' Travels 1672–1681* (London, 1915), I, 62, II, 5, 53.

[76]J. H. Grose, *A Voyage to the East Indies* (London, 1772), I, 148–9.

[77]J. N. Chaudhuri, *Malik Ambar* (Calcutta, n.d.); *Cambridge History*, III, 159, IV, 148. For contemporary paintings of Malik Coomaraswami, *Catalogue of the Indian Collection of the Museum of Fine Arts, Boston* (Boston, 1930), VI Mogul paintings, p. 49, plates XXXVII and XXXVIII; I. S. Stchoukine, *Le peinture indienne* (Paris, 1929, plate 29; K. Khandalavala, "Identification of the Portraits of Malik Ambar," *Lalit Kala* (1956), nos. 1–2.

[78]*Cambridge History*, IV, 180, 203–4. See also Powell-Price, pp. 291–3; Majumdar and others, *Advanced History*, p. 446.

[79]*Cambridge History*, IV, 189, 263–4.

[80]Sansamu-d-Daula Nawas Khan, *The Masiru-e-Umara* (London, 1911–1914), I, 990.

[81]*Cambridge History*, IV, 192–3, 264–5; Samsamu-d-Daula Nawas Khan, *The Masiru-e-Umara*, I, 532, II, 626.

[82]Samsamu-d-Daula Nawas Khan, *The Masiru-e-Umara*, I, 305.

[83]Samsamu-d-Daula Nawas Khan, *The Masiru-e-Umara*, II, 33.

[84]Samsamu-d-Daula Nawas Khan, *The Masiru-e-Umara*, II, 994.

[85]Yazdani, *Bidar*, pp. 14, 49.

[86]Pierre du Jarric, *Akbar and the Jesuits* (London, 1926), pp. 102–6.

[87]Clunes, *Appendix*, p. 38.

[88]Duff, *History of the Marattas*, I, 110; *Gazetteer of the Bombay Presidency*, I, part II, p. 34.

[89]Orme, *Historical Fragments*, p. 80.

[90]H. M. Elliott, *The History of India as Told by her Own Historians* (London, 1877), VII, 289–90; *Gazetteer of the Bombay Presidency*, XI, 437–8.

[91]Elliot, *History*, VII, 290–1. See also Clunes, *Appendix*, p. 24; *Cambridge History*, V, 101.

[92]Orme, *Historical Fragments*, pp. 9–11, 80; *Gazetteer of the Bombay Presidency*, II, 89, IX, 3, XI, 433–4, 436–7, XIII, part II, p. 227; B. V. Gokhale, "Bombay and the Shivaji," *Journal of the Royal Asiatic Society* (1958), XXXIII, 72.

[93]Orme, *Historical Fragments*, pp. 80–1.

[94]R. O. Cambridge, *An Account of the War in India* (London, 1761), p. 216.

[95]Orme, *Historical Fragments*, pp. 32–4, 39, 43, 78; *Gazetteer of the Bombay Presidency*, XI, 437; Gokhale, "Bombay and the Shivaji," 72.

[96]*Gazetteer of the Bombay Presidency*, I, part 1, pp. 71–2, II, 117, XI, 437.

[97]Cambridge, *Account of the War*, p. 216–17.

[98]Orme, *Historical Fragments*, pp. 42–3, 62, 108–9, 152; Crooke, *New Account*, I, 195, 201, II, 18, 57, 63, III, 163; J. Ovington, *A Voyage to Surat in the Year 1689* (London, 1929), p. 10; *Gazetteer of the Bombay Presidency*, I, part 1, pp. 71–2, II, 117, XI, 437.

[99]*Gazetteer of the Bombay Presidency*, XI, 444. See also D. R. Banaji, *Bombay and the Sidis* (London, 1932).

[100]Duff, *History of the Marattas*, I, 231–2; *Gazetteer of the Bombay Presidency*, XII, 498.

[101]*Gazetteer of the Bombay Presidency*, II, 117, XI, 443–4.

[102]Cambridge, *Account of the War*, p. 217.

[103]*Gazetteer of the Bombay Presidency*, II, 250; *Cambridge History*, V, 369.

[104]Clunes, *Appendix*, p. 24.

[105]Foster, *Early Travels*, p. 138.

[106]Crooke, *New Account*, I, 352, II, 5, 53.

[107]Crooke, *New Account*, II, 52.

[108]Duff, *History of the Marattas*, p. 110.

[109]Grose, *Voyage*, I, 58.

[110]Crooke, *New Account*, II, 16, 23; Gray, *Voyage*, II, 223.

[111]*Gazetteer of the Bombay Presidency*, VIII, 161, XI, 447; Clunes, *Appendix*, p. 52.

[112]G. Schouten, *Voyage de Gautier Schouten aux indes orientales commencé l'an 1658 et fini 1665* (Rouen, 1725), I, 108; R. C. Temple, *The Travels of Peter Mundy, in Europe and Asia 1608–1667* (London, 1919), III, part 1, p. 192, part II, pp. 241, 260, 312, 511.

[113]Crooke, *New Account*, I, 62.

[114]Clunes, *Appendix*, p. 24; *Gazetteer of the Bombay Presidency*, XIII, 488.

[115]R. Pankhurst, "The Ethiopian Slave Trade in the Nineteenth and Early Twentieth Century: A Statistical Inquiry," *Journal of Semitic Studies* (1964), IX, no. 1, pp. 220–8.

The African Presence in Portuguese India

Ann M. Pescatello*

Historians concerned with the Portuguese presence in India generally have focused on political or military events to the neglect of social or cultural forces. Due to this predilection followers of Clio have overlooked a curious character: The African slave in India.** This ubiquitous stranger is more than discernible in archival stories of Portuguese India as well as in travel accounts of early European imperial interests. There is not yet sufficient evidence uncovered to write a definitive monograph on the long history of the African in India. But because his appearance forms an intriguing chapter in any recounting of South Asian history, I present here—based on circumscribed materials—a limited discussion on the functions of the African in early Portuguese Indian history and his place in the colonial structure. Before proceeding, however, two major dimensions contributing to the story should be delineated. The first concerns the pre-Portuguese involvement of Africans in Indian societies, including the extent of a slave trade, its location in India, and the relationship of that trade with the general Indian population. The second aspect concerns the structure of sixteenth and seventeenth century Portuguese India into which the African was thrust.

Long before the arrival of da Gama, Albuquerque, and other Lusitanian adventurers, Islamized African communities, called Habshi,[1] existed in India, their ancestors either slaves purchased by Arabs from the African Horn or military slave troops from neighboring Muslim countries. The majority of Africans probably were Abyssinian; the name Habshi means Abyssinian but eventually became applied to all blacks.[2] Later, during Portuguese involvement in India, many so-called Habshi actually were either Bantu or Sudanic Negro.

Our knowledge of the numbers, status, and functions of Habshis prior to the arrival of the Portuguese in South Asia is severely circumscribed and necessarily gleaned from scattered court and travel records. One of our earliest references is Ibn Battuta who, during his travels in India (1333–1342), discovered that Habshis were distributed throughout the subcontinent from North India to Ceylon, and were employed primarily as guards or men-at-arms in land and sea contingents.[3] Other sources indicate that under the Tughluk dynasty in North India, especially in the late fourteenth century, several African slaves or descendants of African slaves either became governors of provinces or were prominent eunuchs in sultanate courts.[4]

African influence, after an initial appearance in the Delhi area, shifted East. Records indicate that from 1459 to 1481, the Bengali Ily s Sh h sultan Rukn al-Din B rbak Sh h maintained some eight thousand African slaves for military service, a few of whom later acquired powers, usurped the throne, and provided a succession of Habshi rulers from 1486 to 1493. In 1493 a successful popular revolt against the last Habshi ruler resulted in the expulsion of these Africans from Bengal, most of whom dispersed to the Deccan, and later to Gujrat, the central and western sections of the subcontinent. They were welcome, for in the Deccan the practice of employing foreigners in state service had begun in the latter half of the fourteenth century and by 1422 Habshi bodyguards were an important factor in determining succession to the throne. Their successes were short-lived, however, for by the end of the fifteenth century they had come into conflict with other foreign mercenaries in the kingdom. Although they were Sunni Muslims, as was the local populace, and although they were also supported by Muwallads,[5] Habshis were not accepted by the lighter-skinned Turks, Persians, and Arabs on the basis of race and color[6] and ultimately lost their positions of power.

In addition to their influence in land posts, Habshis were apparently prominent in Indian navies, first in the Deccan and later, especially, in Gujrat where their power as naval commanders endured until the Marathas rose to supremacy in eighteenth-century western India. Gujrat, however, appears to have received a continuous supply of Habshis not only as exiles from Bengal and the Deccan but also as cargo shipments through several western Indian ports. We are informed that the government of Gujrat in 1376–1377 paid a tribute of four hundred slaves who were "children of Hindu chiefs and Abyssinians," a not uncommon occurrence,[7] while nearly two hundred years later, in 1537, such cities as Ahmadabad, supposedly still counted as many as five thousand Habshis working in government service.[8]

191

Any discussion of the quantity, the functions, or the status of pre-Portuguese African elements in India is based largely on suppositions drawn from isolated references. Numbers of Habshis prominent in Indian court life and service may have been exaggerated and certainly it is only reasonable to suppose that of the thousands of Africans who entered the subcontinent in servile capacities, only a few attained prominence as governors of Bengal, Bihar, and the Deccan.[9] Those who acquired power did so because of the unique avenue of mobility offered by the Janissary-type arm of Muslim militias and not by the structure of Indian society itself. Supposedly, Ethiopian slaves continued to flow into India as late as the eighteenth-century and some scholars believe that this influx may have exerted not only a biological but also a social effect on Indian culture.[10] Since our knowledge of the numerical composition and geographic location of Africans in Islamic India is limited and since our awareness of the daily existence and social circumstances of the ordinary African is severely circumscribed, I shall leave the problem untouched.

Changes in functions of Africans in India possibly occurred with changes in their ethnic composition. Earlier stocks of Africans, primarily of Hamitic and Nilotic peoples, were from markedly different cultural milieux than were Africans carried to India after the fifteenth century by both Arabs and Iberians. This may be attested to linguistically by the decline in usage of the term Habshi as descriptive of all blacks in India.

Because of vicissitudes of war, weather, and worms, documentation concerning the African slave trade to Asia is subject to restricted manuscript collections and extensive speculation. We know that the Arabic trade in African slaves had been a durable and brisk one during the centuries preceding Portuguese occupation in India, for the Arabs had established both commercial and connubial relations with the Bantu in East African coastal settlements from Sofala to Somalia, thus fathering a Swahili "civilization."[11] The Africanized Muslims traded with the Bantu in the interior, exchanging Indian beads and cottons for African gold, ivory, or slaves. Indian residents on the East African coast were closely associated with Arab traders and although they were neither Muslim nor aristocratic much of the ocean-going shipping was owned, manned, and financed by Indians. A bulk of the actual trading also was in Indian hands and direct business relations were maintained between East Africa and the western coast of India.[12]

The Portuguese arrived in East Africa attempting to usurp the role of the Swahili, their viceroy having been enjoined to enslave all Muslim merchants but to leave the local Negroes unharmed.[13] Initially it proved difficult for the Iberians to establish relations with the Bantu but eventually there developed a cordial commerce, the perquisites of which were gold and slaves. It proved a complementary enterprise to Portugal's fairly lucrative Guinea coast trade in Africans, conducted expressly for a chronically underpopulated Portugal and Spain which needed and relied upon "slave" labor for its farms and homes.

Early records are insufficient in supplying more information concerning arrivals of Africans but we can determine that their presence along the western Indian coast was a well-established fact by the end of the sixteenth century. A European traveller, commenting on Abyssinians (and Arabians), noted that "there are many of them in India that are slaves and captives, both men and women which are brought [thither] out of Aetheopia, and sold like other Oriental nations. . . ."[14] He further observed that

> From Mosambique great numbers of these Caffares are carried into India, and many times they sell a man or woman that is growne to their full [strength] for two or three Ducats . . . the cause why so many slaves and captives of all nations are brought to sell in India, is, because everie ten or twelve miles, or rather in every Village and towne, there is a severall King, one of them not like another . . . are in warres, and those that on both sides are taken they keep for slaves. . . .[15]

Other sixteenth century references mention figures from which we can determine the character of the trade of African slaves in the early decades of Portuguese rule in India.[16] Albuquerque's letters mentioned one Garcia de Sousa and his "mulatto man" who fought alongside him in his attack on Aden.[17] Later, on leaving the port of Aden, Albuquerque encountered a Moorish boat with "some Abyssinian women and youths whom the Moors were carrying to sell" and whom, after overcoming the Moors, Albuquerque would not allow to be captives "as they were from the land of Prester John."[18]

Additional sixteenth century references in Goa's historical archives indicate other Africans along the more northerly strip of coast, while there existed yet another group, apparently neither part of recent dispersals from Bengal or the Deccan, nor of new shipments from southern or western Africa.[19] Through oral tradition we know of the African's appearance in other guises all along the western Indian trading coast: the Black Jews of Cochin and Kerala. Descendants of African slaves transferred to Malabar in the seventeenth and eighteenth centuries by so-called White Jews,[20] these Africans were primarily domestic laborers who through the centuries have maintained their position in the Malabar communities despite intermarriage with the local population, including White Jews.

Since the African in India seems to appear most often in the role of "slave," some agreement should be reached as to the actual connotation of "slave" in the societies concerned. As far as I am able to discern, "slavery" as a chattel concept did not exist in sixteenth century India. Those locals who occupied positions of menial responsibilities were socially circumscribed within the context of a complex and elaborate system consisting of four *varna* and thousands of *jatis*, but western or African notions of a person as "chattel" seem to have had no basis in Indian social thought.[20a] Also, European definition had not yet developed from Enlightenment theory. According to Iberian philosophical enquiries and international legal dictates of the time, the concept of "slave" implied a social and economic position rather than a racial subjugation.[21] Thus it would appear that the Africans who lived and labored in India, both during Muslim rule and later in areas specifically subject to Portuguese suzerainty, were a type of "slave" not related in status to the type of chattel laborer we associate with plantation workers on European, African, and American plantations after the seventeenth century.

Having discussed the pre-Portuguese period of African influence in India, the Arabic and later Portuguese-managed slave trade from East Africa to the subcontinent, and definitions of what a "slave" was not, prior to sixteenth century Iberian intrusions, I want to examine briefly the origins of a Portuguese society in an India in which Africans and black slaves were an important presence. Already by the fifteenth century Portuguese seamen were systematically plying the oceans, their ultimate goal to reach sources of spices for European markets. The Iberians arrived at a propitious time, for not only were the numerous kingdoms that they encountered—from Arab trading states to Javanese Majapahit and its neighboring spice islands—politically splintered, but also the great empires of Egypt, Persia and Vijayanagar (South India) possessed no armed shipping and even the Chinese had been confined by imperial decree to navigating their own coastline. Within a few years of their appearance in the Indian Ocean the Portuguese had begun to regulate maritime commerce between Malacca and Moçambique. To order administratively their growing mercantile interests the Portuguese established the *Estado da India* (State of India) at Goa, to supervise their discoveries, conquests, and markets from the Cape of Good Hope in Africa to Japan in the Far East.

Perusal of Portuguese chronicles or early European accounts of Lusitanian expansion in Asia leave the impression that life in the Iberian colonies was one of constant bloodletting and rapacious greed, but this is not a realistic assessment. Recent archival investigations have destroyed some of the myths regarding Iberian actions, derived initially from pietistic Portuguese accounts, and have dusted off the canvas to give us a clearer picture of an active, bustling metropolis. "Golden Goa" had been selected as the *Estado's* capital shortly after its conquest by Albuquerque in 1510 and by 1516 its citizens were exchanging petitions with Lisbon, determining privileges of economic and social consequence. Since the Portuguese crown was eager to promote economic development and political stability as quickly as possible, it granted her married citizens free trading privileges that they requested for themselves, "their business associates, their slaves, and their factors," in all European or Asian provisions or goods, but reserved for itself a monopoly of spices and other special products.[22] The colony prospered and many Portuguese who ventured to India acquired riches and licenses to wealth so that by mid-sixteenth century Goa was a showplace of exquisite homes, retinues of servants, elegant churches, and bustling, flower-bedecked *praças*—a city of beauty!

Throughout the sixteenth century Goa continued its commercial successes and, contrary to previous assessments, was at its apex. In a session of her municipal council on 7 September 1605, pride in the growth and opulence of "this city of Goa, which can nowadays be reckoned as one of the greatest belonging to the Portuguese Crown," was written into the record.[23] All of it was made possible not only by her wealthy citizenry but also by a very large sector of the economy which was organized into workers' guilds. Supposed Portuguese contempt for manual labor also required that other work be relegated to a "vast number" of African, Indian, or foreign-born slaves and servants.

To oversee administrative and political matters shortly after Albuquerque's conquest, a municipal council was established consisting of ten individuals, all with voting rights and probably selected (or elected) from among Portuguese who had taken Albuquerque's advice, married Indian women, and committed themselves to settling in Goa for life. The charter and privileges were closely modeled on those of Lisbon and were jealously guarded; no administrative or judicial official, not even the viceroy, could interfere in daily administrative matters of the council and the rights and privileges of Goa's Portuguese citizens were scrupulously respected.[24] A modern assayor of Imperial Portugal has noted that the council was "one of the principal forces which held the ramshackle State of India . . . together," that it successfully maintained its privileges and was valued by the Crown, for at least three centuries as a check on both viceroys and archbishops.[25]

Economy and polity were not the only areas of imperial interest, for the Crown was concerned with the education, health, and welfare of its citizenry and quickly transplanted to its overseas territories the *Santa Casa da Misericordia*, a charitable order founded in 1498 in Portugal and which was extremely effective in attending to the needs of the poor, sick, widows, and orphans. The *Misericordia* maintained a hospital and other agencies for the spiritual and corporal welfare of Portuguese Indian society, although its later vulnerability to "borrowing" by Goanese gentlemen aided its decline from the eighteenth century.[26]

The *Estado's* military establishment depended on African slaves as soldiers in all its territories; this was the case in Goa as well as Ceylon where Negro slaves were utilized as auxiliary troops. Not surprisingly, the Sinhalese epic *Parangi Hatane* numbers "Kaffirs" among their important opponents.[27] Other evidence suggests a rather numerous contingent of black militia for there were frequent requests from other parts of the empire for blacks, such as that from the governor of Macao in 1651 for a squad of African slaves as part of additional military for the Macaense garrisons; Goa complied.[28]

Portuguese India appears to have been a complex and profitable state whose social structure was a looser version than that of the mother country and was based on the fact that the original Portuguese settlers were almost exclusively male and predominantly military or missionary types. Many married and remained in India, forming a class of *casados* rewarded with profitable perquisites, from offices to trading voyages. Clergy (especially Brothers of the *Misericordia*) and municipal councillors were eminently ranked on the social scale and they and other influential citizens profited from bribery and corruption. Most of the lower classes were composed of Indians with some unfortunate whites and Eurasians joined by Africans.[29] Colonial society remained primarily military, mercantile, and maritime. The *casado* class, which earlier had earned their position and wealth from interport Asian trade, later acquired greater income from lands in the so-called "Provinces of the North," ultimately lost to the Mar th s in the War of 1737–1740. Thereafter the social and

economic situation in India declined. A growing population, an increasingly unhealthy climate, economic decline, and loss of imperial territories forced the removal of the capital to Pangim (Panaji) in 1760, and from there the derelict state of India lethargically merged into the local landscape. Such then was the once-flourishing, gaudy jewel in the Portuguese imperial crown into which the alien African was thrust and to whose functions in the sixteenth and seventeenth century religious, legal, social, and economic life of the *Estado da India* I shall now turn.

Most references for the sixteenth and seventeenth century African presence in the socio-economic structure of Portuguese India are found in archival collections and travel accounts, most of which are housed in India. Because information on sixteenth century South Asia, in general, and Portuguese India, in particular, is so fragmented, the following discussion might appear somewhat anecdotal. I have tried, in light of the available evidence, to tie the aspects of the functions of Africans into the general structure of Portuguese Indian society.

Most specific notices refer to Africans in India in servile roles. Religious men provide a substantive amount of information on this aspect. Their records indicate that these African slaves were Christianized, then sold to other Christians to serve primarily as domestics.[30] That practice apparently became *de rigueur* in the following century.[31] But "accepting" Christianity did not necessarily reward the slaves with benevolent treatment. This is especially evident from correspondence, primarily of secular clergy, who were ordained non-Europeans. (Early in the colonial presence, the regular clergy had erected a color bar against non-Europeans.) Their petitions afford insight not only into the conditions of servitude but also into the attitudes of Church and Crown. Here, as elsewhere in the Empire, for economic reasons the Portuguese Church (and Court) placed itself in opposition to the colonists. The incidents were not so isolated, at least during the sixteenth century. The petitions were applicable both to the African and the indigenous slaves of coastal western India and the petitions indicate that the slavery situation was subject to review by the Portuguese monarch, whose aid was enlisted to alleviate grievances. Priests entreated "His Majesty" to investigate "persons who are cruel to their slaves" and to allow those "who are cruelly treated" to be "sold away from them."[32] Priests claimed that the slaves' "sufferings and torments" were so abominable that "many die" and are interred *"em cazas e quintaes,"* and demanded firmer treatment of offenders.[33] Throughout the seventeenth century the situation scarcely changed if we are to believe other petitions to the Crown to "help the desperate slaves" who are "evidently in danger of dying."[34]

The Catholic clergy also found itself at odds with commercial constituents of the Empire. Due both to sincere ideological controversy over the legal and natural order of slavery (See n. 21) and to conflicting economic interests, the slave became a bandying point. Merchants and colonists sought a source of labor both cheap and tractable; so did the clergy, but they were interested also in the spiritual nature of the slave. Archival accounts in metropolitan Portugal attest to the clergy's duplicity at isolating the servile elements for their own economic aggrandizement while propagandizing to establish their own protective postures with the King. The merchants engaged in similar haggling.

Despite the selfish conflict of Crown, clergy, colonists, and merchant-men over the spiritual and material value of the slaves, there was legal commitment to bettering the conditions of the servile population. There is asserted, in Portuguese documents, an attitude, often reasonable for its time, of great concern about the treatment and material condition of slaves. And, there are annual notices of numbers of slaves freed each year in Portuguese India, although it is difficult to determine whether this was a result of clerical agitation or an annual gesture on the part of the Crown.[35]

Archival records allow us to review the legal policies and established attitudes regarding African slavery in India, but usually it is travellers' accounts that provide insights into local practices. Necessary to a functioning servile labor force is the merchandising of the labor commodity. This was a dimension of slavery frequently commented upon. An early traveller, Linschoten, observed that in the markets "were many sorts of [captives and] slaves, both men and women, young and old, which are daily sold there, as beads are sold with us where everyone may choose which liketh him best, every one at a certain price."[36]

Pietro della Valle also commented on this process. In his descriptions of Goa, della Valle noted of one of the central squares that "in this plaza are sold all sorts of merchandise; and among other things, quantities of slaves."[37] The sellers first performed a thorough examination of the merchandise, then bantered "all their endowments, skills, strength, and health; and the buyers . . . question and examine them, with curiosity, from head to foot, the same with the men as with the women."[38] While, for their own purposes, the slaves "hoping for better treatment with a change of owner, showed their best disposition and are boastful of themselves in order to stimulate the desire of the buyer."[39]

Those in bondage apparently were of a wide range in source and age, and comprised both males and females. Della Valle noted that blacks from both East and West Africa composed slave cargoes to Portugal's possessions (and other mercantile points of interest) in India. The apparent persistence in Portuguese India of both Moçambicans and Guineans indicates not only the transfer of blacks from both major slave areas of Africa, but also presupposes a relatively long existence for barter operations.

Slaves were not solely African but also included Indians and others who had been captured in pirate raids. Della Valle noted some "very beautiful and lovely young girls and women from all lands in India," while included "among these young women . . . very beautiful whites, and lovely, are others swarthy, dark-skinned, and of all colors."[40] But he also observed that "of all those females [the] most pleasing are the servant girls— *Cafres de Moçambique* and [those] from other parts of Africa, who are of black color, very dark and have curly hair, and who are called negresses of Guine."[41]

The diet of the slaves was similar to the everyday foods of the common people and both commoners and slaves were great consumers of Portuguese wines. Of the many wines brought from Portugal was "a white [one] called *Orraca*, worth not more than ten basarucos, and ordinarily used by people of the lowest status and by the slaves, who, from it, are frequently intoxicated. . . ."[42]

Sexual license, a common characteristic of colonization, was a common ingredient in relationships between masters and slaves in Portuguese India. Clerical revulsion of the practice is responsible for our information regarding the practice of Portuguese who "to satiate their passions . . . buy droves of girls and sleep with all of them, and subsequently sell them."[43] Primacy of the male and leniency to mistresses were practices that della Valle observed in relationships of slaves to their masters. According to the Portuguese practice in India, if any man "fathered" a son by his Negress slave, the boy was legitimized and the slave given her freedom.[44]

Abbé Carre also painted a picture of female slaves in their more intimate relationships to the Portuguese gentry. One Dom Pedro de Castro was particularly singled out as a man who "amused himself only with scoundrels and debauchers, and with a troop of women-slaves whom he kept for his sensual pleasures" and, furthermore, that type of living was "one commonly led by all the Portuguese in India."[45] In the Abbé's opinion the other *fidalgos* (gentry) were alike in that they were always "dragging about an appalling number of slaves."[46] And another enclave visit confirmed his opinion of the desolute lives the Portuguese were now leading after two centuries in India, wining, well-dressed, and "followed by a fine troop of slaves."[47]

Next to domestic servants, the largest percentage of slaves either were resold by their owners or were manual laborers who worked at such odd jobs as "conserving fruits and other things; others earned money as carriers and loaders of wares."[48] There were also the young servant girls who were forced into prostitution. They "were called to the houses" and "were made amorous propositions."[49] Some succumbed to the attentions involved in this type of occupation, although many undoubtedly had little choice in the matter. Servant girls and others who labored at menial tasks actually were hired out by their masters and expected to comply with orders issued by temporary employers. This was a common labor policy of the Iberian powers in their American possessions. Any monetary gains acquired by slaves, by whatever means available to them, they "hand it over to their *senhor* (master) or *senhora* (mistress)."[50]

Labor conditions fluctuated with the whims of the *senhors*. Linschoten noted that slaves carried on Portuguese and Dutch ships from Moçambique to India included both men and women . . . "to do their filthiest and hardest labor, wherein they only use them."[51] One of the most common slave tasks was to supply water throughout the various cities or hamlets occupied by the Portuguese. It was noted by della Valle that they "carried it to all the sections in earthenware jugs each of which contained two jars, and sold the jugs at five *basarucos*."[52]

Bondsmen of particular households frequently appeared in public as escorts and bearers to their ladies and gentlemen. Whenever the men ventured out they "never left without taking a slave who carried a large umbrella to guard against the sun," or to carry "veils or hats over them in the rain."[53] Ladies, meanwhile, were borne inside a palanquine "carried by four negro slaves attired in silks . . . and accompanied by many negress slaves . . . all dressed in silks."[54] This lifestyle was not restricted to Europeans; the sultan who "had a Black-guard of some a Dozen slaves," was a not infrequent personage in Portuguese India.[55]

By far the greatest number of African slaves were employed in domestic tasks, and it is about the African's function in this capacity that we have the most information. Both Linschoten and della Valle discerned that the riches of the Goan gentry derived from the great number of slaves that each house possessed and that the Goanese commonly held "five, six, ten, twenty, and some more, some less slaves, both men and women, in their houses. . . ."[56] Accounts depict an affluent gentry, accustomed to service by slaves, and confident in their own position vis à vis their servile population.

On a visit to Daman,[56a] the Frenchman Thevenot commented that "the Portuguese have Slaves there of both Sexes, which work and procreate only for their masters, to whom the Children belong, to be disposed of at their pleasure."[57] He further observed the style of living afforded the Portuguese by their African slaves in Daman: "The Portuguese live very great in India, both as to their tables, clothing, and number of Cafres, or Slaves, to serve them; having some of these to carry them in Palanchines on their Shoulders and other great Umbrelloes of Palm-Tree Leaves."[58] The charges for hiring non-slaves to carry the Palanquines was a perfunctory sum, so "they that have no Slaves, pay four Indians but twelve Coslines of Naples a Month for carrying them."[59] The implication is, of course, that there was an abundance of slaves.

Another traveller, Careri, told the story of a son of a neighboring king who came to visit and had two slaves to accompany him. At the place of the visit there were no chairs available so the princeling "caus'd his two Slaves to squat down and sate upon them."[60]

Abbé Carré's observations concur with these social conditions at the end of the seventeenth century. In Daman "most of the houses are filled with women who make dainties and sweets, with troops of slaves, who have hardly any food but rice and fish."[61] Carré left an elaborate account of the slaves of landholders:

> On Tuesday, 22 November, I had prepared all my equipage to leave at day-break, but received a message from a P. fidalgo, Dom Francisco Gonsalve de St. Paye, one of the richest citizens of Daman, asking me to wait an hour for him, as he wished to accompany me to Tarapur, where, he was going to visit his farms and tenancies. I waited till seven o'clock, when I saw my Portuguese arriving with an escort of slaves armed with matchlocks, javelins, and some sort of blunderbuss . . . I was amazed at the weight of the arms which these Caffres are obliged to carry. . . .[62]

In Goa proper the Abbé considered that practically everyone must have been outfitted with some Negroes and other "large suites of slaves. . . . [Everyone], Bakers, fruiterers, and party-cooks, were in clover; and above all those who dealt in human flesh, with which this town is full, made wonderful profits."[63] He even extended his observations on the master-slave relationship to the Portuguese colony at Madras where the Portuguese men "Day and night... cannot rest themselves without a dozen mosses, i.e. female slaves to massage and knead their bodies."[64]

It appears that black, African slaves were, at various periods, considered a luxury and prestige element, and the Abbé recorded an incident to which others allude as fairly common practice. On the arrival of any gentleman, or nobleman, or person of major rank, the "Noble ladies sent their kafir slaves to escort him."[65] A similar situation was described by Fryer who noted their special role and observed that although cafirs initially arrived as slaves, "they have become as endeared to their Master, who, as they merit, have the first places of Honor and trust imposed upon them...."[66]

There were, however, definite distinctions between the races in legal matters. For example, orphanages and the care of illegitimate and unfortunate children occupied a certain amount of interest among the religious orders and some secular organizations. The reasons were essentially those of acquisition of labor and salvation of souls. Records on the famous Convent of Santa Monica reveal the nuns' complaints that the 120 slaves allotted them was insufficient and pointed out that even European, Eurasian, or mulatto artisans could have "15 or 20 female slaves," or "26 women and girls," while a *juiz ordinaria* (judge) or a *desembargador* (lawyer) held "85 female slaves... and some rich ladies had over 300."[67] These documents indicate vast numbers of slaves in Goa and also are supportive of the Portuguese colonial ideal that maintenance of large slave households lends social status and personal prestige to a person.

Another aspect of slavery seems to have been that particular members of various religious communities were assigned legal responsibilities of guardianship. This practice, in Portuguese communities in India, defined differences in the ethnic composition of the children. For each orphanage, two persons were appointed under an *ouvidor*, (i.e. one who would hear cases and oversee affairs): One man was designated for the whites and another was assigned to the blacks,[68] a practice continued by the British when Cooke assumed control of Bombay from the Portuguese in 1665 (Bombay was part of the dowry of Catherine of Braganza to Charles II of England). Again, we are not certain if this implied *all* non-Portuguese occupying these pockets of western India but it probably does include any African orphans, illegitimate offspring of a relationship which the Master refused to sanction.

The synonymous usage of the term *Cafir* for slave indicates the apparently widespread utilization of Africans as bondsmen in western India's coastal sectors, at least in those areas frequented by the Portuguese. However, the seemingly pittance fees paid to free men to undertake tasks for which there was insufficient slave labor available indicates a rather low economic and social position for workers in general in Portuguese colonial society. Documents and time have supported the Fleming Cleynaerts's assessment of the Iberian contempt for manual labor, that for the *fidalgo* it was less shameful to beg than to work with one's hands, a station in life best filled by foreigners, natives, and slaves.[69]

This contempt for manual labor by the *fidalgo* stratum of society necessitated a goodly supply of servile labor. To this end, in the sixteenth and seventeenth centuries a constant trade in slaves was carried on within India and between India and Africa. The Italian Careri, traveling in the seventeenth century, had himself purchased a slave at a sum low enough to indicate either a sudden decline in the esteem of blacks or, even more likely, an oversupply for the demand. "My Armenian Servant, refusing to go to China, on Wednesday 11th, I bought a Cafre, or Black Slave for eighteen Pieces of Eight."[70] Although the slave was available and willing to accompany Careri, the Italian was forced to obtain a license to ship the slave because the carrier was touching at Malacca [where the Dutch were]. He "went on Thursday 12th, to the Inquisitors to have it Pass'd. They made a great difficulty of granting it... alledging that some Cafres, who had been Shipp'd at other times, being taken, had turn'd Mahometans."[71]

Careri, who travelled at the end of the seventeenth century, supports the contention that African slaves were numerous throughout Portuguese India:

There are also abundance of *Cafres* and Blacks; for there are Portuguese that keep thirty, or fourty, and the "least six or twelve; to carry their umbrella, and Andora, and other mean Employments; nor are they at any other charge to keep them, but a Dish of Rice at Noon, and another at Night; for they have no other Garments but what they brought out of their Mothers Wombs.[72]

The Italian also described the carriage of slave cargoes to India's West Coast: "The Slaves are carry'd to sell at Goa, and all along the Portuguese Towns, by the Company's Ships belonging to Lisborn and India, who buy them at Monbaza, Mozambique, Zofala, and other Ports along the Coast of Africa."[73]

Careri attributed the superfluity of blacks available in Africa, as did most of his contemporaries, to the constant warfare among African tribal groups. He claimed that the "nations" at war captured slaves and sold them; that children were sold into slavery by their parents; and that many adults, in desperation, often sold themselves as slaves. All of those factors are undoubtedly true. There were problems of survival related to population pressure, food deficiencies, and political turmoil. However, Careri and his contemporaries failed to note that the increase in turmoil and the possible increment in tribal conflicts were due in part to the increased awareness by Africans of European and Arabic interest in human cargo. Hence, the more modern view of the availability of African slaves due to tribal conflict correctly places part of the responsibility on the traders themselves. Nonetheless, there was an abundance of slaves for the trade and "They being very cheap, that is, 15 or 20 Crowns of Naples a Head, it is no wonder there should be such numbers of them, and that the very Vintners keep them to sell their Wine. . . ."[74]

Other travellers, in later journeys to Portuguese possessions, left testimonies agreeing with earlier visitors on persisting patterns of slave sale and functions in the Portuguese enclaves.[75] The pervasiveness of the black in his new environs is noticeable in the later archival records. "I declare that all the mosses who are vulgarly called negresses, whom I have in my house, and who have served me for many years are free in becoming New Christians . . ."[76]

In a process of liquidation of losses and other claims filed in the court at Goa city by a family, mention was made of the common practice among the Portuguese in India of the "assistence" of cafre servant boys.[77]

The carrying of slaves on ships plying between the coasts of eastern Africa and western India continued into the nineteenth century. Evidence of this appears in records on the rather steady increase of piracy along the route. In documents devoted to the problem of pirating of slave cargoes between Daman and Mozambique, Portuguese captains lamented that excessive numbers of cafres died in such expeditions and that many of the cargoes (remaining) were sold to the French who were resident in Daman for that purpose![78]

After several centuries of Christian domination the concept of the slave as a piece of merchandise had changed little, despite Pombaline edicts against slavery and prohibition of slave transport "from America, Asia, and Africa to the Kingdom."[79] In 1783–1784 there are records of "black men" sold in Lisbon and other apparently illegal situations according to the cases of formal court charges against such practice.[80] A

few decades later such records as sales of "goods available" included a "Negress called Maria with her two sons"[81] and in another area, in Chimbel, additional notices of goods available included a "Negress with her two sons,"[82] while in court processes of liquidations, etc. a "Negress called Rita" was identified as part of the estate of one Sebastiao Joaquim Monteiro.[83]

One of many court records of the above type listed the proceedings about the death of twenty-six cafres belonging to one Joao Rebelo de Albuquerque, who "were part of the overload of the ship Santo Antonio Triunfo de Africa."[84] The fact that so many slaves were part of a single shipload, and that so many died or were killed for expediency's sake, indicates that the traffic to India in African labor was still an active concern in the early nineteenth century. Ten years later the advertisements of marketplace buying and selling included such items as:

gold and silver
....
four cafres by the names of Ventura, Joze, Passarinho, and Furtuno
one Negress named Junevita
four pigs with ten sucklings
....[85]

There are notices of purchases of freedom by slaves as well as the fairly common practice of slaves being given their freedom by their masters, but the notices are relatively few compared to the instances of court actions and confiscations or selling of Negroes as household merchandise or livestock. Nonetheless, an example of the ability of slaves to purchase and to petition for their freedom is found in requests of slave girls in the royal cloth factory at Polvora, Goa. His Majesty, in his compassion, would free the girls given the price, on their account or another's to "the said Natalia, Dulcine, Genoviva, Anna, Maria, Josefa, Rital, and Maria Chimbel."[86] There are also, in the *assentas baptismo* and *Registos baptismos,* records of the births of many of the Cafirs' children in Daman as well as their marriages and baptisms. There seem to have been rare instances of marriages of Cafirs with Goans except in Salcete and among the very lower classes.

Such is some evidence available in archival records and travellers' accounts of the transfer, presence, and treatment of the African in Portuguese India. The materials offer a number of observations. The first is that Africans not only from the east but also from the west coasts of that continent were utilized as slave labor. It might also be possible to assume, as in instances of the Black Jews in Kerala, that Africans were purchased and utilized, earlier than the

Portuguese presence, as slave labor by the Indians themselves through some trading mechanisms exclusive of Arabic or Portuguese involvement. There is reason to believe that wealthy Indians, who had a practice of slavery as a system of labor among their own peoples and within the strictures of their own caste system, would not ignore the availability of an external labor supply. This would seem quite plausible in view of the flourishing trade in tribal peoples and other groups, as mentioned by Manrique and other travellers, along the eastern coast of India. It can also be assumed from available evidence pertinent to Hindu and Muslim societies that slaves would be held by families of both religious groups.

A second point of observation is that the African was a valued item in trade because he fulfilled a number of tasks which Indians either could not (because of caste restrictions) or would not perform, or for which the Portuguese deemed themselves and the Indians to be unsuited. There are indications also that the African slave enjoyed a rather unusual position, at varying times, as a prestige servant or in the case of females, as suited for amorous duties in a household. The Portuguese treatment of the African in India follows much the same pattern as his actions in Brazil and other territories of empire. Cruelties and inhumane treatment were generally a part of the slave milieu but, as has been seen, in the African's role as a domestic he was often well treated and also highly regarded in relation to the indigenous populations of the places to which he was imported.

A thorough and exhaustive investigation of the socio-racial policy of the Portuguese Crown must be undertaken before postulating a definitive analysis or judgment regarding the position of the African as well as other enthralled peoples in the Portuguese imperial scheme. There are paradoxes in the policy as it was fashioned at the time by Iberian legal codes and Catholic philosophic enquiries. There also are gaps in our knowledge about the existing patterns of conduct, legal and social, by many of the inhabitants of territories visited by the Portuguese. All of these investigations must be undertaken before we can affect modern judgments on centuries-old social and economic relations among the races. Meanwhile, it is hoped that this initial overview of records and accounts will contribute new insights into and add impetus to study a hitherto neglected chapter in South Asian history: the presence of the African in India.

Notes

*The author wishes to thank the University of California, Los Angeles, and the Ford Foundation Grant in International and Comparative studies for funds to conduct the research on this paper. Materials for this paper were gathered during January and February, 1969, in Panaji, Goa, India. For their help in locating documents, I wish to thank the Director of the Arquivo Nacional, Mr. Gune, and his assistant.

The travel accounts and some of the documents consulted are published but for the most part the information in archival sources exists only in MS form in the Goan archives.
**The term African is used in this article to mean anyone from, or whose ancestors were from, the continent of Africa.

---

[1] Habshi means people of Habash, i.e., Abyssinia.

[2] See, e.g., G. Yazdani, *B dar; its history and monuments*, (Oxford, 1947), pp. 82ff. for information on and gathered from tombs of Abyssinian nobles and soldiers scattered throughout this region.

[3] Ibn Battuta, *Travels*, trans. H. A. R. Gibb, (Cambridge, 1929), pp. 224, 229, 236, 260.

[4] For presence of the Habshi as generals, administrators, kingmakers, and in positions of power and prestige, see R. C. Majumdar, H. C. Raychaudri, and K. Datta, *An Advanced History of India*, (London, 1948); and R. Pankhurst, *An introduction to the economic history of Ethiopia*, (London, 1961) Appendix E.

[5] *Muwallads* are mixed bloods: African fathers and Indian mothers.

[6] Henry H. Dodwell (ed.) *The Cambridge History of India*, I-V, (Cambridge, 1928), III, pp. 403–404.

[7] K. K. Basu, *The Tarikh-i-Mubarak Shadi*, (1932).

[8] *H djdj al Dab r, Zafar ul-walih* (n.d.) pp. i., 97, 407, 447. (An official court record assumed to be written by an unnamed court official. The copy is in the Institute Vasco da Gama, Panaji, Goa.)

[9] See the *Ma'athir al-umar'*, the register of Mughal nobility, for biographies of prominent Habshis. Unfortunately, due to the nature of Muslim genealogical historical writing we know practically nothing about the ordinary citizen's daily affairs.

[10] See, e.g., C. F. Beckingham, "Amba Gesen and Asirgarh," *Journal of Semitic Studies*, II, (1957), 182–188.

[11] See Robert I. Rotberg, *A Political History of Tropical Africa*, (New York, 1965), pp. 152–153 for speculation on sources and quantities involved in the African slave trade to Asia.

[12] See S. D. Goitein, "From the Mediterranean to India: Documents on the Trade to India, South Arabia, and East Africa, from the Eleventh and Twelfth Centuries," *Speculum*, XXIX, 2, (1954), pp. 181–197 for the composition of the trade and traders.

[13] *Cartas de Affonso de Albuquerque*, I–VII, (Lisboa, 1884–1935), II, p. 282. See also Alexandre Lobato, *A Expansão Portuguesa em Moçambique de 1488 a 1530*, I–III, (Lisboa, 1954–1960), I, pp. 75, 81.

[14] Jan Linschoten, *Voyage*, I–II, (London, Hakluyt Series 1, 1885), I, pp. 70–71, 264–265.

[15] *ibid.*, I, pp. 275.

[16] *Provisões, alvaras e regimentos*, unpublished documents, bound in two volumes (Evora, 1515–1598), I, fls. 17 vs, 2 March 1520. For a published account on the Portuguese slave trade see K. G. Jayne, *Vasco da Gama and his Successors*, (London, 1910), pp. 22ff.

[17] Commentaries of the Great Affonso de Albuquerque, I–IV, (London, 1774), IV, p. 21.

[18]*ibid.*, IV, p. 28.

[19]*Livro das Monções do Reino*, MS in bound volumes, (Panaji, 1585–1593), V, fl. 34v (in the old numbering it is volume 3B).

[20]The White Jews are supposedly refugees from Spanish and Portuguese persecutions against the "new Christians" or non-convertible Jews of the sixteenth and seventeenth centuries.

[20a]The Indic terms *varna* and *jati* have no precise English equivalents. The term *varna* has been translated as "class," and the term *jati* as "caste," both designations unknown until the arrival of the Europeans. In the Indic sense *varna* and *jati* do not imply the same meanings as class and caste.

[21]According to Basham there was no caste of slaves; the *Artha stra* claims that an individual of any caste might become a slave, while for the Aryan the term *dra* (or lowest of the four *varna*) is explicitly included for slave. The *d sa*, or member of the peoples conquered by the Aryans, was used to indicate slave and Basham says that the word implies bondsman or serf rather than a chattel slave. A. L. Basham, *The Wonder that was India*, (New York, 1954), pp. 151–153. Davis points out for the western and Mediterranean-Middle eastern worlds (as well as Asia) that slaves have generally been defined as chattels personal, unqualified for legal marriage, property ownership, or judicial testimony; but, he also points out, no slave system in history was quite like that of the West Indies and of the southern states of the United States. The various terms to describe "slave" and the contrary nature of other servile institutions is discussed in detail in David Brion Davis, *The Problem of Slavery in Western Culture*, (Ithaca, Cornell University Press, 1966). For Africa, see Basil Davidson, "Slaves or Captives? Some Notes on Fantasy and Fact," in Nathan I. Huggins, Martin Kilson, and Daniel M. Fox, eds., *Key issues in the Afro-American Experience*, I–II, (New York, Harcourt Brace Jovanovich, 1971), I, pp. 54–73.

[22]Charles R. Boxer, *Portuguese Society in the Tropics. The Municipal Councils of Goa, Macao, Bahia, and Luanda, 1510–1800*, (Madison, The University of Wisconsin Press, 1965), p. 13.

[23]*ibid.*, p. 37.

[24]*ibid.*, p. 13.

[25]*ibid.*, p. 40.

[26]José Frederico Ferreira Martins, *História da Misericordia de Goa, 1520–1910*, I–III, (Nova Goa, 1910–1914).

[27]Charles R. Boxer, *The Portuguese Seaborne Empire*, (New York, Alfred A. Knopf, Inc., 1969), p. 302.

[28]*ibid.*, p. 302.

[29]This information can be studied in the various collections of documents of the Câmaras. A partial inventory is listed in Boxer, *Portuguese Society*, Appendixes, pp. 153–218.

[30]*Provisões a favor da Cristandade* (15: 3–1840), I, fl. 42v. Evora, 14 March 1533 (date of the testimonial card: 11 April 1551); fl. 40v., Lisboa, 24 March 1559.

[31]*ibid.*, fls. 98v., Goa, 5 November 1593.

[32]*ibid.*, fls. 113, Madrid, 26 January 1599. The latter was noted from Madrid because during the years 1580–1640 the Portuguese Crown came under the control of Spain. See also, for the sufferings of the slaves, *Livro das Monções do Reino*, I, (1560–1601), 26 January 1599, fl. 95.

[33]*ibid.*, fls. 113.

[34]*ibid.*, fls. 109, Goa, 10 September 1658.

[35]*Provisões e Regimentos*, I–II (1539–1614), I, fls. 107v. Goa, 3 September 1609. On November 31 1592, Viceroy Mathias de Albuquerque proclaimed that slaves of infidels who converted themselves to Christianity would be freed. See Cunha Rivare, ed., *Arquivo Português Oriental*, (1865), Fasc. V, pt. iii, Doc. 983, p. 1300.

[36]Linschoten, *Voyage*, I, 185.

[37]*Viagem de Francisco Pyrard de Laval*, I–II, (Porto, 1944), p. 50. I have used the Portuguese version of this account by the intelligent and knowledgeable Italian scholar who travelled in India in the early seventeenth century. There is an English version entitled *The Travels of Pietro della Valle in India*, edited by E. Grey, in two volumes by the Hakluyt Society, (London, 1892).

[38]*ibid.*, p. 50.

[39]*ibid.*, p. 50.

[40]*ibid.*, p. 51.

[41]*ibid.*, p. 51. The term Negro or Negress from *Guine* designated one who was from the western coast of Africa. *Cafre, cafra*, or *Kafir* usually referred to blacks from the East Coast of Africa. The word *kafir* is a term applied by the Arabs to pagan Negroes and means an infidel, or a nonbeliever in Islam. It was adopted by the Portuguese and later by other Europeans. These designations are minuscule segments of the complex linguistic formulae involved in the sixteenth century philosophical enquiries over the legal and natural condition of pagan and Christian or Muslim man. An interesting singular insight into this situation as it occured in the India trade is the issuance of a *cartaz* (the pass bought from the Portuguese and a prerequisite for trade and travel in Portuguese-controlled waters) on a 1613 voyage from Dabhol to Jiddah: The ship could not transport slaves unless they were from Bijapur and *not* Christian! See J. F. J. Biker, *Colleção de Tratadôs*, (Lisboa, 1921), iv., pp. 181–2.

[42]*Pyrard de Laval*, pp. 56–7.

[43]A letter from the Jesuit Nicolas Lancilotta to Ignatius Loyola, quoted in A. da Silva Rego, ed., *Documentação para a historia das missões do padroado portugues do Oriente India*, I–XII, (Lisboa, 1947), VII, pp. 32ff. See also the report of Padre Valignano in XII, pp. 577–81.

[44]*Pyrard de Laval*, II, 52.

[45]*The Travels of the Abbé Carré in India and the Near East 1672–1674*, I–III, Series II of the Hakluyt Society, XCX–XCVII, (London, 1947), I, p. 242.

[46]*ibid.*, p. 245. *Fidalgo* (or in Spanish *hidalgo*) is derived from the combination *of fil (ho) d'algo*, i.e. the son of someone.

[47]*ibid.*, II, p. 342.

[48]*Pyrard de Laval*, II, p. 52.

[49]*ibid.*, 000.

[50]This supplements evidence from Brazilian sources of the domineering position that the Portuguese wife assumed in the direction of household affairs. In fact, a probable consistency of practice in various Portuguese colonies was that the Negress as slave suffered an uncomfortable existence at the whims of her Portuguese mistress.

[51]Linschoten, *Voyages*, I, p. 32.

[52]*Pyrard de Laval*, II, 55. Five *basarucos* were calculated to equal nearly six *dinheiros* of the day, accurate value

unknown. Twenty-five *basarucos* equalled six *brancos*, value also unknown. The editors of the edition I have used indicate that the six *brancos* possibly equal two *escudos* in the equivalent rate of the Portuguese currency of the time of the edition or about one Indian rupee or 13.5 United States cents.

[53]Linschoten, *Voyages*, I, pp. 193–4. See also, II, p. 257.

[54]*Pyrard de Laval*, II, pp. 58–9. The Palanquine was a type of litter, for one or two persons, and common throughout the interior provinces of India and parts of Asia.

[55]John Fryer, *A New Account of East India and Persia*, I–III, (London, 1909), I, p. 62.

[56]Linschoten, *Voyages*, I, p. 193.

[56a]Portuguese India, other than the occasional territories, consisted of the enclaves of Goa, Daman, and Diu. They lost the so-called Northern Territories in the 1737–1740 war with the Marathas.

[57]S. N. Sen, ed., *Indian Travels of Careri and Thevenot*, (Delhi, National Archives of India, 1949), Chapter XLVIII, p. 116. Jean Thevenot (1633–1667), was a Frenchman and a student of geography and ethnology who travelled in the western areas of India.

[58]*ibid.*, p. 116.

[59]*ibid.*, p. 160. "Coslines of Naples" is from the Italian "cosa-llino," meaning a thing of trifling value and designating the smallest coin in use in Naples at the time.

[60]*ibid.*, p 189.

[61]*Travels of the Abbé Carré*, I, p. 168.

[62]*ibid.*, I, p. 172.

[63]*ibid.*, II, p. 398.

[64]*ibid.*, II, p. 522. The word "mosses" appears to be a Portuguese or French corruption of the French *macer* or *masser*, meaning "to massage" and so designated by another traveller Le Gentil (*Voyage des mers de l'Inde*, I, 128) in 1770. It assumed that the word was used by French colonists in India. It is also conjectured that it is from the Arabic *mass*, to rub or touch, and as a possessive derivative from the Arabic *masis*, one who rubs or touches. The editor of the Carré volume points out that if the last is the case then it is "an incorrect active participle for *mass*."

[65]*ibid.*, III, p. 740.

[66]Fryer, *A New Account . . .*, II, p. 52.

[67]Agostinho de Santa Maria, *Historia do Real Convento de Santa Monica*, (Lisboa, 1699), pp. 263, 358–9, and Francisco de Sousa, S. J., *Oriente Conquistado a Jesu Christo pelos Padres da Companhia de Jesus da Provincia de Goa*, I–II, (Lisboa, 1710), I, pp. 739–40.

[68]*Travels of the Abbé Carré*, I, p. 168, N. 1.

[69]From Cleynaerts' *desamor ao trabalho*, cited in M. Gonçalves Cerejeira, *Clenardo e a sociedado portuguesa do seu tempo*, (Coimbra, 1949), pp. 159–89, 203–21.

[70]Sen, *Indian Travels . . .*, p. 272. Giovanni Gemelli-Careri, a Neapolitan noble and lawyer, travelled along the western coast during the last years of the seventeenth century.

[71]*ibid.*, p. 272.

[72]*ibid.*, p. 188.

[73]*ibid.*

[74]*ibid.*, pp. 188–9.

[75]Other travellers' accounts of value include *The Travels of Sebastian Manrique 1629–43*, I–II, in the Hakluyt Series II, (London, 1926–1927); J. S. Hoyland and S. N. Banerji, eds., and trans., *The Commentary of Father Monserrate*, (London: Oxford University Press, 1922); a book concerned solely with the sixteenth century. Others include Jean B. Tavernier, *Travels in India*, I–II, and the various collections compiled by such men as John Pinkerton, Richard Hakluyt, John C. Locke, Samuel Purchas, et al.

[76]*Feitoria Mandados de prisão e supersedencia*, in one volume (1804–1832). The testament is dated 27 May 1706 in proc. 3, fls. 15, *Arquivo Historico*, Goa. Also see *Livro das Monções . . .*, vol. 117, doc. from 1690.

[77]*Feitoria. Esbulbos; liquidação de perdas, danos, e interesses*, (1723–1834), I, fls. 127 (1723), proc., 1.

[78]*Feitoria. Tomadias*, I–IV, (1772–1834), I, proc. 2, fls. 72 (1776) and fls. 81.

[79]*Livro das Monções do Reino*, CXXXV, fls. 303 (12 October 1761). Pombal was the Chief Minister of Portugal who, from 1750–1777 ruled that empire in the tradition of an enlightened despot.

[80]*Feitoria. Causas de libelo*, I–II (1784–1831), I, proc. 1, fls. 25 (1784) and proc. 2, fls. 25 (1783).

[81]*Feitoria. Inventarios*, I–VII, (1730–1833), III, proc. 2, fls. 109, (1807), fls. 6v.

[82]*ibid.*, proc. 25, fls. 220 (1808).

[83]*ibid. Penhoras e execuções*, I–LXIII, (1735–1834), XXVI, proc. 1, (1809).

[84]*ibid. Justificações*, I–VII, (1717–1833), IV, proc. 2, fls. 52 (1813).

[85]*ibid. Inventarios*, I–VII, (1730–1833), V, proc. 4, fls. 125 (1825).

[86]*ibid. Arrematações*, I, (1736–1834), I, proc. 16, fls. 45, on the auction of these slave girls.

Anti-Black Racism in Post-Mao China*

Barry Sautman

Expressions of anti-black sentiment by Chinese students have caught the world's attention periodically since the end of the 1970s. Demonstrations against African students in Nanjing and other cities between late 1988 and early 1989 received wide press coverage. Because the African population in China is small and transient, some observers saw these events as a manifestation of a vestigial xenophobia, not as part of a developing trend of thought within a key segment of Chinese society. Placed next to the brutal ethnic conflicts that plague much of the world, the episodic, non-lethal incidents in China seemed evanescent, with only fleeting implications for China's foreign policy.

Anti-black racism in China may however have greater importance than was initially apparent. First, reform-era racism calls into question China's credentials as a leader of the Third World. Secondly, because the anti-African clashes created an unprecedented situation where those persecuted were themselves part of the proto-elites of foreign states, there may be long-term consequences for Sino-African relations. Thirdly, Chinese elite involvement in expressions of racial hostility suggests that domestic intolerance may also have a role in moulding external affairs. Policy-makers may consciously or unconsciously hold racial stereotypes, as among some American politicians.[1]

This article will examine the Chinese–African student clashes of the first decade of China's reform and suggest some explanations for them. The results of survey research conducted in several Chinese cities in 1992 will be used to gauge the racial views of students and intellectuals and offer a theory of anti-black prejudice based on an analogous elite disdain for China's peasants.

Precursors

African students first arrived in China in 1960 as part of a Chinese government programme of fully paid university education for the nationals of friendly countries. It was an attempt to "win hearts and minds" and bolster China's Third World credentials in the wake of the Sino-Soviet split. In 1961–62 118 African students came to study in China. They were mostly from elite backgrounds, but encountered a spartan, puritanical and politicized environment in their host country. Although their stipends were many times those of Chinese students,[2] the Africans soon became dissatisfied with their low living standards. While there were no reports of generalized anti-black hostility initially, the March 1962 beating of a Zanzibari by Beijing hotel attendants in a dispute over the sale of cigarettes led to sit-ins and hunger strikes by Africans, most of whom returned home. Africans returned to China in the early 1970s, but in 1972 about a dozen students at the Beijing Railroad Engineering School were so discontented with their living standards that they deliberately burned portraits of Mao Zedong so that they would be deported.[3]

A hostile account by a former African student makes clear that among the factors that caused them to react adversely to their life in Maoist China (including pervasive politics, low living standards and a dearth of social opportunities), racial hostility was the least important.[4] At the same time China backed anti-colonial and revolutionary movements in Africa[5] and anti-racism featured in Mao's pronouncements on Africa and the black diaspora.[6] Red Guards held rallies to support oppressed peoples, including blacks, and no one would have openly expressed hostility to students from developing countries.[7]

The problems that were to plague relations between African students and Chinese in the reform era were of a different order from those of earlier years. Questions of social isolation and living standards continued to play a role in discontent among Africans in the late 1970s and 1980s, but there was also a marked downplaying of Third World themes in the Chinese media and a rise of antagonism toward Africans by Chinese students, expressed in racial epithets and assaults. Incidents of anti-African prejudice were moreover often excused, if not justified, by the authorities.[8]

The Shanghai Incident of 1979

The first major clash between Chinese and African students occurred seven months after the December 1978 Third Plenum of the Eleventh Central Committee of the Chinese Communist Party initiated the post-Mao reform era.[9] An altercation at the Shanghai Textile Engineering Institute in July 1979 set a pattern for a series of conflicts between Chinese and African students that culminated in the 1988–89 Nanjing racial turmoil.

The Shanghai incident began on 3 July, during an examination period. Chinese students complained of loud music played by Africans at

202

night, and referred to them during a confrontation as "black devils" *(hei gui)*. In the ensuing scuffle, a Chinese attempting to mediate was stabbed and injuries were incurred on both sides. The next morning, Africans were stoned and the foreign student hall of residence besieged by Chinese hurling bricks.[10] African students called the police, but officers did not arrive for several hours and failed to intervene as fighting continued throughout the day. Yemeni students who came to the Institute to assist the Africans were attacked by Chinese using iron bars. There were several serious injuries and an ambulance that arrived at 5 p.m. to pick up injured Africans was overturned by Chinese students.

On the evening of 4 July, a Malian was beaten when he emerged from the hall of residence. Deemed "too light" by his attackers, he was doused with ink. The siege continued into the small hours of the morning, when the authorities ordered the hall evacuated. The evacuees—mostly Africans—were attacked as they left and their possessions were destroyed as police stood by. Sixteen foreign students were hospitalized, but as many as 50 foreigners and 24 Chinese may have been injured. Chinese students finally dispersed after a broadcast appeal by Vice-Premier Fang Yi.

The foreign students, who called a strike and complained of police brutality and incitement, were sequestered in a hotel outside the city. Most initially sought repatriation. One Mauritanian was in fact deported after being accused of raping a Chinese woman, charges which other Africans disputed. Some foreigners attributed the fight to Chinese student dissatisfaction with low allowances. Diplomats who travelled to Shanghai were unable to resolve the situation to the satisfaction of the African students.[11]

Two weeks after the incident, 100 Africans demonstrated in Beijing's diplomatic quarter. They called upon African countries to stop sending students to China and noted that there had also been anti-African demonstrations in Shenyang and Guangzhou. Chinese press commentaries admitted that Chinese students had unreasonably refused to be dissuaded from attacking the foreign students, but implied that the Shanghai incident was provoked by an assault on Chinese and reflected a penchant for troublemaking by drunken and womanizing Africans.[12] The clashes resulted in an effort to educate young Shanghainese in "internationalism" and some joint Chinese–African tea parties.[13] The CCP Central Committee issued an internal circular in early 1982 urging greater understanding toward African students in order to safeguard China's image.[14] The insufficiency of these efforts was clear, however, when further clashes between Chinese and Third World students took place in Shanghai in 1980 and 1982.[15]

The Tianjin Incident

In 1982, more than 400 of the 1,800 foreign students in China were Africans. By 1988, there were some 1,500 Africans among 6,000 foreign students.[16] The vast majority were males who took one year of language training and a four to six year technical curriculum. Virtually none had an opportunity for a home visit.

In the 1980s, the theme of tensions over social relations between foreign men and Chinese women, obliquely alluded to by commentators in connection with the Shanghai incident, was raised directly by the authorities through arrests and deportations of Africans (but not whites) who had Chinese girlfriends. Although their friendships with foreign men were not technically illegal, such women were often considered traitors or prostitutes and subjected to loss of employment and arrest, especially where the foreigner was black. Many individual incidents between Chinese and Africans erupted over contact between African men and Chinese women.[17]

African students became acutely sensitive on this and other questions involving racial hostility. For example, a letter that contained racial slurs and threatened Africans who associated with Chinese women circulated on Beijing campuses in January 1987. Although the letter did not emanate from any official organization, African students treated it as expressive of thinking among many Chinese and staged a class boycott and illegal protest march.[18] This harassment was part of a more general bias perceived by Africans, who complained of being ignored by shop assistants and teachers and of experiencing frequent racial taunting. Chinese students reportedly often saw their African colleagues as "uncultured." Many were said to view Africans negatively as peasants because the Chinese media only showed Africans as poor recipients of aid from China.[19]

Instances of hostility led to protests by Africans during the first half of the 1980s. They demonstrated in Nanjing in 1980 after posters appeared in which Chinese students expressed resentment over their government's provision of food and clothing to African students.[20] When a Burundian was beaten by seven Beijing hotel attendants in a dispute concerning the sale of beer in 1983, Africans staged a protest. The authorities arrested two of the attendants, implying acknowledgment that a racial problem existed.[21] In 1985, Africans planned a march in Beijing and Sudanese students struck after two of their number were beaten by Shanghai police during a brawl aboard a bus.[22] These incidents were minor, however, compared with the clash that began at Tianjin University on 25 May 1986.

As in Shanghai in 1979, the Tianjin incident grew out of complaints of loud music. Some 25 foreigners (mostly Africans and Arabs, but including some Americans and Europeans) and three Chinese women were besieged at the campus site of a party held to mark the anniversary of the Organization of African Unity (OAU). The fight began at about 11:30 p.m. after Chinese students preparing for a physics competition asked the foreigners to turn down their music. The Chinese claimed that two Africans attacked them with bottles, injuring seven people. The foreigners asserted that the Chinese engaged in an unprovoked assault and barricaded a university dining hall. It was soon surrounded by 400–600 Chinese, who hurled bricks and bottles, causing much damage and some minor injuries. Police arrived at 5.30 a.m. and removed the foreigners. Twelve African and six Arab and South Asian students were taken to a hotel and detained. They were allegedly told that their release required an admission of guilt.[23]

Chinese officials denied that racism was involved in the incident and proclaimed an end to the "misunderstanding." The 18 students refused, however, to return to campus because of fears for their safety.[24] Their disquiet was fuelled by a march of 500 Chinese on the Tianjin municipal offices on 28 May at which legal action against the foreigners was demanded. About 150 Chinese besieged the foreign halls of residence at Nankai University on 31 May, but were dispersed. They then entered the Tianjin University foreign student hall, kicking in doors in a search for the detainees. Officials told the 18 students that their Chinese classmates were planning an attack. The foreign students fled to Beijing,[25] where a march of 200–300 Africans took place on 6 June. Demands were made of the Ministry of Education for an end to racism and better security. Anti-African incidents at campuses in Nanjing, Shenyang and Xi'an were also reported.[26]

The Chinese authorities denounced the African march and attributed anti-African incidents to "cultural misunderstanding." Tianjin University officials and the State Education Commission (SEC) blamed the incident on the foreign students. Vice-Premier Li Peng told reporters that the incidents reflected the excitability of youth. Some observers ventured that jealousy over better housing—foreign students lived 2–3 to a room, while Chinese students were 5–6 to a room—might have played a role. African students reported that Chinese involved in the Tianjin incident seemed more upset about the presence of Chinese women at the dance than about noise. An anonymous SEC member, however, stated that both cultural factors and racial hostility were involved.[27]

African diplomats who investigated the Tianjin incident were unsuccessful in obtaining security guarantees from the Chinese authorities. Some ambassadors recommended that their governments send fewer students to China until the situation changed[28] and there was adverse commentary in the African media.[29] Most of the 18 detained students returned to Tianjin University at the end of June[30] and a campaign among Chinese students in July to collect relief aid for Africa was widely publicized.[31] The number of black Africans enrolled at Chinese universities nevertheless fell during the 1986–87 academic year.[32]

Anti-African Incidents in 1988–89

In April 1988, Communist Party head Zhao Ziyang stated that racial discrimination was common "everywhere in the world except China."[33] Clashes that began at Nanjing's Hehai University on Christmas Eve 1988, however, involved the most open, mass and sustained display to date of hostility to Africans in China. No fatalities were involved, but at their peak the 1988–89 attacks on Africans had the makings of an incipient pogrom. The clashes at Hehai are well-recorded in Michael Sullivan's accompanying article, and are thus not dealt with in detail here.

If Nanjing had been the only city in late 1988–early 1989 to witness an outbreak of racial hostility, the Chinese government's claim that it was an isolated incident might have convinced observers who lacked a knowledge of past Sino-African student clashes. Soon after the initial altercation in Nanjing, however, anti-African incidents broke out in several other cities.

In Hangzhou on 26 December, some 60 Zhejiang Agricultural University African students began a class boycott to protest against accusations that they were AIDS carriers. Several incidents triggered the boycott. A local newspaper cited the high incidence of the disease in some African countries as grounds for supposing that the African students had AIDS. Blacks were taunted by the monicker *aizibing* (AIDS), even though they had registered negative on the required HIV test and the risk of AIDS in China stems mainly from the lack of a system of detection of HIV in blood donors, not the presence of foreigners.[34] The university reportedly enacted regulations forbidding Chinese to enter the foreign student hall of residence and withdrew its Chinese staff. A university operator allegedly told callers to the hall that the Africans had AIDS.

Three days after the boycott began, a university finance officer visiting the hall was taken hostage and held in an office, from where he escaped after nine hours. The hall was surrounded by police, its water shut off and its canteen closed. Some Africans tried to leave Hangzhou, but were stopped by police. The strike ended on 5 January when authorities accepted the students' demand for a direct telephone link and a public pledge that there was no policy of trying to isolate them by claiming that they had AIDS.[35]

On 2 January, about 300 Chinese students and teachers at the Beijing Language Institute put up posters and demonstrated outside a foreign student hall to demand punishment of a man described as an African who had entered a Chinese women's hall the previous evening and accosted a student. The woman was injured when she fell on glass while fleeing. Leaflets distributed at the protest urged authorities to "protect our women." About 2,000 Chinese students at the Institute boycotted classes. Posters also appeared at Beijing University accusing blacks of lawlessness.

The perpetrator in the harassment incident was described as garbed in a stocking mask that revealed only his eyes. Africans demanded proof that one of their number was involved and charged that the Chinese protest had been staged with official approval in order to justify the anti-African outbreak in Nanjing. Some 500 Africans met to demand the release of colleagues detained in Nanjing, a ban on racial epithets (which had appeared in posters) and a government effort to educate people about Africa and curb abuse of Africans. Some also asked that the Chinese name for Africa (*feizhou*, a homophone for Africa which can be translated as "evil continent") be changed. They noted that the homophones of other countries, such as America (*meiguo* or "beautiful country") and England (*yingguo* or "brave country") were by contrast pleasant.[36] Some 300 Africans studying at the Institute declared their willingness to leave China.[37] Although the Institute's president said that Chinese students were wrong to protest,[38] the African boycott continued until the semester's end in early February.[39] No action was taken on their demands.

In Wuhan, 300 Chinese students threw rocks at the foreign student hall of the Central China University of Science and Technology on 29 December, injuring a Sri Lankan. Posters appeared calling Africans "black devils" and urging them to go home. Chinese students allegedly wrote to a school official saying that they did not want Africans at the college because the latter were "polluting Chinese society with their relations with Chinese women." Local officials initially denied that any disturbances had occurred and asserted that the Sri Lankan was injured as he cleaned up glass from a window broken by a child. All 12 African students were taken on a sightseeing trip. Later, however, Western reports stated that Hubei provincial officials had acknowledged that Chinese students had stoned the hall and injured the Sri Lankan, while an official Chinese source carefully skirted the issue of what was behind the stone-throwing incident.[40]

The Reaction in Africa

There was much negative commentary by governments and opinion leaders in Africa on the situation of their compatriots in China. A Kenyan newspaper termed the racial incidents "not accidental." A Liberian daily spoke of "yellow discrimination." Nigerian radio said the Nanjing conflict occurred because "the Chinese could not bear to see African students mix freely with the Chinese girls." OAU secretary-general Ide Oumarou spoke of an "appalling situation" involving "apartheid in disguise" and called in the Chinese ambassador to the OAU. Gambia protested against the detention of Alpha Robinson, an African charged in connection with the Hehai clashes. The Ghanaian government considered a recall of its student nationals. Liberia offered scholarships to nationals willing to return. Libya decried the "pressure campaign of a racist nature" and offered scholarships to all Africans in China. Benin protested to the Chinese Foreign Ministry and threatened to stop sending students to China.[41] In March 1989, 18 of the 25 Senegalese students in China departed. The remaining seven indicated that they would leave at the end of the semester.[42]

In the midst of this, the Chinese government announced a reduction in interest-free loans and technical assistance to the Third World, most of which had gone to Africa. Chinese aid to Africa had been sharply reduced in 1978, but modestly revived in the early to mid-1980s.[43] The post-1988 emphasis was to be on joint ventures, leases and mutually beneficial projects. This change reflected a contemporaneous downturn in China's economy and the waning of the Sino-Soviet dispute, and was probably planned before the outbreak of anti-Africanism.[44] The move, however, could only have aggravated tensions between China and African countries.

The Nanjing events were the last major outbreak of anti-Africanism in China during the 1980s. This does not mean, however, that hostility has since disappeared. Interviews with Africans in China in 1992 revealed that racial slights continue to be daily experiences. Africans spoke of continuing isolation from Chinese students and a fear of the violence to which some of them have been exposed when venturing off campus on their own. Their overall impression was that they remained the objects of scorn and that neither the Chinese regime nor their own governments were willing to take steps to mitigate the situation.

Non-Racial Explanations for Chinese Anti-Africanism

During the 1988–89 incidents, some commentators referred to non-racial factors as the cause of the conflict. While no cited factor is wholly implausible, some non-racial explanations have logical flaws and others are based on little more than viewpoints ascribed to Chinese participants without any evidence.

The Chinese government contended that the Nanjing events were triggered by a handful of disruptive Africans and that "erroneous slogans" were advanced by only a few Chinese.[45] However, blaming a core of habitual malcontents fails to account for universal African complaints of racial hostility and the frequency of anti-black sentiment expressed by Chinese during and apart from the demonstrations.[46] Claims of an absence of racism in China[47] are belied by the comments of low-level officials not attuned to the necessity of tailoring public pronouncements to the need to mollify foreign opinion. Thus President Liang of Hehai University expressed disgust that white women were living with black men, and All-China Student Federation leaders characterized Africans as undisciplined, drunken womanizers.[48]

Several observers maintained that the clashes reflected a general xenophobia with roots in China's past humiliation at the hands of foreign powers and resentment at the higher living standards of foreigners.[49] Some put it that if there was racism in China, it was against Chinese, who were now second-class citizens in their own country.[50] This analysis is vitiated by statements of Chinese and foreign students during the 1988–89 incidents that whites were seen as contributors to China's development, while Africans were viewed as uncultured suppliants. Interviewees noted that racist assessments of blacks were openly expressed. African businessmen and diplomats reported daily incidents of being refused services accorded others.[51] No Chinese interviewed during the Nanjing events hinted at a general resentment of foreigners or higher foreign student living standards. No actions were directed against white students, who were better-off than their African colleagues.

Other commentators pressed a more sophisticated hypothesis. They argued that Chinese accept that foreigners from developed countries will be well-off in China because they are prosperous at home, but regard Africa as destitute and the comparative wealth of Africans

in China as unjust.[52] This resentment was supposedly expressed in President Liang's statement that African students received a stipend greater than his salary after 30 years of teaching.[53] Liang's statement, however, was offered to show that African students had no cause for complaint. No Chinese suggested that antagonism between indigenous and African students would be overcome by equalizing their living standards. Rather, slogans called for the expulsion of blacks from China.

Several foreign students interviewed during the Nanjing events surmised that Chinese were jealous of the ability of Africans to use their greater wealth to attract Chinese women.[54] It is not clear, however, that they were more likely than other foreigners to have Chinese girlfriends. Africans noted that foreigners of all nationalities had relations with Chinese women, but complaints were not raised where non-Africans were involved.[55] Demonstrators demanded that Chinese womanhood be protected from "corruption" by Africans. In doing so, they almost precisely reproduced against Africans the stereotype of sexual hyperactivity levelled against Chinese males in America a century earlier, and the anger of Chinese males of the same era at sexual contacts between non-Chinese men and Chinese women.[56] As one Hong Kong journal put it, the repugnance expressed against African–Chinese assignations was "the kind of gene-pool protectionism expected from Afrikaners or the Ku Klux Klan."[57]

Protesters interviewed during the Nanjing incident expressed unease not at foreigner–Chinese but at black–Chinese sexual relations. One 25-year-old is quoted as saying: "When I look at their black faces, I feel uncomfortable. When I see them with our women, my heart boils."[58] Another young demonstrator stated: "If a girl goes with a black man, Chinese will want to beat either him or her, and they will curse the girl forever."[59] In contrast, relations between Chinese women and white men are often tolerated because a more prosperous life abroad may result for the woman and her family.

Some correspondents and specialists opined that Chinese students used the Nanjing incident to protest implicitly against poor living conditions and curriculum deficiencies.[60] Because Africans are less than one-tenth of one per cent of university students in China, their presence is unrelated to these problems. "Frustration-aggression" is however commonly offered to explain racial persecution, based on the assumption that persecutors actually concerned with real grievances displace their angst on innocent target groups.[61] Such psycho-social explanations are usually not borne out by analysis.

For example, racial attacks in Germany in 1992 were initially attributed to high unemployment in the former East Germany. It was later determined, however, that most attacks occurred in prosperous ex-West Germany, while mass assaults in the eastern *länder* were often led by middle-class westerners.[62] in the Nanjing events, the absence of references by interviewed Chinese to low living standards and educational deficiencies indicates that the role of frustration with student life was more a matter of supposition than fact.

It was also contended that the Nanjing demonstrations represented an effort to rekindle the student "democracy movement" that flared briefly two years earlier and heralded the movement of 1989.[63] Student "democrats" did attach slogans about human rights and freedom to anti-black exhortations and thus used the events to advance their own agenda by claiming that the regime failed to protect the rights of Chinese against the alleged depredations of Africans. That being said, there is no reason to suppose that the racist component of the slogans was not entirely sincere.

The linkage in Nanjing of concern for universal rights with racial antagonism is incongruous, but not unprecedented. Early 20th-century South African trade unionists protested against the importation of Chinese labourers with banners inscribed "Workers of the World Unite; Fight for a White South Africa." The white workers saw nothing untoward in linking the principle of unity with their Chinese brothers to a demand that the latter remain in China.[64] The mixture of racist and democratic slogans displayed by the Nanjing demonstrators reflects a conceit often present in the majority populations involved in ethnic and religious conflicts: a subordinate group is accused of usurping the rights of a dominant group. Thus, redressive programmes for racial minorities in the United States are attacked as "reverse discrimination."[65] Hindu nationalists denounce India's Muslims as using protective laws to thwart the institutionalization of majoritarian religious principles.[66] Serbian leaders accuse Bosnian Muslims of wanting to repeat the Second World War persecution of Serbs in which some Bosnian Muslims were involved.[67]

While some observers contended that Chinese "democrats" used the anti-African movement to direct protest against the party-state, Africans accused the government of manipulating existing sentiment to scapegoat Africans and channel protest away from the regime.[68] At the very least, the regime gave the demonstrators mixed signals, disapproving of mass protests (which were more or less under the leadership of its critics) while seconding outrage against African "troublemakers." In any case, that the regime and its critics both used the outbursts to promote their own aims does not mean that they did not share anti-African views.

The Racial Explanation

During and after the Nanjing events, some commentators argued that anti-black prejudice provided the impetus for Chinese–African student conflicts.[69] Historical and contemporary evidence that Chinese intellectuals have held notions of black inferiority supports the view that racial animosity was the main element. Anti-black bias can in turn be seen in the context of a recrudescence of elitist values that link and denigrate those who are dark and those who are poor.

Traditional Chinese culture idealized fair skin[70] and, among elites at least, associated it with intellectual endeavour. The most attractive man was a "white-faced scholar" *(baimian shusheng)* whose freedom from manual labour at once implied a high status, potentially leisured life and light complexion. Fair skin continues to be a standard of female beauty. Many urban Chinese women take pains to avoid the sun and some use whitening creams. Chinese, in common with other languages, associates blackness with negative qualities, as in *heixin* (black hearted), *heiren* (black person, but also one who lacks a residency permit), *heishi* (black market), *heishehui* (gangster organization) and *heihua* (bandit argot). Urban Chinese have long associated the dark complexions of manual labourers, particularly peasants, with low economic and cultural status.[71]

Racial stereotyping in China has a long history, ably documented in recent studies by Frank Dikötter. When the Western intrusion began in the mid-19th century, Chinese writers propagated racial typifications that treated all foreigners as inferior. The image of blacks, however, was distinctly worse than other groups. Africans were portrayed as supine natural slaves from the most backward of continents.[72]

At the turn of the century, leading reformist intellectuals, including Liang Qichao and Kang Youwei, adopted a "scientific" racism influenced by Western views. In their racial hierarchy, the white and yellow races were opposed to darker races doomed to extinction by hereditary inadequacies.[73] Blacks were seen as lazy, stupid and incapable of progress. In contrast, some whites (particularly Anglo-Saxons) were considered natural-born rulers. The reformers expressed alarm at the supposedly higher sexual drives of blacks, which Liang cited as underlying and justifying the lynching of African-Americans. Kang advocated the eradication of darker races through dietary change, migration, sterilization and intermarriage. He feared, however, that the last of these methods would run into difficulties because of the natural repugnance of whites and Asians to inferior blacks.[74]

Prominent intellectuals in Republican China also disseminated notions of black intellectual and aesthetic inferiority, while assimilating blacks with subordinate classes in China. One anthropologist whose works were widely distributed in the 1920s described blacks as small-brained racial inferiors who were only as civilized as "stupid peasants" (*yunong*) in China. Advocates of eugenics transferred the idea of a biological hierarchy to classes: intellectuals were the premier elements of a race; intellectual and moral incompetents were found at the lower levels.[75]

The Communist ascension to power in 1949 produced a break with racial hierarchies and the putative link between race and class. Class relations were marked by an ideological inversion. The moral and political qualities of poor peasants were extolled and externalized in the thesis that Asia, Africa and Latin America constituted a revolutionary countryside that would encircle and end the dominance of the developed world.[76] Universalist ideals were illustrated in posters of Third World revolutionaries and a famous photo of Mao surrounded by exchange students of all races.

The promotion of international solidarity and the pre-eminence of the poor faded quickly in the 1980s, replaced by the official laudation of national self-interest, individual enrichment and social restratification. This political change, together with external influences, resulted in a rejection of egalitarianism among students, even as the salience of ideology generally declined and students became increasingly estranged from the party-state.[77] With the change to economic success as a key status marker, those from poorer countries and less well-off classes might be expected to have a low standing in Chinese status hierarchies. The results of survey research show that this is indeed the case.

Attitudes Toward Foreign Peoples and Chinese Social Groups: Survey Results

Contemporary reports are the main evidence available on the question of racism as the animating factor in the Chinese–African clashes. Participant observations contained in these reports help illuminate the origins of the clashes, but remain the end-products of a selection process that reflected the predilections and interests of journalists. The motive of Chinese participants is in any case only one issue raised by the conflicts. A more important question is whether the clashes

were random incidents or reflections of a developing core vision among the country's future elites. That question is best plumbed by survey research, while bearing in mind the problems of such research in China.[78] A 1992 poll suggests that racial hierarchy and social elitism are again part of the world view of the Chinese intelligentsia.

The survey was carried out among 461 persons in 14 diverse sampling populations, primarily students and intellectuals, but also high school pupils, PLA recruits at a normal university, the staffs of two research institutes, a municipal planning office and a provincial foreign trade mission, and technical and managerial personnel employed in a factory.[79] The first questionnaire asked that seven groups of foreigners (Western Europeans, Africans, Japanese, Americans, Southeast Asians, Arabs and Indians) be rated for ten attributes: cultural level (*wenhua*), intelligence (*zhili*), industriousness (*qinfen*), behaviour (*xingwei*), role as models from whom one can learn (*zuo wei women xuexi bangyangde diwei*), attractiveness (*xiyinli*), interest in education (*dui jiaoyu de xingqu*), honesty (*chengshi*), capacity to manage their own political affairs (*chuli tamen zijide zhengzhi shiwude nengli*) and interest in economic development (*dui fazhan jingji de xingqu*). A second questionnaire asked that Chinese peasants (*nongmin*), private entrepreneurs (*siren qiyejia*) and intellectuals (*zhishi fenzi*) be rated for the same attributes. Teachers or staff members administered the surveys, without the presence of outsiders. Respondents were told that the survey's purpose was to gauge their impressions of foreign peoples and Chinese social groups.

The survey results show how Africans and Chinese peasants are rated in relation to other foreign peoples and social groups and allow comparison of the scoring of Africans and Chinese peasants. There are some inconsistencies and anomalies among the results, but also a distinct pattern. Africans were rated worst for nine and peasants worst for eight of the ten attributes. Africans were thought of in relatively positive terms only as to honesty and peasants only as to honesty and behaviour.

Culture and intelligence are among the characteristics most salient to attitudes on race. Racial hierarchization has long been based on claims that the backward cultures and low intelligence of certain peoples brand them as hereditary inferiors.[80] The questions on culture asked for a choice between advanced (*fada*), fairly advanced (*bijiao fada*), average in terms of development (*yiban jiu qi fazhan eryan*), somewhat backward (*you xie luohou*) and very backward (*hen luohou*). Many Chinese equate culture and education, but responses to the questions on interest in education suggest that the equation is not complete. All groups surveyed rated Africans last in culture and most placed their level between somewhat backward and very backward. Using a scale of very interested (*feichang gan xingqu*), fairly interested (*bijiao gan xingqu*), average interest (*yiban xingqu*), little interest (*xingqu bu da*) and no interest (*wu xingqu*), only ten of the 14 groups rated Africans last in terms of interest in education. All but one group scored Africans' interest in education higher than their level of culture and in most cases there were wide differences between the two scores. Concomitantly, all groups rated Western Europeans, Japanese and Americans as the three most cultured peoples; only ten groups did the same for interest in education.

Questions on intelligence gave choices of highly intelligent (*feichang congming*); fairly intelligent (*bijiao congming*); average intelligence (*yiban*); below average intelligence (*diyu yiban*) and unintelligent (*bu congming*). All groups rated Africans last in terms of intelligence, with student groups tending to place them between average and below average and intellectuals usually rating Africans as below average to unintelligent. Western Europeans, Japanese, Americans and South-east Asians were rated highly as to intelligence, suggesting the connection between that attribute and economic level that is often made in racialist thinking.

All groups deemed Chinese peasants to have the lowest "cultural level" among the three social groups. Most considered peasants culturally somewhat backward, but several groups regarded them as very backward. In this instance, the result does indicate a likely equation of cultural levels and educational factors, since all groups rated intellectuals highest, entrepreneurs second and peasants last in terms of interest in education, with large gaps between the three groups. Peasants were uniformly rated as the lowest in intelligence of the three social groups, although all groups scored them higher (and often much higher) in intelligence than Africans. All but one group did the same with culture and interest in education.

Questions on industriousness asked respondents to choose between very hard working (*gongzuo hen nuli*), fairly hard working (*gongzuo bijiao nuli*), average in terms of work habits (*yiban xiangdui yu qi gongzuo xiguan eryan*), not hard working (*bu nuli*) and lazy (*lan*). Half the groups rated Africans as the least industrious of peoples. Others considered Arabs and/or Indians to be less industrious, but in no case were Africans given higher than fifth position. Most groups rated peasants as the least industrious social group, with entrepreneurs consistently receiving the top

rating. Although peasants were rated poorly compared to the other social groups, they were scored much higher than Africans in terms of industriousness. While the former were generally considered average to fairly hard working, the latter were almost always rated as average to not hard working.

On behaviour, respondents were asked to choose between very well-behaved (*pinxing hen duanzheng*), fairly well-behaved (*xingwei bijiao duanzheng*), average in terms of behaviour (*yiban jiu qi xingwei eryan*), not well-behaved (*pinxing bu tai hao*) and criminal or troublemaking (*fanzui huo reshi shengfei*). Most groups placed Africans last in terms of behaviour; a minority put them in fourth, fifth or sixth place.

All groups rated the behaviour of intellectuals, peasants and entrepreneurs in that order, with large gaps between the scores. Peasant behaviour was considered very much higher than African behaviour, on average a full point higher.

Among the ten attributes, Africans and Chinese peasants fared best as to honesty, on a scale that went from very honest (*feichang chengshi*), through fairly honest (*bijiao chengshi*), average honesty (*yibande chengshi*), not very honest (*bu hen chengshi*) and dishonest (*bu chengshi*). There was a wide spread in the ratings of Africans, but on average they were placed somewhere between third and fourth among the seven foreign peoples. This may have been in part because other foreigners were considered dishonest. The vast majority of surveyed groups rated the Japanese as the least honest, in keeping with the common perception that they are not forthright in business dealings and lie about the history of their aggression in China.[81]

The majority of respondents deemed peasants the most honest social group. In all but two cases, entrepreneurs were in third place, an unsurprising result given the universal Chinese complaint that private businesspeople engage in price gouging and bribery. All but one group gave peasants higher scores for honesty than Africans, generally by one-half to one full point.

Using a scale of very important role (*you hen zhong yao diwei*), fairly important role, (*you bijiao zhongyao diwei*), some role (*you yixie diwei*), practically no role (*jihu mei you diwei*) and no role (*wu diwei*), all groups rated Africans and Chinese peasants last as role models. The scores for peasants were in all cases higher than those for Africans. Almost every group gave Africans a rating between practically no role and no role; peasants were rated between some role and practically no role. Japanese, Americans, Western Europeans and South-east Asians were consistently in the top four positions, most often in that order. Intellectuals were uniformly given pride of place as role models, with entrepreneurs second. Economic development levels probably played a significant but not determinative part in the ratings of foreign peoples as role models. Using a scale of very high interest (*xingqu hen gao*), fairly high interest (*xingqu jiao gao*), some interest (*you yixie xingqu*), little interest (*mei duoshao xingqu*) and no interest (*wu xingqu*), Africans were rated last by ten of the 14 groups in terms of interest in economic development. Japanese, Americans, Western Europeans and South-east Asians were in most cases given the top four positions.

It is doubtful, however, that the responses to the questions about the social groups' interest in economic development were strictly influenced by levels of prosperity. Intellectuals were rated first by nine groups and private entrepreneurs by five groups, yet Chinese students and intellectuals are keenly aware that the standard of living of the intelligentsia generally falls below that of entrepreneurs. Peasant interest in economic development was rated lowest by all groups. This was one of two categories in which a majority of groups gave Africans better scores than they gave to peasants and may be related to the publicity given to Chinese aid to African countries.

The questions concerning political capacity are also key indices of racial and elitist thinking, which have historically been linked to claims that a given ethno-racial group or social majority are incapable of managing their own affairs.[82] A scale of very high capacity (*nengli hen gao*), fairly high capacity (*nengli bijiao gao*), average capacity (*nengli yiban*), little capacity (*mei duoshao nengli*) and no capacity (*wu nengli*) was used. Africans were rated last by 12 of the 14 groups, with most scores hovering around the little capacity rating. Chinese peasants were rated lowest by all groups, with large gaps between their ratings and those of intellectuals and entrepreneurs, who were in almost all cases rated in that order. The scores given peasants by all but one sampling group were worse than those given Africans. This may be because Chinese peasants are widely perceived as having a "petty-producer ideology" that bars any interest in politics.

Relative perceptions of attractiveness provide another important indicator of the status accorded racial and social groups. Racial ideology in particular has long counterposed the beauty of one group to the ugliness of the "other."[83] The questions on attractiveness allowed respondents to pick among generally good-looking (*congde jiang piaoliang*), better than average (*haoyu yiban*), average (*yiban*), not good-looking (*bu piaoliang*) and generally ugly (*yiban eryan choulou*).

All groups surveyed rated Africans as the least attractive of the listed foreign peoples; all but one group placed them between not good-looking and generally ugly. Most groups put Western Europeans, Americans, Japanese and South-east Asians in the top four positions—generally in that order—with Arabs or Indians in the fifth and sixth places. That whites were considered more attractive than fellow Asians should not surprise anyone who has seen a Chinese women students' dormitory decorated with magazine cutouts of white women or witnessed the delight displayed by Chinese at the appearance of white children. Chinese and whites have in fact been shown to have the same notions of attractiveness with regard to whites.[84]

Intellectuals were generally considered the most attractive of the three social groups. All groups rated peasants as the least attractive, placing them between average looks and not good-looking, with most ratings closer to the latter category. All groups scored Africans worse than peasants on attractiveness.

In addition to numerical ratings, the questionnaires provided space for short comments about the foreign peoples and social groups. This opportunity, which required respondents to use handwriting, was mainly taken by students, whose observations may not be representative of general attitudes. In fact, this section was intended to elicit the views of the more outspoken.

About half the high school pupil commentators described Africans in purely negative terms, that is as primitive, unclean, backward, and honest but simple-minded. An equal number were marginally more positive. Africans were termed hard working and honest, but lacking the capacity to manage their own countries; ugly, but not lacking in humour; clever, but ignorant and prone to political instability; the inheritors of a rich culture and victimized by the colonial legacy, rapid population growth and diseases, but also slow at development. A few comments were wholly positive: Africans have a fighting spirit, are kind-hearted, generous and honest and arouse sympathy.

High school pupils were scarcely more charitable in comments about peasants, writing that they are bumpkins (*tu*), pitiable, detestable, backward, ignorant, parochial, narrow-minded, lacking in cultivation, disrespectful of science, low-quality, poisoned by feudalism, infused with a petty-producer ideology, resisting birth control, hard to educate, unenterprising, honest but inflexible, and kind-hearted in some cases but cunning, arrogant and fierce in others. A few positive comments were made: peasants are simple, plain and willing to endure hardships, the pillar of China, hard working and down to earth and brave.

The vast majority of university student commentators were more vitriolic. Africans were said to be undisciplined, wild, ignorant, uninhibited, primitive, uncivilized, lazy, foolish, ugly, weak, rude, incapable, backward, troublemakers, nuisances, not welcome, and the least intelligent tribe of black apes. They were held to lack the strength to resist suppression, to project a bad impression and lack a capacity for progress. A few students remarked that Africans are honest, but also simple and backward. Unambiguously positive characterizations were strikingly absent.

Most university students who commented on Chinese peasants also regarded them negatively, as backward, ignorant, stupid, mean, foolish, apathetic, shortsighted, needing improvement, lazy, hapless, lacking in manners, without any idea of democracy or the need to be the master of one's own affairs, and unsatisfactory in contributing to development. Mixed comments included stubborn but humble, kind and tame, and lacking in intelligence, knowledge or shrewdness but pure, simple, frank and warm-hearted. There were only a few unambiguously positive comments. Peasants were said to be honest and respectable, industrious and enduring, and courageous in exploring new ways of making a living.

There were many more positive characterizations of other peoples and groups even where commentators were generally negative in their descriptions. Many saw the Japanese as duplicitous and alluded to sharp business practices and Japan's unwillingness to acknowledge war-time atrocities, but also viewed them as intelligent, hardworking innovators. These same positive characteristics were often attributed to Americans, who were also said to be genially freespirited. Negative comments focused mainly on America's political interference and culture of violence. Western Europeans generally received accolades and escaped critical comment. South-east Asians were much more often praised than blamed. Comments about Arabs and Indians were usually negative, but restricted. Arabs were seen as not knowing what to do with their oil wealth. Indians were largely ignored; those who commented mainly focused on the rapid Indian population growth.

The comments made about Chinese private entrepreneurs focused almost exclusively on their perceived opportunism, manifested in unethical business practices designed to turn a quick *yuan*. The words shrewd (*jingming*), capable (*nenggan*), and cunning (*jiaohua*) were repeatedly applied to entrepreneurs, expressing a mixture of admiration and revulsion. Comments about intellectuals praised their high-mindedness and potential as contributors to development, but deplored their passivity and low economic status. There was little derogation of entrepreneurs or intellectuals, in contrast to an evident disdain for peasants.

Conclusion

The racialized outlook of Chinese students and intellectuals evidenced by the survey supports the inference that racism, not xenophobia, was the driving force behind clashes between Chinese and African students. The bottom-rung ratings given Africans and Chinese peasants, taken together with similar comments about the two groups and an elite tradition of depreciating peasants as dark and backward, lends credence to the claim of African students that Chinese view them as peasants.

That the Chinese intelligentsia may construct an image of Africans based on the peasantry does not preclude other bases for their view, such as analogies to domestic minority nationalities, toward whom "many Hans tend to be disrespectful."[85] In any case, first-hand experience is probably not a basis for views on Africans, with whom, even in academic settings, most Chinese have no contact. In response to queries, Chinese students mention texts used in their primary and secondary educations, news reports, and accounts received from friends who have gone abroad as sources of their knowledge of black people.

An examination of geography textbooks and journals devoted to foreign cultures showed them to be unlikely sources of negative conceptions of Africans. The news media, however, may play a role in debasing the image of black people, as it has in some Western societies.[86] Black students interviewed in China focused on media depictions of Africans as destitute, ignorant and unstable as a key factor in creating perceptions of them. Tendentious reports of the student clashes in the Chinese media can only have reinforced the notion that Africans are unruly and even dangerous.

Anecdotal evidence suggests that Chinese students abroad convey negative impressions of black people to relatives and friends back home. For example, some Chinese studying at urban American universities live in poor minority areas where crime rates are high and cultural interests diverge markedly from those of the Chinese intelligentsia. Most of these students concentrate on science or engineering courses that are populated largely by whites and Asians. Few have contacts with black colleagues and all are exposed to the prejudices of the larger society. The same process is at work with foreign films that feature black people. Many students in China have seen such films and their general effect is to reinforce negative stereotypes.[87] Additional research needs to be done about these and other bases of the racialized thinking of the Chinese intelligentsia, particularly the question of whether the Chinese view of Africans mainly derives from Western stereotypes or is *sui generis*. Interviews in China and with Chinese abroad, a search for memoirs by Chinese economic aid workers who served in Africa and an examination of the depictions of blacks in Chinese literature might be profitable paths to pursue.[88]

Learning more about how contemporary Chinese acquire their views of race may also lead to greater knowledge about the effects of these views. The most important of these involves foreign policy. By the beginning of the 1980s, the turn away from a universalist ideology, the adoption of an open-door policy focused on investments and trade by developed countries, and a receding "Soviet threat" had loosened earlier Sino-African bonds.[89] In essentially excusing the ill-treatment of African students in Nanjing and elsewhere, the Chinese regime signalled a willingness to allow those bonds to fray.

Complex reasons doubtless lay behind the regime's approach to the anti-African outbursts. Internationally, it had a political investment in its claim—dating back to the Bandung Conference of 1955—that racism is uniquely absent in China.[90] In 1988–89 the Chinese government unflinchingly refused to admit that race was a factor in the Nanjing clashes. Domestically, the regime could gain political advantage by using Chinese nationalism to outflank student critics who had taken up the anti-African banner. However important these factors may have been, it nevertheless must be queried whether the countenancing of anti-Africanism also reflected racialized thinking on the part of high-level policymakers.

Anti-black sentiment has not been publicly expressed at the highest levels of the contemporary Chinese state, as it was in 1945 when Chiang Kai-shek tried to block African-American troops from entering China over the Burma Road that they had just built.[91] By the late 1980s, however, most higher-level Chinese officials were college-educated and unlikely to be resistant to factors that have racialized the thinking of the intelligentsia.

While the outlook of Chinese leaders cannot be scrutinized in the way that racial views of Western leaders are studied,[92] more might be learned through surveys and interviews about the thinking of middle-level officials. This would in turn aid in gauging the degree to which Chinese foreign policy may now be influenced by differing conceptions of foreign peoples. In this regard, Chinese policy would not be unique. Racial factors were influential, for example, in the U.S. government's Vietnam policy in the 1960s and in its stance on the Falklands War of 1982.[93]

Finally, the interplay of racial and democratic thinking among Chinese intellectuals needs to be explored. In 1990, the exiled student leader Wuer Kaixi acknowledged that his movement was "ridden with various degrees of xenophobia, including racism."[94] Nothing is known, however, about the degree to which leaders of the anti-African demonstrations in Tianjin in May 1986 and Nanjing in December 1988 also participated in democracy movements in those cities only months after the racial incidents.[95] While racial questions figured not at all in the latter movements, the commitment of their leaders to a democracy that would include China's peasant population has been questioned by some scholars.[96] Deepening understanding of the nature of racial and elitist thinking among the intelligentsia, may add to knowledge of larger political trends among this important sector of Chinese society.

Notes

*I should like to thank Frank Dikötter for his valuable suggestion of the link between anti-African and anti-peasant ideas, and Gerard Mare for his valuable comments.

1. See Alexander DeConde, *Ethnicity, Race and American Foreign Policy* (Boston: Northeastern University Press, 1992).
2. Emmanuel Hevi, *An African Student in China* (London: Pall Mall, 1963), p. 113; Margaret Schott, "Blacks and red faces," *Far Eastern Economic Review (FEER)*, No. 132 (19 June 1986), p. 20; "Backgrounder: about 1,500 African students in China," Xinhua, 31 December 1988 in *Foreign Broadcast Information Service (FBIS)*-CHI-89-002 (4 January 1989), p. 20; Tammy Tam, "Africa policy to continue despite row," *Hong Kong Standard (HKS)*, 5 January 1989, p. 7; Daniel Southerland, "China's long-held image of foreigners fuels racial conflict," *Washington Post (WP)*, 3 January 1989, p. A8.
3. Alan Hutchison, *China's African Revolution* (Boulder: Westview, 1975), pp. 186–89; Alaba Ogunsanwo, *China's Policy in Africa, 1958–1971* (Cambridge: Cambridge University Press, 1974), p. 85; John Burns, "Africans accuse Chinese of racism," *New York Times (NYT)*, 10 June 1986, p. A5.
4. See Hevi, *An African Student in China*, ch. 6.
5. See Bruce Larkin, *China and Africa, 1949–1970* (Berkeley: University of California, 1971).
6. Mao Zedong, "Message of greetings on the occasion of the 45th Annual Conference of the ANC," *Renmin ribao (RMRB)*, 14 December 1957, in *Survey of the China Mainland Press*, No. 1674 (18 December 1957), p. 56; "Statement in

support of the Afro-American struggle against violent repression," *RMRB*, 16 April 1968, in *Peking Review*, Vol. 11, No. 16 (19 April 1968), p. 5.

7. See Gao Yuan, "In China, black isn't beautiful," *NYT*, 25 January 1989, p. A23.

8. Compare, for example, David Shambaugh, *Beautiful Imperialist: China Perceives America* (Princeton: Princeton University Press, 1991), pp. 161–62 and pp. 216–17.

9. An assault by Chinese students in Nanjing on foreign, mainly African, students took place in mid-April 1979, but apparently did not result in serious injuries or demonstrations. See Anthony Barker, "China to take more foreign students despite past tensions," Reuter, 13 December 1984; "Other reports: African students' protest demonstration in Peking:" Agence France Presse (AFP), 18 July 1979 in British Broadcasting Corporation, *Summary of World Broadcasts* (BBC/SWB), FE/6173/A5/2 (21 July 1979).

10. A Soviet source claimed that 2,000 Chinese participated in the attack. "Excesses against Afro-Asian students in China: outcome of chauvinism," Radio Peace and Progress (Moscow), 19 July 1979, in BBC/SWB, SU/6174/A3/7 (23 July 1979).

11. AFP, 8 July 1979, in FBIS-CHI-79-132 (9 July 1979), pp. 02–03; AFP, 9 July 1979, 1527 GMT; AFP, 11 July 1979, in BBC/SWB, FE/6166/BII/19 (13 July 1979); Associated Press (AP), 25 July 1979. Where a source is not otherwise specified, wireservice accounts derive from the Nexis on-line database.

12. Reuter, 18 July 1979; "African students march in China," *WP*, 18 July 1979, p. A20; "Other reports: African students' protest demonstration in Peking," AFP, 18 July 1979, in BBC/SWB FE/6173/A5/2; AP, 25 July 1979; Xinhua, 25 July 1979, in FBIS-CHI-79-145 (26 July 1979), pp. L1–L2; "Unity and friendship come first," *Zhongguo qingnian (Chinese Youth)*, 26 July 1979, in FBIS-CHI-79-145 (26 July 1979), p. L2.

13. Xinhua, 11 August 1979, in FBIS-CHI-79-158, p. 07; Xinhua, 11 September 1979, in FBIS-CHI-79-180, p. 05; "China: Restive Africans," *Africa Confidential*, Vol. 22, No. 24 (1 July 1981), p. 8.

14. Philip Snow, *The Star Raft: China's Encounter with Africa* (London: Weidenfeld & Nicolson, 1988), p. 205.

15. D. Southerland, "Frictions Between Chinese, Africans surface," *WP*, 5 June 1986, p. A33; D. Southerland, "200 African students protest racism in China" *Los Angeles Times (LAT)*, 9 January 1987, p. 6; "Africans reported to attack Chinese in Nanking," AP, 25 December 1988.

16. "Tianjin student incident isolated one: education official," Xinhua, Item No. 0607075 (7 June 1986); "African students in China," Xinhua, Item No. 121528 (15 December 1982); "Foreign students clash with Chinese," AP, 26 May 1986; "Backgrounder: about 1,500 African students in China," Xinhua, 31 December 1988 in FBIS-CHI-89-002 (4 January 1989).

17. Richard Pascoe, Reuter, 23 May 1980, "Arab and African students clash at Chinese school," AP, 13 June 1980; Michael Weisskept, "Simple love story of mixed cultures ends tragically in Peking," *WP*, 8 November 1980, p. A23; Dick Wilson, "A paler shade of yellow," *New Society*, Vol. 70, No. 1136 (11 October 1984), pp. 52–53; D. Wilson, "Black and white view from the Middle Kingdom," *FEER*, No. 126 (13 December 1984), pp. 52–55; United Press International (UPI), 28 May 1986; D. Southerland, "Frictions between Chinese, Africans surface," *WP*, 5 June 1986, p. A33; Robert Thomson, "China looks up and down at the big noses," *Financial Times (FT)*, 12 July 1986, p. 2; R. Thomson, "Overseas students in Peking protest march," *FT*, 7 January 1987, p. 4; Nicholas Kristof, "Chinese in Nanjing hold racist rally," *NYT*, 27 December 1988, p. A1; William Kazer, "Chinese rally against Africans, envoys rush to Nanking," Reuter, 27 December 1988; "African students attacked in China," *Chicago Tribune (CT)*, 27 December 1988, p. 2; Jasper Becker, "China's Africa crisis," *Manchester Guardian Weekly*, 15 January 1989, p. 9; John Pomfret, "African students isolated from angry Chinese," AP, 27 December 1998; D. Southerland, "Chinese isolate Africans for protection," *WP*, 27 December 1988, p. A14; Mark O'Neill, "Chinese–African violence—racism or provocation," Reuter, 30 December 1988; Southerland, "China's long-held image of foreigners fuels racial conflict," p. A8; Yojana Sharma, "China: racial incidents could cloud relations with Africa," Inter Press Service, 4 January 1989; Eve-Ann Prentice, "Bleak celibacy for Africans in China," *Sunday Telegraph*, 8 January 1989, p. 10; Uli Schmetzer, "Africans' privileges rile Chinese," *CT*, 10 January 1989, p. 4; D. Holley, "They face widespread prejudice," *LAT*, 10 January 1989, p. 1.

18. James Miles, UPI, 7 January 1987; M. O'Neill, "Arab and African students protest in Peking," Reuter, 8 January 1987; Edward Gargan, "African students in Beijing march in outrage at a racial slur," *NYT*, 9 January 1987, p. A4; "African students receive assurances, return to classes," AP, 12 January 1987.

19. David Fraser, "Recurrent Chinese campus riots highlight clash of cultures," Reuter, 2 June 1986; D. Southerland, "Frictions between Chinese, Africans surface," *WP*, 5 June 1986, p. A33; D. Southerland, "China denies clash hurt Africa ties," *WP*, 8 June 1986, p. A24; R. Thomson, "Tianjin 4; 'Open door' policy has its problems," *FT*, 20 August 1986, p. 12; James Miles, UPI, 7 January 1987; Southerland, "200 African students protest racism in China," p. 6; Jim Abrams, "Students boycott classes, say request for written guarantees rejected," AP, 9 January 1987.

20. AFP, 28 December 1988, in FBIS-CHI-88-250 (29 December 1988), pp. 2–3; Schmetzer, "Africans' privileges rile Chinese," p. 4; Snow, *The Star Raft*, pp. 201–202.

21. "Troublemakers at friendship hotel arrested," Xinhua, Item No. 100845, 8 October 1983; Reuter, 8 October 1983.

22. "Foreign students in Peking plan police protest march," Reuter, 8 December 1985; Graham Earnshaw, "Peking University quiet with no sign of unofficial gatherings," Reuter, 9 December 1985.

23. "Twenty-five foreigners besieged in Chinese university hall," Reuter, 25 May 1986; Kyodo, 26 May 1986, in FBIS-CHI-86-101 (27 May 1986), p. A1; "Chinese police detain students after five-hour siege," Reuter, 26 May 1986; "Foreign students clash with Chinese," AP, 26 May 1986; UPI, 27 May 1986; I. Chang, "Foreign students held in hotel after conflict," AP, 27 May 1986; Southerland, "Frictions between Chinese, Africans surface," p. A33; AFP, 1 July 1986 in FBIS-CHI-86-127 (2 July 1986), p. G2.

24. "Incident involving African students at Tianjin University a 'misunderstanding'," Xinhua, 28 May 1986 in BBC/SWB, FE/8272/BII/1 (30 May 1986); "Students conflict in Tianjin quietens down," Xinhua, Item No. 0530081, 30 May 1986; "Foreign students said to be refusing to leave Chinese hotel," Reuter, 30 May 1986; "China denies race was factor in clash," UPI, 4 June 1986.

25. J. Abrams, "Government official disapproves of demonstration, denies racism," AP, 7 June 1986; UPI, 2 June 1986; D. Fraser, "Recurrent Chinese campus riots highlight clash of cultures," Reuter, 2 June 1986; R. Thomson, "Peking to investigate clash at student dance," *FT*, 9 June 1986, p. 2.

26. "Africans in Peking hit racial bias," *LAT*, 6 June 1986, p. 2; "Foreign students march in Peking to demand safety," Reuter, 6 June 1986; J. Burns, "Africans accuse Chinese of racism," *NYT*, 10 June 1986, p. A5; AFP, 11 June 1986 in FBIS-CHI-86-115 (16 June 1986), p. I1.

27. J. Abrams, "African students protest racial discrimination," AP, 6 June 1986; D. Southerland, "China denies clash hurt African ties," *WP*, 7 June 1986, p. A24; Jim Mann, "Peking denies racism caused clashes between Chinese and African students," *LAT*, 8 June 1986, p. 16; "Tianjin student incident isolated one: education official," Xinhua, Item No. 0607075, 7 June 1986; "China says no students to be expelled following clash," Reuter, 7 June 1986; "China criticizes foreign student protests," UPI, 7 June 1986; "Beijing denies brawl was caused by racial discrimination," Kyodo, 7 June 1986; Jim Mann, "China tries joining the Third World," *LAT*, 15 June 1986, p. 5:2.

28. "Foreign Ministry promises no punishment, students to return," AP, 12 June 1986; AFP, 13 June 1986, in FBIS-CHI-86-115 (16 June 1986),
p. I2; "Other reports: African ambassadors reportedly called in to settle student dispute in China," Kyodo, 13 June 1986 in BBC/SWB, FE/8281/A5/1 (16 June 1986).

29. See, e.g., Libreville (Gabon) Africa No. 1, 8 June 1986; Lagos (Nigeria) Domestic Service, 8 June 1986, in FBIS-MEA-86-110 (9 June 1986), pp. S1, T6; Lagos Domestic Service, 10 June 1986, in FBIS-MEA-86-111 (10 June 1986), p. T4.

30. "African students sent back to site of campus clash," Reuter, 30 June 1986; AFP, 1 July 1986 in FBIS-CHI-86-127 (2 July 1986), p. G2.

31. "Chinese students leave for Africa to deliver donation," Xinhua, Item No. 1114169, 14 November 1986; "Chinese students donate 500,000 *yuan* for 'African calamities'," Xinhua, 12 November 1986 in BBC/SWB FE 8417/A5/1 (15 November 1986).

32. Chang, "Foreign students held in hotel after conflict"; Yu Yuanchao, "Nation aims to get more students from Africa," *China Daily (CD)*, 5 November 1986, p. 1.

33. W. Kazer, "China keeps silent on charges of torture, hidden apartheid," Reuter, 4 January 1989.

34. "'Expert' says 'high risk' of contracting AIDS in China," *Zhongguo tongxun she*, 19 February 1993, in BBC/SWB, FE/1626/B2, (2 March 1993). Surveys in China show that AIDS is largely conceived as a "foreign problem." See Deidre Godfrey, "China: AIDS threat hangs over world's most populous nation," Inter Press Service, 14 October 1992; John Leicester, "Experts fear China may be downplaying AIDS threat," UPI, 28 September 1992.

35. AFP, 29 December 1988 in FBIS-CHI-88-250 (29 December 1988), pp. 3–4; M. Del Vecchio, UPI, 30 December 1988; AFP, 30 December 1988 in FBIS-CHI-88-251 (30 December 1988), p. 1; A. Roche, "African students seize Chinese teacher after AIDS slur," Reuter, 30 December 1988; "Racial conflict hits second Chinese city," *LAT*, 30 December 1988, p. 2; O'Neill, "Chinese–African violence—racism or provocation"; D. Southerland, "Racial conflict spreads to second Chinese city," *WP*, 31 December 1988, p. A15; T. Luard, "China's racial tension spread by AIDS claim," *Daily Telegraph (DT)*, 31 December 1988, p. 8; J. Pomfret, "African student sentenced without trial to 15 days," AP, 2 January 1989; W. Kazer, "China keeps silent on charges of torture, hidden apartheid," Reuter, 4 January 1989; "Three Africans admit breaking China's law," *LAT*, 5 January 1989, p. 2.

36. AFP, 3 January 1989 in FBIS-CHI-89-001 (3 January 1989), pp. 20–21; J. Pomfret, "Racial tensions spread to Beijing," AP, 3 January 1989; "China racial unrest moves to Beijing," *LAT*, 3 January 1989, p. 2; UPI, 3 January 1989; J. Pomfret, "Chinese students demonstrate after incident with African," AP, 3 January 1989; D. Southerland, "Chinese protests against Africans spread to Beijing, one other city," *WP*, 3 January 1989, p. A16; AFP, 4 January 1989 in

FBIS-CHI-88-002 (4 January 1989), p. 18; Ma Lixin, *CD*, 4 January 1989, p. 3; W. Kazer, "China keeps silent on charges of torture, hidden apartheid," Reuter, 4 January 1989; D. Southerland, "OAU protests to China on attacks on Africans," *WP*, 5 January 1989, p. A27; T. Luard, "China faces diplomatic crisis over race relations," *DT*, 4 January 1989, p. 8; "A detailed account of the demonstration staged by Chinese students at the Beijing Language Institute," *Zhongguo tongxun she*, 4 January 1989 in FBIS-CHI-89-003 (5 January 1989), pp. 14–15; T. Tam, *HKS*, 5 January 1989, p. 7; J. Pomfret, "China claims Africans confess, boycott continues in Beijing," AP, 6 January 1989.

37. K. Wilhelm, "Africans boycott classes, demand protection," AP, 6 January 1989; AFP, 7 January 1989 in FBIS-CHI-89-005 (9 January 1989), p. 21.

38. K. Wilhelm, "Ghana Embassy calls for China to release student," AP, 9 January 1989.

39. AFP, 22 February 1989, in FBIS-CHI-89-038 (28 February 1989), p. 16.

40. AFP, 3 January 1989, in FBIS-CHI-89-001 (3 January 1989), pp. 19–20; A. Roche, "China faces worsening racial tension as conflict spreads," Reuter, 3 January 1989; Kazer, "China keeps silent on charges of torture, hidden apartheid"; N. Kristof, "Africans in Beijing boycott classes," *NYT*, 5 January 1989, p. A12; Southerland, "Chinese protests against Africans spread to Beijing, one other city," p. A16; J. Abrams, "Racial tension spreads to fourth Chinese city," AP, 4 January 1989; D. Holley, "Africans press China on student dispute," *LAT*, 5 January 1989, p. 13; J. Pomfret, "Class boycott ends with school agreeing to letter about AIDS," AP, 5 January 1989; "Wuhan refutes foreign news agencies' fabricated 'news'," Xinhua, 7 January 1989 in FBIS-CHI-89-005 (9 January 1989), pp. 10–11; N. Kristof, "China assails foreign reports of racial strife," *NYT*, 7 January 1989, p. 1:6.

41. "Kenyan paper comments on clashes between African and Chinese students," BBC/SWB ME/0349/ii (4 January 1989); Kazer, "China keeps silent on charges of torture, hidden apartheid"; A. Roche, "African students in Peking start classroom strike," Reuter, 3 January 1989; "China: unbeautiful black," *Economist*, 7 January 1989, p. 30; A. Roche, "China faces worsening racial tension as conflicts spread," Reuter, 3 January 1989; "Three Chinese held over race violence," *South China Morning Post (SCMP)*, 6 January 1989, pp. 1, 17; Hong Kong Commercial Radio Service, 6 January 1989, in FBIS-CHI-89-004 (6 January 1989), p. 16; "Libyan and Nigerian reaction to clashes between African and Chinese students," BBC/SWB ME/0348/11, 3 January 1989; AFP, 4 January 1989, FBIS-CHI-88-002 (4 January 1989), p. 19.

42. Guy Dinmore, "African students say they quit China because of racism," Reuter, 15 March 1989; J. Pomfret, "18 Africans to leave China, saying it's racist," AP, 16 March 1989.

43. Gerald Segal, "China and Africa," *Annals of the American Academy of Political and Social Science*, No. 519 (January 1992), p. 121; "Peking redefines its ties," *Africa*, No. 138 (February 1983), pp. 32–34.

44. T. Luard, "China faces feud with Africa as race row grows," *DT*, 5 January 1989, p. 9.

45. Bao Xin, "There is no racial discrimination on China's school campuses," *Liaowang Overseas Edition*, No. 3 (16 January 1989), p. I in FBIS-CHI-89-013 (23 January 1989), p. 18.

46. Dick Wilson, "Asian racism: cold truths are beginning to surface," *NYT*, 15 April 1992, p. 7.

47. "China says no change in African policy, denies racism," Reuter, 27 March 1989; K. Wilhelm, "Zairean students take over embassy," AP, 24 July 1989.

48. C. W. Fan, "Cultural differences sparked row: students," *HKS*, 6 January 1989, p. 1.

49. N. Kristof, "China's burst of rage: a show of racism and something more," *NYT* 8 January 1989, p. 4:3; M. Del Vecchio, "Unrest reveals face of Chinese racism," UPI, 7 January 1989; Southerland, "China's long-held image of foreigners fuels racial conflict," p. A8.

50. See, e.g., Editorial, "Sino-African student clash and aftermath," *Da gong bao* (Hong Kong), 12 January 1989, p. 2 in FBIS-CHI-89-008 (12 January 1989), pp. 11–12; Weijan Shan, "China's discrimination against . . . Chinese," *Christian Science Monitor*, 18 January 1989, p. 19; Mark Petracca, "In China, only foreign students know comfort," *NYT*, 26 January 1989, p. A22.

51. E. Gargan, "For Chinese, sophisticated Africans are contradictions in cultural terms," *LAT*, 8 January 1989, p. 5; Southerland, "China's long-held image of foreigners fuels racial conflict," p. A8; D. Holley, "They face widespread prejudice," *LAT*, 10 January 1989, p. 1; *SCMP*, 15 January 1999, p. 11, 15–16; M. Del Vecchio, "Unrest reveals face of Chinese racism," UPI, 7 January 1989.

52. N. Kristof, "Black Africa leaves China in a quandary," *NYT*, 30 December 1988, p. A3; J. Pomfret, "*Chinese-African* tensions spotlight racism, disaffection," AP, 8 January 1989; Holley, "Ibey face widespread prejudice," p. 1.

53. O'Neill, "*Chinese–African* violence—racism or provocation."

54. Kristof, "Black Africa leaves China in quandary," p. A3; Gargan, "For Chinese, sophisticated Africans are contradictions in cultural terms," p. 5.

55. "Analysis of Events" (typescript foreign student document, Nanjing, c. January 1989), p. 2; A. Roche, "African student group asks to leave 'racist' China," Reuter, 18 January 1989. The results of the survey discussed below cast doubt on the theory that the Nanjing events reflected a male concern with free-spending Africans. Compared to male colleagues, Chinese female university student respondents

rated Africans marginally worse for such key indicators of sexual worth as attractiveness and behaviour. Both sexes thus could be expected to disapprove of African–Chinese liaisons because of the negritude, not the wealth, of Africans.

56. Stuart C. Miller, *The Unwelcome Immigrant: The American Image of the Chinese, 1785–1882* (Berkeley: University of California, 1969), pp. 184–87; Jerome Cohen, *China and the West: Society and Culture, 1815–1937* (London: Hutchinson, 1979), p. 166.

57. "The shock of recognition," *Asiaweek*, Vol. 15, No. 3 (20 January 1989), p. 18.

58. Pomfret, "*Chinese–African* tensions spotlight racism, disaffection."

59. T. Luard, "China faces feud with Africa as race row grows," p. 9.

60. D. Southerland, "Chinese students continue protests against Africans," *WP*, 30 December 1988, p. A21; W. Raspberry, "In China or the south racism is racism," *WP*, 12 January 1989, p. A19; "Violence at Christmas," *Asiaweek*, Vol. 15, No. 2, (13 January 1989), p. 25.

61. Oliver Melvin and James Johnson, "Inter-ethnic conflict in an urban ghetto: the case of blacks and Latinos in Los Angeles," *Research in Social Movements, Conflict and Change*, No. 6 (1984), pp. 57–94.

62. Ferdinand Protzman, "German attacks rise as foreigners become scapegoats," *NYT*, 2 November 1992, p. A1.

63. Jonathan Wolfman, "In China, racism serves needs of change," *NYT*, 10 January 1989, p. A22.

64. SACHED, *Freedom From Below: the Struggle for Trade Unions in South Africa* (Durban: Durban LACOM, 1988), p. 32.

65. Kent Greenawalt, *Discrimination and Reverse Discrimination* (New York: Knopf, 1982).

66. R. R. P. Singh, *Hindu–Muslim Relations in Contemporary India* (New Delhi: Wisdom Publishers, 1990).

67. Jeri Laber, "Bosnia: questions about rape," *New York Review of Books*, Vol. XL, No. 6 (25 March 1993), p. 6.

68. "Analysis of events," p. 2; "Africans made scapegoat for China's economic woes, student says," Reuter, 23 March 1989.

69. See Raspberry, "In China or the south racism is racism," p. A19; Rushworth Kidder, "No race can be an island," *CSM*, 30 January 1989, p. 13.

70. Harold Isaacs, "Group identity and political change: the role of color and physical characteristics," in John Hope Franklin (ed.), *Color and Race* (Boston: Houghton Mifflin, 1968), pp. 92–93.

71. Snow, *The Star Raft* p. 188; N. Kristof, "In China, beauty is a big Western nose," *NYT*, 29 April 1987, p. C4; Gao Yuan, "In China, black isn't beautiful," p. A23; Pomfret, "Chinese–African tensions spotlight racism, disaffection"; Colina MacDougall, "Racial clashes damage China's Third World standing," *FT*, 5 January 1989, p. 3.

72. Frank Dikötter, *The Discourse on Race in Modern China* (London: Hurst & Co., 1992), pp. 38–39, 49, 91–92.

73. F. Dikötter, "Group definition and the idea of 'race' in Modern China (1793–1949)," *Ethnic and Racial Studies*, Vol. 13, No. 3 (July 1990), p. 424.

74. Dikötter, *The Discourse on Race*, pp. 79, 82–83, 88–91, 93.

75. Ibid. pp. 144, 147–48; Dikötter, "Group Definition," p. 429; "Eugenics in Republican China," *Republican China*, Vol. 15, No. 1 (1990), pp. 1–17.

76. Lin Biao, *Long Live the Victory of People's War* (Beijing: Foreign Language Press, 1965).

77. Stanley Rosen, "Students and the state in China: the crisis in ideology and organization," in Arthur Rosenbaum (ed.), *State and Society in China: The Consequences of Reform* (Boulder: Westview Press, 1992), p. 172.

78. See Stanley Rosen, "Public opinion and reform in the PRC," *Studies in Comparative Communism*, Vol. 22, No. 3 (Summer–Autumn, 1989) pp. 153–70.

79. The numerical data underlying the survey results are available from the author upon request.

80. See, e.g., Carleton Coon, *The Origin of Race* (New York: Knopf, 1962), pp. 655–56. Proponents of the idea of racial differences in intelligence usually extend their views to class. See Cahpour Haghighat, *Racisme Scientifique: Offensive Contre L'Egalite Sociale* (Paris: Editions L'Hamattan, 1988); Elaine Mensh, *The IQ Mythology: Class, Race, Gender and Inequality* (Carbondale: Southern Illinois Press, 1991).

81. Sheryl WuDunn, "China and Japan on path to better ties," *NYT*, 10 August 1991, p. A3.

82. Jan Breman, *Imperial Monkey Business: Racial Supremacy in Social Darwinist Theory and Colonial Practice* (Amsterdam: VU University Press, 1990).

83. bell hooks, *Black Looks: Race and Representation* (Boston: South End Press, 1992). See, e.g., Thomas Jefferson, *Notes on the State of Virginia* (Chapel Hill: University of North Carolina, 1782, 1965), pp. 138–43.

84. Bogdan Krzyk, "'You pay more, big nose,'" *World Press Review* (January 1993), pp. 26–27; Ira Bernstein *et al.*, "Chinese and white concepts of attractiveness," *Bulletin of the Psychonomic Society*, Vol. 18, No. 2 (1981), p. 59.

85. Ma Yin, *Questions and Answers About China's Minority Nationalities* (Beijing: New World Press, 1985), p. 57. Scholars disagree as to whether this attitude involves racism or a mere feeling of cultural superiority on the part of Han Chinese. See A. Tom Grunfeld, "In search of equality: relations between China's ethnic minorities and the majority Han," *Bulletin of Concerned Asian Scholars*, Vol. 17, No. 1 (1985), p. 55 fn. 3.

86. See Paul Gordon, *Daily Racism: The Press and Black People in Britain* (London: Runnymede Press, 1989).

87. See Peter Scheckner, "E. T. and the Beijing Spring Movement: American culture and Chinese values," *Midwest Quarterly*, Vol. 34, No. 2 (Winter 1993), pp. 151–65. On media stereotyping and an antipathy toward the dark-skinned as determinants of Korean anti-black prejudice, see Lucie Cheng and Yen Espiritu, "Korean businesses in black and Hispanic neighborhoods: a study of intergroup relations," *Sociological Perspectives*, Vol. 32, No. 4 (1989), p. 526.

88. For treatments of Japanese anti-black prejudice based on interviews and the explication of literary texts, see Hiroshi Wagatsuma, "The social perception of skin color in Japan," in Franklin, *Color and Race* pp. 149–56; John G. Russell, "Narratives of denial: racial chauvinism and the black other in Japan," *Japan Quarterly*, No. 38 (October–December 1991), pp. 416–28. The same technique has been applied to anti-Chinese prejudice in the United States. See, e.g., Colleen Fong, *Tracing the Origins of a Model Minority: A Study of the Depictions of Chinese-Americans in Popular Magazines* (University of Oregon, unpub. Ph.D. diss., 1989).

89. See George Yu, "Africa in Chinese foreign policy," *Asian Survey*, Vol. 28, No. 8 (August 1988), pp. 849–62.

90. See the statement of Zhou Enlai quoted in George Kahin, *The African-Asian Conference* (Ithaca: Cornell, 1956), p. 60. .

91. Isaacs, "Group identity and political change," p. 93.

92. See George Sinkler, *The Racial Attitudes of American Presidents: from Abraham Lincoln to Theodore Roosevelt* (Garden City: Doubleday, 1971).

93. See, e.g., Roger Morris, *Uncertain Greatness: Henry Kissinger and American Foreign Policy* (New York: Harper & Rowe, 1977), p. 132; Ronald Reagan, *An American Life* (New York: Simon & Schuster, 1990), p. 357; Christopher Hitchens, *Blood, Class and Nostalgia: Anglo-American Ironies* (New York: Farrar, Straus & Giroux, 1990), p. 357.

94. Philip Martin, "Racism and the fight for rights collide in a painful paradox," *LAT*, 23 June 1990, p. B7.

95. Julia Kwong, "The 1986 student demonstrations in China: a democratic movement," *Asian Survey*, Vol. 28, No. 9 (September 1988), p. 970; Richard Lufrano, "Nanjing Spring: the 1989 student movement in a provincial capital," *Bulletin of Concerned Asian Scholars*, Vol. 24, No. 1 (1992), pp. 19–42.

96. Lufrano, "Nanjing Spring," p. 42. For an account of the 1989 movement in one city where leaders tried to dissociate it from the "floating population" of ex-peasants living in the city, see Anita Chan and Jonathan Unger, "Voices from the protest movement in Chongqing: class accents and class tensions," in J. Unger (ed.), *The Pro-Democracy Protests in China: Reports from the Provinces* (Armonk: M. E. Sharpe, 1991), pp. 106–26.

SECTION FIVE:
THE IMPACT OF THE ATLANTIC SLAVE TRADE: THE MIDDLE PASSAGE

Introduction

The fifth section examines one of the most important activities that confronts the African Diaspora experience: the African slave trade. This section seeks to broaden the discussion on the involuntary migration of Africans out of Africa, while not limiting it to the waves of migration of Africans out of Africa, that were orchestrated by fellow Africans, as well as Arab and Islamic slave dealers, who traded across the Sahara Desert and into regions of the Mediterranean world, the Red Sea, and the Indian Ocean.

The first essay is Eric E. Williams's "Origin of Slavery," a very persuasive essay from his 1944 monumental work, *Capitalism and Slavery*, in which he argues that the institution of slavery was devised to facilitate the new economic realities of the colonialists in the Americas and the Caribbean. Williams's argument still creates a healthy debate in many circles and has been at the center of many discussions that have appeared in numerous articles, books, and conferences. He is the author of about a dozen works related to slavery and its aftermath in the Caribbean. Williams's other works include *The Negro in the Caribbean* (1942), *Education In the British West Indies* (1950), *The British West Indies at Westminster* (1954), *The British Historians and the West Indies* (1964), *History of the People of Trinidad and Tobago* (1962, 1967, 1982), *Inward Hunger: The Education of a Prime Minister* (1969), and *From Columbus to Castro: The History of the Caribbean 1492–1969* (1970).

The second essay is the well-known firsthand account of an African experiencing the Middle Passage. It was authored by Olaudah Equiano, who was later known as Gustavus Vassa, one of the leading Black eighteenth-century abolitionists. Equiano was born about 1745 near Guinea (Ibo) Coast (now Nigeria), and was kidnapped and brought forcibly to the Americas.

Written many years after the experience and after he had lived in Barbados, Canada, the United States and England, his story remains compelling. It was published nine times before his death in 1797. The fist edition appeared in 1789 and was called *The Interesting Narrative of the Life of Olaudah Equiano or Gustavus Vassa, the African*. There are many recent reproductions of this twelve-chapter publication, and recent scholars have sought to vindicate the accuracy of this account.

The third essay by David P. Henige is entitled "Measuring the Immeasurable: The Atlantic Slave Trade." This penetrating analysis appeared in the *Journal of African History* (1986) and is a wonderful and clear summation of the ongoing debate regarding the volume of the African population that actually made the centuries-old Middle Passage. After the publication of Philip D. Curtin's *The Atlantic Slave Trade: A Census* (1969) with its assertion that the estimated number of 9.5 million Africans crossed in the Middle Passage, there have been numerous studies, including the works of Walter Rodney (1972), Roger Anstey (1975), Selwy Carrington (1988), Seymour Drescher (1977), and of course Stanley Engerman and Joseph E. Inikori (1992) to list a few, revising the numbers upward. Henige gives a skeptical view of how much can really be determined and documented about this clandestine centuries-long international business and suggests that it may be impossible to ever determine the actual volume of the Atlantic slave trade. He has served as the African Studies bibliographer at the University of Wisconsin, Madison and as editor of History in Africa, a journal on methodology in African history, published by the African Studies Association of the United States. Henige has written widely on many aspects of African history and on demographic issues as they related to historical methodology and oral tradition. He has authored and edited works in American, Latin American, and African Studies. His publications include *Works in African History* (1974–1978), *Catholic Missionary Journals* (1980), *Oral Historiography* (1982), *Working Papers on Columbus (1982), In Search of Columbus* (1991), *The Native American Population* (1992), and *Numbers From Nowhere* (1992).

The fourth essay deals with the Creolization process that transpires within the slave community and produces a new way of life in the Americas and the Caribbean. "Enslaved Africans and their Expectations of Slave Life in the Americas: Towards a Reconsideration of the Models of 'Creolization,'" prepared by Paul E. Lovejoy and David V. Trotman is an insightful work that seeks to investigate the wide range of expectations that African slaves had towards their new experiences in the Americas. This study was originally published in Verene A. Shepherd and Glen L. Richards's, *Questioning Creole: Creolization Discourses in the Caribbean Culture* (2002). Verene A. Shepherd is a Senior Lecturer in history at the University of the West Indies in Jamaica. She is the author and editor of many works on Caribbean history. She co-edited *Caribbean Slave Society and Economy* (1991), *Caribbean Freedom* (1993) and *Caribbean Slavery in the Atlantic World* (2000) all with Hilary McD. Beckles as well as *Engendering History: Caribbean Women in Historical Perspective* with Barbara Bailey and Bridget Brereton (1995).

Paul E. Lovejoy is Professor of History at York University in Canada, and has written extensively on African economic and social history. Among his works are *Transformations in Slavery: A History of Slavery in Africa* (1983), and *Slow Death for Slavery: The Course of Abolition—Northern Nigeria 1897–1936* (1990).

David V. Trotman is associate Professor of History at York University in Canada. He is the author of *Crime in Trinidad: Conflict and Control in a Plantation Society 1838–1900*, (1986) and co-editor of *Trans-Atlantic Dimensions of Ethnicity in the African Diaspora* (2002) with Paul E. Lovejoy.

The Origin of Negro Slavery

Eric E. Williams

Slavery in the Caribbean has been too narrowly identified with the Negro. A racial twist has thereby been given to what is basically an economic phenomenon. Slavery was not born of racism: rather, racism was the consequence of slavery. Unfree labor in the New World was brown, white, black, and yellow; Catholic, Protestant and pagan.

The first instance of slave trading and slave labor developed in the New World involved, racially, not the Negro but the Indian. The Indians rapidly succumbed to the excessive labor demanded of them, the insufficient diet, the white man's diseases, and their inability to adjust themselves to the new way of life. Accustomed to a life of liberty, their constitution and temperament were ill-adapted to the rigors of plantation slavery. As Fernando Ortíz writes: "To subject the Indian to the mines, to their monotonous, insane and severe labor, without tribal sense, without religious ritual, . . . was like taking away from him the meaning of his life. . . . It was to enslave not only his muscles but also his collective spirit."

The visitor to Ciudad Trujillo, capital of the Dominican Republic (the present-day name of half of the island formerly called Hispaniola), will see a statue of Columbus, with the figure of an Indian woman gratefully writing (so reads the caption) the name of the Discoverer. The story is told, on the other hand, of the Indian chieftain, Hatuey, who, doomed to die for resisting the invaders, staunchly refused to accept the Christian faith as the gateway to salvation when he learned that his executioners, too, hoped to get to Heaven. It is far more probable that Hatuey, rather than the anonymous woman, represented contemporary Indian opinion of their new overlords.

England and France, in their colonies, followed the Spanish practice of enslavement of the Indians. There was one conspicuous difference—the attempts of the Spanish Crown, however ineffective, to restrict Indian slavery to those who refused to accept Christianity and to the warlike Caribs on the specious plea that they were cannibals. From the standpoint of the British government Indian slavery, unlike later Negro slavery which involved vital imperial interests, was a purely colonial matter. As Lauber writes: "The home government was interested in colonial slave conditions and legislation only when the African slave trade was involved. . . . Since it (Indian slavery) was never sufficiently extensive to interfere with Negro slavery and the slave trade, it never received any attention from the home government, and so existed as legal because never declared illegal."

But Indian slavery never was extensive in the British dominions. Ballagh, writing of Virginia, says that popular sentiment had never "demanded the subjection of the Indian race *per se*, as was practically the case with the Negro in the first slave act of 1661, but only a portion of it, and that admittedly a very small portion. . . . In the case of the Indian . . . slavery was viewed as of an occasional nature, a preventive penalty and not as a normal and permanent condition." In the New England colonies Indian slavery was unprofitable, for slavery of any kind was unprofitable because it was unsuited to the diversified agriculture of these colonies. In addition the Indian slave was inefficient. The Spainards discovered that one Negro was worth four Indians. A prominent official in Hispaniola insisted in 1518 that "permission be given to bring Negroes, a race robust for labor, instead of natives, so weak that they can only be employed in tasks requiring little endurance, such as taking care of maize fields or farms." The future staples of the New World, sugar and cotton, required strength which the Indian lacked, and demanded the robust "cotton nigger" as sugar's need of strong mules produced in Louisiana the epithet "sugar mules." According to Lauber, "When compared with sums paid for Negroes at the same time and place the prices of Indian slaves are found to have been considerably lower."

The Indian reservoir, too, was limited, the African inexhaustible. Negroes therefore were stolen in Africa to work the lands stolen from the Indians in America. The voyages of Prince Henry the Navigator complemented those of Columbus, West African history became the complement of West Indian.

The immediate successor of the Indian, however, was not the Negro but the poor white. These white servants included a variety of types. Some were indentured servants, so called because, before departure from the homeland, they had signed a contract, indented by law, binding them to service for a stipulated time in return for their passage. Still others, known as "redemptioners," arranged with the captain of the ship to pay for their passage on arrival or within a specified time thereafter; if they did not, they were sold by the captain to the highest bidder. Others were convicts, sent out by the deliberate policy of the home government, to serve for a specified period.

This emigration was in tune with mercantilist theories of the day which strongly advocated putting the poor to industrious and useful labor and favored emigration, voluntary or involuntary, as relieving the poor rates and finding more profitable occupations abroad for idlers and vagrants at home. "Indentured servitude," writes C. M. Haar, "was called into existence by two different though complementary forces: there was both a positive attraction from the New World and a negative repulsion from the Old." In a state paper delivered to James I in 1606 Bacon emphasized that by emigration England would gain "a double commodity, in the avoidance of people here, and in making use of them there."

This temporary service at the outset denoted no inferiority or degradation. Many of the servants were manorial tenants fleeing from the irksome restrictions of feudalism, Irishmen seeking freedom from the oppression of landlords and bishops, Germans running away from the devastation of the Thirty Years' War. They transplanted in their hearts a burning desire for land, an ardent passion for independence. They came to the land of opportunity to be free men, their imaginations powerfully wrought upon by glowing and extravagant descriptions in the home country. It was only later when, in the words of Dr. Williamson, "all ideals of a decent colonial society, of a better and greater England overseas, were swamped in the pursuit of an immediate gain," that the introduction of disreputable elements became a general feature of indentured service.

A regular traffic developed in these servants. Between 1654 and 1685 ten thousand sailed from Bristol alone, chiefly for the West Indies and Virginia. In 1683 white servants represented one-sixth of Virginia's population. Two-thirds of the immigrants to Pennsylvania during the eighteenth century were white servants; in four years 25,000 came to Philadelphia alone. It has been estimated that more than a quarter of a million persons were of this class during the colonial period, and that they probably constituted one-half of all English immigrants, the majority going to the middle colonies.

As commercial speculation entered the picture, abuses crept in. Kidnapping was encouraged to a great degree and became a regular business in such towns as London and Bristol. Adults would be plied with liquor, children enticed with sweetmeats. The kidnappers were called "spirits," defined as "one that taketh upp men and women and children and sells them on a shipp to be conveyed beyond the sea." The captain of a ship trading to Jamaica would visit the Clerkenwell House of Correction, ply with drink the girls who had been imprisoned there as disorderly, and "invite" them to go to the West Indies. The temptations held out to the unwary and the credulous were so attractive that, as the mayor of Bristol complained, husbands were induced to forsake their wives, wives their husbands, and apprentices their masters, while wanted criminals found on the transport ships a refuge from the arms of the law. The wave of German immigration developed the "newlander," the labor agent of those days, who traveled up and down the Rhine Valley persuading the feudal peasants to sell their belongings and emigrate to America, receiving a commission for each emigrant.

Much has been written about the trickery these "newlanders" were not averse to employing. But whatever the deceptions practiced, it remains true, as Friedrich Kapp has written, that "the real ground for the emigration fever lay in the unhealthy political and economic conditions. . . . The misery and oppression of the conditions of the little (German) states promoted emigration much more dangerously and continuously than the worse 'newlander.'"

Convicts provided another steady source of white labor. The harsh feudal laws of England recognized three hundred capital crimes. Typical hanging offenses included: picking a pocket for more than a shilling; shoplifting to the value of five shillings; stealing a horse or a sheep; poaching rabbits on a gentleman's estate. Offenses for which the punishment prescribed by law was transportation comprised the stealing of cloth, burning stacks of corn, the maiming and killing of cattle, hindering customs officers in the execution of their duty, and corrupt legal practices. Proposals made in 1664 would have banished to the colonies all vagrants, rogues and idlers, petty thieves, gypsies, and loose persons frequenting unlicensed brothels. A piteous petition in 1667 prayed for transportation instead of the death sentence for a wife convicted of stealing goods valued at three shillings and four pence. In 1745 transportation was the penalty for the theft of a silver spoon and a gold watch. One year after the emancipation of the Negro slaves, transportation was the penalty for trade union activity. It is difficult to resist the conclusion that there was some connection between the law and the labor needs of the plantations, and the marvel is that so few people ended up in the colonies overseas.

Benjamin Franklin opposed this "dumping upon the New World of the outcasts of the Old" as the most cruel insult ever offered by one nation to another, and asked, if England was justified in sending her convicts to the colonies, whether the latter were justified in sending to England their rattlesnakes in exchange? It is not clear why Franklin should have been so sensitive. Even if the convicts were hardened criminals, the great increase of indentured servants and free emigrants would have tended to render the convict influence innocuous, as increasing quantities of water poured in a glass containing poison. Without convicts the early development of the Australian colonies in the nineteenth century would have been impossible. Only a few of the colonists, however, were so particular. The general attitude was summed up by a contemporary: "Their labor would be more beneficial in an infant settlement, than their vices could be pernicious." There was nothing strange about this attitude. The great problem in a new country is the problem of labor, and convict labor, as Merivale has pointed out, was equivalent to a free present by the government to the settlers without burdening the latter with the expense of importation. The governor of Virginia in 1611 was willing to welcome convicts reprieved from death as "a readie way to furnish us with men and not allways with the worst kind of men." The West Indies were prepared to accept all and sundry, even the spawn of Newgate and Bridewell, for "no goale-bird [*sic*] can be so incorrigible, but there is hope of his conformity here, as well as of his preferment, which some have happily experimented."

The political and civil disturbances in England between 1640 and 1740 augmented the supply of white servants. Political and religious nonconformists paid for their unorthodoxy by transportation, mostly to the sugar islands. Such was the fate of many of Cromwell's Irish prisoners, who were sent to the West Indies. So thoroughly was this policy pursued that an active verb was added to the English language—to "barbadoes" a person. Montserrat became largely an Irish colony, and the Irish brogue is still frequently heard today in many parts of the British West Indies. The Irish, however, were poor servants. They hated the English, and were always ready to aid England's enemies, and in a revolt in the Leeward Islands in 1689 we can already see signs of that burning indignation which, according to Lecky, gave Washington some of his best soldiers. The vanquished in Cromwell's Scottish campaigns were treated like the Irish before them, and Scotsmen came to be regarded as "the general travaillers and soldiers in most foreign parts." Religious intolerance sent more workers to the plantations. In 1661 Quakers refusing to take the oath for the third time were to be transported; in 1664 transportation, to any plantation except Virginia or New England, or a fine of one hundred pounds was decreed for the third offense for persons over sixteen assembling in groups of five or more under pretense of religion. Many of Monmouth's adherents were sent to Barbados, with orders to be detained as servants for ten years. The prisoners were granted in batches to favorite courtiers, who made handsome profits from the traffic in which, it is alleged, even the Queen shared. A similar policy was resorted to after the Jacobite risings of the eighteenth century.

The transportation of these white servants shows in its true light the horrors of the Middle Passage—not as something unusual or inhuman but as a part of the age. The emigrants were packed like herrings. According to Mittelberger, each servant was allowed about two feet in width and six feet in length in bed. The boats were small, the voyage long, the food, in the absence of refrigeration, bad, disease inevitable. A petition to Parliament in 1659 describes how seventy-two servants had been locked up below deck during the whole voyage of five and a half weeks, "amongst horses, that their souls, through heat and steam under the tropic, fainted in them." Inevitably abuses crept into the system and Fearon was shocked by "the horrible picture of human suffering which this living sepulchre" of an emigrant vessel in Philadelphia afforded. But conditions even for the free passengers were not much better in those days, and the comment of a Lady of Quality describing a voyage from Scotland to the West Indies on a ship full of indentured servants should banish any ideas that the horrors of the slave ship are to be accounted for by the fact that the victims were Negroes. "It is hardly possible," she writes, "to believe that human nature could be so depraved, as to treat fellow creatures in such a manner for so little gain."

* * *

Negro slavery, thus, had nothing to do with climate. Its origin can be expressed in three words: in the Caribbean, Sugar; on the mainland, Tobacco and Cotton. A change in the economic structure produced a corresponding change in the labor supply. The fundamental fact was "the creation of an inferior social and economic organization of exploiters and exploited." Sugar, tobacco, and cotton required the large plantation and hordes of cheap labor, and the small farm of the ex-indentured white servant could not possibly survive. The tobacco of the small farm in Barbados was displaced by the sugar of the large plantation. The rise of the sugar industry in the Caribbean was the signal for a gigantic dispossession of the small farmer. Barbados in 1645 had 11,200 small white farmers and 5,680 Negro slaves; in 1667 there were 745 large plantation owners and 82,023 slaves. In 1645 the island had 18,300 whites fit to bear arms, in 1667 only 8,300. The white farmers were squeezed out. The planters continued to offer inducements to newcomers, but they could no longer offer the main inducement, land. White servants preferred the other islands where they could hope for land, to Barbados, where they were sure there was none. In desperation the planters proposed legislation which would prevent a landowner from purchasing more land, compel Negroes and servants to wear dimity manufactured in Barbados (what would English mercantilists have said?) to provide employment for the poor whites, and prevent Negroes from being taught to trade. The governor of Barbados in 1695 drew a pitiful picture of these ex-servants. Without fresh meat or rum, "they are domineered over and used like dogs, and this in time will undoubtedly drive away all the commonalty of the white people." His only suggestion was to give the right to elect members of the Assembly to every white man owning two acres of land. Candidates for election would "sometimes give the poor miserable creatures a little rum and fresh provisions and such things as would be of nourishment to them," in order to get their votes—and elections were held every year. It is not surprising that the exodus continued.

The poor whites began their travels, disputing their way all over the Caribbean, from Barbados to Nevis, to Antigua, and thence to Guiana and Trinidad, and ultimately Carolina. Everywhere they were pursued and dispossessed by the same inexorable economic force, sugar; and in Carolina they were safe from cotton only for a hundred years. Between 1672 and 1708 the white men in Nevis decreased by more than three-fifths, the black population more than doubled. Between 1672 and 1727 the white males of Montserrat declined by more than two-thirds, in the same period the black population increased more than eleven times. "The more they buie," said the Barbadians, referring to their slaves, "the more they are able to buye, for in a yeare and a halfe they will earne with God's blessing as much as they cost." King Sugar had begun his depredations, changing flourishing commonwealths of small farmers into vast sugar factories owned by a camarilla of absentee capitalist magnates and worked by a mass of alien proletarians. The plantation economy had no room for poor whites; the proprietor or overseer, a physician on the more prosperous plantations, possibly their families, these were sufficient. "If a state," wrote Weston, "could be supposed to be made up of continuous plantations, the white race would be not merely starved out, but literally squeezed out." The resident planters, apprehensive of the growing disproportion between whites and blacks, passed Deficiency Laws to compel absentees, under penalty of fines, to keep white servants. The absentees preferred to pay the fines. In the West Indies today the poor white survive in the "Red-legs" of Barbados, pallid, weak and depraved from in-breeding, strong rum, insufficient food and abstinence from manual labor. For, as Merivale wrote, "in a country where Negro slavery prevails extensively, no white is industrious."

It was the triumph, not of geographical conditions, as Harlow contends, but of economic. The victims were the Negroes in Africa and the small white farmers. The increase of wealth for the few whites was as phenomenal as the increase of misery for the many blacks. The Barbados crops in 1650, over a twenty-month period, were worth over three million pounds, about fifteen million in modern money. In 1666 Barbados was computed to be seventeen times as rich as it had been before the planting of sugar. "The buildings in 1643 were mean, with things only for necessity, but in 1666, plate, jewels, and household stuff were estimated at £500,000, their buildings very fair and beautiful, and their houses like castles, their sugar houses and negroes huts show themselves from the sea like so many small towns, each defended by its castle." The price of land skyrocketed. A plantation of five hundred acres which sold for £400 in 1640 fetched £7,000 for a half-share in 1648.

The estate of one Captain Waterman, comprising eight hundred acres, had at one time been split up among no less than forty proprietors. For sugar was and is essentially a capitalist undertaking, involving not only agricultural operations but the crude stages of refining as well. A report on the French sugar islands stated that to make ten hogsheads of sugar required as great an expenditure in beasts of burden, mills and utensils as to make a hundred. James Knight of Jamaica estimated that it required four hundred acres to start a sugar plantation. According to Edward Long, another planter and the historian of the island, it needed £5,000 to start a small plantation of three hundred acres, producing from thirty to fifty hogsheads of sugar a year, £14,000 for a plantation of the same size producing one hundred hogsheads. There could be only two classes in such a society, wealthy planters and oppressed slaves.

The moral is reinforced by a consideration of the history of Virginia, where the plantation economy was based not on sugar but on tobacco. The researches of Professor Wertenbaker have exploded the legend that Virginia from the outset was an aristocratic dominion. In the early seventeenth century about two-thirds of the landholders had neither slaves nor indentured servants. The strength of the colony lay in its numerous white yeomanry. Conditions became worse as the market for tobacco was glutted by Spanish competition and the Virginians demanded in wrath that something be done about "those petty English plantations in the savage islands in the West Indies" through which quantities of Spanish tobacco reached England. Nonetheless, though prices continued to fall, the exports of Virginia and Maryland increased more than six times between 1663 and 1699. The explanation lay in two words—Negro slavery, which cheapened the cost of production. Negro slaves, one-twentieth of the population in 1670, were one-fourth in 1730. "Slavery, from being an insignificant factor in the economic life of the colony, had become the very foundation upon which it was established." There was still room in Virginia, as there was not in Barbados, for the small farmer, but land was useless to him if he could not compete with slave labor. So the Virginian peasant, like the Barbadian, was squeezed out. "The Virginia which had formerly been so largely the land of the little farmer, had become the land of Masters and Slaves. For aught else there was no room."

The whole future history of the Caribbean is nothing more than a dotting of the i's and a crossing of the t's. It happened earlier in the British and French than in the Spanish islands, where the process was delayed until the advent of the dollar diplomacy of our own time. Under American capital we have witnessed the transformation of Cuba, Puerto Rico and the Dominican Republic into huge sugar factories (though the large plantation, especially in Cuba, was not unknown under the Spanish regime), owned abroad and operated by alien labor, on the British West Indian pattern. That this process is taking place with free labor and in nominally independent areas (Puerto Rico excepted) helps us to see in its true light the first importation of Negro slave labor in the British Caribbean—a phase in the history of the plantation. In the words of Professor Phillips, the plantation system was "less dependent upon slavery than slavery was upon it. . . . The plantation system formed, so to speak, the industrial and social frame of government . . . , while slavery was a code of written laws enacted for that purpose."

Where the plantation did not develop, as in the Cuban tobacco industry, Negro labor was rare and white labor predominated. The liberal section of the Cuban population consistently advocated the cessation of the Negro slave trade and the introduction of white immigrants. Saco, mouthpiece of the liberals, called for the immigration of workers "white and free, from all parts of the world, of all races, provided they have a white face and can do honest labor." Sugar defeated Saco. It was the sugar plantation, with its servile base, which retarded white immigration in nineteenth century Cuba as it had banned it in seventeenth century Barbados and eighteenth century Saint Domingue. No sugar, no Negroes. In Puerto Rico, which developed relatively late as a genuine plantation, and where, before the American regime, sugar never dominated the lives and thoughts of the population as it did elsewhere, the poor white peasants survived and the Negro slaves never exceeded fourteen percent of the population. Saco wanted to "whiten" the Cuban social structure. Negro slavery blackened that structure all over the Caribbean while the blood of the Negro slaves reddened the Atlantic and both its shores. Strange that an article like sugar, so sweet and necessary to human existence, should have occasioned such crimes and bloodshed!

The Life of Olaudah Equiano, or Gustavus Vassa the African

Olaudah Equiano

Chapter Two

I hope the reader will not think I have trespassed on his patience in introducing myself to him with some account of the manners and customs of my country. They had been implanted in me with great care, and made an impression on my mind, which time could not erase, and which all the adversity and variety of fortune I have since experienced served only to rivet and record; for, whether the love of one's country be real or imaginary, or a lesson of reason, or an instinct of nature, I still look back with pleasure on the first scenes of my life, though that pleasure has been for the most part mingled with sorrow.

I have already acquainted the reader with the time and place of my birth. My father, besides many slaves, had a numerous family, of which seven lived to grow up, including myself and a sister, who was the only daughter. As I was the youngest of the sons, I became, of course, the greatest favourite with my mother, and was always with her; and she used to take particular pains to form my mind. I was trained up from my earliest years in the art of war; my daily exercise was shooting and throwing javelins; and my mother adorned me with emblems, after the manner of our greatest warriors. In this way I grew up till I was turned the age of eleven, when an end was put to my happiness in the following manner:—Generally when the grown people in the neighbourhood were gone far in the fields to labour, the children assembled together in some of the neighbours' premises to play; and commonly some of us used to get up a tree to look out for any assailant, or kidnapper, that might come upon us; for they sometimes took those opportunities of our parents' absence to attack and carry off as many as they could seize. One day, as I was watching at the top of a tree in our yard, I saw one of those people come into the yard of our next neighbour but one, to kidnap, there being many stout young people in it. Immediately on this I gave the alarm of the rogue, and he was surrounded by the stoutest of them, who entangled him with cords, so that he could not escape till some of the grown people came and secured him. But alas! ere long it was my fate to be thus attacked, and to be carried off, when none of the grown people were nigh. One day, when all our people were gone out to their works as usual, and only I and my dear sister were left to mind the house, two men and a woman got over our walls, and in a moment seized us both, and, without giving us time to cry out, or make resistance, they stopped our mouths, and ran off

with us into the nearest wood. Here they tied our hands, and continued to carry us as far as they could, till night came on, when we reached a small house, where the robbers halted for refreshment, and spent the night. We were then unbound, but were unable to take any food; and, being quite overpowered by fatigue and grief, our only relief was some sleep, which allayed our misfortune for a short time. The next morning we left the house, and continued traveling all the day. For a long time we had kept the woods, but at last we came into a road which I believed I knew. I had now some hopes of being delivered; for we had advanced but a little way before I discovered some people at a distance, on which I began to cry out for their assistance: but my cries had no other effect than to make them tie me faster and stop my mouth, and then they put me into a large sack. They also stopped my sister's mouth, and tied her hands; and in this manner we proceeded till we were out of the sight of these people. When we went to rest the following night they offered us some victuals; but we refused it; and the only comfort we had was in being in one another's arms all that night, and bathing each other with our tears. But alas! we were soon deprived of even the small comfort of weeping together. The next day proved a day of greater sorrow than I had yet experienced; for my sister and I were then separated, while we lay clasped in each other's arms. It was in vain that we besought them not to part us; she was torn from me, and immediately carried away, while I was left in a state of distraction not to be described. I cried and grieved continually; and for several days I did not eat any thing but what they forced into my mouth. At length, after many days traveling, during which I had often changed masters, I got into the hands of a chieftain, in a very pleasant country. This man had two wives and some children, and they all used me extremely well, and did all they could to comfort me; particularly the first wife, who was something like my mother. Although I was a great many days journey from my father's house, yet these people spoke exactly the same language with us. This first master of mine, as I may call him, was a smith, and my principal employment was working his bellows, which were the same kind as I had seen in my vicinity. They were in some respects not unlike the stoves here in gentlemen's kitchens; and were covered over with leather and in the middle of that leather a stick was fixed, and a person stood up, and worked it, in the same manner as is done to pump water out of a cask with a hand pump. I believe it was gold he worked, for it was of a lovely bright yellow colour, and was worn by the women on their wrists and ankles. I was there I suppose about a month, and they at last used to trust me some little distance from the house. This liberty I used in embracing every opportunity to inquire the way to my own home: and I also sometimes, for the same purpose, went with the maidens, in the cool of the evenings, to bring pitchers of water from the springs for the use of the house. I had also remarked where the sun rose in the morning, and set in the evening, as I had traveled along; and I had observed that my father's house was towards the rising of the sun. I therefore determined to seize the first opportunity of making my escape, and to shape my course for that quarter; for I was quite oppressed and weighed down by grief after my mother and friends; and my love of liberty, ever great, was strengthened by the mortifying circumstances of not daring to eat with the free-born children, although I was mostly their companion.

Here follows an anecdote about Equiano's fears after he has accidentally killed a chicken and run off in terror. He is found, however, and his African master, "having slightly reprimanded me, ordered me to be taken care of, and not to be ill-treated."

Soon after this my master's only daughter, and child by his first wife, sickened and died, which affected him so much that for some time he was almost frantic, and really would have killed himself, had he not been watched and prevented. However, in a small time afterwards he recovered, and I was again sold. I was now carried to the left of the sun's rising, through many different countries, and a number of large woods. The people I was sold to used to carry me very often, when I was tired, either on their shoulders or on their backs. I saw many convenient well-built sheds along the roads, at proper distances, to accommodate the merchants and travelers, who lay in those buildings along with their wives, who often accompany them; and they always go well armed.

From the time I left my own nation I always found somebody that understood me till I came to the sea coast. The languages of different nations did not totally differ, nor were they so copious as those of the Europeans, particularly the English. They were therefore easily learned; and, while I was journeying thus through Africa, I acquired two or three different tongues. In this manner I had been traveling for a considerable time, when one evening, to my great surprise, whom should I see brought to the house where I was but my dear sister! As soon as she saw me she gave a loud shriek, and ran into my arms—I was quite overpowered: neither of us could speak; but, for a considerable time, clung to each other in mutual embraces, unable to do any thing but weep. Our meeting affected all who saw us; and indeed I must acknowledge, in honour of those sable destroyers of human rights, that I never met with any ill treatment, or saw any offered to their slaves, except tying them, when necessary, to keep them from running away. When these people knew we were brother and sister they indulged us together; and the man, to whom I supposed we belonged, lay with us, he in the middle, while she and I held one another by the hands across his breast all night; and thus for a while we forgot our misfortunes in the joy of being together: but even this small comfort was soon to have an end; for scarcely had the fatal morning appeared, when she was again torn from me for ever! I was now more miserable, if possible, than before. The small relief which her presence gave me from pain was gone, and the wretchedness of my situation was redoubled by my anxiety after her fate, and my apprehensions lest her sufferings should be greater than mine, when I could not be with her to alleviate them. Yes, thou dear partner of all my childish sports! thou sharer of my joys and sorrows! happy should I have ever esteemed myself to encounter every misery for you, and to procure your freedom by the sacrifice of my own. Though you were early forced from my arms, your image has been always riveted in my heart, from which neither *time nor fortune* have been able to remove it; so that, while the thoughts of your sufferings have damped my prosperity, they have mingled with adversity and increased its bitterness. To that Heaven which protects the weak from the strong, I commit the care of your innocence and virtues, if they have not already received their full reward, and if your youth and delicacy have not long fallen victims to the violence of the African trader, the pestilential stench of a Guinea ship, the lash and lust of a brutal and unrelenting overseer.

I did not long remain after my sister. I was again sold, and carried through a number of places, till, after traveling a considerable time, I came to a town called Tinmah, in the most beautiful country I had yet seen in Africa. It was extremely rich, and there were many rivulets which flowed through it, and supplied a large pond in the centre of the town, where the people washed. Here I first saw and tasted coco-nuts, which I thought superior to any nuts I had ever tasted before; and the trees which were loaded, were also interspersed amongst the houses, which had commodious shades adjoining, and were in the same manner as ours, the insides being neatly plastered and whitewashed. Here I also saw and tasted for the first time sugar-cane. Their money consisted of little white shells, the size of the finger nail. I was sold here for one hundred and seventy-two of them by a merchant who lived and brought me there. I had been about two or three days at his house, when a wealthy widow, a neighbour of his, came there one evening, and brought with her an only son, a young gentleman about my own age and size. Here they saw me; and, having taken a fancy to me, I was bought of the merchant, and went home with them. Her house and premises were situated close to one of those rivulets I have mentioned, and were the finest I ever saw in Africa: they were very extensive, and she had a number of slaves to attend her. The next day I was washed and perfumed, and when meal-time came I was led into the presence of my mistress, and ate and drank before her with her son. This filled me with astonishment; and I could scarce help expressing my surprise that the young gentleman should suffer me, who was bound, to eat with him who was free; and not only so, but that he would not at any time either eat or drink till I had taken first, because I was the eldest, which was agreeable to our custom. Indeed every thing here, and all their treatment of me, made me forget that I was a slave. The language of these people resembled ours so nearly, that we understood each other perfectly. They had also the very same customs as we. There were likewise slaves daily to attend us, while my young master and I with other boys sported with our darts and bows and arrows, as I had been used to do at home. In this resemblance to my former happy state I passed about two months; and I now began to think I was to be adopted into the family, and was beginning to be reconciled to my situation, and to forget by degrees my misfortunes, when all at once the delusion vanished; for, without the least previous knowledge, one morning early, while my dear master and companion was still asleep, I was wakened out of my reverie to fresh sorrow, and hurried away even amongst the uncircumcised.

Thus, at the very moment I dreamed of the greatest happiness, I found myself most miserable; and it seemed as if fortune wished to give me this taste of joy, only to render the reverse more poignant. The change I now experienced was as painful as it was sudden and unexpected. It was a change indeed from a state of bliss to a scene which is inexpressible by me, as it discovered to me an element I had never before beheld, and till then had no idea of, and wherein such instances of hardship and cruelty continually occurred as I can never reflect on but with horror.

All the nations and people I had hitherto passed through resembled our own in their manners, customs, and language: but I came at length to a country, the inhabitants of which differed from us in all those particulars. I was very much struck with this difference, especially when I came among a people who did not circumcise, and ate without washing their hands. They cooked also in iron pots, and had European cutlasses and cross bows, which were unknown to us, and fought with their fists amongst themselves. Their women were not so modest as ours, for they ate, and drank, and slept with their men. But, above all, I was amazed to see no sacrifices or offerings among them. In some of those places the people ornamented themselves with scars, and likewise filed their teeth very sharp. They wanted sometimes to ornament me in the same manner, but I would not suffer them; hoping that I might some time be among a people who did not thus disfigure themselves, as I thought they did. At last I came to the banks of a large river, which was covered with canoes, in which the people appeared to live with their household utensils and provisions of all kinds. I was beyond measure astonished at this, as I had never before seen any water larger than a pond or a rivulet: and my surprise was mingled with no small fear when I was put into one of these canoes, and we began to paddle and move along the river. We continued going on thus till night; and when we came to land, and made fires on the banks, each family by themselves, some dragged their canoes on shore, others stayed and cooked in theirs, and laid in them all night. Those on the land had mats, of which they made tents, some in the shape of little houses: in these we slept; and after the morning meal we embarked again and proceeded as before. I was often very much astonished to see some of the women, as well as the men, jump into the water, dive to the bottom, come up again, and swim about. Thus I continued to travel, sometimes by land, sometimes by water, through different countries and various nations, till, at the end of six or seven months after I had been kidnapped, I arrived at the sea coast. It would be tedious and uninteresting to relate all the incidents which befell me during this journey, and which I have not yet forgotten; of the various hands I passed through, and the manners and customs of all the different people among whom I lived: I shall therefore only observe, that in all the places where I was the soil was exceedingly rich; the pomkins, eddoes, plantains, yams, &c. &c. were in great abundance, and of incredible size. There were also vast quantities of different gums, though not used for any purpose; and every where a great deal of tobacco. The cotton even grew quite wild; and there was plenty of red-wood, I saw no mechanics whatever in all the way, except such as I have mentioned. The chief employment in all these countries was agriculture, and both the males and females, as with us, were brought up to it, and trained in the arts of war.

The first object which saluted my eyes when I arrived on the coast was the sea, and a slave ship, which was then riding at anchor, and waiting for its cargo. These filled me with astonishment, which was soon converted into terror when I was carried on board. I was immediately handled and tossed up to see if I were sound by some of the crew; and I was now persuaded that I had gotten into a world of bad spirits, and that they were going to kill me. Their complexions too differing so much from ours, their long hair, and the language they spoke, (which was very different from any I had ever heard) united to confirm me in this belief. Indeed such were the horrors of my views and fears at the moment, that, if ten thousand worlds had been my own, I would have freely parted with them all to have exchanged my condition with that of the meanest slave in my own country. When I looked round the ship too and saw a large furnace or copper boiling, and a multitude of black people of every description chained together, every one of their countenances expressing dejection and sorrow, I no longer doubted of my fate; and, quite overpowered with horror and anguish, I fell motionless on the deck and fainted. When I recovered a little I found some black people about me, who I believe were some of those who brought me on board, and had been receiving their pay; they talked to me in order to cheer me, but all in vain. I asked them if we were not to be eaten by those white men with horrible looks, red faces, and loose hair. They told me I was not; and one of the crew brought me a small portion of spirituous liquor in a wine glass; but, being afraid of him, I would not take it out of his hand. One of the blacks therefore took it from him and gave it to me, and I took a little down my palate, which, instead of reviving me, as they thought it would, threw me into the greatest consternation at the strange feeling it produced, having never tasted any such liquor before. Soon after this the blacks who brought me on board went off, and left me abandoned to despair. I now saw myself deprived of all chance of returning to my native country, or even the least glimpse of hope of gaining the shore, which I now considered as friendly; and I even wished for my former slavery in preference to my present situation, which was filled with horrors of every kind, still heightened by my ignorance of what I was to undergo. I was not long suffered to indulge my grief; I was soon put down under the decks, and there I received such a salutation in my nostrils as I had never experienced in my life: so that, with the loathsomeness of the stench, and crying together, I became so sick and low that I was not able to eat, nor had I the least desire to taste any thing. I now wished for the last friend, death, to relieve me; but soon, to my grief, two of the white men offered me eatables; and, on my refusing to eat, one of them held me fast by the hands, and laid me across I think the windlass, and tied my feet, while the other flogged me severely. I had never experienced any thing of this kind before; and although, not being used to the water, I naturally feared that element the first time I saw it, yet nevertheless, could I have got over the side, but I could not; and, besides, the crew used to watch us very closely who were not chained down to the decks, lest we should leap into the water: and I have seen some of these poor African prisoners most severely cut for attempting to do so, and hourly whipped for not eating. This indeed was often the case with myself. In a little time after, amongst the poor chained men, I found some of my own nation, which in a small degree gave ease to my mind. I inquired of these what was to be done with us; they gave me to understand we were to be carried to these white people's country to work for them. I then was a little revived, and thought, if it were no worse than working, my situation was not so desperate: but still I feared I should be put to death, the white people looked and acted, as I thought, in so savage a manner; for I had never seen among any people such instances of brutal cruelty; and this not only shown towards us blacks, but also to some of the whites themselves. One white man in particular I saw, when we were permitted to be on deck, flogged so unmercifully with a large rope near the foremast, that he died in consequence of it; and they tossed him over the side as they would have done a brute. This made me fear these people the more; and I expected nothing less than to be treated in the same manner. I could not help expressing my fears and apprehensions to some of my countrymen: I asked them if these people had no country, but lived in this hollow place (the ship): they told me they did not, but came from a distant one. "Then," said I, "how comes it in all our country we never heard of them?" They told me because they lived so very far off. I then asked where were their women? had they any like themselves? I was told they had: "and why," said I, "do we not see them?" they answered, because they were left behind. I asked how the vessel could go? they told me they could not tell; but that there were cloths put upon the masts by the help of the ropes I saw, and then the vessel went on; and the white men had some spell or magic they put in the water when they liked in order to stop the vessel. I was exceedingly amazed at this account, and really thought they were spirits. I therefore wished much to be from amongst them, for I expected they would sacrifice me: but my wishes were vain; for we were so quartered that it was impossible for any of us to make our escape. While we stayed on the coast I was mostly on deck; and one day, to my great astonishment, I saw one of these vessels coming in with the sails up. As soon as the whites saw it, they gave a great shout, at which we were amazed; and the more so as the vessel appeared larger by approaching nearer. At last she came to an anchor in my sight, and when the anchor was let go I and my countrymen who saw it were lost in astonishment to observe the vessel stop; and were now convinced it was done by magic. Soon after this the other ship got her boats out, and they came on board of us, and the people of both ships seemed very glad to see each other. Several of the strangers also shook hands with us black people, and made motions with their hands, signifying I suppose we were to go to their country; but we did not understand them. At last, when the ship we were in had got in all her cargo, they made ready with many fearful noises, and we were all put under deck, so that we could not see how they managed the vessel. But this disappointment was the least of my sorrow. The stench of the hold while we were on the coast was so intolerably loathsome, that it was dangerous to remain there for any time, and some of us had been permitted to stay on the deck for the fresh air; but now that the whole ship's cargo were confined together, it became absolutely pestilential. The closeness of the place, and the heat of the climate, added to the number in the ship, which was so crowded that each had scarcely room to turn himself, almost suffocated us. This produced copious perspirations, so that the air soon became unfit for respiration, from a variety of loathsome smells, and brought on a sickness among the slaves, of which many died, thus falling victims to the improvident avarice, as I may call it, of their purchasers. This wretched situation was again aggravated by the galling of the chains, now become insupportable; and the filth of the necessary tubs, into which the children often fell, and were almost suffocated. The shrieks of the women, and the groans of the dying, rendered the whole a scene of horror almost inconceivable. Happily perhaps for myself I was soon reduced so low here that it was thought necessary to keep me almost always on deck; and from my extreme youth I was not put in fetters. In this situation I expected every hour to share the fate of my companions, some of whom were almost daily brought upon deck at the point of death, which I began to hope would soon put an end to my miseries. Often did I think many of the inhabitants of the deep much more happy than myself. I envied them the freedom they enjoyed, and as often wished I could change my condition for theirs. Every circumstance I met with served only to render my state more painful, and heighten my apprehensions, and my opinion of the cruelty of the whites. One day they had taken a number of fishes; and when they had killed and satisfied themselves with as many as they thought fit, to our astonishment who were on the deck, rather than give any of them to us to eat as we expected, they tossed the remaining fish into the sea again, although we begged and prayed for some as well as we could, but in vain; and some of my countrymen, being pressed by hunger, took an opportunity, when they thought no one saw them, of trying to get a little privately; but they were discovered, and the attempt procured them some very severe floggings. One day, when we had a smooth sea and moderate wind, two of my wearied countrymen who were chained together (I was near them at the time), preferring death to such a life of misery, somehow made through the nettings and jumped into the sea: immediately another quite dejected fellow, who, on account of his illness, was suffered to be out of irons, also followed their example; and I believe many more would very soon have done the same if they had not been prevented by the ship's crew, who were instantly alarmed. Those of us that were the most active were in a moment put down under the deck, and there was such a noise and confusion amongst the people of the ship as I never heard before, to stop her, and get the boat out to go after the slaves. However two of the wretches were drowned, but they got the other, and afterwards flogged him unmercifully for thus attempting to prefer death to slavery. In this manner we continued to undergo more hardships than I can now relate, hardships which are inseparable from this accursed trade. Many a time we were near suffocation from the want of fresh air, which we were often without for whole days together. This, and the stench of the necessary tubs, carried off many. During our passage I first saw flying fishes, which surprised me very much: they used frequently to fly across the ship, and many of them fell on the deck. I also now first saw the use of the quadrant; I had often with astonishment seen the mariners make observations with it, and I could not think what it meant. They at last took notice of my surprise; and one of them, willing to increase it, as well as to gratify my curiosity, made me one day look through it. The clouds appeared to me to be land, which disappeared as they passed along. This heightened my wonder; and I was now more persuaded than ever that I was in another world, and that every thing about me was magic. At last we came in sight of the island of Barbados, at which the whites on board gave a great shout, and made many signs of joy to us. We did not know what to think of this; but as the vessel drew nearer we plainly saw the harbour, and other ships of different kinds and sizes; and we soon anchored amongst them off Bridge Town. Many merchants and planters now came on board, though it was in the evening. They put us in separate parcels, and examined us attentively. They also made us jump, and pointed to the land, signifying we were to go there. We thought by this we should be eaten by these ugly men, as they appeared to us; and, when soon after we were all put down under the deck again, there was much dread and trembling among us, and nothing but bitter cries to be heard all the night from these apprehensions, insomuch that at last the white people got some old slaves from the land to pacify us. They told us we were not to be eaten, but to work, and were soon to go on land, where we should see many of our country people. This report eased us much; and sure enough, soon after we were landed, there came to us Africans of all languages. We were conducted immediately to the merchant's yard, where we were pent up altogether like so many sheep in a fold, without regard to sex or age. As every object was new to me every thing I saw filled me with surprise. What struck me first was that the houses were built with stories, and in every other respect different from those in Africa: but I was still more astonished on seeing people on horseback. I did not know what this could mean; and indeed I thought these people were full of nothing but magical arts. While I was in this astonishment one of my fellow prisoners spoke to a countryman of his about the horses, who said they were the same kind they had in their country. I understood them, though they were from a distant part of Africa, and I thought it odd I had not seen any horses there; but afterwards, when I came to converse with different Africans, I found they had many horses amongst them, and much larger than those I then saw. We were not many days in the merchant's custody before we were sold after their usual manner, which is this:—On a signal given, (as the beat of a drum) the buyers rush at once into the yard where the slaves are confined, and make a choice of that parcel they like best. The noise and clamour with which this is attended, and the eagerness visible in the countenances of the buyers, serve not a little to increase the apprehensions of the terrified Africans, who may well be supposed to consider them as the ministers of that destruction to which they think themselves devoted. In this manner, without scruple, are relations and friends separated, most of them never to see each other again. I remember in the vessel in which I was brought over, in the men's apartment, there were several brothers, who, in the sale, were sold in different lots; and it was very moving on this occasion to see and hear their cries at parting. O, ye nominal Christians! might not an African ask you, learned you this from your God, who says unto you, Do unto all men as you would men should do unto you? Is it not enough that we are torn from our country and friends to toil for your luxury and lust of gain? Must every tender feeling be likewise sacrificed to your avarice? Are the dearest friends and relations, now rendered more dear by their separation from their kindred, still to be parted from each other, and thus prevented from cheering the gloom of slavery with the small comfort of being together and mingling their sufferings and sorrows? Why are parents to lose their children, brothers their sisters, or husbands their wives? Surely this is a new refinement in cruelty, which, while it has no advantage to atone for it, thus aggravates distress, and adds fresh horrors even to the wretchedness of slavery.

Measuring the Immeasurable: The Atlantic Slave Trade

David P. Henige

Conjecture has all the pride and joy of invention, and he that once has started a happy change, is much too delighted to consider what objections may rise against it.[1]

If casting the components of the slave trade in an arithmetical paradigm has the advantage of clearly distinguishing their epistemological bases, it carries the disadvantage of suggesting that finding the value of X is a necessary, or even desirable, goal—however unpromising—of quantitative analyses of the trade. If historians were content to tease out local circumstances through micro-studies, there would be less need to point out the chimerical nature of X. As it happens however, historians of the trade are more frequently succumbing to the temptation to widen their field of vision by contemplating the effects of the trade on West Africa, both *en gros* and in its parts. Success in this particular enterprise depends on a concomitant success in estimating the facets of the trade already discussed, as well as several others (e.g. ratio of males to females; differential regional impact of the trade within West Africa; the counter-active role of newly introduced New World food crops). Both with and without regard to the degree of that success, we can consider what the possibility might be of determining with any useful precision the impact of the trade on West Africa.

The obverse to knowing the number of West Africans killed or transported is to know how many were not, entailing some effort to determine the population of West Africa (or parts of it) during the centuries in question, as well as any trends in it that might be discernible or inferable. If it should be possible to do this, we could at least begin to assess the purely demographic implications of the trade.

Pre-censal populations can be estimated in three ways—carrying capacity, retrojection or projection, and extrapolation. In one way or another each has been employed by historical demographers and historians interested in early African population. Although its limited analytical capabilities are often ignored, carrying capacity is actually a ceiling concept—what the maximum level of a given population *could* have been if a constellation of optimal conditions prevailed. Calculating carrying capacity depends on knowing, or closely estimating, such variables as the amount of land under cultivation and its likely yield, granted a certain technological level; the nutritional value of whatever crops and animal products an area provides; and the nutritional levels required by the inhabitants of the area on a *per capita* basis. It comes as no surprise then to find that most estimates of carrying capacity, even when these data can be reasonably estimated, arouse a chorus of dissent.[2] This disagreement usually extends to opinions as to how close to carrying capacity a given population actually reached; after all, that x people *could* live in area y at any one time is no argument that they ever did.[3]

So far as I am aware, no estimates of past West African population have made extensive use of the carrying-capacity approach in all its fullness, although it is not uncommon for comparisons to be made with modern African or contemporary European population densities.[4] These generally unuseful exercises can never address adequately the problematical relationship between actual and potential population, the host of differing local circumstances, and the like.

Necessarily regarding late colonial population figures as sufficiently accurate for the purpose, several historians have attempted to calculate earlier figures by retrojection. As a result, this is the most popular means of estimating West African population back as far as the sixteenth century, but I defer discussion to the comments on population trends below.

Finally, there is extrapolation, or estimating the whole from one or another of its parts as determined at the same time. This too entails a formidable array of assumptions. Among these are that the portion in question is the "entire part" and, of course, that this part somehow constitutes a fixed and calculable percentage of some desired whole. Any number of extrapolative techniques have been employed by those interested in putting numbers to past populations. At one extreme palaeodemographers use skeletal remains from scattered sites to infer the total population of a given area, but this procedure has naturally given rise to much controversy.[5]

A more common, and seemingly less troublesome, expedient has been to estimate the size of a population from the apparent size of its armed forces, since the latter make many more appearances in the historical record than their civilian counterparts. Such an approach is becoming popular in efforts to calculate New World population and has been used for early India as well.[6] For West Africa Diop has employed the technique on a grand scale and Kea and Johnson on a much reduced scale (but with better evidence).[7]

Successfully using warrior counts to estimate total population involves two assumptions and a calculation. The first assumption is that we can determine just which group of people the armies mentioned in historical sources actually represented; the second is that the cited figures are roughly accurate. About the first little need be said. About the second all too much can be. Let it suffice to point out that there is no type of historical evidence more subject to misrepresentation than battlefield figures. Ramesses II started it all in motion in the thirteenth century BC when he claimed to have slain "hundreds of thousands" from a Hittite force of fewer than 40,000, and the momentum has continued without surcease ever since.[8] War is, after all, the ultimate polemic and we can only expect that each of its aspects will take on similar characteristics.[9]

The calculation involved in dealing with warrior counts relates to the appropriate figure to adopt in order to determine "total" population. Multipliers in the range of four to eight are popular, but much depends on knowing certain socio-political information as well as the circumstances of each particular occasion (e.g. a lower multiplier when national defense is at stake, a higher one when the armed force is no more than a raiding party). In fact historians do not very often know such things for pre-colonial West Africa so that, as usual, the sole criterion remains apparent plausibility.

The multiplicity of discrepant figures in exercises of this nature, and the variety of multipliers, inevitably result in arguments that touch the near edges of abuse. Low figures are rejected as representing only a modicum of a certain diagnostic proportion, while implausibly high figures are accepted without demur. Niane's contention that the typical structure in Gao housed fourteen persons, or his belief that Mahmud Ka'ti's assertion that ancient Mali had 400 towns indicates a population there of forty to fifty million, can emanate only from a predisposition to postulate dense populations there.[10]

In sum, efforts to estimate the size of whole populations on the basis of sundry parts of them are seldom useful surrogates for vital but absent information. Spurred by prospects of discovering indirectly that for which no direct evidence exists, proponents of extrapolative measures tend to outstrip both their data and the uses to which they can be put. The situation for pre-colonial West Africa differs from most other times and places only in that the evidence is even more intractable.

The usual procedure for determining both the levels of and trends in the historical population of West Africa has been to accept figures in colonial censuses and to project them backwards, in the process assuming various rates of natural increase (fertility less mortality) on the one hand, and rates of unnatural decrease (losses from the slave trade) on the other, with each tailored to fit the thrust of particular arguments.[11] Three hypotheses have been mooted: that population remained fairly stable during the period; that it declined slightly in the eighteenth century before recovering slowly; and that it declined continuously throughout. In its own way each of these lines of thought illustrates the ultimate deficiency of the evidence on which it is based.

The argument of long-term equilibrium is of longest standing. It proceeds from belief in a figure of about 100 million for all of sub-Sahara Africa in the sixteenth century, of which West Africa is held to have constituted perhaps one-quarter to one-third. Both of these figures and the idea of stability have been borrowed from the literature of historical demography, where it seems not to be very firmly based. Caldwell has shown, for instance, that at least the figure is no more than a latter-day repetition of a hazard by a seventeenth-century author who, for his part, based it on nothing tangible at all.[12] In turn Caldwell suggests a much lower figure, perhaps no more than 50 million, or about the same as Niane believes Mali alone possessed.[13]

That West African population declined to one degree or another during the course of the eighteenth century is an almost inevitable conclusion from the fact that the Atlantic slave trade in that century constituted fully one-half of its whole. In hopes that technology might be made to intervene between the historian and his evidence to the advantage of the former, Patrick Manning has attempted to estimate what the extent of this decline might have been.[14] Manning does not pretend that the task he has set is a simple one and is careful to make explicit both his postulates and their problematic aspects. In general none of his assumptions is inherently impossible, although some might quibble with at least his premise that males and females were captured in roughly equal numbers and that two of every three females remained in Africa whereas two of every three men did not.[15] At any rate, Manning concludes that West Africa suffered a loss of in the neighborhood of eight million persons from the slave trade, a figure that could not have been offset by natural growth rates.[16]

If Manning's conclusions do not fly in the face of any known evidence, it is more difficult to characterize the views of the advocates of a continuous and even precipitate decline in West African population from the middle of the sixteenth century through the middle of the nineteenth. This argument has been championed most persistently by Inikori, who decides (there is no other word for it) that the mid-nineteenth-century population of West Africa was actually much lower than usually estimated, while that of three centuries earlier was even larger than Riccioli had imagined. Inikori goes so far as to argue that the earlier population was as large as it was because West Africa's land was fertile and its productivity high; its inhabitants were healthy and fecund and serious encounters with disease, famine, and drought were infrequent. On the other hand its later population was as low as it was *because* high levels of natural increase must be projected as far back as the middle of the nineteenth century.[17] Those who feel that they detect a whiff of circularity in all this are not likely to be mistaken.

Indeed, all arguments dealing with West African population trends base themselves to one degree or another on adopting natural growth rates, which tend to be concocted to taste from ranges putatively provided by other pre-industrial societies or by twentieth-century Africa.[18] In no other aspect of West African historical demography does argumentation beg the question more obstinately by confounding what is to be proved with what is to do the proving. The notion that West African population declined dramatically, whether or not as a result of the slave trade, is reminiscent of the current rage to attribute an even more dramatic depopulation to the post-contact New World. Both hypotheses are supported by the same amount of evidence: none.[19]

On the other hand, it is only fair to point out that any other particular interpretation suffers from much the same handicap, and it becomes a nice question whether we are more justified to be moderate without cause than to be extreme without it. The unpalatable truth is that we have not the slightest idea (nor any hope of gaining it) of the population of any part of tropical Africa in the sixteenth or the seventeenth or the eighteenth centuries. Such ineffable ignorance is ordinarily considered an unpromising point from which to move on towards other hypotheses which require just the knowledge we lack.

However, this is clearly not the only recognized view of the appropriate relationship between hypothesis and evidence. A contrary methodology seeks to go beyond reconstructing what was, to dwell on what might have been; we see counterfactual argument recurring more frequently in this field (as in others). Based on widely divergent views of the number of individuals physically lost to West Africa (X in our equation) and linked to determine (for instance) what proportion of these were female, estimates of what *potential* losses resulted inevitably range widely.

The work of M. L. Diop exemplifies one locus of this argument. Diop believes that on the eve of the slave trade Africa (and certainly West Africa) was able to (and therefore did) sustain populations more dense than that of contemporaneous western Europe and nearly as dense as those of "monsoon Asia" and that the population of the continent might have been as great as 270 million if not greater.[20] Startling as this thesis is, even more startling is the manner in which Diop arrives at it. Her conclusion stated,

Diop seeks to legitimate it by arguing that such a dense population *must have* been predicated on agrotechnological capabilities on a par with those of Europe at the time.[21] She supplements this reasoning by arguing that "if [sic] the slave trade involved a loss on the order of 100,000,000 persons," then Africa's population "must have surpassed" the commonly cited figure of 100 million in the seventeenth century.[22]

This dizzying confusion between cause and effect in argument serves as a prelude for her major counterfactual hypothesis: without the slave trade the population of Africa would not be about 1,800 million, or as much as eight times what it actually seems to be.[23] In a similar vein, if on a somewhat smaller scale, Inikori adopts similar arguments for West Africa, concluding that the slave trade resulted in the (potential) loss of nearly 50 million people.[24]

These breezy exercises in helical thinking ignore other constraints on population growth or dismiss them as "Malthusian" and therefore inappropriate. Both Diop and Inikori stoutly deny that disease played an important role in limiting West Africa's population growth before the seventeenth century, and even contend that the well-known climatic constraints of today were all but unknown earlier.[25]

Conversely, taking advantage of the opportunity to base himself on actual evidence, Miller argues that, for West Central Africa at least, drought, famine, and disease were, in aggregate, more effective constraints on population growth than the slave trade.[26] It does appear that from the sixteenth century West Africa became more humid, which should have (and maybe did) reduce the probability of frequent and severe droughts and famines.[27] But any such blessing was not likely to have been unmixed since higher levels of humidity frequently bring with them a higher incidence of such diseases as malaria and plague.[28]

It is no more easy to accept Inikori's contention that the centuries of the slave trade coincided with (and not accidentally) an increasing tempo of warfare in West Africa.[29] To advance this argument is to turn a decidedly blind eye to the evidence of the *ta'rikhs* and other sources for the earlier history of the western Sudan, which are replete with accounts of warfare.[30] Inikori's intuition of a *"Pax Askiana,"* rudely broken at the end of the sixteenth century, is ludicrously at odds with this evidence, which Inikori must impeach if he is to carry his point.[31]

One taste of the heady heights of counterfactual reasoning often leads to another. The slave trade and its possible effects have come to be a cornerstone for those who wish to extend the concept of "underdevelopment" back beyond the colonial period. By lexicography "underdevelopment" is a counterfactual concept, and its proponents necessarily rely on their instincts as to what would have happened had

Africa been allowed to proceed untouched through (in this case) the centuries of the slave trade. Inikori and Suret-Canale have criticized Fage and Curtin for failing to venture suitable opinions on this aspect of the trade, as though such silence constitutes more than a realization of the limitations in pressing such counterfactual arguments.[32] One such misbegotten effort to do just this personifies well the inescapable hazards of adopting a form of argumentation which cannot be linked to evidence in any way.

Becker and Martin attempt to remedy Curtin's oversight for Senegambia by using oral traditions and by "rereading" contemporaneous French accounts of the several polities of the area.[33] They argue that trade in general—and of course the slave trade in particular—had "important consequences in the disorganization of traditional society and the transformation of social, political, and religious structures" of Bawol and Kayoor in the eighteenth century.[34] Arguing that the written sources often "evince the fears" of the French that the two states (which had been part of a larger whole, oral tradition tells us, before the sixteenth century) would reunite, Becker and Martin conclude that "it is possible to regard the frequent attempts" at union as "a form of resistance to European commercial hegemony and foreign encroachment on local political authority."[35]

This argument assumes much, not least that the Senegalese traditional (and non-traditional?) elite were aware of alleged French preferences in the matter (in order to "resist" them) and that unification had not been a goal formerly. About the first we can hardly know, but even the more exiguous sources from the seventeenth century leave no doubt that efforts to unite the two states had then been on the agenda of each.[36] Nor is tradition particularly reticent about the fairly brisk pace of warfare and the constant succession disputes which characterized the fluid Wolof succession system well before the French appeared on the scene.[37] That these earlier efforts at union failed, while those of the eighteenth century frequently succeeded, suggests, that Becker and Martin, that the presence of the French and the trade (perhaps even the slave trade) actually improved chances for success.

To what extent did the slave trade *cause* upheavals in Senegambia? Might it not simply be that the trade brought observers who recorded more details than oral tradition could, or chose to, remember? How do we separate our sources from what they say? Beyond these rhetorical questions, it is fair to observe that Becker and Martin fail utterly to demonstrate that any significantly harmful changes can be attributed solely, or even primarily, to the undoubted intensification of the slave trade. There is no credible evidence for a "multiplication of civil war, pillage, and conflicts with neighbouring states," although we might reasonably suspect that at times this happened.[38]

The game went on as always; only the number of participants increased.

If an area like Senegambia, favored in its contemporaneous documentation, and with an unusually full-bodied oral tradition, cannot provide data to sustain the argument for underdevelopment, it is hard to imagine how any other part of West Africa (with the possible exception of parts of the Guinea coast) could provide much better opportunities. Nor will condemnation of well-considered silence enrich our understanding of the issue. But it is taking another silence too seriously that is the abiding weakness of these arguments. Historians of pre-colonial Africa must resign themselves to operating on the assumption that their sources can never be complete and that in consequence arguments can seldom be advanced on the *absence* of data within a particular body of texts. To argue that the silences of very exiguous oral tradition and written sources are interpretatively significant is to push the always tenuous argument from silence right over the edge.

The few examples discussed here do not generally fall within the more moderate mainstream of work on the effects of the slave trade on African societies. Nevertheless, they were purposely chosen to emphasize two points. First, they exemplify the ease with which argumentation can get out of hand by losing track completely of the importance of tying (or at least tethering) it to the evidence which is available. More to the point in the present reasoning, they illustrate the futility of pushing beyond X in any even remotely quantitative fashion when X itself is completely beyond our knowing.

A third point might be added that relates to the recent abandoning of micro-studies in favor of theorizing on a grand scale. For the moment at least, only micro-studies based on a heavy leaven of primary sources can hope to develop arguments which will stand the test of falsification. Yet the pace with which these have appeared has slackened considerably in favor of argumentation which implicitly accepts both the need and the desirability to rush beyond the secure (if unexciting) domain of evidence into the neighboring wilds of the kingdom of conjecture—and without visas.

> I do not really care whether I have been right or wrong on any point; but I care a great deal about which of the two I have been.[39]

To sum up the reasoning of this paper, the situation with respect to the extent and certainty of our knowledge of the numerical and ancillary aspects of the West African slave trade is that: from *a* to *g* both what we know and what we can know diminishes at each stage, to the point that the possible range of *g* is from very few (or, theoretically, even zero) to many millions. Worse yet, the probability of satisfying Butler's yearning (which should also be ours) is exactly nil. Crucially to our argument, any estimates for b through g can be derived not from evidence but from commensurability.[40] But since there is no demonstrable proportionate relationship between, say d and e, e and f or f and g, commensurable arguments can be no more than a function of particular historians' angles of vision. An unwelcome by-product of this is the drift from one inference to another, each more estranged from incontrovertible evidence.

Historians cannot expect to be unencumbered by doubt (although some are skillful at disguising it), and a healthy skepticism and an eye for incongruities are indispensable tools in their work. Pyrrhonian skepticism does not assert the impossibility of attaining knowledge, but it does question, if only initially and for methodological reasons, the adequacy of our grounds for holding certain beliefs. It puts forward such doubts by way of a challenge to show that they are unjustified and that the beliefs in question are indeed justifiable. Inevitably then, the pyrrhonian critic lays stringent standards on demonstrating success and prefers to suspend judgment until these standards can be reached.[41] It follows that he lays particular weight on understanding that, while inference can render a conclusion credible, it can never *require* that conclusion, because it is never possible—as historians well realize—to be sure that other evidence does not exist which would invalidate even the most persuasive hypothesis.

The pyrrhonian is disquieted when he encounters generalizations that cannot be tested. He regards it as anathema to make a series of less, or even least, likely assumptions, all supporting a given presupposition, for he recognizes this as ideology in embryo. Nor can he comfortably accept far-reaching arguments derived solely from anecdotal evidence. Finally, he is likely to consider it both bad manners and bad policy to regard lack of evidence against a hypothesis to be evidence in favor of it. And, while it would be too much to say that pyrrhonism is a species of pessimism, it is likely that most pyrrhonists, benefiting from experience, would marvel at such confident forecasts as one made in 1978 that "it may take a decade or more" before the number of Africans exported as slaves "can be stated in terms of global figures."[42] Perhaps recalling an even more emphatic closure ventured nearly a century ago, he can only wonder how the future can provide the wherewithal that the past has so signally failed to.[43] If historical facts are found, not made, and if knowledge consists in justifiably believing the facts, then it would seem that historical knowledge is very much in thrall to the success, or lack of it, with which the past has managed to preserve information about itself through time.

Despite these reservations the pyrrhonian critic refrains from rejecting such arguments, attitudes, and practices out of hand because to do so would resemble too closely the dogmatism that epitomizes them. Even so, he realizes that the most worrisome aspect of the questions raised here is not that there are at present no answers to them but that there are no real prospects of answers. At a more operational level, historians should never feel that the unproductive experience of the past, however disheartening, is sufficient reason to abandon the search for new evidence. But it scarcely permits us to proceed as though we have already found it. Pending that happy event, we are more justified to doubt all global estimates of the west African slave trade and its effects than to accept any one of them.[44] For us Kelvin's dictum that

> When you measure what you are speaking about, and express it in numbers, you can know something about it; but when you cannot measure it, when you cannot express it in numbers, your knowledge is of a meagre and unsatisfactory kind

can only seem so remote as to be unreal, so beside the point as to be fatuous, so unsparing as to be incapacitating.[45] It may well be time for historians of the slave trade to break the bonds of this line of thinking in favor of setting objectives that are more congruent with the means available to achieve them.

Summary

No problem has exercised Africanists for so long and so heatedly as the slave trade. Now that any difference of opinion as to its morality has ended, debate tends to concentrate on its economic and political aspects, particularly on its magnitude and regional characteristics. In the past few scholarly generations, sophisticated statistical manipulations have supplied more evidence, but it has been concentrated on the number of slaves who arrived in the New World. Nonetheless, dearth of evidence (sometimes total) regarding the other components of the trade has not seemed to discourage efforts to arrive at global figures and, by extension, to determine its effects on African societies.

The present paper asks why this should be so, and wonders how any defensible conclusions can ever be reached about almost any facet of the trade that can go beyond ideology or truism. It concludes that no global estimate of the slave trade, or of any "underdevelopment" or "underpopulation" it may have caused, are possible, though carefully constructed micro-studies might provide limited answers. Under the circumstances, to believe or advocate any particular set or range of figures becomes an act of faith rather than an epistemologically sound decision.

[1] Samuel Johnson, *Shakespeare* [1765] in Samuel Johnson, *Works of Samuel Johnson* (New Haven, 1958–85), VII, 109.

[2] A recent survey, particularly useful for its bibliography, is Robert E. Dewar, "Environmental productivity, population regulation and carrying capacity," *American Anthropologist*, LXXXVI (1984), 601–14.

[3] An example is Inikori's misinterpretation of Thurstan Shaw's argument; see Inikori, "Introduction" to J. E. Inikori ed., *Forced Migration: The Impact of the Export Slave Trade on African Societies*, (New York, 1982), 29–30. Occasionally, too, when an area's population outstrips its ability to feed itself, it relies on imports, as does Japan today.

[4] However, J. C. Caldwell, "Two comments on Manning," *Canadian Journal of African Studies*, XVI (1982), 127, does argue for the ultimate efficacy of the carrying capacity approach.

[5] Jane E. Buikstra and Lyle W. Konigsberg, "Paleodemography: critiques and controversies," *American Anthropologist*, LXXXVII (1985), 316–33, provides some flavor of the recent debate.

[6] For comments on one such effort see David Henige, "If pigs could fly: Timucuan population and Native American historical demography," *Journal of Interdisciplinary History*, XVI (1985/86) 701–20.

[7] Diop, "Sous-peuplement," 780–803; Ray A. Kea, *Settlement, Trade, and Polities in the Seventeenth-Century Gold Coast* (Baltimore, 1982), 137–46, 379–82; Marion Johnson, "Census, map, and guesstimate: the past population of the Accra region" in *African Historical Demography* I (Edinburgh, 1977), 272–93. Cf. Austen, "Trans-Saharan slave trade," 51–8.

[8] Alan H. Gardiner, *The Kadesh inscription of Ramesses II* (Oxford, 1960), 13, 41; Ahmed Kadry, "Some comments on the Qadesh battle," in *Bulletin du centenaire* [*Supplement* of the *Bulletin de l'Institut français d'archéologie orientale*, 81] (Cairo, 1981), 47–55.

[9] Is it not odd, for instance, that estimates of Fante army sizes decreased as that state became more powerful during the early eighteenth century? See Kea, *Settlements*, 138.

[10] D. T. Niane, "Mali and the second Mandingo expansion," in *UNESCO General History of Africa IV* (Berkeley, 1984), 156, 206n. Niane's discussion embodies the common belief that there is a necessarily correlative relation between dense populations and imperial status so that demonstrating one is seen to enjoin proving the other as well.

[11] A particular ambitious effort along these lines is Thornton, "Demographic effect."

[12] J. C. Caldwell, "Major questions in African demographic history" in *African Historical Demography I*, 7; Walter F. Willcox, *International Migrations, II, Interpretations* (New York, 1931), 53–4, 640–2; A. M. Carr-Saunders, *World Population: Past Growth and Present Trends* (London, 1964), 34–5; Colin Clark, *Population Growth and Land Use* (New York, 1967), 64–6. All derive from Giovanni Baptista Riccioli, *Geographiae Hydrographiae Reformatae* (Venice, 1672), 679–80.

[13] Caldwell, "Major questions," 18.

[14] Manning, "Enslavement," 499–526. Further studies by Manning are forthcoming.

[15] As does Caldwell, "Two comments," 128, whereas Inikori, "Two comments," 135, considers the premise "quite close to historical reality." If nothing else, the idea that most captured females were assimilated by other African societies seems to compromise the notion that the Atlantic slave trade was a radical departure from existing mores unless we accept the idea that integrating extra-societal females occurred to African societies only on seeing them pass on their way to the coast. This is possible, of course, but perhaps more probable (again, if the premise is accepted) is that slave raiding was an age-old feature of African societies, at least with females as the objective.

[16] P. Manning, "Contours of slavery and social change in Africa," *American Historical Review*, LXXXVIII (1983), 850.

[17] Inikori, "Introduction," 29–31; *idem.* "Under-population," 296–301.

[18] Inikori, "Introduction," 32; *idem.* "Under-population," 303, however, prefers to draw the comparison with blacks in the antebellum American South.

[19] This contretemps is discussed in Henige, "If pigs could fly."

[20] Diop, "Sous-peuplement," 730–3; *idem.* "Méthode et calculs approximatifs pour la construction d'une courbe répresentative de l'évolution de la population de l'Afrique noire, du milieu du XVIe siècle au milieu du XXe," in *African Historical Demography II*, 147–9. While I do not suggest that the work of Diop and Inikori necessarily typifies the work being done on West African historical demography, I choose to present their arguments precisely because of their extravagance, in order better to underscore how difficult it is to refute any given line of reasoning in the state of the evidence.

[21] Diop, "Sous-peuplement," 734–5.

[22] *Ibid.*, 738.

[23] *Ibid.*, 744. Perhaps Diop overplays her hand when she argues in support of her thesis that seventeenth-century maps of Africa featured no "lacunae," or refers to "the agriculture practices and mentality of black people," or rhapsodizes about the nutritional superiority of yams, sorghum, and millet. For more, see now *Population* XL (1985), 855–9.

[24] Inikori, "Under-population," 303–4. For all of Africa Inikori ("Introduction," 33) has recently suggested a figure of 112 million for potential losses.

[25] Inikori, "Under-population," 298–300; Diop, "Sous-peuplement," 726–8, believes that droughts, famines, and diseases were probably less common in pre-colonial Africa than in contemporary Europe.

[26] J. C. Miller, "The significance of drought, disease, and famine in the agriculturally marginal zones of west-central Africa," *J. Afr. Hist.* XXIII (1982), 17–61.

[27] Sharon E. Nicholson, "Saharan climates in historic times," in Martin A. J. Williams and Hugues Faure, eds, *The Sahara and the Nile* (Rotterdam, 1980), 178–85; George E. Brooks, *Western Africa to ca. 1860 A.D.: A Provisional Historical Schema Based on Climate Periods* (Bloomington, 1985), 154–96.

[28] Brooks, *Western Africa*, 154–67; Lansiné Kaba, "Archers, musketeers, and mosquitos: the Moorish

invasion of the Sudan and the Songhay resistance (1591–1612), *J. Afr. Hist.* XXII (1981), 457–75.

[29]Inikori, "Under-population," 300–1, 305–6; *idem.* "Introduction," 46–51.

[30]This state of endemic warfare is conveniently summarized in Claude Meillassoux, "The role of slavery in the economic and social history of Sahelo-Sudanic Africa" in Inikori, *Forced Migration,* 76–83.

[31]Inikori, "Under-population," 297–8.

[32]Inikori, "Introduction," 29; *idem.* "Two comments," 131; Jean Suret-Canale, "La Sénégambie à l'ère de la traite," *Canadian Journal of African Studies,* XI (1977), 125–34.

[33]Charles Becker and Victor Martin, "Kayor et Baol: royaumes sénégalais et traite des esclaves au XVIIIe siècle," *Revue française d'histoire d'Outre-Mer,* LXII (1975), 271. Cf. Charles Becker, "La Sénégambie à l'époque de la traite des esclaves," *Revue française d'histoire d'Outre-Mer,* LXIV (1977), 203–24; Becker develops these arguments in "Les effets démographiques de la traite des esclaves en Sénégambie: esquisse d'une histoire des peuplements du 17e à la fin du 19e siècle," Colloque International sur la Traite des Noirs, Nantes, July, 1985.

[34]Becker and Martin, "Kayor et Baol," 272.

[35]*Ibid.* 273.

[36]Becker and Martin, "Les teen du Baol: essai de chronologie," *Bulletin de l'Institut Fondamental de l'Afrique Noire,* sér B, XXXVIII (1976), 464–80.

[37]*Ibid.*

[38]Becker, "Sénégambie," 218.

[39]Samuel Butler, *Further Extracts from the Note-books of Samuel Butler,* ed. A. T. Bartholomew (London, 1934), 158.

[40]Commensurability governs many aspects of historians' work, whether quantitative or not. This is appropriate to the extent that it is necessary, but it bears emphasizing that commensuration is basically another form of interpretation, governed more by the historian's perceptions than by further and independent evidence.

[41]A good survey of the premises of pyrrhonism is Arne Naess, *Scepticism* (London, 1968). See also Richard H. Popkin, "The high road to Pyrrhonism, *American Philosophical Quarterly,* II (1965), 18–32; M. F. Burnyeat, "The sceptic in his time and place," in Richard Rorty, J. B. Schneewind and Quentin Skinner, eds. *Philosophy in History* (Cambridge, 1985), 225–54.

[42]J. E. Inikori, "The slave trade and the African economies, 1571–1870," in *The African slave trade from the fifteenth to the nineteenth century. Reports and papers of the meeting of experts organized at Port-au-Prince, Haiti, 31 January to 4 February 1978* (Paris, 1979), 57.

[43]"Nearly all the [historical] evidence that will ever appear is accessible now." Lord Acton, *Lectures in Modern History* (London, 1907), 315.

[44]I would like to thank Bruce Fetter, Paul Hair, Paul Lovejoy, Joseph Miller, and Donald Wright for providing their own devil's advocacy on an earlier draft of this paper, without necessarily implying that they would agree with the residue.

[45]William Thomson, Baron Kelvin, "Electrical units of measurement," in his *Popular Lectures and Addresses* (London, 1889–94), I, 73.

Enslaved Africans and Their Expectations of Slave Life in the Americas: Towards a Reconsideration of "Creolisation"

Paul E. Lovejoy and David V. Trotman

Discussions of slave life in the Americas have only just begun to see Africans as wholly human and as peoples whose peculiar histories had resulted in their forced migration across the Atlantic. Each individual arrived with his or her own attitudes, ideas, beliefs and expecta-tions, and as Michael Sobel has observed in her discussion of colonial Virginia, "Africans brought their attitudes towards slaves and masters with them to Virginia, suggesting an important but totally unexplored issue." Sobel notes that "their expectations and reactions may well have been an important factor in shaping the character of American slavery." We agree with Sobel that the individual life experiences of the enslaved affected how people responded to their bondage in the Americas. Our purpose here is to explore the range of possible expectations which en-slaved Africans might have had about life in bondage before crossing the Atlantic and also to examine some of the fundamental characteristics of the slave experience in the Americas that differed from preconceived notions of slavery that had been formed in Africa. In this way we hope to comment on the process of "creolisation," as developed by Kamau Brathwaite and others, in relation to the impact of African ideas and expectations on the early culture of slavery in the Americas.

According to Brathwaite, who drew his insights from the Jamaican experience between circa 1770 and the 1820s,

> "Creole" . . . presupposes a situation where the society concerned is caught up "in some kind of colonial arrangement" with a metropolitan European power, on the one hand, and a plantation arrangement on the other; and where the society is multiracial but organised for the benefit of a minority of European origin. "Creole society" therefore is the result of a complex situation where a colonial polity reacts, as a whole, to external metropolitan pressures, and at the same time to individual adjustments made necessary by the juxtaposition of master and slave, elite and labourer, in a culturally heterogeneous relationship.

We follow Brathwaite in defining the cultural action and social process of creolisation as a "response and interaction . . . dictated by the circumstances of the society's foundation and composition—a 'new' construct, made up of newcomers to the landscape and cultural strangers to each other; one group dominant, the other legally and subordinately slaves." Even more specifically, Brathwaite noted,

> . . . here in Jamaica, fixed within the dehumanising institution of slavery, were two cultures of people, having to adapt themselves to a new environment and to each other. The friction created by this confrontation was cruel, but it was also creative. The white plantations and social institutions . . . reflect one aspect of this. The slaves' adaptation of their African culture to a new world reflects another.

The adaptation that was necessary under slavery, which is central to Brathwaite's conception, nonetheless applies to a specific period—from the end of the eighteenth century until emancipation—and therefore not to the whole period of slavery or necessarily to other slave societies in the Americas, without modification.

Our focus is on the period in which enslaved people who were African-born predominated in the population, roughly the first 100 years of colonial settlement in the English and French Caribbean and North America, but including nineteenth-century Brazil and Cuba, when there was a great influx of African-born migrants. In these contexts, there was a significant population of first-generation slaves with roots in Africa, and in our opinion these enslaved Africans, and the periods and places in which they formed a majority or large minority, must be clearly distinguished from the "Creole societies" in which later generations tended to dominate. Taking generations into consideration, the foundations of "Creole society" are to be located in the period in which African-born slaves formed the bulk of the population. Our intention is to explore aspects of the mental map which the enslaved brought with them and subsequently adapted. The contours of those maps relate specifically to the landscape of trans-Atlantic slavery.

Until recently, the tendency has been to homogenise the African experience under slavery and to assign beliefs and actions to an amorphous group without reference to the specific historical circumstances in which individuals found themselves. For Sidney Mintz and Sally Price, the African background became submerged into the "crowds" that filled the slave ships to the Americas, and hence the African background could only have a generalised influence on slave culture, which received its dynamism through the agency of the slaves themselves, responding to the oppressive conditions of slavery.

We contextualise "creolisation" in such a way as to demonstrate the reality and specifics of Africa and the impact that this might have had on the experiences of those enslaved in the Americas. By focusing on the period of heaviest African settlement, and the period in which the African-born predominated in the population, our study attempts to flesh out the African-derived cultural heritage that is crucial to Brathwaite's conception of Creole society. We suggest that many enslaved Africans found ways of extricating themselves from the mentality of the crowded slave ship to reformulate their expectations, adjusting their visions as new experiences challenged their assumptions, whether it was being devoured by cannibals, or whatever. In this way, we suggest that the claim of Mintz and Price that the African background was filtered through the crowd mentality of the middle passage fails to appreciate the extent to which people were able to disengage from the crowd.

In our view, a careful reading of the African context reveals that in the Americas the enslaved were subjected to forms of oppression that were remarkably different in substance from what was generally known in those parts of Africa from which they came, but in our view, a careful reading of the African context reveals that enslaved Africans still interpreted what they confronted in the light of their previous experiences and resulting expectations. We contend that the experience of slavery in the Americas, buttressed by racism, was fundamentally different than what the expectations of the enslaved must have been before leaving Africa. It is possible to assess what people expected in some situations through an examination of the personal histories of individuals who were enslaved. Testimonies of enslaved Africans offer insights into what people knew and what they feared. When we raise the issue of previous experience and expectations, it is not an attempt to suggest that Africans were somehow precon-ditioned for a life of servility in the Americas. Moreover, African notions of slavery were in sharp contrast to the reality of racial slavery in the Americas. Rather, our attempt is to highlight the possible junctures

at which disappointments and oppression would lead to resistance and rebellion.

In virtually every society with which enslaved Africans were familiar, there was a social status and legal category of servility in which people were treated as property and hence could be bought and sold, inherited, or given away. The range of legal and customary obliga-tions varied widely, as did the various terms for different categories of servility in various languages and places. While the different patterns of obligations and responsibilities may or may not have constituted a continuum of relationships, they all included slavery as the extreme form of servility. The available data, and the detailed studies of these data, demon-strate conclusively that virtually everyone who was taken to the Americas as a slave, except the very young, had his/her own understanding of what slavery was supposed to be. Clearly that is not to argue that everyone who crossed the Atlantic was a slave in Africa before their transportation, although many were. Moreover, there was a distinction between recent captives, who might still have hope of being ransomed, and slaves who had been sold on the market. An awareness of the existence of systems of obliga-tions included outright slavery. We contend that the cultural practices of the society from which the enslaved came informed the attitudes and reactions of these individuals to their experience of slavery in the Americas. These attitudes and reactions varied, of course, depending upon the age at which a person was removed from Africa and the extent of exposure to people of similar background in the diaspora, among other factors. The European immigrants to the Americas, although travelling with similar notions of service obligations (serfdom, apprenticeship, impressment, "transportation" of criminals) could expect to use the transition to their "New World" as an opportunity to change their circumstances—for the vast majority of involuntary African migrants this would not be the case. Some did achieve emancipation and even repatriation, but the overwhelming majority found themselves enmeshed in the coils of a system that would require them to plumb the full repertoire of their cultural skills to survive.

Given the large number of children who were taken as captives across the Atlantic, especially in the nineteenth century, the question of age and its relationship to memory and expectations is an important consideration, and a feature that is seldom fully acknowledged in the literature. Although attitudes and expectations were modified, the homeland experiences were never completely removed from the individual's memory bank. The memory of a ten-year-old was significantly different from that of a 24-year-old, but even then children continued to be nurtured within a community that re-enforced traditions of the homeland from where the children had come, or children were effectively adopted and treated as if they were from some other homeland. An Igbo child might well have found him or herself on a plantation in the Americas with a substantial Igbo population, or in a population where Igbo cultural influences might be prominent, or a boy from Mozambique might be adopted by someone who spoke Kikongo or Kimbundu from west-central Africa.

Similarly, gender as well as age also affected the ways in which individuals understood servile status. The range of experiences for enslaved women requires detailed comparison. As the demography of the trans-Atlantic slave trade establishes, enslaved women were more likely to be retained or sold locally in western Africa than sold into the Atlantic trade, and they were quite likely to end up in relationships of marriage or concubinage that were governed by law and custom. Moreover, free females, often girls, could be pawned, which meant that male elders had control over their persons, but not the right to sell them. Instead, marriages could be arranged to cancel debts. Under slavery in the Americas, women seldom ended up in legally constituted marriages with their masters, who might sexually exploit them, but who could also sell them, whether or not they had borne their children. As a slave in western Africa, a woman might well end up in a sexual relationship that was forced upon her, as indeed would likely be her fate in the Americas, too. Her status after bearing children, and indeed the status of her offspring, were carefully regulated but often violated in practice, on both sides of the Atlantic. Unfortunately, there have been few comparative studies of the treatment of women and their offspring that bridge the Atlantic during the period of slavery. In the Americas—certainly Mexico, Brazil, the Caribbean and North America—slaves formed families, but there is virtually no information on slave families in Africa during the same period, only information on the children of enslaved women who inherited the free status of their fathers. A comparison of gender relations and child-rearing in the Americas with marriage customs and residence patterns in western Africa might well demonstrate ways in which trans-Atlantic slavery helped to shape the treatment and therefore the expectations of enslaved women.

In areas where Islamic law prevailed, the status of slave, particular concubine, was clearly defined, and while there was debate and disagreement over how the law should be applied, individuals who were exposed to Islamic law in Africa, whether in countries where Islamic law prevailed or along trade routes controlled by Muslim merchants, people understood slavery in an Islamic setting. The discussion of slavery in this context dates back to the period before the trans-Atlantic slave trade, and the topic remained central to Islamic discourse within West Africa throughout the whole period of the Atlantic trade. Given the nature of Islamic education, whether in the rudimentary form to which most Muslim children were exposed, or in the more learned discussion of written texts and scholarly traditions that was open to the educated elite, there was ample opportunity to explore well-developed and historic arguments about slavery. Inevitably, a comparison with the real world around them followed from such exposure, and dissatisfaction with the treatment of freeborn Muslims was a major grievance within the Islamic community, at least since the early seventeenth century. Muslims even discussed how to behave and what to expect if they found themselves enslaved to Christians.

In non-Muslim regions along the Guinea coast—where slaves also came from and which was a region through which slaves from the Muslim interior had to pass to reach ports of embarkation for the Americas—there were also clearly understood codes of servility commonly observed to be slavery. A clear distinction in theory, at least, was maintained between slaves and pawns, for example. Slaves were individuals who were purchased and could be sold, while pawns were individuals whose kin were using them as collateral for debts. Whereas slaves were considered to be property, pawns were servile dependents subject to contracts that prohibited their sale. While there were many cases in which these distinctions were ignored and many others where the legal rights of pawns were violated, in theory, nonetheless, the distinction between the practices of slavery and pawnship confirms the fact that enslaved Africans from these areas had preconceived views of the distinctions among different types of servility. The slavery of the Americas was a new type based on race.

Although individuals came from areas where slavery and other forms of bondage were well known, the legal, ideological and practical implications of servile status varied considerably. Africans in the Americas did not confront slavery for the first time, but the nature of the institution in the Americas was fundamentally different from what many people could have expected, although at least some reports indicate that enslaved Africans were sometimes aware that this was so. As Thomas Phillips described, the attitudes of captives on board the *Hannibal*, in 1693–1694, people had "a more dreadful apprehension of Barbadoes than we can have of hell". Certainly in Dahomey, which according to Edna Bay was a country "deeply affected by the slave trade," those directly involved in the trade "knew its brutal nature and understood something of the fate that awaited those sent overseas."

Differentiation in status in western Africa, as elsewhere, was not only common but was often fluid. Individuals might well experience a change in status, either through enslavement or through pawnship, marriage or apprenticeship. They were aware that these possibilities were part of life experiences and that fortune, Allah or the ancestral spirits might influence their lives. There are numerous examples of Muslim mer-chants and aristocrats from countries where Islam was widespread who ended up in the Americas as slaves, despite the efforts to protect Muslims. There are also examples of individuals who were sold because they had been convicted of some crime or otherwise were being punished for crimes that they were accused of committing. There are even claims that the number of offenses punish-able by enslavement increased as a result of the trans-Atlantic trade. Lt Hugh Dalrymple, who was at Gorée in 1779, learned that

> Every Person who commits any Sort of Crime is sold for a Slave. Crimes [which were] formerly to be punished in different Ways are now punished by this . . . [whereas] formerly the Punishment for all Crimes was commuted for a certain Number of Cattle or Quantity of Grain, which was either paid by the Offender or by his Family, in case of his Incapacity but, since the Introduction of the Slave Trade, not only all Crimes are punished by Slavery, but even the most trivial Offences are punished in the same Manner.

The experiences of merchants, aristocrats and convicts certainly differed, but the evidence demonstrates that people could experience dramatic changes in their status. The gradations of status and the alterations in fortune were common knowledge and must have been the subject of discussion among the enslaved and, indeed more generally, especially among Muslims and at the slave ports along the coast.

Whether for political or other reasons, the idea that Africans had conceptions of slavery before coming to the Americas has traditionally been downplayed in the study of the adjustments of the enslaved to chattel bondage in the Americas. At best, those studies that have broached the subject have argued that slavery was so different in Africa as to have had no impact on the adjustments of Africans to their situation in the Americas. We would suggest that prior knowledge of slavery and other forms of servitude helped in shaping the range of responses of the enslaved. Moreover, the expec-tations of slaves as to how they should be treated derived from their personal knowledge of slavery in Africa. The forum for debate over expectations and the reality of the Americas was in the fields, mines and manor houses of the Americas, where racial arguments and actions increasingly became the recourse and the discourse of the slave-owning elite in maintaining and explaining their domination. There was pressure from below to conform to expectations, and thereby "soften" slavery. Moreover, individuals came from specific places, not a generic "Africa"; hence to examine expectations and notions of slavery, it is necessary to identify the specific historical circumstances and contemporary attitudes towards enslavement and slavery in those regions of Africa from which the enslaved people originated.

The method of enslavement affected the expectations of individuals. Those who were taken in war might well have expected to be ransomed, although the presence of high-ranking officials and wealthy merchants in the Americas demonstrates that ransoming did not always occur. Frequently, women and children were considered the spoils of war, and while in many cases, soldiers and the political elite might retain many captives, others were still sold as a means of realising the payoffs from war. Those who were too old or too young might be killed, which certainly must have been a greatly feared feature of war. Slave raiding was often connected with on-going political rivalry and friction among states, and hence the harassment caused by raiding must also have shaped the expec-tations of many people who grew up in western Africa during the height of the slave trade across the Atlantic. Kidnapping, though often consid-ered illegal, is reported to have been common in many places, as for example in Igbo country. Equiano's experience is well known, but there are many other such recollections. Kidnapping even blurred into seizure as compensation for some debt or crime. Thus one teenage girl, who was given the name Eve, claimed that she had been enslaved as compensation for a goat that had deliberately been placed in her father's garden—her father was then accused of theft. Un-doubtedly, the uncertainties of an era in which kidnapping was a problem affected people's expectations. The possibilities of enslavement were many, therefore, whether through judicial or religious means, debt-bondage, or capture.

Religious issues, especially in the case of Islam, affected expectations, since Muslims who found themselves slaves to non-Muslims were likely to receive different treatment from those whose masters were also Muslims. Religious or other justification for changes in status also varied, of course, whether or not Islam was a factor. In areas where Islam was not important, slaves might be sacrificed, and hence foreign sale was a source of victims for religious ceremonies. In the Niger delta and the Cross River, areas that were clearly affected by the trans-Atlantic slave trade, slaves were killed at funerals and were also sacrificed at religious rites. To avoid sale and possible execution, outcasts, such as the mothers of twins, became "slaves" of religious shrines, thereby protected from sale or sacrifice but nonetheless ostracised. The possibility of death or total social isolation certainly were known to many people, and this knowledge must have affected the expectations of the newly enslaved and those being sold.

As with other aspects of slavery, we need to consider to what extent the existence of the trans-Atlantic trade became such common knowledge that it formed part of the mental landscape of

Africans. While slavery existed before the Atlantic trade, and slaves had gone across the Sahara, the question is how the Atlantic experience was internalised as one option which the enslaved might be forced to confront. Removal from the social formations of western Africa and sale across the Atlantic were possibilities that faced most people in western Africa because it was impossible to guarantee that people would not be enslaved. It is not always possible to determine when enslavement became a punishment for crimes or the fate of captured warriors and kidnapped women and children, but it is clear that most people could not escape the possibility that they or their relatives might have to be ransomed one day or otherwise be permanently enslaved. It can be assumed that people in the areas that were long in contact with the Atlantic world discussed issues of slavery and the slave trade, just as they responded to the fluctuations in the market, whether in slaves or others goods, and adjusted accordingly. Walter Rodney analysed these changes in terms of the extent and degree of social oppression that can be documented for the upper Guinea coast, and how there seems to have been a correspondence between the scale of the export trade in enslaved Africans and the incidence of slavery, pawnship and other institutions of dependency in those areas affected by the trans-Atlantic market. Rodney's argument has been extended to other parts of Africa. Documenting changes in attitudes and practices is painstaking work, which is far from complete, and it still must be admitted that the degree and timing of change in social institutions is difficult to document, even if the trend seems to reinforce Rodney's thesis.

The role of the *ekpe* society in governing master-slave relations and hence in supporting the slave trade has been reasonably well documented. *Ekpe* was a "secret society," as anthropologists have sometimes labelled this graded association of adult males which was controlled by the most influential and wealthiest men in the interior of the Bight of Biafra. The society was only "secret" in the sense that decisions and enforcement of decisions were determined collectively among the members of the highest grade of the society, and hence individuals could not be held responsible for decisions. The spread of *ekpe* in the interior of the Bight of Biafra in the eighteenth century had important implications for the institutions of slavery and pawnship. In overseeing the enforcement of debt repayment, *ekpe* served to protect pawns from enslavement, except in cases of default, when the society could determine who would be executed or otherwise punished and who would be sold into slavery. Hence, *ekpe* was involved in deciding who was enslaveable and who was not, and therefore had a direct impact on distinguishing between slave and free.

The arbitrary powers of *ekpe* developed in the context of the Atlantic slave trade and implicitly reveal that senior members of the society, at least, had full knowledge of the consequences of the trans-Atlantic trade. Indeed, some of these senior members had been educated in England. They were responsible for the development of a "written" language of over 500 signs that was used to announce decrees and enforce decisions of the elite. Despite the difficulty of demonstrating how slavery changed over time, such developments as the emergence of *ekpe* affected how the enslaved viewed slavery, and specifically what they expected as a consequence of their enslavement and their possible sale to different buyers, including those trading to the Americas.

Expectations were also affected by the abuse of power, and the degree to which individuals suffered from such abuse. In many cases, enslavement itself resulted from war, kidnapping or the reduction of debt pawns to slavery, all of which exploited relationships of power. The extent to which the existence of a slave market encouraged such distortions, is reflected in the discussion over "legal" versus "illegal" enslavement. Hence Muslims debated whether or not enslavement was "just"; efforts to define the status of being a Muslim were articulately explored in the works of Ahmad Baba and Muhammad Bello. Similarly, the Kongo civil war raised issues of who could and should not be enslaved in a Christian context. Jose Curto has recently uncovered a case of "wrongful" enslave-ment in Angola in 1805, in which a Portuguese military expedition raided for slaves among allies and subjects of the Portuguese crown, with the result that the governor freed the prisoners and punished his own soldiers.

We are not suggesting a simple correlation between the growth of the trans-Atlantic slave trade and the corruption of institutions; rather we are suggesting that modifications and adapta-tions of institutions were complex and ultimately contributed to the ongoing supply of slaves for the Americas. There was corruption and distortion of institutions on all sides of the slave trade. Thus, some members of the British legal system contributed to the corruption of justice in England by manipulating the law to facilitate the transportation of prisoners to Barbados and Jamaica in the seventeenth century; and hence the phrase "to be Barbadoed." Similarly in Africa, there are numerous examples of individ-uals wrongly accused of crimes and subsequently enslaved, or simply kidnapped, and there was the practice of "panyarring," the specialised term that was used to describe the practice of holding people collectively responsible for debts or wrong-doing, so that anyone considered to be associated with an act could be seized and enslaved. Although it is not always possible to verify whether or not accounts of "wrongful" seizure are truthful, it is certainly likely that the types of cases that are reported did occur.

The controversy surrounding the abolition of the slave trade and the emancipation of slaves in the Americas affected the expectations of the enslaved. It took Mahommah Gardo Baquaqua only two years to realise the opportunities presented by abolition. From the time he was enslaved near Djougou in circa 1843–1845, until his escape from a Brazilian ship in New York harbour in late June 1847, he had been a slave in Pernambuco and Rio de Janeiro. "Freedom" took on a new meaning once he was under the protection of the New York Vigilance Society and spirited away to Haiti. What is not always recognised is that there was debate on both sides of the Atlantic. Hence in Africa, people debated the meaning of abolition. In Asante, there was general perplexity over the fact that the British, the country with the greatest number of slave ships active on the African coast, should abruptly abolish the trade in 1808. How could a trade that had previously been legal now be illegal? The Asantehene asked one British dele-gation to Kumasi what was to be expected if slaves could not be sold overseas, other than large-scale public executions?. A British mission at the royal court of Benin responded to another set of questions about abolition in 1838. Frustrated by what the Benin government perceived as an "illegal" blockade of the West African coast by the British anti-slave trade patrol, the *oba* attempted to explain the apparently irrational policy of abolition on the basis that Britain had a queen and not a king, or as the *oba* of Benin stated it, "the King of England is a woman.". At Old Calabar, Egbo Young Eyambo, the principal merchant in Duke Town, asked Henry Nicholls, who was there in 1805 on a mission from the African Association, to explain his reasons for visiting the town, since he was not a merchant. Eyambo is reported to have asked Nicholls if he "came from Mr. Wilberforce . . . and eyed me with some little ferocity, saying, if I came from Mr. Wilberforce they would kill me.". Such hostility was justified later with the repatriation of liberated slaves with abolitionist ideas.

Similarly, in the Americas, as historians have observed, the significance of the American and French revolutions take on new meaning when viewed in Atlantic perspective, both representing the triumph of "Creole society," although in different ways. On the one hand, "Creole" North America became a new nation that institution-alised slavery, while on the other hand, Haitian "Creole" emerged as a new nation in which slavery was terminated. Whether through the uprising in St. Domingue or the ongoing struggle against slavery in the United States, the expectations of slaves were clearly affected, but what is sometimes not recognised is that the whole Atlantic was in turmoil in the eighteenth century, at least since 1776. The "creolisation" of the Americas occurred at a time when there was a prevailing mood of resistance and unrest arising from trans-Atlantic slavery. That resistance is first apparent in the baracoons of western Africa and on the slave ships themselves in the form of revolt, suicide and acts of sabotage.. Hence the expectations of the enslaved were always set within a framework of resistance and schemes of freedom. Enslavers everywhere worried about what those enslaved might be scheming, but they could not prevent them from learning about ideas of abolition and emancipation. The discussion around the emancipation of the enslaved in British colonies, for example, infected the enslaved with ideas of freedom. Both the 1824 and 1831 slave rebellions in Jamaica followed the spread of rumours of a general emancipation granted by Queen Victoria that was reputedly being subverted by the local slave owners.. Rebel leaders used the fact that emancipation was inevitable as a crucial element in the mobilisation of support for the rebellions. We admit that these incidents occurred towards the end of the British trade, but what does it mean for Africans who were still being shipped across the Atlantic at this time? Did news of these rebellions and developments filter back to African societies and thereby inform the expectations of those recently enslaved?

As these cases suggest, the idea of slavery was subject to an ongoing, if often blurry, debate, or rather series of debates, in different parts of the Atlantic world, including Africa. The atti-tudes of the enslaved who were sent to the Amer-icas were shaped by these discussions. To what extent was the issue of enslavement as justifiable discussed in Africa, so that individuals had some knowledge/experience in the debates over legitimate servitude and protection of the free population from enslavement. This raises the issue of how the "free" population was defined, and by this we mean the population that was recognised to be protected from enslavement. And it is also necessary to explain how people could be enslaved despite such protection, so that we can determine when this happened in a form that was acceptable to local custom and when there was an abuse of power. Here the debate enters the difficult terrain of subtle distinctions over "legitimate" enslavement and the limitations on enslavement. Moreover, discussions of the rights of slaves and the distinctions among servile categories also affected the expectations of individuals. Unlike traditional views of African slavery, therefore, our view posits a complex range of experiences and expectations that were also affected by age and gender and the extent to which people of similar ethnic and linguistic backgrounds found themselves together under slavery. Moreover, attitudes changed over time—slaves from sixteenth-century Kongo were more medieval in their thinking about slavery than nineteenth-century Yoruba escaping from *jihad*.

In the context of slavery, the enslavement of an individual could realise a financial reward equivalent to the profits acquired through theft. Such opportunities for profit weakened the social fabric, as reflected in the collapse of central authority in the Kingdom of Kongo in the last decades of the seventeenth century. Officials might well threaten enslavement in the hope of financial gain and religious shrines came to accept slaves as compensation and retribution. Determining when institutions succumbed to corruption and officials and merchants abused their power, raises issues of context and place, as Rodney demonstrated for the upper Guinea coast. Social oppression and the corruption of institutions were not, of course, only associated with slavery and the trans-Atlantic slave trade, but inevitably there were institutional responses to trans-Atlantic slavery that increased the level of oppression. We are thinking here of the development of the Aro commercial network in the eighteenth century which supplied slaves to Bonny and Old Calabar, the adaptation of the institution of pawnship to accommodate the commercial requirements of British traders at Old Calabar, and the development of similar commercial practices elsewhere that depended on an interplay between the external demand for slaves and local political and social conditions. Where a strong centralised state controlled the ports, as Dahomey and Oyo did in the Bight of Benin, pawnship was not a feature of the transactions between Europeans and Africans; in the Bight of Biafra, the nature of the political structure was entirely different, so that the use of pawns to guarantee debts that were owed to the captains of slavers became common practice.

The impression often given is that the transactions in slaves occurred in a state of silence; that slaves, as commodities, did not have ears or minds that could intercept and interpret the events around them. In fact, there were numerous people involved in transactions—from captors, merchants, guards, people who provided food along the slave routes and at the ports before embarkation, African sailors, and indeed white sailors and ship captains—with whom slaves had to interact and from whom they gained information or misinformation that went into the construction of their fears and expectations. The enslaved had to distinguish among various types of stories and gossip, whether these were myths of white cannibalism, rumours that someone might be freed because of proof of wrongful enslavement, or conspiracies to seize ships. The fact that relatives and friends did occasionally find one another also has to be taken into account. The period of exposure to conflicting information, thereby leading to uncertainty, was at least a few months from time of capture to delivery in the Americas, and often much longer. The existence and extent of wide and interlocking networks of information flows and informants and hence what was known about the trade and slavery are often ignored or under-appreciated. There were Black seamen in all periods of Atlantic history, from the earliest voyages through the eighteenth century when the slave trade was at its height, and they constituted an important network for the trans-Atlantic and circum-Atlantic flow of information.

Similarly, the existence of con-tinuous interaction between Brazil and western Africa created an important avenue for the circulation of knowledge and hence the formation of expectations. The deportation of criminals, often slaves and mulattoes from Brazil, to the western coast of Africa as punishment began in the late sixteenth century and was a feature of the Brazilian penal system into the nineteenth century. Hence, many of the rebels in the 1835 Male uprising in Bahia were sent to the Bight of Benin. Similarly, the education of the children of African merchants in Europe and the role of Islam as a network of information both challenge the idea that knowledgeable people along the slave routes in Africa were isolated from and hence ignorant of what was going on beyond the Atlantic.

We are suggesting that the degree of isolation of western Africa has been exaggerated. Certainly there was a gap between what mer-chants knew and what the enslaved knew, but it cannot be said that merchants and ruling elites were unaware of the likely fate of the deported population, especially not at the ports and along the trade routes that supplied slaves. How long did it take for those enslaved to find out what was going on? Enslaved people who were retained on the coast certainly learned about the signifi-cance of export, and the fear of being shipped on a European slaver must have often served as an effective means of controlling captives on the coast. It was difficult to trick slaves on board the French ship *Deux Soeurs* in 1825 because there were on board,

> . . . several slaves who had been employed as labourers and boatmen [in Sierra Leone.] These men were aware of the consequences of being taken to the coast which no doubt induced them to have recourse to force to affect their liberation.

The result was an uprising in which seven French sailors were killed. Sometimes, at least, there was reasonably clear knowledge about the fate awaiting slaves being taken to the Americas, which raises the issue of language and ease of communication, including the importance of "trade" languages and the use of common languages on board ships. The fact remains that many people along the slave routes had to know what was going on, although it is not always clear how they interpreted what they saw and what they heard about.

The incidence of attempted suicide both on board ship and on plantations in the Americas raises questions about how such actions reflected the worst expectations of the slaves. Although a persistent feature of the slave trade and slavery, it is not clear how suicide was conceived in different societies in Africa and how specific "African" notions either supported or proscribed such extreme actions. Since some slaves, at least, believed that "Whites" were cannibals, and it may be that such stereotypes were re-enforced by slave owners in Africa as a means of discouraging their own slaves from resisting bondage through the fear of being sold overseas.. Certainly, the autopsies that were performed on board some slave ships must have intensified such fears about the intentions of Whites. As one surgeon, Dr. Falconbridge, told the Parliamentary enquiry into the slave trade in 1790 in London, efforts to discover the causes of deaths were easy to misinterpret, which is why he always conducted autopsies at night, by candle light, so that the slaves below deck would not know what was going on, which may only have had the effect of feeding rumors.. Captains of slave ships at some point began erecting nets on the main decks to prevent people from jumping into the sea. Moreover plantation owners in the Americas complained frequently that suicide was a form of resistance that was directed at destroying the value of their property. Certain ethnic groups, especially Igbo, became identified with suicide, and hence there were efforts to avoid the purchase of enslaved Africans of this background. More often than not, however, the quest for profits dictated that all available slaves be purchased, so that preferences could not always be satisfied.

Similarly, infanticide also reflects the views of some enslaved Africans that the life under slavery was not worth living. While it is clear that infant mortality rates were high, most scholarship has linked these high rates to the conditions of servitude (diet, the labour regime, disregard for pre- and post-natal care), but we cannot ignore the possibility of induced abortions and deliberate infanticide as part of a pattern of what some have called "gynaecological" resis-tance.. The decision to take the life of an unborn or recently born infant is a serious issue, whose discussion would have been cast in particular moral, religious and political terms reflecting the African background. Unfortunately, we know next to nothing about levels of infanticide and abortion in Africa during the period of the trans-Atlantic slave trade and the corresponding differences in attitudes and beliefs in Africa and the Americas. Those enslaved Africans who made the decision to kill children, and there was a significant minority who did, had to take this step with reference to their previous under-standings about the gravity of the act and the likely consequences. While we need to know more about attitudes towards both infanticide and abortion, like suicide, the expectation that conditions of slavery would continue to be intolerable surely shaped the decisions of individuals to commit such acts of desperation.

Our purpose has been to demonstrate the extent to which the enslaved were aware of the world around them and the extent to which movement along the routes that fed the trans-Atlantic trade was a factor in the evolution of slave consciousness. What most enslaved African captives experienced upon being sold to the captains of slave ships was different in ways that were as profound as the crossing of the Atlantic itself. Already along the slave routes, the question of communication had required slaves to learn a common language, and in so doing their identities became tied up with issues of ethnicity and ultimately in religious expres-sion.. However, the alteration in the status of individuals who had been enslaved did not make people forget skills or fail to take advantage of situations in which past experience mattered. The new world of the Americas reinforced ethnicity and the use of common languages, often in pidgin form, as a means of overcoming isolation. Hence, the bonding that characterised slavery in the Americas encouraged the development of a sense of community based on common, and often shared, experience and the ability to communicate beyond the hearing of their enslavers. Such bonding must have been based on expressions of widely divergent emotions and expressions that resulted in shared knowledge of the enslaving past.. This common memory certainly was important later when enslaved people were separated and sold to different enslavers. We have evidence of expressions of relief because someone was not sacrificed at a funeral; hysteria because of a violation of the underlying principle of debt bondage that prohibited further alienation and outright sale; the grief expressed by those who had suffered from "panyarring" because they belonged to a group that was being punished as a collectivity.. Finally, the fate of war prisoners, both combatants and non-combatants, must have been a common subject of discussion during the Middle Passage.

A central issue in understanding how the enslaved adjusted any expectations that they might have had about the nature of slavery and their own plight as slaves to their actual experience and the various warnings that must have been immediately showered on them by other slaves of their new owners in the Americas, relates to what was called "seasoning" and the distinction between the Creole generation and the African-born. It should be noted that in most of the slave societies of the Americas, for most of the period of slavery, the majority of the population had been born in Africa.. The growing importance of a Creole population, born in slavery in the Americas, should not distort the importance of African-derived notions of civility and society, and hence we want to make a sharp distinction in periodisation, emphasising the shift in the demography of slave societies. Second-generation slaves had far different experiences than those born in Africa, and their expectations of slavery varied accordingly.. Moreover, the second generation also included a mixed, "mulatto," population, almost always the result of unrecognised, even illicit, sexual liaisons between White men and enslaved women. Sometimes such liaisons led to the emancipation, effective or legal, of the women, but more often, the offspring of such unions were born slaves and remained so. The violation of enslaved women was a characteristic of the Atlantic crossing, and hence it is not always possible to discern when mulatto offspring were the result of relations with slave owners and other Whites in the colonies and when pregnancy occurred during transit. How did the mothers of children born of such shipboard rapes react, what did they see as their future and the future of their offspring? For a variety of reasons, the existence of mulatto slaves whose paternity was effectively denied suggests that racial distinctions were defined in specific ways. On the one hand, the prosperous slave colonies of the Caribbean experienced a steady growth in the "free" Black population, which was disproportionately mulatto, although there were also mulatto slaves and indeed mulatto slave owners. Racial distinctions were indeed blurry. Similarly, in many parts of Hispanic America, the racial distinctions also became confused, but in a different, although also racially perceived, manner. The process there has often been referred to as the "browning" of the population, as the demographically-dominant Amerindian population absorbed Spanish and African alike. Mulatto/prado and other designations thereby emerged as forms of categorisation that promoted the "racialisation" of slavery. Ethnic identification appears gradually to have given way to racial categories.

In considering the differences between what happened to men and women under racial slavery and other forms of slavery, it should be recognised that the sexual dimension was regulated and violated in different ways. Women in Islamic and in non-Muslim African societies had the possibility of cohabitation, whether voluntary or not, which often led to improved status for children and the women themselves. In the Americas, what did the racial dimension impose on relationships between enslaved women and free men? Enslaved women in Africa could expect that sexual relationships would alter their status and the status of their children, but in the Americas, the racial dimension imposed a barrier that often thwarted such expectations. When children of slave women were recognised, they often attained a higher status, but very often paternity was not recognised in the Americas and children, therefore, continued in bondage. Because the mulatto/free Black popu-lation was descended from such sexual liaisons, this process was imbedded in the society as an ongoing struggle. In the Americas, there were firm lines of racial difference, while under Islam and in non-Muslim African societies, there were no such distinctions. In the Americas, descendants of mixed liaisons between slave and free could aspire to membership in the class of freed Blacks and mulattoes, but not membership in the White class.

There were no such restrictions in Africa or Islamic lands based on race.

In the context of the trans-Atlantic slavery, at what point did Africans begin to recognise the racial dimension of their enslavement? In Africa, the enslaved sometimes recognised their subordination, on ethnic, religious and political grounds—but never on racial grounds. J. K. Fynn has expressed the absence of racism on the Gold Coast in the eighteenth century as follows: "There was no racism then; Black Man cheat; White Man cheat; everyone cheat; no racism.". In the Americas, subordination was not always racial, especially early in the history of some colonies; hence Irish indentured workers and slaves in Barbados and mainland North America sometimes staged coordinated resistance. In Brazil, generalisations about the nature of slave society in seventeenth-century Bahia do not apply to the nineteenth century. Each major economic development, whether the renewed growth of sugar and tobacco in Bahia, the development of the gold mines of Mineas Gerais or the coffee plantations of Sao Paulo, evolved in a specific context. Each phase in development relied on a distinctive grouping of enslaved Africans, who require identification and correlation with the history of their homelands before it can be fully understood what the newly enslaved thought about slavery and how they expected to survive in captivity. We contend that strategies of servility were not crystallised, and while scholarship has usually examined the shift in attitudes from the point of view of the primarily White enslaving class, the expec-tations of the enslaved as to differences in treatment for Black and White servile labour have to be reassessed. Our interest lies in examining these shifts from the point of view of the enslaved. Differences in pigmentation meant that individuals experienced servility as racial domination and therefore at variance with the expectations that would have seemed likely in Africa.

The response of enslaved Africans to racial domination reinforced ethnic loyalties. On the basis of ethnic loyalty, Akan became synonymous with Maroon resistance in Jamaica, as Monica Schuler and others have shown. Similarly, John Thornton has drawn attention to the influence of the Kongo civil wars on events in Haiti and in Georgia/South Carolina and the consolidation of Kongo ethnicity. Ethnic identification, while a vital reflection of how people responded to enslavement in the Americas, nonetheless was ultimately subordin-ated to race, so that over generations the racial dimension superceded and then fully replaced the ethnic. When did slaves perceive maroons, other slaves, freed blacks as racial colleagues and not merely as members of different ethnic com-munities? Categories of identification recognised by the enslavers reflected a nascent community structure among those enslaved that often began on board ship, or even before, and resulted in the acceptance of languages of communication that frequently carried over into the Americas and thereby helped integrate new slaves into a community that had established an ethnic identity—that is, one based on acceptance of common origins and preserving an autonomous means of communication through a shared lan-guage that was not generally understood by members of the slave-owning elite. Shared language and common experience inevitably reinforced a sense of community and confirmed the perceptions of slave owners that slaves recognised ethnic loyalty.

This association of ethnicity with resistance highlights an important transition in the evolution of racialised slavery. The ethnic basis of slave identification is often attributed to the initiative of enslaved Africans themselves, who had to overcome Old World rivalries in order to form pan-ethnic unions to confront New World realities. On the contrary, we understand ethnic identification as a fluid and dynamic process affecting individuals and how they relate to social groups. We are suggesting that what was unique in the Americas was not the development of ethnic associations of slaves but the opposition of such identities with racial categories. In doing so, we are distinguishing between individual resistance and collective resistance, and attempt to examine the differences in terms of what people expected and how they responded when their expectations were not met. We assume that slavery as an institution fosters resistance, but we distinguish the responses of slaves in Africa to bondage from their experiences of the enslaved in the Americas, where racial distinctions became a factor in strategies of accommodation and resis-tance. We want to know when resistance moved from the individual to the collective, and thereby what roles ethnicity, religion and face played in shaping patterns of resistance. We contend that these questions relate to the issue of the expectations of slaves and how those expectations changed along the slave routes to the Americas.

Africans had expectations of how status could be improved under slavery both in Africa and, by extension, in the Americas as well. In Africa, there were various means by which to achieve manumission. Individuals who had been enslaved were successful in achieving freedom or otherwise escaping from slavery through ransom by relatives or other third parties.. Others re-ceived redress in future war, in which they were liberated, but there was also self-purchase through private employment and acts of charity. Moreover, each of these avenues of freedom was possible on both sides of the Atlantic. In the Americas, however, the intensification of chattel status affected the incidence of emancipation, so that avenues of amelioration and liberation became more difficult. In this regard, the racial factor was of course very significant.

Whereas enslavers in widely separated places and with very different cultural and political views shaped the institution of slavery in increasingly racialist terms, the enslaved themselves came to accept racial characteristics as the basis of a collective strategy of accommodation and resistance. Racialist ideas and practices, which varied widely and changed over time, nonetheless introduced a new and powerful weapon in the subjugation of slave populations and implicitly laid the foundations for the emergence of an "African" consciousness in the Creole societies of the Americas. Because of recent scholarship, it is now possible to determine the specifics of the "African" cultural baggage that was taken across the Atlantic. By examining expectations, our aim has been to individualise the slave trade, and hence to demonstrate the importance of personal histories, whether in the form of profiles, autobiographies or oral tra-ditions. These life stories can be used to examine notions of slavery in western Africa and the reality of racialised slavery in the Americas and thereby informs an analysis of identity and consciousness under slavery and how ethnicity, religion and other factors affected the ways individuals adjusted in the Americas.

Brathwaite's notion of adaptation as a crucial element in the process of creolisation is an important starting point in any discussion of the histories of enslaved Africans; for he assigned them an agency that was lacking in much of the previous scholarship. He rescued enslaved Africans from the ahistorical, non-active, unspecified role of victim. They came to life in his poetry more so than in his writing as an historian, for it is in poetry that he allowed Africans and their descendants to express their vibrancy and creativity. We suggest that their real life historical ancestors/counterparts are better understood and their limitations, pos-sibilities and responses better appreciated with a fuller understanding of their expectations. We can only understand these expectations if we ground them in the historical reality of their times. These expectations figured prominently in their adaptation to the reality of enslavement in the Americas. In the process they influenced the system of slavery (even as it influenced them) and over time created Creole societies. Thus, Creole society is not created from the adaptation of a generalised African background but from the specificity of the expectations and actions of identifiable individuals and communities.

[1]Research for this paper was funded by the Social Sciences and Humanities Research Council of Canada. An earlier version was presented at the conference, "Reunion: La Ruta del Esclavo en Hispanoamérica," Universidad de Costa Rica, 24–26 Feb. 1999.
[2]M. Sobel, *The World They Made Together: Black and White Values in Eighteenth Century Virginia* (Princeton: Princeton University Press, 1987), p. 29.

[3]Kamau Brathwaite, *The Development of Creole Society in Jamaica, 1770–1820* (Oxford: Clarendon Press, 1971), p. xv. It should be noted that the book is based on his 1968 Ph.D. thesis.

[4]Ibid., p. 296.

[5]Ibid., p. 307.

[6]Sidney Mintz and Richard Price, *The Birth of African-American Culture: An Anthropological Perspective* (Boston: Beacon Press, 1992).

[7]See, for example, the accounts in Philip Curtin, ed., *Africa Remembered: Narratives by West Africans from the Era of the Slave Trade* (Madison: University of Wisconsin Press, 1967). For an insightful discussion on this, see Richard Rathbone, "Some Thoughts on Resistance to Enslavement in West Africa," *Slavery and Abolition*, 16 (1985), pp. 11–22.

[8]See, for example, the accounts in John W. Blassingame, ed., *Slave Testimony: Two Centuries of Letters, Speeches, Interviews, and Autobiographies* (Baton Rouge: Louisiana University Press, 1977), pp. 225–28, 254–61, 306–20; especially the accounts of William Thomas, John Homrn, Lorenzo Clarke, Maria Rosalia Garcia, Margarita Cabrera, Maria Luisa Macorra, Dolore Real, Luca Martina, and other former slaves from Cuba. Also see the various biographies in Curtin, ed., *Africa Remembered*; and Allan D. Austin, ed., *African Muslims in Antebellum America: A Sourcebook* (New York: Garland, 1984), especially the account of Mahommah Gardo Baquaqua (pp. 585–634). For a general discussion, see Paul E. Lovejoy, "Biography as Source Material: Towards a Biographical Archive of Enslaved Africans," in Robin Law, ed., *Source Material for Studying the Slave Trade and the African Diaspora* (Stirling: Centre of Commonwealth Studies, 1996), pp. 119–40.

[9]For a general discussion of slavery in the African context, see Paul E. Lovejoy, *Transformations in Slavery: A History of Slavery in Africa* (New York: Cambridge University Press, 2nd edn., 2000).

[10]See, for example, the various studies in Suzanne Miers and Igor Kopytoff, eds., *Slavery in Africa: Historical and Anthropological Perspectives* (Madison: University of Wisconsin Press, 1975), Claude Meillassoux, ed., *L'esclavage en Afrique precoloniale* (Paris: Maspero, 1975); Paul E. Lovejoy, ed., *The Ideology of Slavery in Africa* (Beverly Hills: Sage, 1981); and Claire C. Robertson and Martin A. Klein, eds., *Women and Slavery in Africa* (Madison: University of Wisconsin Press, 1983).

[11]Emmanuel Kwaku Senah argues that conditions of servility in West Africa were fundamentally different from European constructs and did not include the full range of meanings attached to European ideas of slavery; see "What Slave? What Chattel?: A Philosophical Critique of Aspects of Caribbean Historical Literature from the Perspectives of Ga, Ewe-Foh, and Akan Culture and Language," paper presented at the 30th Annual Conference, Association of Caribbean Historians, Suriname, April 1998.

[12]Douglas Chambers, "He Is an African But Speaks Plain: Historical Creolisation in Eighteenth-Century Virginia," in Alusine Jalloh and Stephen E. Maizlish, eds., *The African Diaspora* (College Station, TX: Texas A and M University Press, 1996), pp. 100–33; "My Own Nation: Igbo Exiles into the Diaspora," in Paul E. Lovejoy, ed., *Identity in the Shadow of Slavery* (London: Continuum, 2000).

[13]John Hunwick, "Islamic Law and Polemics over Race and Slavery in North and West Africa, 16th–19th Centuries," *Princeton Review* (1999); Paul E. Lovejoy, "Cerner les identités au sein de la Diaspora africaine: L'Islam et l'esclavage aux Ameriques," *Les cahiers des anneaux de la mémoire*, 1 (1999).

[14]Sylviane A. Diouf, *Servants of Allah: African Muslims Enslaved in the Americas* (New York: New York University Press, 1998).

[15]Toyin Falola and Paul E. Lovejoy, eds., *Pawnship in Africa: Debt Bondage in Historical Perspective* (Boulder: Westview Press, 1994); Paul E. Lovejoy and David Richardson, "The Business of Slaving: Pawnship in Western Africa, ca. 1600–1810," *Journal of African History*, 42:1 (2000).

[16]Thomas Phillips, "The Voyage of the Hannibal in 1693–94," in Churchill, *Collection of Voyages and Travels* (London, 1732), vol. 4, pp. 218–19. See the discussion in Rathbone, "Enslavement in West Africa," pp. 17–18.

[17]Edna G. Bay, "Dahomean Political Exile and the Atlantic Slave Trade," proceedings of the UNESCO/SSHRCC Summer Institute, "Identifying Enslaved Africans: The Nigerian Hinterland and the African Diaspora," York University, Toronto, 1997.

[18]Testimony of Hugh Dalrymple, who served on Gorée in 1779 and made frequent excursions to the mainland; see Sheila Lambert, ed., *House of Commons Sessional Papers of the Eighteenth Century. Report of the Lords of Trade on the Slave Trade, 1789*, part 1 (Wilmington, Del.: Scholarly Resources Press, 1975), vol. 69, p. 25.

[19]Mintz and Price, *African American Culture*; Philip Morgan, "The Cultural Implications of the Atlantic Slave Trade: African Regional Origins, American Destinations and New World Developments," *Slavery and Abolition*, 18:1 (1997), pp. 122–45; Morgan and Ira Berlin, *Many Thousands Gone: The First Two Centuries of Slavery in North America* (Cambridge, MA: Harvard University Press, 1998), pp. 102–3.

[20]On the methods of enslavement, see, for example, David Northrup, *Trade without Rulers: Pre-Colonial Economic Development in South-Eastern Nigeria* (Oxford: Oxford University Press, 1978); Lovejoy, *Transformations in Slavery*, pp. 66–87, 135–58; and Robin Law, "Legal and Illegal Enslavement in the Context of the Trans-Atlantic Slave Trade," paper presented at Colloque: Les Héritages du Passé: Cinq Siècles de Relations Europe-Afrique-Amérique, Dakar, 1997.

[21]James Walvin, *An African's Life: The Life and Times of Olaudah Equiano, 1745–1797* (London: Continuum, 1998). Also see various papers presented at the conference on "Repercussions of the Slave Trade: The Interior of the Bight of Biafra and the African Diaspora," Enugu, Nigeria, July 2000.

[22]Account reported by James Arnold, who was at Bimbia in 1787; see Lambert, ed., *House of Commons Sessional Papers of the Eighteenth Century*, vol. 69, p. 50.

[23]For an overview, see Lovejoy, *Transformations in Slavery*, and the references cited therein.

[24]Bay, "Dahomean Political Exile"; Law, "Legal and Illegal Enslavement."

[25]Rodney, "Slavery and Other Forms of Oppression."

[26]Paul E. Lovejoy and David Richardson, "Trust, Pawnship, and Atlantic History: The Institutional

Foundations of the Old Calabar Slave Trade," *The American Historical Review*, 104:2 (1999), pp. 333–55.

[27] Law, "Legal and Illegal Enslavement."

[28] Lovejoy, Situating Identities."

[29] John Thornton, "'I Am the Subject of the King of Congo': African Political Ideology and the Haitian Revolution," *Journal of World History*, 4:2 (1993), pp. 181–214.

[30] Jose Curto, "An Unlawful Prize: Slave Raiding and Luso-African Relations between the Kwanza and Kwango Rivers, 1805," Harriet Tubman Seminar, York University, 1999.

[31] Also see David Eltis, *The Rise of African Slavery in the Americas* (Cambridge: Cambridge University Press, 2000).

[32] Eric Williams, *Capitalism and Slavery* [1944] (London: Andre Deutch, 1964 edn.), pp. 9–19.

[33] Ivor Wilks, *Asante in the Nineteenth Century: The Structure and Evolution of a Political Order* (Cambridge: Cambridge University Press, 1975), pp. 176–78.

[34] John Beecroft, "Account of a Visit to the Capital of Benin, in the Delta of the Kwara or Niger, in the Year 1838," *Journal of the Royal Geographical Society*, 14 (1841), pp. 191–92.

[35] Account of Henry Nicholls, 1804–05, in *Records of the African Association (1788–1831)*, ed. Robin Hallet (London, 1964), p. 197.

[36] Antonio T. Bly, "Crossing the Lake of Fire: Slave Resistance during the Middle Passage, 1720–1842," *Journal of Negro History*, 83:2 (1998), pp. 178–86.

[37] Williams, *Capitalism and Slavery*, pp. 197–208; Michael Craton, *Testing the Chains: Resistance to Slavery in the British West Indies* (Ithaca: Cornell University Press, 1982); Mary Turner, *Slaves and Missionaries: The Disintegration of Jamaican Slave Society, 1787–1834* (Champaign-Urbana: University of Illinois Press, 1982): and Emilia Viotti da Costa, *Crowns of Glory, Tears of Blood: The Demerara Slave Rebellion of 1823* (New York: Oxford University Press, 1994). Also see Eugene Genovese, *From Rebellion to Revolution* (Baton Rouge: Louisiana University Press, 1979); Gary Okihiro, ed., *In Resistance. Studies in African, Caribbean, and Afro-American History* (Amherst: University of Massachusetts Press, 1986).

[38] Rodney, "Slavery and Other Forms of Social Oppression on the Upper Guinea Coast in the Context of the Atlantic Slave Trade," *Journal of African History*, vol. 7, no. 4 (1966), pp. 431–43.

[39] Lovejoy and Richardson, "Old Calabar Slave Trade," pp. 353–55; Lovejoy and Richardson, "Business of Slaving"; and Ugo Nwokeji, "The Biafran Frontier: Trade, Slaves, and Aro Society, c. 1750–1905." Ph.D. thesis, unpublished, University of Toronto, 1999.

[40] Robin Law, "On Pawning and Enslavement for Debt in the Pre-Colonial Slave Coast," in Falola and Lovejoy, eds., *Pawnship in Africa*, pp. 55–70.

[41] W. Jeffrey Butler, *Black Jacks: African American Seamen in the Age of Sail* (Cambridge, MA: Harvard University Press, 1997).

[42] Pierre Verger, *Trade Relations between the Bight of Benin and Bahia, 17th–19th Century* (Ibadan: University of Ibadan Press, 1976); Bellarmin Coffi Codo, "'Les Brésiliens' en Afrique de l'ouest: Hier et aujourd'hui,"

Les Cahiers des Anneaux de la Mémoire, 1 (1999); João Reis, *Slave Rebellion in Brazil: The Muslim Uprising of 1835 in Bahia*, trans. Arthur Brakel (Baltimore: Johns Hopkins University Press, 1993).

[43] Commissioner of Sierra Leone to Canning, April 1825, as quoted in Rathbone, "Enslavement in West Africa," p. 18.

[44] See the testimony of Mark Cook, reporting on Jamaica in 1791, in Lambert, ed., *House of Commons Sessional Papers, Slave Trade 1791 and 1792*, vol. 72, p. 194; also comments of Isaac Wilson, surgeon, who examined slaves who had hung themselves on board ship at Bonny in 1788; in ibid., p. 567. Also see Rathbone, "Resistance to Enslavement," 14; and John Saillant, "Explaining Syncreticism in African-American Views of Death: An Eighteenth Century Example," *Culture and Tradition*, 17 (1995), pp. 25–41.

[45] William D. Piersen, "White Cannibals, Black Martyrs: Fear, Depression, and Religious Faith as a Cause of Suicide among New Slaves," *Journal of Negro History*, 62 (1977), pp. 147–59; Barry Higman, *Slave Populations of the British Caribbean, 1807–1834* (Kingston: UWI Press, 1995), pp. 295, 343–46. For a reference to the fear that Europeans were cannibals, see William Bosman, *A New and Accurate Description of the Coast of Guinea* [1705] (London: Frank Cass, 1967 reprint), pp. 363–65.

[46] Testimony of Falconbridge, in Lambert, *Sessional Papers*, vol. 72, pp. 581, 626.

[47] Barbara Bush, "Hard Labour: Women, Childbirth and Resistance in Caribbean Slave Societies," *History Workshop*, 36 (1993), pp. 83–99; Todd L. Savitt, "Smothering and Overlaying of Virginia Slave Children: A Suggested Explanation," *Bulletin of the History of Medicine*, 49 (1979), pp. 400–4; Michael P. Johnson, "Smothered Slave Infants: Were Slave Mothers at Fault?" *Journal of Negro History*, 62 (1977), pp. 147–59.

[48] Rathbone, "Enslavement in West Africa," pp. 21–22, n. 17, n. 25.

[49] See various studies in forthcoming volume on slavery and memory, edited by Ralph Austen.

[50] See the various testimonies in Lambert, *House of Commons Sessional Papers*.

[51] For the ratio of African-born to American-born in the slave population, see Eltis, *Rise of African Slavery in the Americas*.

[52] Hilary McD. Beckles, *Centering Woman: Gender Discourses in Caribbean Slave Society* (Kingston: Ian Randle, 1999).

[53] Colin Palmer, "From Africa to the Americas: Ethnicity in the Early Black Communities of the Americas," *Journal of World History*, 6:2 (1995), pp. 223–36. Also see Teresa Castello Yturbide, "La Indumentaria de las Castas del Mestizaji," *Artes de Mexico*, 8 (1998), pp. 72–80.

[54] Hilary McD. Beckles, "Female Enslavement in the Caribbean and Gender Ideologies," in Lovejoy, ed., *Identity in the Shadow of Slavery*, pp. 163–82; Beckles, "Sex and Gender in the Historiography of Caribbean Slavery," in Verene A. Shepherd, et al., eds., *Engendering History: Caribbean Women in Historical Perspective* (Kingston: Ian Randle, 1995), pp. 125–40.

[55] *The African Trade*, BBC Timewatch, November 1997.

[56]Monica Schuler, "Akan Slave Rebellions in the British Caribbean," *Savacou,* 1:1 (1970), pp. 8–31; and "Ethnic Slave Rebellions in the Caribbean and the Guianas," *Journal of Social History,* 3 (1970), pp. 374–85.

[57]Thornton, "Subject of the King of Congo"; and *Africa and Africans in the Making to the Atlantic World* (Cambridge: Cambridge University Press, 2nd edn., 1998).

[58]Paul E. Lovejoy, "Murgu: The Wages of Slavery in the Sokoto Caliphate," *Slavery and Abolition,* 24:1 (1992), pp. 168–85; and Lovejoy, "Muslim Freedmen in the Atlantic World: Images of Emancipation and Self-Redemption," conference on "From Slavery to Freedom: Manumission in the Atlantic World," paper presented at the Conference on Manumission, College of Charleston, 4–7 October 2000.

SECTION SIX:
COMPARATIVE SLAVERY IN THE AMERICAS

Introduction

During the centuries of African slavery in the Americas and the Caribbean, most of the millions of slaves worked on plantations, smaller estates, in mines, and others in urban areas for their masters or were hired out. A large group of slaves also did domestic work for their masters and his or her family. While there were similar exploitive experiences that the African slaves encountered in these roles, they were also many differences that transpired as they worked and lived under very restrictive and abusive conditions to produce sugar, tobacco, cacao, precious metals, rice, coffee, and cotton for sale in Europe.

The five essays in section six cover significant elements of any comparative approach to understanding the nature, the forces, and the activities that transpired within the institution of slavery in the Caribbean and across the Americas. Slave societies in the Americas varied according to time, place and numerous other factors. The circumstances and responses of the African slaves also differed remarkably. One of the most important aspects of slave life was the extent to which slaves were allowed to maintain their family ties. Another critical and vital element within the slave society was the role that women played and their contributions to the overall quality of slave life in the Americas. While there is no singular slave experience throughout this vast region, there are elements of a common legacy.

The first segment in this section includes short passages from the autobiography of Frederick Douglass, who became the most well-known and respected nineteenth century former African slave from Maryland. After fleeing slavery he became the voice of the American Abolitionist society and soon felt compelled to write in great detail about his slave experience. His *Narrative of the Life of Frederick Douglass, An American Slave written by Himself* has been recognized as one of the greatest insightful stories penned about American slavery as it reveals the complexities of slave resistance.

This second narrative provides an insightful description of slave society across the Caribbean. Franklin W. Knight's "Social Structures of a Caribbean Slave Plantation Society" is taken from his important work *The Caribbean, the Genesis of a Fragmented Nationalism* (1990). Knight is Professor of History at Johns Hopkins University. He is author of numerous articles on the Caribbean. His other publications include *Slave Society in Cuba During the Nineteenth Century* (1990), *The African Dimensions of Latin American Societies* (1974), *Africans and the Caribbean: Legacies of a Link* (1979), *Atlantic Port Cities, Economy, Culture, and Society in the North Atlantic 1650–1850* (1980), and with Colin A. Palmer (eds.) *The Modern Caribbean* (1989).

Katia M. de Queiros Mattoso's "Charter of Freedom in Brazil" presents a clear and readable analysis of the slave institution taken from the largest population of slaves in the Americas. Brazil was home to more than a third of all the African slaves in the

Americas. The Portuguese were among the first to establish the institution of African slavery and it lasted longer there than anywhere else in the Americas. De Queiros Mattoso has taught at the Catholic University of Salvador in Brazil, the Sorbonne in Paris, the University of Minnesota, and Columbia University, New York. This essay is from the seventh chapter of *To Be a Slave in Brazil 1550–1888*, which was first published in French in 1979 and translated into English in 1986. This chapter is based on extensive archival Brazilian sources. De Queiros Mattoso analyzes the precarious position of the Brazilian slave and explores the inherent problems of the Brazilian liberation process.

Andrew Billingsley's historical review of the general experiences of the African American family is extremely useful in comparing the slave experiences across the Americas. Billingsley is a sociologist by training and in this narrative seeks to show that African American slave families existed but that they were extremely fragile because of the powerlessness of the male-female arrangement granted by their American slave masters. Billingsley is Professor of Sociology in the Department of Family and Community Development at the University of Maryland, College Park. He was president of Morgan State University between 1975 and 1984. He has authored *Black Families in White America* (1868), *Children in the Storm: Black Children and America Child Welfare* (1972), *Climbing Jacob's Ladder: The Enduring Legacy of African American Families* (1993), and *Mighty Like a River: The Black Church and Social Reform* (1999).

The fourth essay provides us with a fascinating picture that in some ways is dissimilar to familiar images of the slave systems that existed in the Caribbean, Brazil, and the United States. Peter Blanchard, Professor of History at the University of Toronto, Canada, focuses on the life of Peru's relatively small slave population immediately after the country achieved its political independence. We view a slave system with many contradictions and contrasts with many larger slave systems from Brazil to that in the U.S. This essay is from Blanchard's more extensive work *Slavery and Abolition in Early Republican Peru* (1992). He also is the author of *Origins of the Peruvian Labor Movement 1883–1919* (1982) and editor of *Markham in Peru: The Travels of Clements R. Markham 1852–1853* (1991).

The final essay in this section unlocks long-held myths about African Argentineans. During the early years of Spanish settlement in the viceroyalty of La Pieta in southern South America, a significant percentage of the population was African slaves. From the time of independence in the early nineteenth century, the African presence seemed to decline significantly. This study is taken from George Reid Andrews's important volume *The Afro-Argentines of Buenos Aires 1800–1900* (1980), which describes in great detail how significant numbers of the African Argentineans continued to live in the country after its independence and contributed to the development and protection of the newly independent South American Republic. Andrews identifies the many reasons that caused their apparent disappearance from the pages of Argentinean history. He has published numerous articles on the African experience in Latin America and is author of *Blacks and Whites in Sao Paulo, Brazil 1888–1988* (1991) and *Afro-Latin America 1800–2000* (2004).

from *Narrative of the Life of Frederick Douglass, an American Slave*

Frederick Douglass

I was born in Tuckahoe, near Hillsborough, and about twelve miles from Easton, in Talbot country, Maryland. I have no accurate knowledge of my age, never having seen any authentic record containing it. By far the larger part of the slaves know as little of their age as horses know of theirs, and it is the wish of most masters within my knowledge to keep their slaves thus ignorant. I do not remember to have ever met a slave who could tell of his birthday. They seldom come nearer to it than planting-time, harvest-time, cherry-time, spring-time, or fall-time. A want of information concerning my own was a source of unhappiness to me even during childhood. The white children could tell their ages. I could not tell why I ought to be deprived of the same privilege. I was not allowed to make any inquiries of my master concerning it. He deemed all such inquiries on the part of a slave improper and impertinent, and evidence of a restless spirit. The nearest estimate I can give makes me now between twenty-seven and twenty-eight years of age. I come to this, from hearing my master say, some time during 1835, I was about seventeen years old.

My mother was named Harriet Bailey. She was the daughter of Isaac and Betsey Baily, both colored, and quite dark. My mother was of a darker complexion than either my grandmother or grandfather.

My father was a white man. He was admitted to be such by all I ever heard speak of my parentage. The opinion was also whispered that my master was my father; but of the correctness of this opinion, I know nothing; the means of knowing was withheld from me. My mother and I were separated when I was but an infant—before I knew her as my mother. It is common custom, in the part of Maryland from which I ran away, to part children from their mothers at a very early age. Frequently, before the child has reached its twelfth month, its mother is taken from it, and hired out on some farm a considerable distance off, and the child is placed under the care of an old woman, too old for field labor. For what this separation is done, I do not know, unless it be to hinder the development of the child's affection toward its mother, and to blunt and destroy the natural affection of the mother for the child. This is the inevitable result.

I never saw my mother, to know her as such, more than four or five times in my life; and each of these times was very short in duration, and at night. She was hired by a Mr. Stewart, who lived about twelve miles from my home. She made journeys to see me in the night, travelling the whole distance on foot, after the performance of her day's work. She was a field hand, and a whipping is the penalty of not being in the field at sunrise, unless a slave has special permission from his or her master to the contrary—a permission which they seldom get, and one that gives to him that gives it the proud name of being a kind master. I do not recollect of ever seeing my mother by the light of day. She was with me in the night. She would lie down with me, and get me to sleep, but long before I waked she was gone. Very little communication ever took place between us. Death soon ended what little we could have while she lived, and with it her hardships and suffering. She died when I was about seven years old, on one of my master's farms, near Lee's Mill. I was not allowed to be present during her illness, at her death, or burial. She was gone long before I knew any thing about it. Never having enjoyed, to any considerable extent, her soothing presence, her tender and watchful care, I received the tidings of her death with much the same emotions I should have probably felt at the death of a stranger.

Called thus suddenly away, she left me without the slightest intimation of who my father was. The whisper that my master was my father, may or may not be true; and, true or false, it is of but little consequence to my purpose whilst the fact remains, in all its glaring odiousness, that slaveholders have ordained, and by law established, that the children of slave women shall in all cases follow the condition of their mothers; and this is done too obviously to administer to their own lusts, and make a gratification of their wicked desires profitable as well as pleasurable; for by this cunning arrangement, the slaveholder, in cases not a few, sustains to his slaves the double relation of master and father.

***

As to my own treatment while I lived on Colonel Lloyd's plantation, it was very similar to that of the other slave children. I was not old enough to work in the field. and there being little else than field work to do. I had a great deal of leisure time. The most I had to do was to drive up the cows at evening, keep the fowls out of the garden, keep the front yard clean, and run of errands, for my old master's daughter, Mrs. Lucretia Auld. The most of my leisure time I spent in helping Master Daniel Lloyd in finding his birds, after he had shot them. My connection with Master Daniel was of some advantage to me. He became quite attached to me, and was a sort of protector of me. He would not allow the older boys to impose upon me, and would divide his cakes with me.

I was seldom whipped by my old master, and suffered little from any thing else than hunger and cold. I suffered much from hunger, but much more from cold. In hottest summer and coldest winter, I was kept almost naked—no shoes, no stockings, no jacket, no trousers, nothing on but a coarse tow linen shirt, reaching only to my knees. I had no bed. I must have perished with cold, but that, the coldest nights, I used to steal a bag which was used for carrying corn to the mill. I would crawl into this bag, and there sleep on the cold, damp, clay floor, with my head in and feet out. My feet have been so cracked with the frost, that the pen with which I am writing might be laid in the gashes.

We were not regularly allowanced. Our food was coarse corn meal boiled. This was called *mush*. It was put into a large wooden tray or trough, and set down upon the ground. The children were then called, like so many pigs, and like so many pigs they would come and devour the mush; some with oyster-shells, others with pieces of shingle, some with naked hands, and none with spoons. He that ate fastest got most; he that was strongest secured the best place; and few left the trough satisfied.

I was probably between seven and eight years old when I left Colonel Lloyd's plantation. I left it with joy. I shall never forget the ecstasy with which I received the intelligence that my old master (Anthony) had determined to let me go to Baltimore, to live with Mr. Hugh Auld, brother to my old master's son-in-law, Captain Thomas Auld. I received this information about three days before my departure. They were three of the happiest days I ever enjoyed. I spent the most part of all these three days in the creek, washing off the plantation scurf, and preparing myself for my departure.

The pride of appearance which this would indicate was not my own. I spent the time in washing, not so much because I wished to, but because Mrs. Lucretia had told me I must get all the dead skin off my feet and knees before I could go to Baltimore; for the people in Baltimore were very cleanly, and would laugh at me if I looked dirty. Besides, she was going to give me a pair of trousers, which I should not put on unless I got all the dirt off me. The thought of owning a pair of trousers was great indeed! It was almost a sufficient motive, not only to make me take off what would be called by pig-drovers the mange, but the skin itself. I went at it in good earnest, working for the first time with the hope of reward.

The ties that ordinarily bind children to their homes were all suspended in my case. I found no severe trial in my departure. My home was charmless; it was not home to me; on parting from it, I could not feel that I was leaving any thing which I could have enjoyed by staying. My mother was dead, my grandmother lived far off, so that I seldom saw her. I had two sisters and one brother, that lived in the same house with me; but the early separation of us from our mother had well nigh blotted the fact of our relationship from our memories. I looked for home elsewhere, and was confident of finding none which I should relish less than the one which I was leaving. If, however, I found in my new home hardship, hunger, whipping, and nakedness, I had the consolation that I should not have escaped any one of them by staying. Having already had more than a taste of them in the house of my old master, and having endured them there, I very naturally inferred my ability to endure them elsewhere, and especially at Baltimore; for I had something of the feeling about Baltimore that is expressed in the proverb, that "being hanged in England is preferable to dying a natural death in Ireland." I had the strongest desire to see Baltimore. Cousin Tom, though not fluent in speech, had inspired me with that desire by his eloquent description of the place. I could never point out any thing at the Great House, no matter how beautiful or powerful, but that he had seen something at Baltimore far exceeding, both in beauty and strength, the object which I pointed out to him. Even the Great House itself, with all its pictures, was far inferior to many buildings in Baltimore. So strong was my desire, that I thought a gratification of it would fully compensate for whatever loss of comforts I should sustain by the exchange. I left without a regret, and with the highest hopes of future happiness.

***

My new mistress proved to be all she appeared when I first met her at the door,—a woman of the kindest heart, and finest feelings. She had never had a slave under her control previously to myself, and prior to her marriage she had been dependent upon her own industry for a living. She was by trade a weaver; and by constant application to her business, she had been in a good degree preserved from the blighting and dehumanizing effects of slavery. I was utterly astonished at her goodness. I scarcely knew how to behave towards her. She was entirely unlike any other white woman I had ever seen. I could not approach her as I was accustomed to approach other white ladies. My early instruction was all out of place. The crouching servility, usually so acceptable a quality in a slave, did not answer when manifested toward her. Her favor was not gained by it; she seemed to be disturbed by it. She did not deem it impudent or unmannerly for a slave to look her in the face. The meanest slave was put fully at ease in her presence, and none left without feeling better for having seen her. Her face was made of heavenly smiles, and her voice of tranquil music.

But alas! this kind heart had but a short time to remain such. The fatal poison of irresponsible power was already in her hands, and soon commenced its infernal work. That cheerful eye, under the influence of slavery, soon became red with rage; that voice, made of all of sweet accord, changed to one of harsh and horrid discord; and that angelic face gave place to that of a demon.

Very soon after went to live with Mr. and Mrs. Auld, she very kindly commenced to teach me the A, B, C. After I had learned this, she assisted me in learning to spell words of three or four letters. Just at this point of my progress, Mr. Auld found out what was going on, and at once forbade Mrs. Auld to instruct me further, telling her, among other things, that it was unlawful, as well as unsafe, to teach a slave to read. To use his own words, further, he said, "If you give a nigger an inch, he will take an ell. A nigger should know nothing but to obey his master—to do as he is told to do. Learning would *spoil* the best nigger in the world. "Now," said he, "if you teach that nigger (speaking of myself) how in read, there would be no keeping him. It would forever unfit him to be a slave. He would at once become unmanageable, and of no value to his master. As to himself, it could do him no good, but a great deal of harm. It would make him discontent and unhappy." These words sank deep into my heart, stirred up sentiments within that lay slumbering, and called into existence an entirely new train of thought. It was a new and special revelation, explaining dark and mysterious things with which my youthful understanding had struggled, but struggled in vain. I now understood what had been to me a most perplexing difficulty—to wit, the white man's power to enslave the black man. It was a grand achievement, and I prized it highly. From that moment, I understood the pathway from slavery to freedom. It was just what I wanted, and I got it at a time when I the least expected it. Whilst I was saddened by the thought of losing the aid of my kind mistress, I was gladdened by the invaluable instruction which, by the merest accident, I had gained from my master. Though conscious of the difficulty of learning without a teacher, I set out with high hope, and a fixed purpose, at whatever cost of trouble, to learn how to read. The very decided manner with which he spoke, and strove to impress his wife with the evil consequences of giving me instruction, served to convince me that he was deeply sensible of the truths he was uttering. It gave me the best assurance that I might rely with the utmost confidence on the results which, he said, would flow from teaching me to read. What he most dreaded, that I most desired. What he most loved, that I most hated. That which to him was a great evil, to be carefully shunned, was to me a great

good, to be diligently sought; and the argument which he so warmly urged, against my learning to read, only served to inspire me with a desire and determination to learn. In learning to read, I owe almost as much to the bitter opposition of my master, as to the kindly aid of my mistress. I acknowledged the benefit of both.

***

Bad is all slaveholders are, we seldom meet one destitute of every element of character commanding respect. My master was one of this rare sort. I do not know of one single noble act ever performed by him. The leading trait in his character was meanness; and if there were any other element in his nature, it was made subject to this. He was mean; and, like most other mean men, he lacked the ability to conceal his meanness. Captain Auld was not born a slaveholder. He had been a poor man, master only of a Bay craft. He came into possession of all his slaves by marriage; and of all men, adopted slaveholders are the worst. He was cruel, but cowardly. He commanded without firmness. In the enforcement of his rules, he was at times rigid, and at times lax. At times, he spoke to his slaves with the firmness of Napoleon and the fury of a demon; at other times, he might well be mistaken for an inquirer who had lost his way. He did nothing of himself. He might have passed for a lion, but for his ears. In all things noble which he attempted, his own meanness shone most conspicuous. His airs, words, and actions, were the airs, words, and actions of born slaveholders, and, being assumed, were awkward enough. He was not even a good imitator. He possessed all the disposition to deceive, but wanted the power. Having no resources within himself, he was compelled to be the copyist of many, and being such, he was forever the victim of inconsistency; and of consequence he was an object of contempt, and was held as such even by his slaves. The luxury of having slaves of his own to wait upon him was something new and unprepared for. He was a slaveholder without the ability to hold slaves. He found himself incapable of managing his slaves either by force, fear, or fraud. We seldom called him "master"; we generally called him "Captain Auld," and were hardly disposed to title him at all. I doubt not that our conduct had much to do with making him appear awkward, and of consequence fretful. Our want of reverence for him must have perplexed him greatly. He wished to have us call him master, but lacked the firmness necessary to command us to do so. His wife used to insist upon our calling him so, but to no purpose. In August, 1832, my master attended a Methodist camp-meeting held in the Bay-side, Talbot county, and there experienced religion. I indulged a faint hope that his conversion would lead him to emancipate his slaves, and that, if he did not do this, it would at any rate, make him more kind and humane. I was disappointed in both these respects. It neither made him to be humane to his slaves, nor to emancipate them. If it had any effect on his character, it made him more cruel and hateful in all his ways; for I believe him to have been a much worse man after his conversion than before. Prior to his conversion, he relied upon his own depravity to shield and sustain him in his savage barbarity; but after his conversion, he found religious sanction and support for his slaveholding cruelty. He made the greatest pretensions to piety. His house was the house of prayer. He prayed morning, noon, and night. He very soon distinguished himself among his brethren, and was soon made a class-leader and exhorter. His activity in revivals was great, and he proved himself an instrument in the hands of the church in converting many souls. His house was the preacher's home. They used to take great pleasure in coming there to put up; for while he starved us, he stuffed them. We have had three or four preachers there at a time. The names of those who used to come most frequently while I lived there, were Mr. Storks, Mr. Ewery, Mr. Humphry, and Mr. Hickey. I have also seen Mr. George Cookman at our house. We slaves loved Mr. Cookman. We believed him to be a good man. We thought him instrumental in getting Mr. Samuel Harrison, a very rich slaveholder, to emancipate his slaves; and by some means got the impression that he was laboring to effect the emancipation of all the slaves. When he was at our house, we were sure to be called in to prayers. When the others were there, we were sometimes called in and sometimes not. Mr. Cookman took more notice of us than either of the other ministers. He could not come among us without betraying his sympathy for us, and, stupid as we were, we had the sagacity to see it.

***

I lived with Mr. Covey one year. During the first six months, of that year, scarce a week passed without his whipping me. I was seldom free from a sore hack. My awkwardness was almost always his excuse for whipping me. We were worked fully up to the point of endurance. Long before day we were up, our horses fed, and by the first approach of day we were off to the field with our hoes and ploughing teams. Mr. Covey gave us enough to eat, but scarce time to eat it. We were often less than five minutes taking our meals. We were often in the field from the first approach of day till its last lingering ray had left us; and at saving-fodder time, midnight often caught us in the field binding blades.

Covey would be out with us. The way he used to stand it, was this. He would spend the most of his afternoons in bed. He would then come out fresh in the evening, ready to urge us on with his words, example, and frequently with the whip. Mr. Covey was one of the few slaveholders who could and did work with his hands. He was a hard-working man. He knew by himself just what a man or a boy could do. There was no deceiving him. His work went in his absence almost as well as in his presence; and he had the faculty of making us feel that he was ever present with us. This he did by surprising us. He seldom approached the spot where we were at work openly, if he could do it secretly. He always aimed at taking us by surprise. Such was his cunning, that we used to call him, among ourselves, "the snake." When we were at work in the cornfield, he would sometimes crawl on his hands and knees to avoid detection, and all at once he would rise nearly in our midst, and scream out, "Ha, ha! Come, come! Dash on, dash on!" This being his mode of attack, it was never safe to stop a single minute. His comings were like a thief in the night. He appeared to us as being ever at hand. He was under every tree, behind every stump, in every bush, and at every window, or the plantation. He would sometimes mount his horse, as if bound to St. Michael's, a distance of seven miles, and in half an hour afterwards you would see him coiled up in the corner of the wood-fence, watching every motion of the slaves. He would, for this purpose, leave his horse tied up in the woods. Again, he would sometimes walk up to us, and give us orders as though he was upon the point of starting on a long journey, turn his back upon us, and make as though he was going to the house to get ready; and, before he would get half way thither, he would turn short and crawl into a fence-corner, or behind some tree, and there watch us till the going of the sun.

Mr. Covey's *forte* consisted in his power to deceive. His life was devoted to planning and perpetrating the grossest deceptions. Every thing he possessed in the shape of learning or religion, he made conform to his disposition to deceive. He seemed to think himself equal to deceiving the Almighty. He would make a short prayer in the morning, and a long prayer at night; and, strange as it may seem, few men would at times appear more devotional than he. The exercises of his family devotions were always commenced with singing; and, as he was a very poor singer himself, the duty of raising the hymn generally came upon me. He would read his hymn, and nod at me to commence. I would at times do so; at others, I would not. My non-compliance would almost always produce much confusion. To show himself independent of me, he would start and stagger through with his hymn in the most discordant manner. In this state of mind, he prayed with more than ordinary spirit. Poor man! such was his disposition, and success at deceiving, I do verily believe that he sometimes deceived himself into the solemn belief, that he was a sincere worshipper of the most high God; and this, too, at a time when he may be said to have been guilty of compelling his woman slave to commit the sin of adultery The facts in the case are these: Mr. Covey was a poor man; he was just commencing in life; he was only able to buy one slave; and, shocking as is the fact, he bought her, as he said, for a *breeder*. This woman was named Caroline. Mr. Covey bought her from Mr. Thomas Lowe, about six miles from St. Michael's. She was a large, able-bodied woman, about twenty years old. She had already given birth to one child, which proved her to be just what he wanted. After buying her, he hired a married man of Mr. Samuel Harrison, to live with him one year; and him he used to fasten up with her every night! The result was, that, at the end of the year, the miserable woman gave birth to twins. At this result Mr. Covey seemed to be highly pleased, both with the man and the wretched woman. Such was his joy, and that of his wife, that nothing they could do for Caroline during her confinement was too good, or too hard, to be done. The children were regarded as being quite an addition to his wealth.

If at any one time of my life more than another, I was made to drink the bitterest dregs of slavery, that time was during the first six months of my stay with Mr. Covey. We were worked in all weathers. It was never too hot or too cold; it could never rain, blow, hail, or snow, too hard for us to work in the field. Work, work, work, was scarcely more the order of the day than of the night. The longest days were too short for him, and the shortest nights too long for him. I was somewhat unmanageable when I first went there, but a few months of this discipline tamed me. Mr. Covey succeeded in breaking me. I was broken in body, soul, and spirit. My natural elasticity was crushed, my intellect languished, the disposition to read departed, the cheerful spark that lingered about my eye died; the dark night of slavery closed in upon me; and behold a man transformed into a brute!

Sunday was my only leisure time. I spent this in a sort of beast-like stupor, between sleep and wake, under some large tree. At times I would rise up, a flash of energetic freedom would dart through my soul, accompanied with a faint beam of hope, that flickered for a moment, and then vanished. I sank down again, mourning over my wretched condition. I was sometimes prompted to take my life, and that of Covey, but was prevented by a combination of hope and fear. My sufferings on this plantation seem now like a dream rather than a stern reality.

***

Mr. Covey entered the stable with a long rope; and just as I was half out of the loft, he caught hold of my legs, and was about tying me. As soon as I found what he was up to, I gave a sudden spring, and as I did so, he holding to my legs, I was brought sprawling on the stable floor. Mr. Covey seemed now to think he had me, and could do what he pleased; but at this moment—from whence came the spirit I don't know—I resolved

to fight; and, suiting my action to the resolution, I seized Covey hard by the throat; and as I did so, I rose. He held on to me, and I to him. My resistance was so entirely unexpected, that Covey seemed taken all aback. He trembled like a leaf. This gave me assurance, and I held him uneasy, causing the blood to run where I touched him with the ends of my fingers. Mr. Covey soon called out to Hughes for help. Hughes came, and, while Covey held me, attempted to tie my right hand. While he was in the act of doing so, I watched my chance, and gave him a heavy kick close under the ribs. This kick fairly sickened Hughes, so that he left me in the hands of Mr. Covey. This kick had the effect of not only weakening Hughes, but Covey also. When he saw Hughes bending over with pain, his courage quailed. He asked me if I meant to persist in my resistance. I told him I did, come what might; that he had used me like a brute for six months, and that I was determined to be used so no longer. With that, he strove to drag me to a stick that was lying just out of the stable door. He meant to knock me down. But just as he was leaning over to get the stick, I seized him with both hands by his collar, and brought him by a sudden snatch to the ground. By this time, Bill came. Covey called upon him for assistance. Bill wanted to know what he could do. Covey said, "Take hold of him, take hold of him!" Bill said his master hired him out to work, and not to help to whip me; so he left Covey and myself to fight our own battle out. We were at it for nearly two hours. Covey at length let me go, puffing and blowing at a great rate, saying that if I had not resisted, he would not have whipped me half so much. The truth was, that he had not whipped me at all. I considered him as getting entirely the worst end of the bargain; for he had drawn no blood from me, but I had from him. The whole six months afterwards, that I spent with Mr. Covey, he never laid the weight of his finger upon me in anger. He would occasionally say, he didn't want to get hold of me again. "No," thought I, "you need not; for you will come off worse than you did before."

This battle with Mr. Covey was the turning-point in my career as a slave. It rekindled the few expiring embers of freedom, and revived within me a sense of my own manhood. It recalled the departed self-confidence, and inspired me again with a determination to be free. The gratification afforded by the triumph was a full compensation for whatever else might follow, even death itself. He only can understand the deep satisfaction which I experienced, who has himself repelled by force the bloody arm of slavery. I felt as I never felt before. It was a glorious resurrection, from the tomb of slavery, to the heaven of freedom. My long-crushed spirit rose, cowardice departed, bold defiance took its place; and I now resolved that, however long I might remain a slave in form, the day had passed forever when I could be a slave in fact. I did not hesitate to let it be known of me that the white man who expected to succeed in whipping, must also succeed in killing me.

From this time I was never again what might be called fairly whipped, though I remained a slave four years afterwards. I had several fights, but was never whipped.

It was for a long time a matter of surprise to me why Mr. Covey did not immediately have me taken by the constable to the whipping-post, and there regularly whipped for the crime of raising my hand against a white man in defence of myself. And the only explanation I can now think of does not entirely satisfy me; but such as it is, I will give it. Mr. Covey enjoyed the most unbounded reputation for being a first-rate overseer and negro-breaker. It was of considerable importance to him. That reputation was at stake; and had he sent me—a boy about sixteen years old—to the public whipping-post, his reputation would have been lost; so, to save his reputation, he suffered me to go unpunished.

My Slave Experience in Maryland
May 6, 1845

Douglass had completed the Narrative approximately one week before this speech, and it is believed to be the first time he divulged specific facts of his slave background.

Frederick Douglas[s] was next introduced to the audience, Mr. Garrison observing that he was one who, by the laws of the South, had been *a chattel* but who was now, by his own intrepid spirit and the laws of God, *a man*. He proceeded:—
I do not know that I can say anything to the point. My habits and early life have done much to unfit me for public speaking, and I fear that your patience has already been wearied by the lengthened remarks of other speakers, more eloquent than I can possibly be, and better prepared to command the attention of the audience. And I can scarcely hope to get your attention even for a longer period than fifteen minutes.

Before coming to this meeting, I had a sort of desire—I don't know but it was vanity—to stand before a New-York audience in the Tabernacle. But when I came in this morning, and looked at those massive pillars, and saw the vast throng which had assembled, I got a little frightened, and was afraid that I could not speak; but now that the audience is not so large and I have recovered from my fright, I will venture to say a word on Slavery.

I ran away from the South seven years ago—passing through this city in no little hurry, I assure you—and lived about three years in New Bedford, Massachusetts, before I became publicly known to the anti-slavery people. Since then I have been engaged for three years in telling the people what I know of it. I have come to this meeting to throw in my mite, and since no fugitive slave has preceded me, I am encouraged to say a word about the sunny South. I thought, when the eloquent female who addressed this audience a while ago, was speaking of the horrors of Slavery, that many an honest man would doubt the truth of the picture which she drew; and I can unite with the gentleman from Kentucky in saying, that she came far short of describing them.

I can tell you what I have seen with my own eyes, felt on my own person, and know to have occurred in my own neighborhood. I am not from any of those States where the slaves are said to be in their most degraded condition; but from Maryland, where Slavery is said to exist in its mildest form; yet I can stand here and relate atrocities which would make your blood to boil at the statement of them. I lived on the plantation of Col. Lloyd, on the eastern shore of Maryland, and belonged to that gentleman's clerk. He owned, probably, not less than a thousand slaves.

I mention the name of this man, and also of the persons who perpetrated the deeds which I am about to relate, running the risk of being hurled back into interminable bondage—for I am yet a slave;—yet for the sake of the cause—for the sake of humanity, I will mention the names and glory in running the risk. I have the gratification to know that if I fall by the utterance of truth in this matter, that if I shall be hurled back into bondage to gratify the slaveholder—to be killed by inches—that every drop of blood which I shall shed, every groan which I shall utter, every pain which shall rack my frame, every sob in which I shall indulge, shall be the instrument, under God, of fearing down the bloody pillar of Slavery, and of hastening the day of deliverance for three millions of my brethren in bondage.

I therefore tell the names of these bloody men, not because they are worse than other men would have been in their circumstances. No, they are bloody from necessity. Slavery makes it necessary for the slaveholder to commit all conceivable outrages upon the miserable slave. It is impossible to hold the slaves in bondage without this.

We had on the plantation an overseer, by the name of Austin Gore, a man who was highly respected as an overseer—proud, ambitious, cruel, artful, obdurate. Nearly every slave stood in the utmost dread and horror of that man. His eye flashed confusion amongst them. He never spoke but to command, nor commanded but to be obeyed. He was lavish with the whip, sparing with his word. I have seen that man tie up men by the two hands, and for two hours, at intervals, ply the lash. I have seen women stretched up on the limbs of trees, and their bare backs made bloody with the lash. One slave refused to be whipped by him—I need not tell you that he was a man, though black his features, degraded his condition. He had committed some trifling offence—for they whip for trifling offences—the slave refused to be whipped, and ran—he did not stand to and fight his master as I did once, and might do again—

though I hope I shall not have occasion to do so— he ran and stood in a creek, and refused to come out. At length his master told him he would shoot him if he did not come out. Three calls were to be given him. The first, second, and third, were given, at each of which the slave stood his ground. Gore, equally determined and firm, raised his musket, and in an instant poor Derby was no more. He sank beneath the waves, and naught but the crimsoned waters marked the spot. Then a general outcry might be heard amongst us. Mr. Lloyd asked Gore why he had resorted to such a cruel measure. He replied, coolly, that he had done it from necessity; that the slave was setting a dangerous example, and that if he was permitted to be corrected and yet save his life, that the slaves would effectually rise and be freemen, and their masters be slaves. His defence was satisfactory. He remained on the plantation, and his fame went abroad. He still lives in St. Michaels, Talbot county, Maryland, and is now, I presume, as much respected, as though his guilty soul had never been stained with his brother's blood.

I might go on and mention other facts if time would permit. My own wife had a dear cousin who was terribly mangled in her sleep, while nursing the child of a Mrs. Hicks. Finding the girl asleep, Mrs. Hicks beat her to death with a billet of wood, and the woman has never been brought to justice. It is not a crime to kill a negro in Talbot county, Maryland, farther than it is a deprivation of a man's property. I used to know of one who boasted that he had killed two slaves, and with an oath would say, "I'm the only benefactor in the country."

Now, my friends, pardon me for having detained you so long; but let me tell you with regard to the feelings of the slave. The people at the North say—"Why don't you rise? If we were thus treated we would rise and throw off the yoke. We would wade knee deep in blood before we would endure the bondage." You'd rise up! Who are these that are asking for manhood in the slave, and who say that he has it not, because he does not rise? The very men who are ready by the Constitution to bring the strength of the nation to put us down! You, the people of New York, the people of Massachusetts, of New England, of the whole Northern States, have sworn under God that we shall be slaves or die! And shall we three millions be taunted with a want of the love of freedom, by the very men who stand upon us and say, submit, or be crushed?

We don't ask you to engage in any physical warfare against the slaveholder. We only ask that in Massachusetts, and the several nonslaveholding States which maintain a union with the slaveholder—who stand with your heavy heels on the quivering heart-strings of the slave, that you will stand off. Leave us to take care of our masters. But here you come up to our masters and tell them that they ought to shoot us—to take away our wives and little ones—to sell our mothers into interminable bondage, and sever the tenderest ties. You say to us, if you dare to carry out the principles of our fathers, we'll shout you down. Others may tamely submit; not I. You may put the chains upon me and fetter me, but I am not a slave, for my master who puts the chains upon me, shall stand in as much dread of me as I do of him. I ask you in the name of my three millions of brethren at the South. We know that we are unable to cope with you in numbers; you are numerically stronger, politically stronger, than we are—but we ask you if you will rend asunder the heart and [crush] the body of the slave? If so, you must do it at your own expense.

While you continue in the Union, you are as bad as the slaveholder. If you have thus wronged the poor black man, by stripping him of his freedom, how are you going to give evidence of your repentance? Undo what you have done. Do you say that the slave ought not to be free? These hands—are they not mine? This body—is it not mine? Again, I am your brother, white as you are. I'm your blood-kin. You don't get rid of me so easily. I mean to hold on to you. And in this land of liberty, I'm a slave. The twenty-six States that blaze forth on your flag, proclaim a compact to return me to bondage if I run away, and keep me in bondage if I submit. Wherever I go, under the aegis of your liberty, there I'm a slave. If I go to Lexington or Bunker Hill, there I'm a slave, chained in perpetual servitude. I may go to your deepest valley, to your highest mountain, I'm still a slave, and the bloodhound may chase me down.

Now I ask you if you are willing to have your country the hunting-ground of the slave. God says thou shalt not oppress: the Constitution says oppress: which will you serve, God or man? The American Anti-Slavery Society says God, and I am thankful for it. In the name of my brethren, to you, Mr. President, and the noble band who cluster around you, to you, who are scouted on every hand by priest, people, politician, Church, and State, to you I bring a thankful heart, and in the name of three millions of slaves, I offer you their gratitude for your faithful advocacy in behalf of the slave.

---

[1] This passage is possibly influenced by Psalm 137 in which during the Babylonian captivity, the children of Israel are asked while "carried . . . away captive" to "sing the Lord's song in a strange land." In his Fourth of July speech in 1852, Douglass quotes from Psalm 137 at length. See "The Meaning of July Fourth for the Negro," Rochester, New York, July 5, 1852, in Philip S. Foner, ed., *The Life and Writings of Frederick Douglass*, vol. 2 (New York: International Publishers, 1950), 189.

Social Structure of Caribbean Slave Plantation Society

Franklin W. Knight

Virginia and Barbados were first peopled by a sort of loose, vagrant People, vicious and destitute of means to live at home (being either unfit for labour, or such as could find none to employ themselves about, or had so misbehaved themselves by Whoring, Thieving, or other Debauchery, that none would set them to work) which Merchants and Masters of Ships by Their Agents (or Spirits as they were called) gathered up about the streets of London, and other places, cloathed and transported to be employed upon Plantations. . . .
—Josiah Child, *New Discourse on Trade,* 1688

Throughout the Caribbean the slave-labor plantation complex inexorably succeeded the faltering attempts to create a viable settler society patterned after the European antecedents. Designed to produce tropical staples for the temperate, mainly European markets, these slave-based plantation complexes eventually evolved from artificial communities to composite societies. But they were societies with some unusual characteristics. Nowhere throughout the plantation Caribbean did enslaved social units procreate and maintain their demographic viability as other social units did in Africa, Europe, and within the indigenous American communities. As a rule, the Caribbean plantation society demonstrated some erratic, eclectic and artlessly contrived traits: predominantly male, predominantly adult, predominantly nonfree, and relentlessly coerced. Nevertheless, it would be a gross exaggeration to assert that these societies were not dynamic, resilient, creative, and strong. By the late eighteenth century, when the Caribbean slave society attained its highest stage of development, it had assumed a distinctive form. Masters and slaves, merchants and shippers, rulers and ruled, free and nonfree, white and nonwhite all constituted a closely integrated, mutually interdependent grouping of distinct castes and classes. In the Caribbean case, however, castes were neither as rigid nor as impermeable as the classic Indian caste system.

Within the plantation complex, no one group—neither the masters nor their slaves—fashioned this strange world all by themselves. Rather, it was a world that developed slowly as a result of the equal participation of both the masters and the slaves. To speak of a "world the slaveholders made" provides a catchy, eloquent phrase but does less than full justice to the confusing reality. Masters and slaves did not, and could not, form two totally independent communities. Together, both masters and slaves formed a curious world apart from the normal original American, African, or European experience. Time and the exigencies of the plantation export economy hallowed their Creolized traditions, calcified their peculiar relationships, and tended to freeze such views as the inhabitants of the region had of themselves and their role in the universe of production and commerce. Thus arose the misleading and static view which many nineteenth-century writers portrayed of the vast, variegated region stretching from the North Atlantic seaboard to the Northeast of Brazil which they deemed "Afro-America." The Caribbean plantation complex formed the center of this spectrum of societies and cultures—and it was a very important economic center until the whole system began to fall apart during the nineteenth century.

Before this prolonged process of disintegration, however, some notorious internal ambiguities and contradictions manifested themselves within these slave societies. And nowhere were these ambiguities and contradictions more pronounced than in the overlapping structures of castes and classes. The caste system represented the most notable aspect of the plantation society. The typical slave society had three legally defined castes stubbornly supported partly by force, partly by custom, and partly by impromptu legal ingenuity. In ascending order of social status (and often population size), these three castes were the slaves, the free persons of color, and the white persons. Each component required a separate set of criteria to define and distinguish it, and this further contributed to the contradictions and ambiguities. Occupation and stipulated legal disabilities patently separated the subordinate slave component from the two free sectors of the society. Slaves were slaves only because they were bought as such and condemned legally to that status. Originally the relationship with African descent was merely coincidental. In the earliest period of constructing the complex, servants and slaves were often interchangeable labels applied indiscriminately to servile Europeans or Africans, but by the end of the seventeenth century, the term "slave" connoted African origin and menial occupation. A narrowing of the definition had already begun to take place. At the same time, within the realm of the free, ethnicity, phenotype, and attributed status largely determined the caste boundaries between the white sector and the other nonwhite sector, subdivided into free blacks and free mulattoes. As far as the distinction could be made, free mulattoes represented the result of inescapable miscegenation within the complex.

This general description of the castes sometimes broke down in specific circumstances. Small islands such as Bermuda, the Caymans, St. Barthélemy, Carriacou and the Grenadines; commercial entrepôts such as Curaçao; or economically undeveloped territories such as Puerto Rico tended to approximate less the classic structure of the plantation society than the larger, more-productive places. The prevailing ambiguities and inherent contradictions of the plantation structure continually operated to undermine rigidity and permitted vagueness, uncertainty, overlap, and social "passing" on a limited scale—most notably along the peripheral penumbra of the two free castes as well as between free colored and slaves. Slaves could become members of the free colored community; and occasionally free coloreds could become members of the white community.

Each caste was further internally subdivided into classes or ranks. Each social class varied in size, function, and consequently in the intensity of its acceptance of, or hostility to, the overall system. And like the definition of castes, class and status designations were also complex. Within the white caste, economic and occupational indices figured prominently in designating individual social position and status. Normally prestige correlated with the ownership of slaves and plantations. Within the intermediate stratum of the free persons of color, race and color—or more precisely complexion and shades of color—determined status and rank. In most cases, free mulattoes were considered (and considered themselves) to be superior in status to free blacks. Race and color distinguished the free groups, and freedom, however tenuously held, separated them from the status of slaves. Among the slaves, occupation probably comprised the most important criterion for social ranking. Skilled and domestic slaves generally enjoyed higher social status than non-skilled field slaves. Each caste therefore had its elaborate pecking order, a factor that might have contributed to internal social mobility either laterally across the vertical divisions of caste or upward through the horizontal divisions of classes or ranks. This internal social mobility contributed to the cohesion and longevity of the slave society, but it also generated enormous discontent within the various segments and eventually contributed to its demise.

The conventional demographic profile of the slave society was that of a narrow-peaked triangle, horizontally divided into three segments. The broad base of this triangle represented the vast majority of slaves. In the fifteenth and early sixteenth centuries, these slaves were entirely African- or Iberian-born, but as the demand grew and the system expanded, an increasing proportion was born in the Americas. Nevertheless, throughout the history of slavery, the society depended more on imports than procreation to maintain its population. Africans constituted the first major immigrant stream to enter the Americas after the fifteenth century, albeit in bondage. African-born slaves were called *bozales* while those born in the Americas were called Creoles or Afro-Americans.

Miscegenation between the imported African slaves and all the other ethnic groups also produced a new mixed-blood substratum of individuals designated mestizo or mulatto who fell into the categories of slave and free. Eventually the mixed population formed the middle band of the triangle, an important, intermediate segment uncomfortably juxtaposed between the upper and the lower orders of society, between the fully free and the thoroughly enslaved, between white and nonwhite. Generally this group was labeled the free people of color, uncharitably referred to by an English colonial governor as "the unappropriated people." The free people of color shared qualities of both the free and the nonfree. Ethnically divided into black and mulatto like the slave sector, they suffered a circumscribed freedom which probably accentuated their ambiguity and contributed to their psychological disorientation. Throughout the eighteenth century and after, the free persons of color fought doggedly to preserve their individual liberty and legal status.

The small apex of the triangle represented the white population. Small in number, diverse in background, varied in original culture, this group possessed the economic and political power within the society and exercised an inordinate influence on local culture. The Caribbean, after all, served the purposes of Europe and the Europeans.

The pyramidal illustration of Caribbean slave societies, however, reflects only the most fully developed systems found primarily in the English and French Caribbean during the eighteenth and early nineteenth centuries. There, the white population represented between 3 percent and 11 percent of the total colonial population. The proportion of slaves and free varied considerably from place to place, reflecting the degree of agricultural development or nature of the local economy. In some places, the whites consistently formed a large group. In the early nineteenth century, the white population comprised 23 percent of the inhabitants of the Bahamas, 48 percent in Bermuda, 44 percent in Cuba, and 51 percent in Puerto Rico. That the presence of plantations played a major role in determining the population composition may be seen in the case of the Dutch Caribbean in the nineteenth century. On the trading islands of St. Eustatius, St. Martin, and Curaçao, the whites accounted for slightly more than 17 percent of the population. By sharp contrast, in the plantation colony of Surinam the whites, although equal to the number in Curaçao, represented slightly more than 4 percent of the population.

By custom and often by law, any person of European birth or ancestry, regardless of economic circumstance, intellectual ability, or educational achievement, enjoyed a social status superior to that of every nonwhite person. As the slave-based plantation economic system matured throughout the eighteenth century, a concomitant social complex based on the mutually reinforcing cleavages of race, color, and occupation not only manifested itself throughout the Caribbean but also became indelible and pervasive. On the plantations as well as in the cities away from the plantations, the color of one's skin immediately and effectively fixed both social position and occupation, with blackness indicating low status and arduous menial labor and whiteness superiority and leisure. Such was the condition of the Caribbean colonies until the later decades of the nineteenth century, when association with the plantation and its occupational structure no longer provided a reliable index of either caste or class. When that occurred, however, the plantation complex was already in an advanced stage of disintegration.

Fully developed plantation societies all exhibited common characteristics. Both the concentration on export agriculture and population composition, indicated the degree of participation in and the stage of maturity of the particular colony within the context of the South Atlantic System. In general, the most vigorous and most mature structures revealed a preponderance of Africans and Afro-Americans. In plantation zones, slaves outnumbered the free by ratios varying between two to one and thirty to one. At the beginning of the nineteenth century, the entire population of the Caribbean islands and their neighboring enclaves of Berbice, Demerara, Essequibo, Surinam, Guiana, and British Honduras (now Belize) amounted to about two million inhabitants, with about two-thirds of that number being slaves.

The size and composition of local populations fluctuated according to the nature and state of the economy. In times of prosperity, the total number of people increased. Economic depressions or shrinking fortunes diminished the community, especially among the white, plantation-owning sector. For example, in 1781 the small Dutch island colony of St. Eustatius (commonly called Statia) was both a flourishing free port and a prominent sugar exporter. Of a total of approximately twenty thousand inhabitants, nearly fifteen thousand were slaves working on a number of sugar plantations. The English captured and sacked the island, and its fortunes rapidly declined. By 1840, the population of St. Eustatius had dwindled to less than four hundred white persons and two thousand slaves. The Spanish island of Cuba presented an opposite change. In 1774, Cuba had a

population of 171,620 of which only 44,333 (25.8 percent) were slaves. By 1827, with the sugar revolution fairly advanced, the total population of the island increased dramatically to 704,487, of whom 286,942 (40.7 percent) were slaves. The common feature of the sugar revolutions in the Caribbean was the rapid increase of a servile black population at the expense of the free-white settler population. The plantation complex changed the focus of agricultural enterprises and the composition of the local population. This created an economic, demographic, and social change of considerable importance.

The Caribbean slave societies were very complex social organizations. Although the slaves formed the lowest castelike stratum of the entire population, they were just as elaborately subdivided for purposes of occupation, management, and rank as the free castes. The most basic division was along lines of color, between the African and Afro-Caribbean slaves (usually referred to as the "black" slaves) on the one hand and the miscegenated or "colored" slaves (most frequently called mulattoes or *pardos* in the Spanish islands) on the other. Slaves of mixed race, however, do not seem to have been a significant factor in the overall slave population before the nineteenth century. The overall decline of the slave trade—facilitated by the abolition of the English transatlantic slave trade in 1808—and normal increases in the birthrate produced an increasing proportion of mulattoes, mestizos, and other persons of mixed blood throughout the region.

In 1800, the mixed slave population on Worthy Park Estate in central Jamaica accounted for only about 5 percent of the estate's slave labor force. This percentage does not seem to vary significantly from the general pattern for agricultural populations recently involved in intensive plantation production. Indeed, Barry Higman, reviewing the situation for the British Caribbean in the early nineteenth century, suggests that "around 1,817 slaves of color made up roughly 12 percent of the total slave population in the first-phase sugar colonies [Antigua, Barbados, Jamaica, Nevis, Montserrat, and St. Kitts], 10 percent in the marginal colonies [Anguilla, the Bahamas, Barbuda, British Honduras, and the Cayman Islands], 8 percent in the second-phase sugar colonies [Dominica, Grenada, St. Vincent, and Tobago], and 4 percent in the third-phase sugar colonies (Berbice, Demarara, Essequibo, St. Lucia, and Trinidad)." In Cuba, as late as 1846, the mulatto slaves accounted for 12,791 of a total slave force of 323,759—slightly less than 4 percent. Higman finds that the slave registers reveal that the overall mulatto slave population might have been between 10 and 12 percent of the total Jamaican slave population in 1820. Such an increased percentage would not necessarily be at variance with the Worthy Park Estate findings of Michael Craton and James

Walvin, since the proportion of mulattoes would have increased after the termination of the English slave trade. Moreover, since colored slaves were more frequently found among domestic and urban slaveholdings than rural ones, the increase could also be explained by an increased urban concentration as the Jamaican sugar economy declined during the nineteenth century.

Urban centers seemed to have produced a greater concentration of persons of mixed blood—slave as well as free—than the plantations. Many travel accounts make this observation. Janet Schaw, the Scottish "lady of quality" who traveled through the West Indies and South Carolina on the eve of the American Revolution, described "crouds [sic] of Mullatoes [sic] ... in the streets, houses and indeed everywhere" in the town of St. Johns, Antigua. Most Caribbean towns would have given a similar impression, especially to the eye that could not discriminate between the free and the slave. In Havana, according to the census of 1828, the colored slaves numbered 1,010, or 12.6 percent of a total slave population of 8,005. By contrast, the free coloreds numbered 8,215 of a total free nonwhite population of 23,562, a proportion slightly less than 35 percent. In the island of Puerto Rico, the free-colored population in 1860 represented 41.3 percent (241,037 persons) of a total 583,181 inhabitants and combined with the colored slaves probably represented the largest component of the population.

Slaves of mixed ancestry were not generally regarded as good field workers. As a result, there was a concentration of these slaves in urban areas and in the domestic, skilled, and artisanal trades. These occupations provided both the exposure and the income that facilitated the movement from slavery to freedom, thereby reinforcing the notion that lightness of skin color lubricated upward social mobility. Consequently, slaves of mixed heritage felt that they were generally superior in rank to African and Afro-American slaves, and this sentiment permeated every society where the norms for grace and beauty were those established by the superordinate white sector.

Other subtle distinctions followed. Slaves born in the Caribbean felt socially superior to their relatives and colleagues who were not. Obviously these Creole slaves had some advantages over their African counterparts. They were physically acclimatized as well as mentally socialized to the conduct and routine of the plantation and local culture, and in some cases they spoke and understood the local languages. Yet familiarity brought few material benefits to Creole slaves. Moreover, the curious Creole Afro-Caribbean sentiment of enhanced status may have been based solely on the reflected impressions and unquestioned acceptance of the prevailing white biases. The white colonists, after all, continuously condemned the Africans as "savages," claimed that exposure to the rigors of the tropical plantation "civilized" them, and in some cases

were willing to pay more for locally born black slaves than for recently imported African ones.

If color provided one criterion for rank among slaves, occupation provided another. Edward Brathwaite, in his study of Jamaica, divided the slaves into five occupational groups based on the convenient distribution of functions on the plantation and in the economy: field slaves, usually called praedial slaves; mechanic and domestic slaves; slaves working as hired hands; and skilled, professional, or semiprofessional and managerial slaves. Some of these categories depended to a great extent on the type of society, the size of the category engaged in the activity, and the number of slaves held by the slave owner. Nevertheless, certain common patterns emerged. Field slaves, as indicated earlier, were generally considered lowest in rank. They were the most numerous group. Edward Long estimated that about 160,000 of the approximately 220,000 slaves in Jamaica in 1787 were field slaves, more than 72 percent. Rural slaves accounted for the vast majority of slaves throughout the Caribbean, although it should be noted that the difference between rural and urban in the nineteenth century could not be sharply defined. In 1855, at the height of the Cuban sugar revolution, about 81 percent of the slaves were registered as rural slaves, indicating an extremely high proportion of field slaves.

But even these field slaves had their own internal social ranking as well as their own preference for certain tasks, and these did not necessarily correspond with those of their masters. Nevertheless, the records of the masters predominate in the historical archives. Slave masters ranked slaves according to their utility in the production process or their personal needs. Ranking, however, was an arbitrary procedure, more common on established, large, specialized estates than on small, multicrop estates. On Irwin Estate in St. James Parish in Jamaica, the slaves were listed in the following order: first gang, second gang, third gang, tradesmen, pen-keepers, domestics, watchmen, grass cutters, invalids, young children. The cattle were also listed in an order that suggested value: working stock, bulls, young working stock, mules, cows, calves, fattening cattle. Slave listing was similar on Peruvian Vale Estate in St. Vincent with the order being: first gang, second gang, third gang, tradesmen, jobbers, domestics, watchmen, stockkeepers, cattle and mule boys, "at works," superannuated, children, and sick. The Peruvian Vale Estate task allocation pattern clearly indicated that some flexibility occurred in assigning tasks, depending on the season and the needs of the plantation routine. When Rose Price took personal control of Worthy Park Estate, Jamaica, in the early 1790s, he divided his 483 slaves into seventeen different categories based on his assessment of their relation to production. This was a refinement of the seven or so categories into which the slaves were divided before his arrival. Slaves and cattle were the perennial concerns of the Caribbean plantation owner: their value, their health, their number, and their disposition.

Field slaves were the backbone of the plantation and the economy. The division into gangs represented the varying degrees of physical strength and permitted the deployment of workers as units, whether the demands were heavy and rigorous, as they were during the crop season when the mill operated, or light and sporadic, as during the planting season and *tiempo muerto*. Gangs maximized productive efficiency as well as facilitated group management. The first gang on any estate comprised the most able-bodied males and females, with subsequent gangs organized according to a descending order of physical strength and ability. Some planters simplified the groupings, as did J. Stewart, who based his descriptions on his experiences in Jamaica:

> The plantation slaves are divided into three classes or *gangs,* as they are called, according to age and condition. The first gang consists of the ablest of both sexes, from sixteen to about fifty years of age, and are employed in the most laborious of the work; the second gang contains the elderly and weakly men and women, and boys and girls of from twelve to sixteen who have lighter work assigned to them; and the third, or what is called *small gang,* consists of the children of about six to twelve, attended by a female driver, and are employed in weeding the young plant-canes, and other easy work adopted to their strength. In most of the jobbing-gangs the different classes, with the exception of children, are improperly blended together. When the slaves are rendered unfit, by age or infirmity, for field labor, they are employed in occupations that require little bodily exertion; the men are placed as watchmen over the canes and provisions, and the women to take care of the children, or in other light employments.

Since a great deal of the labor on any estate—from the basic planting to the harvesting and ultimate preparation of the crop for export—remained repetitive, newly imported Africans could fit into the routine of the plantation without considerable difficulty or dislocation. After a period of seasoning and acclimatization that could last for up to three years, new slaves were placed alongside the older ones to learn the routine of the plantation. Most purchased Africans began and ended the their enslavement working with the field gangs.

One frequently overlooked aspect of plantation slavery was the high degree of participation by women in all aspects of field and factory labor. Plantations in general demanded prime workers and placed their emphasis on able-bodied males in the fourteen-to-forty age category. For a number of reasons, women comprised a large proportion of the workers on the older plantations. Their presence derived from the needs of social control as well as from the natural consequences of differential mortality rates and reproduction or the exigencies of an irregular market supply mechanism. Sexual imbalance was not a pronounced feature of large estates. In Cuba during the middle years of the nineteenth century, male slaves in rural areas outnumbered the females by a ratio of slightly less than two to one. In 1857, the official returns for slaves gave a rural slave force of 193,187 males and 114,188 females. Urban slaves showed a slight majority of females, with 34,762 females and 30,848 males. Barbados, one of the first islands to complete its sugar revolution, consistently had more female than male slaves throughout the nineteenth century. In 1832, the island possessed 43,738 female slaves and 37,762 male slaves, or about 86 male slaves for every 100 female slaves. Until 1817, males outnumbered females in Jamaica. After that date, however, the female population gradually outnumbered the male population. In 1829, Jamaica had 164,167 females and 158,254 males in a total slave work force of 322,421. The predominance of male slaves, then, was a feature of the moving plantation frontier found in rural Trinidad, Demerara, Essequibo, central Cuba, and the Ponce area of Puerto Rico during the nineteenth century. As the system matured, the imbalance tended to redress itself. As soon as the initial task of clearing the virgin forests of the tropical lands was completed, women served just as efficiently as men in the daily routine of cultivation, harvest, and manufacture.

In every colony, women worked alongside the men in the majority of the occupations. In his study of the slave population of the British Caribbean, Barry Higman reported that "females were totally excluded from skilled trades other than sewing, and rarely worked in transportation and fishing, or served as "watchmen" and that "males were excluded only from washing and sewing." For many large established sugar estates women may even have had a proportionately greater share of the arduous field work than men. On the Jamaican Worthy Park Estate, this was certainly the case at the end of the eighteenth century, and there is no reason to believe that the situation did not persist afterwards. In 1789, Worthy Park Estate had a labor force of 339 slaves, 162 female and 177 male. Slightly more than 43 percent of its females (70 slaves) worked in the field gang, while just over 16 percent of the males (29 slaves) did. During the efficient reorganization by Rose Price between 1791 and 1793, the situation remained the same. In 1793, the labor force increased to 528 slaves, 244 women and 284 men. But again almost 44 percent of the women (107 slaves) worked in the fields, while only slightly more than 32 percent of the men (92 slaves) did so.

A similar situation prevailed on La Ninfa Estate in Cuba in the 1820s. This large progressive estate, owned jointly by Francisco Arango y Parreño and the intendant, Pablo José Valiente, had 350 slaves. According to Manuel Moreno Fraginals during the harvest of 1827 "cane was cut and loaded exclusively by women—who cut an average of 300 *arrobas* (3.5 tons) a day."

One curious, though probably typical observation on the female labor force emerged from Higman's study of the Jamaican slave population just prior to emancipation in 1834. Higman found that women worked in the fields much longer, on the average, than men, probably corresponding to their longer life expectancy. He noted that "males were put to a fairly wide range of occupations, whereas females were confined almost entirely to field or domestic tasks." He also found relatively few female slaves of color among the field slaves. Indeed, the recruitment of black women for domestic work declined as soon as female slaves of color could be found. This pattern prevailed throughout the Caribbean and most likely reflected concepts about race, color, and physical ability held by the slave owners.

The slave system was a constantly changing one, but it responded to the demographic patterns. The relatively low percentages of field-labor participation by the two sexes on Worthy Park Estate indicate a regional trend throughout the nineteenth century. The system of slavery did not produce a very efficient process of labor employment. On the typical sugar estate—the largest employers of slaves—only about 50 percent of the workhands were capable, healthy, able-bodied participants in the field-production process. On La Ninfa in Cuba, an 1829 daily register of slaves showed that of 340 slaves, 26.5 percent (90 slaves) were infants, invalids, or deserters, and only 54.4 percent (185 slaves) were employed in the fields. Barbados appeared to be unique in the region for its large gangs of young children working in the fields under the supervision of a female driver. More men than women worked in the factory, however, while an unduly large number of slaves seemed to be in domestic service, especially while the owners were in residence.

Again, the Worthy Park experience was indicative. The great house, while normally vacant, employed two full-time domestics to maintain it. With the owners in residence however, the number increased to a high figure of seventeen slaves. Robert Ellis, the overseer, began with one slave and within six years had a domestic staff of thirty-six slaves to serve only six white persons in 1795. Domestic slaves tended to form a larger category in the Spanish and French colonial societies than in the English, perhaps owing to the relatively larger residential white populations in the former societies. Nevertheless, domestic slaves were not merely servants of the white population, and their lives were not invariably superior to their rural counterparts. In reality, the distinction between domestic and field could be muted among slaves of small holdings, especially holdings in rural areas. On sugar estates in the English Caribbean, about 10 percent of the female slaves were domestics, but about 20 percent of the female slaves among the small holdings of coffee, cotton, cocoa, and ground-provision plantations or grazing pens were domestics.

As the historian Edward Brathwaite points out, domestic slaves sometimes considered themselves to be of a higher rank than field slaves. Some masters reinforced this impression by distinguishing the dress and nurturing the civility of the group and treating—in the most benevolent cases—their domestic slaves as part of a large extended family. Banishment to field labor was utilized as a form of punishment for disobedient or disgraced domestic slaves. One imperial master decreed that his mulatto stable boy be "stripped of his livery, degraded to a field negro" as punishment for some unspecified misdeed. In the Cuban antislavery novel, *Francisco,* written by Anselmo Suárez y Romero, the author has the protagonist whipped and condemned to join the field slaves by a cruel, jealous master. Despite this impression of a great gulf between field and domestic slaves, most domestic slaves served as either cooks or washerwomen, two tasks which could be both arduous and difficult—especially for fastidious owners.

Domestic slaves, like the general category of urban, skilled, or semi-independent slaves, did have certain advantages denied most field slaves. They probably had more leisure time, were under less coercive control, and had more opportunities for self-purchase or *courtución* than their rural companions. Nevertheless, domestic and urban slaves displayed a dislike equal to that of field slaves of the entire system of slavery and demonstrated an equal proneness to flee the system.

Specialist slaves were found in both domestic and field categories and participated in a variety of occupations. They could be skilled, such as mechanics, carpenters, coopers, masons, sugar boilers, rum distillers, potters, weavers, seamstresses, tailors, shoemakers, assorted hired hands, superannuated watchmen, and caretakers of children, the last affectionately called *criolleras* in Cuba. Not all of these skills were practiced full time throughout the year, and not all were necessary on all plantations. Small cocoa, coffee, and spice plantations, for example, often did without the services of skilled slaves of any sort.

Highest in privilege and importance on the estate were the slave drivers and chief sugar makers, whom the Jamaican planter, Matthew Lewis, felicitously called "principal persons." Drivers were a feature of large slaveholdings, normally containing more than fifty slaves, and led the various gangs. Some gangs had two drivers, often referred to as the "head driver" and the "under driver." The order, loyalty, and productivity of slave forces rested almost entirely in the hands of the slave drivers. In most cases, they comprised the crucial managerial force of the entire operation. The drivers not only controlled the daily routine of the plantation but also performed the essential liaison functions between the Europeans and the Africans. Moreover, drivers could administer corporal punishment, with or without the instruction of the white overseer. As long as these low-level supervisory personnel remained satisfied and loyal, coordinated resistance to the system of slavery could not meet with significant success. In recognition of this fact, slave owners tended to bestow special privileges on these male and female slave drivers. Often they had their own residences separate from the community of slaves, greater rations, and more leeway in the ordinary rules and regulations of the plantations. The treatment of the drivers provided a clear illustration of the positive incentives that the system used to maintain social control.

On sugar estates, the skill and experience of the master sugar boiler was equally valuable for the economic success of the enterprise. His keen sense of the proper elaboration of sugar could make the difference between the financial success of the estate and disaster. In terms of purchase price, however, drivers and sugar boilers cost less than those specialists who made possible the reliable, trouble-free operation of the entire machinery of sugar production: carpenters, millwrights, coppersmiths, coopers, sawyers, and masons. Together these groups appeared to constitute a hierarchy among the slaves with a great deal of personal freedom of movement on the estates. Occasionally they were hired out to supplement the income of their owners or to acquire the capital to purchase their own freedom or that of their relatives.

Outside the plantations, a vast number of slaves plied trades, filled occupations, and participated in the two overlapping, symbiotic economies—the export and the domestic economies. Some slaves engaged in huckstering (called "higglering" in the British Caribbean), operating as middlemen between the growers of ground provisions in the rural areas and the consumers in the towns and on the estates. Predominantly female, huckster slaves operated as itinerant or fixed vendors, often competing with the free and white merchants and causing no small degree of inconvenience to the authorities. Slaves also operated small coastal boats and were fishermen, musicians, craftsmen, guides, or rat catchers. In short, any jobs that provided an income and were not, or could not be, adequately filled by the free population, fell to the slaves.

Some of these occupations gave the slaves tremendous control over their time and their activity, eventually blurring the legal and customary distinctions between slavery and freedom. For this reason, runaways found it quite easy to engage in these occupations as one means of survival until more organized connections could be established. These occupations, connecting as they did the internal marketing economy and the export economy, proved a viable way of circulating the wealth of the society throughout the three castes. At any given time, a considerable proportion of the liquid capital in any colony would be in the hands of the slaves, and at the end of slavery, slaves were able to purchase a number of bankrupt estates and establish themselves as peasant farmers.

Runaways and individual slaves working independently or semi-independently merged imperceptibly into the lower ranks of the heterogenous intermediate group identified as free persons of color. This category represented a mélange of somatic-norm images as so many travelers to the Caribbean remarked from time to time. It ran the spectrum from indistinguishably white to unmistakably black. John Stewart, in his anonymously published *Account of Jamaica and Its Inhabitants*, put it this way:

> Between the whites and the blacks in the West Indies, a numerous race has sprung up, which goes by the general name of people of colour: these are subdivided into Mulattos, the offspring of a white and a black; Sambos, the offspring of a black and a Mulatto; Quadroons, the offspring of a Mulatto and a white; and Mestees or Mestisos, the offspring of a Quadroon and a white. Below this last denomination, the distinction of colour is hardly perceptible; and those who are thus removed from the original negro [sic] stock, are considered by the law as whites, and competent, of course, to enjoy all the privileges of a white. Between these particular *castes*, an endless variety of nondescript shades exist, descending from the deep jet to the faintest tinge of the olive; by gradations which it were impossible to mark and to designate.

Stewart's graphic description neither reflected the full legal distinctions of biological and complexional mutations nor accurately portrayed the composition of the free colored in Caribbean society. The Spanish managed to get twenty-five possible hybrid variations in their range of color, although only a small number of descriptions were precise enough to be practically useful. Few outside the esoteric realm of primitive biological specialists bothered to trace bloodlines so carefully. The random selections of genetic transmissions frustrated the general desire to have phenotype conform regularly to genealogical heritage. Combinations of white and nonwhite did not fall neatly into designated categories of shades of color, and a range of characteristics could be found within the same family. For all practical purposes, therefore, most designations were the simple, visually correct but biologically false, categories of mulattoes and Sambos.

But the free colored group was not confined merely to persons of mixed African, European, and American heritage. By the nineteenth century, a large number of blacks had become bona fide members of this group. The free colored group was not uniformly one of freedom in the sense that all members were once slaves. Some were the descendants of successive generations of free individuals of unaltered African ancestry. To describe them as freedmen, with the connotation of a group recently manumitted, is as misleading as describing contemporary Americans as Europeans or Latin Americans as Spanish and Portuguese.

The origins of the free coloreds in the Caribbean rested predominantly in the miscegenated results of the unions of European masters and their non-European slaves. Gradually the group developed its own internal marital affiliations, procreative impulses, and hereditary continuities. With the passage of time, opportunities for self-purchase and other forms of unrestricted freedom allowed fluctuating numbers of African slaves to move into the legal category of free persons, though carefully distinguished from free white persons. Some of these Africans formed biological unions with persons of mixed ancestry or non-Africans, further contributing to the biological mélange. Others preferred their own kind, thereby continuing to reinforce a distinct, and often legally designated, subcategory of free blacks.

As a proportion of the entire population, the free nonwhite sector varied considerably from colony to colony, and even across time within the same colony. The free coloreds comprised a high 43.5 percent of the total population of the Dutch colony of Curaçao in 1833. In plantation Surinam—likewise a Dutch colony—the free population constituted less than 9 percent of the total colonial society. In Puerto Rico, the free coloreds remained 41.3 percent of the island's total population in 1860, about the same proportion as it was in 1830. In Cuba, the percentage of free colored remained likewise virtually constant, changing from 15.1 percent of the total population in 1827 to 16.2 percent in 1860. In the English and French colonies, the proportion varied between the low of 1 percent in Berbice (later part of British Guiana) and a high of 12.6 percent in the Bahamas in 1810. In Barbados, the free coloreds represented 6.5 percent of the island's total population in 1834. In Jamaica, it was 10.2 percent in 1800. In French Saint-Domingue, the free coloreds were 5.3 percent of the total for the colony in 1791; while Martinique had a proportion of 5.4 percent in 1789.

The data presented provide only a frozen "snapshot" view of the demographic profile of the Caribbean. But "frozen" representations, however graphic they may be, cannot reveal the inherent dynamism of the social groups. The history of the free colored population is one of continual response to an ever-varying number of influences through time. One of the most prominent influences on the behavior of the free nonwhite population as a category was the changing economic fortunes of the plantation-based export economy. Fluctuating economic conditions, of course, had an equal impact on all sectors of the colonial society.

A few examples illustrate the vagaries of economy and population. During the eighteenth century, the plantation economy expanded in Surinam until 1788, when the colony had 591 plantations and 50,000 slaves of a total population of 55,000 inhabitants. By 1813, the number of plantations had declined to 369, and in 1863, when slavery was abolished, the number was 210. At the same time, the collapse of the Amsterdam exchange in 1773 began an irreversible process of capital withdrawal from agriculture. In 1863, the total population of the colony was less than in 1830. Other subtle changes also took place. Plantations fell into absentee ownership, with more than 80 percent (297) of all plantations in 1813 in this category. The number of free coloreds, especially in the female mulatto group, increased dramatically. Dutch plantation owners and their families left the colony in large numbers, allowing Jews to become the predominant element among the superordinate white sector. At the same time, bachelor whites sent out from Holland to administer foreclosed estates further accentuated the male-dominant sexual imbalance among the whites. Between 1768 and 1834, the free colored population spurted from about 3,500 to 35,000, a tenfold increase that boosted their proportion from 16 percent of the total free group to about 70 percent. During the period, the white population fell by almost 50 percent; and the number of slaves—by an entirely unrelated coincidence—nearly doubled. In Martinique, where the plantation economy declined precipitately during the Napoleonic wars of the early nineteenth century, the free colored sector increased from 7.1 percent of the total population in 1802 to 24.9 percent in 1835. In Cuba, on the other hand, the plantation economy expanded rapidly between 1774 and 1827, and the free nonwhite sector declined from 20.3 percent to 15.1 percent of the population.

The free nonwhite sector, wherever they were found and regardless of the circumstances under which they flourished, manifested a number of common traits. It tended to be predominantly female, largely urban, and almost self-consciously differentiated from the slave sector. In Trinidad in 1811, 56.7 percent of the free nonwhite population was female, with adult females outnumbering adult males by 2,830 to 1790. Barbados presented a slightly anomalous picture, with females predominating in all three castes. In 1817, for example, females comprised more than 54 percent of the slave and white sectors and more than 51 percent of the free nonwhites. Free nonwhite females outnumbered free nonwhite males in Cuba, too, where in 1841 the 78,843 free nonwhite women outnumbered the free nonwhite men by 3,140 and proportionately exceeded the latter by 51 percent to 49 percent. In the new colonies of Demerara and Essequibo free nonwhite adult females outnumbered free nonwhite males 1,096 to 487; while in small Tobago, the adult free nonwhite women numbered 153 and the free adult nonwhite men 92. The numerical superiority of women among free nonwhite populations did not prevail among children. In most cases, male children outnumbered females in all segments of the Caribbean societies, slave or free.

With some notable exceptions, the residential pattern of the free nonwhites throughout the Caribbean tended to be urban. In the eighteenth century, free nonwhites predominated in the southern departments of French Saint-Domingue. In the nineteenth century, a substantial number of this population continued to exist in the rural areas of Cuba, Puerto Rico, Spanish Santo Domingo, and Trinidad. Even in Cuba, a far heavier concentration of free colored persons lived in the cities of Havana, Santiago de Cuba, Manzanillo, and Trinidad than in the plantation zones of Cárdenas, Colon, and Matanzas. In Barbados the situation was the same. After 1809, about 61 percent of all the free Barbadian nonwhites lived in the parish of St. Michael, and there is a strong indication that the majority of this group resided in or near the capital of the island, Bridgetown. In 1829, in any case, 3,140 of the 5,146 free nonwhites in Barbados lived in St. Michael Parish. A greater number of nonwhites lived in Belize City than anywhere else in British Honduras; and more lived in Kingston than in the rest of the island of Jamaica. Trinidad was the only exception in the British Caribbean, having a larger free colored population in the rural areas than in the towns.

The urban residence pattern fulfilled certain physical as well as psychological conditions for the free colored population. Although some free coloreds figured among the wealthy plantation owners and slave owners—most prominently in Jamaica, Puerto Rico, Spanish Santo Domingo, Saint-Domingue, Martinique, Trinidad, and Surinam—most working free coloreds derived their livelihood from trades and services. The cities provided a far more conducive ambience for the pursuit of these occupations than the rural plantation zones, where they would face some degree of competition from the slave work force. Moreover, like the slaves, the miscegenated free were generally recognized to be less than ideal manual workers on the plantations. Once the magnetic pattern of urban residence and association was established it could not be easily reversed. Towns offered the critical mass necessary to project opportunities for economic gain and social recognition. The rural exodus of the free coloreds might also have had powerful subconscious motivations. The social mores of the Caribbean plantation society consistently denigrated those who did manual and menial labor. For this reason, plantation field slaves represented the lowest social category. And in an atmosphere where the correlation between a black skin and the status of slavery was almost taken for granted, free nonwhites in rural areas faced the unavoidable and continuous problem of proving their freedom. Increasing the social distance between slavery and freedom for the Afro-Caribbean population might have meant increasing the physical distance as well.

Yet the flight to the cities, although providing many opportunities for upward social mobility, created and intensified economic and political competition, especially at the two ends of the spectrum. At the lower end of the economic scale, the free Afro-Caribbean population faced competition from jobbing slaves, often working zealously to purchase their freedom while being indirectly subsidized by their owners. At the upper end of the scale, the free nonwhites competed with the artisan, commercial, and semiskilled service sector of the lower orders of the white group.

The whites often used their political power, or their access to political power, to define and broaden the economic and occupational gap between themselves and the free colored sector. Laws distinguishing comportment, dress, and residence or denying the practice of certain occupations or limiting the material inheritance of the free colored population were commonplace throughout the Caribbean during the early years of the nineteenth century. The constriction of the range of occupations, the personal liberties, and the political rights of the free nonwhite sector tended to run concurrently with the expansion of a plantation economy of a colony. Throughout the eighteenth century, therefore, the French Antilleans sought to restrict intermarriage across ethnic boundaries and curtail nonwhite participation in shipping, commerce, and the military. The Jamaica Assembly passed an act in 1762 restricting the inheritance of any free person of color to no more than two thousand pounds sterling. In 1783, the Assembly of the Virgin Islands passed a law which restricted the amount of land free coloreds could buy to a maximum of eight acres, prohibited them from inheriting lots of more than fifteen slaves, and imposed public whipping as the punishment for striking whites. Similar types of restrictions were introduced in Cuba during the nineteenth century—at the time when the British Caribbean was moving in the direction of removing distinctions within the free population.

One area of colonial life in which the free coloreds found ready opportunities for service was in the military. Slaves had always been impressed for emergency military service and often rewarded with freedom for their military valor in all European colonies in the New World. Gradually free colored males were organized into separate militia units designed to serve alongside the whites in local defense. In Cuba the free coloreds were formally constituted into a separate unit in the military reforms at the end of the sixteenth century, thereby becoming the first colored soldiers recognized by any European state anywhere in the Caribbean. Between 1600 and the late 1800s, the number of free colored militia companies increased from one to sixteen in Cuba, and nearly one-third of all the local militia came from the free colored sector. In the French Antilles, integrated units of whites and free coloreds existed before the end of the seventeenth century. In 1697, a separate free black militia company was recognized in Saint-Domingue, and by 1730, the free nonwhites formed their own companies under white officers. In Jamaica, where the free coloreds were required by law to serve in the segregated island militia, they constituted more than 54 percent of the troops in 1828. The free colored militia not only sought to defend the island against foreign attack but also fought against the Maroons in 1739 and again in 1795 and stood ready to contain slave revolt. Barbados, which had a relatively larger resident white population than Jamaica and which had less to fear from slave revolts or foreign attacks, showed greater reluctance to admit free nonwhite companies into the volunteer militia. Nevertheless by 1833, fully 25 percent of the militia were drawn from the free colored population—a sharp contrast with the less than 5 percent serving at the time of the American Revolution.

The free colored population throughout the Caribbean, then, was a considerably heterogenous group, struggling to assert itself and establish its identity under a variety of ever-changing conditions. In Santo Domingo, the Bahamas, Bermuda, and a number of the smaller islands in the Eastern Caribbean, the local economies remained virtually constant and the social structures reflected this stability in their pattern of slow evolution. Elsewhere the situation was far more volatile, far more dynamic. In 1789, Saint-Domingue erupted at the height of its prosperity, and the society experienced the first thorough revolution in the Western Hemisphere. There change went far beyond a political rearrangement. The slaves destroyed not only their bondage but also the symbols of their servitude—the white masters, the large plantation complex, the whole pattern of latifundium, and the export-oriented economy. In the early nineteenth century, the export economies of a number of the British Caribbean colonies were on the verge of collapse. The politically dominant white minorities waged a determined but futile campaign to forestall the emancipation of their slaves and the gradual political participation of the nonwhite majorities. By 1834, both goals were lost as the British government accepted the abolition of slavery throughout their empire and began to take measures to secure the civil rights of the free nonwhites. In 1844, the Cuban whites, basing their action on a presumed island-wide conspiracy, staged a sort of preemptive massacre that virtually decimated the intellectual and economic leadership of the Afro-Cuban population. That action, called the Conspiracy of the Ladder, signified the highest point of local racial tension during the century.

Despite the monumental handicaps, free colored individuals achieved outstanding successes in many spheres of activity. Where the opportunities presented themselves, members of the free colored community participated ably and enthusiastically. In Trinidad and Puerto Rico, free coloreds comprised nearly one-third of all landowners in the early nineteenth century. Throughout the region, the free coloreds were noted for their participation in the printing trades, in literature, in music, in dance, and in other aspects of local culture, sometimes performing better than the whites. Considerations of class, color, and the inescapable ambiguity of being neither fully free nor plainly servile for so long might have definitely inhibited the cohesion of the nonwhites. Until the nineteenth century, the local white groups tried to marginalize, demoralize, and eliminate this important component of the society. It could not be done. Like the slaves, this sector survived and eventually came into its own.

Like the free persons of color, the white sector was also a quite heterogenous group. Their division along socioeconomic class lines was almost as pronounced as the color divisions within the free colored caste: *peninsulares* and *criollos* in the Spanish colonies; *grands blancs* and *petits blancs* in the French colonies; and "principal whites" and "poor whites" in the English colonies. As indicated before, some of these social attributes derived from the relationship to the plantation structure in the exploitation colonies. In the settler colonies, place of birth assumed some importance, with greater status attributed to whites born in the metropolis. This distinction did not diminish even when the colony was transformed into a plantation colony. By the end of the eighteenth century, colonial-born whites were already becoming so self-conscious that their attitude became a source of some political friction in Cuba and Saint-Domingue.

But the white community was further divided in other ways. Every colony had a mixture of national origins and religious denominations within the white ranks. Sometimes this situation restricted cooperative action on the part of the whites and may have retarded the growth of a local nationalism. Nowhere was this illustrated better than in the island of Trinidad, captured and retained by the English from the Spanish in 1797.

Trinidad had never been an important Spanish colony, lying as it did just off the Venezuelan coast and outside the axis of the Spanish-American empire. During the later half of the eighteenth century, the Spanish had attempted to encourage Catholic settlers to boost the population and had enthusiastically welcomed refugees from war-torn French Saint-Domingue. At the time of its capture, the island already had a mixed population of whites, and the diversity increased. In 1811, the white population of Trinidad numbered 4,353 persons, representing ten different national or regional origins. Indigenous Indians numbered 1,736, constituting the largest white group at about 40 percent of the population. English whites totaled 1,280, or 29.4 percent. The French settlers numbered 681, or nearly 15 percent. The Spanish component was 559, or almost 12.8 percent. In addition, there were 25 Germans, 20 Americans, 20 Corsicans, 18 Italians, 10 Maltese, and 4 Portuguese. National origin and religious affiliation, however, were lesser considerations than merely being white in a colony where color was more important than condition. The English placed the colony under a government that continued to respect Spanish law and custom—but not those laws and customs which supported the civil rights of the nonwhite sector.

Every slave society struggled to preserve its carefully delineated hierarchical order and only reluctantly accepted the unavoidable breaches of social boundaries. This was as true within the white sector as between the races. The genial Lady Maria Nugent, an American Creole born in Perth Amboy, New Jersey, of mixed Scottish, Irish, and Dutch ancestry, a loyalist refugee from the American Revolution as well as the wife of the governor of Jamaica, left a classic description of the colonial society in which she lived for five years. Lady Nugent found Jamaican upper-class conduct a source of exasperation and bemusement and well below her metropolitan expectations:

> In this country it appears as if every thing were bought and sold. Clergymen make no secret of making a traffic of their livings; but General N. [her husband, General George Nugent, governor of Jamaica, 1801–1806] has set his face against such proceedings, and has refused many applications for this purpose. He is determined to do all he can towards the reformation of the church, and thus rendering it respectable. It is indeed melancholy, to see the general disregard of both religion and morality, throughout the whole island. Every one seems solicitous to make money, and no one appears to regard the mode of acquiring it. It is extraordinary to witness the immediate effect that the climate and habit of living in this country have upon the minds and manners of Europeans, particularly of the lower orders. In the upper ranks, they become indolent and inactive, regardless of everything but eating, drinking, and indulging themselves, and are almost entirely under the domination of their mullatto favorites. In the lower orders, they are the same, with the addition of conceit and tyranny; considering the negroes as creatures formed merely to administer to their ease, and to be subject to their caprice; and I have found much difficulty to persuade those great people and superior beings, our white domestics, that the blacks are human beings and have souls. I allude more particularly to our German and other men-servants.
>
> It was curious to observe, when we were entering any town, the number of trunks, band-boxes, & c. that were hurrying to the different houses, and the same at our departure, all going back to the country again, and all on negroes' heads; for whenever the ladies go to town, or are to appear in society, their black maids and other attendants start off with their finery in cases or their boxes, on their heads. Trunks of any size are carried in the same manner. In short, everything is put upon the head, from the largest to the smallest thing; even a smelling-bottle, I believe, would be carried in the same way. I have often, on our tour, seen twelve or fourteen negroes in one line of march, each bearing some article for the toilette on his head.
>
> The creole language is not confined to the negroes. Many of the ladies who have not been educated in England, speak a sort of broken English, with an indolent drawling out of their words, that is very tiresome if not disgusting. I stood next to a lady one night, near a window, and, by way of saying something, remarked that the air was much cooler than usual; to which she answered, "Yes, ma-am, *him rail-ly too fra-ish.*"

Despite its stuffiness, Lady Nugent's remarkably perceptive observations on Jamaican colonial society could be made, *mutatis mutandis,* of just about any other Caribbean colonial society. The "corruption" of clergy and public officials, the laxity of European moral standards, the stereotypical social behavior of mulatto females, the gluttony (always under the guise of generosity), the prodigal use of labor, and the profligate obsession with materialism could be observed equally in Cuba, Martinique, Barbados, or Surinam—in any of the wealthier European colonies in the Caribbean. These were common behavioral traits of the upper classes of whites and nonwhites in the plantation society. They probably were one indication of the effects that the mercantile mentality and occupational servility of slavery had on the Europeans overseas. It was not merely the climate of the tropics but also the process of Creolization within the peculiar socioeconomic structure of their own creation that surreptitiously undermined their original

"Europeanness." By the eighteenth century, this process had led to a marked difference between metropolitan whites and Creole whites.

The two basic social classes within the category of Euro-Caribbean whites formed four distinct social ranks. At the very summit—and closest to what might otherwise be called an elite—were the noble and seminoble families and the wealthy owners of large, successful plantations. In the Spanish and French colonies some of these noble families had titles that ranked among the most distinguished in their respective metropolises. Cuba, for example, had twenty-nine titled families in 1810, including thirteen marquesses and sixteen counts. Most of these families arrived in the island as true settlers in the sixteenth or early seventeenth centuries, although their titles dated only from the eighteenth century. This was true of the Pedroso, González de la Torre, Roxas, Santa Cruz, Cárdenas, Cepero, and Sotolongo families of Havana; the Porcallo de Figueroa, Varona, and Guerra families of Bayamo; the De la Torre family of Puerto Príncipe; and the Estrada family of Santiago de Cuba. Lower members of the nobility also sojourned for various periods in the British islands, brought out by the call of duty, the lure of pleasure, or the desire for profit. William Scarlet, a wealthy landowner in St. James Parish, Jamaica, was knighted on becoming chief justice of the island in the 1720s. He was the brother of Lord Abinger (James Scarlett, 1769–1844, of Duckett's Spring, St. James), attorney general and chief baron of the Exchequer in England. Simon Taylor, the wealthy landowner, left his extensive properties in Jamaica to his nephew, Sir Simon Taylor. Indeed, founding families of the British West Indian plantation societies formed, by the late eighteenth century, a core of old planters, whose advice was often influential in the realm of imperial as well as local politics.

Along with the titled nobility and the old plantocracy came a mixed group of wealthy—sometimes distinctly *nouveaux riches*—planters, bureaucrats, senior officers in the military and naval services, and wealthy merchants, often the proud owners of lavish country estates. The difference between these two strata of the white upper class was not great. Indeed, kin affiliations occurred frequently between the two groups. The most distinguished and dominant Cuban families provided offspring who gave valuable service in the Spanish military, bureaucracy, and clergy throughout the empire. H. P. Jacobs reports in his study, *Sixty Years of Change*, that members of the old plantocracy in the British Caribbean often sent their sons to fight and die in the military service of the British empire in faraway places such as Spain, Egypt, and India, convinced that they were fighting for their monarch and their country. By the nineteenth century, however, a division had developed within the ruling elite. As Jacobs noted: "The old plantocracy had frequently a deep love

for Jamaica and a feeling of responsibility; but they were not completely identified with it. The new plantocracy looked for advancement through Jamaica and through Jamaica alone." Both groups, old and new, formed a powerful alliance stubbornly defending the economic and political interests of the white planting sector against the legitimate aspirations of the nonwhites.

Below the upper group of old and new planters and their bureaucratic peers came the middling merchants and the important professionals, such as doctors and clergymen. These together formed a third rank within the white sector. The expansion of commerce and the complex semibartering nature of the export economy provided opportunities for the expansion of the commercial and professional classes. The plantation society was, above all, a major consumer society importing necessities and luxuries from a variety of sources. Bills of lading for the Port of Havana in 1852 demonstrate the universality of its commercial contacts and the diversity of the imported products. A partial selection of the list included among the imports fine cloths, furniture, and mirrors from England, Holland, France, and North America; flour, wine, spices, olive oil, and shoes from Spain; codfish and salted meat from Newfoundland, New York, Philadelphia, Baltimore, and Vera Cruz; silverware from Manchester and Birmingham; bricks, clay pots, and stones from Toledo in Spain; tiles and ceramic ware from Puebla, Mexico, and Talavera de la Reina in Spain; and timber from neighboring Jamaica. With certain variations in the sources, the selection could have been representative of the commerce for Curaçao, Port-of-Spain, Bridgetown, Point-à-Pitre, or Kingston. The merchant groups were a diverse, sometimes socially well-connected class. Some were the scions of great families. This was particularly noticeable in Cuba in the early nineteenth century. Others, especially in the French colonies, were connected to prominent merchant houses in Nantes, Bordeaux, and La Rochelle. Still others were simple adventurers of uncertain origin. Basques and Catalans virtually controlled the trade of the Hispanic Caribbean during the nineteenth century. Jews, Syrians, and Lebanese were prominent in the Dutch and British colonies. Eventually the most successful merchants that stayed on in the colonies found acceptance into the social circles of the plantation elite. Jews in some British Caribbean colonies, while conceded freedom of worship and movement, suffered from some political disabilities. They could neither vote nor serve in the military services until the general enfranchisement of all free nonwhites, beginning with the Jamaica law of 1830.

Merchants were a large and active part of municipal life throughout the Caribbean. The most successful merchants established impressive urban and rural dwellings and acquired country estates. As a group, they were never generally regarded as the social equivalent of the specialist planting classes, and it is ironic that in the French and British colonies the merchants were sometimes considered as absentee owners and blamed for many of the economic ills of the colony. The nineteenth-century modus operandi of the commercial craft necessitated travel, not just abroad to suppliers and customers but also throughout the interior of the colony. It is perhaps unlikely that a greater proportion of merchants than planters retired abroad. Moreover, the tone of all the large Caribbean cities—Havana, San Juan, Kingston, Bridgetown, Fort-de-France, or Willemstad—was set by the merchant groups that pioneered (albeit with great self-interest) some of the fledgling police and fire protection services that have survived as major municipal occupations. After 1805, merchants comprised more than half of the Kingston Vestry Jurors' Lists.

The fourth rank was the largest white grouping. They were labeled with a variety of terms, some of which, regardless of the language, carried a pronounced pejorative connotation: *petits blancs,* poor whites, "lesser orders," *campesino, guajiro, mambí, jíbaro,* "walking buckra," or "red legs." At one time or another, the category included small independent farmers, petty shopkeepers, lawyers, taverners and hostelers, day laborers, itinerant preachers, teachers, policemen, firemen, bookkeepers, bill collectors, commission agents, gunsmiths, blacksmiths, coppersmiths, goldsmiths, druggists, midwives, nurses, undertakers, hairdressers, seamstresses, porters, cooks, gardeners, bakers, barbers, tailors, coachmakers, coopers, watchmakers and repairers, shoemakers, sailmakers, wharfingers, shipwrights, carpenters, cabinetmakers, bricklayers, masons, printers, and stationers. Since these whites gained their employment mainly in the service occupations, they competed with jobbing slaves and the free nonwhite population, a coincidence that did not enhance their social status. This motley group also included a small number of unskilled, unemployed, and socially unsuccessful that formed a part of the poor white community in every colony. But in general, members of the poorer white classes were employed, industrious, and filled with the hope of enormous pecuniary gain and eventual upward social mobility that helped form the magnetic attraction for their sojourn in the tropics. Moreover, regardless of their economic circumstances, the accidental factor of race and color invested all whites with a superior status in the colonies.

The white segment was not more homogeneous than any other, but it tended to display a far greater cohesiveness and unity than any other group, especially after the revolution in Saint-Domingue. Whites emphasized their racial and color differences, and they dominated all the major institutions of the society. Whites virtually controlled the export economy, monopolized the political structure before the late nineteenth century, and set what they arrogantly presumed to be the cultural norms for the entire society. Nevertheless, the scathing criticisms of visitors and some long-term residents indicated that in most cases local white Creole culture was merely a parody of that in the metropolis. The white subgroup suffered from the class prejudices of the elite, as Edward Long described graphically in his remarkable *History of Jamaica* published in 1774:

The lower order of white people (as they are called here), are, for the most part, composed of artificers, indented servants, and refugees . . . carpenters, who never handled a tool; bricklayers, who scarcely know a brick from a stone; and bookkeepers, who can neither write nor read. Many of these menial servants, who are retained for saving a deficiency, are the very dregs of the three kingdoms. They have commonly more vices, and much fewer good qualities, than the slaves over whom they are set in authority; the better sort of whom heartily despise them, perceiving little or no difference from themselves, except in skin, and blacker depravity. By their base familiarity with the worst-disposed among the slaves, they do a very great injury to the plantations; causing disturbances, by seducing the Negroes [*sic*] wives, and bringing *odium* upon the white people in general, by their drunkenness and profligate actions. In fact, the better sort of Creole Blacks disdain to associate with them, holding them in too much contempt, or abhorrence.

Long's antagonistic attitude was probably not widely held by the majority of upper-class whites who passed their lives in the colonies among a far greater number of enslaved Africans and their descendants. For them, race and color rather than class and nationality became a consoling, fraternal bond. Such were the peculiarities of the plantation slave society that the conventional class divisions and social distinctions of the metropolis largely broke down in the overseas colonies. Even as Long wrote in the later eighteenth century, he was aware that some fundamental changes had already taken place—the autocracy of the plantation owner had yielded to a community of common law, and the colonial society had become, in many ways, a pale reflection of the mother country.

The essentially frontier conditions of the tropical American colonies facilitated a fantastic upward mobility among the whites that often made a mockery of metropolitan class consciousness. But there was more at work than the frontier. Bryan Edwards, the experienced Jamaican planter and member of the British Parliament, wrote apprehensively of white colonial social relations in the 1790s as the French

Revolution engulfed the Continent and the distant colony of Saint Domingue:

> It appears to me [he wrote in 1793] that the leading feature [among the whites] is an independent spirit, and a display of conscious equality throughout all ranks and conditions. The poorest white person seems to consider himself nearly on a level with the richest, and, emboldened by this idea approached his employer with extended hand, and a freedom, which in the countries of Europe, is seldom displayed by men in the lower orders of life toward their superiors. It is not difficult to trace the origin of this principle. It arises, without doubt, from the preeminence and distinction which are necessarily attached even to the complexion of a White Man, in a country where the complexion, generally speaking, distinguishes freedom from slavery.

The simple facts of Caribbean life everywhere permitted sufficient examples of the dramatic rise from dismal poverty and humble status to Croesus-like wealth and the most highly esteemed social rank. It was not impossible for a poor white to become the governor of a colony. Henry Morgan, a poor Welsh indentured servant-turned-buccaneer, ended his fascinating life as a highly respected planter and the lieutenant-governor of Jamaica during the eighteenth century. Julian de Zulueta, a poor semiliterate rural Basque, went out to Cuba in the nineteenth century; entered the slave trade; rose to be a wealthy mayor of Havana, a respectable member of the Spanish nobility, and an advisor to the monarchy of Spain. There was always some degree of initial snobbery, some inevitable snickering, and some understandable unease at accepting new members to the group, but in time all of this could be overcome.

Lady Nugent found it convenient to act "like an invalid, to keep up the character I have politically adopted" on meeting a group of French refugee ladies in Spanish Town until she could clarify their social status and determine "what ladies to receive." Because she was a bit of a prude and an official transient in the Jamaican society, she probably deliberately exaggerated social distance to bolster her husband's position. It is hardly likely that the other white elite ladies would have gone to such extremes to display rank with foreign women of their own color. Within the Caribbean context, color by itself was a ticket of admission.

The mutually reinforcing cleavages of race and color for the minority whites can hardly be overestimated in the Caribbean. Auguste Lacour, writing of Guadeloupe society in the middle of the nineteenth century, described with cutting precision the ranks within the local society as a whole and the congealing effect of color:

Although the island counted among itself a number of the titled nobility, especially younger sons who had come out to the place in pursuit of their fortune, the nobility was not constituted as in France. Within the white group, the nobility did not exist. The only privilege of the nobility was being entitled to a seat in the *Conseil Supérieur,* and the exemption from the head tax for a fixed number of slaves. What constituted the nobility was not parchment, but color. To the white group, to individuals of the European race, were exclusively reserved all public, lucrative and honorific functions.

Color, therefore, delineated the boundaries of caste and highlighted the distinctions between the "we" and "they." To a certain extent, it mitigated the potential class divisions within the white sector, especially after the Haitian Revolution demonstrated the ultimate consequences of placing class interests above racial solidarity. Race, color, and bondage were fundamental ingredients in white thoughts about their precarious world in the Caribbean. Unfortunately, it was sometimes the only thing they thought about—besides markets and profits.

Race, color, and legal status did not, however, preclude some relationships across caste lines. The masters could no more live without their slaves than the slaves could live without their masters. Each group, the free and the enslaved, the masters and the slaves, the Africans and the Europeans, adjusted to life in the tropical world as best they could. And this adjustment included an adjustment to each other. The monopoly of power exercised by the white sector on the plantations, in politics, in law, and in the export economy was more apparent than real. In two ways, the structure that the whites created was both fragile and contradictory. In the first place, their economic success at all levels depended largely on factors entirely outside their control—including the supply of slaves, the price of sugar, and the fortuitous consistency of climate. In the second place, the white master class defined slaves as property but were forced to use them as persons of intelligence and self-will. Whatever the white masters may have confessed about the subordinate nature of their slaves, they encountered in their everyday dealings with them an uncomfortable, unmistakable humanity.

Alongside the continuous proliferation of laws establishing the sanctity of private property in Africans and the vast literature deploring the inherent inhumanity or subhumanity of slaves went an elaborate system of police-protection measures fully conceding the basic humanity of the slaves. The plantation was an artificial construct, but slaves were people. Slaves, after all, demonstrated equally all the qualities of the whites. They could work as hard, administer as efficiently, speak the languages as well, think as subtly, scheme as cunningly, inflict revenge as maliciously, love as passionately, fight as bravely, and subvert society as totally. Other forms of property—land, cattle, equipment, and buildings—could not respond as creatively to their circumstances. Slaves had a life, mind, and culture of their own that induced them to make the appropriate survival response to the situation in which they found themselves.

The exigencies of production, profit, and social order required substantial white supervision of nonwhite society. But this supervision could not take the form of unrelenting coercion or uninterrupted regulation. The white sector delegated authority, recognized cultural differences, encouraged divisions of rank, and employed all types of incentives to minimize the simultaneous disaffection of the majority of the slave sector. The numerical weakness of the master class provided an agent for upward social mobility. The fact that in most territories the whites could not even provide sufficient women for the adequate sexual satisfaction of the males meant that caste-confined relations, even at the most domestic level, had to be relaxed. Slave plantation society, then, held an ideal about race, class, color, and condition that was far removed from the operational reality of day-to-day living.

The practical operations of work and living in the slave society produced a number of contradictions, some of which proved quite dysfunctional to the system. At one level, ideal social stratification clashed with inescapable mobility. This produced explosive pressures of class, color, race, and status. The legal divisions of slave and free were the most sharply defined concepts of status established by the slave society. The society maintained the intrinsic nature of slavery by declaring that the offspring of any slave remained slaves, regardless of the status of one parent who might be free. At the same time, the slave society held freedom as the highest ideal and provided a number of ways in which the status could be achieved by those who were slaves. Slaves could buy their freedom on their own initiative. Masters could independently grant freedom to their slaves for satisfactory service or for private religious motives. Free parents could purchase the freedom of their offspring. Society granted freedom to slaves who fought bravely against foreign invaders or exposed conspiracies among their fellow slaves or had legitimate complaints of excessive cruelty and inhumanity against their masters. Freedom was also granted for idiosyncratic reasons. The Spanish normally granted freedom to foreign-owned slaves escaping from non-Catholic adversarial states to their own territories, provided they claimed they were fleeing from religious persecution. This offered incentives for British and Dutch Caribbean slaves fleeing their Protestant masters but offered cold comfort for nominally Catholic French slaves. Superannuated slaves owned by the Spanish and French monarchs were granted freedom after what was considered a lifetime of royal service; and the French government manumitted slaves who had served seven or more years as drummers for the military troops. During the Ten Years' War (1868–1878) in Cuba, the Spanish government declared slaves of the insurgents to be free, while retaining in slavery those whose masters had loyally supported the Crown.

The slave system was not inflexible. Theoretically, individuals could move upward within the class structure and laterally across the caste divisions. The unskilled field slave acquiring a technical skill could assume a higher status. Slaves polishing their command of English, Spanish, French, Dutch, or Swedish could become a part of the respected domestic staff of the plantation great house or the city residence, improving both their status and their value. Or field slaves could work their ways into urban jobbing gangs, gaining social and occupational mobility and a better opportunity for eventual self-purchase. On the contiguous, overlapping, and frequently ill-defined boundaries of race and status, some "passing" could occur. Urban skilled slaves could successfully run away and become free. Free light-complexioned mulattoes could pass as white (and undoubtedly some wealthy ones did), legitimizing their new status by judicious bribes, calculated marriages, or socially acceptable conduct. Even within the upper stratum, newcomers with money and temerity could break into the ranks of the socially privileged, as did Henry Morgan in Jamaica and Julian Zuleuta in Cuba. The slave society, in short, was similar to any other society faced with widely fluctuating economic and demographic conditions and rapidly changing social norms. The dynamism had internal as well as external sources of stimulation.

Nevertheless, the fluidity of the structure, especially at the free level, engendered the type of internal class and cast friction that contributed to social instability and made the slave society a potentially revolutionary complex. During the nineteenth century, the Caribbean slave society was equally one of ferment and strife. Its potential strengths generated its inherent weaknesses. A divided society, it was simultaneously a divisive society. Tensions existed at all levels. Tensions existed between free and slave as well as within the free groups along lines of color and class. The most potentially explosive were tensions between free and slave and among the white groups. Between slave and free the tensions took the forms of slave revolts, conspiracies, and subversions with varying degrees of success. In French Saint-Domingue, the slave revolt destroyed the colony. In Cuba, most enduring of the Caribbean slave societies, the white group split basically between Spanish-born *peninsulares* and Cuban-born *criollos*. *Criollo* versus *peninsular* antagonism manifested itself in a number of conspiracies throughout the century, flared unsuccessfully during the Ten Years' War, and finally broke the last vestiges of the Spanish-American imperial connection in 1898. In 1788, the rift between *grands blancs* and *petits blancs* on Saint-Domingue—the most extreme case of intracaste antagonism anywhere in the Caribbean—opened the floodgates of revolution, with permanent reversals for French ambitions and the French dream of empire in the Americas. In Jamaica, the political incompatibility between rural whites and urban whites contributed to the constitutional surrender of representative-assembly government after the Morant Bay uprising in 1865.

Class antagonisms paled against the force of racial distrust. The recurring slave revolts and the constant preoccupation with the possibility of slave revolts exacerbated the antagonistic racial divisions in every slave society. The increased exploitation of slaves at the very period when the institution of slavery was undergoing relentless international moral and intellectual attack—and in some cases physical dismantlement—coincided with the increased nineteenth-century awareness of ethnicity, ethnocentricity, and nationalism. The Caribbean societies, too, felt the winds of political change in the nineteenth century and began to articulate—although nowhere as strongly as in Cuba and on the neighboring mainland—a heightened sense of self-consciousness. Their sense of nation, however, clashed with their reality. Cultural, ethnic, and economic diversity appeared patently undesirable to adherents of social engineering infatuated with the current ideas of the other emergent nations.

This steady political awakening before the middle of the nineteenth century in the Caribbean coincided with the development of a lively local literature, drama, and art. While much that was written about the region came from the pens of foreigners, local writers increasingly expressed their ideas about their world. A distinct Caribbean civic culture, rooted in the diverse popular experiences of the various territories, was slowly maturing and beginning to compete with the adopted metropolitan cultures that remained the ideals of the elites. Aided by the expanding presence of the printing press after the eighteenth century and a growing literate readership for newspapers, books, and pamphlets, the various territories produced a vigorous and perceptive type of literature. This fell into three overlapping categories: political analyses, histories, and scientific publications designed to advocate political change and enhance the political position of the local elites; publications determined to defend or to attack slavery; and imaginative literature drawing heavily on stylized versions of local customs and manners. In one way or another, the various writings of authors such as José Agustín Caballero (1762–1825), Francisco Arango y Parreño (1765–1837), Félix Varela y Morales (1788–1853), José Antonio Saco (1797–1879), José de la Luz y Caballero (1800–1862) and Domingo del Monte y Aponte in Cuba; Eugenio María de Hostos (1839–1903) in Puerto Rico; or Richard Hill (1795–1872) in Jamaica all served these purposes. It was almost impossible to write about politics or culture during the nineteenth century without somehow contemplating the role of slavery and its enduring impact on the society in the Caribbean.

The anonymously published *Marly Hill* (1828), a novel about Jamaican society, and the Cuban antislavery book *Francisco* (1937) by Anselmo Suárez y Romero discussed politics as well as the ways in which slavery affected social mores and revealed new local perspectives on the region. Along with the increasing acceptance of local dances, religious customs, music, and plays, the Caribbean Creole elites were, consciously or unconsciously, moving away from their own metropolitan ideals while fostering closer links between the elites and the masses.

The Charter of Freedom in Brazil

Katia M. de Queiros Mattoso

Legal Definition and Description

For the Brazilian slave there was more than one road to much-coveted freedom: flight, death, certain special provisions of the law (in the nineteenth century only), and manumission. The law in Brazil, as in all other slave regimes, provided that the child of a slave mother was born a slave, even if the father was a free man: *Partus sequitur ventrem*. There was one exception to this rule: a child engendered by the master became free after the death of his father, provided the latter recognized him as his child. In the decades prior to the abolition of slavery in Brazil, a few halting efforts were made to legally manumit certain categories of slaves; the 1885 law freeing sexagenarians and above all the law of the "free womb."

The law of 28 September 1871, Law no. 2040 known as the law of the free womb, promulgated by the Imperial Princess Isabelle, regent in the absence of her father Dom Pedro II, granted freedom to children born in Brazil to a female slave. Since it was by then illegal to import slaves from Africa, this meant that there would henceforth be no young slaves to replenish the slave stock, so that slavery would gradually vanish from Brazil. But the law was in reality far less liberal than it appears. The liberty granted to newborns was hedged about with appalling restrictions, such as the stipulation that the minor child remained under the joint authority of the master and its mother, who were supposed to raise it together until it reached the age of eight. After that, the mother's owner had two options. He could accept an indemnity of 600,000 reis from the government or he could use the services of the child until it reached its twenty-first year. In the first case the government took charge of the child. It then generally placed him in a charitable institution, where he was put to work until he reached the age of twenty-one. The 600,000 reis were paid to the master in the form of government bonds paying 6 percent over thirty years. When the child reached the age of eight, the master had one month to make up his mind about which procedure he preferred. In almost all cases he chose to retain the child. This resulted in a new form of slavery, since the law did not specify the maximum work day or minimum health and dietary criteria to which the "free slave" should be subject, thus leaving him entirely at the master's mercy. In a society where any dark-skinned individual was immediately identified as a "slave," his life was scarcely different from that of most slaves. Nor was he likely to fare better if sent to a charitable institution by a master who chose to accept the government indemnity. For after a wrenching separation from his mother and from the slave community the child became an anonymous ward of an impersonal government that exploited him in its own way by putting him to work. Since slavery was abolished in Brazil before any children born under the free-womb law reached age twenty-one, their problems were the same as those of slaves freed by means of conditional manumission.

Manumission was a legal procedure. It could be granted with or without formal proceedings, directly or indirectly, explicitly, tacitly, or presumptively, by contract between living persons or by will of the deceased, under private seal or sworn before a notary, verbally or in writing. In the absence of a written document, witnesses were required to certify that manumission had taken place. Generally manumission was granted by written document, however, signed by the master or by a third party upon request of an illiterate master. To avoid disputes the document customarily was registered with a notary in the presence of witnesses. Several years often elapsed between the grant of liberty and its registration with a notary. Many manumissions were granted by will or at baptism. The owner voluntarily renounced his *manus* on the captive, who became a free man "as if free from birth," as manumission documents often expressed it.

Children who in the eyes of the law have no will of their own therefore could not liberate their slaves. Tutors or guardians of minors were not allowed to dispose of the property of their wards without express authorization of the courts. Similarly, persons possessing slaves "in usufruct," insane persons, "prodigal sons," and slaves who owned another slave were not legally entitled to sign manumission papers. A married woman could sign only with her husband's authorization, except on her death bed, when she became her spouse's equal. Finally, in the nineteenth century, laws were passed authorizing the manumission of so-called national slaves, slaves belonging to the nation as a whole, because they had been smuggled in after the abolition of the slave trade in 1831. These slaves were seized and set free at once. The law, in its far-sightedness, even declared that dead slaves would be resurrected as free men, a Christian view often embroidered upon in pastoral homilies. A more tangible measure here below was a law liberating any slave legally married to a free spouse. Finally, all foundlings were presumed free (and it was quite common to abandon newborns). As mentioned earlier, any slave who found a large diamond (more than twenty carats) was immediately freed, but the government, which received the diamond, paid the master an indemnity of 400,000 reis. Slaves who denounced their masters for smuggling or dealing in commodities on which the government had a monopoly (gold, diamonds, Brazil wood) were also liberated and received a reward of 200,000 reis. Any slave belonging to the confraternity of Saint Benedict who paid the redemption price was immediately set free. A slave who managed to cross the borders of the empire gained his freedom, even if he returned to Brazil. Military service brought manumission: many slaves won their freedom in this way during the war with Paraguay (1864–1869). Through inheritance it was common for a slave to become the property of more than one owner. If any one of these masters decided to grant the slave his freedom, all the others were obliged to go along. Finally, if a slave offered his master the sum required for manumission and the master refused to accept it, the slave could ask for the protection of the courts through an intermediary, a court appointed tutor or guardian (this was necessary since the slave himself possessed no legal personality). After 1831 a slave whose master asked an exorbitant amount for his manumission could be set free by court order, but such judgments were not always easy to acquire.

Some fifteen years prior to abolition, an imperial regulation established a so-called manumission fund. The fund consisted of duties paid on slaves, taxes on transfer of slave ownership, subscriptions, donations, and bequests. The actual endowment was never sufficient. Between 1873 and 1882, 70,183 slaves are said to have been liberated through this fund. To put this figure in perspective, recall that during the same nine years 132,777 slaves died in captivity. It was frequently impossible to call a meeting of the *juntes* who were supposed to decide what slaves were to receive the benefits of the fund, and when they did meet they often gave in to pressure from slave owners: for example, the juntes of São Paulo state met in 1886, two years before the abolition of slavery, and declared that newly freed slaves must faithfully and diligently serve their former masters for five years after receiving their manumission papers.

The law of 28 September 1885, the so-called sexagenarian law which set free all slaves above sixty years of age, also stipulated that the freed slave was required to indemnify his master. If he was unable to do so in cash, he must work for three more years if he was between 60 and 62, or else until he was 65. Now, we know that in the state of São Paulo, only 2,553 slaves were liberated as a result of this law in 1887, and that 2,503 of these were freed under contracts whose terms imposed much longer periods of service than required by the law. Thus the generosity of the laws and regulations was more apparent than real. More than anything else, the laws testify to the efforts of certain masters to delay, by whatever

means were available, the inevitable abolition of slavery, upon which they depended for essential manpower.

Slaves were generally unaware of the laws. They rarely benefited from favorable laws unless they had the support of free men. Such support was hard to come by, especially in the countryside, where slaves lived in a closed world and the law was in the hands of their lords and masters. Sometimes manumission cost nothing, either by dint of legislative act or thanks to a generous slave owner. But more often it was costly. Slaves had to pay for their freedom in hard cash, metal coin or paper money, either in a lump sum or by installments. Some slaves redeemed themselves by giving another slave to their masters. If a master's will stipulated the price of a slave's freedom, then the master's heirs had to abide by that price without question, even though it was generally below the slave's actual market value.

Regardless of whether manumission was bought or granted free of charge, it could be revoked. Therein lay one of the ambiguities of the law as well as of actual practice. The grounds for revocation that slave owners were entitled to present were entirely subjective. If a master suddenly discovered "ingratitude" in his former slave, he could annul his manumission as easily as he granted it. Not until 1865 did the courts declare this procedure unacceptable. Despite this judgment, however, the revocation of manumission on grounds of ingratitude, authorized by Title 13, Book 4 of the Philippine Ordinances of the seventeenth century, remained officially legal. Brazil did not adopt a civil code of its own until 1917. Another ambiguous aspect of manumission was that many documents contained restrictive clauses, specifying time delays or suspensive conditions which in practice nullified manumission. The slave was then free but actually prevented from making use of his liberty. In other words, his liberty was conditional. Only a slave who managed to secure complete and unequivocal manumission, with no second thoughts and no restrictions, really became a "free" citizen.

Still, as we shall see later, even this free citizen did not enjoy full civil rights. But at least he could dispose of his own property as he saw fit. If he died childless and intestate, his inheritance went to his wife or other heirs. If he died unmarried, his property, like that of all free men without heirs, reverted to the state. The slave's former master became his patron after manumission, but the patronage relationship had nothing in common with that of ancient Rome, which imposed numerous obligations on the freed slave. In Brazil the freed slave owed his patrono nothing more than the respect and loyalty of a grateful son. The one restriction was that, in order to bring suit against his patrono, he required special authorization from the court.

Manumission charters are moving documents. Based on models that changed little over the centuries, they recount the sufferings of an entire people desperate for the favors of masters who often showed themselves to be more calculating than generous. Below are the complete texts of two such charters, chosen from among thousands—two brief and quite ordinary examples. Innumerable others are genuine sagas, full of complicated twists and turns. But the simplicity of the two documents cited here shows how little slaveowners were required to justify their actions:

I, Joaquina de Sant'Anna, hereby declare that among my property is a *cabra* slave by the name of Luciana, daughter of the slave Ines of the Angola nation, now deceased, who also belonged to me; and, further, that the said slave Luciana is from this day forth, by virtue of the good service she has rendered me and for the love of having raised her and for value received, the sum of 100,000 reis in cash, free from this day forth and forevermore, as if she were born of free womb, and my heirs shall have no claim, for which I beseech the justice of His Royal and Imperial Majesty. And if in this charter of freedom some clause is lacking, I consider it as having been expressed.

And because I can neither read nor write I have asked Mr. Aleixo Antunes to prepare this document, which he has signed in my place and as witness and in the presence of other witnesses. Bahia, 15 March 1814, Joaquina de Sant'Anna, and as witness and drafter of this act Aleixo Antunes de Carvalho, and the following witnesses:

Manoel Domingos dos Santos Siloa Cavalcanti, Caetano Alberto de Barros Vianna, Francisco Albergaria. Bahia, 16 March 1814, Simoes. I recognize my own writing: Marcelino Soares de Albergaria, Bahia, 22 March 1814.

His Excellency, Doctor and Chief of Police, Registered
30 December 1875
Antonio João Damasio

I, the undersigned, hereby grant liberty as if he were born of free womb to my slave Ramiro, age 19, of creole color [sic], son of my deceased slave Julia, which liberty my aforesaid slave may enjoy from this date forth and forevermore. I beseech the authorities of His Majesty the Emperor to warrant my decision. Bahia, 2 April 1874, signed Maria Custodia. I recognize the above signature. Antonio João Damasio (notary). Bahia, 30 December, 1875.

Generally, manumission charters include such details as the name of the slave to be freed, country of origin, parents if known, color, the reasons for liberation, whether manumission was free, paid for, or conditional, the names of witnesses, and the date of registration with the notary. Occasionally one also finds information about the master's occupation, his place of residence, and the age or occupation of the slave to be freed. Quite clearly, these documents are mirrors in which we see reflected the lives of that privileged group among slaves, those who were destined to be freed. Particularly valuable are the indications of the reasons that led to the grant of freedom as well as the various restrictions that might be imposed on the freed man's liberty. These records give us a vivid and poignant picture of the hopes and illusions of so many men and women who set out to overcome the innumerable pitfalls on the road to freedom.

Who Purchased Freedom?

Though manumission existed in Brazil almost as long as slavery itself, many barriers, some legal, some circumstantial, persistently hindered its development. The law prohibited manumission in four situations. First, some slaves had been sold under contracts that explicitly stipulated they could never be freed. On the other hand, some contracts contained clauses providing that the slave would eventually be set free or could be set free if obliged to engage in prostitution by the new master. Second, manumission could not be granted to the detriment of the master's creditors. Now, a slave who knew nothing of his master's legal incapacity may well have paid out all or part of the sum necessary for his manumission, only to find himself legally barred from recovering any of it. Third, manumissions granted by will were held to be null and void if granted in contravention of the law: a master could use only the "disposable third" of his property in liberating slaves, for example. If he made a mistake in evaluation, a slave liberated in good faith might find himself once more a slave when the heirs succeeded in proving "fraud." The last and most interesting case involves slaves mortgaged or given as collateral. As movable property like any other, usable as collateral without restriction, slaves who were mortgaged could never purchase their freedom. These legal restrictions clearly show that, in the eyes of their masters, slaves were first and foremost commodities, sources of profit. To be sure, masters could not ask a slave to engage in illicit or immoral acts, but their only duty to the slave was to provide food, clothing, and medical care in case of sickness. The master could rent, loan, sell, give, alienate, bequeath, mortgage, or grant a life interest in the slave. Not until 1864 did a law prohibit the mortgaging of slaves belonging to an agricultural enterprise, though they could still be used as collateral. Mortgage and collateral documents were notarized acts, just like any other donation *inter vivos* or for *causa mortis.* Five witnesses were required.

The slave was in fact a commodity. That is why government and religious authorities tried in vain to combat prostitution of slaves as a source of profit for their masters. Indeed, a law inherited from Roman law, which declared free any slave obliged to work as a prostitute, seems never to have been enforced. A slave needed substantial support to gain freedom in such conditions. As late as 1871, a Rio de Janeiro court refused manumission to a female slave compelled to engage in prostitution, "because article 179 of the Constitution of the Empire guarantees ownership in the full sense and because the hypothesis of Roman law invoked here is not applicable."

Some of the circumstances that could prevent a slave from achieving freedom have already been mentioned. The cost of manumission was the most obvious of these. It was fixed by mutual verbal agreement, and many freedom charters stipulate that "the price was decided by both parties." Hence it was a contractual price, but based on an evaluation made by the master: "He was liberated at his proper price," writes the all-powerful master. In the nineteenth century, if agreement between master and slave proved difficult, either because the master was reluctant to free his slave at all or because he felt the price offered was insufficient, the slave could seek out a godfather to take his case to court. The courts usually found in favor of the slave. But how many slaves were able to make use of this procedure? With our current information we cannot answer this question. In any case, most manumission documents proclaim to all and sundry that the slave has been granted his freedom "freely and spontaneously, without compulsion of any kind." There is no reason not to accept this at face value, since no earthly power could "compel" a master to grant freedom to his slave against his own judgment and interest. Thus the redemption price was a contractual price based on the local market price, which, as we saw earlier, depended on the slave's health, age, sex, and qualifications. The evaluation of a slave also depended on another very important factor, whose influence is difficult to gauge: the relationship between master and slave. The degree of intimacy between servant and master was important; such feelings are hard to quantify. The cost of freedom was affected by feelings that ranged from friendship to indifference. One can speak of a sort of secondary market, in which a slave's price declined if his master was inclined to favor manumission and rose otherwise. An esteemed slave could have his freedom for less than the market price.

It was not in the master's interest to free a slave unless he could replace the freed worker with a new slave bought on the open market. He might, for example, wish to purchase a younger slave to replace an older one, worn out by years of work. For the master, then, the price of manumission was a true surplus, a supplementary profit on the capital invested in the slave. Quite commonly a slave would begin making payments as much as six, seven, or eight years prior to actual manumission, which increased the master's profits still more. Many slaves purchased their freedom on the "installment plan," paying part of the cost over a number of years. After 1850, by which time the slave trade had been abolished for almost twenty years, the slave market became very tight and the price of slaves rose. Here again the master stood to benefit. He was entitled to ask a high price for freeing an elderly slave because of the high cost of buying a replacement worker. Other circumstances favored manumission. Repeated crises in the sugar industry, which deeply affected northeastern Brazil in the nineteenth century, encouraged masters to free workers who had become a burden. The first to be freed were the elderly and those in poor health. Unfortunately, the basic research needed for further analysis has yet to be done. Masters certainly were always interested in increasing their income, and manumission provided a way of converting capital into cash that could be reinvested at a higher rate of return. After 1850, for example, it was tempting and even fashionable in Salvador to buy real estate, bank stock, and government bonds. The sale of a freedom charter providing ready cash might have seemed a favorable arrangement to both master and slave.

The reality was certainly more complicated than it may seem, for manumissions were not paid for only in cash. Little is known about the question: for information about certain aspects of manumission contracts we have only three studies of freedom charters in Salvador between 1684 and 1889 and one study of manumissions granted in Paraty (Rio de Janeiro province) between 1789 and 1822 to go on. In Salvador, it seems that paid manumissions at no time exceeded 48 percent of the total, whereas in Paraty the corresponding figure was only 31 percent. We cannot begin to answer the question without further study of conditional manumissions, of which there were more (43 percent) in Paraty than in Salvador. Were such manumissions really "free," as some masters liked to claim, given that they required the slave to remain a slave during the lifetime of the master or his son or his sister or some other family member? Conditional manumissions were dearly bought, in fact, since they could be revoked at any time and made the slave even more dependent than ever, knowing that the slightest quarrel, the slightest provocation of the master could wreck well-laid plans for freedom. In Bahia, conditional charters accounted for only 18 to 23 percent of the total, depending on the period, compared with the 43 percent just mentioned in Paraty. But in Paraty there was a large proportion of creoles and half-breeds and hence more women and children. Now, creoles, half-breeds, women, and children were always heavily represented among the liberated in all parts of the Country. In Bahia these categories accounted for 80 percent of the slaves freed from the late seventeenth century until the middle of the eighteenth century. Only in the nineteenth century did this proportion drop appreciably, to about half of all manumissions. During the eighteenth century the city of Salvador changed dramatically: as activities related to sugar declined, the city became an important commercial center, a way station for imported merchandise. The growth of trade led to all expansion of the middle class, in which creoles and half-breeds found their place. Moreover, newly arrived Africans were primarily sent to the mining regions, where their prices were higher than in Bahia or Rio. All these circumstances favored the manumission of Bahian creoles. By contrast, when agriculture picked up in the second half of the eighteenth century and even more in the nineteenth century, African slaves were in greater demand. They arrived in large numbers until the abolition of the slave trade in 1831. After 1820 the sugar engenhos experienced periods of crisis alternating with comparative prosperity. The ratio of freed Africans to creoles then increased, to 52 percent in Paraty and to nearly 80 percent in Bahia.

In regard to manumissions of women and children, we have the results of studies carried out in Rio de Janeiro, Salvador, and Paraty. Manumissions of women outnumbered those of men in the three cities by two to one. But in the slave population as a whole, men outnumbered women by the same factor. In other words, manumissions were much more readily granted to women, who generally lived in greater intimacy with the master or worked as itinerant merchants. Women also cost less to replace than men and aged more quickly. Thus women were precious commodities if they knew how to please and rapidly depreciating commodities if they didn't and found it relatively easy to gain freedom for themselves and their children. The percentage of freed children was relatively high until 1745 in Bahia and even higher in Paraty. The ensuing decline (1779–1850) occurred in areas where the number of creole slaves did not increase; creoles had more children than Africans, and it was easier for the children of creoles to gain manumission.

Thus masters were more willing to liberate women and children than men. What about elderly slaves? A vast literature in Brazil describes abandoned old people left to beg at church doors, along with invalids of every stripe, blind people, cripples, and others reduced to living on charity. Substantial research has shown, however, that the elderly and disabled nowhere accounted for more than 10 percent of all manumitted slaves. Most masters did not cast useless slaves out into the street, and in any case people died young in yesterday's Brazil, and younger still if they worked as slaves.

In summary, two-thirds of manumitted slaves were women. For the rest, variations in the conditions of manumission were due mainly to economic circumstances and to differences in the composition of the slave population. But everywhere the majority of manumissions—66 to 75 percent of them—were granted either in exchange for payment or under conditions that profited the owner. The freedom charter was usually a commercial document and rarely a record of generosity.

Immediate Freedom

Why was it easier for ganho and domestic slaves to obtain their freedom than it was for their brothers in captivity? Can a fuller appreciation of the extremely subtle relationships that developed between masters and slaves be gained by looking at the process of manumission? Indeed, understanding this process can, I think, help us to understand what "being a slave" really meant. For the condition of the freed slave can be grasped only through comparison with the condition of the slave himself. Just as there were many ways of being a slave, so too were there many ways of being a freed slave. The process of liberation and the conditions under which it was achieved can shed a good deal of light on everyday life under slavery.

Obtaining freedom was usually a question of money, since the slave was a commodity with a market value. In freedom charters purchased for cash, it is striking that many preconditions had to be met before any cash could change hands. These conditions have a ritual air and tell us much about master-slave relations. What themes, what litanies recur frequently in manumission documents? The two key formulas are the following: "For having served me well" and "For the love that I bore him (or her) because I raised him (her)." Very few charters fail to contain one or the other of these formulas. To be freed, then, one must have been a hard-working, loyal, and obedient slave. In other words, masters wished to make it clear that the slave deserved his freedom in order to justify their decision to free him. For society had to be reassured, had to be told that the freed slave would become a good citizen and not a public burden in a country where charity was the responsibility of private individuals. Thus freedom was a reward, even when payment was required, and for many years it was dangled before slaves as an incentive to good behavior. To be sure, it was not enough merely to dangle the carrot of freedom: the slave was not a donkey. Nor was he simply a commodity, an object to be bought and sold, or a mere laborer whose initiative could be ignored. The slave was in fact a complex human being, in the master's view somewhat like a difficult child in need of education and guidance in order to become a functioning adult. The language of the charters says much about the moralistic and paternalistic

TABLE 9.
Distribution of Freed Slaves in Brazil by Age and Sex

	A Salvador 1684–1745 (N = 1,160)		B Salvador 1779–1850 (N = 6,635)		C Salvador 1813–1853 (N = 686)		D Salvador 1819–1888 (N = 12,799)		E Rio de Janeiro 1807–1831 (N = 1,319)		F Paraty 1789–1822 (N = 325)		
		%		%		%		%		%		%		%
Male	384	33.1	2,543	38.3	225	32.7	5,126	41.1	479	36.3	112	34.5		
Female	776	66.9	4,092	61.7	461	67.3	7,673	59.9	840	63.7	213	65.5	156[b]	58
Adult	818[a]	70.5	6,305	88.9	551	80.3	11,430	86.7	1,143	87	213[l]	65.5		
Child	342	29.5	784	11.1	135	19.7	1,697	13.3	176	13	112	34.5	123	41

Source: James Patrick Kiernan, "The Manumission of Slaves in Colonial Brazil," Diss. New York University, 1976, p. 87. Unpublished data from the study, "A carta de alforria como fonte, . . . pp. 149–163, have been added in column D.
[a] Slaves of unknown age included.
[b] Slaves of unknown age not included.

attitudes, more petty than generous, of slave owners toward slaves.

With morality and custom duly taken care of, the charters usually went on to say that the master was freely granting the slave his liberty, without coercion of any kind. But we know that in the nineteenth century some slaves were obliged to seek the help of "godfathers." In 1825, for example, a mulatto woman named Domingas became an object of antipathy to a person acting as guardian for minors whose parents' will stipulated that Domingas should be freed in exchange for a "sum corresponding to her value." The guardian had obtained an evaluation far in excess of the slave's true value. But Domingas successfully called upon the services of the new master to whom she had been hired out, Karl-Gustav Waiss, the Salvadoran vice-consul representing the Hanseatic city of Hamburg, who went to court and obtained a second evaluation favorable to the slave. In this case the promised manumission had to be secured through all-out battle, but this was the exception and not the rule.

Somewhat more numerous were the slaves freed by masters obliged to liquidate their capital in order to survive. Such slaves were set free with great reluctance, and their masters justified their actions to both themselves and their slaves in such passages as the following:

In 1796 Faustina de Santa Teresa de Jesus, widow, freed her slave Theodoro Joaquim de Sant'Anna, half-breed, cobbler by trade, "not only because he aided her, through his trade as a cobbler, in her poverty but also because on various occasions when she had urgent need of money he gave her the sum of 100,000 reis."

João, a creole carpenter, was set free in 1836 by Ana Joaquina de Sacramento, also a widow, for the sum of 380,000 reis, "because, abandoned as she was by her relatives, as is notorious public knowledge, he provided her with food and served her with humility and charity, seeing to it that she wanted for nothing."

The slave Amancio, son of a creole, mulatto, was liberated in 1862 because his master "found himself in a state of great necessity

and needed this money to cure his ailments and contribute to his upkeep."

In 1877, Maria Augusta Mendes da Silva was obliged to liberate a young creole named Maria, age nine, because she found herself "utterly abandoned and in complete poverty after being cast out by her husband . . . and in need of money to live on."

These four examples show us that some masters experienced genuine hardship and explain how slaves could, in certain circumstances, help to support their owners' families, serve with zeal and even affection, and earn enough money through outside work to support an entire household.

Stories like these lead us to raise three questions: How did slaves come by the money required for manumission? In what way were payments made? And finally, if manumission was not paid for in cash, what reasons did the masters give to explain why they were granting it?

Mainly the slaves who shared their daily earnings with their masters are the ones who managed to accumulate enough money to buy freedom. Yet no law ever guaranteed that slaves could freely dispose of what they carried. Strictly speaking, slaves possessed nothing of their own. It was up to the master to decide whether or not to allow the slave to hold on to part of his earnings. By verbal agreement it was settled between master and slave that the slave must pay the master a set sum of money every day or every week. What the slave earned beyond this sum then belonged to him. In other words, the master tacitly deemed the slave capable of owning property, which explains why slaves were allowed to possess not just money but even other slaves, and why some slaves went so far as to draw up wills even though they had no legal personality or right to own property. Customary practices were quite contradictory: it was recognized that slaves were entitled to inherit property and to receive gifts and that masters should not appropriate savings amassed by slaves out of allowances; for food, lodging, and clothes. Masters also usually respected money awarded to slaves as indemnity for injuries.

None of these rules had any real basis in law, but, tacitly accepted, they acquired a practical social value that helped the slave work his way out of slavery. It was then up to the slave to earn the necessary money, or obtain a loan, or receive a bequest or donation, or persuade his master to grant him his freedom for nothing, which came to the same thing, since free manumission was a form of gift. These practices, of benefit mainly to urban slaves, domestic slaves, and slaves working in the mines, worked against the vast majority of slaves: the field hands.

How long did it take for a slave who worked outside the master's home to amass the sum needed for manumission? The question is not easy to answer. Take two examples: workers in Salvador and Paraty, that is, in large cities of the northeast, and workers in a small town in southern Rio de Janeiro. In Paraty between 1791 and 1815, a slave's daily wage was 160 reis. In an as-yet-unpublished thesis, the American historian James Kiernan has calculated that it would have taken seven long years for a slave to earn the average sum required for manumission in this period (94,584 reis)—assuming that he did not spend a single real in all this time and that the master authorized him to keep all his earnings. If we consider not the average price of manumission but the average market price of slaves during this period, we find that it would have taken twelve and a half years to earn the 167,776 reis paid for the average slave on the Paraty market. Now, even when slaves purchased their freedom on the installment plan, the payments were never extended over such a long period. In Salvador the average daily wage of a male slave was 160 reis in 1805, compared with 130 reis for a female slave (the figures are for unskilled slaves working in construction, a trade in which work was halted during the winter and the rainy season). It was customary in Salvador for slaves to pay one-third of their earnings to their masters. Assume that the slave spent nothing of what was left to him. Since the average price of manumission was 100,000 reis for men and 80,000 reis for women, it would have taken four years of work for these slaves to purchase their freedom, and five to six years to save an amount equal to their price on the slave market.

It is hard to compare figures that are not really comparable. The criteria used for the Paraty calculations were not exactly the same as those used in the case of Salvador. One must be careful not to generalize on the basis of this type of example, which could easily lead to distortions. Yet the slave's savings must in general have stimulated productivity, and masters must have authorized and even encouraged slaves to save only when their work capacities began to diminish. We have virtually no information about the age of freed slaves. It is unlikely that slaves could begin to work immediately on their own behalf, especially in Salvador in the nineteenth century, where the number of newly arrived Africans was large. The new arrivals did not speak Portuguese, and it would have taken some time for them to learn a trade and win the confidence of their masters. After a period of time, however, a thrifty, hard-working slave could hope to earn enough at work to purchase freedom. Consider the case of one barber, a "black named Albano" (his master must not have known much Latin to have given him such a name), who was liberated in 1811 for the round sum of 250,000 reis, and whose manumission papers state that he was highly skilled at working with his hands. Or Ana Joaquina, adept at embroidery, originally from Guinea, to whom Francisco Amoroso de Castro sold her freedom for 180,000 reis in 1809. Precisely because these prices are high masters took great care to praise the merits and virtues of the freed slaves. Slaves with no particular skills with which to earn what they needed for manumission could be freed by a family member or godparent or even a friend or workmate. Some were not required to pay the full price of manumission, because their masters took pity on them and decided to help them along the hard road to freedom.

From a thousand examples, I have chosen a few slaves' stories to present. All are Bahian. Some are sordid, others moving, a few comical or surprising in what they reveal of the ins and outs of a practice whose details varied widely from case to case.

In 1855, Francisco Antonio Pereira da Rocha inherited the slave José Joaquim, itinerant fruit and vegetable merchant, whom he set free for just 25,000 reis "because of services rendered to his family for a very long time."

From Fabricio, a Nago, his master declared that he had received in 1857 "only" 400,000 reis and that he "forgave him the rest so that he could trade and earn his living, since he is old."

In 1879, the creole Eugenia, an excellent cook and laundress who worked in the home of her owner in Alagoinhas, a small town in the Bahian *agreste,* obtained her freedom for 1,000,000 reis, although she had been evaluated at 1,200,000 reis.

In 1825, Joaquim Valentin, a mulatto carpenter, had to pay 100,000 reis for his freedom, even though he had lost one arm on the job.

In most cases, if the master seemed willing to grant manumission to a slave who could not amass the required sum, the slave's father, mother, grandparents, sisters and brothers, husband, or godmother hastened to help out as much as they could. The opportunity could not be allowed to pass. It is easy to imagine how eagerly the master's words were scrutinized for the slightest sign that he was willing to free this or that slave on such and such terms. As in the African bush drums beat out the news, which spread as fast as the wind could carry it. In the cantos and confraternities and senzalas, and across the fields, the rumors spread, blood ties were revived, humble savings were pooled, and all sorts of allegiances were called upon for help.

In 1751, Jeronyma da Conceiçao, a widow, freed Marcelianno, a mulatto aged two or three, for the sum of 30,000 reis paid by his father, the adjutant Floriano Alvares Pereira, who must have been a free man.

In 1866, Maria Joaquina de Jesus, in exchange for the sum of 800,000 reis, granted freedom to her creole slave Tomasia, age twenty, and to her daughter Cassiana, age eleven months. The father of little Cassiana, a freed African by the name of Pompeu de Barros, had made a cash down payment of 400,000 reis to secure the two women's freedom. The rest was to be paid in twelve months with an interest of 2 percent on the guarantee of another freed African by the name of João Thomaz.

João, a slave born in Portugal, had his freedom purchased by his mother, who substituted for him an African slave from Mina. The master agreed to set him free "because he suffers from asthma and has crises at every quarter of the moon, which prevents him from serving well, and also because one of his eyes is cloudy."

In 1819, Sister Maria Clara de Jesus, professed nun of the convent of Santa-Clara-do-Desterro, freed a newborn creole for 20,000 reis, payed by his mother of the Gégé nation.

At age seventeen, the slave Emiliana had a daughter, Agostinha. She purchased the child's liberty for 100,000 reis but continued to work as a slave.

A grandmother might wish to liberate her infant grandchild and yet not wish, or be unable, to liberate the child's mother, still a slave. More grandmothers than grandfathers paid for the manumission of their grandchildren, but in one will, dating from 1766, we find the curious case of Felix de Andrade dos Reis, who made the following declaration:

Among the goods that I possess, there is a granddaughter, daughter of my son-in-law Ignacio de Souza, whom I bought for 70,000 reis from Jeronimo Ferreira, who had purchased her at the auction of the property of the fathers of the Company of Jesus and of their *fazenda* at Campinas. My granddaughter is named Clara de Jesus de Andrade Souza, she is mulatto, and I hereby set her free for the sum of 70,000 reis received from her father.

In other words, the child's father paid his father-in-law for the child's freedom; the grandfather set her free, but he did not do so free of charge.

Families tried whenever possible to gain the freedom of newborns prior to baptism. In 1866 a young creole named Alberto had his freedom purchased by his African grandmother Josefa, "so that he could be baptized a free man." His owner added this further declaration: "I did not have him baptized sooner, before the sum at which he had been evaluated was completed, so that he would not receive this sacrament as a slave."

Of 16,403 freedom charters examined in Bahia, none pertained to the purchase of a husband's freedom by his wife. A very few referred to the freeing of a wife by her husband. In 1806, Pedro Alexandrino de Souza Portugal, owner and master of the São Gonçalo sugar engenho, freed his creole slave Felipa "because of her marriage to Bartolomeu de Costa Pinto, a manumitted male mulatto, who will sacrifice his wages as overseer and bookkeeper of his engenho in order to pay the sum of 60,000 reis per year for two years."

Many charters were purchased by close relatives: a son paid for the freedom of Joana, a black woman from Angola, who was set free in 1839 after twenty years of faithful service, during which she raised her master's child. The 100,000 reis were earned during two voyages that Joana's son made from Pernambuco to Angola. The young creole Rosa was set free in 1855 when her elder sister paid her owner money she needed to pay taxes on her late husband's estate. In these official, registered, and notarized documents we witness a parade of relatives and friends coming forward to offer their assistance, sometimes in the most unexpected forms. Especially in the cities slaves found the community ready to support them in many ways. This support was so effective that it sometimes astonished masters, who indicated that the slave's freedom had been purchased by an "unknown" person. . . .

Historical Backgrounds
of the Negro Family

Andrew Billingsley

In their study of the major ethnic groups in New York, Glazer and Moynihan concluded their discussion of the Negro family with the observation that: "The Negro is only an American, and nothing else. He has no values and culture to guard and protect." This statement could not possibly be true. And yet, it represents the prevailing view among liberal intellectuals who study the Negro experience from the outside. Nat Hentoff, who holds a different view, has pointed out that not one of the critical reviewers of Glazer and Moynihan's book took them to task for this generalization. The implications of the Glazer-Moynihan view of the Negro experience are far-reaching. To say that a people have no culture is to say that they have no common history which has shaped them and taught them. And to deny the history of a people is to deny their humanity.

If, on the other hand, the Negro people constitute in some important respects an ethnic subsociety with a distinct history, what are the essential elements of this history? Three facts stand out above all others. The first is that the Negro people came to this country from Africa and not from Europe. The second is that they came in chains and were consequently uprooted from their cultural and family moorings. The third is that they have been subjected to systematic exclusion from participation and influence in the major institutions of this society even to the present time. Because of these factors, "the Jews, Irish, Italians, Poles or Scandinavians who see no difference between their former plight and that of Negroes today are either grossly uninformed or are enjoying an unforgivable false pride."

At the same time, it needs saying that the Negro experience has not been uniform. It has varied according to time, place, and other conditions. The consequences of these experiences have also been varied and complex. Furthermore, not all the history of the Negro people has been negative. There is much in the historical backgrounds of the Negro people which has helped them survive in the face of impossible conditions. This history has produced a most resilient arid adaptive people with a strong appreciation for the realities of existence, as reflected in the ability of Negroes to "tell it like it is," and to "get down to the nitty-gritty" in talking about their life circumstances, at least among their friends, if not always when among their enemies. (Perhaps the increasing ability of Negroes of all social classes to speak out to the wider society about their conditions and "tell it like it is" also

indicates a feeling, or at least a precarious hope, that we are indeed among friends.)

In this chapter, we will set forth some highlights of the historical backgrounds of the Negro people which have helped to shape both the structure and the functioning of Negro families. The family is at once the most sensitive, important, and enduring element in the culture of any people. Whatever its structure, its most important function is everywhere the same—namely, to insure the survival of its people.

Two aspects of Negro history will be considered, their African backgrounds and the impact of slavery. Each of these topics could and should be the subject of full-length books. We can only sketch some of the highlights to show their relevance for a more general understanding of Negro families, and a more comprehensive strategy for the reconstruction of Negro family and community life.

African Backgrounds

Negroes, under the tutelage of white Americans, have long viewed their African background with a sense of shame. To be called an African when I was growing up in Alabama was much worse than being called a "nigger." And, to be called a "black African" was a sign of extreme derision.

Later, when I was a student in a Negro college, we were more sophisticated, but we were no less ambivalent about our heritage. The two or three African students on campus were isolated. They were viewed and treated with great disdain, while the two or three white students were the objects of adulation. The African students represented the deep, dark past, while the Caucasians represented the great white hope of the future. In spite of vast changes which have occurred in the world since World War II, with respect to Africa and its place in the world, large numbers of Negroes still feel just a twinge of inferiority associated with their African heritage. How could it be otherwise, considering the sources of our knowledge about ourselves and our past? Yet the image is changing radically and rapidly. Negroes are taking seriously the questions posed by Lincoln Lynch, formerly of the Congress on Racial Equality: "It is a question of who are we, and where do we come from, and where are we going?"

A careful reading of history and ethnographic studies reveal a pattern of African backgrounds which are ancient, varied, complex, and highly civilized. The evidence suggests that far from being rescued from a primitive savagery by the slave system, Negroes were forcibly uprooted from a long history of strong family and community life every bit as viable as that of their captors. It was a very different type of society from the European-oriented society in the new world.

Several general features of African family life showed great viability. First, family life was not primarily—or even essentially—the affair of two people who happened to be married to each other. It united not simply two people, but two families with a network of extended kin who had considerable influence on the family, and considerable responsibility for its development and well-being. Marriage could neither be entered into nor abandoned without substantial community support. Secondly, marriage and family life in pre-European Africa, as among most tribal people, was enmeshed in centuries of tradition, ritual, custom, and law. "When the Arabs swept into North and West Africa in the Seventh Century," writes John Hope Franklin, "they found a civilization that was already thousands of years old." Thirdly, family life was highly articulated with the rest of the society. The family was an economic and a religious unit.

***

A preliterate people, the West Africans nevertheless had a highly complex civilization. Their patterns of family life were closely knit, well organized, highly articulated with kin and community, and highly functional for the economic, social, and psychological life of the people.

Thus the men and women who were taken as slaves to the New World came from societies every bit as civilized and "respectable" as those of the Old World settlers who mastered them. But the two were very different types of society, for the African family was much more closely integrated with the wider levels of kinship and society. The simple transition of millions of persons from Africa to America would in itself have been a major disruption in the lives of the people, even if it had proceeded on a voluntary and humane basis. As we shall see presently, however, this transition was far from simple, voluntary and humane.

The Impact of Slavery on Negro Family Life

The Negro family in the United States began with Anthony and Isabella, who were among the original twenty Negroes landed at Jamestown in 1619, one year before the Mayflower. Later Anthony and Isabella were married, and in 1624 their son William became "the first Negro child born in English America." These first Negroes were treated essentially as indentured servants. However, after 1690 the bulk of Negroes were brought into the country and sold as slaves.

We have shown that the Negroes brought to the United States were descendants of an ancient and honorable tradition of African family life. While scholars are still in considerable dispute about the relative influence of this heritage on Negro family life today, particularly in the United States, there is no doubt that the breaking up of that tradition by the slave trade has had a major impact on both the form and substance of the Negro family. African slavery, stretching over a period of four centuries and involving the capture of more than 40 million Africans, was, for the European countries, a colossal economic enterprise with effects not unlike those of the discovery of gold. But for the African Negroes, it was a colossal social and psychological disruption.

The transportation of slaves from Africa to the New World completely disrupted the cultural life of the Africans and the historical development of the Negro people. This total discontinuity had a particular impact on the Negro family, because the family is the primary unit of social organization. Some of the ways in which this culture was disrupted may be briefly stated.

First, moving as they did from Africa to the New World, the Negroes were confronted with an alien culture of European genesis. Thus, unlike some of the later migrants, including the Germans, Irish, and Italians, they were not moving into a society in which the historical norms and values and ways of life were familiar and acceptable. Secondly, they came from many different tribes with different languages, cultures, and traditions. Thirdly, they came without their families and often without females at all. In the fourth place, they came in chains. These are all major distinctions between the Negro people and all the other immigrants to this country. Therefore, whatever the nature of the two cultural systems from which they came and to which they arrived, and whatever their capacity for adaptation, they were not free to engage in the ordinary process of acculturation. They were not only cut off from their previous culture, but they were not permitted to develop and assimilate to the new culture in ways that were unfettered and similar to the opportunities available to other immigrant groups.

The Negro slaves in the United States were converted from free, independent human beings they had been in Africa, to property. They became chattel. This process of dehumanization started at the beginning of the slave-gathering process and was intensified with each stage along the way. It should not be difficult to discern that people who, having been told for 200 years—in ways more effective than words—that they are subhuman, should begin to believe this themselves and internalize these values and pass them on to their children and their children's children. Nor is it difficult to imagine how the history and current status of the Negro people might be different if, for all these 200 years, our ancestors had been paid a decent wage for their labor, taught how to invest it, and provided all the supports, privileges, and responsibilities which the New World offered its immigrants of Caucasian ancestry. Conversely, the process of Negro dehumanization provided superior opportunities, privileges, and status to the white majority at the expense of the black minority, and deeply ingrained within white people a crippling sense of superiority.

These are the dynamics of the slave system which must have been in the mind of President Lyndon Johnson when he spoke so eloquently of the need of our society to "heal our history." But the dehumanizing experience of slavery did not come all at once; it came in stages.

Minimum protections of the family were built into the slavery system in the United States, where slaves were often permitted to marry, but only at the discretion of the master. In the United States, the slave husband was not the head of his household; the white owner was the head. The family had no rights that the slave owner was bound to respect. The wholesale disregard for family integrity among the slaves may be suggested by the following quotation from an actual advertisement in a New Orleans newspaper: "A Negro woman, 24 years of age, and her two children, one eight and the other three years old. Said Negroes will be sold separately or together as desired." Another, in South Carolina in 1838, offered 120 slaves for sale of both sexes and every description, including "several women with children, small girls suitable for nurses, and several small boys without their mothers."

The official records of shipping companies also reflected this family disruption. "Of four cargoes, making a total of 646 slaves, 396 were apparently owned by Franklen and Armfield. Among these there were only two full families. . . . There were 20 husbandless mothers with 33 children."

Perhaps the cruelest of all the forms of emasculation of the Negro family was the very widespread practice, perhaps in all the slave states, of breeding slaves for sale as if they were cattle. An enterprising slave master, then, could enjoy not only the emotional advantages accrued from sex relations with his female slaves, but also the economic advantage which accrued from selling his offspring in the open market. Such decadence was much too common to have been confined to a few undesirable or emotionally disturbed white citizens. It was widespread and normative, though of course not all planters engaged in such practices. More common, perhaps, was the practice of breeding slaves among each other. One advertisement of a shipment of slaves claimed that

they are not Negroes selected out of a larger gang for the purpose of a sale, but are prime. Their present owner, with great trouble and expense, selected them out of many for several years past. They were purchased for stock and breeding Negroes and to any planter who particularly wants them for that purpose, they are a very choice and desirable gang.

In the United States, then, contrary to Latin America, the legal system made no provision for, and took no special recognition of, marriage and family life among the Negro slaves. In addition, the slave owners and other whites took frequent sexual advantage of the slave women. Even if she were the wife of a slave, her husband could not protect her. The Attorney General of Maryland observed in one of his reports that "a slave never has maintained an action against the violator of his bed." This statement apparently would apply in other states as well, regardless of whether the violator was slave or citizen. The powerlessness of the Negro man to protect his family for two and a half centuries under slavery has had crippling consequences for the relations of Negro men and women to this very day.

Slavery and Family Life in the United States

Marriage among slaves was not altogether absent in the United States, and was probably more common than has been generally recognized. It was, however, a far different institution with much less structural and institutional support in this country than in Latin America. The strong hand of the slave owner dominated the Negro family, which existed only at his mercy and often at his own personal instigation. An ex-slave has told of getting married on one plantation:

When you married, you had to jump over a broom three times. Dat was de license. If master seen two slaves together too much he would tell 'em dey was married. Hit didn't make no difference if you wanted to or not; he would put you in de same cabin an' make you live together. . . . Marsa used to sometimes pick our wives fo' us. If he didn't have on his place enough women for the men, he would wait on de side of de road till a big wagon loaded with slaves come by. Den Marsa would stop de ole nigger-trader and buy you a woman. Wasn't no use tryin' to pick one, cause Marsa wasn't gonna pay but so much for her. All he wanted was a young healthy one who looked like she could have children, whether she was purty or ugly as sin.

The difficulties Negro men had in establishing, protecting, and maintaining family ties, together with the strong values they placed on family life and responsibilities, are graphically depicted in the correspondence between ex-slaves and their ex-masters. It often happened that the slaves who escaped into freedom by the underground railroad were those who had been treated relatively well by their owners, and who even had been taught to read and write. Often they were the "favorite" slaves of the owners, highly trusted and considered dependable and grateful. Thus, it was not uncommon that when a slave holder found out the whereabouts of an ex-slave, he would write to him, imploring him to return. Three letters by ex-slaves written in response to such appeals will illustrate the damaging consequences slavery had for Negro family life. The first was written by Henry Bibb in 1844, after he had escaped into Canada by way of the underground railroad.

Dear Sir:—I am happy to inform you that you are not mistaken in the man whom you sold as property, and received pay for as such. But I thank God that I am not property now, but am regarded as a man like yourself, and although I live far north, I am enjoying a comfortable living by my own industry. If you should ever chance to be traveling this way, and will call on me, I will use you better than you did me while you held me as a slave. Think not that I have any malice against you, for the cruel treatment which you inflicted on me while I was in your power. As it was the custom of your country, to treat your fellow men as you did me and my little family, I can freely forgive you.

I wish to be remembered in love to my aged mother, and friends; please tell her that if we should never meet again in this life, my prayer shall be to God that we may meet in Heaven, where parting shall be no more.

You wish to be remembered to King and Jack. I am pleased, sir, to inform you that they are both here, well, and doing well. They are both living in Canada West. They are now the owners of better farms than the men are who once owned them.

You may perhaps think hard of us for running away from slavery, but as to myself, I have but one apology to make for it, which is this: I have only to regret that I did not start at an earlier period. I might have been free long before I was. But you had it in your power to have kept me there much longer than you did. I think it is very probably that I should have been a toiling slave on your property today, if you had treated me differently.

To be compelled to stand by and see you whip and slash my wife without mercy, when I could afford her no protection, not even by offering myself to suffer the lash in her place,

was more than I felt it to be the duty of a slave husband to endure, while the way was open to Canada. My infant child was also frequently flogged by Mrs. Gatewood, for crying, until its skin was bruised literally purple. This kind of treatment was what drove me from home and family, to seek a better home for them. But I am willing to forget the past. I should be pleased to hear from you again, on the reception of this, and should also be very happy to correspond with you often, if it should be agreeable to yourself. I subscribe myself a friend to the oppressed, and Liberty forever.

Another letter was written in 1860 by J. W. Loguen who escaped to New England:

Mrs. Sarah Logue: Yours of the 20th of February is duly received, and I thank you for it. It is a long time since I heard from my poor old mother, and I am glad to know that she is yet alive, and, as you say, "as well as common." What that means, I don't know. I wish you had said more about her.

You are a woman; but had you a woman's heart, you never could have insulted a brother by telling him you sold his only remaining brother and sister, because he put himself beyond your power to convert him into money.

You sold my brother and sister, Abe and Ann, and twelve acres of land, you say, because I ran away. Now you have the unutterable meanness to ask me to return and be your miserable chattel, or, in lieu thereof, send you $1000 to enable you to redeem the land, but not to redeem my poor brother and sister! If I were to send you the money, it would be to get my brother and sister, and not that you should get land. You say you are a cripple, and doubtless you say it to stir my pity, for you knew I was susceptible in that direction. I do pity you from the bottom of my heart. Nevertheless, I am indignant beyond the power of words to express, that you should be so sunken and cruel as to tear the hearts I love so much all to pieces; that you should be willing to impale and crucify us all, out of compassion for your foot or leg. Wretched woman! Be it known to you that I value my freedom, to say nothing of my mother, brothers and sisters, more than your whole body; more, indeed, than my own life; more than all the lives of all the slave-holders and tyrants under heaven.

You say you have offers to buy me, and that you shall sell me if I do not send you $1000, and in the same breath and almost in the same sentence, you say, "You know we raised you as we did our own children." Woman, did you raise your own children for the market? . . .

. . . But you say I am a thief, because I took the old mare along with me. Have you got to learn that I had better right to the old mare, as you call her, than Manasseth Logue had to me? Is it a greater sin for me to steal his horse, than it was for him to rob my mother's cradle, and steal me? If he and you infer that I forfeit all my rights to you, shall not I infer that you forfeit all your rights to me? Have you got to learn that human rights are mutual and reciprocal, and if you take my liberty and life, you forfeit your own liberty and life? Before God and high heaven, is there a law for one man which is not a law for every other man?

If you or any other speculator on my body and rights, wish to know how I regard my rights, they need but come here, and lay their hands on me to enslave me. Did you think to terrify me by presenting the alternative to give my money to you, or give my body to slavery? Then let me say to you, that I meet the proposition with unutterable scorn and contempt. The proposition is an outrage and an insult. I will not budge one hair's breadth. I will not breathe a shorter breath, even to save me from your persecutions. I stand among a free people, who, I thank God, sympathize with my rights, and the rights of mankind; and if your emissaries and venders come here to re-enslave me, and escape the unshrinking vigor of my own right arm, I trust my strong and brave friends, in this city and State, will be my rescuers and avengers.

A third letter is from Jourdon Anderson, who was freed by the Union Army Forces during the Civil War.

Sir: I got your letter, and was glad to find that you had not forgotten Jourdon, and that you wanted me to come back and live with you again, promising to do better for me than anybody else can. . . .

. . . I want to know particularly what the good chance is you propose to give me. I am doing tolerably well here. I get twenty-five dollars a month, with victuals and clothing; have a comfortable home for Mandy,—the folks call her Mrs. Anderson—and the children—Milly, Jane, and Grundy—go to school and are learning well. The teacher says Grundy has a head for a preacher. They go to Sunday School, and Mandy and me attend church regularly. We are kindly treated. Sometimes we overhear others saying, "Them colored people were slaves" down in Tennessee. The children feel hurt when they hear such remarks; but I tell them it was no disgrace in

Tennessee to belong to Colonel Anderson. Many darkeys would have been proud, as I used to be, to call you master. Now if you will write and say what wages you will give me, I will be better able to decide whether it would be to my advantage to move back again.

. . . Mandy says she would be afraid to go back without some proof that you were disposed to treat us justly and kindly; and we have concluded to test your sincerity by asking you to send us our wages for the time we served you. This will make us forget and forgive old scores, and rely on your justice and friendship in the future. I served you faithfully for thirty-two years, and Mandy twenty years. At twenty-five dollars a month for me, and two dollars a week for Mandy, our earnings would amount to eleven thousand six hundred and eighty dollars. Add to this the interest for the time our wages have been kept back, and deduct what you paid for our clothing, and three doctor's visits to me, and pulling a tooth for Mandy, and the balance will show what we are in justice entitled to.

. . . In answering this letter, please state if there would be any safety for my Milly and Jane, who are now grown up, and both goodlooking girls. You know how it was with poor Matilda and Catherine. I would rather stay here and starve—and die, if it come to that—than have my girls brought to shame by the violence and wickedness of their young masters. You will also please state if there has been any schools opened for the colored children in your neighborhood. The great desire of my life is to give my children an education, and have them form virtuous habits.

Say howdy to George Carter, and thank him for taking the pistol from you when you were shooting at me.

The Negro family existed during slavery in the United States, but it was a most precarious existence, dependent wholly on the economic and personal interests of the white man, and the grim determination and bravery of the black man.

Interracial Marriage

A fourth respect in which the slave system in the United States differed markedly from that in Latin America relative to family life was in the area of interracial marriage. Marriage between white persons and black persons, particularly between European men and African women, was common, sanctioned, and encouraged in Latin America even under slavery. It was forbidden by law in the United States, not only during slavery, but in modern times as well. Not until 1967 were the last legal supports for such bans were struck down by the U. S. Supreme Court. Even now, however, despite the lack of legal support for such bans on interracial marriage, the customs and norms of the white majority in the country, and to some extent the black minority, make interracial marriage a rare and deviant sort of behavior.

Marriage among peoples of different cultural backgrounds is considered, by many students of assimilation, to be the ultimate test of the process of integration, as well as of whether a caste system exists, separating two peoples into superior and inferior beings. In these respects, then, the question of interracial marriage is more than a matter of personal choice; it is an index of the view and place of different peoples in the national life.

It is not, of course, that miscegenation and other forms of interracial contact have been absent in the United States. In fact, they have been persistent. But they have been more or less illicit, unsanctioned by the wider society. Consequently, the white men who have been the chief exploiters of Negro women in such relationships have escaped the responsibilities associated with these relationships. The manner in which Negro women were exploited by white men during slavery, and the damage these relationships caused to the stability of Negro family life can be seen from two personal accounts provided us by two remarkable Negro women writers, Pauli Murray and Margaret Walker. Both accounts are taken from actual family histories.

Pauli Murray tells of her own great-grandmother, Harriet, who was born a slave in 1819. She was the product of miscegenation and described as mulatto. When she was fifteen, she was sold to a medical doctor in North Carolina who bought her as a housemaid for his own eighteen-year-old daughter. These two women, the slave and the mistress, grew into the most intricate of relationships filled with all the human drama of love, envy, and hate imaginable.

When Harriet was twenty years old, she asked her owner for permission to marry a young mulatto man who was born free, and who lived and worked in the town. It is said that Dr. Smith, her owner, readily agreed. "It was good business. He had no obligation to the husband, and every child by the marriage would be his slave and worth several hundred dollars at birth." Harriet and her husband were not permitted to live together permanently, but he was permitted to visit her in the evenings after she had finished her work in the "big house." After three years, in about 1842, they had a child. Of course, this son became a slave like his mother, and was the property of Dr. Smith.

Sometime after this, Dr. Smith's two grown sons came from college, and both took a special interest in Harriet. "Before long," Miss Murray tells us, "everybody in the house knew that a storm was brewing between the brothers, and that Harriet was the cause of it." The author then describes an encounter between Sydney, one of the Smith sons, and Reuben, Harriet's free Negro husband.

Sydney Smith informed Reuben that he could not be legally married to a slave, and that if he were ever caught visiting Harriet again he would be whipped and thrown in jail. The author continues: "Reuben had to leave without a word to Harriet. That was the last she ever saw of him." It is not, however, that Reuben abandoned his wife, his child, and his rights so easily; he came back to see them one time, but the two Smith brothers saw him.

> The brothers beat Reuben with the butt end of a carriage whip and when they finally let him go, they told him if he ever came back on the Smith lot, they'd shoot him on sight. He disappeared from the county and nothing was heard of him again.

Shortly after Reuben was banished from his wife's cabin, Sydney Smith "had his way with her" in the presence of her little boy.

> He raped her again, again, and again in the weeks that followed. Night after night he would force open her cabin door and nail it up again on the inside so that she could not get out. Then he would beat her into submission.

Sydney's brother Frank was furious at the turn of events. One night he accosted Sydney on his way from Harriet's cabin.

> The brothers had it out once and for all, and there was a terrible fight. Early the next morning, one of the slaves found Sydney lying unconscious in the yard, his clothes soaked with blood and an ugly hole in his head.... He learned his lesson. He never touched Harriet again.

But already Harriet was pregnant with Sydney's child. This child, born on the Smith lot in February 1844, was Pauli Murray's grandmother.

After the baby was born, Sydney's brother Frank "had his way" with Harriet. This time she did not fight back.

This relationship was long and enduring. Over the course of five years, Harriet bore to Francis Smith three daughters. Harriet was now the mother of five children by three different fathers, all growing up on the same plantation but treated according to their father's positions. Julius, the oldest, was almost ignored by the Big House, and his mother was almost a stranger to him. When he was around thirteen, he got lost in the woods during a heavy snowstorm. They found him almost frozen to death. He was severely crippled for the rest of his life.

The girls lived lives of crippling ambivalence.

The Smiths were as incapable of treating the little girls wholly as servants as they were of recognizing them openly as kin. At times the Smith's involuntary gestures of kinship were so pronounced, the children could not help thinking themselves as Smith grandchildren. At other times, their innocent overtures of affection were rebuffed without explanation and they were driven away with cruel epithets.

In *Jubilee* Margaret Walker tells a similar story of her own grandmother Vyry, and her great-grandmother Hetta. Several generations before the Civil War, Hetta, a slave girl, had borne fifteen children by the time she was twenty-nine. She died in childbirth with the sixteenth. Many of them, including Vyry, were by the son of her owner. Vyry is the center of a most fascinating account of that pre–Civil War period in the life of the slaves, freedmen, and masters. Randall Ware, a young freedman, who loved, courted, married, and lost her, is a most remarkable example of black manhood, who, despite the efforts of the system to crush him, managed to survive. There was a man, if only for one brief season! He insisted on exercising his freedom in the plantation South, which conspired to make slaves of all black people. He almost rescued his wife and family from slavery. He escaped to the North by way of the underground railroad and returned to fight in the Civil War. This is not, however, a story of essential triumph. It is a vivid illustration of the tragedy of slavery and the crippling consequences it had for Negro family life.

In summary, it may be said that the slave system had a crippling effect on the establishment, maintenance, and growth of normal patterns of family life among the Negro people. This impact was cruel in all the Americas. It was exceedingly vicious in the United States. There were several facets of this process of personal, family, and social emasculation. First, the family was broken up at the very beginning of the slave trade in the manner in which the slaves were gathered, the disregard the captors showed to family and kinship ties, the preference they showed for selecting young men in the prime of their life, and the consequent underrepresentation of females for hundreds of years, and the inhumane conditions under which the slaves were quartered, worked, and treated.

All these conditions were found everywhere in the slave system, although some evidence suggests that the living conditions were worse in the United States. The particular factors which characterize the impact of slavery on the Negro family in the United States include, in addition to the above, the absence of legal foundation, sanction, and protection of marriage as an institution among the slaves, the exploitation of slave women by white owners and overseers for both pleasure and profit; the systematic denial of a role for the man as husband and father; the willful separation of related men, women, and children and selling them to different plantations. In short, there was the absence, in the United States, of societal support and protection for the Negro family as a physical, psychological, social, or economic unit. This crippled the development, not only of individual slaves, but of families, and hence of the whole society of Negro people. The consequences these conditions wrought for generations of Negroes under the slave system were direct and insidious. The consequences for succeeding and even modern generations of Negroes are, perhaps, less direct, but no less insidious. At no time in the history of this country have Negroes experienced, systematically and generally, the kind of social supports from the society which would even approach the intensity of the negative impact of slavery. Not only has the society not made any massive efforts to undo the damages of slavery and actively integrate the Negro people into the society on the basis of equality, but many of the explicit conditions of slavery still exist at the present time.

The Failures of Reconstruction After the Civil War

It is often said that slavery was a long time ago; that surely the freedom and opportunity granted to the Negro people by emancipation has been sufficient to overcome the ravages of slavery; and that, surely, contemporary white people and institutions bear no responsibility for slavery and reap no benefit from this dark chapter in human history.

But the historical facts are otherwise. The Negro people have never been indemnified, either economically, or politically, or socially, or psychologically for two centuries of bondage. And furthermore, the wider society has not reconstructed itself to any substantial degree in any of these areas of life.

The end of slavery with the Civil War in the United States brought a certain freedom to the slave and the free Negro alike, but it was also a crisis of major proportions. For tens of thousands of Negroes, emancipation meant the freedom to die of starvation and illness. In some communities, one out of every four Negroes died. The destitution and disease among the Negroes, who were now uncared for and had no facilities to care for themselves, was so great that the editor of a famous newspaper observed with considerable glee that "The child is already born who will behold the last Negro in the State of Mississ-ippi." And Mississippi had more Negro slaves than any other state. Nor were such dire straits and predictions confined to one state. The eminent southern scholar, Dr. C. K. Marchall, expressed a similar and more general hypothesis: "In all probability New Year's Day on the morning of the 1st of January, 1920, the colored population in the South will scarcely be counted.".

The survival of the Negro people after such a holocaust can be attributed primarily to the resiliency of the human spirit. It most certainly cannot be attributed in large measure to the efforts of his society to help him survive. For the ingredient most absent to make freedom meaningful was the ingredient which has been most useful to other depressed people, namely opportunity.

There were no national, regional, or other large-scale plans for dealing with the ex-slaves. How could they be integrated into the life of the embattered republic as free men? Uncertainty abounded. There were enlightened voices who put forward suggestions. The most rational package suggested that the nation should give each ex-slave forty acres of land, a mule, the ballot, and leave him alone. Charles Sumner of Massachusetts plugged hard for the ballot, Thaddeus Stevens of Pennsylvania plugged even harder for the forty acres. And several generations before justice Louis D. Brandeis was to expound his famous doctrine of the freedom to be let alone, Frederick Douglass, the ex-slave, echoed the same sentiment.

> The Negro should have been let alone in Africa. . . . If you see him plowing in the open field, leveling the forest, and work with a spade, a rake, a hoe, a pick-axe, or a bill, let him alone; . . . If he has a ballot in his hand, let him alone..

But the nation's response was to be much more limited and temporary. The Freedman's Bureau, probably the first national social welfare administration, during six short years with severely limited funds, administrative imagination and courage, and in the face of apathy in the North and hostility in the South, strove to feed and clothe ex-slaves and poor whites, and to establish hospitals and schools. It did a commendable job under the circumstances, but much too little and over too short a time. President Andrew Johnson's heart was not in the efforts of the Freedman's Bureau, and despite certain efforts of Congress he crushed this program.

John Hope Franklin has summed up the period of reconstruction as follows:

> Counter reconstruction was everywhere an overwhelming success. In the face of violence the 14th and 15th Amendments provided no protection for the Negro citizen and his friends. The federal enforcement laws of 1870 and 1871 proved wholly inadequate, especially when enforcement was left to the meager forces that remained in the South at the time of their enactment. Negroes could hardly be expected to continue to vote when it cost them not only their jobs but their lives. In one state after another, the Negro electorate declined steadily as the full force of the Klan came forward to supervise the elections that

federal troops failed to supervise. . . . The federal government was, more and more, leaving the South to its own devices. Even more important was the enormous prestige that the former Confederates enjoyed. In time they were able to assume leadership in their communities without firing a shot or hanging a single Negro. What they lacked in political strength they made up in economic power. By discharging or threatening to discharge Negro employees who persisted in participating in politics, they could reduce the Negro electorate to a minimum. By refusing to pay taxes to support the expanded and inflated functions of the new governments, they could destroy Radical Reconstruction in a season. But the former Confederates relied on no one method. By political pressure, economic sanctions, *and* violence they brought Radical Reconstruction crashing down almost before it began..

Of course, Emancipation had some advantages for the Negro family. Although family members could be whipped, run out of town, or murdered, they could not be sold away from their families. Marriages were legalized and recorded. The hard work of farming, even sharecropping, required all possible hands—husband, wife, and children.

Emancipation, then, was a catastrophic social crisis for the ex-slave, and Reconstruction was a colossal failure. At the same time, there were some "screens of opportunity" which did enable large numbers of families to survive, some to achieve amazingly stable and viable forms of family life, and a few to achieve a high degree of social distinction.

---

[1]Nathan Glazer and Daniel P. Moynihan, *Beyond the Melting Pot* (Cambridge, Mass.: The M.I.T. Press and The Harvard University Press, 1963), p. 51.

[2]Nat Hentoff, "The Other Side of the Blues," in *Anger and Beyond: The Negro Writer in the United States*, ed. Herbert Hill (New York: Harper & Row, Publishers, 1966), p. 76.

[3]Harold L. Sheppard and Herbert E. Striver, *Civil Rights, Employment, and the Social Status of American Negroes* (Kalamazoo, Mich.: The W. E. Upjohn Institute for Employment Research, June, 1966), p. 47.

[4]John Hope Franklin, *From Slavery to Freedom* (New York: Alfred A. Knopf, Inc., 1956), p. 11.

[5]Lerone Bennett, Jr. *Before the Mayflower: A History of the Negro in America* (Chicago: Johnson Publishing Co. 1964), p. 30.

[6]Frank Tannenbaum, *Slave and Citizen: The Negro in the Americas* (New York: Random House, Inc., 1946), p 77.

[7]*Ibid.*, pp. 77–78.

[8]*Ibid.*, p. 78.

[9]*Ibid.*, pp. 80.

[10]*Ibid.*, pp. 76–77.

[11]Milton Meltzer, ed., *In Their Own Words: A History of the American Negro 1619–1865,* copyright © 1964 by Milton Meltzer (New York: Thomas Y. Crowell Company, 1954; Apollo Edition, 1967), pp. 46–47.

[12]*Ibid.,* pp. 100–101.

[13]*Ibid.,* pp. 120–22.

[14]*Ibid.,* pp. 170–72.

[15]Pauli Murray, *Proud Shoes: The Story of an American Family* (New York: Harper & Row, Publishers, 1956), quotes from pp. 38–48

[16]Margaret Walker, *Jubilee* (Boston: Houghton Mifflin Company, 1968).

[17]Bennett, p. 188.

[18]*Ibid.,* pp. 188.

[19]*Ibid.,* pp. 186–87.

[20]John Hope Franklin, *Reconstruction After the Civil War* (Chicago: University of Chicago Press, 1961), pp. 172–73.

Slavery in Nineteenth-Century Peru

Peter Blanchard

In the first years following independence, Peru's slaves found themselves in as confusing a situation as that confronting the nation as a whole. The liberators' antislavery legislation followed by the slaveholders' countermeasures left a great deal of uncertainty as to whether slavery was going to die a quick death or whether its demise was to be a long, drawn-out affair. Subsequent initiatives on both sides did not resolve the issue. A similar sense of confusion about Peruvian slavery emerges from the historical record. From contemporary observers one gets the impression that it was little more than a system of domestic servitude. The same conclusion might be reached based on an examination of the legal protections enjoyed by the slaves, the opportunities they had for ameliorating their condition and securing their freedom, and the nature of their everyday existence, which seemed to differ little from that of other sectors of society. This evaluation, however, ignores the realities experienced by the majority of Peru's slaves. While they may have had advantages not shared by slaves in neighboring countries, they were still property and still subject to the whims of their owners. They had very little control over their lives, uncertainty pervaded their existence, abuse and exploitation were their everyday companions, and the freedom promised by the liberators remained an unfulfilled dream.

The impression that Peruvian slavery was a more humane system than that found elsewhere in the hemisphere was largely the creation of contemporary observers. British travelers such as Archibald Smith, Robert Proctor, and Clements Markham have left a picture of a happy people and a light work load. Proctor noted how domestic slaves amused themselves when the family was absent, dancing, singing, and playing blindman's buff. He concluded that "the slaves certainly lead a very happy life in Lima. There are generally a great many of them in every house, with little else to do than for one sex to loll on the back of their mistresses' chairs during meals, and the other to do needlework." Smith noted that rural slaves could work as they wished and earn wages like free laborers once their assigned tasks were done. Markham wrote that slaves in the Cañete Valley "appear a happy and contented race, and though their labour is forced, they receive clothing, food, and lodging, and escape the capitation tax of the oppressed Indians of the Sierra." The Swiss scientist J. J. Von Tschudi came to the same conclusion. He wrote that "the treatment of slaves in Lima, especially by the Creoles, is exceedingly mild, and generally much on the same footing as the treatment of servants in Europe," adding that the treatment was so good that blacks preferred to remain enslaved because of the food, clothing, and lodging the owners provided.[1] Another British observer made the same points:

The slave is, generally speaking, both well fed and well treated—his labour is not excessive: he generally receives a small allowance in money: and has the means of accumulating the sum necessary for purchasing his freedom, but seldom avails himself of this privilege, at least not openly, because by becoming legally free he becomes exposed to the levies for the army: he, more frequently pays his own price to the Master, leaving his name on the Register of Slaves, and no instance is known of this confidence having been abused.[2]

Descriptions such as these can be dismissed as the inaccurate observations of individuals who had limited knowledge or preconceived notions of slavery in general, had only superficial contact with Peru's slaves, and were unwilling to criticize the people who had been their hosts. But there may have been a grain of truth in what they wrote: Peruvian slavery may have been less harsh than that elsewhere in the hemisphere. If so, this was the result of years, perhaps centuries, of resistance and accommodation by the slaves, producing what had become "Peruvian slavery." Such a development was common to slavery systems. Although the slaves were property and subject to their owners' wishes, they had some latitude of action which permitted them an opportunity to establish their own lives. In the words of James C. Scott, slaves retained "considerable autonomy to construct a life and a culture not entirely controlled by the dominant class." Eugene Genovese has shown that this was certainly true of the United States.[3] In the case of Peru, the result may have been the "humane" system described by foreign travelers, and it might explain, in part, why it differed in many ways from what might be termed "classical slavery."[4]

The impression of a benevolent system can be derived as well from an examination of the nation's legal system and the various laws that seemed to favor the slaves. Legislation introduced in the first months after independence appeared to indicate that Peru and Peruvians were committed to an early end to the institution and that slaves could easily change their legal status. Today's slave would be tomorrow's freedman. Other laws seemed to protect the slaves. Bolívar's 1825 regulation of coastal haciendas limited their workday to ten hours, so that, although starting hours might vary according to the season, work had to end at 6 P.M. In addition, owners had to supply daily rations of one pound of flour and one pound of beans, as well as an annual clothing allowance of two pairs of shorts, two shirts, and a poncho for men, and two shirts, two fustians, two petticoats, and a mantilla for women, with a blanket and two sheepskins for both.[5] Attempts were made to see that the directive was implemented. In 1827 the provincial intendant instructed the administrator of the state-owned estate of San Javier de la Nazca to begin the work day at 5 A.M. in the summer and 6 A.M. in the winter, and he detailed what was to be the clothing allowance, the weekly ration of meat (from two to four pounds depending on the difficulty of the work), and the allocation of seed corn (to be distributed during the harvest season according to the work done). Children and elderly slaves were to care for the infants of working mothers, pregnant women were not to do any shoveling but could be used in easier jobs, and postpartum mothers were to receive chicken for the first two days after delivery and mutton for the next six. The instructions permitted whipping, but only for the most severe crimes and no more than twelve lashes. Finally, although the workday began early, not all of it was devoted to estate labor: the instructions specified that on the completion of their tasks the slaves were permitted to till their own land and to tend to their animals. Any savings could be applied toward their purchase price, which the slaves knew because they had to be evaluated regularly.[6]

Cognizant of their rights, slaves were not afraid to take their owners to court to defend them, although this may have been more common in the early years of the republic when San Martín's liberal legislation was still fresh, the concept of freedom was a cherished principle, and liberation was an apparently tangible goal. One petitioner, Isabel Verano, was a twenty-two-year-old slave owned by the mayor of Huaura. In 1825 she demanded a new owner because the mayor had been mistreating her, even though she had been born, educated, and married in his house. She pointed out to the court, "We are now constituted in republics with everyone enjoying freedom, and it is not right for you to deny the miserable slave the only freedom [to change owners] the law permits him." She was obviously not intimidated by either her owner or the court, as she threatened to appeal directly to the government if the court refused to act.[7]

The decisions of the courts were another indication that the system was not rigidly set against the slaves. Courts heard cases involving slaves who had been mistreated by being punished unjustly, forced to work excessively, and denied adequate food and clothing. They could decide in favor of the slaves by reducing their value, compelling their sale, or freeing them.[8] Although in most instances they may have been concerned about protecting property rights and so decided against the slaves, they did not differentiate between slave and free in criminal cases, nor did they forego their customarily thorough investigation just because the complainant was a slave. When José Miranda (or Mejía) demanded his freedom through the courts, numerous witnesses were called for both sides. José claimed, first, he should be freed because his former owner had freed him in her will, even though she had sold him before the will was executed. Second, he should be freed because his sales contract had been violated: It stipulated that he could not be sold for more than 140 pesos, yet he had been sold for 206. Witnesses explained that the larger amount was because José was a thief and one of his owners, Gregorio Basallo, had sold him for 140 pesos plus 66 pesos, the value of the goods he had stolen. To arguments that his labor, not his person, had been sold, José replied that if his labor had been for sale, he should have received the wages. Calculating a rate of 8 pesos per month for the more than three years he had worked, he reckoned he had made enough to obtain his freedom. He was accused by some witnesses of having fled from his present owner, stolen a horse, and lured another slave to flee with him, while others claimed that Basallo had threatened to kill him. Eventually a document was found supporting José's original claim. He derived no benefit from it, however, for the court discovered that his old owner was still alive, which meant that her will could not be executed and José, despite his imaginative defense, was still a slave.[9]

The courts also played a role in weakening and even reversing some of the laws that negatively affected the slaves, especially the 1839 decree extending the period of patronal control over *libertos*. Questions were raised concerning the applicability of the law and even its validity. Did the law apply to all *libertos*, or only to those born after the decree? Lawyers argued that in the case of the former interpretation, the decree was being applied retroactively and was thus unconstitutional. In 1846 a court agreed, finding that a *liberta* who had been born in 1823 had been held illegally by her master after she reached the age of twenty-one, and ordered her freed. Other courts concurred, freeing more *libertos* and perhaps giving hope to those born after 1839 that further loopholes might be found to invalidate the law completely.[10]

Freedom was the principal goal of Peru's slaves, despite the contrary belief of foreign observers, and various ways existed for them to become free, providing further evidence of a humane system and a society that was not unalterably committed to the preservation of slavery. Peruvians were willing to free their slaves in repayment for years of faithful service. Manumission might come unexpectedly in a will or be offered as an inducement, as in the case of María Trinidad, an Arequipa slave who after nine months' service was promised her freedom on her owner's death if she continued to serve him with the loyalty she had shown thus far.[11] Many infants were freed on being baptised, perhaps in recognition of the mother's past service.[12] Some of these gestures may have been hollow. María Trinidad's owner may have been in his prime, while the babies may have been sickly and expected to die. Nevertheless, slaves were being freed—and in increasing numbers after 1840—while others were being offered freedom in the not-too-distant future.[13] An Arequipa slave was bought with the condition that she would be a slave for only four more years, until she became twenty-five. A newspaper advertisement in 1840 appealed for a female slave to work outside Lima, offering freedom in return for two years' service. Another offered a woman and her infant daughter for sale, but with the conditions that the woman was to be used as a wet nurse and was to be freed on the completion of her duties. Wet nurses as a group seem to have been particularly successful in obtaining their unconditional freedom after completing their obligations.[14]

If slaves could not depend on a humane or liberal owner to free them or an aged one to show a degree of generosity in his or her will, they had the option of purchasing their own freedom. They had been doing so since the early sixteenth century, and the practice had become institutionalized by the mid-1600s.[15] In the early republic it seems to have occurred far more frequently than owners freeing them.[16] Slaves had the legal right to buy their freedom if they had the necessary funds, and many did. Urban slaves retained some of the wages that they received for their work. Rural slaves earned wages too. Those in the Ica area received the same wage as free laborers, 6 reals per day, when they worked on Sundays and feast days. On the estates of San José and San Javier some slaves received wages instead of rations. Rural slaves also could sell the produce of their individual plots in the local towns or to the estate itself, as happened on the state-owned estates that purchased corn, beans, and other vegetables for distribution as rations. On the Chavalina estate, Clements Markham found that

> all the married slaves and workmen are allowed a piece of ground rent free, where they grow vegetables and breed pigs and poultry, while their children may be seen driving donkey loads of provision towards the town, and sitting before their heaps of fruit and vegetables in the market place of Yca.

They are thus enabled to earn money and live in comparative comfort. One old slave at Chavalina had made several hundred dollars by lending money on usury; and, unable to write, he kept his accounts by notches on a stick.[17]

If slaves could not earn money, they might obtain it by other means such as gambling, stealing, or even through inheritance. When María Fuentepacheco, a free *morena,* died in 1844 she left all her possessions to her husband, a slave.[18] They might receive the required funds from a third party, whom they then served for a set period to pay off the debt. The relationship was formalized by a contract and seems to have involved primarily domestic slaves who had few other means to obtain money.[19]

The accumulation of funds may have been a long and arduous task, with numerous temptations for spending it elsewhere, but many slaves demonstrated a remarkable self-discipline and managed to save enough to purchase either their own freedom or that of family members, or the *patronato* of *libertos.* The records list numerous examples of husbands purchasing wives, wives husbands, parents children, children parents, and other interfamilial combinations. Catalina Colo's daughter paid 250 pesos for her mother's freedom in 1854; María de la Cruz Salazar purchased the *patronato* of her daughter for 150 pesos in 1850.[20] In the late 1820s the state seemed particularly willing to permit its slaves to buy their freedom, in recognition perhaps of the liberators' abolitionist legislation, although more likely in response to its desperate need for cash and a desire to get rid of an unprofitable slave population. Whatever the reason, several slaves managed to free themselves. In 1827 a foreman on the estate of San José paid 500 pesos, a formidable saving, for his own freedom and for that of his daughter. Manuel de los Inocentes, a freedman, paid 100 pesos in 1828 for one of his daughters and 200 pesos the following year for a second. Manuel Sacramento paid 100 pesos for his niece; Agueda Josefa Funés paid 200 pesos for her daughter.[21]

The savings involved so great a sacrifice by the slaves or their families that they were not prepared to have their efforts frustrated. In the 1830s, Melchora Valverde, a free woman, paid 500 pesos to free her husband, a master carpenter. However, he had only just begun to enjoy his new status when the owner of the Palpa estate had him abducted off the street, claiming he had fled the estate two years earlier. Melchora determined to secure his release, even though it might involve "the sacrifice of all my fortune and the product of my work and the work of my husband." She appealed to the courts and eventually obtained a favorable decision, only to learn that her husband had been put in shackles and sent to Palpa. Once again she appealed to the courts, this time to secure his unconditional freedom.[22]

Slaves without the full amount to purchase their freedom had other options open to them. They could arrange to amortize their price over a period of time, paying off a certain amount each month until the full price had been met. Slaves on being sold could pay part of their purchase price to their new owner, thereby reducing their value and the amount they needed to save for their eventual freedom.[23] To improve the possibility of self-purchase, they tried to have their values reduced by appealing either directly to their owners or, if this failed, to the courts.[24] In July 1827 all the slaves of the San José and San Javier estates demanded new evaluations based on their present skills and medical state. Many sought reductions on the grounds of ill health, citing venereal disease, bleeding from the mouth (probably consumption), rheumatism, or simply "chronic illness." The usual reduction requested seems to have been 50 pesos, as was the case with one San José slave who had her value reduced from 250 to 200 pesos because of venereal disease, eye problems, advanced age, and habitual sickness. But the reduction was sometimes more. In 1828 a San Javier slave secured a reduction of 100 pesos because of her poor physical condition, permitting her to buy her freedom.[25] When a claim of poor health was not possible, slaves sought reductions on the grounds of long years of service, injuries suffered while working for their owners, or, in the case of women, their reproductive record. Atanasia de la Cruz, another San José slave, had her price reduced by 50 pesos in recognition of long years of service and the production of six children.[26]

Slaves also benefited from owners setting a maximum sale price for their property and including the figure in sales contracts and other legal documents. This meant that, although a slave's value might increase and his or her owner change, the sale price could not rise. Moreover, since the amount was contractually set, the slaves knew exactly how much they had to save to buy their freedom.[27] A common accompanying condition was that they could not be sold outside the city. In these cases the owners may have wanted to save slaves that they knew from the hard work of a plantation or to prevent the division of families. Whatever the rationale, the courts recognized the condition even though it contributed to the rural labor shortage.[28]

If slaves were unable to obtain the necessary money to purchase their freedom, they had the alternative of changing owners, or masters in the case of *libertos*. They enjoyed this right first under Bolívar's order and later under the 1852 Civil Code. During the earlier period, at least one slave appealed directly to Bolívar himself, demanding a change because his owner had failed to provide the necessities required by law. When Patricia

Sayán sought a new owner, she specified one who would appreciate her weak and sickly state which, she claimed, was a result of pulmonary problems brought on by her present owner's insistence that she work in the fields, even though she had been bought for housework.[29]

The slaves' struggle for change and improvement was part of a day-to-day existence that, in the opinion of many foreign commentators, differed little from that experienced by other sectors of Peruvian society. Neither urban nor rural slaves were confined to their homes or their place of work. They mixed openly with fellow slaves, free blacks, Indians, mulattoes, and other members of the community. They were probably as law-abiding as anyone else, although the records tend to focus on their deviance from the norms set by the white community and leave the impression that they were an antisocial and immoral sector of society. Gambling seems to have been popular among them, and they did not always use their winnings to purchase their freedom, spending it instead on alcohol, entertainment, their notoriously sumptuous clothing, and other goods. Lima residents complained in 1853 that slaves and servants congregated on the street corner of Rifa and San Antonio from six in the morning to six at night, gambling with dice, bothering pedestrians, blocking the sidewalk, and corrupting the students at a nearby school with their example and obscene language.[30]

In their life cycle Peru's slaves closely followed established norms. The church strongly influenced their lives, which may help to explain why they were more successful in preserving their family structure than were slaves elsewhere.[31] Although cohabitation and consensual relationships were common, they seem to have made some effort to legalize their relationships, choosing either free persons or other slaves to marry. Their willingness to marry indicates a confidence that family ties would be respected by their owners. Their willingness also could prove costly. The estate accounts of San Javier and San José for the late 1820s record a fee of 12 pesos for a wedding. The owners—recognizing that family ties served as a means of social control—might have paid the fee, but in many instances the slaves themselves were forced to provide the money from their hard-earned savings.[32] Before marrying, they had to have their owner's permission and provide two witnesses to attest to their unmarried state. Female slaves had to swear that they had not made a vow of chastity or entered a convent, and had no hidden illnesses or defects. Males had to swear to their chastity with regard to certain relatives of the bride. In 1850, Hipólito Moncada, a free black, had to swear that he neither was related to his bride, a slave, nor had had sexual relations with her sister.[33]

When a child was born to slaves, the parents seem to have made an effort to have it baptized. This was true even when the child was illegitimate and the father "unknown" according to the records. In some instances, the father may have been the slave's owner, as was probably the case of two illegitimate baby girls born in the Lima parish of Santa Ana in 1824, whose fathers were listed as Don Agustín Bustamente and Don Ramón Echenique.[34] Baptism was relatively cheap—1 peso at San Javier and San José—yet owners and masters of *libertos* insisted that the mother pay, even though baptism provided written proof of the existence of the offspring. Owners complained that they had already been deprived of their slave's labor for two months or more and now had to feed and clothe a child who was almost free.[35] Slaves were willing to pay for a baptism because it not only satisfied their religious concerns but also provided an opportunity to record any conditions affecting the status of their child. Some slaves used the occasion simply to make the point that the child was free according to San Martín's 1821 decree.[36] That freedom was still circumscribed, but they at least had made a gesture toward securing a better future for their children in both this life and the hereafter.

Death brought with it one final expense for the slave, the cost of the funeral. In the countryside the fee was 6 pesos, 6 reals for adults and 4 pesos, 4 reals for children.[37] Death may have relieved the slaves of their earthly obligations and ended their suffering, but some of the discriminatory distinctions that had accompanied them during their lives pursued them to the grave. The racial terminology that had developed during the colonial period continued to be applied, for death notices still differentiated among them as blacks, *morenos, pardos,* mulattoes, and the like.[38]

These divisions indicate that much of the colonial past had survived the Independence Wars, that Peru's black population still had to contend with widespread racism, and that the favorable picture of slavery presented by foreign observers should be viewed with some skepticism. While examples like the above might suggest that Peru's slaves enjoyed an almost normal existence or, at least, were experiencing some improvements in their daily lives, the reality was quite different. Despite the freedoms and perquisites provided to many of Peru's slaves, despite their various legal rights—which leave the impression that Peruvian slavery had deteriorated so that it was nothing more than the "contractual arrangement between the master and his bondsman," as described by Frank Tannenbaum—slavery in Peru was still extremely exploitative, like chattel slavery elsewhere.[39] Peruvian slaves were harshly treated, they had to overcome enormous obstacles in their struggle for freedom, and they could not guarantee that their legal rights would be recognized by their owners or the state. *Libertos* may have been technically free, but their lives were still circumscribed, and they were considered inferior by many whites. The views of one lawyer, who objected to educating young *libertos* because "*libertos* are not children of a class who need grand comprehensive principles to direct their actions but those that are in keeping with their condition and state," were not atypical.[40]

The interrelationship of color and prejudice was evident in the harassment suffered by all Peruvian blacks, even those who had never been slaves. Free blacks were often arrested and held as runaways. In some instances this may have been a simple case of mistaken identity, but the details from numerous court cases suggest that more often the action was deliberate. Blacks were hounded by individuals who saw them as a means to make money or to obtain workers and who were confident that their illegal actions would succeed. For the blacks, a trial to right this wrong might mean years of litigation and heavy costs. Isabel Urrutia, a freedwoman, was involved in a case that lasted six years. In 1825 her owner promised that in recognition of the past service of her mother she would be freed when she either married or became twenty-one, and she was subsequently freed. However, in 1851 a court decided that she had been legally sold in 1832 and turned her and her two children over to the person claiming to be her owner. Isabel appealed the decision through the *defensor de menores,* charging that the 1832 sale was of another person and that the birth certificate submitted as evidence had been a fake. An appellate court agreed and ordered her freed. The *defensor,* however, was still not completely satisfied and sought a court document for Isabel and her children to prevent further harassment. Another case involved an ex-slave named Francisco Venegas who had been freed in 1822 and who subsequently worked in the congress, earning 15 pesos per month. In 1850 he was abducted by Juan Venegas, who claimed that he had just bought Francisco. The latter appealed through the *defensor,* who demanded that criminal charges be brought against Juan for participating in the sale of a free man. This may have been another case of mistaken identity, but the *defensor* believed that someone was deliberately lying in order to make some money. The court decided in favor of Francisco and ordered that he be paid the wages he had earned while being held in a bakery. His position remained uncertain, however, for Venegas appealed the decision.[41]

Thus, all of Peru's blacks were condemned by the color of their skin and by the nation's continuing commitment to slavery, but those who suffered most were the slaves. They remained property and had little control over their lives. They could be seized and moved to a new owner with no warning or explanation except that some previous sale had not been legal.[42] Many of them existed in an unclear legal position because of the conditions placed on their status. A slave who was promised her freedom when she married but was placed in the charge of another before this occurred seemed to be neither slave, *liberto*, nor free, according to the person who was trying to sell her.[43]

Adding to the uncertainty was the courts' inconsistent interpretation of the laws. Frequently, they found in the owners' favor, protecting property rights and preserving slavery. Some courts, for example, interpreted Gamarra's 1839 decree strictly, insisting that *libertos* remain with their masters until they reached the age of fifty, and even applying it to the children of *libertos*, known as *ingenuos*. In 1843, Inés Salazar sought the court's intercession to secure her own freedom and that of her two-year-old daughter. Inés, a *liberta* who had been born in October 1821, argued that the decree could not be applied retroactively. The court decided, however, that her argument applied only to *libertos* who had reached the age of twenty-one before 1839; others were not affected. The court then took the decree one step further, applying it to her daughter, an *ingenua*, and declaring that she had to remain with the master until she, too, was fifty. Other courts supported this interpretation, adding only the limitations that *ingenuos* could not be sold and that the master had to provide for their education. According to newspaper reports, this interpretation opened *libertos* and their children to illegally extended periods of domination, as masters altered their recorded ages.[44] Slaveholders also followed the time-honored tradition of ignoring legislation. Routinely ignored were the laws that permitted parents to demand a new master or complete freedom for their *liberto* children if a master failed to provide food, clothing, education, and medical assistance. Even when brought to court, owners refused to comply.[45]

With the courts and the laws of questionable use, the slaves had to try other means to alter their status, but these often proved to be equally ineffective. Many slaves who were promised freedom in return for loyal service found the promises hollow. For example, in 1825 a woman commenced a legal action on the grounds that her daughter had been freed in a will that had subsequently been ignored by the dead slaveholder's heirs; she was still in the courts eight years later. In 1854 a slave claimed that she had been promised her freedom in return for eight years of service and that despite mistreatment she had completed the eight years. Now she sought her freedom through the courts but faced one delay after another; eventually, quite likely out of frustration, she took matters into her own hands and fled. Toribio Elmes also turned to the courts to seek compliance with a promise of freedom. He claimed that upon his purchase in August 1853 he had been promised his freedom in one year, plus a

wage of 4 pesos per week, but he had received only 2 pesos per week during his ten months in service. He wanted his back pay (amounting to 90 pesos) and, on the basis of calculations that his value had depreciated over the year so that he was now worth only 33 pesos, 2.5 reals, he offered to buy his freedom. Instead, he found himself in a bakery in irons while his owner explained that his slaves could not make public pronouncements without his consent. The court found in Toribio's favor, but he had to turn to it again one month later, as he was still being held and was still without his back pay of 34 pesos. Once more the court decided in his favor, and finally he was freed.[46]

Slaves also found their chances for freedom limited because they were unable to obtain reductions in their value—even if they could prove poor health—or because a reduction left their price still too high. In 1828 a seventy-five-year-old San José de la Nazca slave was valued at 120 pesos. He managed to produce the funds to buy his freedom, but many others did not. One Lima slave who in 1843 had her value of 350 pesos reduced by 150 pesos—100 pesos for a payment to her owner and 50 pesos for years of good service and the production of four children—was unable to accumulate the remaining 200 pesos in the twelve years before abolition.[47]

Sometimes money was available, but the anticipated reward was snatched from the poor slave's grasp. In 1827 a judge set up a voluntary subscription fund to purchase the freedom of a slave valued at 150 pesos. When 200 pesos were collected, the slave, "dancing with joy," went to secure his manumission, only to be told that the money had been spent. Confronting the judge, he was insulted and then informed that the money was going to be returned to the donors because he was "an insolent scoundrel." Theft of funds also kept two slaves, whose uncle had paid 600 pesos to a middleman, in bondage. Instead of buying their freedom the agent took the money, and the slaves ended up being sold to a new owner. Some of those slaves who obtained loans to purchase their freedom found the interest payments so high that they were unable to pay off the loan, forcing them to work for the creditor for the rest of their lives, with little real change in their status. Furthermore, owners might simply refuse to accept the money, although this was illegal. Josefa Dionisio offered her owner 400 pesos, which was 50 pesos more than a court-imposed valuation, but he refused it, demanding to know where she got the money. Courts, too, ignored the law, returning slaves who had the necessary funds to buy their freedom to their owners. Even an apparently legally completed purchase could prove illusory. In 1850 a court ordered a *liberta* to remain with her master despite the fact that her mother had paid her value. Although a higher court overruled the decision, the case emphasized once again that

Peru's slaves could be certain of virtually nothing.[48]

Attempts by slaves to change owners could be equally unsuccessful, regardless of the law in their favor. In 1854, María Henríquez, complaining of bad treatment and fearful that she was going to be returned to a hacienda, sought a new owner. She found a possible buyer who deposited her purchase price, but her owner, Irene Aria de Henríquez, refused, stating that slaves had no right to alter their dominion on their own, as it set a bad example. She also denied the charge of mistreatment, explaining that she once had sent María to a hacienda for twelve days because of insolence, "licentious living," and misconduct, and as punishment for striking her son, but that otherwise she had treated her "like a daughter." She was backed by the hacendado, who testified that María had been sent to the farm after being arrested for "sleeping in the street," for which her owner had been fined. María denied that she had hit anyone, insisted that she had been at the farm for a month, but agreed that her owner had been caring. The court decided against her and returned her to Irene.[49] Other slaves were equally unsuccessful despite pressure from officials, the courts, and even relatives of slave owners.[50]

Denied opportunities to change their legal position or their owners, slaves had to cope with the harsh realities of their daily existence. Rural slaves faced especially difficult conditions, as the depressed state of agriculture and the limited returns meant that planters sought to make economies, often at their slaves' expense. In some cases the situation was so desperate that even whites felt compelled to comment. In 1845, Cañete Valley residents complained that "the hacienda blacks are wretched; as a result of their very slave state they lack many necessities."[51] Housing was primitive. Proctor noted that plantation slaves lived in cane huts. They were probably clustered "in villages . . . round a plaza generally with a cross in the centre," as Markham found the slave *galpón* or quarters in the Cañete Valley in the 1850s. He added that the "villages are surrounded by high walls, and all must be within by a certain hour." He did not comment on the condition of this accommodation, but elsewhere found at least one hacienda in a dilapidated state, a description that probably applied to the slave quarters as well.[52]

Little money seems to have been spent on food for the slaves. Pablo Macera has written that Peru's slaves were better fed than either the Chinese coolies, who were imported later in the century, or other groups in Peru and elsewhere, but this does not prove that they were eating well.[53] Legislation specified the rations that were to be provided, and the records indicate that owners purchased meat, beans, chickpeas, grapes, and *aguardiente* for their slaves. However, laws were ignored. In 1824 each slave on an estate whose slave population had recently declined from one thousand to four hundred was receiving what observers described as "small" quantities of corn and beans, amounting to less than one liter of each.[54] In 1828, when slaves on San Javier de la Nazca were reported to be searching for food "in the street" because of shortages on the estate, the subprefect had to intervene and increase their rations. Slaves on the sister estate of San José did receive weekly food rations, but not the clothing, tobacco, and medical treatment that they were promised.[55]

The minimal amount spent on slaves was reflected in the estates' maintenance figures. The costs, including food, rented mules, and clothing, totaled 1142.5 pesos for San Javier in 1824 and only 90 pesos for the period from November 1827 to February 1828. On San José the estate paid 426 pesos, 1 real for slave maintenance in 1825 but only 251 pesos the following year. In that same period the slave population remained constant, while total estate expenses rose from 1753.7 pesos to 2997.3 pesos.[56] Providing slaves with a plot of land to grow their own food enabled owners to reduce their costs and avoid their obligations concerning rations. Whether the slaves could grow enough on their plots to meet all their needs is unclear. Some were evidently unsuccessful, as they fled their estates owing to the shortage of food and other basic essentials. In 1836 seven slaves fled the Nepén estate, complaining that they had received no food or clothing, been assigned excessive work, and been punished without cause. They were willing to return to the estate, "for they knew that they were obliged to do so because they were slaves," but they wanted the administrator to be replaced. In court, the owner's widow denied the complaints, stating that each slave received land to cultivate and that rations were distributed each Sunday. The court accepted her version and ordered the slaves returned, but it was not completely convinced, for it directed that the slaves should not be punished for their appeal to the court and absence from the estate.[57]

Because of poor rations, inadequate housing, limited health care, and mistreatment, illness among the slaves seems to have been common. Comparative statistics are not available, and since the coast of Peru was a notoriously unhealthy place all sectors of the population may have been suffering equally. Yet the frequent claims for price reductions on the basis of illness suggest that slaves were a disease-prone group. One of the few sources that examines slave illnesses deals with the state's Nazca holdings. In 1828, 39 (of whom 23 were women) of San Javier's 300 slaves, and 17 of San José's 130 slaves, were listed as having various illnesses. The most common were "blood from the mouth" (probably consumption) and venereal disease, usually syphilis. Other physical complaints included pulmonary typhoid, scabies, leprosy, flatulent colic, piles, gout, hernias, buboes, ruptures, rheumatic pain, loss of limbs, sunken chest, eye inflammation, hysteria, weeping sores from branding, and sore throats. On both estates medicines and medical treatment were lacking, which probably translated into high mortality rates, although the lack of statistics makes it impossible to prove this was the case.[58]

Deficiencies in health care, food, clothing, and accommodation, along with excessive labor demands, were all part of the abuse and exploitation that both urban and rural slaves had to face daily.[59] In addition many were physically confined, as owners tried to control their movements and prevent flight. José Aguirre was kept chained by his owner, who claimed this was a condition of his purchase since José had a reputation for being a fugitive and a pickpocket. This owner may have had some justification for his actions, but others did not. A former San Javier de la Nazca slave accused her new owners of mistreating her by threatening to whip her, tying her to a staircase, chaining her even though she was in the final stages of pregnancy, feeding her badly after the birth, and forcing her to return to work three days after parturition. She wanted to return to San Javier, where she had been born and where her family still lived. A more celebrated case involved the infamous Manuela Pando, a member of Lima's elite who had acquired notoriety for her marriages, her relationship with a priest after the death of her last husband, her role in the separation of her daughter and son-in-law, and her alleged involvement in the poisoning death of her grandson. In 1854, at the age of seventy-three, she was at the center of a new controversy, this time involving a male slave and two young *libertas* whom she was reported to have kept locked away in her house, which she guarded with two loaded pistols. One of the girls, who was fourteen or fifteen, had no idea how long she had been in the house, while the other, a nine-year-old, had been there for four or five months. Locked in their separate rooms and fed either every second day or "once a day badly," they had never met. The slave claimed that he had suffered for two years. A further charge was leveled subsequently, that another slave had fled the house after two years of "incarceration" and had died shortly thereafter. Manuela denied any wrongdoing, but an investigation was begun. While it proceeded, the girls were sent to a convent and the slave was moved out of the house.[60]

Slaves also faced incarceration by the state. With a reputation for criminal behavior, blacks could expect close attention from the authorities for any misdemeanors.[61] However, the frequency of the arrests, the flimsiness of the charges, and the treatment of those detained suggest that goals other than punishing criminals and preventing crime were involved. Slaves were arrested for not having their *boletos* and then accused of being runaways, for being out at night, and for drunkenness, gambling, and making merry in the streets. The real purpose behind the arrests may have been financial, for owners usually had to pay a fine for the release of their slaves. In 1843 the owners of thirty slaves who were arrested for gambling and drinking had to pay 2 pesos for each one. Alternatively, the authorities may have been seeking some unpaid workers, for arrested slaves often were assigned the task of cleaning the barracks while they awaited their owners to claim them.[62]

The prospect of unprovoked arrest must have been worrisome, but a far greater fear of the slaves was to be sold and thus separated from home, family, and familiar surroundings. Many slaves seem to have experienced no stability at all, being sold time and again. Some may have been responsible for their plight, being habitual criminals or fugitives or having some other perceived defect.[63] In other instances, however, the reasons are less clear. One slave, sold in 1829 by a nun who gave the money to her "sisters" and other poor religious, was resold seven more times in the next four years. Another was sold seventeen times between 1826 and 1849, including three times in a ten-day period. A third, who was seven when she was sold in April 1817, was resold nine times by November 1846, and a fourth was sold six times between October 1837 and January 1847.[64]

The sale of a slave not only disrupted his or her life but also could result in the division and separation of families. Husbands lost their wives, parents their children. In the process, the roots of family life were undermined. Children were frequently sold, as newspaper advertisements reveal. They were also given away, often as soon as they were born, to members of the owner's family. A marriage in the owner's family might have the same divisive effect, as slaves and *libertos* were a normal part of dowries. So, too, did the death of an owner, as the slaves would be distributed among the heirs or sold.[65] Thus, separation was a fact of life that afflicted many slaves, and its frequency challenges the image of a harmonious family life among Peru's slave population.

Parents tried to prevent the divisions, but with little success. Rosa Gasteagudo appealed to the court to try to stop the sale of her daughter, Beatriz, to a hacienda distant from Lima on the grounds that Beatriz's bill of sale contained the conditions that she had to remain in Lima and could change owners as she wished. Rosa also claimed that Beatriz suffered from a chest condition and monthly "fatal weaknesses," and asked that her value be reduced from 330 pesos. In reply, the owners noted that the bill of sale contained no such conditions, Beatriz was perfectly healthy, and hacienda air would be good for her. The court agreed, upholding the right of property in slaves and the right of the owner to sell his property.[66]

Most of the cases of this sort involved the separation of *liberto*, and thus technically free, children from their mothers. The separation might take place years after the child's birth, as in the case of Úrsula Fuentes; her former owner demanded her eight-year-old son since Úrsula had been her slave when the boy had been born, which meant that he was her *liberto*. Manuel La Rosa was a twelve-year-old boy who was taken from his mother and the house where they had lived for nine years by the heirs of his mother's former owner.[67] Cases such as these raise questions about the degree of freedom permitted *libertos*. With the decline in the number of slaves and the continuing shortage of labor, the reasons why individuals were prepared to go to virtually any extreme to claim *libertos* years after their parents had been sold or freed are obvious.

Competing demands could leave the mother with a choice that would have tried the wisdom of Solomon. Feliciana was a slave who sought the court's help in returning to her former owner, with whom she had left her two infant children. She claimed her present owner was planning to sell her away from Lima. She was assisted by the *defensor de menores*, who called on the court to respect maternal love. Her owner denied that he intended to sell her, although his defense that there was no law requiring families to remain together raised some doubts. He then offered to buy the *patronato* of the children. Although it would have united the family, Feliciana refused because she thought that the children's present master was a better guardian than her owner.[68]

Following the promulgation of the Civil Code in 1852, with its proviso that slave families were to remain together, slaves were afforded somewhat better protection, as the case of Juliana Rojas indicates. She had been a slave on La Molina estate where, she claimed, she had suffered from hunger, lack of clothing, cruel and unjust punishment, and work beyond her capabilities. Nevertheless, she had managed to save enough to buy her freedom, and for the past four years had been working on a neighboring estate, supporting herself and her four children. Now the renter of La Molina, Juan Pedro Lostaunau, claimed the children as his *libertos*. Juliana argued that, since the estate had neither fed, clothed, nor educated them for over three years, they were legally free. Lostaunau replied that he had provided pabulum after the birth of the two youngest children, as well as food and money for clothing. In 1853 a court agreed that he had not abandoned them; however, it was not prepared to separate minors from their parents and decided that the *patronato* should be sold to a person of the parents' choosing. Lostaunau objected, calling the order prejudicial to his interests and arguing that by law children had to remain with their parents only for their first three years. Juliana and her husband objected, too. They demanded that the children be freed on the grounds of the laws of nature and humanity that prevented the division of families. Their case was still being decided in September 1854.[69]

Not every case ended unhappily for the slaves. Manuela and her two-year-old son, Timoteo, were sold to the subprefect of Caylloma in 1841. Two years later she and her ten-month-old daughter were sold back to Manuela's former owner, but Timoteo remained with the subprefect. Five months later mother and daughter were sold again, but the following day the new owner also purchased Timoteo, reuniting mother and children.[70] This comparatively happy denouement seems to have been one of the few exceptions to the generally tragic rule.

The fate of their children weighed heavily on mothers. While charges that neglect by slave mothers resulted in the death of three quarters of the children born to them were probably exaggerated, abortion and infanticide were not unknown, as slaves sought to save themselves the heartache of separation or worse. Flora Tristán heard from one owner that the incidence of abortion among slaves was high, and she met two slaves who were in jail for starving their children to death. Face to face with them, she speculated that they preferred to have their children dead rather than enslaved. Another observer claimed that slaves suffocated their children rather than see them be victims of cruelty. He added that, on seeing their children whipped, mothers cursed their wombs and the hour they were born.[71]

In addition to the death, loss, and punishment of their children, female slaves had to contend with the sexual demands of their owners. The law tried to prevent this form of exploitation by granting freedom to any slave who could prove it, but only a few of those abused seem to have appealed to the courts. In 1830, Rafaela Marín charged that her owner, who had bought her the previous year for 100 pesos, had promised to free her in return for sexual favors and had forced her to work as a prostitute while continuing to sleep with her. They had even been caught in flagrante delicto by his wife. The court accepted her charge of abuse and ordered her freed.

In another case, Remijia Nuñes had been promised her freedom in her owner's will on her twenty-fifth birthday if she was married; if not, she was to remain the slave of his sister. In 1847, when she was twenty-nine, she sought her freedom but was unsuccessful because she was still single. She appealed through the *defensor de menores*, who testified that at the age of twenty she had been engaged to marry Maximo Rojas but that he had been jailed to prevent the marriage. She then had been raped by her new owner's husband and had borne his child. Nevertheless, Maximo had still been willing to marry her, but again he was jailed to prevent the marriage that would have secured her freedom. The husband denied the charge of rape and accused Remijia of having abandoned herself to "sensual pleasures" at an early age, engaged in prostitution, and been a runaway. However, he did not deny fathering the child, probably because the affair had been common knowledge and the reason why his wife had tried to sell Remijia on one occasion. The court ordered her freed on the grounds of sexual exploitation.[72]

The men involved in cases such as these usually denied the charge of sexual abuse, but occasionally the women could counter with evidence that was the product of the exploiters' actions. Vicenta Urrutia, the slave of Father Manuel Palma, had three children during the nine years she was his slave, one of whom was given to Palma's parents. Obtaining her freedom, Vicenta sought to free her son, claiming he was Palma's illegitimate child, even though his birth certificate stated he was the legitimate child of Vicenta and her husband. Palma denied the charges as "unjust and malicious." Vicenta, however, pointed out that the boy was a *samba obscura* while her husband was a *negro tinto*, so that the boy's father had to be white. Palma continued to deny any paternal relationship, charging that the adultery had occurred "only in the imagination of this unhappy colored woman."[73]

With family life unstable, relations between spouses were bound to suffer. Disempowered by the system, slaves turned to violence as a release for their frustrations. Domestic assaults were numerous and in some cases resulted in death. The slavery system may not have been responsible in every instance, but it and the accompanying tensions were at the root of some cases at least. Was it responsible, for example, for undermining the eleven-year marriage of Luis Castro and his wife? In 1823 he accused her of attacking him once with a machete and twice with a knife before leaving him for another man, who had also attacked him with a knife and had insulted him. He blamed the lover and his wife's owner for the troubles. Less clear are cases such as that of Juan Espejo, a fifty-year-old water seller, who hit his partner on the head after she said she wanted to end their relationship. The injuries were not severe, but Espejo was sentenced to be sold fifty leagues from Lima within a month. Toribio Elmes, a bakery worker, planned to kill his wife, whom he accused of having an affair with another slave, but his attack went astray and he slashed a free black woman who seemed to be trying to protect his wife. The injured woman demanded 34 pesos in compensation for her medical treatment. Petronila Vasquez was arrested for slashing her lover, a slave, but was released after testifying that she had only been defending herself against him when he began hitting her in a drunken stupor.[74]

This same lack of power may help to explain why some slaves resorted to rape. The records may or may not reflect the reality of the situation, but the instances seem to have been few. In 1845, Mateo Ugarte, a shoemaker, was charged with raping a six-year-old orphan. According to the court record, Ugarte threw the girl on a bed and tried to have intercourse with her but failed because of her size. He then sexually assaulted her with his hand, breaking her hymen and leaving her pubis bruised. The court decided that since intercourse had not occurred there had been no crime, but at the same time it found that the girl had been corrupted "in a certain sense" and so levied a fine of 30 pesos, which Ugarte was to pay off by working in a bakery. His owner decided that this was enough to render him valueless and indicated his intention to sell Mateo after the fine was paid.[75]

While the day-to-day existence of Peru's slaves might be seen as a form of punishment in itself, those convicted of crimes were subject to special abuse. Like freedmen they might be fined, jailed, or conscripted into the army. They could also be "exiled" from their homes if the court ordered them sold to some distant spot, a punishment owners resisted since it meant losing their property.[76] A more common form of punishment was to be imprisoned in a bakery and compelled to work. Many bakeries contained holding cells of some sort, along with shackles and chains. Slaves being held for trial might also be deposited in a bakery, with their wages paid to their owner. Archibald Smith described the use of bakeries as the "ordinary mode of punishment." Von Tschudi echoed this observation, adding that corporal punishment was uncommon. Rather, if a slave "requires punishment, he is sent into the *Panaderia* . . . to knead the dough and bake the bread, which work they perform under the supervision of a mayordomo, who is usually a hard task-master. Owing to the heat of the climate, working in the *Panaderia* is more feared by the slaves than any other kind of punishment."[77] Yet, in the eyes of the law, bakery work was not the most severe punishment. A sentence of hard labor in a bakery could be increased to a term in prison, and slaves could be condemned to death.[78]

However, the most common form of punishment for slaves, according to the records and contrary to the views of Von Tschudi and others, was whipping.[79] It was permitted by law and administered by both officials and owners. In the latter case, owners usually justified their actions by claiming that the slaves were lazy and could be compelled to work only with the lash.[80] It was used quite arbitrarily: Slaves were whipped for "grossly" insulting officials, "shameless public conduct," and throwing stones in the street—but not in every case, for the courts might fine the owner a few pesos instead.[81] The severity of this form of punishment was circumscribed by law: The maximum was twelve lashes, blood could not be drawn, certain individuals were exempt, and the owner had to be present at the whipping. Failing to have the owner present could create problems for the person who carried out the whipping. In 1849 the Lima police intendant found himself the target of a congressional inquiry after whipping a slave of José María Lizarzaburu four times. Lizarzaburu was a member of the chamber of deputies, and he sought the chamber's assistance in punishing those responsible. The justice committee complied, deciding that the slave was protected by the constitution "because a slave is also a man, also a member, although a passive one, of society and humanity." It also condemned the police for their actions and for considering themselves "the lash of God."[82]

Despite interventions of this sort, the laws regarding whipping, like other laws, were commonly ignored. Neither sex nor age spared slaves from the lash: Children, pregnant women, and the aged were whipped. Some beatings were so savage that slaves died or had to be hospitalized, sometimes with the expectation that they would not survive. In one case a minor had to be taken to the hospital after he was "cruelly punished" by his owner. On the Pedreros estate an elderly man who was whipped by the majordomo for having stolen some sheep required hospitalization, as his wounds became gangrenous and maggoty. Another slave on the same estate, an aged woman, complained that she had been whipped despite having two daughters and ten grandchildren. She demanded her freedom on the grounds of mistreatment and old age. Another female slave had been whipped more than thirty times. Two female slaves on the San Nicolás estate were reported to have been whipped far more than twelve times, as their wounds still had not healed after twenty days. They were also imprisoned and held incommunicado, all for having demanded that their *liberto* children not be treated as slaves.[83]

Libertos, most of whom were children, were subject to the same punishment. Andrés Castro, whose master accused him of attempting to murder him, was whipped over fifty times and confined in stocks. The whipping produced wounds on his buttocks that were half an inch in depth and took over a month to heal. A *liberta*, a girl of ten or eleven years, had scars on her body from whippings administered by her master's wife. A seventeen-year-old *liberta* from the San Pedro estate was whipped twenty times by the estate foreman for failing to carry out his orders and for associating with known highwaymen. She was accused of being the concubine of the notorious robber Juan de Mata Duanes, a San Pedro slave. She insisted that she had been kidnapped by Duanes and was unable to escape because she was ignorant of the roads.[84]

In cases of excessive whipping, slaves could demand their freedom from the courts. Gerónimo Jauregui, one of the first slaves to use the services of the *defensor de menores*, demanded even more when he complained to a court in 1830 about the punishment meted out to his family. His wife had been whipped twice for fleeing, while his son had received anywhere between six and twenty-five lashes—the evidence differed—for leaving a door open that permitted a *"zambito"* to carry on affairs with other slaves. A doctor testified that the scars from the whipping were still visible in the boy's buttocks a month later. Gerónimo wanted a new owner, as well as his present owner, Juan Pedro Lostaunau, to be considered an enemy of the fatherland since his actions were contrary to the law. Lostaunau's defense was not to deny the whippings but rather to try to discredit the *defensor* and his evidence. His lawyer accused the *defensor* of "seducing" the slave witnesses and causing other slaves to flee and make excessive demands.[85]

These and many other cases show that Peruvian slavery was not the mild institution that contemporary observers claimed. Peru's slaves were an abused and exploited sector of the population. Opportunities for enjoying what might be called a normal life may have existed for some of them, but the vast majority faced uncertainties, frustrations, and tensions that denied any possibility of normalcy. The effects of the abuse, exploitation, and uncertainties were mixed. Many slaves responded by accepting the situation or accommodating themselves to it, waiting for improvements or even emancipation to occur. Some were so completely indoctrinated that they came to accept the dominant sector's attitudes toward slaves and slavery. This may explain the actions of one slave who tried to sell another, claiming to be his owner.[86] The vast majority, however, took advantage of any opportunity that might arise to secure some minimal benefits for themselves and, at the same time, to chip away at the system that kept them in chains. Peru's slaves may have been exploited, but they were not passive. They confronted their owners and the state in various ways, some more violent than others, and in the process proved to be the most effective of the abolitionist forces that were slowly but surely undermining Peruvian slavery.

[1]Markham, *Cuzco and Lima*, 27; Proctor, *Narrative*, 232–34; Smith, *Peru As It Is* 1:110–11; J. J. Von Tschudi, *Travels in Peru, during the Years 1838–1842, on the Coast, in the Sierra, across the Cordilleras and the Andes, into the Primeval Forests*, trans. Thomasina Ross (London, 1847), 107–8.

[2]Enclosure with Adams to Aberdeen, ST5, August 4, 1845, F.O. 84/595. The fear of military conscription prompted some free blacks to obtain slave *boletos*. See *El Comercio*, February 1, 1842, December 13, 1843.

[3]James C. Scott, *Weapons of the Weak: Everyday Forms of Peasant Resistance* (New Haven, 1985), 280, 328; Genovese, *Roll, Jordan, Roll*.

[4]Manuel Burga has approached this point of view from a different perspective, arguing that by the late colonial period the mode of production in Peru had progressed

from a slave mode to more of a feudal mode, so that "classical slavery" did not exist. See Manuel Burga, "La hacienda en el Perú, 1850–1930: evidencias y método," *Tierra y Sociedad* 1 (1978): 17–23.

[5]Sales de Bohigas, *Sobre esclavos*, 123–27.

[6]"Ordenes a instrucciones dadas por la comandancia general e intendencia de Ica a Dn. Miguel Bernales, administrador de las haciendas San Javier y San Pablo de la Nazca," AGN, Temporalidades, San Javier de la Nazca, 1819–1828, Leg. 70, Cuad. 109.

[7]"Expediente sobre los autos seguidos por la esclava Isabel Verano, para cambiar de amo," Huaura, October 17, 1825, BN D12586.

[8]Enclosure with Adams to Aberdeen, ST5, August 4, 1845, F.O. 84/595.

[9]AAL, Causas de Negros, 1815–1855, Leg. 36, LXII:59. For another case illustrating the care taken by a court, in this instance deciding whether a woman was a slave or a *liberta*, see "Promovido por el sindico procurador con la testamentaria del D. D. José Pando, sobre la libertad de la sierva Petronila Pando," June 11, 1853, AGN, CCiV, 1852–53, Leg. 169. The case covers 150 numbered folio pages.

[10]*El Comercio*, July 18, 1846, October 5, 1849, January 27, 1855.

[11]AD-A, Notarial, Francisco de Linares, 1829–1831, Leg. 678, January 10, 1831.

[12]See, for example, AAL, Bautismos de Indios, Esclavos, Mestizos, 1819–1825, Parroquia de San Sebastián, Leg. 11, October 1, 1824.

[13]Engelsen, "Social Aspects," 81, table 4.

[14]AD-A, Notarial, Toribio de Linares, 1844–1846, Prot. 709, April 3, 1845; *El Comercio,* April 10, 1840, April 20, 1849. For more examples see Aguirre, "Agentes," 46–49.

[15]Bowser, *African Slave*, 278–82.

[16]A survey of Lima slaves in the last fifteen years of slavery shows that close to three quarters of them were freed through self-purchase. See Aguirre, "Agentes," 14.

[17]"Información que el prefecto del departamento de Ica mandó levantar en el valle de la Nazca con el fin de pesquisar la conducta del pbro. Dn. Manuel Barreto, administrador de la hacienda San José de la Nazca y tierras anexas, en orden a la recta administración de los dichos fundos," AGN, Temporalidades, Leg. 97, Cuad. 84; "Cuentas de Don Miguel Bernales," AGN, Temporalidades, Leg. 70, Cuad. 111-A; Markham, *Cuzco and Lima,* 42; John Thomas, *Diario de viáje del General O'Higgins en la campaña de Ayacucho,* trans. Carlos Vicuna Mackenna (Santiago de Chile, 1917), 220. See also Markham, "Travels" 1:133–35. Foreign observers used the terms *dollars* and *pesos* interchangeably.

[18]AGN, Notarial, Eduardo Huerta, 1844–45, Prot. 274, October 19, 1844.

[19]Aguirre, "Agentes," 40–42.

[20]For these and similar purchases of slaves and *libertos* see AGN, Notarial, Lucas de la Lama, 1854–55, Prot. 333; AAL, Causas de Negros, 1815–1855, Leg. 36, LXVII: 33; AD-A, Notarial, Francisco de Linares, 1834–35, Prot. 681.

[21]"El prefecto de departamento acompaña el expediente sobre la libertad del esclavo Matías propio de la hacienda de San José de la Nazca," AGN, 1827, P.L. 7-229B; "El prefecto de este departamento participa haber dirigido a los administradores del tesoro público, un libramiento de 382 pesos, 4 reales girado contra la administración de correos de esta capital, cuya suma han recibido por su libertad, Manuel Sacramento y Nolberta, esclavos que fueron de la hacienda de San José de la Nazca," AGN, 1827, P.L. 7-335; "El prefecto de esta capital dando parte de haber entregado a Manuel de los Inocentes, esclavo que fue de la hacienda San José de la Nazca, al sub-prefecto de Ica 150 pesos por la libertad de su hija, Norberta de Jesús," AGN, 1828, P.L. 8-597; "El prefecto de este departamento acompañando el expediente promovido por Agueda Joséfa Funés, sobre la libertad de su hija, Isabel, esclava de la hacienda de San Javier de la Nazca," AGN, 1828, P.L. 8-670; "El prefecto de esta capital sobre la libertad de Gregoria, esclava de la hacienda de San José de la Nazca, y entrega de 100 pesos que ha hecho al sub-prefecto de Ica," AGN, 1828, P.L. 8-714. See also Aguirre, "Agentes," 12–31.

[22]"Expediente promovido por Melchora Valverde sobre la libertad de su marido, José Antonio Rivadeneyra," AGN, CCiv, 1834, Leg. 84.

[23]Aguirre, "Agentes," 36–37.

[24]For cases of this sort in La Libertad see *El Peruano,* October 28, December 30, 1826.

[25]"El prefecto de este departamento acompaña la nota que le ha remitido el intendente de la provincia de Ica, sobre el reclamo que hace la esclavatura de la hacienda de San José de la Nazca, por el excesivo valor en que ha sido tasado," AGN, 1827, P.L. 7-229C; "El prefecto del departamento de Lima acompaña la solicitud de Inocente, Manuel, y otros esclavos de la hacienda de San José de la Nazca sobre que se les dé su carta de libertad, previo el entero que ofrecen de su tasación," AGN, 1827, P.L. 7-425; "El prefecto de esta capital acompañando representación de María Natividad, esclava de la hacienda de San Javier, sobre que se haga de ella nuevo avaluo," 1828, AGN, P.L. 8-715. See also "El prefecto del departamento de Lima acompaña la nota del sub-prefecto de la provincia de Ica sobre la solicitud de la liberta María Libonia, esclava que fue de la hacienda de San Javier de la Nazca sobre su nueva tasación por los motivos que expresa," AGN, 1829, P.L. 9-227; "Gertrudis Atela, esclava de la hacienda de San José de la Nazca, solicitandose el justo precio para reclamar su libertad," AGN, 1829, P.L. 9-31; and "El prefecto del departamento de Lima acompaña el expediente promovido por María del Carmen Valdez sobre la libertad de su hijo, Casimiro," AGN, 1829, P.L. 9-444.

[26]See "El prefecto de este departamento acompaña el expediente relativo a la libertad de Narciso y Simón de los Santos, esclavos de la hacienda de San Javier de la Nazca," AGN, 1827, P.L. 7-143; and "El prefecto de este departamento acompaña la representación de Atanacia de la Cruz, esclava de la hacienda de San José de la Nazca, en que solicita su libertad y rebaja del importe de su tasación," AGN, 1827, P.L. 7-193.

[27]AAL, Causas de Negros, 1815–1855, Leg. 36, LXVII:1.

[28]*Mercurio Peruano,* November 13, 1827.

[29]"Petición presentada por la esclava, Patricia Sayán, para que se proceda a su tasación," Huacho, January 19, 1828, BN D12551; AAL, Causas de Negros, 1815–1855, Leg. 36, LXII:32. For an example of a *liberto* seeking a new master see "Seguidos por sindico D. Francisco Garfias con D. Nicolás Prunedas sobre la libertad de Juan Bautista," AGN, CCrim, 1854, Leg. 612.

[30]*El Comercio*, July 21, 1853. See also "Seguidos contra los reos Francisco Olavid, N. Sambrano, José Alforno

Cabillas y otro por la muerte alevosa ejecutada en la persona del teniente conductor, Don Ambrosio Rojas," AGN, CCrim, 1830, Leg. 529; "Criminales contra Agustín Palacios, Jacinto Muñoz y Bernardo Pino para homicidio Ylavio Mendoza," AGN, CCrim, 1840, Leg. 576; and "Expediente sobre las averiguaciones acerca de la muerte de un criado negro," Huaura, March 16, 1824, BN D12591.

31Macera, "Las plantaciones azucareras," 62.

32"El Dr. D. Silvestre Peñaranda, cura del Ingenio en Ica, solicitando el pago de las pensiones que a su favor gravan sobre la hacienda de San José y San Javier de la Nazca, además de los derechos de obenciones que le corresponden por la esclavatura," AGN, 1828, P.L. 8-32; AGN, Temporalidades, Leg. 70, San Javier de la Nazca, 1819–1828, Cuad. A.

33"Peticiones presentadas por varios negros para que se les expide licencias para que pueden contraer matrimonio," Lima, November 4, 1828, BN D10859; "Expediente sobre la "petición presentada por el Gral. de Brigada José María Lizarzaburu para que se expide el decreto de matrimonio de una esclava a su servicio con un mozo libre," Lima, July 1, 1850, BN D9508. See also AAL, Matrimonios, Indios, Negros, Parroquia de San Marcelo, 1789–1838, Leg. 4; and AAL, Matrimonios, Indios, Negros, Parroquia de Santa Ana, 1795–1824, Leg. 3.

34AAL, Bautismos de Negros y Pardos de la Parroquia de Santa Ana, 1820–1825, Leg. 10. See also AAL, Bautismos de Indios, Esclavos, Mestizos, Parroquia de San Sebastian, 1819–1825, Leg. 11; and AAL, Bautismos de Indios, Mulatos, Negros, Parroquia de San Marcelo, 1810–1828, Leg. 14.

35*Mercurio Peruano*, July 17, 1828. For baptismal fees see "El Dr. D. Silvestre Peñaranda, . . . ," AGN, 1828, P.L. 8-32.

36See the case of María de Jesús, AAL, Bautismos de Indios, Mulatos, Negros, Parroquia de San Marcelo, 1810–1828, Leg. 14.

37"El Dr. D. Silvestre Peñaranda . . . ," AGN, 1828, P.L. 8-32.

38See, for example, AAL, Defunciones, Parroquia de San Lazaro, 1821–1830, Leg. 11; and AAL, Defunciones, Parroquia de San Lazaro, 1831–1843, Leg. 12.

39Tannenbaum, *Slave and Citizen*, 55.

40"Doña Manuela Aguirre sobre el deposito de Isabel Urrutia y sus dos hijos menores," AGN, CCiv, 1851, Leg. 162.

41Ibid.; "Seguidos por el defensor general de menores contra Don Juan Bautista Venegas sobre la libertad de Juan Antonio Iglesias," AGN, CCiv, 1850, Leg. 158.

42See, for example, AAL, Causas de Negros, 1815–1855, Leg. 36, LXII:2.

43"D. José Ascona con Doña Manuela Nuyn sobre la libertad de Matea Martel," AGN, CCiv, 1851, Leg. 162.

44*El Comercio*, October 3, 1843, August 4, 7, 1852; *El Peruano*, September 28, 1850.

45For examples of court cases see "Seguidos por Juliana Rojas con Don Juan Pedro Lostaunau y el sindico de La Molina sobre la libertad de sus hijos, 1852," AGN, CCiv, 1854, Leg. 172; and AAL, Causas de Negros, 1815–1855, Leg. 36, LXVI:38.

46"Autos seguidos por Doña Carmen Loayza con su esclava María Jesús Flores sobre su libertad," AGN, CCiv, 1825, Leg. 20; "Seguidos por Josefa Chunga con Doña María Estebes sobre su libertad," AGN, CCiv, 1854, Leg. 172; "Causa de libertad de Toribio Elmes, esclavo del Doctor D. Luis Ponce," AGN, CCrim, 1854, Leg. 614.

47"El prefecto del departamento de Lima hace presente la consulta del sub-prefecto de Ica sobre la cuota que presenta Carmen Valdez por la libertad de su hijo, esclavo de la hacienda de San José de la Nazca," AGN, 1828, P.L. 8-454; "El prefecto de esta capital comunicando haber entregado al esclavo de la hacienda de San José de la Nazca, José Ugalde, al subprefecto de Ica los 120 p. valor de su tasación," AGN, 1828, P.L. 8-531; "El prefecto del departamento de Lima acompaña el expediente promovido por María del Carmen Valdez sobre la libertad de su hijo Casimiro," AGN, 1829, P.L. 9-444; "D. Rafael Vilsa—dos esclavos," Archivo de la Cámara de Diputados, Lima (hereafter cited as ACD), 1856/1857, Convención Nacional, Leg. 21–25, Junta de Manumisión, 81.

48*El Comercio*, January 23, February 5, November 14, 1846, January 27, 1854; *Mercurio Peruano*, November 3, 1827; "Seguidos por el abogado defensor general de menores con Doña Concepción Malpartida sobre nombramiento de curador de la menor, Petronila Voto," AGN, CCiv, 1850, Leg. 160.

49"D. Luis Monsante, como defensor de la esclava María Henríquez con su ama, Doña Irene Aria de Henríquez sobre variación de dominio," AGN, CCiv, 1854, Leg. 172. See also *Telégrafo de Lima*, July 27, 1833.

50For an example see *Telégrafo de Lima*, July 27, 1833.

51*El Comercio*, June 9, 1845.

52Markham, "Travels," 1:42–43, 46–47, 75; Proctor, *Narrative*, 303.

53Macera, "Las plantaciones azucareras," 253-54, 270–75.

54Thomas, *Diario*, 220.

55"Cuenta de cargo y data que rindió al supremo gobierno en el despacho de hacienda Dn. José Félix Hurtado, administrador de la hacienda San Javier y de su anexa San Pablo, y corre desde el 5 de marzo de 1828 hasta el 21 de setiembre de 1829," AGN, Temporalidades, Leg. 70, Cuad. 113; "Cuenta documenada que rindió al supremo gobierno el administrador de la hacienda San José de la Nazca y corre desde el 24 de noviembre de 1827 hasta el 30 de noviembre de 1828," AGN, Temporalidades, Leg. 97, Cuad. 82; "Información que el prefecto del departamento de Ica mandó levantar en el valle de la Nazca con el fin de pesquisar la conducta del pbro. Dn. Manuel Barreto, administrador de la hacienda San José de la Nazca y tierras anexas, en orden a la recta administración de los dichos fundos," AGN, Temporalidades, Leg. 97, Cuad. 84.

56"Cuentas de Don Francisco Iglesias," AGN, Temporalidades, Leg. 70, San Javier de la Nazca, 1819–1828, Cuad. 6, 7; "Cuentas de Don Miguel Bernales," AGN, Temporalidades, Leg. 70, Cuad. 110-C; "Cuenta que rindió al supremo gobierno D. Juan Bautista Mesa, administrador de la hacienda San José de la Nazca, propia del estado, y corresponde a los años de 1824–1831," AGN, Temporalidades, Leg. 97, Cuad. 83.

57AD-LL, División Judicial, Prefectura, CCrim, 1828–1886, Leg. 613, Exp. 117.

58"El prefecto del departamento de Lima acompaña las diligencias obradas al reconocimiento de la esclavatura de las haciendas de San José y San Javier de la Nazca encomendado al juez de letras de la provincia de Ica," AGN, 1828, P.L. 8-725. For a thorough examination of the issue of slave diseases see Karasch, *Slave Life,* chap. 6.

[59]For an example of a slave complaining about overwork see "Defensa de esclavo," *Revista del Archivo Histórico del Cuzco* 3 (1952): 356–58.

[60]"D. José Reynoso sobre servicia en su esclavo José Aguirre, 1852," AGN, CCiv, 1852–53, Leg. 169; "El prefecto de este departamento acompaña la representación hecha por Don Manuel Carbajal, en que pide se le revalide la venta de dos esclavos de la hacienda de San Javier de la Nazca, propias del Estado," AGN, 1827, P.L. 7-70; *El Comercio,* April 1, 5, 8, 11, October 4, 1854; *El Heraldo de Lima,* March 31, April 6, 1854.

[61]The reasons for this reputation are unclear and a lack of data prevents comparisons with other groups.

[62]For examples see *El Comercio,* May 4, 8, 11, 15, 22, June 22, July 5, August 13, 26, September 2, 3, 23, 25, October 3, 22, December 11, 13, 1839, September 2, 6, 12, October 13, 1843; *Gaceta Mercantil,* July 9, 1834, February 17, 18, 1835; and AD-A, Corte Superior de Justicia, CCrim, 1842, (II), September 23, 1842.

[63]Francisco Zamudio was sold six times between April 1826 and June 1827 and was finally given to the navy for being a thief and fugitive. See "D. Francisco Sánchez, acompaña la boleta de un esclavo de su propiedad y lo cede a favor del estado," AGN, 1827, P.L. 7-239.

[64]AAL, Causas de Negros, 1815–1855, Leg. 36, LXVII:1; "D. Lorenzo Figueroa a nombre de Da. Joaquina Uribe, reclamando el pago del valor de una esclava," ACD, 1855, 1856, 1857, Leg. 15, Expedientes de particulares pasados a la Comisión de Memoriales, 1857, 26; "Da. Isabel Mendoza—dos esclavos," ACD, 1856/1857, Convención Nacional, Leg. 21–25, Junta de Manumisión, 78; "D. Rafael Vilsa—dos esclavos," ACD 1856/1857, Convención Nacional, Leg. 21–25, Junta de Manumisión, 81.

[65]The dowry of Manuel Ravajo y Avellafuentes totaled over 64,916 pesos and included two slaves worth 500 pesos, a boy of ten and a girl of seventeen. See AGN, Notarial, Ignacio Ayllón Salazar, 1825, Prot. 41. See also AAL, Bautismos de Indios, Esclavos, Mestizos, 1819–1825, Parroquia de San Sebastián, Leg. 11; and AD-LL, División Notarial, Escrituras, José V. Aguilar, Leg. 408, August 6, 1845, Leg. 409, 1846–47, May 12 and 13, 1846, 24–27.

[66]"Autos que sigue Rosa Gasteagudo, madre de Beatriz, con Dn. Blas Zavaleta su amo sobre que la venta," AGN, CCiv, 1834, Leg. 84.

[67]AAL, Causas de Negros, 1815–1855, Leg. 36, LXII:24; "Expediente sobre la petición presentada por José García Moreyra, para que se deje libre al liberto Manuel La Rosa, a quien retiene Manuel Lorenzo Casas, pretendiendo ser esclavo," Lima, January 28, 1853, BN D12749.

[68]"Promovido por el defensor general de menores con D. Gerónimo Sanchez sobre la variación de dominio de la esclava Feliciana," AGN, CCiv, 1846, Leg. 141.

[69]"Seguidos por Juliana Rojas con Don Juan Pedro Lostaunau y el sindico de La Molina sobre la libertad de sus hijos, 1852," AGN, CCiv, 1854, Leg. 172.

[70]AD-A, Notarial, Toribio de Linares, 1844–1846, Prot. 709, May 1, 2, 1844.

[71]Tristán, *Peregrinaciones,* 414, 421; *El Comercio,* August 5, 1852.

[72]"Expediente sobre la petición presentada por Rafaela Marín, esclava, para que su amo comply con la promesa de darle libertad," Huaura, February 1, 1830, BN D12785; "Sobre la libertad de una esclava, Remijia Nuñes," AGN, CCiv, 1847, Leg. 149.

[73]AAL, Causas de Negros, 1815–1855, Leg. 36, LXVII:50.

[74]AAL, Causas de Negros, 1815–1855, Leg. 36, LXI:100; "Contra Juan Espejo por heridas," AGN, CCrim, 1840, Leg. 577; "Seguidos contra Toribio Elmes por heridas inferidas a María del Rosario Zapata," AGN, CCrim, 1840, Leg. 574; "Criminales contra Petronila Vasquez," AGN, CCrim, 1843, Leg. 584. See also "Contra Dolores Argote por heridas," AGN, CCrim, 1842, Leg. 581; and *El Comercio,* September 9, 1851. For examples of murders see *El Comercio,* June 11, 12, 1841, January 2, 1845, June 20, 1851.

[75]"Criminales contra Mateo Ugarte por estupro," AGN, CCrim, 1845, Leg. 586; "Homicidio de Manuel Champas," AGN, CCrim, 1851, Leg. 665. For another case of rape, this one involving an estate slave who was hunted down and killed after a second assault, see *El Comercio,* January 2, 1845. A slave participating in a manhunt where the fugitive was another slave could find himself in an impossible situation, unable to refuse his owner but subject to prosecution for his actions. In 1834 a slave helped his owner capture a slave who had stolen some pigs, but injured the thief in the process and was the one charged when the case came to trial. See *Gaceta Mercantil,* January 29, 1835.

[76]For examples see "El prefecto de este departamento acompañando un expediente seguido en el juzgado de derecho de Ica, sobre la necesidad de enajenar al esclavo, Manuel Dionisio, perteneciente a la hacienda San José de la Nazca," AGN, 1828, P.L. 8-145; and "Criminales contra Bernardo Aliaga y José Luis Ulloa, José Cambiaso, y Pedro Pablo Baca a Dn. Pedro Puccio," AGN, CCrim, 1843, Leg. 583. For the punishments meted out to Brazilian slaves at this time see Karasch, *Slave Life,* 113–25.

[77]Smith, *Peru As It Is* 1:108; Von Tschudi, *Travels in Peru,* 107.

[78]AAL, Causas de Negros, 1816–1855, Leg. 36, LXII:63; "Criminales seguido contra Pedro Nolasco y Pablo Bosa por robo a Don Pablo Alzamora, 1843," AGN, CCrim, 1844, Leg. 585.

[79]Proctor wrote that he never saw a whip or a single slave punished. See Proctor, *Narrative,* 234.

[80]Tristán, *Peregrinaciones,* 415.

[81]*El Comercio,* June 5, 1839, February 4, April 4, May 8, 1840.

[82]*El Comercio,* September 4, December 13, 1849; "Mandando someter a juicio a los que cooperara a la vapulación de un esclavo," ACD, 1849–50, Leg. 2, Asuntos Generales Resueltos por esta Cámara, 24.

[83]*El Comercio,* May 20, 1843, March 14, May 30, June 2, 1846, June 18, 1853; *La Miscelánea,* July 23, 1831; "El defensor general de menores en representación de la esclava Dolores Vivanco con su ama Doña Josefa Briseño sobre su libertad," AGN, CCiv, 1846, Leg. 141; AD-A, Corte Superior de Justicia, CCrim, 1842, (II), October 20, 1842; AAL, Causas de Negros, 1815–1855, Leg. 36, LXVII:39; AAL, CCiv, 1848–1851, Leg. 235.

[84] *El Comercio,* February 22, 23, 1853; "La defensoria de menores con D. Pablo Huapaya sobre variación de dominio de la liberta Andrea Ortis," AGN, CCiv, 1850, Leg. 160; "Seguido por el sindico procurador D. Francisco Garfias con D. Manuel Gonzales sobre flagelación al liberto, Andrés Castro," AGN, CCrim, 1853, Leg. 609; "Seguido contra Mauricio Zabala y otros por salteadores," AGN, CCrim, 1854, Leg. 614.

[85] "El defensor general de menores en representación de Gerónimo y Sebastián Jauregui, esclavos, con Don Juan Lostanau, sobre su venta," AGN, CCiv, 1830, Leg. 59.

[86] *El Comercio,* November 15, 1844.

The Black Legions of Buenos Aires, Argentina

George Reid Andrews

The phenomenon of armed black men has always been a troublesome one for the multiracial societies of the Americas. The spectacle of present or former bondsmen, or their descendants, organized into disciplined fighting units inevitably suggests the possibility that those units may acquire institutional autonomy and strike against the very government and society that created them. Armed forces always present this threat, but especially so when the members of those forces belong to a class or social group consistently exploited and confined to a subordinate position. Even if the black soldiers never use their power to redress their legitimate grievances, the fear that they will do so is a constant in the mind of the greater society.

Another drawback of black participation in the armed forces is that the services rendered the state by its black soldiers entitle those men, and the rest of the black population as well, to recognition and repayment of the collective debts owed them by their nation. Black assistance in defending the country against invasion can form the basis for demands that official and unofficial discrimination against black people be ended. This assistance, plus the potential of mutiny or rebellion if the demands are not met, can provide black people with the bargaining power to force societal change.

Thus, while black military units have proved useful and even irreplaceable as defenders of various North, South, and Central American states, their very existence has implied a force potentially hostile to the social bases on which those states rest. The problem of black men serving in the armed forces has therefore proved to be an extremely complex and delicate issue, not only for military policy makers, but for historians as well. To acknowledge black participation in a nation's military history is to acknowledge the contributions which entitle black citizens to equality with whites. Such acknowledgment is obviously undesirable in societies dedicated to maintaining racial inequality.

Perhaps it is for these reasons that the role of the Afro-Argentines in fighting their country's wars remains so little known and poorly understood. Few Argentine historians have failed to mention the importance of black soldiers in the nation's military past, but their participation in that past has been misrepresented in a variety of ways. Inaccuracies abound in the writings on Afro-Argentine military history, ranging from fairly innocuous mistakes concerning which regiments were black and which were white to far more serious misconceptions concerning the nature of segregation in the armed forces, death and desertion rates, and the very existence of the black officer corps. This chapter is an effort to set straight the confused and confusing record of Buenos Aires's black legions.

It is particularly important to correct these inaccuracies because of the pervasive influence of military activity and institutions in the life of Buenos Aires as a whole and its black community in particular. Embroiled in an almost continuous series of foreign and civil wars between 1810 and 1870, Buenos Aires underwent the "militarization" of its society and political system common to most Spanish American states in the postindependence period. Military institutions assumed tremendous importance in the social and political affairs of the province, and black men were disproportionately represented in those institutions, though seldom at very exalted levels. Afro-Argentines were subject not only to the racially discriminatory draft decrees, but also to other laws aimed at rounding up as many of the province's non-elite masses as possible and impressing them into service. Legislation in effect between 1823 and 1872 required all men convicted of vagrancy, gambling, carousing, idleness, or carrying a firearm to serve four-year terms in the regular army, twice as long as terms for volunteers. The embattled Rosas administration, straining to fight simultaneous wars in Uruguay and the interior of Argentina, stretched those terms considerably: its courts regularly handed down sentences of ten to fifteen years of military service, while women convicts could receive sentences of ten years or more as military seamstresses, sewing uniforms for Rosas's troops. Once enlisted, soldiers could be sentenced to additional years of service for infractions of military discipline, and cases of soldiers being illegally forced to reenlist were common.

Given the province's never-ending quest for men to fuel its war machine, military service was an experience that virtually every black man who reached adulthood in nineteenth-century Buenos Aires could count on having. Few indeed are the memoirs of life in the city that do not include a vision of the province's black troopers, and one cannot help but be struck by the way in which the Afro-Argentines themselves dated events in their lives in relation to military happenings. The will of Federico Mendizábal recalled how his wife

Ermenegilda deserted him in 1851 to follow Rosas's army in the Campaign of the South. Mendizábal himself died in 1867 while fighting as a lieutenant in the Paraguayan War. In an 1852 lawsuit brought by the female members of the Mayombé nation against the males, the women recalled that the origins of their dispute dated from the calling up of the men for the 1840 campaign.

Battalions and Regiments

Afro-Argentines served in a succession of units in colonial and nineteenth-century Buenos Aires. As early as the 1660s, black men formed segregated militia units in the province; by 1801 black troops formed 10 percent of the city's 1600-man militia. These troops were easily overcome by a British expeditionary force which occupied the city in 1806, but when the British were driven out six weeks later, free and slave Afro-Argentines fought side by side with white militiamen. A second British invasion a year later was defeated by a defending force of some 5000 men, of whom 876 belonged to the Corps of Indians, Pardos, and Morenos.

Officers and enlisted men from these black militia units went on to fight in the independence wars. Free black troops from Buenos Aires constituted two all-black units in the revolutionary army—the Sixth Infantry Regiment of Pardos and Morenos, and the Battalion of Pardos and Morenos of Upper Peru. Both units distinguished themselves against the Spanish in Uruguay, Bolivia, and northwestern Argentina before being mauled at the Battle of Sipe-Sipe in November 1815. In the worst defeat suffered by Argentine arms during the revolution, over 1000 men were killed, wounded, and captured, while the Spanish suffered 20 dead and 300 wounded. The surviving Afro-Argentines were sent back to Buenos Aires to recuperate; they saw no further action against the Spanish.

Another black unit, the Seventh Infantry Battalion, also fought at Sipe-Sipe, but the Seventh was of a very different type from the free black units, being composed entirely of slaves bought by the state or donated by their owners. In 1813 the government initiated the first of a series of *rescates* (possible translations of this word include ransom, redemption, and exchange), decrees by which owners were required to sell their able-bodied slaves to the state in varying proportions, depending on the economic use to which the slaves were being put. Owners of domestic slaves were to contribute one-third of their holdings, owners of bakeries and fábricas one-fifth, and owners of slaves engaged in agriculture one-eighth. In Buenos Aires province, this draft produced 1016 slave soldiers, who were organized into two battalions, the Seventh and the Eighth Infantry. Subsequent rescates in 1815, 1816, and 1818 yielded 1059 more libertos, who were

aggregated to the Eighth Infantry and the Second Battalion of *Cazadores* (literally Hunters).

When Englishman Emeric Vidal wrote an account of his trip to Buenos Aires, as part of his discussion on the humaneness of porteño slavery he mentioned a particularly benevolent government program by which slaves could be sold to the state as soldiers, whereupon they would be free men. In one respect Vidal was quite right: slaves were free as soon as they entered the armed forces, acquiring liberto status which they would retain for the duration of their military service, afterwards becoming completely free men. This program therefore had obvious attractions for Buenos Aires's male slaves, though there is no record of their responding to it as enthusiastically as the slaves of Santiago, Chile, three hundred of whom hired a lawyer in 1813 to sue the government for their right to enter the army and win their freedom. Instances of slave resistance to the rescate program in Buenos Aires were rare, much rarer than those of owner resistance. After an initial flurry of enthusiasm in which a number of porteño families donated slaves to the state as a patriotic gesture, slave owners began to flood government offices with petitions for exemptions for their slaves, usually based on their economic dependence on the slave's labor. Many owners resorted to the crime of spiriting their slaves out of the city and hiding them in the countryside, where law enforcement was looser. By 1816 the government had decreed the uncompensated expropriation of slaves belonging to any master caught illegally withholding eligible slave males, and an especially long term of service for any slave who failed to turn himself in when called for service. Slaves who informed on such recalcitrant owners would be released from service after a mere three-year term of duty, considerably less than the hitches served by the other libertos.

Vidal's description of the rescate system as a benevolent one is a bit wide of the mark. The libertos' freedom came neither easily nor frequently. Those drafted earliest signed up for the comparatively short term of five years; later decrees required liberto troops to serve until two years after the cessation of hostilities before acquiring complete freedom. To what extent these original terms were honored is unclear. Many libertos died during the campaigns and thus never lived to claim their freedom. The numerous libertos discharged for medical reasons before completing their term of service did not always win their freedom, but rather were frequently returned to their owners—whether as slaves or libertos is not clear.

Many other libertos deserted to escape the miserable conditions of campaign life. Those who succeeded in this enterprise may have won a precarious freedom which conceivably could have proved permanent, but those who were recaptured were usually sentenced to lengthy terms of extra service as punishment. In any case,

Table 1. Enlistees in Selected Military Units from Buenos Aires Province, 1813–60, Tabulated by Race

Unit*	Black	White	Trigueño	Total	Percent Black
Third Infantry Regiment (1813–17)	14	25	36	75	18.6%
Second Infantry Regiment (1813–15)	23	28	37	88	26.1
Tenth Infantry Regiment (1814–18)	65	15	7	87	74.7
Seventeenth Cavalry Regiment (1826–28)	34	60	40	134	25.4
Buenos Aires Artillery Battalion (1824–28)	12	24	49	75	16.0
First Infantry Battalion (1853–60)	200	224	264	688	29.1
Second Infantry Battalion (1853–60)	43	97	80	220	19.5
Third Infantry Battalion (1853–60)	56	91	60	207	27.1
Second Cavalry Regiment (1853–60)	12	26	26	64	18.8
Fifth Regiment of Mounted Grenadiers (1853–60)	10	12	11	33	30.3

Source: Archivo General de la Nación, 3 59-1-1, 59-1-6, 59-2-1, 59-2-4, 59-2-7.

*Dates in parentheses indicate the years for which enlistment records survive.

deserting libertos forfeited hopes of legally winning their freedom through the originally established mechanism of service. There is even serious doubt that the remnants of the revolutionary regiments that made it back to Buenos Aires after years of campaigning were allowed to enjoy the freedom they so richly deserved. An official history of the liberto Eighth Infantry Regiment reports that when its few survivors returned to Buenos Aires in 1824 after eight years of campaigning in Chile, Peru, and Ecuador, they were promptly incorporated into regiments preparing for the approaching War with Brazil, an incorporation which must have been forced on them since it is impossible to imagine that those broken survivors would have gone off voluntarily to fight in yet another war.

Despite the shortcomings of the rescate program from the Afro-Argentines' point of view, it was undeniably successful in furnishing the revolutionary armies with much-needed manpower. Following the destruction of the free black battalions at Sipe-Sipe, the Afro-Argentine representation in the armed forces consisted almost entirely of libertos. When General José de San Martín led his army across the Andes into Chile in 1818 to liberate that country from Spanish rule, half of his invading force consisted of ex-slaves recruited from Buenos Aires and the provinces of western Argentina and organized into the all-black Seventh and Eighth Infantry Battalions and the integrated Eleventh Infantry. San Martín's conquest of Chile and Peru is the stuff of which military legend is made. Leading his small army with a rare combination of skill and luck, he succeeded in throwing off Spanish rule in two centers of royalist resistance and sympathy. Even more remarkable was the career of the black battalions that accompanied him. Between 1816 and 1823 they fought and won battles in Chile, Peru, and Ecuador in an odyssey of campaigning that took them as far north as Quito, thousands of miles from their homes in Argentina. By the time they were finally repatriated, fewer than one hundred fifty men remained out of the approximately two thousand

black soldiers who had crossed the Andes with San Martín.

No other black unit ever experienced a Calvary quite so long and difficult as that suffered by those ill-fated battalions. The only other liberto unit fielded by Buenos Aires, the Second Battalion of Cazadores, sat out the war doing garrison duty in the city. It later saw action against the federalists who invaded the province in 1819 and in the Indian wars of the 1820s. The Fourth Battalion of Cazadores, established in 1826 at the outset of the War with Brazil, also spent the war in Buenos Aires, seeing minor service in the civil disturbances of 1829. Dissolved in 1831, its members were assigned to the Argentine Guard, an all-black battalion of the Rosas period. Other black units prominent in Rosas's army were the Provisional Battalion and the Restorer Battalion, named after Rosas's self-imposed title of Restorer of the Laws.

Following Rosas's fall in 1852, segregation was eliminated in the regular army by the national Constitution of 1353 and the provincial Constitution of 1854, but it continued to exist in the militia. Black militia units remained a constant in Buenos Aires's military establishment throughout the nineteenth century, evolving from the colonial Corps of Indians, Pardos, and Morenos and Battalion of Castes into the Civic Regiment of Men of Color (established in 1811), the Third Battalion of the Native Legion (1820), the Fourth Militia Battalion (1823), the Defenders of Buenos Aires (1830), various units established during the Rosas years, and the Fourth Battalion of the National Guard (established in 1852 and reorganized into the Second Battalion of the Third National Guard Regiment in 1858). A slave militia, the Argentine Auxiliaries, also served during the independence wars.

A focus on the all-black regiments, however, obscures the importance of Afro-Argentines in integrated units. Though segregation of the military was more strictly observed during the colonial period than after independence, there is considerable evidence that even prior to 1810 black and white soldiers served side by side in the local militias. It was not unusual, for instance, for well-to-do merchants or professionals to send their slaves to substitute for them at militia drills and in actual combat, so that a de facto integration resulted through slaves' serving in supposedly all-white units. Sometimes integration was officially condoned. During the English invasions a company of free mulattoes was attached to the First Squadron of Hussars, a prestigious white cavalry unit. At least two petitions survive from black officers in this company appealing to the viceroy to allow them to continue to serve in "this distinguished unit" rather than be transferred back to the Battalion of Castes. So badly did these two men want to stay in the white unit that they both offered to serve without pay, supplying their armament and horses at their own expense. Despite their pleas, both men were reassigned to the Castes.

Given the liberal rhetoric of the revolution, integration of regular army units was almost inevitable. At first the revolutionary junta sought to keep Afro-Argentine companies in separate battalions, allowing only the Indians to serve with the whites, but eventually they relented, and in 1811 several companies of free Afro-Argentines were aggregated to the Second Infantry Regiment. These companies were later separated from the regiment to form the basis of the Tenth Infantry, another integrated unit. The Eleventh Infantry, which accompanied the black Seventh and Eighth Battalions on their eight-year campaign through the Andean countries, was also integrated.

The true extent of integration in Buenos Aires's nineteenth-century regiments is only hinted at by official military legislation. Although several units were established by decrees that explicitly described their integrated or segregated racial nature, the majority were not. Only by studying enlistment records from the period and seeing to which regiments soldiers of given races were assigned can one arrive at an accurate impression of the racial composition of Buenos Aires's army. Such investigation indicates that the province did not field one single battalion or regiment in the 1810–60 period that did not have black soldiers. In some of these units black representation was minimal, 1 or 2 percent. Examples of these would be the Buenos Aires Artillery Division (1853–60), the Ninth Infantry Regiment (1816), the Infantry Legion of Cazadores (1853–60), and the Artillery Regiment of the Fatherland (1814–17). But in other units the representation was substantial, especially when one takes into account the Afro-Argentines probably concealed among the trigueños that appear in the enlistment records. Table 1 is a tabulation of the enlistments recorded for ten units in the 1813–60 period. Those enlistments appeared in five volumes of such documents chosen at random from a total of about twenty. The importance of black soldiers in integrated units, even before integration was instituted in Buenos Aires's army, is obvious. Black troops constituted

more than a quarter of the soldiers in six of the ten units considered; in one of them, the Tenth Infantry Regiment, they made up three-quarters of the enlistments. The trigueño enrollment was even larger, outnumbering the white in four of the ten units, including the largest, the First Infantry Battalion.

There is also evidence that units established as black were in fact integrated, though the number of whites in them was very small. Even the liberto Seventh Infantry Battalion of 1813–15 showed two white enlistees, as did the Fourth Cazadores. In the Rosas period there were instances of white criminals being sentenced to service in such black units as the Restorer Battalion and the Argentine Guard, just as there were black prisoners sentenced to serve in white units. This accounts for a surprising incident in 1847, when the commander of the Restorer Battalion, asked to nominate noncommissioned officers for promotion to two vacant sublieutenancies in the battalion, nominated two white men, both of whom had served in the unit for ten years.

Death, Desertion, and Disease

A potentially explosive question concerned with segregation and the existence of all-black units is the possibility that commanders used them as assault troops in preference to white units, consciously killing off Argentina's black population while achieving military objectives. No Argentine historian has suggested in print that such genocidal policy existed, but several mentioned it in conversation as one explanation for the demographic decline of the Afro-Argentines. Simón Bolívar, the liberator of northern South America, once argued frankly in favor of such a policy.

Is it right that only free men die to free the slaves? Would it not be just for the slaves to win their rights on the battlefield and diminish their dangerous number by this powerful and legitimate means? In Venezuela we have seen the free population die and the slaves remain; I do not know if this is politic, but I do know that if in [Colombia] we do not make use of the slaves [as soldiers] the same thing will happen.

Let it stand to Argentina's credit that there is no evidence of such thought or practice in the country's military history. Although black males were drafted in numbers disproportionate to their representation in the population, it does not appear that they were singled out for consistently hazardous duty. It is true that the Seventh and Eighth Infantry Battalions eventually melted away to nothing during their years of campaigning, but the white units that accompanied them did no better. The First Cazadores was almost completely destroyed at the Battle of Maipú, and very few of the Mounted Grenadiers ever returned from Peru to Buenos Aires. No casualty counts are available for the disaster at Sipe-Sipe but a list of officers killed and captured suggests that the mainly white Ninth Infantry suffered more heavily than the two black regiments combined. The Ninth lost fifteen officers, while the Sixth and Seventh Infantry between them lost six. Or consider the Fourth Cazadores, which quietly sat out the War with Brazil in Buenos Aires while the integrated regiments battled Brazilians and the cold in Uruguay.

A comparison of the 1810–15 roll calls of several battalions on active duty against the Spanish indicates that the white units actually lost more men than the black. Since these roll calls are fragmentary in nature and vary considerably in coverage from month to month, monthly death rates (number of deaths divided by number of men in the unit at the beginning of the month) were computed and the sum of those rates then divided by the number of months to produce a mean monthly death rate for the period in question. That mean monthly death rate was then multiplied by twelve to produce a yearly death rate.

Three units that campaigned together in Bolivia and northwestern Argentina from 1812 to 1814 were the Battalion of Pardos and Morenos of Upper Peru and the white Second and Eighth Battalions of Peru, all Argentine units despite their names. During the 1810–13 period the Battalion of Pardos and Morenos suffered an annual death rate of 91.2 men per 1000, a very high rate indeed. However, the roll calls of the white Second Battalion, which survive only for 1813, show a death rate of 253.2 per 1000. By comparison, the black battalion's death rate in 1813 alone was 114.6 per 1000. The white Eighth Battalion also fought in the 1813 campaign in northwestern Argentina, but roll calls survive for only two of the twelve months of that year, so their results should be treated with caution. They produce an annual death rate of 201.6 per 1000.

Three other units that served together in the northwest were two Afro-Argentine units, the Sixth Infantry Regiment and the Seventh Infantry Battalion, and the white Ninth Infantry Regiment. These units had much lower losses. In an eighteen-month period in 1814–15 (a period which does not include the Battle of Sipe-Sipe; the army was so shattered after its defeat there that no roll calls were taken), the Ninth had an annual death rate of 38.4 per 1000, the Sixth slightly lower at 37.2, and the newly created liberto Seventh Battalion had 27.6.

These losses vary somewhat from the traditional image of Argentina's blacks dying in heaps on the battlefield, going to their deaths by the thousands in the cause of the *patria,* the fatherland. There is no writer on the subject of the Afro-Argentines who does not sound this familiar theme, and some carry it to ghoulish extremes. One Argentine poet and writer of popular history recalls at length how the Afro-Argentines served as cannon fodder from one end of the country to the other, leaving their bleaching bones, which he employs as a recurring image, everywhere they went. The image of the bones is a striking one: as used by that author, who focuses on the contrast between the black skin of the Afro-Argentines and the whiteness of their bones, it becomes a subtle metaphor for the whitening of the Afro-Argentines. They did their duty to their country, died in the process, and left as their memorial a heap of bones, which redeem the memory of the Afro-Argentines not only through the heroism they represent, but also by the fact that the soldiers' blackness has disappeared, replaced by pure and gleaming white.

The bone motif appeared in another of the many popular magazine features that have reinforced the theme of the Afro-Argentines' being killed in the wars. An 1898 interview with a veteran of the independence wars yielded the following grisly anecdote:

> One time we were marching to San Juan, and with me in the advance guard was a black from La Rioja, a slave of the Bazán family. . . . One night he was on guard duty and he went to sleep forever when an enemy scout slit his throat. Well, before leaving we got the body and to save it from the vultures we put it in a huge cave in the hillside, and there we left it, without so much as a wooden cross. After all, the black left nothing on this earth besides his bones—who would ever remember him?

As it turned out, the teller of the story did. Four years later he happened to be campaigning in the same area when a thunderstorm broke and he took refuge in a nearby cave. Surprise of surprises, it proved to be the same one in which they had left the black man's body. "Would you believe that the bones of that poor guy served as fuel to make our fire and keep us dry that night? See what some people are destined for, eh? Some are useful even after they're dead, and others even when they're living are worthless."

Other feature stories on the Afro-Argentines were less gruesome, but they all agree on the recurring theme of the blacks' being killed in the wars. As recently as 1976 a Buenos Aires newspaper article recalling the end of the slave trade went on to discuss how "the blacks fell to the last man in all the battles of the young nation, in the Army of the Andes, in the wars against the Indians, in the marshes of Paraguay."

To what extent is this image of the Afro-Argentines' dying en masse in the country's wars an accurate one? It has more than a kernel of truth, of course, as can be seen from the marked sexual imbalance in the city's black population, documented by the census of 1827. The low death figures registered for the regiments described above should not obscure the fact that all it took was one disastrous battle for a unit to lose more men in an afternoon than it had lost in three years. Though black losses at such battles as Salta (eleven killed), Tucumán and Chacabuco (eight killed) were minimal, clashes such as Ayohouma, Sipe-Sipe, Maipú, Pichincha, Ituzaingó, Caseros, and a host of others levied a hideous toll on the Afro-Argentines, as well as on the whites, Indians, and mestizos unfortunate enough to be drafted into the armed forces.

Even more destructive was the sickness endemic among nineteenth-century armies throughout the world, Argentina being no exception. When the Argentine army invaded Bolivia in 1813 the worst enemy it faced there was the *soroche*, a crippling condition produced by prolonged exposure to the altitude and the bitterly cold weather of the Bolivian *altiplano*. Between December 1811 and July 1812, when the Battalion of Pardos and Morenos of Upper Peru was stationed in the Argentine province of Jujuy, bordering on Bolivia, an average of 22.2 percent of the battalion was sick each month, the majority of them with soroche. When the integrated Río de la Plata Regiment left Lima in 1823 for the Campaign of the Ports, it left behind over one hundred fifty sick men in the city's hospitals; almost all of them died. During the anti-Indian campaign of 1824, the Second Cazadores lost hundreds of men dead or permanently crippled by freezing and frostbite.

Given the miserable conditions of army life, it is amazing that Argentine historians have consistently overlooked the single most important source of losses in the Afro-Argentine regiments. Perhaps attracted by the drama and pathos of the subject, historians have ascribed the losses suffered by those units to battlefield deaths, though a minority do mention the living conditions that caused so many deaths from illness. Only one study has pointed to desertion as a factor in the losses suffered by black regiments, and that study concluded that desertion was relatively infrequent among black troops. This is completely untrue. Blacks and whites alike deserted in droves in all of Argentina's wars, especially the early ones. General Paz's memoirs recalled that during an 1815 march from Buenos Aires to Bolivia, an army of five thousand men was reduced to three thousand by desertions. A draft sent to northwestern Argentina three years later lost two-thirds of its men in a matter of months as a result of desertions.

Afro-Argentines did not hesitate to embrace discretion as the better part of valor, joining their white comrades in wholesale flight from the front. The debilitating effect that these desertions could have on a unit's manpower can be seen in the fact that while the roll calls of the Battalion of Pardos and Morenos of Upper Peru show it losing 47 men through death from 1810 to 1813, it lost 69 men through desertion. The Sixth Regiment lost 18 men dead between October 1814 and August 1815 but 98 men through desertion. Similar figures for the Seventh Battalion (March 1814 to August 1815) are 30 deaths, 189 desertions; the Ninth Regiment (September 1814 to August 1815), 27 deaths, 145 desertions; and the white Second Infantry Battalion of Peru (January through June 1813), 34 deaths, 64 desertions. An obviously discontented unit was the Afro-Argentine Fourth Cazadores, which between November 1827 and October 1829 lost 31 soldiers dead and an astonishing 802 in desertions, many of which must have been multiple, since the battalion at its largest numbered only 715 men. And the same military report that mentions that the Río de la Plata Regiment left one hundred fifty sick men behind in Lima when it departed the city in 1823 adds that it also had to leave behind some three hundred fifty deserters who had not been apprehended by the military police and who remained at large in the city. Therefore, when one reads such accounts as Domingo Sarmiento's description of how he encountered the remnants of an Afro-Argentine regiment at the siege of Montevideo in 1851, reduced to 30 men and commanded by a sergeant, one should not immediately draw the conclusion that Sarmiento implies—that the rest of the regiment was killed in fighting. It is entirely possible that they took the rational course of action and left for home rather than be killed or maimed in the grueling siege.

By claiming an almost complete destruction of the black male population through military service, the nation's historians were able to ignore the fact that many of those soldiers returned alive from the wars to contribute to Buenos Aires's cultural, social, and demographic development. It is significant that the best-known Afro-Argentine military hero is not a historical figure like Colonels Domingo Sosa and José María Morales, who fought in a host of battles, served Buenos Aires heroically for forty or fifty years, and died quietly at home in bed, but rather the mythical Falucho, who, if in fact he ever existed, was killed while suicidally defending the flag of Argentina. Emphasis on the heaps of white Afro-Argentine bones and the pools of red Afro-Argentine blood provides a convenient distraction from the continued presence of black Afro-Argentine skin in the nation's capital. This is not to belittle the disastrous effect that virtually continuous military service over six decades exerted on the city's black population. Many of those deserters clearly never made it back to Buenos Aires and thus were as effectively removed from the black community as they would have been if they had died. Several Argentines who visited Lima in the 1330s and 1840s reported encountering survivors of San Martin's expeditionary force there, and one of the more celebrated anecdotes of nineteenth-century Argentine literature concerns an old black deserter encountered living among the Ranquele Indians by the writer Lucio Mansilla. And many more of the deserters who did make it back to Buenos Aires arrived broken in health, suffering from wounds or the rigors of campaigning. But it is clearly incorrect to say that the Afro-Argentines fell "to the last man" fighting for a country that consistently denied them the rights they were fighting for. To pretend that this was so is to deny them the most elementary common sense or instinct of self-preservation.

When one considers the meager rewards received by the black warriors for their services, the infrequent promotions, the miserable pay, the hardships, the grudging and long-delayed granting of rights promised them during the revolution, one must be amazed at the heroism and endurance the Afro-Argentines consistently displayed. The only major Argentine commander who ever criticized the Afro-Argentines' military performance was Manuel Belgrano, who after presiding over a series of defeats in Paraguay, northeastern Argentina and Bolivia, wrote to General San Martin that "I'm not at all pleased with the libertos; the blacks and mulattoes are a rabble who are as cowardly as they are bloodthirsty, and in the five actions we have been in, they have been the first to break ranks and hide behind walls of bodies." General Paz, a subordinate of Belgrano's who later made brilliant use of black troops in the civil wars, disagreed sharply, once remarking that one black soldier was worth at least three Europeans. Paz and San Martin both preferred liberto troops, whose experience as slaves made them more amenable to military discipline than the whites. When the Seventh Infantry arrived in northwestern Argentina in 1813, Paz was extremely pleased with the way they had mastered their drills: "Along with the Mounted Grenadiers the handsome Seventh Battalion arrived to enlarge the Army of Peru. They came already instructed in modern tactics with which we were unfamiliar, so that they served as a model to the rest of the infantry and cavalry." Generals Rondeau, Viana, Miller, and Guido are also on record as lavishing special praise on Afro-Argentine troops.

The devotion with which thousands of Afro-Argentines fought for their country is a puzzling phenomenon, when one considers the meager rewards they received in return. Perhaps they actually believed the appeals to defend God and country with which their officers fired them before battle, but it is more likely that their bravery and even ferocity in battle sprang from two sources. The first source included the resentments and frustrations they suffered due to their position in Buenos Aires's society. The discontent and rage that they had to repress in the city could be released on the battlefield without fear of punishment, and the occasional testimonials to the "bloodthirstiness" and "savagery" of the Afro-Argentine soldiers suggest that they did not hesitate to take advantage of this opportunity. The fury they displayed on the battlefield was truly above and beyond the call of duty and hints at some deeper motive than mere love of country.

The second source was the hope for promotion: upward mobility in the army and perhaps even in the greater society.

The Officers

Historians writing on the Afro-Argentines have traditionally maintained that it was virtually unheard-of for black men to attain officer rank. José Ingenieros stated unequivocally that the soldiers of the independence wars were always mestizos or blacks, their officers always white. Emiliano Endrek concurred, saying that a few Afro-Argentines may have reached officer level during the post-1820 civil wars, but that black units of the colonial and independence periods were commanded entirely by white officers. José Ramos Mejía maintained that even during the Rosas period, when the government made a policy of courting Afro-Argentine support, it was almost impossible for black men to rise above the rank of sergeant or lieutenant. José Luis Lanuza echoed this statement, and even the normally well-informed Leslie Rout flatly states that "no acknowledged Negroid" held officer rank in the Argentine or Uruguayan colonial militias, and that no black Argentine rose above the rank of captain until after 1820.

The very authors who make these assertions include incidental information which strongly suggests, and in some cases conclusively demonstrates, that black men did in fact reach command positions. In the same essay in which Endrek claims that no blacks served as colonial or independence-period officers, he includes the quotation in which General Belgrano excoriated his black troops as cowardly rabble, a quotation which terminates: "My only consolation is that white officers are coming [to command them], under whom perhaps they can be made of some use." The implication is that at that point they were under the command of black officers. Later Endrek refers specifically to the black officers of Córdoba's Afro-Argentine militia, who were displaced by white officers when the unit was sent off to fight in Bolivia. Another case in point is a thesis written at the University of Córdoba in 1972, whose author asserts that blacks never became officers and then quotes an 1830 decree by General Paz that all liberto prisoners-of-war were to be returned to their owners, with the exception of "those slaves who have served as officers in the invading army"! And there is little question that the above-mentioned authors are familiar with Vicente Fidel López's *Manual de la historia argentina*, one of the most frequently quoted Argentine histories from the nineteenth century. Lanuza, for example, cites it frequently but inexplicably omits López's statement that every officer in Rosas's elite Fourth Battalion was black, with the sole exception of the colonel.

Not only did black men serve as officers in Buenos Aires's army, but some rose to high levels of command. It seems to have been an unwritten rule that no Afro-Argentine could be allowed to reach the rank of general, but at least eleven rose to be full or lieutenant colonels; doubtless more such cases lie concealed in the documentation of the period, waiting to be discovered. Furthermore, Afro-Argentine colonels could hardly have existed in isolation from an even larger number of Afro-Argentines at lower levels in the hierarchy. In order to identify these men and arrive at a coherent representation of the evolution of the black officer corps, I examined the officer staffs of seven all-black battalions in existence between 1800 and 1860. White and integrated units were not included in this study because black officers in those units appear to have been too few in number to justify the expenditure of time and energy involved in searching for them. All seven battalions were infantry; four were regular line units, two were militia, and one, the Restorer Battalion, was a mixed unit of militia and line companies, a common form of military organization under the Rosas administration.

In order to insure comparability between militia and regular officers (who, as will be seen shortly, occupied very different positions in the military establishment), I relied wherever possible on the individual's regular line rank rather than his militia rank. Since almost all of the men in this study held line commissions at one or more points during their lives, it proved possible to compare careers over time using reasonably consistent data.

The names of every officer mentioned in the battalion rolls produced a universe of 186 men. Since roll calls never indicated an individual's race, it was necessary to verify race using other sources. These included military service records and evaluations, which occasionally mention race; enlistment records, which always do; censuses; birth, death, and marriage records; and newspaper articles. Using these data it was possible to establish the race of 104 of the 186 men, somewhat over half.

I tend to suspect that, due to a documentary bias in the data available, the majority of the unknown officers were black. The men for whom it was easiest to get information were those who had the most successful careers and were most prominent in the army and in the society as a whole. For obvious reasons, they tended strongly to be whites. Another complicating factor is the demonstrable tendency on the part of record keepers to cover up evidences of the black officers' African ancestry. Several instances may serve to illustrate this phenomenon. Sublieutenant Bernardo Pintos of the colonial Corps of Indians, Pardos, and Morenos was a successful musician and a rather well-known figure in the city. Histories of colonial Buenos Aires single him out as a renowned black organist, but in the municipal census of 1810 he was counted as white. When he married in 1828, his marriage certificate was filed in the book reserved for whites, despite the fact that the document specifically labeled him as a

pardo. Captain Gregorio Sanfines's 1761 baptism certificate described him as the son of a moreno father and a parda mother. By the time his son José María Sanfines married in 1813, however, the young Sanfines was eligible to be described in the marriage certificate as an *español*, a white. When Sanfines's other son, José Gregorio, married in 1816, no mention was made of his race, but when this son and his wife had a daughter in 1824 (the original captain's grandchild), her baptism record was inscribed in the book reserved for *españoles*. Thus an Afro-Argentine militia captain produced a white Spanish son and granddaughter. Lieutenant Colonel Cabrera's entire family was labeled as pardo in the 1327 census, but by the time his daughter Agueda died in 1891 she had been transformed into a white woman, at least according to her death certificate. Lieutenant Lorenzo Castro of the Restorer Battalion was labeled a pardo in the 1827 census, but the priest who officiated at his 1918 wedding made no mention of his race on the marriage certificate. Castro is described simply as a native of Caracas and a lieutenant in the regular army, though his *porteña* wife is described as a parda.

One can hardly blame the Afro-Argentine officers, who had attained some measure of social standing in the city, for wishing to conceal documentary evidences of their blackness, a guarantee of inferior social status in nineteenth-century Buenos Aires. But coupled with the other documentary bias, this results in its being very difficult to reconstruct the genuine racial composition of the officer corps. This is undoubtedly another contributing factor behind the misconceptions concerning Buenos Aires's black officers.

Table 2 describes the distribution of the sample by race and unit. Of the 104 officers whose race was verifiable, 39, over a third, were black, 61 were white, and 4 were Indian. (The totals in Table 2 exceed these figures due to the fact that several officers in the sample served in more than one unit.) If one is willing to assume that the percentage of black officers among the unknowns was much higher than among the knowns, as seems reasonable, it is probable that black men made up at least half of the officer corps of the Afro-Argentine battalions.

The role of the black officers in Buenos Aires's army changed markedly between 1800 and 1360. The first unit considered, the colonial militia Corps of Indians, Pardos, and Morenos, was officered almost entirely by blacks and Indians, in complete contradiction of traditional claims that no black men achieved officer rank in the colony. Of 23 officers whose race is known, 17 were black, 4 were Indian, and only 2 were white. These free black officers went on to serve in two line units in the revolutionary army, the Sixth Infantry Regiment of Pardos and Morenos, and the Battalion of Pardos and Morenos of Upper Peru. Only the latter was included in this study, and

Table 2. Racial Composition of Officer Corps in Selected Battalions from Buenos Aires Province, 1800–1860

Unit	Indian	Black	White	Unknown	Total	Percent Black[a]
Corps of Indians, Pardos, and Morenos (1808)[b]	4	17	2	7	30	74
Battalion of Pardos and Morenos of Upper Peru (1813)	0	3	5	8	16	38
Seventh Infantry Battalion of Libertos (1814–15)	0	0	25	14	39	0
Second Battalion of Cazadores (1817–20)	0	1	11	7	19	8
Fourth Battalion of Cazadores (1829)	0	0	15	14	29	0
Restorer Battalion (1834–35)	0	6	4	8	18	60
Restorer Battalion (1852)	0	4	0	13	17	100
Fourth Battalion of the National Guard (1853)	0	10	2	12	24	83
Total[c]	4	41	64	83	192	38

Source: Data on the race of individual officers were taken from a variety of sources, including enlistment and service records; parish birth, death, and marriage registers; censuses; and newspaper articles. For citations of sources on each individual, see George Reid Andrews, "Forgotten but Not Gone: The Afro-Argentines of Buenos Aires, 1800–1900" (Ph.D. diss., University of Wisconsin, Madison, 1978), pp. 396–410.

[a]Column calculated excluding unknowns from total.

[b]Dates in parentheses indicate years from which roll call records were taken.

[c]Totals exceed sample totals because several officers served in more than one unit.

very little information could be obtained on its officers, half of whom remain of unknown race. Of the 8 officers whose race could be verified, 5 were white and 3 black. More useful for the purposes of this study would have been the Sixth Infantry, whose roll calls were unfortunately not discovered until after this research project had been completed, at which time it was not possible to subject each name on the rolls to the careful cross-checking in a variety of sources undergone by officers in other units. However, of 39 officers in its 1814–15 rolls, 9 were immediately recognizable as black men who had served at lower ranks in the colonial militia.

Free black troops in the revolutionary army were therefore commanded in large part by black men. This was not the case in the liberto units, represented in this study by the Seventh Infantry Battalion and the Second Cazadores. Only one officer in these two units was verifiable as Afro-Argentine. There are several possible explanations for this dichotomy between the free black battalions and the liberto battalions. First, the government was under no political necessity to make black men the officers of these units. Since the free blacks were accustomed from their colonial experience to serving under black officers, and members of the free black militia had been led to expect that a certain percentage of their number would eventually acquire officer status, the revolutionary government would instantly have alienated free black support by failing to continue this practice. Among the slaves, on the other hand, no such precedent existed. The mere promise of freedom was sufficient to insure their support for the new regime. Since there had never been slave officers, there was no need to elevate libertos into command positions.

Second, and perhaps more important, keeping the liberto regiments officered by whites prevented alliance of any sort between free black officers and the slaves, which the liberto troops in essence still were. In 1806 the town council had described the job of commandant of the Slave Corps (formed during the emergency of the English invasions and disbanded shortly thereafter) as "one of the most delicate positions imaginable." The last thing the upper echelons of the military and the government wanted was to put recently freed black troops under the command of free black officers, producing a potentially explosive convergence of interests between the two.

The destruction of the free black battalions at the Battle of Sipe-Sipe therefore marked the end of a brief five-year period in which many Afro-Argentines enjoyed officerships in the regular army. As free black troops were displaced by libertos, the black officer corps in the regular army withered away and, by 1820, had disappeared almost completely. Regular army Afro-Argentine units from 1815 to 1830 were officered almost entirely by whites, as may be seen in the cases of the Second and Fourth Cazadores. Of 29 officers in the latter unit, 15 are of known race, and every one of them was white.

The color bar preventing Afro-Argentines from reaching officer status was dropped by the Rosas administration. Roll calls of the Restorer Battalion at the beginning and end of its existence (1834–35 and 1852) produce a list of 35 officers, of whom 14 are of known race. Four are white and 10 black. This pattern of black dominance was continued in the post-Rosas Fourth Battalion of the National Guard. Of 24 officers in the unit's 1833 roll calls, 12 are of known race, 2 are white and 10 black, including the commander, Colonel Domingo Sosa.

How does one explain the resurrection of the Afro-Argentine officer corps in the 1830–60 period, after its apparent demise between 1815 and 1830? One explanation must be Rosas's policy of courting Afro-Argentine support for his administration, a policy which did not allow the continued relegation of black men to the lowest ranks of the army. Just as the revolutionary government of 1810 bartered officerships for black political support, so Rosas did the same in the 1830s and 1840s.

Another reason for the return of the black officers may be found in the changing legal status of the black population. The municipal census of 1810 showed that 22.6 percent of the city's black population was free; by 1827 that proportion had risen to 54.8 percent. Following the policy adopted by the revolutionary government in 1810, the Rosas administration recognized that free black men could be impressed into service, but they would not fight well unless there were genuine opportunities for advancement. Since the need for manpower to fight the Indian and civil wars of the 1830s and 1840s was as great as it had been to fight the Spanish in 1810, the government was forced to cede black men the right to rise through the ranks.

When Governor Rosas came to power, he found a readily available supply of potential Afro-Argentine officers in the form of the militia officers. The dearth of black officers in the regular units from 1815 to 1830 can be deceiving, since it hides the fact that black men continued to exercise command in the city's militia units throughout that period. A cursory glance at the 1815 officer list of the Civic Regiment of Men of Color reveals a number of black men from the earlier colonial militia. These officers, later joined by regulars returning from the campaigns in the northwest, continued in the unit well into the 1820s. Black officers who were later to achieve high rank in Buenos Aires's army all served in the black militia during this period in which their access to the regular army was barred. Young Domingo Sosa, after returning from service in the Sixth Infantry, was assigned to duty as a drill instructor in the slave militia, the Argentine Auxiliaries, and in 1828 was called up to serve in the all-black Fourth Militia Battalion. Feliciano Maurino, later to rise to major, served from 1826 to 1833 as an officer in the various black militia units of the city. He then made the unfortunate decision to be an anti-Rosista in the 1833 uprising, for which he was broken to common soldier in the Restorer Battalion. Even the extraordinarily talented Lorenzo Barcala, Argentina's best-known black officer, saw service in the War with Brazil not in a regular unit but in the Fourth Militia Battalion.

Being restricted to the militia set the Afro-Argentines several ranks lower in the military hierarchy than the white regulars. For one, regular officers assigned to mobilized militia units were always elevated one or two ranks above their customary rank. Thus, a regular lieutenant assigned to the militia became an acting captain or even major, with authority over all those officers below him. Black militia officers always came out on the short end of this arrangement. Also, periods of active service in the militia counted toward retirement and pension rights, but periods of inactivity did not. Such slack time did count for regular army officers, enabling them to collect the pensions that often eluded the Afro-Argentines. Finally, regular officers were subject at all times to the *fuero*, military legal jurisdiction, while militia officers were subject to such jurisdiction only when they were on active duty. Being subject to the fuero was considered to be one of the great privileges of military service, since it made one immune to the civilian courts and the police: officers found that their military peers tended to be more lenient in punishing civil offenses than were the civilian courts.

Table 3. Highest Known Rank Achieved by Individuals of Known Race in Selected Buenos Aires Battalions, 1800–1860

	Indian	Black	White	Total
General	0	0	6	6
Colonel	0	2	16	18
Lieutenant colonel	0	5	12	17
Major	1	5	7	13
Captain	1	13	10	24
Lieutenant	0	9	7	16
Sublieutenant	2	5	3	10
Total	4	39	61	104

Source: See Table 2.

Although the Afro-Argentine militia officers do not appear to have been disadvantaged in relation to white militia officers, their inability to acquire line commissions during the 1820s was clearly the result of a policy of racial exclusion. While not every white man could win a position in the regular officer corps, no black man could. It was therefore of concrete benefit to them that Governor Rosas allowed the Afro-Argentines back into the ranks of the regulars.

Once having entered the regular army, however, the Afro-Argentines' race continued to have an adverse effect on their possibilities for advancement. A tabulation of the highest known rank reached by each individual in the sample (Table 3) shows that the average black officer in service between 1800 and 1860 was most likely to end his career as a captain, while the average white officer was most likely to end his as a colonel. No black man achieved the rank of general, whereas 10 percent of the whites did. And the increasing difficulty that black men experienced in winning promotion past the rank of captain can be seen in the fact that there are fewer black majors and lieutenant colonels than captains, and fewer black colonels than lieutenant colonels. Among the whites, there were more lieutenant colonels than majors, and even more colonels than lieutenant colonels.

Military service could and did serve as an avenue of upward mobility for those men skilled and determined enough to make their way to the top. An Afro-Argentine male looking to rise as high in the society as possible was probably best advised to join the army and bend such talents as he had toward acquiring a colonelcy. But such a man would have been a fool not to realize that the odds against his reaching that goal were extremely long, that access to the topmost levels of the hierarchy would be forever closed to him because of his race, and that even if he were lucky enough

320 Section Six: Comparative Slavery in the Americas

to rise as high as a black man could go, his influence and prestige could be cut short at any moment by political reversals or violent death. Men seeking less spectacular but more secure advancement were better advised to master a more reliable and less hazardous trade than that of arms.

The twentieth-century reader may level the charge that the black soldiers and officers prostituted themselves to fight white men's wars. The charge is anachronistic, since it presupposes a political consciousness that simply did not exist in nineteenth-century Buenos Aires, nor in the United States. Many Afro-Argentines sincerely believed in love of country and the principles of heroism, loyalty, and valor, just as thousands of North Americans went to their deaths under similar banners in colonial wars in Mexico and Cuba. Others capitalized on their military service to win the upward mobility denied them by the society at large. The Afro-Argentines lived in a white man's society; the alternatives were either to fight his wars or to suffer the consequences of refusing to do so. While fighting those wars they served not only as followers but also as leaders, and as soldiers and officers they compiled a record of achievement that has been too easily relegated to history's back drawers. Let the record stand corrected.

SECTION SEVEN:
INTERPRETING WOMEN'S STRUGGLES IN THE AFRICAN DIASPORA

Introduction

During the past thirty years, there has been a growing concentrated effort to undertake far more scholarly studies in women's history and gender issues. History's relatively recent focus on the importance of studying social systems and the careful examining of the rise of the Civil Rights and feminist movements, have all led to numerous treatises that show that women's concerns and activities were different from but equally important as those of men. These new gender-awareness studies have led to a variety of approaches in dealing with our revision of history as it relates to better understanding the role of women in the development of societies. The treatment and perspective given women in history have been one of the fastest-growing areas of research and writing in the past two decades.

The role of women in the African Diaspora experience has been systematically studied, beginning with the pioneering work of Lucille Mathurin Mair in her *Rebel Women in the British West Indies During Slavery* (1975). Since then a growing number of scholars have concentrated their efforts on dealing with various aspects, issues, and regions of women in the African Diaspora. Among the most important authors contributing to our better understanding of the gender issues are Debora G. White (1985), Hilary M. Beckles (1988, 1989), Marietta Morsey (1989), Barbara Bush (1990), Darlene C. Hine (1990), David B. Gaspar (1996), Verene Shepherd (1999), and Rosalyn Terborg-Penn (1987). Most of the essays in this section focus on issues that relate to the reinterpretation of the role of women during slavery in the Americas. Since women accounted for roughly a third of the Africans in the Atlantic slave trade and were long considered the weaker sex, they were treated by most early writers and later scholars (most of whom were men) with less than scant attention. The majority of works viewed women's role in the society as not really important. Recent scholarship has clearly demonstrated that the female slaves endured an extra dimension of exploitation, at times far more than men slaves, not only for their labor, childbearing and other domestic responsibilities, but also because they were more often sexually exploited by the slaveholding men and by their male African counterparts. These essays describe the critical role of slave women in the United States, Brazil, and the Caribbean in areas of economics, social interaction, family rearing, and passing on cultural traits.

This section begins with an essay by Rosalyn Terborg-Penn, who clearly outlines the development of the various approaches that authors have used in analyzing and interpreting women's history. Rosalyn Terborg-Penn's essay is extremely useful in placing in bold perspective the theoretical approach necessary in studying, researching and writing about African Diaspora women's history cross-culturally. Terborg-Penn is one of the pioneering scholars in the study of African American women's history and has published extensively on the role of women in the African Diaspora. She helped introduce the teaching of the history of African Diaspora at Morgan State University, where she is Professor Emerita of History. She co-authored *A Special Mission: The Story of Freedmen's Hospital 1862–1962* (1975), and is co-editor of *The Afro-American Woman: Struggles and Images* (1978), *Women in Africa and the African Diaspora* (1987), *Black Women in America: An Historical Encyclopedia* (1993), and *The African American Women in the Struggle for the Vote* (1998). She was coordinator of the Department of History's graduate program until the spring of 2006.

The second essay in this section is Barbara A. Bush's "The Economic Role of Slave Women," which is taken from her book *Slave Women in Caribbean Society 1650–1838* (1990). Bush has been a pioneer in writing about slave women in the Caribbean. She is Senior Lecturer at Parson Cross College, Sheffield, England, and tutor in third world studies at the Open University, London, England. Her other essays include "Towards Emancipation, Slave Women and the Resistance in the British West Indies 1790–1838" from *Slavery and Abolition* (December 1984), "White 'Ladies,' Colored 'Favorites,' and Black Wenches" from *Slavery and Abolition* (December 1981), and "Hard Labor, Women, Childbirth and Resistance in British Caribbean Slave Societies" from *Black Women and Slavery in the Americas* (1996), edited by D. Barry Gaspar and Darlene Clark Hine. This section continues with essays that clearly represent many of the most positive features that women can achieve.

The third essay in this section is authored by Robert Olwell. The narrative focuses on the role of slave women in eighteenth century Charleston, South Carolina. Olwell shows how slave women were able to push the limits usually assigned to their kind in the American South. He raises a number of questions about who really influenced whom during slavery and suggests that a new view be found about the significance of the slave women in the shaping of the American South. Robert Olwell is Associate Professor of History at the University of Texas at Austin. He is author of *Masters, Slaves and Subjects: The Culture of Power in the South Carolina Low Country 1740–1790* (1998).

The fourth essay on women in the African Diaspora experience was written by Robert W. Slenes. He reexamines the negative stereotyping that Brazilian slave women acquired from casual observers as well as from some trained scholars regarding their sexual practices and their attitudes toward their spouses and their families. Slenes's article was included in the anthology edited by David B. Gaspar and Darlene C. Hine, *More Than Chattel: Black Women and Slavery in the Americas* (1996). He is Professor of History at the Universidade Estadul de Campinas in Brazil, and he has written extensively on slavery in Brazil.

The fifth essay in this section examined the methods that historians have used to evaluate feminist consciousness among West African women during the Colonial period. Cheryl Johnson-Odim made a strong case indicating most Western feminist scholars have missed some critical insights in interpreting the role and activities of African women and that their activities were not inspired by western models but their own models. Johnson-Odim's dissertation 'Nigerian Women and British Colonialism: The Yoruba Example' was her first work on the theme. She is the co-author of, *For Women and The Nation: A Biography of Funmilayo Ransome-Kuti of Nigeria* (1997). She has also written articles in *Third World Women and The Politics of Feminism* (1991), and *Nigerian Women in Historical Perspective* (1992).

The final essay in this section brings us into the more contemporary period of the 1920s and is about one of the most important African American women of her time, Amy Jacques-Garvey. The essay narrates the struggles, frustrations, and achievements of Marcus Garvey's wife during this turbulent time. The author of this essay is Ula Y. Taylor, Chairperson and Associate Professor of African American Studies at the University of California at Berkeley. She earned her doctorate in American History from the same university at the Santa Barbara campus. She is co-author of *Panther, The illustrated History of the Story Behind the Film* (1995), and *The Veiled Garvey, The Life and The Times of Amy Jacques-Garvey* (2002). She is soon to publish *Re-Gendering of The Nation of Islam: A History of The Nation of Islam*.

African Feminism: A Theoretical Approach to History of Women in the African Diaspora

Rosalyn Terborg-Penn

To develop a historical theory for the study of women in Africa and the African diaspora entails the surmounting of obstacles erected by traditional historiography cross-culturally, but also poses the challenge of exploring new concepts in women's, African-American, African, Caribbean, and Latin American histories. The methodology, by necessity, is often unorthodox to traditional historians, because the concept, African diaspora women's history, requires nontraditional methods and sources. In addition, traditional sources, those recorded in manuscripts or in official documents, often failed to include the female presence other than in passing. More important, historians of the past often failed to include a female perspective when analyzing the data collected. It is now up to scholars reconstructing African diaspora women's history to reexamine some of the old documents and secondary sources to find the female perspective and to include traditionally neglected sources.

For historians, developing theories for the study of women in the diaspora is crucial at a time when taking an advocacy approach to black women's history has left scholars under attack. It is crucial because during the past few years, criticism has ranged from total rejection of the idea that black women have a history of their own to acknowledgment that we must, to some extent, have a history but that our experiences could not vary that much from that of blacks as a group or of women in general. Among those who at least feel that black women should be discussed historically, questions about why they should be separated from black history or from women's history arise. In both cases, critics assume that black women have always had a history of being victimized, like the stereotyped slave woman, or of being victimizers, like the stereotyped black matriarch. Hence, our experiences are generalized erroneously to fit into Western concepts of the masses of either blacks or women, as being oppressed while passively looking to others for liberation, or as black women pathologically abusing their own. Such theorists look askance at the idea that there have been black women leaders revered by their own people, especially their women, and black women who actively resisted oppression using their own networks. Furthermore, a historical theory that couches these ideas within a time perspective, which can be

exemplified throughout areas of Africa and the diaspora, seems heretical to some.

To the advocates, however, one of the most exciting issues about the emerging field of African diaspora women's history is that it involves interdisciplinary methods, as well as cross-cultural perspectives. Because historians cannot rely upon traditional, written historical sources in order to reconstruct black women's past totally, they turn to the works of other social scientists and humanists. It is not surprising that Filomina Steady, although she is an anthropologist, includes in her book *The Black Woman Cross-Culturally* essays from a variety of disciplines, several of which provided insights for historians.[1] With this in mind, scholars searching for alternative sources on women in the African diaspora may want to examine works about black women written by sociologists, anthropologists, ethnomusicologists, and others.

Whether to use interdisciplinary approaches to historical analysis or not is a debate that reemerges periodically among historians. In the early 1960s historians of American history debated this methodology as American studies programs began to develop across the nation. Similarly, in the early 1970s historians of Afro-American history debated the virtues of black studies programs. In the early 1980s that debate surfaced again among historians of African history, as well as American history. A theory for African diaspora women's history that includes the use of interdisciplinary methods will stimulate this debate even further. Nonetheless, such an approach seems quite viable, and Steady's concept of African feminism lends itself to a historically based theoretical framework. In essence, the theory is used to approach the study of black women's lives through an analysis of their own networks. Beginning with an examination of the values that foster the customs of women in traditional African societies, historians can plot how these customs have changed, even though the values remained somewhat the same as women of African descent were forcibly transported throughout the world, especially to the Western Hemisphere. Perhaps the two most dominant values in the African feminist theory, which can be traced through a time perspective into the New World, are developing survival strategies and encouraging self-reliance through female networks. Historically, this combination has not been present among females of Western, i.e., European origins, but can be traced among women of African descent in New World societies, as well as in Africa.[2]

Although historians have not confronted the issues of African feminism directly, at least two of them have approached the study of black women in such a way that applies well to this theoretical path. Historian Lucille Mathurin has written several works on enslaved women in the British West Indies, especially in Jamaica, which exemplify issues found in the African feminist theory. In addition, historian Bernice Johnson Reagon's work on the culture of traditional black southern women in the United States reflects this approach. Both historians identify black women leaders who provide strength, both physically and spiritually, to their communities. These women are revered in their societies as a whole, but especially by the women. In the case of enslaved women in the British West Indies, Mathurin finds that their rebellious exploits against the slave system are celebrated in song and in oral tradition. In her essay, "My Black Mothers and Sisters or on Beginning a Cultural Autobiography," Reagon finds black southern women to be the "major cultural carriers and passers-on of the traditions of our people." In this case, the culture has been influenced by African survivals. Thus, in both diaspora societies, women, often within networks, provide significant avenues for community survival—past, present, and future. This analytical approach to black women's history clearly reflects the African feminist tradition.[3]

Historical Approaches

African feminism as a theory differs from the other conceptual approaches used to study black women's history from the early 1960s to the early 1980s. A review of these approaches is imperative here. The first stems from the integrationist theory, which fosters a traditional approach by utilizing what historian Okon Uya calls a "white filter."[4] In using this filter, scholars evaluate African or African-American societies in terms of European or Euro-American culture, or from the outside in, rather than from the inside out. The integrationist approach seeks to identify what contributions black women have made to western culture or looks at how black women have been passively victimized by the mainstream society. This historical approach is perhaps the oldest and most commonly used.

An example of this integrationist approach is Sylvia Dannett's *Profiles of Negro Womanhood*, which was published in the mid-1960s.[5] It reflects the integrationist theory in that most of the women selected for discussion attempted to break the barriers of racism in order to integrate into the mainstream. Although this collection of biographical sketches gives much-needed data about black women long forgotten in United States history, their lives are celebrated by Dannett more because of their contributions to America, rather than their contributions to black life.

Other examples of the integrationist approach are Gerda Lerner's documentary collection, *Black Women in White America* and Loewenberg and Bogin's documentary collection, *Black Women in Nineteenth Century American Life*,[6] both of which were published in the 1970s. Although the voices of assertive black women are heard when reading the documents, more often than not the editors' analysis deals with the plight of victimized black women, who are viewed through a "white filter." It is not surprising that the limited historical works to come out about black women in the United States from the 1960s through the mid-1970s would have an integrationist thrust, since much of the early 1960s black freedom movement espoused integration. To some extent, these works were either stimulated or influenced by the movement.

Historical works that analyzed the lives of black women in the United States and that were written by black women themselves began to emerge with a nationalist approach in the late 1970s, again reflecting the changing black mood of the times. *The Afro-American Woman: Struggles and Images,* edited by Harley and Terborg-Penn, was the first of this type.[7] All the essays were written by black scholars who used historical methods and who took a nationalist theoretical stance. Nationalist theory revised the integrationist framework by eliminating the "white filter" and by seeking to find what black women have done in their own communities or organizations to help themselves and others. The nationalist approach deals with victimization fostered by racism but rejects the thesis that black women passively accepted it or looked to others for their liberation. Although racism is seen as the major barrier to black women's self-determination, gender and class oppression are also discussed as obstacles to black female progress.

Similarly, Jeanne Nobles's, *Beautiful, Also, Are the Souls of My Black Sisters* takes a nationalist position. Although the subtitle of Nobles's work is *A History of the Black Woman in America*, she is not a historian, and her book reveals this in its inaccuracies and shortcomings in historical analysis.[8] Nonetheless, her perceptions about black women, especially in contemporary matters, reflects a nationalist view of self-determination and identity with Africa. This can be observed in her quoting of an African proverb: "'You are beautiful, but you cannot eat your looks; you must learn to work,' American black sisters will have to work for what they get."[9]

In addition to the nationalist approach, a Marxist feminist theory has been used in the last few years to assess black women's history. In this analysis, class, race, and gender are the variables discussed in the dynamics of black women's oppression. However, the class struggle is considered to be the major variable. This theory, by its nature, imposes a "white filter," in that the standards of Western feminism, as well as Marxism, are often used to evaluate cultures, values, and oppression. Black women are then compared with other oppressed workers, usually nonblacks, who are struggling against capitalism.

Journalist Stephanie Urdang's work on women of the revolutionary struggle in Guinea-Bissau reflects this approach.[10] Although her writings do not include historical analysis, her perceptions about West African women formerly colonized by the Portuguese have been noted by historians of the Marxist theoretical persuasion. However, her work, like much of the work written from a Marxist feminist perspective about African-American women's history, does not include a cross-cultural perspective.

Perhaps the best historical work about African-American women that uses Marxist theory was published in 1982 by Bettina Aptheker. In her book *Women's Legacy: Essays on Race, Sex and Class in American History*, Aptheker focuses her analysis on the experiences of black women.[11] Interestingly, her book includes autobiographical statements that link her analytical development to political changes in the United States during the 1960s and 1970s. As a result, one can see how the nationalist phase of the black freedom movement replaced the integrationist phase of the movement, of which she was a part. By the late 1960s, when this transformation occurred, the women's movement had been revitalized, mainly among middle class white women. Within this context, white women in the black freedom movement revolted, feeling rejected because of their race and their sex. Aptheker's long relationship with Marxist ideology, however, remains steadfast in her feminist theoretical development. Thus, it is not surprising that she adopted a Marxist feminist approach. Her political activities during the late 1960s intertwined with those of Angela Davis. However, as a black Marxist, Davis flirted briefly with nationalism before taking a feminist posture, and in 1981, she published a collection of essays, *Women, Race and Class*, similar in approach to Aptheker's work. Davis admitted that she was a lay person when she called for a reexamination of black women's history. This is evident. As a result, the ideas she puts forth in the book lack the theoretical, as well as the historical, continuity found in Aptheker's work. Hence, the ideologies in Davis's thirteen essays range from Marxist feminist to nationalist to radical feminist, all reflecting the secondary sources she used, as well as changes in her own political development. Despite the inconsistencies in theory, Davis's essay "Racism, Birth Control and Reproduction Rights" reflects the next step in the theoretical development process—radical feminism.[12]

Although a radical feminist theory has been applied to black women's experiences in books such as *Some of Us Are Brave*, edited by Hull, Scott, and Smith, no historical works have been published in book form.[13] Nonetheless, some attention should be given to this theory. The radical feminist approach may or may not use a "white filter." It seeks to find ways for black women to develop a political female consciousness or to fight gender, for the most part, as well as race and class oppression. The term *radicals* has been interpreted by recent scholars to mean historians who see society ruled by bourgeois liberal apologists using reform as a means to preserve their privileged places.[14] In this sense, then, radical feminist historians reject women's history that omits analytical discussions of women oppressed by male-dominated society or patriarchy.[15] Hence, a radical feminist approach to black women's history would view victimization as the major theme, with patriarchy, whether white or black, as the basis for oppression. An example of this type of analysis can be seen in an essay written by a group of black feminists, The Combahee River Collective, named for the successful campaign led by Harriet Tubman during the Civil War. The essay combines historical materials with autobiographical narrative to present the group's point of view. In describing the origins of the collective, the authors' state, "A combined antiracist and antisexist position drew us together initially, and as we developed politically we addressed ourselves to heterosexism and economic oppression under capitalism."[16]

All of these theories have their merits because they represent various stages in the development of black women's history during the twenty years from the early 1960s to the early 1980s. The African feminist theory, however, seems to be the most viable for the study of African diaspora women's history because it provides three points which the other theories have not. First, it begins with the cosmology common to traditional African women who lived during the era of the slave trade. Because the African heritage of most women indigenous to New World societies originated then, this cosmology provides a common source for historical analysis. Second, the theory eliminates the "white filter" in that it looks to black standards for interpreting culture, values, initiatives, activities, and organizations. In so doing, the theory is uniquely a black women's theory. Third, the theory can be applied cross-culturally through time in order to assess women's roles and activities during and after slavery, as well as women's struggle against human oppression. Here the variables in the liberation struggle are more diverse than in any other theory, because they include race, gender, sexuality, class, religion, and culture, all areas of human activity in which black women have achieved in spite of discrimination.

The Use of the Term *Black*

Before applying the African feminist theory to black women's past, it is important to look at the term *black,* because not all women of African descent identify with this term. In the United States, for example, by law, people with any measurable degree of African ancestry are considered black. As a result, since slavery, women of African descent, regardless of skin color, have been identified, and often have identified themselves, as black. In this sense, *black* symbolizes a cultural milieu, more than it does a color. On the other hand, in many Caribbean and South American societies, women of African descent vary in colors that determine legal status, as well as cultural association. Hence, a mulatto woman in the British West Indies, for example, does not identify herself as black, whereas the same woman born in the United States may choose or be forced to do so by society. Differences in legal and cultural identification by race cause barriers to reconstructing the past, especially for researchers studying countries like Argentina and Brazil, where blacks have not been counted in the population census for several generations. The key to historical reconstruction, then, must rest first upon how women identify themselves and second on how they are identified by the society in which they live. A mulatto woman from South America may emigrate to the United States perceiving her status to be nonblack, but after years of experiencing social and economic proscription based upon race, she will begin to identify with blacks because of her need for a survival network. The necessity for this change in racial orientation may well vary among immigrants due to time of immigration. Hence, in applying the African feminist approach to historical reconstruction of black women's lives, color and cultural perception should be taken into consideration.

Resisting Oppression

African feminism can be applied cross-culturally to black women resisting oppression during the postslavery eras in the United States and in the former Danish Virgin Islands. In both of these cases, the way in which the heroines have been revered and remembered by later generations is important to understanding women's roles in carrying on the culture of black people. In addition, the women leaders in these resistance efforts were over forty years of age and were among groups of women who shared similar oppressive experiences. Hence, age appears to be an important variable among black women leaders. How female leaders were chosen is an important question; however, the historical sources and the oral testimonies that survive rarely deal with this process. Nonetheless, we can assume that women in the African diaspora believed that with age came wisdom and maturity, as did women in traditional African societies. Women who demonstrated leadership ability, then, earned leadership positions because of these qualities. Leadership, nevertheless, appeared to be a practical status for the women discussed in the remainder of this paper, for their daily lives appeared to be much like those of other women with similar status in their communities. Working-class women worked outside of the home to survive. Women of professional or higher economic status often did so, as well. Hence, work, for the most part, was an essential ingredient in the lives of black women leaders. As a result, networking among women was as important a survival strategy as establishing self-reliance imperatives.

In the United States, Harriet Tubman's name has been celebrated since the 1840s. Some conveyed the title "Moses" upon her because of her leadership in the Underground Railroad freedom movement. Although the title is a biblical, male term, Tubman functioned in much the same way as this historical figure, who was said to have delivered his people from slavery via powers divine in source. Likewise, Tubman, a victim of the mysterious disease somnolence, miraculously overcame her handicap to deliver over three hundred people from slavery to freedom. Her accomplishment of this feat was believed by many to have been divinely directed. Over the years, women, especially, have named organizations, schools, homes, and other community institutions in her honor. For example, The Combahee River Collective was named in honor of Tubman's successful military campaign against the Confederates during the Civil War. It is this rarely noted of Tubman's many accomplishments that merits discussion here.

During the Civil War, Tubman took leave from her role as a conductor on the Underground Railroad to assist in the Union Army effort. In 1862 she went to the Sea Islands and attached herself to the forces under Major General David Hunter's command in Beaufort, South Carolina. There Tubman won the respect of the newly freed slaves who had joined the Union Army after Emancipation. In various roles, she brought freedmen's problems to the attention of the military authorities, nursed the sick, and taught the women how to care for themselves, independent of their former masters. Tubman's relationship with these women was one of mutual assistance. Because she received no pay for her work, Tubman found ways to support herself. One was to spend the evenings baking root beer pies, which women in her network sold for her during the day. Tubman also acquired a special reputation for curing dysentery with roots, a remedy surely borrowed from African foreparents via slaves in her native Dorchester County, Maryland.[17]

The roles of nurse, teacher, intermediary, and entrepreneur were not unique to Tubman in comparison with other southern black folks in the United States during these revolutionary times.

Other former slave women, many of whom remain anonymous, assumed similar roles during the Civil War. Among these were Susie King Taylor of South Carolina and Sojourner Truth of New York. Their recollections reveal the strong sense of networking among black women, as well as the development of survival skills among black women and others whose lives were disrupted by the war. Although Taylor was a young woman when she nursed black soldiers and taught them to read, Truth was in her sixties when she provided services to black refugees at the Freedmen's Hospital in Arlington, Virginia.[18]

Tubman's unique quality was her skill as a military strategist. Consequently, Union Army officers prevailed upon her knowledge of guerrilla warfare and espionage, notably in the Combahee River campaign against the Confederate camp in July 1863. Although in January 1863, the Emancipation Proclamation had freed the enslaved in rebelling states such as South Carolina, plantation owners continued to enslave black people in areas held by the Confederacy. Breaking the Confederate control of the Combahee River was assigned to Colonel James Montgomery. Tubman biographer Earl Conrad noted that she selected Montgomery, the leader of three hundred black soldiers, to command this expedition, which in reality Tubman planned and executed. The result was the destruction of millions of dollars worth of Confederate supplies and the liberation of nearly eight hundred slaves, most of whom were women and children. A news dispatch noted that these Union Army forces were "guided" by a black woman, who remained anonymous to readers. Nonetheless, oral traditions and Tubman's recollections of the battle remained. At the time, Tubman was over forty years of age, a significant age among black women chosen to resist oppression.[19]

In her late years, Tubman described the hundreds of freed women fleeing the Confederate lines with their children, their animals, and often with their provisions still cooking in the pots. Although they escaped undaunted, many of them were whipped by plantation overseers. Tubman's description of the scene reveals self-reliant women of African descent creating their own means for survival during and after slavery.[20]

From the extant data we can conclude that Harriet Tubman assumed leadership positions and that the people she led accepted her direction and assisted her in daily survival activities, such as the root beer pie enterprise Tubman established. In short, the women in the camp became part of Tubman's practical network as they exchanged services for survival.

In the Danish Virgin Islands, slavery ended in 1848 as a result of a massive slave revolt on the island of St. Croix. The revolt was precipitated by a gradual emancipation decree the year before. It is believed that the governor of the Virgin Islands was persuaded by his free mulatto mistress, Anne Heegaard, to lobby the Danish king at least for gradual emancipation. However, slaves wanted immediate liberation and took action to achieve it. Soon after their revolt, peonage replaced the slave labor system on the sugar plantations, which dominated the island's economy. By 1878, a generation later, peons realized that the restrictions of the labor regulations legislation virtually bound them to the plantations through yearly contracts. Like the soon-to-be-developed sharecropping system in the United States, peonage in the Virgin Islands was quasislavery. As a result, on October 1, 1878, the day new contracts were to be signed, a labor revolt exploded in Frederiksted, one of two cities on the island. Laborers burned and looted the city. From the town the rebels headed for sugar plantations between Frederiksted and Christiansted, the island's other city, burning nearly all the fields and the plantation estates. Men, women, and children took part in the war that ensued, with several women taking leadership roles. Mary Thomas, known among her people as Queen Mary, led the band of women and children, aided by her lieutenants Queen Agnes and Queen Matilda. In addition, two other women were implicated in the rebellion, Rebecca Frederik and Axelline Salomon, known as "the black Amazon." Their efforts were responsible for the rum and kerosene fires that destroyed most of Frederiksted, including the rum factory that exploded, killing fourteen women. According to accounts of the battles that ensued in the countryside, women led the burning of the sugar estates, or Great Houses, but not the livestock. Some accounts say that this was a labor riot that erupted spontaneously, with no particular leadership, while others discuss a well-organized rebellion of discontented peasants. Nonetheless, in the oral tradition, renditions of the rebellion survive, extolling the efforts of Queen Mary. One such, a Carasou folk song, reads:

> Queen Mary away ya go burn.
> Don't ask me nothin' tall.
> Just give me match and oil.
> Bassin Jailhouse ata we go burn.[21]

The three queens were all imprisoned in the Bassin jail for their rebellious acts. Subsequently, they were sent to Denmark for trial, imprisoned, but later returned to St. Croix. Of the sixty-four persons convicted of criminal acts, twelve men were executed. The others included four women, the only native-born of the conspirators. It is the women's exploits that continue to be celebrated and revered by the common folk of St. Croix.[22]

Significantly, the women leaders of this military campaign had long before earned the title "queen," suggesting their status in their own communities. Such status came with age and ability, as was the case among similar types of women in traditional West African societies. Their roles as the leaders of black women warriors reflected African roots as well, generations after the arrival of their last African foremothers. Thus, the tradition of warrior queens remained in this African-Caribbean society, as one characteristic of a system that encouraged self-reliant women developing survival mechanisms that challenged economic oppression.

All of the women leaders involved in the St. Croix labor revolt worked either in the rum factory or on the sugar plantations. Labor in either circumstance was strenuous, requiring long hours. The fact that the masses of these women brought their children with them into their struggle reveals the close bond between black women and their children. Both on the South Carolina plantations and on the St. Croix plantations women carried their children into the battle and carefully tended the livestock needed for future survival.

A comparison of the armed struggles black women waged during the mid-nineteenth century in the United States and in the Danish Virgin Islands reveals similarities in experiences, resistance strategies, and cultural frameworks. In both societies, plantation slavery had been a way of life that dominated the legal, as well as the economic, status of black women and their ancestors. Despite the attempts to foster docile behavior by the plantation system, women often looked to themselves for survival networks and openly resisted the system. In times of crisis, they selected their own leaders, often older women known for their strength and military prowess. Afterward, the oral traditions of women in the community carried the memory of these heroines on for future generations to revere. Cultural heroines are especially important in societies such as these, because the victories were short-lived. Peonage returned to St. Croix within less than a generation, although in a less oppressive way, and the sharecropping system replaced the plantation slavery system in the southern region of the United States. Survival strategies designed and executed by women remained a major imperative, and women sought various ways to maintain it. Here the African feminist approach to historical analysis is clearly applicable.

The Struggle for Woman Suffrage

The African feminist approach can be applied to the early twentieth century political struggles for woman suffrage among black women in both the United States and the Virgin Islands. The woman suffrage movement was a struggle that involved mainly white middle-class women reformists in Western societies. It is not surprising that black women who championed this cause were usually from the educated and professional class. In both the United States and the Virgin Islands, class, rather than color, determined leadership among black women suffragists. These women ranged from dark brown to light brown in skin color. However, women leaders in the struggle for suffrage championed the right of all

people to vote, not just the women of their class. Organizations and networks of black women effectively mobilized both women and men, using a variety of political strategies, including petitioning legislatures, holding rallies, canvassing churches and neighborhoods, and taking cases to the courts. Many of these efforts were led by black women in black communities, with support, primarily, from black women in their networks, but also from sympathetic black men and white women suffragists.

In the United States, an example of a black women's suffrage network was the Colored Women's Civic and Political League of Rhode Island. This group of Republican party women was politically active, despite their disenfranchisement. Their leaders were professional women and women married to professional men, among them Mary E. Jackson, a Rhode Island state civil servant, Susan E. Williams, a teacher, Maria Lawton, the wife of a government official, and Bertha G. Higgins, the wife of a physician. Of this group, Higgins was the prime mover. A seamstress by training, she had given up her business after marriage to devote her time to homemaking and community service. Higgins was a founder and leader of several women's political organizations, mainly the Political League and, later, the Julia Ward Howe Republican Women's Club. In these associations she fought for woman suffrage and black women's political patronage from 1913 until 1932, when she became disillusioned with the Republican party and led many of her women supporters to the Democratic party.[23]

Before this break, Higgins and women like her saw the hope for black women, both politically and economically, in the right to vote. Like many politically active blacks of the times, Higgins felt that the Republican party could best facilitate this goal. Nonetheless, these women joined a variety of political and civic organizations to foster the networking they felt was necessary for survival. In 1916, for example, Higgins persuaded the Twentieth Century Art and Literary Club, a group of black Providence women, to sponsor a suffrage minstrel show. The funds raised from this event benefited the Providence Woman Suffrage party, a racially integrated association. Subsequent rallies and church affairs were designed not only to support the movement financially but to recruit black women into the cause.[24]

Drawn into the woman suffrage movement for a variety of reasons, Higgins first saw political patronage as a major means to racial uplift for her people. Voting citizens, of course, have greater access to patronage than do others. In addition to patronage as a goal of woman suffrage, votes for women could help reform society through several steps, including prohibiting the use of alcohol, Higgins believed, and she was convinced that "the colored ballot of our mothers, sisters and sweethearts, will purify."[25]

Black women had significant roles not only in helping to pass the Nineteenth Amendment, which enfranchised American women in 1920, but in helping to elect Warren G. Harding to the presidency that year. A black woman went on record as the second member of her gender to register to vote in Rhode Island. In addition, Mary Church Terrell, a leading black suffragist on the national scene, wrote Higgins from Washington shortly before the presidential election calling for black Republican women to reach every woman in the state. The goal was to have them register and vote for the Harding ticket. Terrell noted, "By a miracle the 19th Amendment has been ratified. Colored women all over the country have a weapon of defense which they have never possessed before."[26] The success of this effort was apparent in Rhode Island, where in June 1920, the growing number of black women Republicans organized their own club—The Julia Ward Howe Republican Women's Club—with Bertha Higgins as president. At the time, Higgins was forty-eight years of age. After the November elections, Warren G. Harding sent a message to Higgins, thanking the club members for their efforts in the campaign.[27]

Shortly after the women of the United States received the right to vote, women in the Virgin Islands began lobbying for woman suffrage. The Danish Virgin Islands had been purchased by the United States in 1917, and a decade later Congress passed a law making Virgin Islanders American citizens. From that point on, black women teachers, in particular, took the lead, arguing that as American women they, too, should be enfranchised. Numerous women became active in this campaign, but Edith Williams is the one whose name frequently is associated with the movement. In the 1980s, when Virgin Islanders talk about woman suffrage, they refer to Williams, who was living and ninety-nine years of age in 1986. One of the early black women school teachers on St. Thomas, Williams has been revered as one of the "mothers" of public education on the island. A single woman, Williams worked for nearly fifty years as a teacher. In the Virgin Islands, teachers' salaries were low; however, Williams struggled until she acquired enough money to purchase her own property. In addition, she introduced the school lunch program in St. Thomas, by developing a vegetable garden at her school, where the children grew their own food, prepared some of it for lunches, and sold the rest. Mothers and other teachers participated in this program, revealing the connection between educational and economic goals as priorities in the daily lives of St. Thomas women. The first inductee into the *Virgin Island Education Review* Hall of Fame, Williams was saluted further in 1982, when an elementary school was named in her honor.[28]

In addition to Williams, Mildred V. Anduze was amid the black school teachers esteemed by the people of St. Thomas. Among the few women listed in *Profiles of Outstanding Virgin Islanders,* Anduze was noted as an active civic affairs leader, notably cited for her efforts in the woman suffrage campaign. Unlike Williams, Anduze was a married teacher, who raised several children. She reflected the reality of daily life among many African diaspora women, who not only divided their daily activities among their students and families, but included time for civic and political campaigns, as well.[29]

Like Williams and other women leaders in this struggle, Anduze was an older woman during the final victory of the suffrage battle, revealing again the significant role that women over forty maintained not only in African, but in African-American and African-Caribbean communities. In 1935, when the St. Thomas courts ruled that eligible women should not be restricted from the voter rolls, Williams was forty-eight, and Anduze was forty-four.

The 1935 victory involved a long process, with petitions and court battles, led by a network of teachers, mainly women in the St. Thomas Teachers Association. By November of that year, association president Amadeo Francis had successfully won a legal suit wherein the question was raised about women's right to vote under the United States Constitution. The court ruled that the Danish code, under which local St. Thomas affairs were regulated, never intended to limit the franchise specially to men. As a result of this ruling, women in the St. Thomas Teachers Association decided to test the court decision. Interestingly, the Virgin Islands electoral laws restricted the franchise to literate, property-owning men. A growing movement among the educated Virgin Islanders of African descent questioned this restriction against 90 percent of the population, who were disqualified because they were women, or had no property, or were not literate.[30]

Within a month after the court ruling, Edith Williams applied to vote in the 1936 elections. She had hoped that the Colonial Council, or local legislative body, would take the initiative to inform the Electoral Board of women's right to vote, but the council refused. Hence, the decision to accept her application would be left to the board. Shortly thereafter, twenty-three other St. Thomas and St. John school teachers filed with the board to vote in the next election. When the election officials refused to accept their applications, three of the women, Edith Williams, Anna M. Vessup, and Eulalie Stevens, petitioned the court successfully to open the election process to qualified women. Why were these women selected by their peers to test the system? First, all three were self-reliant, self-supporting women and members of the teachers association. Second, they were residents of the Virgin Islands, property owners, and they were significantly past the required voting age of twenty-five. Hence, aside from gender, they met the restricted qualifications for voters. In addition, they were respected members of their communities whose reputations were beyond reproach. As a result of their struggle, plus a United States congressional law the following year, all literate citizens of the Virgin Islands were enfranchised.[31]

In both the United States and the Virgin Islands, networks of professional women led the way to political reform that eventually brought black women the right to vote. Some of these women were homemakers. Others were single women, whose survival was determined by their personal ability to make a living. Suffrage, then, was not just a right that they sought so that women could be merely politically equal to men. On the other hand, the fight for the ballot was motivated by social and economic reasons—the desire to use political means to improve the quality of life in black communities where, historically, women had been at the bottom of the economic strata.

In a political sense, these women did not hold prestigious positions in government, nor in the economy. However, as leaders they were revered in their own communities because of years of service. With time, the memory of these women has remained in the communities through oral testimonies and institutional landmarks that have kept many of their names alive. It seems that the Virgin Islands women received considerable male support in their networks; however, whenever the legal process toward suffrage broke down, the women mobilized and chose another strategy until victory was theirs.

In comparing the suffrage activities of U.S. and Virgin Islands women of African descent, once again the networks of women seeking to reform not only their status but the conditions of others in black communities are apparent. In addition, these women leaders were older, established women with a tradition of community

service behind them that commanded respect. Undoubtedly, the Virgin Islands women were influenced by the woman suffrage activities and strategies of black women in the United States. By the mid-1920s, many black women's organizations were extending their networks to include women from the Caribbean and Africa. Among such groups were the National Association of Colored Women and the International Council of Women of the Darker Races.[32] In this case the cross-cultural exchange was reversing as African-American women shared their strategies and goals for survival with their sisters in Africa and the diaspora.

Implications for Future Research

Within a broad historical framework, African feminist values and imperatives can be applied to women of African descent cross-culturally—as female networking to assure the survival of human rights. In this essay we have observed the use of networking among black women and the application of survival strategies among formerly enslaved women in two settings—the United States and the Virgin Islands—and in two time periods for each—the late nineteenth and the early twentieth centuries. In all cases, African feminist imperatives were operative in the historical analysis used.

Using African feminism as a theoretical method for analyzing contemporary as well as past events that focus upon women of African descent has many other possibilities. Cross-cultural studies about slavery, colonialism, gender exploitation and women's resistance against these forces are just a few themes for which African feminist analysis can apply.[33] Hopefully, scholars researching past experiences of women in the African diaspora will be challenged to consider the African feminist approach to historical reconstruction.

[1]See Filomina Chioma Steady, "The Black Woman Cross-Culturally: An Overview," in *The Black Woman Cross-Culturally*, ed. Filomina Chioma Steady (Cambridge, Mass.: Schenkman Publishing Co., Inc. 1981), 7–36.

[2]Ibid.

[3]See Lucille Mathurin, *The Rebel Woman in the British West Indies During Slavery* (Kingston: African-Caribbean Institute of Jamaica, 1975); Lucille Mathurin, "The Arrivals of Black Women," *Jamaica Journal* 9, nos 2 & 3 (1975): 2–7; Lucille Mathurin, "Reluctant Matriarchs," *Savacou* 13 (Gemini 1977): 1–6; and Bernice Johnson Reagon, "My Black Mothers and Sisters or on Beginning a Cultural Autobiography," *Feminist Studies* 8 (Spring 1982): 81–96.

[4]Okon Edet Uya, "The Mind of Slaves as Revealed in their Songs: An Interpretative Essay," *A Current Bibliography on African Affairs* 5, series 2 (1972): 3–4.

[5]Sylvia Dannett, *Profiles of Negro Womanhood*, 2 vols. (Yonkers, N.Y.: Educational Heritage, Inc., 1964).

[6]Gerda Lerner, ed., *Black Women in White America: A Documentary History* (New York: Random House, 1972); and Bert James Loewenberg and Ruth Bogin, eds., *Black Women in Nineteenth Century American Life* (University Park: The Pennsylvania State University Press, 1976).

[7]Sharon Harley and Rosalyn Terborg-Penn, eds., *The Afro-American Woman: Struggles and Images* (Port Washington, N.Y.: The Kennikat Press, 1978).

[8]Jeanne Nobles, *Beautiful, Also, Are the Souls of My Black Sisters: A History of the Black Woman in America* (Englewood Cliffs, N.J.: Prentice-Hall, Inc., 1978), 17, 19.

[9]Ibid., 109.

[10]Stephanie Urdang, *Fighting Two Colonialisms: Women in Guinea-Bissau* (New York: Monthly Review Press, 1979).

[11]Bettina Aptheker, *Women's Legacy: Essays on Race, Sex, and Class in American History* (Amherst: University of Massachusetts Press, 1982), 7.

[12] Angela Y. Davis, *Women, Race and Class* (New York: Random House, 1981).

[13] Gloria T. Hull, Patricia Bell Scott, and Barbara Smith, eds., *All the Women Are White, All the Blacks Are Men, But Some of Us Are Brave* (Old Westbury, N.Y.: The Feminist Press, 1981).

[14] Robert F. Berkhofer, Jr., "The Two New Histories: Competing Paradigms for Interpreting the American Past," *OAH Newsletter* 2 (May 1983): 9–11.

[15] Hilda Smith, "Women's History and the Humanities," *OAH Newsletter* 2 (May 1983): 12–14.

[16] The Combahee River Collective, "A Black Feminist Statement," in *Capitalist Patriarchy and the Case for Socialist Feminism*, ed. Zillah R. Eisenstein (New York: Monthly Review Press, 1979), 364, 392.

[17] Earl Conrad, *Harriet Tubman* (New York: Paul S. Eriksson Inc., 1943 and 1969), 160–64.

[18] See Susie King Taylor, *Reminiscences of My Life in Camp* (New York: Arno Press and The New York Times, 1968); and Sojourner Truth, *Narrative and Book of Life* (Chicago: Johnson Publishing Co., Inc., 1970), 139–44.

[19] Conrad, *Harriet Tubman*, 169–72.

[20] Ibid., 174–75.

[21] Florence Lewisohn, *The Romantic History of St. Croix: From the Time of Columbus Until Today* (St. Croix: St. Croix Landmarks Society, 1964), 50–51, 55–57; and Isaac Dookhan, *A History of the Virgin Islands of the United States* (St. Thomas: Caribbean Universities Press, 1974), 227–31.

[22] Lewisohn, *Romantic History*, 54; and Dookhan, *History of the Virgin Islands*, 231.

[23] "Report to Members of the Rhode Island Suffrage Party, and League of Women," November 1919, Bertha Higgins Papers, Rhode Island Black Heritage Society, Providence, R.I.

[24] Newsclipping, "Minstrel Show," *The Providence Sunday Journal*, 14 May 1916, Scrapbook, Bertha Higgins Papers.

[25] Bertha Higgins to "My Dear Madam," n.d., draft, Bertha Higgins Papers.

[26] Mary Church Terrell to Bertha Higgins, October 1920, Bertha Higgins Papers.

[27] Newsclipping, *The Providence Sunday Journal*, 12 June 1920, Scrapbook; and Charles E. Harding to Bertha Higgins, 21 February 1921, Bertha Higgins Papers.

[28] *The Virgin Islands Education Review* 1 (August 1982): 5; and June Lindquist, interview with author, Virgin Islands Bureau of Libraries and Museums, St. Thomas, V.I., 12 January 1983.

[29] Department of Education, U.S. Virgin Islands, *Profiles of Outstanding Virgin Islanders* (St. Thomas: Government of the U.S. Virgin Islands, 1976), 4.

[30] *The (St. Thomas) Daily News*, 27 March 1935; and 11 November 1935.

[31] *The (St. Thomas) Daily News*, 14 December 1935; and 28 December 1935.

[32] Cynthia Neverdon-Morton, "The Black Woman's Struggle for Equality in the South, 1895–1925," in Harley and Terborg-Penn, *The Afro-American Woman: Struggles and Images*, 512–52; and Monroe N. Work, *Negro Year Book*, 1925–1926 (Tuskegee, Ala.: Negro Year Book Publishing Co., 1925), 37.

[33] For further information about contemporary issues, see Josef Gugler, "The Second Sex in Town," in Steady, *The Black Woman Cross-Culturally*, 169–84; Richard E. Lapchick, "The Role of Women in the Struggle Against Apartheid in South Africa," in Steady, *The Black Woman Cross-Culturally*, 231–61; Margaret Randall, "The Story of Monica Baltodana and Zulema," *Black Scholar* 14 (March/April 1983): 48–57; Elizabeth V. Murrell, "Our Children—Their Future: The International Year of the Child—1979," *Freedomways* 19 (First Quarter, 1979): 7–12; and The Women's Committee, International Defense and Aid Fund for Southern Africa, *To Honour Women's Day* (Cambridge, Mass.: The Women's Committee, International Defense and Aid Fund for Southern Africa, 1981).

The Economic Role of Slave Women

Barbara A. Bush

Women in the Formal Plantation Economy

The sole reason for the existence of black women in the Caribbean was their labor value. Although in the early days of slavery planters had made some attempt to promote marriage and healthy patterns of reproduction, with the increasing dominance of sugar monoculture, it was more economically viable to buy fresh slaves from Africa until abolitionist pressure at the end of the eighteenth century threatened the continued supply through the iniquitous middle passage. From the earliest days of the slave trade women were regarded by Europeans as eminently suited to field work because of their perceived "drudge" status in polygynous marriages. A large part of the labor on sugar estates consisted of digging holes for canes, hoeing and weeding—tasks generally accepted in slaving circles as "women's work" in Africa. Planters professed a preference for males and demographic evidence indicates that more males than females were brought to the Caribbean during the eighteenth century (Sheridan, 1985). However, in the complex and hierarchical division of labor that existed on large plantations, men were valued for craftsman skills or work in the semi-industrial processes of the sugar mill and at least half or more of ordinary field gangs were comprised of women, a pattern which was also evident in the French Caribbean (Gautier, 1983).

There was no common experience of female slaves as conditions varied from island to island and changed with the developing of the large-scale plantation system. Barry Higman has provided a detailed breakdown of the diversity of work regimes in the British Caribbean, highlighting the main points of contrast between rural and urban slave, sugar and other types of production on, for instance, coffee and pimento estates or cattle pens. However, when slaves were emancipated in 1834, 68.5 per cent of all employed slaves classified for compensation paid to slave owners were field laborers and inferior field laborers. Slaves employed in agricultural extraction of produce from the land (predial slaves) comprised 85 per cent of the total slave labor force. According to Higman, between 1810 and 1834 the sugar estate played a dominant part in defining the character of slavery and thus discussion of women's role will be restricted primarily to this area of slave economic activity. During the later period of slavery large-scale sugar production occupied 80 per cent of all economically active slaves with the exception of Jamaica where the figure was 53 per cent. The 1834 slave registration returns for 82,807 slaves show that 49 per cent were "labourers in sugar cultivation" and 78 per cent of slaves lived on sugar estates. Cotton or other agricultural production occupied 5.3 per cent of slaves, 11.6 per cent were laborers *not* in agriculture, 13 per cent were domestics and 20.1 per cent had no occupation, being either too young, too old or sick (Higman, 1984).

From the earliest days, West Indian sugar plantations incorporated certain features of the woodland and savanna economies of West Africa, where hoe cultivation predominated. The newly arrived slaves continued the West African traditions of tilling their own kitchen gardens and cultivating provision grounds, in addition to laboring on their master's plantation (Dunn, 1973). In the first stage of colonization of the West Indies, the economy of the islands was mixed; tobacco was grown, smallholdings predominated and owners relied upon white indentured labor to work their holdings. As the planters gradually turned from tobacco to the far more profitable sugar cane, small farms were consolidated into large plantations and owners came to rely more and more upon imported African slaves to meet their labor needs. Plantation management became increasingly more complex as the near monoculture stage of production was approached.

Viable plantation units required a large number of slaves, who came to be differentiated into different classes, with the skilled artisans and drivers forming the elite. After this elite, in descending order, came the domestic servants, the slaves involved in more menial "ancillary" tasks such as washerwomen, the field laborers, the children's gangs and the "unemployable," sick or superannuated. This social hierarchy was further complicated by divisions between black and colored, African and creole.

Within this complex occupational stratification of slaves, the position of the woman slave was generally less favorable than that of her male counterpart. The Jamaican planter, William Beckford, gave a brief outline of occupations ascribed to the different sexes in plantation society:

> A negro man is purchased either for a trade, or the cultivation and different process of the cane—the occupations of the women are only two, the house, with its several departments and supposed indulgences, or the field with its exaggerated labors. The first situation is the more honourable, the last the most independent.

Apart from the midwife, doctoress or chief housekeeper, the slave elite consisted almost solely of men: women in general were restricted to the lower ranks. Richard Sheridan analyzed the occupational pattern of Roaring River Estate, Jamaica, in 1756 and found that, of the 92 women on the estate, 70 were field workers, whereas, of the 84 men, only 28 were working in the cane fields. The women not engaged in field work had a variety of occupations; Creole Phibba and Mulatto Mary were "house wenches," Mulatto Dolly and Juran were cooks and Sue was a washer. Two women were doctoresses (traditional folk healers) and two others carried water to quench the thirst of field negroes; Old Bones took care of the "Piquinio gang" as a driver, supervising the labor of small children (Sheridan, 1974). A similar occupational pattern existed on the Worthy Park Plantation in 1789, where, out of 162 women, 70 worked in the fields, compared with 29 men out of a total of 177 (Craton and Walvin, 1970). The pre-eminence of field work as the slave woman's major occupation is also shown in Richard Dunn's analysis of the occupational pattern of Mesopotamia, Jamaica, in 1809 (Dunn, 1977). Yet, despite the preponderance of women in field work, planters allegedly preferred men. Bryan Edwards wrote:

> I have to observe, that though it is impossible to conduct the business, either of a house or of a plantation without a number of females ... the nature of the slave service in the West Indies (being chiefly field labor) requires, for the immediate interest of the planter, a greater number of males.

In consequence, according to contemporary accounts, only a third of slaves imported were women. The occupational patterns of individual plantations referred to above do not, however, support plantocratic statements on female labor. Plantation lists analyzed by Craton and Dunn reflect neither a marked preference for male field hands nor a high ratio of male to female slaves. On the contrary, such modern research into the occupational distribution of sugar plantations indicates that planters may have exaggerated the adverse sex ratio to play down the exploitation of women slaves as field hands.

Although conditions of labor varied slightly from island to island, it is unlikely that the occupational distribution on plantations changed very much from the development of sugar monoculture, apart from an increase in skilled occupations as plantations became larger and more complex. According to Richard Dunn, a typical labor pattern found in plantation accounts of 1706 indicates that 64 per cent of slaves were field hands, 14 per cent domestics and 12 per cent overseers and craftsmen (Dunn, 1973). By the end of the eighteenth century, in Thomas Atwood's estimation, the proportion of "working field negroes" per plantation was about two-fifths of the total number of slaves, the remainder being "tradesmen, watchmen, stock-keepers, invalids, house servants, nurses and young children."

As the higher occupations were largely restricted to men, women slaves would have comprised a significant percentage of common field hands from the earliest days of slavery. It can be argued that most of the more arduous tasks on the plantation, such as cane-cutting, holing and sugar-boiling, were performed by men, while women undertook the less demanding, though no less essential, tasks. Evidence from the French Caribbean collated by Arlette Gautier indicates that the way tasks were subdivided suggests a clear division of labor. Women cut canes, weeded and manured whilst men cut trees, extracted stones and carried heavy weights. In a symbolic gesture of feeding—traditionally women's responsibility in all cultures—women fed the mill, which could be dangerous work as, for instance, fingers could be trapped in rollers. Only women looked after children and chickens. A similar sexual division of labor existed among domestics. Men were valets and coach drivers, women cleaned and did the laundry. The head overseer, who had considerable power through control of work regimes and many aspects of the lives of slaves, was always a man (Gautier, 1983). The complex sexual division of labor on slave plantations—in the French Caribbean at least—would thus appear to be a combination of traditional African roles, imposed European values about the relative worth of male and female labor, and pragmatic economic calculations which designated all slaves as work units rather than human beings.

In view of the high numbers of women involved in field work, it is unlikely that women were spared the heaviest forms of labor, especially during busy periods, such as crop time. Dallas, who divided slaves into three basic classes, wrote that the first and most important class was comprised of "the most robust of both sexes" whose chief employment consisted of "preparing and planting the soil, cutting the canes, feeding the mill and aiding the manufacture of sugar and rum." This observation, made around 1800, implies little differentiation between men and women, regardless of the nature of tasks undertaken. The only concessions made were for children, who picked grass and weeded, and convalescents and pregnant women, who were given "light labour."

Although conditions of labor and the treatment of female slaves changed in response to the social and economic development of the West Indian sugar colonies, from early sources it would appear that the taxing nature of the work performed by women slaves was an ever-present feature of plantation life. Richard Ligon, who owned a plantation in Barbados, wrote:

The work which women do, is most of it weeding, a stooping and painful work; at noon they are called home by the ring of a bell, where they have two hours repast, at night they rest from six, till six o'clock.

On an average seventeenth-century plantation there was nearly one laborer per acre of cane. Men and women did the work of animals. A negro field laborer had three tools, an ax, a hoe and a bill. Slaves were kept at work all year round, even though sugar-growing was only seasonal (Dunn, 1973). When sugar monoculture was fully established in the eighteenth century, the arduous nature of the field labor intensified. Nonetheless, Beckford's account of the daily routine of a field laborer in the 1780s in Jamaica corresponds relatively closely to Ligon's earlier account of Barbadian plantation life. The slaves, observed Beckford:

> generally turn out at six o'clock in the morning and (after breaks for breakfast and dinner) seldom continue in the field out of crop time after sunset, which is never later than seven; so from this hour, till six the ensuing morning, they may call time their own, part of which they consume in broken sleep, the rest in supper, and in preparation for breakfast.

Women slaves, then, excluded in the large part from the elite occupations, suffered far more than male slaves from inevitable restriction to their ascribed occupations. Confined to the lower ranks, their opportunities of social mobility were severely limited; the favors and privileges accorded the elite slaves were available only to the majority of female slaves through concubinage or the "selling" of sexual favors; a favored slave or the natural daughter of the owner or overseer was often taken into service in the house. The majority of women, however, remained working in the fields, in harsh conditions and maintained by their owners at a bare subsistence level. Demographic analysis by Higman confirms the dominance of women in field gangs after 1800. On sugar plantations only 10 per cent were domestics compared with 20 per cent on coffee and cotton plantations. There were now a larger number of creoles and more females of color were likely to find themselves in the field gang than colored men, although Africans were still regarded by whites as stronger, if less intelligent, than creoles.

Although planters maintained the general treatment of sugar slaves was mild and "indulgent," Higman's data confirm that slave morbidity and mortality were highest and the birth rate the lowest on sugar plantations of the notional optimum size of 250 slaves. Next highest in mortality were the coffee plantations, followed by cocoa, cotton, pimento plantations, cattle ranches or pens, the towns and finally marginal subsistence units (Higman, 1984). Sugar plantations were generally regarded as health hazards by whites and were characterized by unhygienic conditions, accidents, suicides, punishments, poor diets (even famine at times when food imports were disrupted) and endemic diseases such as yaws. The labor regime ensured that women shared the same back-breaking work, miseries and punishments as men. In crop time (four to six months between October and March) slaves were turned out of their quarters at sun-up and worked till sunset with little time to call their own. There was also extended night-work during this period. Higman has estimated that between 1807 and 1832 a typical day worked by field workers was 12 hours in Jamaica and 10 hours in the eastern Caribbean but that was averaged out over the whole year (Higman, 1984). Field workers were treated as the capital stock of the plantation, on a par with animal stock and maintained at bare subsistence level. Though they performed the hardest labor and worked the longest hours, their conditions were far inferior to those of domestics or skilled craftsmen and they suffered from greater ill-health and higher mortality rates. In addition they had to produce food in their free time on slave provision grounds to supplement the often inadequate diets provided by masters.

Despite the fact that slave owners neglected the material welfare of their ordinary field hands, a good profit was extracted from them. The profitability of slaves appears to have been a constant from the beginning of sugar cultivation. Richard Ligon wrote of planters in Barbados:

> they have bought this year no less than 1000 negroes, and the more they be, the better able are they to buy, for in a year and a half they will earn as much as they cost.

Whether the economic value of slaves induced planters to treat them well is, however, debatable. Ligon, for instance, believed that slaves were "preserved with greater care than the [white] servants," as the latter were only indentured for five years, while the slaves were "subject to their masters forever" and thus constituted a lifelong investment. Conversely, one contemporary critic of slavery, William Edmundson, a Quaker, writing of seventeenth-century Barbados, accused planters of keeping their slaves "in ignorance and under Oppression" and of starving them "for want of Meat and Cloaths Convenient." Sir Hans Sloane also regarded the West Indian slave regime as essentially harsh and dehumanizing.

By the 1780s the average cost per annum of maintaining a field slave was about £12 sterling inclusive of food, clothing, medicine, poll tax and insurance. At a slightly later date, Bryan Edwards estimated that the annual profit from one able field hand was £25. It would appear that West Indian planters received a good return on their investments, regardless of the high mortality rates of new African slaves in particular. From an analysis of statistical data for the years 1765 to 1775, Richard Sheridan has estimated that, if a prime field hand in Jamaica labored for twelve years, he (or perhaps, more appropriately, she), would return 6 per cent per annum; fifteen years' labor produced a return of 9 per cent, while, if the slave survived twenty years' labor, he would bring a return of 11 per cent per annum for his owner (Sheridan, 1974).

Whether many ordinary field hands ever survived long enough to verify Sheridan's neat computation is debatable, but there is no doubt that, as the backbone of the plantation economy, they were highly valued assets. In the case of the prime female slave, her utility value is reflected in the price she fetched. Throughout the period of slavery, this was only marginally less than that paid for an able-bodied man. Ligon quoted £30 for a male negro and £25 to £27 for a female. Before the abolition of the slave trade in 1807, the approximate purchase price of a new male slave was between £50 to £70, while a healthy female sold for between £50 and £60. Prices for creole slaves were roughly 20 per cent higher, although Bryan Edwards asserted that these slaves were sometimes twice as expensive as "salt-water" Africans, depending on their particular skills. Men and women were often sold together in "jobbing gangs." A Jamaican advertisement in 1827, for instance, offered a "small gang of effective and well-disposed males, 17 males and 17 females."

Before 1807 there is no indication that fertility increased the worth of women—women of similar ages, with or without children, generally cost the same. After the abolition of the slave trade, an able-bodied field slave cost approximately £180 sterling and Stewart noted that a female slave with a healthy infant was "at least twenty per cent more valuable than she was before it was born," a reflection of a change in attitude towards the woman slave on the part of the planter. The decline in slave numbers after 1807 encouraged a much greater interest in the childbearing potentialities of women slaves, in addition to raising the value of infant slaves to a fifth that of a healthy adult.

Controversial debates still rage, particularly among quantitative historians, as to whether slavery remained profitable after abolition of the slave trade or whether slave conditions improved or deteriorated over time. But one important aspect of the slaves' existence remained constant; labor was extracted via coercion and punishment from the beginnings of sugar cultivation. Work in the fields was hard, monotonous and degrading, with the result that slaves, men or women, gave their labor unwillingly and inefficiently. This often resulted in low productivity linked to various forms of resistance to the regime from individual shirking and malingering to sabotage, arson and more, collective discontents in the gang which rendered control over productivity difficult.

Michael Craton has estimated that Jamaican slaves at the end of the eighteenth century cut only one-fifth as much cane per day at crop time than equivalent modern-day wage earners (Craton and Walvin, 1970). Sheridan disagrees and argues that productivity was good, especially in the case of cane-hole digging where workers were forced to wield hoes in equal time and with equal effect irrespective of sex, age or physical strength (Sheridan, 1985). This debate aside, labor was undoubtedly extracted in the main through coercion. Planters could only squeeze a respectable profit out of their slaves by literally beating it out of them, an unsavory practice, used on men and women alike, which inspired strong resistance on the part of the slaves. The need to keep the slaves in line and suppress insubordination hence became the slave owner's main justification for habitual physical maltreatment, such as whippings and confinement in the stocks. Sir Hans Sloane, a relatively detached observer, wrote that these punishments "were sometimes merited by the Blacks who are a very perverse Generation of people, and though they appear harsh, yet are scarce equal to some of their crimes." Edward Long, in defending allegations of the inhumanity of the planters, asserted that the planter's authority could be equated with that of an "ancient patriarch." There was not a great deal of punishment and cruelty, he wrote, but added that:

> Amongst 3 or 4000 blacks, there must be some who are not to be reclaimed from a savage, intractable humour and acts of violence, without the coercion of punishment.

Long did admit, however, that odd planters did at times exhibit "inhuman tempers."

The vehement denials of the planters apart, punishment and, not infrequently, unwarranted cruelty were an integral part of plantation life from the earliest days of slavery. Sir Hans Sloane wrote that for "Negligence" slaves were usually "whipt by the Overseers with Lance Wood Switches, till they be bloody . . . being first tied up by their hands in the Mill-houses." After these floggings, slave masters sometimes used "several very exquisite Torments" such as rubbing pepper and salt or dropping melted wax on the slave's skin. William Beckford remarked that the "instrument of correction" was to be heard throughout Jamaica, and the Reverend John Riland, despite his Christian views, had to own that his own Jamaican estate "was not worked without the whip." Slaves, both men and women, were thus caught up in a vicious circle. When they reacted to the harsh work conditions with non-cooperation or outright insubordination, they were punished. This punishment only served to make them more resentful of their condition and thus the cycle of non-cooperation, resistance and punishment was indefinitely repeated. As

Beckford astutely observed, "the whip . . . does not correct, but multiply faults."

Women slaves were no less immune to physical punishment than male slaves. There is no hard evidence to suggest that they were more compliant than men. As will be shown in the following section, resistance to slavery was an integral part of the life of the woman slave. The whip constituted an important element in her life. When the first legislation forbidding the whipping of black women was introduced in Trinidad in 1823, it was strongly objected to by planters who felt that women slaves were "notoriously insolent" and only kept in some "tolerable order" through the fear of punishment. One colonial official stated that female slaves "more frequently merited punishment than males." The general consensus of opinion amongst Trinidadian slave owners on the 1823 law was that insolence among women slaves was checked only by the dreaded whip (Brereton, 1974).

Under the overseer's whip neither age nor sex found any favor. "Whether the offender be male or female, precisely the same course is pursued," observed a critic of slavery in 1824, describing the procedure for formal punishment thus:

> The posterior is made bare and the offender is extended prone on the ground, the hands and feet being firmly extended by other slaves; when the driver, with his long and heavy whip, inflicts under the eye of the overseer, the number of lashes, which he may order.

In the case of women slaves in particular, the degradation inflicted by this act was compounded by the fact that frequently a black driver was appointed to carry out the punishment; as his privileged position depended on his ability to conform, overtly at least, to the system, he showed no lenience. John Stedman visited one estate in Surinam where he was appalled by the sight of "a beautiful samboe girl of eighteen" who was tied up by both arms to a tree, naked and "lacerated in such a shocking manner" by the whips of two negro drivers. Although conditions on plantations in Surinam were notoriously harsh, a similar pattern of cruelty undoubtedly existed throughout the British Caribbean.

In respect of physical maltreatments, female domestic slaves were perhaps in a more vulnerable position than the ordinary field slaves. Because of their close proximity to their masters, they were far more frequently the victim of sadistic whims and personal caprice. Henry Coor, giving evidence to the House of Commons inquiry into the slave trade in 1790, recalled how one evening, as a house guest at a Jamaican plantation, he saw the master of the house nail the ear of a house wench to a tree post because she had broken a plate. In the morning the woman had gone, "having torn the head of the nail through the ear." When found, she was severely flogged.

During his sojourn in Surinam, John Stedman noted several incidences of cruelty towards female domestics, who were often expected to perform sexual duties in addition to their official duties. The underlying sexual jealousy this aroused in their white mistresses often resulted in acts of unwarranted cruel treatment. In many ways, then, the apparent comforts and privileges of the domestic slave were canceled out by the precarious nature of her position. Moreover, unlike the ordinary woman slave, the domestic slave could be punished by relegation to field work.

Pregnancy did not guarantee either a lighter work burden or a reprieve from physical punishment. Women were expected to work in the fields until at least six weeks before delivery and return to work no later than three weeks afterwards. In theory, during the early period of slavery a woman was exempted from flogging until after the delivery of her child. In practice little special consideration was paid to the pregnant slave woman. The prime consideration of the planter was the pursuit of profit, not procreation.

As negro prices began to rise in the late eighteenth century, planters introduced measures designed to give better care to pregnant women and slave mothers. However, these measures were often negated by the planter's exploitation of the female slave as a worker. For example, on most large Jamaican plantations in the 1790s, a woman could technically get release from work by producing a large number of children; in effect she usually received little credit for this activity.

When slave owners became increasingly anxious about the threat of the abolition of the slave trade, the slave woman's potential as a breeder of new slaves gained a greater significance. From the end of the eighteenth century, ameliorative laws were passed which, in theory, afforded pregnant women some protection. For instance, women were entitled to perform less arduous labor whilst pregnant. In reality, however, they were expected to work as normal, for a slump in sugar prices motivated planters to extract the maximum profit from their slave work-force. If pregnant women complained about their conditions of labor, they risked a flogging. One abolitionist observer recalled the following incident on a Jamaican plantation in the 1820s:

> Two women, who were pregnant, desired to quit the field during the rain . . . The overseer refused them permission. They went to complain . . . to a magistrate, but were stopped on their way by a neighbouring overseer and by him thrown in the stocks until he sent them back to their own overseer who put them again in the stocks and had them flogged.

Accounting for the propaganda motives of this anecdote, and given that slave women maintained an excessively low fertility rate after the introduction of ameliorative legislation, the above passage indicates that, even during the so-called ameliorative period, pregnant women were no less immune to heavy labor, harsh conditions and physical punishments than other groups of slaves.

After 1807 some provisions were made to exempt pregnant women from floggings, but, even as late as 1826, in Jamaica at least, legislation limiting the number of lashes which could be inflicted upon an individual slave made no special provision for the woman slave, whether or not she was pregnant. Under the 1826 Jamaican law, punishment was "restricted" to 10 lashes, except in the presence of the owner or overseer, when a maximum of 39 lashes could be administered. A second punishment could not be given until "the culprit" was "entirely recovered" from the former one, under a penalty of £20.

In general, the treatment of pregnant slaves, even during the penultimate years of slavery, left much to be desired. Pregnant women were unnecessarily flogged or confined in the stocks, punishments which jeopardized not only the lives of their unborn children but also their own lives. One critic of slavery, Dr. John Williamson, writing of Jamaica in 1817, related the salutary tale of a pregnant woman who was "confined to the stocks for misconduct" and liberated only a few days before delivery. After giving birth, she subsequently died of puerperal fever.

As slave owners and overseers had little regard for women slaves in their reproductive capacity, it is hardly surprising that they suffered from so many gynecological disorders. Hard work and cruel treatment took its toll on their health. "Monk" Lewis, who was genuinely concerned about the welfare of his female slaves, commented strongly on the general atmosphere of callous indifference to the female slaves. Having received several reports of white book-keepers and overseers kicking women in the womb, often crippling them or their unborn children, he felt entitled to state that white overseers and book-keepers "kick black women in the belly from one end of Jamaica to another." Some planters, like Lewis, were without doubt genuinely concerned about the well-being of their female slaves, but, in general, a woman slave, pregnant or not, was too valuable a labor unit to be accorded preferential treatment.

Despite the constant threat of punishment and the additional burden of pregnancy, slave women were far from submissive as workers. Their relative independence as field workers, noted by Beckford, had important implications for resistance, collective and individual. Female slaves took their revenge on their owners through shirking work, shamming illness, lying, stealing and even openly defying and abusing overseers. These forms of slave resistance, often interpreted by slave owners as evidence of the inferiority of blacks, were harshly dealt with by the whites. "The indolent only and the ill-disposed, encounter punishments," remarked William Beckford.

Resistance to punishment itself demanded much courage. Little hard evidence exists to show that slave women in the Caribbean protested against brutal punishment. Thomas Cooper did refer to one particular woman who, when placed in the stocks by her overseer, subsequently complained to the attorney and in consequence received 39 lashes from the same overseer. Such insights into the reactions of slave women, though rare, suggest that similar incidents may not have been as isolated as the absence of evidence indicates. If we can believe John Stedman, slaves in general were "spirited and brave," they met death with "the most undaunted fortitude"; if they believed their punishment unmerited, "immediate suicide" was too often the fatal consequence "especially among the Coromantyn Negroes." Unfortunately it is difficult to substantiate this observation in the context of West Indian slave women. In terms of less dramatic reactions, however, it is possible to glean some useful comparative information from the American South, where a number of references are made in slave narratives to slave women resisting floggings. According to Eugene Genovese, it was not uncommon for women slaves to fight against physical punishment (Genovese, 1974). Slave conditions in the old South were in many respects superior to those in the West Indies, where sugar planting was regarded by one contemporary critic as "not a very slow species of murder." Unless we conclude that female slaves in the Caribbean were more submissive than their American counterparts, it is reasonable to assume that, as well as showing their resentment through more convenient modes of non-cooperation, slave women, if sufficiently provoked, would have resisted actual punishment itself.

Informal Economic Activities: The Provision Ground and the Slave Market

In the words of Lucille Mathurin (1975), in West Indian slave society, "the black women produced, the brown woman served and the white woman consumed." But not only did the ordinary black slave woman make an indispensable contribution to the external economy of the sugar islands, she also participated in the internal marketing system which developed in the slave islands. Arguably it constituted a positive and creative area of the slave's existence. The reluctance of West Indian planters to provide their slaves with sufficient food led to the establishment, at a very early date, of provision grounds on marginal lands from which slaves were encouraged to supply their own food. Paradoxically, this failure on the part of West Indian planters to supply their slaves with the basic material necessities of life was instrumental in the development of a resilience and independence among the slaves which gave their otherwise depressing lives meaning and purpose.

The provision ground was everywhere more important than the master's store with the exception of Barbados, St. Kitts, Nevis, Antigua, Demerara-Essequibo and Berbice (Higman, 1984). In Jamaica, provision grounds came under greater regulation in the Consolidated Slave Act of 1788 and subsequent amendments. Except in crop time slaves were allowed one day per fortnight exclusive of Sundays and public holidays to cultivate their plots. According to Higman, the vast majority of slaves, in the Windward Islands and Jamaica relied heavily on produce of their provision grounds for sustenance although there were some localities, for instance the parish of Vere in Jamaica, where slaves had limited grounds and had to depend on rations provided by slave owners. Under the Jamaican Slave Law of 1816 planters were required to provide rations where no suitable land was available for slaves to cultivate or where drought had caused crop failure. However, as a rule, the only rations provided by planters were salt and pickled fish (Higman, 1984). Internal organization of provision grounds was left largely to the slaves themselves and they were worked by individuals or family groups with men, women and children all performing labor. Planter involvement was limited to the occasional inspections stipulated by the slave laws.

For one and a half days a week, including Sundays, the slave was thus freed from plantation labor to work his or her provision grounds. The slaves took advantage of this free time to engage in other enterprises such as raising poultry or traditional handicrafts. This was customary from the earliest days of slavery. Sir Hans Sloane noted that:

> [the slaves] have Saturdays in the Afternoon and Sundays . . . allowed them for the culture of their own plantations to feed themselves from . . . [the] ground allow'd them by their masters.

Whole slave families were involved in the cultivation of these grounds. They, not their masters, reaped the benefit of their labors. Thus the slaves expended an amazing amount of energy on their "polinks" or provision grounds. On these "polinks" (distinct from the tiny plots, kitchen gardens or yards close to their houses) slaves produced a variety of crops and herbs for medicinal purposes. Crops produced varied with locality but root crops predominated with corn and plantain as subsidiaries. European green vegetable crops were also produced, primarily for sale in the public markets. Pigs and poultry were kept in the slaves' garden plots. Higman argues that slaves in the Windwards and Jamaica played an important part in supplying internal markets but that it is impossible to know how much produce of ground or garden entered the slaves' diet directly or was exchanged at the market for other items, food and non-food, or accumulated as cash (which provided opportunities to buy freedom). The provision ground system was said to be preferred by slaves themselves and created a framework for independent economic activity (Higman, 1984).

Although technically the land which they cultivated belonged to their master, in effect the slaves passed it on as family property, as they did any other possessions they may have had, so that Dallas could note, "Their right of property in what they acquire is never questioned, but seems completely established by custom." Bryan Edwards agreed with Dallas that slaves could dispose at their deaths of "what little property they possess" and "even bequeath their grounds or gardens."

If owners disrespected these customary rights it could elicit a strong response from the individual slave concerned. John Jeremie, a legal expert arguing against the practice of selling slaves off separately when plantations changed ownership, wrote:

> The slave becomes attached to his plantation, to his garden, and to his cottage; but when the strip of land is taken from him, which he has cultivated with care, he becomes discontented and often contracts habits of heedlessness and indolence which render him worthless even to his owner.

John Parry (1955) argues that the origins of the Caribbean peasantry can be traced to slavery when blacks were made to provide their own food. He has argued that the system gave slaves a better diet and a small, independent income, and made them less likely to run away or rebel (although this last point may be disputed). Sheridan (1985) is more circumspect and, although he broadly agrees about the origins of the free peasantry, he points out that questions still remain concerning the performance of the provision-ground system. Were slaves given enough time to cultivate grounds? Did they have enough energy and will? How much time was needed to walk to the provision ground or market (the distance could vary from a few to thirty-five miles)? He is dubious about the impact of produce from provision grounds on slave diet and argues that Caribbean slaves were poorly fed in terms of calorie intake, which was far less than that provided by the typical diet of slaves in the USA on the eve of the Civil War. There was also a serious threat of crop failure through drought or hurricane. Hall also concedes that, although Jamaican slaves grew more food than their counterparts in the Lesser Antilles, for instance, their needs were seldom fully met without imported supplies (Hall, 1962). Controversy over the economic contribution of slave provision grounds and plots still needs to be resolved (Mintz, 1983). But this should not detract from their undoubted importance to the slaves themselves, which was recognized by contemporary observers.

Although contemporary plantocratic and abolitionist sources referred to the fact that it was the duty of all "adult males" to provide for their families, this emphasis on patriarchal family structures reflects a middle-class European perception of gender roles with man as the "provider." On the slave plantation, however, many women were single or providing for children. More importantly, economic organization of slave provision grounds was arguably based on a traditional African rather than European division of labor.

Women in traditional African societies make a significant and indispensable contribution to food production and, in West Africa in particular, gain a degree of economic independence from men (even within marriage) through marketing activities. They thus exhibit a high degree of entrepreneurial skills. Although women are still subordinate to men in social terms, they are not simply the passive drudges of plantocratic mythology. Women carried these skills with them to the Caribbean and, in addition to participating fully in the cultivation of provision grounds, they became prominent as market sellers and "higglers" or commercial intermediaries who sold the crop surplus of other slaves for a small profit. The latter occupation was particularly connected with urban slaves. A runaway slave advertisement in the Jamaican *Royal Gazette*, October 1827, alludes to a whole family of Kingston-based female higglers—Sarah Christian and her daughters Rosetta and Amelia, who also had a female child, Mary. They were described as "very artful and likely to attempt to pass as free persons." Arlette Gautier writes that in the French Caribbean, which developed a slave economy very similar to that of the British Caribbean, women sold agricultural products as they had done in Africa and this gave them a high degree of autonomy. The Sunday markets were dominated by free creoles and slave women as it was difficult for male slaves to get passes (Gautier, 1983).

The public Sunday market was an important institution in the West Indian sugar colonies from the very beginnings of slavery and was later to become anathema to religious abolitionists, who wished to stop it in order that slaves and masters could keep the sabbath. Indeed abolitionists like Thomas Cooper were the main critics of the provision-ground system on the grounds that slaves worked too hard to cultivate their crops adequately and were forced to spend their only day of leisure—Sunday—in cultivation and marketing. However, slaves were not noticeably enthusiastic about Christianity until the last years

of slavery and such commentators may have misread the degree to which cultivation of provision grounds was an added burden, reluctantly taken up out of necessity. Other contemporary writers, such as Edwards, have noted that slaves approached this extra work with enthusiasm as it was they, not planters, who reaped the benefits.

It is debatable whether the importance of the slave woman in the internal marketing system of the British slave colonies was a direct African retention or a result of the new roles she was forced to adopt as a result of enslavement. Mintz and Hall (1970) suggest, however, that through these activities (which are still dominated by women in West Africa and the modern Caribbean), the woman slave contributed significantly to the integration of creole society. In visiting the market, for instance, women could disseminate information amongst the slaves and facilitate communication between different plantations, for, despite the general stringency of the laws regarding the mobility of slaves, this sharp vigilance was relaxed where marketing activities were concerned. For instance, one clause in the Laws of Jamaica, 1826, stated that "no slave except when going to market shall travel about without a ticket, specially worded and signed by his owner." This is perhaps an indication of the importance of the slave market to the entire population of the sugar islands, an importance noted by Bryan Edwards who, reflecting general plantocratic opinion, wrote that the gardening and marketing activities of the slaves were beneficial to both slave and planter, as the former earned extra money and the latter did not have to feed the slaves.

Allowing slaves to grow their own food, then, was an easy way out for the planters. In effect, this lax attitude meant that slaves came to dominate the internal economy of the colonies. Although, as Gautier (1983) notes, more research is needed to establish the extent women were involved in provision ground cultivation and marketing and the degree to which this represents African retentions, it is certain that they were not only vital to the formal economy of the West Indies but also the informal sector. In her work as a field slave, the individual woman had more autonomy and independence than the elite slaves and this was reinforced by the resourcefulness and individual enterprise she developed in the cultivation of her "polinks" and her visits to the market. These unofficial economic activities benefited both the slave community and the white society. Despite the harsh realities of the plantation, the woman slave energetically used her precious free time to cultivate her individual or family "polink." The internal marketing activities of the slave woman represented a valuable contribution on her part to the creation, in the midst of hardship and oppression, of a positive underlife for herself and her fellow slaves.

[1]New slaves from the transatlantic crossing.

[2]Ashanti or Akan-speaking slaves originating in the Gold Coast (modern Ghana) who had a reputation as proud and rebellious slaves.

[3]That is, a parallel sector to the formal production of cash crops for export which was controlled by Europeans. It produced goods for internal production and was organized on a loosely structured, small scale basis by blacks and coloreds separate from but complementing the formal sector.

Slave Women in the Eighteenth-Century Charleston Marketplace

Robert Olwell

Black and White all mix'd together
Inconstant, strange, unhealthful weather
. . . . .
The markets dear and little money
Large potatoes, sweet as honey
Water Bad, past all drinking
Men and Women without thinking
Every thing at a high price
But rum, hominy and rice
. . . . .
Many a bargain, if you strike it,
This is Charles-town, how do you like it?
—A Description of Charleston in 1769[1]

An old Charleston adage holds that a person standing at the intersection of Broad and Meeting streets in the center of the old town can turn about and see embodied in the buildings on each corner of the crossroads the various "laws" that govern the city. On the southeast corner stands St. Michael's Church, representing God's law, on the west side are the Federal Post Office and the Courthouse, representing man's law, and on the northeast corner stands the old Bank of the United States, representing the law of money or the market.[2]

Although most of the present buildings postdate the American Revolution, the adage applied just as well to the same spot in the colonial period. In 1774, for example, an English visitor to the city and to the intersection of Broad and Meeting wrote, "At one of the four corners . . . stands the new English church [St. Michael's], and at another is the State House . . . [while] Opposite to it [on another corner] stands the Town Watch House." The anonymous tourist thought these buildings were "handsome [and] substantial" but noted that on "the fourth corner," where the Bank of the United States would later be built, there "is only a low dirty looking brick market house."[3] Despite the visitor's disparaging opinion of the market house, his account indicates that institutions representing the three "laws" of Charleston were already in place at the crossroads.

Perhaps one reason for the contemporary disregard of the marketplace in descriptions of colonial Charleston lies in the fact that activities in the market could not readily be reconciled with those that prevailed on the other three corners of the junction. In contrast to the subordinate position allotted to African slaves in the church and the law, they played a central role in the Charleston marketplace. In 1741, two years after the market house was built, the clerk appointed to regulate trade there noted that "Negroes went so much to Market."[4] With the exception of butchers and fishermen, the vast majority of the slaves who traded in the market were women. In February 1778 one observer "counted in the market and different corners of this town, sixty-four Negro wenches selling cakes, nuts, and so forth."[5]

Like eighteenth-century tourists, most historians of colonial Charleston have chosen to overlook evidence about the "low and dirty looking . . . market house" for the more "substantial" records provided by the church and state. Consequently, both "God's law," that is, religion and the church, and "man's law," statutes and courts, have received considerable scrutiny from scholars, while the other "law" that governed the colonial metropolis, the "law of the market," and its immediate institutional representative, the town marketplace, have seldom been the subject of historical analysis. Nonetheless, the town marketplace was a place of considerable significance in the day-to-day life of the city, and an examination of activities in the Charleston marketplace reveals much about the nature of colonial South Carolina's society.

To succeed as both an economic and social system, New World slavery constantly had to balance and reconcile the contradictory requirement of patriarchy and the market. A final resolution of the conflict or a simple rejection of one in favor of the other was neither possible nor desirable. Slavery could not long survive in a social order based entirely upon market relations. Similarly, a perfectly patriarchal slave society would not be economically profitable. The fault line that resulted from the slave society's need to respect the dictates of both patriarchy and the market profoundly shaped relations between slaves and masters.

In most cases, whether as individual masters on their plantations or collectively in their churches, law courts, or legislature, eighteenth-century slaveholders sought to employ the metaphors of patriarchy to implement the domination that they exercised over their own slaves and over the slave society in general. According to patriarchal metaphors, slaves were to be completely subordinate and dependent upon their masters. All relations between slaves and masters were to be based upon a reciprocal exchange of duties and rewards, obligations and

343

gratitude. However, early modern patriarchy implied more than the rightful superiority of masters over slaves. It also demanded the subordination of women to men. The patriarch was expected to be a lordly father as well as a fatherly lord. Therefore, in regard to gender as well as race, day-to-day activities in the market defied ordinary rules.

Metaphors of patriarchy, however, were only the means low country slaveholders employed to achieve their profit-making ends. The market house is a reminder that South Carolina slaveholders were merchant capitalists as well as plantation patriarchs. From the plantation "great house," masters sought to use patriarchy to define the slaves' labor in terms of love, gratitude, and obligation; but, at the same time, in the "counting house" of trade and commerce, masters aimed to transform the product of their slaves' labor into economic capital.

In their effort to exercise a profitable domination over their slaves, slaveholder patriarchs had to recognize and concede somewhat to the "law of the market." In this realm, the dictates of property and price rather than those of deference and duty determined relations between slaves and masters. Through the utilization of market relations, slaves could escape the smothering metaphors of patriarchy, assert their own property right, and gain a degree of autonomy and self-control. Conversely, while masters could not completely deny the legitimacy of the market, they constantly strove to restrict its application and to construct master-slave relations in patriarchal terms.[6]

The Charleston marketplace was the crucible of this conflict and struggle. Encounters which took place there every day between slaveholders and slave marketeers offer a glimpse of how the social order of the colonial slave society was constructed and perpetuated. As E. P. Thompson has pointed out, "the market . . . [was] a social as well as an economic nexus" in the preindustrial world.[7] Here town met country and news and gossip were exchanged along with goods and money.

In Charleston, public markets were the creation of both statute and custom. The Charleston marketplace was largely established in 1739, but other markets had long existed, and continued to exist, in the city. In a 1741 petition to the Assembly, the commissioner of the newly established market complained that although the "[Market] Act appoints but one public Market Place . . . there were two in the . . . Town; the one established by Law, the other by Custom."[8]

The Negro Act of 1740 permitted slaves to attend the market to buy or sell on behalf of their masters provided they carried tickets "particularly enumerating" what was to be bought or sold.[9] From the beginning, however, slave marketeers sought to do more. Many worked out an arrangement with their masters by which they not only sold their master's produce but used their earnings to purchase goods in their own right and resell them for their own personal profit. After they paid their master an agreed-upon "wage," these slave marketeers could retain whatever surplus they had earned. Most of the marketeers were slave women, perhaps because other casual work as porters or day laborers was closed to them. As market traders these women took on the roles traditionally allocated to women in West African, Caribbean, and most other preindustrial societies.[10]

In the short term, such commercial arrangements suited slaveowners who could thereby collect a steady income from their slaves and from the market even when they had no work for the slaves to do, or produce of their own to sell. In the long run, however, as slaves came to play an expanding role in the marketplace and increasingly provided the city's inhabitants, white and black, with basic necessities, whites resented both the independence of the slave marketeers and their control over the city's food supply. Thus, even while individual slaveowners allowed their slaves to become "independent" marketeers, white society collectively acted to censure the practice. Attempts to prohibit, or at least limit, the subversive aspects of slave trading go back to the late seventeenth century. In 1686 the South Carolina Assembly enacted a law that prohibited any person from buying goods from servants or slaves.[11] In 1734, the Charleston grand jury complained that "Negroes are suffered to buy and sell, and be Hucksters of Corn, Pease, fowls, &c. whereby they watch night and day on the several wharves, and buy up many articles necessary for the support of the inhabitants and make them pay an exorbitant rate."[12]

The "official" marketplace was established in 1739 partly to "prevent the injurious and illegal Practice of . . . Negro-huckstering." A year later, when the assembly revised the slave code in response to the Stono rebellion, it renewed the prohibition on independent trading by slaves.[13] However, the stern words and prescribed penalties of the new law did not stop the slave marketeers. In 1744 the grand jury again objected that "many Negroes in Charlestown (in defiance of the 31st paragraph of the Negro Act) do openly buy and sell sundry sorts of wares."[14] The recurrent complaints of Charleston grand juries, to give only the most obvious example, indicate that the sight of slave women acting as independent traders in the market was a common and accepted "illegality."[15]

The discrepancy between statute and custom suggests that the constant reassertion of a patriarchal ideal of master-slave relations in the legislature may actually have allowed slaveholders to accept the intrusion of the market into their everyday relations with their slaves. The law may have served as an ideological citadel in which the masters' absolute and patriarchal authority could be secured, while in practice and on the ground the master-slave interactions were conducted on a very different and far more negotiated basis.

Two accounts, a generation apart, provide a fair picture of the nature and extent of the participation of slaves in the Charleston marketplace in the mid-eighteenth century. A 1747 petition to the assembly complained that as a result of the competition of black marketeers "white people . . . are . . . entirely ruined and rendered miserable . . . by the great liberty and indulgence which is given to Negroes and other slaves in Charles Town to buy, sell and vend . . . valuable commodities."[16] The petitioners' description of the slave marketeers is worth quoting at length:

> [Their masters] give them all imaginable liberty, not only to buy and sell those commodities, but also, . . . to forestall the markets of Charles Town by buying up the Provisions, &c. which come to town for sale, at dear and exorbitant prices, and take what other indirect methods they please, provided they pay their masters their wages, which they seldom or never enquire how they came by the same, . . . [further] those Negroes and other slaves, being possessed of large sums of money, purchase quantities of flour, butter, applies, &ca., all [of] which they retail out to the inhabitants of Charles Town, by which means leading lazy lives, and free from the government of their masters.[17]

Another equally vivid portrayal of the market scene, printed in the *Gazette* in 1772, documents the continuing presence of slaves at the market. An anonymous observer wrote that

> almost every day . . . in and near the Lower Market . . . poultry, fruit, eggs, c. are brought thither from the country for sale. Near that market, constantly resort a great number of loose, idle and disorderly negro women, who are seated there from morn till night, and *buy* and *sell* on *their own accounts*, what they please, in order to pay their wages, and get so much more for themselves as they can; for their owners care little, how their slaves get the money, so they are paid.[18]

Similarly, runaway slaves were often described in the colony's newspapers to be "well known in Charlestown" for their activities at the market. One fugitive, Bella, was said to be "almost every day at Market selling diverse things." An advertisement also drew attention to "the widow Brown's old Negro wench, named Lizette, who attends the lower market and frequently has things to dispose of there."[19]

Slave market women "free from the government of their masters" soon outnumbered and displaced white traders and made the Charleston market their own particular domain.[20] By the mid-eighteenth century, in terms of race as well as tolerated illegalities, the public marketplace of Charleston might be justly termed a "black market." The public market was therefore the only "official" institution in the colony where slaves played not only a central but a dominant role.[21]

The slaves' predominance in the market had important social as well as economic ramifications. Much of the produce sold by the slave marketeers "on their own accounts" had been grown by other slaves in their private gardens. In this way, slave market women became an important source of cash and manufactures to their country counterparts, and the marketplace became one of the central crossroads of the slave community. In trade, town and country slaves could cooperate to their mutual advantage. Studies of present-day markets in Jamaica and Haiti have detailed the existence of "trading partnerships" between rural peasant producers and urban market traders.[22] Such economic ties and clientage may have existed among colonial South Carolina slaves. One observer reported that

> [slave market] women have such a connection with and influence on, the country negroes who come to market, that they generally find means to obtain whatever they may chuse, in preference to any white person; . . . I have seen the country negroes take great pains, after having been first spoke to by those women to *reserve* whatever they chose to sell to them only, either by keeping the particular article in their canows [canoes], or by sending them away and pretending they were not *for sale*; and when they could not be easily retained by themselves, then I have seen the wenches so briskly hustle them about from one to another that in two minutes they could no longer be traced.[23]

The numerical predominance of slaves at the Charleston market may have given them an opportunity to collectively defy white authority in ways that would have been impossible individually. According to Thompson, "the market was the place where the people, because they were numerous, felt for a moment that they were strong."[24] Whites in Charleston also may have recognized that in the marketplace the ordinary powers of the slave society were to some extent suspended. In 1770, the commissioners noted that the fish market, where "the business . . . is principally carried out by negroes . . . [was] apt to be riotous and disorderly."[25]

The most common sentiment expressed in the collected grand jury presentments and other white complaints against the slave marketeers was a frustration at the large degree of discretion that market women exercised during transactions in the market and the subsequent powerlessness of white inhabitants. As slaveholders, Carolina whites felt that slaves should be generally subordinate, but as property holders and capitalists they also had to recognize the legitimacy of the market in which sellers had the right to seek the highest price for their goods. In the market, slaves could turn the contradictions of slavery to their own advantage. They could use the "law of the market" to deflect and reject the patriarchal authority under which slaveholders ordinarily sought to contain their relations with their slaves. Despite their patriarchal pretensions, slaveholders were very familiar with the "law of the market" and were bound to respect it. For slaves, the distance which market relations allowed them to create between themselves as unfree laborers and the commodities they produced could be a source of liberation. Behind the mask of a commodity and governed only by the "law of the market," slave marketeers could challenge their masters and assert a de facto equality every time they refused to sell except upon their own terms.[26]

Furthermore, because slave marketeers did not trade themselves (in the form of their labor) but instead merely exchanged goods for money, the relationship between them and the white "customer" ended as soon as the bargain was transacted. Buyer and seller were momentarily equal and no other connection existed or was thereby created. As a result, no reassuring restoration of the proper social hierarchy took place after the threatening equality of the bargaining process was concluded.

For slaveholders, an easy alternative to having to negotiate as an equal with a slave was to send their own slaves to the market to make purchases on their behalf. Doubtless, this course was taken by many if not most of Charleston's white inhabitants. Nonetheless, when their slaves returned and reported having paid a slave marketeer thirty-two shillings for a quarter of a hog, masters may still have felt a sense of humiliation at having been "out-bargained" by a slave.[27]

The grand jurors and others who objected to the "black market" protested most often against this so-called profiteering. That market slaves, "free from the government of their masters," should take profits from the slaveholders' pockets rather than contribute their labor to produce wealth for their masters was a galling contradiction of the social ideal. Black marketeers were accused of selling goods "at 100 or 150 per cent advance" from what they had paid for them.[28] In 1763, Charleston's market commissioners protested that "Negroes and other slaves . . . have of late actually raised the price of almost every necessity of life beyond anything heretofore known."[29]

Through the market, slaves in Charleston appeared to have evaded the basic principles of South Carolina slave society. To many whites, this development may have pricked latent fears that the slaves might begin to assert their independence in other areas of society as well. Consequently, many whites couched complaints about the slave marketeers in terms that seemed to describe a far more direct insubordination and rebellion. One complaint accused slave market women of acting "in open violation and contempt" of the law and of "combining together in the most impudent and notorious manner." After depicting the little regard blacks paid to white supremacy in the market, an observer remarked that *"they* are *your slaves"*—as if the matter was in doubt.[30]

In extreme cases whites spoke of the market as if their world had already been turned upside down. They described their relationship to market slaves in terms that revealed both their unease at slaves' control of the market and their own feelings of dependency. The commissioners wrote of the "manifest oppression . . . of the inhabitants" by the market slaves.[31] Another account was even more explicit: "[i]t plainly appears that we are at the mercy even of the lowest and most abandoned scoundrels, who dispose not only of our fortunes but our lives . . . this is permitted in contempt of government, which ought to exert itself."[32]

Exchange is a cultural as much as an economic phenomenon. It cannot be separated from its social context or from the structures of power within which it is conducted. Even if the transaction itself takes place within a momentary "social vacuum" of de facto equality, each participant can remember what came before and, more importantly, can anticipate what will follow after the exchange is concluded. Therefore a truly "free market" can exist only when both participants in the exchange are in a relation to each other that is genuinely equal.[33]

In Charleston two factors acted to deflect or contain the challenge which the activities of slave market women posed to the authority of the slaveholders. First, the fact that the majority of the market slaves were women may have rendered their challenge to the social order less threatening. Even if black marketeers defied the principle of white supremacy, as women they could still be subordinated under the larger patriarchal social order.[34]

It is interesting in this vein to note the vocabulary that was used to describe slave marketeers. In 1768 jurymen complained of the "many idle negro wenches, selling dry goods, cakes, rice, etc. in the markets." Four years later, market women were similarly described as "loose, idle and disorderly." Some complainants characterized these women as "insolent," "abusive," "notorious," and "impudent." Female slave marketeers were also perceived to be both "free from the government" and contemptuous of it.[35] Such descriptions of women's actions by male authorities were not confined to slave societies. Natalie Davis has noted that similar language and imagery representing "disorderly women" who protested against authority was common in early modern Europe.[36] Market women in eighteenth-century England were portrayed in the same way. A description of bread riots in England in 1807 observed that "women are more disposed to be mutinous; they stand less in fear of law, partly from ignorance, partly because they presume upon the privileges of their sex, and therefore in all public tumults they are foremost in violence and ferocity."[37]

As long as the actions of slave marketeers could be read as a female challenge to male authority and not as a black or slave challenge to white authority, they could be fit into this existing tradition of "unruly women" and contained within the parameters of what constituted acceptable manifestations of social conflict. To some degree, therefore, female market slaves in Charleston may have been "hiding behind their sex" in their defiance of laws and statutes.[38] Their behavior may thus provide an example, in microcosm, of how gender differences in a patriarchal society may have shaped slave resistance. When complainants described the resistance of market women they referred mostly to verbal aggression and linguistic "impudence." Ridicule, bluster, and wit were the market women's strongest weapons. In 1741, the clerk of the market complained that the "insolent abusive Manner" of slave marketeers rendered him "afraid to say or do Anything in the Market" and left him to be made "a Game of."[39]

Female slave marketeers may have been permitted to act in "contempt of government" precisely because white authorities felt confident that their verbal insolence was unlikely to escalate into violent rebellion. A visitor to the market wrote, "I have known those black women to be so insolent as even to *wrest* things out of the hands of white people, pretending they had been bought before, for their masters or mistresses, yet expose *the same* for sale again within an hour after, for their own benefit."[40] A black man would hardly have been permitted to make such an overt challenge to the authority of the slave society. Consequently, only the continuing subordination of the slave marketeers as women may have allowed them momentarily to overcome the limitations imposed by slavery and race.

Occasional public punishment of slave offenders provided the second outlet for the anxieties and resentments that the slaves' domination of the market caused among slaveholders. The laws against slaves' trading "on their own accounts" in the market were never strictly enforced, partly because of the effort required to do so but largely because whites had no ready alternative through which the city could gain a regular supply of fresh food. In the ordinary course of events, the "black market" was permitted to continue and whites merely complained, doubtless largely in conversation but also through the presentments of grand juries, regarding the market slaves' defiant behavior and galling presumption.

Every few years, however, whether sparked by a temporary shortage in which the market slaves' monopoly power became painfully evident or merely by a general feeling among whites that the marketeers were taking their "liberty" too much for granted, the Negro Act's prohibitions against slave trading would suddenly be enforced. In May 1773, for example, the *Gazette* reported that "a large quantity of Earthen ware, &c. was seized from Negro Hawkers in Meeting, notwithstanding the many examples lately made by forfeitures for this atrocious offense."[41] Continued complaints of grand juries indicate that these sporadic efforts to enforce the law had little real effect in limiting slave marketeering.[42] Nevertheless, the momentary and public enforcement of the law asserted the authority of the slave society over the market women and may have placated white anxieties and resentments. By threatening the marketeers with the loss of what they had so painstakingly gained and punishing them with twenty lashes if they stepped too far, such tactics might also have served as a means of keeping prices down.

A similar process may have taken place far too often upon an individual and personal level. In the market, slaveholders could at any time cast their social superiority into the balance to gain an unfair advantage or to remove the humiliation of trading, or worse, of reneging upon a contract with a slave. Slaves engaged in marketplace exchange, but they were still fettered by their inferior social status. They were constantly aware of their lack of any legal right to property and knew that their white "customer" could at any time void all contracts simply by moving the relationship from one of buyer-seller to one of master-slave or white-black. Although slaveholders constantly complained of "profiteering," it seems more likely that with such a constant threat hanging over them, slave market women accepted a smaller margin of profit than genuinely free traders would have done.

Through occasional demonstrations of their power, slaveholders could draw a line around the ordinary "disorder" of the "black market" and remind the slaves and perhaps reassure themselves that the illegality of the market continued only upon their sufferance.[43] Given their very real dependence upon the slave marketeers to gather and distribute the city's food supply, this construction was based largely on wishful thinking. Through periodic punishments, however, authorities could make the point that the dependency was at least mutual. If whites were forced to rely upon the slave market women for their basic necessities, these women were just as reliant upon white forbearance for their de facto "liberty." More importantly, the occasional enforcement of otherwise dormant laws served to remind all members of the slave society where authority lay. By such actions, slaveholders contained the independence of market slaves in the realm of tolerated illegalities.

At most, several hundred slave women regularly engaged in selling "sundry sorts of wares" in the mid-eighteenth-century Charleston marketplace. Slave marketeers therefore comprised a tiny fraction of the colony's slave population. In numerical terms, the threat they posed to the slave society was of small consequence. However, the fact that market slaves posed their challenge in the colonial metropolis of Charleston gave it a significance beyond mere numbers. In Charleston, although slave marketeers were few in number, they "played" to a large audience. Along with the city population, thousands of country residents, white and black, visited the city every day and would have had contact with the "black market." The ability of slave women to dominate the proceedings at the market in the center of the slave society's metropolis and to "escape" the limitations of their condition in such a public way challenged white authority and served as an example to other slaves. The challenge was evidently more symbolic than real, striking at the ideological level against white supremacy rather than at the actual structures of power.

The transactions and encounters which took place every day in the Charleston marketplace provide a glimpse in microcosm of the complex relations which shaped the social order of the colonial slave society. The market straddled the line that divided legal code and customary practice. While the slave market women were a vital part of the domestic economy and colonial social order, the "black market" nonetheless continued to exist outside the law. Its impact on the slave community was also two-edged. By allowing slaves to hold property and accumulate wealth within slavery, the market may have acted to lessen overt slave rebelliousness in the short term. In the longer term, however, marketeers remained a focus of dissent and a challenge to notions of white supremacy and patriarchal authority in the slave society. In the market, buyer and seller negotiated over more than the price of food. They also reckoned and constructed the ongoing relations between master and slave, white and black, men and women, authority and property.

[1]"A Naval Officer's View of the Metropolis, 1769," in *The Colonial South Carolina Scene: Contemporary Views, 1697–1774*, ed. and comp. H. Roy Merrens (Columbia: University of South Carolina Press, 1977), pp. 230–31. An earlier and shorter version of this chapter (under the title "The World Turned Upside Down: Slave Women in the Charleston Marketplace") was presented at the meeting of the Organization of American Historians in Louisville in April 1991. The author would like to thank Sylvia Frey, Colin Palmer, and, in particular, David Barry Gaspar for their helpful criticisms of that paper.

[2]The adage is somewhat spoiled by the fact that the old Bank of the United States building is now the Charleston city hall.

[3]"Charleston, S.C., in 1774 as Described by an English Traveler," *Historical Magazine* 9 (November 1865): 341–47, reprinted in *The Colonial South Carolina Scene*, p. 282.

[4]*Journal of the Common House of Assembly* (hereafter *JCHA*), ed. J. H. Easterby et al. (Columbia Historical Commission of South Carolina, 1953), May 21, 1741, p. 16.

[5]*South Carolina and American General Gazette*, February 19, 1778.

[6]The research presented in this chapter and the thesis briefly sketched out here is developed at greater length in Robert Olwell, "Authority and Resistance: Social Order in a Colonial Slave Society, the South Carolina Lowcountry, 1739–1782," Ph.D. dissertation, Johns Hopkins University, 1991.

[7]E. P. Thompson, "The Moral Economy of the English Crowd in the Eighteenth Century," *Past and Present* 50 (February 1971): 135.

[8]*JCHA*, May 21, 1741, p. 23. The act "for establishing a Market in the Parish of St. Philips Charles Town" was passed on April 11, 1739; *JCHA*, p. 698.

[9]William Simpson, *The Practical Justice of the Peace and Parish Officer of His Majesty's Province of South Carolina* (Charleston, 1761), p. 137.

[10]On this point, Philip Morgan has written, "By the late eighteenth century, then, black women had assumed an important role in the town's daily economic affairs, not unlike the place traditionally held by female entrepreneurs in the trading centres of West Africa." See Morgan, "The Development of Slave Culture in Eighteenth-Century Plantation America," Ph.D. dissertation, University of London, 1977, p. 138. Likewise, Sidney Mintz notes the predominance of women in postemancipation (1838) Jamaican markets (while also noting, due to lack of evidence, that the sex of the Jamaican marketeers during slavery cannot be known). See Mintz, *Caribbean Transformations* (Baltimore: Johns Hopkins University Press, 1984), p. 216.

[11]*The Statutes at Large of South Carolina*, ed. Thomas Cooper and David J. McCord (Columbia, S.C., 1836–41), vol. 2, p. 22.

[12]*South Carolina Gazette*, March 30, 1734, Weber contrib., "Presentment of the Grand Jury," *South Carolina Historical and Genealogical Magazine*, 2512.22 (October 1924), pp. 193–94.

[13]*JCHA*, May 21, 1741, p. 16. The Negro Act of 1740 directed that: "[n]o slave who shall dwell ... or be usually employed in Charles Town, shall presume to buy, sell, deal, traffic, barter, exchange or use commerce for any goods, wares, provisions, grain, victuals, or

commodities, of any sort or kind whatsoever . . . on pain that all such goods, wares, provisions, grain, victuals, or commodities, which by any slave shall be . . . used in commerce, shall be seized and forfeited . . . and moreover . . . every slave who shall be convicted of such offence [is] to be publicly whipped on the bare back not exceeding twenty lashes." (*The Statutes at Large of South Carolina*, pp. 407–8).

14Journal of the Council, October 17, 1744 (microfilm), Library of Congress, Washington, D.C., pp. 527–29.

15Michel Foucault described this process of tolerated "illegalities" in early modern France:

> each of the different social strata had its margin of tolerated illegality: the non-application of the rule, the non-observance of the innumerable edicts or ordinances were a condition of the political and economic functioning of society. . . . Sometimes it took the form of a massive general non-observance, which meant that for decades . . . ordinances would be published and constantly renewed without ever being implemented. Sometimes it was a matter of laws gradually falling into abeyance, then suddenly being reactivated; sometimes of silent consent on the part of the authorities, neglect, or quite simply the actual impossibility of imposing the law and apprehending offenders. The least-favored strata of the population did not have, in principle, any privileges: but they benefited, within the margins of what was imposed on them by law and custom, from a space of tolerance, gained by force or obstinacy. (*Discipline and Punish: The Birth of the Prison*, trans. Alan Sheridan [New York: Vintage Books, 1979], p. 82)

16"Petition of Sundry Inhabitants of Charlestown," *JCHA*, February 5, 1747, pp. 154–55.

17Ibid.

18*South Carolina Gazette*, September 24, 1772.

19*South Carolina Gazette*, December 6, 1751; November 10, 1746; May 31, 1770. Lizette was accused of "contrivance" in a robbery in which sixty-five pounds worth of exchange notes were stolen. The advertiser thought it "very probable, that she [Lizette] may endeavour to exchange some of them [the notes] for goods to sell against."

20*JCHA*, February 5, 1747, pp. 154–55.

21In this regard, Betty Wood has noted that "by the late eighteenth century, the Lowcountry's urban markets were dominated by black vendors"; Wood, "'White Society' and the 'Informal' Slave Economies of Lowcountry Georgia, c. 1763–1830," *Slavery and Abolition* 11 (December 1990): 317.

22In Haiti such "trading partnerships" are known as *pratik*. Sidney Mintz provides a description of their operation: "A buying pratik who knows her selling pratik is coming will wait at the proper place and time, refusing to buy stock from others that she is sure her pratik is carrying . . . to the extent that her stock is committed in such arrangements a selling pratik will refuse to sell to others until she has met her pratik buyer." Quoted in Stuart Plattner, "Equilibrating Market Relationships," in *Markets and Marketing*, ed. Platter (Lanham, Md.: University Press of America/Society for Economic Anthropology, 1985), p. 137.

23*South Carolina Gazette*, September 24, 1772.

24Thompson, "The Moral Economy of the English Crowd," p. 135.

25*South Carolina Gazette*, November 15, 1770. The commissioners decreed that stocks be erected near the fish market and local magistrates be authorized to confine "riotous, disorderly or drunken Negroes . . . buying, selling, or being in and about the said market in the stocks, there to remain for a space not more [than] two hours."

26On this point, Lawrence T. McDonnell writes, "Master and slave confronted each other at the moment of exchange as bearers of commodities, snipped of social dimensions. . . . In this realm each knew perfect freedom and dependence"; McDonnell "Money Knows No Master: Market Relations and the Slave Community," in *Developing Dixie: Modernization in a Traditional Society*, ed. Winfrid B. Moore, Jr., Joseph F. Tripp, and Lyon G. Tyler, Jr. (New York: Greenwood, 1988), p. 34. While accepting McDonnell's idea as important and illuminating, I nonetheless have some significant reservations. Most importantly, I would argue that the market can never be entirely removed from its social context and that therefore market slaves cannot achieve "perfect freedom" (if such a thing ever exists for anyone). The equality of the market is necessarily one of degree, perception, and comparison, and is full of limitations.

27*South Carolina Gazette*, November 26, 1772.

28*South Carolina Gazette*, September 24, 1772.

29*South Carolina Gazette*, October 22, 1763.

30*South Carolina Gazette*, October 22, 1763; September 24, 1772.

31*South Carolina Gazette*, October 22, 1763.

32*South Carolina Gazette*, November 26, 1772.

33James C. Scott gives an example of a contemporary Malaysian agricultural worker who was given less than the expected wage for stacking rice and when asked why he didn't argue about the low rate, replied, "Poor people can't complain; when I'm sick or need work, I may have to ask him again. I am angry in my heart." Scott quotes Karl Marx as calling this dilemma "the dull compulsion of economic relations." See Scott, "Everyday Forms of Peasant Resistance," *Journal of Peasant Studies* 13 (January 1986): 14–15.

34For more on the "patriarchal metaphor" in theory and practice, see Olwell, "Authority and Resistance," chap. 5.

35*South Carolina Gazette*, February 1, 1768; September 24, 1772; October 22, 1763; November 26, 1772. *JCHA*, May 21, 1741, p. 18; February 5, 1747, pp. 154–55.

36Natalie Davis, *Society and Culture in Early Modern France* (Stanford: Stanford University Press, 1975), pp. 124–51.

37Thompson, "The Moral Economy of the English Crowd," pp. 115–16.

38Davis, *Society and Culture in Early Modern France*, p. 146. Wole Soyinka vividly describes the social "power" of contemporary West African market women (who, among other things, led a successful protest against unpopular legislation) in the Nigeria of his childhood; see Soyinka, *Ake: The Years of Childhood* (New York: Random House, 1981), pp. 199–223. For the same phenomenon in present-day Peru, see Linda J. Seligmann, "To Be In Between: The *Cholas* as Market

Women," *Comparative Studies in Society and History* 31 (October 1989): 694–721.

39*JCHA*, May 21, 1741, p. 18.

40 *South Carolina Gazette*, September 24, 1772.

41*South Carolina Gazette*, May 17, 1773.

42The "many examples" of slaves' goods being seized for violation of the law in the spring of 1773 did not prevent the grand jury from complaining on May 21 "that the Huckstering and selling dry goods, cook'd rice and other victuals is still practised about the Markets and streets of Charlestown by Negroes," *Journal of the Court of General Sessions [Charleston], 1769–1776* (South Carolina Department of Archives and History, Columbia, S.C.), p. 241.

43Owing to lack of evidence it is impossible to prove how often (or how seldom) the laws against trading by slaves in the market were enforced. Certainly the impression gained from the presentments, which were generally directed as much at white law office as slaves (for example, a presentment published in the *South Carolina Gazette* on June 8, 1765, complained of "the magistrates and constables of Charlestown . . . not carrying into execution the laws . . . particularly those against . . . negroes hawking and selling . . ."), would indicate that the laws were rarely enforced. This is also indicated by the "surprised" tone adopted in the account of slaves being punished for illicit trading in 1773.

Perceptions of Slave Women in Nineteenth-Century Brazil

Robert W. Slenes

On August 24, 1899, Simão Alves appeared at one of the main parish churches of Campinas, in Brazil's São Paulo state, "to make a new registration of the act of marriage celebrated between Policarpo Salvador and Afra." The witnesses to this new document—Egydio Franco and José Antônio Aranha—declared that Policarpo and Afra were "husband and wife—by virtue of the fact that they were married—the religious act having been celebrated in the church which was the parish seat of this county during the time when the said couple were slaves of Mr. Thomaz Luiz Alves Cruz—more or less in the year 1858–59." Egydio and José Antônio "added that they had been companions [of Policarpo and Afra] in slavery and that for thirty and twenty-four years [respectively] they have known them always as a married couple." The testimony of these men is reliable. Although it is not possible to check their story against the original marriage certificate (perhaps because the register of slave marriages for most of 1858 and 1859 disappeared from the church archives in Campinas—a fact which may provide us with the motive for the "new registration" of 1899), another document confirms its accuracy. On October 19, 1862, a child named Benedicta, aged thirteen days, was baptized in the county; she was identified as "a daughter of Policarpo and Afra, slaves of Thomas Luis Alvares [sic]."[1]

Long and stable marriages like that of Policarpo and Afra were relatively uncommon among Brazilian slaves, if one accepts the arguments of the standard works which address the question. Indeed, for several important authors the conditions of bondage (the excess of men over women, the separation of families in the internal slave trade, the capriciousness and violence of masters) made slave sexual unions so unstable that affective life became virtually normless and family institutions practically nonexistent. Gilberto Freyre referred to the "animality in Negros [who were slaves], their failure to restrain their instincts, and the prostitution that went on within the home"; Emilia Viotti da Costa pointed to "the sexual promiscuity in which the slaves lived" and the "licentiousness of the slave quarters"; Oracy Nogueira noted that "given the occasional and promiscuous character of sexual relations," the slave "barely came to know his or her own mother and siblings"; and Roger Bastide, arguing that "a [slave] woman would sleep, now with one man now with another

as the fancy took her," characterized the sexual life of slaves as "a vast primitive promiscuity."[2] Bastides's assertion, calling attention to the capriciousness of slave women, reveals an assumption that seems to be shared by all of these authors: that a breakdown in sexual norms means, above all, a disruption of controls on female sexuality. From this vantage point, what was distinctive about slave sexual behavior was less the inconstancy of men than the wantonness of women. In the context of these studies, Policarpo and Afra together are certainly exceptions, and Afra seems especially unusual.

Recent studies in slave demography, mostly unavailable in English, suggest however that in many respects the experience of this couple, particularly of Afra, was not uncommon. This chapter briefly reviews the results of this new research, then examines the sources which informed the earlier evaluations of the Brazilian slave's sexual behavior and family life. It argues that the image of slave promiscuity was drawn from an uncritical reading of nineteenth-century accounts left by European travelers and well-to-do Brazilians. The authors of these accounts viewed blacks through an ethnocentric and elitist prism which caused them to overlook or misinterpret the evidence regarding the intimate life and domestic arrangements of slaves. Their distortion of the experience of slave women was particularly severe. An examination of the biases which permeated their writings reinforces the conclusions of recent studies in slave demography. It also opens the way for posing new questions to these same sources, which are replete with information that may be read in a radically different way.

In Brazil, as in the United States, the question of the slave family—or, more precisely, of the stability or instability of the nuclear slave family—has been linked to fundamental issues regarding black acculturation and socialization. The four authors cited above, like virtually all students of the subject since the 1930s, have emphatically rejected racist explanations for slave sexual behavior;[3] nonetheless, if they have lifted the burden of race from the shoulders of blacks, they have replaced it with a sociological burden that is almost as heavy. The affirmation that slaves in general lived in "incentiousness," in "promiscuity," or in "prostitution" leads easily to the argument that they were profoundly marked by that experience. Bastide and Florestan

Fernandes are particularly emphatic in positing that these conditions had an impact on the slaves' religious culture, their sexual and family norms, and even the innermost recesses of their psyches. Bastide asserted that given the impossibility of maintaining the existence of the family—that is, the lineage—over time, the "cult of the ancestors" of slaves of Bantu origin was destined to disappear rapidly or to survive only through "indirect" ways.[4] Fernandes argues that the conditions of slavery, above all the determination of the masters to prevent "all the forms of union or of solidarity of the slaves," not only marked the sexual behavior of slaves but also undermined the norms of their family life. The result was that blacks emerged from slavery in a state of "anomie" or of "social pathology," without the psychological resources and the ties of solidarity among kin that was so necessary for engaging in competition with immigrants and achieving social mobility.[5] Finally, Bastide argued that "racial parental dualism is the most singular phenomenon of slavery," noting that if "the patriarch's son had a white father and a black mother" (the *ama de leite*, equivalent to the figure of the "mammy"), "the slave's son, on the other hand, may have known his mother but often had no idea who his real father was. In the final analysis his real father, if not his biological one, was the white patriarch, the plantation owner." In this "parental dualism" Bastide found the key to explaining the "psychic mechanisms of [the] acculturation" of blacks; "interiorizing" the white father, the black man (and, presumably, the black woman) would have "interiorized his culture, his view of the world and of life, his frames of references and his norms."[6]

We recognize here the voice of authority; the opinions are emphatic, expressed with the assurance of those who have a firm grasp on theory and an intimate acquaintance with the historical sources. Thus it is curious—or perhaps not so curious, in view of the dramatic changes in the historiography on the slave family in the United States since the late 1960s[7]—that recent studies of the slave family in Brazil indicate that the marriage of Afra and Policarpo was not entirely atypical.[8] Indeed, it would appear that sexual unions of "long duration"—not, of course, those which lasted forty years, which would be relatively rare in any society with high mortality rates, but say, those of ten years or more—were rather common among Brazilian slaves. Also common were children who not only knew their father but also passed their formative years in his company. Illustrative data exist for Campinas, a major plantation county (producing mainly sugar in the first part of the nineteenth century, then coffee after midcentury) in the state of São Paulo. According to the manuscripts of the slave *matricula* (registry) of 1872–73 for Campinas, in holdings with ten or more bondmen and women (including perhaps as many as four in every five slaves in the county), 67 percent of women above the age of fifteen were married or widowed, 87 percent of the mothers (with children under fifteen present in the same matricula list) were married or widowed, and 82 percent of children under ten lived in the same holding with both their parents or with a widowed mother or father.[9] Studies of other counties and periods, using different demographic sources, present compatible or similar results.[10]

To be sure, most of the new research focuses on localities in São Paulo, where slave marriages celebrated by the Catholic Church were considerably more common than in other provinces.[11] Nonetheless, other information strongly suggests that the data from São Paulo do not portray family structures radically different from those of slaves in the rest of Brazil, but simply indicate a greater degree of access to religious marriage.[12] In sum, in São Paulo the consensual unions among slaves were sacramented by the church and thus were documented more frequently than in other provinces. One could object that the data, above all the information from censuses, such as the matricula, may have been invented by slaveowners to deceive the authorities, or that they may simply reflect an attempt by masters to instill white standards of "morality" among their workers. In Campinas, however, the nominative linkage of the baptism and marriage registers for slaves with the matricula lists—similar to that effected between the baptism certificate of Benedicta in 1862 and reaffirmation of the marriage of her parents, Policarpo and Afra, in 1899—confirms without a doubt the authenticity of the data from 1872–73.[13] In so doing, this linkage of sources also shows that a substantial proportion of marriages recorded in the matricula had been formed ten, fifteen, even twenty years earlier.[14] Thus another possible criticism of the census data—that they may simply document the existence, at one point in time, of a large number of unions which were fundamentally unstable—is also rebutted.

The new studies about the Brazilian slave family do not aim at making life under bondage seem less harsh; nor do they mean to show that black people adopted the family norms of whites. The indices of marriage among slaves, the proportion of married mothers, and the percentage of children who lived with both parents or with one widowed parent were much lower in small holdings (those with less than ten people) which, because of their size and instability, severely limited a slave's chances of finding a marriage partner or of maintaining her or his nuclear family intact.[15] In major plantation areas like Campinas, these small holdings were relatively unimportant in demographic terms, but there is no doubt that in all of São Paulo—as in

Brazil considered as a whole—they accounted for at least a very large minority of slaves.[16] Furthermore, even on the larger holdings there is no doubt that the separation of families did occur, and that the possibility of such separation was ever present. Recent studies also do not deny the impact of the great disparity between the numbers of men and women (resulting from the African trade and later, in the coffee areas of Rio, São Paulo, and Minas Gerais, from the internal commerce in slaves) on the slaves' chances of forming stable families. They simply show that the negative impact on marriage rates was felt by the men, not the women; in Campinas in 1872–73, in holdings with ten or more slaves, only 30 percent of the male population above fifteen years of age was composed of married men or widowers, a figure that was much below the proportion of married women or widows of that age.[17] Finally, the new research does not indicate that the slaves internalized the sexual family norms of their owners, or that their norms permitted only monogamous marriage. The data—which, one may presume, in the majority of studies portray marriages sanctioned by the church—practically by definition exclude the registration of cases of polygyny, or the union between a man and more than one woman, a practice which was accepted by many African societies. And even if this were not the case, a high frequency of monogamous marriages would not necessarily mean that slaves preferred this type of union. It is important to remember that in Africa polygyny tends to be a sign of relative wealth; in general, only those men who have sufficient means to sustain a larger domestic economy marry more than one woman. In sum, the practice of polygyny could only have been relatively uncommon (regardless of slave norms on the question) among slaves in Brazil, where we may presume that most men confronted an economy of scarcity, not to mention a great lack of women.[18]

What recent studies do indicate is that the weight of slavery, the disequilibrium between the sexes, and the possible (or probable) "survival" of norms favorable to polygyny did not destroy the Brazilian black family as an institution. In addition, and more important, these studies strongly suggest that a stable marital union was a cultural norm among slaves. When conditions of bondage permitted the formation of social relations with a certain continuity over time (as tended to be the case in holdings with ten or more slaves in places like Campinas), slaves opted for this type of union. In sum, there is no apparent reason to characterize the sexual and family practices of Brazilian slave women and men as unregulated, or their system of norms as destructured or in disarray. Thus the conclusions of Bastide and Fernandes, summarized above—with respect to the necessarily rapid disappearance of the cult of the ancestors among slaves of Bantu origin and descent, the prevalence

of "anomie" among slaves and free blacks, and the influence of the white master/"father" or the psyche of the slave—simply have no basis.

And yet, doubts may well persist. How is it possible that researchers of the stature of those cited could have arrived at conclusions at once so emphatic and so wrong? One answer may be that they interpreted their data in the terms of a paradigm that has since been seriously questioned. Brazilian social science from the 1930s to the 1960s was strongly influenced by the sociology of Emile Durkheim, as extended and modified by American functionalism; studies about the slave family, in particular, reflected Robert K. Merton's redefinition of anomie as a concept for studying individual deviance, and also the attempt by Talcott Parsons and others to integrate Freudian thought into functionalist theories of social action, especially theories of social deviance.[19] Furthermore, authors writing on Brazil (especially Bastide and Fernandes) were acquainted with the American literature on the black family produced within the same paradigm.[20] It is not surprising, therefore, that Bastide's discussion of slave psychology, which was based on the supposed absence of the black father, paralleled that of Abram Kardiner and Lionel Ovesey in the United States, even though Bastide may have been unaware of the specific work of these authors on the subject. Nor is it strange that Fernandes independently described the Brazilian black family in terms of "social pathology" in the same year (1965) that Daniel P. Moynihan placed the family, supposedly weakened by slavery, at the center of the "tangle of pathology" in the American black community.[21]

However, if this analysis helps to explain how these students of Brazilian slavery interpreted their data, it does not go very far toward providing a critique of their sources. Is it not conceivable that the information they used—drawn mainly from the accounts of white observers, above all foreign travelers, during the time of slavery—may be more reliable than the demographic data on which recent studies are based? It is certainly true that the opinions expressed in those firsthand accounts form a coherent whole. They coincide in recording a pathological state among slaves, and it is understandable that their unanimity in this sense could have seduced many historians. Nonetheless, a closer examination of these sources reveals that the problem was not, as Bastide would have it, in the ego and superego of the slave but in the eye of the nineteenth-century beholder.[22]

Nineteenth-century accounts of Brazil employed common metaphors to describe black people. Indeed, the images are not only recurrent but also so lurid at times that one begins to suspect they were based more on white prejudices than on black realities. The novel *A Carne* (The flesh), by Júlio Ribeiro, published in 1888 and set on a plantation in western São Paulo during the time of slavery, offers a particularly good example. In one scene the white protagonist, Lenita, observes a bull and a cow mating. Immediately thereafter she witnesses a tryst between two young slave lovers. For Lenita, their encounter "was the reproduction of what had occurred, moments ago, but on a more elevated scale; the instinctive, brutish, wild, instantaneous copulation of the ruminants was followed by the premeditated, lascivious, gentle and deliberate human coitus." The scene foreshadows Lenita's fate. Later in the novel she becomes the lover of Barbosa, the son of her planter host. Lenita was interested in science; in the novel, she and Barbosa first have a platonic relationship as researchers in a laboratory he set up on the plantation where they both reside. Through science, Lenita "had hoped to fly with a bound, to ascend to the clouds"; but "the FLESH [sic] had held her to the earth, and she fell, she submitted herself, she fell like the feral black woman [negra boçal] in the copse, like the tame cow in the field."23

To associate cattle and slaves—not just as chattel, a category codified in law, but as beings with an unregulated sexual life—appears to have been common at the time. Other authors, who did not call themselves writers of fiction, expressed themselves in the same or in similar terms as Ribeiro. On visiting the region of Cantagalo in the province of Rio de Janeiro at the beginning of the 1860s, the Swiss traveler and diplomat Johann Jacob Von Tschudi commented upon the "frivolity and well-known inconstancy of the black in everything which has to do with sexual relations." Among slaves, according to Tschudi, "it is relatively rare to find marriages blessed by the church; but the fazendeiro [planter] permits couples to live together, in accordance as slaves find and choose mates among themselves, and his pronouncement that they be considered man and wife is sufficient for a union that only exceptionally will last a lifetime; normally, black women have children by two or three or even more men. On the majority of estates, even this formality [the pronouncement of the planter] is not observed, and the blacks live in sexual relationships rather like the cattle on the pampas."24

A few years later, in 1867, the jurist (and slaveowner) Agostinho Marques Perdigão Malheiro observed that "slave women, in general, used to live and continue to live in concubinage, or (what is worse) in lechery; only in exceptional cases does marriage guarantee to them the regular propagation of offspring."25 In 1881, Louis Couty, a Frenchman who resided for several years in Brazil and wrote profusely on the coffee economy and slavery, affirmed that many masters, confronted by the difficulty of imposing a moral order on their bondmen and women, had decided they would no longer interfere in their slaves' sexual lives. Consequently, "in the agglomerations [of slaves] on the plantations, the two sexes are allowed to mix during two or three hours every evening; and in the towns, in the case of isolated slaves, no attempt is made to exercise any vigilance whatsoever. As a result, most slave children know only one of their parents, the mother, and she would often be embarrassed if she had to fill in an exact civil register." In addition, according to Couty, "one finds many black women who do not know how many children they have, just as one encounters those who have never bothered themselves to find out what has become of their children." Then too, when slaves did marry, the exploitation of the wife by the husband, who transformed his spouse into "his servant and his property," generally led the woman "to return . . . with usury this lack of affection." The cases of male slaves who died, poisoned by their wives, "came to be so frequent that, on almost all the plantations, it was necessary to prohibit the widows from remarrying, and to prevent them from continuing to have sexual relations."26

Similar declarations can be cited from accounts of the first half of the nineteenth century. Johann Moritz Rugendas, a Bavarian artist who accompanied the Langsdorff scientific expedition to Brazil and remained there from 1822 to 1825, affirmed that "generally the planters encourage marriages among the slaves"; nonetheless, "it cannot be denied that there are many exceptions to this rule, that the slaveowners very often seduce the slaves with their own example of immorality, and that the disproportion between [the numbers of] female and male slaves does not make possible a greater severity on this point and a very strict observance of conjugal fidelity."27 In the same period, Jean Baptiste Debret, a French artist and likewise an acute observer of life in Brazil, noted that "since a slaveowner cannot, without going against nature, prevent his black men from frequenting black women, it is practically the custom, on the large properties, to bestow one black woman on every four men; it is then up to them to reach an agreement as to how to share peacefully the fruit of this concession, which is made as much to avoid any pretext for flight, as with a view toward encouraging procreation so as to counter, some day, the effects of mortality."28

Debret's assertion is somewhat ambiguous—it could be a simple demographic observation or a suggestion of promiscuity—as is also another sentence in his book, in which the black woman is described as "endowed to an extraordinary degree with the ardour of the senses, although [she is] faithful and chaste, in marriage."29 The other authors, however, leave little room for doubt. They created the image of sexual license and unstable families which most later historians accepted as a faithful portrayal of the lives of Brazilian slaves.

It is an image which is suspect, to say the least. Actually, contemporary observations of slavery in Brazil regarding the intimate life of bondwomen and men are short and scarce; worse, on the whole they simply do not stand up to critical examination. Accounts of European travelers, from which most of the citations are drawn, are extremely useful when they describe aspects of material culture which are easily visible and relatively unambiguous (for example, the structure, arrangement, and internal divisions of the slave quarters of the plantation which were seen firsthand). These accounts are much less reliable, however, when they convey opinions about the intimate lives of an entire social group, especially such an "exotic" group as African slaves and their descendants. George Gardner, an Englishman who traveled through the interior of Brazil in 1836, did not restrain his criticism of "voyagers, *en passant,* who have derived their knowledge from others, and not from personal observation. The most ridiculous stories are told by the European residents to strangers on their arrival, as I well know from personal experience."[30] Even careful travelers, like the majority of those cited, would have had difficulty in freeing their observations about the Brazilian slave family from the influence of preconceived ideas, either of their own or of their white informants. Brazilian writers would not have been in a much better position. Although they were not in Brazil *en passant* and thus could recognize and discard "the most ridiculous stories" regarding their country, they were, nonetheless, almost as distant from the slaves in their culture, perceptions, and way of life as European travelers.

What would have been some of the prior images, stamped on the retina, which blurred the vision of white, mostly middle- or upper-class Europeans and Brazilians when confronted with the slave? To begin with, it would be surprising not to find a deformed image of blacks and Africans themselves, because few European travelers or well-born Brazilians could have escaped the influence of racist ideologies of the time. In this regard, it is worth referring again to the case of Louis Couty, who left what is probably the longest account by a contemporary (less than two pages) about the Brazilian slave family. To be sure, even without considering Couty's ideas about race, there is reason to question his reliability as an observer. His Dutch contemporary, C. F. Van Delden Laërne, whose study of the coffee industry in Brazil is remarkable for its careful research and meticulous exposition, complained that "it would lead me to too great a length were I to confute one by one the statements in this work [Couty's *Étude de Biologie Industrielle sur le Café,* published in 1883] which appear to me to be incorrect, nay, even untrue."[31] It is best to leave this criticism aside, however, because it may be seen as the expression of professional envy, the critique of a rival researcher, and instead focus on the paragraphs in Couty's writings which concern the slave family. If the despotic husbands, heartless mothers ("black women," not "slave women"), and murderous wives in the text already cited did not raise the reader's suspicions, let us backtrack a few pages in Couty's account to find his point of departure:

Do not . . . [the] free citizens of Africa [in Africa itself] have a distaste for manual labor, like their slave brethren; do they cultivate the ever-so-fertile lands which are in their possession; has it not been proven that, when they are employed as workers, they provide much less labor than white workers? Do they have ideas of individual liberty, these men who find it natural to be beaten, to be sold, to be killed according to the caprices of a military chief or a despot? Do they have ideas about family or property, these unhappy people who sell their children for a few scraps of gaudily colored cloth, who kill travelers to pillage their goods and consider theft as a [legitimate] means of struggle for life? And is not the study of their societies—[which are] embryonic, transitory, barely cohesive, without manufacturing plants and without production—like the study of their brain or of their cranium, sufficient to permit a suitable reply to those who make social theories with vague words or with a priori ideas?[32]

The explicit and virulent racism of this passage makes Couty's testimony regarding slaves extremely dubious. Unfortunately, it has not kept him from becoming one of the authors most cited on the question of the Brazilian slave family.[33]

Cultural prejudices also almost certainly obstructed or interfered with the vision of white observers in nineteenth-century Brazil. It is important to remember that the great majority of European travelers who wrote about Brazil, especially in the nineteenth century, came not from Spain or Portugal but from Northern and Western Europe (principally from France, Switzerland, the Germanic states, and England). In these countries from the beginning of the sixteenth to the middle of the eighteenth century, procreation practically did not occur outside sexual unions sacramented by the church; and even in the nineteenth century the illegitimacy rate generally did not rise above 10 percent—a figure much below the proportion in the Iberian countries and Latin America. Even so, the enormous increase in illegitimacy after the mid-eighteenth century, especially in the cities (where the proportion of illegitimate births was often considerably more than the national average), caused widespread alarm in Europe and was commonly interpreted as a sign of deteriorating standards of morality.[34] Thus it is not surprising that European travelers in the nineteenth century, when confronted with the very low indices of religious marriage and the very high rates of illegitimacy which prevailed among Brazilian slaves outside São Paulo, would have recorded an impression of social pathology. The distorting lens of their culture practically prohibited a different vision of reality.

In the case of Brazilian observers, one suspects that a different cultural prejudice was more important. Suggestive in this regard is "Lucinda— the *Mucama* [slave lady-in-waiting]," a short novel which forms part of Joaquim Manoel de Macedo's *As Vitimas-Algozes* (The victim-executioners). Published in 1869, this work of fiction transmits the same negative image of the slave woman that we find in Couty, but it offers a sociological, rather than racial, explanation of her character. The novel is an antislavery tract whose theme is the malefic influence of slavery in the very bosom of the white family. In describing how the young white girl, Cândida (representing purity), is corrupted by her slave lady-in-waiting, Lucinda (whose name evokes that of the devil), Macedo reveals his vision of the moral formation of the slave and his conception of how a girl from an honorable family should be brought up. Macedo writes that the slave woman, "abandoned to the scornful neglect of slavery, growing up surrounded by the practice of the most scandalous and repugnant vices, from her childhood, from her very earliest childhood, witnessing lascivious depravities and hearing the turbid eloquence of speech that knows no restraint, becomes perverted long before she is conscious of her perversion." In contrast, "the damsel [*donzela*] is a flower whose blush is a blend of circumspection and shame." In good families, "daughters are given a certain special care, which on the part of their mothers takes the form of a religious cult of love, constantly on guard, like that of the priestesses of Vesta who stood vigil over the fire of purity, and which on the part of their fathers is a sublime source of prudish sensitivity and scruples, a saintly exaggeration of the paroxysms of zealous love."

As a result of parental vigilance, "Cândida had arrived at the age of eleven with the perfect innocence of her early childhood." Unfortunately, her parents then gave her Lucinda as a present, and "[it was] the slave who wrenched her out of her happy and serene ignorance, the fruit of her innocence, and crudely . . . [taught] her sensuous theories about woman's mission." It is clear from all this that Macedo condemns the moral formation of the slave woman because he cannot accept as legitimate any set of norms for a young girl's upbringing other than that adopted by Cândida's parents. Implicit in his praise of this couple's "saintly exaggeration of the paroxysms of zealous love," one finds his condemnation of slave parents and their daughters. The modern reader will ask if it is legitimate to measure the morality of slave women and men—or any other group— by this yardstick.[35]

Macedo's concern for the fires of Vesta, however, is only an extreme manifestation of a cultural prejudice that was probably shared by most well-born Brazilians and Europeans alike. Significantly, when confronted with one of the most visible aspects of black culture in Brazil— slave dances of African origin—most white observers could not help but perceive them, in contrast to their own dances, as extremely sensual, even lewd. Charles Ribeyrolles, a Frenchman who visited the coffee and sugar regions of Rio de Janeiro in 1858, had this to say about a slave dance called the *lundú*: "it is a mad dance in which eyes, breasts and hips provoke; it is a kind of drunken convulsion." Ribeyrolles categorized this and other dances as expressing "coarse joys, indecent sensual pleasures, libertine fevers." He himself may have viewed these performances less as manifestations of African culture than as hideous creations of slavery. But others, who described them similarly, offered a different interpretation. Enrico Giglioli, who visited a coffee plantation in Rio de Janeiro in 1865, witnessed a slave dance in which "the arms and the body . . . moved in a pantomime that was far from being chaste." He went on to observe that "it is well known that the sensual character prevails in African dances." The perception that African culture did not place "civilized" restraints on behavior made it easy for whites to believe (as Lenita and her creator, Júlio Ribeiro, certainly did) that the sexuality and the families of Africans and their descendants were utterly different from those of Europeans or of Brazilians of European extraction. And it was at this point, in an age that frequently viewed acquired traits as transmissible from generation to generation, that what I have called "cultural" and "racial" prejudice in fact merged.[36]

In addition to these stereotypes regarding black character and African culture, one would also expect to find evidence in these nineteenth-century accounts, particularly in the last decades of the period, of an ideology that postulated radical differences in the behavior of slave and free workers. According to the Frenchman Ribeyrolles,

Pale, wan hunger does not enter the dwelling of the slave, and there one never dies of starvation as in White Chapel or the boroughs of Westminster. But families do not exist; there are only broods. Why would a father take to himself the austere and saintly joys of labor? He has no interest whatsoever in the land, in the harvest. Work, for him, is affliction and sweat; it is servitude. Why should a mother keep her hut and children clean? Her children can be taken from her at any moment, like the chicks or the kid-goats of the estate, and she herself is no more than a chattel.

At times, however, distractions and joys exist in these hovels, the brutish distractions and joys of drunkenness, in which one never speaks of the past, which is pain, nor of the future, which is closed off. . . .

In the huts of the blacks, I never once saw a flower: for in them, neither hopes nor remembrances exist.[37]

The reference to the "brutish distractions and joys of drunkenness" among slaves may be an allusion to slave dances, which Ribeyrolles described elsewhere in similar terms; if so, at least there is evidence in his book that he observed these dances at first hand, whatever one makes of his opinions about them. Ribeyrolles documents nothing else in this passage, however, and his reference to kid-goats—rarely found on the cotton plantations of the time, according to data presently available—is quite revealing.[38] Indeed, Ribeyrolles provides us here with a perfect example of how a "reality" can be constructed almost exclusively from preconceived ideas which make it impossible even to think about investigating slave hopes and remembrances by declaring them, a priori, nonexistent.

The ideas brought together by Ribeyrolles—the "saintly," moralizing function of free labor which, in the crux of the happy encounter between necessity and interest, makes possible the formation of the "family," conceived as a project of accumulation—are also expressed, with certain modifications and additions, in *Theses on the Colonization of Brazil*, a report by João Cardoso de Menezes a Souza presented to the Brazilian minister of agriculture, commerce, and public works in 1875. In discussing the possibility of making use of the labor of freedpersons in agriculture, Souza calls attention to the example of "a colony of blacks founded in Goyanna" (presumably French Guiana) after the emancipation of the slaves, where it had been "demonstrated that the African race can be employed usefully in agricultural work, once it has been educated in the shadow of religion and set up on the double base of family and property." Citing a French author on this case, a certain Duval, Souza extends his analysis:

the family, to which [male] slaves paid little attention as long as marriage did not assure them either the privileges of a husband or those of a father, rapidly constitutes itself in the emancipated population. In the wake of the family comes property, in the beginning very small, its measure set by necessities and by ambition; but with children, necessities will increase, with well-being, so too will ambition. The black man . . . will work to enlarge his cabin, where he is king; his plot of land, where nobody gives him orders. Mutual aid societies, preludes to the savings banks, ardently called for, will come to the aid of this movement, revealing habits of order and providence to races which were reputed incapable of them.[39]

In this passage, Souza (via Duval) adds to Ribeyrolles's set of ideas that the family only fully constitutes itself when the man of the household is assured of the privileges of husband and father—that is, his authority before his wife and his children—which (in the supposition of these authors) does not occur under slavery. The passage also attempts to define more precisely the mutual relation between family and property, which is no more than Ribeyrolles suggested (and, incidentally, also Couty, in the paragraph in which he denies the African any "ideas about family or property"). For Souza, "in the wake of the family comes property," because the struggle to assure the welfare of the family also becomes a struggle to increase one's patrimony; but from this initial moment on, property and family march together, hand in hand, one reinforcing the other. What we have here, then, is the clear enunciation of the idea that there was a relation of mutual support between family (defined as a nuclear kin group that is monogamous and patriarchal) and private property. This model of the family will scarcely be new to students of the nineteenth century, a period at once patriarchal and bourgeois. Nonetheless, it is worth emphasizing that those who thought in its terms—as was most likely the case with the majority of travelers and well-born Brazilians in the nineteenth century—would have faced enormous difficulty in perceiving, not to mention interpreting, the family strategies and projects of slaves.

It is also worth noting that this difficulty probably would have increased with time. In the observations of foreigners and Brazilians regarding the slave family, one would expect to find the influence of a disciplinary project that, during the course of the nineteenth century, increasingly associated the stability of the nuclear family and sobriety in sexual life with constancy and diligence in work. In Europe and the United States during this period, dominant social groups and intellectuals and professionals linked to them were commonly concerned with devising strategies for putting discipline in the home, as part of an effort to instill new values among the working classes, thereby permitting a more effective control over their labor.[40] In this, there was a tacit recognition that the *embourgeoisement* of the worker would not occur through a natural process. It depended instead on the tutelage of the bourgeoisie itself and the state. For those who thought this way in Brazil, the problem of transition from slave to free labor, which raised the specter of a profound change in disciplinary practices, probably made it seem especially necessary to adopt such tutelary strategies.[41] It should be noted, in this regard, that at least three books by Samuel Smiles, the Scottish propagandist for the "moral domestic economy" and for the advantages of "subordinating the animal appetite to reason, forethought and prudence," had been translated into Portuguese and published in Rio de Janeiro by 1880.[42] Furthermore, it appears significant that from the 1870s through the decade after abolition in 1888, the "vagrancy" of freedmen and women was a constant subject of political debate, and of the press; and it is particularly intriguing that the supposed refusal of these people to work was frequently attributed to their moral degeneration, as revealed by a whole complex of negative characteristics, among them lasciviousness and the lack of stable family institutions.[43]

In summary, racism, cultural prejudices, and contemporary ideology regarding labor predisposed European travelers and well-born Brazilians in the nineteenth century to see blacks, whose intimate lives apparently did not conform to their rules, as lacking rules altogether. In the second half of the century, when not following the rules seemed to menace labor discipline increasingly, this predisposition probably became stronger. Within this context, the stories told by Ribeiro, Tschudi, Couty, and the other authors I have cited are extremely precarious as historical sources, unless one's purpose is to understand the Lenitas of the time—that is, to capture the perceptions of the elite. To enter the world of the slave, other types of information and methods of analysis are necessary.

Or at least other readings of these nineteenth-century accounts are in order. In fact, the observers of slavery were not as blind as my analysis may have suggested. Their vision was white, but it was not altogether blank. While their writings explicitly portrayed the sexual and family life of slaves as normless, they also registered details (en passsant, while frequently missing the meanings) which can be interpreted in an entirely different way. Indeed, between the lines of these white homilies it is possible to glimpse black homes which *are* consistent with the new demographic data.

To demonstrate this in detail, however, requires another essay.[44] Here I will only point to some of the possibilities and ultimate limits of these sources. The accounts left by white contemporaries about slavery, as it turns out, are quite useful for studying the conjugal family group. They offer particular insights into how the slaves built a domestic economy of their own and attained greater autonomy and security. For example, Tschudi, the Swiss traveler who compared slave sexual life to that of "the cattle on the pampas," also noted that there were married slaves on the plantation he visited and that these couples were permitted to live together in spaces "duly separated" from the barrackslike quarters for single slaves.[45] Other travelers also mentioned in passing the presence of married slaves on the plantations of Rio de Janeiro and São Paulo and confirmed that slave couples were commonly permitted separate living arrangements. Furthermore, it becomes apparent from these same sources that marriage, at least on large properties in this part of Brazil, brought other material advantages: the possession of one's own hearth (a fire maintained in the middle of the slave couple's hut or cubicle for heating and cooking), probably control over the preparation of and participation in at least one of the daily meals (single slaves generally took all their meals together and ate the food prepared by the plantation kitchen), possibly greater access to land for planting garden crops, and certainly greater opportunities to build a domestic economy based upon a division of labor within the household.[46]

These sources, if they are approached with some knowledge of African societies, also provide insights into how slave couples used their cultural heritage to give order and meaning to their domestic economies. For instance, an understanding of traditional patterns of architecture and building use in West-Central Africa—the prevalence there of dwellings that were very small by middle- and upper-class European standards of the nineteenth century, the general absence of windows, the positioning of an oven or hearth in the middle of the dwelling space with no chimney for ventilation—can help one appreciate how slaves in Rio de Janeiro and São Paulo (who were mostly from this part of Africa or descended from people of this region) evaluated the small spaces available to them in the slave quarters and the possibility of obtaining a separate cubicle or hut to share with a mate.[47] At the very least, one will be able to see farther than the German traveler, Ina Von Binzer. On a visit to a coffee plantation in 1881 (in an area in Rio de Janeiro where, only a generation earlier, the large majority of adult slaves had been Africans), she was repulsed by the smoke she saw emerging from a married couple's hut in which a slave woman was preparing the late-afternoon meal, and appalled that slaves would build their cooking fires in quarters that were cramped, windowless, and without chimneys. Binzer's planter host opined that the lack of ventilation in the huts had originated long before planters' attempts to control the slaves who had since grown so accustomed that even when they were freed they built their dwellings without windows.[48] Clearly, planter and traveler in this case, as in so many others, had no idea how to interpret their observations. Nevertheless, Binzer's account provides important information to those who have the skills to read it in a different way.

Ultimately, however, these sources have their limitations. They offer virtually no information on family links beyond the nuclear unit or about the skein of relations between the living and the dead. These kinship ties, so important in African societies, were virtually invisible to travelers *en passant*, like Binzer, or planters *pas pensant*, like her Brazilian host. Almost as invisible to these observers were slave women, even those who were part of a conjugal family. For instance, while the nineteenth-century accounts do suggest that when slave couples cooked for themselves it was the wife who made the meal—and this is not surprising, given African patterns—I know of no white observer who commented on the ingredients, methods of preparation, or condiments that the slave woman used. Such themes could shed light on the cultural preferences and household economies of the slaves.[49] Binzer's lack of interest in this regard—she saw a slave woman making "some sort of food"—is typical.[50] As to the broader division of labor within the household, these contemporary accounts do not permit us to go beyond the information that historian Stanley Stein presented (drawn, apparently, from interviews with ex-slaves) regarding work patterns on Sundays and holidays, when slaves had time for themselves: "where male and female slaves cohabited, men often were accompanied to the roças [garden plots] by their children, while women washed, mended, and cooked, bringing the noon meal to their mates in the field."[51] To apprehend more of the world of women slaves and to understand broader kinship ties, other sources (such as trial records, which abound in local archives) must be explored.

Still, our knowledge of the Brazilian slave family, particularly of the experience of slave women, is substantially greater than it once was. Recent demographic studies indicate that slave marriages were considerably more common and longer-lasting than was previously believed. They show that the majority of slave children, at least on the larger estates of Rio de Janeiro and São Paulo, not only knew who their fathers were but also spent their early years in the presence of both parents. Finally, these studies provide no reason to think that promiscuity was the rule, particularly among women slaves. My criticism of the biases in the accounts of nineteenth-century travelers and well-to-do Brazilians strengthens confidence in the recent demographic data; we may now reject the conclusions regarding slave anomie, deculturation, and impressment into white ways of thinking and feeling that have been so often drawn from the belief that slave sexual life and family life were normless. An alternative reading of these white homilies is clearly one way to move sensitively beyond the new quantitative data to discover meanings that slave women and men themselves conferred on their domestic arrangements and intimate lives. In the search for meanings, an effective approach to these and other sources should surely be to focus on the ways in which Brazilian slaves created an autonomous domestic economy, shaped by their cultural heritage and by their particular conditions of bondage. We must seek to discover the "hopes and remembrances" that the French traveler Charles Ribeyrolles, with his vision fixed on the bourgeois family, so adamantly denied to slaves.

Notes

An earlier version of this chapter appeared in Portuguese as "Lares Negros, Olhares Brancos: Histórias da Família Escrava no Século XIX," *Revista Brasileira de História* 8, no. 16 (March–August 1988): 189–203. All translations from foreign-language sources are mine. I would like to thank Ute Bärnert-Fürst for her assistance in translations from the German.

[1] Marriage and baptism registers, Parish of Nossa Senhora de Conceição de Campinas, in Arquivo da Cúria Metropolitana de Campinas: "Casamentos, Escravos, 1841–1858," fol. 111 ("Termo de Justificação," 8/24/1899), and "Batizados, Escravos, 1861–1867."

[2] Gilberto Freyre, *The Masters and the Slaves: A Study in the Development of Brazilian Civilization*, trans. Samuel Putnam, 2d English-language ed. (Berkeley: University of California Press, 1986), p. 328; Emilia Viotti da Costa, *Da Senzala à Colônia* (São Paulo: Difusão Européia do Livro, 1966), pp. 269–70; Oracy Nogueira, *Comunidade e Família: Um Estudo Sociológico de Itapetininga* (Rio de Janeiro: Centro Brasileiro de Pesquisas Educacionais, INEP, MEC, 1962), p. 262; Roger Bastide, *The African Religions of Brazil: Toward a Sociology of the Interpenetration of Cultures*, trans. Helen Sebba (Baltimore: Johns Hopkins University Press, 1978), p. 61. Stanley J. Stein also states that passing sexual unions prevailed among Brazilian slaves; but unlike the other authors cited, he argues, with Melville J. Herskovits, that these unions represented a redefinition of African traditions of polygyny, not a normless promiscuity. See Stein, *Vassouras: A Brazilian Coffee County, 1850–1900*, 2d ed. (Princeton: Princeton University Press, 1985), p. 155, and Herskovits, *The Myth of the Negro Past* (Boston: Beacon, 1958), p. 168.

[3] Freyre, for instance, in the passage cited is at pains to note that the cause of slave promiscuity was slavery itself or, more specifically, the immorality of white masters; and by "prostitution . . . within the home," he means prostitution within the big house.

[4] Bastide, *The African Religions*, pp. 60–61. The problem was different for Yoruba and Dahoman slaves, according to Bastide (p. 61), since their religion was "simultaneously a lineage religion and a community religion." The first aspect "was bound to disappear," as it was among the bantu; but the community religion "was able to survive by accommodating itself to the framework of 'nations' reestablished by the Portuguese and Brazilian governments for the purpose of fomenting interethnic rivalries. . . ."

[5] See Florestan Fernandes, *A Integração do Negro na Sociedade de Classes*, (São Paulo: Dominus/EDUSP, 1965), vol. 1, p. 35, for the passage cited and esp. pp. 34–38, 110–18, for the general argument.

[6] Bastide, *The African Religions*, p. 72.

[7] See esp. Herbert G. Gutman, *The Black Family in Slavery and Freedom, 1750–1925* (New York: Pantheon 1976).

[8] I define marriage, following Herskovits, as "socially sanctioned mating entered into with the assumption of permanency" (with "permanency" understood as a relative concept defined by each culture); Melville J. Herskovits, *Man and His Works* (New York, 1948), p. 296, cited in Emílio Willems, *Latin American Culture: An Anthropological Synthesis* (New York: Harper, 1975), p. 52.

[9]Data from a sample of 1,975 slaves in Robert W. Slenes, "Escravidão a Família: Padrões de Casamento e Estabilidade Familiar numa Comunidade Escrava (Campinas, Século XIX)," *Estudos Econômicos* 17, no. 2 (May–August 1987): 217–27, and "Slave Family Formation in the Context of Creolization and Crop Change: Campinas, São Paulo, 1776–1872," paper presented at the Conference on Cultivation and Culture: Labor and the Shaping of Slave Life in the Americas, University of Maryland at College Park, April 1989. Data from local Campinas censuses for 1801 and 1829, reported on in the latter paper, are similar.

[10]See, in chronological order, Robert W. Slenes, "The Demography and Economics of Brazilian Slavery: 1850–1888," Ph.D. dissertation, Stanford University, 1976, chap. 9; Richard Graham, "Slave Families on a Rural Estate in Colonial Brazil, *Journal of Social History* 9, no. 3 (1976): 382–401; Iraci del Negro da Costa and Francisco Vidal Luna, "Vila Rica: Nota sobre Casamentos de Escravos (1727–1826)," *Africa* (Centro de Estudos Africanos, Universidade de São Paulo), no. 4 (1981): 105–9; Iraci del Negro da Costa and Horacio Gutiérrez, "Nota sobre Cassamentos de Escravos em São Paulo a no Paraná (1830)," *História Questões a Debates* 5, no. 9, (December 1984): 313–21; Stuart B. Schwartz, *Sugar Plantations in the Formation of Brazilian Society: Bahia, 1550–1835* (Cambridge: Cambridge University Press, 1985), chaps. 13, 14; João Luís R. Fragoso and Manolo G. Florentino, "Marcelino, Filho de Inocência Crioula, Neto de Joana Cabinda: Um Estudo sobre Famílias Escravas em Paraíba do Sul (1835–1872)," *Estudos Econômicos* 17, no. 2 (May–August 1987): 151–73; Alida C. Metcalf, "Vida Familiar dos Escravos em São Paulo no Século Dezoito: O Caso de Santana de Parnaíba," ibid.: 229–43; Iraci del Nero da Costa, Robert W. Slenes, and Stuart B. Schwartz, "A Família Escrava em Lorena (1801)," ibid.: 245–95; Silvia Hunold Lara, *Campos da Violência: Escravos a Senhores na Capitania do Rio de Janeiro, 1750–1808* (Rio de Janeiro: Paz a Terra, 1988), pp. 220–30; Horacio Gutiérrez, "Crioulos a Africanos no Paraná 1798–1830," *Revista Brasileira de História* 8, no. 16 (March–August 1988): 161–88; Kátia de Queirós Mattoso, "O Filho da Escrava (em Torno da Lei do Ventre Livre)," ibid.: 37–56; José Flávio Motta, "A Família Escrava e a Penetração do Café em Bananal, 1801–1829," *Revista Brasileira de Estudos de População* 5, no. 1 (January–July, 1988): 71–101, and "Família Escrava: Uma Incursão pela Historiografia," *História Questões e Debates* 9, no. 16 (July 1988): 104–59; Gilberto Guerzoni Filho and Luiz Roberto Netto, "Minas Gerais: Indices de Casamento da População Livre a Escrava na Comarca do Rio das Mortes," *Estudos Econômicos* 18, no. 3 (September–December 1988): 497–508; Ida Lewkowicz, "Hernança a Relações Familiares: Os Pretos Forros nas Minas Gerais do Século XVIII," *Revista Brasileira de História* 9, no. 17 (September 1988–February 1989): 101–14. See also various studies in Associação Brasileira de Estudos Populacionais [ABEP], *Anais do VI Econtro Nacional de Estudos Populacionais (Olinda, Pernambuco, 16–20 de Outubro,* 4 vols. Belo Horizonte: ABEP, 1988), vol. 3, esp. Francisco Vidal Luna, "Observações sobre Casamento de Escravos em São Paulo (1825)," pp. 215–33. Several papers on the question were presented at the Conference on the Population History of Latin America, Ouro Preto, Brazil, July 2–6, 1989.

[11]See Slenes, "The Demography," p. 420, for the percentage of married slaves by province.

[12]According to provincial censuses circa 1850 and the slave matricula of 1872–73, slave marriage rates in the provinces of Rio de Janeiro and São Paulo were higher in sugar and coffee plantation areas than in non-plantation zones. Nonetheless, the percentage of married slaves was considerably greater in the plantation counties of São Paulo than in those of Rio de Janeiro (even when one compares the São Paulo and Rio sections of the Paraíba Valley), with the highest proportions being found in central-western São Paulo. Since the percentage of married free blacks (the census categories of "blacks" and "mulattoes") was also much higher in São Paulo than in Rio, it seems more likely that the data represent contrasting institutional histories—that is, differential access to church rituals on the part of lower-class persons, slave or free—rather than different family patterns. For more discussion of this question, see Slenes, "The Demography," pp. 445–58.

[13]The consistency of the information in the various sources is so striking that the data, as a whole, could not be the result of an effort to deceive or to create and maintain on paper families which had no basis in reality. See Slenes, "Slave Family Formation."

[14]See Slenes, "Slave Family Formation," table 2, for data on forty-eight marriages (involving slave mothers aged fifteen to forty-four) still existing in 1872–73, in a sample of 1,163 slaves from the matrícula in Campinas. For the fourteen married mothers aged thirty-five to forty-four, the median length of marriage was sixteen years and eight months.

[15]For instance, in Campinas in 1872–73, in holdings with fewer than ten slaves, only 26 percent of women over fifteen and 37 percent of mothers (with children under fifteen) were ever married; furthermore, only 27 percent of children aged one to nine lived with both parents or one widowed parent. Slenes, "Escravidão a Família," 225, 227. (The data on marriage reflect, in the first instance, the small "pool" of potential mates within these holdings and the masters' virtual prohibition of church marriages between slaves of different owners; from what is known about the relative instability of small holdings, however, one suspects that slaves in these properties also had more difficulty maintaining consensual unions across ownership boundaries than bondspeople on the plantations.)

[16]Stuart B. Schwartz, "Patterns of Slaveholding in the Americas: New Evidence from Brazil," *American Historical Review* 87, no. 1 (February 1982): 313–33, and Francisco Vidal Luna and Iraci del Nero da Costa, "Posse de Escravos em São Paulo no Início do Século XIX," *Estudos Econômicos* 13, no. 1 (January–April 1983): 211–21.

[17]Slenes, "Escravidão a Família," 225.

[18]I exclude from the category of polygynous unions serial monogamous relationships, or concomitant unions which are not entered into "with the assumption of permanency." (See Herskovits's definition of marriage in n. 8.)

[19]Robert K. Merton, *Social Theory and Social Structure,* 2d. ed. (New York: Free Press, 1968), chaps. 6, 7; Talcott Parsons et al., *Family Socialization and Interaction Process* (New York, 1955); Marshall B. Clinard and Robert F. Meier, *Sociology of Deviant Behavior* (New York: Holt, Rinehart and Winston, n.d.), chap. 3 (for a review of sociological theories of deviance). Perhaps indicative of the influence of American functionalism on Brazilian

sociology is the success of the textbook by F. A. de Miranda Rosa, *Pathologia Social: Uma Introdução ao Estudo da Desorganização Social*, 5th ed. (Rio de Janeiro: Zahar, 1980), first published in 1966.

[20]See Roger Bastide and Florestan Fernandes, "O Preconceito Racial em São Paulo," *Publicações do Instituto de Adminstraçao* [of the University of São Paulo], no. 118 (April 1951), pp. 44–45 (n. 2); in this joint proposal for research, the authors cite studies on American blacks by E. Franklin Frazier (*The Negro Family in the United States*), Gunnar Myrdal (*An American Dilemma*), and Horace Cayton and St. Clair Drake (*Black Metropolis*), among others.

[21]See Abram Kardiner and Lionel Ovesey, *The Mark of Oppression: Explorations in the Personality of the American Negro*, 2d ed. (New York: World, 1962), esp. pp. 44, 46, 359–61. Bastide, who published the original French version of *The African Religions* in 1960, was aware of Kardiner's work on "basic personality" (Bastide, *The African Religions*, pp. 8, 357, 389) but does not cite this book, first published in 1951. See also Daniel Patrick Moynihan, *The Negro Family: The Case for National Action* (Washington, D.C.: Office of Policy Planning and Research, United States Department of Labor, March 1965), republished in Lee Rainwater and William L. Yancey, *The Moynihan Report and the Politics of Controversy* (Cambridge: MIT Press, 1967), pp. 39–124. It should be noted that Fernandes's concept of anomie seems closer to Durkheim's than to Merton's, in that it points to broader functional and structural factors as causes of deviance, even in situations of apparent social equilibrium rather than simply to the inability of individuals to achieve culturally prescribed goals by culturally accepted means. See Florestan Fernandes, *Esaios de Sociologia Geral a Aplicada*, 2d ed. (São Paulo: Livraria Pioneira Editora, 1971), pp. 143–44. In part because of this, Fernandes's book *A Integração do Negro na Sociedade de Classes* has a much stronger tone of social criticism than Moynihan's work.

[22]See Bastide, *The African Religions*, p. 72, for a discussion of the effects of acculturation on slave egos and superegos. My critique of the accounts of nineteenth-century white observers in Brazil is similar to Gutman's examination of sources of this type in the United States, although the specific bibliography on Brazil has led me to use somewhat different categories of analysis. See Gutman, *The Black Family*, pp. 293–303. See also Barbara Bush, *Slave Women in Caribbean Society, 1650–1838* (Bloomington: Indiana University Press, 1990), chap. 2 ("The Eye of the Beholder"), which came to my attention after this chapter, including this particular line in the text, was written.

[23]Júlio Ribeiro, *A Carne* (Rio de Janeiro: Edições de Ouro, n.d.), pp. 101, 231. In the nineteenth century the word *boçal* was commonly applied to newly arrived Africans, but here it is used to refer to a Brazilian-born slave.

[24]Jochann Jacob Von Tschudi, *Reisen durch Südamerika* (Leipzig: F. A. Brockhaus, 1867), vol. 3, pp. 133–34.

[25]Agostinho Marques Perdigão Malheiro, *A Escravidão no Brasil: Ensaio Histórico, Juridico, Social* (Petrópolis: Editora Vozes, 1976), vol. 2, p. 129.

[26]Louis Couty, *L'Esclavage au Brésil* (Paris: Librairie de Guillaumin, 1881), pp. 74–75.

[27]Johann Moritz Rugendas, *Malerische Reise in Brasilien* (Paris: Engelmann, 1835), p. 11.

[28]Jean Baptiste Debret, *Voyage Pittoresque et Historique au Brésil, ou Sejour d'un Artiste Français au Brésil depuis 1816 jusq' en 1831 Inclusivement* (Paris: Firmin Didot Frères, 1834–1839), vol. 2, p. 84.

[29]Ibid., vol. 3, p. 149.

[30]George Gardner, *Travels in the Interior of Brazil, Principally through the Northern Provinces and the Gold and Diamond Districts during the Years 1836–1841* (Boston: Milford House, 1973), p. 14.

[31]C. F. Van Delden Laërne, *Brazil and Java: Report on Coffee Culture in America, Asia and Africa* (London and The Hague: W. H. Allen/M. Nijhoff, 1885), pp. 253–54.

[32]Couty, *L'Esclavage*, p. 68.

[33]See Stein, *Vassouras*, p. 155; Bastide, *The African Religions*, p. 61; Fernandes, *A Integração do Negro*, vol. 1, p. 36. Couty's belief that slave men mistreated their wives and that black mothers did not provide proper care for their children probably reflected prevailing European stereotypes regarding African women; see Bush, *Slave Women*, pp. 20, 103, for a discussion of these stereotypes within the Caribbean context.

[34]See, for example, Edward Shorter, "Sexual Change and Illegitimacy: The European Experience," in Robert Bezucha, ed., *Modern European Social History* (Lexington, Mass., 1972), pp. 231–69; Edward Shorter, John Knodel, and Etienne Van de Walle, "The Decline of Non-Marital Fertility in Europe, 1880–1940," *Population Studies* 25, no. 3 (November 1971): 375–93; and Peter Laslett, "Introduction to the History of the Family," in Laslett, ed., *Household and Family in Past Time* (Cambridge: Cambridge University Press, 1972), pp. 16–17. On the Iberian peninsula, see Antônio Cândido, "The Brazilian Family," in T. Lynn Smith and Alexander Marchant, eds., *Brazil: Portrait of Half a Continent* (New York, 1951), pp. 300–301, and Willems, *Latin American Culture*, pp. 52–53. According to Willems (p. 53), in Portugal and in Spain "the consensual union . . . was a deep-rooted cultural pattern rather than a deviation; it was certainly transplanted to America, where it found a receptive environment, particularly among the peasantry and the rural laborers."

[35]Joaquim Manoel de Macedo, *As Vítimas-Algozes: Quadros da Escravidão* (Rio de Janeiro: Typographia Perseverança, 1869), citations respectively from vol. 2, pp. 60, 91, 115, 21, 273.

[36]Charles Ribeyrolles, *Brasil Pitoresco: História-Descrições-Viagens-Instituições-Colonização* (Rio de Janeiro: Typographia National, 1859), vol. 3, pp. 47–48 (my translation is from the French text in this French-Portuguese edition); Enrico Hillyer Giglioli, *Viaggio Intorno al Globo della Pirocorvetta Italiana Magenta negli Anni 1865–66–67–68 Sotto il Comando del Capitano di Fregata V. F. Arminjon. Relazione Descrittiva e Scientifica . . .* (Milan: V. Maisner, 1875), p. 59.

[37]Ribeyrolles, *Brasil Pitoresco*, vol. 3, pp. 40–41.

[38]See the detailed data on animals registered in probate inventories in the county of Paraíba do Sul in João Luis Ribeiro Fragoso, "Sistemas Agrários em Paraíba do Sul (1850–1920)—um Estudo de Relaçoes não Capitalistas de Produção," master's thesis, Universidade Federal do Rio de Janeiro, 1983, pp. 56, 58.

[39]João Cardoso de Menezes a Souza, *Theses sobre Colonização do Brasil . . . Relatorio Apresentado ao Ministerio da Agricultura, Commercio e Obras Publicas em 1875* (Rio de Janeiro, 1875), pp. 166, 169–70.

[40]Isaac Joseph, Philippe Fritsch, and Alain Battegay, *Disciplines à Domicile: l'Edification de la Famille,* Thematic Issue of *Recherches,* no. 28 (November 1977); Jacques Donzelot, *La Police des Familles* (Paris: Les Editions de Minuit, 1977).

[41]See the suggestive study by Jurandir Freire Costa, *Ordem Médica e Norma Familiar* (Rio de Janeiro: Graal, 1979).

[42]Samuel Smiles, *Economia Domestica Moral ou a Felicidade e a Independencia pelo Trabalho a pela Economia,* trans. Jacintho Cardoso da Silva (Rio de Janeiro: B. L. Garnier, 1880), p. 19 (my translation from the Portuguese). Two other books by Smiles were advertised by Garnier in this work, with no indication of date of publication: *O Caracter* and *O Poder da Vontade, ou Caracter, Comportamento a Perseverança,* 2d ed.

[43]Sidney Chalhoub, *Trabalho, Lar a Botequim: O Cotidiano dos Trabalhadores no Rio de Janeiro da "Belle Époque"* (São Paulo: Brasilienese, 1986), pp. 39–40; Célia Maria Marinho de Azevedo, *Onda Negra, Medo Branco: O Negro no Imaginário das Elites—Século XIX* (Rio de Janeiro: Paz a Terra, 1987), esp. chaps. 2 and 4; Lília Moritz Schwarcz, *Retrato em Branco a Negro: Jornais, Escravos a Cidadãos em São Paulo no Final do Século XIX* (São Paulo: Companhia das Letras, 1987), pp. 163ff., 224–26, 232–40.

[44]Robert W. Slenes, "Na Senzala, uma Flor: 'As Esperanças e as Recordações na Formação da Famíla Escrava," article in progress.

[45]Tschudi, *Reisen,* vol. 3, p. 133.

[46]Evidence presented in Slenes, "Na Senzala, uma Flor."

[47]On these aspects of architecture in West-Central Africa, see John Vlach, *The Afro-American Tradition in Decorative Arts* (Cleveland: Cleveland Museum of Art, 1978), pp. 124–25, 135; Julius F. Glück, "African Architecture," in *The Many Faces of Primitive Art: A Critical Anthology,* ed. Douglas Frasier (Englewood Cliffs: Prentice-Hall, 1966), p. 225; Luiz Figueira, *Africa Bantú Raças a Tribos de Angola* (Lisbon: Oficinas Fernandes, 1938), pp. 135–36. For a summary of data on the origins of Africans imported into Brazil's center-south region (Rio de Janeiro, São Paulo, and Minas Gerais), see Mary Karasch, *Slave Life in Rio de Janeiro, 1808–1850* (Princeton: Princeton University Press, 1987), pp. 3–28.

[48]Ina von Binzer, *Os Meus Romanos: Alegrias a Tristezas de uma Educadora Alemã no Brasil,* trans. Alice Rossi and Luisita da Gama Cerqueira (São Paulo: Editora Paz e Terra, 1980), pp. 50–51. The plantation visited by Binzer probably was in the Rio de Janeiro section of the Paraíba Valley, near the border with São Paulo (see the preface by Paulo Duarte in ibid., p. 15). An 1850 census showed that 50 percent of all slaves in Rio province were Africans; in the major coffee counties of the Paraíba Valley, the proportion was 70 percent or higher. Similar figures are available for the São Paulo plantation counties, Bananal (78 percent) and Campinas (70 percent), in 1829; in the latter county, where the data can be broken down by age group, Africans accounted for 80 percent of all bondpeople over age fifteen. Sources: *Archivo Estatistico da Provincia do Rio de Janeiro: Primeira Publicação* (Niterói, 1851), table C, annexed to Rio de Janeiro [Province], *Relatório [of the President of the Province],* presented May 5, 1851 (Rio de Janeiro, n.d.); Motta, "A Família Escrava," pp. 82, 97 (n. 18); Slenes, work in progress on the 1829 census manuscripts from Campinas deposited in the Arquivo Publico do Estado de São Paulo, Box 27–27.

[49]See Bush, *Slave Women,* p. 98, on gender roles with respect to cooking in Africa and among slaves in the British Caribbean. Also see the suggestive comments by Charles Joyner, *Down by the Riverside: A South Carolina Slave Community* (Urbana: University of Illinois Press, 1984), pp. 91, 106, on the cultural significance for North American slaves of "the choice of particular foods and particular means of preparation."

[50]Binzer, *Os Meus Romanos,* p. 50.

[51]Stein, *Vassouras,* pp. 170–71, 181.

Actions Louder Than Words:
The Historical Task of
Defining Feminist Consciousness
in Colonial West Africa

Cheryl Johnson-Odim

The term "feminism" is layered with multiple meanings, interpretations, and perspectives. In recent years, primarily due to research and writing emanating from and being conducted in the non-western world, and to the contribution of women of color in the western world, some scholars have begun to speak of feminism in the plural, as feminisms. Others have elected not to use the term feminism at all, but to coin other terms, such as womanist. Still others, as I have done elsewhere, have attempted to redefine feminist philosophy in a way in which women remain integral to it but that includes activity and thought aimed at eliminating structural inequalities (racism, imperialism) that oppress both women and men.

As a result, in recent years much of feminist theory originating in the West has reached out to include analyses of nonwhite, non-western women of varying classes and in various places. Some feminist theory has begun to embrace what historian Joan Wallach Scott has termed "an historicizing approach [that] stresses differences among women and even within the concept of 'women.'" Yet, Scott acknowledges two things. First, that women of color, in both national and international fora, have been responsible for, in her words, "exposing the implicit whiteness of [western] feminism" as well as its essentializing and ahistorical tendencies. And two, that the historicizing and acknowledgment of the salience of difference is still working its way into western feminist theory and is seen as divisive by some western feminist theoreticians.

The tremendous growth (at least if we judge by publications) in post-1960s theories of feminism mostly took place in the United States and western Europe. In part due to the fact that they proliferated as fast as or even faster than specific research, theories of feminism often proceeded from the theoretical to the concrete; hypotheses went in search of examples. Moreover, much of the specific research on which theories were based was undertaken in Western, Christian, industrialized, capitalist societies. This sometimes engendered a reductionist reasoning that resulted in two equally unsatisfactory conclusions vis-à-vis the study of the lives of women outside the West. First, it defined feminism in a cultural context and along a historical continuum that were western. Secondly, it looked to the "Third World" with a western eye in search of examples of western feminism, or anthropological antecedents of women's preindustrial, precapitalist power that could fit someplace along a western historical continuum that could be defined as universal. Nancy Hewitt telescopes the point in observing that

> Without intending to, Western women's historians may become mere raiders of a lost ark—seeking out the telling anecdote, the apparent parallel, the seeming sisterhood; exploring the primitive, the pre-capitalist, the prepatriarchal; searching for either the pre-modern and traditional or the mythic and matriarchal, with which or against which to define ourselves, still at the center. . . .

There were problems with this logic even among some women resident in the West. Among women of color long resident in the West, African American women for example, debate has often ensued over whether race or sex took precedence in African American women's struggles—as if African American women could separate the two, given that they are indivisibly nonwhite and female in a society that locates nonwhites and females at its lowest rungs. For instance, the debate over whether African American women were doing "race work" or "feminist work" in their anti-lynching campaigns seems a false dichotomy, even granted that most victims of lynching were men. The popular perception of the justification for lynching was that Black men had sexually assaulted white women. But the construction of Black men as sexually uncontrolled and savage was linked to the construction of Black women as promiscuous and lascivious. If the struggle of African American women against lynching was "race work," given that it focused on a concern particular to African Americans, was the struggle of white women to pass a white-woman-only suffrage bill also "race work" rather than feminist struggle?

African American and African women share common terrain in relating women's struggle against oppression to the struggles of their communities against oppression. African women who opposed colonialism, for instance, opposed it on the dual grounds of its oppression of their *people* (both male and female) and its rendering of women, to use Fran Beale's phrase of over twenty years ago, as "slaves of slaves." Interestingly enough, when the Nigerian woman's rights and anticolonial activist Funmilayo Ransome-Kuti took her message to London in the 1940s, she accused colonialism of making women slaves.

The historicizing and contextualizing of women's actions allow us to locate "difference" in a useful way—such that it can be understood in relation to conditions. Thus we can make meaningful comparisons about those things that seem to oppress or liberate women and delineate connections between women's different statuses in different places. We can also investigate other models and agendas of feminism beyond those located in the activities of European and Euroamerican women.

In my dissertation, written over fifteen years ago, I went in search of Yoruba women's roles in the anticolonial struggle in Nigeria. I believe I did important work in uncovering women's activity on behalf of women and in elucidating the important and powerful role of the "community of women" in the lives of Yoruba women and girls. Among the precolonial Yoruba (and actually far beyond for most women), it was the community of women that would make as many decisions affecting the lives of girls and women as men. This was primarily a result of the sexual division of labor, women's important roles in the productive and distributive sectors of the economy, the proliferation of dual male and female societies and offices, and a cultural ethos that placed the group above the individual. Still, I paid less attention to the complexity of the web in which women's identities and actions were constructed—including the extent to which women operated (and often continue to operate) in a dialectic of oppression and power.

Africanist scholars have long resisted (and I believe rightly so) the extension to Africa of the public/private dichotomous analysis of women's productivity. Women were (most still are) employed directly in production that crossed such boundaries, and they derived a certain autonomy and status from their roles as cultivators, traders, artisans, and providers of other marketplace services. Yet there is a discrepancy, a contradiction, in the autonomous ways women behaved collectively and in women's obeisance as daughters-in-law and especially as wives. Women are far more subordinated to men privately than publicly, and even to other women such as mothers-in-law or senior wives (wives entering a polygamous marriage before other wives).

More and more I realize the difficulty of describing women's statuses in West Africa in cultures that sometimes simultaneously op-

pressed, venerated, and feared women, in whose economies women were integrally productive workers in both the home and the marketplace, in whose philosophical/spiritual cosmologies women were often centered, and that provided space in which even nonelite women exercised power. Thus, it is no wonder that we so often have contradictory pictures of women in "traditional" West African societies. Whether it is the legendary market women, the women's "wars," or the anticolonial activists, we are presented with ample evidence that ordinary, nonelite women exercised autonomy and planned massive grass-roots responses aimed at directing and controlling their collective and shared destinies.

This contradiction, combined with the historical juncture at which much of West African women's history begins to be produced, affects the way that history is written. In fact, the "modern" (post-1960s) historiography of West African women doesn't seem to have passed through any real "women as victims" stage of development, with the possible exception of some of the recent historiography on the continental enslavement and pawnship of women.

In fact, the idea that writing women's history proceeds along a linear trajectory of development, one defined by the methodological, conceptual, and theoretical models of the devel-opment of women's history in Europe and the United States, is often assumed by western scholars. Nancy Hewitt has observed:

By rendering Western women's history more cohesive and complete in retrospect than it has been in its making we will find it easy to "add 'n stir" . . . other "marginal" women into existing frameworks and will resist their transformative power the way men's history resisted ours.

The writing of the histories of women in West Africa has the opportunity to shape and to gender the writing of West African history at an earlier juncture in the development of that historiography than did that of European or American women's history in the development of those historiographies.

The construction of gender in much of West Africa depended as much on life cycle as it did on sex, wealth, or status. A woman's order as wife in a polygamous marriage (for example, as first or second wife), her ability to bear children, her status as mother and as mother-in-law, or her being postmenopausal resulted in often radically different constructions of "gender privilege" or "gender oppression."

The need for historians of women in West Africa to generate theory and construct paradigms that are rooted in African historical developments, modes of production, and cultures (surely related to the first two) is clear. Given differences in West African settings, this will not essentialize African women's history but rather provide us with the interpretive data to inform gender theories in Africa and elsewhere.

In some arenas, the colonial period in Africa can provide us with a window on the commingling of gender constructions and consciousness. That is, in urban areas where the colonized and the colonizers (both women and men) intermingled regularly and were drawn into one another's worldviews, we can see mutually transformative processes at work. It is useful in such settings to locate "difference" and "sameness" and "hybridity" to aid in our understanding of how gender is constructed and to allow "difference" to inform our theory and paradigms relating to the construction of gender and to models of feminism.

One way of doing this lies in examining West African women's anticolonial protest movements. In these movements a partnership often existed between "traditional" women and "westernized" women. These protests took place under circumstances where colonialism was much in evidence but not *more* so than "traditional" culture and "traditional" socioeconomic and political organization.

There are a number of well-documented studies of such movements, including their leadership. Though arguments are sometimes made that westernized women activists were taking their cue from the West and even from the nationalist men of their cohort group, and that they supplied the real "leadership" to many of these activities, I think this is of limited significance and a false dichotomy. Such an argument ignores the fact that the base of support for most of these movements was among nonwesternized, non-elite women, that these women used "traditional" women's protest tactics such as ridiculing men (both the colonizers and indigenous men whom they considered to be in sympathy with the colonizers) in song and dance, camping en masse in vigils outside the homes and offices of men and refusing to let them pass; that they referred to the "good old days" when they considered that some "traditional" power or right of theirs was being trespassed upon; and that they *assumed*, in a time when political activity by women was disparaged and considered unnatural by the colonizers and their supporters, that they had a right as women to engage in public, political activity. Much of West African women's anticolonial protest arose from a philosophical point of departure that was not anything they learned from the colonizers, and they employed tactics that were historically their own.

My own work has been biographical studies of women leaders. Information uncovered in these studies has led me to rethink interpretations of their evidence and to speculate about uses of biographical evidence, particularly in the colonial West African setting. Doing biographical studies of feminist women in colonial Nigeria identified the extent to which women's leadership revolved around actual interaction with, and empowerment by, other women. I am using the term feminist here based on at least two of its most universally agreed upon components: women who seek to challenge both the restriction of women's rights, and women's marginalization from centers of power and decision making.

What I am suggesting is that we reexamine the biographical approach for things it can tell us about the creation of feminist theory, and moreover, about what *counts* as theory. The relationship between sociopolitical theory and praxis ought to be organic. That is, theory is not only *writing* that emerges from careful observation and analysis of action, but *action* itself is a kind of theory. It is through action that theory is both created and realized. The anti-colonial actions of West African women made a theoretical statement about their gender consciousness, about their definition of feminism. And, it was a theoretical statement rooted in their own traditions rather than being imported from the West.

Even if we examine the "leadership" (where it is identifiable) of women's anticolonial protests, we see that it is tied to a historically indigenous mode of action. That "leadership" is characterized by being at the forefront of all women's protest movements as much, or more, than by any individual interactions with anticolonial organizations led by men, or by individual interaction with foreign and indi-genous members of the colonial hierarchy. Women, especially urban women in direct contact with colonialism, despite their increasing class, ethnic, and religious differences, continued to identify gender qua gender as an important organizing base, as they had done historically. It was not *new* to them to see their collective destiny embodied in gender solidarity, it was *old*. Though not monolithic in their aims, they *assumed* gender as a primary bond and organizing base as they most certainly had for centuries.

The class development, and the ethnic and religious diversity created by the colonial experience provided new challenges to an old way of organizing, but the West had nothing to teach African women about organizing as women. Whether "traditional" or members of the newly emerging westernized elite, women activists looked primarily to their *past* modes of protest to help remake their future. But, looking to the future, they appropriated those aspects of external ideologies that seemed most likely to benefit women. They sought to align themselves closely with ideas that were the most consonant with their own cosmologies—the struggle for women's right to vote, for instance, resonated with the "traditional" notion that women had a role to play in the political sphere.

The struggle against women's taxation separately from their husbands was both a reaction to the transgression of this policy against the family-based taxation of the formerly independent African societies and states, and the desire of women to couple their taxation with the right to vote. The struggle against the power of the colonial bureaucracy to decide the placement of markets and the prices of commodities traded therein was intended to maintain women's power in their roles in production and distribution. Even among the westernizing elite, the struggle for equal pay for equal work, and for access to all grades of the civil service, was an extension of women's historical role of working outside the home, which was as much an obligation of adulthood as a right for most of the women of West Africa.

I will examine, in brief, two women's protest groups of the colonial era in Nigeria. These groups are illustrative of the points I have made above, and they are different from one another.

The first, the Lagos Market Women's Association (LMWA), was an organization of at least ten thousand market women in Lagos, Nigeria. Lagos was the center of the colonial bureaucracy in Nigeria after 1914, when the protectorates of Northern and Southern Nigeria were joined to be the British colony of Nigeria. Though the exact date for the formation of the LMWA is not clear, by the 1920s it was active and a powerful organization that represented the market women before both the "traditional" African authorities such as the various chiefs, and the colonial hierarchy. Guilds predated the organization of the LMWA, which represented a collectivity of markets. In addition, at least as early as 1908, ad hoc groups of market women's guilds had united to protest the imposition of taxes on the selling and use of water in the city. The formation of associations of women representing various markets, and of women's guilds representing various occupations (such as hairdressers, sellers of cooked food, shea-butter producers), predated colonialism by centuries.

The most well-known head of the LMWA during the colonial period was Madam Alimotu Pelewura. A fish trader in Ereko market at least as early as 1900, Pelewura shared several other characteristics of the market women: she was unlettered, a Muslim, and poor. Pelewura was the elected *Alaga* (head) of Ereko market, which in a 1932 colonial government study was reported as one of the most efficiently run markets in Lagos. Shortly after the study, the Commissioner of the Colony publicly lamented the power of market women's guilds such as those at Ereko and advocated that market women's associations should be more "social" in nature. He stated that the degree of power women exercised within certain markets should be "nipped in the bud."

In the 1920s, the LMWA provided a base of power for one of the first nationalist political parties in Nigeria, the Nigerian National Democratic Party (NNDP), founded in 1923. Though some historians have posited that the NNDP founder Herbert Macaulay inspired the formation of the LMWA and was a shadow leader of the Association, several elderly market women informants (in 1975) told this author that Macaulay and Pelewura walked hand in hand, that is to say, as equals. In a speech to a gathering of NNDP members in Abeokuta in 1942, Pelewura opened with the powerful declaration, "I am she who is called Pelewura," and, in noticing an audience of mostly men, added, "We wonder why your womenfolk did not show up here today. Tell me of that thing which men can undertake alone without the help of the women folk?". Furthermore, though the LMWA would solicit Macaulay's help in hiring those with skills LMWA members did not possess, such as lawyers and accountants to aid them in their interactions with colonial authorities, the LMWA long outlasted the NNDP and allied itself with a number of other nationalist political organizations. There is no evidence to support the idea that Macaulay either inspired the founding of the LMWA or was a shadow authority figure in the Association.

By 1932 Pelewura was appointed a member of the *Ilu* committee by the traditional African (Yoruba) authorities of Lagos. The *Ilu* committee was a component of traditional government, a body of chiefs and others who advised the *Oba* (king). With their policy of indirect rule for Lagos (and other parts of Nigeria), the British did not dismantle indigenous political insti-tutions but rather sought to undermine and manipulate them in ways which rendered them primarily titular and consultative when it came to decision making, as well as helpful when it came to implementation of colonial directives. A representative of the market women had historically sat on the *Ilu* to ensure that women's concerns were voiced and considered. At the time of her appointment, Pelewura was a spokeswoman for eighty-four market women's organizations. As will be seen, the *Ilu* would deeply disappoint the colonial authorities when, in a confrontation with the market women, the *Oba* would make it plain that there was no historical precedent for his (or the *Ilu*'s) contravening a decision that the women made about their spheres of power.

Between 1932 and 1951, there were several major confrontations between the market women and the colonial authorities. These had to do with the taxation of women, the location of markets, the price of commodities, and women's right to vote.

In 1932 rumors spread that the colonial government intended to tax women in Lagos. Though a limited tax on women had been inaugurated in the nearby town of Abeokuta in 1918, the market women of Lagos were prepared to resist such taxation. They sent a delegation to see the Administrator of the Colony, C. T. Lawrence, who assured them the government had no intention of taxing women in Lagos. Despite that assurance, in 1940 the colonial government enacted an Income Tax Ordinance which proposed to tax women whose incomes exceeded fifty pounds per annum. Immediately the market women began to organize, and on December 16, 1940, within days of the enactment of the Ordinance, over a hundred women assembled outside the office of the Commissioner of the Colony. The women were adamant that the tax be repealed and, receiving no assurance to that effect, left to report to the *Oba* Falolu. In a petition formulated by the women (drawn up by a hired clerk) and "signed" with over two hundred of their thumbprints, they stated that female taxation had to be repealed because it violated "native law and custom" and was untimely due to the hardship created by World War II. The petition further reported that the *Oba* Falolu and his chiefs agreed with them that female taxation was not only contrary to custom but undesirable.

On December 18, the markets of Lagos were nearly deserted as the women marched in the thousands. They first went to the Office of the Commissioner of the Colony. Receiving no satisfaction there, they then marched to Government House, where soldiers barred the door. Eventually two women, one of who was Pelewura, were admitted by Governor Bourdillon. Pelewura later reported in an interview with the *Daily Times* newspaper that Bourdillon apologized that Lady Bourdillon was out that day and could not receive them. She said she replied they were not particular about reception that day. They delivered their petition and later in the evening held a mass meeting at Glover Memorial Hall. Both Pelewura and the Commissioner addressed the crowd, which ranged in estimates from one thousand to seven thousand women. When the Commissioner, in his address, stated that women in England paid tax, it was reported that Pelewura responded that she was not surprised, since England was where the money was made and that Africans were poor "owing to many factors over which they had no control." She went on to state that "Europeans should not interfere with native custom and impose taxation on women" and, according to official reports, wound up with a Yoruba version of "votes for women or alternatively no taxation without representation."

Within two days, the government raised the ceiling for women's taxation from fifty pounds income per annum to two hundred pounds. Clearly, this meant that almost no market woman would be taxed. A letter was dispatched to the market women and delivered to Pelewura, advising her of the new policy. Pelewura reportedly responded that once the principle of female taxation was conceded, it was only a matter of time before all women had to pay tax. History proved her prophetic.

During the World War II years, the Nigerian colonial government instituted a system of price controls on food that came to be known as the Pullen Marketing Scheme, named after Captain A. P. Pullen, who was appointed as its director in 1941. The Pullen scheme had expanded by 1943 to such an extent that the government not only sought to cap the prices of food sold in the markets but wanted to send agents to buy food outside of Lagos and bring it to Lagos to sell in the market at designated centers at government-set prices.

The Lagos market women had several objections to the Pullen scheme. As the primary distributors and retailers of food, they had historically exercised control over its pricing. Moreover, most of the market women were petty traders operating on the smallest profit margin and were unable to sustain even short-term losses. Government prices for foodstuffs were unrealistic, often amounting to less than retailers had to pay to purchase them for resale. A vigorous black market developed, and by 1944 the official estimate of the number of Lagosians fed by the black market was as high as two-thirds. When arrests were made for black market profiteering, employees of European firms received lesser sentences than market women arrested for the same offense.

The market women were determined to resist the price controls. The women proposed that, rather than prices being set by the government, a committee composed of twelve experienced market women of the LMWA should regulate prices. When the women farina sellers of Ijebu-Ode (a town near Lagos that supplied much of Lagosians' supply of farina) stationed them-selves on the main road between Ijebu-Ode and Lagos and refused to allow any lorries carrying farina to pass, the LMWA supported their actions. Early in 1944, Pelewura was summoned to several meetings with the Deputy Controller of Native Foodstuffs and the Commissioner of the Colony to discuss the possibility of finding a way for the market women to support the price controls. At one such meeting, Captain Pullen proposed that Pelewura assist him and offered to pay her to do so. According to official reports, Pelewura refused and accused Pullen of "seeking to break and starve the country where she was born."

A meeting of the market women (reportedly three thousand of them) with the *Oba* and chiefs was also unhelpful to the colonial authorities. At that meeting, Chief Oluwa informed Pullen that no market woman would go against the LMWA prohibition on abiding by the price controls. The LMWA achieved a limited success in August 1945, when the government agreed to decontrol the price of gari, a staple food of the population of Lagos and the one in greatest scarcity. By September 1945, the government decontrolled food prices. The war was over, the protest was mounting, and there seemed to be no logic to keeping them in place.

Most interestingly, when a widespread general strike occurred in Nigeria in 1945, the marketwomen supported the striking workers and voluntarily suppressed the price of market commodities to demonstrate their solidarity. The LMWA also made generous contributions to the Worker's Relief Fund.

This brief description of some of the activities of the LMWA is indicative of the market women's awareness of the acute frustrations of the colonial period. More importantly, it is evidence that they had in place conceptual formulations and practical mechanisms to represent themselves, and that they drew on their history as much as their present reality of colonialism/westernization to promote their interests in being active agents in decision making about their lives. The assumptions they made about the proper spheres for women's activity were solidly rooted in their history and in fact contravened colonial notions of "woman's sphere."

The second major women's organization in colonial Lagos that I will discuss is the Nigerian Women's Party (NWP). The NWP was founded by a group of women who were members of the newly emerging Christianized, westernized elite. Its most prominent member, and its president from its inception until its demise around 1956, was Lady Oyinkan Ajasa Abayomi. Abayomi's father was the first Nigerian knight (Sir Kitoye Ajasa), and her mother (Oyinkan Bartholomew) was the daughter of first treasurer to the Egba United Government. Abayomi was sent to Britain for postsecondary education. Though both of her parents were relatively conservative, after the death of her first husband, Abayomi married Dr. (later Sir) Kofoworola Abayomi, who was a leader of the Nigerian Youth Movement (NYM), an early nationalist organization founded in 1935. Even before this marriage in 1934, Abayomi had distinguished herself as a freethinker and a political activist who was more radical than her parents, albeit less revolutionary than some other Nigerian women activists. She was among the first women in Lagos to drive a car, and in 1927 had founded the British West African Educated Girls' Club (later the Ladies' Progressive Club) to raise funds for African girls' secondary education. In 1935 Abayomi joined the women's wing of the NYM and became increasingly aware of the problems common among African women of all classes, ethnicities, and religions. She began to exhort elite women to take a more active role in improving the conditions of unlettered, poor women. In an article published in the NYM journal in 1935, she warned that "The uppishness among the few privileged women who have been educated abroad must be killed. Unless the so-called highly educated make themselves open and approachable they will have no one to lead. . . ." She ended the article by sounding a note for women's equality: "women also should be given free chances to develop their faculties for the benefit of the race."

On May 10, 1944, Abayomi held a meeting in her Lagos home to discuss women's political situation. The twelve women gathered there decided to form the Nigerian Women's Party. In an interview the following day in the African-run *Daily Service* newspaper, Abayomi, and another NWP founder, Tinuola Dedeke, addressed the reasons for the founding of the NWP. Abayomi decried the fact that, though women owned property and paid taxes, they had no political representation because they could not vote. She specifically criticized the lack of any women on the Lagos Town Council or the Legislative Council, the two bodies on which the colonial government had allowed some African representation. She also pointed out the lack of government scholarships for girls to study in Britain, comparing the Nigerian situation to that of the British colony of Sierra Leone, where such scholarships existed. Dedeke implored women to "cast away all feelings of religious and tribal differences and present a united front for the sake of their motherland.".

Within a short time, the NWP had drawn up its Constitution that set forth its goals:

The Women's Party makes its strongest appeal to the women of Nigeria irrespective of class or any other distinction, reminding them of their backward and unenviable position among the women of other races and calling them to action. It appeals to those who may be outside the ranks of the Women's Party for sympathy and cooperation:

1. To shape the whole future is not our problem, but only to shape faithfully a small part of it according to rules laid down.
2. To seek by constitutional means the rights of British citizenship in its full measure on the people.
3. To work assiduously for the educational, agricultural and industrial development of Nigeria with a view to improve the moral, intellectual and economic condition of the country.
4. To work for the amelioration of the condition of the women of Nigeria not merely by sympathy for their aspirations but by recognition of their equal status with men.

Though patrons could be adults of any nationality at home or abroad who agreed with the objectives of the Party, membership was open only to women of African descent. An executive committee was formed consisting of a president, vice president, two secretaries, a legal adviser, two treasurers, and seven ex officio members elected from the general membership. One of the duties of the legal adviser was "To study closely all government bills and other measures affecting the people, irrespective of class or any other designation. . . ." There were also three committees established: Health and Education,

Market and Native Industry, and Political and Social.

Though its intentions were to establish branches throughout Nigeria, for a variety of reasons, the NWP's activities were effectively confined to Lagos. One reason was that the party had limited resources. Though estimates of its numerical strength ranged from five hundred to two thousand, the number of truly active members, as opposed to those who aligned themselves with the Party on an ad hoc basis over special issues, was apparently quite small. In addition, though the Party sought to solicit membership among the market women, it was not nearly as successful in recruiting them as members as were the market women's own associations, particularly the LMWA. One prominent market woman, Rabiatu Alaso Oke, who was unlettered and Muslim, did serve on the executive committee of the NWP. Though Pelewura had a working relationship with the NWP and shortly after its founding announced her personal willingness to cooperate with the Party, she never appears to have held any official status and it is not even clear if she was actually a member. There was at least one major disagreement between the NWP and the market women over remarks made by Funmilayo Ransome-Kuti, a leftist and leader of the Abeokuta Women's Union.. Still, the NWP cooperated with the market women during the resistance to the Pullen price controls and conducted free literacy classes in the evening for market women at the CMS Grammar School.

The NWP took up four major issues during its most active phase: (1) girls' education and literacy classes for adult women; (2) the employment of women in the civil service; (3) the right of female minors to trade freely in Lagos; and (4) the securing of women's rights in general, but particularly the right to vote.

Many in the NWP leadership were schoolteachers and were seriously concerned by the lack of educational facilities for girls' education, particularly at the secondary level. Moreover, the NWP fought to have the curriculum offered to girls expanded; they wanted science and foreign languages added to the curriculum. The Party advocated the provision of government scholarships for Muslim girls, who were at a particular disadvantage since both primary and secondary education was dominated by various Christian church denominations. Last but not least, the Party sought to have the government provide adult literacy education, particularly for women.

The second issue, employment of women in the colonial civil service, had been a major concern since the 1930s, when Charlotte Olajumoke Obasa and her Lagos Women's League (defunct by the 1940s) had battled for African women's employment. The NWP argued not only for women's employment but for equal pay with men in the same grade of the service. Female teachers, for instance, were paid 33 percent less than men employed in the same rank. There was other discrimination. Particularly rankling was the apparent preference by the government for hiring European women, usually wives of administrative officers, as nurses and secretaries.

In 1946 the legislature passed the Children and Young Persons Ordinance, which struck at the heart of African traditions. The Ordinance prohibited children under fourteen from engaging in street trading, required parental permission for girls between fourteen and sixteen to trade, and limited to daylight the hours in which young girls were allowed to trade. Though this legislation may have had as its intention the protection of child labor, it was crafted without consultation with the African community and contravened local customs, in which girls were apprenticed to trade for their mothers and other relatives as a kind of vocational training in preparation for economic independence as adult women. The police force exceeded acceptable behavior when it began meeting trains entering Lagos and removing all girl traders who seemed below age, and arresting young girls, including young married women with babies on their backs. In a letter to the *Daily Service*, the NWP expressed the fear that the authorities intended to introduce a pass system similar to that in effect in South Africa. The NWP worked with the market women's associations in succeeding in having the ordinance suspended.

The NWP constantly agitated for the right of women to vote. In 1950 southern Nigerian women were finally enfranchised. That year, the NWP ran four candidates in the Lagos Town Council election. All four NWP candidates lost. After this election, the NWP began its gradual demise. The Party continued to advocate for girls' education and health care reforms, but by 1956 it effectively disappeared when it joined other Nigerian women's groups to establish the National Council of Women's Societies, a decidedly less politically oriented group.

Most of the active membership of the NWP straddled the "traditional" and the "new," the indigenous and the foreign. Though often much acculturated in western ways, these women also maintained an allegiance to their own culture. They were that middle strand who sometimes opted for slower and less radical change by exhorting colonialism to improve itself rather than end immediately. It was particularly in their advocacy of women's rights that they were a thorn in the side of the colonizers, and often in the side of African men as well. The NWP was clearly a champion of women's rights, especially those of poor women. While there may have been some noblesse oblige in their actions, they were sincere in their desire to see all women treated as equals with men. Their notion of the political sphere as a proper arena for women's activity was certainly nothing they learned from the West.

These two organizations, the Lagos Market Women's Association and the Nigerian Women's Party, are examples of feminist activity in the colonial setting in the capital city of the most populous British colony in Africa. The feminist activity they represent was inspired not by western models, but by their own models. Though their activity may have gone unnamed as

feminism, and unarticulated in ideological terms, their modes of organization and their language of protest are transparent in their advocacy of women's equal status with men and women's right to power over their own lives and participation in the general political sphere. In actions louder than words, they created theory.

---

[1] Alice Walker appears to be among the first to use this term. In her book *In Search of Our Mother's Gardens* (New York: Harcourt, Brace, Jovanovich, 1983) she describes a womanist as a Black feminist or feminist of color and says, "womanist is to feminist as purple is to lavender."

[2] Cheryl Johnson-Odim, "Common Themes, Different Contexts," in Chandra T. Mohanty, Ann Russo, and Lourdes Torres, eds., *Third World Women and the Politics of Feminism* (Bloomington: Indiana University Press, 1991).

[3] Joan Wallach Scott, "Introduction," in Joan Wallach Scott, ed., *Feminism and History* (New York: Oxford University Press, 1996), 1.

[4] Ibid., 6.

[5] Nancy Hewitt, "Uneven Developments: Women's History Reaches Puberty," unpublished paper delivered at the Social Science History Association Conference, Minneapolis, 1990. A version of this paper has been published as "Reflections from a Departing Editor: Recasting Issues of Marginality," *Gender and History* 4, no. 1 (Spring 1992): 3–9.

[6] Joan Wallach Scott writes, "Some kind of analysis is needed of a complicated and highly specific relationship of power. . . . Does race take priority over class and class over gender, or are there inseparable connections among them?" See Scott, "Introduction," 8.

[7] For a brilliant discussion of this connection, see Angela Davis, "Rape, Racism and the Myth of the Black Rapist," in Angela Davis, *Women, Race and Class* (New York: Random House, 1981). See also Cheryl Johnson-Odim, "Common Themes, Different Contexts."

[8] Fran Beale, "Slave of a Slave No More: Black Women in Struggle," *Black Scholar* 6, no. 6 (March 1975): 2–10.

[9] See the quotation in the British newspaper the *Daily Worker*, 10 August 1947. Funmilayo Ransome-Kuti is among the most important women leaders in Nigeria's history. She was the most radical Nigerian woman of the colonial period. For more on her, see Cheryl Johnson-Odim, "On Behalf of Women and the Nation: Funmilayo Ransome-Kuti and the Struggles for Nigerian Independence and Women's Equality," in C. Johnson-Odim and M. Strobel, eds., *Expanding the Boundaries of Women's History* (Bloomington: Indiana University Press, 1992); and Cheryl Johnson-Odim and Nina Mba, *For Women and the Nation: A Biography of Funmilayo Ransome-Kuti of Nigeria* (Urbana: University of Illinois Press, 1997).

[10] Cheryl Johnson, "Nigerian Women and British Colonialism: The Yoruba Example with Selected Biographies" (Ph.D. dissertation, Northwestern University, Evanston, IL, 1978).

[11] See, for example, Ife Amadiume, *Male Daughters, Female Husbands* (London: Zed Press, 1987); Niara Sudarkassa, *Where Women Work: A Study of Yoruba Women in the Marketplace and in the Home* (Ann Arbor:

University of Michigan Press, 1973); Kamene Okonjo, "The Dual-Sex Political System in Operation: Igbo Women and Community Politics in Midwestern Nigeria," in N. Hafkin and E. Bay, eds., *Women in Africa* (Stanford: Stanford University Press, 1976), 45–58; Karen Sacks, *Sisters and Wives* (Westport, CT: Greenwood Press, 1979); Simi Afonja, "Land Control, A Critical Factor in Yoruba Gender Stratification," in C. Robertson and I. Berger, eds., *Women and Class in Africa* (New York: Holmes and Meier, 1986), 78–91; Leith Mullings, "Women and Economic Change in Africa," in Nancy J. Hafkin and Edna G. Bay, eds., *Women in Africa* (Stanford: Stanford University Press, 1976), 239–64; and Nancy J. Hafkin and Edna G. Bay, "Introduction" to *Women in Africa*, 1–18.

[12] I do not include in this discussion the explosive literature on female circumcision/genital mutilation since this is a literature not primarily written by historians and frequently not even historicized.

[13] Hewitt, "Uneven Developments."

[14] By "traditional," I mean the way people did things before the arrival of colonialists external to the region who brought western culture. For an important discussion of false dichotomies between "traditional" and "modern," see Cheryl Johnson-Odim and Margaret Strobel, "Conceptualizing the History of Women in Africa, Asia, Latin America and the Caribbean, and the Middle East," *Journal of Women's History* 1, no. 1 (Spring 1989): 36–37.

[15] See, for example, Nina Mba, *Nigerian Women Mobilized: Women in Southern Nigerian Political History 1900–1965* (Berkeley, CA: Institute of International Studies, 1982); Cora Ann Presley, "Labor Unrest among Kikuyu Women in Colonial Kenya," in Robertson and Berger, eds., *Women and Class in Africa*, 255–73; Cora Ann Presley, *Kikuyu Women, the Mau Mau Rebellion and Social Change in Kenya* (Denver, CO: Westview Press, 1993); Jean O'Barr, "Making the Invisible Visible: African Women in Politics and Policy," *African Studies Review* 18, no. 3 (1975): 19–27; Judith Van Allen, "Sitting on a Man: Colonialism and the Lost Political Institutions of Igbo Women," *Canadian Journal of African Studies* 6, no. 2 (1972): 168–81; and Cheryl Johnson-Odim, "Madam Alimotu Pelewura and the Lagos Marketwomen," *Tarikh* 7, no. 1 (1981): 1–10.

[16] For more information on Pelewura, see Johnson-Odim, "Madam Alimotu Pelewura and the Lagos Market-women," in *Tarikh*, 7, no. 1 (1981): 1–10.

[17] Colonial Secretary's Office Files #248/24 at the National Archives, Ibadan, Nigeria.

[18] Pelewura's speech is in the file "Political Parties in Abeokuta," at the Abeokuta Archives, Abeokuta, Nigeria.

[19] *Daily Times*, 18 December 1940, cited in Johnson-Odim, "Madam Alimotu Pelewura."

[20] Macaulay Papers Collection, University of Ibadan Manuscripts Collection, Box 13, File 5, Ibadan, Nigeria.

For further discussion of the struggle between Pelewura and Pullen, see *Daily Service* newspaper for 23 September 1942, National Archives, Ibadan, and Colonial Secretary's Office Files #2516 and #2686, National Archives, Ibadan.

[21] For more information on the strike and the market women, see Wale Oyemakinde, "The Nigerian General Strike of 1945," *Journal of the Historical Society of Nigeria* (December 1974): 693–710.

[22] For more information on Abayomi, see Cheryl Johnson-Odim, "Lady Oyinkan Abayomi: A Profile," in Bolanle Awe, ed., *Nigerian Women in Historical Perspective* (Lagos, Nigeria: Sankore Publishers, 1992).

[23] The most radical Nigerian woman of the colonial period was certainly Funmilayo Ransome-Kuti. For her story and that of the Abeokuta Women's Union that she founded see Johnson-Odim, "On Behalf of Women and the Nation"; Johnson-Odim and Mba, *For Women and the Nation.*

[24] Lady Oyinkan Ajasa Abayomi, "Modern Womanhood," *NYM [Nigerian Youth Movement] Journal,* the Macaulay Papers Collection, University of Ibadan Manuscripts Collection, Box 73, File 7, Ibadan, Nigeria.

[25] *Daily Service* newspaper, 11 May 1944, National Archives, Ibadan, Nigeria.

[26] The NWP's Constitution was among the private papers of Tinuola Dedeke in Lagos, Nigeria. I am uncertain as to what happened to this collection following her death in the 1990s. The Constitution is also cited in Johnson-Odim, "Nigerian Women and British Colonialism," and in Mba, *Nigerian Women Mobilized.*

[27] Cited in the NWP's Constitution; see note 26.

[28] For details, see Johnson-Odim, "Lady Oyinkan Abayomi." The bulk of the research on which this chapter is based was done in Lagos, Ibadan, and Abeokuta, Nigeria, in 1975–76 and in 1989. I used several Nigerian newspapers, particularly the *Daily Service, Daily Times,* and *West African Pilot;* the Colonial Secretary's Office Files and the Commissioner of the Colony Files at the National Archives, Ibadan; the Macaulay Papers Collection at the University of Ibadan Manuscripts Collection; the private papers of Tinuola Dedeke and Funmilayo Ransome-Kuti (the Ransome-Kuti papers are available at the University of Ibadan Library); and interviews with Oyinkan Abayomi, Tinuola Dedeke, and Funmilayo Ransome-Kuti. For additional references, please refer to Johnson-Odim, "Nigerian Women and British Colonialism."

"Negro Women Are Great Thinkers As Well As Doers": Amy Jacques-Garvey and Community Feminism in the United States, 1924–1927

Ula Y. Taylor

Amy Jacques-Garvey (1896–1973) was the second wife of Marcus Mosiah Garvey and unofficial leader of the Universal Negro Improvement Association (UNIA), the largest Pan-African movement in the twentieth century. Jacques-Garvey mastered what Taylor calls community feminism. Community feminism allowed black women to function within their communities as both helpmates and leaders. An examination of Jacques-Garvey's editorials published in the Negro World, *the propaganda newspaper for the UNIA, reveals her brand of community feminism and how her choices were political—transforming her from a personal secretary, editor, and wife into an indispensable UNIA leader during the 1920s.*

The 1920s marked the decade of the "new Negro," and nowhere was this more pronounced than in New York City. It was in Harlem that an intelligentsia, representing a range of organizations, produced layers of political commentary. Settled within the cauldron of activism was the Universal Negro Improvement Association (UNIA), the largest Pan-African organization in the twentieth century.[1] Led by Marcus Mosiah Garvey and commonly known as Garveyism, this movement was based on the idea that the needs and interests of people of African descent throughout the diaspora were linked to Africans on the continent, since the collective identity of both groups lay in Africa.

In 1923, the UNIA was a thriving organization of six million members and at least nine hundred branches worldwide.[2] The black masses had responded to Marcus Garvey's platform, which highlighted the necessity of generating global economic connections and redeeming Africa from European colonists. However, the organization suffered a setback in July of that year, when Garvey was convicted of mail fraud in New York and sentenced to five years in federal prison. During Garvey's prison term, his second wife, Amy Jacques-Garvey (1896–1973), was an unofficial but fundamental leader of the UNIA.[3]

The incarceration of her husband created a new set of circumstances for Jacques-Garvey. Up until this point, the married couple had been guided by their traditional Jamaican upbringing, which stipulated that wives were to be compromising helpmates. Jacques-Garvey was proud to claim the identity of helpmate to Garvey; but after his conviction, she became the focus of public attention, and, in time, the unofficial head of the organization. In rising to this challenge, she revealed herself to be a highly capable and charismatic leader and intellectual in the Pan-African struggle.

This article examines Jacques-Garvey's thinking on black nationalism and feminism, based on editorials she wrote for the UNIA's newspaper, the *Negro World,* from 1924 to 1927. By placing the UNIA's nationalist ideas within a feminist paradigm, Jacques-Garvey was able to keep her husband's incarceration crisis at the center of her world without shifting her intellectual self completely to the periphery. The difficulty, however, as literary scholar Carole Boyce Davies has pointed out, is that "Afrocentric feminism sounds like a contradiction in terms, for if it is Afro-centered then the feminine/feminism is already an appendage, an excess, easily expelled or contained within."[4] In Jacques-Garvey's editorials, nonetheless, she expressed her feminism as a cornerstone of the UNIA's platform. Although Garveyites imagined a gendered community inherently grounded in a system of differences, Jacques-Garvey contested the socially constructed categories and roles that limited women's personal and intellectual development; her feminism became not only a means to critique black men but it also served as a linchpin to unite all black women to reach their full potential for the imagined black nation. Overall, Jacques-Garvey's writings exemplify how one woman maneuvered between what most contemporary observers view as intrinsically oppositional forces—nationalism (a doctrine that first and foremost advocated popular freedom and sovereignty in order to achieve self-determination) and feminism (a doctrine of equal rights for women that challenged women's oppression and subordination)—and brought them together in one theoretical construct, ultimately producing what I call community feminism.

While Jacques-Garvey's personal life and choices have kept many feminists and Garvey scholars from recognizing her as an ideal feminist, her writings suggest that she was an early and significant community feminist. In essence, community feminists are women who may or may not live in male-centered households; either way, their activism is focused on assisting both the men and women in their lives—whether husbands or sisters, fathers or mothers, sons or daughters—along with initiating and participating in activities to uplift their communities.

Despite this helpmate focus, community feminists are undeniably feminists; their activism discerns the configuration of oppressive power relations, shatters masculinist claims of women as intellectually inferior, and seeks to empower women by expanding their roles and options. Best understood through poststructuralist ideas of relativism and difference, community feminism challenges a macropolitical model that implies there is something inherently pure or essential in feminist theory.[5] A decentering of feminist epistemologies allows us to move away from an ahistorical interpretation of feminism and toward a more dynamic understanding that embraces the multiple identities of black women. In addition, communitarian ideas—the rejection of self-interest and the autonomous individual in lieu of a view of the self as collective, interdependent, and relational—take center stage.[6] The concept of community feminism is essentially an effort to expand the historical meaning of feminism. Located within a particular historical moment (the 1920s), community feminism challenges the notion that helpmate and leadership roles exist in contradiction. The interplay between helpmate and leadership roles appears repeatedly in Jacques-Garvey's writings.

Jacques-Garvey's notion that women ought to be both helpmates and leaders within the Pan-African struggle tussles with the common view that, historically, men have exclusively constructed female activities within nationalist movements. Political scientist Cynthia Enloe has explored women's relationships to nationalist movements internationally; she correctly has posited that even though women have suffered abuses, "they have been treated more as symbols than as active participants by nationalist movements organized to end colonialism and racism." Enloe has observed that men frequently urged women to fulfill the roles of "ego-stroking girlfriend, stoic wife or nurturing mother."[7] These traditional identities are nonthreatening to male nationalists; therefore, women who refuse to be confined by these roles have an uneasy relationship with men. Enloe has concluded that the majority of anticolonial and antiracist movements throughout the world are "patriarchal nationalisms."[8]

Similar perspectives emerged among advocates of Black Power during the 1960s freedom struggles in the United States, when nationalist rhetoric, as Davies has accurately stated, continued to operate "from a singularly monolithic construction of an African theoretical homeland which asks for the submergence or silencing of gender."[9] Historian E. Frances White has concurred that "the ideology of complementarity and collective family needs continues to work against the liberation of black women."[10]

Enloe, Davies, and White have presented sound collective arguments regarding the marginalization of women in nationalist movements, largely caused by the symbolic creation of "nation" as a patriarchal construct. Garvey's Pan-African struggle was also based on assigning women and men particular roles. He constructed them to meet his expectations of nationhood; Garvey argued that his male-dominated movement benefited women by allowing them to develop their God-given talents, making the home a haven of comfort and place to nurture children—the future generation. Historian Barbara Bair has pointed out that these roles were not "separate and equal but separate and hierarchical."[11] Men and women were advised to wield proper influence and authority over their respective spheres, public and private. Garvey believed that men should function as providers and protectors and women should be in charge of familial matters. These designated roles, he argued, replicated the lifestyles of other successful and powerful people worldwide.

Jacques-Garvey, nonetheless, labored to give feminist impetus to a nationalist movement, which, at times, countered her husband's nationhood structure. She had migrated from Jamaica in 1917, become affiliated with the UNIA in New York in 1919, and married Garvey in 1922. Jacques-Garvey's private life is relevant to the ideas she presented in her editorials; one of the most salient features in Jacques-Garvey's editorials was her assertion that women must claim their equality to men, even though she lived in a male-dominated marriage. We need to consider whether Jacques-Garvey's personal choices—perhaps not as politically correct or appropriate as present-day feminists with narrow-minded conceptions of feminism would prefer—unfairly prevents scholars from seeing her as a feminist writer and thinker.

It is my contention that Jacques-Garvey simultaneously rejected and accepted codes of patriarchy. In the Garvey household, as in most homes during the 1920s, the parameters for the wife, helpmate, mother, and daughter were based on patriarchal principles.[12] While a universal and transhistorical idea, patriarchy was diverse in its specific structures and effects. For example, capitalist patriarchy was so pervasive in the United States that, in some cities, married women were barred from working in certain professions, such as teaching, because it was assumed that their husbands should maintain their status by being the primary breadwinners.[13] Social norms dictated that women, in particular middle-class women, function as self-sacrificing nurturers who deferred to their husbands' and fathers' wishes, making their family obligations the priority in their lives.

Moreover, "race women" believed they had an additional moral obligation to be efficient housewives, because their domestic responsibilities to their husbands and children were of paramount importance for racial progress. According to historian Stephanie J. Shaw, even professional black women were not excused from performing household duties, and they devoted as much energy to their communities as their families. Black women perceived their public and private roles and work as "complementary rather than contradictory."[14] In an Afrocentric community, to borrow from historian Elsa Barkley Brown, "community is family."[15] Thus, Jacques-Garvey's domestic behavior should not be seen as a reflection of her inability to challenge patriarchy wholeheartedly or take a critical stand against her husband, but more as a strategic expression of her talent to maneuver between her family and the larger world. In doing so, Jacques-Garvey along with other race women mastered community feminism.[16] An examination of Jacques-Garvey's editorials reveals her particular brand of community feminism and how her familial choices were political and ultimately led to her transformation from personal secretary, editor, and wife into an indispensable leader within the UNIA during the 1920s.

Soon after her marriage to Garvey, Jacques-Garvey began giving public speeches and was noted for being a skilled secretary. Her editorials, however, were her forte. In them, we see the clearest account of her feminism. Jacques-Garvey's diverse writings were the embodiment of the concept of community feminism, as they advocated all-encompassing roles for black women who sought participation in a Pan-African movement. Between 1924 and 1927, she served as associate editor of the *Negro World* and introduced the woman's page, "Our Women and What They Think."[17] T. Thomas Fortune, editor of the newspaper during the woman's page run, was genuinely impressed with Jacques-Garvey's editorial "knack," which he believed "just seem[ed] to come natural to her." He further stated that she must have been "born with genius to do it."[18] Her "genius," however, does not shine through each weekly edition. On first glance, the woman's page appears to be a hodgepodge of intellectual sentiments regarding women. A comprehensive evaluation, though, reveals an eclectic pattern; writers hammered home the need for women to work as political agents and they also made statements that explained why they had to perform as helpmates, acknowledging the difficulties related to this nurturing role. While debating different strategies on the most appropriate means of achieving the movement goal, the goal was still the same—empowerment through self-determination and nationhood in Africa.

During the mid-1920s, despite the proliferation of the "Negro Press," most women's sections in newspapers were merely columns highlighting the fine points of etiquette and fashion alongside food recipes and household hints.[19] Jacques-Garvey balked at the frivolity of these discussions, saying that "fashions and [housewives'] topics only" were poor "reflections on the intelligence of our women."[20] Believing that "men have a higher appreciation of us when they read our ambitions and achievements, and more help would be given us," she opted, instead, to create an open forum in which women could share their ideas and opinions on serious matters.[21] She wrote, "In this way we will be able to command a respectful hearing before the world, and prove that Negro women are great thinkers as well as doers."[22]

Jacques-Garvey called on women to participate in the Pan-African movement by contributing "to this page, whether in the form of news articles, poems, or otherwise." Since the *Negro World* had an international readership, her appeal to "all Negro women of all climes" recognized that regional and class differences stood in the way of a united race movement; thus, she instructed women who "cannot express [them]selves on paper [to] get someone who is better equipped to clothe [their] sentiments in proper language and send them into our office." It is common knowledge, she believed, "that some of the most beautiful sentiments and lofty ideas emanate from the brains of women who have [had] very little education."[23] By celebrating the genius of poor black women, Jacques-Garvey turned W. E. B. DuBois's popular mantra of the "talented few" on its elitist head.[24] It was Jacques-Garvey's "aim to encourage Negro women to express their views on subjects of interest to their communities and particularly [those] affecting our struggling race."[25] She led the way by writing nearly two hundred editorials that situated feminist proclivities within black nationalism; her commentary represents a struggle on behalf of women within this context of masculinist discourse.

Jacques-Garvey's feminism was entrenched in her confidence that an actualized Pan-African agenda (itself based on a romantic imagining of a modern black nation) would minimize divisive differences among black people, since "the nation is always conceived as a deep, horizontal comradeship." She defended her political position with an array of international examples. Jacques-Garvey paralleled the UNIA's call for an "Africa for the Africans at home and abroad" with discussions of the struggles of China and India to be free from "European Powers," and she applauded the Moors' willingness to engage in warfare to keep the French and Belgians out of North Africa. The combination of these struggles, she wrote, weakened "our common oppressor and strengthened the prestige of one of the members of the family of darker peoples of the world in the field of achievement and world power."[26]

Jacques-Garvey was not alone among women in her attempts to fuel a discussion that connected the political aspirations, racial histories and cultures, and potential for collective "world power" among non-European people. A few active members of the National Association of Colored Women, led by Margaret Murray Washington, were also spreading information on "people of color the world over" in order to secure cooperation and appreciation of the "darker races of the world." In 1920, a new organization—the International Council of Women of the Darker Races of the World (ICWDRW)—was formed. The ICWDRW was short-lived, but during its heyday, in 1924, one hundred fifty American and fifty women of color from other countries constituted Committees of Seven to study conditions in order to promote race literature in schools in order to stimulate "a greater degree of race pride for their achievements."[27] The UNIA and cultural nationalists placed the study of race history high on their agendas, and Jacques-Garvey may well have applauded the efforts of the ICWDRW; but it is unlikely that they would have ever extended membership to her. Although they had similar intellectual goals, the elite pedigree of the ICWDRW placed such women as Jacques-Garvey (those without college degrees) on the outskirts.[28] In contrast, the UNIA and its woman's page provided an avenue for all black women, regardless of class or caste, to participate as intellectuals in the Pan-African struggle.

While Jacques-Garvey did not flatly reject armed struggle, she was convinced that black people could most efficiently free themselves from the clutches of colonialism and rise to their highest potential by acquiring the "knowledge that has made other races great." In Jamaica, the Jacques family's middle-class resources gave them the means to send their daughter to Wolmers, an elite secondary school, and her father often gave her exercises to increase her knowledge and develop her literary skills.[29] She later maintained that intelligence, particularly as it related to the modern sciences and capitalist business, was a globally respected virtue that was rewarded with material wealth and power. To be sure, some leaders used information deviously; it took shrewd minds to rob, steal, and cheat entire nations out of their natural resources, labor power, and possessions. Nevertheless, Jacques-Garvey warned her readers about the far-reaching hazards of ignorance by writing, "When the mind is enslaved, physical slavery, in one shape or another, soon follows."[30] Jacques-Garvey believed that, under these circumstances, the first preparatory step for all Garveyites had to be intellectual development and education.

Jacques-Garvey's fundamental premise was that "women have been endowed with the same mental faculties as men." As a connoisseur of international news, Jacques-Garvey regularly compared the "new Negro woman" to other women in the world.[31] She commented that women of the "East" (India, Egypt, and Turkey) were becoming educated and no longer considered themselves "slaves to their husbands," but rather as "intelligent, independent human beings [able] to assert and maintain their rights in co-partnership with their men."[32] In this discussion and others, Jacques-Garvey connected the worldwide "awakening of women" to their intellectual achievements, which "enhance[d] the prestige of their own nations and race."[33] Not only was education pivotal to the redemption of Africa, but it would also lead to women's personal freedom from marital bondage and colonial oppression. She wrote, "Africa does not want illiterate people now"; it needs "job makers not job hunters. The fellow who is looking for a job had better stay right here and keep looking."[34]

Careful to keep her equality rhetoric within the prescribed gender conventions, Jacques-Garvey commented in another article that while it was "common knowledge that women are not as physically strong as men," the creator—"God Almighty"—gave women other natural gifts to "repay" them for their "physical weakness." These attributes included "graciousness and keenness of mind" and the ability to "control and order things systematically and economically." On this point, Jacques-Garvey's discussion is reminiscent of 1890s black club women.[35] Take, for example, Anna Julia Cooper, a well-respected, formally educated, middle-class club woman. Her text, *A Voice from the South,* literary scholars commemorate as the "unparalleled articulation" of black feminist thought. Cooper averred, "As you know that she is physically the weaker of the two, don't stand under and leave her to buffet the waves alone." Girls needed encouragement and scholarships, she continued, although "not the boys less, but the girls more."[36] Jacques-Garvey helped to renew these philosophies in the 1920s, but, as a Pan-Africanist, she could only go partway with her distinguished foremothers and contemporaries who struggled to uplift their race primarily through formal education and Victorian morals. Jacques-Garvey respected and agreed with their moral ideas, but not their method for transforming society. It was inconceivable to her that the "new Negro," by being well-mannered and accommodating, could sway white America into sharing its resources. She considered any covenant with whites impossible, because racism was too entrenched in U.S. society and colonizers were selfish imperialists who would never share power with people whom they considered inferior.

In addition to focusing on the need for education, Jacques-Garvey's editorials also highlighted the interplay between the familial and public lives of women. She instructed black women to be competent mothers and affirm men in the movement for self-determination. At the same time, Jacques-Garvey went beyond a relational view of self; she anchored her discourse to a refashioning of gender roles that would enable women to do their part as political leaders in building the black nation. Although emphasizing a maternal role for women, Jacques-Garvey differed from most of her peers in her belief that nurturing leadership traits allowed women to run not only their homes and communities efficiently but also their countries, if indirectly.

Dedicated to the idea that women could reorder the gender practices of their communities in feminist directions, in the editorial "Women's Function in Life," Jacques-Garvey addressed "whether woman's place is in the home, in business, in politics or in industry." She understood that countries were different and women's status varied; however, "present-day events convince us that women, lovely women if you please, are making their presence felt in every walk of life." She maintained that the "woman of today has a place in nearly all phases of man's life," and "where such a place is not yet properly established her voice is heard in that regard."[37]

To make sure that her readership recognized her position as distinct from her husband's traditional views of patriarchy, Jacques-Garvey restated in numerous editorials that women must not be denied roles as intellectuals and political architects. For instance, in "No Sex in Brains and Ability," Jacques-Garvey wrote, "some men declare that women should remain in the homes and leave professions and legislation to men, but this is an antiquated belief, and [it] has been exploded by women's competency in these new fields and further by the fact that their homes have not suffered by a division of their time and interest."[38]

Jacques-Garvey continued to publicize her opinion by answering the question "Will the Entrance of Woman in Politics Affect Home Life?" with the claim that men tend not to realize the value of women in the home until they decide to enter electoral politics and political movements; then they cry "Our homes will be broken up, our children will be rejected."[39] Despite the highly charged disapproval of some men, Jacques-Garvey declared that family life had not been neglected by women's entry into politics but had benefited from it, because legislative policies affected the home, communities, and nation. In conclusion, she announced that the only pertinent query to be addressed was how much time a woman should spend in her home and how much devoted to politics. Without hesitation, she wrote, "This is a matter for the individual and women are rational and reasonable enough to give as much time in the home as the exigencies of the hour demand. Woman's inherent self-sacrifice and love will influence her decision in this direction."[40]

Following this June 1924 editorial, Jacques-Garvey published a variety of responses to her opinion. As an intellectual committed to the exchange of ideas, Jacques-Garvey included the thoughts of her peers by reprinting stories and clippings from local newspapers and magazines on activities and issues as they related to women on the woman's page.[41] Her strategy to allow conflicting perspectives on the woman's page was an effort to foster agitation, although she never shifted from her political position that women had the right to act as political beings. She hoped that controversy would encourage women to develop analytically their own viewpoints and inspire men to take notice of and respect their ideas. Because Jacques-Garvey identified the sharing of ideas— theorizing—as a form of activism, she pushed black women to understand that contributions to the Pan-African struggle could come from the use of a pen or typewriter. Although readers submitted a range of contributions, Jacques-Garvey used her editorial power to control the spectrum of debate. Maintaining a community feminist agenda, she printed comments that detailed the necessity of women's involvement in the political arena as well as statements that explained to women why they should act as helpmates.

Jacques-Garvey wanted her readership to understand that a helpmate role did not debilitate women, but it instead gave them authority to wield influence over men. In the editorial "Woman as Man's Helper," she stated that if it were not for women, "men would plunge more deeply in the mire of mistakes than they do. What great man has ever done any profitable thing without the help of some good woman?"[42] She offered this question not only to generate dialogue but also to reveal the empowering nature of a woman's relationship to a man, which further served to put men at ease with women's expanding roles. She concluded, "However great a thing may be, or whatever other men are consulted, even if it is clandestinely done, bank on it, there is a woman in the case before all consultations come to a close."[43] Even though a woman may not occupy the limelight or a position of visible influence, Jacques-Garvey contended that she emphatically shaped the outcome of important decisions. She reiterated this idea in her editorial "The Joy of Living," in which she wrote, "A woman may be born into this world for the purpose of mothering and training the President of a nation; another may be born to be the wife of a great statesman, whose single word could decide the destinies of millions of people."[44] To speak of women being "born" was another way for Jacques-Garvey to create a narrative around certain presumed intrinsic qualities in women. The idea that specific traits (good judgment, mother wit) were ingrained in the female mind and could be used for covert and overt purposes served to celebrate women's infinite possibilities.

In another editorial, "Man's Inspiration Is Woman," Jacques-Garvey described how a helpmate "may be a mother, sister, wife, or sweetheart, but it is she who wakened in him his latent powers, and inspired him to achieve greatness."[45] As fierce supporters, women had to motivate and extract from men the service and commitment necessary to achieve the Pan-African goal: "black women, we appeal to you, get behind your men and keep them moving on the road to progress and nationhood."[46]

Although Jacques-Garvey encouraged black women to be guided by an African consciousness and to let their voices be heard in political and civic affairs, by no means did she want them to be liberated from all gender-specific roles. She believed, as did Garvey, that these were innate roles and beneficial to both women and men, hence the community. Women were particularly suited to be nurturers, Jacques-Garvey said, despite the fact that this role set a restrictive standard for appropriate behavior. Jacques-Garvey's discussion of a black woman's relational self, however, does call into question the contemporary perception that helpmates consistently occupy a second-class status.

The social construction of the term "helpmate" has been inaccurately reduced, largely by Western academics, to imply passivity. Political philosopher Jean Bethke Elshtain argues that too often feminists, radicals, and reformers analyze traditional community and family as "reactionary by definition" and "repressive by nature."[47] By doing so, they obfuscate rather than illuminate how women grapple with and refashion family and community in advantageous ways. For example, at the turn of the century, historian Deborah Gray White avers, black club women fiercely debated women's place in the uplift movement and many concluded that "a woman exercised her greatest influence on behalf of the race in her role as wife, mother, and teacher." For them, "this did not imply notions of woman's inferiority to man," because, as club woman Alice White points out, "woman is man's equal intellectually."[48] Moreover, most black women during the 1920s did not passively surrender to the will and whims of black men. The history of black female and black male ideological and relational differences, which extended across class and geographical lines, is a testament that black women were active and assertive in varying ways.

Jacques-Garvey's feminism must be understood within this historical and cultural paradigm. Certainly, cultural essentialism is haunting, and a totalizing vision of black people is also problematic; nonetheless, for Garveyites, submissive and docile behavior was not only an antithesis to a progressive black identity (based on phenotype and a cultural commitment to the black world) but to nation-building, which required purposeful agency—a combination of leaders and supporters—from all its members. As a community feminist, Jacques-Garvey assisted black women in reconciling these two paths, helpmate and leader, by exposing the underlying unity of their roles.

One of the reasons that Jacques-Garvey was able to expend so much energy in the Pan-African struggle during the 1920s was that she had not yet become a mother to children of her own, although she may have seen herself as a mother to the race. Her writings on motherhood most closely resemble those of black club women of the period.[49] Together, their words articulate the need for properly reared children. Jacques-Garvey observed that "ill-bred children are a menace to any country because they develop into individuals who take on vices that often wreck their homes and endanger the safety of their communities."[50] She viewed proper guidance of children as important not just for race betterment, as black club women preached, but to bring character, dignity, and skills to their future nation in Africa. It was primarily the mother who shaped the minds of her children, and—not surprisingly—Jacques-Garvey maintained that the most efficient, organized, and prepared woman to handle this monumental task was an educated woman.

When Jacques-Garvey wrote about the educated mother, she repeated her cry that women should "be given every opportunity to develop intellectually so that their off-spring may inherit such a quality."[51] Nevertheless, educational opportunities for the masses of black women were few and far between. Jacques-Garvey responded to this reality with suggestions on how women could create avenues to learn, as well as gather information and share it with their children. For example, she was an avid reader and instructed women to cultivate a "taste for serious reading." Women were told not to throw away newspapers but to "put a wrapper on it and mail it to others."[52] Books should be sent as gifts, and mothers should tell children stories from their own reading material. Reading should become a family event. Jacques-Garvey knew from her own childhood experience that this was possible for all families. Her father had stimulated her intellect, and she believed all parents, particularly mothers, had the same obligation to their children.[53] In one editorial, she noted, "Meek docile women usually rear puny, effeminate men, and ignorance certainly begets ignorance."[54] As a community feminist, Jacques-Garvey advocated educating mothers not for self and personal privilege but community advancement.

Jacques-Garvey's child-rearing advice was similar to the strategies developed within middle-class African-American families of the period. These young women, who believed they had unlimited possibilities, were expected to be "self-confident, high achieving, socially responsible adults" and to link "individual success to community development."[55] Jacques-Garvey recognized that working-class black women, the rank-and-file membership of the UNIA, lacked the individual resources to overwhelmingly change their reality, so her advice served as a means to empower the women who were most constrained.

Jacques-Garvey clearly had opinions about all areas connected to Pan-African thought and the redemption of Africa. And while most of her editorials addressed the roles of women, she knew she also had to deal directly with men. Motivating black men could be a difficult task, Jacques-Garvey believed, because they lacked faith in themselves and their potential. She wrote that they had lost the "incentive to achieve big things and produced an over burdened womanhood" and the race was that "much poorer because of their slothfulness."[56] And while Jacques-Garvey was sympathetic to black men's plight, she gave them little room to excuse or justify counterproductive behavior and lack of action. Her chastisement of black men, at times, was harsh and aggressive.

Never short on demonstrative descriptions of black men, many of Jacques-Garvey's editorials refer to them with such words as "selfish," "unappreciative," "lazy," "parasites," and "petty."[57] Deborah Gray White has called attention to the fact that club women, although they challenged patriarchy, never mounted "a malevolent attack against black men."[58] Jacques-Garvey, to the contrary, pitched an assault from every possible angle, ranging from their inability to provide for and protect black women to their lack of appreciation for their mothers and wives. Simultaneously, she consoled black women who suffered because of "the lethargy of [black] men, who are content to be servants, dependents all their lives, and lack the pluck to go out and create positions for themselves."[59] One interpretation of this vehemence is that Jacques-Garvey's ultimate goal was to motivate black women to stay on course in the redemption of Africa, and she believed that black men were failing to honor their women in this task. In the editorial "Listen Women!" Jacques-Garvey hoped to inspire women by counseling them not to let the "apathy of your men discourage you, as black women bore the rigors of slavery so will you bear the hardship preparatory to nationhood."[60]

As Jacques-Garvey unleashed her volley against black men, she often fell into the trap of comparing them to white men. Although she identified white men as oppressors, she too frequently wanted black men to emulate their behavior because she (like her husband) believed it would be advantageous for the race. In one editorial, she stated, "White men are the greatest pioneers of the age. They will brave hell itself to satisfy their women; this desire to please them is actuated by their love and respect for them." If black men "would place the right value on their women, they, too, would feel that there is nothing on God's green earth too good to give them."[61]

To understand this attitude, we need to remember that the UNIA was also a procapitalist movement, and Jacques-Garvey wanted black women to reap the same material benefits that she believed white women had. She projected this position with the following statement, "White men . . . idolize their women and for them they will dare anything in order to merit their looks of admiration." She continued, "They have braved the tropical jungles, slain black men, in order to get gold and diamonds with which to adorn their women; they have ventured forth into the Arctic regions so that she may have beautiful furs to keep her warm; they have exterminated the red Indians in North America, and build up a great republic, so that their women may live in comfort and luxury."[62]

Jacques-Garvey's editorials suggest that she joined other black women—more precisely, 1920s classic blues singers—who connected grand attire with power. Literary scholar Hazel V. Carby has contended that the physical presence of these performers was a "crucial aspect of their power." One way that they reclaimed their "female sexuality from being an objectification of male desire to a representation of female desire" was to wear glittered dresses, furs, and diamonds.[63] Jacques-Garvey was not known as a woman who draped herself with jewelry and expensive clothes; nonetheless, she believed that the devaluation of black womanhood was a global issue that called for redress. Accordingly, she wrote that black women were entitled to everything the world had to offer, including what adorned the bodies of elite white women, and, in some instances, successful women blues singers. Her raw description of the alleged motivation of white men seeking wealth undoubtedly had to capture her readership's imagination and encouraged them to think about why they were impoverished in the midst of abundance.

Jacques-Garvey's opinions of black men in many ways expose the contradictions of the UNIA in general. Although she criticized white men for being "racially selfish," she wanted black men to have similar zeal in pursuing the redemption of Africa. She was adamant that men, just like women, had to fulfill certain gender-specific roles. "Black men you are failing on your jobs! Measure height of achievement and breadth of usefulness with others, and be honest enough to admit your laziness." The world "expects men to play a man's part and is fed up on your whining and 'can't-be-done' moans. Be real men, honest, sincere, determined and straight away the race will be lifted up in the estimation of others who respect those who respect themselves."[64]

While Jacques-Garvey's stance is not completely out of step with the attitudes of other UNIA women, it is one that blames black men (which included Garvey), as opposed to racism and colonialism, and appears inconsistent at points.[65] It is puzzling, for example, that she called on black women to support the same men whom she frequently described as unworthy and inept.

In addition, she continually expressed her desire for black men to read the woman's page and respect the ideas put forth there—but no man would want to be bombarded by such scathing, generalized attacks (nor would such opinions be likely to convince them of women's intellect).

No doubt Jacques-Garvey had an ambivalent relationship with patriarchal traditions. As we have seen, she rebuffed notions that women should be confined to the domestic sphere, but she based her idea of male roles exclusively on white patriarchal standards. Men should be breadwinners, she put forth, so that women would have the choice not to work outside the home. She further observed that "white women have greater opportunities to display their ability because of the standing of their men."[66] She wrote that "black women [would] come out of Miss Ann's kitchen, leave her washtub, and preside over their own homes," if their men would "bring home the bacon."[67] Understanding the economic state of the black diaspora and Africa was not enough to squash her repulsion toward the black man who "is always out of a job because he is too lazy to go out and make a job for himself; he prefers to hang around the white man's factory doors begging for a job, and oftimes [sic] gets what he deserves—a kick."[68] Jacques-Garvey's statements against black men moved beyond the anger expressed by some blues singers whose lyrics critiqued male infidelity and desertion. Her rage was not just about intimate personal relationships, but, moreover, an indictment against all black men who fell below her standards. In essence, not only were her words a message for black men, but they also instructed women readers to refashion the helpmate role, empowering them to critique their husbands' behaviors.

Similar to many journalists, Jacques-Garvey's writings were largely shaped by current events and circumstances. She published the majority of her editorials while Garvey was in jail on mail fraud charges. In her effort to make sure the UNIA remained a formidable organization, Jacques-Garvey had heated confrontations with acting UNIA president-general William Sherrill in addition to conflicts with other male leaders whom she believed lacked respect for her intellectual prowess. When she was not writing, she served as the chief organizer in the campaign to release her husband from prison. Jacques-Garvey explained, "I had to do everything possible to get money for his defense fund, which was not only to pay legal expenses, but to keep him in the Southern prison in a manner that made his confinement tolerable."[69] When the Garveys realized they needed a "device" to clear his negative reputation and raise money, she edited and published two volumes of *The Philosophy and Opinions of Marcus Garvey* (1923 and 1925). She also lectured across the country to garner public support for him and the UNIA. Decades later, Jacques-Garvey added her husband to her list of

men who lacked appreciation for noble women. As she wrote in her memoir, *Garvey and Garveyism* (1970), "The value of a wife to him was like a gold coin—expendable, to get what he wanted, and hard enough to withstand rough usage in the process."[70]

In addition to the physical and emotional stresses and demands of keeping up with this schedule while her husband was jailed, Jacques-Garvey had to cope with challenges to her involvement from men within the UNIA. She believed that the designated male leaders were not carrying out their duties and that she had to pick up their slack. These tensions with black male leaders carried over into her writings. She was angry and hurt that they did not appreciate her diligent work on behalf of the organization.

Jacques-Garvey's resentfulness and anger can be better understood by examining an earlier written exchange with male UNIA leaders and drawing on the writings of journalist Anne Witte Garland. Garland documented how anger can be a principal motivator underlying activists' thinking and behavior. After interviewing a number of contemporary activists, she concluded that "anger is often at the center of their transformations from private actors in restricted universes to encompassing all the important issues of the day."[71] Jacques-Garvey created a space to release her indignation through her editorials. While at times her attack was venomous, she must be commended for never doubting that she deserved a place in the movement as a leader and a critic of chauvinistic men.

When Jacques-Garvey stepped outside her role as wife and took a leadership position within the UNIA, she provoked criticism from some of the organization's disgruntled male membership. Although she was never elected to a UNIA office, she clearly controlled the organization's affairs. Soon after Garvey's first arrest in 1923, Jacques-Garvey was forced to defend publicly her expanded role within the organization. Several men detailed their—and perhaps others'— dissatisfaction with her in a published commentary entitled, "Look Out for Mud." The snipe, dated 14 July 1923, stated that Garvey "had designated three men among the chosen officers of the association to be responsible heads during his absence. Mrs. Garvey is not part of this committee. Mrs. Garvey is not an officer of the association. Mrs. Garvey doesn't actively or passively control the organization." They concluded, "It is beneath the dignity of common decency to attempt to drag the name of an innocent and helpless woman into an arena where she cannot properly defend herself."[72]

In a not-too-roundabout way, these men were, in effect, charging that Jacques-Garvey was functioning as an elected official, but they cloaked their concern in language that appeared to be defending her character as a woman. By raising objections to her role, these men (who espoused self-determination and self-reliance for the "nation" but expected the opposite in gender relations) demonstrated their conviction that politics was men's territory. The piece further defended the male leaders' status within the UNIA.

Jacques-Garvey replied in a letter to the editor, saying "that you have characterized me as helpless. . . . I am innocent of the honor of having the UNIA turned over to me by my husband, but I am not innocent of the depths to which colored men can stoop to further their petty schemes even at the expense of a downtrodden race such as ours." She concluded, "with my unusual general knowledge and experience for a young woman, may I not ask if the word 'helpless' is not misapplied?"[73] Her statement not only publicly questioned the attitude and behavior of male leadership but also focused on her confidence in her skills and intelligence to lead the organization. By placing the onus back on the men, Jacques-Garvey conveyed her sentiments in a way that forced them to rethink their accusations of her stepping beyond her presumed place as a woman.[74] More important, while Jacques-Garvey accepted what she identified as marital responsibilities to Garvey, she refused to allow other men to occupy a position of authority over her. Jacques-Garvey's community feminism empowered her to establish personal parameters regarding her public and private roles, and only her husband had the right to question her decisions.

In sum, Jacques-Garvey's editorials reflected her opinions on black women's multiple roles within the Pan-African movement. Throughout her editorials, she identified innate qualities in black women that enabled them to fulfill a host of duties. Not surprising, perhaps, she possessed the majority of these traits. She consciously personified the epitome of the type of black woman that the UNIA needed—an intelligent, industrious woman, willing to sacrifice self to better her home, community, and nation.

Jacques-Garvey also generalized from her own experience in identifying her expectations for others. Unwavering as a helpmate to her husband, she expected all women to fulfill this role, even if it caused them discomfort. She suffered as the wife of the movement's leader, so she expected other women to bear similar crosses. For instance, producing the woman's page "certainly [was] a hardship." She had "to put in eighteen hours of work daily and sometimes [got] only three hours of sleep."[75] Lack of rest magnified her other ailments, and she often complained of eye trouble and was "handicapped" by prolonged illness; eventually, she had an unspecified minor operation. Jacques-Garvey knew that it was difficult to grieve in silence, and she urged women to "find an outlet for one's woes"; however, "strive always to show a calm exterior, thereby you will command [black men's] respect and gain their sympathy."[76]

This advice may sound manipulative and counterproductive. One would think that she shuddered at the thought that someone wasted energy on pity. Based on her record, Jacques-Garvey should have preferred that vigor be placed into productive action for nationhood. Her statement may be out of character, but it reveals a vulnerable side that she labored to keep private. Jacques-Garvey was a sensitive human being despite the no-nonsense image she constructed for the world.

One cannot ignore that occasionally Jacques-Garvey's personal decisions did taint her theory. She too often labored on behalf of Garvey until her physical health was compromised. Similar to other committed activists, she consciously and unconsciously became a sacrificial lamb for Garvey's needs and the UNIA's goals. Jacques-Garvey's acts of self-subordination unfolded in many forms, and these circumstances require that we create concepts to grapple with seemingly problematic forms of feminism that are endemic to a historical moment. The concept of community feminism (which at times resembles a tug-of-war between feminism and nationalism) gives us a channel through which we may observe the larger implications of both Jacques-Garvey's personal choices and her political activism.

Despite Jacques-Garvey's efforts to balance feminism and nationalism—with the coterminous link of the principle of self-determination—her espousal of a liberation narrative that granted women equal status was too often constrained by a rigidly bound nationalistic expression. What took precedence for Jacques-Garvey was an unflinching commitment, both emotionally and ideologically, to the idea that oppressed people of color must claim the divine right to control their homeland's resources, and it did not matter whether men or women took the lead in pursuing the goal.

The pace involved in producing the woman's page and heading the defense committee to pardon Garvey eventually took its toll on Jacques-Garvey. "Our Women and What They Think" ended abruptly on 30 April 1927; Jacques-Garvey remained an associate editor of the *Negro World* for two additional months and a contributing editor thereafter. During her journalistic heyday, Jacques-Garvey's acuteness and skills were top rank and her grasp of international affairs outclassed many renowned intellectuals of the period. Her thoughts about women as leaders and helpmates deserve a place not only in the black intellectual tradition but also early twentieth-century feminist thought. Equally significant, her personal relationship with Garvey, and other black men, generated ideas that both rebuffed male dominance and embraced aspects of patriarchy. For Jacques-Garvey, "real men" were at the very least breadwinners, and true race women possessed a consciousness that allowed them to celebrate a distinct women's culture and femininity, but not be limited by it, in order to develop the black nation.

As a community feminist pledged to a Pan-African movement, Amy Jacques-Garvey served as a journalist and editor, rallied support on behalf of Marcus Garvey, gave public speeches, and maintained UNIA affairs. As a female black nationalist, she was not simply a symbol within a movement but an active participant who refused to be silenced and manipulated. Her legacy is recorded in her prolific editorials—written words pregnant with multiple meanings, and just as eclectic as the diaspora of black people whom she loved.

Notes

[1]"Pan-African" and "black nationalism" are interchangeable terms within the context of this article. There is a broad spectrum of debate among scholars who define these terms in relation to the UNIA during the 1920s. Some writers characterize the UNIA as Negro Zionism, a psychological back-to-Africa movement in the United States. For a discussion of the UNIA as a Zionist movement, see John Hope Franklin, *From Slavery to Freedom: A History of Negro Americans*, 3d ed. (New York: Vintage Books, 1969), 492; and Theodore Draper, *The Rediscovery of Black Nationalism* (New York: Viking Press, 1970), 50–56. Other scholars see the UNIA as a full-fledged Pan-African nationalist movement, a universal and international confraternity among black people to end white imperialism. See Theodore G. Vincent, *Black Power and the Garvey Movement* (Berkeley, Calif.: Ramparts Press, 1971), 165–85; and Tony Martin, *Race First: The Ideological and Organizational Struggles of Marcus Garvey and the Universal Negro Improvement Association* (Westport, Conn.: Greenwood Press, 1976), 41–62, 110–40.

Recent evidence supports the notion that during the peak years of the UNIA, in the United States, the movement was a Pan-African movement with political parallels close to Zionism. The UNIA had not only international membership but the philosophy of black political and economic empowerment and an end to white domination and exploitation, with the goal of an African Palestine: Liberia. For a discussion of recent scholarship, see Robert A. Hill and Barbara Bair, eds., *Marcus Garvey, Life and Lessons: A Centennial Companion to the Marcus Garvey and Universal Negro Improvement Association Papers* (Berkeley: University of California Press, 1987), lii–lvi, and Robert A. Hill, ed., *The Marcus Garvey and the Universal Negro Improvement Association Papers*, vols. 3–7 (Berkeley: University of California Press, 1984–1988). See appendixes in these volumes for listings of the national and international membership of the UNIA.

[2]Martin, *Race First*, 14–16.

[3]Amy Jacques-Garvey used a hyphenated last name because Garvey's first wife was also named Amy; thus, she used it to clarify the difference.

[4]Carole Boyce Davies, *Black Women, Writing, and Identity: Migrations of the Subject* (New York: Routledge, 1994), 50.

[5]For a discussion on why the poststructuralist vocabulary emerged in response to macropolitical thinking, see Donna Landry and Gerald MacLean, eds.,

The Spivak Reader: Selected Works of Gayatri Chakravarty Spivak (New York: Routledge, 1996), 49 n. 14.

[6]Penny A. Weiss, "Feminist Reflections on Community," in *Feminism and Community*, ed. Penny A. Weiss and Marilyn Friedman (Philadelphia: Temple University Press, 1995), 3–18, esp. 3.

[7]Cynthia Enloe, *Bananas, Beaches, and Bases: Making Feminist Sense of International Politics* (London: Pandora, 1989), 42, 62.

[8]Ibid., 62.

[9]Davies, *Black Women, Writing, and Identity*, 172.

[10]E. Frances White, "Africa on My Mind: Gender, Counter Discourse, and African-American Nationalism," *Journal of Women's History* 2, no. 1 (1990): 73–97, quotation on 75.

[11]Barbara Bair, "True Women, Real Men: Gender, Ideology, and Social Roles in the Garvey Movement," in *Gendered Domains: Rethinking Public and Private in Women's History*, ed. Dorothy O. Helly and Susan M. Reverby (Ithaca, N.Y.: Cornell University Press, 1992), 154–66, quotation on 155.

[12]Of course, there is no single, monolithic form of patriarchy, but common factors include male control over female labor power, sexist ideology, and gender hierarchy in which men are authoritarian and aggressive.

[13]Stephanie J. Shaw, *What a Woman Ought to Be and to Do: Black Professional Women Workers during the Jim Crow Era* (Chicago: University of Chicago Press, 1996), 119.

[14]Ibid., 111.

[15]Elsa Barkley Brown, "Mothers in Mind," in *Double Stitch: Black Women Write about Mothers and Daughters*, ed. Patricia Bell-Scott et al. (New York: Harper Perennial, 1991), 86–89, quotation on 87.

[16]Many scholars have described this phenomenon without naming it community feminism. See, for example, Patricia Hill Collins, *Black Feminist Thought: Knowledge, Consciousness, and the Politics of Empowerment* (New York: Routledge, 1991); and Katie G. Canon, *Black Womanist Ethics* (Atlanta, Ga.: Scholars Press, 1988).

[17]The *Negro World*, established in January 1918 and published in Harlem, New York, was the UNIA's most effective weekly propaganda newspaper. The UNIA published other weeklies, but not at the same time.

[18][T. Thomas Fortune], "Mrs. Garvey Confined to Her Home," *Negro World*, 29 November 1924, 8.

[19]For example, see the woman's column in both the *Chicago Defender* and *New York Age* for the period between 1920 and 1928.

[20]Amy Jacques-Garvey, "Our Page Is Three Years Old," *Negro World*, 12 February 1927, 7.

[21]Amy Jacques-Garvey, "Send in Your Articles for This Page," *Negro World*, 6 February 1926, 7.

[22]Jacques-Garvey, "Our Page Is Three Years Old," 10.

[23]Amy Jacques-Garvey, "Have a Heart," *Negro World*, 7 June 1924, 7.

[24]W. E. B. DuBois, *The Education of Black People: Ten Critiques, 1906-1960* (Amherst: University of Massachusetts Press, 1973), 32.

[25]Jacques-Garvey, "Have a Heart," 7.

[26]Amy Jacques-Garvey, "Can Ghandhi's Fasting Unite Moslems and Hindus?" *Negro World*, 4 October 1924, 6.

[27]Eleanor Hinton Hoytt, "International Council of Women of the Darker Races: Historical Notes," *Sage* 3, no. 2 (1986): 54–55, quotations on 54.

[28]Deborah Gray White, *Too Heavy a Load: Black Women in Defense of Themselves, 1894–1994* (New York: Norton, 1999), 134, 135.

[29]Wolmers School, *Wolmers Bi-Century Souvenir, 1729–1929* (Kingston, Jamaica: Committee, 1929); and Amy Jacques-Garvey, "The Role of Women in Liberation Struggles," *Massachusetts Review* 13, no. 1/2 (1972): 109–12, quotation on 110.

[30]Amy Jacques–Garvey, "Enslave the Mind and You Enslave the Body," *Negro World*, 20 June 1925, 7.

[31]Jacques-Garvey combined the popular 1920s terms "new woman" and "new Negro" to celebrate the expansion of opportunities and roles for black women during the period. Garveyite women believed that the "new Negro woman" was to "(1) work on par with men in the office and on the platform; (2) practice thrift and economy; (3) teach constructive race doctrine to children; (4) demand absolute respect of the race from all men; [and] (5) teach the young to love race first." Mark D. Matthews, "'Our Women and What They Think': Amy Jacques Garvey and *The Negro World*," *Black Scholar* 10, no. 8/9 (1979): 2–13, quotation on 5.

[32]Ibid.

[33]Amy Jacques-Garvey, "Lifting Up Filipino Women," *Negro World*, 22 November 1924, 8; and Amy Jacques-Garvey, "Have Scientific Achievements of Negroes Benefitted Our Race?" *Negro World*, 8 November 1924, 10.

[34]Amy Jacques-Garvey, "Going to Africa?" *Negro World*, 16 April 1927, 7.

[35]Amy Jacques-Garvey, "No Sex in Brains and Ability," *Negro World*, 27 December 1924, 8. See the works of Paula Giddings and Dorothy C. Salem for a discussion of black women activists, most of whom were identified with the black club movement of the period. Paula Giddings, *When and Where I Enter: The Impact of Black Women on Race and Sex in America* (New York: Morrow, 1984); and Dorothy C. Salem, *To Better Our World: Black Women in Organized Reform, 1890–1920* (Brooklyn, N.Y.: Carlson, 1990).

[36]Mary Helen Washington, "Introduction," to Anna J. Cooper, *A Voice from the South* (1892; reprint, New York: Oxford University Press, 1988), xxvii–liv, quotation on xxvii; and Cooper, *Voice from the South*, 78–79.

[37]Amy Jacques-Garvey, "Women's Function in Life," *Negro World*, 19 December 1925, 7.

[38]Jacques-Garvey "No Sex in Brains and Ability," 8.

[39]Amy Jacques-Garvey, "Will the Entrance of Woman in Politics Affect Home Life?" *Negro World*, 14 June 1924, 12.

[40]Ibid.

[41]Reprints came from a variety of newspapers and magazines, including: *Chicago Tribune, New York Evening Post, New York American, Chicago Daily Worker, New York Daily Worker, New York New Republic,* and *Pennsylvania Survey Graphic.*

[42]Amy Jacques-Garvey, "Woman as Man's Helper," *Negro World*, 28 February 1925, 7.

[43]Ibid.

[44]Amy Jacques-Garvey, "The Joy of Living," *Negro World*, 21 June 1924, 12.

[45]Amy Jacques-Garvey, "Man's Inspiration Is Woman," *Negro World*, 25 June 1927, 4.

[46]Amy Jacques-Garvey, "Why K.K.K. Honors Jews," *Negro World*, 6 September 1924, 16.

[47]Jean Bethke Elshtain, "Feminism, Family, and Community," in *Feminism and Community*, 259–72, esp. 260.

[48]White, *Too Heavy a Load*, 44.

[49]The black women's club movement of the 1890s to 1920s encompassed a variety of activities ranging from offering protection from exploitative employers to bourgeois teas. For a discussion of the black club movement, see Salem, *To Better Our World*; Mildred I. Thompson, *Ida B. Wells-Barnett: An Exploratory Study of an American Black Woman, 1893–1930* (Brooklyn, N.Y.: Carlson, 1990); Beverly Washington Jones, *Quest for Equality: The Life and Writings of Mary Eliza Church Terrell, 1883–1954* (Brooklyn, N.Y.: Carlson, 1990); and White, *Too Heavy a Load.*

[50]Amy Jacques-Garvey, "Duties of Parents to Children," *Negro World*, 9 May 1925, 7.

[51]Amy Jacques Garvey, "Women as Cannon Fodder," *Negro World*, 9 February 1924, 10.

[52]Ibid.

[53]Jacques-Garvey, "Role of Women in Liberation Struggles," 110.

[54]Jacques-Garvey, "Women as Cannon Fodder," 10.

[55]Shaw, *What a Woman Ought to Be and to Do*, 10.

[56]Amy Jacques-Garvey, "Listen Women!" *Negro World*, 9 April 1927, 7.

[57]See, for example, Ibid., and Amy Jacques-Garvey, "The Negro Race Needs Trained Men," *Negro World*, 3 July 1926, 5.

[58]Deborah Gray White, "The Cost of Club Work, The Price of Black Feminism," in *Visible Women: New Essays on American Activism*, ed. Nancy A. Hewitt and Suzanne Lebsock (Urbana: University of Illinois Press, 1993), 247–69, quotation on 253.

[59]Jacques-Garvey, "Negro Race Needs Trained Men," 5.

[60]Jacques-Garvey, "Listen Women!" 7.

[61]Amy Jacques-Garvey, "Are Negro Women More Easily Satisfied than White Women?" *Negro World*, 9 May 1925, 7.

[62]Jacques-Garvey, "Listen Women!" 7.

[63]Hazel V. Carby, "'It Jus Be's Dat Way Sometime': The Sexual Politics of Women's Blues" *Radical America* 20, no. 4 (1986): 9–22, quotations on 20.

[64]Jacques-Garvey, "Negro Race Needs Trained Men," 5.

[65]Tony Martin, "Women in the Garvey Movement," in *Garvey: His Work and Impact*, ed. Rupert Lewis and Patrick Bryan (Trenton, N.J.: Africa World Press, 1991), 67–72; and Honor Ford-Smith, "Women and the Garvey Movement in Jamaica," in Ibid., 73–83.

[66]Amy Jacques-Garvey, "Women as Leaders Nationally and Racially," *Negro World*, 24 October 1925, 7.

[67]Jacques-Garvey, "Are Negro Women More Easily Satisfied than White Women?" 7.

[68]Jacques-Garvey, "Listen Women!" 7.

[69]Amy Jacques-Garvey, *Garvey and Garveyism* (New York: Collier Books, 1970), 166.

[70]Ibid., 169; and Amy Jacques-Garvey, ed., *The Philosophy and Opinions of Marcus Garvey* (New York: Universal Publishing House, 1923–1925).

[71]Anne Witte Garland, *Women Activists: Challenging the Abuse of Power* (New York: Feminist Press, 1988), xvi–xvii.

[72]"Look Out for Mud," *Negro World*, 14 July 1923.

[73]Amy Jacques-Garvey, "Mrs. Garvey Replies to the Negro World—Defends Herself against References to Her Being Helpless," *Negro World*, 21 July 1923.

[74]No more articles appeared in the *Negro World* concerning Jacques-Garvey as a UNIA leader after her reply was published.

[75]Amy Jacques-Garvey, "Do Negro Women Want to Express Themselves?" *Negro World*, 11 April 1925, 7.

[76]Amy Jacques-Garvey, "The Busy Have No Time for Tears," *Negro World*, 18 June 1927, 4.

SECTION EIGHT:
SLAVE RESISTANCE AND ABOLITION

Introduction

There has been a growing trend among scholars of slavery in the Americas to debate the impact of slave resistance methods and the whole process that led to the abolition of slavery in the Americas. The complexities of the long history of slave colonies, have led to many academic discussions and a more lively debate among scholars. In some areas, Emancipation Day was ushered in by government decree; in others, it was in conjunction with independence movements. In some slave societies, abolition came immediately; in others, the process was gradual—taking years and sometimes decades. While there may be a wide variety of opinions on the overall effectiveness of one method of resistance over another, it is abundantly clear that the slaves' resistance contributed significantly to the ending of the institution of slavery in all regions of the Americas.

Scholars have argued that African slave emancipation across the Americas was the result of various reasons. The essays in this section examine the critical role that Maroonage and slave revolts had contributing to abolition.

There are two new essays in this section; both deal with Maroonage in the Americas. Anderson re-evaluates the 1965 pioneering essay in English of R. K. Kent entitled "Palmares: An African State in Brazil" written to commemorate the tercentenary anniversary of the death of Nzumbi, the last leader of the Palmares society in the late seventeenth century in northeast Brazil. At the time of the publication, Anderson was a visiting professor of Romance Languages at the University of North Carolina at Chapel Hill. The second essay is Patrick Carroll's "Mandinga: The Evolution of a Mexican Runaway Slave Community, 1735–1827," and describes the most carefully researched Maroon society in Colonial Mexico. Carroll is Professor of History at Corpus Christi State University in Texas and the author of *Blakes in Colonia Vera Cruz: Race, Ethnicity and Regional Development, 1570–1830* (1991).

The third essay in this section on slave resistance and abolition highlights the leading circumstances that led to the Haitian Revolution, which evolved from the Saint Domingue slave revolt of 1791, the only truly successful slave revolt in which the slaves overthrew their masters. The ex-slaves' actions eventually led to the creation of the first independent African Diaspora nation established in the Western Hemisphere, in 1804. David P. Geggus's "The Haitian Revolution" is one of the most concise and compelling essays on this monumental step taken by former slaves. Geggus is Professor of History at the University of Florida at Gainesville and author of many insightful works related to Haitian history. Geggus was Hartly Research Fellow at the University of Southampton,

England, and held fellowships at Oxford University, the British Academy, the Guggenheim Foundation, and the Woodrow Wilson Center. He has been writing about the Haitian Revolution and its effects in the Caribbean for about twenty years. He is author of *Slavery, War, and Revolution: The British Occupation of Saint-Domingue 1793–1798* (1982). His most recent work is co-edited with David B. Gaspar and entitled *A Turbulent Time: The French Revolution and the Greater Caribbean* (1997).

The fourth essay is by Michael L. Conniff and Thomas J. Davis and is entitled "The Abolition of the Atlantic Slave Trade," a highly readable essay that captures the intensity and drama that eventually led to the ending of the official slave trade among the many European nations between 1807 and 1850. This essay was taken from their work *Africans in the Americas: A History of the Black Diaspora (1994*). Conniff is Director of the Institute for Latin American Studies at Auburn University, and his other works include *Black Labor on a White Canal: Panama 1904–1981* (1985), *Urban Politics in Brazil* (1981), *Modern Brazil: Elites and Masses in Historical Perspective* (1989), and *Panama and the United States' Forced Alliance* (1992). Davis was formerly at the State University of New York at Buffalo and is now teaching at Arizona State University. His works include *The New York Conspiracy* (1971) and *A Rumor of Revolt: The "Great Negro Plot" in Colonial New York* (1985).

The fifth essay is Rebecca J. Scott's "Gradual Abolition and the Dynamics of Slave Emancipation in Cuba 1868–1886." Scott's narrative is a carefully argued description of the circumstances that characterized the long, drawn-out process that led to the eventual abolition of slavery in most slave-holding colonies in Latin America. This article first appeared in *Hispanic American Historical Review* (1983). However, Scott presents a more detailed treatment of the Cuban slave experience in her work *Slave Emancipation in Cuba: The Transition to Free Labour 1860–1886* (1985), which is based on her dissertation. Scott is co-author with Frederick Cooper and Thomas C. Hold of *Beyond Slavery: Explorations of Race, Labor and Citizenship in Post Emancipation Societies* (2000). She continues to be one of the leading authorities on emancipation issues in the Americas and has written extensively on this theme.

The last study in this section introduces one of the popular themes on which African Diaspora scholars have been focusing in their attempt to better understand Africans in exile and the forces that shaped their identity. Kim D. Butler's "Abolition and the Politics of Identity in the Afro-Atlantic Diaspora: Toward a Comparative Approach" attempts to compare the common experiences of Africans' response to abolition across the Americas and shows how they moved toward what she called "new collective identities." She examines as case studies the experiences of Afro-Brazilians in Sao Paulo and Salvador. Butler has written extensively about the Afro-Brazilian experience. Her work is an outgrowth of her first book, *Freedoms Given, Freedoms Won: Afro-Brazilians in Post Abolition Sao Paulo and Salvador* (1998).

The Quilombo of Palmares: A New Overview of a Maroon State in Seventeenth-Century Brazil*

Robert Nelson Anderson

Abstract. This article offers a new perspective on the history of the maroon state of Palmares in northeastern Brazil. It adds information and interpretation to R. K. Kent's ground-breaking article "Palmares: An African State in Brazil" published in 1961. The present essay gives an historical narrative summary with commentary on the historiography, describing Afro-Brazilian aspects of the history of Palmares. The purpose is to review and expand upon the historical, linguistic, and cultural context of Palmares and on the sources for the emerging epic material of Zumbi of Palmares.

A epopéia negra hoje é narrada[1]

The twentieth of November 1995 marked the tercentenary of the death of Zumbi, the last leader of the maroon state—or *quilombo*—of Palmares, in northeastern Brazil. This date has loomed large in the popular imagination, since for many Brazilians, especially those of African descent, Zumbi embodies the strongest resistance to the slave-based colonial regime, and, consequently, the struggle for economic and political justice today. The last leader of Palmares has enjoyed an apotheosis as an ethnic hero. The term "apotheosis" is not simply metaphorical here. More than a secular hero, Zumbi is viewed as an ancestor, antecedent in what the outsider might see as a fictive lineage. According to this view, which is African in origin, his spirit is inherently divine and immortal, and is thus worthy of respect from those who consider themselves his descendants. This belief is such that the tercentenary celebrated three hundred years of Zumbi's *immortality*.[2]

Since the establishment of 20 November as National Black Consciousness Day in 1978, popular discourse has increasingly treated Zumbi not only as the premier Afro-Brazilian hero but also as the exemplar of antiracist and anticolonial dogma and praxis.[3] The importance of the tercentenary is widely recognised—seen in the fact that Salvador, the capital of the northeastern state of Bahia, "capital" of Afro-Brazil, and currently host to the world's largest pre-Lenten festival in terms of numbers of tourists, chose Zumbi as the theme for the 1995 *carnaval*. In November 1995 events were held around the country, including a pilgrimage to the site of Palmares in the state of Alagoas, with Brazil's President Fernando Henrique Cardoso speaking in the Municipal Hall in União dos Palmares, the Congresso Continental dos Povos Negros das Américas in São Paulo, and the Movimento Negro Unificado's march on Brasília. These events have underscored the mythic status of Zumbi of Palmares. The significance of this anniversary has also captured the attention of the national and international press.[4]

Scholars interested in Palmares have, however, struggled with a dearth of sources, either primary or secondary. The situation is acute for the English-speaking public: of the few primary and major secondary sources published in Portuguese, Dutch, or Latin, almost none have been translated into English.[5] The Palmares Excavation Project, led by Pedro Paulo A. Funari of the State University of Campinas and Charles E. Orser, Jr., of Illinois State University have conducted preliminary excavations at the site of Palmares. This project promises to illuminate our understanding of the *quilombo*, and presumably its findings will be published in English.[6] However, since R. K. Kent's 1965 article "Palmares: An African State in Brazil," no synopsis of what is known of Palmares has been published in English.[7] Kent's article was groundbreaking in that it was the first scholarly overview of what was known about Palmares available to the English-reading public. Working from primary and secondary sources published in Portuguese or Dutch, Kent summarised information about Palmares. His contribution was to argue, based on historical and linguistic evidence, that Palmares was a successful adaptation of several models of Central African statecraft to the Brazilian context. Kent stated in his conclusion:

> [T]he most apparent significance of Palmares to African history is that an African political system could be transferred to a different content; that it could come to govern not only individuals from a variety of ethnic groups from Africa, but also those born in Brazil, pitch black or almost white, latinized or close to Amerindian roots; and that it could endure for almost a full century against two European powers, Holland and Portugal.[8]

Kent's article was and still is an important starting point for the reader without access to the sources published in Portuguese. It nevertheless contains numerous flaws; as Stuart Schwartz reports, "his translations and ethnographic discussions cannot always be trusted."[9] Schwartz's "Rethinking Palmares" offers new and useful interpretations, especially regarding the etymology of the term "quilombo," tracing the word and the institution back to their Angolan origins.[10] The present essay augments Kent's article with further linguistic, historical, and ethnological interpretation, and corrects several faulty translations. This article also incorporates Schwartz's analysis, adding to the narrative history and linguistic interpretations. It elaborates several issues raised by Schwartz, further describing the Afro-Brazilian character of Palmares. It is hoped that this new exposition will give a firmer foundation for assessing the modern significance of Palmares.

Most of what we know about Palmares comes from accounts of the Dutch and Portuguese campaigns against the quilombo, including those of Bartholomeus Lintz (1640) and Roelox Baro (or Rodolpho Bareo, 1643).[11] In 1645 Captain Johan (or João) Blaer led an expedition against the quilombo, chronicled by his Lieutenent Jurgens Reijmbach, who took over the expedition when Blaer became ill. The Fernão Carrilho expeditions of 1676–77 and contemporary events generated documents from the town council of Alagoas and the captaincy government. The final campaigns against Palmares, including those of Domingos Jorge Velho (1692–94), have also provided information.

One or other combination of these official documents and eyewitness accounts by would-be invaders are the basis for subsequent Brazilian historiography and ethnography, each in turn informed by the ideology and intellectual biases of its time.[12] It is worth noting that, in a tentative way, Zumbi has become a national hero. While primary sources by colonial officials and secondary sources from Rocha Pitta to the present day have tended to see Palmares as a threat to Portuguese colonial sovereignty, and the quilombo's defeat as basically a patriotic victory, even white commentators have lionised the Afro-Brazilian state on occasion. The colonial Rocha Pitta himself refers to Palmares as "a rustic republic, in its way, well-ordered," drawing classical parallels and speaking of the election of its "prince," Zumbi.[13] Taking his cue from Rocha Pitta, Oliveira Martins waxed poetic with republican fervour, expanding the classical analogies, as in the following passage: "Of all of the historical examples of slave protest, Palmares is the most beautiful, the most heroic. It is a black Troy, and its story is an Iliad."[14] Thus, a revisionist view crept into the elite discourse, culminating with Freitas, as suggested by this quote from his conclusion: "These rustic black republics reveal the dream of a social order founded on fraternal equality, and for this reason are incorporated into

the revolutionary tradition of the Brazilian people."[15]

As for the other commentators on Palmares, one may refer to Afonso de Escragnolle Taunay's Preface to Ennes:

If one were to collect all that our historiographers, ancient, modern and contemporary, have written about Palmares, there would be material comparable in volume to an encyclopedia of exceeding dimensions. But the vast majority of these very copious pages is no more than repetition, often most inelegant, on the part of the authors, professionals at taking advantage of the work of others or mere candidates for remuneration of so much per page.[16]

Carneiro, nine years later, put it more succinctly: "Historians in general . . . have limited themselves to repeating the errors of Sebastião da Rocha Pitta."[17] It is safe to say that, aside from the contributions of the authors mentioned above, very little new has been said about the history of Palmares since the middle of the twentieth century. While seeking to avoid the faults identified by Taunay and Carneiro, the synopsis that follows brings some of this material together.

From the earliest time in which Africans were brought forcibly to the New World they resisted bondage by flight, or marronage.[18] It seems that from the earliest arrival of Africans in the captaincies of Alagoas and Pernambuco in Portuguese America slaves had fled to the interior.[19] Towards the end of the sixteenth century, according to Freitas, but no later than 1606, according to Kent, a trickle of runaway slaves had made their way to the interior and there established a mocambo, or maroon settlement, of some reputation.[20] The area of settlement straddled a mountainous area of the coastal forest zone some 30 to 90 kilometres from the coast of present-day northern Alagoas and southern Pernambuco. The region came to be known as "Palmares" due to the preponderance of wild palms there.[21]

In the 1630s the Palmares region received a greater number of fugitive slaves thanks in part to the Dutch invasion of northeastern Brazil.[22] During the Dutch dominion and after the Portuguese reconquest of Pernambuco, completed in 1654, there were occasional incursions into Palmares, without great success. Of special interest are the expeditions that generated the documents mentioned above. At the time of the Lintz expedition, there were two large mocambos and any number of smaller ones.[23] By the time of the Blaer-Reijmbach expedition of 1645 there was at least one large mocambo; another large mocambo had been abandoned three years earlier. The diary of the expedition describes the large "Palmares": It was surrounded by a double palisade with a spike-lined trough inside. This "Palmares" was half a mile long, its street six feet wide. There was a swamp on the north side and large felled trees on the south. There were 220 buildings in the middle of which stood a church, four smithies, and a council house.[24] From captives, they learned something of the ruler of that place:

Their king ruled them with severe justice, not permitting sorcerers among his people, and when some blacks would flee, he would send natives [native blacks] on their trail, and when they were caught, they would be killed, such that fear reigned among them, especially the blacks from Angola. The king also has a house two miles away, with a very abundant farm. He had this house built upon learning of our coming. . . . We asked the blacks how many of their people were there, to which they responded that there were 500 men, in addition to the women and children. We presume that there are some 1,500 inhabitants, according to what we heard from them.[25]

The narrative also includes description of farms and foodstuffs, uses made of the palm, and crafts such as work in straw, gourds, and ceramic. As was so often the case in the long history of wars against Palmares, the soldiers found the settlement virtually abandoned when they arrived; the Palmarinos would receive advance word of expeditions from their spies in the colonial towns and sugar plantations, or *engenhos*.[26]

The external history of Palmares from the expulsion of the Dutch in 1654 to the destruction of Palmares in 1694 is one of frequent Portuguese incursions—sometimes more than one a year—and Palmarino reprisals and raids. Although the "Relação das guerras feitas aos Palmares," from the term of Governor d. Pedro de Almeida, is a troublesome document, as Carneiro states, it is clear from it that in the period 1654 to 1678 there were at least 20 expeditions against Palmares—hardly the "twenty-seven years of relative peace" referred to by Kent.[27] In the internecine peace, Palmarinos traded with their Portuguese neighbours, exchanging foodstuffs and crafts for arms, munitions, and salt.[28] The trade with Palmares was such that many colonials opposed war with the Palmarinos, and in the 1670s there was widespread opinion that establishing peace with Palmares was the best way to achieve stability in the colony.[29] Nevertheless, many local planters feared the predatory raids by Palmarinos, real or potential. They also wished to eliminate the lure of escape that Palmares constantly represented to the plantation slaves. In spite of much vacillation, colonial leaders opted again for the destruction of the *quilombo* and sent militia captain Femio Carrilho against them. Carrilho's campaign of 1676–7 was not only one of the more

devastating, but it also gave us the most substantial descriptions of Palmares.

The "Relação" reported that campaign, mentioning several *mocambos* that constituted Palmares: Zambi, Acotirene or Arotirene, Tabocas, Dambrabanga, Subupira, the royal compound of Macaco, Osenga, Amaro, and Andalaquituche.[30] The Portuguese, as was their wont, named at least some of these towns for the title-holders living there: Zambi (probably Zurnbi), Andalaquituche, brother of "Zambi," and Aqualtune, the mother of the king.[31] Subupira was the *mocambo* of Gana-Zona, brother of the king, a "valorous black man, recognised among those brutes as king as well."[32] Part of the description is worth citing extensively:

They acknowledge themselves to be obedient to one called Ganga-Zumba, which means Great Lord. This one is held to be king and master by all of the rest, both natives of Palmares as well as those who come from the outside. He has a palace, houses for his family, and is attended by guards and officials that royal houses usually have. He is treated with all of the respect of a king and with all of the honours of a lord. Those who come into his presence put their knees to the ground and clap their hands as a sign of recognition and protestation of his excellence. They address him as Majesty and obey him out of admiration. He dwells in his royal town, which they call Macaco ["Monkey"], a name derived from the death dealt to one of these animals in that place. This is the principal town among the remaining towns and settlements. It is wholly fortified by a palisade with embrasures from which they could safely attack combatants. All around the outside was sewn with iron caltrops and such cunning pitfalls that it had imperilled our greatest vigilance. This town occupies a broad area; it is made up of more than 1,500 houses. There is among them a Minister of Justice for the necessary actions, and all of the trapping of any republic is found among them.

And although these barbarians have so forgotten subjugation, they have not wholly lost recognition of the Church. In this town they have a chapel to which they resort in their need, and statues to whom they commend their petitions. When this chapel was entered, there was found a quite well-made statue of the infant Jesus, another of Our Lady of the Conception, and another of Saint Blaise. They choose one of their most *ladinos* whom they venerate as pastor, who baptises them and marries them. The baptism, however, is without the form prescribed by the Church, and their weddings are without the particulars required by natural law. Their appetite is the rule of their choice. Each one has the wives he wants. They are taught some Christian prayers, and the precepts of the faith are observed which are within their capacity. The king who resided in this town was living with three wives, one mulatto and two native [black] women. By the first he had many children, by the others none. The way of dress among them is the same as is observed among us—more or less clothed as the possibilities allow.

This is the main town of Palmares. This is the king who rules them. The other towns are in the charge of potentates and chiefs who govern and reside in them. . . . The second town is called Subupira. In this one governs the king's brother, who is called Zona. It is all fortified with wood and stones [and] comprises more than 800 houses. It occupies an area of nearly one league in length. It is well-watered because the Cachingy River flows through it. This was the place where the blacks prepared for the combat against our assaults. It was wholly circled with pitfalls and to block (in the way of) our thrusts, it was sewn with caltrops.[33]

This excerpt is cited at length, not only for the wealth of information it contains, but because the translation in Kent is riddled with errors and omissions that obscure the meaning of the text. Therefore, Kent's translation should be carefully re-read in light of the present version.[34] First, the architecture of Macaco and Subupira suggests that Palmares was on a constant war-footing. Both towns were surrounded by trenches or pitfalls and caltrops, Subupira had a wood and stone battery, and Macaco had palisades with embrasures. D. Pedro de Almeida's chronicler does not, however, state that the parapets had caltrops.[35] Subupira was a site of military training, but the chronicle makes no mention of arms being forged there.[36] Macaco's fortifications seem to have employed features of both the Buraco de Tatu *mocambo* and the Angolan palisaded *quilombo* which Schwartz contrasts in his article on Bahian *mocambos*.[37] That is, the Palmarino capital made use of the pitfalls and caltrops found in Buraco de Tatu as well as the palisades found in Angola.[38]

The religion of the polity was probably a syncretism of Christian and African belief and practice, and this is conveyed in Kent's translation, despite its shortcomings. I want to clarify the character of this syncretism.[39] Macaco had a chapel to which the Palmarinos resorted when in need, containing statues of apparently Christian figures before which they brought petitions. The Palmarinos did not go to church "whenever time allow[ed]" as Kent states, nor does the chronicler say that the statues were worshipped as such. The pastor was probably *ladino* in the sense that he was at least nominally Catholic, spoke Portuguese, perhaps knew prayers, and was otherwise "acculturated." He may or may not have been "crafty," as Kent renders. The description of the practice of polygamy certainly did not conform to

Portuguese norms. However, for Kent to state that it was "singularly close to the laws of nature" rather than "without the particulars required by natural law" misses an important theological point, i.e., that natural law, as understood by the Church, ordains monogamy, sanctioned by sacramental marriage. The other particulars of belief and practice of African origin that must have been present are not stated. Their presence must be inferred from the sense of distortion or imperfection of Catholic practice sensed and relayed by the chronicler.[40] It is indeed a reasonable hypothesis that Palmares was a diverse and dynamic community as regards religion.

The religious evidence of a creolised Afro-American culture is reinforced by a parallel phenomenon in dress, according to the chronicle: the Palmarinos dressed more or less like the colonials, within their capacity to do so. The description of the royal Palmarino envoy to D. Pedro de Almeida mentions "barbarians" wearing both animal skins and cloth, with various hair styles, including braids, bearing both bows and arrows and firearms.[41] Despite the chronicler describing this as "usual" dress, it is reasonable to assume that on such an occasion the Palmarinos would be in their most festive and martial attire. Fuller details of Palmarino dress and its significance can only be glimpsed and compared with better studied periods and places in Brazil. Engravings and photographs from as late as the nineteenth century reveal a mix of African and European dress among Brazilian slaves.[42] Recently Sílvia Hunold Lara has begun analysing the complex significance of female dress and adornment in colonial Brazil, concluding that this visual language, which signified racial and power relations to the white slave-owning class, had other cultural meanings for the African.[43]

As regards government, the "Relação" clearly refers to Ganga-Zumba as "rei" ("king") and to his residence as a "palácio" ("palace"); the "guards and officials" are those customary for a "royal house," not having "by custom, *casas* which approach those of royalty."[44] The point here is that Kent's translation mitigates the perception held by the Portuguese, not to mention the Palmarinos, that the leaders of Palmares were viewed in some sense as royalty, even if that sense was more African than European. In a gesture of respect towards royalty Palmarinos knelt and clapped hands. They did not beat palm leaves, as Kent states. This gesture was repeated by the Palmarino envoy in Recife.[45] Luís da Câmara Cascudo has commented on praise greeting by prostration and hand clapping in Africa.[46] It would also appear that the principal town of Palmares was christened by and on the occasion of the sacrifice of a monkey. Kent mentions "site initiation with animal blood" in passing in his conclusion, but in no way connects it with the name of the capital town.[47] Thus, a number of errors in transcription and translation muddle intriguing data about what appear to be non-European civil and religious practices.

More seriously, though, the flaws in this translation seem to have affected the nuance of Kent's interesting conclusion, that "Palmares was a *centralized* kingdom with an elected ruler" and that "Ganga-Zumba *delegated territorial power* and *appointed to office*."[48] Admittedly there is nothing in Kent's evidence or analysis that is inconsistent with a view of Palmares as a paramount chiefdom or kingdom along Central African lines, as he has argued. In fact, Kent's assertion that "the political system [of Palmares] did not derive from a particular Central African model, but from several" prefigures Schwartz's later inquiry.[49] What is troubling is that the Portuguese version of the "Relação" suggests a political organisation more complex, even more contradictory than a "centralised" state with "delegated" power imagined by Kent. The "potentates and chiefs" of the other towns, did not govern "in [Ganga-Zumba's] name," as Kent renders; the chronicle says no such thing. In fact, the chronicle suggests confederation and tributary relations among the Palmarino towns, reinforced by what also appear to be lineage or family relations.

The "Relação" states that Palmares had "all the trappings of any Republic."[50] Yet the descriptions of Palmares as a republic with an elective kingship, as though chosen by general suffrage, found in Rocha Pitta, Oliveira Martins, Santos, and Freitas, have scant foundation in the primary sources.[51] Perhaps "republic" should be taken to mean "state," as Nina Rodrigues suggested,"[52] and the election of the king could derive from descriptions of chiefly and bureaucratic checks on the power of the king and the lack of hereditary succession, all of which might look "republican" to the Euro-Brazilian observer. Nothing in this supposition, however, precludes the possibility that the principal chief was elected by the chiefs of the constituent villages or even by popular acclaim, as among the Imbangala of seventeenth-century Angola.

It was Schwartz who noted the connection between the *quilombo* of Brazil and the institution by the same name in Angola (KiMbundu *kilombo*).[53] He synthesised his knowledge of maroons in colonial Brazil with the history of state formation in seventeenth-century Angola as related by Joseph C. Miller.[54] While the more general word for maroon settlement in colonial Brazil is *mocambo* (Kimbundu *mukambo*, "hideout"),[55] the word *quilombo*, referring to the same thing, gains currency only in the late seventeenth century, and then only at first in connection with Palmares.[56] Kent is right to point out that *quilombo is* not the usual designation for "maroon settlement" until the present century. That the term *quilombo* is rarely applied to maroon settlements other than Palmares prior to this century has implications for the arguments concerning African structure of the polity of

Palmares proposed by Kent and subsequent scholars.

In Angola the *kilombo* was originally a male initiation camp and, by extension, a male military society. During the seventeenth century the territory the Portuguese called Angola was disrupted by factors that included the pressure of the Portuguese slave trade and occupation of the coast, by the collapse of states such as the Kingdom of the Kongo to the north, and by invasions principally from the northeast. The people of central Angola responded by coalescing under the name "Imbangala." In contrast to prior states in the area, which crystallised around a royal lineage of divine kings, the nascent Imbangala states gathered together diverse peoples in a lineageless community. Since these communities existed in conditions of military conflict and political upheaval they found in the institution of the *kilombo* a unifying structure suitable for a people under constant military alert.[57] It is clear that the wars in Angola were feeding the slave trade to the northeast of Brazil, a market that expanded to recoup the losses during the Dutch occupation. It is reasonable to assume that many, if not most, of the Palmarinos were the descendants of slaves from Angola, and many may have been recent arrivals from among the Imbangala.[58] Indeed, the residents of Palmares called it Angola Janga, supposedly "Little Angola."[59]

Yet, whatever the Central African presence in Palmares, by the second half of the seventeenth century it was clearly a multiethnic and mostly creole community. The population of Palmares in the 1670s appears to have been largely native-born and of African descent.[60] The balance of the population would have been runaway slaves, slaves and free persons captured in raids, colonials who had suffered political reversals as a consequence of the Portuguese reconquest of Pernambuco, and poor free immigrants of all racial backgrounds.[61] Preliminary results of the Palmares Excavation project also confirm a strong indigenous American presence, presumably among the women.[62]

During this time the paramount chief of Palmares was Ganga-Zumba, probably a title rather than a proper name. As Schwartz and Miller have noted *nganga a nzumbi* was a religious title among the Imbangala, one whose responsibilities included relieving sufferings caused by an unhappy spirit of a lineage ancestor.[63] In a fundamentally lineageless society like the Imbangala—or the colonial maroon—this official would have great importance, as it would fall to him to appease those ancestral spirits who had been cut loose from their descendants and had therefore been deprived of family propitiation. Schwartz speculates that Ganga-Zumba of Palmares held such an office. Despite the title and apparent official function of Bantu origin, the Ganga-Zumba known to history may have been a native Palmarino of the Ardra nation, identifiable with the Ewe-speaking Allada state on the Slave Coast.[64]

Zumbi was the war commander of Palmares under Ganga-Zumba. Freitas gives a biographical portrait of Zumbi which has often been repeated as fact, while raising doubts among scholars about its veracity.[65] The suspicion is justifiable: although Freitas cites numerous published and manuscript sources in his bibliography, there is little rigour in citation of sources in the narrative. For example, Freitas works from "various letters" written by Priest Antônio Melo, without giving the disposition of those letters. However, journalists reporting from Portugal for the Folha de São Paulo tentatively corroborate the existence of Father Melo's letters: one in the Arquivo Historíco Ultramarino and several in the possession of Graziela de Cadaval, Countess of Schonborn, not seen by the reporters but copied with permission by Freitas.[66] Freitas writes that Zumbi was born in 1655. That same year Brás da Rocha Cardoso led the first Portuguese attack on Palmares after the expulsion of the Dutch. During that otherwise ineffective and unremarkable attack, a baby boy, native to Palmares, was captured and later given to Father Melo in the coastal town of Porto Calvo. The boy, baptised Francisco by the priest, was raised as the priest's protégé and instructed in Portuguese, Latin, and other subjects. At the age of fifteen, in 1670, the youth ran away to Palmares, although he later continued to pay the priest secret visits.

Francisco reemerges in Governor d. Pedro de Almeida's chronicle as "Zambi," the "general das armas" of Palmares.[67] During the campaign led by Sergeant-Major Manuel Lopes (Galvão) in 1675–76, "Zambi" suffered a leg wound that left him with a limp.[68] He is described as a "black man of singular valour, great spirit, and rare constancy. He is the overseer of the rest, because his industry, judgement, and strength to our people serve as an obstacle; to his, as an example."[69] A document received by the Conselho Ultramarino, partially cited in Freitas, attributes Palmares's resistance to "military practice made warlike in the discipline of their captain and general, Zumbi, who made them very handy in use of all arms, of which they have many and in great quantity—firearms, as well as swords, lances, and arrows."[70]

The historical record has helped to confuse the issue of proper names at Palmares. It is uncertain whether "Zumbi" was a proper name, title, epithet, or praise name. Freitas advances the idea that it was not a title but a given name or even nickname, since there is only one person known to history as Zumbi, and his name occurs in the record only between 1675 and 1695.[71] This is notwithstanding the account of the Carrilho expedition which mentions the capture of a "Zambi," "a son of the king," who was patently not the general "Zambi" wounded two years earlier.[72] However, there could be confusion here with one Matias Dambi mentioned later, referred to somewhat ambiguously as Ganga-Zumba's father-in-law.[73] The question arises as to whether or not we are dealing in fact with a family name or title, especially where the notorious difficulty of translating kinship terms and titles could have muddled the historical record. In the official documents, the name appears variously as "Zumbi," "Zambi," "Zombi," and "Zomby." Earlier orthography did not indicate stress consistently, so it is possible that the name was stressed on the penultimate syllable, as in KiMbundu, rather than the last, as is customary today.

The seemingly petty uncertainty about the vowel and stress reveals a tangle of uncertainty about the significance of the name. Nzambi is the usual KiMbundu name for the Supreme Being. In KiKongo nzambi means "spirit," and is qualified when referring to the Supreme Being as Nzambi Mpungo or "Highest Spirit."[74] The Brazilian forms of both names Zâmbi and Zambiampungo occur to this day in the Bantu-influenced religions of Brazil.[75] Therefore, deification of Zumbi would appear to be set in motion by his very name. But the situation is more complex yet. In KiMbundu, while Nzambi refers narrowly to the Supreme Being, the word nzumbi means "ancestral spirit," as noted in connection with the religious title nganga a nzumbi above. The nzumbi is similar, if not identical, to the category of spirit that the BaKongo call in the singular n'kulu.[76] In Central African culture a nzumbi demands special propitiatory attention, lest it disturb its descendants. Often European observers have only partially understood the nature of this spirit. For example, Albino Alves gives the following definition of "ndjumbi": "spirit of a person who, murdered without blame, later enters the body of the children of the murderer and kills them, until it is placated by a sacrifice."[77] For this reason, the KiMbundu nzumbi has often been mistranslated as "evil spirit." It is this sense that is usually meant in Brazil by zumbi.[78] Colloquially in Brazil zumbi also refers to someone with nocturnal inclinations.[79] We could also compare the etymology of the word to the cognate Haitian zombi and all of the meanings and connotations that "zombie" has acquired in English.[80] It is a matter of speculation how Zumbi came to receive his name, but there can be little doubt that his compatriots viewed the name within the paradigm of the cult of ancestors. Perhaps, if Freitas's biography is accurate, Francisco/Zumbi had figuratively returned from the dead when he returned to Palmares. To the sugar plantation owners and colonial officials, however, Zumbi was surely the "evil spirit" of folklore, descending at night to wreak havoc on their patrimony. This polysemy of the name Zumbi, born of cultural difference, continues to the present.

A similar confusion surrounds the name "Ganga-Zumba." While this is probably the Imbangala religious title *nganga a nzumbi,* as stated above, "Ganga-Zumba" is usually rendered incorrectly in the Portuguese sources as "Great Lord."[81] The KiMbundu title for respectful address is *ngana,* approximately "sir," "lord," or nowadays, "mister." It is not clear however how "Zumba" could translate "great." A KiMbundu epithet for the Supreme Being is *Ngana Nzambi,* the Christian translation of which is "Lord God" (cf. *Nzambi* above). Héli Chatelain records a story in which the character Ngana Fenda Maria is accosted by a voice from the sky while travelling, to whom she replies, "inga u mutu, inga u nzumbi, inga eie Ngana Nzambi, ngaiola (Whether thou be a person, whether thou be a ghost [sic], whether thou be the Lord God, I am going")." [82] The similarity between these names might lead one to equate Ngana Nzambi with Ganga-Zumba. In fact, sources occasionally give the Palmarino king's name as "Ganga-Zumbi," thus utterly confusing the names (or titles) of the only two leaders of Palmares known to history. In any case, confusion of these two names with names for the Supreme Being and other supernatural beings of the Central African ethos have contributed to the apotheosis of Ganga-Zumba and Zumbi in much of the subsequent cultural production of an epic or heroic nature.

Ganga-Zumba was wounded in an attack on the *mocambo* of Amaro in November 1677, and a number of his sons, nephews, and grandchildren were captured.[83] The destruction wrought by Carrilho must have had an effect. In 1678, Ganga-Zumba, tired of war, accepted terms of peace from the governor of Pernambuco, which affirmed his sovereignty over his people on the condition that he return any fugitive slaves and move his people from Palmares to the Cucaú Valley.[84] Sometime thereafter, Ganga-Zumba and his followers relocated to the Cucaú Valley, closer to the watchful eye of the colonial government.

However, Ganga-Zumba's treaty did not gain peace. An opposition faction preferred resistance to removal. A bann from Sergeant-Major Manuel Lopes, dated 1680, called on "Captain Zumbi" and other rebels to cease their uprising, to adhere to the terms of the treaty, and to join his uncle, Gana-Zona.[85] The document also affirms that in 1680 Zumbi or his partisans had poisoned their king "Ganazumba." Kent viewed this last act as a "palace revolt."[86] Clearly, Ganga-Zumba's concessions had provoked a rift in Palmares, but the death may also be viewed as the widespread African practice of sanctioned regicide, the severest penalty for royal weakness or abuse of power. Zumbi, until then a chief and military commander, occupied the capital and was proclaimed supreme chief. He immediately set about prosecuting the defensive war against the Portuguese, ruling Palmares with dictatorial authority.[87] Zumbi thus ruled Palmares from the time of Ganga-Zumba's move to Cucaú to the destruction of Palmares in 1694.

The broken peace eventually precipitated the enlistment of the aid of the "Bush Captain" Domingos Jorge Velho.[88] This *bandeirante*—or wilderness tamer—from São Paulo, and his irregulars joined forces raised in the northeast for an assault on Palmares in 1692. In late 1693, after the defeat the year before, a new combined expeditionary force gathered in Porto Calvo. When they reached the heavy fortification of the royal compound of Macaco, they laid siege for 22 days. The attackers were building a counter-fortification in order to move their canon within range of the compound palisade when the Palmarinos began abandoning their positions, either to attack from the rear or in order to flee through a break in the opposing fortification.[89] In the ensuing battle on 5–6 February 1994, Jorge Velho took some 400 prisoners. Another 300 died in battle, while some 200 hurled themselves or were forced from the precipice at the rear of the compound. In all, some 500 Palmarinos were killed and over 500 total were taken prisoner in the campaign.[90]

Zumbi had escaped this fatal battle. He continued to skirmish with the Portuguese for over a year, until one of his aides revealed his location. There Zumbi and a small band of followers were ambushed and killed. His mutilated body was identified in Porto Calvo. Then his head was taken to Recife, the capital of Pernambuco, and displayed as proof against claims of his immortality.[91] Jorge Velho fixed the date of Zumbi's death at 20 November 1695.[92]

These events recorded and republished in the historical record over the last four centuries provide the epic material of Zumbi of Palmares. Since the seventeenth century later accretions and variants have been incorporated into the textual tradition. A case in point is the alternate version of Zumbi's death, in which Zumbi allegedly hurled himself from the precipice during the final assault on Macaco to avoid capture. The story was committed to history by Rocha Pitta, who claimed to have learned it from a survivor. This romantic episode has been repeated by several secondary sources, and has been incorporated into some artistic works on Palmares. The version has its basis in the statements by eyewitnesses that a number of Zumbi's compatriots met a similar fate. While the secondary sources coincide in great measure of their detail, they also contain internal contradictions and ambiguities. Together the primary and secondary sources have woven the text that became the authorised history of Palmares, at times describing the state in ahistorical terms that obscure the fact that *quilombos* existed in the Palmares region for at least 150 years. This ahistorical conflation of detail has contributed in effect to the mythification of Palmares.

The historiography of Palmares is necessarily elite historiography. We do not know of any surviving accounts of Palmares by Palmarinos. The record of popular oral history is scant although it certainly exists. Notable is a report by Arthur Ramos on a popular pageant performed in Pilar, Alagoas, as late as the 1930s.[93] Also Carolina Maria de Jesus recalls her unschooled grandfather telling her of Zumbi's battle against slavery.[94] The Bahian *afoxés* of the turn of the century celebrated Zumbi as a hero.[95] In the absence of more information, however, it is impossible to say how much the existing works about Palmares owe to oral literature uninformed by erudite scholarship. These historiographic facts mean that nowadays activists, artists, and scholars desirous of avoiding Eurocentric accounts have had to rely on documents written by outsiders. This has not prevented them from appropriating that elite discourse, and doing so frequently. One could argue that they have little choice in the matter, and that such a strategy is nevertheless subversive.

However, I would add that the historical record offers ample evidence within a small corpus that at least suggests creole Brazilian alternatives, many ultimately of African origins. While subsequent generations have added interpretations and mythic accretions to this record, they have not necessarily contradicted the Afro-Brazilian character of the community that was Palmares. It would appear then that in mature Palmares Central African titles and political and public ritual practices prevailed among a heterogeneous creole population. This seeming incongruity is explained by the very continuity of the *kilombo/quilombo* discussed by Schwartz. The flexibility of the institution of the Kilombo as a mechanism for integrating a lineageless community engaged in warfare and self-defence, as was Palmares, explains why some adaptation of the Imbangala institution would thrive in Brazil, even if only a minority of Palmares's inhabitants were actually Imbangala. It has been faulty logic to assume that because Bantu evidence exists in titles, toponymy, and cultural practices, that Central African-born Bantus necessarily predominated in Palmares, and that Palmares was conservatively Central African. Whatever the ethnic composition of Palmares at any given time, one can make the case that certain African cultural forms and practices lent themselves to adaptation to the problematic of the New World. In this instance, the Central African solution of the *quilombo* served the Brazilian maroons, uniting *malungos*, or comrades, from diverse ethnic backgrounds, not on the basis of lineage, but for the purposes of commodity production, raiding, and self-defence. The persistence and adaptation of African cultural elements such as the *quilombo* to the Afro-Brazilian creole context, in fact, demonstrates the continuity of African and African Diasporic cultures in the process of New World transculturation.[96]

Such has been the grist for the mills of historians, ethnographers, artists, and activists, regardless of their ideological formations and pragmatic aims. Better descriptions of the continuity and elaboration of Central African cultural forms in the Brazilian *quilombo* depend on future primary research on Palmares and other Brazilian maroons. Doubtless we all stand to learn much from the efforts of those in disciplines such as folklore, oral history, and archaeology. Archives in Brazil, Portugal, and Angola have a wealth of information yet to yield. In the meantime, activists, artists, and intellectuals concerned with the experience of the African in Brazil have made a bounty of a poor man's charity. Appropriating the historical record they have undertaken to fashion the epic of Zumbi of Palmares.

Notes

*This work was made possible in part by funds from the Tinker Foundation, the Mellon Foundation, and the US Department of Education Title VI, administered by the Duke University of North Carolina Program in Latin American Studies. I am grateful to John Charles Chasteen and two anonymous referees for their comments on earlier versions of this article.

[1]Xuxu (Edson Carvalho), "Negros de luz," in Ilê Aiyê (ed.), *América negra: "o sonho africano* (Salvador, 1993), p. 28

[2]Bujão (Raimundo Gonçalves dos Santos), personal communication. Full discussion of the mythification of Zumbi or its representation in artistic production is beyond the scope of this essay. See Robert Nelson Anderson, "The Muses of Chaos and Destruction of *Arena conta Zumbi*," *Latin American Theatre Review*, vol. 29, no. 2 (forthcoming 1996); "O mito de Zumbi: Implicações culturais para o Brasil e para a Diáspora Africana," *Afro-Asia*, no. 17 (forthcoming 1996).

[3]Originally called Zumbi Day. See George Reid Andrews, *Black and Whites in São Paulo, Brazil, 1888–1988* (Madison, 1991), pp. 216–18; Abdias do Nascimento and Elisa Larkin do Nascimento, "Pan-Africanism, Negritude, and the African Experience in Brazil," in *Africans in Brazil: A Pan-African Perspective* (Trenton, N.J., 1992), pp. 81–117.

[4]E.g.: Vilma Gryzinski, "O mais novo herói do Brasil," *Veja*, 22 Nov. 1995, pp. 64–80; articles in *Folha de São Paulo*, 12 Nov. 1995, sec. 5 ["Mais!"]; James Brooke, "Brazil Seeks to Return Ancestral Lands to Descendants of Runaway Slaves," *New York Times*, 15 Aug. 1993. sec. A, p. 12; "From Brazil's Misty Past, a Black Hero Emerges," *New York Times*, 23 Nov. 1994, sec. A, p. 4.

[5]On Richard M. Morse's translations of documents about the destruction of Palmares see note 11 below.

[6]Ricardo Bonalume Neto, "O pequeno Brasil de Palmares," *Folha de São Paulo*, 4 June 1995, sec. 5 ["Mais!"], p. 16.

[7]R. K. Kent, "Palmares: An African State in Brazil," in Richard Price (ed.), *Maroon Societies: Rebel Slave Communities in the Americas*, 1st ed. (Garden City, N.Y., 1973), 2nd ed. (Baltimore, 1979), pp. 170–90. Originally published in *Journal of African History*, no. 6 (1965), pp. 161–75.

[8]Kent, "Palmares," p. 188.

[9]Stuart B. Schwartz, *Slaves, Peasants, and Rebels: Reconsidering Brazilian Slavery* (Urbana, Ill., 1992), p. 134, n. 65. The English translation of Roger Bastide's *Les Religions Afro-Brésiliennes* includes a short section on Palmares. The historical summary uses the same sources as Kent, and the text concentrates on ethnological interpretation, much of which is interesting. However, as with Kent, some of the linguistic arguments are weak. See Roger Bastide, *The African Religions of Brazil: Towards a Sociological Interpretation of Civilizations*, Helen Sebba (trans.), (Baltimore, 1978), pp. 83–90. Originally published in Paris in 1960.

[10]In Schwartz, *Slaves, Peasants, and Rebels*, pp. 122–36.

[11]Information from the Lintz and Baro expeditions was compiled by Caspar Barlaeus (Gaspar Barleus) and translated into Portuguese by Cláudio Brandão as *História dos feitos recentemente praticados dwante oito anos no Brasil* (Rio de Janeiro, 1940). Originally published as *Rerum per octenium in Brasilia* (1647). The account of the Blaer-Reijmbach expedition was translated from the Dutch and published by Alfredo de Carvalho under the title "Diário da viagem do Capitão João Blaer aos Palmares" in the *Revista do Institute Arqueológico Pernambucano* and reprinted in Edison Carneiro, *O qmilombo dos Palmares 1630–1695*, 1st ed. (São Paulo, 1947), pp. 231–9. Documents from the second *Livro di Vereações da Câmara de Alagôas*, providing additional information about the Carrilho campaign and Zumbi's revolt, are in Carneiro under the title "Os sucessos de 1668 a 1680," pp. 207–30, originally published in *Revista do Instituto Histórico Alagoano* (1875). The "Relação das guerras feitas aos Palmares de Pernambuco no tempo do Governador d. Pedro de Almeida, de 1675 a 1678" is from the Torre do Tombo in Lisbon, reprinted in Carneiro, pp. 187–206, originally published in *Revista do Instituto Histórico Geográfico Brasileiro*, vol. 22 (1959), pp. 303–29. The first edition and the second edition (São Paulo, 1958) of *O quilombo dos Palmares* reproduce the primary sources as an appendix. The third edition (Rio de Janeiro, 1966) is a version of the edition in Spanish, *Guerra de los Palmares* (Mexico, 1946), neither of which includes the appendix. All citations from Carneiro are from the first edition, including references to the documents published therein. Ernesto Ennes published documents spanning 1684 to 1697, dealing with Zumbi's rebellion against Ganga-Zumba and the Portuguese Governor, the destruction of Palmares by Domingos Jorge Velho, and the death of Zumbi in *As guerras nos Palmares: Subsídios para a sua história*, vol. 1, *Domingos Jorge Velho e a "Tróia negra," 1687–1700* (São Paulo, 1938). On the verso of the title page of this edition a second volume is promised, titled "Os primeiros quilombos"; to my knowledge it was never published. Five of the documents in the Ennes collection appear in English translation under the title "The Conquest of Palmares," in Richard M. Morse (ed.), *The Bandeirantes: The Historical Role of the Brazilian Pathfinders* (New York, 1965), pp. 114–26. In citing these and all other sources, the orthography of the published source is maintained.

[12]Notable among these secondary sources are Sebastião da Rocha Pitta, *Historia da América Portugueza desde o anno de mil e quinhentos do seu descobrimento até o de nil e setecentos e vinte e quatro*, 2nd ed. (Lisbon, 1880), originally published in Lisbon (1730), book 8, paragraphs 25–40; Joaquim Pedro de Oliveira Martins, *O Brasil e as colonias portuguezas*, 3rd ed (Lisbon, 1920), originally published in Lisbon (1880), pp. 63–6; Raimundo Nina Rodrigues, *Os africanos no Brasil*, 2nd ed. (São Paulo, 1935), pp. 115–50; Ernesto Ennes, "As guerras nos Palmares," the introduction to his collection of documents; Carneiro, *O quilombo dos Palmares*; Clóvis Moura, *Rebdeliões da senzala: Quilombos, insurreições e guerrilhas* (Rio de Janeiro, 1972), pp. 179–90; Joel Rufino dos Santos, *Zumbo* (São Paulo, 1985); Décio Freitas, *Palmares: a guerra dos escravos*, 5th ed. (Rio de Janeiro, 1982); Benjamin Péret, *O Quilombo de Palmares: Crónica da "República dos Escravos," Brasil, 1640–1695* (Lisbon, 1988), originally published as "O que foi o Quilombo de Palmares?" in *Anhembi* (April and May 1956). Forthcoming are João José Reis and Flávio dos Santos Gomes (eds.), *História do quilombo no Brasil*, as well as Gomes's new documentary history of Palmares. Both Freitas and Gomes have used archival material from the Torre do Tombo, bringing this primary material to a wider public.

[13]Rocha Pitta, *Historia da America Portugueza*, paragraphs 28–9. All translations are mine. The original text follows: "uma república rústica, a sua maneira, bem ordenada."

[14]Oliveira Martins, *O Brasil e as colonias portuguezas;* p. 64. , "[D]e todos os exemplos históricos do protesto de escravo, Palmares é o mais bello, o mais heroico. É uma Troya negra, e a sua história é uma Illiada."

[15]Freitas, *Palmares*, p. 210. "Estas rusticas repúblicas negras desvendam o sonho de uma ordem social alicerçada na igualdade fraternal e estão por isso incorporadas à tradição revolucionária do povo brasileiro."

[16]Taunay, Preface, in Ennes, *As guerras nos Palmares*, pp. 1–2. "Se se coletasse tudo que os nossos historiógrafos antigos, modernos e contemporâneos escreveram sobre Palmares haveria material comparável, pelo volume, a uma enciclopédia de avantajadas dimensões. Mas é que a imensa maioria dessas páginas copiosíssimas não passa de repetição, frequentemente a mais deselegante, por parte de seus autores, profissionais do aproveitamento de alheio esfôrço ou meros candidatos a remuneraço a tanto por página."

[17]Carneiro, *O quilombo dos Palmares*, p. 182. "Os historiadores em geral ... se limitaram a repetir os errores de Sebastião da Rocha Pita."

[18]Price, Introduction, in *Maroon Societies*, p. 1.

[19]Carneiro, *O quilombo dos Palmares*, p. 188.

[20]Freitas, *Palmares*, p. 15 ; Kent, "Palmares," p. 175. On *mocambo* vs. *quilombo*, see below.

[21]Carneiro, *O quilombo dos Palmares*, p. 188. *Palmar* means "palm grove" in Portuguese; plural *palmares*.

[22]Ibid., pp. 33–34.

[23]Kent, "Palmares," p. 177. Notwithstanding the etymology of Palmares given above, the early chronicles appear to use the term "palmar(es)" to signify "*mocambo.*" It is intriguing to speculate how this usage came to be, given that "Palmares's in the early literature also refers to the palm-covered region. In fact, Nieuhof states that there were two forests, one called "Palmares pequenos," with some 6,000 black inhabitants, and the other, "Palmares grandes," with some 5,000 scattered black inhabitants. Johan Nieuhof, *Memorável Viagem maritima e terrtstre ao Brasil*, Moacir N. Vasconcelos (trans.), José Honório Rogrigues (ed.) (São Paulo, 1942), pp. 18–19. Translated from the English and reconciled with the original Dutch *Gedenkweerdige Brasiliaense Zee-en Lant-Reize* (Amsterdam, 1682).

[24]Carneiro, *O quilombo dos Palmares*, pp. 235–6. Kent's translation (p. 177) neglects to mention that the trees to

the south were felled, suggesting clearing for cultivation or defence.

[25]Carneiro, *O quilombo dos Palmares*, p. 236. "[S]eu rei os governava com severa justiça não permitindo feiticeiros entre a sua gente e, quando alguns negros fugiam, mandavalhes creoulos no encalço e, uma vêz pegados, eram mortos, de sorte que entre êles reinava o temor, principalmente os negros de Angola; o rei também tem uma casa distante dali duas milhas, com uma roça muito abundante, casa que fez construir ao saber da nossa vinda. . . . [P]erguntamos aos negros qual o número da sua gente, ao que nos responderam haver 500 homens, além das mulheres e crianças; presumimos que uns pelos outros há 1,500 habitantes, segundo dêles ouvimos." For reasons that are not clear, Kent leaves many words untranslated and unglossed, not to mention mistranscribed. Some of these, such as *grandes* [sic] (p. 178) would be evident to the general reader, but others (*feticeiros* [sic], *crioulos* [sic], ibid.) would not. Carvalho probably followed colonial usage in using "creoulo"/"crioulo" to refer broadly to "native," and more narrowly to "Brazilian-born black." Without the Dutch original it is impossible to determine the exact sense in the context of Palmares. Kent's translation also errs in not stating that the Palmarinos reported their number to be 500 *men, not including* children and women.

[26]Ibid., p. 236.

[27]Ibid., pp. 81–93; Kent, p. 178.

[28]Freitas, *Palmares*, p. 73.

[29]Ibid., pp. 73–5; 105–6.

[30]Carneiro, *O quilombo dos Palmares*, pp. 188. "Subupira" and "Macaco," not "Subupuira" and "Macoco," as in Kent, "Palmares," p. 178. Kent attempts to construct etymologies for these place names, seeking Bantu and indigenous American roots for them (pp. 180–81). His etymologies, though, are unscientific and uncorroborated, and in the cases of Macaco (in fact, Portuguese for "monkey") and Amaro (the name of the *mocambo's* chief), clearly wrong. Such a task is difficult at best, and should not lead to hasty conclusions. Yeda Pessoa de Castro affirms that some Palmarino place names, including Osenga, are of Bantu origin. Castro, "Dimensão dos aportes africanos no Brasil," *Afro-Ásia*, no. 16 (1995), p. 28. I have not yet seen the sources in which she explains their etymologies.

[31]Carneiro, *O quilombo dos Palmares*, p. 197.

[32]Ibid., p. 202. "[N]egro valoroso, e reconhecido daquêles brutos como rei também."

[33]Ibid., pp. 189–90. "[R]econhecem-se todos obedientes a um que se chama o Ganga-Zumba, que quer dizer Senhor Grande; a este têm por seu rei e senhor todos os mais, assim naturais dos Palmares, como vindos de fóra; tern palácio, casas da sua família, é assistido de guardas e oficiais que costumam ter as casas reais. É tratado com todos os respeitos de rei e com todas as honras de senhor. Os que chegam à sua presença põem os joêlhos no chão e batem as palmas das mãos em sinal de reconhecimento e protestação de sua excelência; falam-lhe por Majestade, obedecem-lhe por admiração. Habita a sua cidade real, que chamam o Macaco, nome sortido da morte que naquêle lugar se deu a um animal destes. Esta é a metrópole entre as mais cidades e povoações; está fortificada toda em uma cerca de pau a pique com treneiras [sic] abertas para ofenderem a seu salvo os combatentes; e pela parte de fóra toda se semêa de estrepes de ferro e de fojos tão cavilosos que perigara nêles a maior vigilância; ocupa esta cidade dilatado espaço, fórma-se de mais de 1,500 casas. Há entre êles Ministros de justiça para as execuçoes necessárias e

todos os arremêdos de qualquer República se acham entre êles.

E com serem estes bárbaros tão esquecidos de toda sujeição, não perderam de todo o reconhecimento da Igreja. Nesta cidade têm capela a que recorrem nos seus apertos e imagens a quem recomendam suas tenções. Quando se entrou nesta capela achou-se uma imagem do Menino Jesús muito perfeita; outra de N. S. da Conceição, outra de São Braz. Escolhem um dos mais ladinos, a quem veneram como pároco, que os batisa o os casa. O batismo porém, é sem a fórma determinada pela Igreja e os casamentos sem as singularidades que pede ainda a lei da naturesa. O seu apetite é a regra da sua eleição. Cada um tem as mulheres que quer. Ensinam-se entre êles algumas orações cristãs, observam-se os documentos da fé que cabem na sua capacidade. O rei que nesta cidade assistia estava acomodado com três mulheres, uma mulata e duas creoulas. Da primeira teve muitos filhos, das outras nenhum. O modo de vestir entre si é o mesmo que observam entre nós. Mais ou menos enroupados conforme as possibilidades.

Esta é a principal cidade dos Palmares, este é o rei que os domina; as mais cidades estão a cargo de potentados e cabos móres que as governam e assistem nelas. . . . A segunda cidade chama-se Subupira. Nesta assiste o irmão do rei que se chama Zona. É fortificada toda de madeira e pedras, compreende mais de 800 casas. Ocupa o vão de perto duma legua de comprido. É abundante de águas porque corre por ela o rio Cachingy. Esta era a estância once se preparavarn os negros para o combate de nossos assaltos. Era toda cercada de fojos e por todas as partes, por obviar (vias aos) aos nossos impulsos, estava semeada de estrepes."

[34]See Kent, "Palmares," pp. 179–80.

[35]See also Carneiro, *O quilombo dos Palmares*, p. 197.

[36]See ibid.

[37]Schwartz, "The *Mocambo*: Slave Resistance in Colonial Bahia," in Price, *Maroon Societies*, pp. 202–26. Originally published in *Journal of Social History*, no. 3 (1970), pp. 313–33.

[38]See description and figures, ibid., pp. 220–1.

[39]The notion of "syncretism" has an ancient history in the scholarship on religion and more recently scholars have sought to give the term more rigour. See Carsen Colpe, "Syncretism," in Mircea Eliade (ed.), *The Encyclopedia of Religion*, 16 vols. (New York, 1987), vol. 14, pp. 218–27. For the Brazilian context, see Bastide, *The African Religions of Brazil*, passim. Recently, Leslie Gérald Desmangles used Bastide's categories, renaming the phenomena "symbiosis" by way of describing the nature of Haitian syncretism. Desmangles, *Faces of the Gods: Vodou and Roman Catholicism in Haiti* (Chapel Hill, N.C., 1992), pp. 7–11. There are modes of syncretism, related to the social processes that engender it. For example, syncretism may arise when the hegemonic religious tradition is a protective façade, in which case the metaphor of "veneer" is appropriate. Often, however, the juxtaposed religious traditions are complementary avenues to power and experience, both temporal and metaphysical, as has often been the case in Brazil and Haiti. Finally, there are cases of genuine fusion—the operative metaphor here is amalgam—which have arisen historically. What is sometimes missing in the debates on sociology of religion is that a community may be multimodal in its syncretism. Given the difficulty of interpreting the artifacts of belief and practice from a distant time, which affects research of the prehistory of Afro-Brazilian religions, "syncretism" affords the elasticity necessary to describe the data

without speculating recklessly on the particularities of the phenomena.

[40]See Bastide, *The African Religions of Brazil*, pp. 83–90.

[41]Carneiro, *O quilombo dos Palmares*, p. 203.

[42]Mary Karasch, *Slave Life in Rio de Janeiro, 1800–1850* (Princeton, 1987), passim; Robert Levine (prod.), *Faces of Slavery* (Miami, 1990). Videocassette.

[43]"Sob o signo da cor: Trajes femininos e relaçoes raciais nas cidades de Salvador e Rio de Janeiro," paper delivered at the meeting of the Latin American Studies Association, Washington, D.C., Sept. 1995.

[44]Kent, "Palmares," p. 179.

[45]Carneiro, *O quilombo dos Palmares*, p. 203.

[46]Luís da Câmara Cascudo, "A saudação africana," in *Made in Africa: Pesquisas e notas* (Rio de Janeiro, 1965), pp. 82–9. Carneiro noted the existence of a hand-snapping gesture in West Africa as a sign of vassalage that was also used in the cult of Xangô. Carneiro, p. 43, n. 2.

[47]Kent, "Palmares," p. 188.

[48] Ibid., p. 187. Emphasis added.

[49]Ibid., p. 188.

[50]Carneiro, *O quilombo dos Palmares*, p. 189, cited above. This phrase is very loosely translated by Kent as "their office is duplicated elsewhere."

[51]See Bastide, *The African Religions of Brazil*, p. 87.

[52]Nina Rodrigues, *Os africanos no Brasil*, pp. 120–1.

[53]Schwartz, *Slaves, Peasants, and Rebels*, pp. 122–36.

[54]*Kings and Kinsmen: Early Mbundu States in Angola* (Oxford, 1976).

[55]Antônio Geraldo da Cunha, *Dicionário etimológico Nova Fronteira da língua portuguesa* (Rio de Janeiro, 1982), p. 526.

[56]Schwartz, *Slaves, Peasants, and Rebels*, p. 125. Although as Schwartz points out, colonial choniclers used the phrase "kingdom and quilombo" to refer to Matamba and other Imbangala-influenced polities in seventeenth-century Angola, such that "[q]uilombo was becoming a synonym for a kingdom of a particular type in Angola" (ibid., p. 128).

[57]Schwartz, *Slaves, Peasants, and Rebels*, pp. 125–77; Miller, passim.

[58]Bastide, *The African Religions of Brazil*, pp. 84–5; Schwartz, *Slaves, Peasants, and Rebels*, p. 125.

[59]Ennes, *As guerras nos Palmares*, doc. 54, article 11. I have been unable to confirm the sense of *janga* as "little" in KiKongo or KiMbundu. My best hypothesis is that Angola Janga is from KiMbundu *ngola iadianga*, "first Angola."

[60]Carneiro, *O quilombo dos Palmares*, p. 189; Kent, "Palmares," p. 180.

[61]Freitas, *Palmares*, pp. 182, 185.

[62]Funari, quoted in "Neto."

[63]Miller, pp. 254–5; Schwartz, *Slaves, Peasants, and Rebels*, p. 127. KiMbundu *nganga*, "priest"; *nzumbi*, "ancestor spirit."

[64]Freitas, *Palmares*, p. 102. Freitas, however, does not give the source of this information.

[65]Ibid., pp. 125–7.

[66]Aureliano Biancarelli and Jair Battner, "Pistas dispersas: Milhares de documentos aguardam catalogação," *Folha de São Paulo*, 12 Nov. 1995, sec. 5 ["Mais!"], p. 6; "Arquivo revela que Zumbi sabia latim," ibid., p. 7, initialled "B.A.," presumably Aureliano Biancarelli as well.

[67]Carneiro, *O quilombo dos Palmares*, p. 193.

[68]Freitas, *Palmares*, p. 100; Carneiro, *O quilombo dos Palmares*, p. 193.

[69]Ibid., pp. 193–4. "[N]egro de singular valor, grande ânimo e constância rara. Este é o espectador dos mais, porque a sua indústria, juizo e fortalesa aos nossos serve de embaraço, aos seus de exemplo."

[70]Freitas, *Palmares*, p. 111. "[P]ratica militar aguerrida na disciplina do seu capitão e general Zumbi, que os fez destríssimos no uso de todas as armas, de que têm muitas e em quantidade assim de fogo como de espadas, lanças e flechas."

[71]Ibid., p. 126.

[72]Carneiro, *O quilombo dos Palmares*, p. 199.

[73]Ibid., p. 201.

[74]Wyatt MacGaffey, *Religion and Society in Central Africa: The BaKongo of Lower Zaire* (Chicago, 1986), p. 78.

[75]Bastide, *The African Religions of Brazil*, pp. 194–5, 201–2.

[76]MacGaffey, *Religion and Society*, pp. 63–5. Plural *bakulu*, "ancestors."

[77]Albino Alves, *Dicionário etimológico bundo-português* (Lisbon, 1951), p. 865. Espírito de pessoa que, assassinada sem culpa, entra depois no corpo dos filhos do assassino e os mata, enquanto não é aplacado com um sacrifício."

[78]Luís da Câmara Cascudo, "Noticia do Zumbi," in *Made in Africa*, p. 113.

[79]Ibid.

[80]Wade Davis agrees with Wyatt MacGaffey in deriving *zombi* from KiKongo *nzambi*. Davis, *Passage of Darkness: The Ethnobiology of the Haitian Zombi* (Chapel Hill, N.C., 1988), p. 57. There is no reason to discount several cognate Bantu sources for the Haitian word. Haitians distinguish the corporeal *zombi* (Davis's *Zombi corps cadavre*) and the spirit *Zombi* (Davis's *Zombi astral* or *Zombi ti bon ange*), ibid., pp. 183, 190–3. See also Alfred Métraux, *Voodoo in Haiti*, Hugo Charteris (trans.) (London, 1959), pp. 258, 281–5.

[81]Carneiro, *O quilombo dos Palmares*, p. 199.

[82]*Folk-tales of Angola* (Boston, 1894), p. 33.

[83]Carneiro, *O quilombo dos Palmares*, p. 199.

[84]Ibid., pp. 203–5 ; Kent, "Palmares," pp. 183–6; Freitas, pp. 118–21.

[85]Carneiro, *O quilombo dos Palmares*, pp. 228–9.

[86]Kent, "Palmares," p. 186.

[87]Freitas, *Palmares*, p. 124.

[88]"Capitão-do-mato," a field commander charged with fighting Indians and capturing runaway slaves. For a discussion of this office, see Schwartz, "The *Mocambo*," pp. 212–3.

[89]For drawings of how these opposing fortifications may have looked, see Joel Rufino dos Santos, pp. 44–5. After visiting the site of Macaco on the Serra da Barriga or " Belly Ridge," it is my opinion that Jorge Velho's diagonal wall was built to protect the cannons and troops in their difficult ascent of the flank of the ridge; it was not built on level ground, as the pictures suggest.

[90]Accounts of the destruction of Palmares are found in Freitas, *Palmares*, 168–9; Carneiro, *O quilombo dos Palmares*, 140–6; Ennes, *As guerras nos Palmares*, docs. 24, 26, 92–95.

[91]Ibid., doc. 38. See also Morse, *The Bandeirantes*, p. 121.

[92]Carneiro, *O quilombo dos Palmares*, pp. 150–1.

[93]Arthur Ramos, *O folclore negro do Brasil: demopsicologia e psicanálise*, 2nd ed. (Rio de Janeiro, 1954), pp. 60–7.

[94]Carolina Maria de Jesus, *Diário de Bitita* (Rio de Janeiro, 1986), p. 58.

[95]Daniel J. Crowley, *African Myth and Black Reality in Bahian Carnaval* (Los Angeles, 1984), pp. 23, 29.
[96]For the general conceptual framework on which these conclusions are based, see Sidney W. Mintz and Richard Price, *The Birth of African American Culture: An Anthropological Perspective* (Boston, 1992).

Mandinga: The Evolution of a Mexican Runaway Slave Community, 1735–1827

Patrick J. Carroll

Most runaway slave communities in the Americas were quickly overcome by whites. However, a good many of those communities not only survived but became legally recognized towns whose residents eventually blended into the surrounding population. The first part of this article attempts to demonstrate that, although whites managed to eventually destroy most New World fugitive slave settlements, a surprising number of them managed to survive. The second section analyzes the social, demographic, and economic changes that one such community, called Mandinga, went through in evolving from a runaway hideout to a legal township.

Maroonage was the condition of living as a fugitive slave, under constant threat of recapture.[1] Black slaves fled their masters throughout the New World. Bands of runaways formed and settled in remote strongholds from which they raided, pillaged, and harassed their neighbors. They performed these acts for a number of reasons. As fugitives it was difficult for them to establish stable economic bases for their communities. To survive, the maroons often seized the produce and stores of farms, plantations, and merchant packtrains. They also attacked or terrorized free settlers in their area in order to drive them away: seclusion was vital to the survival of the hideout. Once discovered, it became easy prey to the anti-maroon forces.

Escaped slaves may have expressed hostility toward others for a third reason—one that has been referred to as a "violent and aggressive ethos."[2] This was a type of slave attitude which was "crafty, artful, . . . not often grateful . . . , but frequently deceitful and overreaching."[3] Rebels who formed maroon communities were supposed to have had this type of disposition. If this were so, then they might have engaged by choice in hostile activities toward others, because such patterns of behavior were consistent with their personalities.[4]

Another reason why maroons raided and pillaged was to acquire women. Most slaves who ran off to the forest were adult males. Once they secured their freedom they began to think about other needs, and women placed high on their priority list.

Freedom was difficult to maintain. A settlement of rebellious slaves was razed on Hispaniola in 1522.[5] In Peru, Gonzalo Pizzaro sent a force to conquer 200 maroons who were living in a marshy area just north of Lima. In 1545, a bloody battle was fought in which every one of these blacks was killed.[6] In 1795, a large band of Venezuelan slaves from the Serranía de Coro region rose in revolt and established a close-knit chain of mountain retreats. Expeditions sent out by the Spanish quickly subdued them.[7] A group of local planters reduced a runaway community near Mobile, Alabama, in 1827. The fugitives had inhabited the site for "years" prior to its destruction.[8]

In some cases whites were simply unable to forcibly overthrow maroon settlements, and those communities retained their fugitive character until abolition legitimatized them. The British never entirely subjugated descendants of shipwrecked Africans and native Amerindians on the island of St. Vincent.[9] In the sixteenth century, Spaniards on the Isthmus failed to overcome the runaway community (or *palenque* as it was called in Spanish) of Castilla de Oro which was built atop the overgrown ruins of the old white settlement of Santa María la Antigua in the jungles of the interior.[10] French forces sent against strongholds which dotted rugged mountain ranges of the parish of Cayes de Jacmel on Guadeloupe in 1702, 1717, 1728, 1733, 1746, 1757, 1761, 1777, and 1781, met with little success.[11] Of course, the most notable example of black resistance on the French islands involved the Haitian struggle for independence.[12]

The individual experience of each of these communities depended on a variety of factors. The ability of its residents to defend it was important. Equally important was the degree to which the runaways fused culturally, economically, and racially with surrounding peoples. The Mosquito "Indians" of Central America were the offspring of runaway slaves who had interbred with local Indians.[13] The Croatons of North Carolina, the Redbones of South Carolina, the Moors of Delaware, and the Melungeons of West Virginia were all North American Indian tribes which heavily mixed with United States maroons.[14] Finally, residents of the well known Ecuadorian *palenque* of Esmeraldes were not killed or captured by their white pursuers; they interbred with Indians and were absorbed but never conquered.[15]

Other maroon communities solicited treaties from whites which recognized the freedom of the runaways and which in many instances allowed them to found legally sanctioned towns. The former maroons promised to live in peace with their neighbors, and to aid in the apprehension of other fugitive slaves. At times these treaties were honored; at other times they were not.

Palmares, located in the hinterland of Pernambuco, in northeastern Brazil, became probably the largest maroon stronghold in the Americas. It took the Portuguese nearly 100 years to destroy this cluster of settlements whose total population contained up to 10,000 runaways. During the latter part of the seventeenth century the ex-slaves were ruled by an African named Ganga-Zumba. On June 18, 1668, he signed a treaty with whites which recognized the liberty of the residents of Palmares, and ended the fighting. The blacks swore fealty to the king of Portugal and promised to help capture future runaways. But the treaty contained a flaw. The territorial boundaries of Palmares were not defined, and white settlers soon began to move onto lands which the freedmen considered to belong to them. Within a year hostilities resumed, and eventually the rebel kingdom was destroyed.[16]

Bumba was the name of a fugitive black hideout near Santiago, Cuba. When repeated attempts to reduce it failed, white authorities offered the rebels a treaty much like that signed by the maroons of Palmares, with the exception that the Bumba group was to settle on a specific site somewhat removed from their old settlement. Although the maroons initially agreed to the move, they later refused to go. The Spaniards contributed to the downfall of the agreement by breaking the peace on several occasions. Ignoring the peace provisions of the treaty, the whites continued to send armed expeditions against the freedmen. In the hostilities that ensued after the treaty's collapse, Bumba was destroyed.[17]

Despite such instances of failure, enough documented examples to the contrary exist to indicate that in a great many cases these treaties were upheld. The experiences of this group of maroon communities prove that this type of slave resistance was often much more effective than has previously been realized. In South America, nearly all the "Bush Negro" communities of Dutch Surinam won lasting treaties during the 1760s.[18] In the Trombates region of Amazonia a group of mixed Indians and maroons under the leadership of a Negress named Filippa María Aranha became so powerful that the Portuguese decided to negotiate rather than fight with them. Descendants of the band continue to guide white travelers down the Tocantins rapids.[19]

San Blas and San Basilio were two maroon communities in New Granada near Cartagena. In the eighteenth century they both signed treaties with the Spanish government, and the descendants of the freedom fighters of the two groups still dwell in the subsequent towns they founded.[20]

History records several examples of lasting treaties between maroons and whites on the Caribbean islands, the best known of which was between the Leeward blacks of Jamaica and the English government. When the British captured the island from the Spanish in 1655, most of the slaves followed their Iberian masters into the mountains, and together they carried on a guerrilla war against the invaders. The Spanish half of the resistance broke down within five years, but most of the blacks continued to fight against British domination. The rebels' numbers grew from natural increase and a steady flow of new runaways from the island's slave population. The whites constantly tried to suppress the blacks, but were never able to do so. In 1739, a treaty was signed with the most formidable group, the Leeward maroons. These blacks were given their freedom, lands, and permission to found a town. For their part, they promised to hunt down other runaways.

The Leeward freedmen were later forced by the English to resettle in Nova Scotia, but they complained of the cold climate, and the whites agreed to transport them to Sierra Leone, where they landed in 1801. Despite their removal from Jamaica they never lost the free status that had been guaranteed in their treaty after over eighty years of fighting.[21]

The Jamaican maroons signed other treaties. A few of the black fugitive bands did not join the Spanish in opposing the English, but ratified treaties with the newcomers. Juan Bolas' group signed one of these agreements. Nine years later, while hunting down another band of fugitives, Juan and most of his men were killed.[22] The "Pelinco negroes," under the command of a black called Lubola, were freed under the same conditions as the blacks led by Juan Bolas. They too were killed while fighting maroons.[23]

At least four cases exist of Cuban maroon settlements that negotiated permanent treaties with the island's Spanish rulers. Carlos Rojas, in the province of Matanzas, and Palenque, near Havana, are two examples. A third is the settlement of Poblado del Cobre in Oriente province. The origins of this last community went far back to the beginning of the seventeenth century. For two hundred years its inhabitants thwarted Spanish attempts to destroy them. In 1800, the blacks signed a treaty of freedom with the whites. The town they established is still occupied today.[24]

The last known treaty involving Cuban maroons was signed by the stronghold of San Andrés, also in Oriente province. Negotiations took five years. During that time a number of other fugitive bands united with San Andrés so that they could share in the benefits of the impending agreement. Between 1815 and 1819, the population of San Andrés grew from sixty to 314. When the treaty was finally approved the original residents and the newcomers established the village of Caujerí, which is still in existence.[25]

There are three documented instances in which maroon groups in Mexico were parties to enduring treaties with white authorities. The first recorded example is a treaty agreed to in 1609, between Spanish officials from the port of Veracruz and a group of blacks under the leadership of an African named Yanga. As in all the previously cited cases, the whites agreed to this type of accommodation only after repeated failures to reduce the blacks. The treaty declared the maroons free men, and gave them a royal license to found a town, which they named San Lorenzo, or Yanga. The blacks promised to assume the role of runaway-slave catchers.[26]

The second instance concerns the runaway community of Cuijla, which is located on the west coast of Mexico in the present state of Guererro. This maroon stronghold was established sometime in the sixteenth century. In 1579, Viceroy Don Martín Enríquez launched a vigorous but unsuccessful military campaign against the town. Later expeditions also failed. It is not known exactly when a treaty was ratified, but in the military census of 1792, the inhabitants of Cuijla were listed as free black tributaries, indicating that the maroons had officially received their liberty, and that their town had a royal charter.[27] These changes could only have come about through a treaty between the whites and the black fugitives.

The above twelve examples demonstrate that although most maroon settlements could not withstand prolonged white military pressure, a surprising number of exceptions exist to this generalization. These exceptions indicate by their frequency and extent that maroonage was a relatively effective form of slave resistance. They also demonstrate a variety of relationships between runaway slave communities and the general populations in their differing local settings. The range and strength of these relationships were crucial in shaping the particular experience of each of these communities.

The remainder of this article will deal with the history of one runaway slave settlement called Mandinga. It was located on the Veracruz-Oaxacan border in late colonial Mexico. Over a period of nearly one century it evolved from a runaway slave hideout to a legally recognized township. The intervening demographic and economic changes, plus the shifting social relationships between the members within the settlement, and the relationships between the community and the larger surrounding population without, suggest a great deal about the nature of the general experiences of other runaway communities throughout the Western Hemisphere.

In 1735, a group of runaway slaves began to roam the mountainous region between the modern states of Veracruz and Oaxaca. These maroons escaped from sugar and tobacco growing districts of Córdoba and Orizaba, Veracruz. During the eighteenth century alone, both districts were shaken by major slave uprisings in 1725,

1735, 1741, 1749, and 1768.[28] According to local planters, most of the members of this particular band bolted during the second of these revolts, which was fomented by a group of earlier runaways after planter opposition had successfully blocked their efforts to secure a treaty with Spanish authorities.[29]

The 1735 rebellion cost a great deal in property and lives. Militia companies came from Córdoba, Orizaba, and Jalapa, along with royal troops from the port of Veracruz. It took five months to crush the revolt. The uprising left the region in near financial ruin. Many of the rebellious slaves were either killed or captured, but a large number managed to escape. They worked their way east along the Blanco River, turned south in the direction of Cosamaloapan, then headed southwest, ending their flight at an old maroon sanctuary, the mountains of Mazatiopa, within the Oaxacan district of Teutila.[30] There they established six settlements: Rosario, Mata de Anona, San Antonio, San Martín de Mazatiopa, Breve Cosina, and the Palacios de Mandinga.[31] This study deals with the last of these strongholds.

The word "Mandinga" is undoubtedly of African origin. The Mandinga nation inhabited the upper Niger River Valley in West Africa, and slaves of Mandinga origin were often associated with rebellion in the New World. During the sixteenth century a large proportion of the slaves imported into New Spain were Mandingas.[32] The choice of name for the community could have represented an African cultural holdover, or it might have merely been a symbolic rallying point for resistance.

Eight years after the foundation of Mandinga, its inhabitants petitioned the royal *audiencia* for freedom, and submitted a census of the entire settlement. This document may not have included all of the original founders. During the interim some of the residents were undoubtedly lost to disease or the slave catchers. A few may have simply moved to another site. However, the list is complete enough to reveal the composition of the fledgling society. In 1743, a total of 23 persons lived in the hideout. Two of them were recent arrivals from the 1741 revolt.[33] Fifteen had escaped during the 1735 uprising. Judging from the ages and the length of time the remaining six had been at large, it is probable that they had not participated in the rebellion, but were already settled on the Mandinga site when the rebels arrived. Most of these six were in their 70s or 80s, and had been maroons for over 40 years.[34]

Of the six pre-1735 settlers, two had belonged to Don Juan Urrieta, who owned a plantation called Maracallo; three had escaped from Don Lope de Iribas' estate near Córdoba; and Joseph Alarcón had been a former body servant of a lieutenant in the royal army.[35] These early runaways had escaped individually or in pairs. However, the 1735 arrivals did not slip off in the

400 Section Eight: Slave Resistance and Abolition

night, or take advantage of an unguarded moment to steal their freedom; they fought for it and left *en masse*. Eleven of the 1735 rebels who came to Mandinga had escaped from Don Miguel Navarro's sugar plantation near Córdoba. The other four were all from nearby estates.[36]

The relationships the blacks maintained in their mountain stronghold seem to have been extensions of those they had held as slaves. Couples who had lived together on the plantation continued to do so in the palenque. Carlos Joaquín and his wife Eugenia Antonia fled together in 1735, and remained together at Mandinga. The same was true of Antonio Francisco and his wife, Francisca de la Encarnación, and of Isidro Joseph and his wife, María Gerónima.[37]

Of the 23 persons residing at Mandinga in 1743, only five were women: the three wives already mentioned, and two 80-year-old widows.[38] It is not surprising that there were no children among the inhabitants. There was actually only one female of childbearing age, Isidro Joseph's wife, Maria Gerónima, who was in her twenties.[39] Fifteen of the remaining eighteen residents were single adult males.

After 1735, the planters conducted numerous expeditions against the maroons, but their efforts invariably ended in failure. At best one or two blacks would be captured at the expenditure of considerable sums of money. Usually, government forces had to be content with destroying the huts and gardens of owners who deserted them at the whites' approach.[40] From their mountain retreats maroons could see a hostile force in plenty of time to flee into the surrounding forests.

In 1750, the planters tried to remedy the problem by launching an ambitious, privately financed road-building project into the nearly inaccessible Mazatiopa range. When the undertaking became too costly it was abandoned. Instead, the owners decided to raise a less expensive slave patrol of 25 men to police the region for runaways. Thus, the goal of the whites had moderated from hostility to coexistence with the maroons.[41]

In the end, all the whites' measures proved ineffective. The rugged wilderness surrounding Mandinga was too vast and impenetrable to overcome. In addition, the maroons were mounted and had developed an intricate system of informants at nearly all levels of the local population. The livestock-feed gatherers from the port city of Veracruz who foraged along the coastal savannas periodically rendezvoused with the runaways. Most of the gatherers were slaves themselves. They accepted booty from the maroons, and sold it in the port for a commission. They also purchased requested supplies for the fugitives, and notified them of impending slave-catching expeditions.[42]

Depositions from the negotiations leading up to the foundation of the free community give ample evidence of contact between the maroons and the surrounding free population. Prudente de Arellano, a mestizo blacksmith from Teutila, testified that he had been dealing with the Mandinga group for many years. He was on intimate terms with several of the black captains, and swore to their good character.[43]

Francisco Vargas was a mestizo carpenter from the Indian village of Soyaltepec, also within the district of Teutila. He too was very familiar with the blacks, as were Joseph Ruíz, a mulatto muleteer, and Joseph Badilla, a mestizo farmer.[44]

Even Teutila's white elite worked out mutually useful relationships with the maroons. The district magistrate, Don Andrés Fernández Otañes, was involved with the blacks in a variety of ways. He refrained from deploying the district militia against them, was a constant source of information, and supposedly even provided them with arms. Fernández Otañes also acted as the runaways' extra-official intermediary with the crown, drafting and forwarding their petitions to the royal audiencia in Mexico City.

In return, the blacks performed a number of services for the district magistrate. They acted as his agents in dealing with Indians involved in the local vanilla-gathering trade. They also served as armed guards for the district's cotton warehouses.[45]

More than in any other capacity, however, the maroons were used by powerful local whites to intimidate various sectors of the district's population. Fernández Otañes utilized them to harass rival merchants who tried to break his monopoly of the area's vanilla trade.[46] Working through the district magistrate, the owner of one of the largest cattle haciendas in the area, Carlos Ribadenyra, commissioned the blacks to drive Indians off a parcel of land adjacent to his hacienda. Earlier he had tried to acquire the land by legal means, but after a protracted litigation with the Indian village of Soyaltepec, the audiencia ruled in favor of the Indians. In the maroons, Ribadenyra had a more effective tool than the viceregal court. Working in cooperation with the hacienda's resident manager, the blacks had soon driven the Indian farmers off the land, which was reoccupied by Don Carlos' cattle.[47]

In 1762, the runaways dealt with the viceroy himself. The government was preparing to defend the coast against an imminent British naval attack. The viceroy sent out a call for men, and the maroons seized the opportunity to bring a petition for freedom directly to the highest authority in New Spain. They rode to the port of Veracruz and volunteered. The tactic worked, and the viceroy gave them licenses of freedom in recognition of their service during the crisis, in the black company of Mounted Lancers of Jaliscoya (Yanga).[48] Unfortunately for the blacks, law and practice often followed divergent courses in New Spain. The maroons had been granted freedom at a time when authorities needed their aid. Once that need was removed, officials had little reason to enforce their decision over the objections of slave owners. The owners refused to recognize the runaways' liberty, and continued to try to reduce them to their former slave status.[49] But the myriad socioeconomic ties that the blacks held with the larger population offset the persistent hostility of their former masters.

With the passage of time the maroon community began to change. The group grew larger both through natural increase and through the steady influx of fugitives from the periodic rebellions that took place in the Córdoba-Orizaba districts. The society became less homogeneous. At least two factions began to develop, one formed of the older maroons and their families, the other consisting of the newer arrivals. The latter group, led by a former slave named Macute, was committed to maroonage and non-accomodation with the whites. Mostly young unattached males or married men with wives and children still in the slave quarters, they refused to compromise. The earlier residents, on the other hand, who were led by Fernando Manuel, had established most of the previously mentioned ties with the surrounding free population. Their families were either with them, or they had long since started new ones. Their ties to the plantations and to the slaves on them had loosened. They were ready for integration into the free society. With the aid of Fernández Otañes, they renewed their petition for freedom and the right to found a township. Tensions mounted between the two groups to the point of open hostility. In the ensuing battle the outnumbered followers of Macute were defeated. The victors turned over what captives they had to the authorities in Córdoba as a gesture of good will.[50] Fernando Manuel and his people then moved off the secluded hilltop where Mandinga had been located to a lower, more exposed site on the bank of the Amapa River.[51]

Finally, after a year of petitioning, and with the financial and legal backing of the district magistrate, they succeeded in winning their case over the protests of the Córdoba-Orizaba planters. At 8:00 a.m. on the morning of June 6, 1769, they met with authorities at the modest hut of a small farmer named Juan González. Suspicious to the end, the maroons refused to negotiate in the district capital. Fernández Otañes acted on behalf of the crown; the blacks were represented by the foremost fighters in the band: Captain Fernando Manuel, his lieutenants, Pablo de los Reyes, Santiago Joaquín, Joseph Francisco, and an escort of 20 other armed men.[52]

The fugitives agreed to terms that had been offered to them five months earlier. They were given their freedom and permission to establish a town on the site they had chosen on the Amapa. For their part, the blacks swore allegiance to the king, vowed to obey the district authorities, pledged to serve in the coastal militia, and promised to pay the tribute which the crown imposed on free blacks. But the most crucial condition from the point of the shifting roles of the members of the community was the group's agreement to capture future runaways and return them to their masters. For each fugitive they returned they were to receive 25 pesos from the owner. In order to accomplish this mission, the new freedmen promised to make bi-annual patrols into the mountains in search of runaways.[53] Lastly, the former maroons were prohibited from visiting any estate's slave quarters without the written permission of the owner or of a crown official. This restriction did not apply to those freedmen who still had families living as slaves on the plantations. The blacks then proceeded to found their new town, which they christened Nuestra Señora de Guadalupe de Amapa.[54]

The former maroons lived up to their agreement. They were at least partially successful in curbing the number of runaways in their area. Fourteen blacks who escaped from the plantations of San Antonio and Toluquilla near Córdoba were the first to be recaptured by the new slave catchers from Amapa. Diego de Bringas, who owned the runaways, had been one of the staunchest opponents of the founding of Amapa. He must have paid the 350 peso bounty with mixed emotions.[55] By the end of 1771, Fernando Manuel and his men had turned in 44 maroons, and were in the process of tracking 8 more from the plantation of Rosario near Orizaba.[56]

The Mandinga-Amapa blacks had changed a great deal, from fugitive slaves in 1735 to fugitive slave catchers in 1769. Up to this point two factors which contributed to this drastic reversal of roles have been described. A third factor involved the changing configuration of the community itself.

Table 1
Population Breakdowns of Mandinga-Amapa: 1743, 1769, 1827

Date	1743	1769	1827
Male-Female Ratio	4:1	3:1	1:1
Married Couples of Childbearing Age	1	11	23
Percentage of Adult Population Married	30	51	82
Children Under Twelve Years of Age	0	17	92
Total Population	23	52	148

Sources: Archivo General de la Nación de México, Ramo de Tierras, exp. 1, fol. 7–7v, 67v–69v; José María Murguía y Galardi, "Extracto general que abraza la estadística toda en su 1ª y 2ª parte del estado de Guaxaca (Oaxaca), 1827," G428 of Genaro García Collection, University of Texas Latin American Collection, exp. 2, fol. 1.

Table 1 shows Mandinga's population at three times: 1743, 1769, and 1827. The first date represents the early formative period in the community's history, just eight years after its establishment. It was an all adult population, one in which males outnumbered females by four to one. The men devoted most of their energy to marauding while the few women cultivated small garden patches. The group was highly mobile, capable of picking up at a moment's notice and melting into the forest. There was little familial structure, most of the blacks being single males. In the absence of kinship ties, the society's principal cohesive force was defense against the maroon hunters and opposition to the institution of slavery. In a sense, the group's marginality held it together. Devoid of a self-sustaining economy and socio-economic ties with the rest of the inhabitants in the area, and threatened by recapture, the community was committed to engaging in maroonage and promoting slave rebellion for its very survival.

By 1769, the internal structure of the community had undergone significant modification. The male-female ratio had changed to three to one. Over 50 percent of the adults were married, as opposed to only 30 percent in 1743. The number of couples of child bearing age—that is, where the female was between 14 and 50—had substantially increased. As a result, children had begun to appear among the group. The population was becoming demographically and socially more balanced.

This balance meant that the group was no longer as mobile as it had been. Women and children could not flee so easily as unattached males, nor conduct the guerrilla raids and ambushes for which the maroons were so notorious. The blacks were now supplementing the provisions they obtained directly or indirectly from plundering by planting their own agricultural crops. Adopting the local Indian method of *milpa* plots on the slopes of the mountains, they grew corn, manioc, beans, peanuts, and chili. They even started an illicit trade in these products, selling to travelers as they passed through the district along the royal roads.[57] In 1735, the blacks would have obtained money at lance or musket-point instead of through commercial exchange.

Free persons from the surrounding area began to filter into the palenque. The wife of a runaway named Mateo Joseph was a free Negress from Córdoba.[58] María Carbajal, a mestiza from Orizaba, was also married to one of the maroons. Joseph Ignacio, a free Afro-mestizo, was the husband of Pablo de los Reyes' daughter. The girl, like many of the other younger blacks, had never even experienced the onus of slavery.[59]

As the group's demographic stability increased, its commitment to maroonage decreased. The greater balance in the male-female ratio, the growing percentage of married adults, and the appearance of children among the population indicated that the nuclear family was replacing the bringing in of new recruits as the most important factor of social unification within the society.

Socio-economic ties with outsiders were increasing and were exemplified by the instances of inter-marriage with members of the free population and the roadside commerce which the blacks were conducting. And the maroons were also engaging in larger-scale milpa agriculture. The Mandinga residents were in the process of integrating into the general population. They were more sedentary; they were less mobile; and they were less marginal. Maroonage was becoming more inappropriate and less necessary to their best interests. By 1769 and thereafter the majority of the residents had less to gain and more to lose by continuing to be maroons. They petitioned for their freedom just as other blacks under similar circumstances had undoubtedly done before them. Those within the group who opposed this action were eliminated. Royal officials, realizing from past experience that the group could not be reduced by force, granted its petition.

The treaty was just one more step in an ongoing process of fusion with the local population. After 1769 the town did not always enjoy amicable relationships with its neighbors. Later that very same year the blacks were accused of sacking a nearby Indian village. During the raid, they abducted women and destroyed the village church along with 60 huts. Friction between the freedmen and local Indians had been building since 1767, when Spanish authorities decided to seize lands from the Soyaltepec Indians to provide a site for Amapa.[60] To make matters worse, indigenous laborers were pressed into service to construct the new town's public buildings. Some of the Indians had to travel as many as fifteen leagues to Amapa, and remained separated from their families and fields for long periods of time. While the Indian men were working without compensation in the black community, some of the Amapa freedmen visited their villages and raped their women.[61]

Even Don Carlos Ribadenyra, who had supported the foundation of Amapa, became disenchanted with the blacks when their freedom failed to reduce the number of cattle periodically stolen from his hacienda. He even went so far as to accuse them of being responsible for some of the losses.[62]

The Amapa residents also engaged in an illegal sugar brandy trade. Their bootlegging operations not only drew criticism from Spanish authorities but from Indian village leaders as well. The blacks had a tendency to use liquor as a medium of exchange instead of coin when dealing with the local indigenous population. As a result Indian leaders complained that the freedmen were corrupting the morals, undermining the health, and usurping the property of their people.[63]

Finally, in spite of the anti-maroon activities of the Amapa group, the level of runaway depredations in the region remained high: Fugitives continued to accost travelers along the highways. In 1771, the situation became so critical that authorities even considered closing the road from the port up through Córdoba and Orizaba.[64]

With time, however, the former runaways settled deeper and deeper into the same life style as their non-black neighbors. By 1827, the population of the community had grown to 148 persons. The inhabitants were no longer a group of feared warriors. Demographically and economically Amapa had become similar to the other small rural villages which were located in the area. Its male-female ratio had finally evened-off. A full 80 percent of the adult residents were married, and most of these couples were of childbearing age. As a result, the number of children increased from an average of one per nuclear family unit in 1769, to an average of four per nuclear family unit in 1827.

Economically, the group had added pigs and cotton to its list of products. Twenty riding and five cargo mules could be counted in the village, indicating that at least some of the residents might have supplemented their agricultural produce with some pesos in freight fees which they could make as muleteers not only within the district but also along the east-west trade route between the cities of Veracruz and Mexico.[65]

By the eve of Independence, the region, like the rest of New Spain, had largely converted to free labor. The census of 1791 showed that less than 30 percent of the blacks in the Orizaba district were slaves.[66] Those blacks who did remain bondsmen, however, continued to resist the system of slavery just as vehemently as had their ancestors. When Miguel Hidalgo issued the call for Independence, his movement received little support from the Veracruz slaves. However, as the news spread of Hidalgo's emancipation proclamation issued at the end of 1810, slaves began to enlist in the revolutionary ranks. By the following year they were deserting their masters in droves. Don Mariano de las Fuentes Alarcón, the curate of Maltrata, organized many of the runaways from the Córdoba-Orizaba districts into a single fighting force which saw action in most of the major engagements taking place all along the Gulf coast.[67]

When Iturbide issued a proclamation freeing all slaves who had fought in the insurgent ranks, the Veracruz freedom fighters reacted much as the Mandinga-Amapa blacks had acted in 1762 and 1769—suspiciously and cautiously. They remained in their mountain hideouts, and refused to come into the white settlements. They continued in this marginal state, in a self-imposed seclusion from the rest of the national society which they had fought for several years to establish. Some began to come down out of the mountains in 1824, others remained in hiding until 1829, when slavery was legally abolished in Mexico.[68]

Common outward characteristics were present in each of the twelve previously cited instances of fugitive slave communities that eventually managed to survive and become legally, socially, and economically integrated townships. They all went through the same transformations that the Mandinga-Amapa group did. They changed from runaway slave strongholds to legal townships to ordinary communities within their separate local settings. The roles of their inhabitants shifted from runaway-slave abettors to runaway-slave catchers to ordinary citizens. But only in the Mandinga-Amapa account is there presently enough data to illustrate the combined internal and external social, economic, and demographic shifts which contributed to these common external sets of changes.

When they were merely escaped slave strongholds, they were almost totally populated by adult males who had few social bonds with each other. The primary cohesive force was the threat of recapture. They all derived their sustenance from pillaging and forest gathering.

For the next stage, or the foundation of a legal township and the assumption of the slave-catching role, information exists for Mandinga-Amapa and eight other cases.[69] After 20 to 100 years had elapsed, and the settlements had managed to withstand the repeated assaults of anti-maroon forces, their populations eventually became demographically balanced. More women and some children began to appear among the residents. Kinship and social ties began to develop, and their economic bases started to broaden into areas such as agriculture and limited commerce.

The Mandinga-Amapa case is, at present, the only source of evidence on the last in this series of transformations, namely the integration of the townships into their surrounding regions. Their male-female ratios evened-off , and the number of children per nuclear family unit reached the average for the area and period. Crime decreased to levels consistent with those of neighboring towns. The residents of the former fugitive settlements began to rely almost exclusively on agriculture, gathering, and trade for a livelihood.

After reviewing the Mandinga-Amapa experience in light of the experiences of other runaway slave communities it is apparent that groups of fugitive blacks were often able to form and maintain their own communal identities and eventually integrate into their larger surrounding populations. The evidence concerning the similar outward transformations that these settlements went through suggests that the Mandinga-Amapa case was probably representative of the changes which took place in many similar communities throughout the Western Hemisphere.

Notes

[1]"Maroon" is the root of the word maroonage which is based upon the French word *marron*. The French term represents an adaptation of the Spanish word *cimarron*, which, in itself, is derived from the Spanish word *marron*, meaning wild, and the Latin word *cyma*, meaning summit, or mountain top. The word cimarron, therefore, literally meant wild on the mountaintop. Additional meanings have been ascribed to the term. In French, Italian, and other Southern European languages derivatives of *maroon* came to denote a particular type of chestnut, or simply chestnut in color. During the seventeenth and eighteenth centuries the word took on three more meanings: to put a person ashore and abandon him or her on a desolate coast or island; to escape from slavery; and one of a class of Negroes, chiefly fugitive slaves or their descendants living wild in the mountains and forests of some of West Indian islands and in Guiana, especially Surinam. *The American Heritage Dictionary of the American Language* (Boston: American Heritage Publishers/Houghton Mifflin, 1969); *Webster's Third New International Dictionary* (Springfield, Mass.: G. & C. Merriam Company, Publishers, 1971); *The Oxford English Dictionary* (13 vols.; London: Oxford University Press, 1933).

[2]Gonzalo Aguirre Beltrán, *Cuijla: Esbozo etnográfico de un pueblo negro* (México: Fondo de Cultura Económica, 1958), p. 12.

[3]Edward Brathwaithe, *The Development of Creole Society in Jamaica, 1770–1820* (London: Oxford University Press, 1971), p. 12.

[4]*Ibid.*; Aguirre Beltrán, *Cuijla*, p. 12.

[5]Carlos Federico Guillot, *Negros rebeldes y negros cimarrones* (Buenos Aires: Fariña Editores, 1961), pp. 80–85.

[6]Frederick P. Bowser, *The African Slave in Colonial Peru, 1524–1650* (Stanford: University of Stanford Press, 1974), pp. 187–88; James Lockhart, *Spanish Peru, 1532–1560* (Madison: University of Wisconsin Press, 1974), p. 189.

[7]Pedro Arcaya M., *Insurrección de los negros de la Serranía de Coro* (Caracas, Venezuela: Instiuto Panamericano de Geografía e Historia, Publicación núm. 7, 1930), pp. 23–49.

[8]Herbert Aptheker, "Maroons Within the Present Limits of the United States," in *Maroon Societies*, edited by Richard Price (New York: Anchor Press/Doubleday, 1973), 159–60.

[9]Sir William Young, *An Account of the Black Caraibs in the Island of St. Vincent's* (London: J. Sewell, Cornhill and Knight and Triphook, Booksellers, 1795), pp. 123–25.

[10]Guillot, *Negros rebeldes*, pp. 137–38.

[11]Shelby McCloy, *The Negro in the French West Indies* (Louisville: University of Kentucky Press, 1969), pp. 41–42.

[12]*Idem.*; Roger Bastide, *African Civilizations in the New World*, translated by Peter Green (New York: Harper and Row, Publishers, 1971), pp. 46–47.

[13]Bastide, *African Civilizations*, pp. 49–50.

[14]Edward Bryan Reuter, *The American Race Problem*, 2nd edition (New York: Thomas Y. Crowell Company, 1966), p. 126.

[15]Guillot, *Negros rebeldes*, pp. 242–46; Magnus Mörner, *Race Mixture in the History of Latin America* (Boston: Little, Brown and Co., 1967), p. 20.

[16]R. Kent, "Palmares: An African State in Brazil," in *Maroon Societies*, pp. 184–85.

[17]José Franco, "Maroons and Slave Rebellions in the Spanish Territories," in *Maroon Societies*, p. 55.

[18]Melville Herskovits and Frances Herskovits, *Rebel Destiny* (New York: McGraw-Hill Book Co., Inc., 14), p. vii; Johannes King, "Guerrilla Warfare: A Bush Negro View," in *Maroon Societies*, p. 291.

[19]Roger Bastide, "The Other Quilombos," in *Maroon Societies*, p. 197.

[20]Aquiles Escalante, "Palenques in Colombia," in *Maroon Societies*, p. 79; "Notas sobre el palenque de San Basilio, una comunidad negra en Colombia," in *Divulgaciones Etnológicas*, III, núm. 5 (junio, 1954), 207, 228–31.

[21]R. C. Dallas, *The History of the Maroons* (2 vols.; London: T. N. Longman and O. Rees, 1803), I, pp. 1–65; Bryan Edwards, "Observations on the Disposition, Character, Manners, and Habits of Life, of the Maroon Negroes of the Island of Jamaica . . ." in *Maroon Societies*, pp. 230–42; Orlando Patterson, "Slavery and Slave Revolts: A Socio-historical Analysis of the First Maroon War, 1665–1740," in *Maroon Societies*, pp. 273–81; Cary Robinson, *The Fighting Maroons of Jamaica* (Jamaica: William Collins and Sangster Ltd., 1969), pp. 9, 12, 16–25, 31, 82–85, 140, 152.

[22]Edwards, "Observations on . . . , the Maroon Negroes of . . . Jamaica," in *Maroon Societies*, pp. 231–32.

[23]Patterson, "Slavery and Slave Revolts," in *Maroon Societies*, p. 254.

[24]Francisco Pérez la Riva, "El Negro y la Tierra, El Conuco y el Palenque," in *Revista Bimestre Cubana*, LVIII, núms. 2–3 (septiembre–diciembre, 1946), 106–07; Franco, "Maroons and Slave Rebellions," in *Maroon Societies*, pp. 54–55.

[25]Pérez la Riva, "Negro y la Tierra," in *Revista Bimestre Cubana*, 114–28.

[26]David Davidson, "Negro Slave Control and Resistance in Colonial Mexico, 1519–1650," in *Maroon Societies*, pp. 94–97; Enríque Herrera Moreno, *El Canton de Córdoba* (Córdoba, México: Prensas de R. Valdecilla Compañía, 1892), pp. 82–93; Octaviano Corro, *Los Cimarrones en Veracruz y la fundación de Amapa* (Jalapa, México: Imprenta Comercial, Veracruz, 1951), pp. 11–13.

[27]Aguirre Beltrán, *Cuijla*, pp. 59–63.

[28]México, Archivo General de la Nación, Ramo de Tierras, Vol. 3543, expediente 1, fol. 81–82v. (Hereinafter this archive will be cited as AGN). William B. Taylor, "The Foundation of Nuestra Señora de Guadalupe de Amapa," in *The Americas*, XXVI (April, 1970), 442.

[29]AGN, Tierras, Vol. 3543, exp. 1, fol. 76v.

[30]AGN, Tierras, Vol. 3543, exp. 1, fol. 15v–16, 29–30, 76v–78v.

[31]AGN, Tierras, Vol. 3543, exp. 1, fol. 1–1v, 17v; Herrera Moreno, *Cantón de Córdoba*, pp. 126–27.

[32]Gonzalo Aguirre Beltrán, *La población negra de México* (México: Fondo de Cultura Económica, 1973), pp. 128, 241; Ward Barrett, *The Sugar Hacienda of the Marqueses del Valle* (Minneapolis: University of Minnesota Press, 1970), p. 133; Patrick Carroll, "Mexican Society in Transition: The Blacks in Veracruz, 1750–1830," unpublished Ph.D. dissertation, University of Texas at Austin (December, 1975), p. 229.

[33]AGN, Tierras, Vol. 3543, exp. 1, fol. 67v–70.

[34]AGN, Tierras, Vol. 3543 , exp. 1, fol. 68, 69.

[35]AGN, Tierras, Vol. 3543, exp. 1, fol. 67v–69.

[36]*Ibid.*

[37]*Ibid.*

[38]*Ibid.*

[39]AGN, Tierras, Vol. 3543, exp. 1, fol. 69.
[40]AGN, Tierras, Vol. 3543, exp. 1, fol. 14–14v, 16, 23v, 30.
[41]AGN, Tierras, Vol. 3543, exp. 1, fol. 30; AGN, Tierras, Vol. 3543, exp. 2, fol. 13v–14.
[42]AGN, Tierras, Vol. 3542, exp. 2, fol. 12v, 16.
[43]AGN, Tierras, Vol. 3543, exp. 2, fol. 12–13v.
[44]AGN, Tierras, Vol. 3543, exp. 2, fol. 14–15v, 17–21.
[45]AGN, Tierras, Vol. 3543, exp. 2, fol. 79, 87v; AGN, Tierras, Vol. 3543, exp. 1, fol. 139–139v, 141.
[46]AGN, Tierras, Vol. 3543, exp. 1, fol. 139v.
[47]AGN, Tierras, Vol. 3543, exp. 3, fol. 13–14.
[48]AGN, Tierras, Vol. 3543, exp. 1, fol. 27v–28, 57–57v.
[49]AGN, Tierras, Vol. 3543, exp. 1, fol. 3–3v, 27v–28.
[50]AGN, Tierras, Vol. 3543, exp. 1, fol. 2v–3; AGN, Tierras, Vol. 3543, exp. 2, fol. 7–7v; Taylor, "Foundation of Amapa," in *The Americas*, 440.
[51]AGN, Tierras, Vol. 3543, exp. 1, fol. 10.
[52]AGN, Tierras, Vol. 3543, exp. 2, fol. 58–58v, 121–124.
[53]AGN, Tierras, Vol. 3543, exp. 2, fol. 29v–30; Taylor, "Foundation of Amapa," in *The Americas*, 440–41.
[54]AGN, Tierras, Vol. 3543, exp. 2, fol. 30–30v.
[55]AGN, Tierras, Vol. 3543, exp. 2, fol. 126.
[56]AGN, Tierras, Vol. 3543, exp. 2, fol. 127v.
[57]AGN, Tierras, Vol. 3543, exp. 1, fol. 12v, 14.
[58]AGN, Tierras, Vol. 3543, exp. 1, fol. 7.
[59]AGN, Tierras, Vol. 3543, exp. 1, fol. 7v.
[60]AGN, Tierras, Vol. 3543, exp. 3, fol. 11, 13, 14v–15.
[61]AGN, Tierras, Vol. 3543: exp. 3, fol. 14v–15.
[62]AGN, Tierras, Vol. 3543 exp. 3, fol. 14v.
[63]AGN, Tierras, Vol. 3543, exp. 3, fol. 10v, 15v.
[64]AGN, Tierras, Vol. 3543, exp. 3, fol. 7v, 13.
[65]José María Murgía y Galardi, "Extracto general que abraza la estadística toda en su 1ª y 2ª parte del estado de Guaxaca (Oaxaca), 1827," G428 of Genaro García Collection, University of Texas Latin American Collection, exp. 2, fol. 1.
[66]AGN, Padrones, Vol. 19, fol. 392–425.
[67]Herrera Moreno, *Cantón de Córdoba*, pp. 162–70.
[68]Herrera Moreno, *Cantón de Córdoba*, pp. 295–96; Mörner, *Race Mixture*, p. 152.
[69]The eight cases referred to include: the Bush Negroes of Surinam, plus the former runaway slave settlements of San Blas and San Basilio of New Granada, Yanga and Cuijla in Mexico, Poblado del Cobre and San Andrés on Cuba, and the Leeward communities of Jamaica. In order of their above listing see the following sources for these eight settlements: Herskovits and Herskovits, *Rebel Destiny*, and King, "Guerrilla Warfare," in *Maroon Societies*; Escalante, "Palenques en Colombia," in *Maroon Societies* and Escalante, "Notas sobre el palenque de San Basilio," in *Divulgaciones Etnológicas*; Davidson, "Slave Control and Resistance in Colonial Mexico," in *Maroon Societies*; Herrera Moreno, *Cantón de Córdoba*; Corro, *Cimarrones en Veracruz*; and Aguirre Beltrán, *Cuijla*; Pérez la Riva "Negro y la Tierra," in *Revista Bimestre Cubana* and Franco, "Maroons and Slave Rebellions," in *Maroon Societies*; Dallas, *History of the Maroons*; Robinson, *Fighting Maroons of Jamaica*; and Edwards, "Observations on . . . , the Maroon Negroes of . . . Jamaica," in *Maroon Societies*.

The Haitian Revolution

David P. Geggus

Racial equality, the abolition of slavery, decolonization, and nationhood first came to the Caribbean with the Haitian Revolution. Between 1791 and 1803 the opulent French colony of Saint Domingue was transformed by the largest and most successful of all slave revolts. After twelve years of desolating warfare, Haiti emerged in 1804 as the first modern independent state in the Americas after the United States. For slaves and slave owners throughout the New World, the Haitian Revolution was an inspiration and a warning. The most productive colony of the day had been destroyed, its economy ruined, its ruling class eliminated. Few revolutions in world history have had such profound consequences.

Saint Domingue in the 1780s

In the period between the American and French revolutions, Saint Domingue produced close to one-half of all the sugar and coffee consumed in Europe and the Americas, as well as substantial amounts of cotton, indigo, and ground provisions. Though scarcely larger than Maryland, and little more than twice the size of Jamaica, it had long been the wealthiest colony in the Caribbean and was hailed by publicists as the "Pearl of the Antilles" or the "Eden of the Western World." Moreover, it was still expanding. In the long-settled coastal plains, the number of sugar plantations grew only slowly but the mountainous interior was the scene of bustling pioneer activity, where new coffee estates were being cut out of the mountain forests to meet rising demand in Europe and North America.

By 1789 Saint Domingue had about 8,000 plantations producing crops for export. They generated some two-fifths of France's foreign trade, a proportion rarely equaled in any colonial empire. Saint Domingue's importance to France was not just economic, but fiscal (in customs revenue) and strategic, too, since the colonial trade provided both seamen for the national navy in wartime and foreign exchange to purchase vital naval stores from northern Europe (hemp, mast trees, saltpeter). In the Môle Saint Nicolas, the colony also contained the most secure naval base in the West Indies.

Although colonial statistics are not very reliable, Saint Domingue's population on the eve of the French Revolution consisted of approximately 500,000 slaves, 40,000 whites (including transient seamen), and over 30,000 free coloreds, who constituted a sort of middle class. In broad outline, Saint Domingue society thus conformed to the three-tier structure common to all sugar colonies. However, there were some significant differences.

The tiny white community was united by racial solidarity but also divided to an unusual degree along class lines. The resulting tensions pitted sugar and coffee planters against each other as well as against merchants and lawyers, and separated all of these from the turbulent *petits blancs*, or poor whites, an amorphous group that included plantation managers, artisans, clerks, shopkeepers, seamen, and peddlers. Such tensions reflected the wealth and diversity of Saint Domingue's economy. Also, because France was a much more populous country than Great Britain or Spain, and possessed fewer colonies, Saint Domingue inevitably attracted uncommonly large numbers of indigent young men seeking employment. The richest planters, on the other hand, were able to reside in Europe living off their revenues. This was typical of West Indian sugar colonies. At the same time, however, the extent of less profitable secondary economic enterprises such as coffee, indigo, and cotton meant that Saint Domingue also possessed a sizable resident planter class, like the southern United States or Cuba. Residence in the colony, its competitive position in the world market, and its ability to produce much of its own food were factors that encouraged some planters to envisage its eventual independence.

Saint Domingue's free colored sector was exceptional both for its size and its wealth. Elsewhere in the Caribbean free coloreds were generally a very small minority and they rarely rose above the position of prosperous artisan. In Saint Domingue, however, the *gens de couleur* outnumbered the whites in two of the colony's three provinces, and they included in their number rich and cultivated planters who had been educated in France. In Saint Domingue anyone with a black ancestor, no matter how remote, was subject to the humiliating restrictions of the legal system of separation typical of all slave colonies in the eighteenth century. Free coloreds were banned from public office and the professions, and forbidden to wear fine clothing, ride in carriages, or sit with whites in church or when eating. They were not only unequal before the law but also suffered extralegal harassment, especially from poor whites with whom they competed for jobs.

The gens de couleur thus covered an extremely broad social range, from recently freed black slaves to rich landowners and tradesmen who were almost indistinguishable in appearance or culture from their white counterparts. They constituted merely a legal category (those neither slave nor white) rather than a class. Probably a majority of the men were artisans or smallholders.

The women were usually petty traders or white men's mistresses. As most were of mixed racial descent, the term "mulatto" was often applied to the entire free colored community. Many had both whites and slaves for relatives. Their position within Saint Domingue society was therefore highly ambiguous. Though held in subjection by the whites, they were often slave owners themselves or acted as slave catchers in the rural police force.

Despite the spread of liberal ideas in Europe, the laws governing the free coloreds in France, as well as Saint Domingue, grew increasingly severe in the late eighteenth century—a paradox of the French Enlightenment. At the same time, the free coloreds grew rapidly in number, and in wealth as they profited from the coffee boom. By the 1780s they not only dominated the rural police force but in addition formed the backbone of the colonial militia.

Saint Domingue's slave population was easily the largest in the Caribbean. It was nearly twice the size of Jamaica's, its closest rival. The imbalance between slave and free, black and white, was not unusually extreme, but for most of the 1780s the number of slaves grew at a faster rate than probably anywhere else. During the period 1785–90 over 30,000 manacled Africans were imported each year. Despite the influx of white immigrants and the growing community of free coloreds, Saint Domingue was actually becoming increasingly African. Young men around twenty years old comprised a significant proportion of the black population.

The slave community was not at all homogeneous, being even more segmented than the white and free colored groups. Split up into small units, tied six days a week to plantation labor, the slaves constituted a random agglomeration of individuals from diverse cultures, speaking different languages and at different stages of assimilation into colonial society. On a typical sugar estate of two hundred slaves there would be Africans from twenty or more different linguistic groups. Mountain plantations were much smaller and even more isolated. Everywhere in Saint Domingue, however, Bantu slaves known as "Congoes" constituted the largest of the African groups, and formed a third of the population in the plains and well over half in the mountains.

On the lowland sugar plantations about half the adults were Creoles—that is, individuals born locally and raised in slavery; they made up perhaps one-third of the total slave population. Accustomed to producing their own food and marketing the surplus, they tended to be better off than the Africans. Fluent in the local creole tongue, superficially Christianized, and united by at least limited family ties, they constituted the slave upper class. From their ranks were chosen the domestics, artisans, and slave drivers who formed the slave elite. Elite slaves would have some familiarity with French, the language of the master class, and a few could read and write.

Little is known about how these groups interrelated. Plantation labor, social interaction, and the common experience of slavery inevitably imposed some sort of solidarity, which was symbolized in songs of call and response, networks of fictive kin, and a strong sense of locality. Moreover, slaves from different estates could meet at weekly markets, at Saturday night dances, and in more secret assemblies associated with the Voodoo cult. Voodoo apparently served to integrate different religious traditions—West African, Bantu, and Christian—and doubtless helped release anomic tensions. Nevertheless, the diversity of the slave community must be accounted one reason why, in a comparative context, Saint Domingue's slaves seem to have been remarkably unrebellious. It is true that in the twenty years before the American Revolution poisoning scares swept the colony, but these had as much to do with white paranoia as with real resistance; in the 1780s little was said about poison. Compared to the British or Dutch colonies, organized, violent resistance in Saint Domingue was relatively slight.

This paradox underlying the greatest of all slave revolts has received little scholarly attention. The planters themselves tended to attribute the absence of slave revolts to Saint Domingue's military-style government, which precluded the democratic dissensions of the self-governing British colonies, and which placed far more stress on militia training. Certainly the slaves seem to have been no better treated than in any other sugar colony. Perhaps most importantly, the colony's size and low population density meant that slave discontent was most easily channeled into running away to the mountains and forests. Other slaves fled over the frontier into the even more sparsely populated Spanish colony of Santo Domingo, as well as to towns such as Port-au-Prince and Cap Français. While some runaways formed armed bands which attacked travelers or isolated plantations, they were never very numerous and the 1780s saw a definite downturn in such activities. Although this is a controversial area, it seems clear that desertions were usually short-term and offered little threat to the system. Moreover, in 1777 an extradition treaty was signed with Santo Domingo. As new settlements spread into the remaining frontier regions, and as the colony's forests were felled, it was becoming increasingly hard to be a successful maroon. It may be, therefore, that by the 1780s slave dissidents were coming to see revolt as a more viable alternative.

The Influence of the American Revolution

Vulnerability to slave rebellion and foreign invasion made all West Indian colonies especially dependent on their mother countries for military and naval protection. Nevertheless, the desire for self-government had a long history in Saint Domingue, and among a minority of radical planters it was notably strengthened after the North America colonists won their independence from England. Apart from its ideological impact, the American Revolution gave Saint Domingue a tempting taste of free trade. When France intervened in the conflict, it opened the colony's ports to Yankee traders, who supplied its needs more cheaply than could French merchants. These commercial contacts were sustained after the war through a new system of free ports, but the trade was heavily taxed and subject to frustrating prohibitions. Moreover, smuggling was severely curtailed by new measures reminiscent of British action in North America twenty years before. Such conflicts of interest encouraged planters to think of themselves as "Americans" rather than Frenchmen.

The War of Independence, perhaps, had its greatest impact on the free colored community. A special regiment of free coloreds was raised and sent to Georgia to fight alongside the rebel colonists. It included André Rigaud, Jean-Baptiste Chavannes, J. B. Villatete, Henry Christophe, Jean-Pierre Lambert, and Louis-Jacques Beauvais; its muster roll reads like a roll call of future revolutionaries. These men returned to Saint Domingue with military experience and a new sense of their own importance. Leading mulattoes secretly drew up a report attacking the caste system and in 1784 sent a representative to France. The government, however, for fear of offending the whites or exciting the slaves, dared not yield an inch.

The abolition of slavery in Massachusetts and other northern states must have been discussed in Saint Domingue by American seamen and local whites, but it is not known how this affected the slaves. By the end of the 1780s news was anyway arriving from France itself of a French antislavery society, the Amis des Noirs. At the same time, government reforms aimed at limiting abuses on the plantations outraged the planter class. Hitherto, whites had presented a solid front on the question of slavery. Now cracks were starting to appear in what had been a monolithic white power structure.

The Impact of the French Revolution, 1789–1792

Historians do not agree on just how close Saint Domingue came to having a revolution in the 1780s. Whether the whites' desires for autonomy, the free coloreds' for equality, or the slaves' for liberty would of themselves have led to violent conflict must remain a matter for speculation. No one doubts, however, that the French Revolution of 1789 precipitated the colony's destruction. If Saint Domingue was a dormant volcano, as contemporaries liked to say,

it needed only the shock waves of the political earthquake in Paris to provoke its eruption.

The ideological impact of the French Revolution is not easy to distinguish from its political impact. The ideals of liberty, equality, and fraternity proclaimed by the revolutionaries in Paris were peculiarly dangerous for Caribbean societies, which represented their complete negation. But at the same time, the overthrow of the Old Regime in France also directly undermined the traditional sources of authority in the French West Indies—governor, intendant, law courts, garrison, militia, police. The French Revolution thus enflamed social and political aspirations, while weakening the institutions that held them in check.

The influence of the French Revolution was felt first at the peak of the social pyramid and thereafter worked its way inexorably downward. Although colonists were not invited when the States-General was summoned in 1788 to recommend sweeping changes in French government, wealthy planters in both Paris and Saint Domingue met in secret committees to elect deputies and ensure their representation. Their activities in fact merged with movements already under way to protest against recent government reforms in the colonies. It was the fall of the Bastille, however, and the creation of a National Assembly in the summer of 1789 that overturned the Old Regime in Saint Domingue as well as France. While mobs of poor whites adopted the tricolor cockade and celebrated riotously the news from Paris, planters, merchants, and lawyers became politicians and elected assemblies in each of the colony's three provinces. In many parishes and towns, elected committees and municipalities emerged alongside or replaced local military commanders. The militia was converted into a National Guard dominated by the plantocracy. The intendant, former strongman of the administration, was driven out of the colony, and the governor, uncertain of support from France, was forced to accept what he could not prevent.

From April to August 1790, a Colonial Assembly met in the town of Saint Marc. Though illegal, it declared itself sovereign and boldly drew up a constitution severely restricting French control even over matters of trade. Its most radical deputies openly discussed the idea of independence. The extremism of these *Patriotes* brought about a backlash, which temporarily united the Assembly of the North with the governor and military. In 1789 the elegant northern capital of Cap Français had been in the forefront of the revolution. Thereafter its big merchants and establishment lawyers became a moderating influence, and sprawling and shabby Port-au-Prince took over as the center of colonial radicalism. Lower-class whites came to exercise increasing control over its politics, notably after its garrison mutinied in March 1791 and caused the governor to flee to Le Cap.

Colonial politics was an affair of factions and demagogues. Without previous political experience, Saint Domingue's whites threw up local leaders of ephemeral fame who maintained the Creole's reputation for turbulence and impulsive egotism. Divided by regional, class, and political loyalties, colonists disagreed as to what degree of autonomy Saint Domingue should seek, how much militancy they should employ, what classes of whites should vote and serve together in the militia, and whether the colony should be represented in the National Assembly or cooperate directly with the king's ministers. The great majority agreed, nonetheless, on two things—that no one should tamper with the institution of slavery, and that the system of white supremacy should be rigorously maintained. Increasingly, however, the revolution in France came to be seen as a threat to both these pillars of colonial society.

In 1789 the society of the Amis des Noirs gained new prominence as the revolution provided a platform for its leading members (Mirabeau, Brissot, Condorcet). It campaigned only for the abolition of the slave trade and for equal rights for free coloreds, and disclaimed any desire to interfere with slavery. However, to the colonial mind which saw racial discrimination as an essential bulwark of slavery, such action endangered white lives in the West Indies. Encouraged by the Amis des Noirs, free coloreds in Paris demanded that the National Assembly live up to its Declaration of the Rights of Man. Were they not men, too? At the same time, the autumn of 1789, free colored property owners in Saint Domingue also gathered to demand equal rights with whites. Some also seem to have called for the freeing of mixed-race slaves, and those in Paris spoke of an eventual, though distant, abolition of slavery. In general, however, the free coloreds acted like the slave owners they were and were careful not to have their cause confused with that of the black masses.

In a few parts of the colony, the early days of the French Revolution saw free coloreds and whites attending meetings together and sitting on the same committees, but this was rare. The mulattoes' request to adopt the tricolor cockade created great unease among whites. Before long they and their few white allies became the victims of intimidatory acts of violence, including murder. Fears for the stability of the slave regime reinforced deep-seated prejudice, so that by 1790 it was clear that the colonists were determined to maintain the status quo and keep the free coloreds out of politics. The Assembly of the West even demanded from them a humiliating oath of obedience. Faced by mounting persecution, some now fortified their plantations, but a small armed gathering in the spring in the Artibonite plain was easily dispersed. The free colored militia joined the governor's forces which suppressed the Colonial Assembly, but the administration proved no more willing than the colonists to grant concessions.

Meanwhile, however, the mulattoes were acquiring leaders from among wealthy nonwhites now returning from France, men who had been accustomed to equal treatment. These included Villatte, J. B. Lapointe, and Pierre Pinchinat, but it was the light-skinned Vincent Ogé (an unsuccessful small merchant) who decided to force the whites' hand. He had been a prominent spokesman of the free colored activists in Paris, where he had tried and failed to gain the cooperation of the absentee colonists. One of his brothers apparently was killed in the skirmish in the Artibonite. In October, Ogé secretly returned to his home in the mountains of the North Province. With Jean-Baptiste Chavannes he rapidly raised an army of over three hundred free coloreds and demanded that the governor put an end to racial discrimination. Despite the urging of Chavannes, Ogé refused to recruit any slaves. Free coloreds were not numerous in the North; and though they initially created great panic among the whites, Ogé's men were soon routed. Mass arrests and a lengthy trial followed. Twenty rebels were executed, Ogé and Chavannes suffering the excruciating punishment of being broken on the wheel. In the West and South, free coloreds had also taken up arms but there they were peaceably persuaded to disperse by royalist officers. Military men were often more sympathetic to the mulattoes' cause, if only because they saw them as a counterweight to the colonial radicals. In the North, all free coloreds were disarmed except a few fugitives from Ogé's band who remained in hiding in the forests.

Up until now the National Assembly in Paris had maintained an ambiguous silence on the color question. France's Revolutionary politicians were extremely embarrassed by events in the Caribbean and the issues that they raised. Colonial self-government, racial equality, and freedom for the slaves all posed serious threats to France's prosperity. The news of the barbarous execution of Ogé and Chavannes, however, shocked the National Assembly into making a compromise gesture. On May 15, 1791, free coloreds born legitimately of free parents were declared equal in rights to whites. Although the measure concerned a very small population of free coloreds, news of the Assembly's vote created a violent backlash in Saint Domingue. Whites, now meeting to elect a second colonial assembly, seemed determined to resist the decree with force. A few talked of secession. When the governor announced he would not promulgate the decree, the patience of the free coloreds was exhausted. In August, those of the West and South began to gather in armed bands in the parishes where they were strongest. At the same time, news arrived from France that King Louis XVI had revealed his hostility to the revolution by attempting to flee from Paris.

It was in this rather complicated political situation, with civil war brewing between whites and free coloreds, with tensions rising between conservatives and radicals, with rumors circulating of secession and counterrevolution and a new assembly gathering in Cap Français, that the slaves took everyone by surprise. At the end of August 1791, an enormous revolt erupted in the plain around Le Cap. Beating drums, chanting, and yelling, slaves armed with machetes marched from plantation to plantation, killing, looting, and burning the cane fields. From the night it began, the uprising was the largest and bloodiest yet seen in an American slave society. Spreading swiftly across the plain and into the surrounding mountains, the revolt snowballed to overwhelming proportions. Whites fled pell-mell from the plain, and military sorties from Cap Français proved ineffective against the rebels' guerrilla tactics. By the end of September, over a thousand plantations had been burned and hundreds of whites killed. The number of slaves slaughtered in indiscriminate reprisals was apparently much greater, but this merely served to swell the ranks of the insurgents. Nevertheless, a cordon of military camps managed to confine the revolt to the central section of the North Province.

Most slave conspiracies in the Americas were betrayed before reaching fruition, and most rebellions were quashed within a few days. The circumstances surrounding the August uprising are therefore of great interest. The divided and distracted state of the whites and the alienation of the free coloreds probably explain much of the rebels' success, both in gathering support and in overcoming opposition. Their aims, however, are less clear. Many slaves appear to have believed they were fighting to gain a freedom already granted them by the king of France but which the colonists were withholding. They in fact rebelled, not in the name of the Rights of Man, but as defenders of church and king. How far this was a deliberate ploy (perhaps designed to win aid from their conservative Spanish neighbors), is hard to say, but the influence of French Revolutionary ideology on the revolt would seem slight. Since 1789 slaves had called the tricolor cockade the symbol of the whites' emancipation, but in revolt they adopted the white cockade of the royalists. Rumors of a royal emancipation decree had circulated in Saint Domingue in the autumn of 1789, along with news of an insurrection in Martinique, which was itself prompted by similar rumors that may have had their roots in late ancien régime reforms. The Saint Domingue uprising was one of the first of a new type of slave revolt, soon to become typical, in which the insurgents claimed to be already officially emancipated. Apparently beginning with the Martinique rebellion of August 1789, this development probably owed more to the antislavery movement than to French Revolutionary ideals.

Contemporary interrogations of captives revealed that the slave revolt was organized by elite slaves from some two hundred sugar estates. Later sources connect their meetings with the voodoo cult. The colonists, however, refused to believe that the slaves acted alone. Royalist counterrevolutionaries, the Amis des Noirs, secessionist planters, the remnants of Ogé's band, and the free coloreds in general were all accused by one group or another in the devastating aftermath of the rebellion. However, if any outside elements were involved, they soon found that the slaves were determined to decide their own fate. Their early leaders, Jean-François and Biassou, imposed an iron discipline on the disparate bands that they formed into armies. Yet, when they attempted, fearing famine and defeat, to negotiate in December a sell-out peace with the planters, their followers forced them back onto the offensive.

Free coloreds from the parishes of Ogé and Chavannes certainly did join the slave rebels when the northern mountains were overrun, but in this they had little option. Elsewhere in the North, free coloreds fought against the slaves until they learned that the May 15 decree had been withdrawn. This was a fatal move by the wavering National Assembly. Although civil war between whites and free coloreds had broken out in the western and southern provinces, the whites had been swiftly compelled to accept the mulattoes' demands in these regions where the free coloreds predominated and showed exceptional military skill. Now, however, fighting began all over again. The towns of Port-au-Prince and Jacmel were burned and, as in the North, fearful atrocities were committed by all sides, making future reconciliation the more difficult. In parts of the West, white and colored planters combined to fight urban white radicals. In the South, they divided along color rather than class lines, while in the North free coloreds joined the slave rebels. All sides began to arm slaves to fight for them, and plantation discipline slackened. Slave revolts broke out intermittently in the West and South, but the rebels were usually bought off with limited concessions, so that in general the slave regime remained intact though shaken.

Beginning in December 1791, troop reinforcements started to arrive in small numbers from strife-torn France. The soldiers died rapidly, however, from tropical diseases, and, needed everywhere in the colony, they had little impact on an enemy that avoided pitched battles. Not until France finally granted full citizenship to all free persons in April 1792 did the situation begin to stabilize. Prejudice and resentment remained strong; but in most areas outside the main towns, white and mulatto property owners now grudgingly came to terms and turned their attention to the slaves. However, the civil commissioners who arrived in September to enforce the decree rapidly alienated most sections of the white population. Léger-Félicité Sonthonax and Etienne Polverel were dynamic and zealous radicals who scorned colonial opinion and who immediately adopted the cause of the Republic on learning that the French monarchy had been overthrown. After deporting the governor, they dissolved the Colonial Assembly, all municipalities, and political clubs. Royalist officers, autonomist planters, and racist small whites were imprisoned and deported in large numbers, and free coloreds were promoted to public office in their stead.

Separated from the race war, the slave rebellion assumed more manageable proportions. The 6,000 troops and National Guards who came out with the civil commissioners were left inactive for months, but the northern plain was nonetheless easily retaken in November 1792. When a full offensive was eventually mounted in January 1793, Jean-François and Biassou were driven from one after another of their mountain camps, and thousands of slaves surrendered. By this time, however, the new French Republic was being propelled by its leaders into a world war that would leave Europe and Saint Domingue irrevocably changed.

War and the Rise of Toussaint Louverture, 1793–1798

By refuting the ideology of white supremacy and destroying the governmental structure that imposed it, the French Revolution thus brought the free coloreds to power in most parts of Saint Domingue in alliance with the Republican officials from France. This transfer of power to the free coloreds also gained impetus from the outbreak of war with England and Spain in the spring of 1793. The colonists looked to foreign invasion to free them from the civil commissioners, who in turn grew intolerant of any white in a position of power. Port-au-Prince was bombarded into submission by Sonthonax and its jails were filled with recalcitrant colonists. The southern coast was already a free colored stronghold, but, following a massacre of whites in Les Cayes in July, it became effectively autonomous under the mulatto goldsmith André Rigaud. In the plain of Arcahaye the ruthless J. B. Lapointe established himself as a local dictator, while in the plain of Cul-de-Sac behind Port-au-Prince, Pinchinat, Lambert, and Beauvais became the dominant influences. At Cap Français, Villatte would achieve a similar local dominance after the burning of the town in June and the flight of some 10,000 whites to North America.

With the white colonists eclipsed and the slave revolt close to suppression, the spring of 1793 represents the high point of mulatto control in Saint Domingue. The rest of the colony's history, indeed that of independent Haiti, may be viewed as a struggle between the emergent power of the black masses and the predominantly brown-skinned middle class. Whether the slave revolt in the North could actually have been suppressed, and whether slavery on the plantations of the South and West would have continued as before, of course no one can say. However, the onset of war quite clearly transformed the situation not only of the veteran fighters in the northern mountains but also of all the blacks in Saint Domingue.

As soon as war was declared, both the Republican French and the Spaniards, preparing to invade from Santo Domingo, began competing to win over the black rebels. They offered them employment as mercenaries and personal freedom for themselves. Both in Europe and Saint Domingue, the fortunes of the new Republic were at their lowest ebb. Half of the soldiers sent to the colony in 1792 were already dead, and no more could be expected from a France racked by civil war and itself facing invasion. The civil commissioners' rhetoric about Republican virtues therefore had little impact on Jean-François, Biassou, and the other black chiefs. They preferred to take guns, uniforms, and bribes from the Spaniards and continued to attack Frenchmen and free coloreds in the name of the king. Increasingly, Sonthonax and Polyerel were compelled to turn to the masses in general to shore up Republican rule. First they liberalized the plantation regime, then freed and formed into legions slaves who had fought in the civil wars. To forestall a counterrevolution by the new governor, they offered rebel bands the sack of Cap Français; and when an English invasion was imminent, they abolished slavery completely on August 29, 1793.

The decree of General Emancipation was felt in the colony like an electric shock. It was greeted with hostility by mulatto and white planters and with some skepticism by the blacks; Sonthonax had acted unilaterally and might yet be overruled by the French government. Sonthonax's intention was to convert the slaves into profit-sharing serfs, who were to be tied to their estates and subject to compulsory but remunerated labor. Almost nothing is known about how this system of forced labor functioned, either in 1793 or later years, but among the decree's initial effects were a disruption of plantation discipline and an increasing assertiveness on the part of the blacks. The hitherto powerless began to fully appreciate their latent power.

British and Spanish troops, sent from the surrounding colonies and welcomed by the planters, were to preserve slavery in most of the West and part of the South, but in some of the districts they occupied their arrival itself provoked uprisings and the burning of the plantations. Even without such militant action a social revolution was quietly proceeding, for where planters abandoned the countryside, work in the fields ceased and the blacks adopted a peasant life-style centered on their provision grounds. Moreover, to supplement their scanty forces the British, like the Spanish, were to recruit thousands of blacks as soldiers, further weakening the plantation regime. Above all, to repel the invaders, the Republican forces were also, during five years of warfare, to arm thousands of former slaves who until then had not left their plantations. As to the psychological effects of participating in a war of liberation, one can only guess, but in military terms the results were obvious. The civil commissioners in the North and West, André Rigaud in the South, the Spanish, and eventually the British all came to rely on armies predominantly made up of blacks.

One may argue, therefore, that though the Spanish and British occupations were intended to save the slave regime and the plantation economy, they had precisely the opposite effect. The outbreak of the European war greatly extended the effects of the slave revolt, breaking down the mental and physical shackles of slavery and plantation habit, and enabling the ex-slaves to develop the military skills with which to defend their freedom. At the same time, it made the former free coloreds increasingly dependent on the martial ability of the blacks. More than this, foreign intervention completely divided the *anciens libres* (as the free coloreds were now called) and isolated the large communities of the West from their cousins in the North and South. Slave emancipation was a fatal dilemma for the members of this classically unstable class. The Republic had guaranteed their civil rights but then took away their property and offended their prejudices. Many, therefore, opted to support the Spanish and British, though of these a large number soon changed their minds. Rigaud and Vilatte remained committed to the Republic, but friction between them and Sonthonax and the French general Laveaux mounted as the latter looked more and more to the blacks for support.

While this gradual shift in the internal balance of power lay in the logic of the political situation, it also came to acquire enormous impetus from the meteoric career of a single black general, Toussaint Bréda, who in August 1793 adopted the name Louverture. A few months before, he had joined the Spaniards independently of Jean-François and Biassou, under whose command he had served. During the next ten years, he was to emerge as a military commander, diplomat, and political leader of consummate ability. He would achieve international renown and be acknowledged in some quarters as one of the great men of his day. Of the previous fifty years of his life little can be said with certainty.

Like the majority of slave leaders who achieved prominence, Toussaint was a Creole who had belonged to the slave elite. He had been a coachman and in charge of the livestock on the Bréda estate just outside of Cap Français, whose manager appears to have favored him. At some point he had become a devout Christian. Though his command of French would always remain fairly basic, he had learned to read, and late in life

(between 1779 and 1791) to write his name. Despite his degree of acculturation, Toussaint did not lose touch with his African roots. He is said to have spoken fluently the language of his "Arada" father—apparently the son of a chief—and to have enjoyed speaking it with other slaves of his father's ethnic group. He seems also to have become skilled in the medicinal use of plants and herbs. Such slaves who lived at the interface between white and black society needed to know the ways of both worlds. To maintain their standing in both communities, they had to be shrewd observers of human nature and skilled performers of a number of roles. It is not so surprising, then, if among Toussaint's dominant characteristics in later life were his ability to manipulate and his virtuoso use of deception. The plantation house was in this respect a good school.

This is perhaps one reason why it has only recently been discovered that Toussaint was no longer a slave at the time of the French Revolution. He had actually been freed around the age of thirty. While he appears to have maintained a close connection with the Bréda estate and its manager, he also owned and rented at different times both slaves and small properties. He thus belonged to the class of free colored slaveholders, into whose lower ranks he and his children married. One gets a picture, then, of a man of diverse experience, who was at home in various social milieus: among the white colonists, who thought well of him; among creole slaves and free blacks; and among *bossales* newly arrived from Africa.

Two versions exist of Toussaint's behavior during the August 1791 insurrection, both shakily supported by contemporary documentation. Most historians suppose that Toussaint had nothing to do with the uprising and at first protected the Bréda plantation, until after a few months he threw in his lot with the rebels. Others suggest that Toussaint himself secretly organized the rebellion. They claim he acted as an intermediary for counterrevolutionary whites, using his contacts among leaders of the slave community but remaining shrewdly in the background. Similar puzzles exist with regard to many other events in his life. It is certain, however, that within three months of the August uprising he had achieved prominence among the rebel blacks and was apparently one of Biassou's advisers. He interceded successfully for the lives of white prisoners, and, as one of the free colored negotiators used by the slave leaders, he transmitted their offer to the whites to help suppress the rebellion in return for the freedom of a few score leaders. Despite the amnesty France offered to free coloreds in rebellion, Toussaint stayed with the slave rebels through the dark days of 1792. His relations with Jean-François, who called himself the "Grand Admiral," and with Biassou, self-styled "Generalissimo," seem to have been stormy, but he remained one of their leading subordinates commanding a small force of his own with the rank of field marshal.

After he joined the Spaniards around June 1793, Toussaint's star rose rapidly. In the great jumble of mountains of the North Province, he immediately won a series of startling military victories against the French and free coloreds. These early campaigns reveal at once a leader of acute intelligence, who was adept at ambush and at totally confusing his opponents. They also reveal a man both ruthless and humane, capable of making barbarous threats but of sparing even those who had double-crossed him. This policy reaped rewards. White and mulatto property owners surrendered to him, knowing his reputation for mercy. As arms and ammunition fell into his hands, so his tiny army grew. Lances and machetes were exchanged for muskets. Free colored and even French soldiers joined its ranks and helped train its levies. If the essence of things creole is creative adaptation, this was truly a creole army. In nine months, it grew from a few hundred to several thousand men.

Meanwhile, the Spanish troops stayed cautiously on the Santo Domingo frontier, paralyzed by a series of epidemics. The forces of Jean-François and Biassou, for their part, gave up campaigning for quarreling among themselves and for living it up outrageously at the expense of the king of Spain. The Spaniards soon realized that they had bitten off far more than they could chew. Such successes as they had, they owed almost entirely to Toussaint. The handsome Jean-François they found vain and fickle, and the impetuous Biassou, gross and overbearing. But in Toussaint, Spanish officers recognized a military commander of ability and a man of honor and personal dignity. They were also much impressed by his piety and the hours he spent in church. Nonetheless, however much the Spanish might respect piety, honor, and military ability, they found themselves stuck with Jean-François and Biassou and compelled to recognize them as principal commanders.

This raises the difficult question of Toussaint's volte-face, his sudden desertion of the Spaniards in the spring of 1794 and his rallying to the French Republic. According to one interpretation, it was frustrated ambition and increasing friction with Biassou that led Toussaint to leave the Spanish and seek promotion under the French. Others attribute the changeover to a desire to win freedom for all the blacks in Saint Domingue. Specifically, they link his change of direction to the decree of February 4, 1794, by which the French government ratified Sonthonax's actions and abolished slavery in all France's colonies. However, though it would seem logical that these two great events were connected, the decree was not in fact known in the colony until long after Toussaint began negotiating with the French general Laveaux, and not for at least a month after he had turned on his Spanish allies.

Even so, Toussaint's volte-face was not a simply self-interested affair. His concern for the liberty of the blacks was genuine. Although in 1791–92 he was prominent among the chiefs who offered to force their followers back into slavery on the plantations, this was at moments when defeat seemed certain. Unlike Jean-François and Biassou, Toussaint never rounded up plantation blacks for sale to the Spaniards, and at least by mid-1793 he had become associated with the idea of General Emancipation. There is some evidence that his delay in joining the Spaniards was specifically due to his attempts to get the French to declare slavery abolished. His refusal to join the French thereafter was probably attributable to the Republic's precarious position. Anyway, having joined the Spanish, Toussaint played a double game, fighting to preserve the plantation regime but at the same time speaking to the blacks of liberty and equality. This doubtless helps explain why his army grew so rapidly. It was also at this time that he adopted the name Louverture ("the opening") with its cryptic connotation of a new beginning.

Matters came to a head early in 1794. After Spanish troops had arrived from Cuba and Venezuela, hundreds of French refugees began returning to the occupied districts. Only now, after almost a year of inaction, could the Spanish seriously contemplate restoring slavery on the plantations and launching an attack on Cap Français. Resistance came from various quarters— from plantation blacks who had not taken up arms but who refused to be coerced back into the fields, from free coloreds disenchanted with their treatment by the Spanish, and from some of the black mercenary troops as well. It was behind this movement that Toussaint decided to fling his weight as of the beginning of May 1794. For several months, nevertheless, he kept up his astonishing double game while he assessed the political situation. Though he told the French general Laveaux he was fighting hard for the Republic, he remained largely on the defensive, assuring the Spaniards that such hostilities as occurred should be blamed on his disobedient subordinates. At the same time, he tried to allay the suspicions of Jean-François and he also promised his allegiance to the British forces who were threatening him from the south. In the meantime, news trickled through from Europe of Republican victories and of the abolition of slavery, while in Saint Domingue the spring rains brought fevers that decimated the Spanish and British troops. Cunningly choosing his moment, Toussaint then fell on each of his opponents in turn with devastating effect.

Whether motivated by idealism or ambition, Toussaint's volte-face was therefore tortuous, cautious, and protracted, and it was not a single-handed initiative. It was nonetheless the turning point of the Haitian Revolution. Now associated with the ideology of the French Revolution, black militancy became unequivocally directed toward the complete overthrow of slavery for perhaps the first time in the Americas. The balance of power tipped against the alliance of slave owners and foreign invaders, and French rule in Saint Domingue would be saved for another decade; but having gained a leader of genius, the movement for black self-liberation henceforth held center stage.

The next four years were a period of almost constant warfare. For much of this time, Toussaint's ragged soldiers, "as naked as earthworms" as he graphically described them, were perpetually short of food, clothing, and ammunition. They died by the hundreds in their attacks on the well-entrenched positions of the British and Spanish, but in the process was forged a formidable army. The development should not be taken for granted. Unlike the free coloreds, who had a reputation as horsemen and sharpshooters, few slaves can have had much experience of firearms or antillery, even if they had been warriors in Africa. Since 1791 they had shown themselves skillful in their use of surprise and in exploiting terrain, capable of great endurance, and difficult to pin down. To these qualities Toussaint added the ability to maneuver in large numbers, heightened esprit de corps, and a tactical brilliance few could equal. He gathered around him an experienced officer corps, which was mainly black and ex-slave but included many mulattoes and a few whites as well. Already prominent by the end of 1794 were the youthful Moise, whom Toussaint called his nephew, and the vigorous and stern Jean-Jacques Dessalines.

By then, the Spaniards and their black auxiliaries were almost a spent force in Saint Domingue. They had lost half of their conquests and even their own frontier towns of San Raphael and San Michel on the grassy central savanna, stormed by Toussaint in October. They held the strategic northeastern seaport of Fort Dauphin, but the massacre there of 800 French colonists by Jean-François's soldiers, smarting from defeat, had ended all hopes of reviving the plantation regime. Instead, Spanish and black officers cooperated in stripping the sugar estates and sending their slaves and equipment to Cuba. Defeated in Europe and the Caribbean, Spain withdrew from the war in July 1795 and became an ally of the French Republic the following year. Santo Domingo, Spain's oldest colony, had become untenable and was surrendered to France, which for the time was too weak to occupy it. Jean-François and Biassou with 800 of their followers went into pensioned exile in different parts of the Spanish Empire. In the mountains of the northeast, however, many of their soldiers fought on in the name of the king until 1797.

Toussaint's forces occupied a cordon of some thirty camps stretching from the central mountains of the North Province along the fringe of the Artibonite plain to the port of Gonaives. He thus controlled access from the North to the West. Most of the northern littoral, however, was in the hands of Villatte and other semi-independent mulatto leaders. Laveaux, now governor, was confined with his few surviving white troops to the northwestern port of Port-de-Paix. The broad flood plain of the Artibonite became something of a no-man's land, but the whole of the West Province to the south of it eventually fell to the British and their planter allies, although independent bands of blacks continued to harry them from various mountain strongholds. The British also held the naval base of the Môle Saint Nicolas and, at the tip of the southern peninsula, the prosperous coffee-growing region of the Grand Anse. The rest of the southern peninsula was a mulatto fief ruled from Les Cayes by André Rigaud. Launching successive attacks against the Grand Anse and Port-au-Prince, Rigaud, like Toussaint, built up an army mainly consisting of ex-slaves. By 1798 he commanded some 10,000 soldiers and Toussaint around 20,000.

Up to 1796, the British government had hoped to conquer Saint Domingue and add it to its tropical empire. Thereafter, it became resigned to failure but dared not withdraw for fear the black revolution would be exported to its own colonies. During their first two years in Saint Domingue (the only time they had any prospect of success), the British forces averaged barely 2,000 men. Though they were massively reinforced in 1796, British commanders continued with a mainly defensive strategy that condemned most of their troops to die in the seaports of epidemic diseases. Throughout these years of war, yellow fever flourished in the Caribbean, fueled by the huge influx of nonimmune European troops and their concentration in the region's ports. During the five-year occupation of Saint Domingue, the British lost 15,000 of the 25,000 soldiers they sent there. The British also gravely blundered early on by alienating the free coloreds, many of whom deserted them. Even so, the most valuable part of the occupied zone was the plain of Arcahaye, where the local commander, the ancien libre Lapointe, kept the plantations in full production. By 1798 the costs of occupation were found to be prohibitive; and under mounting pressure from Toussaint and Rigaud, the British staged a gradual evacuation. Only then for some 60,000 to 70,000 blacks did slavery come to an end.

During these years Toussaint's position within the Republican zone grew steadily more dominant. Early in 1796, Villatte and the anciens libres of the North Province attempted to overthrow Governor Laveaux in an apparent bid for independence, which seems to have been secretly supported by André Rigaud in the South. According to some sources, Toussaint knew of the planned coup and with supreme cunning actually encouraged its instigators. But once it had broken out, he intervened in force and crushed it. The French government was left in no doubt on whom it depended for keeping Saint Domingue in French hands. Toussaint, the ex-slave, was proclaimed deputy-governor.

For the time being, however, the Republican position remained precarious. Not only were the British now pouring troops into the colony, but also dissension was rife in the Republican zone. Having fled to France in 1794, Sonthonax returned to Saint Domingue in May 1796 with four other civil commissioners and 900 white soldiers. Their attempts to centralize control of both the war effort and the economy of the Republican parishes quickly made enemies. As Laveaux had found, mulatto leaders who had become accustomed to complete local autonomy resented attempts to take over abandoned property they themselves were exploiting. Efforts to raise the productivity of the surviving plantations also spread fears among the ex-slaves (now called "cultivators") of a restoration of slavery. This was especially true of the northwestern peninsula, where the plantations had suffered relatively little, and whose coffee was sold to American traders for food and munitions, as in the mulatto South. From the failure of Villatte's coup to the end of 1796, the Northwest witnessed a succession of uprisings by black cultivators, in which were killed the few remaining white colonists in the region. Local mulattoes were probably behind at least some of these revolts. They show, nevertheless, that even in these districts least affected by the slave revolution a complete break with the past had by now occurred in the minds of the rural blacks. This did not mean, however, that such blacks were willing to defend their freedom by leaving their homes and becoming soldiers in Toussaint's army. Sonthonax had distributed guns to plantation workers; but when in a moment of crisis he tried to conscript all young males for military service, the extent of rebellion increased. At the same time, the mulatto South broke away from French rule, when the tactless commissioners sent to Les Cayes were expelled by André Rigaud and more whites were massacred.

The Republic was to weather these crises but only at the cost of seeing more and more power pass into the hands of Toussaint Louverture. It was his homespun diplomacy that finally pacified the blacks of the Northwest. The African General Pierre Michel, hero of the northeastern campaigns and a favorite of Sonthonax, was then arrested. Earlier rivals of Toussaint had already disappeared. With the aristocratic Governor Laveaux, Toussaint had formed a remarkably close friendship, referring to him in his correspondence as "Papa," though the two men were about the same age. Even so, by the autumn of 1796 Toussaint was intimating that Laveaux could best serve Saint Domingue if he were in Paris, where angry planters were demanding the restoration of West Indian slavery; Laveaux was promptly elected a deputy for Saint Domingue and returned home to France. Next it was the turn of Commissioner Sonthonax. In the summer of 1797, Toussaint suddenly accused him of plotting to make Saint Domingue independent. Though still popular with the blacks, he also was forced to depart.

Smitten with life in the West Indies and threatened by political reaction in Paris, Sonthonax may indeed have wished to see Saint Domingue sever ties with France. Nevertheless, Toussaint's accusation suggests a neat sense of irony. While continuing to play the role of a loyal servant of the French Republic, he eliminated one by one all his rivals within the colony. The French government was becoming alarmed and in 1798 dispatched a new representative, General Hédouville. In six months, he, too, was deftly outmaneuvered, though with all due courtesy, and driven out of Saint Domingue by a supposedly spontaneous uprising. Whether or not Toussaint was aiming for independence, or even supreme power, at this time, historians will probably never agree. However, the growth of Toussaint's power was inexorable.

The Ascendancy of Toussaint Louverture, 1798–1802

Toussaint's expulsion of Sonthonax facilitated a rapprochement with Rigaud, which enabled the two men to cooperate in driving out the British. Thereafter, only Rigaud himself stood between Toussaint and complete domination of Saint Domingue. Rigaud now controlled all the southern peninsula; Toussaint all the North and West. Once their common enemy had been eliminated, relations between them rapidly deteriorated. Even today, the conflict between Toussaint and Rigaud is regarded by Haitians as one of the most sensitive topics in their history. It has become known as the War of Knives. Although it was in essence a regional power struggle, it tended to divide the light-skinned anciens libres from the new class of black military officers, though most of the troops on both sides were black ex-slaves. Many of Toussaint's light-skinned officers, though they had been with him for years, sided with Rigaud; and when Toussaint invaded the South, they staged rebellions against him. The fighting was desperate, and Toussaint's reprisals were brutal, although prudently delegated to subordinates. The details are disputed, but the black general Dessalines had been accused of waging something like a war of genocide against the southern mulattoes. Toussaint later reproved him: "I ordered you to prune the tree not to uproot it." Rigaud and most of the leaders fled to France.

By the middle of 1800, Toussaint ruled supreme in Saint Domingue and of necessity was recognized as its governor. A small, wiry man, very black, with mobile, penetrating eyes, he greatly impressed most who met him, even those who thought him ugly. He had lost in battle his upper set of front teeth and his ears were deformed by wearing heavy gold earrings, but his presence was commanding and suggested enormous self-control. Whether socializing with white planters or pacifying angry plantation workers, his manner was reserved but dignified. In private, the whites might mock his rusticity (his headscarf, his limited French) or his "pretensions" (his huge watch chains, his moralizing piety), but in his presence no one laughed. Though Toussaint maintained the external pomp of previous colonial governors and he acquired much landed property, his private life was frugal. Wary of being poisoned, he ate little, and he slept only a few hours each night, invariably working late with his secretaries. His prodigious activity astonished people, as did the air of mystery he deliberately cultivated. Still an excellent horseman, he often rode over one hundred miles a day, making frequent changes of direction so that no one could be sure where he would appear next.

With the war ended in the south, Toussaint could now set about rebuilding the colony and restoring its shattered economy. Although fiercely committed to the liberty of the blacks, he believed it essential that the plantation regime be revived in order to restore Saint Domingue's prosperity. With no export economy, there would be no revenue to maintain his army of 20,000 to 40,000 men. And without the army, the gains of the revolution would be at the mercy of France's unstable politics. Toussaint therefore continued with the schemes of Commissioner Sonthonax, whereby the ex-slaves were compelled to work on the plantations in return for a share of the produce. It was a difficult policy to implement, for increasingly the blacks preferred to establish smallholdings of their own and had little desire to work for wages. This was especially true of the sugar estates, which depended on regimented gang labor and where the working day was long and arduous. Already accustomed to marketing their own food crops, most blacks preferred to concentrate on extending their family provision grounds, cheerfully letting the fields of cane and coffee choke with weeds. Toussaint, however, refused to break up the great estates. He used the army to impose the regime of forced labor and sanctioned the use of corporal punishment; he even supported the reintroduction of the slave trade to make up the loss of manpower. As most estates had been abandoned by their owners, they were leased out usually to army officers and other privileged figures in the new regime. In addition, Toussaint also encouraged the return from exile of the white planters to take charge of their properties and to work toward the creation of a new Saint Domingue.

The return of the planters, of course, raised grave suspicions among the plantation blacks and also among some of Toussaint's officers. They also resented the white advisers he appointed, and the pleasure he evidently took in inviting planters and merchants to his social gatherings. A naturally taciturn man, he seemed to be becoming increasingly remote. These tensions were given violent expression when the very popular General Moise staged a revolt in the northern plain, which caused the deaths of several of the returned planters. When Toussaint had him executed, many thought his policies were going awry. It is usually argued that Toussaint thought the technical expertise of the whites and their social polish were necessary to the rebuilding of the colony, and that he therefore was committed to a multiracial Saint Domingue. Recent work, however, has stressed that, although Toussaint encouraged the whites to return, he rarely gave them back their estates. These tended to remain in the hands of his army officers who constituted a new, black, landholding class. The return of the planters served to camouflage this development, and also to provide hostages.

It is by no means clear how successful Toussaint was in reviving the plantation economy. Export figures for the twelve months following the war against Rigaud (1800–1801) show coffee production at two-thirds the 1789 level, raw sugar down by four-fifths, and semirefined sugar, the most valuable item, almost nonexistent. On the other hand, it is likely that trade figures were deliberately understated to allow the amassing of secret funds and the stockpiling of munitions. The administrative confusion and the autonomy of local army commanders, of which white officials complained, probably fulfilled the same function. According to his critics, Toussaint kept his generals' loyalty by allowing them to amass personal fortunes. Their troops went unpaid but the soldiers in turn were allowed to exercise a petty tyranny over the cultivators, whose provision grounds were subject to army requisitions. Only on the generals' plantations, however, were the labor laws effectively applied. Other commentators painted a more enthusiastic picture of the regime, insisting that a new spirit was abroad in the colony. Race prejudice was diminishing fast. Towns were being rebuilt. Justice was administered impartially. Even some schools were established (though this was a French initiative). All one can say with certainty is that the new regime was given very little time to prove itself.

Late in 1799, France, like Saint Domingue, also acquired a military strongman for a ruler. Napoleon Bonaparte and Toussaint Louverture had much in common. Both were seen as defenders of basic revolutionary gains of the previous decade, particularly of new land settlements. Both were autocrats who extinguished all political liberty in the respective countries. Both were destroyed by their own ambition. In July 1801, shortly before Napoleon proclaimed himself consul for life, Toussaint promulgated a constitution for Saint Domingue which flagrantly concentrated all power in his hands and which made him governor for life with the right to choose his successor. Drawn up by planters with a secessionist background, the document came within a hairbreadth of a declaration of independence. Toussaint had anticipated by 160 years the concept of associated statehood. Napoleon was infuriated. However, the first consul had already determined that French rule should be restored in what had been France's most valuable possession.

There was, nevertheless, nothing inevitable about the epic clash between Toussaint and Napoleon. Although he was constantly under pressure from vengeful planters, merchants, and colonial officials, Bonaparte had resisted for well over a year their clamor for a military expedition. His original policy was to leave Toussaint in control of Saint Domingue and to use the colony as a springboard for expanding French power in the Americas. Black troops would be sent to conquer the slave colonies of France's rivals. As part of the plan, Louisiana was purchased from Spain. However, by the spring of 1801 it was apparent that, under its black governor, Saint Domingue would be of little use to France; it was de facto already an independent state. Though France was at war with Great Britain, and unofficially with the United States, too (the Quasi-War of 1798–1800), Toussaint had made a secret commercial treaty and non-aggression pact with both these powers. This involved expelling French privateers from the colony. His purpose was to preserve the trade on which Saint Domingue, and his army, depended. The United States supplied vital foodstuffs, livestock, and munitions; the British navy controlled the sea-lanes and would otherwise have blockaded Saint Domingue. This is why, when the French and mulattoes tried to foment a slave rebellion in Jamaica, and sent agents there from Saint Domingue, Toussaint betrayed the plot to the Jamaican administration. Whatever his interest in black liberation, he needed to keep on good terms with his neighbors so as to preserve his autonomy.

In spite of Toussaint's independent foreign policy and his ambiguous behavior toward the planters, Napoleon's intention remained down to March 1801 to work with the black leader, not against him. However, the last straw for Napoleon came when Toussaint suddenly annexed without reference to France the adjoining colony of Santo Domingo, which was then French territory. The ex-slave thereby became master of the entire island of Hispaniola. It was the high point of his career. Suspicious of French intentions, Toussaint aimed to deny a potential invasion force use of Santo Domingo's harbors. But it was precisely this event that persuaded Napoleon that an invasion was necessary. Toussaint's new constitution merely enraged him further. Nevertheless, the fatal decision to attempt to restore slavery in Saint Domingue was not taken for another year, long after the invasion force had landed. Although usually presented as an act of vicious megalomania, the Napoleonic invasion of Saint Domingue was more like a last-ditch attempt to keep the plantation regime in French hands.

Toussaint had grossly miscalculated. If he was willing to antagonize Napoleon to this degree, some say, he should have gone all out and declared complete independence, rallying the black masses behind him. Instead, he kept up the fiction of loyalty to France, sending envoys to Napoleon to explain each act of defiance. He continued to assure local whites of his goodwill and to admonish the blacks on the necessity of hard work. The ambivalence of his double game was to critically weaken black resistance to the coming invasion. Toussaint's failure to declare independence was doubtless due to a number of factors. Caution, the need for white administrative personnel, and the fear of alienating the slaveholding Americans and British were probably the most important. By stopping short of de jure independence, Toussaint evidently thought that Napoleon would negotiate rather than fight. Perhaps he overrated the military lessons he had taught the Spanish and British. Or perhaps he believed that the British navy would prevent a French fleet from crossing the Atlantic.

The British, however, would support the black governor's rule only so long as it weakened France's war effort, and the Anglo-French war was now drawing to a temporary close. The British government feared both Toussaint and Napoleon, but regarded the latter as the lesser of two evils. To see the two embroiled in internecine conflict would be a perfect compromise solution to a threatening situation. In October 1801, as soon as peace preliminaries were signed, the British gave their assent to an invasion of Saint Domingue.

The War of Independence, 1802–1803

Napoleon's brother-in-law, General Leclerc, landed in Saint Domingue at the beginning of February 1802 with some 10,000 soldiers. By sending out a large force in the healthy winter months and deploying it rapidly, Napoleon avoided the worst mistakes of the British and Spanish. His troops were also far superior to those previously sent there, and their numbers were doubled within two months. Leclerc's orders were nevertheless to seize the colony by ruse, winning over where possible the black generals. Only later, once he had allayed their suspicions, was he to disarm their soldiers and then deport all the black officers. The plantations would be returned to their owners. Slavery would be restored in Santo Domingo, where it had never been officially abolished, but in Saint Domingue the forced labor regime would be retained. Leclerc both said and thought he was reestablishing French rule but not slavery.

Uncertain of French intentions, the blacks failed to offer any concerted resistance and Leclerc quickly occupied all the colony's ports. Cap Français, under the eye of Toussaint, was burned by its commander, Henry Christophe, as was Saint Marc by Dessalines, but several of the generals surrendered without a fight. They were now planters themselves and had property to protect. Toussaint, Christophe, and Dessalines, however, took to the mountains, fighting heroic rearguard actions and destroying all that they left behind. Battle casualties were heavy and from the beginning the war was marked by frightful atrocities on both sides. Fearing the return of slavery, the rural population rallied to the black army and produced guerrilla leaders of their own. However, as successive generals surrendered, their troops were turned against those who still held out. Through the month of April Toussaint kept up a vigorous guerrilla campaign with great persistence but dwindling resources. He surrendered early in May and retired to private life on one of his plantations. Christophe, Dessalines, and the other generals were maintained in their posts and used by the French to mop up remaining guerrilla resistance.

It may be that all three leaders were biding their time. Leclerc's army was already severely weakened and the blacks well knew that during the summer it would be decimated by disease. Nevertheless, when within a month Toussaint was accused of plotting rebellion, it was Dessalines and Christophe who helped denounce him. The old leader was kidnapped, hastily deported, and died in a French dungeon in April 1803. Despite this devious maneuvering by the military chiefs, small bands of insurgents fought on in the mountains in the tradition of the maroons. As Toussaint declared on leaving the colony: the French had felled only the trunk of the tree of liberty; it had strong roots and would grow again.

The situation changed dramatically in July 1802, when it was learned (by the blacks and Leclerc almost simultaneously) that the French government had decided to restore slavery in all France's colonies. Attempts to disarm the rural population now met with massive resistance, just when hundreds of French soldiers each week were dying of yellow fever. The campaign of terror launched by Leclerc proved counterproductive. As thousands of black prisoners, men and women, went stoically to their deaths, a new sense of unity was forged based on racial solidarity. By the autumn, the French were fighting the entire nonwhite population of Saint Domingue. Even the free coloreds who had fled the South in 1800 and returned in Leclerc's army now combined with their former opponents. Led by Rigaud's protégé, Alexandre Pétion, they accepted the overall leadership of Jean-Jacques Dessalines, who finally deserted the French in late September. As Toussaint's inspector of agriculture, the conqueror of the mulatto South, and then Leclerc's chief collaborator, Dessalines had been responsible for the deaths of very many blacks and anciens libres. However, he was the ideal person to lead the struggle to expel the French, and not only because

he was the senior general. A menial slave under the old regime, he had none of the liking for white society which Toussaint, and the former domestic Christophe, shared with the mulattoes. He spoke only *Créole*, the language of the cultivators. And he was possessed of demonic energy, his battle cry being, "Burn houses, cut off heads!"

After Leclerc himself died of yellow fever, the repugnant General Rochambeau openly waged a war of genocide against the black population, but to no avail. No one can say how far Napoleon would have gone in this hopeless venture, but once war was resumed with Great Britain in May 1803 he had to admit defeat. Until then he had sent 44,000 troops to Saint Domingue. Thereafter the British navy prevented any reinforcements from crossing the Atlantic. Napoleon's western design was at an end. Louisiana was sold to the United States. With British ships blockading the coast of Saint Domingue, and Dessalines's forces besieging the coastal towns, the remains of the French army evacuated the colony in November. Since 1791, some 70,000 European soldiers and seamen had died in the attempt to maintain slavery. Of the few thousand whites who optimistically stayed behind, most died in a series of massacres in the following months.

International Repercussions

On January 1, 1804, Dessalines declared Saint Domingue independent and gave it the aboriginal Amerindian name of "Haiti." "I have given the French cannibals blood for blood," he proclaimed. "I have avenged America."[1] During the war of independence some of the blacks referred to themselves as "Incas" (perhaps an echo of the Peruvian uprising of 1780), and some European writers also fancifully depicted the ex-slaves as avenging the Arawaks exterminated in the sixteenth century. Archaeological finds probably made for a general awareness among the blacks of these fellow victims of colonialism, whose patrimony they were now inheriting. While anchoring the new state to the American past, the country's new name meant above all a symbolic break with Europe. All whites were henceforth forbidden to own land in Haiti.

Having destroyed the wealthiest planter class in the New World and defeated the armies of France, Spain, and England, the former slaves and free coloreds now went about making laws for themselves and erecting a state apparatus. In a world dominated by Europeans and where slavery and the slave trade were expanding, the new state was a symbol of black freedom and a demonstration of black accomplishments. For both abolitionists and the proslavery lobby, Haiti was a great experiment, a crucial test case for ideas about race, slavery, and the future of the Caribbean. In Haiti itself, publicists and statesmen spoke out against racism, colonialism, and enslavement. Nevertheless, all the early Haitian statesmen took pains to disclaim any intention of intervening in neighboring colonies. Like Toussaint, they wished to do nothing that might provoke a maritime blockade or an invasion by the slaveholding powers. The exception to this policy was the annexation of Santo Domingo, which Dessalines attempted in 1805 and was finally accomplished in 1822. As in the 1790s, rumors about the activity of Haitian "agents" continued to circulate, and these are given credence by some historians, but official involvement in any of the slave conspiracies or rebellions of the post-1804 period has yet to be proven. The only clear case we have of subversive proselytizing is by agents of the French Republic during the 1790s, most particularly by Victor Hugues, who from Guadeloupe helped foment rebellions among the French-speaking free coloreds of Grenada and Saint Vincent. Haiti nonetheless did make a major contribution to the abolition of slavery (and to decolonization) in the New World. This was in 1815, when Alexandre Pétion gave vital assistance to Simon Bolívar that enabled him to relaunch his campaign for South American independence. Pétion demanded as payment that the planter aristocrat declare slavery in his homeland abolished, which he did on his return to South America.

From 1792 onward laws were passed all around the Caribbean and in North America restricting immigration from strife-torn Saint Domingue. Even when the likelihood of direct interference was not considered strong, slave owners feared the revolution's inflammatory example. Within a month of the August 1791 revolt, slaves in Jamaica were singing songs about the uprising, and before long whites in the West Indies and North America were complaining uneasily of a new "insolence" on the part of their slaves. Several plots and insurrections were partly inspired by events in Saint Domingue and the Emancipation Decree of 1794. Most notable of these were the conspiracies organized by free coloreds in Bahia (1798), Havana (1812), and Charleston (1822). However, many factors were at work in the slave rebellions of the period, and to suppose that mere inspiration from abroad was critical in provoking resistance would be to underestimate the difficulties confronting dissidents in this age of strong colonial garrisons.

France did not abandon its claims to its former colony until 1825, when the Haitian government agreed to pay a large indemnity to the expelled colonists. The debt the country thereby incurred was among the factors retarding its growth in the nineteenth century, and the concessions then given to French merchants further shifted the export economy into foreign hands. Britain and the United States had early established trade relations with the new state (later interrupted by Jefferson as a favor to Napoleon), but full diplomatic recognition was withheld by these countries until they had abolished slavery and no longer deemed Haiti a threat.

The Legacy of Revolution

Created from a unique experience of slavery, war, and revolution, Haiti was to be like no other state. The fledgling black republic began life with its towns and plantations in ruins and under constant threat of another French invasion. Its population had been decimated; it was severely lacking in technical skills and almost totally without experience in administration or government.

Despite the attempts to maintain production on the plantations, the ex-slaves had for a decade been building new lives for themselves as either soldiers or peasant cultivators. Fear of invasion and institutional self-interest were to burden Haiti with an exceptionally large army for the rest of the century. The earliest governments, particularly that of Henry Christophe (1806–20), continued the struggle to revive the sugar plantations with forced labor. However, the masses' desire for land and hatred of estate work, and the falling world price of sugar, forced the attempt to be finally abandoned by 1830. Haiti became essentially a country of peasant smallholders who grew food crops and a little coffee, either on land distributed by the government or on which they squatted. The postwar population was presumably young and mainly female, and therefore grew rapidly. The relative abundance of land meant that the peasants probably lived reasonably well in the nineteenth century. The Voodoo religion, though persecuted by all the early leaders as subversive to authority, became entrenched in the countryside.

Government revenues came primarily from taxing coffee exports. As in colonial times and during the revolution, the government remained military and authoritarian in character, though constitutional forms were to vary widely and regimes change rapidly. After declaring himself emperor, Dessalines was assassinated in 1806 and for the next fourteen years Haiti was divided between a mulatto republic in the South and West and a northern state, ruled by Henry Christophe, which became a monarchy in 1811. Dessalines had made great efforts to preserve the fragile wartime alliance between blacks and anciens libres but tensions continued to run deep, even after the reunification of the country in 1820. Haitian politics developed as a struggle between the uneducated black officer corps which controlled the army, and the brown-skinned professional and business class which made up most of the country's elite.

This conflict was mirrored more broadly in the elaboration of two competing ideologies, one "black," the other "mulatto." In Haitian society the color line was not at all absolute, but these two opposing camps, fronted by the Liberal and National parties, tended to be divided by phenotype as well as by culture, religion, and attitudes toward national development and toward the country's revolutionary past.

[1]Archives Nationales Paris, Cols., CC9B/23, proclamation of 28 avril 1804.

The Abolition of the Atlantic Slave Trade

Michael L. Conniff and Thomas J. Davis

1780s	Peak of the trans-Atlantic slave trade.
1803	The Danes abolish the slave trade, the first ban by a modern nation.
1807	British and U.S. nationals barred from the slave trade.
1831	French slave trade finally suppressed.
1841	Quintuple Agreement (England, France, Russia, Prussia, and Austria) declares slave trading piracy and allows searches.
1845	Aberdeen Act permits the British to inspect Brazilian and flagless vessels suspected of carrying slaves.
1845	Spanish law forbids slave trading by nationals.
1850	Brazilian law forbids slave trading by nationals.
1856	Last documented arrival of slave ship in Brazil.
1862	Anglo-American antislave trade agreement.
1867	Arrival of last slave ship in Cuba marks end of Middle Passage.

The trans-Atlantic slave trade dominated migration to the New World for almost as long as the trade lasted. As late as the 1880s, more immigrants to the Americas had left Africa under duress than had left Europe voluntarily. The traffic brought death to hundreds of thousands in Africa long before slavers received their human cargo and ensured a short life for millions more in passage. By almost any standards, it was probably the most appalling long-distance mass migration that ever occurred. Free migrants, indentured servants, and even transported convicts rarely faced the horrendous conditions, extended duration of travel, loss of life, and sheer human misery that were routine for Africans in the Middle Passage.

Like slavery itself, the slave trade did not simply wither away. It ended because of an arduous campaign that began in the 1780s as the traffic reached its peak, with over nine hundred thousand Africans shipped during the decade. Another eight hundred and fifty thousand or so embarked in the 1790s. In all, from 1780 to 1867, when the traffic was supposedly winding down, over five million persons—or about half of all those who landed in the traffic—began the Middle Passage. In the face of this enormous forced migration, with its economic importance, its longevity, and its indifference to humanity, explaining the purposeful abolition of the traffic in the 1800s challenges modern historians.

Ending the traffic was not easy. Despite restrictions and resultant high prices, slave trading expanded in two of the three major plantation economies in the Americas as late as the 1850s. Cuba continued to import slaves to grow its sugar. Brazil also continued the trade for its coffee regions. Only in the United States did expansion not feed on the traffic, as the South's cotton grew with only a domestic slave trade. Yet during the U.S. Civil War (1861–1865), the South itself came close to reopening the trade. Demand for Africans continued in the Americas, and access to them made a significant difference among plantation economies in the 1800s.

Ending the slave trade required abolition and suppression. The first was a formal prohibition, the second an actual cessation. By whichever means, a restructuring of the Atlantic economy was heralded, particularly in the plantation Americas, and the prospect of such drastic change raised the specter of widespread resistance. Force or threat of force accompanied the process everywhere.

The timing proved crucial to the future complexion of the Americas. If the slave trade had not ended when it did, the transportation revolution might have transformed the traffic, as it did North Atlantic passenger shipping. A large share of the mass trans-Atlantic migration in the 1800s might then have been enslaved Africans rather than free Europeans. Employers probably would have found ready use for plentiful slaves in an ever-widening range of nonplantation occupations unless the ideological climate changed drastically from that of the 1700s. Thus, stopping the flow of coerced labor from Africa in the early 1800s ensured that the Americas would become predominantly white rather than predominantly black.

Like modern narcotics trafficking, slave trading was an international activity; yet international law never outlawed it, and so the force used to suppress slave trading sometimes violated international law. While force was necessary, it was not sufficient, for ending the traffic required international cooperation. As was demonstrated time and again, one nation acting alone might shift the traffic's course, but it would not stop the flow. Slavers simply chose other routes to evade the interdicting nation. They eluded its forces by smuggling, or they denied its authority by sailing under a different flag. Only nations acting together could effectively end the traffic.

Great Britain led the way. It initiated the first serious restriction on the traffic in 1787 when it ordered British slavers to reduce their slave-per-ton ratios. In 1792 Denmark became the first nation to abolish the trade, although its actual part in the traffic continued until 1803. Britain continued to show the strongest commitment to ending the traffic and outlawed it in 1807. As the world's foremost maritime power, its actions proved the most effective, although national trade rivalry also impeded cooperation.

Britain's act of 1807 outlawed slave traffic by its nationals and barred slave ships to and from any of its territories. In the next seventeen years Parliament added fourteen supplemental acts to close loopholes in enforcement. Liverpool, London, and Bristol traders, who ranked among the world's foremost slavers, quickly switched their vast fleets to other businesses.

Not all British hands abandoned the slave traffic so quickly. British bankers lent handsome sums that kept slavers thriving. They furnished mortgages for plantation owners to buy slaves in the traffic, and they advanced credit to outfit and sponsor slavers not flying the British flag. In addition, British merchants furnished goods and services to slavers. They sold ships to slavers and insured their voyages. In short, while no longer doing the actual hauling, some Britons willingly supplied the means to support the traffic long after 1807.

Getting Britons totally out of the traffic required more than statutes. Mercantile prowess, industrial development, and imperial reach made British business and financial interests nearly ubiquitous in the Atlantic economy of the 1800s. At some point British goods or services touched almost every significant series of Atlantic transactions. Thus, any continued traffic almost by necessity carried some British connection. However, it often proved difficult to ferret out the actual identity of the British firms or individuals involved. With enormous profits at stake, secrecy, misdirection, espionage, bribery, and worse thwarted law.

Enforcement: The British Experience

Even when the Britons' activities seemed clearly contrary to law, successful prosecution proved difficult. Conviction required proof not merely of the illegal but also of illegal intent. Showing that a British merchant sold goods or services used in slave trading was not enough. To convict the merchant required showing that he knew or should have known the customer's purpose to use the goods or services in the slave trade. Not surprisingly, prosecutors found the standard hard to meet, and so the British courts were not able to produce even a single conviction for the crime of supplying slavers.

While seeking to bring its own nationals into line, Britain also attempted to move other nations to eliminate the slave trade. Its efforts began with force during the Napoleonic Wars (1804–1815). Like other combatants, Britain claimed the right to search and seize ships at sea with contraband cargo, and so it directed its navy to seize slavers whenever and wherever it found them. In addition, in 1808 it dispatched a squadron to Africa with the sole purpose of interdicting the traffic. Thus began its sixty-year campaign against non-British slave traders.

The cover of war was incomplete and temporary. Taking their opponents' slavers or other ships as prizes was routine business; searching and seizing allied and neutral ships was not. So when Britain seized and sank Portuguese or Spanish slavers, it acted illegally. The same was true when it stopped U.S. ships. To uphold its right of freedom of the seas, the United States went to war with Britain in 1812. The Iberian powers pursued damage claims and received large reparations. With the arrival of peace in 1815, British search and seizure became naked aggression. Britain persisted, however, and paid dearly. Attacks on French slavers provoked outrage and further expensive damage claims. Between 1808 and 1824, Britain paid millions of pounds sterling to settle claims for damages its ships inflicted on slavers.

Britain's direct and unilateral attack on traffickers proved expensive—and not only in monetary terms. It generated ill-will that threatened to drive rivals into a hostile alliance against Britain. The international balance of power was at stake. Neither custom nor international law backed Britain's position. For centuries Europeans had plied the slave trade as a business like any other. Not only had Christians of most sects sanctioned it, but also international law never banned it. Therefore, Britain stood alone in its initial campaign, and even with its enormous power was incapable of halting the traffic alone.

Mutual Rights Pacts

International cooperation was imperative. Because Britain needed to persuade other nations to join in suppressing the traffic, it launched diplomatic initiatives to accompany its naval campaign. Promoting a network of bilateral and multilateral treaties, Britain became a party to every international pact signed to suppress the slave trade. By the 1850s, when the campaign peaked, the British-backed network featured four types of agreements aimed at blocking the export of slaves at their sources and at barring the arrival of slaves at their destinations.

In the main, all the treaties dealt with problems of national sovereignty that international law posed for antislaving activities. The crux was that the international law never made slaving into an act of piracy. Had it done so, slavers would have been punished under the laws of whichever country seized them. Nationality would have furnished no protection. As it was, however, international law permitted seizing a slaver only on the high seas where no nation had sovereignty, and even then, it required the consent of the nation under whose flag the ship sailed. The treaty network conveyed consent for suppression to overcome sovereignty issues.

Britain tended to favor pacts that provided mutual rights of search. Any nation, of course, had the power to search any ship flying its flag. Signatories to mutual rights pacts were permitted to search each other's ships. If inspection uncovered evidence of slaving, the ship became subject to detention. Its fate then depended on courts of mixed commission which were empowered to act under the signatories' joint authority. These early agencies of international law brought together jurists of the participating countries to try shippers accused of violating antislave trade agreements. Such courts exercised no jurisdiction over persons, for countries balked at subjecting their nationals to foreign laws. Thus, captains and crews were off limits. The mixed commission courts had jurisdiction only over property. The mutual rights pacts allowed them to dispose of ship and cargo, and under that guise they gained power over one class of persons—the human cargo paradoxically logged as property.

Britain signed mutual rights pacts with Spain, Portugal, and the Netherlands in 1817 and 1818; with Sweden in 1824; with Brazil in 1826; and, eventually, with the United States in 1862. The early pacts established mixed commissions at Freetown in the British West African colony of Sierra Leone; at Rio de Janeiro in Brazil; at Havana, Cuba; and at Paramaribo in Dutch Suriname. In time, the mixed commission courts ringed the Atlantic from New York City to Capetown, South Africa.

Mutual rights pacts gave Britain the authority to police shipping among the signatories, and the activity remained overwhelmingly British. The mixed commission in Sierra Leone adjudicated 80 percent of all captures under the mutual rights pacts. Elsewhere the pacts encountered serious problems. Judges often bickered and split along national lines, resulting in the release of seized ships. Moreover, the pacts laid narrow grounds for condemnation. Slavers initially had to be caught in the act with slaves on board to warrant condemnation. Yet the main problem was simply getting the pacts in place. Nations such as the United States long refused to agree and thus allowed their flags to shield slavers.

Detention and Self-Policing Pacts

Many nations refused to surrender jurisdiction of either persons or property under their flag. Thus, they shunned mutual rights pacts with mixed commission authority. Several countries, however, France, for example, were willing to join the suppression effort, and Britain developed a second type of treaty with them. The Anglo-French pacts signed in 1831 and 1833 illustrated the typical terms. Under these agreements, France permitted Britain to detain ships flying its flag, but the British had to release the suspected slaver to French domestic tribunals.

The so-called Quintuple Agreement of 1841 marked the acme of the detention pacts like the Anglo-French treaties of the 1830s. In all, Britain signed fourteen such agreements before 1850, but not all of them worked as well as the one with France. The treaty with Sardinia, for instance, became nearly worthless. The western Mediterranean island kingdom released most of its ships that the British detained. The law of states like Sardinia continued to shield slavers from ultimate condemnation; nevertheless, the pacts deterred the slave traffic by allowing British policing.

Before the Anglo-American mutual rights pact of 1862, the United States exemplified a third treaty approach to international suppression. The United States denied any other nation's authority to detain or search and seize any ship flying its flag. It agreed only to maintain its own squadron on the African coast to interdict slavers flying the U.S. flag.

After its 1830s pacts expired, France switched to the self-policing form of agreement and at one time had twenty-eight ships, or about 15 percent of its total naval resources, stationed off West Africa. The measures worked well enough to remove the French flag from the traffic and to make the French a major force in suppression. At their peak in the 1840s, the suppression squadrons of Britain, France, Portugal, and the United States averaged over sixty ships on African duty.

The mutual rights, detention, and self-policing pacts wove a net that covered most of the Atlantic, but traffickers continued to find shelters. Brazil and Portugal, for example, continued to shield slavers, despite their mutual rights pacts. The British responded with two parliamentary acts named after foreign secretaries Lord Palmerston and Lord Aberdeen. The Palmerston Act applied to Portuguese ships between 1839 and 1842, and the Aberdeen Act applied to Brazilian ships after 1845. Both laws directed the British navy to detain Portuguese and Brazilian slavers for adjudication in British courts. As clear assaults on Portuguese and Brazilian sovereignty, these provocative acts offered cause for war and undoubtedly would have prompted fighting with stronger powers. The acts also authorized British naval ships to detain carriers with no papers and thus no flag to which to answer. They, too, were hauled into British courts.

Suppression Activities

With the sea lanes covered by the first three treaty types and parliamentary acts, the British turned to inland sources for the fourth treaty type—Anglo-African suppression pacts. Ultimately, Britain signed forty-five African powers to agreements that required the Africans to end the slave trade in their territories or suffer British incursions to suppress the trade. More than anything else, these pacts provided Britain with a pretext for the sequel to the slave trade in Africa— direct colonization. Under the guise of attacking slave trading, Britain landed expeditions that made inroads in the European scramble beginning in the 1880s.

To monitor and coordinate suppression activities, Britain maintained a foreign office section called the Slave Trade Department which surveyed and scrutinized domestic and foreign laws and diplomatic dealings with a bearing on slaving. With eyes, ears, and hands around the Atlantic, it was first and foremost an intelligence agency gleaning information everywhere it could. Then it disseminated the knowledge where it thought best to aid suppression.

Since the Foreign Office's Slave Trade Department acted as something of a brain, the Admiralty formed the backbone of suppression. At least ten ships and a thousand men were usually assigned specifically to antislaving duties. At peak strength in the mid-1840s, the commitment reached thirty-six ships and forty-four hundred men—about 20 percent of British naval resources. The Crimean War (1853–1856), the Indian Mutiny of 1857, and other events slashed the British commitment. Yet, between 1815 and 1865, Britain spent over 7 million pounds on naval antislaving activity.

Naval expenditures were only part of the cost Britain paid for suppression. It paid a host of other direct costs: damages for its illegal search and seizure of foreign shipping; financial inducements to get Spain and Portugal to sign early suppression pacts; maintenance of the mixed commission courts under the mutual rights treaties; and bounties for landing recaptured slaves alive. In sum, between 1807 and 1865, Britain paid at least 12 million pounds on suppression—an amount comparable to the total profits British slave traders earned between 1760 and 1807.

The full cost of suppression greatly exceeded the 19 million pounds Britain spent in its naval expenditures and other direct payments. Indirect costs abounded. For example, suppression meant higher prices to British consumers for sugar, cotton, coffee, and other slave-produced commodities. Even so, the total cost could have consumed only a small share of British national income.

Evaluating the success of suppression is more difficult than counting its monetary cost. Based on measures such as slavers captured and condemned, suppression appeared a greater failure than success. Between 1807 and 1867, for example, traffickers launched about 7,750 trans-Atlantic slaving expeditions. At least 1,635 of the ships—about one in five—were caught and condemned or otherwise disposed of at a loss to traffickers. British admiralty courts, rather than the courts of mixed commission, accounted for most of the loss. Still, for every one caught, four slavers eluded the international suppression effort.

Efforts to Elude Suppression

Traffickers accepted the risk of interception as a cost of doing business and devised artful dodges to minimize losses. The risks merely raised the rewards. The lucrative returns on a successful voyage induced slavers in the 1860s to send out ships in sections for assembly, loading, and launching in isolated inlets along Central Africa's Zaire River. Ships bearing such parts to Africa could pass inspection as freighters, for they carried no contraband. They sailed at liberty.

Slavers worked to decrease exposure to capture primarily by cutting sea time. Speedier voyages with quicker ships were significant aids in evasion. Slavers even entered steamships in the traffic. Most emphasis, however, fell not on time under sail but on time at anchor. The stress lay where most interception occurred—not out in the Atlantic but on the African coast. That pushed slavers to enter and exit quickly in loading their human cargo.

Before 1800, ships had commonly waited on the coast to load groups of slaves until the holds were full. After suppression began, slavers stopped lingering, and they usually loaded no slaves until they had assembled a full cargo. Then they loaded and left, all within a few hours. Quickly in and quickly out were the ways slavers usually tried to skirt even the tightest naval blockades.

In order to cope with the risk of capture, suppression era slavers pushed every voyage to the utmost margin of profitability. Thus, they tended to pack captives tightly. The *Minerva*, a 21-ton bark measuring 36.5 feet from stern to stern, offered an appalling illustration of the extremes to which this could be carried. In 1842 the *Minerva*, a little ship for little people with little space, carried slaves from Ambriz, Angola, to Salvador, Brazil. When intercepted, it held 126 children; half sat exposed on deck, while the other half lay below deck in a 14-inch crawl space. So close were the conditions on board that they could neither stand nor even shift position by rolling over. Although atypical, the *Minerva* episode revealed the effects of profit-taking in the later years of the trade.

While crowding did not increase shipboard deaths, mortality on the Middle Passage was higher in the nineteenth century than it had been earlier. The major causes were dysentery and other gastrointestinal diseases. The greater morbidity was probably associated with the increased time captives spent confined in shore-based barracoons. Slave ships spent less time at sea than in earlier times, but they carried people who had been subjected to greater epidemiological stress. The net result of suppression on shipboard mortality was to increase it.

As a result of suppression, traffickers altered their routes. Before 1800, the typical slaver sailed from Europe to Africa to the Americas and back to Europe; after 1800, the trip usually went from the Americas to Africa and then back to the port of origin. Thus, while England's Liverpool and France's Nantes dominated the early traffic, Cuba's Havana and Brazil's Rio de Janeiro became headquarters for the later traffic.

Suppression also exaggerated the slavers' profits. By increasing the risks, it pushed profits up during the illegal phase of the slave trade higher than during the legal era. Profits were probably never so high as in the 1850s and 1860s—the trade's last two decades. Traffickers suffered losses, of course, but the margins of return greatly favored their continuing business.

Bluntly put, suppression at sea was a woeful failure in its intent to destroy the traffic. At best it probably reduced the amount of slaving after 1807 by about 12 percent. Its greatest success was in driving up prices in slave markets in the Americas. It raised distribution costs almost everywhere in the receiving regions. Of every $1,000 paid in Brazil and Cuba for a newly arrived African in the 1860s, about $660 went for premiums due to suppression risks. The excess fattened slavers' profits and fed bribes that corrupted government officials throughout the Atlantic Basin.

Suppression Efforts in the Americas

Internal political pressure rather than external pressure in the form of naval suppression ended the trans-Atlantic slave trade. It died when importing regions in the Americas closed their shores to the traffic. In the colonies of the British Caribbean, the French Americas, and Dutch Suriname, the end came when popular sentiment demanded an end. The same was true in the United States where popular attitudes demanded a halt to slaving, as they did later to slavery. Brazil and Cuba proved different situations.

Brazil reflected most clearly the combination of internal and external pressure. British agents bribed Brazilian government ministers, infiltrated the Brazilian customs service, and covertly funded Brazilian newspaper campaigns against the traffic. Under the 1845 Aberdeen Act, Britain took captured Brazilian slavers into British courts for condemnation. Furthermore, in the mid-1850s, the British Royal Navy took advantage of a revolt in

Pernambuco that occupied Brazilian forces in the north to sail into Brazil's southern waters and destroy every slaver found.

Brazilian public opinion, which was sympathetic owing in part to the secretly funded antislaving propaganda, applauded rather than condemned the British aggression. Before long, Brazil began to enforce and strengthen its own antitrafficking provisions. As a result, when an importing region's sovereign power finally stopped its people from buying slaves, importers stopped selling slaves there.

Cuba reflected a different mix of external and internal pressures for suppression. As Spain's main Caribbean colony, the island enjoyed protection that deterred the kind of action Britain used in Brazil. Moreover, direct British action would have provoked hostility not only with Spain but also with the United States, where the slaveholding South coveted the island. As the notorious Ostend Manifesto of 1854 showed, the South wanted to annex Cuba. And if it could not claim the island outright, the South wanted to keep Cuba as something of a slave auxiliary.

Only the outbreak of the U.S. Civil War in 1861 changed official U.S. thinking. Indeed, during the war the United States for the first time took an unequivocal stand for suppression. The South's defeat and the abolition of slavery in the United States in 1865 dealt a hard blow to Cuba's slave trade. The fall of the largest slaveholding regime suggested that slavery elsewhere in the Americas had little future. As a consequence, slave prices everywhere plummeted. Indeed, after 1865 prices were too low in Cuba to make slaving imports viable. In that context, genuine cooperation developed among Britain, Spain, and the United States to end the island's traffic.

Suppression and the Plantation System

In the 1760s almost all plantation produce in the Americas came from five sectors: the British Caribbean, the Dutch West Indies, the French West Indies, and the colonies of the two Iberian powers—Spain and Portugal. The rise of the United States added a sixth by the 1780s. Each sector attempted to produce a wide range of plantation products and aimed at self-sufficiency. The French and English led as the most developed and dominant sectors; the Portuguese and the Spanish, in particular, lagged as the least developed. All areas had open land frontiers and the capacity to absorb more labor from seemingly limitless Africa. Nothing then signaled any slackening of the slave traffic or any shift in rank among the plantation economies.

By 1860 the major features of the plantation system of the 1700s had largely disappeared. Neither Cuba, Brazil, nor the United States, the three dominant plantation regions in 1860, had been of more than marginal importance in the 1700s. Then they had all sat on the periphery of the core plantation zone in the French and British

West Indies. Moreover, the three new regions each specialized in producing a single crop on an almost unprecedented scale. By 1850, 80 to 90 percent of the exports of Cuba, south-central Brazil, and the U.S. South were made up of sugar, coffee, and cotton, respectively. Although each dominated the world markets for its product, in 1760 none of these commodities was of much importance in these regions. Three new systems had emerged.

The pattern of rise and fall among the Americas' various plantation regions during the 1800s reflected the effects of suppression. Denmark ended the traffic to its colonies in 1803; Great Britain followed four years later; and the United States abolished the trade effective 1 January 1808. The French Revolution (1789–1799) and the Napoleonic Wars (1804–1815) curtailed the Dutch traffic. The Haitian Revolution (1791–1804) and other wars had the same effect on the French traffic, although it was revived again between 1814 and 1831. As the flow of fresh labor from Africa ended in most of these areas, their economies declined.

The British plantation colonies exemplified the fall. In 1800 the British Caribbean—led by Jamaica—stood atop plantation producers, producing nearly two-thirds of the world's sugar exports, half the coffee, and a third of the cotton exports. The abolition of the British slave trade in 1807 marked the start of a precipitous slide. The abolition of slavery itself in 1833 pushed the downturn further into stagnation. Only in the 1850s, when the flow of indentured workers from Asia became significant in Trinidad and British Guiana, did the British colonies see economic growth again.

After 1800 the Danish, Dutch, and French colonies also slipped relative to Cuba and Brazil, but the process was slower than in the British islands because each of these areas preserved slavery longer than did the British plantation colonies. The Dutch sugar-growing area of Suriname in northeastern South America never matched its dynamic performance during the 1700s when the slave trade was open. The loss of St. Domingue following Haitian independence crippled French Caribbean production. Only after the 1820s did the French islands again respond to expanding European demand.

Brazil and Cuba stood apart from their declining neighbors, with each boasting considerable natural advantages. Yet the signal difference between them and other nations was their access to labor from Africa. The continued Portuguese and Spanish trade drove the rapid expansion of coffee and sugar production after 1800; their chief competitors lacked that edge.

Only the United States managed to dominate a world market for a plantation product without access to fresh labor from Africa. It had an expanding domestic supply, and by 1860 it was producing over half the global exports of raw cotton. The United States was an exception that confirmed the general pattern. It joined Barbadoes and one or two smaller areas as the only regions in the Americas where the slave population experienced high rates of natural increase. Between 1800 and 1860, the U.S. slave population increased from about one million to about four million and had become a very effective substitute for the slave trade.

Impact of Changes in the Slave Trade

Even in Brazil, Cuba, and the United States, the growing restrictions on the Atlantic slave trade triggered major changes. Indeed, the impact reverberated in all slave societies. The restrictions tightened the supply of slaves while demand for slave plantation produce soared. As a result, slave prices also soared after 1800. The increased cost and increased profit potential induced planters to move slaves into the most productive regions and tasks.

Thus, major new slave migrations occurred, as internal traffic replaced the old Middle Passage. In Brazil, for example, holders moved slaves from the older, northeast cotton and sugar provinces to the south-central Paraíba Valley coffee-growing areas. Cuba's western provinces, like Brazil's upper Paraíba Valley, acted as a magnet and drew slaves from the rest of the island. In the United States, slaves flowed from the older tobacco lands in Virginia, Maryland, and Kentucky to the frontier cotton lands in Alabama, Louisiana, and Mississippi.

Changes in occupation coincided with changes in location. As slaves became more expensive, they were increasingly concentrated in the highest earnings areas. Thus, Brazil, Cuba, and the United States claimed increasing shares of the hemispheric slave population, for they dominated the export sectors producing profits in the 1800s. They became specialized for the sake of efficiency, and their per capita output rose at a rate comparable to that of contemporary British textile factory workers.

With the ending of the slave trade, blacks throughout the Americas suffered more than changes in location and occupation. Their connections with Africa were disrupted, and they increasingly lost a sense of commonalty with African societies. The result was that they became much more isolated from their old world than their white counterparts from Europe. Without fresh reminders from the motherland, customs, language, and religion became less African. Except among scattered and isolated maroon communities, distinctive African American forms emerged, and Euro-American influences also increased.

The Effect of Abolition on Africa

Abolition of the slave trade affected Africa, too, though the impact was probably smaller than in the Americas. Until the 1850s no drastic decline occurred. Contraband carriers offset much of the early Danish, Dutch, British, and United States withdrawal, but the results differed by region. Early suppression most affected areas north of the equator. In Senegambia, the most northerly of the provenance zones, the traffic was already a trickle before any formal abolition occurred. The traffic died in the Gold Coast by the 1820s and in the Bight of Biafra by the early 1840s. It lasted longest in the Bight of Benin and in southeast and west-central Africa. The Zaire River was the focal point of the traffic after 1850. Throughout the 1800s, then, the center of the slave trade steadily shifted southward.

Africa's political response to abolition of the trade also differed by region. North of the Slave Coast the infamous kingdom of Dahomey diminished in power as the slave trade declined, yet its capacity to export slaves did not apparently lessen. Down the coast near the Bight of Benin, the great Oyo empire of the Yoruba collapsed between 1800 and 1850, but the fall resulted from no drastic drop in traffic, because slave exports had been declining since the 1720s. Further south in the Angolan area, the abolition of the trade apparently triggered massive change. No clear common pattern emerged, however. In southern Africa, as in West Africa, diverse local conditions and developments mitigated the impact that ending the trade had on indigenous power bases and structures.

The economic impact of abolition was clearer and relatively smaller in Africa than in the Americas or Europe. The main reason was that the Atlantic trade, including the slave traffic, was tangential to the commerce and income of most African economies. Key slave-trading enclaves such as Cabinda, near the Zaire River, and Efik trader towns in the Niger and Cross River deltas, suffered lost incomes in the declining traffic. Outside such centers, however, few Africans lost income, for most never partook in, let alone profited from, the traffic. Indeed, the larger Atlantic trade hardly touched most Africans and was always of relatively small value to Africa in monetary terms. Among Atlantic Basin participants, Africa reaped the lowest per capita revenues from trade.

With fewer slavers to the Americas, fewer Africans were enslaved. The trans-Saharan slave trade increased to the east as slave prices declined on Africa's Atlantic coast during the 1800s, but the volume paled in comparison with the Atlantic flow. Domestic slavery made up for the smaller numbers being shipped to the Americas. As the trans-Atlantic traffic declined, however, total enslavement decreased, and with that decline came fresh economic development.

Africa enlarged its Atlantic trade in commodities as the traffic in human beings declined. Already by the end of the 1700s, for example, Senegal gum had risen to commercial importance. Between 1800 and 1850 palm oil and palm oil kernels became important in the Bight of Biafra. In the 1840s products did not rapidly replace the slave trade; some involved slave labor, and in no sense did they squeeze out the slave trade. Neither the earlier Atlantic trade nor the later commodities absorbed more than a minuscule share of African resources.

Throughout the era of the slave traffic, Africans engaged overwhelmingly in domestic economic activities; Atlantic activity remained tangential. Africa's large population and sophisticated economies allowed it to supply its basic needs while producing substantial surpluses for trade and tribute. West Africa was especially self-reliant. The continent as a whole was self-sufficient in contrast to Europe and its colonies in the Americas; thus, the abolition of the slave trade disturbed Africa less than it did Europe and the Americas.

Gradual Abolition and the Dynamics of Slave Emancipation in Cuba, 1868–1886

Rebecca J. Scott

The abolition of slavery in Cuba is usually examined as a series of discrete legal and political events, viewed either as the expression of increasing contradictions within the Cuban economic system or as the result of domestic and international pressures exerted on the Spanish government. The sequence of events begins with a declaration of emancipation by Cuban insurgents rebelling against Spain in 1868, followed by the passage of the Moret Law by the Spanish Cortes in 1870, then by the establishment of the *patronato,* or apprenticeship, in 1880, and finally by the termination of the *patronato* in 1886. This article will focus instead on the developing interaction of individuals and classes during this process of change, in an effort to determine the social dynamics that underlay these legal and political events.

The gradualness of abolition in Cuba provides an unparalleled opportunity to analyze the disintegration of chattel bondage in a plantation society. The legal structure of slavery in Cuba was dismantled piece by piece. Young children and the elderly were legally freed and the use of the whip banned in 1870; meager wages were introduced, but corporal punishment maintained, in 1880; stocks and chains were prohibited in 1883. Social and economic relationships changed as legal ones altered, in turn producing further change, all within a context of warfare, pacification, and economic adaptation. This process, I will argue, involved a complex hybrid of resistance and accommodation by both slaves and masters, whose actions then helped to shape the further course of emancipation.

In October 1868, in the Eastern Department of Cuba, a group led by small-scale planters, frustrated at Spain's multiple failings as a metropolitan power and provoked by economic hardship and new taxes, rose in rebellion. Some freed their own slaves and incorporated them into the rebel army, and the insurgents' platform called for the eventual indemnified emancipation of all slaves. The rebel leaders planned for this abolition to come after the triumph of the revolution, however, and in the meanwhile decreed the death penalty for anyone caught inciting slaves to revolt. Later, under pressure from within their ranks, and aware of the need for international support, they declared immediate emancipation. The effects of this emancipation were limited, though, by the

enactment in July 1869 of a restrictive Reglamento de Libertos that required forced labor of former slaves. Only at the end of 1870, when these regulations were revoked, did the rebels take up a position of genuine abolitionism.

The Cuban scholar Raúl Cepero Bonilla, in an essay published more than thirty years ago, argued that the class position and the political aims of the leaders of the 1868 rebellion caused them to move toward abolition with great hesitation. Cepero Bonilla's analysis of the ideology of the rebel leaders is perceptive, but to understand the impact of the rebellion on slaves, one must also turn to sources that reflect conditions in areas under insurrectionist control or near the fighting. Some such records—transcripts of court cases, correspondence of prefects, complaints from masters and *libertos* (as former slaves were called by the rebels)—were captured by the Spaniards and preserved. These documents make clear that insurgent administrators obliged some *libertos* to remain with their former masters, ordered others from place to place as forced labor, compelled *libertas* to work as their personal domestic servants, and made invidious distinctions within the army among whites, creole *libertos,* and Africans. Both wartime exigency and the class and cultural differences between officers and *libertos* led officers to view freed slaves as useful but dangerous and to impose controls drastically limiting their freedom.

Other aspects of insurgent policy, however, had opposite effects. As a military measure, many *libertos* were drafted into the fighting force. This had unintended consequences for the maintenance of slavery. The *liberto,* now a soldier, became potentially disruptive, a symbol of freedom and a walking challenge to the institution of slavery. In one revealing case, a planter tried to keep a *liberto* soldier named Florentino away from his former home. A physical confrontation resulted, and the record of the ensuing court case reflects both the master's desire to prevent Florentino from returning to visit his *compañeros* who were still servants, and the dramatic effect of the *liberto's* appearance in the cookhouse of his old plantation. The master had been willing to free the troublesome slave and contribute him to the rebel cause as a soldier, but he had no intention of allowing Florentino to come back to the plantation to display his rights as a free man. In a letter to the rebel authorities, the planter complained bitterly that the remaining servants on his estate had little affection for him and had come to view Florentino as their protector.

While the insurgent leaders used emancipation to provide themselves with recruits, they assumed that former slave women would remain at work, generally in agriculture. Once freedmen went into the army, however, some freedwomen refused to remain on estates, preferring to accompany their friends, husbands, sons, or brothers into the *monte*. One official wrote with exasperation in March 1869 that a group of women alleged "that the emancipation decree has declared them free and in virtue of their independence they resist returning to that estate. . . ." The logic of the women's position was clear, as was the frustration of the administrator. He advised the estate's owner to appeal to the military court to recover the recalcitrant *libertas*.

The use of abolitionism by the rebels as a rallying cry, even when in practice abolition was heavily compromised, had its own effects. It encouraged slaves outside the rebellion, and *libertos* within it, to become more assertive. Some *libertos* chose to view the revolutionary prefects as their potential defenders and, when mistreated, fled their masters to demand justice. The prefect might be unsympathetic, but raising the issue could be disruptive all the same. It brought masters before a court to answer for their behavior toward *libertos*, something no former slaveowner could view with equanimity.

Outside the area of insurrectionist control, the rebellion posed a threat to Planters with estates near the front lines. Slaves who fled plantations could now go not only to the hills, but to the rebels; pursuing runaway slaves might lead to engaging rebel forces. The presence of the revolutionary alternative made the maintenance of plantation discipline a delicate matter—even though, in extreme cases, it brought new forms of control, as the Spanish military became directly involved in keeping the peace on estates in contested zones.

Thus, the impact of the insurrection on slavery went beyond the initial intentions of its leaders. Rebel policy itself evolved under pressure toward a less qualified abolitionism, particularly as the participation of free persons of color and *libertos* in the army increased. At the same time, *libertos* learned to make use of even partial and opportunistic concessions by the rebel leaders.

Though the majority of Cuba's slaves were in the West, not directly touched by the war, pacification of the island nevertheless required the colonial government to come to terms with the issue of abolition. However ambivalent the initial insurgent commitment to abolition, that commitment put Spain on the defensive, both within Cuba and internationally. Spain could hardly afford to appear the retrograde defender of slavery in the eyes of the United States, a potential ally of the insurgents, or in the eyes of potential Black recruits to the insurrection. Yet neither could the government afford to take steps that might damage sugar production or betray loyal planters who were still terrified by the notion of an abrupt abolition.

The Moret Law, passed by the Spanish Cortes in 1870, attempted to meet these conflicting needs. It was a "preparatory bill for the gradual abolition of slavery" that freed children born since 1868 and all slaves over the age of sixty, while promising that an indemnified emancipation of the rest would be introduced once Cuban delegates were seated in the Cortes—something to be expected only with the end of the war. The bill outlawed the use of the whip and provided that any slave proven the victim of "excessive cruelty" was to be freed. Juntas Protectoras de Libertos, one half of whose members were to be slaveholders, were established to oversee enforcement.

Colonial authorities portrayed the Moret Law as wise and judicious, the logical outcome of the Spanish revolution of 1868, and a measure to which even slaveowners would consent. In practice, however, slaveholders criticized it and sought to block its enforcement. As a result, the law turned out to be both less and more than it seemed, and its history reflects the complex dialectics involved in reforming or ameliorating slavery.

It was less than it seemed in that the freedom it granted was limited, compromised, and, in many cases, quite illusory. Children were freed, but they owed unpaid labor to their masters until they reached the age of eighteen, which meant that even when parents won freedom, they could not automatically take their children with them. The aged were declared free, but since ages were much in dispute, there was the possibility of widespread fraud. Unregistered slaves were legally free, but owners' petitions for the inclusion of names in the registers continued for years, stalling actual manumission. Thus, although the number classified as slaves fell sharply in the 1870s, the law did not change as many lives as the numbers suggest.

The Moret Law was also a bit more than it seemed, however, because its provisions led to institutional changes that tended to disrupt the social order of slavery. When the law was being discussed in 1870, one powerful planter, Francisco Ibáñez, recommended that the law avoid the "intervention of Agents of Authority" to carry it out, for such intervention could cause abuses and could "discredit" (*desprestigiar*) masters on their estates. The very existence of the Juntas Protectoras nonetheless created the possibility that slaves could take the initiative of bringing complaints against their masters before outside judges.

Given their membership, the Juntas were unlikely in practice to serve as champions of slaves. In the aftermath of the passage of the

Moret Law and the outbreak of insurrection in the eastern end of the island, however, some slaves were emboldened to press for concessions. In this, they sometimes used the older institutions of the *sindicatura* ("office of the *síndico,*" the appointed "defender of slaves") and of *coartación* ("gradual self-purchase"). Several kinds of evidence suggest a trend toward greater self-assertion. First, the records of the *sindicaturas* indicate an increased volume of activity in the 1870s, including requests for the lowering of the appraised price for self-purchase and permission to change masters. Second, some of the texts of appeals for freedom to the Juntas have survived, conveying a sense of the nature of the demands and the persistence of the slaves who made them. Finally, there is a general tone of embattled frustration in many slaveowners' petitions during this period. They appealed to the government to be more restrictive in interpreting the rights of *coartados* and the role of the *síndico,* and they tried in various ways to delay enforcement. These protests were a response both to uncertainty about the legal future of slavery and to increased initiatives by slaves.

The Moret Law by itself did not free significant numbers of slaves of working age, but by multiplying regulations and establishing the Juntas, it did create an additional lever—a small, fragile, and awkward one—that some slaves could use to help bring about their own emancipation. Because of the reluctance of the government to enforce the law and the opposition of masters to changes in their relations with slaves, appeals for freedom were difficult to file and even more difficult to win. The government, for example, acquiesced in the planters' desire not to have the order of the plantation disturbed, and instructed local officials to enter estates and speak to slaves only under special circumstances and not for routine inquiries. Successful appeals tended to come from the relatively privileged—for example, urban domestic slaves, personal servants who had been in Europe with their masters, or *coartados,* slaves partially free by virtue of having made a down payment on their purchase price.

A representative case suggests the ambiguities of the situation. An urban slave named Luisa appealed for her freedom on the grounds that she was not properly registered. The Junta agreed, but her master intervened to stall the case, and meanwhile sent her to the countryside, presumably to punish her and to block her access to outsiders. Her brother, the literate slave of another master, appealed to Madrid on her behalf, and won the case. The incident illustrates the way in which the Moret Law raised expectations and encouraged slave initiatives, which in turn could be blocked by masters. Only with access to someone literate, urban, and daring was Luisa able to counter her master's tactics.

Other factors besides the Moret Law were at work in the 1870s to alter the importance of slavery. Planters had long recognized that the Cuban slave population did not fully reproduce itself, and would inevitably decline once the slave trade was ended, as it was in the 1860s. Chinese contract laborers, who worked alongside slaves and were treated much like them, had provided one alternative source of plantation labor. The importation of indentured Chinese workers declined, however, and was finally abolished in the 1870s. As their eight-year contracts ran out, some Chinese in Cuba were organized into work gangs. Chinese contractors provided *cuadrillas,* whose members worked in the fields or the mill for fixed terms, maintained themselves, received their pay, and then left the plantation. This was a particularly flexible form of labor for planters, and one that no longer quite so closely resembled slavery.

Growing numbers of white workers also labored on estates, particularly as the Ten Years' War (1868–78) drew to a close, and demobilized Spanish soldiers remained in Cuba. Account books reflect the increasing heterogeneity of the labor force, listing slaves owned by the estate, slaves rented on an annual or monthly basis, white and Black wage laborers, *cuadrillas* of Chinese, and a few *colonos,* or tenants. Forms of payment were correspondingly diverse. Some laborers were paid daily and others weekly; gangs were paid by the day and by the task; even slaves might receive a *jornal* if they worked on Sunday.

The use of these additional forms of labor did not, however, eliminate planters' dependence on slavery. The returns of the 1877 agricultural census suggest that at least 72 percent of the workers in the *dotaciones* of sugar plantations were still slaves owned by the planters for whom they worked. Free workers, rented slaves, and Chinese made up the remaining 28 percent. Furthermore, slave prices stayed high, indicating that slavery was not in a state of internal collapse. The war and the Moret Law were nonetheless making the direction of change clear, and adaptations on the plantation undermined planters' claims that sugar could survive only if slavery remained utterly unaltered.

In 1878 and 1879, pressures increased for another step toward resolving the issue of slavery. Irregular concessions had been made on several fronts. The pact that ended the Ten Years' War granted freedom to *libertos* among the insurgents—a tactical necessity if these fighters were to be persuaded to lay down their arms. The Spaniards had already been forced to give freedom to slaves who had served the loyalist cause, and to some *libertos* who had surrendered earlier. Then, unexpectedly, the remaining slaves of Santiago de Cuba Province directly challenged their masters, refusing to work unless abolition were granted. Although the details of the confrontation are not clear, there was apparently widespread passive resistance from slaves demanding their freedom "como los convenidos," like those freed by the peace treaty. In September

1879, the governor-general wrote to Madrid that slaves were deserting in large numbers and that it had become necessary to guard them with troops.

The events in the eastern end of the island, something between *marronage* ("flight of slaves") and a strike, were given added urgency by postwar unrest. Blacks in the hills, in conjunction with those on the plantations, were able to obtain from a frightened slaveowning class concessions that the government was not yet prepared to grant. Eastern planters apparently feared that they would never again be able to control their work force, even with the aid of the military, and so struck a bargain with their slaves. They conceded that slavery would continue only four more years, and that during those years the slaves would receive a wage. Although the agreement did not have the force of law, its seriousness was indicated by the advice of the senator from Santiago de Cuba to the Spanish government in 1879. Though he himself favored more gradual abolition, he warned that if the existing agreement were ignored, it would be extremely difficult to impose any solution on that province.

At the other end of the island the government-ordered posting of slave registers, long delayed, was having its effect. Those whose names did not appear on the lists were legally free, and in some areas this included large numbers of individuals held as slaves. From local authorities in Pinar del Río came complaints of passive resistance among slaves, and fears that soon those not freed would rise up to demand their liberty. In Sagua la Grande, Santa Clara Province, the posting of the lists produced "great excitation" among proprietors. For a decade, masters had been debating the completeness of slave registers with the government, but now the posting of the lists brought the dispute into the open and made direct challenges from slaves much more likely.

All of these developments helped to force the general issue. Economically, they made it difficult for planters to obtain credit; politically, they undermined the government's control. Desertions, passive resistance, cane burning, and the omnipresent threat of a new insurrection made the cost of keeping slavery seem ever higher. This did not make planters into abolitionists, for many feared that the cost of abolition would be higher still, but it made them eager for some "resolución de la cuestión social."

A logical next step was to eliminate slavery in name while maintaining key elements of its substance. The vehicle for this was the institution of the *patronato*, established by a law passed in the Spanish Cortes in 1880. It represented an intermediate stage between slavery and freedom during which former slaves would owe labor to their former masters, but would receive a token wage in return. Under the law, one quarter of the remaining *patrocinados* were to obtain their full freedom each year, in descending order of age,

beginning in 1885, with the *patronato* finally to end in 1888.

The *patronato* was based on a belief in gradualism, in the necessity of making haste slowly. Planters raised specters of Haiti, of Radical Reconstruction in the United States, and of a lapse into barbarism, to argue that only a gradual transition could avoid such evil consequences of abolition. The *patronato* also involved a denial of conflicting interests, a claim that the needs of former slaves and of former masters could be mediated and compromised to the benefit of both; hence the use of imagery of tutelage and guardianship.

The 1880 law nonetheless left in place the fundamental relations of slavery. Though the owner was now to be called *patrono* and the slave *patrocinado*, the master still had the right to the labor of the former slave, and could transfer that right through sale. He could mete out corporal punishment, and runaways were to be returned to him. The obligations of masters toward *patrocinados*, however, were somewhat greater than those owed to slaves. In addition to maintenance, *patronos* were to provide education to the young, and to pay each *patrocinado* a small stipend. The law also allowed for freedom through "mutual accord" of the *patrono* and *patrocinado*, and through "indemnification of services," or self-purchase.

Although reciprocal responsibilities were spelled out, the relationship was by no means a contractual one. It was not a matter of choice whether one became a *patrocinado*, and *patrocinados* had few of the rights of free workers. They could not refuse to labor, seek another employer at will, or leave an estate without permission. They could be ejected from the master's property if he unilaterally renounced his rights over them. As in the case of free workers, however, their pay could be docked for the time they were ill or being punished.

The law in some ways resembled a liberalized slave code. In one crucial respect, however, it was different: it held that certain infractions of the rules by masters would be punishable by the termination of the *patronato* and the freeing of the *patrocinado*. New Juntas de Patronato were to oversee enforcement of these rules. The irony is that the specification of slaveowner obligations, even though the obligations might differ little from general practice under slavery, converted these practices into entitlements on the part of the slave and established a form of redress if these rights were violated. An example may serve to illustrate the point. Masters were in the habit of feeding and clothing their slaves, and it was in their interest to do so. The law introduced nothing new when it obliged them to maintain their *patrocinados*. It did introduce something new, however, when it held that a *patrocinado* could bring the charge of failure to provide food and clothing before a Junta and, if the charge were proven, obtain his or her freedom. The effects emerged in an unusually dramatic way on a plantation in Güines where local authorities ordered 185 patrocinados freed on the grounds that they had not been adequately fed and clothed. The master refused; the patrocinados mutinied; and the army was called in to suppress them. The case was an extreme instance—the plantation was bankrupt, and the overseer unable to guarantee order. Nevertheless, the patrocinados were ordered freed rather than simply transferred to another owner, and this order was the result of their own complaints and of enforcement of provisions of the 1880 law..

The government did not set out to undermine the power of masters. On the contrary, it was thoroughly solicitous of their interests. But once rights were set out explicitly, and the state claimed responsibility for enforcement, and, moreover, a sanction was created that was so attractive to potential complainants (freedom for the patrocinado), social relations were inevitably altered.

To understand what actually went on between patrocinados and patronos, one must recognize that the patronato, as an attempt to eliminate the tensions and contradictions of gradual abolition, was an ambiguous institution. To the extent that the law tried to resolve these contradictions, it either denied legal freedom, thus undermining the distinction between slave and patrocinado, or granted new rights, thus giving patrocinados increased potential leverage over the course of emancipation. The contradictory nature of the institution meant that neither patronos nor patrocinados saw it as functioning fully in their interests, even while both attempted to use it to defend or advance their positions.

[1] Among the historians who have analyzed aspects of the abolition of slavery in Cuba are Raúl Cepero Bonilla, in Azúcar y abolición (Havana, 1948); Arthur Corwin, in Spain and the Abolition of Slavery in Cuba, 1817–1886 (Austin, 1967); Ramiro Guerra y Sánchez, in Guerra de los diez años, 1868–1878, 2 vols. (Havana, 1950–52); Franklin Knight, in Slave Society in Cuba during the Nineteenth Century (Madison, 1970); and Manuel Moreno Fraginals, in El ingenio: Complejo económico social cubano del azúcar, 3 vols. (Havana, 1978).

[2] Cepero Bonilla, Azúcar y abolición, chaps. 11–17.

[3] A group of insurgents' documents, titled the Colección Fernández Duro, is to be found in the Library of the Real Academia de Historia, Madrid (hereinafter RAH, FD). The evidence that libertos were treated as labor gangs rather than as free individuals is abundant. See, for example, the orders given by M. Quesada in June and July of 1869, in RAH, FD, leg. 4, docs. 432, 635, 713, and 720. On the use of libertas as domestics, see J. Agustín Bora to C. Prefecto del Partido Porcayo, Nov. 25, 1869, RAH, FD, leg. 2, carpeta 11, doc. 484. An example of the racial distinctions made appears in an order distributing the men of a particular unit: "De los hombres que él tiene destine U. los blancos á las armas y los libertos con raras escepciones a la agricultura. . . . Order from M. Quesada, July 12, 1869, RAH, FD, leg. 4, doc. 616.

[4] For the testimony in the case of Florentino, see RAH, FD, leg. 1, doc. 5.

[5] Libertos, Mar. 12, 1869, RAH, FD, leg. 2, carpeta 11, doc. 376.

[6] For an example of a liberta appealing to a prefect, see the dispute between Rosa and Francisco Socarrás, RAH, FD, leg. 3, doc. 1, Sumarios.

[7] Contemporary observers, both sympathetic and unsympathetic, were agreed on the large proportion of persons of color in the rebel army. See, for example, James J. O'Kelly, The Mambi-Land or Adventures of a Herald Correspondent in Cuba (Philadelphia, 1874), p. 221. He estimated that only one-third of the fighting men were white. Rebel documents bear out these estimates. See Thomas Jordan to Eduardo Agramonte, Dec. 16, 1869, RAH, FD, leg. 1: "In my inspection of the troops here as well as in the Oriente, I have been surprised to find much more than half of them negroes (including many Africans) and Chinese. . . ." (original in English).

[8] For analyses of the politics of passage of the Moret Law, see Knight, Slave Society, chap. 6, and Corwin, Spain and the Abolition of Slavery, chaps. 12–13. The text of the Moret Law can be found in Fernando Ortiz, Los negros esclavos (Havana, 1916), Appendix.

[9] For the debate on the Moret Law, see Knight, Slave Society, chap. 6, and Corwin, Spain and the Abolition of Slavery, chaps. 12–13. The text of the Moret Law can be found in Fernando Ortiz, Los negros esclavos (Havana, 1916), Appendix.

[10] Reliable statistics on the slave population and the number freed during the ten years of the Moret Law are difficult to obtain. The two censuses of the era suggest that the slave population fell from around 368,550 in 1861–62 to 199,094 in 1877, some of which, of course, is accounted for by deaths. Between the enactment of the Moret Law in 1870 and the end of 1877, official figures showed 61,766 children declared free by virtue of having been born after 1868, 21,032 slaves freed for being over age 60, and 9,611 freed because they were not registered. For the results of the census taken in 1861–62, see Cuba, Centro de Estadística, Noticias estadísticas de la isla de Cuba en 1862 (Havana, 1864), and for 1877, see Fe Iglesias García, "El censo cubano de 1877 y sus diferentes versiones," Santiago (Santiago de Cuba), 34 (June 1979), 167–214. For official reports on the numbers freed, see Estado demostrativo de los esclavos . . . , Mar. 15, 1878, in Archivo Histórico Nacional, Madrid (hereinafter AHN), Sección de Ultramar, leg. 4882.

[11] Acta de la Junta de hacendados, propietarios y comerciantes para tratar de la cuestión social, June 17, 1870, AHN, Ultramar, leg. 4881, tomo 1.

[12] Expediente promovido . . . para conocer las operaciones practicadas en todas las sindicaturas de la Isla durante el quinquenio de 1873 a 1877, Archivo Nacional de Cuba, Havana (hereinafter ANC), Miscelánea de Expedientes (hereinafter ME), leg. 3814, exp. A.

[13] Some appeals reached Madrid and are in AHN, Ultramar, particularly leg. 4759. Records of local cases

are scattered through ANC, ME. For governmental rulings on the *síndicos* and on *coartación,* see Bienvenido Cano and Federico de Zalba, *El libro de los Síndicos de Ayuntamiento y de las Juntas Protectoras de Libertos* (Havana, 1875), pp. 65, 67. See also AHN, Ultramar, leg. 4882, tomo 3, exp. 75, for masters' protests.

[14]For the ruling on estates, see Cano and Zalba, *El libro de los Síndicos,* p. 244. For examples of appeals, see AHN, Ultramar, leg. 4759.

[15]El pardo Faustino, esclavo de Dn. Pedro Prado, solicita la libertad de su hermana Luisa, esclava de D. Elías Núñez, AHN, Ultramar, leg. 4759, exp. 74.

[16]On the Chinese in Cuba, see Duvon C. Corbitt, *A Study of the Chinese in Cuba, 1847–1947* (Wilmore, Ky., 1971); Juan Pérez de la Riva, *Para la historia de las gentes sin historia* (Barcelona, 1976); Juan Jiménez Pastrana, *Los chinos en las luchas por la liberación cubana (1847–1930)* (Havana, 1963); Denise Helly, *Idéologie et ethnicité. Les Chinois Macao à Cuba: 1847–1886* (Montreal, 1979); and this author's review essay on Helly in *Revista/Review Interamericana* (San Juan), 9 (Summer 1979), 324–327.

[17]On the labor gangs, see Corbitt, *A Study,* p. 91. Official figures suggest that in 1872 there were approximately 34,000 Chinese contract laborers still serving their eight-year terms, 8,000 runaways, and 14,000 free. See *Estado resumen del padrón general de asiáticos . . .,* in AHN, Ultramar, leg. 87. By 1877 the figures were 25,000 under contract and 22,000 free. See Iglesias García, "El censo cubano."

[18]For a profile of the labor force on a specific plantation, see the Libro Diario del Ingenio Delicias, 1872–82, in ANC, Miscelánea de Libros (hereinafter ML), num. 10802.

[19]The returns of the agricultural census of 1877, which record 90,516 slaves, 20,726 "libres y alquilados," and 14,597 Chinese working on sugar plantations, are not complete, and there are some ambiguities in the categories that compose the *dotaciones.* The totals for "libres y alquilados" seem to include some young and elderly slaves legally free under the Moret Law, as well as rented slaves and wage workers. The proportion of active sugar workers who were slaves was thus probably higher than the 72 percent recorded in the category "esclavos." For the aggregate statistics, see *Revista de Agricultura* (Havana), 3 (Mar. 31, 1879), 75.

[20]Detailed work on slave prices in the 1870s remains to be done. For estimates, see Hubert H. S. Aimes, *A History of Slavery in Cuba, 1511–1868* (New York, 1907), p. 268, and O'Kelly, *The Mambi-Land,* p. 64. For an analysis of prices in the preceding decades, see Manuel Moreno Fraginals, Herbert S. Klein, and Stanley L. Engerman, "The Level and Structure of Slave Prices on Cuban Plantations in the Middle of the Nineteenth Century: Some Comparative Perspectives," unpublished.

[21]Telegram from the Governor-General to the Minister of Ultramar, Sept. 11, 1879, AHN, Ultramar, leg. 4882, tomo 3, exp. 76.

[22]See the opinion of José Bueno y Blanco in *Documentos de la Comisión . . . 1879,* AHN, Ultramar, leg. 4883, tomo 5.

[23]See the petitions and reports in AHN, Ultramar, leg. 4882, tomo 3, exp. 75.

[24]The text of the law and its Reglamenio can be found in *Código penal vigente en las islas de Cuba y Puerto Rico* (Madrid, 1886), pp. 233–266.

[25]Don Nicolás de Cárdenas y Ortega to the Governor-General, Oct. 1880, AHN, Ultramar, leg. 4884, tomo 7, exp. 101, and Don Nicolás de Cárdenas suplica . . ., AHN, Ultramar, leg. 4528, 1°, exp. 167. See also Rafael M. de Labra, *Mi campaña en las Cortes españolas de 1881 a 1883* (Madrid, 1885), p. 301.

Abolition and the Politics of Identity in the Afro-Atlantic Diaspora: Toward a Comparative Approach

Kim D. Butler

In a world shaped by slavery and racism, the retention of identity and personhood by people of African descent was an essential mechanism of survival. Self-determination became the ultimate political act of resistance against a system that defined human beings as commodities. The multiple forms of resistance through self-determination have long been recognized as an integral facet of slavery. Yet the long tradition, on one hand, of elites seeking to manipulate one segment of the population for their own benefit and, on the other, rejection of that manipulation by the exploited, did not suddenly end with the declaration of emancipation.

Abolition is often viewed as a terminal point signaling the end of one era and the start of a new one. In fact, final abolition typically came after years of intermediate legislation outlawing slave trading and specific categories of enslavement. Thousands of slaves throughout the Americas also achieved their own liberation through such mechanisms as self-purchase, escape, or war. However, any analysis of abolition must go beyond the question of civil status to address the social relations of power undergirding the concept of slavery itself. By exploring beneath the veneer of de jure abolition, it becomes increasingly clear that abolition was but one point in a protracted transitional era in the Afro-Atlantic world during which patterns of hegemony established under slavery were transposed into the new conditions of post-emancipation societies.

The ability of elites to dictate the terms of abolition has generally been taken for granted; most abolition studies examine elite initiatives and their effect on people of African descent. However, African descendants were not simply passive objects of this transition. For them, abolition held the promise of self-determination and self-fulfillment. The majority of freed-persons were more than willing to close a painful chapter of the past and start on the road to complete and equal participation in national life. Herein lies the dialectic of abolition repeated throughout the Americas and the Caribbean. It was only the former slaves who talked of "freedom." Ruling elites intended to continue, to the extent possible, the socioeconomic relationships of slavery and the attendant benefits derived from the exploitation of blacks. For them, abolition was but one phase of an extended process of solidifying an exclusionary barrier around their ranks comprised of social, economic, psychological, and political restrictions on most people of African descent. However, manipulations to transform abolition into a tool of hegemony were met by the equally powerful drive by African descendants to give practical meaning to freedom. Resistance against elite attempts to restrict the roles of African descendants in national life was not only omnipresent, but black initiatives during this period of contestation played a major role in shaping race relations in the Atlantic world in the twentieth century.

Thus, abolition may be conceived not as a static historical event but, rather, as a dynamic process in which conflicting objectives were negotiated. The comparative framework on which this article is based explicitly addresses the historical circumstances of the Afro-Atlantic diaspora during the abolition and post-abolition era. This can be defined nationally as individual communities responded to specific conditions under which slavery ended. Simultaneously, abolition was a transdiasporan phenomenon in which individual abolitions had repercussions affecting the entire Afro-Atlantic world begin-ning with the start of the Haitian Revolution in 1791 and ending with Brazilian abolition in 1888. Abolition occurred in a variety of ways. Slavery ended in Haiti during the violent war that lasted from 1791 to 1804. Haiti invaded the neighboring Dominican Republic in 1822 and ended slavery there. Formal abolition was followed by apprenticeship programs regulating the lives of freed-persons in the British Caribbean (1833–1838) and Cuba (1880–1886). The French and Dutch abolished slavery in their Caribbean colonies in 1848 and 1863. In the continental Americas, newly independent governments declared emancipation only after the majority of their slave populations had already attained freedom through individual manumission, self-purchase, or escape. This process began with Chile, Mexico, and Central America in the 1820s and, in mid-century, was joined by most of South America: Colombia (1851), Ecuador (1852), Argentina and Uruguay (1853), Peru and Venezuela (1854). Yet despite the fact that abolition occurred under various circumstances over nearly one hundred years, basic commonalities of Atlantic slave societies yielded similarities in modes of response that bear further analysis. If the factors affecting the political ideologies and activities of African descendants after abolition may be identified, they may illuminate patterns heretofore obscured by conventional boundaries of national histories and yield new insights derived from an Afro-Atlantic perspective.

While a full comparative framework is beyond the scope of the present essay, it is possible to explore a single but important hallmark of the Afro-Atlantic response to abolition—the strategic use of identity. Identity is not a fixed variable; multiple identities are possible and subject to change depending on the socio-historical context. The fluidity of ethnic identity is often obscured by the apparent permanence of racial ideologies developed under slavery. Yet not only is identity largely a matter of choice within contextual constraints, race itself is a social construct not supported by genetic reality. Thus both oppressors and oppressed were able to reshape identities and give new social meanings to existing ones.

In the Afro-Atlantic world identity has had a long history as a tool of social control. Slave-holders fomented ethnic differences to impede the development of solidarity, creating instead heterogeneous groups of many smaller communities. Additionally, stereotypes about the attributes of specific groups, labeling slaves according to their port of departure in Africa, and preferences amongst slaveholders for particular ethnic groups all contributed to a sense of ethnic heterogeneity. Thus any given diasporan society began as mixtures of Angolans and Congos and Minas, American-born and African-born, browns and blacks, freedmen and slaves. While creolization, or the development of shared African diasporan cultures, began almost immediately, the broad conceptualizations of "blackness" or "Africanity," which eventually became commonplace in the late twentieth century, were not universal throughout the Afro-Atlantic diaspora. Depending on specific historical and demographic conditions, the emergence of widely shared diasporan creole cultures began relatively early, as was the case in the United States, or as late as the twentieth century in Brazil.

One of the hallmarks of the abolition era is that it helped speed the demise of the smaller ethnic categories and the emergence of new broad-based ethnic categories across the Afro-Atlantic diaspora. This happened for a number of reasons. First, slavery had instituted clearly defined social categories that served as a rationale for the exclusion of large segments of the population from the political, economic, and social prerogatives of local elites. The absence of slavery forced elites to articulate new bases for social exclusion. No longer able to use the civil status of slave versus free to differentiate between segments of the African-descended population, exclusionary practices in the post-abolition era typically extended to larger groups identified as "blacks" or "Africans."

Second, abolition was a nineteenth-century phenomenon that coincided with the emergence of Darwinism, Positivism, and the belief in biological determinism, doctrines fervently embraced by American elites. The blanket condemnation of all blacks as a single, inferior race provided whites with a justification for discrimination. Ironically, it also held for blacks the potential for mobilization and ethnic solidarity, which they too could use to their advantage.

Politically oriented responses to the new bases of exclusion did, in fact, prove to be another important factor in the increasing ethnic solidarity among African descendants, a phenomenon which is the focus of the present essay. However, the process had already begun because of the demographic changes taking place under slavery. Despite the efforts of enslavers to foment discord, cohesive forces were at work within the African-descended population from as early as the Middle Passage. Relationships established on slave ships or in communal living quarters, and shared cultural elements such as colonial languages, set in motion the creation of African diasporan cultures. As the slave trade dwindled by the nineteenth century, cultural and demographic changes had seriously weakened many of the internal divisions among persons of African descent in Atlantic diasporan communities. The most important changes were the declining numbers of the African-born and the pervasiveness of the ideology of race.

The rising proportion of the African-descended population born in the Americas was a significant factor in increasing cultural commonality. In some cases, especially in those regions in which slaves were a minority population, persons of African descent adopted dominant national cultures. In other cases, cultural solidarity was reinforced by the emergence of creole cultures based upon an African matrix. Culled from the distinct traditions of insular communities, new cultures bridged the barriers between various segments of the African-descended population. Monica Schuler describes this process in Jamaica. Under slavery, recently arrived Africans from numerically stronger ethnic groups relied on their homeland affiliations for survival in a hostile environment. African national identity became central to distinct Afro-Jamaican ethnicities. Thus, early in the eighteenth century, slave revolts were typically led by Akan or other large ethnic communities. However, by the end of the century, when the number of African-born slaves had diminished to 25 percent, there was a greater tendency toward interethnic cooperation. This trend was reflected in the slave revolt of 1798, led by a coalition of Akan, Kongo, and Mandinka people. A form of Africanized Christianity known as Myalism was of central importance in forging a pan-African culture, drawing as it did from the many ethnic traditions of Afro-Jamaicans. By the 1830s and 1840s, Myalism had become one of the central anchors of the Creole community. A similar process took place with such syncretic cultural expressions as santeria in Cuba and candomblé in Brazil. In each of these communities, creole cultural blends were gradually forging a sense of shared ethnic identity and greater homogeneity within the African-descended population.

Religion and language were not the only institutions facilitating the development of interstitial relationships within Afro-Atlantic communities. In post-abolition Cuba, where *cabildos de nación* had served as mutual aid societies during slavery, new advocacy organizations emerged to address the social and political concerns of Afro-Cubans. These pan-Afro-Cuban societies brought together individuals of diverse African ethnic origins, representing the new importance of race as the organizing principle of ethnicity. Elsewhere, people of color used political entities such as Venezuela's Acción Democrática party to attack prejudice and discrimination, although not explicitly construed as "racial" organizations.

While it is clear that Afro-Atlantic communities were moving toward broad-based ethnicity, how and why those ethnicities took shape as they did is far more difficult to discern. It also remains to be seen how the specific conditions of abolition may have affected the choices of African descendants in relation to the strategic politics of ethnicity.

To explore this issue, I have used a case study of two cities in Brazil, the largest of all Afro-Atlantic diasporan populations. Both moved toward new collective identities, albeit by strikingly different paths. Their contrasting experiences provide a clear example of the ways in which ethnic identity was politicized and transformed in the new context of the post-abolition period, which I have defined in Brazil as the fifty years following final emancipation in 1888. Although they shared a common national culture, Afro-Brazilians experienced discrimination differently based upon local social, economic, and historical conditions. As a result, in some regions Afro-Brazilians mobilized on the basis of membership in a "black" race, whereas in others, they formulated a sense of group identity around shared African cultural heritage.

In the southern city of São Paulo, racial discrimination became a focal point for Afro-Brazilian activism. At the time of abolition, less than 3 percent of the state's Afro-Brazilian population lived in the capital. As the city of São Paulo quickly developed into South America's industrial hub, it attracted thousands of new arrivals. Most of these were Europeans, some coming directly from overseas, but the majority were former contract laborers who had originally been hired by Brazilian planters to replace former

slaves and assist in the building of a technological infrastructure. Among the Italians, Portuguese, Spaniards, Germans, and others were Afro-Brazilians, mostly from neighboring rural communities, whose numbers increased from 10,000 in 1890 to over 100,000 by 1940. Nonetheless, they comprised a very small segment of the city's population, ranging between 8 and 12 percent during this period.

The earliest black communities in the city were formed around hometown networks. Many black men worked for the railroads as manual laborers, and families took advantage of this fact to travel back and forth, especially to hometown festivals, and maintain strong ties between the capital and the countryside. But these hometown identities were soon overshadowed by the blanket racial discrimination affecting all Afro-Brazilians in São Paulo.

Blacks were formally barred from employment in such institutions as the state police. They were discouraged from frequenting such public sites as the skating rinks or downtown plazas. The lucrative jobs that had attracted many to the capital proved to be inaccessible, and even factory work was monopolized by immigrants employed by fellow nationals. Moreover, in their zeal to impose social order, the police had targeted the tenements and bars where blacks gathered, resulting in a disproportionate arrest and imprisonment rate for Afro-Brazilians.

Such obstacles were unacceptable to a community dominated by highly motivated individuals who had staked their futures on relocating to São Paulo. They were particularly offended by their lack of opportunity as Brazilians vis-à-vis European immigrants, especially since many blacks of their grand-parents' generation had fought for Brazil in the Paraguayan war. Words of protest began appearing in the social newspapers circulated by recreational clubs. And more and more, the younger generation was using the word *negro* to describe themselves, instead of *prêto*, which was considered the "polite" way to identify a dark-skinned person in Brazil.

Given the context in which they lived, appropriating the concept of negritude was a revolutionary departure. Until then, the word *negro* had been employed as an insulting term equated with slavery. People of color typically used a host of other terms along a finely calibrated spectrum of racial identity—*prêto, moreno, mestiço, clarinho, pardo*—to avoid the *negro* epithet. Essentially, however, traditional racial categories grouped all Afro-Brazilians into the two large and distinct categories of blacks and mulattoes. Afro-Brazilians in São Paulo had begun to reject this distinction in favor of the broader-based negro identity in response to the discrimination they suffered collectively as nonwhites.

It soon became apparent that blackness held great potential as the organizing principle for a political constituency with which to address social inequities. The first experiment of this type took place in 1926, with the creation of the Palmares Civic Center. Headed by a group of approximately twenty young men, Palmares protested the exclusion of black officers from the state police force, and succeeded in having the ban revoked by São Paulo's governor. Five years later, a former Palmares member founded the Brazilian Black Front (Frente Negra Brasileira), the first national Afro-Brazilian civil rights organization. The Front targeted cases of overt discrimination, engaged in activism to desegregate public spaces, and created training programs to enable Afro-Brazilians to compete effectively in the labor market. Impressed by their early successes and their objectives of promoting "the moral, intellectual, artistic, technical, professional and physical advancement of the Black people," Afro-Brazilians flocked to the Front in record numbers. They quickly became a force to be reckoned with. Aware of its political potential, the Brazilian Black Front registered as a formal political party in 1933.

The significance of the Brazilian Black Front is sometimes minimized because it was unsuccessful in electing candidates and was ultimately dissolved by the political coup of 1937 that signaled the beginning of a presidential dictatorship. Yet the Afro-Brazilians of São Paulo shaped an identity of negritude that became the cornerstone of subsequent black activism throughout the twentieth century.

In the northeastern region of the country, the situation was apparently quite different. The idea of a black identity as captured in the term *negro* had not caught on, and attempts at establishing a chapter of the Brazilian Black Front had not met with success in Salvador, a city populated predominantly by people of African descent. There, the parameters of ethnicity had developed along a trajectory based in the recent slave past. In the beginning of the nineteenth century, enslaved West Africans had come to Bahia in record numbers. A series of slave revolts led by Yorubas and Hausas, in which Muslims played a predominant role, had resulted in a severe backlash against Africans and the repression of African culture. In the wake of that revolt, African cultural manifestations were cast as acts of potential sedition, suspected of providing Africans with secret forums for hatching new plots against the Brazilian state. In the "us versus them" polemic that ensued, Afro-Brazilians stood ambiguously, having to choose between casting their lots as "Brazilians" or "Africans." The polarity thus established was not one of race, as in São Paulo, but of culture.

The anti-African sentiment of the early nineteenth century continued as the century progressed, developing a new ideological underpinning as the historical context changed. By the time of abolition, concern was not about rebellion, but rather the possibility that Afro-Bahian culture would become dominant. Influenced by the concepts of environmental and biological determinism, white Bahians became alarmed at the apparent proliferation of "barbaric" Africanisms, a trend diametrically opposed to what they viewed as the "progressive" regions of the industrialized southern states. One senator went so far as to characterize Afro-Brazilians as "an imminent danger weighing down our future." In a country in which modernization was equated with physical and cultural Europeanization (*embranquecimento*, literally, "whitening"), this meant the suppression of Africanisms in a city where most of the population was of African descent.

Private homes and public streets alike became the battlegrounds of the Culture wars of post-abolition Salvador, where elites began a campaign to rid the city of what they perceived to be excessive displays of African culture. The Afro-Brazilian religion of candomblé was an early target. Sacred gatherings were raided by clandestine police forces who arrested priests and confiscated religious artifacts. Carnival groups with African themes, welcomed when they first appeared in the 1890s, quickly incurred the wrath of influential citizens fearful of presenting a public image of Salvador as an African city. Local newspapers launched an editorial attack on the African clubs. "Once again, we remind the police of the necessity, in the name of civilization and to the credit of Bahia, to put a stop to these degrading parades of an entirely African character," complained one newspaper in 1902. The following year, a letter to the editor clearly identified the cause of alarm: "If someone from outside were to judge Bahia by its Carnival, they could not help but place it on a par with Africa. . . . That part of the population which is civilized [should protest against] this savage festival." In 1905, African clubs were banned from Carnival. Despite the prohibition, Afro-Bahians continued to assert a right to social space for African culture. This struggle came to focus on candomblé.

Over the course of the nineteenth century, candomblé had emerged as the basis of pan-Afro-Bahian culture in a process similar to those noted in Jamaica and Cuba. With the decline of the African-born population, candomblé houses adapted to incorporate the Brazilian-born masses, changing principles of initiation so that one could join an African ethnic circle by affiliation rather than birth. This change opened candomblé to non-Africans and facilitated its spread into popular culture. Candomblé religious leaders created allegiances with influential politicians, academics, and artists and, in 1938, formed the Union of Afro-Brazilian Sects under the leadership of Edison Carneiro and Martiniano de Bomfim. Visionaries such as Eugenia Anna dos Santos moved candomblé out of the shadows by opening the doors of her terreiro, to the international community. Despite the intense efforts to repress African culture in Bahia, the authorities were ultimately outmaneuvered. They had outlawed candomblé, African carnival, the martial art of capoeira; the Catholic Church tried to weed out Africanisms in religious festivals and practices. Yet of all the cities of the African diaspora, today Salvador is among those most closely associated with African retentions. The cultural autonomy for which they fought provided people of African descent with an alternative space to develop a sense of their own worth and human dignity, and thus they subverted the intentions of an oppressive society that had institutionalized discrimination against Africa and African people. Their actions ultimately had important political repercussions; Afro-Bahians created a mode of social struggle deeply rooted in cultural nationalism that characterized collective activism throughout the twentieth century.

The two cases of São Paulo and Salvador were very different in political orientation, yet they both took similar paths toward broader-based collective identities that could mobilize new constituencies and effect social change. While elites were taking advantage of the malleability of ethnicity and using it as a strategy to protect the insularity of their group, people of African descent also began to manipulate imposed identities as a strategy of their own. Discrimination against "blacks" or "Africans" intensified the cultural homogenization already accelerated with the cessation of the slave trade. Use of broader ethnicities emphasized greater levels of inclusion; for the first time, the notion of blackness in São Paulo now included mulattoes, and the concept of Africanity in Salvador came to embrace all adherents regardless of birthplace or even skin color. This understanding of identity not as a fixed variable, but as a social strategy, refines the research question by directing it toward a search for patterns of response that are obscured by external differences of form.

Regardless of their political orientations and specific objectives, African diaspora peoples such as those of São Paulo and Bahia were confronting issues shared across the Americas and the Caribbean at abolition. They challenged the hegemonic paradigms that threatened the potential of their freedom. Their actions forced power and social spaces to be negotiated rather than dictated.

In terms of establishing broader frameworks for the comparison of the strategic use of identity during the post-abolition era across the Afro-Atlantic diaspora, the Brazilian case suggests some possible patterns for exploration. The exclusionary ideologies imposed upon African descendants seem to have been embraced and used by them as a basis for solidarity and political mobilization to address discrimination. The development of broader ethnicities was due in part to such factors as demographic shifts and the ongoing process of creolization. Yet the conscious choice to establish collective identities for purposes of political strategy was equally important. It should also be noted that this process began transcending national boundaries with the re-migrations of African descendants throughout the Atlantic world in the aftermath of abolition, and improvements in communications and transportation technologies that permitted the Afro-Atlantic diaspora to form a sense of themselves as a cultural community of shared history and social concerns. The process reached its fullest expression in Marcus Garvey's Universal Negro Improvement Association, but was also reflected in smaller-scale Afro-Atlantic movements such as the *negritude* of the 1930s, and more recently Black Power and Rastafarianism, for example.

It is important to situate black agency in the consideration of the subsequent evolution of race relations in the diaspora. What is presented here is but one potential avenue for comparative analysis across Afro-Atlantic communities, one facet of a historical era in which people of the Afro-Atlantic diaspora seized the opportunity to define themselves and their relationship with their former enslavers. For among the many experiences that unify the Afro-Atlantic diaspora, the struggle to achieve what Jamaicans called "full free" is one of the strongest, and continues to unite descendants as shipmates into the twenty-first century.

---

[1] The author wishes to thank Dr. Monica Schuler for her valuable comments on this paper.

[2] The term "Afro-Atlantic" refers to that portion of the African diaspora sent to the Americas and the Caribbean in the Atlantic slave trade. As a reference to the trade specifically, it also includes Afro-American populations along the Pacific coast.

[3] Many scholars of specific abolitions in the Afro-Atlantic world have concluded that they did not bring about profound revolutionary changes but, rather, merely altered the parameters of oppression. See, for example, Eric Foner, *Nothing but Freedom: Emancipation and Its Legacy* (Baton Rouge: Louisiana State University Press, 1983); Peter Blanchard, *Slavery and Abolition in Early Republican Peru* (Wilmington, DE: Scholarly Resources, 1992), xviii, 212; O. Nigel Bolland, "Systems of Domination after Slavery: The Control of Land and Labor in the British West Indies after 1838," *Comparative Studies in Society and History*, 23:4 (October 1981); Aline Helg, *Our Rightful Share: The Afro-Cuban Struggle for Equality, 1886–1912* (Chapel Hill: University of North Carolina Press, 1995); John V. Lombardi, "The Abolition of Slavery in Venezuela: A Nonevent," in Robert Brent Toplin, ed., *Slavery and Race Relations in Latin America* (Westport, CT: Greenwood Press, 1974); Walter Rodney, *A History of the Guyanese Working People* (Baltimore: Johns Hopkins University Press, 1981).

[4] Rebecca Scott, "Comparing Emancipations: A Review Essay," *Journal of Social History* 20:3 (1987), 565–83; Nancy Naro, "Revision and Persistence: Recent Historiography on the Transition from Slave to Free Labor in Rural Brazil," *Slavery and Abolition* (UK) 13:2

(1992), 68–85; Stanley L. Engerman, "Slavery and Emancipation in Comparative Perspective: A Look at Some Recent Debates," *Journal of Economic History* 46 (June 1986), 317–39.

[5]The specific post-abolition strategies of elites in the Afro-Atlantic world are summarized in Herbert S. Klein and Stanley L. Engerman, "The Transition from Slave to Free Labor," 255–269; Francisco A. Scarano, "Labor and Society in the Nineteenth Century," in Franklin W. Knight and Colin A. Palmer, eds., *The Modern Caribbean* (Chapel Hill: University of North Carolina Press, 1989), 51–84; Eric Foner, *Nothing but Freedom: Emancipation and Its Legacy* (Baton Rouge: Louisiana State University Press, 1983), 10–28.

[6]Michael L. Conniff and Thomas J. Davis, eds., *Africans in the Americas: A History of the Black Diaspora* (New York: St. Martin's Press, 1994), 175–188; Franklin W. Knight and Colin A. Palmer, "The Caribbean: A Regional Overview," in Knight and Palmer, eds., *The Modern Caribbean*, 8.

[7]Ashley Montagu, *Man's Most Dangerous Myth: The Fallacy of Race* [1942], 5th ed. (New York: Oxford University Press, 1974).

[8]Sidney Mintz and Richard Price, *The Birth of African-American Culture: An Anthropological Perspective* (Boston: Beacon Press, 1992).

[9]Despite the heterogeneity of African origins in the United States, slave communities developed shared cultures at a markedly quicker rate than in Brazil, where new arrivals from Africa well into the nineteenth century helped reinforce distinct identities based on African "nations" (*nações*). Sterling Stuckey, *Slave Culture: Nationalist Theory and the Foundations of Black America* (New York: Oxford University Press, 1987); Charles Joyner, *Down by the Riverside: A South Carolina Slave Community* (Urbana: University of Illinois Press, 1984); Gwendolyn Midlo Hall, *Africans in Colonial Louisiana: The Development of Afro-Creole Culture in the Eighteenth Century* (Baton Rouge: Louisiana State University Press, 1992); Eugene Genovese, *Roll, Jordan, Roll: The World the Slaves Made* (New York: Vintage Books, 1972). On the persistence of Afro-Brazilian ethnic heterogeneity, see João José Reis, *Slave Rebellion in Brazil: The Muslim Uprising of 1835 in Bahia*, trans. Arthur Brakel (Baltimore: Johns Hopkins University Press, 1993), 139–59; Mary C. Karasch, *Slave Life in Rio de Janeiro, 1808–1850* (Princeton: Princeton University Press, 1987), 3–28; Mieko Nishida, "Gender, Ethnicity, and Kinship in the Urban African Diaspora: Salvador, Brazil, 1808–1888," Ph.D. diss., Johns Hopkins University, 1991, 197–211.

[10]George Reid Andrews traced this process in Argentina, where a diverse community of Afro-Argentine "nations" and consciousness of civil status under slavery evolved into a community defined by race in the post-abolition period. "To the present day, they call themselves *la clase de color* (the colored class) . . . reflecting their own historical experience of having been shunted aside in the porteño class structure solely on the basis of their race." George Reid Andrews, *The Afro-Argentines of Buenos Aires, 1800–1900* (Madison: University of Wisconsin Press, 1980), 204.

[11]E. Bradford Burns, "Cultures in Conflict: The Implication of Modernization in Nineteenth Century Latin America," in Virginia Bernhard, ed., *Elites, Masses and Modernization in Latin America, 1850–1930* (Austin: University of Texas Press, 1979). Winthrop Wright examines the interaction of Positivist ideas and the politics of ethnicity in Venezuela in *Café con Leche: Race, Class and National Image in Venezuela* (Austin: University of Texas Press, 1990).

[12]Sidney Mintz and Richard Price, *The Birth of African-American Culture: An Anthropological Perspective* (Boston: Beacon Press, 1992).

[13]Monica Schuler, *Alas, Alas Kongo: A Social History of Indentured African Immigrants into Jamaica, 1841–1865* (Baltimore: Johns Hopkins University Press, 1980), 33–34; 65–70.

[14]Kim D. Butler, "Identity and Self-Determination in the Post-Abolition African Diaspora: São Paulo and Salvador, Brazil, 1888–1938," Ph.D. diss., Johns Hopkins University, 1995, 317–351; Roger Bastide, *The African Religions of Brazil: Toward a Sociology of the Interpenetration of Civilizations*, trans. Helen Sebba (Baltimore: Johns Hopkins University Press, 1978), 58–77; Roger Bastide, *African Civilisations in the New World*, trans. Peter Green (New York: Harper and Row, 1971); George Brandon, *Santeria from Africa to the New World: The Dead Sell Memories* (Bloomington: Indiana University Press, 1993); Fernando Ortiz Fernandez, *Hampa Afro-Cubana: Los Negros Brujos. Apuntes para um estudio de etnologia criminal* (Madrid, 1906).

[15]The *cabildos* were vital institutions in the Cuban slave community, and membership was closely linked to African ethnicity. They performed such practical functions as providing for burial, care of the sick, purchase of manumission, and savings. Philip A. Howard, "The Spanish Colonial Government's Responses to the Pan-Nationalist Agenda of the Afro-Cuban Mutual Aid Societies, 1868–1895," *Revista/Review Interamericana* 22:1–2 (1992), 151–67; Aline Helg, *Our Rightful Share: The Afro-Cuban Struggle for Equality, 1886–1912* (Chapel Hill: University of North Carolina Press, 1995), 36–43. See also George Reid Andrews, *The Afro-Argentines*, 138–55.

[16]Winthrop Wright, *Café con Leche*, 98–100.

[17]The full analysis of these two Brazilian post-abolition communities is contained in Kim D. Butler, *Freedoms Given, Freedoms Won: Afro-Brazilians in Post-Abolition São Paulo and Salvador* (New Brunswick, NJ: Rutgers University Press, 1998).

[18]This is true for individuals as well as collectives, although only the latter are addressed here.

[19]Brazil, *Recenseamento Geral da População*, 1890; 1940.

[20]The city's population grew from 64,934 in 1890 to 1,326,261 in 1940. Brazil, Ministerio da Agricultura, Industria e Comercio, Diretoria Geral de Estatística, *Anuario Estatistico do Brasil*, Anno I (1908–1912), vol. 1, 260–61; 268–69.

[21]José Carlos Gomes da Silva, "Os Sub-Urbanos e a Outra Face da Cidade. Negros em São Paulo, 1900–1930: Cotidiano, Lazer e Cidadania," M.A. thesis, Universidade Estadual de Campinas, 1990; Iêda Marques Britto, *Samba na Cidade de São Paulo, 1900–1930: um exercício de resistencia cultural* (São Paulo: FFLCH-USP, 1986), 37–41.

[22]For a full discussion of social conditions facing Afro-Brazilians in post-abolition São Paulo, see George Reid Andrews, *Blacks and Whites in São Paulo, Brazil, 1888–*

1938 (Madison: University of Wisconsin Press, 1991); Florestan Fernandes, *A Integração do Negro na Sociedade de Classes,* 2 vols. (São Paulo: Editora Atica, 1978); Kim D. Butler, "Identity and Self-Determination in the Post-Abolition African Diaspora: São Paulo and Salvador, Brazil, 1888–1938," Ph.D. diss., Johns Hopkins University, 1995, 122–156.

[23] Although the exact number of Afro-Brazilians to serve in the war has been a matter of debate, the perceived ingratitude with which they were treated lingers even today in the public memory. Andrews, *Blacks and Whites in São Paulo,* 220–21. See also Hendrik Kraay, "Soldiers, Officers, and Society: The Army in Bahia, Brazil, 1808–1889," Ph.D. diss., University of Texas at Austin, 1995.

[24] Historian Mary Karasch noted that the word *negro* "was almost synonymous with *escravo* (slave)." Mary C. Karasch, *Slave Life in Rio de Janeiro, 1808–1850* (Princeton: Princeton University Press, 1987), 5.

[25] Butler, "Identity and Self-Determination," 195–219; see also Michael Mitchell, "Racial Consciousness and the Political Attitudes and Behavior of Blacks in São Paulo, Brazil," Ph.D. diss., Indiana University, 1977; Florestan Fernandes, *A Integração do Negro na Sociedade de Classes,* vol. II (New York: Atheneum, 1971).

[26] For a complete discussion of these revolts and their repercussions, see João José Reis, *Slave Rebellion in Brazil: The Muslim Uprising of 1835 in Bahia,* trans, Arthur Brakel (Baltimore: Johns Hopkins University Press, 1993); Reis, "Slave Resistance in Brazil: Bahia, 1807–1835," *Luso-Brazilian Review* 25:1 (1988), 111–38.

[27] Raymundo Nina Rodrigues documented this phenomenon in Bahia in *O Animismo Fetichista dos Negros Bahianos* (Rio de Janeiro: Civilização Brasileira, 1935).

[28] Fidelis Reis, *Paiz a Organizar* (Rio de Janeiro: Coelho Branco, 1931).

[29] *Jornal de Noticias* (Salvador, Bahia), 22 January 1902.

[30] *Jornal de Noticias,* 23 February 1903.

[31] Edison Carneiro, *Candomblés da Bahia,* 3d ed. (Rio de Janeiro, 1961), 57.

[32] For a complete discussion of the politics of culture in post-abolition Salvador, see Kim D. Butler, *Freedoms Given, Freedoms Won* (New Brunswick, NJ: Rutgers University Press, 1998), ch. 6.

[33] Bonham C. Richardson, "Caribbean Migrations," in Franklin W. Knight and Colin A. Palmer, eds., *The Modern Caribbean* (Chapel Hill: University of North Carolina Press, 1989), 203–28.

SECTION NINE:
THE ROLE OF RELIGIONS
IN THE AFRICAN DIASPORA

Introduction

Over the many centuries of the Atlantic slave trade, millions of Africans arrived as slaves in the Americas. The Africans brought with them their culture, folkways, ideas about their world and strong views about their African religions. Their European masters mostly ignored, marginalized and outlawed the African's religious beliefs referring to them as "heathen," and "devilish cults." Determined to maintain as much of their way of life as was possible, most slaves retained whatever they could under the slave conditions. The slavemasters deliberately attempted to discourage the close association of large numbers of slaves with similar ethnic backgrounds. Consequently the African religions that emerged are in many cases amalgams of various African belief systems. Scholars who have studied the religions that flourished in the Americas refer to them as "New World religions." Most of these religions are essentially syncretic in nature and seek to assist followers in coping with slave life, preserving African culture and thought, maintaining a community closeness, and resisting the master's attempt to have them view their slave experience from their master's perspective.

There were many "new African belief systems" that emerged over the centuries across the Americas during slavery. However, certain conditions allowed some of these belief systems to grow and flourish and become major religious forces within specific regions in the Americas. Among the most successful New World religions are Vodoun in Haiti, Candomble in Brazil, Santeria called Lukumi in Cuba, Myalism in Jamaica, Maria Lionza in Venezuela, Garifuna in Honduras, Shango in Trinidad, and numerous others. These religions developed strong roots in these societies and continue to have strong followings in these countries' present day societies. Scholars in various fields from anthropology to sociology have been carefully studying, researching and writing about various aspects of these religions indicating the very significant role these religions played in the lives of the slaves and their descendants. The essays in this section will introduce some of these religions to readers and show how these religions have survived and continue to attract large numbers of believers in recent times.

The first essay was prepared by two outstanding anthropologists, Sidney Mintz and Michel-Rolph Trouillot on "The Social History of Haitian Vodou." Vodou is probably the best known and least understood of the African religions and is based on a wide cross section of West African belief systems from concepts out of the Arada system and a dozen others including Nago, Ibo, Fon, Dahomean, Wolof, Hausa, and Mandingo.

441

Sidney Mintz held the position of Williursh Straus, Junior Professor of Anthropology at the Johns Hopkins University for over thirty years. He is author of numerous articles and books on various aspects of Caribbean life, including *Worker in the Cane, Caribbean Transformations, Sweetness and Power*, co-editor of *Caribbean Contours* with Sally Price, and with Richard Price *The Birth of An African American Culture*. Michel-Rolph Trouillot is Krieger-Eisenhower Professor of Anthropology at the Johns Hopkins University, and his books include *Peasants and Capital: Dominica in the World Economy*, and *Haiti: State Against Nation and Silencing the Past*.

The second essay is William Bascom's "The Focus of Cuban Santeria" in which the reader is introduced to the basic elements of beliefs and practice of Cuba's largest African religion. Bascom clearly explains the religion's historical development and importance in Cuban society. Bascom published this essay in 1950 in a leading American anthropological journal and had recently studied the Santeria/Lucumi religion in Cuba based on a Wenner-Gren Foundation Grant. Bascom was also an authority on Nigeria's Yoruba religion. He was the first Ph.D. student to complete the degree under Melville Herskovits. He graduated in 1939 and joined the faculty at Northwestern University immediately afterwards.

The third essay is about the establishment of Jamaica's Rastafarian religion in the 1930s. Many scholars have since written extensively about this religion that presently has believers of all races around the world from Europe to Australia. Scholars frequently point out the similarities of this movement to that of the Nation of Islam in regards to its Black nationalist views. This article deals with its early years as well as with his basic beliefs and worldwide appeal. "Rastafarianism as an African Diaspora Phenomenon" is written by Michael Barnett, who was Professor of Sociology and Anthropology at Florida International University and more recently has been affiliated with the University of the West Indies, Mona campus. Among his most recent studies on this theme are his "Differences and Similarities Between the Rastafari Movement and the Nation of Islam" in the *Journal of Black Studies,* Vol. 36, no. 3, 2006, and his presentation at Temple University's 2007 Cheikh Anta Diop International Conference in mid October 2007 when he spoke on the theme "Rastafari: A Continuation of Ancient Wisdom."

Essay four in this section focuses on Candomble, the African religion in the Americas with the largest following. The article entitled "Candomble and the Reterritorializaton of Cultures" is written by Abil Trigo, a distinguished Humanities Professor of Latin American Cultures in the Department of Spanish and Portuguese at the Ohio State University. He has published widely on the effects of globalization in Latin Americam societies. He is co-editor of *The Latin American Cultural Studies Reader* (2004).

The fifth essay is "The Orisha Religion in Trinidad Today" which presents a clean up-to-date view of Trinidad's Shango religion. It is authored by Frances Henry, Professor Emerita from the Department of Anthropology at Canada's York University in Toronto. She is also the author of several books and articles on a wide range of themes regarding ethnicity and multiculturalism across the Americas.

The final essay in this section is Martin Holbraad's "Religious Speculation: The Rise of Ifa Cults and Consumption in Post Soviet Havana." This study focuses on the evolutionary role of the African belief system in contemporary Cuba that has for decades been denied a prominent role for organized religions in any form. Holbraad studied anthropology at Pembroke College at the University of Cambridge. He has also in recent years worked in the Department of Anthropology at the University College in London. He also published a similar essay entitled "Expending Multiplicity: Money in Cuban Ifa Cults" in the *Journal of the Royal Anthropological Institute*, Vol. II in 2005, and is co-author of *Thinking Through Things, Theorizing Artifacts in Ethnographic Perspective* (2007).

The Social History of Haitian Vodou

Sidney Mintz & Michel-Rolph Trouillot

voodooism also voudouism n-s (1): a religion originating in Africa as a form of ancestor worship, practiced chiefly by Negroes of Haiti and to some extent other West Indian islands and the U.S., and characterized by propitiatory rites and use of trance as a means of communicating with animistic deities— called also vodun; compare OBEAH (2): the practice of black magic: conjuring, witchcraft.

Webster's Third New International Dictionary.

The term Vodou, as used here, is one of a group of related terms (vodun, vodoun, vaudoux, "voodoo," "hoodoo," etc.) which are names for a religious system, as Webster's definition suggests. Each word embodies a cluster of meanings and associations as used by nonbelievers. The terms carry a geographical and a racial association as well. Understandings about little-known events that once occurred on the Caribbean island of Hispaniola (of which Haiti is a part) in the seventeenth and eighteenth centuries are mentally condensed in the imagery associated with Vodou. In the words of one of the more thoughtful students of the religion, "Qui dit Haiti, pense 'Vaudoux,' c'est un fait devant lequel on doit se contenter d'émettre une vaine protestation."[1]

Most Americans and Europeans think they know what "voodoo" means. The meaning of the phrase "voodoo economics," for example, associated with ex-president George Bush, appears to be understood and is clearly recognized as pejorative, even though it has never been defined. The apparent collective assurance that the meaning of such words and phrases is already known makes it unusually difficult to write informatively about the history of Vodou and about problems connected with the label. There are many experts on Vodou and they do not all agree. In fact, it is easier to provide a sober ethnographic account of a contemporary ceremony than it is to make good sense of the religion's history.

Vodou was created by individuals drawn from many different cultures. It took on its characteristic shape over the course of several centuries. It has never been codified in writing, never possessed a national institutional structure—a priesthood, a national church, an orthodoxy, a seminary, a hymnal, a hierarchy, or a charter. It runs no day camps, athletic contests, or soup kitchens. And until the creation of the organization called ZANTRAY, explicitly for the defense of the Haitian cultural tradition, Vodou has never had "public relations" either. It is widely dispersed nationally, in the form of what

appear to be local cult groups. It has no geographical center or mother church. Its practice seems to be highly variable locally. Though lacking a national apparatus of any kind, so widely is Vodou practiced and so powerful are the premises of its underlying cosmology that it is usually considered by the Haitians themselves to be the national religion.

Subtle political elements are also involved in the image that Vodou projects. A strong ideological current among Haitians centers on the idea of Vodou's importance in the revolutionary creation of the Republic of Haiti, nearly two centuries ago.[2] The religion continues to be lauded (and sometimes damned) in contemporary accounts of all sorts.

Since its beginnings in the New World, Vodou has always stood in some counterposed dialectical relationship to other (European) religions, particularly Catholicism. It appears never to have excluded these other faiths from its own means for organizing belief, and for squaring life with the demands of the daily world. But there are differences of opinion concerning the contribution of Catholicism to Vodou, and at least some authorities who discount that contribution.

To document the history of Vodou is to define as much as to explain it. Yet because that history is murky—shrouded not only in myth but also in a million printed pages written by non-practitioners, both infatuated and violently hostile—a comprehensive picture is elusive. Before Haiti became independent, a few observers described aspects of the slaves' religious behavior. But once freedom came, the social context of religious expression changed radically. Hardly any outsiders observed what was happening, or reported on their observations. During half a century following the Revolution, there was no formal signing of a Concordat with the Vatican; and though there were some Catholic priests in Haiti during that period,[3] their collective effect upon Haitian belief was probably negligible.

Yet in the wider world there was some interest in "The Black Republic," its people and their religion. This interest was a coefficient of Haiti's stormy revolutionary history, the (partly) African origins of its leaders and citizens, and its successful war for freedom. Hence various accounts of Haiti's religious life appeared even before the Concordat was signed and finally put in place, in 1860. Though most of these accounts are open to doubt, it is easy to explain why we have them. Surely no other "religion of Negroes" has ever received so much attention, nor was it ever as important to demean its content. That slaves would fight their colonial masters—that masses of uneducated black slaves would wage war against Napoleonic and French dominion—was thought to be morally hideous. But that these "gilded Africans"[4] would win was absolutely intolerable.[5] When they did, their religion (as well as their presumed failure to survive without European guidance) had to be exposed. The manner in which independent Haiti appeared upon the world scene inevitably colored everything written about it thereafter; and to some extent this is still true, even today. Its popular religion received similar treatment. Hence what follows is written in the absence of any adequate objective history of this New World belief system.

We cannot initiate a discussion of an historically particular body of belief and behavior (as denoted by the term Vodou) as if we knew at the outset what it stood for. Therefore, we shall comment briefly on the nature of the religion itself, and what scholars have written about it. First, however, it may be useful to state broadly the highly specific conditions under which the religious beliefs of enslaved Africans and their descendants in the New World must have evolved. Scholars are not often prepared to analyze religious systems that have had to undergo reconstitution on a wholly new basis, after near-total dissolution. In the last five centuries, this sort of dissolution has occurred frequently in non-Western areas, particularly in those regions subjected to extreme pressures of the sort that result in depopulation, geographical resettlement or expulsion of large numbers of people, radical changes in the political order, and widespread loss of civil rights. In causing such changes, the West has figured importantly.

The rapid and highly destructive expansion of European society across the Great Plains of North America, for example, led to the decimation of some Native American populations, to war against most, and to the active missionization or proselytization of still others. Disease and war often killed off so many of the ceremonial leaders that large segments of religious practice were lost—if not forever, then at least in their earlier, "authentic" form.[6] The extreme nature of such cases makes it appear that total destruction was followed by entirely new beginnings. But in fact the analyses of what actually happened leave no doubt that older materials could be carried forward within the new religions. It would be unhistorical and incautious to claim that the religious systems in such cases always "vanished," or were wholly destroyed.

The case of enslaved Africans is more radical still. The vast majority of Africans who reached the New World were fated to spend the remainder of their lives outside communities of those who spoke their own language and practiced their own religion, even though they found themselves among other Africans. Slaves on the plantations had to forge common cultural practices out of their highly diverse pasts and within the constraints imposed by their living conditions. Enslavement, transportation, and life under servitude in the New World was a fundamentally *individualizing* experience.[7] A slave's prior status and the rhythms of his daily life in the society of origin were traumatically broken by enslavement, the Middle Passage, the acculturative process called "seasoning," and the awful demands of the new existence as slave. The old life and culture were now remote, even if not forgotten.

At the same time, this trauma was also an intensely drastic resocializing process: drastic because it proceeded under the constant threat of violence and even death; resocializing because it demanded the learning of wholly different behavioral patterns by its subjects and victims. The "seasoning" of which the planters and slavers spoke was specific to their preparation for work. But in fact the seasoning process actually covered much more. The simplest acts—of eating, of elimination, as well as of dressing and toilette, not to mention courting, establishing kinship ties, or managing life-crises such as birth and death—had to be relearned to fit the new (and mostly very oppressive) circumstances, in the absence of one society governing principles[8] based on cultural content. The "right way" to fall in love, to give birth, to bless, to bury had, in this situation, to be fashioned through social acts. The slaves could not bring with them the material apparatus that sustained their institutions at home, such as ritual objects, particular foods or beverages, distinctive items of dress, weapons, equipment, tools. Even though many of these items might be faithfully reproduced (and doubtless were), to do so required innovativeness, motivation, and probably stealth. Nor could they bring the personnel of any such institution, such as a group of priests, a group of artisans, or a royal family. Coming as they did from many different societies, the enslaved did not share a common language, a common religion, or a single political system. The culturally specific practices that usually enable us to distinguish individuals from one society from individuals coming from another—Frenchmen, say, from Russians—varied among the enslaved as well, but it tended to vary from individual to individual. It is because of this inescapable variability, created by the history of slavery, that we believe that "one-society governing principles" were absent.

On the other hand the heterogeneity was not as thoroughgoing as commonly supposed. Persons from the same group did on occasion find each other in the same locale, and many broad principles of traditional cultural orientation, principles underlay the culture-specific differences and were in fact conserved.[9] Indeed, recent work[10] documents the significance of preexisting cultural connections. Despite the lack of a common culture, the enslaved often shared certain fundamental orientations—a "substratum"—toward the universe and toward each other that helped them in reestablishing common cultural ground. But that did not make the pressure less.

Accordingly, it can be taken as an initial premise that the evolving religious life of the slaves in the New World depended on their success in (re)constructing religious systems that successfully "patched" what had been believed to what *would* be believed. In order to do so, they were obliged to employ the various memories, insights, practices, and beliefs available, from that heterogeneous group of individuals who would be living in one place, or on one plantation. The initial period of contact among the enslaved on the estates to which they were transported was of crucial importance.[11] In the case of the firstcomers, many acts may still have been practiced; and many of those that could not were still vividly remembered. Words, objects, songs, gestures, associations, specific beliefs about nature or agency may be expressed and thereby contributed to a kind of common fund of cultural "knowledge." From this fund, all may draw, so to speak, until certain specific behaviors become normative—until, that is, such material takes on some common characteristics that all group members acknowledge behaviorally. Particular behavioral features—gestures, words, ways of dressing and undressing, addressing and redressing—thus become embodied in group behavior as norms.

The perpetuation of those features, however, does not rest only upon wide individual recognition, but also upon the emergence of some kinds of specialized personnel: priests, priestesses, healers and herbalists, midwives, soothsayers, ritual assistants, craftsmen such as drum makers, musicians, and so on. In effect, the allocation of tasks and responsibilities among persons who come to be recognized as ritual figures is the ongoing institutional accompaniment to the emergence of a body of coherent and accepted practice.

Until an institutional form becomes visible, even a body of belief that has been transferred coherently has nowhere to attach itself. If we think of an institution as a social instrument for addressing a problem—including under "problems" such things as birth, maturity, sexual union, parenthood and death—its emergence is determined in large part by the readiness of group members to agree on how best such a problem can be handled. It is for this reason that we can speak of group behavior as extending itself along the latticework of institutions that, together, make up a society's "solutions." (An event such as birth is always a "problem"; in the same sense, an act such as baptism or circumcision, the choice of godparents or of ritual presiders is always a "solution.")

While the slave sector of New World societies was not a separate (and separable) society in its own right—materials of all kinds were clearly transmitted across the status and other boundaries that divided the masters from the slaves—these were social groups deeply divided from each other, ideologically and in good measure culturally, even though they were in intimate daily contact. The ancestral cultures from which their members came were certainly different in nearly every way.

Indeed the dichotomy between these two groups, and between their religious legacies, has been a persistent theme of the scholarship to date on Vodou. Analytic work such as that of Herskovits (1936), Bastide (1967), Desmangles (1992), Larose (1977), and de Heusch (1989) suggests the following points. There is a general recognition that Vodou took on its characteristic shape through whole series of events occurring during slavery and after freedom came, as half a million Africans (and their descendants) brought a new religion into being in the French colony. Authors identify meaningful distinctions of various sorts reflecting the evolution of the religious system itself, over time, and the playing-out of various influences (e.g., the Rada-Petwo duality); new religious ideas (as in the analysis of Petwo by de Heusch); contests over authenticity (as in Larose's discussion of Guinea), and other processes of change. In nearly every study mentioned, the operative word is "juxtaposition,"[12] since this makes it possible to speak of two systems or subsystems of belief, operating within reach of each other but not assimilated to each other. That, in short, is how most observers see Vodou, since it contrasts organizationally and in content with nearly everything that is Catholic. De Heusch contends that the presence of Catholic elements in Vodou is largely inconsequential. Most other students see the two religions as interactive in Haitian life, even if they cannot be said to form a single body of belief.

Yet missing from most accounts is the study of the relations between this Vodou/Catholic duality and dualities of class. It is in any event clear that what Vodou means, and how it is employed, varies enormously from the bottom of the Haitian class system to the top. These variations throw special light on the perception and denigration of Vodou as witchcraft.

On Vodou, Witchcraft, and Politics

Many outsiders, in observing or commenting on Vodou, reduce its compass from what they would call "religion" to "witchcraft." By "witchcraft" is commonly meant "black magic," or the harnessing of malevolent forces with the object of causing harm to other human beings. This conception of Vodou often highlights the racism or ethnocentrism of such distant observers, foreigners and Haitians alike (see, for example, William Seabrook's *The Magic Island*, published in 1929); but their prejudices are also nourished by the significance of transformative practices associated with Vodou in Haitian life.

Almost all religions include what some anthropologists call "transformative practices," that is, acts which, when performed properly by humans, mobilize "supernatural" forces in order to affect human life. Such transformative practices appear to most outsiders as "magic" regardless of their ethical value—whether they have benign consequences (such as purification) or bad ones (such as the death of an enemy). An American Indian rain dance is an obvious transformative practice; so is a Roman Catholic mass. When a Christian family gathers around the bed of a sick child to pray for her recovery, family members engage in a transformative practice. Likewise, a Christian wedding or a Jewish circumcision can be considered transformative practices. Of course, most transformative practices, like all rituals, require in different degrees the right words, the right setting, the right movements and, especially, the right attitude from the participants. As such, they are also demonstrative practices. Better said, many religious rituals throughout the world have a transformative and a demonstrative aspect.

Two facts signal the significance of transformative practices in Vodou. First, such practices are more common than they are in religions such as Islam, Judaism, Buddhism, or Christianity; and even rituals that are primarily demonstrative tend to have a strong transformative aspect. Second, in Vodou, the moral divide between good and evil in the performance of transformative practices is based as much on the goals as on the knowledge of the performers. That is, in Vodou, a transformative ritual is thought to belong to sorcery rather than religion *primarily on the basis of what it does to other human beings.* This second point is relevant to the relation between Vodou and state politics in Haiti.

The abundance of transformative practices is not due, as often believed, to Vodou's dubious association with animism. Anthropologist Alfred Métraux was right when he argued that "vague animist beliefs are to be found floating, so to speak, on the margin of Vodou."[13] But it must be remembered that the world of Vodou is peopled by numerous spirits, such as the *Marasa* (the Twins), *lemò* (the dead), *mistè* (the mysteries) and especially the lesser gods or *lwa*. All of these stand hierarchically and theologically below the supreme deity, the God recognized by Christians (*Bondye*); but they, rather than He, interact with humans. In practice, this means that the servant of the gods has access to an abundance of forces to solicit.

Indeed, the more nonhuman forces (gods, spirits, saints, angels, etc.) inhabit the spiritual world, the higher the interaction between them and humans, and the higher the number of transformative practices. This is a general tendency of all religions. Gods, spirits, saints, and angels do things for us and we do things for them.

The more gods, saints, spirits or angels, the more we are likely to do things for them or with them. Early Christian reformers such as Luther publicly reproved this tendency. They sought to reduce both the number—and the power—of beings with whom humans could interact (the Virgin Mary, saints, angels). At the same time, they condemned the high number of transformative practices associated with these spirits, such as the purchase of indulgences. Today, in many Catholic countries, the large number of saints and the fact that some of them, and particularly the Virgin Mary, come under more than one persona contribute to an increase of transformative practices (e.g., novenas). It can be argued that the Haitian people "inherited" aspects of many spiritual beings from French Catholicism, probably at least as many as from Africa. To these, however, they added numerous native—which is to say, Creole—ones.

Most of these spirits are inherently neither good nor bad, although some do more good than others, and some are primarily malevolent. Moreover (in theory at least), anyone has access to these largely neutral forces. The difference between good and evil depends on the ways in which one validates access to them and the purposes for which they are put to use. *Lwa erite* (inherited spirits) generally perform good deeds; *lwa achte* (bought gods) perform most malevolent ones. Similarly, to serve the gods "with the right hand" is to call upon their forces to do good, whereas to serve them "with the left hand" is to do evil. In short, the difference between good and evil is realized in practice rather than through some essential manicheism as in Christianity Quintessential Evil and its manifestations (such as Lucifer, the fallen angel, or the "devil" figure, *djab*) are among Vodou's most Christian legacies—an ironic inheritance, given Vodou's diabolical reputation among Christians.

Given the limited presence of quintessential evil, it is not surprising that there is no generalized word for "sorcery" in Haitian Creole. if we defined "sorcery" as a transformative practice fundamentally oriented toward evil and recognized as such by the practitioners ("bad magic"), the closest Haitian is *fe mal*, which literally means to do bad but is not restricted to the use of supernatural forces. The noun *chochè* (sorceror), which may be as recent as the turn of the century, applies more often to females than to males. Both *chochè* and *bòkò* may be used for a practitioner who serves exclusively "with the left hand," but *bòkò* in particular may refer to an individual otherwise recognized as a legitimate priest. Further, taken in context, no clear line of knowledge separates the priest (*oungan*) from the sorcerer, even though some sorcerers engage in practices—and may belong to secret societies—shunned by genuine oungans. Most often, the *bòkò* is only an oungan "who serves with both hands," "who appears to fulfill his priestly functions" but turns to *lwa achte* when it suits him.[14]

This premium on practice does not mean that Vodou theology does not distinguish between religion and sorcery but, rather, that it does not set them up as exclusive domains. As with most religions, Vodou sustains its practitioners with ethical parameters, but the difference between good and bad is realized, more often than not, on the basis of the deeds performed and the characteristics of action. In that context, one key characteristic of sorcery is expediency.

The absence of a clear ontological line between good and evil spirits and of a publicly recognized division of knowledge between priests and sorcerers has contributed greatly to many foreigners' inclination to reduce Vodou to witchcraft. More important, since the line between religion and sorcery is defined by practice, Vodou has always been left open to exploitation by outsiders of all kinds, especially members of the Haitian urban elites.

The manipulation of Vodou as sorcery by Haitian urbanites stems in part from the historical ambivalence of the Haitian elites vis-à-vis that religion. Herskovits's statement that the two ancestral elements of Haitian civilization have not completely merged may apply more to the elites than to the majority of Haitian peasants. At any rate, few fieldworkers have noted any reluctance among Haitian peasants to acknowledge the importance of Vodou in their daily lives, in spite of two nationwide campaigns of repression. The story is quite different among the elites, whose behavior and values have also directly influenced the urban middle and lower classes. Vodou-related practices have never been socially sanctioned in the urban sphere. This means that most urban families have engaged in such practices only with reluctance, regardless of belief. Vodou rituals were held secretly and only when it would have been detrimental not to do so. Transformative practices were used only when everything else had failed.

This history of ambivalence has encouraged urban—and especially elite—families to use Vodou only as it fits their needs: whenever Vodou's abundance of transformative practices seems immediately convenient and practical. Medical emergencies are such occasions, especially since medicine and religion overlap in Haiti as they do in many other countries.[15] Few Haitians would label such practices "sorcery," just as few fundamentalist Christians would so label a vigil for a sick friend. The relationship is inherently manipulative, however, and characterized primarily by expediency. Quite unlike a Haitian peasant who serves the lwa, or a fundamentalist Christian, the Haitian elites commonly view such religious practices as deeply contradictory to what they claim to be. Few would acknowledge daily and publicly their allegiance to the bedrock of religious beliefs upon which the healing practice is based. Instead, the transformative aspect of Vodou is appropriated for what are only limited practical goals.

It is important to note that this manipulative aspect of the relation between the Haitian elites and Vodou does not depend much upon the strength of internal beliefs among urbanites. Rather, it inheres in the fact that Vodou has never been socially sanctioned in the urban space. While their goals are not always malevolent, Haitian elites engage in Vodou as if it were sorcery But when the goals are malevolent, such as in the fields of politics, the manipulation of both supernatural forces and of the religious beliefs of the majority become most visible.

The manipulations of Vodou by Haitian politicians are of two kinds, and can be traced back to the nineteenth century. On the one hand, politicians have been known to turn to transformative practices in order to gain or secure control of the state apparatus. On the other, they have used the public's knowledge of their engagement in such practices to further sustain that control, irrespective of their own beliefs in supernatural efficiency. These two kinds of manipulation overlap in practice, but they constitute different forms of religious exploitation.

First, unlike healing practices that aim at the well-being of individual minds and bodies, those aiming to influence state politics are viewed as malevolent by most Haitians. They involve secret and dishonorable alliances. They engage humans with forces bought with money—*lwa achte*, undue promises, and undeserved privileges. In other words, they clearly cross the line into sorcery, as drawn by Vodou practitioners themselves.

Secondly, and more important, as such practices are flaunted by politicians aiming to use the beliefs of the majority to instill fear or awe, they also contribute to the reinforcement of the perception of Vodou as sorcery. In that sense, the use of Vodou by urban politicians is not just a benign example of the cultural appropriation that typifies social history generally. It goes further than the potentially exploitative use of Vodou by foreigners and urbanites facing medical emergencies or other life crises. It is, to a large extent, a cultural embezzlement.

Embezzlement suggests intent, willful misappropriation. Symbolic of the politicians' will to manipulate Vodou as a foreign object is their apparently contradictory behavior. They never hesitated to condemn Vodou publicly, even while secretly engaged in their "bad magic"; yet they make sure that most people do come to learn their "secret." Pressured in part by the Roman Catholic clergy, successive Haitian governments repeatedly banned Vodou practices on the pretext that they were, indeed, equivalent to sorcery. At the same time, the power holders of the day would entertain rumors alleging their involvement in some of the very practices they condemned. That some of these rumors were sometimes false matters less than the fact that they were always perceived as beneficial by the politicians involved. This dual manipulation blurred both in words and in practice the distance between Vodou and sorcery; it also legitimated the public condemnation of Vodou as magic and sorcery. There is a Janus-like quality in a religious system that means one thing to its popular practitioners, and quite another to those higher in the class system who only appropriate bits of its peripheral practice for their personal, instrumental ends.

Santo Domingo-St. Domingue: Early History

In the preceding discussion of basic concepts in Vodou practice and their inflection according to differences in class position and power, we have not so far tried to link the argument to historical events; not enough is known at this time to make that possible. We try now to provide a more historical account. But the reader should keep in mind that any exact linkage between event and historical process is still beyond reach.

No easier is the task of declaring when we might begin to speak of *a* religion, rather than of a widely-scattered series of local cults *in ovo*, not yet coherent enough to be called a (single) religion by outsiders. We can enumerate and comment on those sparse markers in order to comment on each of them. We aim to report what others have described as Vodou, through time, and to infer, as have so many before us, what *their* inferences mean. Before we can even address these issues, we need some historical background, against which to describe how this new religion is believed to have grown.

When he set sail for Lisbon to return from his first voyage on January 16, 1493, Columbus left thirty-nine men in an infant north coast settlement in Santo Domingo, which he had named Navidad. He sailed again for the New World nine months later. After reaching Samaria Bay on the north coast on November 22, he headed for Navidad, but learned from the Indians with whom he spoke beforehand that all of the people in the Navidad settlement were dead.

During the ensuing three decades the Spaniards founded settlements in all of the Greater Antilles. It is not absolutely certain when the first enslaved Africans reached the islands. Some authors have suggested 1501, others 1502[16]; and yet others still later dates. There is no doubt, however, that by 1510, there were enslaved Africans on all of the large islands. Soon enough there were sugar mills on all of them, as well; the strange link between sugar and African slavery had been perpetuated across the ocean. But the sugar industry pioneered in the Caribbean by Spain was not to flourish and, indeed, neither were the Spanish colonies there for several centuries. The link between slavery and overseas commerce was vital. The presence of Africans in the New World was closely linked to the rise—and fall—of the plantation system.

Though Santo Domingo was the Old World's oldest colony in the New, and got off to a good start with the arrival of Governor Ovando in 1502, it lost population after the discovery of Mexico. The twin attractions of mineral wealth and large exploitable native populations made the mainland irresistible. Therever after the Spaniards were hard put to maintain adequate populations in the islands.

In the second and third decades of the seventeenth century, at that very time when the North European powers were beginning to challenge Spain head-on in the Lesser Antilles, their governments witnessed to their satisfaction a movement of European dissenters to the disputed margins of the Spanish Caribbean empire, from which they would challenge Spain more and more impudently. These strange frontiersmen—for this region still contained a frontier—were a motley lot: military deserters, Huguenots, Lutherans, Irish and Welsh resisters, Catholics ejected from Britain, and no doubt many criminals. The "refuse" of many lands and many conflicting policies, they found common ground in Santo Domingo, where effective territorial control by the Spaniards was limited. They established themselves in the sparsely populated northwestern region of the island. When chased by the Spaniards, they took refuge on Ile à Tortue (Tortuga, off the northwestern, coast). These interlopers, the ancestors of the buccaneers, constituted the first successful territorial aggression against Spain on the Greater Antilles. Their success culminated in the cession of the western third of Santo Domingo to France by the treaty of Ryswick (1697), out of which the French colony of Saint Domingue was created.

Although France had illegal settlers in this part of the country—and had even dispatched administrative officials there as early as 1639—the official colony dates from 1697. Though the New World sugar industry began in Spanish Santo Domingo, it remained little developed before about 1680. And though there were many people of part-African ancestry in Santo Domingo, slavery before 1680 had proved to be of little economic consequence.[17] From about 1680 onward, however, under French stimulus—illegal, of course, until 1697—the plantation economy of the west began to grow. That growth is demonstrated by the rapid increase in sugar production (and soon enough, the production of other tropical commodities), as well as by the swiftly mounting number of enslaved Africans. Figures for the immediate pre-1697 period are practically nonexistent. But Fick, citing Stein, suggests that during the initial period of growth (1690–1720), the number of slaves increased from a little over 3,000 to well over 47,000.[18] Galloway claims that St. Domingue's slave population in 1680 was 4,000, and in 1791, 480,000.[19] During those 111 years, it is believed that 864,000 enslaved Africans were imported. These figures document the vertiginous rise in the number of slaves, and help us to imagine the terrible conditions under which they lived. They also make clear that the ratio of African-born slaves to "creole" (colony-born) slaves remained high throughout. By 1789, Fick tells us, two-thirds of the nearly one-half million slaves in St. Domingue were African-born.[10] We can only guess at the impact of this ratio on the outbreak and nature of the Revolution and on the development of Vodou itself. Suffice it to say here that our stress on the importance of the initial contact period on culture-building in no way denies the constant addition of new materials by slaves freshly embarked from Africa.

Yet some would argue that, at least as important as the African origins of the slaves in making the Revolution that would follow, was the adjoining presence of the nearly-empty, undeveloped Spanish colony of Santo Domingo, which shared the island with French St. Domingue. Twice the area of French St. Domingue, scantily populated and of little interest to Spain, Santo Domingo was an internal frontier of which rebellious slaves took rich advantage. Even the boundary between the two colonies was imprecise, until fixed by agreement in 1777. The runaway slave *(marron)* bands, which had developed on the island long before the Spanish cession of the western third, continued their activities as the plantation colony grew. By the early eighteenth century, the French had formed a permanent runaway-chasing body (the *maréchaussée)*; and toward the end of that century, they were compelled to sign a peace treaty with one of the maroon bands. It is difficult—without looking at the small islands, such as Barbados, where *marronnage* could never really occur, or at the undivided larger islands in which police power was extended islandwide, such as Jamaica—to give proper weight to the situation in Hispaniola. Without extending its power over the entire island, the French colony was unable to regulate movement. This counted heavily against local authorities, during the scant century between the creation of the colony and the start of internal war.

So much has been written concerning the Haitian Revolution that it is unnecessary to review here the social, political, and economic situation of the colony in 1791, at the moment of the outbreak. Instead we need to turn back, to take note of the events of 1757–58, concerning the slave named Makandal. Makandal has often been referred to as a harbinger of the Revolution, though the events in question took place almost half a century before the outbreak. Makandal's history matters here because of the place Vodou is claimed to play in his story.

A great deal of imaginative reconstruction surrounds François Makandal's personal history He is thought to have been of "Guinea" origin—some claim of the Muslim faith. It is said that he was enslaved at the age of twelve. (There is to our knowledge no conclusive evidence for any of this.) On reaching Saint Domingue, he was sold to a plantation owner in the north, named Lenormand de Mézy. Years later Makandal escaped and became a runaway, and the leader of a maroon-band. (The circumstances surrounding his flight are not really known; there are many fanciful stories.) Makandal is described as eloquent, highly intelligent, and resourceful. He was also said to have had a large number of followers, and to be an expert manufacturer of poisons. To him was imputed a grand plot to poison the white planters of Saint Domingue (particularly and at first, those of Cap François), and to free the colony of its colonial and slavery yoke. It appears that there were numerous victims of poisoning, both slaves and masters; some historians have interpreted such poisonings as political in motivation, the work of Makandal's followers. Makandal himself was eventually captured and burned at the stake, in 1758.

The presence and importance of Vodou in his story is suggested by the words of a contemporary, the *lieutenant-juge* of the town of Port-de-Paix:

> This colony is swarming with slaves, so-called soothsayers and sorcerors who poison and who, for a long time, have conceived the plan of insensibly wiping out all the whites.... These blacks are of a sect or a new kind of religion formed by two leaders, old Negroes, who for many long years have been fugitive and whose names are Macandal and Tassereau: These two sectarians have fortunately been arrested ..., but unfortunately they have a considerable number of sectarians and disciples; there are currently over two hundred in the prisons of le Cap: We have roughly a dozen in those of Port-de-Paix since instructions have been delivered a fortnight ago, and twenty-two more have been denounced; and I have reason to believe that those who remain to be discovered in the various quarters of this department are equal in number to those at le Cap.[21]

Unfortunately, the story of Makandal is shrouded in considerable uncertainty, aggravated by imagination. We know that he was put on the rack and burned to death because of the alleged widespread plot to poison people, both white and black.

Milscent, writing in 1791, recalled Makandal's conspiracy, but saw no link to the claim of others that a revolution was brewing, and that it had its roots in the past. It is clear, though, that by the mid-eighteenth century, there was grave trouble in the colony. The mortality rates among the slaves were horrifyingly high; the slaves struggled against their condition. Violent acts of resistance, both by slaves and by the maroon bands, became increasingly common. Such violence against the system was occurring in spite of the application of organized terror by the planter class and its servant government.

But in Saint Domingue, of course, the issue was not simply that of slavery. Serious students of the Revolution take note of the deep cleft between the colonial whites of all class levels, and those of color. The great power of the free people of color (*affranchis*) greatly threatened the whites, particularly the poor or landless whites; and numerous laws were passed to circumscribe the power of colored free persons. it was in the context of this Political struggle that slave resistance flourished. In crisis, the potential political usefulness of Vodou may have become more evident to the slaves.

The French Revolution altered the balance of forces in St. Domingue. Though opinions differ somewhat about the influence of the Revolution on later events in the colony, once the Revolution began in France, events in St. Domingue were inevitably affected. We cannot attempt to touch these matters here, however. We turn instead, briefly, to the famous August 1791 "ceremony at Bois Caïman" and the role of the slave called Boukman Dutty.

As in the case of Makandal, much hearsay and imagination enter into the description of events at Bois Caïman.[22] It is said to have been both a religious ceremony and a political event; allegedly, some of the revolt leaders who had gathered earlier near the plantation of Lenormand de Mézy to schedule their revolt for August 22 are said to have attended. Boukman presided in the role of *oungan* (priest), supposedly together with an African-born priestess. A pig was sacrificed, an oath taken, and Boukman and the priestess spoke to exhort the listeners to fight bravely against their oppressors. Only days later, the Haitian Revolution began.

The difficulties with even this bare outline of the Bois Caïman ceremony are many. Despite the lengthy and detailed accounts provided by, for example, Fick (in 1990) and Deren (in 1953), there is absolutely no reliable historical basis for the story at all.[23] David Geggus, for example, remarks, "The details of what happened at Bois Caïman . . . remain elusive, beyond the fact that a pig was sacrificed by a priestess in some sort of religious ceremony in preparation for war."[24] He argues persuasively that there is no evidence that, before the Revolution, what we now call Vodou "was not in fact a series of separate ethnic or local cults," a view with which we are strongly inclined to agree. Palmié discusses the chant allegedly sung at Bois Caïman, and demonstrates that the lyrics (which appear in print for the first time in Moreau de St.-Méry's work in 1797–98) not only do not mean what has been claimed, but were being sung by descendants of Bantu-speaking slaves in western Cuba before the Cuban revolution of 1959.[25] In this instance, deconstruction has left us with little we can rely on.[26]

But most important in our view is to recognize that the role of Vodou in the Revolution, and in Haitian life generally, has from the first been subject to nonreligious, ideological influences of all sorts. Though we would firmly contend that Vodou was important in the emerging struggle of the slaves against slavery and of the Haitian people against their French rulers, it seems to us simplistic to make of religious belief the linchpin of the resistance. It is probably more important to try to document the complex social organization of the colony on the eve of the Revolution, before speculating about the importance of religion in the formation of the slaves' resistance to slavery. We believe that the religious orientation of many or even most of the slaves played a part in their resistance to the horrors of slavery. But there were doubtless many individuals and some groups for whom Vodou was not important, perhaps even some who actively rejected it as their religion, yet who played immensely important roles in the Revolution, and in the development of the Republic thereafter.

From the Revolution's end until the signing of the Concordat in 1860, the Catholic clergy in Haiti, though not entirely unrepresented, remained practically inactive.[27] During those nearly sixty years, the ideological and emotional relationship between formal Catholicism and Vodou changed radically. What is more, it was during that period that the Vodou religion became stabilized in significantly different form. Forced immigration from Africa, as represented by enslavement, had ended. The economic status of the masses, at first only painfully, but more rapidly by mid-century, began to change for the better.

In their new capacity as peasant landholders, the Haitian people were now able to link their own genealogies directly to the control of land. The declaration of independence in 1804 had been followed by the beginnings of land distribution by the state, particularly under President Boyer, in the period 1827–43. Over time, the lands on hundreds of sugar and coffee plantations were occupied by the Haitian people. It is accurate to say that from about 1825 until mid-century, the second republic of the Western Hemisphere was transformed into a nation of peasants. We mean by this that most land in the Haitian countryside was subdivided into relatively modest holdings that became the property of individual families. Such families grew most of their own food, but sold some part of their product to have the means to buy those things they needed which they could not produce for themselves.[28] Such small-scale cultivators mostly used family labor or exchanged labor with their neighbors. Their technical means for working the land were severely limited; even the use of the plough was rare. Peasants needed to purchase cloth or clothing, most tools and other metal objects, any fuel other than wood, all china, many medicines, and much else.

To do so meant producing salable (and usually, exportable) commodities, such as coffee, vetiver, goats' horns, beeswax, etc. The spread of a peasant mode of existence assumed a typical shape, in which a senior male and his wife, together with several grown sons with their wives and children and perhaps one or two aged, indigent, and landless relatives or strangers occupied a single plot of land. Residence in a compound was typically patrilocal; sons brought their wives into their father's compound. But descent was traced through both father and mother. Inheritance was supposed to be equal among siblings. The children of unmarried secondary wives (*plase*) of the senior male were discriminated against in inheritance. Since Napoleonic law was followed, family lands were commonly divided on the death of the senior male. Over time, average holdings decreased rapidly in average size; meanwhile, population continued to grow. Attached to the house of the senior male was some land with a place of worship and ceremony. This ancestral homestead (*lakou*) was also a burying ground for descendants in the patriline. The Vodou lwa who were ceremonially invoked were familial in character, lived in the family's land, and played an active part in family life. Thus land, kinship, and cult were intertwined in belief, in ritual construction, and in practice.

From about the third decade of the nineteenth century onward, this (admittedly idealized) picture came to typify a substantial proportion of the Haitian peasantry. It was subjected increasingly to stress by the declining economic base of rural life, however, and could no longer be reported as typical by the time that scholars such as Herskovits (1937), Bastien (1951) and Métraux (1959) were writing. We believe, then, that there was a peak period in the history of Vodou as a familial system of ancestral belief, tied to the land and, through the land and through the lwa, to the past. This rooted aspect of Vodou, however, authentic in 1850 and still functioning in 1900, was to undergo considerable change. By the late nineteenth century—and even though land was more widely distributed than in any other country in the Americas—the peasant economy was already in some trouble. But there was worse to come.

Historical Summary: 1915–1990

The occupation of Haiti by the U.S. Marines put an abrupt end to Haiti's long nineteenth century. It directly affected the Haitian elites, including their assessment of themselves, their country and its people. It directly affected the way of life of most peasants, their social and economic organization, their sense of place and mobility. It also affected the relation between elites and peasants. In all of these ways, the occupation indirectly yet profoundly affected Vodou.

What Haitian elites called "Le Choc" ("The Shock")—the United States Occupation—was above all the irretrievable destruction of the world of 1804. The Haitian intelligentsia (and, in their own way, the people of Haiti) had long believed that the revolutionary victory had meant an eternal vindication of the black race. But despite sincere pronouncements by Haitian intellectuals about the equality of all humankind, they were more interested in their equality with the elites of Europe than they were in the equality of the Haitian masses with themselves. The Haitian elite had always considered the social norms that supposedly distinguished them from the peasant masses as more important than those which unified them as a nation. The U.S. Occupation forced upon Haiti's privileged classes a painful reevaluation of their own beliefs.

Large segments of the urban middle and upper classes blamed the cultural chasm that divided Haitians from each other for the country's most visible failures, and advocated a more positive assessment of peasant beliefs and practices. To be sure, the "indigenist movement," which arose after 1915, amounted to much more than a simple reaction to the reality of whites in power on Haitian soil. The roots and aims of this movement were not simply ideological: the cultural reevaluation that it called for resonated with the slow but significant changes in Haiti's urban landscape, notably a small but notable rise of the black middle classes.[29] But reevaluation there was, and Vodou benefitted from it, notably with the rise of Haiti's first generation of self-trained ethnologists. The professionalization of Haitian ethnology meant that the religion of the masses was no longer taboo. Instead, it became an object of study, of display, and of praise, for many educated Haitians and at least some foreigners.

Given that official responses to Vodou in the nineteenth century oscillated from indifference to persecution, the achievement was considerable. Henceforth, public denigration of Vodou would always face at least a minimal challenge from some members of the urban classes. But there was also a backlash, sometimes in the form of state-sponsored terrorism against the servants of the gods. That backlash occurred after the Marines left Haiti; but its particular brutality stemmed from various legacies of the Occupation.

Whereas the Occupation did not seriously undermine the material conditions of life for the urban elites (except for a tiny group of merchants of German origin and their immediate kin and associates), it profoundly disturbed life in the countryside. Small-scale landholders in particular suffered expropriation, and induced and coerced migration to the Dominican Republic and Cuba, where they became migrant laborers on U.S.-owned sugar plantations. At home, the most dreadful form of oppression was the *corvée*, organized by the Marines. At its peak, this infamous forced labor system, enforced under U.S. supervision, saw thousands of peasants tied together by ropes while performing "voluntary" labor on the roads. Understandably, peasant irregulars comprised the bulk of the guerrilla bands that fought the Marines under the leadership of Charlemagne Péralte, a landowner and former officer of the Haitian army. Péralte's troops may at times have numbered as many as 15,000 peasants. They were crushed by the new Haitian army trained by the Marines, with as many as 2,000 fatalities.

The U.S. Occupation both reduced and increased the distance between the peasantry and the urban elites. On the one hand, the indigenist movement publicly called for a reevaluation of peasant culture, in part as the response to the Marines' presence. On the other, the corvée and the military campaigns seasoned some Haitians (and most notably the new Haitian army) to the commission of brutal and repressive acts against the peasantry

The sudden presence of North Americans in the country also amplified Haiti's bad press abroad. The Vatican and the resident Roman Catholic clergy, composed almost exclusively of French priests, fueled U.S. prejudices and racism. The Bishop of Cap Haïtien testified to Senator Medill McCormick that Vodou's influence on the Haitian masses had increased since the beginning of the Occupation. He added that oungans "were the soul of the insurrection" against the Marines.[30] Once the Marines left, the Catholic Church in Haiti made use of the legacy of recent repression and the indifference of most urbanites to attack Vodou openly, launching two nationwide campaigns against it. In September 1935, under pressure from the Church, the Haitian government promulgated a decree condemning "superstitious beliefs" and forbidding associated practices. Only a few urbanites protested.[31] The church and the government renewed their attack in 1941–42. Both campaigns did great damage to Haiti. Peasants were coerced to renounce (rejete) their beliefs in public and to destroy sacred objects and animals. Tens of thousands of objects were destroyed, causing an irreparable loss to Haitian culture.

However brutal the backlash, the ideological and social momentum of the cultural nationalism associated with the indigenist movement and the black middle classes was simply too strong to be set aside. In 1946, the army deposed Elie Lescot (1940–1946), the mulatto president who had ordered the second "anti-superstition" campaign. With the regime of noiriste Dumarsais Estimé (1946–1950), the Haitian state became a promoter of cultural and racial "authenticity." Purified versions of Vodou—performances, art, music, and songs tied to the religious and social complex of which it was the core—were displayed to local urbanites and sympathetic foreigners in search of the exotic. Vodou became folklore; and folklore could be sold.

To put it this way is not to impute commercialism to all of the government officials, artists, and entrepreneurs who launched Haiti's exotic tourist industry in the 1940s and 1950s, or to the Haitians and foreigners now involved in a transnational industry of "Vodou as performance." Rather, it is to emphasize that the relation between Haitian elites and Vodou has always been marked by expropriation. Seen in that light, the new approach set by Estimé and reinstituted now by his current avatars fits a century-old pattern of condescending use. Furthermore, no religion or the practices and beliefs associated with it can remain untouched, when it becomes display for nonpractitioners. Elements of its practices and beliefs inevitably become somewhat disassociated from their origins, acquiring a life of their own. This is as true of Gregorian chants or gospel music as it is of Vodou rhythms. In that latter case, touristic commercialization may have both helped and hurt Vodou practices. Thus, the regime of Paul Magloire (1950–1956), which had no official commitment to Haitian popular culture, for example, promoted the acceptance of some art forms associated with Vodou, mainly for the benefit of U.S. tourists. Such official acceptance reflected positively upon the entire religious complex. Yet one wonders about many practitioners' discovery that aspects of their rituals could be manipulated and sold to others, independent of their beliefs.

The coming to power of François Duvalier ushered in a change in the perception and the practice of Vodou, both in Haiti and abroad. Duvalier was a self-trained ethnologist and, since at least the late 1920s, a vocal advocate of cultural nationalism. Long before coming to power, he had repeatedly praised Vodou as the authentic religion of the masses, the necessary cement of racial identity among Haitians. More importantly, like many Haitian politicians, he was rumored to be an initiate who also served "with both hands."[32]

Like many chiefs of state before him, François Duvalier willfully entertained such rumors, but in this domain as in many others, he thoroughly systematized the traditional flaws of Haitian politicians. Because of Duvalier's manipulation of Vodou as sorcery, many Haitians and foreigners perceived his government as a champion of the Vodou religion. Nothing could be further from the truth. There is not a single official act by François Duvalier's government that purported to champion the religion of the Haitian masses. Rather, while manipulating the Vodou-witchcraft association, the Duvalier regime tried in fact to solidify the ties between the Roman Catholic church and the Haitian state.

Until the 1950s, Haiti had no Roman Catholic seminary. The Petit Séminaire Collège Saint-Martial (C.S.S.P), one of the most prestigious schools in the country, also functioned as a clearing house for boys who intended to join the priesthood. Haitian priests, who were few and primarily of elite background, completed their training abroad. A year after taking the oath of office, Duvalier enacted a convention between the Haitian government and the Jesuits in order to enhance their project of establishing a national seminar. Duvalier gave the Catholic order many financial incentives, including moving expenses from Canada whence most of the Haiti-bound Jesuits came.[34] In 1964, Duvalier's new Constitution, the very one that made him President-for-Life, renewed the discarded nineteenth-century tradition that had made Catholicism the state religion. Roman Catholicism deserved special treatment, "given the faith and the religion of the majority of the Haitian people."[34] Duvalier extended his special interest to Haitian Roman Catholic priests in particular, two of whom he appointed to his Cabinet, a first in the history of the Haitian state. Duvalier's early overtures miscarried primarily because the Catholic church, mired as was the Haitian bourgeoisie in the regime's inflammatory rhetoric of cultural and racial authenticity, failed to see these conciliatory gestures for what they were. The vast majority of the French-born clergy had always been distant from most Haitians, both culturally and socially. Their few Haitian friends and acquaintances were among the elites. Understandably, the church apparatus had supported mulatto candidate Louis Déjoie, and most white clerics perceived Duvalier and his cronies as backward and illegitimate leaders. When the regime first increased its repressive tactics in the late 1950s and early 1960s, Duvalier quickly moved to dissipate the previously unchallenged political power of the high clergy. In 1960 Duvalier expelled the French Archbishop of Port-au-Prince and a number of priests, including the director of Saint Martial. Four years later, he expelled the Bishop of Gonaïves, and banned the Jesuits.

The 1960s saw what Duvalier repeatedly described as the most important achievement of his regime: the 1966 Rome Protocol and the nationalization of the Haitian Catholic clergy. Article 4 of the 1860 Concordat between Haiti and the Holy See gave Haitian presidents the right to name bishops and archbishops, pending the Vatican's canonical blessing. In part because of the lack of Haitian priests, in part because of a desire to please, previous governments had hardly exercised that right. But Duvalier actively reclaimed it in 1966, and supervised the consecration of five new bishops. Officiants in the ceremonies included one former Bishop of Cap-Haïtien who had repeatedly denounced Vodou and participated in the anti-superstition campaign. Was Rome returning a favor when, years later, the Vatican declared void Michèle Bennett's first marriage, thus clearing the way for the canonical blessing of her wedding to Jean-Claude Duvalier?

Yet it may not be useful to ask how genuinely pro-Vodou or pro-Catholic was the Duvalierist state. As a state form with totalitarian ambitions, Duvalierism had a long track record in breaking down hierarchical systems and rebuilding them to fit its own purposes. It did so with the Haitian army. It did so with most of the institutions of Haitian urban civil society, including the school and university systems. Its dealings with Roman Catholicism could be read in the light of that record. Duvalierism could not subdue Vodou's national hierarchy, simply because Vodou never had such an organized leadership. Beyond rumors that the Duvalierist state tried in vain to create such hierarchy, it is certain that it did successfully induct many oungans to its political networks. The aim of that state was the total absorption of civil society: it left little room for independent networks and hierarchies and left no civil institution untouched.[35]

It was unfortunate, then, and highly symbolic of Haitian cultural warfare that the fall of the Duvaliers' dictatorship ushered in the last and most massive repression to date of Vodou priests in the Haitian countryside. That an undisclosed number of oungans were members of either the secret police or the civil militia is a fact. But their association with the dictatorship was no deeper than (and certainly not as profitable to them as) that of members of the merchant class, of lawyers, judges, medical doctors, army officials, or high officials of the Christian churches. Yet many Christians used François Duvalier's early rhetoric of cultural nationalism and the widespread rumors of sorcery among officials of the fallen regime to launch a vendetta against Vodou leaders.

The fall of the dictatorship was followed by what Haitians call *dechoukaj* (uprooting). Mobs went around the country attacking alleged pillars of the regime, but in fact molesting primarily—and killing only—members of the lower classes, some of whom were indeed known as Duvalierist thugs. The Protestant radio station, Radio Lumière, used the violent climate to call for the uprooting of all oungans as pillars of the dictatorship. In the countryside, Christian missionaries of all origins and denominations, Roman Catholics as well as Protestants, foreigners and Haitians alike, passively watched—and sometimes encouraged—the slaughter. Joan Dayan reports: "Temples were desecrated, priests killed—hacked to death or forced to swallow gasoline and set afire."[36] As the uprooting went on, a number of prominent Haitian intellectuals, a minority of Roman Catholic priests and a few Vodou priests launched a national campaign to stop the repression. By then, estimates of the number of oungans killed in 1986–87 had reached as high as 400.[37]

The repression modified Vodou's position in Haitian society in irreversible yet unpredictable ways. First, a few influential Roman Catholic priests openly denounced either the violence against oungans or the denigration of Vodou as sorcery. Second, and even more important, a few Vodouists from Port-au-Prince—some from well respected middle-class or elite families—came out of the closet, openly claiming their allegiance to the religion. More importantly, some of these urbanites joined a number of oungans from the major towns and from the most important Vodou centers of the countryside to create the first nationwide organization for the defense of Vodou, ZANTRAY. The acronym stands for Zenfan Tradisyon Ayisyen (Children of the Haitian Tradition). The Haitian word *zantray* itself means "entrails" (literally) and "heart" (figuratively). Vodoun's first official recognition followed, with the popular vote for the 1987 Constitution. In 1991, Father Jean-Bertrand Aristide, a Roman Catholic priest and Haiti's first freely elected president, publicly welcomed Vodou priests to the national palace, where they took part in ecumenical ceremonies celebrating his ascent to nower.

Conclusions

The history of Haitian Vodou has been a reflection, in large measure, of the history of the fate of the Haitian masses. If the emerging religious complex of Vodou was a source of inspiration and faith for most Haitian slaves, it was also a belief system without much interest to Dessalines, Louverture or Christophe. Pétion and Boyer as well were uninterested in it; their successors went to some lengths to restore Catholicism as the state religion. But during the period 1803–1860, while Catholicism languished and the state struggled to increase its power, the Haitian people gained access to land, established themselves in families, and developed their religion on a national scale, though without a national church. By the time that official Catholicism returned to Haiti, the national religion had certainly become Vodou.

From the middle of the nineteenth century onward, however, Vodou has become less and less the people's religion, and more and more something else. Its sociology today is a function not only of the meaning of life for the peasantry and the urban poor, but also of Haiti's present and future as a tourist retreat, of its capacity to attract the jaded with exotica. What was once a people's religion is now two other things besides: a political divertissement for Haitian political leaders, and a side show for tourist hotels.

Notes

[1]Comhaire 1949.

[2]In what is probably the most thoughtful and sensitive account we have of the runaway slaves (maroons) of Haiti, it is striking that Manigat (1977, pp. 420–438)

makes only the most minor reference to the role of religion in the Revolution.

[3]Desmangles 1992, pp. 42–47.

[4]Napoleon's words, in his letter to his brother-in-law General LeClerc—he was referring to the general's uniform worn by Toussaint Louverture and other black officers, who had sided with France against her foreign enemies, but were now fighting for independence and freedom.

[5]Mintz 1972, Trouillot 1991.

[6]Lesser 1933.

[7]Mintz & Price 1992.

[8]In a schematic formulation, a phrase such as "no one-society governing principles" sounds pretentious. But such jargon is hard to avoid because we still have no vocabulary that is adequate to describe the social conditions produced by enslavement and transportation.

[9]Mintz & Price 1992.

[10]See, for instance, Thornton 1992.

[11]One of us has long been arguing for the significance of the initial contact period, when the enslaved and the planters met, for understanding African-American culture-building.

[12]Desmangles 1992, p. 8; de Heusch 1989, p. 292; Bastide 1972, p. 155 ["coexistence between disparate objects"], Glazier 1985.

[13]Métraux 1972, p. 153.

[14]Métraux 1972, p. 267.

[15]See Farmer 1990a & b & 1992.

[16]The year 1501 is suggested by Bourne 1902, Ch. xviii; Scelle 1906 Vol. I, Bk. I, Chs. i–iii, and Newton 1933, Ch. v. But Parry & Sherlock (1965, p. 16) suggest 1502.

[17]Curtin (1969) estimates that Santo Domingo received some 30,000 slaves in all, "during the entire period of the slave trade" (Curtin 1969, pp. 46–47). Though he concedes that the error may be as high as 50%, the period of which he speaks in this instance stretches from about 1501 or 1502 until at least 1810—that is, more than three centuries. If the 30,000 figure is used, that works out to less than 100 slaves per year. Keep in mind that Curtin is referring to Spanish Santo Domingo.

[18]Fick (1990, p. 280) citing Stein 1979.

[19]See Galloway 1989, p. 115, citing Curtin 1969. The more accurate figure is probably Frostin's, pp. 465, 429. Frostin 1975, p. 28.

[20]Fick 1990, p. 25.

[21]Fick 1990, p. 66.

[22]Fick (1990, p. 91 et seq.) writes: "The story of this ceremony has long since passed into legend, rendering all the more difficult the separation of actual fact from the elaborated mythology that later developed around the event." That is an understatement.

[23]The first "authority" on Bois Caïman, Dalmas—writing in 1814!—seems to have two different locales in mind; several careful students of the period doubt that a place of such a name existed. In his own review, Hoffmann has not only called into doubt the many elaborate details others have recorded, but even the historical reality of the event itself. In doing so, he has carefully documented the obvious invention of many "details." He concludes with this wise and sympathetic comment: "Comme chacun sait, l'histoire est un genre littéraire, un moule idéologique, l'expression du désir de l'homme bien plus qu'une science exacte. La cérémonie du Bois-Caïman aurait très bien pu avoir eu lieu mais, s'il me semble valoir la peine de montrer qu'en toute vraisemblance ce ne fut pas le cas, c'est qu'il importe à la liberté des peuples de savoir comment sont nés et comment peuvent être manipulés les mythes sur

lesquels ils fondent leur identité" (Hoffmann 1990, p. 29).

[24]David Geggus, for example, arrives at a conclusion that is not altogether different, but leaves the event "intact," so to speak: "The details of what happened at Bois Caïman thus remain elusive, beyond the fact that a pig was sacrificed by a priestess in some sort of religious ceremony in preparation for war." Geggus 1991a, p. 50. See also Geggus 1992.

[25]Palmié 1993. See Fick 1990, pp. 58, 104, and Geggus 1991a.

[26]Long before the current controversies about Bois Caïman, one of us argued that the difficulties in interpreting the role of religion in the Revolution stem as much from lack of empirical evidence as for analysts' assumptions that "religions" and "politics" are logically and practically unrelated. Trouillot 1977, pp. 73–74.

[27]Cf. Desmangles 1992, pp. 42–47.

[28]Moral 1961, Leyburn 1941, Mintz 1989.

[29]Trouillot 1993.

[30]Bellegarde-Smith 1990, p. 20.

[31]Roumain 1937.

[32]Roumain 1942.

[33]Duvalier 1966, p. 49.

[34]Duvalier 1969, p. 191.

[35]Trouillot 1990.

[36]Dayan 1988, p. 309.

[37]Bellegarde-Smith 1990.

The Focus of Cuban Santeria[1]

William R. Bascom

The worship of African deities, as it is practised in Cuba today, is known as *santeria*. The deities and the men and women who work with them are known by the Spanish words *santos*, *santeros*, and *santeras*, or by the Yoruba words *orisha, babalorisha*, and *iyalorisha*. Santeria is a vital, growing institution, practised throughout the entire length of the island, in both rural and urban areas; in the latter, in fact, it is probably the strongest. In recent years it seems to have been expanding, recruiting additional members from the Negro, the mixed, and even the white population.

The African elements of santeria are predominantly Yoruba, or Lucumi, as the Yoruba of Nigeria are called in Cuba. In the town of Jovellanos, Matanzas province, where most of the material on which this paper is based was gathered,[2] the importance of Yoruba religion in santeria is clearly apparent. The Yoruba influence is also recognizable throughout Cuba, despite regional variations, in the names of the Yoruba deities, in similarities to Yoruba ritual, in the Yoruba cities named by Cuban Negroes as homes of their ancestors, and in individuals who can still speak the Yoruba language. On a quick trip in the summer of 1948, more than eighty years after slavery, it was possible to find Cuban Negroes in towns from one end of the island to the other, and in Havana itself, with whom I could talk in Yoruba.

Certain features of santeria have become well known through the work of Herskovits and other scholars in the field of New World Negro studies. In Cuba they have been discussed in the valuable contributions of Ortiz and of Lachatanere, Castellanos, and Martin. These features include the syncretism of African deities with Catholic saints, commonly represented by chromolithographs; the African pattern of possession which has attracted interest as a psychological phenomenon; and the retention of animal sacrifices and African drumming, singing, and dancing in the New World Negro rituals. All of these are important elements in Cuban santeria, but in the mind of the cult members in Jovellanos, those which are the foundations of their form of worship are the stones, the blood, and the herbs.

In discussing these basic elements of santeria, there are two problems in the field of acculturation to be considered. First, are they derived from Africa or from Catholicism? And secondly, if the traits themselves are African in origin, is their position as the essential elements of the Afro-Cuban cults also African, or has it developed in Cuba under a situation of culture contact? A final answer to the second question may have to wait on a fuller knowledge of West African cultures, but it is of far greater theoretical importance. It will show whether or not the "focus" of an institution or culture pattern—to transfer a term from culture as a whole to a part of culture—has been retained, in addition to the retention of individual cultural traits or items. This point is of more than academic interest, since the preponderance of African retentions in the field of religion among the New World Negroes, over all other aspects of culture, has been interpreted as evidence that religion is the focus of African culture.

The fundamental importance of the stones in Cuban santeria was stressed consistently by informants. While chromolithographs and plaster images of the Catholic saints are prominently displayed in the shrines and houses of the santeros, they are regarded only as empty ornaments or decorations, which may be dispensed with. The real power of the santos resides in the stones, hidden behind a curtain in the lower part of the altar, without which no santeria shrine could exist. The stones of the saints are believed to have life. Some stones can walk and grow, and some can even have children. Informants told of their own experiences with stones which they had thrown into the streets or otherwise disposed of, only to have them reappear in the house. The most powerful stones are said to have been brought from Africa by the slaves, who concealed them in their stomachs by swallowing them.

The power of the stones is conceived as an invisible fluid, whose force at times can be felt. This is the power which protects the santero and the members of his cult house, and through which the "guardian angel" or saint manifests its blessings. This miraculous power is given to the stones by treating them with the two other essentials of santeria, herbs and blood. This treatment is known as "baptism" (*bautismo*). Stones which have not been prepared in this way, as well as any item of cult paraphernalia which has not been "baptized," are called "Jewish" (*judia*); they are said to be distasteful to the saints, as well as completely powerless.

458

When he acquires his stones, each santero takes an oath to protect them constantly and to feed them at least annually. When the saints are fed, the warm blood of the sacrificial animals is allowed to flow onto the stones. The blood must be *caliente* or warm, so that the invisible fluid of the stones may be increased. Following the blood sacrifices there is drumming, singing, and dancing, usually for three successive nights, during which the possessions take place. A large number of possessions is desirable because it is a sign that the saints are well fed and satisfied, and also because the fluid and power of the stones are increased by the presence of saints in possession. The major cult rituals of santeria center about the annual feeding of the saints through the stones.

Resguardo or protective charms are also prepared with herbs and blood in direct contact with the stones from which they acquire some of the invisible fluid. By wearing prepared strings of beads or other objects on the body, the protective power of the saints can be kept nearby at all times. Before and after the annual feeding of the saints, the stones are washed in herbs and the *resguardo* of the cult members may be washed at the same time. The cult members themselves are prepared for possession by washing their heads with herbs and "feeding" their heads with blood. The head may be washed at other times without herbs, but before it can be "fed" it must be treated with herbs. Herbs are also used for brews and baths, and for the cleansing of the house that follows the annual feeding of the saints. A knowledge of the properties and uses of the herbs is as important to a santero as a knowledge of the rituals, the songs, or the language.

To strengthen the fresh mixture of herbs and water used in washing or baptizing the stones and the *resguardo*, a little of the infusion containing the herbs and blood from the sacrifices made in previous years may be added. This infusion, known by the Yoruba name *omi ero*, is the most powerful liquid in santeria, and is said to contain all seven *"potencias."* It is added to after each annual feeding and preserved for future washings and baptisms, for removing evil influences, and for washing the hands of the *matador* and his assistant before they begin the killing of the sacrificial animals. Unless the hands of the *matador* have been washed in *omi ero*, and unless his knife and the stones themselves have been washed in herbs, the gods will not drink the blood through the stones.

Each saint has its own particular herbs, its own type of stone, and special animals which are its favorite food. The function of the herbs is to cleanse and refresh and to prepare individuals or objects for contact with the saints. The blood is the food of the saints. The stones are the objects through which the saints are fed, and in which their power resides. One might perhaps find parallels to these three elements in the consecrated stone (*el ara*) in the Catholic altar, in the blood of Christ as symbolized in the Eucharist, and in the burned palm leaves used on Ash Wednesday. The differences, however, are so marked that one may safely say that the blood, the stones, and the herbs as they are employed in santeria are foreign to Catholicism.

Among both the Lucumi in Cuba and the Yoruba in Africa there are certain saints for whom objects other than stones are actually fed, e.g. Ogun, for whom iron is used. The Cuban concept of the stones (*piedras*) is equivalent not to the Yoruba *okuta* (stone) but to the Yoruba *iponri*, which is the material object which represents the power of a deity and to which its sacrifices are actually presented. The place of blood sacrifices in African religion and of herbs in African magic is widely recognized, although the use of herbs in the worship of the African deities is less well documented. Nevertheless, "the three hundred and seventy-six different kinds of leaves which are used for the making of a *vodu*" are mentioned for Dahomey, with the following footnote

> whatever the exactitude of the figure, that leaves are of great importance in the *vodu* cult has been seen in the description of the making of a *vodu* and in the quoted phrase, "If you knew the story of all the leaves of the forest, you would know all there is to be known about the gods of Dahomey."[3]

Until further work has been done on the religious use of herbs in Africa, it is not possible to show specific similarities between Africa and Cuba in the particular herbs associated with each saint comparable to those found in the types of stones and the animals whose blood is most appropriate for individual saints. Specific correspondences are also to be seen in the types of beads and colors associated with the individual saints; the names, characteristics, and mythological interrelationships of the saints; the techniques of divination; the prayers and songs in the Yoruba language; as well as in the patterns of drumming, dancing, and possession previously mentioned. The details of these and other elements of santeria ritual and belief, however, do not concern us here.

We may then, take the use of stones, blood and herbs in santeria as African in origin and turn to the second and more important problem. Is the emphasis on these three elements as the focus of Cuban santeria also derived from Africa? Here we can speak with less assurance in terms of our present knowledge of West Africa. On the basis of my own field work among the Yoruba, stones (or *iponri),* blood, and herbs do not seem to assume the importance that they hold in the minds of Jovellanos worshippers. The mythology or theology of the gods, the prayers and the verbal formulæ, and the rituals themselves seem of equal, if not greater importance. In the full reports of Herskovits and Rattray on the neighboring Dahomeans and Ashanti these three elements are discussed, but again not in such a way as to indicate their importance as the focus of religion.

We may here be confronted by an illustration of a point made by Herskovits,[4] that the study of Negro cultures in the New World not only provides leads for further research in Africa, but also throws into relief the important values of the African cultures from which they are derived in a way that cannot be seen in Africa because of the wealth of institutional and ritual detail. It is possible, but not highly probable, that the real focus of West African ritual has so far escaped the scholars working in Africa, while it stands in clear relief in Cuba. This can be finally settled only by a reexamination of the importance of stones, blood, and herbs in Africa through further field work.

Another possibility, however, presents itself: that in contact with Catholicism, the distinctive features of African religion, which set santeria apart from the rituals of the Church, have been given additional emphasis and have come to be regarded as the core of the religion. In other words, the focal elements of Cuban santeria may not represent a carry-over of the focus of West African religion, but a shift in emphasis which has occurred as a result of culture contact. In this instance, acculturation would have resulted, not in a coalescence of beliefs, such as is represented by the syncretism of African deities and Catholic saints, the use of plaster images, chromolithographs, candles, and holy water, or the recitation of the Lord's Prayer and Hail Mary in santeria rituals, but a shift in the opposite direction.[5] The present evidence is largely negative, but this interpretation is at least plausible.

If it is correct, an interesting psychological point is raised, since the members of santeria cults regard themselves as Catholics. All informants, without exception, stated unqualifiedly that they were Catholics, yet they stressed the importance of those very elements of their faith and ritual which set it apart from that of the Catholic Church. This would seem to be another illustration of Herskovits' concept of ambivalence in New World Negro cultures. While Catholicism is outwardly embraced, it is inwardly rejected; and the stones, the blood, and the herbs have become, perhaps unconsciously, a rallying point for the defense of the African religious tradition.

Notes

[1]Read before the meeting of the American Anthropological Association in Toronto, Canada, December 30, 1948.
[2]Field work in Cuba for three months during the summer of 1948 was made possible by a grant from the Viking Fund, which also assisted in the preparation of this manuscript. Field work among the Yoruba in 1937–38 was made possible by the Social Science Research Council of New York City. The sponsorship of both of these field trips by Northwestern University is also acknowledged.
[3]Melville J. Herskovits, *Dahomey* (New York, 1938), p. 195.
[4]Melville J. Herskovits, *The Contribution of Afroamerican Studies to Africanist Research* (American Anthropologist, vol. 50, pp. 1–10, 1948).
[5]This would be no less significant as far as the dynamics of culture is concerned if further work in Cuba should show that it is not true throughout the island, or even elsewhere in the New World.

Rastafarianism As an African Diasporic Phenomenon

Michael Barnett

Rastafarianism can best be described as an afrocentric-oriented, Judeo-Christian influenced, religious social movement, that originated in Jamaica in the early 1930s. It was inspired by the crowning of Haile Selassie I as Emperor of Ethiopia in 1930. Haile Selassie I was formerly known as RasTafari Makonen before he was crowned Emperor of Ethiopia, hence it is clear that the movement was inspired by him. *His Coronation was an elaborate and majestic one. In fact it has been heralded as one of the grandest affairs ever to take place on the continent, and was reported to have been graced with representatives from as many as 72 nations.*

Haile Selassie I is widely considered, (by Rastafari and Ethiopians alike), to have a lineage that is traceable to King Solomon of Israel and Queen (Makeda) of Sheba from Ethiopia. He is cited as being 225th in a line of Ethiopian monarchs that stretches back to King Solomon (see the Kebra Negast by Miguel Brooks). As a result it is argued that he is a descendent of King David, as well as Jesus Christ of Nazareth, a necessary criterion that the returned Messiah must satisfy according to many Biblical scholars.

When Prince Tafari (Ras Tafari) was crowned Emperor Haile Selassie I, he was bestowed the titles: King of Kings, Lord of Lords, Conquering Lion of the Tribe of Judah, Elect of God and light of the World. These titles according to the early Rastafari leaders in Jamaica in the 1930s, (the founders of the movement), proved their assertion that biblical prophecy such as that articulated by Revelations 5:2–5, had been fulfilled with Haile Selassie's ascension to the throne. Revelations 5:2–5 reads:

> 5:2 And I saw a strong angel proclaiming with a loud voice, Who is worthy to open the book, and to loose the seals thereof?
> 5:3 And no man in heaven, nor in earth, neither under the earth, was able to open the book, neither to look thereon.
> 5:4 And I wept much, because no man was found worthy to open and to read the book, neither to look thereon.
> 5:5 And one of the elders saith unto me, Weep not: behold the Lion of the tribe of Juda, the Root of David, hath prevailed to open the book, and to loose the seven seals thereof.

In other words Haile Selassie I was the one which this chapter in Revelations was referring to. He was the one who had come to loose the seven Seals. Additionally Revelations 17:4 reads:

> 17:4 These shall make war with the Lamb, and the Lamb shall overcome them: for he is the Lord of lords, and King of kings: and they that are with him are called, and chosen, and faithful.

This chapter and verse was used in conjunction with Revelations 5:2–5 along with other biblical chapters and verses to assert that Haile Selassie I was the returned Christ that many Christians were still waiting for.

The founders of the movement were Leonard Howell, Joseph Nathaniel Hibbert, Robert Hinds, Archibald Dunkley and Altamont Reid, who preached (tirelessly around the Island of Jamaica), that Haile Selassie I was the returned Messiah that the Bible spoke about in Revelations. Remarkably, all of them preached this message independently of each other (except for Robert Hinds who was effectively Leonard Howell's Lieutenant).

Out of all these pioneering Rastafari preachers, Leonard Howell was clearly the most prominent, and in hindsight was the most successful of the early Rastafari proponents. Leonard was so prominent in fact, with his teachings, he quickly came to the attention of the then colonial Jamaican Government. He was arrested in Kingston, (the capital of Jamaica), in December 1933, for using what was considered seditious and blasphemous language to boost the sale of pictures of Haile Selassie I. He was sentenced to two years in prison, but upon his release went right back to preaching the divinity of Haile Selassie I (Rastafari). (Smith et al., 1960: Chevannes, 1994).

Leonard Howell was born on June 16th 1898 at May Crawle in the Bull Head mountain district of Upper Clarendon (Hill 1981). He was the oldest of ten children. His father, Charles Theophilus Howell, was an independent peasant cultivator and a tailor, while his mother, Clementina Bennett, was an agricultural laborer (Hill 1981). Howell was a former seaman, who had been part of a Jamaican contingent to Colon, Panama, during World War I. He traveled back and forth between Jamaica and Panama a few times, before traveling to New York, in the States, in 1918. He remained there for several years becoming a member of Garvey's UNIA, and noting Garvey's organizational techniques. He then returned to Jamaica in 1932, whereupon he immediately started preaching the divinity of H.I.M. Haile Selassie I (Hill 1981).

Joseph Nathaniel Hibbert, another one of the early proponents of divinity of Haile Selassie L and a co-founder of the Rastafari movement, was born in Jamaica in 1894, but traveled to Costa Rica with his adopted father in 1911. In 1924 Mr. Hibbert joined the Ancient Mystic Order of Ethiopia, a Masonic Society based in Panama, which didn't become formally incorporated until 1928. Mr. Hibbert became a Master Mason of this order, before he returned to Jamaica in 1931, when very notably he started to preach that Haile Selassie was the returned Messiah and the King of Kings (Smith et al., 1960).

Mr. Dunkley, another early proponent of Rastafari, was formerly a Jamaican seaman on the Atlantic Fruit Company's boats, until he quit the sea on the 8th of December, 1930, when he landed at Port Antonio off the S.S. St. Mary. Upon his arrival at Kingston, Dunkley studied the Bible for two and a half years on his own to determine whether Haile Selassie I was the returned Messiah whom Garvey had prophesied. Ezekeil 30, Revelation 17 and 19, and Isaiah 43 finally convinced him. In 1933 Dunkley opened his mission, preaching Ras Tafari as the King of Kings, the Root of David and the Messiah (Smith et al., 1960).

Mr. Altamont Reed also preached the divinity of Ras Tafari in the early thirties, but did not remain long in the movement. He relinquished his position in 1940 to become Mr. Norman Manley's bodyguard, turning over his following to a Mr. Johnson. Robert Hinds, as mentioned earlier, was essentially considered to be a deputy of Howell, although he did actually preach to groups by himself on occasion and founded his own Mission (Chevannes 1995) in the late thirties.

The development of Rastafarianism in Jamaica then was essentially the growth of independent Rastafari communities each influenced by one of the early proponents of Rastafari. Archibald Dunkley's group interestingly enough had no actual headquarters, nor officers or constitution, but still met often. Dunkley however, confined his preaching to Kingston.

Because his ideas had much in common with Hibbert, Dunkley was able to speak on Hibbert's platform on one or two occasions. However he lacked Hibbert's Masonic background, thus he restricted his teachings to that of the King James I Bible, in contrast to Hibbert who used extracts of the Ethiopic Bible, St. Sosimas, as well as the Ethiopia Dascalia (Apostolic Constitution), along with the King James I Bible for the instruction of his followers.

Out of all the early proponents of Rastafari, Howell was undoubtedly the most successful. He moved between Kingston and Morant Bay until 1940 with Robert Hinds as his deputy in Kingston. He had the largest following and was the most effective propagandist (Smith et al., 1960). In 1940

Leonard Howell purchased an old estate outside Spanish Town and was joined by many hundreds of faithful Rasta. This initial settlement, dubbed "Pinnacle" lasted little more than a year before the police raided the place in July 1941 and arrested many Rastas including Howell who went to jail for a further two years. Upon his release from prison in 1943, Howell returned to Pinnacle, leading a much subdued existence hardly known to authorities. In 1954 Pinnacle was again raided by the police and was broken up permanently. Many Rastas who had been living at Pinnacle came to Kingston as a result, and took up residence there (Smith et al.).

Rastafarianism is widely considered to be a continuation (and natural evolution) of Ethiopianism, which had been refined and widely disseminated in the nineteen teens by the Right Honorable Marcus Garvey (Jamaica's first National Hero). Ethiopianism in a very fundamental sense is an interpretation of Psalm 68:31 which reads: "Princes shall come out of Egypt and Ethiopia shall soon stretch forth her hands unto God." The key interpretation of this piece of biblical scripture by Garvey was: glory was soon to come to the Blackman and woman, and redemption for Africa and Africans was at hand, (Barnett, 2003).

An important stage in Garvey's development of Ethiopianism came at the historic U.N.I.A convention of 1920, where the anthem "Ethiopia, Thou Land Of Our Fathers" was accepted.

Ethiopia, thou land of our fathers,
Thou land where the Gods love to be,
As storm clouds at night suddenly gather,
Our armies come rushing to thee.

We must in the fight be victorious,
When swords are thrust outward to gleam;
For us will the victory be glorious,
When led by the Red, Black and Green.

Chorus
Advance, advance to victory
Let Africa be free;
Advance to meet the foe
With the might of the Red, Black and Green.

In sharp contrast to the popular songs of the time, this Ethiopian anthem was a call for the military preparations in anticipation of a struggle for Black liberation. Although other Pan-Africanists such as Wilmot Blyden incorporated the ideology of Ethiopianism, it was in Garvey that the spirit of Ethiopianism came into full blossom (Barrett 1997).

In addition to providing an Ethiopianist ideology which provided the theological and ideological foundation for the Rastafari movement, Garvey also developed a political ideology, when he stated, "Africa for the Africans at home and abroad," (Garvey 1986). This helped to lay the foundational basis for the principle of Repatriation that is so central to the Rastafari belief system.

The Rastafari movement from its very early stages has always been a polycephalous, heterogeneous, decentralized movement. It consists of various denominations, better known as Houses or Mansions of Rastafari. The largest and most pervasive Mansions are: 1) The Twelve Tribes of Israel, 2) The Nyahbinghi House, and 3) The Boboshante House, known officially as the Ethiopia Africa Black International Congress. There are key differences between these mansions as detailed below:

Ethiopia Africa Black International Congress

This house established and founded by the venerable Prince Emmanuel 1958, also has the distinction of being a highly organized and disciplined house. When its Shanty-Town headquarters on Spanish Town road was bulldozed during the destruction of Back-O-Wall in 1966, the congress relocated to Davis Lane in Trench Town, Kingston (Tafari 1995; Barrett 1997; Chevannes 1994). They were then forced to move elsewhere in Trench Town until finally in 1972, in the face of more bulldozing, they moved to Bull Bay in the Parish of St. Andrew where this their main camp (often referred to as Zion Hill) still remains today. Boboshante camps outside of Jamaica are located in Trinidad, the Bahamas and the United States. The Boboshante are outwardly easily distinguishable from other Rastas, by the wearing of tightly wrapped turbans, long flowing black or white robes and sandals (Chevannes 1994). Generally speaking all male Bobos are either "prophets" or "priests." The function of the prophets is to reason, while the function of the priests is to move around the altar, that is to conduct their services. Their religious services are arguably closer to revivalism than those of other Rastafari houses in terms of the greater exuberance that goes into the singing, drumming and dancing (Chevannes 1994).

The Boboshante belief system is centered on the Holy Trinity which for them consists of Prophet, Priest and King. The Prophet is Marcus Garvey, while the "High Priest" is Prince Emmanuel, and the King is Haile Selassie I. Interestingly enough, however, Prince Emmanuel is perceived to be Jesus himself by his followers, while Haile Selassie is regarded as the Almighty, and Marcus Garvey is regarded as John the Baptist (Barnett 2005). The general rules of conduct of the Boboshante House are shaped by the laws of the Old Testament, with a particular emphasis on the Nazerine vow, just as is the case of the Nyahbinghi House. (Greater detail regarding the Nazerine vow is given below in the discussion of the Nyahbinghi House.)

The Nyahbinghi House/Order

This Mansion is the oldest of the previously mentioned in that it has its roots strongly connected to those of the vintage Rastafari (Tafari 1995). The Nyahbinghi order is the most orthodox organization within the broader Rasta movement variously known as the House of Nyabinghi or the Theocratic Government of Rastafari, Haile Selassie I, or even the Theocratic assembly (Tafari 1995, Barnett 2000).

The term Nyahbinghi, according to Campbell (1987:72), came from the anticolonialist movement of Kigezi in Uganda which called for death to Black and white oppressors. The University of the West Indies Report, (Smith et al., 1960) details that on the 7th of December 1935 the *Jamaica Times* published an account of the Nyahbinghi Order in Ethiopia and the Congo. According to this account in the *Times*, the Ethiopian Emperor was head of the Nyahbinghi Order, the purpose of which was to overthrow the white domination of Ethiopia, (by the Italians), by racial war. According to Smith et al., (1960), the term Nyahbingi came to mean in Jamaica, for many Rastafari, death to Black and white oppressors. Those who were in accord with this ideology quickly adopted the title, Nyah-men (alternatively spelt as Niyamen). What is clear from the University Report (Smith et al., 1960) is that Leonard Howell's followers at Pinnacle were perceived by the researchers to be the most prone to violence of all the Rastas in Jamaica; they further argue that from 1933 Howell had been preaching violence, thus surmising that it was mainly Howell's followers who adopted the name, Nyahmen, and who appropriated a countenance that was consistent with the name. Howell's followers are also credited by the University Report (Smith et al., 1960) to have been the first dreadlocked Rastamen (locksmen) in the history of the movement, appearing on the scene with the second installation of the Pinnacle camp in 1943. However Barry Chevannes (1995) credits the Youth Black Faith group as the first Locksmen in the movement. He does this on the basis of a personal interview with Bongo Wato a co-founder of the group. Thus the development of Dreadlocks, which is now a key characteristic of the Rastafarians, may be attributed to the Youth Black Faith group which arose in Kingston in the late 1940s. It was this group which laid the key theological foundations for the Nyahbinghi House. Additionally, they have been credited for building the first Tabernacle and hosting the first Nyahbinghi ceremony. For the Nyahbinghi House, Haile Selassie I represents the entire Trinity, the Father, the Son and the Holy Ghost. They make great reference to the significance of his name, which when translated into English stands for "Power of the Trinity."

The Nyahbinghi house in general terms has rules of conduct which are determined by the theocratic laws of the Bible. Identifying as Hebrew Israelites, the laws for behavior prescribed through much of the Old Testament apply (Nicholas 1979). For instance the wearing of uncut, unkempt locks is prescribed by Leviticus 21:5 which reads:

> They shall not make baldness upon their
> head, neither shall they
> shave off the corner of their beard,
> nor make any cuttings in
> their flesh.

It is also supported by the Nazarite vow which is detailed in Numbers 6:5 which reads:

> All the days of the vow of his separation
> there shall no razor come
> upon his head: until the days be fulfilled,
> in which he separateth himself unto the lord,
> he shall be holy, and shall let the locks
> of the hair of his head grow.

The vegetarian diet of the Nyahbinghi is determined by Leviticus 11:41–42 which reads:

> And every creeping thing that creepth upon
> the earth shall be an abomination;
> it shall not be eaten
> Whatsoever goeth upon the belly, and
> whatsoever goeth upon all four,
> or whatsoever have more feet among all
> creeping things that
> creep upon the earth,
> them ye shall not eat;
> or they are an abomination.

The Nazerite vow from Numbers 6 is also considered such that Nyabinghi do not eat grapes, dried or moist, or anything else that grows from the vine tree. For instance Numbers 6: 3–4 reads:

> He shall separate himself from wine and
> strong drink, and shall drink no
> vinegar of wine, or vinegar of strong drink,
> neither shall he drink any liquor of grapes,
> nor eat moist grapes, or dried.
> All the days of his separation shall he eat
> nothing that is made of the vine
> Tree, from the kernels even to the husk.

A controversial practice among the brethren and the sistren of the Nyahbinghi house is that they do not attend funerals, even if it is their close kin such as their mother or father, and in general do not concern themselves with matters of the dead. This is justified by that part of the Nazarite vow which corresponds to Numbers 6:6–7 which reads:

> All the days that he separateth himself unto
> the lord he shall come at
> no dead body.
> He shall not make himself unclean for his
> father, or for his mother,

> for his brother, or for his sister when they
> die, because the consecration
> of his God is upon his head.

In general then the laws of the book of Leviticus coupled with the Nazarite vow of Numbers 6 determine the laws of conduct in the Nyahbinghi house, just as they do in the Boboshante House). Living a lifestyle in which one strictly adheres to these biblical laws of conduct is known as livity in the Nyahbinghi house, and is the ideal way of conducting oneself. Upholding the Nazarite vow means committing oneself to a holy lifestyle; a lifestyle which engenders separation from the ways of the west, and to the Lord, God, Jah Rastafari (Barnett 2005).

The Twelve Tribes of Israel House

The founder of the Twelve Tribes of Israel was Vernon Carrington, who was born in the month of November in Matthews Lane, Kingston, Jamaica. Vernon was the head of Charter 15 of the Ethiopian World Federation, which was based in Trench Town, Kingston; thus when the Twelve Tribes house was initially founded in 1968, it was simultaneously functioning in the name of the federation and in the name of the Ethiopian Orthodox Faith (Tafari 1995). The Twelve Tribes of Israel were initially regarded as the most centralized, most disciplined Rastafari house when they first emerged, but this is no longer the case (Tafari 1995). This organization had shortly after its inception a complete executive body, consisting of twelve male executive members (Firsts), twelve female executive members (Firsts), as well as twelve male stand-in executive members (Seconds) and twelve stand-in female executive members (Seconds). Each set of the twelve executive members represented the twelve months of the year, the twelve Apostles of the Messiah and the Twelve tribes of Israel (Tafari 1995).

After four or five years of operation, the organization discovered that its charter, Charter 15, which was issued from out of Chicago, was in fact null and void (Tafari 1995). As a result the group functioned primarily under the banner of the Twelve Tribes of Israel, and to a lesser extent under the banner of the Ethiopian Orthodox Faith, while still pursuing the objectives of the Ethiopian World Federation, which was migration of New World Africans (who in this case were Rastafarians) to Shashamane, Ethiopia (Tafari 1995).

The Twelve Tribes of Israel house is first distinguished by the following practices of beliefs: first, that each member should read a chapter of the Bible daily, and must finish reading the complete Bible in three and a half years; second, that the number 12 is pivotal. There are twelve tribes mentioned in the Bible, as well as twelve disciples. There are twelve signs of the Zodiac and in fact this house believes that there are twelve human tendencies and faculties (Barrett 1997). Third is that each person entering the movement is given a name based on the month in which he or she was born, and which corresponds to the tribe to which they are associated. Thus April corresponds to the name Reuben and is associated with the color silver. May is Simeon and is associated with the color Gold; June is Levi whose color is purple; July is Judah, whose color is brown; August is Issachar, whose color is Yellow; September is Zebulun, whose color is pink; October is Dan, whose color is blue; November is Gad, whose color is Red; December is Asher, whose color is gray; January is Naphtali, whose color is green; February is Joseph whose color is white; and March is Benjamin, whose color is Black.

The fourth characteristic of the Twelve Tribes house is that like the Jehovah's witnesses and the Unification Church, there is a belief that the chosen (who are to live in God's kingdom) are limited to 144,000. The fifth characteristic is their foundational belief that Jesus Christ was manifested in his second coming in the person of Jah Rastafari, Haile Selassie I. The sixth characteristic is that repatriation is an objective of the organization. The seventh is that marijuana is a religious sacrament. The eighth is that the Twelve Tribes of Israel mansion considers Vernon Carrington, who was also known as Gad-man as their Prophet and reference point, even though he is now no longer alive. (In this respect they are similar to the Bobshante House, for whom Prince Emmanuel is their guiding star and reference point, but unlike the theocracy Nyahbinghi Order, who do not have one specific leader.) The Ninth characteristic is that formal membership is in the form of the payment of dues. Tenth, unlike most of the other mansions of Rastafari, a monthly reggae music session is almost a ritual. Because of their strong attachment to reggae music, it should be no surprise that many of the prominent Rastafari Reggae musicians are members of this house. Bob Marley and Dennis Brown, for instance, were some of their most revered members. Presently the Rastafari artists Morgan Heritage and Luciano are holding the Twelve Tribes of Israel banner high. The eleventh and very distinguishing characteristic is that this house has no racial barriers. Membership consists of all races. Finally, the twelfth and equally distinguishing feature is that men and women have equal roles in the house. In fact this house has been considered the trend-setter Rastafari in terms of women's equality within the movement (Barrett 1997).

What also notably distinguishes this House from the other main Houses of Rasta is that members are not required to adhere to the Nazerine vow, and thus do not have to wear or grow dreadlocks. (Hence the popular song by Morgan Heritage—Don't Haffi Dread to be Rasta—which was released in 1998.) Yet another distinguishing feature is that some members eat meat, including curry goat, chicken and beef, (although pork is still taboo).

Though there is clearly doctrinal diversity between the mansions, (greater detail is provided in the article, The Many Faces of Rasta: Doctrinal Diversity within the Movement-Barnett 2005), there are some principles that are common to all of the Rastafari mansions.

These common principles have perhaps been detailed most comprehensively by the Rastafari scholar, Ras Ishon, (Winston Williams 2000) in an essay entitled, "The Seven Principles of Rastafari." This writer has determined, however, that there are additional principles that apply to the movement as a whole, and as such has compiled a list of ten fundamental Rastafari principles.

The first principle is that Emperor Haile Selassie I is divine. The second principle is that Marcus Garvey is a prophet and patriarch, (in the case of the Boboshante House [the E.A.B.I.C.] he is considered to be divine). The Third is that the Rastafari movement is committed to the fight against oppression worldwide, wherever it may be and against whomever may be committing it, whether they be Black, Brown, Red, Yellow or White. This principle clearly reveals a political dimension to the movement, illustrating that Rastafari is more than a religion; it is also a social movement. Additionally, from this principle comes the concept of "Babylon," which for Rastafari is a term that epitomizes all agents of oppression, whether they are nation-states, a group of nation-states, the state, an oppressive organization of the particular society, the police, the military, or any other agents of the state. The fourth principle is that Ethiopia is a holy and sacred land (the equivalent of Jerusalem for Christians). Ethiopia is also considered to be the cradle of civilization and the birthplace of humanity. The Fifth principle concerns repatriation and the almost inseparable concept of reparations. Repatriation is another central and pivotal aspect of the Rastafari belief system. Most Rastafari consider their real and natural home to be Africa, which they refer to synonymously as Ethiopia, (the land from which their ancestors were forcibly taken, only to experience the tortuous journey of the Middle Passage). They refer to it as Zion, the promised land, that was promised by God to his chosen people. As such Rastafari members strive to repatriate to the continent en mass. (In order to facilitate this, some are agitating for reparations from the former European Colonial powers as well the United States; while some are seeking moral and logistical assistance from the African Union.) The sixth principle is that of Itality, otherwise known as livity, which is essentially striving to live a natural lifestyle, especially with regards to one's diet, (which is generally termed an Ital diet). It should be emphasized, however, that there are various degrees of variation of the diet among the various houses and branches of Rastafari. Thus not every Rasta is a vegetarian, (as is the case for the Twelve Tribes of Israel House); however pork is strictly prohibited among all Rasta.

The seventh principle is that of Africanity, of having an Afrocentric identity orientation, both inwardly and outwardly. The most obvious outward expression is in the wearing of the hair. Hair must be natural for both men and women. Not necessarily in dreadlocks (although dreadlocks are required for much of the movement). Hair straightening and perming is prohibited for any men and women who seek to be Rasta. The wearing of African clothes and robes is strongly promoted in the movement. Rastafari adherents identify as Africans in every sense of the word. Specifically Rastafari identify as Ethiopian (African) Israelites.

The eighth principle is that of the I and I concept. For Rastafari, a divine essence is considered to lie in everyone. All one has to do is tap into that essence to realize their potential Godliness. The divine essence is considered to constitute the large I for Rasta, while the small I is considered to constitute one's base physical self.

The ninth principle is that Marijuana is a holy sacrament for Rastafari, (as opposed to being a recreational drug). Rastafari adherents smoke it, drink it, or even eat it to facilitate the connecting of the small I with the large I (Barnett 2000).

The tenth principle is the way of Reason. This is the way many Rastafari reach the Inter-subjective truth and come to a consensus on important community issues. (Reasoning highlights the collective aspect of the movement.)

The Rastafari movement is deemed to be afrocentrically oriented, (by this writer), because it puts Africa at the center of its world view, and is ostensibly preoccupied with reconnecting New World Africans of the Diaspora with Africa and its inhabitants. The fundamental philosophical and ideological orientation of the Rastafari movement is firmly rooted in the concept of the African Diaspora as a displaced populace, whose homeland and geographical base is Africa. The continent of Africa is not only central to Rastafari from a geographical perspective; it is also central in terms of the formulation of an identity, that essentially purges its adherents of the lingering effects of colonialism. Rastafari adherents located outside the continent of Africa generally see themselves as displaced Africans, and in many specific cases as Ethiopian Israelites.

In this respect, this is why the Rastafari movement has such an overwhelming impact in the Caribbean. Firstly, it is a movement that is indigenous to the Caribbean, secondly, and very importantly, it facilitates the embracing of one's African past and heritage in a very direct way, such that many of the Eurocentric orientations that have been firmly entrenched in the Caribbean region due to its colonial past, are directly confronted and counteracted. The strong

identification of many Rastafari adherents with Mother Africa, this author would argue, is most visible and apparent with their emphasis on wearing their hair as dreadlocks, or simply natural (for both men and women).

As simple as this may appear to be, this is in fact a very political act, particularly in the Caribbean, which is still fighting to overcome the lingering effects of European colonialism. As Barry Chevannes himself notes in his edited book: *Rastafari and other African Caribbean World-views* (Chevannes 1995:105), hair to this day in Jamaica is either good or bad. Good hair is soft and fine, while bad hair is knotty or nappy. As Chevannes further notes, (1995:107), firmly ideologically rooted ideas which upheld the racial superiority of Whites and the racial inferiority of Blacks in Jamaica's racially stratified society are responsible for these attitudes towards hair. Thus for the Rastafari adherents who first institutionalized the wearing of beards by men in Jamaica and then the wearing of dreadlocks, this was a clear symbolization of nonconformity and a rejection of any notions of racial inferiority to Whites. It was a rejection of Eurocentric orientations in favor of Afrocentric orientations. Thus, if for nothing else, Caribbean societies, and indeed the whole of the African diaspora, can thank the Rastafari movement for providing this counter-hegemonic worldview.

References

Barnett, M.A. 2000. *Rastafarianism and the Nation of Islam as Institutions for Group-Identity Formation Among Blacks in the United States: A Case Study Comparing their Approaches.* Dissertation. Florida International University.

Barnett, M.A. 2003. "Intra-Racial Encounters in Defining African Identity in the Americas" A Comparative analysis of Black leadership and Social Movements. In *Ideaz.* Vol 2(1). Mona, Kingston, JA, U.W.I. Press.

Barnett, M.A. 2005. The Many Faces of Rasta: Doctrinal Diversity within the Rastafari Movement. In *Caribbean Quarterly.* Vol 51 (2). Mona, Kingston. J.A.: UWI Press.

Barrett, Sr., Leonard E. 1997. *The Rastafarians.* Boston: Beacon Press.

Campbell, Horace. 1987. *Rasta and Resistance: From Marcus Garvey to Walter Rodney.* Trenton, NJ: Africa New World Press

Chevannes, Barry. 1994. *Rastafari: Roots and Ideology.* New York: Syracuse University Press.

Chevannes, Barry. 1995. The Phallus and the Outcast: The Symbolism of the Dreadlocks in Jamaica. In *Rastafari and other African-Caribbean Worldviews.* Ed. Chevannes, Barry. New Brunswick, NJ: Rutgers University Press.

Garvey, Amy Jacques. 1986. *The Philosophy and Opinions of Marcus Garvey.* Dover, MA: The Majority Press.

Hill, Robert. (1981). Dread History: Leonard P. Howell and Millenarian Visions in Early Rastafari Religion in Jamaica. *Epoche,* 9: 30–71.

Nicholas, Tracy. 1979. *Rastafari: A Way of Life.* New York: Anchor Press Doubleday.

Smith, M. G., Augier, Roy, & Nettleford, Rex. 1960. *The Rastafari Movement in Kingston, Jamaica*. Mona, Jamaica: University of the West Indies.

Tafari, I. Jabulani. 1995. *A Rastafari View of Marcus Mosiah Garvey*. Kingston, JA: Great Company JA. Ltd.

Williams, Winston. 2000. The Seven Principles of Rastafari. In *Caribbean Quarterly, Rastaftri Monograph 2000*. Mona, Jamaica: University of the West Indies.

Candombe and the Reterritorialization of Culture

Abril Trigo

Despite the fact that Uruguay is known for its Europeanized culture, the black minority, which constitutes about two percent of the population, has exercised an influence on urban popular culture that greatly exceeds its numbers. *Candombe,* an Afro-Uruguayan rhythm and dance rooted in carnival festivities, has become a main component of Montevidean music over the years, and is in fact, one of its foundations. *Candombe's* continuity, however, was severely jeopardized during the 1970s when the military dictatorship attacked every manifestation of popular culture not adhering to its ideological framework. *Candombe,* once the cultural expression of a minority, then folklorized and duly acculturated by hegemonic society (Certeau, *Heterologies* 124–25), suddenly became politicized; what was once a well-tamed and almost fossilized manifestation of Uruguayan liberalism reterritorialized Uruguayan culture in an unprecedented manner. In its itinerary from the peripheral to center stage, and in the context of a more ample carnivalization of culture, *candombe* developed into a symbol of resistance to neofascism; thus its popularity transcended the boundaries of its minority audience and/or the framework of traditional carnival, to become the foremost representation of Montevidean popular culture.

The Roots of *Candombe*

According to musicologist Lauro Ayestarán, there are four folklore strata in Uruguay: rural platense, with ties in Argentina; northern, associated with southern Brazil; old European; and that of the *"dramatic dances of the African slaves* from which *candombe* was derived in the 19th century, and which survive in the present-day *Comparsas* (masquerades) of carnival and the very rich *Llamadas* (Calls) or batteries of drums that go through the streets of Montevideo in summertime" (*Folklore* 8). Although the word *candombe* was first recorded around 1830 in a celebratory poem of Independence by Francisco Acuna de Figueroa, author of, among other delicacies, the national anthem and an "Apología del carajo" ("Apology to the Prick"), *candombe* can be traced back to the 18th century and, as Ayestarán points out, originally designated all black dances, as did *tango* (*Folklore* 162). Figueroa's poem enumerates the different African nations who take part in the Independence celebration, and mimics the *bozal* pronunciation of African slaves: "Compñelo di candombe / Pita pango e bebe chicha. / Ya le sijo que tienguemo / No se puede sé cativa" ["Candombe buddy / Smoke weed and drink chicha. / The children we already have / Cannot be captive anymore"] (Lira I, 229–30).

Candombe, a relative of the Brazilian dances pertaining to the Bantu cycle of *macumba, cucumby, congada, maracatú,* and *batuque,* as well as to the Colombian *diablitos,* Peruvian *cofradías,* and Cuban *cabildos,* was by the mid 19th century a "choreographic pantomime" that had been performed during the Christmas season (ending January 6 on the Feast of the Epiphany) since earlier times (Ayestarán, *Música* 101–07). It represented the coronation of the Congo kings, under the aegis of Saint Benedict. Its choreography consisted of a procession, longways, *ombligada* (belly bumping), soloist's improvisation, round formation, and *entrevero* (mix-up), when the whole choreographic order disintegrated into free improvisational dance: the climax of *candombe* (Ayestarán, *Música* 84–86). When the dance was over, the participants would go in procession to the altar of Saint Balthazar in the cathedral and afterwards would pay a visit to civil and religious authorities. From this matrix, already in extinction by the 1870s, are derived almost all of the characters, choreographic figures, rhythms, and instruments of present-day carnival *comparsas* (Ayestarán, *Folklore* 145). As a matter of fact, this extinct ceremony represents both the origin of present-day *candombe* and, simultaneously, the mature product of an evolution, that is, an acculturated and syncretic dramatization signifying some sort of integration of the black community into hegemonic society.

We can thus recognize at least three stages in the historic evolution of *candombe,* which register the progressive loss of original religious sources: the dramatic and ritual dances brought by Afro-Brazilian slaves, equivalent to *congada* and *cucumby;* the previously described choreographic pantomime dramatizing the coronation of the Congo kings (somewhat between *congada* and *batuque*); and its final evolution—or degeneration, according to Bottaro—into modern *candombe,* a purely recreational dance perpetuated through

468

carnival (Ayestarán, *Música* 101–09). In the first stage, secret religious rituals known only to the initiates could have coexisted along with the previously mentioned "dramatic dances" related to public festivities (Ayestarán, *Folklore* 162–70). These were performed in old shanties or in public places such as the Market square and the Recinto, as registered by Isidoro de María (I, 278ss). The *bámbula* of this period, described by Alcides d'Orbigny in 1827 (Carvalho-Neto, *Negro* 294), was a kind of collective war dance from which *la buena,* a confrontational dance similar to Brazilian *capoeira* still practiced in the 1900s, may have developed (Pereda 153). The chica, on the other hand, a dance of loose couples, would be the nucleus of *zemba* (a funeral dance). Building on these foundations, dramatic *candombe* fused both the collective and loose-couple dances, which had been progressively acculturated by catholicism, official censorship or outright prohibitions (Plácido 35–58), and the choreography of European contradance (Ayestarán, *Folklore* 149–52). It was an acculturation so overwhelming that, by 1857, a local chronicler observed that "the new generation, most of all women, despise those memories of their ancestors (and prefer) polka, mazurka, varsoviana" (Carvalho-Neto, *Negro* 297).

The *salas,* ball-rooms supported by the African nations, became an oven where "out of the practice of a native cult, and the reminiscences of a far-away home, there was created the trade of cheap-jacks" (Bottaro 320). *Candombe* became a spectacle, to the point that, according to Lino Suárez Pena, "people liked those festivities so much, that in those days *(candombes)* were a fashionable entertainment of Montevidean society" (Carvalho-Neto, *Negro* 308). It is difficult to ascertain whether, in their origins, these ball-rooms were closed religious societies devoted to the preservation of African beliefs, as sustained by Bottaro and Rossi, but it is undeniable that public curiosity and general success accelerated the erosion of their original africanness and carried out a certain rudimentary commodification. *Candombe* became mimicry, a mode of representation that constructs "a subject of a difference that is almost the same, but not quite" (Bhabha 126). This is the *candombe of the 1870s,* whose continuous accommodation to and whose final acceptance by the dominant culture ended by annihilating most of its original traits. In other words, this is the final product of an acculturation, of the erosions and distortions suffered by a culture exposed to compulsory penetration (contact-impact) by another more powerful one which imposes its own models, erases heterogeneity, and deprives the subaltern of one of its own distinctive traits. This definition

differs sharply from the one established in 1936 by Redfield, Linton, and Herskovits, and provides a more adequate account of the Latin American arena, in conjunction/contrast to Fernando Ortiz' concept of *transculturation,* which refers to the molding of a neoculture through the (re)combination of diverse and sometimes contradictory sources. Within this conceptual framework Carlos Rama has written that in Uruguay "there are not, as is typical in Brazil, Cuba, Haiti, etc., important phenomena of transculturation, but on the contrary, the characteristic is a rapid acculturation" (18). Unlike Uruguay, those countries pertain to Darcy Ribeiro's category of "New Peoples" precisely because they were or are able to develop a neoculture based on their double African and European heritage. Uruguayan blacks, meanwhile, did not have the demographic or cultural strength to overcome the hegemonic culture. In effect, colonization of the Platense region began at a very late date, impelled by the necessity of territorial defense as well as by the capitalist Bourbonic policies of 18th century Spain; slaves were brought in small numbers to serve as servants, cooks, laundresses, water carriers, and only in very rare circumstances performed directly productive labor, such as cattle-ranching. Contrary to the labor-intensive plantation system, the *estancias* demanded very little personnel, primarily *gauchos,* who where perfectly adapted to the vast and open frontier the *estancias* occupied. This same geography, on the other hand, would have posed a constant invitation to *cimarronaje* (runaway) for the slaves. For this reason, the Afro-Uruguayans, who never exceeded twenty six percent of the population, worked as housekeepers and lived in the cities, in very close proximity to their masters, both physically and culturally: exactly the opposite picture of the plantation economy (Rama 15–17). In addition to this, and despite the fact that Afro-Uruguayans belonged to different African ethnic groups (Carvalho-Neto, *Negro* 77), great numbers of slaves were not imported directly from Africa, but were re-exported to Uruguay from Bahia and Río de Janeiro, and thus arrived already acculturated (Rama 12; Pereda 28–29). All these reasons explain why slavery in Uruguay had such liberal traits in comparison with that of areas developed through the massive injection of African blood, and why the caste system, which had always shown a very weak profile, began its total decomposition circa 1800 (Rama 58).

The revolutionary wars and the following civil wars opened to blacks the doors of the armies, which then became the principal mechanism of social ascent (legal freedom and social status) and of their subsequent assimilation. Although abolitionist sentiments were very widespread in patrician circles (Rama 43–44) and despite the fact that blacks and mulattos had formed whole battalions since colonial times, giving an outstanding performance during the wars of Independence, the vicinity of Brazil, the world's largest slave market in the 19th century, retarded abolition until 1842–1846. Then the need for manpower among the opposing armies during the "Great War" pushed through the legal abolition of slavery and the simultaneous draft of former slaves (Rama 53–56). This forced conscription, which would provoke a deeper assimilation in the long run, and meant the use of the black male population as cannon fodder for the political-military factions in the short term (Arredondo I, 85): "a remnant of the slaver's colonial mind," as Pereda Valdés put it (118). At any rate, their acceptance into the military (one of the principal sources of black employment, even today), alongside wide miscegenation (Cabral 317; Rama 26), was another important step in the long process of black acculturation. This acculturation, which has prevented the Afro-Uruguayan from developing any syncretic religion and which even makes Afro-Uruguayan culture difficult to describe in terms of a subculture (as Wagley and Harris define it), is what has made the undermining of hegemonic culture possible. If Afro-Uruguayans had been segregated from the hegemonic society, they would most probably have produced some sort of minor culture (Deleuze), but because of their assimilation, their cultural threads had to be smuggled into the fabric of hegemonic culture and reprocessed through its interstices in order to colonize it: this is the significance of *candombe's* reterritorialization of Uruguayan culture.

Candombe and Carnival

The most accepted etymology of carnival leads us to the Italian *carnevale*, and refers to the season in the Catholic liturgical calendar before Lenten fasts and the prohibition of meat (Caro 34). It is a period in which an apparent inversion of order (the medieval "upside-down world") is allowed precisely in order to preserve it: a controlled, temporary transgression of the *status quo*, an exhaust valve for social tensions (Caro 27, 50). Carnality, sensuality, sexuality and all the worldly pleasures chastised by Christian morals—as well as madness—are implied in carnival, when irrationality reverses the orderliness of civilization (Caro 51).

A true history of carnival would be, therefore, the history of spontaneous and erratic popular behavior (nurtured by tradition), and its control (manipulation/repression/instrumentation) by

the social order. The first notice we have of Montevidean carnival is stated in an edict signed by the Governor in 1799, which bans water-battles, as well as the throwing of water and rotten eggs on passers-by (Plácido 51), all traditional ways in which the lower classes of Madrid celebrated carnival (Caro 65), and which persisted in Montevideo in spite of all prohibitions, well until the end of the 19th century. In 1832, *comparsas* (masquerades) are mentioned for the first time and, among them, those of "the blacks and their tango" (Plácido 57; Pereda 171). It is a black wedge in a white, European carnival, whose cornerstone will continue to be the parade of *comparsas* that ends with the "burial of carnival" (Plácido 69; Caro 127). This prehistoric phase of carnival will last until the 1870s, when the street stages and black *comparsas* characteristic of today were definitively incorporated. In 1874, a new *comparsa* called "Negros Lubolos," integrated by upper-class white youths dressed and made-up as blacks, stormed the scene (Plácido 71; Pereda, 173), disputing the space occupied by ten black *comparsas* (Plácido 124). The role played by these "white blacks" is arguable. According to Plácido they "carried out an important folkloric reconstruction in the field of Afro-Uruguayan dances" (123), but in fact they made palatable for broad consumption, a dish too highly flavored and spicy for the general taste, from which resulted "a simpler choreography, merely evocative" of the original (Plácido 123). In a double paradox, black *comparsas* have been called *lubolos* ever since, and are considered, by the same token, the most authentic component of carnival (Plácido, 159; Carvalho-Neto, *Carnaval* 10). At precisely the moment when the dramatic *candombe* of the ball-rooms—at that time performed only by older people—was vanishing, *candombe*, appropriated and corrupted by urban culture, found itself a space for survival in carnival.

Modern carnival takes shape between the 1870s and the 1920s, a formative period coinciding with the Uruguayan *belle époque*. Nurtured by immigration, urban development, and economic progress (under English tutelage), the country enters into modernity, establishing the foundations of the "Switzerland of America," so christened by Anatole France himself. First there were *lubolos* and street-stages, then the *murga* (from "musga," alteration of "música": a street band which plays light music, originally from Spain, concretely related to Cádiz' carnival), which appeared around 1906 (Capagorry 7).

It is astonishing how carnival reproduces the country's socio-political history, because, as a reflection of the final consolidation of modern institutions and civil society, Montevideo's carnival evolves, in these years, into the rigid institutionalization of its classic period, when it reaches the height of pomp and splendor, as did Uruguayan soccer, in a symbiosis which left us some of the classic songs of all times. This classic period crystallizes three different combined carnivals: the carnival of parades, the carnival of night-balls, and the representational carnival, with *comparsas* performing on street-stages reaching a peak number of almost two hundred (Plácido 160; Carvalho-Neto, *Carnaval* 10). Montevideo's carnival practically became a one month theatre season, which explains its contained nature. Instead of a brief, intense festivity where people actively participate, it is a long spectacle produced for passive consumption by a public of middle-class mindset that "applauds in a very urbane manner. It doesn't sing, it doesn't dance; it eats, laughs and chats": a commodity (Carvalho-Neto, *Carnaval* 174). After all, the Uruguayan cultural system "has been organized to function by consuming culture, rather than by creating it" (Sambarino 28). A bourgeois carnival, closely regimented and scrutinized by the authorities during the happy and reckless years when the "Switzerland of America" became the world's first (prekeynesian) welfare state, and carnival one of its social programs: "In the last century it was, in reality, a festivity of the people; in the present one, it has been and still is a festivity *for* the people" (Plácido 157).

Although secularization or bureaucratization of carnival is not an exclusively Uruguayan phenomenon (Caro 25, 157), it is at least paradoxical that in a country praised for its uncompromising liberalism, carnival became so tightly controlled by the government. Censorship was implemented mainly through a contest whose prizes escalated five thousand percent in twenty-five years, with no significant inflation involved (Carvalho-Neto, *Carnaval* 169). In order to participate in the contest, *comparsas* had to adapt to the rules, which banned, among many other things, "sad or melodramatic scenes and disguises that do not belong to carnival" and took special care in preventing "all indecent words, gestures, or allusions" (Carvalho-Neto, *Carnaval* 118). Besides official censorship, a more effective self-censorship affected lyrics and pantomimes, establishing an unwritten code that washed-up the provocativeness of parody and socio-political satire.

In spite of this bureaucratization, which determined an unstable hybrid between mass and popular cultures (defined by the prevalence of either the exchange or the use value of their products [Margulis 43]), *murgas* and *lubolos* continued to be the backbone of carnival. The classic *murga,* of about twenty members led by a director performing the dancing-miming role, and a battery of cymbals, bass drum, and drum, was officially codified as a *comparsa* that satirizes the outstanding events of the year, through the parodical use of well-known melodies and grotesque dancing. *Murga's* "criticism . . . is supposed to be a caricature and never a destruction of social values" (Capagorry 11).

But, while *murga* is the queen of the stage, *lubolos* are the kings of the parade. The old characters of dramatic *candombe* still reign there: the *gramillero* (old herb-seller) with his picaresque trembling; the *mama vieja* (old mama) and her phlegmatic dignity; the *escobero* (master of ceremonies) who does contortions and juggles with a small broom. All of them have fixed costumes and a very rich choreography, spiced by their free improvisations. The *mama vieja*—the matriarch of carnival—is a living testimony of the colonial laundress or pastry cook; the *gramillero,* of the magician and wise-man; the *escobero,* of the ancient warriors. A *comparsa lubola* would have three or so of each of them, as well as several trophy carriers, standard bearers, and dancers, and a set of between twenty and forty drums of a barrel-like design which, according to Ayestarán, correspond to the human vocal registers: "chico," "repique," "piano," and "bombo" (*Música* 96). The natural habitat of today's *candombe* is the street, the stage where *llamadas* originated in the 19th century, when early in the morning, blacks began to gather and then, in groups, beating the drums, would call to those who stayed behind at the ball. When two groups faced each other, they saluted but, if rivals, they would perform a ritual war. The *escoberos* of each group danced "a la buena," trying to throw their rivals down to the ground. After one group's ritual defeat, both would engage in a street fight that could even end in death (Carvalho-Neto, *Carnaval* 18, 37). This is the original setting for the large banners and flags they still carry to salute the spectators along the sidelines of the parade. While free in the streets, on stage the *lubolos'* formations are tightened-up, not just due to the size of the *comparsa* (around seventy members), but also because the stage imposes a certain discipline, a scenic formation that emphasizes elements borrowed from the variety show, such as the dancers or the Caribbean rhythms superimposed on *candombe* (Carvalho-Neto, *Carnaval* 34–35). In reality, the climax of the *lubolos'* stage show is off stage: that is, their entrance and exit, when they parade from and back to a block away from the stage, through the audience, where the drums play the leading role. A set of drums that overflows the street and strikes to the bones while buildings seem to collapse, the air vibrates, and the floor crumbles underfoot: you're called to dance. Like a magnet. This is the electrifying atmosphere of the *llamadas*, a strictly *lubolo* parade carried out in the narrow, steep, warm streets of Palermo and Sur, traditional black neighborhoods. *Llamadas* kept alive, under the orderly framework of the classic period, the participatory and transgressive essences of carnival, which would promote the resurrection of popular culture under, paradoxically, the most severe of circumstances.

Territorial Politics

The economic decline that began in the late 1950s brought the end of an epoch. Liberal democracy along with economic and social stability, progressively wore out and wore down; their disintegration culminated in the neofascist coup of 1973. Neofascism tried, unsuccessfully, to implement its own ideologic and political agenda. Although unable to attract a distinguished intellectual team, it was able to disrupt popular culture. In spite of its ultranationalistic rhetoric, the regime sold out national resources, implementing the neoliberal recipes of the "Chicago boys" that, as happened in other southern countries, consolidated the privileges of the monopolistic and financial sectors while widening the gap between consumers and producers (Varela 157–61). Among other "progressive" measures, neoliberalism promoted a gentrification process with massive demolitions of historic sites, including the few black "shrines," such as the tenement house Medio Mundo (Half the World) and the Ansina neighborhood, one of Montevideo's architectonic jewels and a densely populated, lower class, black area. It is pointless, of course, to say that these demolitions were racially motivated; their motive was economic, and included as well a hidden strategy of the dismantling of all strongholds of popular culture (see Graceras 21ss): a cultural policy supported by market ideology. This same strategy became explicit when the military prohibited the *llamadas* in their traditional setting of Palermo and Sur neighborhoods—adducing architectonic security reasons—and moved them to a more sterilized location on a main, wide avenue. Evidently, this was part of a policy of imposing an already sanitized location on the *lubolos*, who would then lose much of their strength, and would become hindered in their subversive tactics of fragmentation in the tightened scenario of the official parade. The *llamadas*, as well as Medio Mundo and Ansina, were, because of their demographics and history, symbols of endurance, cultural catalysts for a minority menaced by virtual extinction: if the black population

constituted about twenty-five percent of the total during colonial times, its proportions have decreased continually ever since. Although there are no official figures, because population censuses do not discriminate ethnic or racial information, some calculations made during the 1950s arrived at a figure of about 40–60,000 (most of whom were mulattoes), a meagre two or three percent of the total population (Graceras 9; Rama 74, 81). Great numbers of this black population belong to the lower classes who perform menial or blue-collar jobs; only a few are able to climb to the liberal professions. Even though Uruguay does not show signs of racial segregation, and it can be accepted that the inferior status of blacks is due more to social than to racial mechanisms, there is a diffuse racial discrimination (Pereda 201) that under the military stirred up a few minor incidents in downtown cafes and restaurants. As Pereda Valdés said, "our society has put the black question under a decorous semi-darkness" (197). The destruction of Medio Mundo and Ansina partially brought the question to the foreground.

Such attacks on the people and their cultural expressions, an integral part of neofascist market ideology, profoundly affected the social fabric, but also awoke resistance and a redefinition of the *popular*, in the sense of a culture "in which the *masses* cease to be submissive spectators of a representation contrary to their interests and become the active subject of cultural experience linked to their own project of liberation" (Mattelart 56). Since most of the cadres of the old *intelligentsia* were imprisoned, exiled, or reduced to oblivion, the "ghost generation" (Moraña 220) had to reinvent popular culture: from new channels of communication, to a new, sometimes cryptic language. This is the culture of *insile* (exile within the country's borders): a counterculture that mushroomed under the panoptic system of terror and social alienation implemented by neofascism for the sole purpose of dissociating the individual—not a citizen anymore but a consumer—from the social corpus, thus stretching the threshold of domination beyond the real possibilities of State policing (Caetano 147; Perelli 90–91). However, *insile* did not only alienate people; it also pushed creativity to its limits, and so became the matrix of an authentic renaissance of popular culture: *candombe* and *canto popular* (popular song) would remap the city.

Despite the efforts of some of its members to highlight its connection with the *nueva canción* (new song) movement of the 1960s, *canto popular* departed from the other's overtly socio-political message (Béhague), and replaced it with the apparently more modest intent of being a liturgical agglutinative for those young people pushed to the margins of history. So, with the obscure task of developing a new social imaginary (Castoriadis) to the compulsory acculturation fostered by the market model, musicians and poets nucleated in *canto popular* made of it an aesthetically heterogeneous compendium of genres, from rural folklore, to urban tango; from vernacular jazz and rock (even atonalism and minimalism), to the carnival expressions of *murga* and *candombe*. The 1980s explode in a literal carnivalization of popular music and, through it, a carnivalization of society as a whole that goes well beyond previous occasional incursions, and seeks to erode the puritan-puristic itches of a conservative mentality.

Candombe permeated the urban cultural atmosphere so successfully that it erased the limits between "respectable" popular artists and carnival performers, who began to crossover and collaborate in recording sessions and recitals, while professional artists mounted the carnival stages: *bricoleurs*. This exchange had enormous significance, because it shook the predominant cultural stratification which distinguishes, even inside the "popular" field, between "mesomusic"—authentic art—and folk music (Vega; Masliah): cannibalization led to calibanization. This revolutionary interinfluence disposed of the old concept of the "popular," and dramatically transformed both popular song and carnival. While the former gained a new world of possibilities the latter became extremely sophisticated. A fine example is "Ta' llorando" ("It's crying"), a very cadenced *candombe* by *Los olimareños* that became the paramount symbol of exile:

> Este cielo no es el cielo de mi tierra, / esta luna no brilla como aquella . . . otros vagan sin consuelo por el mundo / ay, paisito, mi corazón ta' llorando. [This sky is not the sky of my land, / this moon doesn't shine like that one . . . others wander around the world without consolation, / ay, sweet country, my heart is crying].

The powerful, deeply political lyrics of "Ta' llorando" notwithstanding, *candombe*, deprived of a poetic tradition of its own and bound by its predominantly musical and rhythmic features, could not compete with *murga* in providing the ground for satirical lyrics. They usually do not surpass the thematics of customs and manners, or the nostalgic remembrance of traditional— sometimes disappeared—characters or places. "Juana con Arturo" by Rubén Rada, is probably the only *candombe* that directly addresses the military coup and the counterculture of *insile* that resisted it, by way of a parable:

> Era un pueblo libre, se dijo una vez, / que tenía de todo y algo más también, / y que de repente, Juana con Andrés, / perdieron la risa por un coronel. . . . Un candombe libre quisiera cantar, / que cambie los males de la sociedad, / y que para siempre todos puedan ver /juntos de la mano el amanecer. [They were a free people, it was once said, / who had everything and a little more besides, / and all of a sudden Juana and Andrés lost their smile—a colonel's fault. . . . I would like to sing a free candombe that changes society's ills / and so that everyone could always see the dawn together].

Such strong lyrics are a rarity, and never exceed the comment between the lines, like these in "La cumparsa" by Chichito Cabral: "Llama que te llama la noche de llamadas / repican los morenos su esperanza . . . como fuego los tambores / la libertad los alienta" ["Calling and calling the night of Calls / the blacks beat their hope. . . . The drums like fire / freedom inspires them"]; or the subtle irony of "Candela" ("Candle") by Ricardo Pidraita, which joyously states that "el candombe es de los negros / pero gozan los demás" ["candombe belongs to the blacks / but others enjoy it"].

The peaks in *candombe's* inroad into popular song are Chiche Cabral and Jorginho Goularte, whose mother, Martha Goularte—an institution in and of herself is a legendary star of classic carnivals. Both Cabral and Goularte always work accompanied by an outstanding group of musicians. Their *candombes*, nurtured on Rubén Rada's candombe-rock of the 1970s, combine a solid percussion, simultaneously traditional and innovative, with harmonic jazz arrangements. But the basis of this music continues to be solidly rhythmic. This is hot dance music, which explains its tremendous success, practically storming Montevideo's ball-rooms: these heirs of the old *llamadas* realized the candombization of popular dance, once dominated by caribbean rhythms and several varieties of rock.

While Goularte and Cabral journey from carnival *candombe* to popular music, Jaime Roos and the band "Repique" accede to *candombe* from *canto popular*. Jaime Roos, evolving out of the vernacular rock of the seventies (the legendary Fattoruso brothers and others collaborate regularly in his recordings), represents in 1990 the only true survivor of *canto popular*. While many other creative artists rest in oblivion, Roos enjoys an unparalleled popularity. His music, a decanted blend of urban rhythms, has the nostalgic cadence of tango and milonga, the spicy irony of *murga*, and the relentless beat of *candombe*. Upon this amalgam, his lyric—allusive, elliptic, reminiscent of concrete poetry—communicate a tamed anguish, an elegy for the disappeared characters of a lost Uruguay, that Arcadian "Switzerland of America" never mentioned, whose memory still haunts the collective imaginary:

> Oyes la historia / Ya la conoces / pyes las notas / Las reconoces / Oyes el coro / Las mismas voces / Una vez más / Te encontraré en la barra / No creo que hayas cambiado de lugar.... [You listen to the story / You already know it / You listen to the notes / You recognize them / You listen to the chorus / The same voices / Once again / I will find you at the bar / I don't think you have changed places.... ("Una vez más")].

Roos' success signals to us the wandering trajectory Uruguayan culture is taking, its shortcomings and possibilities, the clearing of new paths. As recipients of the frustration caused by the failure of liberal democracy, and the horrific neofascist experience, his songs recreate Uruguayan culture by resorting to *murga* and *candombe*, whose rhythms, fused in a new music, penetrate the social imaginary and inhabit daily life, "bringing forth sounds that have been taken for crude hooting, but which are, in reality, racial poetry" (Baker 394). Carnival culture, traditionally kept on the margins of a Europeanized society, thus acquires a legitimacy that transcends the physical and chronological boundaries of carnival. *Candombe* was to be danced and listened to all-year round, in every ball-room, on any radio, on any street corner. *Candombe* trespassed the secluded boundaries of the Palermo and Sur neighborhoods (its cradle, yes, but also its assigned, safe location, in a clear strategy of containment) and reterritorialized the whole city (Deleuze 19). And while *candombe* permeated popular music, traveling back in time, the *llamadas* recovered the summer: they broke up in small bands—hordes—of drummers who once again invaded downtown Montevideo flooding the streets with their music, stopping passers-by and breaking into cafes and restaurants in demand of a few *pesos* "for the boys." Beggars, nomads, gypsies who bring the periphery to the heart of the city, remapping it through wandering trajectories obeying their own logic (Certeau, *Practice* XVIII), or no logic at all. "Tacticians" who take their war to the master's place, to inhabit it, to reterritorialize it by means of their music ("sound and motion ... and rhythm is its soul" [Hanslick

67, 66]) and reshape it into their own space. The serious, elegant, pretentious place of businesses and banks, boutiques and coiffeurs, is transformed into a market where the unemployed offer all kinds of contraband, a fair that installs the informal economy of the marginal on the doorstep of the department-store: tactics of survival that parallel the informal culture smuggled in by *candombe*. Under the magic of the drums, the bureaucrat's and the store employee's feet start tapping, and their steps draw a new street, a new time, a new space: polyrhythms. The order of the city, the panoptic imposed by spacialization and repression, limitations and precepts, is repudiated and disintegrated by these guerrilla drummers who transform the hegemonic place of sameness into an open, everchanging space of heterogeneity; the time of orderly work and productivity, into a carnival: literally, in a pre-Bakhtinian sense, Montevideo is carnivalized, candombezed. Brandishing its negative connotations as a weapon, *candombe* (political conspiracy and social upheaval [Guarnieri]) takes over Montevideo. Deprived of their own space by gentrification and poverty, the drums (those "damn drums (whose) monotonous noice torments the passersby" as a socialite wrote in 1893 [Plácido 135–36]) began once again ascending on downtown, and spread throughout the city in order to rewrite it in their own syncopated score. *Candombe* proved that the panoptic of and its machinery of terror are incapable of controlling the heterogeneous: entropy emerged from beneath the discourse and practice of hegemony: a territorial conquest.

Under the imposition of silence, faced with the politics of apoliticism, *candombe* enacts the politics of polyglotism: political demonstrations are staged—to the beat of the drums—in front of the Ministry of Foreign Relations, to demand the breaking off of diplomatic ties with South Africa. The classic designs that adorned the drums are replaced by Nelson Mandela's face. *Candombe* confronts the policy-makers with its own (inter)national politics; its music reflects a body politic, a kinetics that re-establishes the body as the mapper of space. The place of the city, the place of the ball-room, the place of the airwaves, the place of culture, all are reterritorialized by that old *candombe* step written by "the movement and the muscular tension of the arm which produces the sound" (Ayestarán, *Música* 52). A step now elevated to a socio-political *gestus* (Brecht II, 26) only fully understood "in the context of a larger defeat" (Chambers 613), that is, in the panoptic of the terror machine and its politics of *insile,* where a new concept of the popular emerged. It was not the socio-political protest of the 1960s anymore, it went beyond that, because its intent was to dismantle the manichean foundations of the hierarchical stratification between Culture and popular culture, its ancillary byproduct (JanMohamed 82):

> The idealization of the "popular" is made all the easier if it takes the form of a monologue. People may not speak, but they can sing. The fashion for popular songs . . . is one more sign of this confiscation of a lost treasure. It is precisely the pleasure provided by the "popular" halo of these "natural" melodies that formed the foundation for an elitist conception of culture. The emotion derives from the very distance that separates the auditor from the presumed composer. (Certeau, *Heterologies* 122)

That distance—difference, denial of coevalness (Fabian 30)—is what makes elite culture possible. That distance is the alibi of ethnography and folklore (entrenched in Tylor's deceptive concept of "survivals"), whose object of study "can only be grasped in the process of vanishing" (Certeau, *Heterologies* 131). In other words, people's culture becomes folklore and a commodity precisely upon its elimination, a fundamental irony stamped on the *lubolos*, whose spurious birth demonstrates that in order to be accepted, the old black *comparsas* first had to be confiscated by Europeanized culture. It is an ambivalence traceable to the very origins of modern *candombe*, "which the public pretended to consider magnificent, while in reality believing (it) to be ridiculous" (Bottaro 319). These old cultural premises that understood people's culture as an intermediary between the "primitive" and the "modern" that kept it as folklore, as a frozen, dead property to be enjoyed by the same public who despised it, while replacing it with their own folkloric products, had to be blown-up. And they were.

This is the meaning of the reterritorialization of culture carried out by carnival and *candombe*. It is a response to the deterritorialization suffered by the old 19th century dramatic *candombes*, and goes beyond the denunciatory and confrontational ruptures of *nueva canción* (Reyes 449–50). The vanishing black minority, unable to respond with a minor culture of its own due to the profound and intensive process of acculturation suffered throughout two centuries, sneaked *candombe* into hegemonic, mainstream culture, in order to fertilize it: the politics of the collective. It shattered the barriers that kept the popular as a subservient product of hegemonic culture and thus initiated an authentic phenomenon of "polyculturality" (Uspenskij 18), or, in Latin American terms, of

transculturation. In Ortiz' sense, this involves the creation of a new culture from the free selection and dialectical combination of different and confrontational roots (97–103). Precisely because of its high degree of acculturation, *candombe* was able to permeate the whole of Uruguayan popular culture and become one of its most characteristic features. In spite of Chakravorty Spivak's contention to the contrary, the subaltern *candombe* could speak through its reinscription into hegemonic culture. As an agent of transculturation, it began a process that will lead, eventually, to the complete transfiguration of Uruguayan culture: to a *neoculture*. Truly, a new territory.

Works Cited

Acuna de Figueroa, Francisco. *Nomenclatura y apologia del carajo*. Montevideo: s/e, 1922.

Arredondo, Horacio. *Civilización del Uruguay*. Montevideo: Instituto Histórico y Geográfico, 1951.

Ayestarán, Lauro. *El folklore musical uruguayo*. Montevideo: Arca, 1967.

———. *La música en el Uruguay*. Montevideo: SODRE, 1953.

Bhabha, Homi. "Of Mimicry and Man: The Ambivalence of Colonial Discourse." October 28 (1984).

Béhague, Gerard. "Popular Music in Latin America." *Studies in Latin American Popular Culture* 5 (1986).

Bottaro, Marcellino. "Rituals and < *Candombes* >." *Negro. An anthology*. Ed. Nancy Cunard. New York: Frederick Ungar Pub., 1970.

Brecht, Bertolt. *Escritos sobre teatro*. Buenos Aires: Nueva Visión, 1970.

Cabral, Elemo. "The Negro Race in Uruguay." *Negro. An anthology*. Ed. Nancy Cunard. New York. Frederick Ungar Pub., 1970.

Capagorry, Juan, and Nelson Rodríguez. *La murga Antología y notas*. Montevideo: Cámara Uruguaya del Libro, 1984.

Caro Baroja, Julio. *El carnaval. (Análisis histórico-cultural)*. 2nd ed. Madrid. Taurus, 1979.

Carvalho-Neto, Paulo de. *El carnaval de Montevideo. Folklore, historia, sociología*. Sevilla: Universidad de Sevilla, 1967.

———. *El negro uruguayo (hasta la abolición)*. Quito. Editorial Universitaria, 1965.

Castoriadis, Cornelius. *The Imaginary Institution of Society*. Cambridge: Polity Press, 1987.

Certeau, Michel de. *Heterologies. Discourse on the Other*. Minneapolis: University of Minnesota Press, 1986.

———. *The Practice of Everyday Life*. Berkeley: University of California Press, 1984.

Chakravorty Spivak, Gayatri. "Can the Subaltern Speak?" *Marxism and the Interpretation of Cultures*. Ed. Cary Nelson and Lawrence Grossberg. Urbana: University of Illinois Press, 1988.

Chambers, Iain. "Contamination, Coincidence, and Collusion: Pop Music, Urban Culture, and the Avant-Garde." *Marxism and Interpretation of Culture*. Ed. Cary Nelson and Lawrence Grossberg. Urbana: University of Illinois Press, 1988.

Deleuze, Gilles, and Felix Guatari. *Kafka. Toward a Minor Literature*. Minneapolis: University of Minnesota Press, 1986.

France, Anatole. *L'Uruguay et ses progrès*. Montevideo: Lit. Oriental, 1909.

Graceras, Ulises, et al. *Informe preliminar sobre la situación de la comunidad negra en el Uruguay*. Montevideo: Universidad de la República, 1980.

Guarnieri, Juan Carlos. *Diccionario del lenguaje rioplatense*. Montevideo: EBO, 1979.

Guerra, José Luis. "Ta' llorando," performed by *Los Olimareños in Antología del candombe 2*. Orfeo, 91007-1, 1989.

Hanslick, Eduard. *The Beautiful in Music*. London: Norello and Co., 1891.

JanMohamed, Abdul R. "The Economy of Manichean Allegory: The Function of Racial Difference in Colonialist Literature." *"Race," Writing and Difference*. Ed. Henry Louis Gates. Chicago: University of Chicago Press, 1986.

Lira, Luciano. *El Parnaso Oriental o Guimalda Poética de la República Uruguaya*. Facsimilar. Montevideo: Biblioteca Artigas, 1981.

Margulis, Mario. "La cultura popular." *La cultura popular*. Ed. Adolfo Colombres, et al. México: Premiá, 1982.

Maria, Isidoro de. *Montevideo antiguo*. Montevideo: Biblioteca Artigas, 1957.

Masliah, Leo. "La música popular. Censura y represión." *Represión, exilio, y democracia La cultura uruguaya*. Comp. Saúl Sosnowski. Montevideo: EBO/Universidad de Maryland, 1987.

Mattelart, Armand, and Seth Siegelaub, eds. *Communication and Class Struggle 1. Capitalism, Imperialism*. New York: International General, 1979.

Moraña, Mabel. "Autoritarismo e inhibición crítica en el Uruguay." *Ideologies & Literature* 16 (1983).

Ortiz, Fernando. *Cuban Counterpoint. Tobacco and Sugar*. New York: Alfred A. Knopf, 1947.

Pereda Valdés, Ildefonso. *El negro en el Uruguay. Pasado y presente*. Montevideo: Instituto Histórico y Geográfico, 1965.

Perelli, Carina, and Juan Rial. *De mitos y memorias políticas*. Montevideo: EBO, 1986.

Piedraita, Ricardo. "Candela." *Candombe pal' 1/2 e' la calle*. Chichito Cabral, interpreter. Orfeo, 90771, 1985.

Plácido, Antonio D. *Carnaval Evocación de Montevideo en la historia y la tradición*. Montevideo: Imp. Letras, 1966.

Prado, Jorge do. "La cumparsa" *Candombe pal' 1/2 e' la calle*. Chichito Cabral, interpreter. Orfeo, 90771, 1985.

Rada, Rubén. "Juana con Arturo." *Antología del candombe 2*. Orfeo, 91007-1, 1989.

Rama, Carlos M. *Los afro-uruguayos*. Montevideo: El Siglo Ilustrado, 1969.

Redfield, Robert, Ralph Linton, and Melville J. Herskovits. "Memorandum for the Study of Acculturation." *American Anthropologist* 38 (1936): 149–52.

Reyes Matta, Fernando. "The < New Song > and Its Confrontation in Latin America." *Marxism and the Interpretation of Culture*. Ed. Cary Nelson and Lawrence Grossberg. Urbana: University of Illinois Press, 1988.

Ribeiro, Darcy. *Las Américas y la civilización*. Buenos Aires: CEDAL, 1972.

Rossi, Vicente. *Cosas de negros*, Córdoba: Casa Argentina, 1926.

Sambarino, Mario. *La cultura nacional como problema*. Montevideo: Nuestra Tierra, 1970.

Uspenskij, B. A., et al. "Theses on the Semiotic Study of Cultures (as Applied to Slavic Texts)." *Structure of Texts and Semiotics of Culture*. Ed. Jan Van der Eng and N. Grugar. The Hague/Paris: Mouton, 1973.

Varela, Rafael. "Autoritarismo y dominación de clase en la cultura del Uruguay militarizado." *The Discourse of Power: Culture, Hegemony and the Authoritarian State in Latin America*. Ed. Neil Larsen. Minneapolis: Ideologies & Literature, 1983.

Vega, Carlos. "La mesomúsica." *Polifonía* 131–32 (1966).

Wagley, Charles, and Marvin Harris. "A Typology of Latin American Subcultures." *American Anthropologist* 57 (1955): 428–51.

The Orisha Religion in Trinidad Today

Frances Henry

When Nezer of Moruga walked this earth
Mighty Babalorisha,
Papa Nezer
Father to them all,
And still remembered . . .
            —Eintou Pearl Springer, "The Yard"

The Orisha religion in Trinidad is historically derived from the complex of religious beliefs found among the Yoruba people of Nigeria.[1] Its religious system is syncretic; that is, elements of Catholicism have become fused with native African beliefs. This is most striking in the identification of African gods with Catholic saints; for example, Shango, the Yoruba god of thunder, has become identified with John the Baptist. In more recent times, elements of Hinduism have also found their way into the religion, and some scholars suggest that Kabbalistic elements can also be found in the practices of a few leaders.[2] Orisha worship is found throughout the Caribbean but only in those countries that were colonized by the Spanish or the French, who brought Roman Catholicism with them. The syncretism between Orisha and Catholicism developed in part because of the multiplicity of saints who could be identified with Orisha deities.[3] Similar syncretic belief systems have been described in Haiti,[4] Brazil[5] and Cuba.[6] It is thought that the Orisha religion began in the middle of the nineteenth century in Trinidad, as slaves from Yoruba lands were sent there in significant numbers.[7] More recently, Orisha worship derived from the Caribbean or from Africa directly is a rapidly growing religion among African Americans and migrants from the Caribbean.[8] Recent studies of these religions in the United States include works by George Brandon, Kamari Clarke and Marta Vega.[9]

The annual ceremony performed by active leaders was formerly called a "feast" or "sacrifice" but today the Yoruba term *Ebo*, meaning "sacrifice," is in common usage. This takes place in the courtyard of the leader's home. In earlier times, leaders were sometimes called priests or more often just addressed as "leader." Today the terms *baba* and *iya* are often used. The courtyard is now called a "shrine" and, in the more progressive groups, the Yoruba *Ile* is used. It is composed of the leader's house, a separate kitchen, the *palais*, *chapelle* and the "tombs." The *palais*, where the major part of the ceremony takes place, is an area of approximately thirty by thirty feet that used to be covered by a palm thatched or "carrat" roof, supported by four or more upright log beams planted in the ground. Today, it is more usual to find corrugated tin or galvanized roofing. The beams are interconnected by rough boards reaching about one-third of the distance from the ground to the thatched roof. The boards, serving as partial walls about five feet in height, have extensions built into the *palais* area. These board extensions serve as benches for the spectators. In two corners of the structure there is an opening that serves as a door. The floor is made of packed earth in order to ensure greater contact with the spirit world. In more modern *palais* the structure tends to be more elaborate, with whitewashed walls and real benches. In one well-known shrine, there is a separate seating gallery for visitors and the entire compound is considerably larger than most others.

The *chapelle* is a small (approximately ten by ten feet) one- or two-room "church" with wattle and daub or wooden walls; the ground consists of packed or flattened earth. The *chapelle* is generally located near the *palais* and contains altars, lithographs of the saints and the implements used by the gods. There are usually three to five altars dedicated to various important gods that hold both Catholic and African symbols. Crosses, rosaries, colourful holy statues and thunderstones (Carib or Arawak celts), obi seeds and axes are mingled in profusion. Chromolithographs of the saints hang on the walls, while various implements of the gods lay scattered in corners on the earthen floor. On feast days large coloured flags are hung in the *chapelle*. Despite the attempts at Africanization and the removal of syncretic Christian elements, most *chapelles* still contain pictures of Catholic saints.

Near the gate or entrance to the courtyard (or, in some cases, scattered about the *chapelle*) is a small secluded area. Here the "tombs" (also called "stools" or "pere-oguns" or "memorial stones") to the Orisha are placed. There are five to seven such "tombs" dedicated to the major gods. These are generally flat, raised, cement platforms (but sometimes merely mounds of earth) on which are placed candles, flowers, pottery jugs, bottles of olive oil and other sacred items. Protruding from the centre of each "tomb" is an implement that is associated with the particular god. When these are metal they are charred or burned. Two of the gods

(Ogun-St Michael and Shakpana-St Jerome), as well as others, have flags of their sacred colour set on long bamboo poles waving over their "tombs." Shakpana-St Jerome has a forked branch with a burned pottery jug resting in the fork implanted in his "tomb." Leaders, who are more often today designated by the title *Baba* or the feminine *Iya* or the honorific title of "elder," hold a major feast once a year, usually beginning after Easter or around Christmas time. *Ebos* are sometimes scheduled on a particular saint's day venerated by the leader. The feast begins on a Tuesday evening and continues uninterrupted until the final animal sacrifice on Saturday morning. Following an interval of one week, and if the leader can afford the expense, another feast is held from Wednesday evening until Saturday morning. This is known as "the return" and is explained thus: "when you give somebody something, it's nice to get a return." The "return" does not appear to be practised much today; a one-week ceremony usually suffices. Sometimes a leader will depart from the Tuesday schedule and begin a feast on a Sunday evening if divining or a dream has said to begin on that day. Occasionally some leaders give one- or two-day feasts to commemorate special events at odd times during the year, for example, on New Year's Day.

A typical feast begins anywhere between nine and eleven in the evening. In earlier times, approximately twenty-five to fifty people were seated in the *palais* on rough wooden benches and a comparable number circulated about the courtyard. Today the numbers attending a feast have dropped markedly; there can be as few as ten. At this time the atmosphere is rather casual: people joke with each other, renew friendships, eat dinner, play with children and the like. Despite the mood of jocularity, the air is filled with tension and suspense. Occasionally a few people in the *palais* begin singing, with or without the accompaniment of the drums. As soon as the leader and the *mongba* (teacher) who leads the singing enter, the latter frequently holding a rosary and a candle, and kneel in the centre of the *palais*, people come to attention. The *mongba* begins chanting the Lord's Prayer, Hail Marys, sometimes the Catholic Litany of the Saints and other Catholic prayers. He recites line by line as the audience responds with antiphonal chants. At times he interrupts the prayers to sprinkle water from a pottery jug into the four corners of the *palais*. The same prayers are constantly repeated and the entire prayer period can last as long as two hours. (In some *Ebos* today there is an attempt to eliminate, or at least reduce, the number of Christian prayers chanted. In one *Ebo* given by a well-known elder, however, the prayers lasted for

well over an hour with worshippers kneeling throughout this lengthy period.) At some of the progressive *iles*, the evening begins with Yoruba song followed by Yoruba prayers to each of the major deities being honoured at the feast. If a member can pronounce the Yoruba, the prayers are read in that language and an English translation is then provided.

During this time more and more people enter the *palais*. As the prayer period comes to an end a hymn may or may not be sung, depending in large part upon the whim of the leader. After this, one or more members, "servants to the powers," place a candle flanked by two calabashes containing water and ashes, respectively, at the centre of the *palais*. A circle of olive oil is drawn around it by slowly pouring the oil from a bottle. The three drummers and the *chac-chac* players enter and sit at one end of the *palais*; the leader is in front of them, often resting on a chair. He begins the first song to Eshu, the trickster deity, who in earlier times was also identified as the devil. The drums pick up the beat and the audience begins singing. At the same time a circle of approximately twenty people, mostly women, forms. The women begin to dance in a slow shuffle around the candle and calabash. This dance is said to ensnare or encircle Eshu to keep him from coming to the *Ebo* and disrupting the procedures. One leader recently referred to this practice as "Eshuing." Seven songs are sung to Eshu and each new song is marked by a reversal of the dancing circle. At the conclusion of the sixth song the candle and calabashes are thrown out by the same "servant to the powers." The circle procedure is known as "getting rid of the devil" or "giving him his due." However, few people today refer to Eshu as the devil.

Immediately following the last song to Eshu singing begins to Ogun, who is identified as St Michael, the leading deity in the Orisha pantheon. At least seven songs must be sung to Ogun to equal the number sung to the devil, because "the saints are higher than the devil."

Usually, after three or four songs to Ogun, the first possession manifesting the characteristics ascribed to Ogun begins. (Possessions today are generally known as "manifestations." In earlier times, "getting the power" was the more usual description.) Generally a woman dancing in the circle begins violently swaying back and forth. Her eyes become glazed and dilated and her face undergoes a radical transformation, becoming quite masculine, with lips and chin protruding. She falls back and is supported by several bystanders, thereby breaking the circle of dancers. Singing and drumming cease temporarily. One bystander ties a red (Ogun's colour) headband about the possessed woman's head, another ties a sash underneath her stomach, and her jewellery and shoes are removed. During this dressing period the possessed woman is held by others so that the god or "power" may be dressed properly and given a chance to "settle." This "power" then breaks away and begins dancing in the *palais*. Meanwhile the drumming and singing have resumed. At times the "power" may run into the *chapelle* and kneel on the floor or run to the "tomb" area or anywhere about the courtyard. The "power" calls for his implements, a sword or cutlass in Ogun's case, and dances with them. Ogun greets the audience, generally in a mixture of English and patois, for example, "Bon Soir, tout monde, good night all." He may bless all present by distributing olive oil either to drink or to be rubbed onto the head and face. The singing to Ogun continues either until Ogun decides that he has had enough songs or until the leader sings to another power. After the arrival of Ogun-St Michael, different powers "manifest" upon other individuals.[11]

Most active Orisha participants have one or more special patrons who "manifest" upon them regularly. Such individuals are often, even today, termed "horses" or "saint horses" and identified as "she Ogun [St Michael] horse," or "she take Ogun [Michael]," "Ogun [Michael] manifest on her." Among modern worshippers, the Yoruba Orisha name is more likely to be used, but older members still tend to refer to the saints' names. The more patrons one has, the greater the prestige, so that the leaders can and do "take any power" or "have many manifestations."

Singing, drumming and spirit possessions continue until three to five o'clock in the morning. The duration depends to some degree upon general fatigue. People then go to sleep for a few hours, finding themselves berths anywhere in the courtyard. Many leave to go home to rest briefly and then go to work. When dawn comes, activities begin again. At sunrise, selected animals are washed and sacrificed to the powers, with the accompaniment of drums. The killing, preceded by the casting of obi seeds to determine if the powers will accept the sacrifice, takes place in the *chapelle*, and the blood of the animals is splashed over the "tombs." More drum beating and manifestations may take place following the sacrifice until about ten in the morning. People who have regular jobs leave sometime in the morning and return again the following evening. Today, more people tend to leave for their workplaces during the day. One or two of the women remain and spend the day cooking the sacrificed animals. Some food is cooked without salt and this is offered to the powers on large leaves, in front of their particular "tombs." The rest, cooked with salt, is eaten by the participants.

At approximately the same time on the next evening the entire ceremony begins again until its conclusion on Saturday morning.

Occasionally, during the late afternoon, one of the water powers may "manifest" upon his or her "horse" and call for a special river ceremony. Then a procession, sometimes dressed in white, marches to the river. Food is placed on the banks of the river and singing and drumming to the particular water power takes place. This only occurs when the leader's courtyard is situated near a river. However, several leaders now routinely hold ceremonies dedicated to the water goddess Oshun. At one such ceremony, as many as 250 people attended the beach ceremony during which flags were placed on the beach and the congregants sang as they formed concentric circles. There were also several short manifestations of Oshun. A high point of the water ceremony was the placing of food sacrifices in the water as offerings to Oshun. The tide is supposed to carry them out but it did not appear strong enough, so several participants waded out into the water and pushed the offerings out.

With the increasing Africanization of this religion, more Yoruba festivals are being recreated. Recently, a ceremony honouring the rain was started by one prominent leader and another held a special festival honouring the Orisha Olukun.

Orisha Cosmology

The Orisha, gods or "powers" inhabit the heaven and are called "heavenly powers." Other powers exist, but these are the powers of darkness and evil that inhabit the "nether" regions. In my first Orisha study, a well-known leader talked about evil powers: "It have plenty. Not here, you know. It have its place—circle work Joe Steele, Skull and Crossbones, Prince of Darkness. It have plenty who say they giving Shango dance, but call evil. They do all kinds of wrong, say they do Orisha work, but use the black hand."

The reference here is clearly to Kabbalistic practices, which then, as today, are widely performed. Occasionally during an *Ebo* such an evil spirit can appear despite the fact that he has not been summoned. These evil spirits are then exorcized by the major heavenly powers, usually Ogun-St Michael. Groups working with these supposed evil powers are greatly feared. There appears to be a relationship between the familiarity of the "horse" to the group and this interpretation. Thus, unfamiliar "horses" were frequently accused of manifesting evil spirits or non-recognized powers.

The deities or powers are believed to lead ordinary lives in heaven. Indeed, it seems that the powers are looked upon as if they lived on earth, "always around working." The chief deity is Oludumare, the supreme being, who is thought of as "everything," while the rest of the Orisha are deities who control and protect aspects of the environment and, at the same time, are able to influence the lives of people. While, theoretically, the Orisha live in heaven, the concept of heaven as home for the powers is vague and nebulous. The Orisha may arrive with or without being summoned, especially in the latter case, when they have "work to do." The nature of this work, aside from dancing at feasts, appears to be diagnosing and suggesting cures for ills and delivering messages to "warn of something going wrong or something going [to] happen." The specific behaviour of an Orisha is said to be a function of what activity he or she was engaged in at the time of being summoned. For example, if Ebejee-St Peter calls for a dagger when he arrives, this means that he has been fishing. If, however, he calls for a key, he has just been opening or closing the heavenly gate. Similarly, Ogun-St Michael will call for a cutlass if he has merely been protecting heaven and his dancing and activity will be relatively subdued. If he has been fighting he will call for a sword and dance violently and behave aggressively.

The Orisha can "manifest" on any person. Generally a "horse" will have one or two special patrons who regularly manifest upon him or her. Indeed, an Orisha is recognized after his arrival not so much by his behaviour, but by the regularity of the manifestation on the same person or "horse." The deities are free to choose their "horses," and very frequently individuals become "overshadowed" with a power. They do not fall into the deep trancelike state of active spirit possession but may become dizzy, fall down or shake violently for a few moments and then return to normal. When this occurs it is said to be a power trying to find a "horse" to settle upon.

This may happen, for example, to two or three individuals at the same time, and then a fourth individual may suddenly become completely possessed. In order to receive a power the "horse" must be "living clean" or abstaining from sexual activities and from consuming alcohol two to three days prior to and during the feast. Rejected individuals, that is, those who do not "manifest or catch power," are assumed to have lived "unclean" and are considered "not proper horses." In at least one orthodox Orisha shrine or yard, women who are menstruating are not allowed into the ceremonial area because they are said to be unclean. It is feared that this condition will prevent the Orisha from attending and blessing the *Ebo*.

At the time of first possession, or when a person first "falls under a power or manifests an Orisha," the leader at whose shrine this event takes place interprets to the new person the name of the god who possesses him. The behaviour of a newly possessed person is erratic. For example, he may call for several conflicting implements or use different dance steps. When this occurs it is said that several powers are competing for the new "horse"; that is, one power says to the other, "See what a nice new horse I have." The other powers become jealous and attempt to compete for possession of the new "horse." Newer and younger Orisha members recognize that this signifies the beginning or learning of a manifestation.

The powers of Orisha are said to come in threes. Thus, for example, three individuals may simultaneously be possessed by Shango-St John. However, each is possessed by a different form of St John, for example, the Baptist, the Evangelist and of the Cross. While, in theory, this is supposed to occur with all powers, it was noted in the earlier study that only Saints John and Francis have multiple manifestations, as might be expected in view of the fact that the several saints bearing these names respectively are particularly well known. No multiple manifestations were observed at more recent *Ebos*.

In earlier times most Orisha worshippers had little knowledge concerning the African origins of the deities. The major leaders and a handful of active participants (those who became possessed frequently) were able to cite African names; the rest seemed more comfortable referring to and following the Catholic saints. Respondents spontaneously talked about the saints rather than the African gods. To illustrate this point, one major leader was asked if Shango and Oya were married. His reply was, "St John the Baptist never married." On the whole, most of the participants were primarily concerned with the feasting, singing, drumming and possession aspects of the ceremonies and indicate little knowledge of, or concern with, the theology underlying the practices that they accepted and shared unquestioningly.

Today the African origins of the Orisha are understood by many more worshippers. The supreme deity, Oludumare, is mentioned often and more of the original Yoruba Orisha are now recognized. The role of the ancestors and ancestor worship is also being brought into the religion by innovating individuals.[12] Many more worshippers have been taught Yoruba words and phrases, and a great deal is now known about the Orisha in their original Nigerian home. Some elders have travelled to Africa and have been ordained there, bringing a considerable degree of knowledge back with them.

The Social Organization of Orisha

The Orisha religion was and remains very individualistic. There was no centralized administration or authority structure. In earlier times there was no official head of the religion, although Pa Neezer (Ebenezer Elliott, a great leader and healer who lived in the Fifth Company Village in southern Trinidad) held that position unofficially because of the respect members had for him. During the 1970s and 1980s Isaac "Sheppy" Lindsay was also acknowledged by many as an unofficial head because of the extent of his knowledge of the faith. Today Iyalorisha Melvina Rodney and Baba Clarence Forde are recognized as the heads of the religion because their organizations were officially registered with the government and the Council of Elders was incorporated. The two are therefore automatically central leaders. This is a recent development.

Despite these developments, the religion can still be characterized as individualistic rather than formally organized. Any person can become a leader by opening a shrine, furnishing it with the proper implements and convincing a group of followers that he or she has been called by the Orisha to a position of leadership. This rather fluid method of leadership means that shrines rise and fall depending upon the health, wealth and general position of the leader. Shrines often close upon the death of the leader. At present, it is estimated that there are about sixty shrines with about five thousand active members; twenty of the shrines have registered with the newly formed National Council of Orisha Elders.

There is no real attempt at the centralization of ritual and activity. Although younger modern members are calling for some sort of standard, ritual, beliefs and behaviour may vary from shrine to shrine. This is especially apparent today as some innovators are attempting to eliminate Christian elements. Similarly, some leaders incorporate a few elements of Hinduism while others maintain Christianity. Some leaders practise both Orisha and Spiritual Baptism, and sometimes elements of both religions are found in the same ceremonial. A number of Orisha shrines include a Christian church or sanctum on the compound. Today, on some compounds, there is a concerted attempt to Yorubanize the lyrics of the songs whereas in more traditional compounds, the songs still contain English, French, patois and sometimes merely vocal sounds. While these differences are particularly evident today, some differences were evident previously.[13]

If one examines the structure of the Orisha religion in the country it becomes apparent that there has been some significant change. In earlier times there were distinct networks of Orisha leaders, joined together primarily because they were all the spiritual children of one particular leader or they lived in close proximity. The network that Pa Neezer worked in, for example, included about one dozen or so leaders whose compounds or shrines he would visit and at whose feasts he would officiate. The spiritual kinship that bound a "child" to his or her spiritual father or mother created bonds of ritual kinship between members. They would regularly attend each other's feasts, travelling together in a kind of circuit, and an informal attempt would be made to schedule feasts so that they would not overlap.

Today Orisha leaders and their shrines seem to operate quite independently of each other. There are still a few networks but little attempt is made to avoid conflicting schedules. There is also a much greater tendency towards the independent operation of each shrine, nor do members of one shrine travel to the feasts of other leaders. A few people still attend more than one, especially if the feasts are taking place in close geographical proximity. However, the attachment to one's own shrine and leader seems far more intense today than it was in former times. The newly formed Council of Elders is attempting to standardize the calendar of *Ebos* or feasts. In 2000 Baba Forde complained that there were several feasts taking place at the same time as his, although his feast day of Osain is well known and should, he thought, be respected by others.

There was always a rather strong division between the city of Port of Spain and the countryside, especially the south. This division was also found in Orisha observance and it is still quite evident. There are shrines operating in the south—Siparia, Fyzabad and Gasparillo—that are relatively out of touch with the modernizing dynamic affecting the religion today. Their ritual practices are relatively unchanged and they have not been influenced by the movement away from Christianity. There is also little movement or contact between groups operating in various parts of the country.

One result of this atomized social organization is that there is much competition among leaders for members and other resources. There is also a considerable amount of "bad talking" of leaders by each other. A leader will always mention one or two others who "don't do it right" and whose members are not being taught correctly. The behaviour of people at feasts is also strongly criticized. Leaders exert their influence to keep their members faithful to them. They discourage their attendance at other feasts, telling the members they will learn negative things from them. Another important reason for the increased individualism of the religion is that some shrines that have introduced more Yoruba ritual have suffered a drop in membership. Iyalorisha Rodney, the co-leader of the religion, used to have substantial attendance at her feast, but this has dropped off considerably because of the absence of Christian prayers. (The day of the feast honouring cattle was very well attended, however.) This competition and ill-will among leaders brings about "disunity." The plea is often made publicly that "we need to stop our differences, we need to pull together, we need to respect the ancestors." The cry for unity is the single most important discourse in the religion today. What is meant is not so much the unity between the two Orisha groups (now only one) as between individual leaders, their shrines and their membership.

During the late 1950s and 1960s the social stratification of each shrine or compound was quite evident. Observations about the stratification patterns in 1965 are still relevant today:

> The relatively small group, or more accurately, clique of high status people form a non-permeable, tightly-knit group and are virtually cut off socially from other members. Most people fall into the intermediate class, those who have some measure of status but are constantly striving to increase it. The third group of people, those with extremely low status, is small and often quite transitory. Finding little reinforcement or little need satisfaction, these people either leave or attend feasts sporadically. Members of this latter group have minimal communication with other members and their often, somewhat pathetic, efforts at possession are generally ignored and sometimes ridiculed. The people constituting this group are in the unfortunate position of being relatively unknown in the group and thus do not have the prior knowledge of cult proceedings needed to become a known participating member. They may come from villages quite distant, or from other cities or their familial background may be unknown. Occasionally, such an individual receives a "lucky break" in some way thereby giving him higher status in the group. For the most part, the vicious circle of status leading to more status is in operation and these people have no foundation upon which to build.
>
> One sees status operating most significantly in the intermediate group in which there are the most active status strivers; the individuals who actually count the number of possessions and patrons that a particular person may have, and who often imitate the behavior of high status people even in the non-possessed state. The high status group consists predominantly of leaders and very active followers, those persons who become possessed frequently. Respect, admiration, and complete obedience, both in the possessed and non-possessed state are commanded by this group. The behaviour of the high status people in possession is extremely self-confident, authoritarian and often quite aggressive. They control and take command of the situation so thoroughly that other gods of lesser status yield to them. Power, which may be considered a major behavioral referent of status, is the outstanding characteristic of this small clique; there are little or no restrictions upon their behavior and they are free to structure any situation according to their own wishes. . . .
>
> This division of members into several different groups seems related to other important patterns which have significant influences upon the way in which interpersonal relations are structured. One such pattern is a type of ritual kinship whereby a spiritual family is formed among the high status leaders and their followers. One of the functions of the leader is to interpret to a person possessed for the first time or to an already established follower who manifests a new god, the name of the god who is possessing him and also the behaviors which are appropriate to that god. The new person then considers the leader to be his spiritual mother or father and the two often will call each other by the appropriate terms. "Children" of the same leader consider themselves to be spiritual siblings and the spiritual family may take on major numerical proportions. Often this family is socially and psychologically more significant to the individual than his actual biological family. Leaders attempt to compete with each other for new followers since this too enhances their own positions. Similarly, a new person may approach a well-known and high status leader to serve as his mentor, thereby attaining membership in a more important spiritual family. Friendship patterns to a great extent follow the lines of the spiritual family and friendship across status lines was never observed.[14]

It has been observed today that fewer persons seem to "manifest" power or become possessed than in earlier times. One reason for this might be the increase in middle-class members wearing well-made and -designed African style clothing. Perhaps such persons feel that being in the state of possession might soil their clothing. Another possible reason might be the apparent decrease in the number of high-status persons who surround the leader. Today this high-status group, while always relatively small in the past, appears to have decreased even further. This means fewer people manifest the high-status deities and more of the middle and observer group tend to participate in the ceremonial only to demonstrate their belief and support, but without "manifesting" Orisha power. What has also been observed today is that, as each evening's Orisha is sung to and invoked, that Orisha may appear in the head of the leader or a close follower but no other Orisha grace the evening by their presence. Several evenings were observed in which the evening's Orisha was diligently sung to but the leader, perhaps for reasons of fatigue or ill-health, did not become possessed and neither did any other member present. This appears to add some validity to the notion that it is really only the small number of high-status persons who do manifest power.

Of greater significance, however, in limiting manifestations is that as the religion attracts more members from the middle class, time and the demands of occupation cut into Orisha attendance, as well as the draining and tiring experience of possession. As more members, including women, are employed, they no longer have the time or energy to manifest the vigorous possessions of the deities. There is also more interest among new and younger members in the cosmology of this African religion, and less emphasis on old rituals such as possession.

* * * * *

The Orisha "Powers" or Deities

In the following section the major deities and their characteristics, implements, days, sacrifices and sacred colours are listed. Since there is a great deal of variation in Orisha theology from group to group, this list records those identifications and characteristics heard most often in my earlier period of fieldwork. This variation may also account for the discrepancies between this list and similar ones constructed for Trinidad. Today there is still some variation among shrines.

Ogun

Christian counterpart: St Michael

Characteristics: God of war and iron; highest deity in the Orisha pantheon since he is the "chief angel." He is so powerful that "he can move mountains."

Ogun is generally the first power to arrive and it is said that no power can arrive before him at a feast. In practice, however, another power can arrive first but the reason is then given that Michael used another power as a messenger, being too busy to come himself.

His behaviour is generally aggressive; he does a good deal of violent dancing, using large steps, with his hands on his hips. Much of his time is spent in diagnosing ailments and solving problems. He uses great quantities of olive oil, which he distributes as blessings or scatters about the *palais*. He most frequently "manifests" on large, stout women.

Implements: Cutlass, sword when angry

Colours: Red, white

Day: Wednesday

Food: Goat, black-eyed peas, rice, corn, rum

Osain

Christian counterpart: St Francis

Characteristics: God of the jungle and bush, a herbalist or "bush doctor." He has three manifestations: Osain Kiribejii, identified as St Francis of Assisi; Osain Demolay, identified as St Francis Xavier; and Osain Metaphi who is known simply as St Francis.

He is a quiet power.

One form of Francis dances bent at the waist, using a slow shuffle step. Another walks on his toes, sometimes with a candle lit at both ends clamped between his teeth. Occasionally he throws himself to the ground and rolls on the earth. He "manifests" on both men and slim young women.

Implements: Pestle (thick vine), "checheray broom," lance, turtle carapace. For Osain Kiribejii: "checheray broom"; Osain Demolay: cross; Osain Metaphi: candle lit at both ends in mouth.

Colour: Yellow

Day: Thursday

Food: Muracoy (land turtle), black-eyed peas and rice

Aireelay (Ajaja)

Christian counterpart: "St" Jonah

Characteristics: "Master of the sea." He has two names because Jonah "died twice." He is revered as a "grim, serious man, no time for play." He paces back and forth with his hands on his hips or behind his back. When he dances, he throws his feet forward and spins on one heel. He is very authoritative and generally delivers a sermon or gives various orders, for example, to clean the *palais*. He is called by many "the crab." Only three Aireelay "horses" were observed, two men and one woman.

Implements: Bamboo rod called "roseau," dagger, great deal of olive oil
Colours: Blue, mauve belt
Day: Thursday
Food: Guinea bird, black-eyed peas, rice, corn

Shakpana

(Zewo, although the latter is sometimes considered to be the son of Shakpana and identified with St Vincent de Paul)
Christian counterpart: St Jerome
Characteristics: This power "gets rid of evil and disease." He does little dancing; his activity is confined to pacing about swishing his broom. When he "manifests" upon a woman, a red dress is worn. This is tied between the legs to form trousers. He is feared by some people because of his connection with disease, evil and prophecy.
Implement: "Checheray broom"
Colour: Red
Day: None
Food: Cock, pigeon, black-eyed peas, rice, corn

Shango

Christian counterpart: St John the Baptist
Characteristics: The god of lightning and thunder. He does little in the ritual other than dancing actively. He uses large steps and waves his arms, swinging his axe above his head. He is the only power who is "fed." At odd intervals, on Friday night, twenty-four small bits of cotton are rolled to form small balls, put on a plate, drenched with olive oil and lighted. The power then swallows this mixture. Only one specific Shango "horse" performs this feat currently.
Implements: Axe, pestle, cross. For Shango (John the Baptist): axe; Allado (Evangelist): pestle; Amado Shango (John of the Cross): cross.
Colours: White, red
Day: Friday
Food: Sheep, black-eyed peas, rice, corn

Aba Koso

Christian counterpart: St John the Baptist after beheading
Characteristics: The activity of this power is limited to pacing and stamping about with hands on hips. He grunts and groans continually, all the while shaking his head, which is thrown back. The grunting indicates that he has no head and is thus unable to talk. This makes him seem angry and "vexed" and he is often not taken seriously by other people. Only two people, both young men, were observed to be Aba Koso "horses."
Implement: Usually none, sometimes the axe
Colour: Red
Day: Friday
Food: Usually no sacrifice

Aba Lofa or Elofa

Christian counterpart: Eternal Father or "God Himself"
Characteristics: This power was another patron of Pa Neezer and then, as now, was much revered. He has only been seen at Neezer's feasts since he was the only known Aba Lofa "horse" in Trinidad at that time. Occasionally, if at another feast a cattle (bull) has been sacrificed and if the big leader was present, Aba Lofa may "manifest" upon him. I have not heard of any Aba Lofa manifestations in recent times, although Iyalorisha Rodney holds a "cattle feast" every leap year.

This power does not "manifest" suddenly but comes with a slow gradual shaking of the head. This becomes faster and faster, the hands are clasped and eyes closed. As the power comes the "horse" rises but keeps the hands clasped and the eyes closed. The power is an old man and must walk slowly and haltingly, sometimes with a cane. He dresses in white trousers, white shirt, white headband and a white bed sheet that is draped over the shoulders to form a cloak. He dances slowly, manipulating the cloak about him, and holds a freshly killed cattle head on his own head. After a while he holds the cattle head in the crook of his arm and dabs blood on the heads of all people present as a blessing. He also holds a ritual for children, which generally takes place on the third evening. Huge loaves of specially baked bread are brought out of the *chapelle* and are distributed in small pieces by Aba Lofa to all children present.
Implements: Stick or cane, cattle head, three candles, bottle of oil
Colour: White
Day: Monday or Tuesday
Food: Beef or whole cattle, black-eyed peas, rice, corn

Omira

Christian counterpart: St Raphael
Characteristics: This power is sacred to hunters and is more important as a chief archangel than as a hunter. He does little dancing, but generally walks about carrying a wooden gun. He dresses in a pink and lilac dress, carrying a hamsack "for his lunch" over his shoulder and sometimes a "flambeau," a candle, in his hand, since "hunters need a light."
Implements: Gun, candle, hamsack

Colours: Pink and lilac
Day: Wednesday
Food: Fowl, black-eyed peas, rice, corn

Ebejee

Christian counterpart: St Peter
Characteristics: He is a fisherman. As is the case with Raphael, he is more important in Christian terms than as an African deity. He is especially revered by one of the leaders, who calls Peter her chief patron. She is the only individual who manifests this power.
Implements: Keys, dagger, may wear a crown of leaves on head
Colours: Red, yellow, mauve
Day: None
Food: Drake, black-eyed peas, rice, corn

Yemanja (Amanja, Manja)

Christian counterpart: St Anne
Characteristics: Is a water power and lives in the sea. This power is either "saintly"—for example, simply walks about praying and blessing people—or quite actively going through the manoeuvres of rowing a boat. This is done by sitting on the ground and sliding across it while at the same time she carries a calabash of water in one hand and a "pa-gye" or oar with which she imitates the motion of rowing in the other. Yemanja is considered to be one of the most powerful of the female deities.
Implements: Oar, calabash of water
Colours: Blue and white
Day: Thursday
Food: Duck, pullet, peas, rice

Oya

Christian counterpart: St Catherine
Characteristic: She "lives in the air and comes with the breeze." Oya is closely identified with Shango and some individuals speak of them as married. She does a good deal of vigorous dancing, which looks very similar to the dancing of Shango, and occasionally holds her left ear when dancing. This is interpreted as "listening to the breeze."
Implement: Hatchet
Colours: Green, red
Day: Friday
Food: Fowl, pigeon, peas, rice, corn (the only female power who is offered corn, but her active vigorous behaviour resembles that of the masculine powers more than that of the females).

Oshun

Christian counterpart: St Philomen
Characteristics: This deity is a river goddess and "lives in the river." Her dancing is very delicate and often she balances a filled goblet (pottery jug) of water on her head without a head pad and dances with it for as long as thirty minutes without spilling its contents. At special river ceremonies, Oshun wades into the water and offers food to the river. (At one such ceremony the food, which was placed in a calabash, drifted out onto the water and could not be recovered, as it normally is. This was interpreted as the will of Oshun, who was angry at not receiving enough sacrifices.) She is considered by some to be the female counterpart of Aireelay.
Implements: Anchor, goblet
Colours: Blue and white
Day: Thursday
Food: Fowl, pigeon, black-eyed peas, rice

Omela (Mama Latay)

Christian counterpart: Mother of the Earth. This deity is supposed to accompany Ogun-St Michael, and is generally sung to after Ogun. She does not dance but sits on her knees and slides across the floor distributing water in a calabash to the people present and to the four corners of the *palais*. She is supposed to be an old, stooped woman.
Implement: Calabash of water
Colour: Brown
Day: Wednesday
Food: Ground provisions (such as potatoes)

Lesser-known Powers

Lesser-known powers or those who rarely "manifest" are listed below:

Bayanni (St Anthony)—implement: three candles, bottle of oil

Oromeelay (St Joseph)—implement: carpenter square

Mayadu (St Theresa)—implement: crucifix, flowers; colour: brown, blue

Da Lua (St Jude); Da Logee (St Simon). These two (Da Lua and Da Logee) are "twins."

Obatala (Mary)

Abatala (Jesus)

Zopah (St Benedict)

Ojah (St Mark)

Ajakba (Mother of All Nations)

Mahabil (St Michael) was recognized by only one Orisha leader, who called him the "Indian King." He was an Indian god who was met by Christ in India and baptized as St Michael. In behaviour he is similar to Ogun, uses the sword or cutlass and dresses similarly. He has an altar and a "tomb" in the establishment of this one leader, but is not recognized outside of her immediate circle.

Today there are a number of shrines in which possession by Indian Hindu deities also takes place.[15] In one such, the goddess Shakti was said to manifest on its leader. In at least one shrine, several new Orisha not traditionally associated with the worship have been added to the ritual. These include Olukun and Egede, whose presence has come about as a result of the increased Yorubanization of the movement.

Notes

1. The traditional Yoruba religious system is complex and multilayered. Their cosmos consists of a supreme deity, Olodumare or Olorun, many hundreds of lesser divinities called "Orisa," spirits of deceased ancestors and other spiritual beings. Some Orisa control the forces of nature while others are heroes who have become divine. The Orisa have cults devoted to their worship that are sometimes based on kinship-related descent groups, or a particular divinity may have their centre of worship in a region, town or village. The main Orisa are associated with distinctive dress, colours, foods and rituals. Some are derived from elemental forces of nature that they are believed to control, while others are folkloric heroes who have become divine. Rituals include those that are practiced on an individual basis, those associated with the shrines of the Orisa and, finally, large-scale annual festivals. Divination is a central feature of Yoruba religion as is ancestor worship. See W. Bascom, *Ifa Divination: Communication between Gods and Men in West Africa* (Bloomington: Indiana University Press, 1980); also many Internet sites devoted to Yoruba culture and religion.

2. James Houk, *Spirits, Blood and Drums: The Orisha Religion in Trinidad* (Philadelphia: Temple University Press, 1995).

3. This is not to suggest that African-derived religions are not found in the Protestant Caribbean. In Jamaica, for example, several African-derived groups flourish—among them the Convince Cult and Pocomania. See D. Hogg, *The Convince Cult in Jamaica*, Yale Publications in Anthropology, 58 (New Haven: Yale University Press, 1960); Kenneth Bilbey, "Neither Here nor There: The Place of Community in the Jamaican Religious Imagination," in *Religion, Diaspora and Cultural Identity: A Reader in the Anglophone Caribbean*, ed. J. Pulis (Amsterdam: Gordon and Breach, 1999).

4. Older ethnographic sources include: M.J. Herskovits, *Life in a Haitian Valley* (New York: Knopf, 1937); M.J. Herskovits, "African Gods and Catholic Saints in New World Negro Beliefs," *American Anthropologist*, no. 39 (1937): 635–43; George Simpson, "The Vodun Service in Northern Haiti," *American Anthropologist*, no. 42 (1940): 236–54; George Simpson, "The Belief System of Haitian Vodun," *American Anthropologist*, no. 47 (1945): 35–56. More recent works include: George Brandon, *Santeria from Africa to the New World* (Bloomington: Indiana University Press, 1993); Maureen Warner-

Lewis, *Guinea's Other Suns: The African Dynamic in Trinidad Culture* (Dover: Majority Press, 1991).

5. Donald Pierson, *Negroes in Brazil: A Study of Race Contact in Bahia* (Carbondale, Ill.: Southern Illinois University Press, 1942); M.J. Herskovits, "The Southernmost Outposts of New World Africanisms," *American Anthropologist*, no. 45 (1943): 495–510. More recent works include: Robert Voeks, *Sacred Leaves of Candomble: Magic, Medicine and Religion in Brazil* (Austin: University of Texas Press, 1997).

6. John Mason, *Four New World Yoruba Rituals* (Brooklyn: Yoruba Theological Archministry, 1993).

7. David Trotman, "The Yoruba and Orisha Worship in Trinidad and British Guinea," *African Studies Review* 19, no. 2 (1976): 1–17. See also Philip Sher, "Unveiling the Orisha: African Religions and Public Relations in Trinidad," in *Africa's Ogun: Old World and New*, ed. Sandra Barnes (Bloomington: Indiana University Press, 1997).

8. In *The Lost Orisha*, Conrad Mauge claims that an ancestor of his, Ifayomi, a slave, was transported from Guinea to Martinique and thence to Trinidad in 1808 where he and his master settled in what is today Princes Town in southern Trinidad. He credits him with re-establishing the Orisha religion there a few years later. It then spread during the nineteenth century throughout the country, as more Yoruba were brought to Trinidad. Unfortunately, Mauge does not provide any historical sources for this story, so its authenticity is open to question.

9. See George Brandon, *Santeria from Africa to the New World* (Bloomington: Indiana University Press, 1993); Kamari Clarke, "Genealogies of Reclaimed Nobility: The Geotemporality of Yoruba Belonging" (Ph.D. diss., Temple University, 1995).

10. Supposedly the order in singing is from Ogun, Omela, Omira, Gabriel, Shakpana, Osain, Shango, Aireelay. In actual fact, the singing order is quite flexible and almost any power can be sung to at any time, with the exception of the singing to Eshu and Ogun at the beginning of the ritual.

11. Possessions, or manifestations as they are now called, ranged from two to twenty-four in one evening during my earlier fieldwork. During the present fieldwork period, far fewer manifestations were observed.

12. See chapter 6 for more detail on the Africanization of the religion.

13. For more on Yoruba songs in Orisha ritual and elsewhere in Trinidad, see Maureen Warner-Lewis, *Yoruba Songs from Trinidad* (London: Karnak House, 1994).

14. Frances Henry, "Social Stratification in an Afro-American Cult," *Anthropological Quarterly* (April 1965). There is now a new class of membership composed of high-profile, notable

people from the artistic and professional communities who have recently and publicly affirmed support for the religion.

15. N. Mahabir and A. Majaraj, "Hindu Elements in the Shango/Orisha Cult of Trinidad," in *Indenture and Exile: The Indo-Caribbean Experience*, ed. Frank Birbalsingh (Toronto: TSAR, 1989).

Religious "Speculation": The Rise of Ifá Cults and Consumption in Post-Soviet Cuba*

Martin Holbraad

Abstract. With an ethnographic focus on the prestigious cult of Ifá, this article seeks to account for the recent effervescence of Afro-Cuban cult worship in urban Cuba. It is argued that, since worship involves a marked emphasis on ritual consumption, the cult's rise can be related to wider transformations that have taken place in the field of everyday consumption in Havana during the economic crisis that has followed the collapse of the Soviet bloc. In particular, Ifá has provided an arena for what *habaneros* call "especulación," a style of conspicuous consumption that has become prevalent among so-called "marginal" groups in recent years.

Conducting ethnographic fieldwork among practitioners of the Afro-Cuban diviner cult. Ifá in Havana at the turn of the century, I was struck by a paradoxical situation that seemed to be the source of much anxiety among cult practitioners. On the one hand, since the collapse of the Soviet bloc in 1989–1990, Cubans have experienced a dramatic and generalised drop in their standard of living and well nigh universally consider this period as one of relative poverty. On the other hand, this same period has seen a veritable explosion of Afro-Cuban cult activity. Intriguingly this intensification, characterised by more and more young neophytes becoming initiated in lavish ceremonies, has gone hand in hand with an extraordinary price-hike in the fees charged by cult members for initiation ceremonies and other ritual services. The central question that motivates this article, then, is this: why, in a situation in which people feel that money is harder to come by than ever since the socialist Revolution of 1959, should more and more people be willing to pay inflated prices for increasingly lavish initiations and other ritual services? How can these two phenomena—generalised poverty and ritual inflation, so to speak—go together?

The line of argument advanced here might best be described as "economistic" in style. In order to shed light on some of the more important reasons that have led to the unprecedented growth of Ifá cults in recent years, issues pertaining to cult worship will be linked with certain transformations that have taken place in the field of everyday consumption more generally in Havana. In particular, it is argued here that a new brand of initiates, whose emergence is central to the rise and transformation of Ifá in recent years, can be associated with a style of conspicuous consumption which has become a salient model of and for behaviour among so-called "marginal" groups in inner-city Havana of the post-Soviet period, a stereotype of ostentatious spending that *habaneros* call colloquially "especulación." Drawing critically on Day, Papataxiarchis and Stewart's argument that, placing a premium on "living for the moment,"[1] such apparently imprudent behaviours on the part of marginal groups constitute strategies of ideological contestation, I propose to defend two main points. First, that because Ifá cults have always and inherently emphasised luxury expressed in uncalculating monetary expenditure, they have provided an apposite arena for the performance of *especulación*, this peculiar phenomenon of the 1990s. Second, that "religious *especulación*" (as people in Havana sometimes call it tongue-in-cheek), in other words, the conspicuous consumption of ritual services in the cults, provides a way for young initiates to overcome the problem of vulnerability that the happy-go-lucky hedonism of *especulación* ordinarily implies. By way of conclusion, the point is made that while the affinities between Ifá and *especulación* may help to account for the rise and transformation of cult practice in recent years, the two are nevertheless uncomfortable bedfellows, to the extent that their common emphasis on luxury and unplanned spending is motivated differently in each case: while *especulación* implies ostentatious spending on one's desire as a means of transcending poverty "in the moment," Ifá is meant to involve luxurious expenditure in an ethos of submission to deities who obligate initiates through oracular demands.

A couple of preliminary points are in order here, one on scope, the other on method. It will be evident from the tenor of the above summary that in seeking to identify salient causes for the recent rise and transformation of Ifá in certain practices that are peculiar to the life of the cult, I am effectively treating Afro-Cuban religious manifestations separately from the activities of the Catholic church and various Protestant denominations, all of which have also been on the rise in post-Soviet Cuba. As discussed below, the advantage of limiting the scope of the argument in this way is that it allows one to gauge the peculiar features of the effervescence of Afro-Cuban cult activity, and particularly some of the ways in which worship has changed over this period. Nevertheless, it should be made clear that treating the cults separately from the activities of the institutional churches is to a certain extent artificial, since the two are connected in a number of ways. For a start, the relative freedom that cult worshipers have begun to enjoy in recent years can be seen partly as an effect of a more general opening on the part of the Cuban State towards religious expressions of all kinds, including Christian denominations (see below). Moreover, there are substantive links that connect the cults to the churches both ritually and sociologically, so it could be argued that their respective fortunes are intertwined. The most obvious example of this has to do with the so-called "syncretic" character of Ifá and Santería, in other words their "creolisation" in the New World context of Cuba, whereby cult worship came to incorporate a number of important Catholic elements.[2] Since these elements include substantial ritual connections, such as the fact that the worship of individual cult deities involves regular visits to Catholic churches on annual saint-days it could be argued that the rise of Ifá in recent years can be seen in the context of a wider ecclesiastical renaissance. Conversely, it may also be noted that the intensification of Afro-Cuban cult activity is taking place in a context of increasingly vigorous competition from a variety of new Protestant denominations.[3] These have tended to adopt an exclusive stance vis-à-vis the Afro-Cuban traditions, actively discouraging their members from continuing to practice "heathen" forms of worship. So it could also be argued that an exhaustive analysis of the circumstances of the rise of Ifá would need to take this form of dynamic competition into account as well.

Notwithstanding the relevance of such contextual factors, this paper proceeds on the assumption that the internal dynamic of cult worship—and particularly the peculiar role of consumption within it—is worthy of analysis in and of itself. Indeed, it would be risky to treat the recent rise of Ifá as just an instance of a more general religious upsurge. Such an approach might not only miss the peculiar character of contemporary Ifá, but could also underestimate the significance of such cults as dominant religious forces. It would be useful to be able to illustrate the significance of Ifá and other Afro-Cuban traditions by providing a quantitative estimate of their distribution across the population. Unfortunately, however, this issue is still politically sensitive in socialist Cuba, so the data is scanty and unreliable.[4] Nevertheless, as my account below indicates, there can be little doubt that Afro-Cuban religious manifestations are a dominant presence in the everyday lives of ordinary *habaneros*, particularly in the mainly non-white inner-city areas of Havana, such as Centro Habana where I collected the bulk of my material.

This brings me to a second point, on methodology. As already mentioned, the material presented in this paper is drawn mainly from my own ethnographic research among cult practitioners in Havana, with whom I worked for a total of 16 months. Much of my time in Havana was spent observing and participating in the activities of one particular group of Ifá initiates (*babalawos*) who were linked to each other through relations of ritual kinship,[5] ordinary family ties, or simply friendship or acquaintance. In view of the urban context of Havana, as well as the open structure of Ifá cult organisation (see footnote 5), the notion of a "group" here should not be taken in too strict a sense. A large proportion of my material was collected by spending protracted periods in the house of two *babalawos* (Javier Alfonso and his son Javierito), participating in their ritual activities, conducting more or less formal interviews, and generally following the rhythm of the comings and goings of clients, friends, relatives and so forth. As my acquaintance with their network grew, I was able to follow up on many of the relationships I established in Javier's home, accompanying a number of informants as they went about their business (ritual or otherwise) in the city. In this way I was able to complement the more in-depth research conducted in the house of Javier with material collected from a total of approximately 15–20 *babalawos* from varied backgrounds, as well as a large number of uninitiated practitioners from different walks of life, including clients and practitioners of Santería. Since Ifá is an exclusively male cult, it is probably fair to say that my material tends to concentrate more on the male perspective on ritual life, as does the argument outlined here, although the views of female non-initiates are also considered.

Poverty, "Struggle" and *Especulación*

The "economically informed" argument regarding the rise and transformation of Ifá cults during the crisis of the 1990s may be introduced by means of a brief account of the radical economic transformations that Cuba has undergone as a result of the collapse of the Soviet bloc. It is well documented that the flagship, and indeed momentous, achievements of Castro's socialist Revolution in Cuba (including guaranteed subsistence, housing, health-care, and education for all citizens) were made possible partly by Soviet backing.[6] Partly in reaction to a bellicose US trade embargo, Cuban economic policy was from an early stage founded on two pillars: export primarily of sugar and nickel to the Soviet Union and COMECON countries on trade terms that were extremely advantageous relative to the world market; and rouble "debt-financing" from the USSR that allowed Cuba to run persistent balance-of-payment deficits. During the period from 1989 till 1991 both of these pillars were shattered. First the COMECON countries and then the USSR itself cancelled deals with Cuba one by one, and began to demand debt payments in hard currency. In 1990 Fidel Castro declared that the country was entering a "Special Period in Times of Peace," and by 1992 the economic crisis was so deep that 70 per cent of the country's purchasing power had been lost.[7]

The regime reacted to the crisis by instituting drastic austerity measures on the one hand, and relentlessly pursuing hard currency on the other. As a result of cuts in all forms of energy use in the early 1990s (as well as curtailments of the labour-force itself), agricultural and industrial outputs plummeted. This had an immediate impact on the population, since many of the goods and services that were previously provided at affordable prices by the state became increasingly difficult to procure or, in many cases, disappeared altogether. During my fieldwork in the late 1990s, people's most urgent complaints related to the rationing system, which throughout the Revolution had formed the back-bone of house-hold consumption: while "before" the crisis families could live adequately off the goods provided on the rations-book *(la libreta)*, "now" rations tended to last only for 10 days in every month. On the other hand, cutbacks were accompanied by reforms that would have been unimaginable a few years earlier. In the early 1990s, on the slogan "capital yes, capitalism no," the regime courted hard currency not only by opening up to foreign investors (not least in the tourist sector, which has expanded rapidly throughout the 1990s), but also by tapping into dollars which were already circulating inside Cuba illegally, largely due to remittances sent by relatives in the USA and elsewhere.[8] In 1993 the government decriminalised the possession of dollars, thus incorporating a significant slice of the black market which was rife at the time. With Fort Knox-like security measures, more and more state shops were opened to sell retail goods in dollars. By the time I arrived in 1998, vast arrays of products (including basics like cooking-oil and detergent) were only available in dollar-shops (or, as Cubans call them, *la chopin*—from the English "shopping").

This encroaching dollar market has effectively divided Cuban society in two. There are those who are lucky or clever enough to possess dollars. Depending on the quantity at their disposal, these people are able to live relatively comfortably, and in some cases may even be able to afford luxuries such as a car or a colour TV. Then there is the majority who still have to make do with pesos. Although estimates vary, average wages run at roughly 200 pesos per month (less than $10), an entirely inadequate figure if one considers, for example, that one litre of vegetable oil costs $2.15. During my time in Havana, practically everyone I met would either supplement or replace salary payments through some form of illegal activity or other. A laboratory assistant rented a room in her

flat by the hour to couples, a truck driver bred poultry in his yard, an intellectual dreamed of becoming a porter in a big hotel. The most prized commodity among this large and dispossessed segment of Cuban society is, of course, *el dólar* itself. During fieldwork I became accustomed to hearing the same sociological observation from different informants and in a variety of contexts. "In Cuba today we have two classes: those who have dollars, and those who don't. It wasn't like that *antes* (before the Special Period). It isn't easy!" Indeed, it is worth noting that with the steep drop in people's purchasing power implied by the relative demise of state provision and parallel proliferation of expensive dollar goods, even those who do have access to dollars share in the bitterness of such statements. "These days *no-one* has enough for their needs," is a statement that well nigh everyone assents to in post-Soviet Havana (that is to say, dollar-haves as well as dollar have-nots). Listening to *habaneros* talk about their current "poverty" or "need" (the term that they use is *necesidad,* which amalgamates the two connotations),[9] one gets an image of a people suspended in a kind of economic no-man's land, between a half disintegrated socialist system of state provision, and a world of capitalist plenty which is nevertheless practically beyond reach, for, as *habaneros* often say with a tinge of Revolutionary irony, dollars are the object of "struggle" *(la lucha por el dólar).*[10]

It is within this context of "necesidad" and "struggle" that a peculiar stereotype of consumptive behaviour that *habaneros* colloquially refer to as "especulación" has emerged as a seemingly paradoxical phenomenon, one which, by *habaneros'* account, has become a sign of the times in the 1990s. In socialist discourse "especulación" (literally "speculation") refers to spurious profiteering associated particularly with middlemen who take advantage of workers.[11] On the streets of Havana, however, *especulación* is used as a slang term in reference to a certain stereotype of behaviour that has more to do with consumption than with production. The typical image that *especulación* conjures up for *habaneros* is of a man, normally black or mulatto, in designer sports-wear and heavy with golden bracelets and neck-chains, looking for excuses to show off his wad of dollar notes: dollar beers, dollar rum and dollar women will all be consumed on protracted and ostentatious spending-sprees, starting perhaps in a dollar cafeteria and moving on later to a dollar night-club, deep into the night.

Especulación is not an unambiguously positive term. In fact *habaneros* are generally loath to own up to being *especuladores* ("speculators"). For example, when a young mulatto friend of mine criticised his cousin for being too prudent with his dollar income (earned at a hotel), I asked him how he would prefer to spend the money:

None of this saving up to buy spectacles business. . . . I'd rent a TUR [cars designated for tourist rental], fill it up with whores, and hit the clubs! [Question:] So you'd speculate? [laughing:] No man! You've just got to enjoy life (*vacilar la vida*).

Given such usages, it might seem prudent to consider *especulación* as some kind of discursive caricature, which it surely is in certain senses.[12] Yet, living in Havana, it is striking how often the behaviour of *habaneros* conforms to the *especulación* stereotype. On visits to dollar cafeterias or clubs, one certainly becomes familiar with the sight of groups of men drinking loudly around tables covered with uncleared beer cans and Havana Club rum bottles. Indeed, armed with my own dollars, I was able on numerous occasions to accompany friends and acquaintances on such outings. What was generally remarkable was the ostentatious style with which "luxury" goods were consumed. Dollar-notes would be held out in display as large orders of food and drink were shouted in the waiters' direction, and pretty girls were invited to sit on the understanding that they too could order to their heart's content. On such occasions, the objective seemed invariably to be to create an atmosphere of opulence: the more glamorous and expensive the goods consumed, the more successful the outing. Indeed these are precisely the elements that are emphasised most when men think back, in conversation, to memorable nights. Teasing me for having declined an invitation the previous evening, a 35-year-old male friend of mine described:

Forty beers man! [. . .] Chichi and I really caned it (*apretamos*). I don't know how we left Las Vegas [a dollar nightclub] with all those women sitting on us [indicating his crotch] . . . look! I've got the bottle [taking out a half-empty bottle of 5-star Havana Club]. . . .

The negative connotations of "*especulación*" can be traced partly to the fact that the term evokes groups who in many contexts are considered to be marginal. Not only are *especuladores* typically imagined as being non-white ("whites don't speculate," as a black female friend told me), but they are also—by definition—expected to be involved in some kind of shady economic activity—be it hustling, pimping or dealing on the black-market. Speaking about the behaviour of her brother, a "runner" (*corredor*) for an illegal real estate operation with whom I had been out on several occasions, a middle-aged black informant of mine (Gisel let's call her) explained:

Look, if we had an opportunity to travel, or to make investments, or do whatever we dream of doing, we wouldn't be spending our money the way we do. But as here everything is illegal, and frowned upon, well we just take our money and spend it as we please. Of course we're not like you foreigners, always planning everything. For us this doesn't make sense. If we did that, we'd only draw attention to ourselves, and the police would be constantly on our case in the neighbourhood. So what we do when we have $100 in our pocket is speculate.

The connection between marginality and conspicuous consumption has been explored in anthropology at least since Oscar Lewis listed the "[in] ability to defer gratification" as a defining trait of the "culture of poverty."[13] The theme has been picked up more recently in a seminal collection of essays entitled *Lilies of the Field: Marginal People who Live for the Moment*. In the introduction the editors make a case for looking at "anti-economic" behaviour, such as conspicuous consumption, as part of a repertoire of practices through which marginal groups construct ideologies that are antithetical to the mainstream. In this context it is suggested that anti-economic behaviour can be understood as a distinctive relation to time, which in turn, constitutes a crucial site of "ideological" contestation. The latter proposition owes much to Bloch's Marxist idea that ideology is constructed on symbolic negations of temporal duration,[14] while the former is reminiscent of Parry and Bloch's perspective on the ideological significance of long-term deployments of money.[15]

Along these lines, the editors of *Lilies of the Field* mobilise examples from various ethnographic settings to show how radical forms of short-termism in the consumption of money facilitate a departure from dominant ideological structures, since the latter rely on long-term economic notions about planning, saving, stable labour organisation and so forth. In sum, the efficacy of "anti-economic" deployments of money as "oppositional ideology" is rendered here as a double negative. On the one hand practices such as conspicuous consumption straightforwardly negate mainstream ideological emphases on longer-term economic prudence, and hence may be branded as "oppositional." On the other hand, such practices are also "ideological" since they rely on negating notions of temporal duration. What distinguishes mainstream from oppositional ideology is that while the former constructs "timelessness" with reference to symbolic representations of a permanent order, the latter does so like a pointillist painting, by privileging representations of the present at the expense of the past and the future. As Michael Stewart puts it in his article on the Rom's opposition to Magyar socialism, marginal ideology is premised on the idea that "it is possible to live on a continuous unfolding present in which life is a process of becoming."[16]

Especulación bears out the idea of "living for the moment" in a rather interesting way. In Gisel's words on the subject, the idea of "anti-economic" behaviour and that of an oppositional stance from a marginal perspective emerge clearly. In the hands of the *especulador,* money becomes the ultimate consumable, and the moment of its consumption is celebrated for its purchase on desire: beer, rum, women and "you've got to *enjoy* life." To a snapshot of the *especulador's* protracted night-time of hedonics, one could well append the lottery-winner's *spend! spend! spend!* There is a huge difference, however. While the English lottery-winner may spend "like there is no tomorrow" because she knows that tomorrow she can spend again, the *especulador* spends in the same manner for the *opposite* reason, as Gisel explained. For, in fact, the *especulador's* "unfolding present" never lasts very long. *Qua* marginal, *especuladores* are as subject to *la necesidad* (poverty) as everyone else, so "tomorrow" for them, like "yesterday," is a day of "struggle" once more. The paradox in *especulación* is that as a concerted effort to hold the misery of empty pockets in abeyance by privileging notions of desire albeit "for the moment," this type of behaviour is itself motivated by the conditioning force of poverty and life on the margin of things. And, as the editors of *Lilies of the Field* also point out, ideologies of "living for the moment" also contribute to marginal peoples' very real vulnerability, which in the case of Cuban *especuladores* takes the form not only of a bad hangover, but also of an empty fridge and angry and most likely hungry wives and children.

The central proposition of this article is that the style of conspicuous consumption associated with *especulación* has been an important ingredient in the rise of Ifá worship in the 1990s, and has contributed to certain salient transformations that cults have undergone during this period. Making such an argument, will involve three tasks. First, the claim that Ifá (along with other Afro-Cuban cults) has become increasingly prominent in the 1990s is briefly substantiated. With the caveat that the argument about economic behaviour is put forward only as part of the explanation for the rise of Ifá, the ways in which initiates have sought to dispense ritual services under the new circumstances associated with dollarisation and *la necesidad* are then charted ethnographically. The central theme here is the tension between strictures of ritual propriety and temptations to "commerce" (*comercio*). Finally, the argument is sealed by turning from supply to demand, as it were, in order to show that a crucial factor in the increased popularity of Ifá has been the emergence of a new breed of dollar-wielding practitioners. The central hypothesis is that with its well-established emphasis on "uncalculating" luxury, Ifá furnishes an arena for the kind of conspicuous consumption associated with *especulación*.

The Rise of Afro-Cuban Cults in the Special Period

The history of Ifá and Santería in Cuba is in large part a story of persecution and clandestine worship. Based primarily on elements brought to Cuba by Yoruba speaking slaves from West Africa during the nineteenth century, the cults evolved fluidly in the poorer and predominantly non-white neighbourhoods of Havana, Matanzas and Cárdenas, incorporating elements associated with Catholicism and Spiritism, as well as practices from a variety of West African tribes.[17] Although the rich devotional universe of Ifá and Santería did capture the imagination of intellectuals and artists from the first decades of the twentieth century onwards, and the prestige conferred upon initiates within their own communities accounted for a certain amount of electoral wooing on the part of some politicians, it is fair to say that, from a mainstream point of view, cult practice remained heavily laden with connotations of backwardness and marginality following the abolition of slavery in the late nineteenth century.[18] This situation did not change substantially after Fidel Castro's Revolution in 1959. Notwithstanding significant successes in redressing the racial injustices of previous times in important areas of social policy, the new regime made few attempts to accommodate Afro-Cuban religious practices within the Marxist-Leninist frame of official revolutionary ideology.[19] Throughout the 1960s, 1970s and 1980s, Afro-Cuban cults were practised with muffled drums, so to speak, and behind closed doors.

During the 1990s, however, cults like Ifá and Santeria became arguably more visible and widespread than ever before in recent Cuban history. It is practically impossible to quantify the change. Published statistics are too scanty to form the basis for a reliable synthesis, and those commentators who have remarked on the change often do not disclose sources.[20] Nevertheless, available material does suggest a marked increase in Afro-Cuban ritual activity starting from the mid-1980s and peaking in the mid-1990s at the height of the Special Period. For example, Cuban scholar Lacien Zamora cites a long-term study showing devotees' participation in the annual pilgrimage to the sanctuary of San Lázaro on 16 and 17 December, one of the high points of the ritual calendar. The study records an almost steady rise in the number of pilgrims from 34,444 in 1983 to a high of 94,109 in 1995, dropping slightly to 83,776 in 1998.[21] Quoting results of studies by the same state agency, Díaz and Perera report a marked increase in assistance to "religious festivals" by "the young" (without defining either category), from 31.5 per cent in 1984 to 46 per cent in 1993, with a high of 53.6 per cent in 1991.[22]

Practitioners' own perception resonates with these data. "Don't be fooled," a middle-aged *babalawo* told me when I commented on his busy ritual schedule, "before *(antes)* things were not as you see them now." Certainly, signs of cult activity are ubiquitous in Havana these days. Walking around the less grand neighbourhoods of the city, even the most uninterested visitor must perforce become familiar with the sounds of ritual drumming *(tambores)* emanating from packed flats, or with the sight of whitely clad and colourfully beaded neophytes *(iyawós)* going about their daily business on the street.[23] Bright and chunky initiation-bracelets *(iddé)* weigh down the wrists of young initiates all over town.

There is no doubt that many factors have contributed to this palpable change. The most obvious are political, and relate to the state's gradual relaxation towards religious manifestations in general (including Catholicism and rising Protestant denominations as well as Afro-Cuban cults) at least since 1992, when a new Constitution declared Cuba a "lay" rather than "atheist" state.[24] Explanations for the State's relative *rapprochement* both with the historically dominant Catholic Church and with newer Protestant denominations abound in the literature.[25] The new visibility of Afro-Cuban practices has been less explored, although the authorities' recent permissiveness on this matter can perhaps be seen as part of the government's more general attempts in the early 1990s to relieve some of the pressures on the population in view of the danger of social unrest during the crisis.[26] This would make sense considering that, despite their well-publicised gains under the Revolution, many non-whites (including many initiates) count themselves among the hardest hit by the recent crisis.[27]

Nevertheless, explaining the new vigour of the cults in "hydraulic" terms as a function of the relief from political pressures is inadequate by itself. Crucially, such approaches do not in themselves account for certain salient *transformations* that cult worship has undergone in recent years, or not at least in a way that resonates with practitioners' own experience. An insight into what is really at stake for them can be gained by quoting an extract from one of many interviews that I conducted with Javier Alfonso, a 78-year-old *babalawo* who was initiated in the 1960s. And talk of "stakes" here is not out of place since, as Javier's ambivalent words show, the issue turns mostly on economic concerns with money and its expenditure.

[Our religion] used to be for slaves and now it is for the rich. Recently I was buying coffee there in front and I heard someone saying that Ifá is an exploitation. I asked him: "Are you an initiate yourself? No, you just talk from what you hear. These days it takes a lot of money to make Ifá [in other words to conduct an initiation]. [. . .] I agree that it's an exploitation. But it is not the initiates doing the exploiting. It is the traders who sell the animals [for ritual sacrifices], the *chopin*, and the food is very expensive, for none of the things we use can be bought on *la libreta* [the rationing system]. Above all when we do an Ifá we live it up, we do a ceremony for a king. We have to prepare three full dinners for all the *babalawos*, and beer for everyone throughout the week, and that is very expensive. [. . .] It is this society that we're living in that has made things like this, not the *babalawos*. These people who criticise don't look for the reasons behind the situation. [. . .] Before, even to the most senior *babalawos* they'd give 50 pesos. But now even the young ones need 100 pesos as a minimum for the week.[28] Today the luxury is of course even grander: beautiful *iyawó* [neophyte] clothes from abroad and all the rest of it. When I was an *iyawó* I would dress in flour sacks because of our poverty. People today are ashamed to walk in such clothes. [. . .] In the old days [. . .] a housemaid would save up for years and years. Now in many cases people just get initiated because the money came in, say for people who get dollars sent from the North [remittances from the USA]. Certainly, if you don't have a good income it is hard to be initiated.

It is worth noting that, as a defence against the *babalawos'* retractors, Javier's rhetoric turns on an intriguing double premise. On the one hand, by casting his rant in terms of the opposition of "before" v. "now"—*habaneros'* generic idiom for reflecting upon the everyday travails of the Special Period—Javier is effectively appealing to the self-evidence of *la necesidad*. Connecting the price-hike within the cult with the general deterioration in people's purchasing power during the Special Period, he is able to heap the blame for "exploitation" on to "this society that we're living in." The message is one that his neighbour, like anyone in Havana, can recognise: "it isn't easy these days."

On the other hand, Javier's case also relies on a tacit premise that has less to do with contingent economic circumstance, and more with the nature of Ifá worship as such. As a respected *babalawo*, Javier can vouch for the fact that the hefty purchases associated with Ifá initiation (sacrificial animals, ceremonial dinners, beer, and the like) are ordained by liturgical order rather than personal choice, as accusations of "exploitation" would have it. While recent price-hikes may be a matter of general regret, the emphasis on luxury as such is not, since luxury is integral to the ritual exigencies of initiation, quite properly considered as the "birth of a king." Indeed, it is important to note here that the requirement for liturgical propriety in Ifá (including expenditures for all manner of rituals) is rendered a matter of divine necessity by the practice of divination. One of the hallmarks of *babalawos'* prestige is that, unlike initiates of other Afro-Cuban cults such as Santería, they are able to ascertain the will of Orula, the patron-deity of divination, by means of their privileged access to the oracle of Ifá, through which Orula "speaks," as it is said. While the undisputed prestige of the oracle of Ifá enhances *babalawos'* standing, enabling them to use their divinatory expertise for the benefit of uninitiated clients in exchange for fees, the oracle also plays a crucial role in regulating matters of worship within the cult itself. One might say that Ifá worship is premised on a thoroughgoing divinatory logic, inasmuch as ceremonies (with their inevitable expenditures) are in each case *prescribed* by the oracle itself. Sacrifices, consecrations, magical remedies, or—indeed— initiations, are only properly performed if they have first been sanctioned by the oracle, so that Orula himself may establish what task ought to be performed, when, how, by who or on whom. As in all matters, Orula's will on ceremonial issues is compelling, since it is understood that to "disobey" him ("caer en la desobediencia," as practitioners say) is to risk all manner of personal misfortune. Indeed, ritual propriety in accordance with the oracles' temporary and unpredictable demands is an abiding source of anxiety for practitioners in these expensive times. Certainly the difficulty of bridging the gap between divine necessity and mundane *necesidad*, as it were, is one that *babalawos* like Javier are well aware of. As he explained to me once:

> These days people go to a *babalawo* and it turns out they need to do an *ebbó* (sacrifice), [...] a chicken to Elegguá[29] maybe. Who can afford that? I always begin by asking [Orula, through the oracle] about simpler things: a bath, whatever. People can't afford even a simple *addimú* (offering). Elegguá wants three sweets and they buy one for five pesos and then cut it in three pieces and give it to him.

Now, although Javier's good faith in such matters is by no means unique, one can only understand the subtext of his case by taking into account his status as an elderly *babalawo*—perhaps representing a bygone era—as well as his undisputed reputation in cult circles for honesty and humility. For the argument from divine compulsion may apply to his own case, but, as his disillusioned neighbour probably would attest, not all *babalawos* are like him. One worry that Javier's words do not quite address is that *babalawos* might *abuse* their role as mouthpieces of Orula, exacting expenditures that go beyond the call of ritual propriety. Indeed, knowing Javier, I suspect that in a less defensive mood he might agree with the view expressed to me by Lázaro, his 34-year-old nephew. Lázaro is initiated to *Santería* and has for a number of years been

waiting for the financial opportunity to be initiated to Ifá, as the oracle had ordained at an earlier ceremony. Working on and off at a shoe shop, his chances looked bleak. I asked him whether he felt that the "moral crisis" of the 1990s had affected Ifá:

> I don't worry about that. My family has a long tradition in the religion, I have trustworthy people. [QUESTION: So not everyone is trustworthy?] Of course not! If you don't know, the *babalawo* tells you "do this," "no, buy this," they argue about the food, or steal the things [that are bought for the ceremony]. [...] Let me explain it to you. The problem is commerce (*el comercio*). Everyone wants to be a *babalawo* and they are all doing their own thing, inventing (*están en lo suyo, inventando*).[30]

Certainly, it is not difficult to find instances that give the truth to Lázaro's suggestion. Just as an example, one might mention the case of Agustín (not his real name), a *babalawo* who had acquired a reputation for having amassed a large number of "godchildren" (by presiding over their initiation) during recent years. Now, although having many godchildren is generally considered a mark of prestige, it is interesting that Agustín has become something of an *ur*-object of criticism in the circles that I moved in. Often recounting cases, and with no special axe to grind as far as I can tell, informants disapproved of the speedy and indiscriminate way in which Agustín recruited his godchildren. The comments of one middle-aged *babalawo* were typical:

> Look, there is Ifá and there is the gang (*la banda*). Agustín and his people get you and if they see you have money they put you in the room [referring to the initiation ceremony] and you come out a *babalawo* no matter what happens. The guy is tremendous, if you don't have the [financial] conditions he won't bother with you. He likes to walk around with all this gold. . . . But he doesn't know much, he just wants to get you into the room!

Although I never got a chance to get Agustín's own views on the matter, I did see him twice and admittedly he fit the stereotype—golden bracelets, dollar beers and all. Certainly one would expect him to deny these accusations, perhaps putting them down to "envy" (*la envidia*), as practitioners often do in such disputes. Yet, for our purposes what is important is that practitioners *are* anxious about so-called "commerce" in Ifá, and that they consider it a sign of the times.[31] The question then becomes why the anxiety about *comercio* and the "trustworthiness" of initiates has become so heightened in the 1990s? Furthermore, to what extent is the rise in the number of *babalawos* relevant, as suggested by Lázaro and the case of Agustín?

An important part of the answer is quite straightforward. Given that monetary transactions have always been a legitimate component of Ifá practice, it is not surprising that, in times of *necesidad*, initiates should be using their influence over clients as a weapon in their own "struggle" for dollars. And insofar as this "struggle" has unpalatable connotations for everyone, it makes sense that *babalawos* too might be tempted to cross normative boundaries, even going as far as to mask their own calculating "inventions" with the alibi of divine stricture. Indeed, to understand the temptations of *comercio* it is crucial to consider how much the financial stakes have risen with dollarisation.[32] The point is that the price-hike in initiation fees since the onset of the Special Period is directly related to the distinction between dollar "haves" and "have nots," as Javier's reference to "dollars from the North" would also suggest.

Indeed, my own ethnographic data confirm this point. During fieldwork I was involved in four full initiation ceremonies and was told details regarding over a dozen more (both Ifá and Santería). With prices ranging from $450 to over $2,000, the pattern was invariably the same: whether the neophyte had been planning years in advance or simply taken advantage of an opportunity that had arisen unexpectedly, every ceremony had been funded either entirely or in large part by a windfall of dollars—in many cases a one-off windfall. In most cases initiations were funded entirely by dollar remittances sent by relatives in the USA, Spain or Italy. The most striking example was occasioned by a Spaniard's brief visit from Madrid with his Cuban wife. He himself was initiated to Ifá together with his brother-in-law, who lives in Havana, and he also paid for the Santería initiation of his wife's teenage daughter and niece, also locals. Although I was not able to ascertain the exact figures, I was told that the whole affair cost the Spaniard $5,000 or $6,000.[33]

The rest of the cases involved hefty amounts of dollars earned in more or less illicit activities (black market deals, hustling foreigners, money smuggled in from a trip abroad, and so forth), and often pooled together with remittances. The case of Arsenio (not his real name) is typical. A talented woodcarver, he had managed in 1996 to obtain a licence to sell his work at a dollar street-market for tourists. "I didn't know much about Ifá then," he told me. There he met a number of *babalawos* and soon he got interested in the religion, as he explained. In 1998 he found more lucrative work at a storage house connected to the port of Havana, where he still worked when I met him in 2000. Here there were good opportunities to do "deals" (as he called them) involving imported containers of foodstuffs. Within a year he had found the money to make Ifá (about $1,200). When I asked why he got initiated, he gave me the standard response: "for health and development" (*por salud y desenvolvimiento*).[34] To my question whether he now practises as a diviner, his reply was more cagey: "no, not yet." Indeed, although he was clearly proud to wear his initiation bracelet, Arsenio did admit that he was not actively involved in worship.

In light of this material, which may be taken as representative of dominant trends in recent years, it may be concluded that the intensification of Ifá "commerce" is intimately related to the emergence of dollar-wielding worshipers in the 1990s. More precisely, if the advent of *comercio* can be said to characterise the *supply* of ritual services in recent years, then one must also appreciate that it has gone hand in hand with changes in the field of *demand*. In quantitative terms, the change in demand is both stark and simple: on the one hand, the pool of potential neophytes has become smaller, with a vast proportion of practitioners—like Lázaro—having no access to the kind of money now required for initiation; on the other hand, the pool has also become deeper, since the income differential between those who can and those who cannot afford initiation fees is massive.

So why then should the demand for expensive ceremonies in this shrunken market be so pronounced—so much as to sustain initiation fees at forbiddingly high levels? Why, in Lázaro's words, does "everyone want to be a *babalawo*"? We saw that *la necesidad* is experienced as an abiding condition *across* the dollar/peso divide, so that even those who have access to dollars feel they do not have enough to meet their "needs." How is it, then, that some of these people consider it feasible to splash out on initiation ceremonies, the cost of which represents many months if not years of comfortable living? Here, I would argue, the phenomenon of *especulación* becomes relevant.

Religious *Especulación*

Considering the inordinately positive associations that initiation has for practitioners, it may not seem surprising that people are willing to spend their precious dollars on Ifá. In fact, when asked to comment, informants were despondent: how, after so much investigation, could I still fail to appreciate the sheer value of initiation? That those who can afford it should go ahead with it requires no explanation: Ifá gives "health and development." Moreover, everybody knows that the benefits of initiation are overwhelming in financial terms too: "Orula compensates you for everything" (*Orula te lo recompensa todo*), people often say, in shorthand reference not only to the fees that *babalawos* can expect to earn by providing ritual services to clients, but also to the more vague metaphysical notion that Ifá consecration enhances one's personal fortune (*iré*) in all senses, including the economic.

Nevertheless, there are grounds for looking a little deeper into the eagerness with which young initiates have entered Ifá in recent years. The relevance of *especulación* in particular, as a factor in the rising demand for Ifá initiation, becomes apparent if one probes the subtext of informants' statements. Return, for example, to Javier's comments on the changes of recent years. It is hardly accidental that he juxtaposes initiates' recent taste for "luxury" and "clothes from abroad" with a contrast between "before," when prospective initiates would spend years saving up for the ceremony, and "now," when people often get initiated "just because the dollars came in." Arguably Javier's tacit association of heightened luxury with a spontaneous or "anti-economic" manner of spending on it corresponds closely to the trademark behaviour of so-called *especuladores*. Indeed, more explicit references to *especulación* do feature prominently in practitioners' commentaries on the new breed of dollar-wielding initiates, often coming as part of a cluster of criticisms regarding, for example, the rise of criminality among the new generation of *babalawos*. Nor are such comments just the product of cantankerous or "envious" minds. Much like Agustín or Arsenio, plenty of initiates—especially the younger ones—very much fit the bill. Not only do many of them lead just the showy, "hard fun" lifestyle associated with *especulación*, but, more significantly perhaps, they also give the impression that for them being *babalawos* is an *ingredient* of that lifestyle. One might go as far as to say that among many inner-city dwellers, Ifá initiation has come to acquire a new kind of street-credibility as the kind of thing one can show off, not unlike a motorbike, gold accessories, or cool Nike gear.

As an indicator consider the use of initiation insignia. As already mentioned, at initiation *babalawos* are given a consecrated bracelet (*iddé*) of green and yellow beads, which they are encouraged to wear permanently as a mark of their new status as *babalawos*. Now, traditionally bracelets for such daily use have a single line of beads, while bracelets intended for certain ceremonial purposes may be much thicker, consisting of a "bunch" of interwoven beaded strings (*iddé de mazo*). Interestingly, however, in recent years it has become increasingly common for young *babalawos* to use their *iddé de mazo* as permanent initiation insignia, a practice much derided by people like Javier. "It's their way of 'speculating' (*su forma de especular*); they want everyone to know that they are *babalawos*," an uninitiated friend of mine observed. And, sure enough, *iddé de mazo* are very much on show "on the street" in Havana these days, not least in the dollar bars.

For purposes of the present argument, it is crucial to note the way in which the *especulador's* macho desire for luxury resonates with the ethos of Ifá, which emphasises the regal dignity of *babalawos* as priests of Orula. This is not only a matter of the character of Ifá initiation itself, as an occasion for men to "live it up" in celebration of the "birth of a king." As we saw earlier, in *especulación* the desire for luxury is an integral expression of the impulse to "live for the moment," since *especuladores'* disregard for *la necesidad*, macho and momentary, is made visible in the conspicuous magnitude of expenditure. This connection—between high expenditure and "the moment"—is integral also to the divinatory logic of Ifá worship. As we have seen, practitioners' obligation to the deities in general—and Orula in particular—is expressed in terms of a series of ceremonious expenditures, each of which is made necessary through the temporary (or "momentary" if you like) commands of the oracle. Furthermore, practitioners' standing within the cult depends largely on their position on an escalator of expenditure—from uninitiated clients' humble offerings, to the "kingly" extremes of full initiation—, and the movement of the escalator, so to speak, is dictated by Orula's oracular demands, which are as unpredictable as they are compelling.

This parallel provides an insight into why *habaneros* who lead the kind of lifestyle associated with *especulación* find the regal prestige of Ifá so attractive. As already argued above, *especulación* presents a paradox: as an attempt to keep "need" and "struggle" at arm's length by revelling "for the moment," *especuladores* heroically subvert mainstream ideological strictures; but falling straight back into *necesidad* once the cash is spent, they are as vulnerable as the moment of their desire is short. Ifá arguably provides a way out of this paradox. On the one hand, it furnishes a recognisably prestigious arena for just the kind of conspicuous consumption "for the moment" that *especuladores* thrive on. For, while the ostentatious character of the *especulador's* spending is well suited to the regal opulence of Ifá worship, the wilfully unplanned expenditures of *especulación* can be similarly accommodated to the divinatory logic of Ifá worship, insofar as this too is premised on the unpredictable character of the oracle's prescriptions. On the other hand, it is understood that—unlike dollar bar-outings, motorbikes, or gold bracelets—Ifá initiation bestows a *permanent transformation* on those who undergo it. Rather than just behaving *as if* they were kings, *especuladores* who become *babalawos* are re-borne *as* kings, through consecration. "Ifá gives you *fundamento* in life," initiates explain, the term understood both in the colloquial sense as "foundation"—with its connotations of permanence—, and in a technical sense as a synonym for consecration. Effectively, Ifá provides a way for *especuladores* to make virtue of their *necesidad*, by turning the logic of *especulación* on its head. While the gestures of "living for the moment" are ultimately an index of the *especulador's* vulnerability, initiation to Ifá provides a way of rendering those same gestures as trappings of a permanent regal status. Indeed, if *babalawos* have always displayed the permanence of their transformed status by means of their initiation-bracelets, it is indicative that *especuladores* should render just these insignia as conspicuous as possible.

Conclusion

I have sought in this article to shed some light on the popularity of Ifá during the crisis of 1990s Cuba by looking mainly at issues relating to money and the consumption of ritual services, emphasising some of the key transformations that Ifá has undergone as part of the process of its rise. In a rather obvious way these results make sense. Insofar as *habaneros'* concern with money and its expenditure has indexed momentous transformations in Cuban society (with abiding notions of "need" and "struggle" in the post-Soviet era), it is hardly surprising that by focusing on these issues we should have come to gauge key transformations in cult practice also. Indeed, with its connotations of continuity, the notion of "transformation" takes the parallel further. Just as *habaneros'* complex stance with regard to money and *la necesidad* has its roots in the "before" of discourse (when "everyone had enough"), so the intensified trends towards *comercio* and *especulación* in Ifá are sustainable, as argued here, because they are congruous with the way initiates have "always" done things.

Nevertheless, there is a crucial slippage in the analogy between Ifá and *especulación*, one that helps explain the ambivalence with which many practitioners view the phenomenon of "religious *especulación*." For there is a conflict between the *especulador's* urge to spend indulgently on his *own* desire for luxury, and the *babalawo's* commitment to spend luxuriously on the *deities'* oracular demands. Crudely put, the difference is between self-assertive vanity and submissive dignity. Indeed, there is considerable unease among some *babalawos* about the religious credentials of the new *babalawos-especuladores*, as may be gleaned from some of the quotes from my informants. Given the respect that *babalawos* feel they owe to each other, this unease is expressed mainly through innuendo. But, in tenor, practitioners' comments often intimate doubts as to whether those *babalawos* who like to parade their chunky *iddé*, and spend their days doing deals and "caning" dollar beers, are entirely dedicated to "serving Orula," not least in view of the expectations placed on young initiates in terms of their commitment to acquiring ritual expertise. And, as Arsenio's half-embarrassed admission that he did "not yet" practise Ifá actively would indicate, this kind of conflict of ends is by no means a fiction.

Notes

Martin Holbraad is R. A. Butler Research Fellow at Pembroke College, University of Cambridge.
*The author is grateful to the Economic and Social Research Council for funding his fieldwork, and to the Centro de Antropología for its hospitality in Havana.

[1]S. Day et al. (eds.), *Lilies of the Field: Marginal People Who Live for the Moment* (Boulder, 1999).

[2]For a definitive study of this process, see G. Brandon, *Santeria from Africa to the New World: The Dead Sell Memories* (Bloomington and Indianapolis, 1993).

[3]Although quantitative data are unavailable, it is probably fair to say that a large proportion of recent Protestant converts come from non-white and less well-heeled parts of Cuban society, which is also the traditional constituency of the practitioners of Afro-Cuban cults.

[4]For an indication of how politicised this quantitative question still is in Cuba, see Hagedorn's extract from her interview with María Teresa Linares (a leading Cuban folklorist), which appears as part of Hagedorn's pioneering study of Afro-Cuban music and religion in socialist Cuba; K. J. Hagedorn, *Divine Utterances: the Performance of Afro-Cuban Santería* (Washington and London, 2001), pp. 173–9. For a couple of tentative (and rather vague) estimates in recent Cuban research, see A. Díaz Cerveto and A. C. Perera Pintado, *La religiosidad en la sociedad cubana* (La Habana, 1997), and J. Ramírez Calzadilla and O. Pérez Cruz, *La religión en los jóvenes cubanos* (La Habana, 1997).

[5]Initiation into the cult of Ifá engenders series of ritual kin ties. Potential neophytes are brought into the cult (so as to "become Ifá," as initiation is referred to— *hacerse Ifá*), by soliciting the favour of an already established initiate in exchange for money, various ritual goods and services and, in principle, life-long respect and subordination. This ritualised relationship between the neophyte and the presiding initiate is conceived in terms of godparenthood: godchild (*ahijado*) to godfather (*padrino*). Once initiated, a neophyte can himself become godfather to further recruits, who then become great-godchildren to his own godfather. In this way cult membership is organised in terms of ritual lineages (referred to as *ramas*—branches), which can be extended indefinitely across successive generations. Ritual lineages also extend horizontally since initiates who share a godfather become ritual siblings (*abbures*), and are considered to owe each other mutual support in both ritual and mundane contexts.

[6]S. E. Eckstein, *Back from the Future: Cuba Under Castro* (Princeton, 1994), pp. 31–59, A. Kapcia, *Cuba: Island of Dreams* (Oxford, 2000), pp. 203–4, H. Thomas, *Cuba: The Pursuit of Freedom* (London, 2001), pp. 1011–2, cf. W. M. LeoGrande and J. M. Thomas, "Cuba's Quest for Economic Independence," *Journal of Latin American Studies*, vol. 34 (2002), pp. 325–63.

[7]Eckstein, *Back from the Future*, p. 93.

[8]L. Barberia, "Remittances to Cuba: An Evaluation of Cuban and US Government Policy Measures," http://web.mit.edu/cis/www/migration/pubs/rrwp/15_remittances.pdf. [cited 15 February 2003]

[9]On concepts of "necesidad" in Mexico see Miguel Díaz Barriga, "*Necesidad*: Notes on the Discourses of Urban Politics in the Ajusco Foothills of Mexico City," *American Ethnologist*, Vol. 23, part 2 (1996), pp. 291–310.

[10]For a comparison with a post-socialist case, see Lemon's account of "currency apartheid" in 1990s Russia (Alaina Lemon, "'Your Eyes are Green Like

Dollars': Counterfeit Cash, National Substance, and Currency Apartheid in 1990s Russia," *Cultural Anthropology*, vol. 13 part 1 (1998), pp. 22–55.

[11]J. F. Pérez-López, *Cuba's Second Economy: From Behind the Scenes to Center Stage* (New Brunswick, 1995), p. 88.

[12]For a subtle treatment of a similar dilemma with respect to the notion of "scrounging" among working-class people in N. Ireland, see Leo Howe, "Where is the Culture in the 'Culture of Poverty?'," *Cambridge Anthropology*, vol. 20. part 1–2 (1998), pp. 66–91.

[13]O. Lewis, *La Vida: A Puerto Rican Family in the Culture of Poverty—San Juan and New York* (London, 1965), p. xliv.

[14]Maurice Bloch, "Cognition to Ideology," in his *Ritual, History and Power: Selected Papers in Anthropology* (London, 1989), and M. Bloch, *From Prey into Hunter* (Cambridge, 1992).

[15]Maurice Bloch and Jonathan Parry, "Introduction," in Jonathan Parry and Maurice Bloch (eds.), *Money and the Morality of Exchange* (Cambridge, 1989).

[16]Michael Stewart, "'Brothers' and 'Orphans': Images of Equality among Hungarian Rom," in S. Day et al. (eds.), *Lilies of the Field*, p. 41, cf. Michael Stewart, "A Passion for Money: Gambling, Luck and the Ambiguities of Money amongst Hungarian Gypsies," *Terrain*, vol. 23 (1994), pp. 45–62.

[17]Brandon, *Santeria from Africa to the New World*, pp. 59–99.

[18]Brandon, *Santeria from Africa to the New World*, pp. 82–5, Hagedorn, *Divine Utterances*, pp. 173–202, cf. R. Moore, *Nationalising Blackness: Afrocubanismo and Artistic Revolution in Havana, 1920–1940* (Pittsburgh, 1997).

[19]A. Argüelles and I. Hodge, *Los llamados cultos sincréticos y el espiritismo* (La Habana, 1991), pp. 141–71, Natalia Bolívar, "El legado africano en Cuba," *Papers*, vol. 52 (1997), p. 165, Teresita Pedraza, "'This Too Shall Pass': Religion in Cuba, Resistance and Endurance," *Cuban Studies*, vol. 28 (1998), pp. 16–39.

[20]Eckstein, *Back from the Future*, p. 122, Rafael L. López Valdéz, "Los Orishas *resuelven*. Antropocentrismo y redes informales en los sistemas religiosos de origen africano en Cuba," in A. Núñes Jiménez (ed.), *Conferencia Internacional Presencia de Africa en América* (La Habana, 1995), p. 95.

[21]L. Zamora, *El culto de San Lázaro en Cuba* (La Habana, 2000), p. 245. The study was carried out by members of the Department for Socioreligious Studies (Academy of Sciences of Cuba). It should be noted that the pilgrimages that these findings describe involve ordinary Catholic devotees as well as practitioners of Afro-Cuban cults, although, as Zamora notes, the Afro-Cuban element is very pronounced (*Ibid.* pp. 259–62).

[22]Cerveto and Perera Pintado, *La religiosidad en la sociedad cubana*, p. 18, cf. Ramírez Calzadilla and Pérez Cruz, *La religión en los jóvenes cubanos*. For contrasting data from the 1980s see Argüelles and Hodge, *Los llamados cultos sincréticos y el espiritismo*, pp. 150–8.

[23]In Santería initiation—usually a prerequisite for Ifá initiation—the neophyte is required to spend a year dressed only in white.

[24]P. Schwab, *Cuba: Confronting the US Embargo* (London, 1999), p. 117, cf. Rhoda Rabkin, "Ideological Responses to the Era of Socialist Crisis," *Cuban Studies* 22 (1992), pp. 31–49, Aurelio Alonso Tejada, "Catolicismo, política y cambio en la realidad cubana actual," *Temas*, vol. 4 (1995), pp. 23–32.

[25]J. M. Kirk, *Between God and the Party: Religion and Politics in Revolutionary Cuba* (Tampa, 1989), Pedraza, "'This Too Shall Pass,'" pp. 20–24, Schwab, *Cuba*, pp. 103–31.

[26]Juan M. del Aguila, "The Party, the Fourth Congress, and the Process of Counter-reform," *Cuban Studies* 23 (1993), pp. 71–90, Fransisco León, "Socialism and *socialismo*: Social Actors and Economic Change in 1990s Cuba," in Miguel A. Centeno and Mauricio Font (eds.), *Toward a New Cuba? Legacies of a Revolution* (Boulder, 1997).

[27]Alejandro de la Fuente and Laurence Glasco, "Are Blacks 'Getting out of Control?' Racial Attitudes, Revolution, and Political Transition in Cuba," in Centeno and Font (eds.), *Toward a New Cuba?*, Juan A. Alvarado Ramos, "Relaciones raciales en Cuba. Notas de investigación," *Temas* 7 (1996), pp. 37–43. It is indicative that a large proportion of the *balseros* (rafters), whose mass exodus towards Florida in the summer of 1994 probably marked the most tense period of the 1990s in terms of popular unrest, were Afro-Cubans (see Holly Ackerman, "The *Balsero* Phenomenon: 1991–1994," *Cuban Studies*, vol. 26 (1996), pp. 169–200). Indeed, many of the accounts of that fateful summer told to me by relatives and friends of the departed included references to hastily organised Santería rituals, mostly dedicated to Yemayá and Olokun, goddess of the sea and deity of deep waters respectively.

[28]Javier's rhetorical figures are well on target. For his own initiation in 1967, he was charged 700 pesos in fees (*derecho*) by the initiates who conducted the ceremony. His son Javierito, initiated in 1988, paid 1,800 pesos. In 2000 the going rate for Cubans was quoted in dollars at roughly $300 (equivalent to 7,800 pesos at the time). Note that these figures do not include the even more substantial costs involved in purchasing numerous sacrificial animals, food and drink for the week-long ceremony and ritual paraphernalia of various sorts.

[29]Elegguá is the trickster deity of the Yoruba pantheon, thought of as the gods' messenger.

[30]The slang term "inventar" refers to improvised (usually illicit) ways of making money, or "resolving problems," as *habaneros* like to say more generally.

[31]Note that Ifá "commerce" is not a new phenomenon. Guanche, for example, recounts similar concerns in pre-Revolutionary times (J. Guanche, *Procesos etnoculturales de Cuba* (La Habana, 1983), pp. 362–4, cf. Stephan Palmié, "Against Syncretism: 'Africanizing' and 'Cubanizing' Discourses in North American Òrìsà-Worship," in Richard Fardon (ed.), *Counterworks: Managing the Diversity of Knowledge* (London, 1995), p. 79). Nevertheless, the present argument relies on the idea that the inordinate price-hike of recent years, as well as the rising number of new initiates, suggests that "commerce" has become increasingly prevalent and important.

[32]This argument on *comercio* is offered as an addition to a well-established body of literature on similar phenomena in other ethnographic regions; see C. C. Taylor, *Milk, Honey and Money. Changing Concepts in Rwandan Healing* (Washington, 1992), Christian Krohn-Hansen, "Magic, Money and Alterity Among Dominicans," *Social Anthropology*, vol. 3, part 2 (1995), pp. 128–46, Judith Farquar, "Market Magic: Getting Rich and Getting Personal in Medicine After Mao," *American Ethnologist*, vol. 23:2 (1996), pp. 239–57, Laurel Kendall, "Korean Shamans and the Spirits of Capitalism," *American Anthropologist* vol. 98 (1996), pp. 512–27, Jean

Comaroff and John L. Comaroff, "Occult Economies and the Violence of Abstraction: Notes from the South African Postcolony," *American Ethnologist* vol. 26:2 (1998), pp. 279–303.

[33]The increasing influx of foreigners (as well as Cuban-Americans) who wish to be initiated in Cuba has also contributed to the recent price-hike. Some initiates now dedicate themselves entirely to these lucrative ceremonies (cf. Hagedorn, *Divine Utterances*, pp. 219–33).

[34]"Desenvolvimiento" is ordinarily translated from the Spanish as "development" or "disentanglement." In cult circles in Cuba, however, the term is habitually used to refer to an improvement in one's financial fortunes (such as a better job or a windfall of money).

SECTION TEN:
THE CHALLENGES OF
FREEDOM AND LIBERTY

Introduction

The early decades of the post-emancipation period were filled with deep disappointment and frequent frustrations for the African Diaspora community. New laws were introduced and old ones were revived in many former slave societies to impede the African Diaspora populations from achieving their desired hope of self-improvement and, eventually, self-determination. Many African Diaspora populations were frequently forced to create and maintain their own separate social, economic, and even political institutions since they were not readily accepted or encouraged to assimilate fully into the mainstream of the societal and socioeconomic structure.

While there is a great body of literature that covers this important post-emancipation period, there are few works that seek to capture the overall African Diaspora spirit and that challenged and confronted the leading thinkers and activists across the Diaspora during the late part of the nineteenth and early twentieth centuries. The leaders and proponents of African Diaspora in Brazil, the Caribbean, Europe, and the United States sought to have their views heard and their messages articulated before a world unaccustomed to most of these views. The accompanying activities in a real sense were intended to rehabilitate the conventional thinking about Africa and Africans. However, very few within the African Diaspora responded to these ideas. Although the Black nationalist message was largely ignored by the majority within the African Diaspora communities, their ideas often prompted improvements that eventually benefited the wider African Diaspora society.

In this tenth section, seven essays have been selected that survey this era of new consciousness for many within the African Diaspora community. These articles carefully document the evolution of Black nationalism and Pan-Africanism. One of the very interesting movements of Africans within the Diaspora experience was the gallant Back-to-Africa effort of those who were born away from the motherland but decided to settle in Africa. In part, the struggle to sustain and develop what became the West African Republic of Liberia was the result of the emerging views of Black Nationalism and Pan-Africanism. This segment begins with a review of the work of one of the outstanding pioneers in the effort to create the enclave that would become a nation for Africans. The early settlement was organized by the American Colonization Society, which was made up mostly of white Americans, but the eventual tasks of making the effort successful were in the hands of persons of African descent such as Elijah Johnson, Lott Cary,

Daniel Coker, Joseph J. Roberts, Edward W. Blyden, John B. Russwurm and many others. Carl Patrick Burrowes described the significant role of Hilary Teage, one of the early journalists in Liberia and editor of the *Liberian Herald* from 1834 to 1850. Burrowes examined the major themes that Teage used in motivating his readers and inspiring greater confidence in the development of this ambitious experiment.

Burrowes was formerly Chairperson of the Communications Department at Morgan State University, and Associate Professor of Mass Communications in the School of Communications at Howard University. He worked in Liberia and has written extensively on the Liberian experience. He has co-authored, with Amos Beyan and Elwood Dunn, *The Historical Dictionary of Liberia* (2000) and wrote *The Americo-Liberian Ruling Class and Other Myths: A Critique* (1989).

The second narrative in this section was authored by one of the most influential spokespersons for African Americans during the late nineteenth century, Booker T. Washington. Washington became well known as a result of his particular views, approach, and successful work at the Tuskegee Institute in Alabama; his 1895 Atlanta Exposition address, which appealed to southern whites; and his popular autobiographical work *Up From Slavery* (1900). Born in Virginia on April 5, 1856, he was educated at Hampton Institute and twenty years later became principal of Tuskegee where he introduced his version of Black nationalist and Pan-African ideas. These segments recall his early days, incorporate some of his views and challenges, and feature his famous Atlanta speech.

The third narrative is new to this edition and deals with the many issues of Pan-Africanism. It is authored by Jeremiah I. Dibua, who is professor of History at Morgan State University and coordinator of the Department of History's Graduate Program. He has researched and written extensively on various African historical and political developments. He studied in Nigeria and received his B.A and M.A. from the University of Ibadan and his Ph.D. from the University of Benin. His most recent published work is *Modernization and the Crisis of Development in Africa: The Nigerian Experience* (2006).

Colin Legum was editor of the London Observer when he prepared "Back to Africa, 1958–1962." This easily readable essay explores the tensions that engulfed the Pan-African movement when greater attention was being focused on political developments in the African motherland during the period of early African political independence. This essay is taken from Legum's *Pan-Africanism: A Short Political Guide* (1965), still one of the best texts for introducing students to the major issues involved in the Pan-African movement. Legum is probably the most prolific writer included in this volume, having authored or edited more than thirty publications. His publications include *South Africa, The Early Years* (1949), *Must We Lose Africa?* (1954), *Nationalist Movements and Pan-Africanism* (1963), *Ethiopia, The Fall of Haile Selassie* (1975), *Africa in the 1980s* (1979), *Vorster's Gamble for Africa* (1976), *The Battlefronts of Southern Africa* (1988), and *The Horn of Africa* (1992).

The fifth essay is Tony Martin's "Marcus Garvey, The Caribbean and the Struggle for Black Jamaican Nationhood." This sweeping view of Garvey places his activities at the center of three distinct struggles: Black nationalism, Pan-Africanism, and Caribbean nationhood. Martin is one of the leading authorities on the significance of Garvey's message and its contributions to the struggle of African persons between World Wars I and II. Martin is Professor of Black Studies at Wellesley College in Massachusetts, and he also taught at the Universities of Minnesota and Michigan, Brandeis University, Colorado College, St. Mary's College and the Cipriani Labour College in Trinidad. He has published *Literary Garveyism: Garvey, Black Arts and the Harlem Renaissance* (1983), *The Pan-African Connection* (1983, 1984), *Marcus Garvey Hero: A First Bibliography (1983)*, *Race First: The Ideological and Organizational Struggles of Marcus Garvey and the Universal Negro Improvement Association* (1976, 1986), *The Caribbean and Africa* (1981), *Amy Ashwood Garvey, Pan Africanist* (1988), and *African Fundamentalism: A Literary and Cultural Anthology of Garvey's Harlem Renaissance* (1991).

The sixth reading in this section is taken from selected passages of Malcolm X's 1964 autobiography, published with the collaborative efforts of Alex Haley, a decade before the publication of Haley's own celebrated bestseller, *Roots, An American Saga* (1974). Malcolm X's narrative has long been considered one of the classics of African American literature. The honest, courageous, and independent-minded thinking and views expressed in its pages capture the times, mood, and struggles of the Civil Rights period. These passages also give vivid insights into the rationale that motivated one of the most charismatic Black nationalists of the twentieth century anywhere in the Diaspora. These paragraphs are selected excerpts from four chapters: one, sixteen, eighteen, and nineteen. They highlight many of the major influences and changes in Malcolm X's life. Just months after the publication of his autobiography, Malcolm X was assassinated in New York City on February 21,1965. Although he had become well known before his death as a spokesperson for the Nation of Islam (until his break with that organization in March 1964), his sudden death made him into a martyr, especially throughout the African American community. An even larger segment of America's population desired to know more about his life, his ideas, and the circumstances surrounding his death. However, during his years as a leading spokesperson on Black nationalist ideas, Malcolm X had written very little but had made countless speeches. The demand warranted the publication of a new book *Malcolm X Speaks* (1965). This is a collection of most of his recorded speeches after his break with the Nation of Islam. These speeches expand on certain themes of his autobiography.

The seventh and final essay is W. Arthur Lewis's "Colonial Relations." Lewis was a leading economist on Colonialism who won the 1974 Nobel Prize in Economics, becoming the first person of African descent to win a Nobel Prize in a field other than Peace. He was educated in his homeland of St. Lucia in the eastern Caribbean and earned his B. Sc. (1937) and Ph.D. (1940) in Industrial Economics from the University of Manchester in the United Kingdom, where he became a full professor in 1948. He received the Nobel Prize for his pioneering research into economic development research with particular consideration of the problems of developing countries, consisting of two models that describe and explain the problems of developing countries. This work was first published in his 1954 *The Theory of Economic Growth*. He joined the faculty of Princeton University in 1963 during the same year he was knighted by Queen Elizabeth and continued at Princeton University until his retirement in 1983.

"In Common with Colored Men, I Have Certain Sentiments": Black Nationalism and Hilary Teage of the *Liberia Herald*

Carl Patrick Burrowes

As editor of the Liberia Herald *from 1835 to 1850, Hilary Teage exerted a profound influence on events in Liberia and his reputation reverberated among blacks across the Atlantic. In addition to writing Liberia's declaration of independence, he published over 100 articles, editorials, poems, sermons and speeches. Three persistent and pervasive themes in Teage's writings were: aesthetic romanticism; black nationalism, an ideology that emerged during the era of the early American republic; and liberal republicanism, with its emphasis on empirical analysis and limited government.*

Born in 1805 at the lowest rung of Virginia slave society, Hilary Teage emigrated at age 17 to West Africa where he went on—in the words of one of his contemporaries—to make the single greatest personal contribution to the "framing and establishment" of the Republic of Liberia. Founded in 1820, Liberia was operated by the American Colonization Society (ACS), an organization of powerful and influential whites, as a colony for American free blacks until 1847, when the repatriates declared their independence.

While Liberia was a colony, it encompassed nine scattered coastal towns with a population of 2,390. Only 27 percent of the people were locally born, including some indigenous persons who had adopted Liberian ways. By 1868, the country had expanded to encompass a two-mile strip along the coast, and the population had increased to 15,000, consisting of 12,000 emigrants and 3,000 indigenous Africans. Through the end of the 19th century, the country attracted some 19,000 blacks from various parts of Africa and its Diaspora. Over this commonwealth, Teage cast a long shadow, as Baptist minister, merchant, elected official, president of the Liberia Lyceum, and especially as editor of the *Herald* (1835–1850), which he used to spearhead the drive for Liberia's independence.

In serving as editor of the *Liberia Herald* for 15 years, Teage left a detailed, colorful and rare record of journalistic conditions in 19th century Africa. In addition, he had what probably was the longest journalism career of any black in the antebellum era. In contrast, John B. Russwurm, who proceeded Teage as editor of the *Herald* and is better known for having co-founded the first African American newspaper *(Freedom's Journal)* had a journalistic career of seven years. Even Samuel Cornish, who edited four newspapers—a record for any African American during that period—only served a combined five years and two months in journalism.

Extended the Enlightenment to Africa

More important than longevity of service, Teage made a distinctive intellectual contribution by applying Enlightenment ideas to the black race and extending them to the continent of Africa, both of which had been viewed as beyond the scope of the humanities. Also evident in his writings are all the defining elements of an ideology known as black nationalism.

As the author of Liberia's declaration of independence, Teage was called "the Jefferson of Liberia," a comparison that was intended to be flattering but nonetheless was diminutive because it consigned him to the shadows of a republican slaveholder, without recognition for his own distinctive contribution to the struggle for human liberty. Despite Teage's myriad accomplishments, his ideas, his contributions and his reputation have faded over the years, like the newsprint through which they were realized.

The Search for a Recurring Pattern

This study seeks to rescue Teage from undeserved obscurity by providing a sketch of his life, along with an analysis of a major theme in his writings. Data was assembled by examining every surviving issue of five periodicals that reported intensively on 19th century Liberia, along with a similarly exhaustive examination of letters from African American repatriates to their relatives, friends and former masters in the United States in two published collections. In addition to many items by a variety of authors on the life of Teage, this search process uncovered 112 substantive documents written by the subject, including 71 news articles and editorials, six poems, two sermons, two major speeches, a treatise on self-government by blacks, and—his magnum opus—Liberia's declaration of independence.

Among his works that apparently did not survive were a journal in which he kept records of his travels, a contemplated history of Liberia and copies of sermons. Some 20 research collections with holdings on African colonization, Liberia and Baptist history were searched, of which eight yielded significant primary materials. Sources were selected on the basis of availability, relevance and reliability. To guard against unconscious or deliberate biases, each document or set of documents was checked against others drawn from different individual, political and institutional sources.

But this study goes beyond a recounting of events to concern itself with "the thought within them" which, as journalism historian James Carey has suggested, should be the goal of cultural historians. To achieve this objective, Teage's writings were subjected to "discourse analysis," meaning the search "to uncover the codes, constructions, cultural assumptions, connotations, values, and beliefs embedded in the text by locating correspondences between a text and social structures and identities, noting recurring patterns, such as the repetition of certain themes, phrases, rhetoric, and so on in the discourse."

Black Nationalism a Consistent Theme

One persistent and pervasive theme uncovered in Teage's writings was black nationalism. This ideology emerged during the era of the early American republic, when the contradiction between the revolutionary sentiments of America's founders and their willingness to compromise with slavery engendered a black reaction against white rejection, a sense of racial identity and a belief that people of African descent share a historical mission. In the early 19th century, the phrase "black nationalism" was not used to describe what was then an emerging phenomenon; nonetheless a sense of racial identification among blacks was common. When the American Colonization Society's president wrote Teage in 1841 to complain about an "offensive" article in the *Herald*, for example, the editor responded:

> In common with colored men, I have certain sentiments . . . I should be altogether un-worthy of your confidence and respect, if I should at any time forget for a moment that this is my indefeasible right, or so base and mean-spirited as not to claim to exercise it whenever circumstances should demand it.

Undergirding this response was the essence of black nationalism, evident in his reference to "certain sentiments" that he shared with other people of color. Given the anomalous situation of African Americans, consisting of geographic dispersal across the country, coupled with legal segregation from others on the basis of race, their "nationalism" has always been racially defined,

"premised on the assumption that membership in a race could function as the basis of a national identity." Because of its racial composition, black nationalism easily elides into the kindred ideology of pan-Africanism which, in its broadest interpretation, refers to a "general sense of sympathy and mutual supportiveness among Africans and peoples of African descent."

Like other nationalisms, however, black nationalism is anchored in the belief among a group of people that they are "bound together by ties of kinship, history and heritage," which distinguishes them from others by their commonly held beliefs, behaviors and ways of thinking. As a belief system that was consciously elaborated during a time of social strain and, over time, achieved integration, black nationalism has all the characteristics of an "ideology," as defined by anthropologist Clifford Geertz, who contributed considerably to focusing scholarly attention on the concept during the past several decades.

Rising in the State of Being

Teage was born in 1805 to slave parents on a plantation in Goochland County, Virginia, halfway between Richmond and Charlottesville, not far from the home of Thomas Jefferson. Two years later, his artisan father, Colin, was sold to the owners of a saddle and harness factory in Richmond, a move that significantly widened the family's vistas. By 1819, Colin had paid $1,300 to purchase his family of three and, one year later, held property in Henrico County, outside the city limits.

In Richmond, the Teage family attended the racially mixed but segregated First Baptist Church, where in 1815 a tri-weekly night school was organized for about 17 leading black members, including Colin. Several white Baptist tradesmen and merchants, who had supported Colin in his quest for manumission and literacy skills, also assisted in the creation of the Richmond African Baptist Missionary Society in 1815 and the ACS Richmond auxiliary in 1823. This was the context in which Colin opted in 1821 to become a missionary to Africa, taking his wife, Frances; Hilary, then age 16, and a 15-year-old daughter, Colinette, all of whom were literate.

Two years before leaving for Africa, Hilary and his sister were described as having "been to school considerably." Their education was organized in part by William Crane, a fellow Baptist and native of Newark, New Jersey, who had coordinated a night school for their father and other black adults. At this time, schooling for blacks was frowned upon in Virginia, and there were no public schools, even for whites. The curriculum of private schools in Richmond then included Latin, Greek, mathematics, history, geography and natural philosophy. Hilary later showed some familiarity with all of these subjects.

Teage brought considerable intellectual powers and energy to his various pursuits, including a trading business, which he inherited after his father's death in 1838 and quickly expanded. By 1845 he owned five buildings in Monrovia, was earning an annual commission of $7,000, and had five warehouses along the coast worth $30,000, with about $20,000 in trade stock. Between 1827 and 1853, he owned at least eight vessels that were engaged in the West African coasting trade..

However, his commercial fortunes declined in the late 1840s, as he poured his energies into the campaign for independence.. Teage was elected colonial secretary in 1835, a member of the colonial council and commissioner for Montserrado County five years later, member of the Constitutional Convention in 1847, and senator for Montserrado County one year later. In addition, he served as attorney general (1850–51) and secretary of state (1852–1853), with a stint in May 1852 as acting chief executive, while President Joseph Jenkins Roberts was abroad..

Pride of Place Among Liberian Intellectuals

During the crucial period of 1830 to 1847, when Liberia moved from being a colony to a republic, Teage occupied—by virtue of his age, activities and early arrival in the colony—pride of place among local intellectuals. His contemporaries in 1845 elected him the first president of the Liberia Lyceum, which until about 1850 sponsored public speeches and debates as a means of energizing and educating the larger community.. He was said to have been "remarkable for his abilities, his acquisitions and his influence,". "one of the ablest and best read men in Liberia,". and one of Liberia's "brightest and most cultivated intellects.". West African writer Edward Wilmot Blyden (who would come to be better known through the hundreds of essays and countless letters he wrote to a large and influential circle of correspondents in Africa, England and the United States) described Teage as having "genius.".

As pastor of the Providence Baptist Church in Monrovia, Teage filled his days with such routine ministerial cares as preaching, ordaining and meeting with his flock and other clergymen. From his warehouse on the riverfront, he had a direct view of the St. Paul River, which was also the site on many Sundays of the deep immersion baptisms preferred by emigrants from the South. In 1848 alone, he baptized 61 people—more than any other minister in the country.. Teage was what sociologist Antonio Gramsci termed an "organic intellectual," being the thinking and organizing element of a particular social group. More than a mere eloquent mover of feelings on a momentary basis, he was a "permanent persuader.".

Although Teage was rigid in his commitment to the cause of republicanism and repatriation, he displayed none of the acerbity and self-righteousness that characterizes many ideologues.

A traveling companion on a sea trip from the United States to Liberia noted, "He was never disposed to urge his opinions upon others, well knowing that the best and most thorough converts to the truth usually become such through the force of their own reflections and convictions.". He described Teage as "highly accomplished in his manners, very agreeable, various, and winning in his conversations; of a kind, obliging and generous disposition, and earnestly intent upon building up the cause of civilization and Christianity in Africa." About Teage's personality, he said, "Amid trying reverses in his pecuniary affairs his vivacity and cheerfulness continued without abatement.".

Teage As Romantic Empiricist

Teage's tenure as editor of the *Liberia Herald* began in 1835, following the resignation of John B. Russwurm, the paper's founding editor and one of the first blacks to graduate from an American college.. Four years later, Teage acquired ownership of the paper from the ACS, which led the editor of the rival *Luminary* to comment, "We speak advisedly when we say that the editor, who is also publisher and proprietor, is making new and judicious effort to improve it in every respect.". In an editorial, Teage described the newspaper office as quaint and somewhat rustic:

> a little sooty apartment of six by eight. Beneath (the editor's) dingy foolscap a portion of deal lies supinely on an empty barrel. A few odds and ends of books and newspapers lie in hopeless confusion around. At his side an inkstand, not of china, nor of bronze, but the small end of a cow's horn, on his left a quiver of quills rifled from the upper surface of a porcupine. . . . The walls are duly chalked, not with mechanical design, nor geometrical diagrams, but with mathematical momentos of the kroos. of potatoes of which he has relieved the farmer. This is his blotter; ledger, he keeps none..

True to the temper of the times, Teage's writing showed the impact of two dominant intellectual orientations. On the one hand, his social perspective was anchored by 18th century liberal republicanism, with its emphasis on empirical analysis, free enterprise economics and limited government. On the other hand, his aesthetic was linked to romanticism, the leading Western literary trend from about 1789 to 1839.. His commitment to objectivity was rooted in an empiricist theory of knowledge—then emerging as the *sine qua non* of scientific thought. As Teage explained in an 1845 lecture to the Lyceum, "Knowledge is derived from without. After all that has been said about innate ideas and principles, it will, I think, be no easy matter for anyone to show, that we have one single idea that we did not originally receive by perception or sensation." Later he added: "The object of the modern philosophy is to collect facts, unlike the ancient which was to explain phenomena."

In keeping with his scientific cast of mind, Teage's reports in the Herald were detailed and colorful. He distinguished between various types of local termites on the basis of physical characteristics and used a microscope to scrutinize such oddities as the "witch" recovered by a traditional African healer. Among English-language writers, he admired the "vigor, precision or copiousness" of John Milton, Edmund Burke, Sir Isaac Newton, Sir James Hall, and "the almost immortals that signed the Declaration of American Independence." Teage was modernist even in his choice of type for the newspaper, which consisted of pica and bourgeois faces, in contrast to the Old English and various classical faces favored by other editors of the *Herald*.

Eclectic, Sardonic and Witty

Concerning aesthetics, he was eclectic, finding value and pleasure in sources as diverse as American oratory, African cuisine and 18th century British poetry. His own poetry, mostly on nature and patriotic themes, contained many allusions to Africa's past grandeur. One of the poets most often cited by Teage was England's Edward Young, whose work—like some of his own—was laced with tinges of melancholy and meditations on mortality. But Teage's most masterful pieces were his speeches, which combined systematic argumentation and flourishes of poetry delivered with the full powers of a Baptist pastor. These often were laced with poetic repetition, as in a section of a speech on the displacement of a martial ethos by a civil era:

> He who would embalm his name in the grateful remembrance of coming generations—he who would secure for himself a niche in the temple of undying fame—he who would hew out for himself a monument of which his country may boast—he who would entail upon heirs a name which they may be proud to wear, must seek some other field than that of battle as the theatre of his exploits.

Taken as a whole Teage's works reveal a knowledgeable and witty writer who could be self-deprecating at times yet devastatingly sardonic, if crossed.

In picturesque, self-mocking terms, Teage described an editor's duties in his poverty-stricken society:

> the boy comes for copy. He draws on a well backed trestle, for which he is indebted to the carelessness of the carpenter, and seats himself in front of the barrel. Seizing the fearful quill, he thus begins:

'The press, the omnipotent press, is the most powerful engine which it has ever been the lot of mortals to possess. It is the scourge of tyrants, the pillar of religion and the Palladium of civil liberty. From it, as from an impregnable rampart, the fearless independent editor. . . .'

But this self-congratulatory rumination by the editor is suddenly interrupted by the copy boy, whose concerns are more mundane:

> *There is no cassado for breakfast, sir.*
> Well, go and get some, and don't bother me.
> *I have no money, sir.*
> Well go and collect some money.
> *I have carried out the bills, sir.*
> Have you collected any money?
> *No sir.*
> Why?
> *Mr. — says he has no money, and you need not be afraid of the small amount. Mr. — says he don't like the paper now; you are too polite. Mr. — says your paper is scurrilous. Mr. — says there is too much religion in it and too little politics. Mr. — says there is too much politics and too little religion, and Mr. — says you have insulted his father's tenth cousin. They say they will not make the paper any longer, and they will pay when they get the money.*
> That will do; go and call again in an hour for copy.

With this dismissal, the editor briefly resumes his rumination:

> And though there is no class of men to whom the world is under more immense obligation, yet, there is none. . . .
> *Jambo has come to get his pay for the palm oil, sir.*
> Be gone, sir, don't you see I am engaged . . . there is none we respect that is doomed to a more hopeless . . .
> *The ram has gnawed the rollers, sir.*
> Well, cast another.
> *We have no molasses, sir.*
> Well, shut up the office, and go to dinner.

In keeping with journalistic standards in an era when copyright conventions were not strictly observed, Teage published samples from his diverse readings. The November 7, 1845 issue of the *Herald*, for example, carried a letter from a correspondent in Haiti, along with articles culled from the Republican-leaning *New York Tribune*, published by Horace Greeley; the Federalist *Evening Post*, founded by Alexander Hamilton; the *New York Sun*, the first successful penny press and an ally of the Democratic Party; London's iconoclastic *Punch;* and England-based *Westminster Review,* an outlet for the writings of Jeremy Bentham and James Mill, two founders of British utilitarian economics.

Adhered to Journalistic Standards

Stemming from his avid reading, Teage revealed a keen understanding of journalistic standards of his day. In an appeal to his patrons for support, he noted differences between the news environment of Africa and more industrialized countries, bemoaning the absence in Liberia of "the privilege of arraigning and abusing public men and measures." This was lacking, he noted:

> not perhaps from a virtuous disposition in us, or that we write with a pen less wayward than others, that we do not make occasional drafts on this fruitful subject, but rather because our men and measures are known within a circle so circumscribed that any thing we could say with respect to them, would be uninteresting to our distinct readers.

Also absent from his environment were those "striking events" that journalists of the day considered newsworthy, events which:

> vary and enliven the dull and monotonous narration of ordinary life. No mobs affording columns of matter in accounts of heads broke, houses rifled, magistrates resisted, laws defied, or any other of those brilliant events which generally mark the reign of mobocracy.

"To this degree of refinement," he added with no small measure of sarcasm, "the citizens of Liberia have not as yet arrived; it is left, therefore, to some more fortunate Editor to describe them, when futurity shall bring them forth." The type of society promoted by Teage was one rooted in reasoned consensus, which could be achieved only through "free and dispassionate discussion." Enlightenment would result, he argued, from vigorous public debate, the kind sponsored by the Liberia Lyceum and conducted in the pages of the *Herald:*

> Let the whole popular mind, with its 'Press' and various civil institutions, concentrate on any one subject, and truth will rise prescient. For proof, notice the progress which the subject of slavery has made. As soon as public attention is fixed itself upon the evils and dangers it is likely to entail on the American people, a great and prevailing change was evident to all. This general and popular agitation may throw up much strife and delusion, but, nevertheless, error, whose certain fate is inevitable, will sink and give place to truth.

The Grand Object of a Republic on Africa's Soil

As Liberians moved to declare their independence in 1847, Teage—the man who had done more than any to further the process—cited the planting of "a nation of colored people on the soil of Africa, adorned and dignified with the attributes of a civilized and Christian community" as the "grand object which at first brought us to Africa." Evident in this passage is a defining element of 19th century black nationalism as identified by historian Wilson J. Moses, which was a desire for independence and "absolute control over a specific geographical territory, and sufficient economic and military power to defend it." As noted by Moses, other essential features of classical black nationalism include: 1) dissatisfaction with conditions in the United States; 2) "an invariable belief that the hand of God directed (the) movement" of blacks; 3) a quickness "to claim an ancestral connection with Egypt and Ethiopia," while showing "little enthusiasm for the cultural expressions of sub-Saharan Africa."

Although Teage is said to have made the most important personal contribution to the "framing and establishment of Liberia," his "nationalism" always retained a racial dimension, in keeping with its origin in the American environment. He regarded with anguish the "opprobrious epithets" and "contempt" meted out by northern blacks against Liberians. Unlike many black leaders in the United States who viewed emigrants and abolitionists as antagonists, he saw the two communities as "companions in tribulation" and "co-laborers in different compartments of one structure." In keeping with Teage's republican aspirations, he published in 1844 a historical sketch of the Liberian colony in which he criticized European control over Sierra Leone and called in contrast for black self-government in Liberia.

Dissatisfaction with life in the United States is clearly evident in the Liberian Declaration of Independence—Teage's best known work—which detailed the American racism that had both shaped his world view and driven him to Africa, along with other members of the Liberian repatriate community. It reads in part:

> We were everywhere shut out from all civil office.
> We were excluded from all participation in the government.
> We were taxed without consent.
> We were compelled to contribute to the resources of a country, which gave us no protection.
> We were made a separate and distinct class, and against us every avenue to improvement was effectually closed. Strangers from all lands of a color different from ours, were preferred before us.

Also displayed in the language of this declaration is his skill as a writer, as evident in the poetic use of repetition, combined with a poignant recounting of grievances.

Liberia "Favour'd of God"

Teage's black nationalism was clearly anchored in his religious faith, specifically a covenant theory of history, which held that "God periodically chose certain nations to play the role of his chosen people." Just as American Puritans believed that they had inherited the Biblical covenant from the Old Testament Israelites, many African Americans, including Teage, thought the role of God's chosen people had devolved to blacks, due to the involvement of white Americans in the slave system.

This theory was evident in his poem "Wake Every Tuneful String," where he claimed Liberia to be "Favour'd of God." The interpenetration of his religious and political ideas was facilitated by the absence of a firm division between the secular and sacred in African American cosmology, which one scholar characterized as one of "the most important links between African culture and African American Christianity." Writing 19 years before the Civil War culminated in the abolition of slavery, he drew upon a certainty derived from religious faith in predicting:

> The accursed system is tottering to its fall — All its aiders, abettors and apologists—all its protecting powers in the New World— intellectual and brutal, cannot long sustain it against the advance of liberal and religious principles. The day of darkness has passed. The hosts are mustering for battle. God himself is in the midst.

As Liberians faced the uncertain prospects of independence, Teage sought to reassure his doubtful compatriots by comparing them to a group in the Old Testament that had been elected to be saved from the destruction of an immoral civilization, noting, "Like the wanderers from Sodom, we shall find it certain death to remain here or to return to the city. Hope can be indulged only in going forward."

In their flight from "Sodom," the territory to which many, if not most, 19th century black nationalists sought to escape was Africa, their ancestral home and a land to which many retained cultural ties, having been recently removed. During Teage's childhood in the United States, blacks still referred to and thought of themselves as "Africans," and the names they gave to hundreds of churches and other institutions, such as the *African* Methodist Episcopal Church, reflected this identification with the continent of their origin. Similarly, emigration by the Teage family and others to the area that became Liberia reflected a privileging of Africa—above such alternative sites as Canada and Haiti. To describe

their mission, supporters of African colonization appropriated the phrase from Psalm 68 of the Old Testament, "Princes shall come out of Egypt; Ethiopia shall stretch out her hands unto God."

By appealing to a vision of Africa that was both ancient and awe-inspiring, Teage also sought to empower his audiences with a sense of certainty about achieving their collective goals. Speaking one year before the colony severed its ties to the ACS, he challenged his audience:

> And will the descendants of the mighty Pharaohs, that awed the world—will the sons of him who drove back the serried legions of Rome and laid siege to the "eternal city"—will they, the achievements of whose fathers are yet the wonder and admiration of the world— will they refuse the proffered boon, and basely cling to the chains of Slavery and dependence? Never! never!! never!!!

Similarly, his poem "Land of the Mighty Dead" employed references to a more glorious and orderly African past to inspire action toward self-government by his contemporaries:

> Land of the mighty dead! Here science once displayed, And art, their charms; Here awful Pharaohs swayed Great nations who obeyed, Here distant monarchs laid Their vanquished arms.
>
> They hold us in survey, They cheer us on our way They loud proclaim—From Pyramidal hall—From Carnac's sculptured wall—From Thebes they loudly call—Retake your fame!

Teage regarded those indigenous societies then engaged in the slave trade to be debased, fallen from a higher state. The involvement of several African chiefs in the slave trade notwithstanding, he was against the expropriation of land from them without just compensation. As noted in his poem "Wake Every Tuneful String," the independence of Liberia was but the harbinger of a *return* for all Africa to an earlier state of freedom:

> Shout the loud jubilee Afric once more is free
>   Break forth with joy;
> Let Nile's fettered tongue, Let Niger's join the song, And Congo's loud and long
>   Glad strains employ.

Since all humanity had contributed to "civilization," Teage reasoned, all could aspire to partake of its offerings, including indigenous Africans, whose religious and cultural conversion he justified as a racial duty. The pan-racial element in his thinking led him to welcome indigenous Africans into the polity, but his commitment to Christianity and republicanism made him critical of those African customs linked to servile relations.

Challenged Some African Social Practices, Enjoyed Others

For example, he regarded the status of women, trial by ordeal and some other features of contemporaneous African societies as morally reprehensible and requiring change, if not excision.. Toward other features of African culture, he maintained a non-judgmental attitude, a display of relativism that was rare in the 19th century. He took to eating local cuisine, sent a suit made from African cotton cloth for display at an industrial fair in New York, and found African hospitality and several cultural practices worthy of praise.. For a Baptist minister, he adopted a surprising moral indifference toward conjuring, which he was able to describe without denunciation, perhaps conditioned by previous exposure to similar practices in Virginia..

Teage's works highlight the significant role of Southern blacks in the forging of black nationalism—a position advanced by social historians Eugene Genovese, Sterling Stuckey and others.. His writings also support the argument of Moses that "classical black nationalism brought together the apparently contradictory ideas of cultural assimilation and geopolitical separatism." According to Moses, who has done more than any other scholar to historicize the subject, racial consciousness among African Americans was in its "protonationalist" phase from the late 1770s to 1830, then entered its classical nationalist expression in the years from 1850 to 1925..

Given this periodization, Teage was one of the earliest black nationalists, working as he did between 1830 and 1850. Paradoxically, the racial ideology he articulated helped give rise to a narrow Liberian nationalism and, through the efforts of his protégé Edward Wilmot Blyden (1832–1912), to an all-encompassing pan-Africanism.. Twenty-seven years Blyden's senior, Teage had employed the younger man as his clerk while serving as secretary of state and *Herald* editor, positions which Blyden would eventually come to occupy.. Teage's mentoring role calls into question a historical chronology that credits the ideas of Blyden as being the most important historical progenitor of pan-Africanism.".

During the 19th century, Teage's reputation and ideas reverberated deeply in Liberia and broadly across the Atlantic. While he was editor, the *Herald* maintained a small but continuous circulation in the United States, through a network of business associates and pro-colonization agents, including William Crane, the white Baptist businessman who had guided his early education.. In addition, his writings were regularly reprinted in the *African Repository*, published monthly by the American Colonization Society in Washington, DC, and in the bi-monthly *Maryland Colonization Journal* of Baltimore. In 1848, one of his speeches, along with an address by radical abolitionist Henry Highland Garnet of New York, was included in a booklet published in London that was intended to refute the "calumny" that blacks were incapable of higher education..

When Teage died on May 21, 1853, after a long and painful illness,. his passing was noted by *Frederick Douglass' Paper*, . which had been a worthy adversary to the colonization cause over the years, but not to those individuals who had opted to emigrate. A *Herald* correspondent reported the passing of "the chiefest luminary in our political sky," and said that through Teage "the melancholy spirit of every Liberian was raised from deep despair to hope.". A letter from Liberia reporting the closing of his meteoric career noted, "A great star has fallen in this Republic.".

Committed to Modernism & Black Nationalism

From the lowest rung of Virginia slave society, Hilary Teage emigrated to Liberia, where he became a successful merchant, Baptist pastor, elected official and influential editor. Although lacking a formal education, his writings showed a deep commitment to an emerging modernism, in the form of republican politics, literary romanticism and epistemological empiricism. Also evident in his writings were the hallmarks of 19th century black nationalism, from criticisms of America for failing to extend republican liberties to blacks, through a covenant theology that confidently assumed God to be "in the midst" of the struggle against slavery, to evocative images of Ancient Egypt meant to inspire and empower his audiences.

In elaborating what was a racially based ideology, he channeled it into both a specifically Liberian nationalism and a broader pan-Africanism. By campaigning relentlessly through the *Liberia Herald*, which he edited for 15 years, this former slave helped to achieve his "grand object," which was the creation of a "nation of colored people on the soil of Africa."

---

[1]"The Late Hilary Teage, of Liberia," *Maryland Colonization Journal*, 1853, 71.

[2]P. J. Staudenraus, *The African Colonization Movement, 1816–1865* (New York: Columbia University Press, 1961).

[3]The original towns and their populations were: Bassa Cove, 52; Edina, 67; Marshall, 68; Monrovia, 463; Sinoe, 40; Bexley, 50; Caldwell, 138; Millsburg, 95; and New Georgia, 121; see C. Abayomi Cassell, *Liberia: History of the First African Republic* (New York: Fountainhead Publishers, 1970), 103, 111–12, 250, 264, and U.S. Senate, *U.S. Navy Department, Tables Showing the Number of Emigrants and Recaptured Africans Sent to the Colony of*

Liberia by the Government of the United States . . . Together with a Census of the Colony of Liberia and a Report of its Commerce, etc. September, 1843, Senate Document No. 150, 28th Congress, 2d session (Washington, DC: Government Printing Office, 1845).

[4]For black literary and organizational activities of the antebellum era, see R. J. M. Blackett, *Building an Antislavery Wall* (Cornell University Press, 1983); James Oliver Horton, *Free People of Color* (Washington, DC: Smithsonian Institute Press, 1993); M. E. Dunn, *The Black Press, 1827–1890* (New York: G. P. Putnam's Sons, 1972).

[5]"Reward of Merit," *Maryland Colonization Journal*, August 1846, 220–221; Cassell, Liberia.

[6]*Africa's Luminary*, a semi-monthly newspaper published by the Methodist Episcopal Mission in Monrovia from 1839 to 1841; Vols. 1–3 (15 March 1839–17 December 1841) original in Yale Divinity School Library; microfilm produced for the American Theological Library Association Board of Microtext, Chicago, by Dept. of Photoduplication, University of Chicago Library, 1970; 1 reel, 35 mm; the *African Repository*, the monthly journal of the ACS, published from 1825 to 1892, vols. 1–68 (March 1825–January 1892) available on microfilm from University Microfilms, Ann Arbor, Michigan; Vols. 1–25 known as the *African Repository and Colonial Journal*; Vol. 10 contains an index to Vols. 1–10; the *American Colonization Society Annual Report*, 1818–1908/10, with a reprint available from Negro University Press, New York, 1969; *Liberia Herald*, a bi-monthly newspaper published by the colonial government from 1830 to 1839, when it reverted to private ownership, available in the following locations: Library Company of Philadelphia (15 February 1830; 3 May 1843), Library of Congress (6 April 1830; 6 June 1830; 22 April 1831; 22 June 1831; 22 July 1831; 22 February 1832; 7 June 1832; 1 August 1833; 4 September 1833; 20 November 1833; 24 December 1833; 24 January 1834; 24 February 1834; 7 June 1834; 27 December 1834; Oct., 1839) and Maryland Colonization Society Papers (24 January 1844; 30 March 1844; 24 January 1845; 15–31 March 1845; 31 May 1845; 5 September 1845; 7–28 November 1845; 3–17 July 1846; 1 January 1847; 5 March 1847; 2 April 1847; 4 June–30 July 1847; 26 August–17 December 1847; and the *Maryland Colonization Journal*, a monthly journal published in Baltimore, Maryland, from May 1835–May 1841; new series, June 1841–May 1861; available in the papers of the Maryland Colonization Society (an auxiliary of the ACS), on microfilm reels 28–29 from Scholarly Resources, Wilmington, Delaware; 31 rolls of 35 mm, with guide.

[7]Randall M. Miller, ed., *Dear Master: Letters of a Slave Family* (Athens, Georgia: University of Georgia, 1991); Bell I. Wiley, ed., *Slaves No More: Letters from Liberia, 1833–1869* (Lexington: The University Press of Kentucky, 1980).

[8]"Liberia Herald," *Liberia Herald*, 15 March 1845, 46.

[9]"The Late Hilary Teage, of Liberia," *Maryland Colonization Journal*, October 1853, 72.

[10]These include "The Proceedings of the Liberia Providence Baptist Association," which, according to the *Africa's Luminary*, 19 April 1839, was a recently published pamphlet that contained a pastoral address by him, along with the proceedings of the Liberia Providence Baptist Association Conventions of 1837 and 1838.

[11]The eight most important collections were the American Colonization Society Papers, Manuscript Division, Library of Congress (also available on microfilm through the Library of Congress, Photoduplication Service, Washington, DC; 331 reels); Rare Book and Special Collections Division, Library of Congress; Library Company of Philadelphia, Philadelphia, Pennsylvania; Historical Society of Pennsylvania, Philadelphia, Pennsylvania; Maryland Colonization Society Papers, Maryland Historical Society, Baltimore; Library of Virginia Archives, Richmond; Virginia Historical Society, Richmond; and the Southern Baptist Historical Library and Archives, Nashville.

[12]James Carey, "The Problem of Journalism History," in Eve Stryker Munson and Catherine A. Warren, eds., *James Carey: A Critical Reader* (Minneapolis: University of Minnesota Press, 1997), 86–94, especially p. 89.

[13]Janet M. Cramer, *Woman as Citizen: Race, Class, and the Discourse of Women's Citizenship, 1894–1909*, Journalism & Mass Communication Monograph, no. 165 (Columbia, S.C.: Association for Education in Journalism & Mass Communication, 1998), 13.

[14]John C. Miller, *The Wolf by the Ear: Thomas Jefferson and Slavery* (New York: The Free Press, 1977); also Joyce Appleby, *Capitalism and a New Social Order: The Republican Vision of the 1790s* (New York: New York University Press, 1984), 102; Winthrop D. Jordan, *White Over Black: Attitudes Toward the Negro, 1550–1812* (New York: Pelican, 1971), 429–481; Robert McColley, *Slavery and Jeffersonian Virginia* (Urbana: University of Illinois, 1973); Ira Berlin and Ronald Hoffman, *Slavery and Freedom in the Age of the American Revolution* (Urbana: University of Illinois, 1986).

[15]For black nationalism generally, see Wilson J. Moses, *Classical Black Nationalism: From the American Revolution to Marcus Garvey* (New York: New York University, 1996), 41, 5, 36 n. 2; also John H. Bracey, Jr., August Meier, and Elliott M. Rudwick, eds., *Black Nationalism in America* (Indianapolis: Bobbs-Merrill, 1970); E. U. Essien-Udon, *Black Nationalism: A Search for an Identity in America* (Chicago: University of Chicago Press, 1962); Eugene D. Genovese, *Roll, Jordan, Roll: The World the Slaves Made* (New York: Vintage, 1976), xv; Sterling Stuckey, *Slave Culture: Nationalist Theory and the Foundations of Black America* (New York: Oxford University Press, 1987), 3–97.

[16]"Letter from Mr. Teage to Hon. S. Wilkeson dated Monrovia, 10 December 1840," *African Repository*, 5 March 1841, 95.

[17]Imanuel Geiss, *The Pan-African Movement* (New York: Holmes & Meier, 1974).

[18]Clifford Geertz, "Ideology as a Cultural System," in David Apter, ed., *Ideology and Discontent* (New York: Free Press, 1964), 47–76.

[19]"William Crane to the Rev. O. B. Brown, 28 March 1819," in J. B. Taylor, *Biography of Elder Lott Cary, Late Missionary to Africa* (Baltimore: Armstrong and Berry, 1837), 17–18.

[20]United States Census Office, *Fourth Census of the United States* (Washington, DC, 1820), Roll #132, 95, 98.

[21]Ralph R. Gurley, *The Life of Jehudi Ashmun* (James C. Dunn, 1835), 147–148; Taylor, *Biography of Elder*, 13, 19.

[22]Philip Slaughter, *The Virginia History of African Colonization* (Richmond: 1855); John H. Russell, *The Free Negro in Virginia, 1619–1865* (Baltimore: The Johns Hopkins University Press, 1913), 73; Marie Tyler-McGraw, "Richmond Free Blacks and African Colonization, 1816–1832," *Journal of American Studies* (Great Britain) 21 (2): 207–224, especially p. 217; D. R. Egerton, "'Its Origin is Not a Little Curious': A New Look at the American Colonization Society," *Journal of the Early Republic* 5 (1985): 463–480.

[23]Tom W. Shick, *Emigrants to Liberia: 1820 to 1843: An Alphabetical Listing* (Newark, DE: University of Delaware, 1971), 96.

[24]Taylor, 19. For the role of Crane in Hilary's education, see William A. Poe, "Not Christopolis but Christ and Caesar: Baptist Leadership in Liberia," *Journal of Church and State*, 23 (3): 535–551, especially p. 538.

[25]Tyler-McGraw, "Richmond Free Blacks," 213; Marie Tyler-McGraw, "'The Prize I Mean is the Prize of Liberty': A Loudon County Family in Liberia," *Virginia Magazine of History and Biography*, 97 (1989), 355–374; Virginius Dabney, *Richmond: The Story of a City* (Garden City, N.Y.: Doubleday and Co., 1990), 77.

[26]Dwight N. Syfert, "The Origins of Privilege," *Liberian Studies Journal* 6 (Fall 1975), 109–128; Dwight N. Syfert, "A History of the Liberian Coasting Trade, 1821–1900" (Indiana University, Ph.D. dissertation, 1977), 280–281; Robert W. July, *The Origins of Modern African Thought* (New York: Praeger, 1967), 96.

[27]Syfert, "The Origins of Privilege," 114–6, 126–7; Syfert, "A History of the Liberian Coasting Trade," 271, 280–281, 283; July, *The Origins of Modern African Thought*, 93–100, especially p. 96.

[28]"The Election," *Africa's Luminary*, 3 Jan. 1840; Syfert, "A History of the Liberian Coasting Trade," 280–281; Edith Holden, *Blyden of Liberia* (New York: Vantage, 1966), 36. According to an author who worked at the Liberian State Department and had full access to official records, Teage also served as the country's first secretary of that department; see Nathaniel Richardson, *Liberia's Past and Present* (London: Diplomatic Press, 1959), 59, n *.

[29]"The Lyceum and the Lectures" and "For Africa's Luminary: The Liberia Lyceum," *Africa's Luminary*, 7 Aug.. 1840, 38–39; Tom W. Shick, "Rhetoric and Reality: Colonization and Afro-American Missionaries in Early Nineteenth-Century Liberia," in Sylvia Jacobs, *Black Americans and the Missionary Movement in Africa* (Westport, Conn.: Greenwood, 1982), 162, n. 50; Wiley, 29–30, Letter 15.

[30]"The Late Hilary Teage, of Liberia," *Maryland Colonization Journal*, 1853, 71–72.

[31]"Death in Liberia," *Maryland Colonization Journal*, 1853, 47.

[32]"Death of Hon. Hilary Teage," *Maryland Colonization Journal*, 1853, 47.

[33]Edward W. Blyden to William Coppinger, 3 June 1878, in Lynch, *Selected Letters*, 270.

[34]"Additions to the Baptist Churches in the Last Five Months," *African Repository*, August 1848, 234; Poe, 535–551.

[35]Antonio Gramsci, *Prison Notebook* (New York: International Publishers, 1973), 5–23.

[36]"The Late Hilary Teage, of Liberia," *Maryland Colonization Journal*, 1853, 71.

[37]"The Late Hilary Teage, of Liberia," *Maryland Colonization Journal*, 1853, 72.

[38]For the role of John B. Russwurm in Liberian politics and the events that led to his resignation as editor of the *Liberia Herald*, see Carl Patrick Burrowes, "Press Freedom in Liberia, 1830–1847: The Impact of Heterogeneity and Modernity," *Journalism and Mass Communication Quarterly* 74, 2 (1997): 331–347.

[39]"From the Liberia Herald," *Africa's Luminary*, 18 Oct. 1839.

[40]A unit of measure in nineteenth century Liberia that was equivalent to six imperial gallons or 3 kg.

[41]"An African Editor," *Liberia Herald*, 17 March 1842, 19.

[42]Geoffrey Tillotson, Paul Fussell and Marshall Waingrow, *Eighteenth-Century English Literature* (New York: Harcourt Brace Jovanovich, 1969), 18.

[43]"Address Delivered Before the Liberia Lyceum, in the Council Chamber on May 21, 1845," *Liberia Herald*, 31 May 1845, 9–10.

[44]"Liberia Herald," *Liberia Herald*, 26 Nov. 1842, 8; "A Conjurer and Conjuration," *Liberia Herald*, 3 July 1846, 70.

[45]"Republican Legislature," *Liberia Herald*, 29 Dec. 1849, 10. Although Teage used only last names, these writers were probably intended, given their popularity at the time.

[46]Hilary Teage to R. R. Gurley, Monrovia, 20 March 1839, ACS Papers.

[47]Stephen Cornford, *Edward Young "Night Thoughts"* (Cambridge: Cambridge University Press, 1989), ix; also Russell Noyes, *English Romantic Poetry and Prose* (New York: Oxford University Press, 1967), xxiii. For a reference by Teage to "Night Thoughts," see "Liberia Herald," *Liberia Herald*, 1 Jan. 1847, 22–23. According to Cornford, Young's "Night Thoughts" was not only "one of the most influential, praised and well known poems of the English language during the nineteenth century, but it was also revered by some Christians as a 'standard devotional work,' second only to the Bible.

[48]"Anniversary Speech," *Liberia Herald*, 18 December 1846, 17–18, and "Anniversary Speech (continued)," *Liberia Herald*, 5 February 1847, 29–30.

[49]For examples, see "Liberia Herald," *Liberia Herald*, 21 Jan. 1843, 11, and "The Luminary," *Liberia Herald*, 11 February 1843.

[50]In the nineteenth century, "cassado" was a common spelling of cassava, the root of a shrubby tropical plant that is a staple food in parts of Liberia and many areas of the tropics.

[51]"An African Editor," *Liberia Herald*, 17 March 1842, 19.

[52]Alvin Sullivan, ed., *British Literary Magazines: The Romantic Age, 1789–1836* (Westport, Conn.: Greenwood, 1983), 424–433; Richard A. Schwarzlose, *Newspapers: A Reference Guide* (Westport, Conn.: Greenwood, 1987).

[53]"Liberia Herald," *African Repository*, April 1837, 131–132.

[54]"Our Affairs," *Liberia Herald*, 18 Dec. 1846, 19.

[55]"Liberia Herald," *Liberia Herald*, 7 Nov. 1847.

[56][Hilary Teage,] "The *Liberia Herald* with Regard to Independence," *Thirteenth Annual Report of the ACS,* 1847, 21.

[57]Moses, 1–42. For the religious foundation of black nationalism, see Genovese, 280–284.

[58]"The *Weekly Elevator,*" *Liberia Herald,* 30 March 1844, 2; also Hilary Teage to the Rev. J. B. Pinney, Monrovia, 27 August 1852, printed in ACS *Annual Report,* January 1853, 17–18.

[59]"Death of Hon. Hilary Teage," *Maryland Colonization Journal,* 1853, 47; Hilary Teage, "The Colony of Liberia [Part 1]," *African Repository,* September 1844, 257–61; Hilary Teage, "The Colony of Liberia [Part 2]," *African Repository,* January 1845, 13–17.

[60]Republic of Liberia, *The Independent Republic of Liberia: Its Constitution and Declaration of Independence . . . Issued Chiefly for Use by the Free People of Color* (Philadelphia: William F. Geddes, 1848).

[61]Michael Lienesch, *New Order of the Ages: Time, the Constitution and the Making of Modern American Political Thought* (Princeton: Princeton University Press, 1988), 197.

[62]Poe, 535–551; C. Eric Lincoln and Lawrence H. Mamiya, *The Black Church in the African-American Experience* (Durham: Duke University Press, 1990), 22.

[63]"Wake Every Tuneful String," *Liberia Herald,* 26 August 1847, 76.

[64]Donald G. Mathews, *Religion in the Old South* (Chicago: University of Chicago Press, 1977), 190.

[65]"The *Weekly Elevator,*" *Liberia Herald,* 30 March 1844, 2.

[66]"Address Delivered Before the *Liberia Lyceum,*" *Liberia Herald,* 18 December 1846, 17–18, and *Liberia Herald,* 4 February 1847, 29–30.

[67]"Anniversary Speech, December 1st, 1846," *Liberia Herald,* 18 December 1846, 17–18, and *Liberia Herald,* 4 February 1847, 29–30.

[68]"Land of the Mighty Dead," *Liberia Herald,* 23 December 1842, 8. This poem was reprinted as "Specimen of Liberian Poetry," *African Repository,* June 1843, 191–102, and *Maryland Colonization Journal,* July 1843, 32, with the note, "sung to the tune 'Bermondsey.'"

[69]"*Liberia Herald,*" *Liberia Herald,* 16 October 1846, 2.

[70]"Wake Every Tuneful String," *Liberia Herald,* 26 August 1847, 76; reprinted in *African Repository,* February 1848, 58.

[71]e.g., "Internal Improvement," *Liberia Herald,* 3 Mary 1843, 25.

[72]"*Liberia Herald,*" *Liberia Herald,* 30 September 1843, 31; "Tender Mercies of Heathenism," *Liberia Herald,* 30 September 1843, 31.

[73]See various references to "cassado" as part of his cuisine in "An African Editor," *Liberia Herald,* 17 March 1842, 19; "Hard Times," *Liberia Herald,* 31 May 1845, 11; "Scarcity," *Liberia Herald,* 4 June 1847, 62.

[74]Hilary Teage to R. R. Gurley, Monrovia, 12 April 1839, ACS Papers.

[75]"A Beautiful Custom," *Liberia Herald,* 28 July 1848, 38; "Excursion," *Liberia Herald,* 19 April 1842, 22; "African Belief," *Liberia Herald,* 30 March 1844.

[76]"A Conjurer and Conjuration," *Liberia Herald,* 3 July 1846, 70.

[77]For information on conjuring among Virginia blacks, see Charles L. Perdue, Jr., Thomas E. Barden and Robert K. Phillips, eds., *Weevils in the Wheat: Interviews with Virginia Ex-Slaves* (Bloomington: Indiana University Press, 1976); Mechal Sobel, *The World They Made Together: Black and White Values in Eighteenth-Century Virginia* (Princeton: Princeton University Press, 1987), 41–43, 338.

[78]Genovese, xv; Stuckey, 3–97.

[79]Moses, 2.

[80]For the black nationalist antecedents of pan-Africanism and of African micro-nationalisms, see Hollis R. Lynch, *Edward Wilmot Blyden: Pan-Negro Patriot, 1832–1912* (New York: Oxford University Press, 1970); Henry S. Wilson, *Origins of West African Nationalism* (New York: St. Martin's, 1969). For Teage's contribution to African thought, see July, *The Origins of Modern African Thought,* 85–109.

[81]Lynch, *Edward Wilmot Blyden,* 492. For Blyden's invocation of a poem by Teage during a visit to the pyramids in Egypt, see Holden, *Blyden of Liberia,* 141.

[82]Lynch, *Edward Wilmot Blyden,* 251; also Holden, *Blyden of Liberia;* Hollis R. Lynch, *Selected Letters of Edward Wilmot Blyden* (Millwood, N.J.: KTO Press, 1978).

[83]William Crane, Esq., served for several years as the agent of the *Herald* in Baltimore, Maryland (e.g., "From the *Liberia Herald,*" *Liberia Herald,* 18 October 1839, and "Agents for the *Liberia Herald,*" *Liberia Herald,* 28 February 1849).

[84]E. Wilson Armistead, *Calumny Refuted by Facts from Liberia* (London: 1848).

[85]Two years before his death, he ended a letter to an ACS official with "I now close, by soliciting an interest in your prayers. Yours, in affliction" (Hilary Teage to J. B. Pinney, Monrovia, May 17, 1851, printed in *African Repository,* September 1851, 269).

[86]*Frederick Douglass' Paper,* 3 June 1853.

[87]Daniel B. Warner, "Letter to the Editor," *Liberia Herald,* 15 June 1853, 86.

[88]"Death in Liberia," *Maryland Colonization Journal,* 1853, 47.

Pan-Africanism

Jeremiah I. Dibua

Pan-Africanism grew out of the appalling experiences of slavery among both continental Africans and those who were forcibly dispersed from the continent. It was a reaction to the shared feelings of brotherhood and unity among people of African descent all over the world. The movement became more systematized and formalized in the twentieth century. During this period, there were two clearly discernible phases in the Pan-African movement. The first phase, largely characterized by romanticism and idealism, was dominated by diasporan Africans, and lasted until 1945. The second phase, which lasted from 1945 to 1963, was dominated by continental Africans. One of the main catalysts for the development of this phase was the Italian invasion of Ethiopia in 1935–1936. This phase associated Pan-Africanism with the liberation of the African continent from European imperialism. It also was concerned with the promotion of African unity. The formation of the Organization of African Unity (OAU) in 1963, in certain respects, marked the culmination of this phase.

Pan-Africanism is one of the most momentous and unifying developments that has occurred during the historical experience of peoples of African descent all over the world. The injustices, inhumanity, exploitation, and racism associated with the European slave trade, European imperialism in Africa, and racism in the Americas created a collective feeling of resentment among people of African descent all over the world. It also fostered the desire and determination to struggle against oppression and degradation. Pan-Africanism can, therefore, be seen as a collective effort on the part of African peoples worldwide to promote unity and solidarity of people of African descent, and to liberate them from various forms of European domination and oppression. Although the most visible aspect of Pan-Africanism is manifested on the political front, it is a multifaceted approach that includes political, economic, cultural, and religious aspects in the struggle for the unification, rehabilitation, and regeneration of peoples of African descent in all parts of the world.

Most scholars agree that the origin of Pan-Africanism can be traced to the era of the European slave trade when enslaved Africans, whether en route to the New World or already in the New World, grieved and longed to unite with their kin on the African continent. This implies that the origin of Pan-Africanism is related to the activities of African descendants in the diaspora. Michael Williams, however, has argued that the origin of Pan-Africanism can equally be traced to the African continent during the period of the slave trade. Africans in Africa who lost relatives and members of their ethnic groups to slavery "manifested a pristine desire for Pan-African unity by grieving for their relatives' safe return to Africa." This perspective points to a Pan-Africanism that was characterized by mutual duality originating from the dispersion of Africans as well as from those who were dispersed.[1] Nevertheless, the most visible players in the Pan-African movement up to World War II were Africans in the diaspora. After World War II, continental Africans started acting in much more visible roles in the Pan-African movement, and the eradication of colonial rule from all parts of Africa became one of their major concerns.

This chapter is mainly concerned with the post–World War II Pan-African movement in Africa that culminated in the formation of the Organization of African Unity (OAU) in 1963. Although, as has already been pointed out, Pan-Africanism was manifested in various dimensions, the main concern here is with the political and institutional aspects of the movement, especially in the form of the organization of congresses/conferences. In order to situate the discussion in a proper historical perspective, I will begin with a brief examination of the Pan-African movement before World War II and will examine the immense significance of the Italian invasion of Ethiopia in 1935–1936 for the Pan-African movement.

Pan-Africanism before World War II

One of the earliest manifestations of Pan-Africanism was the expression of a desire to emigrate to Africa. Although the best known cases of emigration involved the establishment of Sierra Leone and Liberia, the movements responsible for the creation of these countries, were not really part of the Pan-Africanist movement. White-dominated groups championed the establishment of these settlements—the Abolitionist movement in Britain in the case of Sierra Leone and the American Colonization Society in the case of Liberia. These organizations were not moved by Pan-Africanist sentiments but saw the formation of the territories as a way of getting rid of the free blacks in their societies. On the other hand, the nineteenth-century emigration efforts by prominent blacks like Paul Cuffe, Martin Delany, and Henry McNeal Turner were motivated largely by Pan-Africanist sentiments.

Perhaps the best known Pan-Africanist advocate who espoused the emigration sentiment was Marcus Garvey. Although his movement has been unfairly portrayed as being primarily concerned with the "Back to Africa" philosophy, Garvey was not just an emigrationist; he was thoroughly Pan-Africanist. His United Negro

Improvement Association (UNIA) was committed to the promotion of the unity of people of African descent in all parts of the world, the restoration of the dignity of the black person, the economic empowerment of black individuals, and liberation from all vestiges of colonialism. According to Vincent Thompson,

> Garvey's programme included four principles which are among the guiding light of contemporary Pan-Africanism: first, the common destiny of all Africans and the need for continental unity as a prerequisite for dealing with the numerous problems; second, the "Negro or African personality," third, the repudiation of all foreign rule and control and the eradication of all its vestiges which are retarding the growth of African man; and, fourth, social change including cultural regeneration and reactivation of the world's cultures.[2]

The various business enterprises of Garvey's movement, including the Black Star Shipping Line, the *Negro World*—the fiery and uncompromising newspaper of the movement and the annual congresses Garvey organized in New York from 1920 onward, were avenues for the attainment of these objectives. Garvey's charisma, his organizational and oratorical skills, and the popularity and effectiveness of the *Negro World* in both exposing the degradation of black folk and mobilizing African peoples all over the world in the struggle against racism and colonial domination, caused him to be viewed as a serious foe by imperialist forces. The effectiveness of Garvey's Pan-Africanist ideals and anti-colonial sentiments were such that his movement and the *Negro World* were banned in British colonies. Nevertheless, branches of the UNIA were formed in various cities in the United States and in different parts of the Caribbean and Africa. All this turned him into a marked man. It is therefore not surprising that various attempts were made to silence him. However, despite Garvey's imprisonment and eventual deportation from the United States in the late 1920s, the impact of his movement was such that its ideals remained the focal points for various Pan-Africanist organizations.

Prior to World War II, Pan-Africanism was also manifested in the convening of Pan-African conferences. The first such conference was convened by the Caribbean lawyer, Henry Sylvester-Williams, and it took place in London in 1900. The achievements of this conference were modest. It is nevertheless significant that for the first time, a meaningful attempt was made to bring people of African descent (although most of the participants came from Europe and the New World) together to discuss their common fate and to foster the idea of cooperation and unity among them. The conference was able to draw attention to the evils of European imperialism and racism directed against African peoples. In addition, it promoted a genuine interest in African history and culture. This congress laid the pattern for future conferences that were to become an important feature of the Pan-African movement in the period leading up to the formation of the OAU.

The next Pan-African congresses were those organized by W. E. B. DuBois. Between 1919 and 1927, he organized four congresses which met in various Western nations. The opportunity for the 1919 Pan-African congress was provided when the National Association for the Advancement of Colored People (NAACP) sent DuBois to Paris in December 1918 to investigate reports of discrimination against and maltreatment of black soldiers in the United States army who were stationed in France. He was also to ensure that African interests were addressed at the impending Versailles Peace Conference. DuBois equally intended to use this opportunity to revive the Pan-African congresses. But on the advice of the United States government, the French government sought to prevent him from holding a congress. However, through the assistance of Blaise Diagne, the Senegalese deputy in the French parliament, the French authorities allowed him to organize his congress with the understanding that there would be no sharp criticism of the colonial governments. The resolutions of this congress, which was held in February 1919, were therefore rather timidly moderate. Among other things, the resolutions demanded the improvement in the living conditions of Africans and peoples of African descent; the abolition of some harsh aspects of the colonial system, like corporal punishment and forced labor; the provision of access to education; protection from land expropriation and economic exploitation; and the gradual involvement of Africans in the administration of their territories, especially at the local level.

The resolutions of the next three congresses were equally moderate. They reiterated the demands of the 1919 congress, demanding absolute equality for people of all races, access to education in the widest sense, tolerance of all forms of society, however different from one's own, and local self-government for "backward groups" which, over time, would develop into complete self-government. Thus the main preoccupation of these congresses was the reform of the colonial system. The idea of self-determination was not an immediate or serious concern. Although during this period, Garvey's movement was gaining a great deal of popularity in the African continent, disagreements between Garvey and DuBois and the opposition from liberal white supporters of the Pan-African congresses prevented Garvey from being invited to attend these congresses. This was in spite of the attempts by some of his supporters to secure his invitation. Yet the limitations of Garveyism notwithstanding, the immense popularity of his movement, his emphasis on the empowerment of the common black folk, his uncompromising attitude toward racism and colonial exploitation, and his solid Pan-Africanist credentials would have complemented the goals of these congresses. DuBois believed in an intellectual-led gradualist Pan-African movement while Garvey believed in a radical, mass-based movement that, if necessary, should not discount the use of force to achieve the liberation of African colonies. The feud between DuBois and Garvey made the Pan-Africanist movement split into two rival camps, the radical camp (led by Garvey and the UNIA) and the moderate camp (led by DuBois).[3]

Continental Africans equally formed some Pan-African organizations. The National Congress of British West Africa (NCBWA) and the West African Students Union (WASU) were two of the most significant ones. Although restricted to West Africa, both organizations were transterritorial and transnational. The NCBWA, which was founded in 1920 through the efforts of Joseph Casely-Hayford of Ghana and Akiwande Savage of Nigeria, had as one of its aims the promotion of unity among the people of British West Africa. The NCBWA demanded the reform of the colonial system and that educated Africans gain more access to the institutions of government. In line with the spirit of Pan-Africanism, the NCBWA further advocated the establishment of a West African university and a West African court of appeal; they also resolved to set up a West African Press Union. On the other hand, the WASU, which was established in Britain in 1925 through the untiring efforts of Ladipo Solanke, had among its aims the provision of a hostel for students of African descent; the presentation to the world of a true picture of African life and philosophy, thereby showing African contributions to world civilization; and the promotion of a spirit of goodwill, better understanding, and brotherhood between all persons of African descent. WASU also collaborated with various Pan-African organizations and maintained contacts with Pan-Africanists like Garvey and his wife, Amy Garvey. Nevertheless, as was the case with the Pan-African congresses, the anticolonial politics of the NCBWA and WASU were moderate and broadly concerned with the reform of the colonial system and not the immediate termination of colonial rule.

The Pan-Africanist movement before World War II was generally infused with romanticism and was more concerned with transcontinental collaboration and unity. It was against racism but believed that Africans had to undergo a process of education in the Western system of government and that power should gradually be devolved to them. The movement's immediate concern was with reform and not termination of the colonial system. Thus while during this period, Pan-Africanism spoke to the issue of cooperation and unity, it did not, save for Marcus Garvey's UNIA,

develop a perception of Pan-Africanism as a serious and fundamental instrument for the liberation of the African continent from European imperialism. The Italian invasion of Ethiopia in 1935, however, radicalized the movement, bringing to the forefront the liberation aspect of Pan-Africanism, which came to full fruition in the post–World War II period.

Italian Invasion of Ethiopia, 1935–1936

Prior to the Italian invasion of Ethiopia there had been a considerable decline in the momentum of Pan-Africanism. The jailing and deportation of Garvey led to the virtual collapse of the UNIA. After 1927, DuBois did not organize any other Pan-African congress. But the invasion of Ethiopia led to an upsurge in the Pan-African movement, marking a turning point in the development of Pan-Africanism. It made Pan-Africanism uncompromisingly committed to the liberation of African countries from the clutches of European colonialism. This commitment to liberation reached its peak at the Manchester Pan-African Congress of 1945. Incidentally, it was in the area of liberation that Pan-Africanism would achieve its greatest success.[4] The invasion of Ethiopia had this far-reaching impact for a number of reasons.

Ethiopia had immense symbolic, sentimental, and even religious importance for black people all over the world. As the only country that was able to escape European conquest during the partitioning of Africa, decisively repulsing the Italian attempt to colonize it at the Battle of Adowa in 1896, independent Ethiopia became a source of pride and hope for millions of Africans all over the world. The independence of Ethiopia symbolized the aspirations of a future Africa, one free from the shackles of European imperialism. Moreover, for the vast majority of Africans in the diaspora, Ethiopia represented their heritage and was a source of identity as exemplified in the use of the name "Ethiopia" to prefix many diasporan institutions, especially cultural and religious ones. Furthermore, for the Rastafarians, Ethiopia had religious significance: they deified Emperor Haile Selassie and adopted his previous title, Ras Tafari. In short, "Ethiopia had great appeal among African peoples and . . . historically the consciousness of the Ethiopian heritage had inspired a redemptive ideology which continued as a recurring force of identity and solidarity in Africa and the diaspora."[5]

The timid way in which the European countries reacted to the invasion and the lame-duck reaction of the League of Nations further helped to bring into sharp focus the evils of European imperialism in Africa as well as the danger posed by fascism. The reaction of the League also helped to convince many Africans that, contrary to the belief of some of the moderate Pan-Africanists, the League of Nations was not in a position to defend the interests of Africans. Moreover, many Africans came to see it as an institution that existed to defend the imperial interests of European nations. Africans all over the world therefore came to the conclusion that they should take their fate into their own hands and that the only way to defend Africa's interest was through the eradication of colonialism from the African continent. The struggle to free Ethiopia from Italian occupation was seen as the first step toward the attainment of this goal, and it became the rallying point of Pan-Africanists.

The invasion provoked a massive reaction among blacks all over the world. They launched various activities aimed at putting an end to the Italian occupation. Mass rallies were organized, Ethiopian liberation funds were launched, and organizations devoted to pursuing the Ethiopian cause were formed. Furthermore, blacks all over the world volunteered to enlist in the Ethiopian liberation army. Public demonstrations were held in various African countries and in the diaspora while newspaper editorials and articles supportive of the Ethiopian cause were written. For instance, the Baltimore-based *Afro-American*, one of the leading black newspapers in the United States, consistently tried to rally blacks behind the Ethiopian cause. In Nigeria, an Abyssinian Association that included many prominent individuals was formed to mobilize people in support of the Ethiopian cause. The United States government proclaimed its neutrality and prohibited Americans from participating in the war, even though many African-Americans expressed eagerness to join the Ethiopian army. Despite the ban on participation, two African-American pilots, Hubert Julian and John Robinson, still went to Ethiopia to join in the war effort.[6]

A number of organizations aimed at providing moral and material support to Ethiopia emerged in the United States. One of these organizations was the Friends of Ethiopia (FOA), which was organized by Willis Huggins, an African-American teacher. The FOA organized joint fund-raising programs with the International African Friends of Ethiopia in London. Within a year, the FOA had branches in nineteen states and 106 cities. In 1937, the Ethiopian World Federation (EWF) was formed under the leadership of Malaku Bayen, Emperor Haile Selassie's emissary to the Western hemisphere. The organization was committed both to instilling black pride in the black world and to the creation of a United States of Africa. In the same year and under the leadership of Max Yergan, an African-American, the International Committee on Africa (ICA) was formed. The ICA was transformed into the Council on African Affairs (CAA) in 1941. The objectives of this organization included the promotion of the political liberation of African countries; the advancement of the social and economic well-being of Africans through the dissemination of relevant and current information and facilitation of training for Africans in Europe

and America; and the arrangement of mutual exchanges of visits and cooperation among African people.[7]

There was equally widespread condemnation of the attack by Africans in Britain. WASU, for example, joined forces with other African organizations to condemn the attack. WASU saw the invasion as a racial war, and the organization's opposition to all forms of European imperialism in Africa was heightened. From September 1935, WASU started holding weekly religious services to "invoke divine intervention" in the conflict. In the following month, it launched an Ethiopian Defence Fund to raise money to defend the people of Ethiopia against the Italian invasion. For WASU, the invasion brought into sharp focus the need for greater unity among people of African descent, and it showed the need for a "Black United Front" against the common front presented by European imperialism.[8]

In 1936, C. L. R. James and a number of blacks in Britain came together to form the International African Friends of Ethiopia (IAFE). The following year, this organization joined forces with other pro-Ethiopian groups and individuals to form the International African Service Bureau (IASB). The new organization was designed to promote the political, economic, and educational empowerment of blacks in Britain and it successfully married local issues with the Ethiopian crisis. The IASB published a paper known as *International African Opinion*, and the wide appeal of this paper gave the organization a number of followers and sympathizers outside Britain. In 1944, the IASB aligned with twelve other active black welfare, students', and political organizations to transform itself into the Pan-African Federation (PAF). This federation published a journal known as *Pan-Africa* through which Pan-African sentiments were disseminated throughout the black world. The objectives of the PAF were to promote the well-being and unity of African peoples and peoples of African descent throughout the world; to demand the independence of Africans and other subject races from the domination of powers proclaiming sovereignty and trusteeship over them; and to secure equality of rights for African peoples and the total abolition of all forms of racial discrimination. In short, the invasion of Ethiopia became a "catalyst which united many Afro-Americans, West Indians and Africans residing in Britain."[9]

The PAF included among its leading members Kwame Nkrumah and Jomo Kenyatta (who were to play pivotal roles in the politics of decolonization in Africa) as well as George Padmore, C. L. R. James, and Peter Abrahams, who organized the Manchester Pan-African Congress of 1945. This congress was to radically transform the nature of the Pan-African movement and anticolonial politics in Africa. The opportunity to organize this conference was created when the British Trades Union Congress invited representatives of labor from the colonies, mainly Africa and the West Indies, to a conference of the World Federation of Trade Unions (WFTU) in February 1945. The PAF used the opportunity to invite these labor representatives to a conference in Manchester at which it was decided that a Pan-African congress should be convened in October 1945, coinciding with the next WFTU meeting.

A "Special International Conference Secretariat" was set up to prepare for the Pan-African congress. The members of this body included Dr. Peter Milliard of British Guiana, chairman, T. R. Makonnen of Ethiopia, treasurer, George Padmore of Trinidad and Kwame Nkrumah of the Gold Coast, joint secretaries, Peter Abraham of South Africa, publicity secretary, and Jomo Kenyatta of Kenya, assistant secretary. By August 1945, arrangements for the conference had been finalized and the agenda was generally approved.

The Manchester Pan-African Congress

This congress was unique in a number of ways. It was the first one attended and dominated by people from the colonies, including Africa. The congress was attended by over 200 delegates from the black world. DuBois and Milliard jointly chaired the conference on the first day, but in recognition of the contributions that DuBois had made to the Pan-African movement, he was made the chair for the rest of the conference. The conference went beyond the realm of idealism that had characterized the previous congresses. It jettisoned the moderate tone of the previous congresses and adopted a more militant and radical stance. It was uncompromisingly committed to the total liberation of Africa from foreign economic and political control. It clearly warned that if the Europeans were still determined to rule their African colonies by force, Africans would have no other choice than to use force to achieve their freedom. Thus for the first time Pan-Africanism was linked to African nationalism, and the need for well-organized and coordinated liberation movements as a *sine qua non* for African liberation was stressed. It was recognized that the liberation of Africa was a necessary step toward the restoration of the dignity of the black man and the promotion of African unity.

Most of the resolutions of the congress centered on the abolition of European imperialism in Africa. In their declaration to the colonial powers, the delegates stated their belief in peace but made it abundantly clear that if the colonial powers were "still determined to rule mankind by force, then Africans, as a last resort, may have to appeal to force in the effort to achieve freedom." They then went on to demand "autonomy and independence; so far and no further than it is possible in this 'One World' for groups of people to rule themselves subject to inevitable world unity and freedom." It was emphasized that the struggle for political power by colonial and subject peoples was "the first step towards, and the necessary prerequisite to, complete social, economic and political emancipation."[10] The delegates called upon the urban and rural masses and the intellectuals and professionals of Africa to unite and organize themselves effectively so that independence might be won. The Congress further demanded the immediate abolition of all racial and other discriminatory laws; the abolition of forced labor and the introduction of equal pay for equal work; the freedom of speech, press, association, and assembly; and the right of every man and woman over the age of twenty-one to vote and be voted for.

The Manchester Pan-African Congress can be seen as the greatest moment of the Pan-African movement. According to Kwame Nkrumah, the congress "provided the outlet for African nationalism and brought about the awakening of African political consciousness."[11] Pan-Africanism and nationalism now became a mass movement of Africans for Africans. In assessing the impact of the Manchester Pan-African Congress on the development of Pan-Africanism, Edem Kodjo and David Chanaiwa wrote that

By the end of the . . . Congress, pan-Africanism finally had been turned into a mass ideology of Africa, by Africans and for Africans. It had grown from a reformist, protest ideology for the peoples of African descent in the New World into a nationalist ideology for the continental liberation of Africa. The global pan-Africanism of DuBois, the militant self-determination and self-reliance of Garvey, and the cultural restoration of Cesaire had then become integral elements of African nationalism. . . . The constitutions of all nationalist movements included pan-Africanist clauses.[12]

The Manchester Congress marked a turning point in the Pan-African movement. It propelled the movement from the realm of idealism into the realm of practical politics in which Pan-Africanism was now effectively associated with the demand for the total liberation of the African continent from European imperialism. The movement now placed its emphasis on ending colonialism on the continent as the first step toward the achievement of the Pan-African goal. In place of the global Pan-Africanism that had previously characterized the movement, primacy was now placed on promoting unity within the African continent as the necessary stepping stone toward global Pan-Africanism.

In line with the Manchester Conference's emphasis on liberation as a necessary condition for the eventual unity of the African countries, a number of West African students in Britain came together to establish the West African National Secretariat (WANS) in December 1945. WANS had Wallace Johnson as its chairman and Nkrumah as its secretary-general. The organization was expected to be the nerve center for directing and coordinating the struggle against imperialism in West Africa. It aimed to work with nationalist organizations in West Africa to build unity in order to realize the dream of creating "a West African Front for a united West African National Independence." The organization saw itself as the vanguard in the struggle not only for "absolute independence for all of West Africa" but also for uniting West Africa as "one country."[13] Toward this end, WANS convened the West African National Congress of August 1946, which pledged to promote the concept of a West African federation as a first step toward the ultimate achievement of a United States of Africa. Although this organization was extremely active, it had a short life span. It collapsed after Nkrumah, the energetic secretary-general of the movement, departed for the Gold Coast in 1947 to assume the position of secretary-general of the United Gold Coast Convention (UGCC). It was not until 1957 that there was a revival of the Pan-African movement. This time the movement was geared mainly to the promotion of African unity and the spirit behind this new phase of Pan-Africanism was Nkrumah.

Kwame Nkrumah and the New Pan-Africanism

Between 1957 and 1958, Nkrumah dominated the Pan-African movement, working tirelessly toward the realization of a United States of Africa. After leading Ghana to political independence in March 1957, Nkrumah stated that the independence of Ghana would not be complete unless it was linked with the total liberation of the African continent from colonial domination. Nkrumah then devoted his energy and the resources of Ghana to the eradication of colonialism from the continent and the promotion of African unity. He did this through the provision of material assistance and the convening of conferences.

In pursuance of these goals, Nkrumah convened two conferences in Ghana in 1958, marking the formal launching of the Pan-African movement on African soil. The first was the Conference of Independent African States, held in Accra in April 1958. This conference was attended by the leaders of the eight independent African states (Ghana, Ethiopia, Libya, Liberia, Morocco, Tunisia, Sudan, and the United Arab Republic [Egypt]). The conference aimed at discussing issues of common interest and working out policies covering political, economic, social, and cultural matters. Among other things, the conference was to discuss the continuing problem of colonialism in Africa, exchange views on foreign policy and the relationship of African countries with the United Nations and other international regional bodies, discuss ways of promoting economic cooperation among African states, formulate ways of promoting cultural exchange among African countries, and discuss the establishment of permanent machinery for consultation on foreign policy. This conference was a demonstration of the transformation of Pan-Africanism from the realm of idealism to that of pragmatism.

The resolutions of this conference were moderate in terms of their attitudes to a strong union among African states. But the conference did advance the cause of Pan-Africanism by proclaiming unity and cooperation among the independent African states in such areas as foreign policy, the fight against colonialism, and economic, cultural, and technical developments. In terms of foreign policy, the heads of state resolved "to pursue a common foreign policy with a view to safeguarding the hard-won independence, sovereignty and territorial integrity of the participating States." They went on to express their determination to "assert a distinctive African Personality which will speak with a concerted voice" in the area of foreign policy.[14] They condemned the continued presence of colonialism in Africa, declared their solidarity with the just struggle for self-determination by colonial subjects, and resolved to offer all possible assistance to nationalist movements in their struggle to achieve self-determination and independence for their territories. A non-voting status was accorded to the representatives of the Algerian National Liberation Front, which was engaged in an armed struggle for political independence from French colonial rule. They condemned racism and apartheid in South Africa and called on the United Nations to intensify its efforts at combating and eradicating this ignoble and inhuman practice. They resolved to cooperate with one another in safeguarding their independence, sovereignty, and territorial integrity, and in their economic, technical, and scientific developments with a view to raising the standard of living of their citizens. Toward this end they agreed to set up a joint Economic Research Commission. Foreign ministers and other ministers or experts from the states were to meet from time to time to study and deal with particular problems of common concern to the African states. The Conference of Independent African States was to be reconvened every two years.[15]

The second conference that was held in 1958, the All African People's Conference (AAPC), was more radical and in many respects similar to the 1945 Manchester Pan-African Congress. This conference, which was held in Accra in December 1958, was attended by over 300 representatives of political parties from all over Africa. In his opening address, Nkrumah reminded the participants that there were four hurdles that had to be crossed before the final objective of Pan-Africanism could be achieved. The hurdles were the attainment of freedom and independence by every African state; the consolidation of that freedom and independence; the creation of unity and community between African states; and the economic and social reconstruction of Africa.[16] The resolutions of this conference were less restrained than those of the conference of the heads of states. The views of this conference with regard to the eradication of colonialism and the promotion of Pan-Africanism were uncompromisingly radical.

In the case of the struggle against imperialism, the conference, among other things, vehemently condemned colonialism and imperialism in whatever shape or form; deplored the continued political and economic exploitation of Africans by imperialist Europeans and stated that the exploitation should cease forthwith; and enjoined independent African states to pursue, in their international policy, principles that would expedite and accelerate the independence and sovereignty of all dependent and colonial African territories. The conference declared "its full support to all fighters for freedom in Africa, to all those who resort to peaceful means of non-violence and civil disobedience as well as to all those who are compelled to retaliate against violence to attain national independence and freedom for the people."[17] This stance on liberation is particularly significant because it reaffirmed the radical anticolonial position of the 1945 Manchester Pan-African Congress.

The conference gave its full backing to the goals of Pan-Africanism and African unity by calling for the creation of a commonwealth of African states. In this regard, the conference made the following resolutions: it endorsed Pan-Africanism and the desire for unity among African peoples; declared that its ultimate objective was the evolution of a commonwealth of free African states; called upon the independent states of Africa to lead the peoples of Africa toward the attainment of this objective; and expressed the hope that the day would dawn when the first loyalty of African states would be to an African commonwealth. Thus, the AAPC unlike the conference of heads of states unreservedly endorsed Nkrumah's desire for a strong African union. Since the delegates were representatives of political parties and not heads of state, they did not have the considerations, interests, and restraints of the heads of state.

With regard to the international boundaries of African countries, the AAPC denounced the artificial boundaries drawn by the imperialist powers to divide the people of Africa; demanded for the abolition or adjustment of such frontiers at an early date; and called upon independent African states to support a permanent solution to the boundary problem based upon the true wishes of the people. In addition, the conference called for the establishment of a permanent secretariat to organize the All African People's Conference on a permanent basis. This secretariat was also to help in promoting understanding and unity among peoples of Africa, accelerate the liberation of Africa from imperialism and colonialism, mobilize world opinion against the denial of political rights and fundamental human rights to Africans, and develop the feeling of community among the peoples of Africa with the object of the emergence of a United States of Africa.[18]

Apart from the radical nationalist and Pan-Africanist resolutions of the AAPC, the conference significantly affected the pace of decolonization struggles, especially in those territories where nationalist activities had been lukewarm, like the Belgian Congo. Due to the extremely harsh and inhumane policies of the Belgian colonial authority, nationalism had been unable to attain a firm footing in this territory. Based on the resolutions of the conference, Patrice Lumumba, one of the Congolese delegates, returned home determined to effect the liberation of his country from Belgian colonial domination. At a rally held on December 28, 1958, Lumumba, citing the resolutions of the Accra conference, demanded independence as a right for the Congolese people. He declared that his objective was the unity and organization of the Congolese people in order to improve their lot. The Belgian authorities were jolted out of their previous complacency and in a panic hastily arranged a decolonization process, the outcome of which plunged the Congo into serious political turmoil that was unfortunately to claim the life of Lumumba.

After the 1958 conferences, Nkrumah initiated steps that he hoped would lead to the eventual realization of a commonwealth of African states. On November 23, 1958, after talks in Accra between Nkrumah and Sékou Touré, the Prime Minister of the newly independent Guinea, the leaders announced that the two countries had decided to form a union, which would constitute the nucleus of a Union of West African States. Both countries agreed to adopt a Union flag and harmonize their policies in the areas of defense, foreign affairs, and economic affairs. In May 1959, during a state visit to Guinea by Nkrumah, both leaders not only reaffirmed the friendship, fraternity, and solidarity between the two countries, they produced a draft constitution for the Union of Independent African States. This draft was to be submitted to the governments of independent African states and those countries that would soon achieve their political independence, for their consideration.

In reaction to the proposed union between Ghana and Guinea and the draft constitution for a Union of Independent African States prepared by the two countries, President Tubman of Liberia decided to convene a meeting of the heads of state of Liberia, Ghana, and Guinea. This meeting, which took place at Sanniquellie, Liberia, in July 1959, discussed issues like African unity, liberation struggles, racial discrimination in South Africa, nuclear tests in the Sahara, and a future conference of independent African states. Although Nkrumah and Sékou Touré insisted that concrete decisions should be taken regarding the nature and specific form that African unity should take, Tubman was of the opinion that such far-reaching and intricate decisions could not be taken until most African states had become independent. Nevertheless, the leaders agreed to the formation of "the Community of Independent African States" with a view to achieving unity among independent African states. Each member state of the community was to maintain its own national identity and constitutional structure. In addition, each member accepted the principle of non interference in the internal affairs of other members. The community was to set up an economic council, a cultural council, and a scientific and research council. Membership was open to any independent African state. The conference resolved to assist, foster, and speed up the liberation of dependent African territories. It was proposed that a special conference of independent African states and non independent states which had dates fixed for independence should be held in 1960 to write a charter which would help to achieve the ultimate goal of unity between independent African states.

Both the Ghana-Guinea Union and the Sanniquellie meeting marked a further advance in the Pan-African movement. They clearly put the issue of African unity on the table at a point when the majority of African states were on the verge of attaining political independence. In certain significant respects, the union and the Sanniquellie meeting set the tone for the conferences and debates that occurred between 1960 and 1963 regarding the form that African unity should take.

Pan-Africanist activities flourished in 1960, the year in which the majority of African countries attained their political independence. Among the Pan-African activities of this year were the second AAPC and Independent African States conferences. The first Pan-Africanist activity to be organized was the second All African Peoples Conference, held in Tunis in January. While emphasizing the political, economic, and cultural aspects of Pan-Africanism, the conference stressed the need for African unity. The conference fixed the objectives of Pan-Africanism as follows: promotion of understanding and unity among the peoples of Africa; development of a feeling of one community among the African people; acceleration of the liberation of Africa from imperialism and colonialism; mobilization of world opinion in support of African liberation; and intensification of efforts toward the emergence of a United States of Africa. With regard to the struggle for Algeria's independence, which was to be one of the issues that caused cleavages in the Pan-African movement, the conference called on all independent African states to recognize the provisional government of Algeria and give material, financial, and military assistance to the Algerian liberation movement. Furthermore, the conference demanded the withdrawal of soldiers from other French African territories fighting on the side of the French imperialist forces against the Algerian liberation fighters.

The second Conference of Independent African States held at Addis Ababa in June 1960 was not as widely attended as had been anticipated. Although invitations were extended to countries that were already independent and those countries whose dates for independence had been fixed, most countries under French colonial rule did not attend. At the conference there was general agreement on the need for African countries to establish some form of unity. But the nature of this unity was greatly in dispute. Ghana, supported by Guinea, pushed for a political union and urged that the Sanniquellie declaration be used as the basis for the achievement of a union of African states. The opposing group, led by Nigeria and Ethiopia, was against this type of strong union but favored cooperation in the economic field while moving gradually toward some form of loose political cooperation. In the words of Maitama Sule, the leader of the Nigerian delegation:

> (W)e must not be sentimental: we must be realistic. It is for this reason that we would like to point out that at this moment the idea of forming a Union of African States is premature. On the other hand we do not dispute the sincerity and indeed the good intentions of those people that advocate it. But we feel that such a move is too radical—perhaps too ambitious—to be of any lasting value.[19]

Nigeria and the other members of this group therefore advocated a gradual and functional approach to African unity. This difference was to characterize the approaches to African unity in subsequent Pan-African conferences.

Nevertheless, there was consensus on the need for more economic cooperation among African countries, the need to eradicate colonialism from the continent, and the need to remove the apartheid system from South Africa. Although there was consensus over supporting the Algerian liberation movement, the conference failed to explicitly recognize the Algerian provisional government as Ghana and Guinea demanded. Instead it recommended that France and Algeria should enter into negotiations.

After the Addis Ababa Independent African States meeting, two major blocs, representing the differing positions on African unity, emerged. These blocs were later to be known as the Casablanca group, representing the radical perspective, and the Monrovia group, representing the moderate/conservative perspective.[20] The Casablanca group emerged from a conference that was held in Morocco in January 1961. The conference was attended by the heads of state of Ghana, Guinea, Mali, Morocco, and the United Arab Republic, including a representative of the Algerian provisional government and the foreign minister of Libya. One of the main issues discussed at the conference was the Congo crisis. Contrary to the stand of the Brazzaville conference, where delegates praised the role the United Nations (UN) was playing in the crisis, this group was highly critical of the UN's role. With regard to Pan-Africanism, the conference decided on the establishment of an effective form of cooperation in the economic, social, and cultural fields. It was resolved to create an African consultative assembly as soon as conditions permitted. This consultative assembly was to be made up of representatives of every African state and was to meet periodically. In the interim, the conference recommended the setting up of a political committee, an economic committee, a cultural committee, and a Joint African high command. To ensure effective cooperation among these organizations, a liaison office was to be established and to be entrusted with the organization of a meeting of experts.

Meanwhile, as a practical way of demonstrating their commitment to Pan-African unity, the heads of state of Ghana, Mali, and Guinea announced the formation of the Ghana-Guinea-Mali Union in December 1960. The union was to make it possible for them to harmonize and coordinate their policies on important foreign affairs, as well as promote cooperation in the economic and monetary fields. In April 1961, they published a "Charter for the Union of African States" and changed the name of their union to "the Union of African States." They regarded this union as the nucleus of a United States of Africa.

The Monrovia group emerged from the conference of heads of state that was held in Liberia in May 1961. The conference was ostensibly convened to bridge the gulf that was emerging in the Pan-African movement and work out ways of fashioning an acceptable form of African unity. However, most members of the Casablanca group refused to attend the conference, partly because of the failure to invite the Algerian provisional government. The conservative and moderate groups dominated the conference. This was clearly reflected in the resolutions that were passed regarding the issue of African unity. It was emphasized that what African states needed was not a political union but unity of aspiration and cooperation in various fields. Other resolutions were: absolute equality and sovereignty of African states; non interference in the internal affairs of other states; respect for the sovereignty of each state and its inalienable right to existence; and promotion of cooperation based upon tolerance, solidarity, and good-neighborliness, periodical exchange of views, and non acceptance of any leadership.

The delegates urged the Algerian provisional government and the French government to expedite an agreement that would put an end to the war of liberation and grant independence to Algeria. In the case of the Congo crisis, the delegates reaffirmed their belief in the ability of the UN to effectively resolve the situation. It was decided that another conference to be attended by all African heads of state would be held in Lagos, in January 1962.

Although the Lagos conference, which was held in January 1962, was expected to bridge the gap between the competing groups, this was blocked by the refusal of members of the Casablanca group to attend. They based their refusal on the fact that arrangements for the conference were made without input from their group and that the representatives of the Algerian provisional government were not invited. In fact, this failure to invite the representatives of Algeria even caused disagreement within the Monrovia group, leading to the refusal of three members of this group (Tunisia, Libya, and the Sudan) to attend the conference. As a result, no North African country was represented at the conference.

The Lagos conference resolved to set up an Inter-African and Malagasy Organization. It adopted in principle a draft charter, which was to become the charter of the organization. This draft charter stressed the need for greater economic cooperation among member states, as well as cooperation in areas like education, culture, politics, and foreign affairs. It stressed the equality of all sovereign African states and non interference in the internal affairs of member states. The charter was to be submitted to all the governments for detailed comments and subsequently considered by a committee of representatives of all the governments concerned. The committee was expected to meet within three months and incorporate all the comments in a revised charter to be submitted to the next conference of heads of state. The documents produced by this committee became known as the Lagos Charter.

By now, the two distinct blocs within the Pan-African movement, the Casablanca group and the Monrovia group, had definitely emerged. Each of these groups had its own idea about the form that African unity should take as articulated in their respective charters. Paradoxically, the events that were to lead to the demise of these two groups and the subsequent formation of a body representing all African countries started at the Lagos conference. This was largely due to the statesmanlike efforts of Emperor Haile Selassie of Ethiopia.

Formation of the Organization of African Unity

In the midst of some of the divisive speeches at the Lagos conference and the reactions from members of the Casablanca group, Emperor Haile Selassie decided to act as a unifier. In the conciliatory speech he delivered at the Lagos conference, he said that:

Ethiopia is committed to the principle of political unity among African states—indeed, we believe that we all are, and that we differ only in our assessment of the speed with which this most desirable of goals can be attained. The task now is to devise the means whereby this basic agreement may be most rapidly advanced.... Ethiopia considers herself a member of one group only—the African group.... We contend, accordingly, that no wider and unbridgeable gap exists between the various groupings which have been created. It is our belief, to the contrary, that a close and careful analysis of the policies adopted by the African nations today on a wider range of questions emphasises, not the differences among them, but the larger number of views which they share in common. We urge that this conference use this as its starting point, that we emphasise and lay stress on the areas of similarity and agreement rather than upon whatever disagreements and differences may exist among us.[21]

After the Lagos conference, Emperor Haile Selassie devoted much of his energy toward convening a meeting of all African heads of state at Addis Ababa during which the issue of African unity would be discussed. At the same time, some members of the two opposing camps started adopting a more conciliatory approach and calling on all African heads of state to sink their differences for the sake of African unity. State visits between African heads of state and bilateral meetings at which the issue of African unity was discussed were intensified. Haile Selassie was determined to hold a meeting of African heads of state in Ethiopia in 1963. He invited all African leaders to the proposed conference and dispatched his foreign minister, Ato Ketema Yifru, on a mission to these countries in order to work out the details of the conference with them. These efforts finally resulted in general agreement, and so the conference was fixed for May 1963.

The meeting of the heads of state was preceded by that of the foreign ministers, which began at Addis Ababa on May 15, 1963. The meeting had the responsibility of producing a draft charter and an agenda for the forthcoming summit of the heads of state. But because of disagreements between ministers from states belonging to the opposing camps, the foreign ministers were unable to agree on a draft charter, although they were able to draw up a comprehensive agenda. When the summit began on May 22, 1963, there was a fear that the disagreement might hinder the formation of a united organization. Nkrumah and some other members of the Casablanca bloc insistently demanded a stronger union of African states while most members of the Monrovia bloc were strongly opposed to such a strong union.

However, the passionate opening address of Emperor Haile Selassie set the tone for a compromise. He emphasized that Africa needed a united platform on which Africans could collaborate in solving Africa's problems, settle inter-African disputes, promote common defense and economic and social programs, and speak with one voice to the rest of the world. As a result, he emphasized that "this conference cannot close without adopting a single African organisation.... If we fail in this, we will have shirked our responsibility to Africa and to the people we lead. If we succeed, then and only then, will we have justified our presence here."[22] One of the most difficult issues that confronted the conference was the form that African unity should take. Nkrumah insisted on a continental union government but this received only scant support. By May 25th, however, the charter of a proposed organization had been prepared, debated, and accepted by the summit. The African leaders decided to form an organization which was titled the Organization of African Unity (OAU). With the formation of this organization, the Casablanca and Monrovia blocs ceased to exist.

This organization was not the type of union government advocated by Nkrumah but a loose association of states in line with the stand of the conservative group. The OAU was a child of compromise although the nature of the organization was generally closer to the position of the conservative group. This was to be expected because the Monrovia group was larger than the Casablanca group. The nature of the organization notwithstanding, the fact that all African countries were able to come together in a single organization marked some form of victory for Pan-Africanism. The objectives of the OAU were the promotion of unity and solidarity among African states and peoples; the achievement of a better life for the peoples of Africa; the defence of their sovereignty, territorial integrity and independence; the eradication of all forms of colonialism from Africa; and the promotion of international cooperation.

The principles of the organization included the sovereign equality of member-states; non interference in the internal affairs of states; respect for the sovereignty and territorial integrity of each state and for its inalienable right to an independent existence; and peaceful settlement of disputes by negotiation, mediation, conciliation, or arbitration. There was also a commitment to the policy of non alignment with regard to all major power blocs.

Conclusion

Pan-Africanism grew out of the gruesome and inhuman experiences of slavery that led to the forced dispersion of a large number of Africans from the mother continent. There were two clearly discernible phases in the growth of the Pan-African movement. The first phase, in the period before World War II, was dominated by Africans in the diaspora and characterized by a great deal of idealism and romanticism. The two leading protagonists of Pan-Africanism during this period were W. E. B. DuBois, with his Pan-African congresses, and Marcus Garvey, who adopted a more radical and multifaceted approach to African unity.

The Italian invasion of Ethiopia in 1935–1936 set in motion forces that led to the second phase of Pan-Africanism. This phase was much more radical and adopted a pragmatic approach to African unity. Continental Africans dominated it and they emphasized liberation from colonialism and the promotion of continental cooperation and unity. This phase successfully linked Pan-Africanism with African liberation and nationalism. Although it was very successful in its liberation agenda, the same cannot be said in terms of its promotion of African unity. The quest for continental unity was bedeviled by a number of divisions resulting in the formation of antagonistic blocs. Nevertheless, the fact that the various blocs were eventually able to compromise and come together to form the OAU can be regarded as some form of victory for the Pan-African movement. Unfortunately, as a product of compromise, the OAU was a rather deformed child from its birth, and it negated some of the hopes and aspirations of genuine and committed Pan-Africanists.

Notes

1. Michael Williams, "The Pan-African Movement," in *Africana Studies: A Survey of Africa and the African Diaspora*, Second Edition, ed. Mario Azevedo (Durham, NC: Carolina Academic Press, 1998), 170.
2. Vincent Bakpetu Thompson, *Africa and Unity: The Evolution of Pan-Africanism* (London: Longman, 1969), 38.
3. Adekunle Ajala, *Pan-Africanism: Evolution, Progress and Prospects* (London: Andre Deutsch, 1973), 7.
4. See Edem Kodjo and David Chanaiwa, "Pan-Africanism and Liberation," in *UNESCO General History of Africa: vol. VIII: Africa since 1935*, eds. Ali A. Mazrui and C. Wondji (Paris: UNESCO, 1999), 744–66.
5. Joseph E. Harris and Slimane Zeghidour, "Africa and Its Diaspora since 1935," Mazrui and Wondji, *Africa since 1935*, 709.
6. Ibid., 709.
7. Ibid., 709–14.
8. Hakim Adi, *West Africans in Britain 1900–1960: Nationalism, Pan-Africanism and Communism* (London: Lawrence & Wishart, 1998), 67–70.
9. Thompson, *Africa and Unity*, 31–3.
10. Ibid., 58–60.
11. Quoted in Ajala, *Pan-Africanism: Evolution, Progress and Prospects*, 11.
12. Kodjo and Chanaiwa, "Pan-Africanism and Liberation," 746.
13. Adi, *West Africans in Britain 1900–1960*, 128–31.
14. Thompson, *Africa and Unity*, 345.
15. For a complete reproduction of the resolutions, see Ibid., 342–50.
16. Ajala, *Pan-Africanism: Evolution, Progress and Prospects*, 17–8.
17. Thompson, *Africa and Unity*, 352.
18. For a complete reproduction of the resolutions, see Ibid., 350–8.
19. Quoted in Ibid., 167.
20. There was a third group (the Brazzaville group) made up mainly of ex-French colonies. This group took a conservative stand and was later to merge with the Monrovia group.
21. Quoted in Thompson, *Africa and Unity*, 175; see also Ajala, *Pan-Africanism: Evolution, Progress and Prospects*, 48.
22. Quoted in C. O. C. Amate, *Inside the OAU: Pan-Africanism in Practice* (New York: St. Martins Press, 1986), 56–7.

Back to Africa, 1958–1962

Colin Legum

The Pan-African political movement came home in 1958; but its cultural wing remained in Europe and the New World. At the time of its transplantation Pan-Africanism possessed a program of ideas and action which can be summed up in nine points.

1. "Africa for the Africans": complete independence of the whole of Africa. Total rejection of colonialism in all its forms, including white domination.
2. United States of Africa: the ideal of a wholly unified continent through a series of inter-linking regional federations within which there would be a limitation on national sovereignty.
3. African renaissance of morale and culture: a quest for the "African personality"; a determination to recast African society into its own forms, drawing from its own past what is valuable and desirable, and marrying it to modern ideas. Modernism is heavily accentuated.
4. African nationalism to replace the tribalism of the past: a concept of African loyalty wider than "the nation" to transcend tribal and territorial affiliations.
5. African regeneration of economic enterprise to replace colonial economic methods: belief in a non-exploiting socialist or communalistic type of socialism; International Communism is rejected outright.
6. Belief in democracy as the most desirable method of government based on the principle of "one man one vote."
7. Rejection of violence as a method of struggle, unless peaceful methods of struggle—*Positive Action*—are met with military repression.
8. Solidarity of black peoples everywhere, and a fraternal alliance of colored peoples based on a mutual history of struggle against white domination and colonialism.
9. Positive neutrality (as it was then called): non-involvement as partisans in power politics, but "neutral in nothing that affects African interests."

The Afro-Arab-Asian Front

Two important events intervened between the last Pan-African Congress (1945) and the first Conference of Independent African States (1958). The first was Egypt's February 23 Revolution (1952) which marks the breakthrough of modern Arab nationalism; the second was the Bandung Conference (1955) which was symptomatic of Asia's arrival on the world scene.

The Pan-Africans played no real part in the Bandung Conference. Ethiopia was the only non-Arab independent African state represented; the then Gold Coast sent observers. Nevertheless, the Bandung Declaration quickly became absorbed into Pan-African thinking.

Col. Nasser's ideas about Egypt's and the Arabs' role in Africa are described in his important brief work on *The Philosophy of the Revolution*. He sees The Revolution linked to three circles—the Arab circle, the African continent circle, and the circle of "our brethren-in-Islam." Of the African circle he writes:

". . . We cannot under any condition, even if we wanted to, stand aloof from the terrible and terrifying battle now raging in the heart of that continent between five million whites and two hundred million Africans. We cannot stand aloof for one important and obvious reason—we ourselves are in Africa. Surely the people of Africa will continue to look to us—we who are the guardians of the continent's northern gate, we who constitute the connecting link between the continent and the outer world. We certainly cannot, under any condition, relinquish our responsibility to help to our utmost in spreading the light of knowledge and civilisation up (*sic*) to the very depth of the virgin jungles of the continent."

Col. Nasser thus clearly saw Egypt playing a leadership role in the continent; a view that he still strongly holds. Cairo became a home for African exiles; Radio Cairo developed special programs to encourage the liberation struggle; and the city put itself forward as a political capital for African independence movements. Islamic teaching was used to expand the "African circle" but it is much less of a political factor than is often thought. It has been more of a factor in, say Somalia, than in Nigeria.

Cairo's political links were mainly organized through the Afro-Asian Solidarity Movement whose first conference was held in Cairo in the closing days of 1957. This conference deviated strongly from the tradition of the Pan-African movement and from the canons of the Bandung Declaration by inviting to full participation—both in the conference itself and in the movement's subsequent work—one of the two sides involved in the cold war. Seeking to justify the participation of the Russians and the Chinese, an official Egyptian statement listed four factors. First, that the effectiveness of the policy of positive neutrality had become more evident. Second, that the socialist bloc had given proof of great superiority in the strategic and scientific fields, thus doubling the chances for peace and freedom in the world. Third, that the struggle between the powers of imperialism and the people of Asia and Africa had crystallized. And fourth, that the fortunes of colonialism had suffered a sharp decline.

But the Afro-Asian Solidarity Movement never became either a successful movement or a happy one, despite some excellent Egyptians on its staff. Few African countries have contributed to the working of the organization notwithstanding promises to do so. The Egyptians themselves have been concerned, from the start, to isolate the influence of the Russians and the Chinese whose participation (tenuous as it has been) has been a source of weakness and embarrassment to them. Egyptian agreement to this heterodox partnership must be explained, not by the rather naïve reasons already quoted, but by the sense of obligation felt at the time for Russia's agreement to build the Aswan dam. Significantly, Col. Nasser did not himself open the first conference. His spokesman was Anwar el-Sadat whose keynote address made a mockery of the structure of the movement:

> "We in Egypt believe in neutralism and non-alignment. This principle has been adopted by many of our friends in Asia and Africa. We believe that by adopting this attitude we ward off the shadow of war, narrow the area facing conflicting blocs and establish a wide area of peace which will impose its existence gradually on the whole world. The neutralism in which we believe means that *we should keep aloof from international blocs* and at the same time make efforts to bring about a rapprochement between those blocs." [Author's italics.]

How does one explain the relationship between Pan-Africanism—with its *black consciousness*—and the Arabs and Asians? The answer, I think, is that although blacks identified themselves emotionally with their skins, they were always intellectually willing and able to identify themselves with peoples of other colors who were in the same boat as themselves—victims of white superiority, of colonialism, of imperialism, and of discrimination. Black regeneration was one aspect of the struggle for emancipation; the wider struggle against colonialism and injustice demanded wider alliances. That is why, in his famous statement, Dr. duBois spoke of "the problem of the Twentieth Century" as "the problem of the colour-line—the relation of the darker to the lighter races of men in Asia and Africa. . . ." He explored this question fully in his prolific writings. In the earlier stages of Pan-Africanism, Duse Mohammed Ali, editor of the anti-imperialist *African Times and Orient Review*, identified himself with the struggles of Marcus Garvey and other Pan-Africanists. He was an Egyptian nationalist of Sudanese descent and an ardent supporter of Zaghloul Pasha, the Wafd leader.

The practical expression of the color struggle also led quite naturally to the Sixth Pan-African Congress (1945) expressing the hope "that before long the people of Asia and Africa would have broken their centuries-old chains of colonialism. Then, as free nations, they would stand united to consolidate and safeguard their liberties and independence from the restoration of Western imperialism, as well as the danger of Communism."

However much, therefore, blacks feel as *blacks,* their color-consciousness has found political expression in associations with peoples of other colors and, indeed, also with Europeans who have been willing to identify themselves with their struggle for emancipation. "Anti-imperialism knows no color," Mr. Kofi Baako, Ghana's Minister of Defense, has said in discussing Nkrumahism. In its wider political context, therefore, Pan-Africanism has not remained racially exclusive, even if the emotional feelings associated with blackness have not necessarily altered in quality.

First Conference of Independent African States, Accra, 1958

The formal launching of the pan-African movement was auspicious. Except for South Africa, all eight independent States met in Accra in April, 1958. Only two—Ghana and Liberia—belonged to Black Africa; five were predominantly Arab and Muslim Egypt, Tunisia, Libya, Sudan and Morocco; the eighth, Ethiopia, was making its official debut in the wider stream of African politics; the Emperor could no longer afford to maintain his policy of isolation in an Africa that was discovering itself.

The Accra conference immediately proved the validity of one of the concepts of Pan-Africanism: a bond of color did exist between former colonial peoples. It proved that neither Islam nor the Sahara constituted an insuperable barrier. In fact, at the first conference and since, it has emerged that some black African States have much more in common, politically, with some Arab States, than either have with their own immediate neighbors. The only divisive factor between the Arab and non-Arab African states has been the question of

Israel: but even on this point the Islamic black States have refused, in their practical affairs to be drawn into the Arabs' war against Israel.

The Accra conference committed the Independent African States to direct involvement in securing the emancipation of the continent: they declared war on colonialism and on South Africa and gave full support to the FLN struggle in Algeria. Henceforth, the colonial struggle was to obtain direct support and encouragement from within Africa. In foreign affairs there was the beginning, too, of a new policy of non-alignment as between "the two antagonistic blocs" in the world; and a determination to establish "an African Personality" in world affairs by working for "a fundamental unity" between African States on foreign questions. This unity was to be based on the Bandung Declaration, the Charter of the UN, and on loyalty to UN decisions. The resolution on racialism not only condemned its practice by others but recommended to African States that they themselves "should take vigorous measures to eradicate, where they arise, vestiges of racial discrimination in their own countries." All the members agreed to observe each other's political and territorial integrity, and to settle their differences, if any, by conciliation and mediation within the African community.

The All African Peoples Organization (Accra, 1958; Tunis, 1960; Cairo, 1961)

There was no mention at the first Accra conference of the United States of Africa, nor of regional federations. It is when we come to the first All African Peoples Conference a non-governmental conference of political parties, which was held in Accra in December, 1958 that we find a resolution in support of the ultimate objective of a Commonwealth of free African States. It is worth noting in passing that this concept has never been endorsed by any of the several conferences of Independent African States (Accra, 1958; Addis Ababa, 1960; Brazzaville, 1961; Casablanca, 1961; Monrovia, 1961). But it usually found a place in the resolutions passed by conferences of non-governmental organizations such as the AAPO.

The first AAPO conference illustrated three other elements in Pan-Africanism. The question of violence was raised, mainly on the insistence of the FLN. After serious debate the conference rejected violence as a means of struggle: it recognized that national independence could be gained by peaceful means "in territories where democratic means are available"; but it pledged support equally to those who "in order to meet the violent means by which they are subjected and exploited, are obliged to retaliate."

The second element relates to inter-racial cooperation. White delegates from South Africa were fully accredited as delegates; these included the Rev. Michael Scott representing Chief Hosea of the Hereros, Mr. Patrick Duncan of the South African Liberal Party, and Mrs. Louise Hooper as a representative of the South African National Congress. This practice was also followed at the second AAPO conference in Tunis in 1960; but at its third conference in Cairo in 1961 neither Indians nor whites managed to get full accreditation. This, it was said, was due to local organizational factors and was not attributable to a change of policy. Accreditation is in the hands of both a Steering Committee and an Accreditation Committee; which did not work very well at the Cairo meeting.

In his welcoming address to the first AAPO conference Dr. Nkrumah declared:

". . . We are not racialists or chauvinists. We welcome into our midst peoples of all other races, other nations, other communities, who desire to live among us in peace and equality. But they must respect us and our rights, our right as the majority to rule. That, as our Western friends have taught us to understand it, is the essence of democracy."

At this conference, the question of the Pan-Africanist slogan "Africa for the Africans" was raised. The Accra conference chairman, Mr. Tom Mboya, announced from the platform, "Once the principle of 'one man, one vote' is established, we will not practice racism in reverse." Dr. Nkrumah went further: "When I speak of Africa for the Africans this should be interpreted in the light of my emphatic declaration that I do not believe in racialism and colonialism. The concept—'Africa for the Africans'—does not mean that other races are excluded from it. No. It only means that Africans, who naturally are in the majority in Africa, shall and must govern themselves in their own countries."

Mr. Julius Nyerere and other leaders have since spoken along the same lines.

Dr. Azikiwe has said: ". . . it should be obvious that unless we accept a broad definition of terms there can be no worthy future for Africanism. That being the case I would like to speak of the peoples of Africa in general terms to include all the races inhabiting that continent and embracing all the linguistic and cultural groups who are domiciled therein."

A third element peeped out briefly at the Accra conference. "The independence of Ghana," Dr. Nkrumah said, "will be meaningless unless it is linked up with the total liberation of Africa." At one time many believed this was not to be taken seriously; but it has recently become quite clear that Ghana's President is in earnest when he says he will commit all the resources and energies of Ghana towards achieving Africa's independence and unity. We will return to this point.

Among the little-known delegates who made their bow at this conference were Mr. Patrice Lumumba and Mr. Joseph Gilmore, better known as Roberto Holden. Mr. Lumumba returned from the Accra meeting to address a mass meeting in Leopoldville which was followed by an outbreak of serious rioting in the city that helped precipitate the decision to give the Belgian Congo its independence. Mr. Holden, the leader of the Union of the Peoples of Angola (UPA), launched his violent liberation campaign just two years later after having "done the rounds" of the African capitals to obtain moral and financial support for his movement. Another delegate who did not accept the non-violent philosophy of the conference was Dr. Felix Moumie, the colorful and loquacious leader of the *Union of the Peoples of the Camerouns (UPC)* who, until he was poisoned in Zürich in 1960, was one of the most active of Africa's itinerant politicians, traveling tirelessly from one African capital to the other and putting in frequent appearances in Moscow and Peking as well. He symbolized the left-wing revolutionary young African leader for whom national independence means more than an exchange of black government for white administration. Leaders who share these feelings are often driven towards alignment with the communists.

The Conakry Declaration

The next important event to be noted is the Conakry Declaration of May 1, 1959, when Guinea and Ghana "solemnly agreed to seal the Ghana-Guinea Union in practice." But the Conakry Declaration went further: it envisaged the Ghana-Guinea Union as the beginning of a *Union* of Independent African States. The use of the term *Union* as opposed to regional federation or association, alarmed Liberia's President Tubman.

The Sanniquellie Declaration

Dr. Tubman took the initiative in calling a meeting with M. Sékou Touré and Dr. Nkrumah at Sanniquellie, a small Liberian village, where they produced the Sanniquellie Declaration of July 19, 1959. It formulates six principles for the achievement of *The Community of Independent African States:* no longer any mention of *Union.* The crucial point is the third principle:

Each state and federation, which is a member of the Community, shall maintain its own national identity and constitutional structure. The Community is being formed with a view to achieving unity among independent African States. It is not designed to prejudice the present or future international policies, relations and obligations of the States involved.
"Pan-Africanism," said Mr. Sule, "is the only solution to our problems in Africa. . . . No one in Africa doubts the need to promote Pan-Africanism. . . . But we must not be sentimental; we must be realistic. It is for this reason that we would like to point out that at this moment the idea of forming a Union of African States is premature. On the other hand, we do not dispute the sincerity and

The Sanniquellie Declaration marks a new phase in the argument between Pan-Africanists about the best way of developing African unity.

Second Conference of Independent African States, Addis Ababa, 1960

This division came into the open when the Sanniquellie Declaration was raised at the Second Conference of Independent African States in Addis Ababa in 1960. Its membership, meanwhile, had increased from eight at the first meeting to fifteen: Algeria Provisional Government, Cameroun, Ethiopia, Ghana, Guinea, Libya, Liberia, Morocco, Nigeria, Somalia, Sudan, Tunisia, United Arab Republic. (Togo and Congo Leopoldville failed to attend.)

Ghana's Foreign Minister, Mr. Ako Adjei, was at great pains to spell out in detail the ideas which Dr. Nkrumah had been advocating with increasing urgency in the latter part of 1959 and early 1960. Commending the Sanniquellie Declaration for adoption he said:

"It is clear from this declaration of principles that the Union of African States which the three leaders discussed and agreed upon is intended to be a political Union. Such a political Union in their view, will provide the framework within which any plans for economic, social and cultural cooperation can, in fact, operate to the best advantage of all. To us in Ghana the concept of African Unity is an article of faith. It is a cardinal objective in our policy. We sincerely believe that the Independent African States can, and may some day, form a real political Union—the Union of African States . . . It does not matter whether you start with an Association of African States or whether with economic or cultural cooperation . . . we must start from somewhere, but certainly the Union can be achieved in the end.

Apart from Guinea this view received little support; the main opposition to it came from the leader of the Nigerian delegation, Mr. Yussuf Maitima Sule. His speech is important for several reasons: firstly because of its disagreement with the Ghana approach; secondly, because of its unveiled attack on Dr. Nkrumah—something new to African assemblies; and thirdly because it demonstrates that Nigeria is no stranger to Pan-Africanist ideas:

indeed the good intentions of those people who advocate it. But we feel such a move is too radical—perhaps too ambitious—to be of lasting benefit. Gradual development of ideas and thoughts is more lasting . . . it is essential to remember that whatever ideas we may have about Pan-Africanism it will not materialize, or at least it will not materialize as quickly as we would like it to if we start building from the top downwards. We must first prepare the minds of the different African countries—we must start from the known to the unknown. At the moment we in Nigeria cannot afford to form union by government with any African States by surrendering our sovereignty . . . President Tubman's idea of the association of states is therefore more acceptable for it is as yet premature to form a Union of States under one sovereignty."

He then went on to make his much-publicized warning that "if anybody makes the mistake of feeling that he is a Messiah who has got a mission to lead Africa the whole purpose of Pan-Africanism will, I fear, be defeated."

In this exchange between Mr. Ako Adjei and Mr. Sule we have the crystallized views of two sides contesting the right way towards unity: Nigeria played the role of the Fabian, arguing from the standpoint of the federalist seeking to build from the bottom upwards; Ghana, the revolutionary unafraid to impel change from the top—a spirit in consonance with ideas of centralist democracy and unitarianism.

These attitudes have become two poles in the Pan-Africanist world; they divide the unitarians from the federalists (this was the tragic argument between Lumumba and Kasavubu in the Congo); the revolutionaries from the reformists, in economic as well as in social questions; and the promoters of a "political union" from those who favor a slower, functional approach.

The Conference of Independent African States did not endorse the Sanniquellie Declaration. In the end they merely requested the President of the conference to address Heads of African States to initiate consultations through diplomatic channels with a view to promoting African unity, and to consider the item at their next meeting in 1962.

Quarrels and Rivals

But this issue was not the only divisive factor between the Independent States. At the Addis Ababa Conference the Cameroun Republic—the first former French territory to join the Conference of Independent African States—mounted a bitter attack on Guinea for harboring the rebel headquarters of Mr. Moumie's UPC at Conakry. Somalia and Ethiopia are unreconciled over "the Somali lands." Tunisia and Egypt have grown steadily apart. For a time their relations were completely ruptured following an unsuccessful attempt to assassinate M. Habib Bourguiba, which he blamed on Cairo. Togo and Ghana quarreled over the question of Ewe reunification and despite attempts at conciliation have remained on bad terms. Relations between Nigeria and Ghana have remained at the level of polite restraint.

What is as significant as the disagreements is that despite them, until roughly October 1960, the Independent African States continued to share a common platform through the Conference of Independent African States, through the Secretariat of the African Group at the United Nations, and even through the AAPO. As late as August 1960, the "Little Summit" conference of thirteen African States was able to reach agreement in Leopoldville (with only Guinea dissenting) on their policy of support for the United Nations in the Congo.

Then everything changed. The five main events associated with this change are: the independence of Nigeria; the sudden independence of the thirteen French territories; the quarrel between Morocco and Mauritania which led to a rift between Morocco and Tunisia because of the latter's support for Mauritania's separate independence; the breakdown in the Central Government of the Congo; and the role of the International Confederation of Free Trade Unions in Africa.

The limited scope of this survey does not allow for a full discussion of all these factors. The serious divisions over the ICFTU, are discussed later. Before their independence, many of the leaders of the French-speaking territories had come to be looked upon by the African States in control of the Pan-African organization as "stooges." It was alleged against them that they had failed to stand against French policy in Algeria—some were even supplying troops to help fight the FLN; that they had not come out against French atomic tests in the Sahara; that they had openly sided with Western policies in contravention of the Pan-Africanist convention of non-commitment; that several states, such as the Cameroun and Togo, had signed treaties for the supply of French troops to defend their governments. As a result, Accra, Rabat, Conakry and Cairo gave open support to exile groups from the French-speaking territories, so that Pan-African organizations (especially the AAPO) had become committed to the opponents of some of the governments in the pre-independent French territories, notably the Cameroun and Niger. In the affairs of the former Belgian Congo, the French territories—led by Congo (Brazzaville)—had openly worked against the Lumumbaists in support of Mr. Tshombe and President Kasavubu. Here, in a nutshell, were the elements making for strong antagonisms against leaders of the emerging French speaking states.

The second event was the belated arrival of an independent Nigeria on the African—and especially West African—scene. By the time of her independence there was, as we have already seen, a division between herself and Ghana on the right approach to African unity. Many of the Nigerian leaders had also come to resent the dominant role assumed by their dynamic neighbor.

The third event was the Congo disaster. Until the fissure opened in the Central Government between Lumumba and Kasavubu, the African states in the United Nations enjoyed their finest hour. They worked in unison, compelling the

Security Council to operate effectively; they staved off the incipient "cold war" threat in the Congo. The presence of Africa as a force in the councils of the world had been made real for the first time in history. There is a great deal still to be written about that period: about Ghana's role as mediator and moderator; about Guinea's role as irritant and militant, outflanking Ghana on the left; about the French African leaders' negotiations with Mr. Tshombe and President Kasavubu; and about Nigeria's incursion through Mr. Jaja Wachuku's chairmanship of the UN Conciliation Commission. But for our purposes it is enough to record that faced with its first major test in an African crisis, the African states were disunited. Nor was it the French-speaking Africans against the rest; the divisions were much more fundamental. In the end one group of African states recognized the Gizenga Government in Stanleyville; another recognized the Kasavubu Government in Leopoldville. And around this division—but for a wider variety of reasons—there grew up two groups, the Casablanca Powers and the Monrovia States.

It is against this background that one must examine the rival groupings that emerged towards the end of 1960.

The Brazzaville Group

The Brazzaville Group—or to give it its official title, *The Union of African States and Madagascar*—grew out of a meeting summoned by the Ivory Coast in Abidjan in October 1960 primarily to discuss the possibility of the French African territories mediating between France and Algeria. The need for such an initiative had become urgent in view of their approaching application for membership of the United Nations. At a subsequent meeting in Brazzaville in December 1960 the decision was taken to form a more permanent association, and this decision was implemented at a meeting in Dakar in January 1961.

The Brazzaville Powers are Congo (Brazzaville), Ivory Coast, Senegal, Mauritania, Upper Volta, Niger, Dahomey, Chad, Gabon, the Central African Republic, Cameroun and Madagascar. Not all the members have agreed to join the French Community; and Togo has not joined the group.

The Brazzaville Declaration called for peace in Algeria by 1961; favored mediation in the Congo; and upheld Mauritania's independence. While opposing political union in the sense of establishing integrated institutions, it nevertheless accepted a permanent Inter-State Economic Secretariat.

This development introduced two new elements into African politics: for the first time invitations were extended to a restricted list of independent states, and a deliberate attempt was made to create a bloc of African states (as opposed to regional groupings).

The Casablanca Powers

Brazzaville led to Casablanca. The group of African states which had adopted a clear-cut Lumumbaist line in the Congo had for some time felt the need to co-ordinate their policies. They had become a minority in the African Group at the United Nations and they were anxious to reassert the initiative taken by them in the earlier stages of Pan-African developments, Morocco, reacting to the Brazzaville Group's sponsorship of Mauritania, took the initiative in calling the Casablanca Conference in January 1961. The list of invitations was again a restricted one. Although more states were invited than finally came, the sponsors have kept their original list of invitations secret. Seven African delegations—Morocco, Ghana, Guinea, Mali, the UAR, Libya, and the Algerian Provisional Government—as well as Ceylon—were represented.

Apart from discussions on a constitutional framework for the Casablanca Powers, four issues dominated the conference: Mauritania, Congo, Israel and the concept of political union. This last point is taken up more fully later in this chapter.

Libya, Ghana and the Algerians had not at first supported Morocco's attitude to Mauritania. Ghana had, in fact, favored her admission to membership of the United Nations. But for the sake of "greater unity" they subsequently reversed their previous stand. (Libya once again changed her position at the subsequent Monrovia Conference.)

On the Congo question the argument was mainly between Ghana and the rest. Only Ghana had refused to withdraw her troops from the UN Command in the Congo (a position she has steadily maintained). On this point she was notably out of step not only with the Casablanca Powers but with her own allies in the Ghana-Guinea-Mali Union. Nor did Dr. Nkrumah favor the suggestion that direct military aid should be given to Mr. Gizenga's Stanleyville regime. He argued at great length against a military adventure because, as he insisted, the "logistics" of keeping Stanleyville supplied would ensure its failure. By all accounts he took a tremendous hammering from many of the other delegations because of this attitude. But in the end his view prevailed.

Ghana was the only member which could have resisted the UAR's demand for branding Israel as an "imperialist base," as it had done at other conferences. But after the Congo debate, Dr. Nkrumah was unwilling to isolate himself on yet another point. Casablanca was the first occasion where a group of African States agreed to the UAR resolution on Israel.

The broad principles of agreement reached at the Casablanca Conference were subsequently incorporated into the Casablanca Charter; its Protocol was signed at a meeting of Foreign Ministers in Cairo in May 1961. Libya did not sign the Protocol. The nineteen articles of the Protocol regulate the executive machinery of the Charter and provide for four permanent committees to be established—political, economic, cultural and a Defense Supreme Command. The Political Committee consists of the Heads of State, or their representatives, and is scheduled to meet "periodically" to co-ordinate policies. The Economic Committee is composed of the Ministers of Finance of member-states, and the Cultural Committee of the Ministers of Education. The Supreme Command consists of the Chiefs of Staff of the various Armed Forces. Bamako, Mali's capital, is designated as the headquarters for the secretariat, with a Moroccan as Secretary-General.

The Charter prohibits accession to foreign military pacts and lays down that all signatories shall strictly adhere to policies of non-alignment. Any independent African state can accede to the Charter.

The Monrovia States

In the same way as Brazzaville had led to Casablanca, so Casablanca in its turn led to Monrovia. The Conference of twenty states that opened in the Liberian capital on May 8, 1961, included the twelve Brazzaville States; as well as Liberia, Nigeria, Somalia, Sierra Leone, Togo, Ethiopia, and the Casablanca deviate, Libya. Tunisia came but chose observer status. The Sudan stayed away as she had from Casablanca. Her official objection was to Mauritania's presence. Neither Congo (Leopoldville) nor the Stanleyville regime of Gizenga was invited to either of the two Conferences.

The Monrovia Conference was originally initiated by Dr. Leopold Senghor, Senegal's President, who had become increasingly concerned about his own country's isolation. Although Senegal belongs to the Brazzaville Powers it is not altogether secure in this association. Not wishing to take the lead himself Dr. Senghor approached Togo's President, Mr. Sylvanus Olympio. After consultation with Liberia's President Tubman and Nigeria's Premier, Sir Abubakar Tafawa Balewa, the three agreed together to act as sponsors, and persuaded the Ivory Coast and Cameroun to join as co-sponsors. At one stage they persuaded Guinea and Mali to act as co-sponsors as well, but under pressure from Ghana these two withdrew on the grounds that the meeting was inopportune and that it should consist only of Heads of State.

In his welcome address to delegates President Tubman indicated some of the aims of the Conference as well as the anxieties that had led up to its being convened:

"It should be crystal clear to every leader that Africans cannot live in isolation if they expect to allay suspicion, fear and tension. The idea of *primus inter pares*, first among equals, is destructive of African Unity and Peace. . . . The sense of oneness should be deeply rooted in the breast of every African. But the whirls of circumstances and ambition can make it difficult for us to fit ourselves into the picture of a unified Africa, the foundation for which we hope will be laid before this Conference closes. I come now to the question of leadership of Africa. . . . In this connection I have observed that there seems to be three schools of thought on this subject. There are those who feel that Liberia should assume leadership based on the fact that she is the oldest African Republic and is riper in political experience; but it will require more than age and political experience to assume leadership of Africa. There are others who assume that Ghana should assume that role because she is physically more developed and embraces larger territories. It will require more than development and larger territory to assume leadership of Africa. And there are yet those who opine that Egypt with its rich traditions dating back to the remotest antiquity should do so. It will require more than rich traditions of antiquity. It will require, in my opinion, the aggregate of the best that is in all compounded in such a manner as to represent the divisibility of Africa indivisible."

The Monrovia Conference has so far been the largest single gathering of African states. For the first time the whole of the French-speaking states joined with a majority of the English-speaking states. On questions affecting the principles of colonialism it spoke with the same sharp voice as the AAPO and other militant Pan-Africanist groupings. It faltered, however, on the atomic tests in the Sahara; its resolution condemning tests in general took note of French assurances that tests in the Sahara would cease. And on Algeria, it accepted a tepid compromise expressing goodwill for the negotiations between the two sides that were about to take place. It backed economic sanctions against South Africa, and promised material support for the Angolans. It expressed full support for the Congo Central Government, but deleted a resolution condemning the assassination of Mr. Lumumba.

The Monrovia approach to the question of co-operation and unity is discussed in the next section. The Conference regretted the absence of the Casablanca Powers and left open the door for them to join at a follow-up conference to be held in Lagos where the machinery of co-operation was to be discussed in greater detail. By the end of the Conference Togo's President, Sylvanus Olympio, was able to say: "At last we are beginning to think of ourselves as Africans and not simply *as extensions* of the European Powers."

No event did more to flutter the dovecotes in Africa's capitals than the Monrovia Conference. Ghana's Press was livid. Having published nothing about the Conference, except to refer to the absence of this or that Head of State, the pro-government papers opened a campaign to show how "bogus" the Conference was. "The very moment the BBC and other imperialist broadcasting brassbands began their phoney adulation of the so-called virtues of the Monrovia slave-mentality operated slogan (*sic*) of 'unity without unification,' students of African history suspected with considerable concern the genesis of this new brand of His Master's Voice, just to discover that it was only the hand that was of Esau." This article in the Ghana *Evening News* went on to suggest that "the imperialists chose Monrovia because they believed that Liberia is still pulling the economic apron-strings." Liberia is referred to as being "in the economic mess-pot with her split, deformed and distorted personality;" and President Tubman is called upon to admit that he is "an American first, African second."

The Nigerian Press was incensed by this language. The *West African Pilot* (the paper started by Dr. Azikiwe and which has always expressed his policies) wrote on May 18, 1961:

"One single parliament for all Africa would be the ideal thing but, unlike Dr. Nkrumah, we would not strive to attain the unattainable. The Ghanaian leader talks sense most of the time but when he goes amiss he does so in a big way. We know that he is a great advocate of African unity but that does not mean that he is always right in his approach to African affairs. Dr. Nkrumah launched a blistering attack on the Monrovia Conference the other day. He was not there and yet this was an opportunity for all leaders of Africa to get together. Dr. Nkrumah is an advocate of unity. He was not there because he and his minority group could not, as they planned, impose their will on the conference. Dr. Nkrumah says Pan-Africanism means nothing unless it transcends the artificial barriers and boundaries imposed by colonialism. Ghana is in union with Guinea. They do not yet have one parliament or currency. Ghana is a very different country indeed, from Guinea, and the so-called union remains a scrap of paper. The Ghanaian Messiah has not yet succeeded in removing 'artificial barriers imposed by colonialism.'"

"As an advocate of unity, Dr. Nkrumah has failed to rally the Ashanti region of Ghana behind him. The lash of the Preventive Detention Act has created an artificial unity. Without his police and para-military groups such as the Builders' Brigades and the Young Pioneers, Dr. Nkrumah knows he will be facing a revolt any day. Yet this is the man who goes before the world, preaching unity. Dr. Nkrumah chooses to believe that the Monrovia powers do not represent the majority of African States. Twenty-one [*sic*] States were represented at Monrovia. There are only five countries in the Casablanca bloc. THE TRUTH IS THAT DR. NKRUMAH MUST BE AT THE HEAD OF ANYTHING OR OUTSIDE IT because he must always lead. He is the Messiah and no camp follower, this man. Dr. Nkrumah must be told that his reckless pursuit of his ambitions for expansion will lead him nowhere. His real aim is to swallow up little Togo and chew off parts of Ivory Coast. This talk of an African parliament and an Africa without boundaries is merely a cloak to conceal his aims. No matter how much we may admire the Ghanaian leader, it is our duty to warn him to desist from the pursuit of false principles."

In another editorial attack the *West African Pilot* said that in pursuance of "cold war tactics" in Africa a struggle for leadership has already developed. "Until recently it was a tournament between Nasser and Nkrumah but Africa today contains many stars and meteorites, all of them seeking positions of eminence."

Politicians joined in the Press war; the NCNC issued a special Press statement appealing to Ghana, Guinea and Mali to join in the discussions with the Monrovia States. In the end, Dr. Nkrumah himself ordered that the Ghana Press should "unilaterally" end its campaign. The importance of this spilling of ink was that for the first time many of the things that had previously only been said in private were now a matter of public discussion with the benefits that go with open disagreements openly discussed.

Pan-African Unity: The Crucial Question

Brazzaville, Casablanca and Monrovia have broken the charmed circle of Pan-African unity. But nobody who has closely followed the interplay of African forces can believe that the present divisions are permanent. Alliances and relationships are still extremely fluid in the Continent. As recently as 1959, Ghana and Guinea signed the Sanniquellie Declaration with Liberia; yet less than two years later the Ghana Press was busy denouncing the Liberians as "western agents of America." But Liberia had not changed. The Tubman of the Monrovia Conference was the same Tubman of Sanniquellie. It is a feature of the contemporary game that friendships and enmities change fast. Nowhere in the Continent have politics or alliances had sufficient time to solidify.

It is not yet possible to make a confident assessment of the fundamental differences that divide the Casablanca Powers from the Monrovia States. Casablanca was for Gizenga's regime; now (like the Monrovians) they are for the Congo Central Government. They support Morocco's claim on Mauritania; Monrovia is opposed to it. On the other hand both groups have declared themselves emphatically against the remnants of colonialism and against *apartheid*. Casablanca is on record for non-commitment; Monrovia is silent on this point. But it would be misleading to tag all the Monrovians as "pro-Western": they represent many different attitudes, ranging from Somalia's strict non- alignment to Madagascar's Francophilism. Is there a clear-cut division then between the two groups on the crucial question of how best to achieve African unity?

The Monrovia declaration on promoting better understanding and co-operation among African states defines five principle's: recognition of each state's equality and sovereignty; freedom from annexation; the right for any state freely and voluntarily to join with another without hindrance; respect for the principle of noninterference in each other's internal affairs; respect for territorial integrity, and condemnation of any state harboring dissident elements who might wish to carry on subversive activities against another state.

Monrovia accepted the idea of promoting cooperation throughout Africa, conditioned by *"non-acceptance of any leadership."* The key to their attitude on Pan-African unity reads: "The unity that it is aimed to achieve at the moment is not the political integration of sovereign African States, but unity of aspirations and of action considered from the point of view of African social solidarity and political identity." Also, they accept, in principle, that an inter-African and Malagasy *Advisory* Organization shall be created. Committees of technicians have been set up to plan cooperation in the economic, educational, cultural, scientific, technical and communications field.

How does all this compare with Casablanca's proposals for African unity? The Casablanca Charter goes only so far as to "affirm our will to intensify our efforts for the creation of an *effective form of co-operation* among the African States in the economic, social and cultural domains." While it provides for the immediate establishment of four joint Committees—political, economic, cultural and a military command—these are purely consultative and have no power of any kind. It is completely vague on the crucial question of what is intended by "an effective form of cooperation." There is no mention of abandoning sovereignty, nor of political union. In fact, although Dr. Nkrumah argued strongly at the Casablanca Conference for political union, his proposal was not accepted. In its closing stages Dr. Nkrumah made his own position admirably clear: "The future of Africa lies in a political union—a political union in which the economic, military and cultural activities will be co-ordinated for the security of our Continent." But he spoke for himself; Casablanca was silent on political union.

Political union is an idea of which Dr. Nkrumah has become the leading and, indeed, virtually the only prominent exponent in Africa; even Guinea and Mali are less specific, except in their approach to the Union of West African States. Dr. Nkrumah's latest book, *I Speak of Freedom,* is, significantly, dedicated to "Patrice Lumumba, late Prime Minister of the Republic of the Congo, and *all those who are engaged in the struggle for the political unification of Africa."* [Author's italics.] To all the disturbing problems in Africa—poverty, neo-colonialism, balkanisation, disunity, cultural and language differences—Dr. Nkrumah offers one recipe: "strong political unity" and "the African race united under one federal government."

"The emergence of such a mighty stabilizing force in this strifeworn world should be regarded," he writes, "not as the shadowy dream of a visionary, but as a practical proposition which the peoples of Africa can and should translate into reality. There is a tide in the affairs of every people when the moment strikes for political action. We must act now. Tomorrow may be too late. . . ."

The debate over *political union* (or as it is sometimes called *organic union)* and *regional association* (or *functional co-operation)* has become a lively issue not only in the higher spheres of Pan-African politics but in national parliaments and on the political hustings as well. Nigeria's official Opposition, the Action Group which is led by Chief Obafemi Awolowo introduced a motion into parliament in September 1961, to promote the idea of a Union of West African States. Opening for the Opposition, Chief Tony Enaharo attacked government policy for advocating "functional co-operation among African States at a time when the climate of progressive opinion throughout Africa is overwhelmingly in favor of organic union."

But neither he nor his leader, Mr. Awolowo, appear to subscribe to the idea of political union as advocated by Dr. Nkrumah. This emerges clearly from a Press Statement made by Chief Awolowo on behalf of the Action Group in June 1961. It is in many ways a remarkable document, coming as it does from a great and influential party which has always been counted in the past among the reformers and traditionalists. It illuminates the strength of feeling about blackness. "The first principle which I advocate is that, in the present context of the world, the black man *qua* the colour of his skin, is confronted with certain knotty and intractable problems which are peculiar to him."

It calls for the creation of an Organization for the African Community which must be "first and last a revolutionary body . . . it must openly advocate the overthrow of all white rule in Africa, whether such rule is by white settlers or by white colonial powers."

But while it makes a number of concrete proposals to achieve African unity, these do not amount to *political union.* It concedes that *confederation* might be considered.

I am not here concerned with the charges leveled against Mr. Awolowo that his plan is only intended to make "political propaganda." The significant fact is that the idea of unity is considered to be sufficiently important to encourage an influential political party to adopt it as its platform in opposition to the Nigerian Government's foreign policy.

What do other Nigerian leaders think? The Governor-General, Dr. Nnamdi Azikiwe, is of course the doyen of the Pan-African leaders in West Africa. In an address delivered in London in August 1961 he put forward his idea for what he called "a concert of African States."

"Granted that political union is desirable," he said, "the question arises whether it should be in the form of a federation or a confederation. If the former, should it be a tight or a loose one, in which case it will be desirable to know whether it is intended to surrender internal or external sovereignty, or both? In this context we cannot overlook the struggle for hegemony as indeed has been the case in the last few years. Hand in glove with the struggle for hegemony goes the manoeuvre for the control of the armed forces for the effective implementation of policy."

Dr. Azikiwe's successor as Premier of the Eastern Region of Nigeria, Dr. M. I. Okpara, was even more concrete in the proposals he outlined for an African Union in London in August 1961 at the end of an extensive tour through Asia and Europe. His proposals envisage: firstly, that Africa should be organized into five Economic Regions (North, East, Central, South and West) with common customs, currency, transport and research organizations; secondly that these economic regions should be welded into political unions; and thirdly, that the five political units should form either a Federation or a Confederation, or even a Common Market.

"My contacts during my journeys through Asia and Europe have confirmed my view that the Union of African States will make for rapid economic advance on this Continent. Its political advantages will be enormous, as the Continent will be completely liberated, and a source of constant temptation to the Imperialist will be removed. . . . Unless there is a rapid and complete change of policy such as we have seen on the West Coast [of Africa], the West will definitely lose Africa. To hasten this change Africans must band themselves together into a Union. . . . It is important that we should carry all along with us if we are to arrive at the goal of a United Africa in peace and not in pieces. Only by the fullest discussion and persuasion is this possible. Coercion or precipitate action will achieve nothing; indeed it might imperil this vital objective of African unity. This is the lesson of Nigerian unity."

But this argument is not confined only to West Africa; it is going on everywhere in the Continent. In an invaluable pamphlet, Mr. Dunduza K. Chisiza, Parliamentary Secretary to the Minister of Finance in Nyasaland and one of Dr. Hastings K. Banda's most effective lieutenants, writes:

"Pan-Africanism, as a strategy for emancipation, is unquestionably effective, but we must build from down upwards, not from up downwards: the fabric of the regions must be knitted together not merely tacked. As a unifying agent for regional co-operation Pan-Africanism is superficial; it is an 'operation roof-top'. This is not a counsel for gradualism in the attainment of independence, which must come quickly, but of realism after it. Ideas about stages vary with writers not only in politics but also in other disciplines such as economics. The writer suggests the following: 1. Attainment of independence. 2. Vigorous modernization of economies. 3. Encouragement of regional economic co-operation and regional consciousness. 4. Political regrouping of neighboring countries."

Non-Alignment and Belgrade (1961)

Non-alignment has become a second major divisive factor between the African states. All believe in non-alignment, or at least profess to do so. There is, however, a wide difference between the *positive neutrality* of Bandung or the *non-commitment* of the first Conference of Independent African States in 1958, and the policy demanded by the Conference of Non-aligned Countries in Belgrade in 1961.

Of Africa's twenty-eight independent states, only ten went to Belgrade: Congo (Leopoldville), Ethiopia, Ghana, Guinea, Mali, Morocco, Somalia, Sudan, Tunisia and the UAR. And of these only two—Somalia and Ethiopia—are members of the Monrovia States. Two others—Tunisia and the Congo—lean towards Monrovia. On the other hand, all the Casablanca Powers were at Belgrade. They had played a leading part in the earlier work of the preparatory committee which met in Cairo in June 1961 to plan the non-aligned conference. Only three non-Casablanca Powers attended this meeting from among the African States: Sudan, Ethiopia and Somalia.

The Cairo preliminary meeting decided two important questions. It defined for the first time what was meant by non-alignment; and, in the light of its definition, it recommended which states should be invited. To be non-aligned a country must: 1. Pursue an independent policy based on peaceful co-existence. 2. Not participate in multilateral military alliances (e.g. NATO, the Warsaw Pact, SEATO or CENTO). 3. Support liberation and independence movements. 4. Not participate in bilateral military alliances with Great Powers; nor should they have foreign military bases on their territory, set up with their agreement.

What is a military alliance? Does it rule out, for example, defense agreements for training local armies? No precise definitions were agreed; this led to bitter controversies both about Latin American and African membership. The Brazzaville Powers were not even seriously considered, but Nigeria was—and it was decided not to invite her (or Tunisia), despite strong protests from such countries as India, the Sudan and Ethiopia. After "the battle of Bizerta" Tunisia was invited; and as a result of a special initiative by Ethiopia a belated invitation went to Nigeria. Her government angrily rejected it, not without bad blood.

"It is a matter of prestige," Nigeria's Foreign Minister, Mr. Jaja Wachuku told Parliament when questioned why the Government had not accepted the invitation. "An African country spent all its time fighting against Nigeria attending this conference. . . . Nigeria is not going to beg for a thing that she is entitled to. . . . If we had the same time as these people have had, perhaps twelve months from today, it may be that all those who have been making the noise will find themselves very backward in international affairs."

Until nearly the end of 1960 the newly-independent African states were, generally-speaking, "neutral on the side of the West." (Two exceptions were Guinea and the UAR; each had good reasons for its attitude.) Even though criticisms of Western policies were voiced everywhere in the Continent, the African leaders continued to shop for aid and ideas almost exclusively in the West. By the end of 1961 this picture had largely changed: no African countries were pro-Communist; none was overtly anti-West; but fewer were "neutral on the side of the West;" and a great number were genuinely non-aligned.

These attitudes are not only reflected in the policies of governments; they are even more strongly shown in the attitudes of political leaders, and especially among the African youth.

Even if Western policies were attuned to the real feelings and needs of Africa it is doubtful whether the drift into non-alignment could have been stopped. Indeed, it is questionable whether Western policies would have been well served by trying to stop it but that is another question. Nevertheless, Western mistakes contributed greatly to its changing fortunes in Africa. The

tragedy of the Congo, and Western pressures in the United Nations (both in the Security Council and in the lobbies) probably did more than anything else to harden sentiment in favor of a more strict application of non-alignment: for one thing it helped to produce the Casablanca Conference with its rigid insistence on members being genuinely non-aligned. But French policy in Africa—the Sahara bomb-tests, the method of surrendering power in some of the French-speaking territories, the Algeria war and Bizerta, as well as her voting record at the United Nations on such questions as South-West Africa and South Africa—also played its part. France's allies in NATO could not escape sharing responsibility for her policies once they refused to disassociate themselves publicly from the French nuclear tests (which were carried out in defiance of the moratorium on testing); and when they tacitly agreed to NATO arms being shipped to Algeria. Once rebellion broke out in Angola, anti-NATO (hence anti-Western) feelings became further hardened, although the uncompromising position adopted by the United States towards the Salazar régime possibly made things less bad than might otherwise have been the case.

These developments occurred at a time when independence was bringing both frustration and fresh opportunities to African states. For the first time many of them had political freedom to negotiate for economic aid where and with whom they chose. At the same time they needed vastly increased technical and financial aid to carry forward the impetus independence gave to development. For these reasons alone the period 1960–62 would unquestionably have witnessed a "breakthrough" of the Communists' economic and technical aid programme into Africa; and this must inevitably have led to some change of attitudes. The Communists' "arrival" as a competitor in Africa should not be connected with Western policies, even if their apparent strength in one or two countries is almost certainly due to Western reluctance to help.

This coincidence of a period of disillusionment, with the West and the appearance of the Communists fresh on the African scene, gave a much sharper edge to African attitudes on non-alignment. While this impact was strongest on militant elements in the Pan-African movement, it had its effect also on such countries as the Sudan, Ethiopia, Tunisia and Somalia.

[1] Padmore, in *Pan-Africanism or Communism*, offers a useful comparison for this summary.

[2] Dr. Nnamdi Azikiwe's phrase.

[3] The Russians were not regarded as being "Asians" qualifying for Bandung membership.

[4] For an earlier reference to this subject by DuBois see p. 24.

[5] This view is not apparently accepted by Chief Awolowo. See Appendix 24.

[6] For a text of its resolutions see Appendix 4.

[7] For the constitution and standing orders of the AAPO see Appendix 22, A, B and C.

[8] For a full text of the resolutions passed see Appendix 22 D.

[9] Ghana sponsored a conference on Positive Action and Security in Accra in April, 1960 to discuss methods of non-violent resistance. The Rev. Michael Scott and other Satyagraha exponents were prominently identified with this conference. In opening it Dr. Nkrumah said: "By our concerted non-violent positive action, we can help

to ensure that this march forward is a swift and peaceful one. . . ."

[10]For a text of the resolutions passed at the Tunis conference see Appendix 22 E.

[11]For a text of the resolutions passed at the Cairo conference see Appendix 22 F.

[12]For text see Appendix 6.

[13]For text see Appendix 7.

[14]For a text of resolutions passed see Appendix 5.

[15]The admission of the Algerians as full members marks the growing success of their effective pressure at Pan-African conferences for unqualified support for their struggle.

[16]Mr. Adjei's speech is given in greater detail in Appendix 10.

[17]For those who wish to refer to the original document it is important to note that the speech of Ghana's Foreign Minister as circulated was altered in some important respects at the time of its delivery.

[18]The countries attending this conference in Leopoldville at the request of the late Mr. Lumumba were Algeria, Congo, Ethiopia, Ghana, Guinea, Libya, Liberia, Morocco, Sudan, Togo, Tanganyika, Tunisia and the U. A. R. The conference disagreed with Mr. Lumumba in his attack on the policies of the U. N. and unanimously agreed to send a message of appreciation to Dr. Bunche. They emphasized the importance of "harmonizing" all aid in the Congo within the U. N. programme. While condemning the "secession and colonialist maneuvers" of Katanga, and pledging support for the integrity of the Congo, they did not agree on a policy for dealing with Mr. Tshombe.

[19]These included Ghana, Guinea, Mali, the U. A. R. and Morocco.

[20]For French and English texts of the Brazzaville Declaration see Appendix 13.

[21]Decision taken at Yaounde in March 1961 where Madagascar's President Tsiranana was elected first president of the organization.

[22]For a text of the resolutions passed at the conference see Appendix 15.

[23]Col. Nasser tried to get support for the Casablanca resolution at the Belgrade Conference of Non-aligned States in September 1961, but failed.

[24]For text of the Casablanca Charter and Protocol see Appendices 15 and 16.

[25]For text of resolutions see Appendix 17.

[26]Extracts from this statement are reproduced as Appendix 25.

[27]For a summary of this speech see Appendix 25.

[28]Algeria's Provisional Government attended the Belgrade Conference as a full member; it was accorded *de jure* recognition by a number of the other countries attending the Conference.

from *Up from Slavery* and 1895 Atlanta Speech

Booker T. Washington

A Slave Among Slaves

I was born a slave on a plantation in Franklin County, Virginia. I am not quite sure of the exact date or exact place of my birth, but at any rate I suspect I must have been born somewhere and at some time. As nearly as I have been able to learn, I was born near a cross-roads post-office called Hale's Ford, and the year was 1858 or 1859. I do not know the month or the day. The earliest impressions I can now recall are of the plantation and the slave quarters—the latter being the part of the plantation where the slaves had their cabins.

My life had its beginning in the midst of the most miserable, desolate, and discouraging surroundings. This was so, however, not because my owners were especially cruel, for they were not, as compared with many others. I was born in a typical log cabin, about fourteen by sixteen feet square. In this cabin I lived with my mother and a brother and sister till after the Civil War, when we were all declared free.

Of my ancestry I know almost nothing. In the slave quarters, and even later, I heard whispered conversations among the coloured people of the tortures which the slaves, including, no doubt, my ancestors on my mother's side, suffered in the middle passage of the slave ship while being conveyed from Africa to America. I have been unsuccessful in securing any information that would throw any accurate light upon the history of my family beyond my mother. She, I remember, had a half-brother and a half-sister. In the days of slavery not very much attention was given to family history and family records—that is, black family records. My mother, I suppose, attracted the attention of a purchaser who was afterward my owner and hers. Her addition to the slave family attracted about as much attention as the purchase of a new horse or cow. Of my father I know even less than of my mother. I do not even know his name. I have heard reports to the effect that he was a white man who lived on one of the nearby plantations. Whoever he was, I never heard of his taking the least interest in me or providing in any way for my rearing. But I do not find especial fault with him. He was simply another unfortunate victim of the institution which the Nation unhappily had engrafted upon it at that time.

The cabin was not only our living-place, but was also used as the kitchen for the plantation. My mother was the plantation cook. The cabin was without glass windows; it had only openings in the side which let in the light, and also the cold, chilly air of winter. There was a door to the cabin—that is, something that was called a door—but the uncertain hinges by which it was hung, and the large cracks in it, to say nothing of the fact that it was too small, made the room a very uncomfortable one. In addition to these openings there was, in the lower right-hand corner of the room, the "cat-hole,"—a contrivance which almost every mansion or cabin in Virginia possessed during the ante-bellum period. The "cat-hole" was a square opening, about seven by eight inches, provided for the purpose of letting the cat pass in and out of the house at will during the night. In the case of our particular cabin I could never understand the necessity for this convenience, since there were at least a half-dozen other places in the cabin that would have accommodated the cats. There was no wooden floor in our cabin, the naked earth being used as a floor. In the centre of the earthen floor there was a large, deep opening covered with boards, which was used as a place in which to store sweet potatoes during the winter. An impression of this potato-hole is very distinctly engraved upon my memory, because I recall that during the process of putting the potatoes in or taking them out I would often come into possession of one or two, which I roasted and thoroughly enjoyed. There was no cooking-stove on our plantation, and all the cooking for the whites and slaves my mother had to do over an open fireplace, mostly in pots and "skillets." While the poorly built cabin caused us to suffer with cold in the winter, the heat from the open fireplace in summer was equally trying.

The early years of my life, which were spent in the little cabin, were not very different from those of thousands of other slaves. My mother, of course, had little time in which to give attention to the training of her children during the day. She snatched a few moments for our care in the early morning before her work began, and at night after the day's work was done. One of my earliest recollections is that of my mother cooking a chicken late at night, and awakening her children for the purpose of feeding them. How or where she got it I do not know. I presume, however, it was procured from our owner's farm. Some people may call this theft. If such a thing were to happen now, I should condemn it as theft myself. But taking place at the time it did, and for the reason that it did, no one could ever make me believe that my mother was guilty of thieving. She was simply a victim of the system of slavery. I cannot remember having slept in a bed until after our family was declared free by the Emancipation Proclamation. Three children —John, my older brother, Amanda, my sister, and myself—had a pallet on the dirt floor, or, to be more correct, we slept in and on a bundle of filthy rags laid upon the dirt floor.

I was asked not long ago to tell something about the sports and pastimes that I engaged in during my youth. Until that question was asked it had never occurred to me that there was no period of my life that was devoted to play. From the time that I can remember anything, almost every day of my life has been occupied in some kind of labour; though I think I would now be a more useful man if I had had time for sports. During the period that I spent in slavery I was not large enough to be of much service, still I was occupied most of the time in cleaning the yards, carrying water to the men in the fields, or going to the mill, to which I used to take the corn, once a week, to be ground. The mill was about three miles from the plantation. This work I always dreaded. The heavy bag of corn would be thrown across the back of the horse, and the corn divided about evenly on each side; but in some way, almost without exception, on these trips, the corn would so shift as to become unbalanced and would fall off the horse, and often I would fall with it. As I was not strong enough to reload the corn upon the horse, I would have to wait, sometimes for many hours, till a chance passerby came along who would help me out of my trouble. The hours while waiting for some one were usually spent in crying. The time consumed in this way made me late in reaching the mill, and by the time I got my corn ground and reached home it would be far into the night. The road was a lonely one, and often led through dense forests. I was always frightened. The woods were said to be full of soldiers who had deserted from the army, and I had been told that the first thing a deserter did to a Negro boy when he found him alone was to cut off his ears. Besides, when I was late in getting home I knew I would always get a severe scolding or a flogging.

I had no schooling whatever while I was a slave, though I remember on several occasions I went as far as the schoolhouse door with one of my young mistresses to carry her books. The picture of several dozen boys and girls in a schoolroom engaged in study made a deep impression upon me, and I had the feeling that to get into a schoolhouse and study in this way would be about the same as getting into paradise.

So far as I can now recall, the first knowledge that I got of the fact that we were slaves, and that freedom of the slaves was being discussed, was early one morning before day, when I was awakened by my mother kneeling over her children and fervently praying that Lincoln and his armies might be successful, and that one day she and her children might be free. In this connection I have never been able to understand how the slaves throughout the South, completely ignorant as were the masses so far as books or newspapers were concerned, were able to keep themselves so accurately and completely informed about the great National questions that were agitating the country.

***

I cannot remember a single instance during my childhood or early boyhood when our entire family sat down to the table together, and God's blessing was asked, and the family ate a meal in a civilized manner. On the plantation in Virginia, and even later, meals were gotten by the children very much as dumb animals get theirs. It was a piece of bread here and a scrap of meat there. It was a cup of milk at one time and some potatoes at another. Sometimes a portion of our family would eat out of the skillet or pot, while some one else would eat from a tin plate held on the knees, and often using nothing but the hands with which to hold the food. When I had grown to sufficient size, I was required to go to the "big house" at meal-times to fan the flies from the table by means of a large set of paper fans operated by a pulley. Naturally much of the conversation of the white people turned upon the subject of freedom and the war, and I absorbed a good deal of it. I remember that at one time I saw two of my young mistresses and some lady visitors eating ginger-cakes, in the yard. At that time those cakes seemed to me to be absolutely the most tempting and desirable things that I had ever seen; and I then and there resolved that, if I ever got free, the height of my ambition would be reached if I could get to the point where I could secure and eat ginger-cakes in the way that I saw those ladies doing.

Of course as the war was prolonged the white people, in many cases, often found it difficult to secure food for themselves. I think the slaves felt the deprivation less than the whites, because the usual diet for the slaves was corn bread and pork, and these could be raised on the plantation; but coffee, tea, sugar, and other articles which the whites had been accustomed to use could not be raised on the plantation, and the conditions brought about by the war frequently made it impossible to secure these things. The whites were often in great straits. Parched corn was used for coffee, and a kind of black molasses was used instead of sugar. Many times nothing was used to sweeten the so-called tea and coffee.

The first pair of shoes that I recall wearing were wooden ones. They had rough leather on the top, but the bottoms, which were about an inch thick, were of wood. When I walked they made a fearful noise, and besides this they were very inconvenient, since there was no yielding to the natural pressure of the foot. In wearing them one presented an exceedingly awkward appearance. The most trying ordeal that I was forced to endure as a slave boy, however, was the wearing of a flax shirt. In the portion of Virginia where I lived it was common to use flax as part of the clothing for the slaves. That part of the flax from which our clothing was made was largely the refuse, which of course was the cheapest and roughest part. I can scarcely imagine any torture, except, perhaps, the pulling of a tooth, that is equal to that caused by putting on a new flax shirt for the first time. It is almost equal to the feeling that one would experience if he had a dozen or more chestnut burrs, or a hundred small pin-points, in contact with his flesh. Even to this day I can recall accurately the tortures that I underwent when putting on one of these garments. The fact that my flesh was soft and tender added to the pain. But I had no choice. I had to wear the flax shirt or none; and had it been left to me to choose, I should have chosen to wear no covering.

***

I pity from the bottom of my heart any nation or body of people that is so unfortunate as to get entangled in the net of slavery. I have long since ceased to cherish any spirit of bitterness against the Southern white people on account of the enslavement of my race. No one section of our country was wholly responsible for its introduction, and, besides, it was recognized and protected for years by the General Government. Having once got its tentacles fastened on to the economic and social life of the Republic, it was no easy matter for the country to relieve itself of the institution. Then, when we rid ourselves of prejudice, or racial feeling, and look facts in the face, we must acknowledge that, notwithstanding the cruelty and moral wrong of slavery, the ten million Negroes inhabiting this country, who themselves or whose ancestors went through the school of American slavery, are in a stronger and more hopeful condition, materially, intellectually, morally, and religiously, than is true of an equal number of black people in any other portion of the globe. This is so to such an extent that Negroes in this country, who themselves or whose forefathers went through the school of slavery, are constantly returning to Africa as missionaries to enlighten those who remained in the fatherland. This I say, not to justify slavery—on the other hand, I condemn it as an institution, as we all know that in America it was established for selfish and financial reasons, and not from a missionary motive—but to call attention to a fact, and to show how Providence so often uses men and institutions to accomplish a purpose. When persons ask me in these days how, in the midst of what sometimes seem hopelessly discouraging conditions, I can have such faith in the future of my race in this country, I remind them of the wilderness through which and out of which, a good Providence has already led us.

Ever since I have been old enough to think for myself, I have entertained the idea that, notwithstanding the cruel wrongs inflicted upon us, the black man got nearly as much out of slavery as the white man did. The hurtful influences of the institution were not by any means confined to the Negro. This was fully illustrated by the life upon our own plantation. The whole machinery of slavery was so constructed as to cause labour, as a rule, to be looked upon as a badge of degradation, of inferiority. Hence labour was something that both races on the slave plantation sought to escape. The slave system on our place, in a large measure, took the spirit of self-reliance and self-help out of the white people. My old master had many boys and girls, but not one, so far as I know, ever mastered a single trade or special line of productive industry. The girls were not taught to cook, sew, or to take care of the house. All of this was left to the slaves. The slaves, of course, had little personal interest in the life of the plantation, and their ignorance prevented them from learning how to do things in the most improved and thorough manner. As a result of the system, fences were out of repair, gates were hanging half off the hinges, doors creaked, window-panes were out, plastering had fallen but was not replaced, weeds grew in the yard. As a rule, there was food for whites and blacks, but inside the house, and on the dining-room table, there was wanting that delicacy and refinement of touch and finish which can make a home the most convenient, comfortable, and attractive place in the world. Withal there was a waste of food and other materials which was sad. When freedom came, the slaves were almost as well fitted to begin life anew as the master, except in the matter of book-learning and ownership of property. The slave owner and his sons had mastered no special industry. They unconsciously had imbibed the feeling that manual labour was not the proper thing for them. On the other hand, the slaves, in many cases, had mastered some handicraft, and none were ashamed, and few unwilling, to labour.

Finally the war closed, and the day of freedom came. It was a momentous and eventful day to all upon our plantation. We had been expecting it. Freedom was in the air, and had been for months. Deserting soldiers returning to their homes were to be seen every day. Others who had been discharged, or whose regiments had been paroled, were constantly passing near our place. The "grape-vine telegraph" was kept busy night and day. The news and mutterings of great events were swiftly carried from one plantation to another. In the fear of "Yankee" invasions, the silverware and other valuables were taken from the "big house," buried in the woods, and guarded by trusted slaves. Woe be to any one who would have attempted to disturb the buried treasure. The slaves would give the Yankee soldiers food, drink, clothing—anything but that which had been specifically intrusted to their care and honour. As the great day drew nearer, there was more singing in the slave quarters than usual. It was bolder, had more ring, and lasted later into the night. Most of the verses of the plantation songs had some reference to freedom. True, they had sung those same verses before, but they had been careful to explain that the "freedom" in these songs referred to the next world, and had no connection with life in this world. Now they gradually threw off the mask, and were not afraid to let it be known that the "freedom" in their songs meant freedom of the body in this world. The night before the eventful day, word was sent to the slave quarters to the effect that something unusual was going to take place at the "big house" the next morning. There was little, if any, sleep that night. All was excitement and expectancy. Early the next morning word was sent to all the slaves, old and young, to gather at the house. In company with my mother, brother, and sister, and a large number of other slaves, I went to the master's house. All of our master's family were either standing or seated on the veranda of the house, where they could see what was to take place and hear what was said. There was a feeling of deep interest, or perhaps sadness, on their faces, but not bitterness. As I now recall the impression they made upon me, they did not at the moment seem to be sad because of the loss of property, but rather because of parting with those whom they had reared and who were in many ways very close to them. The most distinct thing that I now recall in connection with the scene was that some man who seemed to be a stranger (a United States officer, I presume) made a little speech and then read a rather long paper—the Emancipation Proclamation, I think. After the reading we were told that we were all free, and could go when and where we pleased. My mother, who was standing by my side, leaned over and kissed her children, while tears of joy ran down her cheeks. She explained to us what it all meant, that this was the day for which she had been so long praying, but fearing that she would never live to see.

For some minutes there was great rejoicing, and thanksgiving, and wild scenes of ecstasy. But there was no feeling of bitterness. In fact, there was pity among the slaves for our former owners. The wild rejoicing on the part of the emancipated coloured people lasted but for a brief period, for I noticed that by the time they returned to their cabins there was a change in their feelings. The great responsibility of being free, of having charge of themselves, of having to think and plan for themselves and their children, seemed to take possession of them. It was very much like suddenly turning a youth of ten or twelve years out into the world to provide for himself. In a few hours the great questions with which the Anglo-Saxon race had been grappling for centuries had been thrown upon these people to be solved. These were the questions of a home, a living, the rearing of children, education, citizenship, and the establishment and support of churches. Was it any wonder that within a few hours the wild rejoicing ceased and a feeling of deep gloom seemed to pervade the slave quarters? To some it seemed that, now that they were in actual possession of it, freedom was a more serious thing than they had expected to find it. Some of the slaves were seventy or eighty years old; their best days were gone. They had no strength with which to earn a living in a strange place and among strange people, even if they had been sure where to find a new place of abode. To this class the problem seemed especially hard. Besides, deep down in their hearts there was a strange and peculiar attachment to "old Marster" and "old Missus," and to their children, which they found it hard to think of breaking off. With these they had spent in some cases nearly a half-century, and it was no light thing to think of parting. Gradually, one by one, stealthily at first, the older slaves began to wander from the slave quarters back to the "big house" to have a whispered conversation with their former owners as to the future.

Boyhood Days

After the coming of freedom there were two points upon which practically all the people on our place were agreed, and I find that this was generally true throughout the South: that they must change their names, and that they must leave the old plantation for at least a few days or weeks in order that they might really feel sure that they were free.

In some way a feeling got among the coloured people that it was far from proper for them to bear the surname of their former owners, and a great many of them took other surnames. This was one of the first signs of freedom. When they were slaves, a coloured person was simply called "John" or "Susan." There was seldom occasion for more than the use of the one name. If "John" or "Susan" belonged to a white man by the name of "Hatcher," sometimes he was called "John Hatcher," or as often "Hatcher's John." But there was a feeling that "John Hatcher" or "Hatcher's John" was not the proper title by which to denote a freeman; and so in many cases "John Hatcher" was changed to "John S. Lincoln" or "John S. Sherman," the initial "S" standing for no name, it being simply a part of what the coloured man proudly called his "entitles."

As I have stated, most of the coloured people left the old plantation for a short while at least, so as to be sure, it seemed, that they could leave and try their freedom on to see how it felt. After they had remained away for a time, many of the older slaves, especially, returned to their old homes and made some kind of contract with their former owners by which they remained on the estate.

My mother's husband, who was the stepfather of my brother John and myself, did not belong to the same owners as did my mother. In fact, he seldom came to our plantation. I remember seeing him there perhaps once a year, that being about Christmas time. In some way, during the war, by running away and following the Federal soldiers, it seems, he found his way into the new state of West Virginia. As soon as freedom was declared, he sent for my mother to come to the Kanawha Valley, in West Virginia. At that time a journey from Virginia over the mountains to West Virginia was rather a tedious and in some cases a painful undertaking. What little clothing and few household goods we had were placed in a cart, but the children walked the greater portion of the distance, which was several hundred miles.

I do not think any of us ever had been very far from the plantation, and the taking of a long journey into another state was quite an event. The parting from our former owners and the members of our own race on the plantation was a serious occasion. From the time of our parting till their death we kept up a correspondence with the older members of the family, and in later years we have kept in touch with those who were the younger members. We were several weeks making the trip, and most of the time we slept in the open air and did our cooking over a log fire out-of-doors. One night I recall that we camped near an abandoned log cabin, and my mother decided to build a fire in that for cooking, and afterward to make a "pallet" on the floor for our sleeping. Just as the fire had gotten well started a large black snake fully a yard and a half long dropped down the chimney and ran out on the floor. Of course we at once abandoned that cabin. Finally we reached our destination—a little town called Malden, which is about five miles from Charleston, the present capital of the state.

At that time salt-mining was the great industry in that part of West Virginia, and the little town of Malden was right in the midst of the salt-furnaces. My stepfather had already secured a job at a salt-furnace, and he had also secured a little cabin for us to live in. Our new house was no better than the one we had left on the old plantation in Virginia. In fact, in one respect it was worse. Notwithstanding the poor condition of our plantation cabin, we were at all times sure of pure air. Our new home was in the midst of a cluster of cabins crowded closely together, and as there were no sanitary regulations, the filth about the cabins was often intolerable. Some of our neighbours were coloured people, and some were the poorest and most ignorant and degraded white people. It was a motley mixture. Drinking, gambling, quarrels, fights, and shockingly immoral practices were frequent. All who lived in the little town were in one way or another connected with the salt business.

***

Perhaps the thing that touched and pleased me most in connection with my starting for Hampton was the interest that many of the older coloured people took in the matter. They had spent the best days of their lives in slavery, and hardly expected to live to see the time when they would see a member of their race leave home to attend a boarding-school. Some of these older people would give me a nickel, others a quarter, or a handkerchief.

Finally the great day came, and I started for Hampton. I had only a small, cheap satchel that contained what few articles of clothing I could get. My mother at the time was rather weak and broken in health. I hardly expected to see her again, and thus our parting was all the more sad. She, however, was very brave through it all. At that time there were no through trains connecting that part of West Virginia with eastern Virginia. Trains ran only a portion of the way, and the remainder of the distance was travelled by stage-coaches.

The distance from Malden to Hampton is about five hundred miles. I had not been away from home many hours before it began to grow painfully evident that I did not have enough money to pay my fare to Hampton. One experience I shall long remember. I had been travelling over the mountains most of the afternoon in an old-fashioned stage-coach, when, late in the evening, the coach stopped for the night at a common, unpainted house called a hotel. All the other passengers except myself were whites. In my ignorance I supposed that the little hotel existed for the purpose of accommodating the passengers who travelled on the stage-coach. The difference that the colour of one's skin would make I had not thought anything about. After all the other passengers had been shown rooms and were getting ready for supper, I shyly presented myself before the man at the desk. It is true I had practically no money in my pocket with which to pay for bed or food, but I had hoped in some way to beg my way into the good graces of the landlord, for at that season in the mountains of Virginia the weather was cold, and I wanted to get indoors for the night. Without asking as to whether I had any money, the man at the desk firmly refused to even consider the matter of providing me with food or lodging. This was my first experience in finding out what the colour of my skin meant. In some way I managed to keep warm by walking about, and so got through the night. My whole soul was so bent upon reaching Hampton that I did not have time to cherish any bitterness toward the hotel-keeper.

***

When I had saved what I considered enough money with which to reach Hampton, I thanked the captain of the vessel for his kindness, and started again. Without any unusual occurrence I reached Hampton, with a surplus of exactly fifty cents with which to begin my education. To me it had been a long, eventful journey; but the first sight of the large, three-story, brick school building seemed to have rewarded me for all that I had undergone in order to reach the place. If the people who gave the money to provide that building could appreciate the influence the sight of it had upon me, as well as upon thousands of other youths, they would feel all the more encouraged to make such gifts. It seemed to me to be the largest and most beautiful building I had ever seen. The sight of it seemed to give me new life. I felt that a new kind of existence had now begun—that life would now have a new meaning. I felt that I had reached the promised land, and I resolved to let no obstacle prevent me from putting forth the highest effort to fit myself to accomplish the most good in the world.

As soon as possible after reaching the grounds of the Hampton Institute, I presented myself before the head teacher for assignment to a class. Having been so long without proper food, a bath, and change of clothing, I did not, of course, make a very favourable impression upon her, and I could see at once that there were doubts in her mind about the wisdom of admitting me as a student. I felt that I could hardly blame her if she got the idea that I was a worthless loafer or tramp. For some time she did not refuse to admit me, neither did she decide in my favour, and I continued to linger about her, and to impress her in all the ways I could with my worthiness. In the meantime I saw her admitting other students, and that added greatly to my discomfort, for I felt, deep down in my heart, that I could do as well as they, if I could only get a chance to show what was in me.

After some hours had passed, the head teacher said to me; "The adjoining recitation-room needs sweeping. Take the broom and sweep it."

It occurred to me at once that here was my chance. Never did I receive an order with more delight. I knew that I could sweep, for Mrs. Ruffner had thoroughly taught me how to do that when I lived with her.

I swept the recitation-room three times. Then I got a dusting-cloth and I dusted it four times. All the woodwork around the walls, every bench, table, and desk, I went over four times with my dusting-cloth. Besides, every piece of furniture had been moved and every closet and corner in the room had been thoroughly cleaned. I had the feeling that in a large measure my future depended upon the impression I made upon the teacher in the cleaning of that room. When I was through, I reported to the head teacher. She was a "Yankee" woman who knew just where to look for dirt. She went into the room and inspected the floor and closets; then she took her handkerchief and rubbed it on the woodwork about the walls, and over the table and benches. When she was unable to find one bit of dirt on the floor, or a particle of dust on any of the furniture, she quietly

remarked, "I guess you will do to enter this institution."

I was one of the happiest souls on earth. The sweeping of that room was my college examination, and never did any youth pass an examination for entrance into Harvard or Yale that gave him more genuine satisfaction. I have passed several examinations since then, but I have always felt that this was the best one I ever passed.

I have spoken of my own experience in entering the Hampton Institute. Perhaps few, if any, had anything like the same experience that I had, but about that same period there were hundreds who found their way to Hampton and other institutions after experiencing something of the same difficulties that I went through. The young men and women were determined to secure an education at any cost.

The sweeping of the recitation-room in the manner that I did it seems to have paved the way for me to get through Hampton. Miss Mary F. Mackie, the head teacher, offered me a position as janitor. This, of course, I gladly accepted, because it was a place where I could work out nearly all the cost of my board. The work was hard and taxing, but I stuck to it. I had a large number of rooms to care for, and had to work late into the night, while at the same time I had to rise by four o'clock in the morning, in order to build the fires and have a little time in which to prepare my lessons. In all my career at Hampton, and ever since I have been out in the world, Miss Mary F. Mackie, the head teacher to whom I have referred, proved one of my strongest and most helpful friends. Her advice and encouragement were always helpful and strengthening to me in the darkest hour.

***

After having been for a while at Hampton, I found myself in difficulty because I did not have books and clothing. Usually, however, I got around the trouble about books by borrowing from those who were more fortunate than myself. As to clothes, when I reached Hampton I had practically nothing. Everything that I possessed was in a small hand satchel. My anxiety about clothing was increased because of the fact that General Armstrong made a personal inspection of the young men in ranks, to see that their clothes were clean. Shoes had to be polished, there must be no buttons off the clothing, and no greasespots. To wear one suit of clothes continually, while at work and in the schoolroom, and at the same time keep it clean, was rather a hard problem for me to solve. In some way I managed to get on till the teachers learned that I was in earnest and meant to succeed, and then some of them were kind enough to see that I was partly supplied with second-hand clothing that had been sent in barrels from the North. These barrels proved a blessing to hundreds of poor but deserving students. Without them I question whether I should ever have gotten through Hampton.

When I first went to Hampton I do not recall that I had ever slept in a bed that had two sheets on it. In those days there were not many buildings there, and room was very precious. There were seven other boys in the same room with me; most of them, however, students who had been there for some time. The sheets were quite a puzzle to me. The first night I slept under both of them, and the second night I slept on top of both of them; but by watching the other boys I learned my lesson in this, and have been trying to follow it ever since and to teach it to others.

I was among the youngest of the students who were in Hampton at that time. Most of the students were men and women—some as old as forty years of age. As I now recall the scene of my first year, I do not believe that one often has the opportunity of coming into contact with three or four hundred men and women who were so tremendously in earnest as these men and women were. Every hour was occupied in study or work. Nearly all had had enough actual contact with the world to teach them the need of education. Many of the older ones were, of course, too old to master the text-books very thoroughly, and it was often sad to watch their struggles; but they made up in earnestness much of what they lacked in books. Many of them were as poor as I was, and, besides having to wrestle with their books, they had to struggle with a poverty which prevented their having the necessities of life. Many of them had aged parents who were dependent upon them, and some of them were men who had wives whose support in some way they had to provide for.

The great and prevailing idea that seemed to take possession of every one was to prepare himself to lift up the people at his home. No one seemed to think of himself. And the officers and teachers, what a rare set of human beings they were! They worked for the students night and day, in season and out of season. They seemed happy only when they were helping the students in some manner. Whenever it is written—and I hope it will be—the part that the Yankee teachers played in the education of the Negroes immediately after the war will make one of the most thrilling parts of the history of this country. The time is not far distant when the whole South will appreciate this service in a way that it has not yet been able to do.

The Reconstruction Period

It could not have been expected that a people who had spent generations in slavery, and before that generations in the darkest heathenism, could at first form any proper conception of what an education meant. In every part of the South, during the Reconstruction period, schools, both day and night, were tilled to overflowing with people of all ages and conditions, some being as far along in age as sixty and seventy years. The ambition to secure an education was most praiseworthy and encouraging. The idea, however, was too prevalent that, as soon as one secured a little education, in some unexplainable way he would be free from most of the hardships of the world, and, at any rate, could live without manual labour. There was a further feeling that a knowledge, however little, of the Greek and Latin languages would make one a very superior human being, something bordering almost on the supernatural. I remember that the first coloured man whom I saw who knew something about foreign languages impressed me at that time as being a man of all others to be envied.

Naturally, most of our people who received some little education became teachers or preachers. While among these two classes there were many capable, earnest, godly men and women, still a large proportion took up teaching or preaching as an easy way to make a living. Many became teachers who could do little more than write their names. I remember there came into our neighbourhood one of this class, who was in search of a school to teach, and the question arose while he was there as to the shape of the earth and how he would teach the children concerning this subject. He explained his position in the matter by saying that he was prepared to teach that the earth was either flat or round, according to the preference of a majority of his patrons.

***

During the whole of the Reconstruction period our people throughout the South looked to the Federal Government for everything, very much as a child looks to its mother. This was not unnatural. The central government gave them freedom, and the whole Nation had been enriched for more than two centuries by the labour of the Negro. Even as a youth, and later in manhood, I had the feeling that it was cruelly wrong in the central government, at the beginning of our freedom, to fail to make some provision for the general education of our people in addition to what the states might do, so that the people would be the better prepared for the duties of citizenship.

It is easy to find fault, to remark what might have been done, and perhaps, after all, and under all the circumstances, those in charge of the conduct of affairs did the only thing that could be done at the time. Still, as I look back now over the entire period of our freedom, I cannot help feeling that it would have been wiser if some plan could have been put in operation which would have made the possession of a certain amount of education or property, or both, a test for the exercise of the franchise, and a way provided by which this test should be made to apply honestly and squarely to both the white and black races.

Though I was but little more than a youth during the period of Reconstruction, I had the feeling that mistakes were being made, and that things could not remain in the condition that they were in then very long. I felt that the Reconstruction policy, so far as it related to my race, was in a large measure on a false foundation, was artificial and forced. In many cases it seemed to me that the ignorance of my race was being used as a tool with which to help white men into office, and that there was an element in the North which wanted to punish the Southern white men by forcing the Negro into positions over the heads of the Southern whites. I felt that the Negro would be the one to suffer for this in the end. Besides, the general political agitation drew the attention of our people away from the more fundamental matters of perfecting themselves in the industries at their doors and in securing property.

The temptations to enter political life were so alluring that I came very near yielding to them at one time, but I was kept from doing so by the feeling that I would be helping in a more substantial way by assisting in the laying of the foundation of the race through a generous education of the hand, head, and heart.

The Atlanta Exposition Address

Mr. President and Gentlemen of the Board of Directors and Citizens.

One-third of the population of the South is of the Negro race. No enterprise seeking the material, civil, or moral welfare of this section can disregard this element of our population and reach the highest success. I but convey to you, Mr. President and Directors, the sentiment of the masses of my race when I say that in no way have the value and manhood of the American Negro been more fittingly and generously recognized than by the managers of this magnificent Exposition at every stage of its progress. It is a recognition that will do more to cement the friendship of the two races than any occurrence since the dawn of our freedom.

Not only this, but the opportunity here afforded will awaken among us a new era of industrial progress. Ignorant and inexperienced, it is not strange that in the first years of our new life we began at the top instead of at the bottom; that a seat in Congress or the state legislature was more sought than real estate or industrial skill; that the political convention or stump speaking had more attractions than starting a dairy farm or truck garden.

A ship lost at sea for many days suddenly sighted a friendly vessel. From the mast of the unfortunate vessel was seen a signal, "Water, water; we die of thirst!" The answer from the friendly vessel at once came back, "Cast down your bucket where you are." A second time the signal, "Water, water; send us water!" ran up from the distressed vessel, and was answered, "Cast down your bucket where you are." And a third and fourth signal for water was answered, "Cast down your bucket where you are." The captain of the distressed vessel, at last heeding the injunction, cast down his bucket, and it came up full of fresh, sparkling water from the mouth of the Amazon River. To those of my race who depend on bettering their condition in a foreign land or who underestimate the importance of cultivating friendly relations with the Southern white man, who is their next-door neighbour, I would say: "Cast down your bucket where you are"—cast it down in making friends in every manly way of the people of all races by whom we are surrounded.

Cast it down in agriculture, mechanics, in commerce, in domestic service, and in the professions. And in this connection it is well to bear in mind that whatever other sins the South may be called to bear, when it comes to business, pure and simple, it is in the South that the Negro is given a man's chance in the commercial world, and in nothing is this Exposition more eloquent than in emphasizing this chance. Our greatest danger is that in the great leap from slavery to freedom we may overlook the fact that the masses of us are to live by the productions of our hands, and fail to keep in mind that we shall prosper in proportion as we learn to dignify and glorify common labour and put brains and skill into the common occupations of life; shall prosper in proportion as we learn to draw the line between the superficial and the substantial, the ornamental gewgaws of life and the useful. No race can prosper till it learns that there is as much dignity in tilling a field as in writing a poem. It is at the bottom of life we must begin, and not at the top. Nor should we permit our grievances to overshadow our opportunities.

To those of the white race who look to the incoming of those of foreign birth and strange tongue and habits for the prosperity of the South, were I permitted I would repeat what I say to my own race, "Cast down your bucket where you are." Cast it down among the eight millions of Negroes whose habits you know, whose fidelity and love you have tested in days when to have proved treacherous meant the ruin of your firesides. Cast down your bucket among these people who have, without strikes and labour wars, tilled your fields, cleared your forests, builded your railroads and cities, and brought forth treasures from the bowels of the earth, and helped make possible this magnificent representation of the progress of the South. Casting down your bucket among my people, helping and encouraging them as you are doing on these grounds, and to education of head, hand, and heart, you will find that they will buy your surplus land, make blossom the waste places in your fields, and run your factories. While doing this, you can be sure in the future, as in the past, that you and your families will be surrounded by the most patient, faithful, law-abiding, and unresentful people that the world has seen. As we have proved our loyalty to you in the past, in nursing your children, watching by the sick-bed of your mothers and fathers, and often following them with tear-dimmed eyes to their graves, so in the future, in our humble way, we shall stand by you with a devotion that no foreigner can approach, ready to lay down our lives, if need be, in defence of yours, interlacing our industrial, commercial, civil, and religious life with yours in a way that shall make the interests of both races one. In all things that are purely social we can be as separate as the fingers, yet, one as the hand in all things essential to mutual progress.

There is no defence or security for any of us except in the highest intelligence and development of all. If anywhere there are efforts tending to curtail the fullest growth of the Negro, let these efforts be turned into stimulating, encouraging, and making him the most useful and intelligent citizen. Effort or means so invested will pay a thousand per cent interest. These efforts will be twice blessed—"blessing him that gives and him that takes."

There is no escape through law of man or God from the inevitable:—

The laws of changeless justice bind
Oppressor with oppressed;
And close as sin and suffering joined
We march to fate abreast.

Nearly sixteen millions of hands will aid you in pulling the load upward, or they will pull against you the load downward. We shall constitute one-third and more of the ignorance and crime of the South, or one-third its intelligence and progress; we shall contribute one-third to the business and industrial prosperity of the South, or we shall prove a veritable body of death, stagnating, depressing, retarding every effort to advance the body politic.

Gentlemen of the Exposition, as we present to you our humble effort at an exhibition of our progress, you must not expect overmuch. Starting thirty years ago with ownership here and there in a few quilts and pumpkins and chickens (gathered from miscellaneous sources), remember the path that has led from these to the inventions and production of agricultural implements, buggies, steam-engines, newspapers, books, statuary, carving, paintings, the management of drug-stores and banks, has not been trodden without contact with thorns and thistles. While we take pride in what we exhibit as a result of our independent efforts, we do not for a moment forget that our part in this exhibition would fall far short of your expectations but for the constant help that has come to our educational life, not only from the Southern states, but especially from Northern philanthropists, who have made their gifts a constant stream of blessing and encouragement.

The wisest among my race understand that the agitation of questions of social equality is the extremest folly, and that progress in the enjoyment of all the privileges that will come to us must be the result of severe and constant struggle rather than of artificial forcing. No race that has anything to contribute to the markets of the world is long in any degree ostracized. It is important and right that all privileges of the law be ours, but it is vastly more important that we be prepared for the exercises of these privileges. The opportunity to earn a dollar in a factory just now is worth infinitely more than the opportunity to spend a dollar in an opera-house.

In conclusion, may I repeat that nothing in thirty years has given us more hope and encouragement, and drawn us so near to you of the white race, as this opportunity offered by the Exposition; and here bending, as it were, over the altar that represents the results of the struggles of your race and mine, both starting practically empty-handed three decades ago, I pledge that in your effort to work out the great and intricate problem which God has laid at the doors of the South, you shall have at all times the patient, sympathetic help of my race; only let this be constantly in mind, that, while from representations in these buildings of the product of field, of forest, of mine, of factory, letters, and art, much good will come, yet far above and beyond material benefits will be that higher good, that, let us pray God, will come, in a blotting out of sectional differences and racial animosities and suspicions, in a determination to administer absolute justice, in a willing obedience among all classes to the mandates of law. This, this, coupled with our material prosperity, will bring into our beloved South a new heaven and a new earth.

---

[1]Washington quoted from John Greenleaf Whittier's "At Port Royal." Whittier (1807–1892) was a widely read nineteenth-century poet and an outspoken abolitionist from Massachusetts. A lifelong friend of abolitionist William Lloyd Garrison, Whittier was editor of the *New England Review* and a cofounder (in 1839) of the Liberty party, an abolitionist party.

from The Autobiography of Malcolm X

Malcolm X

Chapter One:
Nightmare

When my mother was pregnant with me, she told me later, a party of hooded Ku Klux Klan riders galloped up to our home in Omaha, Nebraska, one night. Surrounding the house, brandishing their shotguns and rifles, they shouted for my father to come out. My mother went to the front door and opened it. Standing where they could see her pregnant condition, she told them that she was alone with her three small children, and that my father was away, preaching, in Milwaukee. The Klansmen shouted threats and warnings at her that we had better get out of town because "the good Christian white people" were not going to stand for my father's "spreading trouble" among the "good" Negroes of Omaha with the "back to Africa" preachings of Marcus Garvey.

My father, the Reverend Earl Little, was a Baptist minister, a dedicated organizer for Marcus Aurelius Garvey's U.N.I.A. (Universal Negro Improvement Association). With the help of such disciples as my father, Garvey, from his headquarters in New York City's Harlem, was raising the banner of black-race purity and exhorting the Negro masses to return to their ancestral African homeland—a cause which had made Garvey the most controversial black man on earth.

Still shouting threats, the Klansmen finally spurred their horses and galloped around the house, shattering every window pane with their gun butts. Then they rode off into the night, their torches flaring, as suddenly as they had come.

My father was enraged when he returned. He decided to wait until I was born—which would be soon—and then the family would move. I am not sure why he made this decision, for he was not a frightened Negro, as most then were, and many still are today. My father was a big, six-foot-four, very black man. He had only one eye. How he had lost the other one I have never known. He was from Reynolds, Georgia, where he had left school after the third or maybe fourth grade. He believed, as did Marcus Garvey, that freedom, independence and self-respect could never be achieved by the Negro in America, and that therefore the Negro should leave America to the white man and return to his African land of origin. Among the reasons my father had decided to risk and dedicate his life to help disseminate this philosophy among his people was that he had seen four of his six brothers die by violence, three of them killed by white men, including one by lynching. What my father could not know then was that of the remaining three, including himself, only one, my Uncle Jim, would die in bed, of natural causes. Northern white police were later to shoot my Uncle Oscar. And my father was finally himself to die by the white man's hands.

It has always been my belief that I, too, will die by violence. I have done all that I can to be prepared.

I was my father's seventh child. He had three children by a previous marriage—Ella, Earl, and Mary, who lived in Boston. He had met and married my mother in Philadelphia, where their first child, my oldest full brother, Wilfred, was born. They moved from Philadelphia to Omaha, where Hilda and then Philbert were born.

I was next in line. My mother was twenty-eight when I was born on May 19, 1925, in an Omaha hospital. Then we moved to Milwaukee, where Reginald was born. From infancy, he had some kind of hernia condition which was to handicap him physically for the rest of his life.

Louise Little, my mother, who was born in Grenada, in the British West Indies, looked like a white woman. Her father was white. She had straight black hair, and her accent did not sound like a Negro's. Of this white father of hers, I know nothing, except her shame about it. I remember hearing her say she was glad that she had never seen him. It was, of course, because of him that I got my reddish-brown "mariny" color of skin, and my hair of the same color. I was the lightest child in our family. (Out in the world later on, in Boston and New York, I was among the millions of Negroes who were insane enough to feel that it was some kind of status symbol to be light-complexioned—that one was actually fortunate to be born thus. But, still later, I learned to hate every drop of that white rapist's blood that is in me.)

Our family stayed only briefly in Milwaukee, for my father wanted to find a place where he could raise our own food and perhaps build a business. The teaching of Marcus Garvey stressed becoming independent of the white man. We went next, for some reason, to Lansing, Michigan. My father bought a house and soon, as had been his pattern, he was doing free-lance Christian preaching in local Negro Baptist churches, and during the week he was roaming about spreading word of Marcus Garvey.

He had begun to lay away savings for the store he had always wanted to own when, as always, some stupid local Uncle Tom Negroes began to funnel stories about his revolutionary beliefs to the local white people. This time, the get-out-of-town threats came from a local hate society called The Black Legion. They wore black robes instead of white. Soon, nearly everywhere my father went, Black Legionnaires were reviling him as an "uppity nigger" for wanting to own a store, for living outside the Lansing Negro district, for spreading unrest and dissension among "the good niggers."

As in Omaha, my mother was pregnant again, this time with my youngest sister. Shortly after Yvonne was born came the nightmare night in 1929, my earliest vivid memory. I remember being suddenly snatched awake into a frightening confusion of pistol shots and shouting and smoke and flames. My father had shouted and shot at the two white men who had set the fire and were running away. Our home was burning down around us. We were lunging and bumping and tumbling all over each other trying to escape. My mother, with the baby in her arms, just made it into the yard before the house crashed in, showering sparks. I remember we were outside in the night in our underwear, crying and yelling our heads off. The white police and firemen came and stood around watching as the house burned down to the ground.

*****

Chapter Sixteen:
Out

. . . I had been trying to explain how I honestly evaluated my own qualifications to be worthy of presenting myself as an independent "leader" among black men.

In the end, I reasoned that the decision already had been made for me. The ghetto masses already had entrusted me with an image of leadership among them. I knew the ghetto instinctively extends that trust only to one who had demonstrated that he would never sell them out to the white man. I not only had no such intention—to sell out was not even in my nature.

I felt a challenge to plan, and build, an organization that could help to cure the black man in North America of the sickness which has kept him under the white man's heel.

The black man in North America was mentally sick in his cooperative, sheeplike acceptance of the white man's culture.

The black man in North America was spiritually sick because for centuries he had accepted the white man's Christianity—which asked the black so-called Christian to expect no true Brotherhood of Man, but to endure the cruelties of the white so-called Christians. Christianity had made black men fuzzy, nebulous, confused in their thinking. It had taught the black man to think if he had no shoes, and was hungry, "we gonna get shoes and milk and honey and fish fries in Heaven."

The black man in North America was economically sick and that was evident in one simple fact: as a consumer, he got less than his share, and as a producer gave *least*. The black American today shows us the perfect parasite image—the black tick under the delusion that he is

progressing because he rides on the udder of the fat, three-stomached cow that is white America. For instance, annually, the black man spends over $3 billion for automobiles, but America contains hardly any franchised black automobile dealers. For instance, forty per cent of the expensive imported Scotch whisky consumed in America goes down the throats of the status-sick black man; but the only black-owned distilleries are in bathtubs, or in the woods somewhere. Or for instance—a scandalous shame—in New York City, with over a million Negroes, there aren't twenty black-owned businesses employing over ten people. It's because black men don't own and control their own community's retail establishments that they can't stabilize their own community.

The black man in North America was sickest of all politically. He let the white man divide him into such foolishness as considering himself a black "Democrat," a black "Republican," a black "Conservative," or a black "Liberal" . . . when a ten-million black vote bloc could be the deciding balance of power in American politics, because the white man's vote is almost always evenly divided. The polls are one place where every black man could fight the black man's cause with dignity, and with the power and the tools that the white man understands, and respects, and fears, and cooperates with.

*****

Chapter Eighteen:
El-Hajj Malik El-Shabazz

It was there in the Holy Land, and later in Africa, that I formed a conviction which I have had ever since—that a topmost requisite for any Negro leader in America ought to be extensive traveling in the non-white lands on this earth, and the travel should include many conferences with the ranking men of those lands. I guarantee that any honest, open-minded Negro leader would return home with more effective thinking about alternative avenues to solutions of the American black man's problem. Above all, the Negro leaders would find that many non-white officials of the highest standing, especially Africans, would tell them—privately—that they would be glad to throw their weight behind the Negro cause, in the United Nations, and in other ways. But these officials understandably feel that the Negro in America is so confused and divided that he doesn't himself know what his cause is. Again, it was mainly Africans who variously expressed to me that no one would wish to be embarrassed trying to help a brother who shows no evidence that he wants that help—and who seems to refuse to cooperate in his own interests.

The American black "leader's" most critical problem is lack of imagination! His thinking, his strategies, if any, are always limited, at least basically, to only that which is either advised, or approved by the white man. And the first thing the American power structure doesn't want any Negroes to start is thinking *internationally*.

I think the single worst mistake of the American black organizations, and their leaders, is that they have failed to establish direct brotherhood lines of communication between the independent nations of Africa and the American black people. Why, every day, the black African heads of state should be receiving direct accounts of the latest developments in the American black man's struggles—instead of the U.S. State Department's releases to Africans which always imply that the American black man's struggle is being "solved."

*****

Chapter Nineteen: 1965

I understood it better now than I had before. In the Holy World, away from America's race problem, was the first time I ever had been able to think clearly about the basic divisions of white people in America, and how their attitudes and their motives related to, and affected Negroes. In my thirty-nine years on this earth, the Holy City of Mecca had been the first time I had ever stood before the Creator of All and felt like a complete human being.

In that peace of the Holy World—in fact, the very night I have mentioned when I lay awake surrounded by snoring brother pilgrims—my mind took me back to personal memories I would have thought were gone forever . . . as far back, even, as when I was just a little boy, eight or nine years old. Out behind our house, out in the country from Lansing, Michigan, there was an old, grassy "Hector's Hill," we called it—which may still be there. I remembered there in the Holy World how I used to lie on the top of Hector's Hill, and look up at the sky, at the clouds moving over me, and daydream, all kinds of things. And then, in a funny contrast of recollections, I remembered how years later, when I was in prison, I used to lie on my cell bunk—this would be especially when I was in solitary: what we convicts called "The Hole"—and I would picture myself talking to large crowds. I don't have any idea why such previsions came to me. But they did. To tell that to anyone then would have sounded crazy. Even I didn't have, myself, the slightest inkling. . . .

In Mecca, too, I had played back for myself the twelve years I had spent with Elijah Muhammad as if it were a motion picture. I guess it would be impossible for anyone ever to realize fully how complete was my belief in Elijah Muhammad. I believed in him not only as a leader in the ordinary *human* sense, but also I believed in him as a *divine* leader. I believed he had no human weaknesses or faults, and that, therefore, he could make no mistakes and that he could do no wrong. There on a Holy World hilltop, I realized how

very dangerous it is for people to hold any human being in such esteem, especially to consider anyone some sort of "divinely guided" and "protected" person.

My thinking had been opened up wide in Mecca. In the long letters I wrote to friends, I tried to convey to them my new insights into the American black man's struggle and his problems, as well as the depths of my search for truth and justice.

"I've had enough of someone else's propaganda," I had written to these friends. "I'm for truth, no matter who tells it. I'm for justice, no matter who it is for or against. I'm a human being first and foremost, and as such I'm for whoever and whatever benefits humanity *as a whole*."

Largely, the American white man's press refused to convey that I was now attempting to teach Negroes a new direction. With the 1964 "long, hot summer" steadily producing new incidents, I was constantly accused of "stirring up Negroes." Every time I had another radio or television microphone at my mouth, when I was asked about "stirring up Negroes" or "inciting violence," I'd get hot.

"It takes no one to stir up the sociological dynamite that stems from the unemployment, bad housing, and inferior education already in the ghettoes. This explosively criminal condition has existed for so long, it needs no fuse; it fuses itself; it spontaneously combusts from within itself. . . ."

They called me "the angriest Negro in America." I wouldn't deny that charge. I spoke exactly as I felt. "I *believe* in anger. The Bible says there is a *time* for anger." They called me "a teacher, a fomenter of violence." I would say point blank, "That is a lie. I'm not for wanton violence, I'm for justice. I feel that if white people were attacked by Negroes—if the forces of law prove unable, or inadequate, or reluctant to protect those whites from those Negroes—then those white people should protect and defend themselves from those Negroes, using arms if necessary. And I feel that when the law fails to protect Negroes from whites' attack, then those Negroes should use arms, if necessary, to defend themselves."

"Malcolm X Advocates Armed Negroes!"

What was wrong with that? I'll tell you what was wrong. I was a black man talking about physical defense against the white man. The white man can lynch and burn and bomb and beat Negroes—that's all right: "Have patience" . . . "The customs are entrenched" . . . "Things are getting better."

Well, I believe it's a crime for anyone who is being brutalized to continue to accept that brutality without doing something to defend himself. If that's how "Christian" philosophy is interpreted, if that's what Gandhian philosophy teaches, well, then, I will call them criminal philosophies.

I tried in every speech I made to clarify my new position regarding white people—"I don't speak against the sincere, well-meaning, good white people. I have learned that there *are* some. I have learned that not all white people are racists. I am speaking against and my fight is against the white *racists*. I firmly believe that Negroes have the right to fight against these racists, by any means that are necessary."

But the white reporters kept wanting me linked with that word "violence." I doubt if I had one interview without having to deal with that accusation.

"I *am* for violence if non-violence means we continue postponing a solution to the American black man's problem—just to *avoid* violence. I don't go for non-violence if it also means a delayed solution. To me a delayed solution is a non-solution. Or I'll say it another way. If it must take violence to get the black man his human rights in this country, I'm *for* violence exactly as you know the Irish, the Poles, or Jews would be if they were flagrantly discriminated against. I am just as they would be in that case, and they would be for violence—no matter what the consequences, no matter who was hurt by the violence."

White society *hates* to hear anybody, especially a black man, talk about the crime the white man has perpetrated on the black man. I have always understood that's why I have so frequently been called "a Revolutionist." It sounds as if *I* have done some crime! Well it may be the American black man does need to become involved in a *real* revolution. The word for "revolution" in German is *Umwälzung*. What it means is a complete overturn—a complete change. The overthrow of King Farouk in Egypt and the succession of President Nasser is an example of a true revolution. It means the destroying of an old system, and its replacement with a new system. Another example is the Algerian revolution, led by Ben Bella; they threw out the French who had been there over 100 years. So how does anybody sound talking about the Negro in America waging some "revolution"? Yes, he is condemning a system—but he's not trying to overturn the system, or to destroy it. The Negro's so-called "revolt" is merely an asking to be *accepted* into the existing system! A *true* Negro revolt might entail, for instance, fighting for separate black states within this country—which several groups and individuals have advocated, long before Elijah Muhammad came along.

When the white man came into this country, he certainly wasn't demonstrating any "non-violence." In fact, the very man whose name symbolizes non-violence here today has stated:

"Our nation was born in genocide when it embraced the doctrine that the original American, the Indian, was an inferior race. Even before there were large numbers of Negroes on our shores, the scar of racial hatred had already disfigured colonial society. From the sixteenth century forward, blood flowed in battles over racial supremacy. We are perhaps the only nation which tried as a matter of national policy to wipe out its indigenous population. Moreover, we elevated that tragic experience into a noble crusade. Indeed, even today we have not permitted ourselves to reject or to feel remorse for this shameful episode. Our literature, our films, our drama, our folklore all exalt it. Our children are still taught to respect the violence which reduced a red-skinned people of an earlier culture into a few fragmented groups herded into impoverished reservations."

"Peaceful coexistence!" That's another one the white man has always been quick to cry. Fine! But what have been the deeds of the white man? During his entire advance through history, he has been waving the banner of Christianity . . . and carrying in his other hand the sword and the flintlock.

You can go right back to the very beginning of Christianity. Catholicism, the genesis of Christianity as we know it to be presently constituted, with its hierarchy, was conceived in Africa—by those whom the Christian church calls "The Desert Fathers." The Christian church became infected with racism when it entered white Europe. The Christian church returned to Africa under the banner of the Cross—conquering, killing, exploiting, pillaging, raping, bullying, beating—and teaching white supremacy. This is how the white man thrust himself into the position of leadership of the world—through the use of naked physical power. And he was totally inadequate spiritually. Mankind's history has proved from one era to another that the true criterion of leadership is spiritual. Men are attracted by spirit. By power, men are *forced*. Love is engendered by spirit. By power, anxieties are created.

I am in agreement one hundred per cent with those racists who say that no government laws ever can *force* brotherhood. The only true world solution today is governments guided by true religion—of the spirit. Here in race-torn America, I am convinced that the Islam religion is desperately needed, particularly by the American black man. The black man needs to reflect that he has been America's most fervent Christian—and where has it gotten him? In fact, in the white man's hands, in the white man's interpretation . . . where has Christianity brought this *world*?

It has brought the non-white two-thirds of the human population to rebellion. Two-thirds of the human population today is telling the one-third minority white man, "Get out!" And the white man is leaving. And as he leaves, we see the non-white peoples returning in a rush to their original religions, which had been labeled "pagan" by the conquering white man. Only one religion—Islam—had the power to stand and fight the white man's Christianity for a *thousand years!* Only Islam could keep white Christianity at bay.

The Africans are returning to Islam and other indigenous religions. The Asians are returning to being Hindus, Buddhists and Muslims.

As the Christian Crusade once went East, now the Islamic Crusade is going West. With the East—Asia—closed to Christianity, with Africa rapidly being converted to Islam, with Europe rapidly becoming un-Christian, generally today it is accepted that the "Christian" civilization of America—which is propping up the white race around the world—is Christianity's remaining strongest bastion.

Well, if *this* is so—if the so-called "Christianity" now being practiced in America displays the best that world Christianity has left to offer—no one in his right mind should need any much greater proof that very close at hand is the *end* of Christianity.

Are you aware that some Protestant theologians, in their writings, are using the phrase "post-Christian era"—and they mean *now*?

And what is the greatest single reason for this Christian church's failure? It is its failure to combat racism. It is the old "You sow, you reap" story. The Christian church sowed racism—blasphemously; now it reaps racism.

Sunday mornings in this year of grace 1965, imagine the "Christian conscience" of congregations guarded by deacons barring the door to black would-be worshipers, telling them "You can't enter *this* House of God!

Marcus Garvey, the Caribbean and the Struggle for Black Jamaican Nationhood

Tony Martin

There have been several movements to federate the British West Indian Islands, but owing to parochial feelings nothing definite has been achieved. Ere long this change is sure to come about because the people of these islands are all one. They live under the same conditions, are of the same race and mind and have the same feelings and sentiments regarding the things of the world.

—Marcus Garvey 1913

The Honorable Marcus Mosiah Garvey (1887–1940) is undoubtedly one of the most important figures in West Indian history. At a time when African peoples all over the world were colonized, disfranchised and subjugated, he provided hope and helped sow the seeds for nationalist struggles in Africa, Afro-America, the West Indies and elsewhere. His Universal Negro Improvement Association (UNIA), founded in Jamaica in 1914 and re-established in the United States around 1917, in the process became the largest Pan-African movement in history. By the mid-1920s it boasted approximately 1,120 branches in over 40 countries.

Within the West Indies, Garvey's UNIA stands out as one of the few Pan-Caribbean political movements in our history, and probably the most successful. For there were UNIA branches in Cuba, Trinidad, Jamaica, the then British Guiana, the Dominican Republic, Barbados, the then British Honduras, the Bahamas, Antigua, Bermuda, Dominica, Suriname, Grenada, Haiti, Nevis, Puerto Rico, St. Kitts, St. Lucia, St. Thomas, and St. Vincent. This was therefore a genuine Pan-Caribbean mass movement, cutting across political and linguistic barriers. Cuba had more branches (52) than any other territory in the West Indies, and indeed more than any country other than the United States. Trinidad had at least 30 branches. Jamaica had 11, British Guiana 7 and the Dominican Republic 5.

In addition to the large number of branches in the West Indies proper, West Indian emigrant workers made up a very large percentage of UNIA members in such Latin American countries as Panama, Costa Rica, Honduras, Colombia, Guatemala and Nicaragua. Many West Indians also joined the movement in other countries, especially in such United States cities as New York, Boston, and Miami, which were major destinations for West Indian emigrants.

The rapid spread of Garvey's movement may be attributed to several factors. For one thing, the World War I period was a time of worldwide radicalism. African peoples were also at their most desperate point in history and so needed vigorous leadership. Garvey himself was a tireless and exceedingly able organizer, in addition to being an exceptional orator and a strongly charismatic figure. His ideological position also appealed to masses of people. He urged Black people to be self-reliant, to put their racial interest first in a world which universally oppressed them, and to strive to build a strong nation in Africa, strong enough to compel world respect and lend support to African people everywhere.

The UNIA's impact on West Indian affairs was almost immediate. Garvey's agents traversed the area establishing branches and spreading the word of nationalism and anti-colonialism. Some were deported from, and/or refused permission to land in certain territories. The UNIA weekly newspaper, the *Negro World* was widely distributed in the area practically from its inception late in 1918. Several of the British colonial governors responded by banning it, illegally in 1919, and from 1920 on by means of hastily introduced Seditious Publications Ordinances. Despite these measures the paper found its way in, sometimes through the mail, sometimes smuggled in by seamen. Copies intercepted by the authorities were burned.

By 1919 the UNIA in the West Indies was firmly entrenched enough to figure prominently in the labor riots and racial unrest that swept the area. The British colonialists blamed the *Negro World* for the upsurge of race consciousness which formed a backdrop to the disturbances. In Trinidad, many of the leaders of the Trinidad Workingmen's Association, the major organization involved in the stevedores' strike of December 1919, were also members of the UNIA. It was reported that Garvey's editorials were read aloud at their meetings. In British Honduras, S. A. Haynes, one of the major figures involved in the riots, was a Garveyite. He later became a high-ranking UNIA official in the United States.

After 1919 the UNIA maintained its links with the budding West Indian labor movement. A. Bain Alves of Jamaica, members of Hubert Critchlow's

British Guiana Labour Union and D. Hamilton Jackson, leader of the St. Croix Labour Union, were among those who established contact with the UNIA in the 1920s. Indeed, Basil Brenthol Blackman, former secretary-treasurer of the Caribbean Congress of Labour, once said that most of the working class leaders coming to power in the 1930s in the West Indies had been influenced by involvement at some level in Garvey's UNIA. Garvey himself founded a Jamaican Workers and Labourers Association after his deportation from the United States in 1927.

Garvey's impact generally on progressive elements in the West Indies, both within and without the labor movement, can be said to have been substantial. Grenada's T. A. Marryshow wrote favorably of him in his *West Indian* newspaper; in Trinidad the *Argos* and the *Labour Leader* (organ of the Trinidad Workingmen's Association) regularly supported him; in Barbados Clennel W. Wickham endorsed Garveyism in the pages of the *Barbados Weekly Herald*.

By the 1920s the UNIA had become, in several greater Caribbean territories, the virtual representatives of the black population. At a time when most black people in the area were denied the right to vote, and in an age mostly predating mass political parties, the UNIA often performed the function of quasi-political party as well as mutual aid organization. It was a major, sometimes the major, organized group looking after the interests of the mass of black people. In 1923 the British government seriously considered recognizing the Cuban UNIA as the body representing the British West Indian population in that island. To this day in Costa Rica the UNIA enjoys a position of importance among the black section of that country.

And when mass-based party politics did come to the West Indies, Garvey and the UNIA were again in the vanguard. For Garvey's Peoples Political Party, formed in Jamaica in 1929, was a pioneer in its class, at least for the British West Indies. A West Indian federation with dominion status was among its aims.

Garvey, in his travels in the West Indies, fared little better than his lieutenants, being occasionally barred from some areas. At various times he was refused permission to land in Bermuda, Cuba, the Canal Zone and Trinidad. Yet on other occasions he was received by such persons as the governor of Oriente province in Cuba, the president of Costa Rica, and the governor of British Honduras. His most extensive trip to the British Caribbean came in 1937, three years before his death. On that occasion he was prevented by the British authorities from holding open air meetings in Trinidad. Nor was he permitted to refer to the labor struggles which had erupted there. Indeed, were it not for the personal intervention of Captain A. A. Cipriani, he may not have been allowed to land at all.

By 1927 Garvey was, of course, no stranger to Jamaican politics. Through workers' struggles, through his participation in the National Club, and through his leadership of the UNIA in Jamaica from 1914, he had amassed a wealth of experience prior to emigrating to the United States in 1916. And during his almost twelve years in the U.S. he maintained contact with Jamaica. In 1921 he suggested that Jamaican workers should unionize and elect their own representatives to the legislative council.[1] In 1923 the Kingston UNIA formed The Jamaica Political Reform Club which, though under UNIA auspices, was open to anyone wishing to take an active part in Jamaican politics. Fifty-four people were reported to have enrolled at its first meeting.[2]

The fear of a Garvey return to Jamaica had plagued some British colonialists, both in Jamaica and in London, for several years. In 1921, shortly after Garvey, on a visit home, had experienced difficulty in obtaining re-entry into the United States, a British Colonial Office official wrote, "Garvey is a very dangerous man . . . Unfortunately he is a native of Jamaica and from that Colony we could not deport him.[3] In 1926, with Garvey's deportation from the United States seemingly imminent, the governor of Jamaica made an unsuccessful attempt to have London intercede with the U.S. officials against sending Garvey home.[4] Garvey sought to allay the fears of the colonialists on his return home by promptly disavowing any intention of seeking election to the legislative council.[5] He soon changed his mind though, and Governor R. E. Stubbs moved quickly to try and head him off. In February 1928, "after a long talk with Garvey," he set forth his position in a dispatch to the Colonial Office. He compared Garvey with Sun Yat Sen of China. His observations are a singular mixture of sound insight and a colonialist mentality. He wrote:

> [Garvey] reminds me curiously of San Yet Sen. There is the same devotion to an idea— possibly spurious but, if so, wonderfully well counterfeited—: in Sun's case the unification and independence of China; in Garvey's the improvement of the status of the black races. They both have the same magnetic power over men, even quite intelligent men, and in each case there is the same childish vanity, incessant talk of "my organization," "my party," "my ideals" etc. In both cases I got the same impression that while the man was genuinely zealous for the cause, he would rather see it fail under himself than success under anyone else. In both cases this vanity had led the man into absurdities: Garvey as Emperor of Africa; Sun as President of the Southern Republic. The main difference is that Sun was honest in money matters; . . . .

Stubbs thought that Garvey himself was not a particularly harmful character but his "followers, being mostly men by no means so well educated as himself or so skilled in the meaning of words," might misinterpret his pronouncements as a call to violence. The governor at this point was undoubtedly confused by Garvey's ability to uncompromisingly champion the cause of the disenfranchised Jamaican masses while simultaneously employing the rhetoric of loyalty to the British empire. In any event he proposed amending existing laws specifically to remove any possibility of Garvey being elected to the legislative council. Under his proposals ex-convicts would be debarred from voting (and therefore, under existing legislation, from running for office) regardless of whether the sentence had been served or not. Alternatively, such persons would be ineligible to hold public office for ten years, regardless of where the imprisonment had taken place. (Garvey, of course, had been jailed in the United States on a trumped up charge of mail fraud.) Such legislation was deemed necessary because Garvey on the legislative council would be "bound to take up the position that the negro is being kept out of his rights and a series of speeches to that effect will pre-dispose the lower classes to violent action if, as must be expected, there comes a bad year for crops and they feel the pinch of hard times."[6] By this time there were ample precedents in the Indies and Africa for laws passed by British administrations specifically to deal with Garvey and Garvey-inspired activities. Among them were Seditious Publications ordinances passed in several West Indian territories in the early 1920s and laws such as the 1924 Undesirable Persons (Prevention of Immigration) Ordinance introduced into Sierra Leone to forestall Garvey's projected African tour.[7]

On this occasion, however, the Colonial Office officials were uniformly against the idea of special legislation. They agreed that such a strategem would be tactically unwise and from their arguments it would appear that they were not entirely aware of the existing precedents. One official argued: "There is no precedent for a disqualification such as that proposed . . . it would be regarded as being "The Marcus Garvey (disqualification from election) Law" . . . It is extraordinary that a man of Sir R. Stubb's intelligence should not see this."[8] Another official, E. R. Darnley, argued that "Legislation ad hoc and obviously if not ostensibly *in personam*" would be an unpalatable admission of fear on the part of the British administration. He alluded to Garvey in terms unusually favorable for one in his position and reminiscent of Stubb's own observations. Clearly Garvey was able to win the respect of at least some colonialist functionaries, even as they plotted to crush him. Darnley wrote,

> I cannot follow the Governor in his indiscriminate condemnation of convicts. The list of them includes Jesus Christ, Bradlaugh, Parnall and innumerable others who will be

remembered when Sir Edward Stubbs is forgotten, although, no doubt, they were highly inconvenient to the Government of the day. Imprisonment is the common penalty of the more drastic political and social reformers and other innovators, but if it were not for such innovators we should never have excelled the monkey.

Marcus Garvey specially excluded from the council and provided with a marketable grievance might well be more dangerous than Marcus Garvey on the Council, and if the electors of Jamaica emulated those of the United Kingdom in the case of John Wilkes, the Colonial Government would find itself involved in difficulties mainly attributable to its own unwisdom.

Darnley's condemnation of the Jamaican governor was a little too strong for the Secretary of State at the Colonial Office and he was forced to clarify his statement. "I am sorry that the Secretary of State should have believed that I meant to show contempt of Sir Edward Stubbs," he explained, "I have always reckoned him in the first rank of West Indian Governors. My remark was merely intended to indicate that he is not a conspicuous historical character like Parnell or Bradlaugh."[9]

The Colonial Office eventually turned down Stubb's request, but with regrets. "I am sorry not to be more helpful," wrote whoever drafted the official reply. "I wish I could, as I know well what a d_____d nuisance Garvey will be if he gets into the Council."[10] Yet the local ruling class did not give up the struggle. One year later Garvey reported an attempt, obviously aimed at him, by the legislative council to deprive of citizenship anyone who had ever applied for citizenship elsewhere, even if such foreign citizenship had not actually been obtained. Garvey commented, "Some people really think that they own the world and that by owning the world they may sell it to their friends."[11] As late as October 1929, shortly before Garvey's first electoral contest, local newspapers were spreading the rumor that he could not be elected due to his conviction in the United States.[12]

In April 1928 Garvey left Jamaica on a seven month trip which took him to Europe, Canada (where he was arrested), Bermuda (where he was not allowed to land) and the Bahamas. By this time the prevailing view at the Colonial Office seems to have been one of resignation to an inevitable Garvey victory at the next general elections.[13] But events were to show, again, that the local ruling class and its British allies on the spot were much less inclined to prematurely concede defeat.

Shortly after his return home Garvey announced the formation of a Peoples Political Party. Dismissing as nonsense the frequently expressed opinion that party politics could not work in Jamaica, he argued that the government and its non-elected minions acted like a de facto party in the legislative council, so it was time for elected members to organize in a similar fashion.[14]

Simultaneous with his active entry into Jamaican politics, Garvey advanced three major demands. The first was for black majority rule. On this point his *Blackman* newspaper editorialized:

**It is an Axiom that other things being equal
THE MAJORITY MUST RULE
and we shall see that other things are equal.**[15]

The second demand flowed from the first and consisted of no less than a call for political independence for Jamaica. The expression used, "dominion status," was simply the terminology then utilized within the British empire to denote the de facto independence soon to be granted to the "white" colonies of Canada, Australia, New Zealand and South Africa. It implied, for the white "dominions," (and for most of the Black and brown British colonies which became independent many years later) a continued ceremonial allegiance to the British crown. Garvey had no problems with this. Hence his expressions of loyalty to the colonial thrust. Besides, it was good tactics. And this anti-colonialism went back at least two decades to his days in the National Club. In 1913, before the formation of the Universal Negro Improvement Association, he was already railing against "the red-tapists, who pull the strings of colonial conservatism from Downing Street, with a reckless disregard of the interests and wishes of the people."[16]

The difference between Garvey's pro-empire statements and his anti-colonial actions were well illustrated during the Empire Day celebrations in 1929. He greeted the occasion with a lot of God Save the King rhetoric, which did not prevent him from sharply attacking Governor Stubbs, who, during the Empire Day celebrations at the Ward theatre, had interrupted the speech of a Black Rev. J. T. Hudson. Stubbs ordered Hudson to shut up when he mildly criticized the British empire. Garvey reprinted the whole speech in the *Blackman*.[17] This paper, begun as a daily on March 30, 1929, greatly facilitated Garvey's entry into Jamaican politics.

Garvey's third basic demand was for a West Indian federation, a logical step for one who had long advocated the unity of African peoples and the linking of Third World struggles. In May 1929 the *Blackman* editorialized: "Federation of the West Indies with Dominion status is the consummation of Negro aspiration in this Archipelago."[18]

These three basic demands reflected the tendency to long-range planning that had characterized Garvey's North American period. The first phase of this West Indian plan would involve a PPP foothold in the Jamaican legislative council. Phase two would call for the democratization of the political system and majority rule, leading to phase three, dominion status for Jamaica. Phase four would see an independent Jamaica launching an initiative throughout the islands to stimulate their own drives towards majority rule and incorporation within the West Indian federation. This West Indian plan was similar to that which Garvey had earlier intended to put into effect in Africa, using Liberia as a base. It is similar to the Pan-African plan that Kwame Nkrumah, an admirer of Garvey, used with partial success operating out of Ghana nearly three decades later. Garvey's West Indian federation would reach out to embrace the non-English speaking islands. In the UNIA, which had branches throughout the Caribbean area (English, French, Spanish and Dutch speaking), Garvey had a ready made vehicle to push for federation, and he intended to use it for this purpose when the time was ripe.[19]

The PPP received its first opportunity to engage in electoral activity several months before the 1930 general election, its major target. In April 1929 the Rev. Dr. F. G. Veitch, described by the *Blackman* as a PPP candidate, won a legislative council bye-election for the Hanover seat by forty-six votes. His opponent campaigned under the slogan of saving Hanover from Garveyism.[20] A mere two months later the PPP won its second victory, this time at a bye-election for the Kingston and St. Andrew Corporation council's No. 2 Urban Ward. The PPP's John Coleman Beecher led with 238 votes, followed by a Mr. Sheerwood, 107, Cyril B. Wilks, 87, T. A. Gayle, 37, and A. Bain Alves, 37.[21] Beecher's association with Garvey dated back to the National Club, and he, like Garvey, had been influenced by the pioneer black nationalist, Dr. J. Robert Love. He had run for election before but had been badly beaten at the polls.[22] Following his victory Garvey had cause to score his perennial adversaries at the *Gleaner* for commenting that "Voters of the Class Higher Up Kept Away from the Polling Stations."[23]

Fresh from these two victories, the Garvey machine rolled on, two months later, to the spectacular Sixth International Convention of the Negro People of the World, held in Kingston throughout the month of August. Of Garvey's status as a world leader there could by this time have been no doubt. However, this convention could not help but bring it home, in a most pertinent way, to all and sundry. Twenty-five thousand people representing "nearly every Negro organization on earth" were said to have participated in the five mile long parade marking the opening of the convention. Ninety thousand were estimated to have lined the parade route.[24] With this kind of momentum going, and with the general elections less than half a year away, Garvey now loomed as a massive threat to the stability of British colonialism on the island. The British administration therefore reacted swiftly and ruthlessly. In the United States the courts had been a major device for harassing, and finally jailing and deporting Garvey. There he had been arrested and/or harassed for one thing or another during practically all of his international conventions.[25] The British colonialists now set out to emulate their North American co-thinkers, and within six months Garvey would be fined twice and imprisoned once for contempt, sentenced to six months for seditious libel (this conviction was overturned on appeal) and the courts would wrongfully sell the Kingston Liberty Hall.

As a preliminary to judicial harassment the authorities mounted a show of force. At the beginning of the convention extra police were placed in readiness with an extra ten rounds of ammunition each. They were augmented by British troops, the Argyle and Sutherland Highlanders, armed for the occasion with machine guns.[26] The convention had barely begun before the chief justice, Sir Fiennes Barrett Leonard, threatened to jail Garvey forthwith for contempt if he did not produce the books of his organization within half an hour.[27] This was in the case of G. O. Marke vs UNIA where Marke, a former UNIA depute potentate, was suing to satisfy a judgment against the UNIA awarded in New York. Despite the fact that the books of the local UNIA were not technically in Garvey's possession he was summarily fined 25 pounds for contempt. The fine was paid by delegates to the convention.[28] The case itself dragged on for the whole of the convention month. To coincide with the end of the convention the chief justice ordered the Kingston Liberty Hall sold. Many foreign convention delegates were present when it was auctioned for 1,005 pounds.[29] This action was eventually overturned by the supreme court but it was over two years before the UNIA regained its Liberty Hall.[30]

Less than a week after the confiscation of Liberty Hall, the *Blackman* announced that the first PPP meeting for the upcoming general election (now less than five months away) would be held shortly. "It is to arouse the peasant to the consciousness of his power," the paper editorialized, "that the Peoples Political Party has come into being."[31] The meeting took place on September 9, 1929 at Cross Roads in St. Andrews parish, and Garvey delivered a major speech. He recalled his days in the National Club, when "Men like the late Mr. S. A. G. Cox, Alexander Dixon, Mr. H. A. L. Simpson, Mr. DeLeon and myself fought . . . to break down the power of the plantocracy, and we succeeded, but another class took control of the Council . . . " He announced that the PPP would soon be holding a national convention at Edelweis Park (his headquarters) to let the people nominate fourteen candidates to contest the elections. The convention would also formulate a platform which would have to be endorsed by all fourteen candidates. In the meantime, he presented an interim fourteen point platform which he hoped would be endorsed at the convention. Much of the speech was taken up

with presentation of the fourteen points together with his explanations of each point. The points and his explanations can be summarized as follows:

1. A "larger modicum of self-government for Jamaica." This could be either through direct Jamaican representation in Parliament at London (as in the French colonies) or dominion status.
2. Protection of native labor.
3. Minimum wage legislation.
4. "The expansion and improvement of . . . urban areas, without the encumbrances or restraint of private proprietorship." This was aimed at big landowners who held idle lands adjacent to towns.
5. Land reform. The bulk of the land, he said, was owned by one percent of the population. He would tax huge landowners and force them to make unused land available to small holders. His uncle, a sharecropper, had been chased off his land on a trumped up charge before harvesting his crops. This kind of thing was still happening. He planned to change all that.
6. The United Fruit Company and other large corporations would be forced to contribute (e.g. hospitals, universities, docks) to the areas where they were extracting their billions.
7. The "promotion of Native industries," to end unemployment and its reluctant emigration, leading to suffering in such places as Cuba.
8. A university and polytechnic with night courses.
9. "A National Theatre in Jamaica, where we can encourage Negro arts."
10. The impeachment of judges who abuse their authority.
11. Legal aid.
12. A law against procuring votes by duress, especially where this involved an abuse of the employer/employee relationship.
13. Granting Montego Bay and Port Antonio "the Corporate rights of Cities."
14. Upgrading the Kingston Race Course into a National Park.[32]

The next step on Garvey's well-organized campaign was to be a ten day tour of all of the country's fourteen parishes. He would take his program directly to the people and lay the groundwork for the national convention which would select candidates and endorse a platform. Before these plans could be put into effect, however, the colonialists struck again. Just over a month after being fined for contempt, and less than two weeks after the loss of Liberty Hall, Garvey was summoned to court to face new contempt charges. This was on the very first day of his country wide tour. This time the judges claimed to be peeved over "scurrilous abuse of the Court" and remarks capable of "inciting disaffection in the minds of the King's Subjects," arising out of Garvey's explanation of point 10 on his draft manifesto.[33] The judges were armed with affidavits by police inspector John Courtenay Knollys and reporter Oscar Joseph Durant, both present at the PPP's first election meeting.[34] Garvey's alleged contempt was contained in the following remarks:

A law to impeach and imprison such judges who enter into agreements and arrangements with lawyers and other persons of influence to deprive other subjects in the realm of their rights in such Courts of Law over which they may preside; forcing the innocent parties to incur the additional costs of appeals and other legal expenses which would not have been but for the injustice occasioned by the illicit arrangements of such judges with their friends.

Now, this is an evil that Jamaica has suffered from for a long time, and we have not been able to tackle it. The time has come now for us to bring changes, and if we cannot settle it in Jamaica, we are going to settle it in England. We are not going to have judges here who can meet their friends and others in their club houses and connive and conspire to take away an innocent man's property or his rights simply because they want to satisfy their friends . . . There is no man who is above the law, and if a judge breaks the law he can be dealt with as any other man who violates the law.

. . . the rich man sits beside the judge and the poor man cannot get his rights.[35]

At the contempt trial the supreme court asked for and received a written apology from Garvey, even though he insisted that his statement was not aimed specifically at this court. The three judge panel, with one dissenting, then imposed a sentence of three months in jail and a hundred pound fine, and admonished him for being a "hot headed and foolish man." The dissenting judge favored a heavier fine and no jail.[36] The wrath of the judges was so great that they transgressed one of the rules of colonial etiquette and fined Garvey's white lawyer, Lewis Ashenheim, 300 pounds on two charges of contempt. He was ordered to pay the costs of a third charge. His offense had been to caution against meddling with UNIA property.[37] Representatives of the legal profession approached the chief justice at the exclusive white club where he was wont to hang out, in a vain attempt to stay his action against Ashenheim. He threatened to cite the delegation for contempt too.[38]

Garvey's trial and imprisonment took care of three and a half of the four and a half months remaining to the election campaign. The fine meant a further depletion of campaign funds. But these types of trials and tribulations were nothing new to Garvey, who had been subjected to all manner of harassments and who had been jailed twice during his stay in the United States, not to mention jailed (it is thought) in Costa Rica, arrested in Canada and barred from entering several areas. Once again he manifested that indomitable spirit that had kept him steadfast on his program of racial emancipation through all vicissitudes. On the same day that he was sentenced to jail for contempt, he announced that he would run for the vacant seat in the No. 3 urban ward of the Kingston and St. Andrew Corporation council. The campaign would be handled by the PPP's Councillor John Coleman Beecher.[39] He would thus be running for both municipal and national office at the same time, and from jail.

A few days after entering jail Garvey was officially nominated for the KSAC seat at a PPP conclave attended by 5,000.[40] A month later he was elected. *Blackman* headlines summed up the situation thus: "Marcus Garvey, Negro Leader, Now Prisoner, Is Elected To Represent No. 3 Urban Ward in Corporation Council—An Event Without Precedent In The Political History of The World!". The voting was Garvey, 321 votes and F. W. Bailey, 102 votes.[41]

Almost two months still remained before Garvey's release from jail, however. And as the day drew near, the exact date of his release became a matter for new maneuvering on the part of the British administration. No matter was too small to escape attention if it involved the possibility of harassing Garvey. An unsigned secret memo from the governor's residence to the Colonial Office tells his story:

[Garvey] was due to come out of prison on the 24th December but we learnt that his release on Christmas Eve would mean that he would be hailed as a "Black Messiah" and a monster procession from the goal at Spanish Town to Kingston a distance of 12 miles, with bands and all the rest of it, was being organized. That, of course, would not have done at all, so with a secrecy which was highly applauded throughout the Island, Mr. Garvey was released about three or four days before the proper time. He was shown the door of the prison at a moment's notice and found his own way back to Kingston. I think he came back in a Police car which we sent out to assist him![42]

Upon his release Garvey took his oath of office on the KSAC council and was able to attend a few meetings before the powers that be (this time with the local ruling class taking the initiative) struck again. His seat was declared vacant since he had missed three consecutive meetings while in jail, and this though his application from jail for leave of absence had been refused. The council was dominated by the class that Garvey opposed and, buttressed by the opinion of their counsel, Norman Washington Manley, they had their way.[43] At this point the legislative council elections were less than three weeks away.

Simultaneous with these problems on the KSAC council, Garvey was trying his best to pick up the pieces of his election campaign. Within days of his release he resumed his tour of the parishes, cut short by the judges three months earlier. He also opened election headquarters at 107 Water Lane.[44] Then came a revised twenty-six point manifesto, consisting of the earlier fourteen points plus an additional twelve. The new points can be summarized as follows:

1. Workmen's compensation.
2. At least sixty percent of local labour to be employed on "all industrial, agricultural and commercial activities. . . . "
3. An eight-hour working day.
4. Free secondary and night school education in each parish.
5. A public library in each parish.
6. The appointment of official court stenographers.
7. A government loan of at least three million pounds to develop Crown lands and thereby create "employment for our surplus unemployed population, and to find employment for stranded Jamaicans abroad"; also to purchase ships to facilitate the marketing of local produce.
8. The expansion of electrification "to such growing and prospering centres as are necessary."
9. Prison reform.
10. Health outreach programs for rural areas.
11. Decent low priced housing for the peasantry.
12. An end to profiteering "by heartless land sharks" "in urban and suburban areas to the detriment of expansion of healthy home life for citizens of moderate means."

Garvey's manifesto was progressive by any standard. At least twelve of the twenty-six planks spoke directly to the immediate needs of workers and peasants. Another eight planks spoke to areas of broad social concern (free education, libraries, etc.), designed to raise the educational and cultural levels of the broad mass of Jamaicans. The oppressed classes obviously stood to benefit most from these. At least four planks directly sought to curb the power of multi-national corporations, landowners and the local capitalist class. In addition most of the twenty-six provisions could only succeed at their expense. The provisions for self-government and the impeachment of judges were of course direct challenges to British colonialism.

The crowd which was on hand to hear Garvey present his twenty-six points cheered repeatedly. Cheering was reportedly loud and long for the planks dealing with the minimum wage, eight-hour day, free secondary education, legal aid, an end to procuring votes by duress, the government loan to increase employment, the National Park for Kingston, cheap housing for the peasantry, and a move against the land sharks. Cheering was "almost deafening" for the planks calling for workmen's compensation and a minimum of 60% local labor in all areas of employment.[45]

The coincidence of class and color in Jamaica became a focal point of Garvey's campaign, since his main opponent for the St. Andrew seat which he contested was both white and mayor of Kingston up to two weeks before the election, making him an important member of the class that had harassed Garvey, both in and out of the KSAC council. In his campaign speeches Garvey therefore harped on the principle of race first, as a means of countering the historic injustices heaped upon black people by the white race. "When you look at [Seymour's] face and lanky, overbearing personality," Garvey declared, "you see there the brutal slave master. . . ." He could not understand why, in 1930, "such men have the audacity to come to you and ask you—you the sons of the slaves whom they treated like brutes . . . to allow them . . . to exploit you." The question of white rulers over black people naturally struck at the heart of Garvey's demand for black majority rule. He noted that "The Legislative council for several terms past [was] made up chiefly of men of Seymour's race . . . "[46] The Council, during the term before the one that has just come to an end, was made up of men purely of his race. The task facing voters was clear: "There must not be one white man on the elected side of the House in January. We have white men on the official and nominated side. But the side which the people elects must be represented by themselves."[47]

A few days before the election Garvey came up with a slate of twelve candidates whom he supported. Among them, perhaps surprisingly, was a Mr. R. Ehrenstein, a white man contesting the St. Thomas seat. This was not the first time that Garvey supported a white person he considered a renegade from his own race.[48]

To add to his imprisonment, the loss of his KSAC council seat, and all his other myriad problems during the campaign, Garvey also had to deal with sundry other election malpractices engineered by his opponents. He complained that people were telling taxpayers in Mavis Bank and Guava Ridge in St. Andrew that taxes were going up because of him. At a mass meeting a few days before the election he protested that Herbert George DeLisser, editor of the *Gleaner*, and D. T. Wint, a black political opponent, were suggesting that he now had black Jamaicans in a state of disorder similar to the 1865 Morant Bay uprising. For some days prior to the elections rumors were circulating that Garvey had been arrested and jailed again.[49] And to crown this incredibly relentless campaign of pressure, the judges struck again in the last days of the campaign, this time charging him with seditious libel.[50]

The elections were held on January 29, 1930, and Garvey lost. The results in St. Andrew were Seymour—1,677, Garvey—915 and Dillon (Black)—269.[51] One of the governor's aides wrote, in a secret memo:

> Garvey lives in the parish of St. Andrew a select residential area, where is also King's House, and he appeared as a candidate for the parish against a very well-known landowner, the sitting member who had recently been Mayor of Kingston . . . Garvey's people . . . were responsible for rowdyism and attempts to break up meetings. But the result was that all the decent people in St. Andrew rallied to the support of the sitting member—many bedridden old ladies going down to record their votes for him—and Garvey was very heavily defeated.[52]

Garvey's initial response to the loss was to angrily blame the voters for having sold themselves for a mess of pottage. He could not afford to spend on rum and transportation to the polls like the other candidates, he said. He had based his campaign solely on his program.[53] There were factors militating against Garvey, however, which were beyond his control. A *Blackman* editorial addressed itself to these:

> In Jamaica there is no universal suffrage. The bulk of the population is Negroes, with a very small proportion of them enjoying the franchise. According to the last census, there are 900,000 people in the island, of which 700,000 are Negroes. We will be very near correct in saying that of the 900,000 population only about 112,000 are registered . . . The supporters of the Universal Negro Improvement Association, we are told, are the voteless unit, and that being so, a paltry eighty or ninety thousand Negroes voting at a general election (although they did not all vote for the successful candidates), is no evidence whatsoever that [Garveyism] is on the wane.[54]

As for Garvey himself, his disappointment at his election reverse did not last very long. He bounced back with his accustomed resiliency and was soon explaining that this was only a retreat, not a defeat. The PPP had fared better, despite everything than the British Labour Party on its first election bid. And his paper noted, correctly, that reform is, in general, in advance of its time ". . . yet, such movements eventually succeed. Not today, not tomorrow, perhaps, but eventually."

And the leaders of such movements are acclaimed, their country prospers and their names go down in succeeding generations."[55]

In this post-election period Garvey also defended two of the major charges brought against him by the Jamaican ruling class. The first was the charge of racism. On this the *Blackman* editorialized: "It is unfortunate that in this country the proletariat or common people belong to a group that is ethnologically described as Negroes, and when one stands up for their economical, social or industrial advancement, the cry goes up that racial antagonism and colour prejudice are being disseminated among the people."[56] The other charge was that his manifesto was socialistic. On this Garvey retorted: "The United Fruit Company makes millions of dollars every year through the banana industry. Why could not your government do the same? You would say that would be socialistic. Is it not socialistic for the government to run the Railway?" He continued, "If the government can plant bananas on the Prison Farm and sell to the United Fruit Company, the government can plant bananas on a larger scale throughout the country and thus find employment for the people of the country."[57] Governor Stubbs thought Garvey's proposals to be so "grotesque" that they "could not bear even looking into, still less encouraging."[58]

Such election post mortems did not have Garvey's undivided attention, however, for the seditious libel case, initiated before the election was tried shortly thereafter from February 12 to 21, 1930. The judges based their case on a *Blackman* editorial entitled "The Vagabonds Again," which took the KSAC council to task for refusing to hear a lawyer whom the burgesses of Garvey's No. 3 ward had retained, at their own expense, to fight the council's determination to unseat Garvey. The editorial further suggested that the council, a "group of vagabonds," was campaigning for Mayor Seymour, and that as a result of their actions confidence in government was being "sorely tried."[59]

Charged along with Garvey were the PPP's John Coleman Beecher, business editor of the *Blackman*, and Theophilus Augustus Aikman, literary editor of the paper and national secretary of the PPP. (Garvey's official position in the PPP was chairman.) The presiding judge was A. K. Agar, Kingston resident magistrate. He refused the defendants a jury trial.[60] Although the editorial had actually been written by Aikman, Garvey received the longest sentence. Indeed so carried away was the judge by his hatred for Garvey that he sentenced him to six months' hard labor. He had to be reminded by the crown solicitor that hard labor could not legally be imposed for such an offense. Aikman was sentenced to three months and Beecher, who had nothing to do with editorial matters, was acquitted. Garvey and Aikman appealed successfully.

Garvey wrote both Governor Stubbs and Phillip Snowdon, the British chancellor of the exchequer with whom he had corresponded while in England, setting forth his objections to these libel proceedings and other harassments. His imprisonment for contempt, he wrote, was a "political dodge." He had learned in advance of the chief justice's intention to convict him from the chief justice's chauffeur, a UNIA member. (The chief justice, according to Garvey, ordered the chauffeur to stop attending UNIA meetings.) As for the libel case, Garvey argued that the judge used the courtroom to direct propaganda against UNIA members. The whole thing he saw as a "conspiracy" to prevent him from representing "the interest of the poor working and labouring classes and give them a voice that may probably help them to improve and better their conditions."[61]

The libel charge was designed to do several things—first it was a "dirty trick" timed to do maximum harm to Garvey's campaign for the legislative council; second, it was part of the general campaign to tie up as much of Garvey's time and money as possible in court cases; third, if successfully prosecuted it would have put Garvey behind bars again for six months; and fourthly, if Garvey went to jail he would once more have lost his seat on the KSAC council.

On the same day that the libel case began the *Blackman* announced that Garvey had decided to enter the bye-election for his former KSAC council seat. The two other candidates, Cyril B. Wilks and E. A. Walters, therefore withdrew and Garvey was returned unopposed.[62] This was a mere two weeks after the legislative council elections. The swearing in ceremony took place a few days after the end of the trial and was marked by anti-Garvey filibustering and much general harassment. Garvey was warned that he was not qualified to sit on the council and much was made of the libel conviction.[63] He nevertheless could not be stopped this time, so in September 1930 the colonialists dissolved the whole council for a year using as a pretext an investigation into corruption on the part of some other councillors. Garvey and the PPP held protest meetings and the *Blackman*, none daunted by the recent libel proceedings, decided that the time for self-government had come, since the forcible dissolution of the council was "a most despotic act."[64]

Garvey was re-elected to be a reconstituted council in 1931 while away in Europe and served until late 1934 when he declined to seek further re-election due to his impending relocation to England.[65] During this period he welcomed the formation of the Kingston Civic Voters League,[66] gave some qualified support to former members of the British West Indies Regiment who were demanding the vote,[67] and continued to make favorable utterances on the subject of socialism.[68]

Garvey's last few years in England (where he died in 1940) coincided with the workers' struggles in Jamaica which ushered into existence the Peoples National Party (PNP) and the Jamaican Labour Party (JLP), the two parties that have dominated Jamaican political life ever since. The strikes and riots met with his approval, as did the appointment of a British royal commission into the matter. He disapproved, however, of the appointment of his old adversary, Sir Reginald E. Stubbs, as chairman, while welcoming the inclusion of the Labour Party's Sir Walter Citrine.[69] Eight years earlier, during Stubbs' administration, Garvey had called for a royal commission to investigate his persecution.[70] He submitted a memorandum to the 1938 commission.[71]

With Norman Washington Manley, who later emerged as head of the PNP, Garvey had had some unusual contact. For Manley, a prominent lawyer during the life of Garvey's PPP, became something of a fixture in legal proceedings against Garvey and the UNIA. In 1929 he appeared for the applicants in the case of *Bourne vs. UNIA*.[72] When Garvey was unseated by the KSAC council in 1930 it was partly on the opinion of Manley, who was retained by the council in that matter.[73] Later that year Manley represented the plaintiff, Mrs. Barnes Haylett, in a libel suit against Garvey and the *Blackman*. She was awarded thirty pounds on a claim for a thousand pounds. Garvey defended himself.[74] Yet Garvey approvingly called him "our popular barrister" and "a first rate man" when Manley became a king's council in 1932.[75] Garvey's Edelweis Park headquarters in 1939 became PNP headquarters.[76] In August 1941 a PNP meeting chaired by N. N. Nethersole stood in silence for a few minutes as a mark of respect for the fallen hero.[77] In 1938 Garvey welcomed the entry of the JLP's Alexander Bustamante into politics.[78]

As in the case of his activities in North America Garvey's political struggles in Jamaica were both a failure and a success. He can be said to have failed in so far as he was thwarted in his bid to consolidate his party and move towards black majority rule, self-government and West Indian federation. But this is to take a very narrow view. He successfully demonstrated that political parties could work in Jamaica and in the process indoctrinated and politicized the workers and peasants on a scale probably more massive than they had experienced before. The hundreds and thousands who followed Garvey and attended his meetings were well-represented among the rioters and strikers of the late 1930s. In a way the leaders who emerged from these later struggles were more fortunate than Garvey. For one thing, they could build on foundations already laid by him. And people like Bustamante and Manley were able to reap the benefits of widespread and violent challenges to British colonialism. Garvey often cautioned his followers, at least in public, to be "constitutional," but there is no telling what may have happened if he had been fortunate enough to walk into a ready made situation of mass unrest, such as was the case in 1938. The fact that the post-Garvey violence was Pan-Caribbean in nature and came at a time when British imperialism was about to be severely weakened as a result of World War II, are also objective advantages that Garvey could certainly have used.

S. J. Garrick, a JLP organizer, was correct when he observed in 1941 that "if there wasn't a UNIA there could be no PNP or JLP . . ."[79]

[1] *Daily Gleaner*, June 2, 1921, p. 6, quoted in Adolph Edwards, *Marcus Garvey* (London: New Beacon, 1967), p. 15.

[2] *Negro World*, September 1, 1923, p. 4.

[3] Minute, July 28, 1921, CO 318/364, Colonial Office records Public Record Office, London. On Garvey's 1921 efforts to re-enter the U.S. see Martin, *Race First*, pp. 184–87.

[4] Destroyed file, March 31, 1926, register of correspondence for the West Indies, 1926, OAG/8674, Colonial Office records; ibid., destroyed file May 6, 1926, FO/8674.

[5] Lenford Sylvester Nembhard, *Trials and Triumphs of Marcus Garvey* (Kingston: The Gleaner Co., Ltd., 1940), pp. 116–117.

[6] Governor R. E. Stubbs to [Sir S.] Wilson, Colonial Office, February 24, 1928, CO 318/391/56634.

[7] Martin, *Race First*, pp. 94–96, 115.

[8] Minute by R. R. Sedgwick [?]. March 12, 1928, CO 318/391/56634. Of course he could have been correct if he meant that despite general precedents of special laws against Garvey, there was no precedent for the specific facts of this case, namely denying a person the right to run for office. See also, ibid., minutes by S. H. [E.?], March 15, 1928, J. S. R., March 15, 1928, and G. G. March 16, 1928.

[9] Minutes by E. R. Darnley, March 13, 30, 1928, CO 318/391/56634.

[10] Draft of reply from Colonial Office to Sir. R. E. Stubbs, March 27, 1928, ibid.

[11] *Blackman*, April 18, 1929, p. 7. Garvey had taken out his first citizenship papers in the United States.

[12] *Blackman*, October 14, 1929, p. 7, quoting the *Jamaican Mail* of October 8 and the *Gleaner* of October 9, 1929.

[13] Draft of Colonial Office to Lord Snowdon, June 14, 1928, CO 318/391/56634.

[14] *Blackman*, April 12, 1929, p. 3.

[15] Ibid., April 16, 1929, p. 2.

[16] Marcus Garvey, "The British West Indies in the Mirror of Truth," *Africa Times* and *Orient Review*, October 1913, p. 159.

[17] *Blackman*, May 28, 1929, p. 2, May 28, 1929, p. 1.

[18] Ibid., May 2, 1929, p. 2. See also ibid., May 16, 1929, p. 2, *New Jamaican*, September 9, 1932, pp. 1, 5.

[19] Amy Jacques Garvey, *Garvey and Garveyism* (Kingston: A. J. Garvey, 1963), p. 204; Nembhard, *Trials and Triumphs*, p. 92. For Garvey's Liberian plan see Martin, *Race First*, pp. 122–137; for a list of UNIA branches in the West Indies (and the world) see ibid., pp. 15, 16, 359–73.

[20] *Blackman*, April 25, 1929, p. 1, April 26, 1929, p. 7.

[21] Ibid., June 27, 1929, p. 1.

[22] Ibid., June 4, 1929, pp. 1, 7, November 6, 1929, p. 2.

[23] Ibid., June 28, 1929, p. 1. He called the *Gleaner* "the unofficial Government of Jamaica"—ibid., July 8, 1929, p. 1.

[24] *Negro World*, August 10, 1929, p. 1; *Blackman*, August 2, 1929, p. 1.

[25] Martin, *Race First*, p. 187.

[26] *Blackman*, August 5, 1929, p. 1.

[27] Ibid., p. 4.

[28] Ibid., August 8, 1929, p. 1, August 13, 1929, p. 5. For more on this case see Garvey, *Garvey and Garveyism*, pp. 193–94.

[29] *Blackman*, September 4, 1929, p. 7.

[30] Ibid., August 30, 1930, p. 2; December 13, 1930, p. 5; October 24, 1931, p. 8.

[31] Ibid., September 7, 1929, p. 4.

[32] Garvey, *Garvey and Garveyism*, p. 196, lists the fourteen points. The embellishments can be found in *Blackman*, September 11, 1929, p. 7, September 12, 1929, pp. 1, 7.

[33] *Blackman*, September 13, 1929, p. 1.

[34] Ibid., September 14, 1929, p. 3.

[35] Ibid., September 12, 1929, p. 7.

[36] Ibid., September 26, 1929, p. 7, September 27, 1929, p. 1. The judges were Chief Justice Sir Fiennes Barrett Lennard, Mr. Justice C. E. Law, and Mr. Justice Adrian Clark, dissenting.

[37] Ibid., October 1, 1929, p. 1, September 14, 1929, p. 4.

[38] Interview with Mrs. Amy Jacques Garvey, Kingston, March 6, 1972.

[39] *Blackman*, September 27, 1929, p. 1.

[40] Ibid., October 1, 1929.

[41] Ibid., October 31, 1929, p. 1.

[42] Secret unsigned memo from King's House, Kingston, June 30, 1930, CO 318/399/76634. See also *Blackman*, December 20, 1929, p. 1.

[43] *Blackman*, December 31, 1929, p. 1, January 6, 1930, pp. 1, 7, January 14, 1930, pp. 1, 7, January 13, 1930, pp. 1, 2; Garvey to Rt. Hon. Phillip Snowdon, Chancellor of the Exchequer, February 27, 1930, CO 318/399/76634.

[44] *Blackman*, December 20, 1929, p. 1, December 24, 1929, p. 7.

[45] Ibid., January 2, 1930, p. 8. The twenty-six points are at ibid., p. 2. They are reproduced in Amy Jacques Garvey, "Political Activities of Marcus Garvey in Jamaica," op. cit.

[46] *Blackman*, January 8, 1930, p. 1.

[47] Ibid., December 28, 1929, p. 14.

[48] Ibid., January 25, 1930, p. 1, January 23, 1930, p. 1. Ehrenstein's platform was similar to Garvey's and his manifesto appeared several times in the *Blackman*. It is not clear whether all twelve persons on Garvey's slate were actually PPP members. For other examples of Garvey's occasional support of renegade whites see Martin, *Race First*, pp. 31, 233.

[49]*Blackman*, September 10, 1929, p. 1; ibid., January 25, 1930, p. 13, Garvey to Sir Reginald E. Stubbs, February 7, 1930, CO 318/399/76634; *Blackman*, January 28, 1930, p. 1.

[50]Garvey to Rt. Hon. Phillip Snowdon, February 27, 1930, CO 318/399/76634.

[51]*Blackman*, January 31, 1930, p. 1.

[52]Unsigned secret memo from King's House, Kingston, June 30, 1930, CO 318/399/76634.

[53]*Blackman*, February 1, 1930, p. 1.

[54]Ibid., February 4, 1920, p. 2.

[55]Ibid., February 15, 1930, p. 12, February 2, 1930, p. 2.

[56]Ibid., February 12, 1920, p. 2.

[57]Ibid., March 29, 1930, p. 13.

[58]Unsigned secret memo from King's House, Kingston, June 30, 1930, CO 318/399/76634. According to the memo, Garvey "saw Sir Edward Stubbs two or three months ago" to put forward his proposals.

[59]*Blackman*, January 14, 1930, p. 2.

[60]Ibid., February 13, 1930, p. 1.

[61]Garvey to H. E. Sir Reginald Edward Stubbs, governor of Jamaica, February 21, February 22, 1930, CO 318/399/76634; ibid., Garvey to Rt. Hon. Phillip Snowdon, Chancellor of the Exchequer, February 27, 1930. In this correspondence Garvey expressed a desire to appeal the libel case all the way to the privy council, if necessary. Somebody at the Colonial Office commented (on the libel case) that though Garvey was "a danger to good order" he should not be subjected to such blatant persecution—minute, June 30, 1930, CO 318/399/76634.

[62]*Blackman*, February 12, 1930, p. 1.

[63]Ibid., February 24, 1930, p. 1, February 26, 1930, p. 7.

[64]Ibid., August 30, 1930, p. 4, September 13, 1930, p. 1, September 27, 1930, p. 1, November 29, 1930, p. 4.

[65]*Ethiopian World*, May 26, 1934. According to this report Garvey would not be contesting the November elections because he would be departing for England where he planned to become a Labour Party member of parliament for West Kensington.

[66]*New Jamaican*, January 16, 1933, p. 1. The League was formed by a Mr. Vivian Durham and others.

[67]Ibid., January 13, 1933, p. 1.

[68]Ibid., October 12, 1932, p. 1, November 1, 1932, p. 2, November 23, 1932, p. 2. Included here are statements by Garvey as well as editorials in his newspaper. For a discussion of the complete relationship between Garvey, communists and communism, and working class struggles in Jamaica and elsewhere, see Martin, *Race First*, pp. 221–272.

[69]*Black Man* (magazine, not to be confused with the *Blackman* newspaper), III, 10 July 1938, pp. 5–7, III, 11 November 1938, p. 19.

[70]Garvey to Rt. Hon. Phillip Snowdon, February 27, 1930, CO 318/399/76634, Garvey thanked the Colonial Office for acceding to his request, but they expressed puzzlement since no royal commission was being contemplated at that time—*Blackman*, August 23, 1930, p. 1; Garvey to Secretary of State, Colonial Office, via the Officer Administering the Government, Jamaica, September 4, 1930, CO 318/399/76634; ibid., Secretary of State, Lord Passfield to OAG, Jamaica, September 18, 1930. In January 1930 Garvey and nine others had presented a petition "On behalf of the Labourers of Jamaica" to a visiting West Indian Sugar Commission, led by Lord Oliver—*Blackman*, January 11, 1930, p. 2.

[71]Garvey, Memorandum to West India Royal Commission, September 24, 1938, CO 950/44. The memorandum traced the history of Black West Indians after emancipation—the importation of foreign labour to depress wages, the consequent migrations to Panama, Cuba, etc. in search of work, the usurpation of commercial activity by Chinese, Syrians, etc. It also dealt with the race/class question in the islands and the persecution of popular black leaders.

[72]*Blackman*, October 25, 1929, p. 1. Manley was instructed here by J. H. Cargill. Mr. N. N. Ashenheim appeared for the respondents.

[73]Ibid., January 14, 1930, pp. 1 and 7.

[74]Ibid., November 1, 1930, p. 10.

[75]*New Jamaican*, September 19, 1932, p. 5.

[76]R. N. Murray, ed., *J. J. Mills—His Own Account of His Life and Times* (Kingston: Collins and Sangster, 1969), pp. 110–111.

[77]*National Negro Voice*, August 23, 1941, p. 8.

[78]*Black Man*, July 1938, p. 6.

[79]National Negro Voice, August 30, 1941, p. 5.

Colonial Relations

W. Arthur Lewis

From the economic standpoint, colonialism is a system for improving the terms of trade in favor of the metropolis. There have been other purposes. The word comes to us from the Greeks, who planted colonies of their own race, not for trade but to dispose of surplus population. Other metropoles have demanded annual tribute. The Spaniards went in search of precious metals. Colonies have been held for military purposes, as military bases. But by the end of the nineteenth century, trade was the central purpose of holding colonies, and more favorable terms of trade were the central expectation. Race is not a necessary element in colonialism, nor is forced labor.

Force becomes a necessary element if there is a shortage of labor to work with the colonial settlers, especially if the aboriginal inhabitants are wiped out, as in the Americas, Australasia, and parts of Africa. Then slavery is introduced, in its stronger or weaker versions, including indentured labor from India or China. If the colony is already well populated, it is not necessary to import labor. The government may force the farmers to deliver specified amounts of produce, as the Dutch did in Java; or trade with the natives may be relied on, if a regular flow of trade at favorable prices seems assured, as in West Africa at the turn of this century. Some investment in transport facilities may be required to open up the colony for easy movement of produce in and out. Prices may be manipulated, with ceilings placed on the prices of exports. Imports can be stimulated by keeping import tariffs low and discouraging local production of manufactures; down to the First World War the government of India bought supplies only in England and not from competing sources in India. Some colonial powers, notably France, made preferential arrangements, giving themselves special terms for imports or exports in preference to other trading nations. Some writers see India's market as a source of foreign exchange used by the British to balance their own triangular payments, but without India, Britain would have had to find other markets, so this is another aspect of the terms of trade.

Much is made of the colony's role as a source of strategic materials, and we would expect to find the search for raw materials playing a major role in the search for colonies. But this was not so in the heyday of colonialism, before 1914. Until then the only raw material the British were concerned about was cotton. In this century oil has played a significant role in Middle East politics; and chrome, we are told, is the principal tie binding the United States to the white side in the Union of South Africa. Control over raw materials is important in wartime; in peacetime it makes little difference if the international commodity markets are working normally.

An alternative explanation associates colonialism with a drive to invest on the part of imperial powers. Two different versions are given. In one, a deficiency of purchasing power leads to a surplus of goods in the imperial economy's market, with equilibrium restored only by overseas investment. It cannot be restored simply through more trade, because the surplus of goods is not reduced if extra exports are matched by extra imports. In the other version, profits fall as the economy matures, and saving is deflected to foreign investment in order to keep up the profits ratio. This will not occur if a steady flow of innovation produces a flow of profitable investment opportunities; it is therefore feasible for an economy in the lead, but not for a follower. Neither of the two leaders in foreign investment at the end of the nineteenth century, Britain and France, was technologically in the lead at that time, so their overseas investment levels could not have been forced on them by domestic maturity.

In any case, even if there were domestic forces driving these countries to invest overseas, it is not clear why they would decide to invest in underdeveloped areas. Some capital would be spent on opening up colonies with transportation facilities and other forms of investment that would bolster colonial exports of primary products and colonial imports of manufactures. Beyond this, there was little interest in investing in colonies, even if this yielded one percentage point more in interest, and indeed the bulk of foreign investment by metropolitan countries did not go to their colonies. We face the same situation today. A great deal of attention is paid to multinational corporations in the Third World. But in fact, apart from oil, most of the investment of such corporations is not in the Third World; it is in Europe and North America. Investment flows more naturally toward developed areas than to the less developed.

Race is not a necessary element in colonialism. Colonialism acquired a racial element when the Spaniards imposed themselves on the South American Indians in the sixteenth century, but most colonials were white in 1750, and white colonialism did not end until successive tides were turned by North American independence, by Latin American independence, the Monroe Doctrine, and the spread of nationalism in Central and Eastern Europe. By 1920 practically all European peoples had become independent, while practically all non-Europeans, with the exception of the Chinese and Japanese, were colonials. Colonialism, although not so originally, had become a racial system.

As the colonial system became more racial, it also became more racist. Small European military and administrative forces were required to govern vast territories, including hundreds of millions of people of different languages, religions, and customs. Thus, India was governed by an army that had only one soldier per thousand of population. This task was accomplished by means of a twofold strategy. First, the imperial powers attracted, allied themselves with, and supported local power centers that would work with them. Chiefs, kings, rich merchants, and mining companies were supported by the government and in turn supported it. Secondly, the doctrine of racial superiority was promulgated. There was to be no socializing between black and white, and the blacks were to be persuaded of the innate superiority of the whites. Thus, through fear, superstition, and ignorance, it became possible for handfuls of military and administrative white men to keep large numbers of indigenous peoples in subjection.

Such a system could be stable only if the natives could be kept out of secondary schools and universities. Where young people were receiving the same education as that of the rulers, while being denied employment in government jobs or big business corporations on grounds of color, resentment and frustration built up to levels where it could no longer be constrained. Whatever may have been the economic reasons for abandoning the colonies, the revolt of the young educated natives was an independent factor making its own explosion. This revolt had reached an advanced state in India; other colonies were at varying distances behind.

Metropolitan powers varied in their application of the color bar to native intellectuals and professionals. In West Africa the British disliked educated natives and refused to socialize with or hire them. Africans were not eligible for college-level positions in the British Territories, thus giving semblance to Bernard Shaw's gibe that the British Empire was a system of outdoor relief for the British middle classes. By contrast, in the colonies or at home the French treated educated Africans as fully French, gave them jobs, and married them to their sisters. Yet each policy was inconsistent. The French seemed to act without prejudice, but so little provision for native education at any level was made that it was easy to assimilate the few educated Africans. The British, on the other hand, encouraged the missionaries to provide education up to the secondary level and further encouraged Africans to train for professions—even while making it clear that on completion, they would not be employed in the government service. This caused frustration and anger. At independence, power passed to these educated people, with their

affection for the French and their dislike of the English. This is one reason why France and her ex-colonies have collaborated closely over the past twenty years, whereas Britain and her African ex-colonies as well as India have drifted apart.

Another important difference is that the British kept working- or lower-middle-class persons out of their colonies, while the French flooded theirs with *petits blancs*. This was how the education system worked. The British missionaries provided enough education for Africans to fill most jobs at the secondary level, apart from skilled craftsmen. The French did not and imported French men and women for such low-level jobs as domestics, waitresses, shop assistants, and semi-skilled workers. Why this difference existed is not clear. Since France was short of labor, and importing labor from around 1890 onward, and since she trumpeted *la mission civilisatrice*, it is odd that she was so stingy with elementary and secondary education for her native subjects.

Did the colonial system pay the metropolitan powers? This is a hard question to answer. Of course it paid some individuals, while others lost; and presumably those who won had disproportionate influence on the making of metropolitan policy. The difficulty arises when one tries to assess profit and loss for the country as a whole. Adding private and public returns, did it make a profit or a loss on its colonies?

On the surface, each metropolis acquired millions of acres of land, much of it desert, but some of it rich in gold or silver or copper, and some to be bitterly disputed between incoming white settlers and native occupants. Most of the acquisition could not be developed without major infusions of capital. These were for the most part not forthcoming. Depending on the effort made, colonialism paid in some places but not in others. It clearly paid the Dutch in Java during the period of the Culture System, when produce requisitioned from farmers was sold at a net profit of $330 million (U.S.) over this period (1830–1870). It probably paid the British in India during the second half of the nineteenth century, when the Indians paid the entire cost of the Indian government as well as of wars outside India fought by the Indian army. On the other hand, it seems highly improbable that Spain made much profit in the Philippines, or that Indochina yielded France any profit comparable with the cost of the war of conquest. Who benefited from settling Frenchmen as farmers in Algeria, or Englishmen in Kenya, would be hard to assess.

Earlier in this book I asked the question, Why does the landowner exploit the tenant when it may be more profitable to invest in developing his productive capacity? Part of the answer is that many policies that would enrich the colony will not benefit and may even harm the metropolitan power. The latter is interested only in policies that improve his trade. Still, this means that he is interested in agricultural and mineral development, and we would expect to find colonial governments active in this field. But this was not so. The Dutch were very active in developing their colonies throughout the nineteenth century. The British were uneven, except in promoting cotton cultivation and the plantation enterprises of Southeast Asia (tea, coffee, rubber, sisal, and so on). France, active in planting settlers in Algeria, was dormant elsewhere. The other metropolitan powers (Portugal, Spain, Turkey) were not interested in development at home, and reflected the same lethargy abroad. Colonialism is identifiable with neglect to an even greater extent than with exploitation.

But how about the terms of trade? Actually colonialism made little difference to the terms of trade, except insofar as it helped to keep supplies of colonial produce growing about as fast as demand, and the terms of trade made little difference to colonial income per capita, within the narrow range in which they moved. On top of all this the imperial governments held no unique opinion about terms of trade. The British wanted higher prices for coffee and rubber, which their colonies sold to the United States, and lower prices for tea and cotton, which their colonies sold to Britain. Strict identification of the terms-of-trade issue as a colonial versus metropolitan issue would therefore be misleading. Nevertheless, the topic lies at the heart of today's tensions between white and nonwhite nations.

The factors that determined the terms of trade for tropical produce had little to do with government manipulation in the form of tariffs, preferences, or other discrimination. The dominant element was the supply price of tropical labor in comparison with the supply price of labor in Britain and other industrial countries. Throughout the nineteenth century the supply price of tropical labor was less than a shilling a day for migrant labor, and as little as sixpence a day for labor in India. The price was determined presumably by the low marginal productivity of Indian farmers in growing food. Their annual output of food per farm person was about one-fifth that of a British farm worker. The factoral terms of trade, which is to say the ratio of British to Indian earnings, had to be no less than five to one.

About 30 million Indians emigrated between 1850 and 1930 to work in other tropical countries. Many millions of Chinese did the same. Employers in tropical countries could get all the cheap labor they needed, while employers in the temperate countries had to pay a multiple of these wages. These factoral terms of trade, then, set the relative prices of commodities, known as the commodity terms of trade.

This outcome did not depend entirely on Indian and Chinese migration. In any tropical country the farmer could choose between growing food and growing a commercial crop for export. If he produced for export he would expect to earn at least twice as much as if he grew food. (I assume twice as much to allow for extra risks or unfamiliarity with the export crop.) So one way or the other the basic determinant of the supply price for tropical labor or tropical produce would be the marginal productivity of the tropical food farmer. This continues today. The migration of Chinese and Indian labor on indentures has ended, but the low marginal productivity of food producers in the tropics still yields a low supply price for tropical labor.

Now suppose that the export crop is tea, and that productivity in tea doubles. Then its price will halve: twice as much tea will be needed for a fixed quantity of food. If the price does not fall by as much as half, more tea will be offered; if it falls by more than half, less tea will be offered. It follows that research designed to increase productivity in tea does not benefit tea producers. If successful, it merely reduces the price they get for tea. The terms of trade are fixed by the amount of food that the farmer could otherwise produce. In this model the farmers benefit if their own productivity rises in food, or if the productivity of the industrial countries rises in the goods that the farmers import, but the farmers gain nothing from greater productivity in their own exports.

This the colonial powers recognized. They spent a great deal of money on research into the commercial export crops—especially tea, cocoa, rubber, sugar, and oil palm—which yielded dividends in lower export prices, but they spent next to nothing on research in tropical foodstuffs. The large international research stations devoted to tropical foodstuffs were all created after 1950.

Third World leaders have attacked commodity prices as being immorally low; defenders of the status quo have responded that the prices are determined by demand and supply in open competitive markets and must therefore be correct. Essentially the sugarcane laborer says: "the sugar production in which I am engaged is one of the finest arts, embodying the latest in chemistry, biology, and engineering; no other industry is more advanced technologically. Therefore, I should earn at least as much as a steelworker. Instead, you tie my wage to that of the least advanced small farmer, offering me 700 pounds of grain, on the ground that this is what I would be growing if I were not producing sugar." The same argument is used by the women's movement. A woman's job, they say, should be rated according to the demands it makes on skills, strengths, and other qualities, when compared with the median man's job. Women should be paid according to the comparable worth of jobs measured by what is required of the performer, rather than by the supply price of an overcrowded market for female labor. "Not so," replies the market economist. "People are paid, and should be paid, according to their supply price and not according to the use that will be made of their labor." Actually the policy rule for internal trade is equal pay for equal work, it being assumed that departures from this would be eliminated by competition. But tropical producers receive instead pay based on alternative cost. The two rules give the same result in internal trade (discrimination apart), but equal pay for equal work does not operate in external trade because immigration is controlled. Neither rule is more "moral" than the other, except that alternative cost is sustained only by keeping immigrants out.

The situation is not static. The fact that tropical labor has a low supply price in comparison with temperate labor enables tropical labor to compete with the temperate world in everything that both countries can do, as long as the difference in productivity does not exceed the difference in wages. Ultimately the big difference in wages will force temperate countries to surrender to the tropical countries all subtropical agricultural crops, all labor-intensive manufacturing, and all those minerals where tropical production can supply world demand.

Sugar and cotton are good examples. Beet sugar has always cost more to produce than cane sugar; it has survived, therefore, in the temperate countries only with the aid of subsidies or protection, The case of cotton is more complex. Cotton production should not have survived in the United States after 1870. It was being produced in India, Brazil, Mexico, Egypt, and many other places, and the expansion of cotton in these countries was held down by cotton production in the United States. At the same time these countries held down wages in the American cotton regions. Productivity was higher in the United States, but not high enough, when combined with low wages elsewhere, to leave room for a reasonable wage for southern cotton growers. Why did the industry continue? Because black labor remained in the South instead of migrating to other parts of the country, where wages were much higher. It is not absolutely clear why black labor remained in the South, not starting its northward trek in significant numbers until the First World War. It was not illegal to emigrate to another state, though one might be harassed by the police. A high level of indebtedness tied people to their localities, as did uncertainty about jobs and housing at the other end. Emigration takes a long time to gain momentum because it usually depends on pathfinders who go first and prepare the way for those who follow. It was the certainty of jobs during the First World War that really started the mass migration of blacks. Meanwhile their failure to migrate had created a circular situation. These southern blacks had to accept low wages to meet other tropical wages, and at these low wages other tropical countries could not compete with them in growing cotton.

It was not necessary to "own" colonies in order to share in the fruit of colonialism. For insofar as colonial powers refrained from giving themselves preferences in the commodity markets, the terms of trade were the same for all. Denmark could buy tea at the world price and not concern itself with how that price came to be the world price.

Instead of fighting to win colonies, a country could simply struggle for nondiscrimination, which was agreed to at Berlin in 1885, though not then fully honored. The British had the biggest colonial area, and though they succeeded in controlling most of the brokerage and shipping and insurance charges, they were reexporting colonial produce throughout Europe at free market prices. The best reason for owning colonies was fear that other colonial powers would discriminate. If colonial markets were open to all countries on equal terms, the principal spur to intercolonial rivalry would be removed. By the end of the Second World War this principle was fully understood by the leading powers.

By 1920 relations between the white and the colored peoples were conducted entirely within the framework of the colonial system. Not so today; within a short period after the Second World War one colony after another became politically independent. There were political and economic reasons for the drastic change. For the British the crucial colony was India; if it was not worthwhile holding India, no other colony was worth holding. Were there economic reasons in 1945 for holding India? The country had been declining since the First World War; national income per head was probably lower in 1947 than it had been in 1911. Throughout the nineteenth century the British had striven to hold down Indian manufacturing, especially of cotton textiles and of iron, but by 1913 even these constraints had been thrown off. It is doubtful that the ability to manipulate India's terms of trade had ever been worth much; the economic forces we have examined kept the terms of trade unfavorable to India anyway; the colonial system would make little difference to this. Perhaps it was possible to squeeze economic gains out of colonialism in 1900, but by 1945 the developed countries had decided against preferential manipulation of colonial prices. A few colonies were thought to have value as military bases, and interest in oil sources was growing, but in 1945 these were not yet the obsessions that they later became.

India's economic problems were more difficult than those of many other colonies, but India was relatively free from what would in practice be the most difficult problem in decolonization: what to do about the European settlers. This complication arose from the fact that the Europeans had acquired the best lands, in terms of rainfall and soil fertility, and had in force policies that stimulated an adequate flow of cheap native labor. In many cases the settlers had become the effective government of the colony, and they were especially prone (more so than the urban whites) to discrimination in social relations and in employment. The settlers were a major source of conflict. If not protected, they would probably be driven out and, not being able to take either the land or their houses with them, would have lost their principal capital.

What would the metropolitan governments do for the settlers? Would they just write them off? This was what Britain did in East and Central Africa, after testing the water in Kenya and learning that even small guerrilla groups could reduce government almost to a standstill. France took longer to learn, and bloodied herself in Algeria and Indochina; but she learned. Belgium and Portugal took longer still, and ultimately made the most destructive transfers to their successors. The Union of South Africa will be the last to learn, but its time has not yet come.

One major problem remained in 1945. I said that by the end of the Second World War the colonial system had lost its function as a protector of imperial powers against each other's policies. However, its function as a protector of the property of investors against predatory acts, public or private, remained, and the abandonment of the system, in the years immediately following the Second World War, implied some degree of confidence that the successor states would assume these protective functions. This outcome could not be guaranteed. Leaders of the new governments came to power by denouncing colonialism in general and their former colonial power in particular. Investors were close to the old governments and had in many cases intervened against the politicians who were now in power; they were suspect and open to attack. In the new situation the corporations had money but little political power, and the ministry had power but little money. Ways of bringing money and power together were worked out, resulting in what is sometimes called neocolonialism, because some part of the role of the former governments has been inherited by the corporations instead of by the ministers.

The system has not worked smoothly, or all in one direction. There have been major battles some of which the corporations have lost—in Peru, Zambia, Guyana, and elsewhere. As a result of such battles the flow of foreign investment into Third World countries has declined, to the point where in the next decade a shortage of some minerals is possible. A United Nations committee has been designing a code of behavior for multinational corporations since 1977, but progresses slowly. Ultimately some modus vivendi will be reached because the two parties have the same interests: the corporations to dig more minerals and the governments to have the additions to national income generated thereby. Joint private and government explorations are the most likely step.

SECTION ELEVEN:
AFRICANS IN THE GLOBAL COMMUNITY: REACHING BACK

Introduction

Before the end of the Atlantic Slave Trade, there was a growing number of powerful voices on both sides of the Atlantic speaking emphatically about having Africans in the Diaspora return to the motherland in order to help shape a new Africa. Throughout the nineteenth century there were even more powerful voices, activists, and organizations supporting the Back-to-Africa movement. The most prominent were Thomas Peters around 1796, Paul Cuffee by 1815, James Forten during 1817, John Brown Russwurm in the 1820s, Dr. Martin R. Delany in the 1850s to the 1860s, Henry M. Turner in the 1870s and the 1880s, Chief Alfred Sam in 1913, and Marcus Garvey in the 1920s. Of course the British and Foreign Abolition Society and the American Colonization Society were among the early organizations that espoused these ideas. The last mass appeal for peoples of African descent to return in significant number to Africa disappeared with the decline of Marcus Garvey's Universal Negro Improvement Association activities. Nevertheless, there continues to be a sustained interest in the future development of Africa from a wide cross section of leaders and communities in the African Diaspora.

Over the past two decades, a series of innovative steps have been made, especially from organizations in the United States. Many of the activities in the 1990s have been sponsored by organizations like Africare, TransAfrica, the South African Work Project, and the International Foundation for Education and Self-Help. These organizations have sponsored projects, tours, conferences, and workshops in attempts to bring about dialogue and interaction between African Americans and their brothers and sisters in Africa. Among the most widely publicized have been periodical visits of Louis Farrakhan, the leader of the Nation of Islam, and the series of high-level meetings of some African American leaders in the African American/African summits with various political and other leaders of West Africa.

During the late twentieth century, a cadre of African American leaders have sought to identify closely and develop meaningful linkages with the newly politically independent countries in Africa. Among the leaders best known for their serious, committed attempts at reaching back are Congressmen Charles Diggs and Mickey Leland; Rev. Jesse L. Jackson, President of the Rainbow/Push Coalition; Rev. Leon H. Sullivan, Chairman of O. I. C. of America; Randall Robinson, and many others.

The first essay in this section is Edwin Dorn and Walter Carrington's "Three Centuries Removed: Black Americans and Their African Connections" from their work

Africa in the Minds and Deeds of African-American Leaders (1991). This essay chronicles and highlights the most significant and meaningful overtures made by African Americans over this period. Since the publication of this essay, Walter Carrington, a former director of the International Affairs Department of Howard University, was appointed by ex-President Clinton to serve as U.S. ambassador to Nigeria. Dorn is the author of *Rules and Racial Equality (1979), Who Defends America?* (1989), and other works from the Washington DC-based Joint Center for Political and Economic Studies.

Essay two in this section deals with one of the increasingly widely discussed themes, the historical involvement and the increasing interest of larger percentages of Africans and persons of African descent in the practice of Islam. One of the most highly respected of African scholars of the past thirty years, Ali A. Mazrui, wrote a short but insightful essay in the volume *The African Diaspora: African Origins and New World Identities* (2001) that we include for your examination.

Ali A. Mazrui has been Distinguished Professor and Director of the Institute of Global Cultural Studies at the State University of New York, Binghamton, as well as Senior Scholar of Africana Studies at Cornell University and the Walter Rodney Distinguished Professor at the University of Guyana. He has had a long career with many leading institutions of higher learning researching and teaching aspects of the African experience.

Mazrui was Research Professor at the University of Jos in Nigeria before becoming Professor of Political Science and Africa and African American Studies at the University of Michigan, Ann Arbor. He has also served as Vice President of the International Political Science Association and the International Congress of Africanists. He has co-authored volume eight of *UNESCO General History of Africa Since 1935* and is the author of the widely acclaimed television series and monograph *The Africans: A Triple Heritage* (1986), as well as dozens of other works on Africa. He holds three concurrent faculty positions at the University of Jos, Cornell University, and as Chancellor of the Jomo Kenyatta Universisty of Agriculture and Technology. He is also a special advisor to the World Bank and on the Board of the American Muslim Council in Washington, DC.

The third essay in this section was prepared by Ethan Michaeli, a journalist who researched his subject with great care. This study entitled "Another Exodus: The Hebrew Israelites from Chicago to Dimona," was part of a more lengthy anthology published by Yvonne Chireau and Nathaniel Deutsche in 2000 called *Black Zion: African American Religious Encounters with Judaism*. Michaeli deals with an interesting religious group of African Americans that sprang up in Chicago during the 1960s. Its members first migrated to Liberia and eventually settled in Dimona, Israel, a region regarded by them as part of Africa.

The fourth essay was prepared by Keith B. Richburg entitled "American in Africa: A Black *Journalist's Story,"* which appeared in the March 26, 1996 edition of the *Washington Post* magazine. The essay is a synopsis of Richburg's more recently published experience during his tenure as the chief correspondent for the African Bureau of the *Washington Post*. During these years, he covered the recent civil wars in Liberia, Somalia and Rwanda. His more detailed account of his tenure in Africa is recorded in his book *Out of America: A Black Man Confronts Africa* (1997) in which, as in his essay, he writes honestly and passionately about his personal conflict, coping with the culture shock in Africa, as well as with the personal greed and recklessness of many modern-day African political leaders. Richburg's analysis of conditions in Africa has been recognized as extremely provocative and has inspired heated discussions. Richburg attended the University of Michigan and received his B.A. in 1980, M.Sc. from London School of Economics. He won the 1993 National Association of Black Journalists International Reporting Award, and he was a finalist for the 1994 Pulitzer Prize Award for his reporting on the numerous challenges facing the African continent. He won the 1996 George Polk Award for Economics reporting on the Asian economic crisis. He has been the *Washington Post's* foreign editor, and since 2000, the Paris Bureau chief. The author's views also highlight the widely differing and often ambivalent views of Africans in the Diaspora towards their understanding of, and appreciation for, the African motherland.

Essay five in this section deals with one of the most hotly debated subjects related to the African Diaspora experience in the past several years. The discussion about reparations has been going on since the end of slavery and has not been restricted to any region that participated in the Atlantic slave trade. However, since U.S. Congressman John Conyers co-sponsored the U.S. House of Representatives Bill 4p of 1997 that deals with the Reparations issue, some heated and sustained debate has continued to the present with little movement towards a solution. Recent dialogues have taken place mostly in classrooms, forums, and the media and has developed with greater success in Europe and some developing countries. There have been recent international conferences on the issue from South Africa to Barbados, but the U.S. general public has not really become involved so far. Morgan State University's Raymond A. Winbush's recent publication *Should America Pay? Slavery and the Raging Debate on Reparations* (2003) has brought invaluable insights regarding the long struggle that has already taken place to have this issue come under serious consideration at the U.S. governmental and corporate levels.

Molefi Kete Asante, one of the most highly respected African American educators of the past thirty years, has written provocatively on this subject. In the essay, Asante makes a strong case for the American public to get involved in a healthy discussion regarding totally understanding the full range of matters related to Reparations. He shows why after all these years America needs to "come to terms, with the basis for reparations" and "begin to overcome the legacy of its slave experience."

Asante received his Ph.D. in 1968 from the University of California at Los Angeles in Communication Studies. At 30 years of age, he became a full professor at the University of Buffalo. He later was the Founding Director of the African American Studies Department at Temple University and the author of numerous works including *The Afrocentric idea* (1987) and *Kemet: Afrocentricity and Knowledge* (1990). He has appeared in many documentaries including "The Faces of Evil" and "500 Years Later." He is still Professor in the Department of African American Studies at Temple University.

The final essay is authored by Uzadinma Iweala, a young African American journalist. Iweala is the author of a highly acclaimed novel *Beasts of No Nation* (2005) that was based on his thesis work at Harvard University, where he graduated in the class of 2004 magna cum laude in English and American Literature. The main plot in the novel is about a child soldier in a war-torn fictitious African country. He received excellent reviews for his work in *Time* magazine, the *New York Times Magazine*, and *Rolling Stone Magazine*. He is currently working at Columbia University and was named among the best young American novelists during 2007. He was also awarded the 2006 Barnes & Noble Discover Award for his work. His short essay "Stop trying to 'save' Africa," is an excellent example of the view of many close observers who are of African descent regarding how many non-Africans are presently misreading the solutions that can assist Africans deal with the continent's present daily challenges.

Three Centuries Removed: Black Americans and Their African Connections

Edwin Dorn and Walter Carrington

What is Africa to me?
Copper sun or scarlet sea,
Jungle star or jungle track,
Strong bronzed men or regal black
Women from whose loins I sprang
When the birds of Eden sang?
One three centuries removed
From the scenes his father loved,
Spicy grove, cinnamon tree,
What is Africa to me?

—Countee Cullen, "Heritage"

To Countee Cullen, a leading light of the Harlem Renaissance of the 1920s, Africa was an Eden lost. His was perhaps the most idyllic of many images of Africa that black Americans have offered—or had forced upon them—since the first slaves arrived on American shores in 1619.

It is the manner of their coming that sets blacks apart from all the other groups which emigrated to America. Upon their arrival in the New World, Africans were stripped of remembrances of the land of their birth. They were detribalized, forbidden to speak their native languages or practice their traditional religions—and they were dehumanized, prohibited from marrying and powerless to prevent the breakup of their families.

To succeeding generations of African-Americans, Africa became a distant memory. It was a place to which they could never return and in time would have little desire to return, even if they could discover the nation, tribe, or village from which their forefathers had been uprooted. Their destiny was to be in a place where, for many decades, they had no rights which the white man was bound to respect.

Much has been written about the long struggle of American blacks to achieve first class citizenship in the United States. Less has been written and understood about the struggle that has long existed within the person and community of blacks—the conflict between their African heritage and their American inheritance. W. E. B. DuBois set forth the dilemma in 1903: "One ever feels his two-ness—an American and a Negro; two souls, two thoughts, two unreconciled strivings; two warring ideals in one dark body. . . ."

At times of deepest despair over their future in America, many blacks followed those who argued, as did Martin R. Delany, that blacks were part of a "broken nation"; they could only be made whole again by separating from their white oppressors. Unwelcome in white churches, blacks formed their own denominations and christened them with names like African Methodist Episcopal, African Methodist Episcopal Zion, and Abyssianian Baptist churches. Early on, these new black churches saw their relationship with Africa primarily in terms of helping to Christianize their "heathen" brethren in Africa; by the late 19th century, however, black churches began to champion Africans' complaints against colonial exploitation.

American blacks took the lead in protesting against Belgian atrocities in the Congo. Along with blacks in other parts of the diaspora, they formed the Pan-African Movement and saved the German colonies from being swallowed up by the victorious Allied powers at the end of the First World War. America's black colleges educated generations of African leaders, from the founders of the African National Congress to the first heads of state of independent Ghana, Malawi and Nigeria.

In contemporary times, black Americans helped to move the American government away from complicity with the apartheid regime in South Africa; they also urged this country to provide relief for the drought-stricken Sahel and Horn regions. Even as they were struggling to hold onto the gains they themselves had made during the Civil Rights Movement of the 1950s and 1960s, black Americans were exhorted to help their Motherland.

The Back to Africa Debate

Although small pockets of free blacks lived in the South prior to Emancipation, much larger free black communities existed in the North where slavery was outlawed. It was among free Northern blacks and white abolitionists that a debate began over whether the black man had a future in the United States.

Early on, the debate was dominated by whites. Many saw slavery as a curse contrary to Christian teaching which could be exorcised only by returning all blacks to Africa. They formed the American Colonization Society (ACS) in the early 19th century and purchased land in West Africa which they named Liberia. Emulating the British experiment in Sierra Leone, the ACS began in 1822

573

the voluntary repatriation to Liberia of free blacks. From its inception, this scheme was highly controversial among blacks. The ACS was regarded, even by many blacks who favored a return to Africa, as a subterfuge by paternalistic whites to evade rather than solve the race question in America.

Those free blacks who were most pessimistic about their future in America sought a solution in emigration back to Africa. Those who felt that blacks had as much a claim upon this country as did whites saw emigration as a shunning of their major responsibility—the freeing of their American brothers in bondage. Thus was joined an intellectual argument that has raged ever since: Was identification with Africa a diversion from the central issue of blacks' role in America, or a complement to it?

Paul Cuffe was among the first blacks to promulgate Africa as a place for blacks to seek the opportunities denied to them in America. He promoted self-reliance through the establishment of mutual benefit societies. Central to this doctrine of self-help was the exploration of opportunities for blacks to better their fortunes by returning to Africa. From money he had earned as a shipbuilder, Cuffe outfitted one of his boats, and underwrote the costs of transporting nine families, a total of 38 free blacks, to Sierra Leone. This was in 1815, seven years before the American Colonization Society's settlement of Liberia. So popular was Cuffe's first venture that he had a waiting list of over 2,000 for his second; but he died before he could transport another group of emigres. It would be nearly forty years before strong black leadership again emerged to promote a return to Africa.

In the meantime, free blacks focused on setting their own domestic agenda. They organized the National Negro Convention, which first met in 1830. For the next two decades, this was the dominant forum for free blacks to press for civil rights. The Convention Movement held meetings throughout the North and passed resolutions for black advancement, but it gave no support to those who felt that advancement could better be realized outside America.

The Convention proved a useful forum for drawing together the most militant free blacks of the day, but all of its resolutions proved inadequate to change materially the condition of Northern Negroes. As pessimism deepened that slavery would ever be abolished or that former slaves could become part of the American polity, advocates of emigration began to be heeded more and more.

Martin Delaney and the Rise of Black Nationalism

The black nationalist strain in American intellectual thought can be traced back to Martin Delany, a graduate of Harvard Medical School. In an age when black was considered anything but beautiful and the black race was held mentally and morally inferior to all others, Delany preached racial pride. Frederick Douglass said of him: "I have always thanked God for making me a man, but Martin Delany always thanked God for making him a black man."

Central to Delany's thought was the belief that blacks formed a nation within a nation: "a Broken Nation of four-and-a-half millions . . . as the Poles in Russia, the Hungarians in Austria, the Welsh, Irish and Scotch in the British dominions . . . who still retain their native peculiarities of language, habits, and various other traits. The claims of no people, according to established policy and usage, are respected by any nation, until they are presented in a national capacity. . . ."

Delany proposed the calling of a Confidential Council that would appoint Commissioners to go to East Africa "to make researches for a suitable location on that section of the coast, for the settlement of colored adventurers from the United States and elsewhere." He disparaged the American Colonization Society's Liberian experiment. He denounced the ACS as "anti-Christian in its character and misanthropic in its pretended sympathies" and ridiculed Liberia as "not independent—but a poor miserable mockery—a burlesque on a government."

In contrast to that "mere nominal nation," Delany dreamed of building a great state in Africa, and believed that money for the venture could be raised from England and France. What they had been willing to do for Liberia, he thought, they

[sh]ould be willing and ready to do, for five millions, if they be but authentically represented in a national capacity. What was due to Greece, enveloped by Turkey, should be due to Us, enveloped by the United States. . .

And, there would be practical reasons for England and France to support the scheme:

The Eastern Coast of Africa has long been neglected, and never but little known, even to the ancients, but has ever been our choice part of the Continent. Bounded by the Red Sea, Arabian Sea, and Indian Ocean, it presents the greatest facilities for an immense trade with China, Japan, Siam, Hindoostan, in short, all the East Indies—of any country in the world. With the settlement of enlightened freemen, who with the immense facilities, must soon grow into a powerful nation.

Delany exhorted his followers: "The land is ours—there it lies with inexhaustible resources; let us go and possess it. In Eastern Africa must rise up a nation, to whom all the world must pay commercial tribute."

That adventure, first proposed in 1852, was never funded; but it laid the groundwork for the

National Emigration Convention's 1854 decision to send Delany to head the Niger Valley Exploring Party. White abolitionists objected to the expedition, arguing that blacks were not ready for such an undertaking. Delany responded with derision; but criticism from whites made fund-raising difficult, so the expedition wound up being smaller than originally planned.

It was symbolic that this pioneer black nationalist took his Niger Valley Exploring Party to Africa in 1859 on a ship owned by three African merchants. His one-year stay resulted in the signing of treaties with western Nigerian chiefs, giving American blacks the right to settle in their areas. Delany returned to the United States as the Civil War was breaking out. He put aside his emigration schemes and joined the Union Army, where he was commissioned a brevet major and assigned to recruit blacks. After the war ended, Delany worked in Reconstruction agencies. In 1874, he tried electoral politics, losing as a Republican candidate for governor of South Carolina.

The Missionary Imperative

The abolition of slavery and the Fourteenth Amendment's grant of citizenship gave hope that there might be a future for blacks in this country after all, and put to rest for half a century any major efforts to return to Africa. Instead, black Americans concentrated on improving the spiritual and temporal condition of Africans. A deeply religious black American population came to believe that they were part of a "providential design." In the words of Bishop Henry McNeal Turner of the African Methodist Episcopal (AME) Church:

> The Negro was brought here in the providence of God to learn obedience, to work, to sing, to pray, to preach, to acquire education . . . and imbibe the principles of civilization as a whole, and then return to Africa, the land of his fathers, and bring her his millions..

Bishop Turner's church was established in 1793 as blacks seceded from the racism of the white-dominated Methodist Church. Eventually, the AME Church became the largest black American religious organization in Africa, growing to a quarter of a million members, most of whom are in Southern Africa.

As early as 1820, Lott Cary had set off for Africa under the sponsorship of the Baptist Board of Foreign Missions of the United States. Cary was recruited at a time when it was felt that blacks would be more successful than whites in converting Africans and would be better able to adapt to the climate and resist tropical diseases.

The early black missionaries proved their benefactors to be all too right as to their effectiveness. These missionaries went beyond ministering to the spiritual needs of their African brothers and took a keen interest in their economic development. In doing so, they were suspected of preaching politically subversive doctrines. The early enthusiasm of white missionary societies for black evangelists soon withered, as settlers and colonial governments let it be known that black Americans would not be welcome.

In 1897, black Baptists, increasingly alarmed over the absence of black missionaries, decided to take matters in their own hands and formed an independent missionary body of their own—the Lott Cary Foreign Missions Convention. Along with the AME Church and the African Methodist Episcopal Zion Church (AMEZ), black Baptists exerted great influence on Africa from the early 19th to the mid-20th century.

Even the least political of them were subversive to European colonial interests, because their very presence provided examples of what black men were capable of achieving. Unlike most of their white counterparts, the black missionaries resisted the expanding European colonial presence and the increasing white domination of African societies. The AMEs were blamed for the 1906 revolt in Durban, South Africa, during which Africans shouted the slogan that Bishop Henry McNeal Turner had made his anthem when in South Africa: "Africa for the Africans." In 1915, black missionaries were accused by the British Colonial Office of being involved in the armed revolt of John Chilembe and his followers in Nyasaland.

Following the Durban disturbances, the *Natal Mercury,* a South African newspaper, declared: "An evil star rose in the American firmament and sent its satellites to preach sedition in Natal." One witness testified that.

> Natal natives were being sent to colleges in America. Over 150 young natives were recently sent from South Africa including twenty from Natal. This was one of the greatest dangers to the standing of the white men in South Africa.

How great a danger, even the *Mercury* could not then know. Three years earlier, two of those "Natal natives" had returned from the United States to begin organizing the African National Congress. Pixley Seme, the ANC's chief founder, and John Dube, its first president, undoubtedly were influenced during their college years in the United States by black Americans' campaigns against racist laws and practices that were very similar to those in South Africa—campaigns that led to the establishment of the NAACP in 1909 and the National Urban League in 1910. The ANC was established in 1912.

Dube and Seme were but two of thousands of Africans who came to black colleges in the United States to receive an education often denied to them at home. No greater contribution was made by black Americans to their ancestral homeland in the century between American Emancipation in the 1860s and African Liberation in the 1960s than the education of young Africans in this country and the American black churches' development of educational facilities in Africa.

The list of future leaders trained at Historically Black Colleges and Universities (HBCUs) is impressive. Lincoln University in Pennsylvania graduated the two most important African nationalists of their time—Kwame Nkrumah, whose Ghana became the first Sub-Saharan state to become independent of colonial rule, and Nnamdi Azikiwe, who became Nigeria's first president. Hastings Banda received his medical training at Meharry and later returned home to lead the breakup of Cecil Rhodes' pride and joy, the Central African Federation. Banda took colonial Nyasaland to independence as Malawi, thereby laying the groundwork for the later transformation of the other two members of the Federation, Northern and Southern Rhodesia, into Zambia and Zimbabwe.

The Ambivalence of Black Leadership

The most influential black leader of the late 19th and early 20th centuries was Booker T. Washington. From his position as president of Tuskegee Institute in Alabama, Washington wielded more power than any black man ever had in America. He discounted the growing demands of other black leaders for civil and political rights, and concentrated instead on providing blacks industrial training so they could develop the skills they needed to compete economically with whites. A former slave, Washington realized that the freedman's greatest handicap was that, unlike the Russian serfs who had been set free at about the same time as they, the American slaves were left landless. The promise of "forty acres and a mule" was never fulfilled.

Washington's emphasis on vocational skills and his accommodationist racial views won him wide acceptance in the white community and overseas. Colonial administrators, wary of the militant gospel being preached by black missionaries, sought to apply his methods in the training of Africans under their charge. His approach seemed to offer the best of both worlds: blacks would get the training they needed to become productive workers, but would eschew agitating for a change in their social and political position. He was to have a huge influence on the education of Africans. His counsel was sought by the leading African educators of the day such as J. K. Aggrey of Achimota College in the Gold Coast and J. L. Dube of the Ohlange Institute in Natal, South Africa.

Ironically, Washington's model was rejected in turn-of-the-century South Africa. White workers feared competition from blacks with vocational training, so government officials and labor leaders joined forces to promote job reservation laws that limited the skilled trades to whites.

While Washington's involvement with Africa was mainly focused on replicating the Tuskegee model, he did become engaged in one major issue of African policy of the day—the Congo Free State. In 1890, George Washington Williams, the leading black historian of his time (also a minister, a lawyer, and the first black member of the Ohio legislature) was sent to the Congo by the United States Congress to investigate the growing charges of brutality. In a scathing report addressed to his "Good and Great Friend" the King of the Belgians, Williams presented a bill of particulars supporting the allegation that "Your Majesty's Government is engaged in the slave-trade, wholesale and retail. It buys, sells, and steals slaves."

Williams's report persuaded Washington to join the growing agitation for reform in the Congo. To that end, Washington became vice president of the Congo Reform Association and helped to rally American public opinion against Leopold's continued administration of the colony.

W. E. B. DuBois and the Rise of Pan-Africanism

While Washington's approach enjoyed support among whites, it was coming under increasing criticism among blacks. The leading critic, William Edward Burghart (W. E. B.) DuBois, argued that vocational skills alone were insufficient to enable the black man to claim his rightful place in the world. He argued for rigorous academic training to produce a "talented tenth" intellectually capable of leading the race.

Early in his long and productive career, DuBois saw an identity of interest among peoples of color everywhere in a white-dominated world. His writings and his life work influenced more black leaders and intellectuals than those of any other black person. He was a founder of the National Association for the Advancement of Colored People (NAACP) and the principal American architect of the Pan-African Movement.

The term "Pan-African" was coined by a West Indian barrister, Henry Sylvester Williams, during the 1900 London conference on Africa that he had organized. The 32-year-old DuBois, who was the conference's secretary, prepared "An Address to the World" for the new Pan-African Association which was formed to carry on the work of the conference. It was in that address that DuBois first made his famous statement that "The problem of the twentieth century is the problem of the color line." If that was so, he reasoned, then Pan-Africanism was the key to African liberation and black redemption.

DuBois foresaw in the fall of the Kaiser at the end of the First World War a unique advantage to Africa. He persuaded the NAACP to send him as an observer to the Peace Conference at Versailles. There, with the assistance of Blaise Diagne, the Senegalese member of the French parliament, he called the first Pan-African Conference. Its goal was to influence the Versailles deliberations, and to that end the Pan-Africanists submitted 11 resolutions to the Peace Conference.

Most of the demands on behalf of African nationalism did not fare well. The one exception concerned the fate of former German colonies. DuBois and his fellow Pan-Africanists urged that they not be turned over to other colonial powers but instead be placed under international control until their inhabitants could determine their own future. This led to the establishment of the Mandates Commission, under which the League and later the United Nations Trusteeship Council kept South West Africa (now Namibia) from being incorporated into South Africa.

Three other Pan-African conferences were held under DuBois' leadership in the 1920s. Then, in 1945, sensing once again the opportunities the ending of a world war offered for African liberation, a fifth Pan-African conference, chaired by DuBois, was held in Manchester, England. This, in many ways, was the most important of all the gatherings. It was attended by future African heads of state such as Nkrumah and Kenyatta, who used the meeting as a springboard for the independence movements which brought about, at long last, the liberation of the continent from colonial rule.

Marcus Garvey and the Raising of Mass-Consciousness

The Pan-African movement united black intellectuals in the Americas and Africa, but it left the masses of blacks in the diaspora largely unmoved. While the Pan-Africanists were convening in various European capitals, the condition of the Negro in the United States was deteriorating. The end of the First World War had brought the mandate system to Africa, but in America there was a rising tide of racial oppression. Jim Crow laws had taken firm hold in the South; mobs of whites rioted against blacks who had migrated North to work in the automobile and steel factories. Once again, blacks were beginning to despair that they could ever hope to live in dignity and security in white America.

It was during this increasingly desperate period that Marcus Garvey arrived from Jamaica to become the greatest mass leader black America had yet known. Garvey came with much more modest ambitions: he wanted to start a Tuskegee type school in Jamaica and had arranged an appointment with Booker. T. Washington. However, Washington died before the two could meet.

Garvey went to Harlem in 1916 to talk about his recently established Universal Negro Improvement Association (U.N.I.A.). His doctrine of "Africa for the Africans at home and abroad," which he preached with charismatic appeal, caught on quickly. He instilled in the dispirited

black masses a pride of self and heritage, and called for a return to Africa—of which he named himself provisional president. At the height of his influence in the early 1920s, Garvey had a following of more than a million people. In 1923, however, he was indicted on controversial mail fraud charges, and in 1927 he was deported.

Garvey never visited Africa himself and his settlement plans did not succeed; but he nevertheless had a great influence on the continent and on ordinary black Americans' attitudes toward Africa. His book, *The Philosophy and Opinions of Marcus Garvey*, influenced a broad spectrum of African thinking. Kwame Nkrumah once wrote that, of all the literature he had studied, none did more to fire his enthusiasm for the liberation of his country than Garvey's *Philosophy*.

Reaction to Mussolini's Invasion of Ethiopia

The consciousness about Africa which Garvey had resurrected among the black masses did not disappear with his deportation. The embers of that fire flamed up again in the mid-1930s when Mussolini's Italy invaded Haile Selassie's Ethiopia. Racial pride erupted as never before when the Emperor of Abyssinia stood before the League of Nations and warned of the holocaust to come if the nations of the world did not come to his country's aid and stop Fascist Italy in its tracks.

The Ethiopian war became the main topic of conversation wherever blacks gathered. A championship boxing match took on mythic proportions as Joe Louis's fists became the instruments of a race's vindication as he delivered a beating to the Italian, Primo Carnera. In northern cities where black neighborhoods abutted Italian-American neighborhoods, un-refereed fist fights broke out. Volunteers were recruited to go fight alongside their African brothers. Black Americans united in the face of threats to the sovereignty of an African nation.

Ethiopia's occupation and Emperor Haile Selassie's flight into exile in London was a deep wound to black pride. Ethiopia was one of two independent states in Africa, the only independent black kingdom, and a land of biblical fulfillment ("Ethiopia shall stretch forth her hands unto God"). Many black Americans saw its destruction as the beginning of a genocidal plan to annihilate the entire race.

Organizing to Influence American Policy

Ethiopia's fate led many blacks into anti-Fascist activity in America. In the run-up to the Second World War, blacks supported President Roosevelt's war preparedness measures when they were being strongly opposed by Americans of German, Italian, and Scandinavian descent. More and more blacks concerned about Africa began to realize that they had to organize to apply political pressure on their government in order that Africa would fare better at the peace conference following World War II than it had in 1919.

In 1937, a year after the Italian invasion, Max Yergen organized the Council on African Affairs (CAA), the first black-led group dedicated to influencing American policy toward Africa. The Council established close working relationships with African nationalists and labor leaders and lobbied on their behalf with the American government. It paid special attention to South Africa and forged links with the African National Congress. As the end of the war approached in 1945, the Council unsuccessfully urged the State Department to convince the British, French, and Belgians to give up their African colonies, or at least to put them under some sort of international supervision as was previously done with the German colonies. The Council's potential was curtailed in the post-war years by the rise of McCarthyism.

Even while the CAA floundered, anti-colonial agitation in Africa in the 1950s was catching the attention of more and more American blacks. Two important but short-lived groups, the American Society for African Culture (AMSAC) and the American Negro Leadership Conference on Africa (ANLCA), emerged in the 1950s and 1960s. AMSAC was formed by American delegates to a conference of black intellectuals in 1956. It brought important African leaders to the United States, held regular conferences on African issues, published a journal, *African Forum*, and helped black colleges develop African programs and courses. The ANLCA was founded by major black groups in the United States and, through an office in Washington, it lobbied the White House, Congress, and the State Department.

Just as the Council on African Affairs ran afoul of the anti-communist hysteria of the 1950s, AMSAC and the ANLCA were unable to survive revelations in the 1960s that they had accepted funding from the CIA. With the demise of the ANLCA, African issues became less a matter of priority with the mainstream civil rights organizations.

Linking Black Power and African Liberation

The decade of the 1960s was marked by a growth in the number of independent African nations. A new American President, John F. Kennedy, was determined to reverse the policies of his predecessor, Dwight Eisenhower, who saw the winds of change sweeping through Africa as a "destructive hurricane."

However, Kennedy soon found himself saddled with one of the legacies of Eisenhower's Africa policy. The old issue of the Congo re-emerged in 1959 when Belgium suddenly granted it independence. The Eisenhower administration branded the Congo's popular leader Patrice Lumumba a communist, an act which brought the cold war to the heart of Africa.

It was widely believed that the United States conspired in Lumumba's overthrow and subsequent murder. When Lumumba's death, in the late days of Eisenhower's term, was revealed in the early days of the Kennedy presidency, black nationalists staged a riot at the United Nations that interrupted a speech by America's new U.N ambassador, Adlai Stevenson. The tumult was a watershed event. America's mainstream leaders, black and white, were taken aback by the passions that Lumumba's death had unleashed.

Those same leaders also were slow to appreciate the mass appeal of a fiery young Muslim minister who called himself Malcolm X. Even as the energies of black Americans were being turned inward and southward during the civil rights movement of the 1960s, the more militant among the young were flirting with nationalist and Pan-African concepts as they sought to link the American struggle with that of people of color around the globe. Malcolm X helped them make that connection when, in 1964, he made a pilgrimage to Mecca. While abroad, he made his first visit to Africa and attended a meeting of the Organization of African Unity where he equated the racist practices of the United States with those of South Africa. Upon returning home he formed the African-American Unity Organization.

Malcolm, who by the mid 1960s was second only to Martin Luther King, Jr., in popularity among American blacks, was invited by Stokely Carmichael and others in the Student Non-violent Coordinating Committee (SNCC) to speak in Selma, Alabama. The militants soon took over the leadership of SNCC; Carmichael was elected to replace John Lewis, the organization's more traditionally integrationist head. Chafing at the strictures that Martin Luther King's ethic of non-violence placed upon them, SNCC took up Carmichael's cry of "Black Power" in 1966. A delegation of SNCC leaders visited Africa and returned home to step up their nationalist rhetoric.

Militant activists and intellectuals began using colonial metaphors to explain the condition of black America. Central cities were viewed as colonies, local police forces as foreign occupiers. The liberation struggle required that the occupiers be forced out and that blacks take control of local institutions. One battleground in this new liberation struggle took place in schools of the Ocean Hill-Brownsville section of Brooklyn in 1968. Along with taking political control of local schools, the community's leaders developed courses that presented African politics and culture from a black nationalist perspective. Around the same time, black college students began to agitate for a curriculum that was more "relevant" to their needs and more in keeping with their cultural heritage.

Meanwhile, Martin Delany's old concept of "the broken nation" was being revived. Robert Williams, a former NAACP leader in North Carolina who argued that blacks had the right to take up arms in self defense, returned from exile in Africa to proclaim the Republic of New Africa. Community control of the decaying cities of the North was not enough on which to build a new nation, Williams argued, so he claimed the five southern states with the largest black American populations—Alabama, Georgia, Louisiana, Mississippi, and South Carolina—as the "National Territory of the Black Nation." The attempt to carve a black nation out of the black belt never got much beyond the dedication, in March 1971, of a parcel of land in Mississippi as "the first African capital of the northern Western Hemisphere." Efforts to relocate American blacks within the borders of the United States were no more successful in the 20th century than the efforts to resettle them in Africa were in the 19th century.

Black nationalist sentiment inevitably spilled over into academic and foreign policy institutions. African independence movements had opened up new opportunities for American scholars. But while African studies programs were developing at major universities, lonely black pioneers in the field like Rayford Logan and Leo Hansberry at Howard University found themselves marginalized. White Africanists established a new African Studies Association (ASA); black scholars gained only token representation in the ASA's top leadership. Just as black missionaries had been squeezed out of colonial Africa, so black scholars felt shunted aside in America's relations with independent Africa.

It had been blacks like Horace Mann Bond and Leo Hansberry who had founded the Institute of African-American Relations in 1953 to establish ties with the emerging leadership of Africa's independence movement. The organizers turned to whites for financial assistance and soon found the Institute under white control, moved to New York and renamed the African-American Institute. The AAI became the leading private organization promoting ties between African and American leaders. Its board was overwhelmingly white and it did not appoint its first black president until 1989.

Black resentment of white hegemony in African affairs led to a major conflict at the 1969 annual meeting of the ASA in Montreal. There, a group of militant black scholars led by Acklyn Lynch presented a set of non-negotiable demands intended to replace "European" control of the Association with "African" control. When the demands were not met, most of the black delegates walked out and soon thereafter formed the African Heritage Studies Association under the leadership of one of the patriarchs of black historiography, John Henrik Clarke.

Uniting on South Africa

By the 1970s, a strategy to eliminate apartheid had become a major point of debate within the black community. Pushing for sanctions against South Africa were student groups on college campuses, liberation support committees being organized throughout the country, and, perhaps, most important of all, black members of the United States Congress.

The passage of the Voting Rights Act in 1965 had moved the civil rights movement from the streets to the polling booths. A critical mass of blacks was now in the House of Representatives, and, under the leadership of Representative Charles Diggs of Detroit, they organized the Congressional Black Caucus. Diggs himself had risen to the chairmanship of the House Subcommittee on African Affairs and had become the most important spokesman on African issues in the nation.

In 1972, the Caucus sponsored a meeting on Africa at Howard University. It turned out to be the largest black American conference on Africa ever held in the United States. At the top of the conference's priority list was the mobilization of black Americans to press for the elimination of white rule from the Portuguese colonies and southern Africa. Success in doing this depended on blacks being able to mount lobbying efforts as effective as those of white ethnic groups on behalf of their ancestral homelands.

Under the leadership of Randall Robinson, a leader of student demonstrations on behalf of sanctions and a former staff aide to Diggs, TransAfrica opened its doors in 1978. Robinson quickly moved to mobilize the black community to defeat efforts to lift sanctions against Southern Rhodesia. He persuaded the leaders of major black organizations to go on record in support of sanctions and rallied black voters in key congressional districts. Sanctions were maintained and TransAfrica, in existence for less than a year, was credited with engineering the first major foreign policy victory ever attributed to the direct political intervention of the black community.

Drought and famine in the West African Sahel had aroused black American concern as much as had the political problems of Southern Africa. To address issues of relief and long-term development aid, another important Africa-oriented organization, Africare, also was founded in the 1970s. C. Payne Lucas, a former Peace Corps official, became director of Africare. Working closely with the President of Niger, one of the drought-stricken countries, Lucas began a relief effort centered in the black community. He tapped ordinary black Americans in a way they had not been solicited for an Africa-related cause since the days of Garvey. From all over the country, contributions to help African famine victims poured into Africare's headquarters in Washington. Over time, Africare moved from relief to long-term development and is now recognized as the leading American organization of its kind.

The victory of Jimmy Carter in 1976 brought black Americans into the foreign policy mainstream as never before. Partly because of his personal friendship with the President, Andrew Young was able to transform his ambassadorship to the United Nations into a politically powerful post. Young and his deputy, Donald McHenry, initiated the strategy that finally led to Namibia's independence, in spite of its repudiation for many years by the Reagan Administration.

The 1980s saw a elimination of black influence on foreign policy formation in the executive branch. The number of black ambassadors, for example, declined from a high of 15 during the Carter administration to seven during the Reagan administration. The one historic appointment Reagan made was that of then-Lieutenant General Colin Powell as National Security Adviser, the highest post ever held by a black American in the foreign policy field; Powell scored another first in 1989, when President Bush appointed him chairman of the Joint Chiefs of Staff.

During the 1980s, black political influence was exerted primarily through the legislative branch. The Free South Africa Movement, which TransAfrica helped establish soon after the 1984 elections, mobilized the public and lobbied Congress to pass the Comprehensive Anti-Apartheid Act of 1986. The CAA was the most important legislative victory blacks had achieved since the civil rights laws of the sixties, and it demonstrated that blacks could harness their political power in support of international as well as domestic priorities.

In the 1980s international issues claimed more and more of the attention of mainstream black organizations. Typical is the Joint Center for Political and Economic Studies, founded in 1970 to support the efforts of black Americans and their elected representatives to participate more effectively in the political life of the country. As the Joint Center moved more and more into economic issues it became clear how inextricably the welfare of black Americans was linked to economic and political currents worldwide. It was increasingly producing occasional studies on international issues and in late 1990 established an international program with a major focus on the problems of governance and democratic change in Africa.

Three centuries removed, many blacks still feel an affinity for Africa. They adopt (or adapt) African cultural trappings—names and styles of dress and grooming. Inspired by Alex Haley's novel *Roots*, thousands of blacks each year make pilgrimages to see their ancestral homeland. Famine relief efforts and the anti-apartheid movement provide further evidence of blacks' strong interest in Africa. In the recently freed ANC leader Nelson Mandela, black Americans also have found a hero; they identify with his suffering and his aspirations as if the land he seeks to free were their own.

[1]Countee Cullen, *On These I Stand: An Anthology of Selected Poems*, (New York: Harper, 1947).

[2]W. E. B. DuBois, *The Souls of Black Folk, Essays and Sketches* (Greenwich, Connecticut: Fawcett Publications, 1961), p. 17.

[3]Quoted in Martin Kilson and Adelaid Hill, eds., *Apropos of Africa*, (New York: Anchor, 1971), p. 25.

[4]Martin Delaney, *The Condition, Elevation, Emigration and Destiny of Colored People of the United States, Politically Considered*, (Philadelphia, 1852), reprinted in Kilson and Hill, *op. cit.*, p. 26.

[5]*Ibid.*, p. 26.

[6]Quoted in John Hope Franklin and Alfred A. Moss, *From Slavery to Freedom: A History of Negro Americans*, sixth edition, (New York: Alfred A. Knopf, 1988), p. 157.

[7]Kilson and Hill, *op. cit.*, p. 28.

[8]*Ibid.*, p. 28.

[9]*Ibid.*, p. 30.

[10]Quoted in Peter Duignan and H. L. Gann, *The United States and Africa: A History* (New York: Cambridge University Press, 1987), p. 256.

[11]Quoted in Elliot Skinner, *Afro-Americans and Africa: The Continuing Dialogue*, (New York: Urban Center, 1973), p. 7.

Islam and the Black Diaspora: The Impact of Islamigration

Ali A. Mazrui

Hinduism is partly predicated on the doctrine of the transmigration of the soul after death. Islam is partly predicated on the migration and physical motion of the *body* in life *before* death. Hinduism is sometimes a salute to absolute motionless and stillness. Islam is sometimes a salute to purposeful movement.

The Muslim formal prayer is one of the most physical forms of prayer among world religions. Five times every day hundreds of millions of Muslims bend, kneel, and prostrate themselves in physical worship. The Muslim rituals during the pilgrimage in Mecca go to the extent of symbolically *stoning* the evil spirit. Most other world religions believe that God is best ap-proached by motionless postures, sometimes even by solemn silence and stillness. While Islam does allow for moments of silence and stillness, the five compulsory prayers are still *physically active* forms of worship.

When were these prayers commanded by God? Muslims believe that they were commanded when the Prophet Muhammad was physically transported first from Mecca to Jerusalem, and then physically transported from Jerusalem to the Heavens, where he met all the preceding great prophets, and where he came into the presence of the Almighty Himself. All this took place in a single miraculous night—the night of the Mi'raj.

Originally God demanded fifty rather than five physical prayers a day. It was Moses who convinced Muhammad to go back to the Almighty and beg for a reduction of the number of physical prayers for Muhammad's followers. Islam was indeed intended to be a religion in *motion* rather than stillness. It was intended to be a religion not of the transmigration of the soul but of the movement of the body and the migration of the person. The concept of Islamigration captures this paradox. The word "Islam" itself means sub-mission (to the will of God), and submission implies *passivity*. "Migration," on the other hand, is an active principle of *movement*. This essay hopes to demonstrate that it is precisely this quality of Islam as movement and migration which gives it a special relationship with Global Africa. We define Global Africa as Africa plus, firstly, the *diaspora of enslavement* (such as African Americans) and, secondly, the *dias-pora of colonialism* (such as twentieth-century African migrants to Europe and the Americas). Both diasporas involve migration and movement.

As the twentieth century comes to a close the world has over one billion Muslims. About a quarter of those are in Africa (including north Africa) and the African diaspora. There are more Muslims in Nigeria than in any Arab country, including Egypt. The Muslims of Nigeria, Egypt, and Ethiopia alone probably account for a quarter of the population of the African continent (over 130 million Muslims in the three countries).

The United States in 1996 has approximately as many Muslims as Jews. Forty-two percent of the U.S. Muslims are African Americans. It is expected that if present trends continue African American *Muslims* will outnumber American Jews by 2020 C.E. or soon thereafter. (At the moment the whole population of African Americans out-number the population of the Jews of the whole world added together, including the Jews of Israel).

But what is the link between Islam as motion and Africa as migration? Let us look more closely at both the dynamics and the dialectic. To further understand the dynamics of *Islami-gration*, let us take a closer look at the two great Hs in Islam—the *Hijrah* and the *Hajj*. The Hijrah was the migration of the Prophet Muhammad himself from Mecca to Medina to escape persecution. The Hajj is the annual move-ment of hundreds of thousands of Muslims from all the four corners of the world to make the pilgrimage to Mecca. Both the Hijrah and the Hajj involved people on the move. The original Hijrah was a displacement of people for reasons of their new religion. The Hajj is an annual reunification of people on the basis of their shared religion.

The theme of migration is at the heart of this entire dialectic. When did the Islamic Era begin? Once again *migration* rears its fascinating head.

The Hijrah is the beginning of the Islamic Calendar. The era *begins* not when the Prophet Muhammad was born in 570 C.E. Nor does it begin when he became a prophet in 610 C.E. The Islamic calendar does not begin when Muhammad died in 632 C.E. The whole *Islamic era is deemed* to begin when Muhammad was forced to migrate from Mecca to Medina in 622 C.E.—*beginning July 16, 622.* Migration inaugurates the Islamic era. The prophet moved under persecution from Mecca to go to a freer exile. *In the beginning was migration.*

Mecca and migration have entered some of the mythologies and histories of Black people, both Muslim and non- Muslim. The Yoruba possess more than one myth of ancestry. One of those ancestral legends traces Yoruba origins to Arabia. The Yoruba are thus seen as the remnant of the children of Canaan, who were of "the tribe of Nimrod."

In a book by the distinguished Yoruba historian and sociologist N. A. Fadipe, published by Ibadan University Press in 1970, a case is made that the Yoruba arrived in West Africa from Arabia via the Nile Valley:

> The cause of their establishment in West Africa was . . . in consequence of their being driven by Yarrooba, son of Kahtan, out of Arabia, to the Western coast between Egypt and Abyssinia. From that spot they advanced into the interior of Africa till they reached Yarba, where they fixed their residence.

According to a related Oyo mythological tradition, the Yoruba migrated from Mecca to their present abode, having been forced out of *Mecca* following a civil war involving Oduduwa, son of King Lamurudu of Mecca. Oduduwa became the common ancestor of the Yoruba as an African people, and Ile-Ife became the *Yoruba equivalent of Medina*—the place from which the African phase of Yoruba culture flowered. Parts of what is today the Sultanate of Oman had a dynasty hundreds of years ago named the *Yaaruba* dynasty. There is speculation as to whether the name of this dynasty contributed to the Arabized version of the Oyo myth of ancestry.

During the Prophet Muhammad's own life-time there was also movement of persecuted *Muslims* from Arabia to Africa. Especially noteworthy historically was the migration of persecuted Muslims to Ethiopia in the early seventh century C.E. seeking religious asylum. This event is celebrated in Ethiopia to the present day as a kind of pre-Hijrah.

Then there is the case of Farrad Muhammad, the founder of the Nation of Islam, the black Muslim movement in the United States. Accord-ing to known history Farrad was born in Mecca in 1877. He arrived in the United States in 1930 and established the Detroit Temple of Islam. This was a nationalist version of Islamigration. Farrad told his followers that Christianity had been kidnapped by slave owners, that a racial war was coming and Blacks should prepare for it, that their own moral superiority would ulti-mately prevail—and they must begin by ceasing to call themselves "Negroes." Farrad had under-taken a lifelong migration from Mecca (where he was born) to Detroit (where he gave birth to a new religious movement). Then Farrad performed the ultimate case of physical migration. He totally disappeared without a trace in 1934, almost like the Hidden Imam of Shiite Islam.

Theories about pre-Columbian Black crossings of the Atlantic also include Muslims on the move. In 1962 the official organ of the NAACP published an article by Harold G. Lawrence entitled "African Explorers of the New World." In the article Lawrence referred to Abubakari II of Mali as having employed Arab navigators and equipped them with a whole armada of ships and African sailors to venture westward:

> We can now positively state that the Mandingoes of the Mali and Songay Empires, and possibly other Africans, crossed the Atlantic to carry on trade with the western hemisphere Indians and further succeeded in establishing colonies throughout the Americas . . . Abubakari II (1305–1307) did not believe that it was impossible to conquer the limits of the neighbouring ocean.

Twenty years after Lawrence's article, Pathe Diagne, a Senegalese scholar, initiated a project about Mansa Bakary II (another version of the name Abubakari II) and whether his armada crossed the Atlantic before 1312 C.E. Columbus's trans-Atlantic crossing was in 1492. Pathe Diagne argued,

> Both Bakary II and Christopher Columbus learned from the African navigators of Senegambia and the Gulf of Guinea about
> (1) trans-oceanic traffic and trade (2) the existence of a corridor fed by North Equatorial winds and (3) the existence of a current that was easy to navigate during the summer and fall and that led to the rich Maya, Olmeque, Aztec and Inca Kingdoms and civilizations. Neither Bakary II nor Christopher Columbus were ready to share this geopolitical secret with [rivals].

According to this theory, Islam therefore arrived in the Americas at least a century-and-a-half before Christianity. Mansa Bakary II was himself a Muslim, and his sailors and navigators were either Muslim or followers of indigenous African religions. But Islam does not seem to have either spread or taken root in the Americas of pre-Columbian times. This seems to have been a case of Islamigration which was still-born.

Islam's second coming to the Americas was also linked to Black people—but this time through the enforced migration of slavery rather than the Islamic concept of *hirjah*. Alex Haley made his grandfather, Kunta Kinte, a Muslim. Haley made Islam part and parcel of Kunta Kinte's *roots*.

The history of Islam in Trinidad is traced to enslaved Mandingos, who began to be imported into the sugar plantations of Trinidad in the 1770s. According to a study by Omar Hasan Kasule:

> In the 1830s, a community of Mandingo Muslims who had been captured from Senegal lived in Port of Spain. They were literate in Arabic and organized themselves under a forceful leader named Muhammad Beth, who

had purchased his freedom from slavery. They kept their Islamic identity and always yearned to go back to Africa.

In the twentieth century the majority of Muslims in Trinidad were East Indians who had originally been imported as indentured laborers, but there were also some Afro-Trinidadian Muslims. On July 27, 1990, members of a radical Afro-Muslim group known as Jamaat al-Muslimeen invaded the parliament building and held hostage Prime Minister A. N. R. Robinson and most of the cabinet for nearly a week. Next to the Million Man March in the U.S. in 1995, the 1990 capture of Trinidad's government was the most spectacular piece of Black diaspora action in the 1990s.

We said that the Senegalese adventurer who undertook the pre-Columbian trans-Atlantic crossing before 1312 was called Abu Bakari II. Who led the Muslimeen in Port of Spain, Trinidad, in 1990? One is tempted to call him Abu Bakari III. His name was indeed Abu Bakr (another version of the same name). His first name was Yasin. Abu Bakr demanded a govern-ment in Trinidad more sensitive to the needs of the poor and more tolerant of religious pluralism. Prime Minister Robinson agreed to some of the demands of the Muslimeen, and also agreed to grant them amnesty. The policy demands were never really implemented, but the courts decided that the amnesty to the hostage-takers was legally binding. So the Muslimeen were never punished. The amnesty was even confirmed by the Privy Council.

But the first of all Muslim Abu Bakars was the first caliph of Islam after the death of Muhammad—Abu Bakar As-Siddiq. Among his advisors was a Black man who had also been an advisor to the Prophet Muhammad before him. The Black man's name was *Bilal*, and he had won his freedom as a result of Islam. In history Bilal was Islam's first link with Africa's diaspora. He was an Ethiopian at the birth of Islam—a migrant in Arabia, originally enslaved by non-Muslims, freed by a Muslim. In the twentieth century Bilal's name has been used by African Americans for their children, sometimes for their publications, at other times for their restaurants. Bilal is a Black Muslim name in history.

Bilal's voice is also part of the history of Black vocal power in human affairs—from Bilal to Paul Robeson and beyond. Robeson's voice made history in song and on the stage. Bilal's voice made history from the minaret—calling believ-ers to prayer. He was the first great muezzin in the history of Islam—calling believers to those five physical forms of submission. Bilal (son of Rabah) used his Black vocal chords to call Muslims to their physical worship. Physicality and motion were once again intertwined in the history of Islam.

Is Louis Farrakhan a latter-day Bilal? As the author of the Million Man March of October 1995 in the United States, Farrakhan once again linked Islam to *movement*. I and other colleagues spent five hours with him at his home in Chicago in January 1996. He discussed a triad of tours—to Africa, to the Muslim world, and to different parts of the United States. Tours are also within an Islamic paradigm of movement.

Inseparable from the history of Islam is this link with the passions of the African diaspora. This is the dialectic of *Islamigration* as it has unfolded across space and time.

---

[1] N. A. Fadipe, *The Sociology of the Yoruba* edited by Francis Olu Okedji and Oladeji Okedji (Ibadan, Nigeria: Ibadan University Press, 1970), p. 31.

[2] Harold G. Lawrence, "African Explorers of the New World," *The Crisis* (Organ of NAACP, USA) June–July 1962, pp. 2–4. Lawrence was Chair of the Research and Education Committee of the Detroit branch of the Association for the Study of Negro Life and History.

[3] Project Outline, Africana Studies and Research Center, Cornell University, 1990.

[4] Omar Hasan Kasule, *Muslims in Trinidad and Tobago* (Port of Spain, Trinidad: Pamphlet, 1978).

Another Exodus: The Hebrew Israelites from Chicago to Dimona

Ethan Michaeli

From their birthplace in the ghettos of Chicago's South Side to their current home in the modern state of Israel, the Hebrew Israelites have been propelled by a powerful combination of religious and racial identity. In this essay I will examine recent developments within the Hebrew Israelite community. My work is based on a series of interviews I conducted with Hebrew Israelite leaders in the United States and Israel (many while I was a reporter for the *Chicago Defender*), on my visit to the Dimona community in 1996, and on my attendance at a number of Hebrew Israelite events in Chicago over the course of the 1990s. Though limited to official sources, my research reveals that the Hebrew Israelites are currently experiencing a number of significant political and ideological shifts, including a better relationship with the Israeli government and a more inclusive attitude toward Jews.

My insights into the Hebrew Israelites were both enhanced and limited by my role as a reporter for the *Chicago Defender*, an African American-owned daily newspaper which has been published for nearly a century. Because of the newspaper's historic role within the African American community, I was privileged with unique access to the Hebrew Israelite leadership and their supporters throughout African American Chicago and when I traveled to Israel. The readership and editorial staff of the *Defender*, moreover, were highly interested in continuing coverage of the Hebrew Israelites, allowing me to revisit the topic over a period of several years. My research was largely defined, however, by the constraints of daily newspaper reporting in that I had relatively little access to rank-and-file Hebrew Israelites or to the group's literature, nor is my perspective that of a scholar of religion but rather that of a journalist with long experience in the African American community.

In 1969 the Hebrew Israelites began arriving in Israel—which they referred to as Northeast Africa—from Liberia, where they had established a community during the 1960s. The Hebrew Israelites claimed the right to Israeli citizenship under the nation's Law of Return, which guarantees automatic citizenship to any Jewish individual. Like many immigrants to Israel at the time, the Hebrew Israelites requested settlement in Jerusalem. However, using policies designed to expand the Israeli presence in outlying areas with new immigrants, the Israeli government instead settled them in the Negev Desert town of Dimona.

In 1973, Israeli officials ruled that the Hebrew Israelites did not have the right to Israeli citizenship and denied the group work permits and state benefits.

The Hebrew Israelites retaliated with a campaign in the United States which accused the Israeli government of racist discrimination against the group. Throughout the 1970s and 1980s Prince Asiel Ben Israel, the Hebrew Israelites' "International Ambassador" and the highest-ranking Hebrew Israelite in the United States, organized protests and enlisted black political figures, community activists, and other figures—including Nation of Islam leader Louis Farrakhan—in the Hebrew Israelites' cause. Ben Ammi, the leader of the Hebrew Israelites, claimed publicly that Jews had usurped the mantle of being "God's chosen" from African Americans. American Jewish organizations—in particular the Anti-Defamation League of B'nai Brith—responded to the Hebrew Israelites' actions with a media campaign which portrayed the Hebrew Israelites as a racist movement in the same vein as the Nation of Islam and various white supremacist groups.

Though the Israeli government never officially moved to deport the Hebrew Israelite community as a whole, a number of individuals were returned to the United States after being arrested for working illegally. Ultimately, the Hebrew Israelites renounced their American citizenship in an effort to prevent further deportations. During the same period the Hebrew Israelites faced other challenges. For example, in 1986 the U.S. Attorney's Office in Chicago brought charges of various financial misdealings against Prince Asiel Ben Israel. He and three others were found guilty and served several years in prison.

In October 1990, Illinois state legislators brokered an agreement with the Israeli government that settled—albeit temporarily—the Hebrew Israelites' legal status in Israel. They are now permitted to hold jobs and receive access to social services and housing. Members of the group reclaimed their American citizenship and received support from the American government that allowed them to build a school and expand housing.

Hebrew Israelite settlements in Dimona and Arad, another Negev town, have a combined population of over 2,000. The Hebrew Israelite gospel choir tours throughout Israel, and the community owns restaurants in several Israeli cities. The settlement with the American and Israeli governments has allowed the Hebrew Israelites to expand their housing and develop a specialized school that combines an education in modern Hebrew, science, math, and Israeli civics with Hebrew Israelite spiritual tenets. Within its compound, the group operates a clinic, communal kitchen, and organic farm.

The rhetorical conflict that marked the previous decades of the Hebrew Israelites' tenure in Israel appears to have evaporated. According to Israeli government sources, the community's two decades in Israel have dispelled Israeli fears that acceptance of the Hebrew Israelites would encourage an exodus of millions of African Americans. Despite aggressive proselytizing in African American neighborhoods across the country, Hebrew Israelites have little more than trickled into Dimona and the other, smaller communities.

In the United States the Hebrew Israelites have established communities in a number of major cities, including Chicago, St. Louis, and Washington, D.C. In addition to bringing in new members, the group's American branches seek to play a grass roots political role in many African American neighborhoods. Characteristic of these efforts was their part in brokering a truce between rival street gangs in Chicago's infamous public housing developments in the fall of 1993.

Beliefs and Rituals

The distinct identity forged by the Hebrew Israelites—visible in their beliefs, rituals, and lifestyle—fuses their particular interpretation of biblical religion with aspects of African American culture. Hebrew Israelite clothing, for example, combines West African styles with biblical traditions. Men wear long African print shirts with the biblically prescribed fringes known in Hebrew as *tsitsit*, as well as head coverings called *kippot*. Women wear long, modest dresses and follow the biblical rules concerning menstruation, known as *niddah*. Following the biblical example—one that was also accepted in some Jewish communities into the twentieth century—Hebrew Israelite men are allowed to have more than one wife.

The community has a strictly vegan diet, which it derives from its exegesis of Genesis 1:29, "And God said: Behold, I have given you every herb-yielding seed, which is upon the face of all the earth, and every tree, in which is the fruit of a tree yielding seed—to you it shall be for food." The Hebrew Israelites refer to their diet as "Edenic" (derived from the Garden of Eden) and consider dietary prescriptions that appear later in the Bible, such as the rules of Leviticus, as concessions or accommodations to human weakness and not binding on their own community. The Hebrew Israelites also characterize their diet as an antidote to the unhealthy lifestyle they associate with African American inner city communities. Reflecting their

own roots in these communities, however, the Hebrew Israelite communal kitchen in Dimona serves vegan versions of traditional African American dishes, such as corn bread and gravy, along with tofu products the group makes in its own factory.

The community considers its leader, Ben Ammi, to be the messiah and view themselves as locked in an apocalyptic struggle with the forces of evil. In this struggle the Hebrew Israelites play a biblically ordained, redemptive role and will eventually gather in the righteous to Jerusalem. Although they do not have a substantial physical presence in Jerusalem, members of the group visit the city often. In addition, the community's ritual leaders are known as *kohanim*, the Hebrew word for the priests who served in the ancient Temple in Jerusalem. Unlike contemporary Jewish *kohanim*, who claim to be actual descendants of the biblical priests, the Hebrew Israelites choose individuals to become priests on the basis of their spiritual characteristics rather than ancestry.

The Hebrew Israelites observe the Sabbath from Friday to Saturday night and celebrate other biblically ordained holidays such as Yom Kippur and Passover. Following another biblical tradition, the group celebrates the New Year in spring rather than in the fall, when contemporary Jews celebrate the New Year festival of Rosh Hashanah. The Hebrew Israelites combine African American religious traditions, such as gospel songs and call and response, with prayers in Hebrew composed by members of the community, often employing biblical verses, in particular the Psalms. The Hebrew Israelites characterize their history in biblical terms and depict their journey from the ghettos of the United States to Israel as a reenactment of the ancient Israelites' Exodus from Egypt.

In a 1995 interview in Chicago, Ben Ammi said he knew Liberia was an interim stop for the group. He described the Hebrew Israelites' abbreviated tenure there as a tropical, coastal metaphor for Moses' 40-year sojourn in the Sinai desert. Ben Ammi emphasized that the travails of the last quarter century had tested, transformed, and finally revised key doctrines of the Hebrew Israelites' faith. Most notably, he recently modified his earlier assertions that African Americans are the only true descendants of biblical Israel and that Jews are "imposters." In an April 1996 interview with me in Dimona, Ben Ammi explained that the quarter century of contact with Israeli Jews was necessary to free his mind from the narrow vision of Jews and Judaism that he had brought with him from Chicago.

Ben Ammi and other Hebrew Israelite spokespeople currently espouse the view that not all African Americans or all Jews are physical descendants of biblical Israel but that many members of both groups, as well as some individuals from other groups, can trace their ancestry to the tribes of Israel who were exiled from the land of Israel. In current Hebrew Israelite ideology, an individual's righteousness, rather than his or her skin color or ethnic origin, is the true sign of Hebrew Israelite ancestry. Reflecting this new ideological development, the Hebrew Israelites now have a number of non-African American members.

Ben Ammi: Return to Chicago

In 1993 Ben Ammi traveled to Chicago and appeared at a South Side church whose pastor had long been involved in black nationalist causes. As a reporter for the *Chicago Defender*, I covered his appearance. The chill from the brisk Sunday morning and the desolate surroundings of Garfield Boulevard belied the enthusiastic, colorful crowd inside the church. Craig Hodges, a former Chicago Bulls basketball star, joined dozens of community activists and local leaders. The crowd included men in their Sunday suits and women in resplendent outfits as well as numerous individuals in African style clothes. By the time Ben Ammi began to speak, the church was filled to capacity.

Ben Ammi took the podium dressed in robes and turban. A thin, graceful man with blazing blue-gray eyes and a sparse beard, he began his speech slowly and methodically. As he delved deeper into religious topics from both the Hebrew Bible and the New Testament, Ben Ammi began to rock forward and make stiff, powerful gestures. He traced the origin of all religious life to the Middle East and discussed a number of prophets, from Ezekiel to Jesus. He described the Hebrew Israelites' Dimona settlement as a community that had freed itself from the evils of African American urban life—no drugs, no crime, no drive-by shootings. He encouraged African Americans to accept their destiny as God's chosen people and begin a new life in the Middle East. Ben Ammi listed the names of dozens of individuals who had been to Dimona and could testify that it was an idyllic, moral community of devout African Americans in the Holy Land.

In 1995 Ben Ammi visited Chicago again and made high-profile appearances in both the African American and Jewish communities. During his visit I interviewed him for the *Chicago Defender*. Ben Ammi declared that the political settlement had allowed the Hebrew Israelites in Dimona to stabilize and thrive. Although the original Hebrew Israelite settlers all came from Chicago, new waves of immigrants had arrived from African American communities across the United States. The community now included members who had been reared in Detroit, Atlanta, Washington, D.C., and New York City.

According to Ben Ammi, the agreement between the Hebrew Israelites, the American government, and Israeli officials paved the way for the community to expand in both concrete and philosphical terms. The years of conflict with the Israeli government had been hard years, Ben

Ammi admitted. His people were not allowed to work legally, and those who worked and were caught were deported. They lived in a few extremely crowded apartments and suffered even as a new generation of Hebrew Israelites was being born in the Holy Land. The group's morale was low and the tensions sometimes turned to anger. Ben Ammi emphasized that only the kindness and generosity of Dimona's Israeli residents had ensured that the Hebrew Israelites did not starve; Israelis respected the Hebrew Israelites' determination to stay in a nation that was still developing.

"We have never had a problem with the people," Ben Ammi said. "The differences we have had have always been political differences."

In addition to solidarity with the Israelis, Ben Ammi said his community had emerged from the hard years in Dimona with an increased strength in their resolve. The community had not descended into drug abuse, violence, and despair, characteristics of the neighborhoods that they had left. The Dimona Hebrew Israelites had maintained the diet, lifestyle, and faith that had brought them across the ocean. Ben Ammi saw this success as evidence of the righteous nature of the community.

In the spring of 1995 Ben Ammi and Prince Asiel attended the Israeli Independence Day celebration in Chicago. Held every year in the elegant Cultural Center in the heart of Chicago's business district, the event typically saw the gathering of a variety of Jewish leaders and intellectuals, Israeli residents of the area, and politicians demonstrating their solidarity with the State of Israel. Ben Ammi and Prince Asiel, dressed in African-style robes and carrying wooden staffs, mingled easily with the crowd, greeting journalists, dignitaries, and well-wishers amid trays of pita bread, humus, and babaganoush. The party-goers included many of the state legislators, both Jewish and black, who had brokered the deal that legitimized the Hebrew Israelites' presence in Israel.

Privately, Israeli government officials from the local consulate expressed general satisfaction with the Hebrew Israelites, but they also revealed that they had learned that during his current tour of America, Ben Ammi had met with Louis Farrakhan and other African American figures whom they considered to be hostile to Jews and the State of Israel. Ben Ammi's public statements had nevertheless remained friendly to Israel and Jews in general, the consulate officials said, and the Israeli government had not regretted its decision to support the Dimona community.

Ben Ammi repeatedly described his group as uniquely qualified to serve as a bridge between African Americans and traditional Jews on both sides of the ocean.

Unlike the Ethiopian Jews, who had been brought to Israel in dramatic airlifts during the 1980s and 1990s, for example, the Hebrew

Israelites had roots within the African American community. Buoyed by the success of his visit to America, Ben Ammi was ebullient about the prospects of playing a central role in improving relations between African Americans and Jews.

Dimona

I visited the Hebrew Israelites' Dimona community on the last day of Passover in the spring of 1996. Since the Hebrew Israelites' arrival in Israel, the country had become a prosperous, industrialized state. Development had not, however, occurred evenly throughout the nation. Whereas Tel Aviv, Haifa, and other coastal areas had become thriving cosmopolitan centers, smaller towns in the Negev like Dimona had not benefited proportionately.

The road to Dimona from Tel Aviv demonstrates the diversity of the Israeli geography. The fecund, humid coast of Tel Aviv gives way to the farms and orchards of central Israel. Minutes later the greenery evaporates along the gradual decline into the sun-baked Negev. Mountains of red and gold stone, barren in their lunar beauty, spread out through the horizon. The last stop before Dimona is Beer Sheva, Israel's desert metropolis, a one-time Bedouin market that has sprouted businesses, factories, and apartment high-rises.

Dimona is located several kilometers beyond Beer Sheva. The main street is lined with Israeli low-rise dwellings, many with red-tiled roofs. When I arrived, the boulevard's only other traffic was a lone donkey, lazily driven in a slow meander by a youth with a twig. At the periphery of the Hebrew Israelite compound I was greeted by a young Hebrew Israelite boy wearing a knitskull cap and African print robes.

I asked him in Hebrew, "Excuse me, where is Ben Ammi's house?"

The boy looked at me and pointed into a complex of houses. "Over there," he answered in Hebrew, "through those houses."

The gateway to the Hebrew Israelite compound was ringed by a waist-high wall of khaki round stones. I walked along a stone-paved path through the small, one-level houses that typify Israeli immigrant settlement communities. A group of tall, thin young men, dressed in crisp white robes and wearing white knit skullcaps, stood in the shade of a tall tree. I explained to them that I had an appointment with Ben Ammi, and one of the youths quickly guided me to the home of another community leader.

Elegant in his comfortable cotton robe, Prince Elkannan stroked his luxuriant white beard as he offered me a cold, sweet fruit drink. The living room was spare: concrete, cool, and airy as most Israeli homes are, though Elkannan's home lacked the air conditioner and television set that are common in Israeli homes. A native of one of Detroit's most impoverished neighborhoods, Elkannan said his decision to become a Hebrew

Israelite arose from a desire to shed a life destined for corruption, poverty, and misery in favor of everlasting paradise. African Americans from similar places around the country—ghettos in New York, Baltimore, Philadelphia, and other cities—had come for similar reasons. All of them believed that the Hebrew Israelite lifestyle would afford them immortality. Elkannan assured me that no one had ever died in the Hebrew Israelite community. He saw everlasting life as the product of the Hebrew Israelite's comprehensive, philosophic approach to life, a matrix that coded their daily behavior.

The land of Israel was the only environment in which the Hebrew Israelite community could thrive, according to Elkannan. He continued to emphasize that the Hebrew Israelite community had never seen and would never see a funeral; illness and malnutrition had been eliminated in Dimona, he insisted. Moreover, the Hebrew Israelites had eliminated the violent deaths that claim a disproportionate number of young African Americans. Elkannan said that the illegal drug trade and its consequences—addicts, dealers, drive-by shootings, and incarceration—were all unknown to those members of the Dimona community who had grown up there. The Hebrew Israelites had developed a quasi-Zionist ideology that made living in Israel a precondition to eliminating the perceived evils of the African American world they had left behind.

All of the inhabitants of the Dimona Hebrew Israelite community dressed in gender-indicative African print cloth. The women wore ankle-length robes and layered head scarves, while older men wore two-piece suits with brimless cylindrical caps. Younger men tended to wear knit caps. My guides through the Dimona community informed me that space was extremely tight. Although the community's yards and homes maintained a neat outward appearance, families were packed into the few houses. The guides said the community was quiet because of Passover, but the stone paths between the homes teemed with groups of young children playing in groups. The children bowed and greeted the adults who passed them. In general, the community was gender-segregated, with strict separation between unmarried young people and even between unaccompanied married adults of the opposite sex.

The Dimona community contained a number of communal facilities. The Conquering Lion of Judah Health Center was operated by Crown Brother Abir. Abir described a training curriculum that included martial arts and yoga, weights, and isometric equipment as well as use of a Jacuzzi and massage facilities. The physical regimen included intensive stretching, breathing, and other holistic exercises, Abir explained, with separate classes and schedules for men and women. The Hebrew Israelite health clinic was staffed by a team of midwives and spiritual physicians who dealt with a wide variety of illnesses and conditions. The midwives boasted that over 600 children had been born successfully through their techniques. Serious injuries such as broken bones were treated at local hospitals, however.

The school compound, financed through the arrangement with the U.S. and Israeli governments, had been built at the edge of the Hebrew Israelite settlement. Although only Hebrew Israelite children attended the school, Israeli school system teachers were employed there as instructors of modern Hebrew, with Russian immigrants as science and math teachers, and Hebrew Israelite teachers for religion and culture.

Many of the community's services were organized along the lines of communal Israeli settlements known as *kibbutzim*. The community's cafeteria was known as a *chadar ochel* after the dining space in the *kibbutzim*. The cafeteria's head cook explained that the community's younger children ate two meals daily at the *chadar ochel*, prepared according to the strict vegan diet prescribed by Hebrew Israelite beliefs. Like many agricultural *kibbutzim*, much of the food used in the *chadar ochel* was grown in communal plots. At the community's clothing store, Hebrew Israelite seamstresses assembled and sold robes, dresses, and turbans that the community members wore, but they also geared their designs for sale to Israeli and foreign consumers.

Hebrew Israelites referred to Ben Ammi as *abba*, the Hebrew word for "father." Ben Ammi received me in the Prince Asiel International Spiritual Center, a modest office decorated with newspaper and magazine articles and photographs depicting the African American singer Stevie Wonder's tour of the Dimona community, along with magazine articles about the community in *Teva Dvarim*, the Israeli version of *National Geographic*. Several of the articles featured the Hebrew Israelites' talented choir.

Ben Ammi described a Hebrew Israelite community that was planted firmly in the modern nation of Israel and the politics of the Middle East. Ben Ammi proclaimed that the Hebrew Israelites had changed their orientation and needs after a quarter century spent in Israel. He referred to Israel as "The Land," a translation from the Hebrew *ha'aretz*, the word employed by Israelis. Ben Ammi acknowledged that geography and experience had created a set of concerns entirely different from those of other African American leaders.

"I would be more concerned with getting an audience with [then Prime Minister Shimon] Peres than with getting an audience with Bill Clinton. The position of Peres is more essential to my life and well-being than the position of Bill Clinton. Naturally, that puts us in a very unique position," Ben Ammi said. "No intended disrespect but it's a question of priorities. Our destiny is tied to the State of Israel."

Ben Ammi emphasized that the Hebrew Israelites' experience in Israel had transformed their perspective concerning Jews. Where he had once been suspicious of Jews and denied their legitimacy, Ben Ammi now included at least some Jews in his collective "Chosen People." Ben Ammi attributed part of the change in perspective to the political agreement that had eased their living conditions. But the single most powerful agent of the Hebrew Israelites' change was the conduct of the Israeli residents of Dimona. Dimona residents had provided food, work, and other necessities for the Hebrew Israelites when the political situation prevented official support of any kind.

"Our problems have always been political. Our people have always been great. In Dimona, we've never had any problems. No one has ever lifted up a finger against us. We haven't lifted a finger against anyone. In times of emergency, we all go out together.

"We're very thankful because, once again, we want to become more involved with what's taking place here."

The Hebrew Israelites' appreciation for their Israeli neighbors was heightened during the Persian Gulf War. When the notoriously imprecise Iraqi SCUDS targeted the Dimona nuclear reactor, the Hebrew Israelites hid in bunkers alongside their Israeli neighbors. In Ben Ammi these experiences generated a feeling of solidarity, inclusion, and loyalty. Ben Ammi contrasted these feelings with the exasperation and helplessness that he had experienced in Chicago.

"We were ready to go to Iraq. Anything that we could have done to stop those SCUDS, we would have been ready to do that and we view that differently from the violence in the neighborhood. We don't want violence in Chicago neighborhoods, but our priorities are quite different here because, again, we're part of the state of Israel," Ben Ammi said. He emphasized that the Hebrew Israelites were committed to pursuing full citizenship and would recognize military and other obligations.

"We want the whole load. When it's time to cry, we will weep together. When it's time to rejoice, we will rejoice together."

Ben Ammi's priorities have placed the Hebrew Israelites on the right of Israeli politics. He supports continued Israeli occupation of the West Bank on religious grounds and urges all Jews to adhere to biblical principles and morals.

"Our priorities are quite different from those of African American communities. These are the things that we seek in our vision. We see the redemption of our people there, in Israel, and all humanity as coming via the achievements and the redemption of the children of Israel," he said. "We were chosen to be a light unto the nations."

Ben Ammi saw a distinct, grand role for the Hebrew Israelites and for himself in modern Israel. Theologically oriented, Ben Ammi saw himself as the broker for the salvation of both Jews and blacks. Arguing that many blacks and Jews were descended from a common heritage, Ben Ammi said that his role would be to catalyze this realization in both communities. He hoped to serve as the "spiritual prime minister" of an Israel that would welcome both Jews and African Americans.

The Hebrew Israelites alone had the ability to exploit this potential alliance, Ben Ammi argued. He saw the Hebrew Israelites as the only group capable of bridging the considerable gaps between Jews and African Americans. Conscious that most Jews and African Americans do not believe that they share a common ancestry and birthright, Ben Ammi said the Hebrew Israelites' unique understanding of both cultures was the necessary ingredient to forge a union of Zionist Jews and Pan-Africanist blacks.

"We represent another paradigm and we are telling all Jews, Israelites, that you're Africans. They're not really ready to accept yet that Israel is a part of Africa historically. That means that if you're a Jew, an Israelite, you're not a European," Ben Ammi told me.

"I'm not trying to make you like me. I'm an Israelite. I'm an African. Israelites are, were, and always will be African as far as the continent. Because of the old indoctrinations, there is a fear of that."

I asked Ben Ammi to reflect on the country and community he had left behind. Ben Ammi was disappointed in the conditions in poor African American neighborhoods, which he felt were far worse than at the time of his departure. The efforts of African American leaders—albeit well intentioned—had failed to disrupt a tide of poverty, drug abuse, and depravity, Ben Ammi argued. To Ben Ammi, African Americans' circumstances would not improve until they acknowledged their Israelite identity and sought out the Promised Land.

Sound and the Kidnapped Afrikan

From disparate, sometimes contradictory motivations and experiences, the Hebrew Israelites have developed a complex worldview. The Hebrew Israelites have followed their religious vision—which combines traditional African American identification with biblical Israel and Pan-African philosophy—to the modern state of Israel. The Hebrew Israelites believe that the redemption of African Americans can be accomplished only through an exodus to the Promised Land. In trying to motivate other African Americans to join their exodus, the Hebrew Israelites have articulated their worldview in literature, music, and other creative endeavors.

Perhaps most compellingly, since 1995 the Hebrew Israelites have toured the United States with a musical drama called *Sound and the Kidnapped Afrikan*. The play depicts the harsh conditions of life in inner city communities as

divine punishment. Like the Old Testament Israelites, African Americans are portrayed as a chosen people temporarily out of favor. The play traces African American history from a time of regal prosperity in Africa, to slavery on Southern plantations, to self-destructive behavior on the streets of Northern cities. In the play, musical ability functions as a metaphor for divine selection. In each scene of the performance, African Americans perform music to transcend their miserable circumstances. The songs reflect the continuous ability of the African people to produce beauty, even during the agony of their exile.

In Chicago *Sound and the Kidnapped Afrikan* was performed on several weekends in February 1997 at the AFC Theater on 79th and Ashland, the desolate heart of the Englewood neighborhood. Once a thriving commercial district, Englewood today is a lonely landscape of vacant lots, long-abandoned storefronts, and run-down single-family homes. Originally built as a movie theater, the AFC Theater now serves mainly as the headquarters of an evangelical Protestant church. Although the play had taken over the actual performing space, most of the building's storefronts were in use as prayer halls even on the night of the play. The building's corner store, which must have been in a prime location in the theater's heyday, now housed a store selling religious paraphernalia.

On the night I attended *Sound and the Kidnapped Afrikan*, the audience's many affluent-looking members appeared to have come from beyond blighted Englewood. The parking lot was filled with late-model, expensive vehicles. Well-dressed men in long leather coats escorted women in furs and boots through the howling Chicago winds into the theater's lobby. Prince Asiel stood at the theater's entrance, greeting many of the arriving community leaders. Entrance to the theater was controlled by a phalanx of large, tight-suited security men. In the hallway immediately outside the theater, Hebrew Israelites from Dimona offered books by Ben Ammi as well as clothing and jewelry.

The theater's interior typified the once-grand style of Chicago's inner-city neighborhoods. The previous weekends' performances had been sold out, although the performance I attended was approximately three-fifths filled with an entirely African American crowd. The start of the play was delayed by a quarter hour, apparently to facilitate the arrival of a special guest. Just before the lights dimmed, a small group of suited men hustled to the front two rows. At their center was Nation of Islam Leader Louis Farrakhan, dressed in a white fur coat, a bowler cap, and his trademark amber-tinted, gold-framed glasses. Farrakhan glanced quickly back at the crowd and flashed a broad smile.

Farrakhan's presence at the performance of *Sound and the Kidnapped Afrikan* suggested that the

Nation of Islam and the Hebrew Israelites continued to enjoy at least a cordial relationship since the days when Farrakhan had lent support to the Hebrew Israelites in their lobbying efforts. This view was supported by an earlier event I attended in June 1996, in which Ben Ammi gave a lecture entitled "Our Prophetic Geo-Political Position: Israel–America–Africa: Hebrewism, Christianity, and Islam;" at Kennedy–King College, a public institution on Chicago's South Side. Farrakhan's wife, Khadijah, was one of several African American community leaders who joined a group of prominent Hebrew Israelites on stage.

During my interview with Ben Ammi in Dimona, I had asked him about the Million Man March organized by Farrakhan in Washington, D.C. Ben Ammi took exception to the Nation of Islam's description of the event as a "A Day of Atonement." Referring to the Jewish holy day Yom Kippur, Ben Ammi said the march's theme was a misappropriation of an Israelite tradition and therefore, despite the march's positive aspects, he was unable to endorse it:

> The Day of Atonement—that's a special kind of event. [The Million Man March] wasn't the Day of Atonement and the danger would have been for me to give the impression that it was the Day of Atonement.
>
> You know what's going to happen now. That's going to become a tradition and I've been warned about the traditions of men.
>
> They need a Day of Atonement but that wasn't it.
>
> The Muslim world is looking for some inroads to form an alliance between the Muslim community and the African American community and to move into the political arena—Muslims, African Americans, and Arabs.
>
> And we look up and see it is working. First of all, they gave an address. In the midst of the African American community, they said, here is the address to make inroads.
>
> They're making inroads because the African American community again is lacking in understanding. First of all, lacking in understanding of the problems that are there and lacking in understanding of the tools that they have at their disposal to neutralize the multiplicity of problems that exist today between the African American and the Jewish communities.

From his comments, it was clear that Ben Ammi felt a connection to Farrakhan because of their shared goal to improve the spiritual and material conditions of African Americans. He also respected the Nation of Islam's efforts to raise the issues of responsibility and atonement within the African American community. Yet, because of the Hebrew Israelites' position within the State of Israel, Ben Ammi was concerned about any alliance between African American, Muslim, and Arab groups that might jeopardize the security of Israel and, by extension, the Hebrew Israelite community. Moreover, Ben Ammi appeared troubled by the tension between the Nation of Islam and the American Jewish community and hoped that African Americans would awaken to the positive role that the Hebrew Israelites could play in improving relations between the two groups.

After watching Farrakhan enter the theater, I greeted Zockriel Ben Israel, whom I had met several times with Prince Asiel. Zockriel, who served as the play's narrator, explained that this tour was the play's second in two years. Last year, he said, *Sound and the Kidnapped Afrikan* had been performed in more than a dozen cities in just a few weeks. Zockriel boasted that this year's performance was enhanced by a new metallic backdrop on which giant slides were projected and other sets mounted.

The play opened with a lone woman in colored robes performing an elaborate dance. Zockriel, his voice amplified across the theater, explained that the dancer was "Sound," an expression of the God of Zion's love for the African people. While Sound performed, Zockriel declared that God created the world with the African people as his chosen, most beloved subjects. The stage was changed into a court during the golden age of African civilization. Drums heralded the arrival of a king, for whom a troupe of women danced passionately.

Zockriel declared that God had become disappointed with the African people. To punish them, God sent the ships of white slavemasters to take them into exile. The king of the scene entitled "Afrikan Glory" now found himself in the center of the stage, bound by chains. Still surrounding him, the dancers sang a wailing lament. On the backdrop a large image of a slave ship alternated with a portrait of brutal Africans beating the terrified slaves.

The set then transformed into a field on a Southern plantation. The actors who had portrayed the African royal court now took on the roles of slaves. After this portrait of Southern slavery, the play focused exclusively on the lives of African Americans in the urban North. In one scene an unscrupulous minister led an identically dressed choir in a song about Jesus and the salvation of his congregation. The minister's cohorts effected a passing of the hat through the audience. When they had finished with the mock collection, the minister greedily turned his back on the singing choir to count the money.

Later scenes portrayed the depravation of life on the inner-city streets. As pop songs filled the theater, the performers acted out scenes in which they drank themselves into oblivion, shot heroin into their veins, and smoked marijuana. The African king of old, now dressed in a lemon yellow jumpsuit and matching wide-brim hat, pimped a beautiful woman and sold drugs on the street until they both collapsed, overcome with debauchery.

In the opening sequence of the final scene, three African American men took the stage in a procession. An economically successful African American man, with the shadow of the Capitol building to his back, posed with his briefcase and informed the audience about his concern for his personal success—to the detriment of his community. A minister and a street hustler emerged next, proclaiming their efforts to corrupt and exploit the poor neighborhoods where they dwelled. Suddenly the desperation of these figures was interrupted by the arrival of a different type of man. Young, healthy, and handsome, this figure walked onto the stage dressed in white robes with a white cap. The personification of Hebrew Israelite manhood, he offered the audience an alternative to the triple vision of corrupted masculinity. The Hebrew Israelite spokesman exhorted the audience, rather than continuing to live a defiling life in America, to relocate to "Northeast Africa" (i.e., Israel), the original home of the African exiles. Before a painted backdrop of a black family dressed in African-style clothing boarding a jetliner, the performers shed their American street clothes in favor of Hebrew Israelite dress and began a triumphant dance as "Sound" joined them on the stage. This final scene recalls a classical Zionist image: the various diasporic Jewish populations—Yemenite, Ethiopean, Soviet—which arrived in Israel on the "wings of an eagle,"—that is, a jet plane.

Conclusion

The Hebrew Israelites travel on the same currents in African American thought that have made Malcolm X and Louis Farrakhan leaders for many African Americans. They float on the same river that carried Jamaican-cum-New Yorker Marcus Garvey and the members of the United Negro Improvement Association. The Hebrew Israelites also find kinship, common rhetoric, and musical solidarity with Rastafarians, who draw on many of the same biblical associations and traditions. But Ben Ammi took the Hebrew Israelites in a unique direction when he brought his followers to the modern state of Israel in the 1960s. The Hebrew Israelites' resolve to establish a thriving community in Israel has inexorably altered their philosophy and practice.

In several interviews Ben Ammi explained to me that the Hebrew Israelites came to Israel with deep suspicions about the nature and birthright of Jews. These views complicated and sometimes inflamed relations with their new Israeli neighbors, and particularly with the Israeli government. Today, with their status in Israel at least temporarily resolved, Ben Ammi preaches a common heritage for African Americans and Jews. Indeed, he sees a special role for himself and the Hebrew Israelites in unifying Jews and African Americans in Israel and the United States. To that end, the Hebrew Israelites currently seek out allies in American Jewish groups and Israeli political organizations. The Hebrew Israelites' aspirations also depend on a continued presence in African American communities. Branches in Chicago and other American cities operate businesses, recruit new members, and actively work to improve conditions in inner-city neighborhoods.

By establishing their home in Dimona, Ben Ammi's Hebrew Israelites have sailed into uncharted waters. They have developed an international organization with roots in both Israeli and African American soil. Overall, the Hebrew Israelites appear to be successfully navigating between African American groups such as the Nation of Islam, American Jewish organizations, and the Israeli government—groups that are often embroiled in conflict with one another. Moreover, the Hebrew Israelites have demonstrated that all borders are porous by adding Israeli political and cultural views to their core of African American religious beliefs.

As I was leaving the compound in Dimona during my 1996 visit, I noticed three young men walking together in an alley. Two premilitary Israeli youths, with the short cropped hair typical of their age group, walked next to a young Hebrew Israelite wearing a traditional knit skullcap and print tunic—but also a pair of blue jeans. The Hebrew Israelite community will continue to be influenced by Israeli society, even as the Hebrew Israelites make their own contributions to the broader Israeli community.

American in Africa:
A Black Journalist's Story

Keith B. Richburg

Continental Divide

I watched the dead float down a river in Tanzania. Of all the gut-wrenching emotions I wrestled with during three years of covering famine, war and misery around Africa, no feeling so gripped me as the one I felt that scorching hot day last April, standing on the Rusumo Falls bridge, in a remote corner of Tanzania, watching dozens of discolored, bloated bodies floating downstream, floating from the insanity that was Rwanda.

The image of those bodies in the river lingered in my mind long after that, recurring during interminable nights in desolate hotel rooms without running water, or while I walked through the teeming refugee camps of eastern Zaire. And the same feeling kept coming back too, as much as I tried to force it from my mind. How can I describe it? Revulsion? Yes, but that doesn't begin to touch on what I really felt. Sorrow, or pity, at the monumental waste of human life? Yes, that's closer. But the feeling nagging at me was—is—something more, something far deeper. It's a sentiment that, when uttered aloud, might come across as callous, self-obsessed, maybe even racist.

But I've felt it before, that same nagging, terrible sensation. I felt it in Somalia, walking among the living dead of Baidoa and Baardheere—towns in the middle of a devastating famine. And I felt it again in those refugee camps in Zaire, as I watched bulldozers scoop up black corpses, and trucks dump them into open pits.

I know exactly the feeling that haunts me, but I've just been too embarrassed to say it. So let me drop the charade and put it as simply as I can: *There but for the grace of God go I.*

Somewhere, sometime, maybe 400 years ago, an ancestor of mine whose name I'll never know was shackled in leg irons, kept in a dark pit, possibly at Goree Island off the coast of Senegal, and then put with thousands of other Africans into the crowded, filthy cargo hold of a ship for the long and treacherous journey across the Atlantic. Many of them died along the way, of disease, of hunger. But my ancestor survived, maybe because he was strong, maybe stubborn enough to want to live, or maybe just lucky. He was ripped away from his country and his family, forced into slavery somewhere in the Caribbean. Then one of his descendants somehow made it up to South Carolina, and one of those descendants, my father, made it to Detroit during the Second World War, and there I was born, 36 years ago. And if that original ancestor hadn't been forced to

make that horrific voyage, I would not have been standing there that day on the Rusumo Falls bridge, a journalist—a mere spectator-watching the bodies glide past me like river logs. No, I might have instead been one of them—or have met some similarly anonymous fate in any one of the countless ongoing civil wars or tribal clashes on this brutal continent. And so I thank God my ancestor made that voyage.

Does that sound shocking? Does it sound almost like a justification for the terrible crime of slavery? Does it sound like this black man has forgotten his African roots? Of course it does, all that and more. And that is precisely why I have tried to keep the emotion buried so deep for so long. But as I sit before the computer screen, trying to sum up my time in Africa, I have decided I cannot lie to you, the reader. After three years traveling around this continent as a reporter for *The Washington Post*, I've become cynical, jaded. I have covered the famine and civil war in Somalia; I've seen a cholera epidemic in Zaire (hence the trucks dumping the bodies into pits); I've interviewed evil "warlords," I've encountered machete-wielding Hutu mass murderers; I've talked to a guy in a wig and a shower cap, smoking a joint and holding an AK- 47, on a bridge just outside Monrovia. I've seen some cities in rubble because they had been bombed, and some cities in rubble because corrupt leaders had let them rot and decay. I've seen monumental greed and corruption, brutality, tyranny and evil.

I've also seen heroism, honor and dignity in Africa, particularly in the stories of small people, anonymous people—Africans battling insurmountable odds to publish an independent newspaper, to organize a political party, usually just to survive. I interviewed an opposition leader in the back seat of a car driving around the darkened streets of Blantyre, in Malawi, because it was then too dangerous for us even to park, lest we be spotted by the ubiquitous security forces. In Zaire, I talked to an opposition leader whose son had just been doused with gasoline and burned to death, a message from dictator Mobutu Sese Seko's henchmen. And in the Rift Valley of central Kenya, I met the Rev. Festus Okonyene, an elderly African priest with the Dutch Reformed Church who endured terrible racism under the Afrikaner settlers there, and who taught me something about the meaning of tolerance, forgiveness, dignity and restraint.

But even with all the good I've found here, my perceptions have been hopelessly skewed by the bad. My tour in Africa coincided with two of the world's worst tragedies, Somalia and Rwanda. I've had friends and colleagues killed, beaten to death by mobs, shot and left to bleed to death on a Mogadishu street.

Now, after three years, I'm beaten down and tired. And I'm no longer even going to pretend to block that feeling from my mind. I empathize with Africa's pain. I recoil in horror at the mindless waste of human life, and human potential. I salute the gallantry and dignity and sheer perseverance of the Africans. But most of all, I feel secretly glad that my ancestor made it out—because, now, I am not one of them.

First, a little personal background that may be relevant to the story at hand.

I grew up as a black kid in 1960s white America, not really poor, but not particularly rich either. Like most blacks who settled in Detroit, my father had come up from the South because of the opportunities offered in the automobile plants, which in the 1940s were gearing up to meet the demands of America's World War II military machine. He joined the United Auto Workers, and stayed involved in union politics for more than 40 years.

There were actually two black Detroits while I was growing up, the east side and the west. The dividing line was Woodward Avenue, our own version of Beirut's infamous Green Line. But the division was more psychological than geographic, centering mainly on black attitudes, the strange caste system in black America at the time, and where you could place your roots in the South. Roughly put, the split was between South Carolina blacks on the west side and Alabama blacks on the east. These were, in a way, our "tribes."

It sounds strange even to me as I look back on it. But those divisions were very real to the black people living in Detroit when I was young, at a time when the city was transforming itself from predominantly white to predominantly black. It was drummed into me that South Carolina blacks, like my family, owned their homes and rarely rented. They had small patches of yard in the front and kept their fences mended. They came from Charleston, Anderson, Greenville, sometimes Columbia. They saved their money, went to church on Sunday, bought their kids new clothes at Easter and for the start of the school year. They kept their hair cut close, to avoid the nappy look. They ate turkey and ham and grits and sweet potato pie. They were well-brought-up, and they expected their children to be the same.

Don't cross Woodward Avenue, we were told, because those blacks over there came up from Alabama. They talked loudly, they drank heavily, and they cursed in public. They had darker skin and nappier hair. They didn't own homes, they rented, and they let the grass in the front run down to dirt, and their fences were all falling apart. They ate pigs' feet, and often had more than a dozen relatives, all from Alabama, stacked up in a few small rooms. They were, as my father would have called them back then, "niggers"—South Carolina blacks being good colored people. The greatest insult was: "He ain't nothin'—he just came up here from Alabama!"

Detroit can get oppressively hot in the summers, and those little houses that black families owned then didn't have anything like air conditioning. So to stay cool, my brother and I would walk (you could walk in those days) down Grand River Avenue to the Globe Theater, where for less than a buck you could sit all day, watching the same movie over and over in air-conditioned splendor until it was time for dinner. I especially remember when the movie "Zulu" was playing, and we watched Michael Caine lead a group of British soldiers against attacking Zulu tribesmen in what is now South Africa. We took turns cheering for the British side and the Zulus. But neither of us really wanted to cheer for the losers. Whoever was rooting for the Africans would usually sit sullenly, knowing what fate held in store. Then came the credits and the heady knowledge that when the movie played again, after a cartoon break, you would be able to cheer for the British once more.

Beyond what I learned from "Zulu," I can't say I had much knowledge of Africa as a kid. I probably couldn't have named a single African country until high school. The word "black" came into vogue in the 1960s, thanks to, among others, James Brown. In 1967, Detroiters burned a large part of the city to the ground, and then all the white people I knew in my neighborhood starting moving out to suburbs that seemed really far away. A lot of the people my father called "black radicals" took to wearing African-style dashikis, and stocking caps in red, black and green, the colors of African liberation. But, when you were a kid from a quiet, South Carolina family growing up on the west side, these seemed like frightening symbols of militancy, defiance, even violence. Any connection to a strange and unknown continent seemed tenuous.

Why am I telling you all this? What does Detroit more than a quarter-century ago have to do with contemporary Africa? Maybe I'm hoping that bit of personal history will help explain the attitude of many black Americans to the concept of their own blackness, their African-ness.

You see? I just wrote "black Americans." I couldn't even bring myself to write "African Americans." It's a phrase that, for me, still doesn't roll easily off the tongue, or look natural on the screen of the computer terminal. Going from "colored" to "black" took some time to get used to. But now "African American"? Is that what we really are? Is there anything African left in the descendants of those original slaves who made that long journey over? Are white Americans whose ancestors came here as long ago as the slaves did "English Americans" or "Dutch

Americans"? Haven't the centuries erased all those connections, so that we are all now simply "Americans"? But I am digressing. Let's continue with the story at hand.

Somewhere along the line, I decided to become a journalist. It was during my undergraduate years at the University of Michigan, while working on the school newspaper, the *Michigan Daily*. My father would have preferred that I study law, then go into politics. Blacks in the 1970s were just coming into their own in politics, taking over city halls across the country and winning congressional seats in newly defined black districts. And that's what articulate, well-educated black kids did: They became lawyers and politicians.

But I wanted to write, and to travel. The travel urge, I think—a longing to cross an ocean—is shared by a lot of mid-westerners. I became a reporter for *The Post*, and would take trips overseas whenever I could save up the money and vacation time. Paris. Morocco. Brazil. London for a year of graduate school. Train journeys across Europe. Trips to Hong Kong, Taiwan, later Japan and China.

But never sub-Saharan Africa (defined as "black Africa"). Whenever friends asked me why, in all my travels, I had avoided the continent of my ancestry, I would usually reply that it was so big, so diverse, that it would take many weeks if not months. I had studied African politics in school, even written a graduate school thesis on the problem of single-party states in Africa. I considered myself a wide-eyed realist, not given to any romantic notions about the place.

The real reason I avoided Africa had more to do with my personal reaction—or, more accurately, my fear of how I would react. I knew that Africa was a continent with much poverty and despair. But what would it be like, really like, to see it as a black person, knowing my ancestors came from there? What if I found myself frightened or, worse, disgusted or repulsed?

And what would it be like, for once in my life, not to stand out in a crowd? To be just one of a vast number of anonymous faces? For better or for worse, a black man in America, or a black man in Asia, stands out.

A friend of mine in Hawaii, a fourth-generation Japanese American, told me once of her fear of traveling to Japan. "I don't know what it would be like to be just another face in the crowd," she said rather innocently. It was a sentiment I immediately shared. When, in early 1991, my editors at *The Post* asked me if I wanted to cover Africa, that same feeling welled up inside me. I was in Asia on vacation when I got the assignment, and I sought out a Reuter reporter named Kevin Cooney who was based in Bangkok but had spent several months working in Nairobi. He put it to me bluntly. "In Africa," he said, after we both had a few too many beers, "you'll be just another nigger."

It was a well-intentioned warning, I would find myself recalling often over three sometimes-tumultuous years.

"Where are you from?" The Zairian immigration officer asked suspiciously in French, fingering through the pages of my passport.

I found the question a bit nonsensical, since he was holding proof of my nationality in his hand. I replied in French, "United States."

"I think you are a Zairian," he said, moving his eyes from the passport photo to me to the photo again. "You look like a Zairian."

"I'm not a Zairian," I said again. I was tired, it was late, I had just spent the day in the Rwandan border town of Cyangugu, just across from Bukavu in Zaire. And all I wanted to do was get back to my room at the Hotel Residence, where, at least if the water was running, a shower awaited. "Look," I said, trying to control my temper, "that's an American passport. I'm an American."

"What about your father—was he Zairian?" The immigration man was not convinced.

"My parents, my grandparents, everybody was American," I said, trying not to shout. "Maybe, 400 years ago, there was a Zairian somewhere, but I can assure you, I'm American."

"You have the face of a Zairian," he said, calling over his colleague so they could try to assess which tribe, which region of Zaire, I might spring from.

Finally, I thought of one thing to convince him. "Okay," I said, pushing my French to its limit. "Suppose I was a Zairian. And suppose I did manage to get myself a fake American passport." I could see his eyes light up at the thought. "So, I'm a Zairian with a fake American passport. Tell me, why on earth would I be trying to sneak back into Zaire?"

The immigration officer pondered this for a moment, churning over in his mind the dizzying array of possibilities a fake U.S. passport might offer; surely, using it to come into Zaire was not among the likely options. "You are right," he concluded, as he picked up his rubber stamp and pounded in my entry. "You are American—black American."

And so it went around Africa. I was constantly met with raised eyebrows and suspicions upon explaining that I really was, really am, an American. "I know you're a Kenyan," said one woman in a bar—a hooker, I think, in retrospect. "You're just trying to pretend you don't speak Swahili."

"Okay," I told her, "you found me out. I'm really a Kenyan."

"Aha!" she said. "I knew it!"

Being able to pass for an African had some advantages. In Somalia, for example, when anti-Americanism was flaring as U.S. Cobra helicopters were bombing militia strongholds of Gen. Mohamed Farah Aideed, I was able to venture into some of the most dangerous neighborhoods without attracting undue attention. I would simply don a pair of sunglasses and ride in the back seat of my beat-up white Toyota, with my Somali driver and AK-47-toting bodyguard up front. My biggest worry was getting caught in the cross hairs of some U.S. Army marksman or helicopter gunner who would only see what, I suppose, we were: three African-looking men riding around Mogadishu's mean streets in a car with an automatic weapon sticking out one of the windows.

But mostly, I concluded, being black in Somalia was a disadvantage. This came home to me late in 1993. I was one of the reporters at the first public rally Aideed had held since coming out of four months of hiding. The arrest order on him had been lifted, and the Clinton administration had called off the humiliating and futile manhunt that had earlier left 18 U.S. soldiers dead in a single encounter. The mood at the rally was, predictably, euphoric. I was among a group of reporters standing on the stage awaiting Aideed's arrival.

Suddenly, one of the Somali gunmen guarding the stage raced up to me and shoved me hard in the chest, forcing me down onto my back. I looked up, stunned, into his wild eyes, and he seemed to be pulling his AK-47 off his shoulder to take aim at me. He was shouting in Somali, and I couldn't understand him. A crowd gathered, and there was more shouting back and forth. Finally, one of Aideed's aides, whom I recognized, helped me to my feet. "I apologize," the aide said, as others hustled my attacker away. "You look like a Somali. He thought you were someone else."

Being black in Africa: I had to fight myself to keep my composure, to keep from bursting into tears.

Many months later, I found out it wasn't only black Americans who felt the way I did. That was when I ran across Sam Msibi, a black South African cameraman for Britain-based Worldwide Television News. I was stuck in Gikongoro, in southwestern Rwanda, and I needed a ride back to Bukavu in Zaire. Msibi was driving that way and gave me a lift.

Msibi had started out in the early 1980s at the South African Broadcasting Corp., then joined a German station, and had worked for a while as a cameraman for the TV station in the "independent" homeland of Bophuthatswana. Since joining WTN, he had covered the worst of South Africa's township wars, back when the African National Congress and the Zulu-based Inkatha Freedom Party were still battling for political dominance.

Msibi knew better than I what it was like to be a black journalist amid Africa's violence; he had been shot five times, in Tokoza township, and managed to live to tell the tale. "It's a problem in Africa," he said, as he navigated the winding mountain road. "When you're black, you have to worry about black-on-black violence."

"Sometimes I want to stop to take pictures," he said, surveying the scene of refugees on the move toward the border, often with their herds of cattle and goats in front, always with small children trailing behind. "But I don't know how these people will react." I explained to him, naively, that I had just traveled the same road a week or so earlier with a Belgian TV crew that had no problem filming along the highway. "Yeah, but they're white," Msibi said. "These people might think I'm a Hutu or something."

I grew quite fond of Msibi during that nearly four-hour drive; I found that he, a black South African, and I, a black American, were thinking many of the same thoughts, venturing together into the heart of an African tragedy that was about as different from downtown Johannesburg as it was from Detroit or Washington, D.C.

"Africa is the worst place—Somalia, Zaire," Msibi said, more to himself than to me. "When you see something like this, you pray your own country will never go this way. Who wants to see his children walking like that?

"I feel I'm related to these people. I feel they're my own people. I pity them—and not just here. In Kenya, Zambia, in Angola. I always feel pain in my heart to see this."

"In South Africa," he said, "you hear on the radio that a million people got killed somewhere in Africa, and there you are brushing your teeth, and it doesn't mean anything to you." Then he added, "It's like in America."

Are you black first or a journalist first?

The question succinctly sums up the dilemma facing almost every black journalist working for the "mainstream" (read: white) press. Are you supposed to report and write accurately, and critically, about what you see and hear? Or are you supposed to be pushing some kind of black agenda, protecting black American leaders from tough scrutiny, treating black people and black issues in a different way?

Many of those questions were at the heart of the debate stirred up a decade ago by my *Post* colleague, Milton Coleman, when he reported remarks of Jesse Jackson referring to Jews as "Hymie." Coleman was accused of using material that was off the record; more troubling, he was accused of betraying his race. For being a hard-nosed journalist, he suffered the wrath of much of the black community, and even had to endure veiled threats from Louis Farrakhan's henchmen.

I have had to deal with many of the same questions over the years, including those asked by family members during Thanksgiving or Christmas gatherings in Detroit. "Let me ask you something," my favorite cousin, Loretta, began once. "Why does the media have to tear down our black leaders?" She was referring to Marion Barry and his cocaine arrest, and to Coleman Young, the longtime Detroit mayor who was always under a cloud for something or other. I tried to explain that journalists only do their job and should expose wrongdoing no matter if the wrongdoer is black or white. My cousin wasn't convinced. "But they are the only role models we have," she said.

It was an argument that couldn't be won. And it was an argument that trailed after me as a black reporter covering black Africa. Was I supposed to travel around looking for the "good news" stories out of the continent, or was I supposed to find the kind of compelling, hard-hitting stories that I would look for any other place in the world? Was I not to call a dictator a dictator, just because he happened to be black? Was I supposed to be an apologist for corrupt, ruthless, undemocratic, illegitimate black regimes?

Apparently so, if you subscribe to the kind of Pan Africanism that permeates much of black American thinking. Pan Africanism, as I see it, prescribes a kind of code of political correctness in dealing with Africa, an attitude that says black America should bury its head in the sand to all that is wrong in Africa, and play up the worn-out demons of colonialism, slavery and Western exploitation of minerals. Anyone who does, or writes, otherwise is said to be playing into the old "white conspiracy." That attitude was confirmed to me in Gabon, in May 1993, when I first met C. Payne Lucas of Africare, a Washington based development and relief organization. "You mean you're a *black* man writing all of that stuff about Africa?" he said.

Lucas was in Gabon for the second African-American Summit, a meeting bringing black American civil rights activists and business leaders together with African government officials and others. It was an odd affair, this "summit," for at a time of profound change across Africa—more and more African countries struggling to shed long-entrenched dictatorships—not one of the American civil rights luminaries ever talked about "democracy" or "good governance" or "political pluralism" in my hearing. These same American leaders who were so quick off the mark to condemn injustice in South Africa, when the repression was white-on-black, suddenly lost their voices when the dictatorships were black.

Instead, what came out was a nauseating outpouring of praise from black Americans for a coterie of some of Africa's most ruthless strongmen and dictators. There were such famous champions of civil rights as Jesse Jackson heaping accolades on the likes of Nigeria's number one military thug at the time, Gen. Ibrahim Babangida, who had just shut down a critical newspaper and was about to renege on his pledge to transfer his country to democratic rule. There was speaker after speaker on the American side complimenting the host, Omar Bongo, a corrupt little dictator in platform shoes who at that very moment was busy shutting down his country's only private (read: opposition) radio station.

But the most sickening spectacle of all came when the baby dictator of Sierra Leone entered the conference hall. Capt. Valentine Strasser, a young

tough in Ray-Ban sunglasses, walked in to swoons and cheers from the assembled American dignitaries, who were obviously more impressed by the macho military figure he cut than by the knowledge that back home Strasser was summarily executing former government officials and opponents of his new military regime.

I had seen that kind of display before around Africa: black Americans coming to the land of their ancestors with a kind of touchy-feely sentimentality straight out of *Roots*. The problem is, it flies smack into the face of a cold reality.

Last March in the Sudanese capital of Khartoum, I ran into a large group of black Americans who were also staying at the Khartoum Hilton. They were there on some kind of a fact-finding trip, and being given VIP treatment by the Sudanese regime. Some of the men went all-out and dressed the part, donning long white Sudanese robes and turbans. Several of the women in the group covered themselves in Muslim wrap.

The U.S. ambassador in Khartoum had the group over to his house, and the next day, the government-controlled newspaper ran a front-page story on how the group berated the ambassador over U.S. policy toward Sudan. Apparently, some members of the group told the ambassador that it was unfair to label the Khartoum regime as a sponsor of terrorists and one of the world's most violent, repressive governments. After all, they said, they themselves had been granted nothing but courtesy, and they had found the dusty streets of the capital safer than most crime-ridden American cities.

I was nearly shaking with rage. Couldn't they see they were being used, manipulated by one of the world's most oppressive regimes? Human Rights Watch/Africa—hardly a water carrier for U.S. policy—had recently labeled Khartoum's human rights record as "abysmal," and reported that "all forms of political opposition remain banned both legally and through systematic terror." And here were these black Americans, these willing tools, heaping praise of an unsavory clique of ruling thugs. I wanted to confront them, but instead I deliberately avoided them, crossing to the other side of the lobby when I had to, just to avoid the temptation of shouting some sense into them.

I went back to my room at the Hilton, turned on CNN—and learned that my Italian journalist friend, Ilaria Alpi, and her cameraman had been slain in a shootout in Mogadishu, left to bleed to death in their bullet-riddled car. I couldn't go get a drink—alcohol is forbidden in Sudan. I didn't want to go pace the bleak lobby and encounter those instant Sudan experts with their romanticized notions. So I stayed there in my room, alone, and cried for Ilaria.

Do I sound cynical? Maybe I am. Maybe that's because, unlike some of the African American tourists who have come out here on a two-week visit to the land of their roots, I've *lived* here.

Do you think I'm alone in my view? Then meet Linda Thomas-Greenfield, and hear her story.

Thomas-Greenfield is a black American diplomat at the U.S. Embassy in Nairobi, her third African posting; she spent three years in Gambia and 2½ in Nigeria. After completing her studies at the University of Wisconsin, she had spent time in Liberia, and she remembers how elated she felt then making her first voyage to her ancestral homeland. "I remember the plane coming down," she said. "I couldn't wait to touch down."

But when I talked to Thomas-Greenfield last summer, she had just finished nine months in Kenya. And she was burned out, fed up and ready to go home.

Her house in Nairobi had been burglarized five times. She had had an electric fence installed. "When they put up the electric fence, I told them to put in enough volts to barbecue anybody who came over." When she continued to complain that even the fence didn't stop the intruders, the local Kenyan police station posted two officers on her grounds. But then the police began extorting payment for their services. "I've gotten to the point where I'm more afraid not to give them money," she said "They're sitting outside with automatic weapons."

Now she was having a higher, 10-foot tall fence built around her grounds. And she had become so exasperated, she told me, that "I'm ready to sit outside myself with an AK-47."

In April, Thomas-Greenfield traveled to Rwanda for an embassy assignment. She had been in the country only a day when the presidential plane was shot down and an orgy of tribal bloodletting began. Most of the victims were Tutsi, and Thomas-Greenfield, a towering 6-foot-plus black woman, was immediately mistaken for a Tutsi. She recalls cowering in fear with machine guns pointed in her face, pleading repeatedly: "I don't have anything to do with this. I'm not a Rwandan. I'm an American."

In the end, it was not just the crime and her close call in Rwanda but the attitude of the Africans that wore down even this onetime Africa-lover. Thomas-Greenfield had never been invited into a Kenyan home. And doing the daily chores of life, she had been met constantly with the Kenyans' own perverse form of racism, under which whites are granted preferential treatment over blacks.

"There's nothing that annoys me more than sitting in a restaurant and seeing two white people getting waited on, and I can't get any service," she said. Once, at a beach hotel on the Kenyan coast, she complained to the manager about the abysmal service from the waiters and staff. The manager explained to her, apologetically, "It's because they think you're a Kenyan."

"I think it's an absolute disadvantage" being black in Africa, said Thomas-Greenfield, who, at the time we talked, said she was considering cutting short her assignment. "Here, as anywhere else in Africa, the cleavages are not racial, they are ethnic. People think they can tell what ethnic group you are by looking at you. And if there's any conflict going on between the ethnic groups, you need to let them know you're an American."

She added, "I'd rather be black in South Africa under apartheid than to go through what I'm going through here in Kenya."

This is not the story I sat down to write. Originally, I had wanted to expound on Africa's politics, the prospects of freedom and development, the hopes for the future. My tour in Africa, after all, came during what was supposed to be the continent's "decade of democracy"— after the fall of one-party communist states of Eastern Europe, the argument went, and the consolidation of democracy in Latin America, could Africa's one-party dictatorships and military regimes be far behind? At least this was the view of many Africa analysts, and of hopeful African democrats themselves, when I began the assignment.

But three years of following African elections, in countries as diverse as Nigeria, Cameroon, Kenya, Ethiopia, Malawi and Mozambique, has left me—and many of those early, hopeful African democrats—far less than optimistic. I've seen elections hijacked or stolen outright, elections canceled, elections bought and elections that have proved to be essentially meaningless. How can you talk about elections in countries where whole chunks of territory are under the sway of armed guerrillas? Where whole villages get burned down because of competing political loyalties? And where traditional belief runs so deep that a politician can be charged in public with casting magic spells over poor villagers to force them to vote for him?

African autocrats are proving far more entrenched, far more brutal and far more adept at the matriculation of state machinery than their Eastern European communist counterparts. Africa's militaries—as compared with those in, say, South America— are proving less willing to return to the barracks and bow to the popular will. In country after country, even oppositionists demonstrate themselves to be grasping, quarrelsome and in most cases incapable of running things if they ever do manage to make it to power. Politics in Africa is about lucrative spoils and fresh opportunities for corruption, and much of opposition politics across the continent consists of an out group wanting its turn at the feeding trough.

It's become a cliché to call tribalism the affliction of modern Africa, but, unfortunately, my years of covering African politics has convinced me that it is true. Tribalism is a corrosive influence impeding democratic change and development. In Kenya, where the opposition had perhaps the best chance of any in Africa to wrest power from a strongman (Daniel arap Moi), it splintered along ethnic lines in the December 1992 elections. One well-educated Kikuyu woman, a secretary working for a foreign news agency, told me she would never vote for the man then considered the lead opposition candidate, Jaramogi Oginga Odinga, for the simple reason that Odinga was a Luo, and Luos, you see, traditionally do not circumcise. "I will never live under a Luo president," she told me, explaining the importance of this operation to "manhood." For want of a circumcision, an election was lost. Moi was reelected with barely a third of the vote, in a split field that saw two Kikuyus dividing the Kikuyu vote and Odinga winning Luoland.

Even in places where opposition parties have managed to overcome the odds and win power in democratic elections, the results so far have been mixed. In Zambia's case, the 1991 election of Frederick Chiluba was supposed to herald a beginning of a new democratic era. But what I found there last year was a country reeling from corruption and incompetence. Government officials have been implicated in drug dealing, others have resigned in disgust claiming the old democratic movement has lost its direction. In a depressing sign of the times, the autocratic former leader, defeated president Kenneth Kaunda, took the opportunity of my visit to announce to me his intentions to launch a comeback bid.

And finally, finding hope becomes even more difficult when you look at the basket cases—places like Zaire, which is in perpetual meltdown; Liberia, still carved up between competing armies; Sudan, ground down by seemingly endless civil war; Rwanda, which was convulsed by one of the worst episodes of tribal genocide in modern times; and Somalia, poor Somalia, which has virtually ceased to exist as a nation-state.

My final journey in Africa was to Somalia—fittingly, I thought, because it was the place I spent most of my time over the past three years. I found it fascinating to cover a country in which all forms of government had collapsed, and to watch as the most ambitious post-Cold War experiment in aggressive peacekeeping tried to patch it together. I was one of those on the early bandwagon for intervention; all Somalia needed was a few Marines and some international aid, I thought, and the gunmen and militias would fade into the background. Somalia got the Marines, 12,000 of them, plus about 15,000 other U.S. troops, and upwards of $4 billion in international aid. But the place today is as violent and chaotic as when the troops first landed more than two years ago. And

now the world has withdrawn, closed the door and turned out the lights, leaving what essentially is a blank spot on the northeastern tip of the continent, a violent no man's land, a burial ground for one of the most costly and ultimately futile interventions in the history of "peacekeeping."

My final journey was to Somalia. But I found that in my time on the continent, the most important journey I took was the one inside my own mind and soul.

In trying to explain Africa to you, I needed first to try to explain it to myself. I want to love the place, love the people. I can tell you I see hope amid the chaos, and I do, in places like Malawi, even Mozambique. But the Rwandas and Somalias and Liberias and Zaires keep intruding into my mind. Three years—three long years—have left me cold and heartless. Africa is a killing field of good intentions, as Somalia alone is enough to prove.

And where does that leave the black man who has come "home" to Africa? I write this surrounded by my own high fence, protected by two large dogs, a paid security guard, a silent alarm system and a large metal door that I bolt shut at night to keep "Africa" from coming across the yard and bashing in my brains with a panga knife for the $200 in my desk drawer. I am tired and, like Linda Thomas-Greenfield, ready to go.

Another black American, writer Eddy L. Harris, the author of *Native Stranger*, ventured into the dark continent, to discover that the place where he felt most at home was South Africa, that most modern, most Western of African countries. So I'll end this journey there too, recalling my last trip to Cape Town, Africa's southern tip. I traveled the wine route, and sat and drank what I'd purchased while the sun set over the beautiful sand beaches. Cape Town is one of the world's most beautiful cities, and one can feel perfectly at peace on the veranda of the Bay Hotel. But all I remember thinking was: Imagine all the horror that lies between here and Cairo, in that vast stretch of earth we call black Africa.

So, do you think I'm a cynic? An Africa-basher? A racist even, or at least a self-hating black man who has forgotten his African roots? Maybe I am all that and more. But by an accident of birth, I am a black man born in America, and everything I am today—culture, attitudes, sensitivities, loves and desires—derives from that one simple and irrefutable truth.

The African American Warrant for Reparations: The Crime of European Enslavement of Africans and Its Consequences

Molefi Kete Asante

Until lions have historians, hunters will be heroes.
—Kenyan Proverb

In his 1993 monograph *Paying the Social Debt: What White America Owes Black America,* Richard America makes a forceful argument that reparation for Europe's enslavement of Africans in the United States is an idea whose time has arrived. Almost a decade before the powerful book *The Debt: What America Owes to Blacks,* written by Randall Robinson in 2000, America laid out the economic bases of the debt owed to African Americans. While the argument for reparations is a Pan-African one, we are most interested in this essay with the discourse surrounding the enslavement and its consequences in the American society. There are those who will immediately say that the people of the United States will never accede to reparations. I am of the opinion that the discussion and debate surrounding reparations has only recently occurred in any serious way; therefore, this essay is offered as an attempt to raise some of the philosophical ideas that might govern such a discourse.

Randall Robinson's *The Debt* has been one of the most popular and important books written on the subject so far because he has captured the warrants for reparations in very clear and accessible language. What he has demonstrated is that while a national *paralysis* of will may exist at the present time, there is no lack of national *guilt* and interest in this theme. There is every reason for the United States to shape and frame the culture of reparations that shall become an increasingly powerful moral and political issue in the twenty-first century. The highest form of law exhibits itself when a system of law is able to answer for its own crimes. Nothing should prevent men and women of moral and political insight from making an argument for an idea whose legitimacy is fundamental to our concept of justice. We must act based on our own sense of moral rightness.

When Raphael Lemkin started in 1933 to gain recognition of the term "genocide" as a crime of barbarity, few thought that it would soon become the language of international law. When genocide was adopted as a convention in 1948 with an international criminal court to serve as the home for judging genocide it was a victory for those who had fought to put genocide on the world agenda. My belief is that the current discussions about reparation undertaken by scholars, political activists, and the United Nations will advance our own plan to place reparations at the front end of the agenda for redress for African Americans.

The Grounds of the Argument: Moral, Legal, Economic, and Political

The argument for reparations for the forced enslavement of Africans in the American colonies and the United States of America is based in moral, legal, economic, and political grounds. Taken together these ideas constitute an enormous warrant for the payment of reparations to the descendants of the Africans who worked under duress for nearly 250 years. The only remedy for such an immense deprivation of life and liberty is an enormous restitution.

When one examines the nature of the terms amassed for the argument for reparations it becomes clear that the basis for them is interwoven with the cultural fabric of the American nation. It is not un-American to seek the redress of wrongs through the use of some form of compensatory restitution. For example, the *moral* ideas of the argument are made from the concept of rightness as conceived in the religious literature of the American people. One assumes that morality based in the relationship between humans and the divine provides an incentive for correcting a wrong, if it is perceived to be a wrong, in most cases. Using *legal* ideas for the argument for reparations, one relies on the juridical heritage of the United States. Clearly, the ideas of justice and fair play, while often thwarted, distorted, and subverted, characterize the legal *ideal* in American jurisprudence. Therefore, the use of legal strategy in securing reparations is not only expected but required by Africans receiving compensatory redress for their enslavement. The Great Enslavement itself showed, however, how legal arguments could be twisted to defend an immoral and unjust system of oppression. Nevertheless, justice is a requirement for political solidarity within a nation and any attempt to bring it about must be looked upon as a valid effort to create national unity. Simply put, no justice, no peace.

Recognizing that justice may be both retributive and restorative, it seeks to punish those who have committed wrong and it concerns itself with restoring to the body politic a sense of reconciliation and harmony. *I believe that the idea of reparations, particularly as conceived in my own work, is a restorative justice issue.*

The *economic* case is a simple argument for the payment to the descendants of the enslaved for the work that was done and the deprivation that was experienced by our ancestors. To speak of an economic interest in the argument is typically American and an issue that should be well understood by most Americans. Simply put, Africans in America are owed back wages for nearly 250 years of uncompensated work by their ancestors and another 130 years for laws and behavior that continue to affect them economically.

Finally, the *political* aspect of reparations is wrapped in the clothes of the American political reality. In order to insure national unity reparations should be made to the descendants of Africans. It is my belief as well as that of others that the underlying fault in the American body politic is the unresolved issue of enslavement. Many of the contemporary problems in society can be thought of as deriving from the unsettled issues of enslavement. A concentration on the political term for reparations will lead to a useful argument for national unity.

Why Reparations?

One of the ironies of the discourse surrounding reparations for the enslavement of Africans is that the arguments against reparations for Africans are never placed in the same light as those about reparations in other cases. This introduces a racist element into the discourse. For example, one would rarely hear the question, Why should Germany pay reparations to the Jews? Or, Why should the United States pay reparations to the Japanese who were placed in concentration camps during World War II? If someone were to try to make arguments against those forms of reparations the entire corpus of arguments from morality, law, economics, and politics would be brought to bear on them. This is as it should be in a society where human beings respect the value of other humans. Only in societies where human beings are considered less than humans do we have the opportunity for enslavement, concentration camps, and gas chambers. It should be noted that when humans are considered the same as other humans no one questions whether compensatory measures should be given to an oppressed group. We expect all of the arguments for reparations to be used in such cases. This is why the recent rewarding of reparations to Jews for the Nazi atrocities is considered normal and natural. In Nazi Germany, Jews were considered

inferior, and had Germany *won* the war, any thought of reparations to Jews would have been unthinkable. It is because Nazi Germany *lost* the war and other humans with different values had to make decisions about the nature of reparations that any were made at all. One can make the same argument for the Japanese Americans who lost their property and resources during World War II. A new reality in the political landscape made it possible for the Japanese to receive reparations for their losses. Eminent African and Caribbean scholars such as Ali Mazrui, author of *The Africans*, Jamaican ambassador Dudley Thompson, and others have argued for an international examination of the role the West played in the slave trade and the consequent underdevelopment of Africa. This is a laudable movement and I believe it will add to the intensity and seriousness of the internal discourse within the United States.

A strong sense of moral outrage has continued to activate the public in the interest of reparations. In early 2001 a lawsuit brought against the French national railroad in the Eastern District of New York Court charged the Société Nationale des Chemins de Fer with transporting 72,000 Jews to death camps in August 1944. The case was brought to the court on behalf of the survivors and heirs. In another case, a French court held that French banks that hoarded assets of Jews had to create a fund of $50 million for those individuals with evidence of previous accounts (*New York Times*, June 13, 2001, A-14). Similarly, on May 30, 2001, the German Parliament cleared the way for a $4.5 billion settlement by German companies and the government to survivors or heirs of more than one million forced laborers. This is in addition to much larger awards to Israel and the Jewish people for the Holocaust. The Swiss government has agreed to pay $1.25 billion to those Jewish persons who can establish claims on bank accounts appropriated during World War II.

Whenever people have been deprived of their labor, freedom, or life without cause, other than their race, ethnicity, or religion, as a matter of group or national policy, they should be compensated for their loss. In the case of Africans in the American colonies and the United States, the policy and practice of the ruling white majority in the country was to enslave only Africans after the 1640s. Prior to that time there had been some whites who had been indentured as servants and some native peoples who were pressed into slavery. However, from the middle of the seventeenth century to 1865, only Africans were enslaved as a matter of race and ethnic origin.

A growing consensus suggests that some form of reparations for past injustice on a large scale should not be swept under the table. We have accepted the broad idea of justice and fair play in such massive cases of group deprivation and loss; we cannot change the language or the terms of our contemporary response to acts of past injustice.

The recognition of reparations in numerous other cases, including the Rosewood, Florida, and the Tulsa, Oklahoma, burning and bombing of African American communities in the early 1920s, means that we must continue to right the wrongs of the past, so that our current relationships as citizens will improve through an appreciation of justice.

The Brutalities of Enslavement

Africans did not enslave themselves in the Americas. The European slave trade was not an African venture, it was preeminently a European enterprise in all of its dimensions: conception, insurance, outfitting of ships, sailors, factories, shackles, weapons, and the selling and buying of people in the Americas. Not one African can be named as an equal partner with Europeans in the slave trade. Indeed, no African person benefited to the degree that Europeans did from the commerce in African people. I think it is important to say that no African community used slavery as its principal mode of economic production. We have no example of a slave economy in West Africa. The closest any scholar has ever been able to arrive at a description of a slave society is the Dahomey kingdom of the nineteenth century that had become so debauched by slavery due to European influence that it was virtually a hostage of the nefarious enterprise. However, even in Dahomey we do not see the complete denial of the humanity of Africans as we see in the American colonies.

Slavery was not romantic; it was evil, ferocious, brutal, and corrupting in all of its aspects. It was developed in its greatest degree of degradation in the United States. The enslaved African was treated with utter disrespect. No laws protected the African from any cruelty the white master could conceive. The man, woman, or child was at the complete mercy of the most brutish of people. For looking a white man in the eye the enslaved person could have his or her eyes blinded with hot irons. For speaking up in defense of a wife or woman a man could have his right hand severed. For defending his right to speak against oppression, an African could have half his tongue cut out. For running away and being caught an enslaved African could have his or her Achilles tendon cut. For resisting the advances of her white master a woman could be given fifty lashes of the cowhide whip. A woman who physically fought against her master's sexual advances was courting death, and many died at the hands of their masters. The enslaved African was more often than not physically scarred, crippled, or injured because of some brutal act of the slave owner.

Among the punishments that were favored by the slave owners were whipping holes, wherein the enslaved was buried in the ground up to the neck; dragging blocks that were attached to the feet of men or women who had run away and been caught; mutilation of the toes and fingers; the pouring of hot wax onto the limbs; and passing a piece of hot wood on the buttocks of the enslaved. Death came to the enslaved in vile, crude ways when the angry, psychopathic slave owner wanted to teach other enslaved Africans a lesson. The enslaved person could be roasted over a slow-burning fire, left to die after having both legs and both arms broken, oiled and greased and then set afire while hanging from a tree's limb, or being killed slowly as the slave owner cut the enslaved person's phallus or breasts. A person could be placed on the ground, stomach first, stretched so that each hand was tied to a pole and each foot was tied to a pole. Then the slave master would beat the person's naked body until the flesh was torn off the buttocks and the blood ran down to the ground.

I have written this brief description to insure the reader that we are not talking about mint juleps and Sunday-afternoon teas with happy Africans running around the plantation while white people sang and danced. Africans on the plantations were often sullen, difficult as far as the whites were concerned, hypocritical because they would smile on command and frown when they left the white person's presence, and plotting.

Some Numbers

It became popular in the 1980s to speculate over just how many Africans were captured, marched, shipped, and sold during European enslavement. Henry Louis Gates of Harvard has placed the number between 10 and 12 million, as has Philip Curtin. It is not my intention to enter the debate over these numbers, although I find the numbers quite conservative given the esti-mates made by other scholars and given the fact that Curtin particularly has demonstrated a penchant for minimizing African agency in the struggle against slavery and colonialism in his widely read book *The Atlantic Slave Trade*. The figure has reached as high as 100 million in the estimation of some scholars, such as W. E. B. Du Bois in his 1920 book *Darkwater*. I believe that the numbers are only important to ascertain just how deeply the Transatlantic Slave Trade affected the continental African economic, social, physical, and cultural character. However, for purposes of reparations the numbers are not necessary since there can be no adequate compensation for the enslavement and its consequences. The broad outline of the facts is clear and accepted by most historians. We know, for instance, that the numbers of Africans who landed in Jamaica and Brazil were different from those of Haiti and the United States. Furthermore, the establishment of concrete numbers of those captured and enslaved throughout the *Maafa* and in the United States, though difficult, will ultimately be achieved because of better data-gathering techniques and the lawsuits now emerging that will research such numbers. I believe it is necessary, however, to ascertain something more about the *nature* of the Africans' arrival in the American nation. At the end of the Civil War in 1865 there were about 4.5 million Africans in the United States, which means that there had been a steady flow of Africans into the American nation since the seventeenth century. *These Africans and their descendants constitute the proper plaintiffs in the reparation case.* Hundreds of thousands of Africans labored and died under the reign of enslavement without leaving any direct descendants. We cannot adequately account for these lost numbers, which include those who died resisting capture in Africa, those who died on the forced marches to the beach barracoons, those who died awaiting to enter the ships, those who died aboard ships, and those who continued to resist throughout 250 years of enslavement. We can, however, account for most of those who survived the Civil War and their heirs. In fact, some of the 187,000 who fought in the Civil War did not survive, but their descendants survived. These also constitute a body of individuals (class?) who must be brought into the discussion of reparations. Thus, two classes of people, those who survived the Civil War and their heirs and those who fought and died in the Civil War and their heirs, are legitimate candidates for reparations. Indeed, the consequences of the residual effects of the enslavement must be figured in any compensation.

The Nature of the Loss

One of the issues that must be dealt with is, how is loss to be determined? Since millions of Africans were transported across the sea and enslaved in the Caribbean and the Americas for more than two centuries, what method of calculating loss will be employed? It seems to me that loss must be determined using a multiplicity of measures suited to the variety of deprivations that were experienced by the African people. Yet the overarching principle for establishing loss might be determined by ascertaining the negative effects on the natural development of people, that is the physical, psychological, economic, and educational toll must be evaluated. What were the fundamental ways in which the enslavement of Africans undermined not only the contemporary lifestyles and chances of the people but also destroyed the potentialities for their posterity? I believe all of the issues of educational deficit, economic instability, poor health conditions, and the lack of estate wealth are directly related to the conditions of enslaved Africans both in the United States and throughout the world. What is called for is a national purpose to confront the historical abuse of Africans.

Given the fact that African Americans constitute the largest single ethnic-cultural grouping in the United States and will maintain this position into the future, reparations for the enslavement of Africans will have positive benefits on the American nation. African Americans number approximately 35 million people.

Occasionally one reads in the newspaper that the Hispanic or Latino population will soon outstrip the African population in the United States. While it is true that taken together the number of Spanish-speaking Americans will soon outnumber the absolute number of African Americans, the Spanish-speaking population includes more than twenty different national origin groups, plus individuals who identify with African, Caucasian, and Native American heritages. One finds, for example, among the Spanish-speaking population, people from Mexico, Cuba, Puerto Rico, Dominican Republic, El Salvador, Honduras, Costa Rica, and numerous South American countries. Many of these people will self-identify as white; others will self-identify as Black or African.

Africans are an indispensable part of the American nation in terms of its history, culture, philosophies, mission, and potential. It is insane to speak of America without the African presence, and yet the deeper we get into the future the more important the nature of the relation-ship of Africans to the body politic will become. Reparations would insure: (1) recognition of the Africans' loss, (2) compensation for the loss, (3) psychological relief for both Blacks and whites in terms of guilt and anger, and (4) national unity based on a stronger political will. These are intrinsic values of reparations.

Toward a Basis for Reparations

Reparations are always based on real loss, not perceived loss. Take the case of the Japanese Americans who were taken from their homes in California and other Western states during World War II. They were removed against their wills from their homes, their property confiscated and their children taken out of schools. The Japanese Americans lost in real terms and were consequently able to make the case for reparations. Their case was legitimate and it was correct for America to respond to the injustice that had been done to the Japanese Americans.

The case of the Africans in America has some of the same characteristics, but in many ways is different and yet equally significant as far as real loss is concerned. What is similar is the uprooting of Africans against their wills. Also similar is the racism whites had against Africans, who they considered cultural and intellectual inferiors. From this standpoint it was easy to brutalize, humiliate, and enslave Africans since, as whites had argued, blacks were inferior in every way. What is different about the reparations case for African Americans is that it is much larger than the Japanese American situation, it has far more implications for historical transformation of the American society, and it is rooted in the legal foundations of the country.

It is possible to argue for reparations on the following grounds: (1) forced migration, (2) forced deprivation of culture, (3) forced labor, and (4) forced deprivation of wealth by segregation and racism. However, these four constituents of the argument for reparations are buttressed by several significant factors that emerged from the experience of the enslaved Africans. In the first place, Africans often lost their freedom because of their age. Most of the Africans who were robbed from the continent of Africa were between the ages of fifteen and twenty years—robbery of prime youth. A second factor is based on the loss of innocence where abuse—physical, psychological, and sexual—was the order of the day in the life of the enslaved African, as Trinidadian scholar Eric Williams detailed in his famous 1961 speech "Massa Day Done." Thirdly, one has to consider the loss in transit that derived from coffles and the long marches, the dreaded factories where Africans were held sometimes as long as seven months while the Europeans waited for a transport ship, and the severe loss of life in transit, where death on board the ships or in the sea further deprived a people. Fourthly, the factor of loss due to maimed limbs, that is, the deprivation of feet, Achilles tendons, and hands. Insurance companies such as Aetna understood the hazards of slavery and provided policies for slaveholders that allowed for premiums to be paid to them if death or maiming occurred to their slaves. Needless to say, none of the slaves received any benefits from this hideous business practice, but the effects lasted for generations, including sterility in women and castration in men.

Thus, to have freedom, will, culture, religion, and health controlled and denied is to create the most thorough conditions for loss of ancestral memory. The Africans who were enslaved in America were among the most deprived humans in history. It is no wonder that David Walker's 1829 "Appeal to the Colored Citizens of the World" argued that the enslaved Africans were the most abject people in the world. He also stated in his Appeal that "the White Christian Americans" were the most cruel and barbarous people who have ever lived.

The Reparations Remedy

One way to approach the issue of reparations is to speak about *money* but not necessarily about *cash*. Reparations will cost, but it will not have to be the giving out of billions of dollars of cash to individuals, although it will cost billions of dollars. While the delivery of money for other than cash distributions is important, it is possible for reparations to be advanced in the United States by a number of other options. Among the potential options are educational grants, health care, land or property grants, and a combination of such grants. Any reparations remedy should deal with long-term issues in the African American community rather than be a onetime cash payout. What I have argued for is the establishment of some type of organization that would evaluate how reparations would be determined and distributed. For example, a National Commission of African Americans (NCAA) would be the overarching national organization to serve as the clearinghouse for reparations. The commission would investigate reparations as a more authentic way of bringing the national moral conscience to bear on the education of African Americans. Rather than begin in a vacuum, the NCAA would study various sectors of society, education, health and welfare, or economics and see how Africans were deprived by two and a half centuries of enslavement. For example, by the time Africans were freed from bondage in 1865, whites had claimed all land stretching from sea to sea, and had just about finished the systematic "cleansing" of indigenous people from the land, pushing thousands to Oklahoma in the Trail of Tears or, as in the case of the Oneida, to Wisconsin in a trail of sorrow. Furthermore, there were already five hundred colleges teaching white students, this during a time when it was a crime for Africans to learn and illegal for whites to teach Africans to read or to write. One likely answer to the reparations issue is free public and private education to all descendants of enslaved Africans for the next 123 years, half the time Africans worked in this country for free. Students who qualified for college would be admitted and have all of their expenses covered by the government. Those who qualified for private schools would get government vouchers to cover the costs of their education.

The present educational deficit is not an individual but a collective and national deficit. This is not the same as saying that Kim Su or Ted Vaclav came to this country and could not read, but they made it by pulling themselves up by the proverbial bootstraps. Immigrants who choose to come to America are in no way enslaved and have different motivations for their immigration including economic, emotional, and political ones. Our coming was different and our struggle was epic because we were brought on slave ships and often worked nearly to death.

Despite the curious attempt to claim for all Americans the same heritage and the same history, the record of the country speaks for itself. From education to prison, the evidence of racial bias in interpretation of data as well as the data themselves show that African Americans have been treated unfairly due largely to the previous condition of servitude. Thus we have been underdeveloped by the very society that supposedly set us free.

At the head of America's race relations problems are the unresolved issues surrounding the institution of slavery. At the root of this irresolution is the belief that Africans are inferior to whites and therefore do not deserve compensation for labor or anything else. Indeed, it is this feeling that fuels the attacks on reparations for Africans as well. How whites feel about the condition of servitude forced on Blacks and how we feel about that condition or how we feel about the attachment of whites to the perpetration of that condition are the central issues affecting race relations in this nation. Once we have come to terms with the basis for reparations we can begin to overcome the legacy of slavery.

Maafa (pronounced Ma-AH-fa). A Kiswahili word meaning "disaster." It is used to describe over five hundred years of warfare and genocide experienced by African people under enslavement and colonialism and their continued impact on African people throughout the world. Until now words such as "diaspora" and "holocaust" had been appropriated from outside African culture and therefore do not embody the experiences of the African reality. The term was first popularized by the author Marimba Ani in her book *Yurugu: An African-Centered Critique of European Cultural Thought and Behavior* (1994), Africa World Press, and will be used throughout this book.

Stop Trying to "Save" Africa

Uzadinma Iweala

Last fall, shortly after I returned from Nigeria, I was accosted by a perky blond college student whose blue eyes seemed to match the "African" beads around her wrists.

"Save Darfur!" she shouted from behind a table covered with pamphlets urging students to TAKE ACTION NOW! STOP GENOCIDE IN DARFUR!

My aversion to college kids jumping onto fashionable social causes nearly caused me to walk on, but her next shout stopped me.

"Don't you want to help us save Africa?" she yelled.

It seems that these days, wracked by guilt at the humanitarian crisis it has created in the Middle East, the West has turned to Africa for redemption. Idealistic college students, celebrities such as Bob Geldof and politicians such as Tony Blair have all made bringing light to the dark continent their mission. They fly in for internships and fact-finding missions or to pick out children to adopt in much the same way my friends and I in New York take the subway to the pound to adopt stray dogs.

This is the West's new image of itself: a sexy, politically active generation whose preferred means of spreading the word are magazine spreads with celebrities pictured in the foreground, forlorn Africans in the back. Never mind that the stars sent to bring succor to the natives often are, willingly, as emaciated as those they want to help.

Perhaps most interesting is the language used to describe the Africa being saved. For example, the Keep a Child Alive/"I am African" ad campaign features portraits of primarily white, Western celebrities with painted "tribal markings" on their faces above "I AM AFRICAN" in bold letters. Below, smaller print says, "help us stop the dying."

Such campaigns, however well intentioned, promote the stereotype of Africa as a black hole of disease and death. News reports constantly focus on the continent's corrupt leaders, warlords, tribal conflict, child laborers, and women disfigured by abuse and genital mutilation. These descriptions run under headlines like "Can Bono Save Africa?" or "Will Brangelina Save Africa?" The relationship between the West and Africa is no longer based on openly racist beliefs, but such articles are reminiscent of reports from the heyday of European colonialism, when missionaries were sent to Africa to introduce us to education, Jesus Christ and "civilization."

There is no African, myself included, who does not appreciate the help of the wider world, but we do question whether aid is genuine or given in the spirit of affirming one's cultural superiority. My mood is dampened every time I attend a benefit whose host runs through a litany of African disasters before presenting a (usually) wealthy, white person, who often proceeds to list the things he or she has done for the poor, starving Africans. Every time a well-meaning college student speaks of villagers dancing because they were so grateful for her help, I cringe. Every time a Hollywood director shoots a film about Africa that features a Western protagonist, I shake my head—because Africans, real people though we may be, are used as props in the West's fantasy of itself. And not only do such depictions tend to ignore the West's prominent role in creating many of the unfortunate situations on the continent, they also ignore the incredible work Africans have done and continue to do to fix those problems.

Why do the media frequently refer to African countries as having been "granted independence from their colonial masters," as opposed to having fought and shed blood for their freedom? Why do Angelina Jolie and Bono receive overwhelming attention for their work in Africa while Nwankwo Kanu or Dikembe Mutombo, Africans both, are hardly ever mentioned? How is it that a former mid-level U.S. diplomat receives more attention for his cowboy antics in Sudan than do the numerous African Union countries that have sent food and troops and spent countless hours trying to negotiate a settlement among all parties in that crisis?

Two years ago I worked in a camp for internally displaced people in Nigeria, survivors of an uprising that killed about 1,000 people and displaced 200,000. True to form, the Western media reported on the violence but not on the humanitarian work the state and local governments—without much international help—did for the survivors. Social workers spent their time and in many cases their own salaries to care for their compatriots. These are the people saving Africa, and others like them across the continent get no credit for their work.

Last month the Group of Eight industrialized nations and a host of celebrities met in Germany to discuss, among other things, how to save Africa.

Before the next such summit, I hope people will realize Africa doesn't want to be saved. Africa wants the world to acknowledge that through fair partnerships with other members of the global community, we ourselves are capable of unprecedented growth.